GEOGRAPHICAL DISTRIBUTION
OF FINANCIAL FLOWS
TO DEVELOPING COUNTRIES

REPARTITION GEOGRAPHIQUE
DES RESSOURCES FINANCIERES MISES A LA DISPOSITION
DES PAYS EN DEVELOPPEMENT

DISBURSEMENTS - COMMITMENTS - EXTERNAL DEBT
ECONOMIC INDICATORS

VERSEMENTS - ENGAGEMENTS
DETTE EXTERIEURE - INDICATEURS ECONOMIQUES

1977/1980

ORGANISATION FOR ECONOMIC CO-OPERATION AND DEVELOPMENT
ORGANISATION DE COOPERATION ET DE DEVELOPPEMENT ECONOMIQUES

PARIS 1981

L'Organisation de Coopération et de Développement Économiques (OCDE), qui a été instituée par une Convention signée le 14 décembre 1960, à Paris, a pour objectif de promouvoir des politiques visant :

— à réaliser la plus forte expansion possible de l'économie et de l'emploi et une progression du niveau de vie dans les pays Membres, tout en maintenant la stabilité financière, et contribuer ainsi au développement de l'économie mondiale ;
— à contribuer à une saine expansion économique dans les pays Membres, ainsi que non membres, en voie de développement économique ;
— a contribuer à l'expansion du commerce mondial sur une base multilatérale et non discriminatoire, conformément aux obligations internationales.

Les Membres de l'OCDE sont : la République Fédérale d'Allemagne, l'Australie, l'Autriche, la Belgique, le Canada, le Danemark, l'Espagne, les États-Unis, la Finlande, la France, la Grèce, l'Irlande, l'Islande, l'Italie, le Japon, le Luxembourg, la Norvège, la Nouvelle-Zélande, les Pays-Bas, le Portugal, le Royaume-Uni, la Suède, la Suisse et la Turquie.

The Organisation for Economic Co-operation and Development (OECD) was set up under a Convention signed in Paris on 14th December 1960, which provides that the OECD shall promote policies designed:

— to achieve the highest sustainable economic growth and employment and a rising standard of living in Member countries, while maintaining financial stability, and thus to contribute to the development of the world economy;
— to contribute to sound economic expansion in Member as well as non-member countries in the process of economic development;
— to contribute to the expansion of world trade on a multilateral, non-discriminatory basis in accordance with international obligations.

The Members of OECD are Australia, Austria, Belgium, Canada, Denmark, Finland, France, the Federal Republic of Germany, Greece, Iceland, Ireland, Italy, Japan, Luxembourg, the Netherlands, New Zealand, Norway, Portugal, Spain, Sweden, Switzerland, Turkey, the United Kingdom and the United States.

***

TABLE OF CONTENTS — TABLE DES MATIÈRES

SECTION A

Summary tables — Tableaux résumés

SECTION B

Tables for Individual Recipient Countries and Territories — Tableaux par pays et territoire bénéficiaires

INTRODUCTION

1. This report, the second in a new series dealing with the volume and sources of the external financial resources provided to individual developing countries, presents detailed data on the geographical distribution of:

- net and gross disbursements;
- commitments;
- debt;
- debt service and
- terms;

for each of over 100 developing countries for each of the four years 1977/1980. These data are supplemented with background economic and social data to provide perspective in interpreting the resource flow information for each country listed. The aim has been to achieve, within the compass of two pages, a comprehensive presentation of the external financing of each country shown.

2. The data show the transactions of each country with:

i) DAC Member countries (individually or as a group)
ii) multilateral agencies (individually or as a group)
iii) Members of the Organisation of Petroleum Exporting Countries (OPEC) (as a group), and of the Council for Mutual Economic Assistance (CMEA), as a group.

The Member countries of the OECD Development Assistance Committee for which data are presented are: Australia, Austria, Belgium, Canada, Denmark, Finland, France, the Federal Republic of Germany, Italy, Japan, the Netherlands, New Zealand, Norway, Sweden, Switzerland, the United Kingdom and the United States. Data for the Commission of the European Communities, which is also a Member of the DAC, are included under "multilateral agencies"; a further separate line (EEC + Members) gives the data for flows from the EEC as an institution and its DAC Member countries combined. The data on financial flows from multilateral sources cover the World Bank, the International Finance Corporation (IFC), the International Development Association (IDA), the Inter-American Development Bank (IDB), the African Development Bank (Af.D.B.), the African Development Fund (Af.D.F.), the Asian Development Bank (As.D.B.), the Caribbean Development Bank (Car.D.B.), the International Fund for Agricultural Development (IFAD), the Arab Fund for Economic and Social Development (AFESD), the Special Account of the Organisation of Arab Petroleum Exporting Countries (OAPEC), the Special Arab Aid Fund for Africa (SAAFA), the OPEC Fund for International Development, Arab Fund for Technical Assistance to African and Arab Countries (AFTAAAC), Arab Bank for Economic Development in Africa (BADEA); Gulf Organisation for the Development of Egypt (GODE), Islamic Development Bank, Islamic Solidarity Fund, and the Technical Assistance and Relief Agencies of the United Nations. The latter cover mainly the following programmes or agencies: regular programme of United Nations Technical Assistance (UNTA), United Nations Development Programme (UNDP), United Nations High Commissioner for Refugees (UNHCR), United Nations Relief and Works Agency for Palestine Refugees in the Near East (UNRWA), United Nations Children's Fund (UNICEF) and the World Food Programme (WFP). Financial flows from OPEC Members are shown as a combined total for the following countries: Algeria, Iran, Iraq, Kuwait, Libya, Nigeria Qatar, Saudi Arabia, the United Arab Emirates and Venezuela[1]. Flows from CMEA countries are shown as a combined total for Bulgaria, Czechoslavakia, German Democratic Republic, Hungary, Poland, Romania and the USSR.

3. For a number of items, coverage goes beyond the sources listed above. The figures on debt and debt service relate to all creditors, including other developing countries and "international". The figures on changes in bank sector claims, given for information (see Annex paragraph A.16), are for countries reporting to the Bank for International Settlements[2] and the affiliates in offshore centres of banks resident in these countries.

Sources of Data

4. DAC bilateral flow figures are based on replies from Member countries to questionnaires issued by the OECD Secretariat. The data on multilateral flows are compiled from published reports of the agencies concerned, supplemented by additional information received directly from them. The bilateral aid figures for OPEC Member countries are based on information provided by the Abu Dhabi Fund for Arab Economic Development, the Kuwait Fund for Arab Economic Development, the Saudi Fund for Development, the General Board for the South and Arabian Gulf and the Central Bank of Venezuela as well as certain information from the Ministries of Finance of Kuwait and of the United Arab Emirates. The remaining data are based on secondary sources and OECD Secretariat estimates. The data for OPEC and CMEA countries have been classified and processed as far as possible according to DAC norms and definitions[3]. Data on economic

1 Ecuador, Gabon and Indonesia, also OPEC Member countries, provided no bilateral assistance in the period 1977/1980.
2 All DAC countries except Australia, Finland, New Zealand and Norway.
3 See Annex: Definition of Concepts used in this Report.

aggregates are derived from IBRD materials (including some estimates by the OECD Secretariat) and IBRD's Debtor Reporting System is an important source for much of the information shown on debt (see paragraphs 13-19). Reserves and balance of payments data are drawn from the IMF, and the trade data are derived from OECD's foreign trade questionnaires.

Comprehensiveness

5. The resource flow data shown are based on records that are comprehensive for the majority of the individual categories shown. The omissions are essentially as follows: (*i*) private sector transactions by residents of OPEC countries; also the data on OPEC non-concessional official flows are incomplete; (*ii*) flows from countries that are neither developing countries nor members of the DAC (e.g., South Africa, Ireland, Luxembourg); (*iii*) net flows from CMEA countries. In addition, only limited data are available on intra-LDC flows. For developing countries combined, the net effect is nil, since inflows to one country are outflows of another. However, it could be misleading, for an individual recipient country, to show the incomplete figure corresponding to the data collected, since it would inevitably be treated as if it were the true total. The decision was taken to show no figures for a country's receipts from other developing countries until a satisfactory level of coverage has been achieved.

Unallocated Amounts

6. A figure that is a comprehensive total reported by a source may include a substantial "geographically unallocated" component. A portion of the amounts reported to DAC as geographically unallocated is in fact properly classified thus e.g., amounts spent in the donor country on research performed for the benefit of developing countries (e.g., tropical diseases). Another portion reflects defective data collection procedures. The major part however stems from the effect of confidentiality restrictions in preventing a reporting country from disclosing the name of a partner country. For ODA and official sector transactions by DAC Members and multilateral organisations, geographically unallocated amounts are too small in aggregate to cause a risk that the figure for a given recipient country will be substantially understated. But for some OPEC donor countries, there are substantial amounts in 1977, 1978 and 1979, and this could involve distortion for some recipient countries. For certain categories of private sector flows, in particular private investment, there is a risk that the understatement of a given country's net inflow may be fairly large. This is true of (*a*) countries hosting investment in the oil sector; (*b*) countries whose investment inflows are derived in large part from source countries whose reporting includes large amounts not allocated by country. These source countries include in particular Canada, Denmark, Finland, New Zealand, Sweden and Switzerland.

Presentation

7. The report consists of two sections:

Section A

8. This section contains eight tables covering the period 1974 to 1980. The first six show the receipts of each developing country, including countries not shown separately in Section B, from DAC countries combined and all sources combined respectively, of:

i) Official Development Assistance, net disbursements.
ii) Official Development Assistance, commitments.
iii) Total net resource flows, net disbursements.

The last two show the receipts of each country from multilateral agencies combined of net disbursements of Concessional Assistance ("multilateral ODA") and total net disbursements.

Section B

9. The tables in this Section treat each developing country individually[4], showing its resource receipts by type and by donor, with separate sub-totals for DAC Members, multilateral agencies and OPEC donors, with additional data on CMEA countries. These tables are supplemented by a series of tables of identical format showing the same information as totals or averages for groups of developing countries (see Annex paragraph 19).

Coverage

Detailed Tables by Source

10. The page layout in Section B is identical. Two pages are used for each country. They include in the left-hand and central panels tables showing the following types of flow by source:

- Total receipts, net.
- Total ODA, gross and net.
- ODA commitments.
- Grants (included in ODA), of which Technical Co-operation Grants (disbursements data).
- ODA Loans, Net.
- ODA Loans, Gross.
- Other Official (non-concessional) Flows (OOF), gross and net.
- Total official flows, gross and net.

11. In each block within a table, flows from individual DAC Members and multilateral agencies are shown separately along with sub-totals for DAC Members and multilateral agencies, for OPEC donors combined, and for the European Economic Community and its Members combined. The data for OPEC donors are treated as comparable with the figures for DAC Members and multilateral agencies, although there are some differences in the coverage and quality of the data. The total reached in this way excludes financial flows from the IMF (other than loans by the IMF Trust Fund), Member States of the Council for Mutual Economic Assistance (for which commitments and gross disbursements data are however shown separately in the top right hand blocks: see Main Aggregates below), other developing countries, and grants by voluntary private agencies. Loans by banks resident in each DAC Member country are included indistinguishably in the "total receipts net" block. The amount thus included for DAC Members combined falls short of the memorandum figure under Main Aggregates shown for "(bank sector loans)" by the amount of lending out of offshore centres in developing countries.

4 The reader will find in Section A the main aggregates for countries not shown individually in Section B.

Main Aggregates

12. Further data for each recipient country are shown for a number of resource flow aggregates for which detailed information by source is not given in the other blocks of the table. The aggregates have been chosen so as to complete the picture for the country concerned, in terms of the analytical and policy uses of the figures. The additional data cover the main classes of private sector transactions of DAC Member Country residents, the commitments by the official sector of (OOF + ODA), the terms of ODA commitments from DAC Members combined and from all sources, and gross disbursements and commitments by CMEA countries as a group.

Indebtedness

13. The data on debt in this section in principle represent the fullest and most comparable information presently available on the total debt position of each country shown vis-à-vis all its creditors. The figures shown relate to disbursed debt outstanding and debt service (principal and interest payments combined) of each country shown, identifying separately the amounts paid to the main creditor groups (DAC countries, international organisations, CMEA countries, other creditors). For DAC countries, separate data are presented for ODA, export credit, other private market debt and debt service.

14. These data are drawn from:

- The "Creditor Reporting System" (CRS) sponsored by OECD and the World Bank. Under this system, DAC creditors report on officially extended or guaranteed debt of some 150 developing countries and territories, arising from Official Development Assistance, (ODA), Other Official Flows (OOF), (mainly official export credits), and Officially-guaranteed Private Export Credits (OGPEC), extended by DAC countries.
- The World Bank's "Debtor Reporting System" (DRS). Under this system, 97 developing countries report on their external debt to all creditors, incurred or guaranteed by their public sector, usually referred to as "External Public Debt".
- Other sources are used in order to present as complete a picture as possible of the total debt and debt service of all developing countries including, in particular, debt owed by the private sector which is guaranteed in neither the debtor nor the creditor country. This is done by drawing on official data from Central Banks of debtor countries, the World Bank and other Multilateral Development Lending Institutions, the IMF and BIS. The figures for some categories of debt (e.g., non-DAC credits to non-DRS countries) are the Secretariat's estimates.

15. The statistics cover all types of debt, public and private, bilateral and multilateral, concessional and non-concessional. Private flows to developing countries channelled through offshore banking centres are included in the final recipient's debt. The debt shown for developing countries which are "offshore centres" or "flag of convenience" shipping centres refers solely to credits used by the domestic economies of those countries. Debt with an original maturity of under one year and official debt arising from military transactions, in principle, is excluded. Also excluded is debt to the IMF.

16. For the developing countries and territories covered by both the DRS and CRS, for ODA, OOF and OGPEC debt to DAC countries, the CRS figures are usually taken (since they are generally more comprehensive than the corresponding data reported by debtors under the DRS). For private debt to DAC countries, the data from the DRS are taken and complemented by information derived from other sources. For debt to non-DAC countries and to international organisations, the DRS figures are generally taken.

17. For the 53 developing countries and territories not covered by the DRS, the CRS data are used, complemented by information derived from other sources.

18. To avoid double counting of debt and debt service arising, respectively, from export credits and bank loans, the amounts shown under private debt exclude, to the extent possible, OGPEC from banks and other financial institutions. With respect to OGPEC, for several DAC Members the CRS-reported debt includes undisbursed amounts and capitalised interest (to be paid over the lifetime of the credit); adjustments are made to show only the disbursed principal debt. The reader is invited to consult the technical notes to "External Debt of Developing Countries" (OECD, 1982) for further information.

19. In view of the differences in coverage between the debt and resource flow statistics, and the different sources addressed to develop the two sets of data, the net flow estimates that can be derived from the debt aggregates may vary considerably from the net resource flow data shown. The differences may be aggravated by the fact that the debt figures, shown in dollars, are converted at the end-of-year exchange rate, whereas the flow figures are converted at the annual average exchange rate. Work on the methodology of reconciliation is going on.

Economic Indicators

20. These data, which appear in the bottom table of each right-hand panel, can be related to the financial flow statistics and include the following indicators for the years 1977 to 1979 or 1980, depending on availability.

21. All these items are as defined in the source from which the figures are taken (see paragraph 4 above), and to which the reader is referred.

22. The product of the population and GNP per capita figures (Atlas Basis) usually differs from the figure for GNP in current prices. The latter is estimated by converting GNP in national currency to US dollars at the current average exchange rate, and is therefore in the same units as the financial flow data in the body of the table. By contrast, the figures for GNP per capita in US dollars in the World Atlas are estimated by converting national currency GNP in constant (1978/80) prices to US dollars at the average exchange rate for 1978 to 1980. The result of this computation is rebased using the change in the GNP price deflator for the USA between the base period and the year of reference, and divided by the population estimate to obtain GNP per capita. The figure thus reached is the best that can be constructed, given available information, for purposes of ranking countries by per capita income level, but it is not comparable to the ostensibly similar figure derived by converting per capita GNP at current prices to US

INDICATOR	ABBREVIATION	UNITS
Gross National Product current	GNP curr.prices $m.	Million US dollars at current prices and exchange rates
Real Gross National Product	Real GNP 1976=100	Index 1976=100
GNP per capita	GNP/cap curr.prices $	Dollars at current prices and exchange rates
GNP per capita 1978/80	GNP/cap Atlas basis $	1978-80 average prices and exchange rates expressed in US dollars at current prices*
Real GNP per capita	Real GNP/cap 1976=100	1976 = 100
Population	Population	Million
Current account deficit	Curr. A/c. deficit (-)$m.	Million US dollars
Exports and private transfers, balance of payments basis	BOP exp and trans.$m.	Million US dollars
Exports to OECD (cif basis)	Exp. to OECD cif $m.	Million US dollars
(of which) Exports of Manufactures	Manufact.	Million US dollars
Imports from OECD (fob basis)	Imp. from OECD fob $m.	Million US dollars
Reserves less Gold**	Reserves ex. gold $m.	Million US dollars

* The OECD Secretariat is indebted to the World Bank for this information, which was, however, provisional for 1980 at the time of going to press, and in a few instances was complemented by OECD Secretariat estimates. For some countries, therefore, the data shown here may differ from those in World Bank documents.

** Gold, which is officially demonetised, has been omitted in the absence of a standard figure for valuation purposes. Data on each country's holdings in ounces are shown monthly in the IMF's International Financial Statistics, which also includes a separate table in which total reserves are shown.

dollars at the current exchange rate. Population data are mid-year estimates. The deficit on current account excludes government unrequited transfers; DAC practice is to consider these transfers as part of the capital account. Exports to OECD cif are those presented in other OECD reports as OECD imports cif from the countries concerned. Similarly, the figures for imports from OECD are actually those for exports (fob) to the country. Manufactures include SITC items 5 to 9, but exclude pearls, precious stones, pig iron and non-ferrous metals.

Concepts and the Interpretation of Data

23. A note on the main concepts used in this report and remarks on specific particularities of the data will be found at the end of the volume.

Timing of Reporting

24. National data were supplied by Members up to 9th November 1981.

N.B. It is recalled that the DAC list of developing countries is designed for statistical purposes, not as guidance for eligibility for aid or other preferential treatment. The names or geographical classification of countries or territories shown in the publication should be construed as having strictly geographical or functional meaning and do not have political implications or imply any expression of view regarding juridical status. The designation "developing countries" is used as a generic term in its own right which does not carry any special meaning as to the political or legal classification of the recipients concerned.

INTRODUCTION

1. Ce rapport, le deuxième dans une série traitant du volume des ressources financières de provenance étrangère reçues par chaque pays en développement récapitule les données détaillées sur la répartition géographique

- des versements bruts et nets;
- des engagements;
- de l'endettement, du service de la dette, et des conditions dont sont assorties les ressources fournies;

pour chacun d'une centaine de pays en développement au cours de chacune des quatre années 1977 à 1980.

Ces données sont supplées par des données statistiques permettant de rappeler les caractéristiques essentielles de la situation économique et sociale de chaque bénéficiaire, qui devraient permettre d'interpréter les données sur les apports de ressources dans une perspective plus large. L'objet du rapport est de dépeindre, par le biais d'une présentation synthétique en deux pages, un tableau aussi complet que possible de financement externe de chacun des pays étudiés.

2. Les données indiquent l'apport de ressources financières à chaque pays selon leur origine :

i) les pays Membres du CAD, séparément et en groupe
ii) les institutions multilatérales, séparément et en groupe
iii) les Pays membres de l'Organisation des Pays Exportateurs de Pétrole (OPEP) en groupe, et les Pays membres du Conseil d'Assistance économique mutuelle (CAEM), également en groupe.

Les pays Membres du Comité d'Aide au Développement de l'OCDE pour lesquels les données sont présentées sont les suivants : République fédérale d'Allemagne, Australie, Autriche, Belgique, Canada, Danemark, Etats-Unis, Finlande, France, Italie, Japon, Norvège, Nouvelle-Zélande, Pays-Bas, Royaume-Uni, Suède et Suisse. Les données relatives à la Commission des Communautés Européennes, qui est aussi un Membre du CAD, sont comprises dans la rubrique « institutions multilatérales »; par ailleurs, une ligne supplémentaire (« EEC + Members ») présente les données relatives au total des apports en provenance de la CEE elle-même et de ses pays Membres qui font aussi partie du CAD. Les données relatives aux apports financiers provenant de sources multilatérales se rapportent notamment aux organismes suivants : Banque Mondiale, Société Financière Internationale (SFI), Association Internationale de Développement (IDA), Banque Interaméricaine de Développement (BID), Banque Africaine de Développement (B.Af.D.), Fonds Africain de Développement(F.Af.D.), Banque Asiatique de Développement (B.As.D.), Banque Caraïbe de Développement (B.Car.D.), le Fonds International pour le Développement Agricole (FIDA), Fonds Arabe de Développement Economique et Social (FADES), Compte spécial de l'Organisation des pays Arabes Exportateurs de Pétrole (OPAEP), Fonds Arabe Spécial d'Aide à l'Afrique (FASAA), Fonds de l'OPEP pour le Développement International, Fonds Arabe d'Assistance technique aux Pays Arabes et Africains (AFTAAAC), Banque Arabe pour le Développement Economique de l'Afrique (BADEA), Organisation du Golfe pour le Développement de l'Egypte (GODE), Banque Islamique du Développement, Fonds de Solidarité Islamique, et les Organismes d'Assistance technique et de Secours des Nations Unies. Ces derniers comprennent essentiellement les programmes ou organismes suivants : le programme régulier et les autres programmes d'assistance technique des Nations Unies (ATNU), le Programme des Nations Unies pour le Développement (PNUD), le Haut Commissariat des Nations Unies pour les Réfugiés (UNHCR), l'Office de secours et de travaux des Nations Unies pour les réfugiés de Palestine dans le Proche-Orient (UNRWA), le Fonds des Nations Unies pour l'Enfance (FISE) et le Programme Alimentaire Mondial (PAM). Les apports de ressources financières des Membres de l'OPEP sont indiqués globalement pour les pays suivants : Algérie, Arabie Saoudite, Emirats arabes unis, Irak, Iran, Koweit, Libye, Nigeria, Qatar et Venezuela[1]. Les apports en provenance des pays Membres du CAEM sont indiqués globalement pour la Bulgarie, la Tchécoslovaquie, la République Démocratique allemande, la Hongrie, la Pologne, la Roumanie et l'URSS.

3. Pour certaines rubriques, l'ensemble est plus large que celle indiquée plus haut. Ainsi les chiffres relatifs à l'endettement et au service de la dette concernent-ils la totalité des créanciers y compris d'autres pays en développement et « international ». Les chiffres relatifs à la variation des créances du secteur bancaire, donnés pour mémoire (voir Annexe, A16), concernent les pays faisant des déclarations à la Banque des Règlements Internationaux (BRI)[2] ainsi que les affiliés dans des centres « offshore » de banques dont le siège se trouve dans ces pays déclarants.

1 L'Equateur, le Gabon et l'Indonésie, qui sont également les Pays Membres de l'OPEP n'ont fourni aucune aide bilatérale au cours de la période 1977/1980.

2 Tous les Pays membres du CAD, à l'exception de : Australie, Finlande, Norvège et Nouvelle-Zélande.

Sources des données

4. Les chiffres concernant les apports bilatéraux du CAD ont pour origine les réponses des pays Membres aux questionnaires diffusés par le Secrétariat de l'OCDE. Les données sur les apports multilatéraux sont puisées dans les rapports publiés par les institutions intéressées et complétées par des informations supplémentaires communiquées directement par ces institutions. Les chiffres relatif à l'aide bilatérale en provenance des pays Membres de l'OPEP se fondent sur des renseignements qu'ont bien voulu fournir le Fonds d'Abu Dhabi pour le Développement Economique Arabe, le Fonds du Koweit pour le Développement Economique Arabe, le Fonds Saoudien pour le Développement, le General Board for the South and Arabian Gulf, la Banque Centrale du Vénézuela, ainsi que sur certaines informations mises à disposition par les Ministères des Finances du Koweit et des Emirats arabes unis.Ces chiffres ont été complétés par des renseignements en provenance de sources secondaires et par des estimations du Secrétariat de l'OCDE. Dans la mesure du possible, les données présentées pour les pays de l'OPEP et du CAEM ont été classées et traitées conformément aux normes et définitions du CAD[3]. Les données sur les indicateurs économiques sont celles élaborées par la BIRD, supplées en tant que besoin par des estimations du Secrétariat de l'OCDE. De même, le Système de Notification des Débiteurs de la Banque Mondiale représente une source importante qui recouvre une grande partie des informations présentées relatives à l'endettement (voir les alinéas 13 à 19). Les statistiques des réserves et de la balance des paiements sont tirées des bulletins publiés par le FMI, celles du commerce extérieur des déclarations des pays Membres à l'OCDE.

Etendue des chiffres

5. Les données relatives aux apports des ressources financières dans ce rapport sont tirées de soumissions qui recouvrent la quasi-totalité des opérations comprises dans chacune des catégories présentées. Les omissions sont essentiellement les suivantes : *(i)* les données sur les apports de l'OPEP excluent les opérations entreprises par le secteur privé pendant toute la période étudiée et, à partir de 1979, sous-évaluent les apports en provenance du secteur public aux conditions du marché ; *(ii)* les apports en provenance de pays qui ne figurent ni dans la liste de pays en développement du CAD ni dans celle des pays Membres (Afrique du Sud, Irlande, Luxembourg par exemple) ; *(iii)* les apports nets en provenance des pays du CAEM (mais des estimations sont présentées pour les versements bruts et les engagements de ces pays). En outre seules quelques données fragmentaires sont disponibles en ce qui concerne les apports de ressources d'un pays en développement à un autre. Pour l'ensemble des pays en développement, cette dernière catégorie s'auto-annule, puisque le montant d'un apport en provenance d'un pays est le même que celui reçu par son partenaire. Néanmoins, aucun chiffre n'est montré au niveau d'un pays bénéficiaire. En effet, les renseignements disponibles étant incomplets, le chiffre s'il était présenté, risquerait d'être retenu comme correspondant au vrai total. Aussi, la décision a-t-elle été prise d'omettre tout chiffre relatif aux apports de ressources en provenance d'un autre pays en développement jusqu'à ce qu'un niveau satisfaisant de couverture ait été atteint.

3 Voir l'Annexe « Définition des concepts utilisés dans ce rapport ».

Montants non-alloués

6. Un total déclaré dans une source statistique lui-même complet peut comprendre une composante parfois importante « non alloué sur le plan géographique ». Il est vrai qu'une partie des montants déclarés au CAD sous la rubrique « non alloués » appartient réellement à cette catégorie, par exemple les dépenses effectuées dans le pays donneur au titre de la recherche effectuée au profit d'un ensemble des pays en développement (exemple : maladies tropicales). Uneautre partie est à attribuer à des procédés de recensement défectueux. Cependant, la partie la plus importante des montants inscrits dans la catégorie « non alloués » s'y trouve en raison du statut confidentiel des renseignements, les dispositions législatives en vigueur interdisant aux autorités déclarantes de révéler le nom du pays partenaire pour certains types d'opérations. Au niveau de APD et des autres opérations entreprises par le secteur public des pays du CAD et les organismes multilatéraux, les montants qui ne font pas l'objet d'une répartition géographique nominative sont trop petits dans l'ensemble pour créer un risque que le chiffre pour un pays bénéficiaire donné subisse une sous-estimation significative. Toutefois, pour certains pays donneurs de l'OPEP, les montants non-alloués en 1977 et 1979 sont conséquents, et ceci pourrait impliquer une distortion pour certains bénéficiaires. Pour certaines catégories des apports en provenance du secteur privé, et ce plus particulièrement en ce qui concerne les investissements privés directs, il existe le risque que la sous-estimation de l'apport net en provenance d'un pays donneur puisse être relativement important. Ceci est surtout le cas *(a)* des pays où des investissements sont effectués dans le secteur pétrolier *(b)* des pays dont une partie importante des investissements proviennent de pays d'origine dont la notification comporte des montants « non-alloués » importants. Dans cette dernière catégorie se trouve en particulier les déclarations faites par le Canada, le Danemark,la Finlande, la Nouvelle-Zélande, la Suède et la Suisse.

Présentation

7. Le rapport se divise en deux sections :

Section A

8. Cette section contient huit tableaux, chacun se référant aux années 1974 à 1980. Les six premiers tableaux indiquent pour chaque pays en développement (y compris ceux qui ne font pas l'objet d'une page à part dans la suite du document) d'une part, pour l'ensemble des pays du CAD, et d'autre part pour l'ensemble des origines recensées :

i) l'aide publique au développement : versements nets,
ii) l'aide publique au développement : engagements,
iii) l'apport total de ressources : versements nets.

Ils sont suivis de deux tableaux qui présentent pour chaque pays ses apports en provenance des organisations multilatérales de versements nets d'aide à des conditions libérales (« APD multilatérale ») et de versements nets totaux.

Section B

9. Les tableaux de cette section concernent chacun un seul pays en développement[4] et indiquent les ressources qu'il a reçues,

4 Un certain nombre de petits pays bénéficiares ne font pas l'objet d'une page à part. On trouvera les données principales les concernant dans les tableaux de la Section A.

ventilées par type et par donneur, avec des sous-totaux pour les Membres du CAD, les institutions multilatérales et les donneurs de l'OPEP. Ces renseignements complétés par des données sur les pays du CAEM. Les tableaux par pays sont suppléés par une série de tableaux qui présentent dans le même format les totaux ou les moyennes pour certains groupes de pays en développement (voir Annexe A19).

Contenu du rapport

Ventilations détaillées

10. La présentation des pages de la section B est normalisée. Chaque couple de pages contient dans la section de gauche et la section centrale des tableaux où sont ventilées les catégories d'apports suivantes par sources :*

- APD, brut et net.
- APD, engagements.
- Dons (inclus dans l'APD), y compris : dons de coopération technique (versements).
- Prêts d'APD, nets.
- Prêts d'APD, brut.
- Autres apports du secteur public (AASP) (aux conditions du marché) bruts et nets.
- Apports totaux du secteur public (bruts et nets).

11. Dans chaque pavé de ces deux sections, les apports des différents Membres du CAD et des institutions multilatérales sont indiqués séparément, avec des sous-totaux concernant respectivement les Membres du CAD, l'ensemble des Membres de l'OPEP, l'ensemble des institutions multilatérales, et la Communauté Economique Européenne et ses Membres en tant qu'ensemble. Les données relatives aux pays de l'OPEP ont été élaborées sur la même base que les données relatives aux pays du CAD et des institutions multilatérales bien que la couverture et la qualité de ces données soient quelque peu différentes. Le montant total obtenu de cette façon ne comprend ni les apports financiers en provenance du FMI (à part les prêts du «fonds fiduciaire» (Trust Fund), ni ceux des états membres du Conseil pour l'Assistance Economique Mutuelle (pour lesquels, toutefois, les données relatives aux engagements et versements bruts sont présentées dans le pavé du haut à droite : voir Principaux aggrégats ci-dessous), ni les apports d'autres pays en développement, ni les dons versés par des organismes bénévoles du secteur privé. Les prêts consentis par les banques ayant la qualité de résident dans chaque pays Membre du CAD sont inclus indistinctement dans les données du pavé «apports totaux nets reçus». Toutefois, le montant ainsi inclus pour l'ensemble du CAD est inférieur aux chiffres apparemment correspondants dans le pavé «aggrégats principaux» relatifs aux prêts du secteur bancaire («Bank Sector Loans»); en effet, cette dernière rubrique comprend également les prêts bancaires consentis à partir des Centres offshore dans des pays en développement.

Principaux aggrégats

12. Le pavé «principaux aggrégats» présente, pour chaque pays étudié, des renseignements supplémentaires relatifs à certaines catégories significatives d'apports qui ne sont pas ventilés en détail dans les autres pavés. Les rubriques ont été choisies de manière à compléter les renseignements relatifs aux différents pays, eu égard à l'utilisation des données à des fins analytiques ou pour la mise en œuvre de politiques de coopération. Les données supplémentaires concernent les types principaux d'opérations entreprises par des résidents des pays Membres du CAD relevant du secteur privé; les engagements (APD+AASP) souscrits par le secteur public; les conditions dont sont assortis les engagements totaux du secteur public ou d'APD souscrits soit par l'ensemble des pays du CAD, soit par l'ensemble des sources d'aide, et les versements bruts et engagements en provenance des pays du CAEM en tant que groupe.

Endettement

13. Les données présentées dans cette section constituent en principe un ensemble de renseignements sur la situation de l'endettement de chaque pays étudié envers la totalité de ses créanciers, le plus complet et le plus comparable actuellement disponible. Les chiffres portent sur l'encours de la dette versée (c'est-à-dire non compris les montants qui ne deviendront exigibles que lorsque les versements en attente sur des engagements déjà souscrits auront été effectués) et le service de la dette (total des remboursements du principal et des versements d'intérêts) de chaque pays étudié. Sont présentés séparément les créances des pays et le service de la dette versé aux principaux-groupes de créanciers (pays du CAD, institutions internationales, pays du CAEM, autres créanciers). Par ailleurs, pour les pays du CAD, des rubriques séparées sont consacrées respectivement à l'APD, les crédits à l'exportation et l'ensemble de la dette autre qu'au titre des crédits à l'exportation envers le marché privé (dette et service de la dette).

14. Les statistiques d'endettement présentées dans les tableaux proviennent de deux sources principales :

- Le «Système de notification des pays créditeurs» (SNPC). Dans le cadre de ce système, les pays du CAD créanciers notifient les données sur la dette contractée par environ 150 pays et territoires en développement au titre de crédits accordés ou garantis par le secteur public des pays du CAD : APD, autres apports du secteur public (essentiellement crédits publics à l'exportation) et crédits privés à l'exportation garantis par le secteur public (CPEG).

- Le «Système de notification des pays débiteurs» (SNPD) de la Banque Mondiale : dans le cadre de ce système 97 pays en développement notifient les données sur leur dette publique et celle garantie par le secteur public envers tous les pays créanciers; cette dette est habituellement appelée «Dette extérieure publique».

- En outre, pour présenter un tableau aussi complet que possible du total de la dette et du service de la dette de tous les pays en développement, y compris leur dette privée ne bénéficiant d'une garantie ni dans le pays débiteur ni dans le pays créancier, le Secrétariat a utilisé les autres sources d'informations que constituent les données officielles des banques centrales des pays débiteurs, celles de la Banque Mondiale et des autres organisations multilatérales de prêt en faveur du développement, ainsi que celles du FMI et de la BRI.

* Du fait que la totalité des tableaux a été élaborée en recourant à un système de photocomposition, il n'a pas été possible de préparer un document bilingue. Le lecteur trouvera le texte français des tableaux sur la dépliante à l'avant-dernière page de ce document.

Le Secrétariat a en outre établi des estimations pour certaines catégories de dette (notamment les crédits octroyés par des pays non Membres du CAD à des pays non couverts par le SNPD).

15. Les statistiques couvrent tous les types de dettes, c'est-à-dire la dette publique et privée, la dette bilatérale et multilatérale, la dette contractée à des conditions libérales et aux conditions du marché. Les chiffres comprennent la dette due aux pays en développement qui font office de centres bancaires « offshore » ou de centres de pavillons de complaisance. En revanche, l'endettement de ces pays n'est répercuté dans les données présentées que dans la mesure où il résulte de crédits utilisés par l'économie intérieure des intéressés. Les prêts à échéance initiale de moins d'un an et la dette publique résultant de transactions militaires sont en principe exclus de ces statistiques. Est également exclue la dette envers le FMI.

16. A ce jour, 96 pays et territoires en développement sont couverts à la fois par le SNPC et le SNPD. En ce qui concerne la dette contractée envers les pays du CAD au titre de l'APD, des autres apports du secteur public et des crédits privés à l'exportation garantis par le secteur public, le Secrétariat a habituellement retenu les chiffres du SNPC (puisqu'ils sont en général plus complets que les données correspondantes notifiées par les débiteurs dans le cadre du SNPD). Dans le cas de la dette privée contractée envers les pays du CAD, le Secrétariat a utilisé les chiffres provenant du SNPD en les complétant par des renseignements provenant d'autres sources. Dans le cas de la dette envers les pays non Membres du CAD et envers les organismes internationaux, ce sont normalement les chiffres du SNPD qui sont retenus.

17. Pour les 53 pays et territoires en développement non couverts par le SNPD, on a utilisé les données du SNPC en les complétant par des renseignements provenant d'autres sources.

18. Pour éviter un double comptage de la dette et du service de la dette au titre respectivement des crédits à l'exportation et des prêts bancaires, on a fait en sorte, dans la mesure du possible, que les montants figurant au titre de dette envers des créanciers privés, ne comprennent pas les crédits privés à l'exportation garantis par le secteur public (CPEG), accordés par les banques et autres organismes financiers. En ce qui concerne les CPEG, les données notifiées dans le cadre du SNPC sur la dette comprennent, dans le cas de plusieurs pays Membres du CAD, les montants non versés et les intérêts sur le capital (à payer pendant toute la durée du crédit) : un ajustement a été opéré afin de présenter une estimation du seul principal versé. Pour plus de détails, le lecteur consultera utilement « La Dette externe des Pays en Développement », OCDE, 1981.

19. Eu égard à la différence de couverture des statistiques relatives respectivement à la dette et aux apports de ressources, ainsi qu'aux sources différentes utilisées dans l'élaboration des deux ensembles de données, les estimations de l'apport net que l'on peut établir à partir des chiffres de l'endettement ne coïncident pas avec les données élaborées à partir du recensement direct de cet apport net. Les écarts peuvent être importants, et parfois sont aggravés par le fait que les données sur l'encours de la dette, présentées en dollars, ont été converties au taux en vigueur à la fin de l'année, alors que les statistiques relatives aux apports sont converties en appliquant le taux moyen annuel. Des études

INDICATEUR	ABREVIATION	UNITES
PNB	GNP curr. prices $ m.	Millions de dollars aux prix et taux de change courants
PNB réel	Real GNP 1976=100	Indice 1976=100
PNB par habitant	GNP/cap curr. prices $	Dollars, aux prix et aux taux de change courants
PNB par habitant	GNP/cap Atlas basis $	Prix et taux de change moyen 1978-1980 exprimés en dollars aux prix des Etats-Unis de l'année concernée*
PNB réel par habitant	Real GNP/cap 1976=100	Indice 1976=100
Population	Population	Millions
Compte courant, déficit	Curr. A/c deficit (-) $ m.	Millions de dollars
Exportations et transferts privés, selon la balance des paiements	BOP exp and transf. $ m.	Millions de dollars
Exportations vers l'OCDE (cif)	Exp. to OECD cif $ m.	Millions de dollars
(dont) Exportations de produits manufacturés	Manufact.	Millions de dollars
Importations en provenance de l'OCDE (fob)	Imp. from OECD fob $ m.	Millions de dollars
Réserves de change hormis l'or**	Reserves ex. gold	Millions de dollars

* Le Secrétariat de l'OCDE exprime sa gratitude à la Banque Mondiale d'avoir bien voulu lui communiquer ces données, qui étaient toutefois provisoires en ce qui concerne les valeurs pour l'année 1980 au moment de la mise sous presse. Dans un nombre limité de cas, par ailleurs, le Secrétariat de l'OCDE a complété les renseignements de la banque Mondiale par ses propres estimations. Ainsi, pour certains pays, les données dans le présent rapport ne seront pas identiques à celles que le lecteur trouverait dans des documents publiés par la Banque Mondiale.

** L'or, qui a été démonétisé, a été omis de cette ligne en raison de la non-disponibilité d'une base d'évaluation normalisée. Le Bulletin Mensuel du FMI International Financial Statistics présente des chiffres pour la quantité d'or, exprimée en ounces, détenus par chaque pays. Par ailleurs, un tableau spécial dans ce bulletin présente des estimations des réserves totales, y compris l'or.

sont actuellement en cours en vue d'élaborer une méthode permettant la reconciliation des deux ensembles de données.

Indicateurs économiques

20. Ces données qui sont portées dans le pavé en bas et à droite de chaque tableau peuvent être rapprochées des statistiques sur les apports financiers et comprennent les indicateurs suivants pour les années 1977 à 1979 ou 1980, selon la disponibilité des renseignements statistiques.

21. Tous ces chiffres sont calculés conformément aux définitions de la source dont ils sont tirés (voir paragraphe 6 ci-dessus) et auxquels le lecteur pourra utilement se référer.

22. Le chiffre obtenu en multipliant la population par le PNB par habitant tiré de l'Atlas de la Banque Mondiale diffère d'habitude du chiffre du PNB exprimé aux prix courants. Ce dernier est une estimation calculée en convertissant en dollars des Etats-Unis, au taux de change moyen courant, le PNB exprimé en monnaie nationale ; il est donc exprimé dans la même unité que les données sur les apports financiers qui figurent dans les autres pavés du tableau. En revanche, le chiffre du PNB par habitant en dollars des Etats-Unis dans l'Atlas est estimé en convertissant le PNB aux prix de la période 1978/80 en monnaie nationale en dollars des Etats-Unis au taux de change moyen de la période. Le résultat de ce calcul est exprimé aux prix de l'année de référence à partir de la variation de l'indice implicite des prix du PNB observée aux Etats-Unis entre la période de base et l'année de référence. Il est ensuite divisé par le nombre d'habitants, donnant ainsi le PNB par tête présenté dans les tableaux. Le chiffre final ainsi obtenu est le meilleur que l'on puisse calculer, avec les informations disponibles, si l'on souhaite classer les pays en fonction du niveau de revenu par habitant, mais il n'est pas comparable au chiffre, à première vue analogue, que l'on obtient en convertissant en dollars des Etats-Unis, au taux de change courant, le PNB aux prix courants. Les données relatives à la population se rapportent à la situation en mi-année. Le solde du compte courant est calculé compte non tenu des transferts gouvernementaux effectués sans contrepartie. En effet, ces transferts sont assimilés dans la pratique du CAD à des transferts sur compte capital. Les exportations vers l'OCDE (c.a.f.) sont les données statistiques qui apparaissent dans d'autres rapports de l'OCDE sous l'intitulé « importations (c.a.f.) de l'OCDE en provenance de.... ». De même, les chiffres présentés pour les importations d'un pays en provenance de l'OCDE sont les données déclarées (f.o.b.) par les pays de l'OCDE relatives à leurs exportations vers ce pays. A noter que la rubrique « manufactures » correspond aux rubriques 5 à 9 du C.T.C.I., à l'exclusion des perles, pierres précieuses, fonte et métaux non ferreux.

Concepts utilisés dans ce rapport et interprétation des données

23. Le lecteur trouvera en fin de volume une note qui récapitule les principaux concepts utilisés, ainsi que des remarques portant sur des aspects particuliers des données contenues dans le rapport.

Date de notification

24. Les données nationales ont été fournies par les Pays Membres jusqu'au 9 novembre 1981.

N.B. Il est rappelé que la liste des pays en développement adoptée par le CAD est destinée à servir des fins purement statistiques, et non à orienter le choix des pays pouvant bénéficier d'une aide ou d'un autre traitement préférentiel. Les noms ou le classement géographique des pays ou territoires mentionnés dans cette publication doivent être pris au sens strictement géographique ou fonctionnel ; ils n'ont aucune signification politique et ne reflètent aucune opinion sur le statut juridique desdits pays ou territoires. L'expression « pays en développement » est utilisée comme une appellation générique à laquelle ne s'attache aucun sens particulier pour ce qui est de la catégorie politique ou juridique dans laquelle se classent les bénéficiaires en cause.

SECTION A

BASIC SUMMARY TABLES

TABLEAUX RESUMES DE BASE

	1974	1975	1976	1977	1978	1979	1980
EUROPE							
Cyprus	6.1	4.9	19.9	49.3	24.3	16.5	30.9
Gibraltar	6.6	3.0	3.0	4.5	3.5	6.5	11.2
Greece	-16.3	7.6	-15.1	5.4	60.2	5.5	19.5
Malta	15.1	29.9	26.2	19.1	27.2	3.3	2.8
Portugal	-2.0	-4.7	57.3	88.7	65.7	122.0	108.1
Spain	-10.1	-12.4	-7.4	1.4	9.9	-7.0	21.7
Turkey	27.9	23.7	31.3	24.9	154.0	458.8	713.8
Yugoslavia	62.0	24.1	29.6	5.0	-47.7	-32.0	-19.4
Europe Unallocated	4.5	6.6	6.8	5.7	7.5	8.7	5.4
TOTAL	*93.8*	*82.8*	*151.5*	*203.9*	*304.6*	*582.1*	*893.9*
NORTH OF SAHARA							
Algeria	100.7	106.4	128.8	112.7	118.8	97.6	117.6
Egypt	105.9	249.7	428.1	617.0	860.2	1011.6	1187.0
Libya	10.4	0.5	6.4	5.3	4.0	1.9	9.9
Morocco	81.7	170.9	147.4	158.7	180.4	168.8	187.8
Tunisia	123.8	113.7	150.5	164.2	252.7	151.1	157.7
North of Sahara Unall.	16.3	6.0	6.2	6.2	8.2	14.9	3.0
TOTAL	*438.8*	*647.2*	*867.4*	*1064.1*	*1424.3*	*1445.9*	*1663.0*
SOUTH OF SAHARA							
Angola	0.3	4.0	10.6	7.9	28.9	29.4	35.8
Benin	18.5	29.1	27.5	26.6	30.3	48.6	35.7
Botswana	29.9	38.5	40.6	38.1	55.1	73.6	83.5
Burundi	18.7	26.4	25.9	28.8	38.6	44.1	59.7
Cameroon	48.0	64.6	88.0	122.5	117.2	183.8	171.4
Cape Verde	–	2.1	6.8	15.8	25.0	27.2	39.0
Central African Rep.	18.6	33.3	25.7	30.2	29.7	51.2	75.1
Chad	37.9	28.2	43.2	49.6	70.9	49.4	20.2
Comoros	27.1	17.5	8.4	1.8	1.8	6.3	13.4
Congo	21.3	38.1	46.0	32.7	44.7	50.1	55.4
Djibouti	28.3	34.1	28.1	32.7	29.3	19.0	32.0
Equatorial Guinea	–	–	–	–	–	0.1	1.2
Ethiopia	79.8	72.9	72.8	59.0	56.0	70.5	91.4
Gabon	22.8	37.6	30.3	23.6	36.9	26.8	49.1
Gambia	3.7	3.5	5.4	12.6	14.8	13.2	16.5
Ghana	25.7	104.4	34.0	52.0	57.2	88.6	107.1
Guinea	6.7	5.5	4.4	5.1	9.9	14.2	32.5
Guinea-Bissau	0.1	8.1	11.8	26.1	36.8	33.9	34.4
Ivory Coast	51.6	71.7	75.6	75.2	85.7	138.6	151.9
Kenya	99.4	104.4	137.0	121.2	186.7	283.8	276.6
Lesotho	12.6	14.7	18.0	20.7	29.1	43.7	59.6
Liberia	7.2	10.7	21.2	21.7	22.0	30.4	60.0
Madagascar	31.0	34.4	29.2	32.6	39.6	73.5	90.8
Malawi	30.5	47.1	46.2	54.1	56.4	92.0	75.6
Mali	60.2	55.7	53.3	60.9	93.0	93.9	131.4
Mauritania	25.5	12.8	17.8	24.8	39.6	35.4	53.5
Mauritius	14.6	15.6	10.7	12.5	18.1	24.3	25.2
Mayotte	–	–	–	6.9	12.9	18.2	22.7
Mozambique	0.6	11.5	34.3	65.9	75.3	114.3	114.8
Niger	82.6	80.2	80.1	59.4	77.7	116.7	105.0
Nigeria	56.0	67.0	46.3	28.7	23.7	10.6	17.3
Reunion	210.0	250.8	301.0	317.0	371.4	391.8	486.7
Rwanda	31.6	53.7	56.6	61.4	78.9	88.4	96.6
St. Helena	2.6	2.8	2.8	4.2	7.1	8.4	8.8
Sao Tome & Principe	–	0.0	0.8	1.6	1.8	1.4	1.2
Senegal	62.8	83.0	81.6	89.3	121.6	148.8	181.9
Seychelles	8.4	7.3	6.9	10.2	15.8	22.0	18.3
Sierra Leone	4.5	9.8	7.5	12.0	13.5	28.2	56.8
Somalia	7.3	23.3	20.1	25.2	46.8	49.8	139.4
Sudan	33.2	60.2	54.4	55.8	113.0	149.3	271.6
Swaziland	11.9	8.4	9.0	21.6	33.1	31.8	32.5
Tanzania	140.2	234.7	212.0	257.3	332.3	457.4	523.1
Togo	23.0	23.5	20.5	42.4	66.5	68.9	52.1
Uganda	6.8	4.7	9.6	3.8	7.5	16.1	42.3
Upper Volta	50.2	53.1	60.1	71.7	96.6	132.0	151.1
Zaire	153.1	154.1	148.7	170.9	204.0	288.7	316.8
Zambia	52.1	67.5	55.6	95.5	164.5	211.9	233.8
Zimbabwe	1.6	3.9	6.2	6.7	8.5	12.4	110.4
East African Community	16.0	21.9	19.2	6.7	12.5	3.4	5.5
DOM/TOM Unallocated	-17.6	3.1	0.8	24.9	–	–	–
EAMA Unallocated	85.1	83.7	4.6	85.7	123.4	130.1	94.7
South of Sahara Unall.	13.9	14.0	71.6	34.9	53.6	51.9	48.8
TOTAL	*1755.8*	*2236.9*	*2228.5*	*2548.3*	*3315.4*	*4198.0*	*5009.9*
Africa Unspecified	46.3	39.9	42.0	71.1	95.5	114.4	141.5
AFRICA TOTAL	***2240.8***	***2924.1***	***3137.8***	***3683.5***	***4835.2***	***5758.4***	***6814.4***
N.& C. AMERICA							
Bahamas	0.1	0.1	0.1	0.2	0.1	0.3	0.2
Barbados	3.0	2.7	4.0	3.2	7.6	4.0	2.0
Belize	4.7	6.6	8.5	5.8	11.7	20.3	11.0

	1974	197
Bermuda	0.0	0.
Costa Rica	14.0	17.
Cuba	11.6	14.
Dominican Republic	11.1	16.
El Salvador	7.7	11.
Guadeloupe	99.2	143.
Guatemala	20.3	26.
Haiti	9.4	24.
Honduras	14.5	28.
Jamaica	18.9	18.
Martinique	104.6	160.
Mexico	16.2	9.
Netherlands Antilles	25.1	21.
Nicaragua	23.8	18.
Panama	13.9	20.
St. Pierre & Miquelon	8.2	15.
Trinidad & Tobago	2.2	3.
Anguilla	–	1.
Antigua	2.7	1.
Cayman Islands	1.6	0.
Dominica	2.7	3.
Grenada	1.5	1.
Montserrat	2.6	4.
St. Kitts-Nevis	3.5	1.
St. Lucia	6.9	7.
St. Vincent	3.3	5.
Turks & Caicos Isl.	2.4	3.
Virgin Islands (BR)	1.6	2.
West Indies Unall.	1.1	7.
DOM/TOM Unallocated	–	
N.& C. America Unall.	6.9	12.
TOTAL	*445.3*	*610.*
SOUTH AMERICA		
Argentina	12.3	5.
Bolivia	37.0	32.
Brazil	118.0	115.
Chile	8.8	104.
Colombia	70.5	61.
Ecuador	21.0	25.
Falkland Islands	2.8	3.
Guiana, French	43.6	44.
Guyana	8.6	7.
Paraguay	15.3	12.
Peru	62.5	53.
Surinam	42.5	48.
Uruguay	1.8	1.
Venezuela	2.1	1.
South America Unall.	7.6	13.
TOTAL	*454.3*	*530.*
America Unspecified	67.3	65.
AMERICA TOTAL	***966.8***	***1206.***
MIDDLE EAST		
Bahrain	0.7	0.
Iran	1.4	-16.
Iraq	0.4	30.
Israel	115.1	466.
Jordan	64.8	108.
Kuwait	0.1	0.
Lebanon	5.4	6.
Oman	0.5	0.
Qatar	–	0.
Saudi Arabia	1.3	0.
Syria	5.5	22.
United Arab Emirates	0.1	0.
Yemen	27.4	15.
Yemen, Dem.	5.0	6.
Middle East Unall.	8.3	11.
TOTAL	*235.9*	*651.*
SOUTH ASIA		
Afghanistan	16.9	32.
Bangladesh	344.2	703.
Bhutan	0.3	0.
Burma	60.0	29.
India	602.2	819.
Maldives	0.2	2.
Nepal	20.5	28.
Pakistan	265.2	375.
Sri Lanka	58.2	100.
Indus Basin	21.8	12.

1976	1977	1978	1979	1980
0.0	0.0	0.0	0.0	0.1
11.7	14.5	34.1	25.5	22.8
26.0	29.7	17.4	23.9	11.1
20.0	10.5	9.4	36.8	57.2
12.8	20.0	26.3	26.6	49.5
162.6	157.6	188.7	231.3	85.0
43.7	37.2	26.3	33.5	33.5
32.1	39.6	49.8	48.5	62.8
23.0	22.9	33.9	41.7	47.7
17.9	22.7	97.8	80.6	83.5
187.3	201.7	232.6	294.9	563.8
9.9	5.8	8.4	49.4	55.0
44.7	39.5	44.5	54.0	86.9
18.6	18.7	26.5	73.8	116.6
27.4	22.9	18.7	17.7	18.3
13.9	19.8	20.5	27.8	27.9
2.5	0.7	0.7	0.5	1.4
1.1	1.1	2.3	2.3	2.3
2.6	4.4	2.7	3.1	2.6
1.0	1.0	0.5	0.6	1.0
2.1	3.5	6.1	8.3	8.4
1.4	2.1	0.7	0.4	0.5
3.1	2.9	1.2	1.3	3.1
1.9	1.3	1.6	1.6	2.7
5.0	2.7	1.3	1.8	2.7
3.6	2.7	3.9	5.5	2.0
3.7	3.4	2.7	2.2	2.9
2.5	2.0	1.1	1.7	2.9
3.1	1.2	3.0	3.9	6.6
–	–	-0.3	–	–
29.9	26.9	15.4	14.0	12.6
727.6	*727.9*	*897.0*	*1137.3*	*1386.4*
6.6	8.9	9.8	18.4	32.1
45.7	57.6	85.6	105.3	99.0
78.1	57.8	75.7	53.8	58.3
4.6	2.2	-14.0	-34.7	-13.2
57.7	31.4	51.7	29.4	31.8
37.2	22.9	23.5	50.0	23.3
2.7	2.0	4.1	1.9	2.3
61.8	85.1	77.6	90.7	109.3
9.6	7.1	17.7	15.8	12.5
17.5	25.2	20.8	16.7	25.3
54.3	72.4	120.1	175.1	176.6
101.5	87.3	62.3	93.1	77.1
2.9	2.1	2.2	4.4	5.3
-16.6	-10.4	-18.4	5.9	15.1
18.4	15.7	18.7	18.9	5.3
482.1	*467.0*	*537.3*	*644.7*	*659.9*
53.3	49.2	53.4	60.1	62.1
1262.9	**1244.1**	**1487.6**	**1842.1**	**2108.4**
0.7	0.9	0.9	0.8	0.7
-16.4	25.8	93.7	4.1	30.8
5.8	69.7	40.0	13.2	5.7
640.9	797.0	899.4	1184.4	892.1
118.9	106.9	119.0	93.3	96.3
0.2	0.4	0.6	0.5	7.5
13.3	28.0	22.1	18.3	24.9
0.7	0.6	0.6	0.9	1.8
0.9	0.2	0.1	0.1	0.4
0.5	2.2	2.5	7.1	8.9
38.3	45.6	35.1	89.2	61.7
0.6	1.3	0.6	5.5	1.7
11.3	34.2	37.1	51.0	78.5
9.0	6.9	12.9	4.7	4.1
12.7	14.2	19.3	26.2	3.1
837.3	*1133.7*	*1283.9*	*1499.3*	*1218.1*
34.8	27.6	32.0	47.0	11.4
319.8	384.0	666.5	775.0	850.4
1.0	0.6	0.7	1.2	1.7
39.2	54.6	156.8	259.1	231.3
725.3	481.6	670.2	769.0	633.4
0.6	1.2	3.7	0.9	1.9
29.2	37.5	39.7	82.4	84.0
352.2	321.8	379.4	417.8	339.2
94.9	119.4	216.3	232.0	296.1
33.0	-3.0	-3.0	-3.0	-3.0

	1974	1975	1976	1977	1978	1979	1980
South Asia Unall.	2.3	4.8	3.3	3.5	4.2	6.4	1.0
TOTAL	*1391.8*	*2109.1*	*1633.4*	*1428.7*	*2166.5*	*2587.7*	*2447.3*
FAR EAST ASIA							
Brunei	0.1	0.1	0.1	0.1	0.1	0.1	0.0
China	–	–	–	–	–	4.3	22.2
Hong Kong	0.8	-1.4	2.5	2.0	2.1	3.2	3.6
Indonesia	539.8	526.6	523.7	398.9	541.0	631.8	844.2
Kampuchea	305.5	79.7	0.5	0.2	0.2	25.0	48.6
Korea, Rep.	220.7	213.3	181.1	171.7	136.1	99.8	117.3
Laos	57.3	32.6	24.0	26.7	42.6	26.4	16.7
Macao	–	–	–	–	–	0.0	0.1
Malaysia	63.0	92.9	57.1	59.2	66.8	90.3	106.2
Philippines	132.9	160.1	161.0	143.9	164.7	170.4	205.4
Singapore	19.7	10.0	10.0	11.3	5.2	3.8	9.4
Taiwan	-17.6	-19.6	-20.6	-16.9	-14.1	-14.1	-4.6
Thailand	63.5	70.9	70.8	83.6	149.2	279.3	305.0
Viet Nam, Soc. Rep.	702.1	279.9	160.9	200.0	208.3	229.5	151.9
Mekong Delta Project	4.0	7.1	0.3	0.3	0.9	0.5	–
Far East Asia Unall.	17.1	35.9	15.4	24.7	31.6	36.8	13.8
TOTAL	*2108.9*	*1488.2*	*1187.2*	*1105.7*	*1334.6*	*1587.5*	*1840.4*
Asia Unspecified	24.9	29.4	40.4	15.3	25.6	57.4	61.0
ASIA TOTAL	***3761.4***	***4278.2***	***3697.9***	***3683.4***	***4810.5***	***5731.5***	***5566.3***
OCEANIA							
Cook Islands	5.6	5.4	6.5	7.3	6.7	7.3	9.9
Fiji	14.1	17.8	20.9	19.4	24.0	25.9	31.7
Kiribati	5.5	5.5	3.8	6.0	10.0	8.8	18.6
Nauru	–	0.0	–	0.0	–	0.0	0.0
New Caledonia	62.1	64.7	46.5	76.6	114.3	148.1	197.7
Niue Island	2.9	2.3	2.8	3.3	4.1	4.8	3.4
Pacific Islands (U.S.)	75.1	81.1	89.1	91.1	100.6	111.1	108.5
Papua New Guinea	257.5	297.5	232.3	241.4	270.9	269.4	286.8
Polynesia, French	36.1	71.0	77.1	83.0	90.6	143.9	159.5
Solomon Islands (Br.)	11.6	21.6	18.9	16.0	24.1	23.1	31.0
Tokelau Islands	0.9	0.2	1.2	1.2	0.9	1.8	1.8
Tonga	2.9	2.9	3.7	4.9	8.0	20.4	13.0
Tuvalu	–	–	2.9	2.4	2.5	4.1	4.5
Vanuatu	15.9	12.1	30.5	12.6	18.4	37.7	43.3
Wallis & Futuna	4.8	1.9	4.8	3.6	2.5	7.7	8.3
Western Samoa	4.3	8.8	7.3	11.1	11.3	20.7	13.7
Tom Oceania Unall.	0.5	0.6	–	8.3	21.4	–	–
Oceania Unallocated	2.5	3.7	3.4	5.3	23.6	9.5	16.4
TOTAL	*502.3*	*597.0*	*551.4*	*593.3*	*733.8*	*844.1*	*948.2*
LDC's Unspecified	665.7	704.6	702.6	672.3	951.8	1159.2	1309.2
TOTAL,ALL LDC'S	***8230.9***	***9793.3***	***9504.1***	***10080.5***	***13123.4***	***15917.5***	***17640.3***
INCOME GROUPS							
LLDCS	1181.7	1747.4	1351.8	1533.0	2196.6	2729.2	3222.2
OTHER LICS	3125.2	3086.2	2932.6	2910.9	3984.0	4877.6	5301.7
CHINA	–	–	–	–	–	4.3	22.2
MICS	2365.7	3342.7	3643.0	3973.2	4863.2	6077.7	6636.4
NICS	403.7	346.8	332.0	340.9	311.4	302.8	401.0
OPEC11	160.2	185.4	177.8	253.5	302.3	212.7	270.0
UNALLOCATED	994.5	1084.9	1067.0	1068.9	1466.0	1713.3	1786.8

	1974	1975	1976	1977	1978	1979	1980
EUROPE							
Cyprus	21.3	30.7	56.9	95.9	48.7	29.8	52.6
Gibraltar	6.6	3.0	3.0	4.5	3.5	6.5	11.2
Greece	-14.5	9.4	-12.6	6.6	62.0	40.4	40.1
Malta	21.1	33.7	30.2	19.8	27.6	26.5	16.3
Portugal	-2.0	-2.6	62.7	109.6	67.8	136.1	112.1
Spain	-9.1	-11.5	-6.4	1.7	10.4	-4.1	23.3
Turkey	50.1	83.1	137.5	93.4	178.0	584.8	1002.5
Yugoslavia	63.9	25.6	31.2	7.0	-45.0	-29.2	-16.9
Europe Unallocated	4.5	7.1	6.8	5.8	11.2	12.7	6.6
TOTAL	*142.0*	*178.5*	*309.3*	*344.1*	*364.2*	*803.4*	*1247.7*
NORTH OF SAHARA							
Algeria	127.9	175.5	136.9	124.6	132.5	104.5	178.8
Egypt	1014.2	2417.6	1828.8	2627.8	2266.9	1433.3	1387.5
Libya	13.6	4.6	10.3	11.1	11.8	4.8	16.7
Morocco	114.9	273.6	209.4	273.9	276.4	623.2	654.5
Tunisia	159.3	210.7	210.1	202.2	290.4	219.2	233.2
North of Sahara Unall.	16.3	6.1	6.3	6.3	8.2	15.0	3.1
TOTAL	*1446.2*	*3088.1*	*2401.9*	*3246.0*	*2986.2*	*2399.9*	*2473.8*
SOUTH OF SAHARA							
Angola	0.4	4.8	17.7	47.7	47.0	47.1	52.6
Benin	33.2	54.4	51.9	48.7	61.1	84.6	90.4
Botswana	36.6	51.3	47.6	47.5	69.0	99.7	106.1
Burundi	37.5	48.1	44.5	48.2	74.5	94.8	117.2
Cameroon	62.3	125.3	134.2	175.6	177.7	269.9	266.4
Cape Verde	–	8.7	24.1	26.4	33.2	33.4	64.4
Central African Rep.	36.7	56.8	38.1	42.1	57.3	88.9	111.0
Chad	79.1	65.2	62.3	83.1	119.0	79.6	35.3
Comoros	27.3	21.7	25.7	17.2	12.4	16.7	42.4
Congo	38.0	56.4	73.0	48.6	81.1	85.6	92.1
Djibouti	29.1	34.4	28.1	46.2	96.2	23.2	145.5
Equatorial Guinea	15.9	2.2	0.4	0.9	0.6	2.7	9.3
Ethiopia	121.1	134.5	140.5	114.1	139.5	174.4	211.8
Gabon	24.6	63.4	34.0	27.6	43.9	36.7	55.8
Gambia	10.3	8.1	11.9	24.0	35.2	36.4	54.4
Ghana	36.6	125.6	64.0	91.2	113.9	168.8	191.6
Guinea	29.9	15.2	12.0	22.4	60.3	54.5	89.4
Guinea-Bissau	3.3	18.6	22.5	37.7	50.1	52.7	59.5
Ivory Coast	76.0	100.6	108.2	106.3	131.4	161.5	210.3
Kenya	117.6	128.6	161.7	162.6	247.5	350.6	396.2
Lesotho	20.9	30.1	30.1	38.8	50.1	64.2	90.3
Liberia	15.6	21.1	26.9	33.7	48.0	80.8	97.9
Madagascar	62.8	84.9	63.2	61.1	90.9	128.0	200.2
Malawi	41.7	63.8	63.3	79.4	98.5	141.8	143.4
Mali	117.7	144.7	89.0	112.8	161.6	193.4	252.1
Mauritania	88.4	58.8	167.5	164.7	216.7	178.6	159.3
Mauritius	25.1	29.1	17.1	22.4	43.8	32.2	33.0
Mayotte	–	–	–	6.9	12.9	18.2	22.7
Mozambique	0.7	20.5	69.9	80.3	105.1	155.7	159.1
Niger	136.9	140.0	129.3	96.8	156.5	173.5	170.2
Nigeria	73.4	82.1	53.4	42.8	42.7	26.8	35.7
Reunion	214.1	259.6	307.9	319.0	376.9	392.9	495.1
Rwanda	46.6	90.8	79.3	95.9	125.3	148.3	155.3
St. Helena	2.6	2.8	2.8	4.2	7.1	8.4	8.8
Sao Tome & Principe	–	0.8	11.7	3.1	4.1	3.1	3.9
Senegal	138.9	132.7	126.8	123.0	226.8	307.4	263.0
Seychelles	8.5	7.5	7.4	10.9	16.5	25.2	21.7
Sierra Leone	10.5	18.1	15.1	26.2	40.2	53.2	88.6
Somalia	81.5	150.9	108.8	255.7	196.7	207.4	434.3
Sudan	137.6	288.5	383.0	231.0	337.7	560.5	682.9
Swaziland	15.9	16.4	15.1	29.4	44.6	50.4	49.9
Tanzania	162.5	295.4	267.6	340.1	424.1	588.3	658.0
Togo	38.7	41.8	43.0	64.2	102.5	109.7	91.0
Uganda	30.1	39.0	25.2	22.2	21.3	42.3	119.2
Upper Volta	96.8	89.1	84.1	110.3	159.4	198.4	212.3
Zaire	180.5	204.5	193.6	260.6	316.9	416.4	446.0
Zambia	57.5	86.8	62.1	108.5	184.6	277.1	295.4
Zimbabwe	1.6	4.0	6.3	6.7	9.2	12.5	162.4
East African Community	16.0	21.9	19.2	6.7	12.5	3.4	5.5
DOM/TOM Unallocated	-17.6	3.1	0.8	24.9	–	–	–
EAMA Unallocated	85.1	85.8	11.3	85.7	123.4	130.1	94.7
South of Sahara Unall.	33.5	46.3	100.8	47.9	69.8	53.7	91.1
TOTAL	*2739.4*	*3684.6*	*3684.2*	*4133.7*	*5477.4*	*6743.5*	*8144.7*
Africa Unspecified	53.1	48.4	44.5	89.7	137.8	240.0	175.0
AFRICA TOTAL	***4238.7***	***6821.1***	***6130.6***	***7469.3***	***8601.4***	***9383.4***	***10793.4***
N.& C. AMERICA							
Bahamas	0.6	0.7	0.6	0.6	1.3	1.4	2.1
Barbados	3.9	5.4	7.6	5.8	11.3	11.1	13.9
Belize	6.2	8.7	11.6	9.6	18.2	20.7	14.7

	1974	197
Bermuda	0.0	0.
Costa Rica	23.3	30
Cuba	16.3	20.
Dominican Republic	21.2	30
El Salvador	29.6	41.
Guadeloupe	100.9	150
Guatemala	26.7	39.
Haiti	14.3	59
Honduras	31.8	52.
Jamaica	26.1	25
Martinique	106.3	164
Mexico	53.9	61
Netherlands Antilles	28.8	33
Nicaragua	46.9	41
Panama	24.8	33
St. Pierre & Miquelon	8.2	15
Trinidad & Tobago	5.7	5
Anguilla	–	1
Antigua	3.0	2
Cayman Islands	1.7	1
Dominica	3.6	7
Grenada	1.8	2
Montserrat	2.7	4
St. Kitts-Nevis	3.6	1
St. Lucia	7.5	8
St. Vincent	3.7	6
Turks & Caicos Isl.	2.4	3
Virgin Islands (BR)	1.7	2
West Indies Unall.	1.1	8
DOM/TOM Unallocated	–	
N.& C. America Unall.	6.9	12
TOTAL	*615.1*	*883*
SOUTH AMERICA		
Argentina	36.3	23
Bolivia	61.8	56
Brazil	168.7	165
Chile	24.4	128
Colombia	108.9	86
Ecuador	46.0	70
Falkland Islands	2.8	3
Guiana, French	46.2	45
Guyana	27.2	10
Paraguay	35.2	37
Peru	80.9	74
Surinam	48.3	52
Uruguay	11.3	12
Venezuela	8.5	18
South America Unall.	7.6	15
TOTAL	*713.9*	*799*
America Unspecified	93.5	100
AMERICA TOTAL	***1422.6***	***1784***
MIDDLE EAST		
Bahrain	29.0	25
Iran	9.9	-5
Iraq	4.7	66
Israel	117.6	467
Jordan	274.5	383
Kuwait	1.3	1
Lebanon	123.9	14
Oman	132.7	205
Qatar	0.6	1
Saudi Arabia	5.2	6
Syria	591.4	586
United Arab Emirates	0.6	10
Yemen	131.3	177
Yemen, Dem.	44.9	51
Middle East Unall.	26.7	27
TOTAL	*1494.3*	*2020*
SOUTH ASIA		
Afghanistan	60.3	75
Bangladesh	521.6	1017
Bhutan	0.6	2
Burma	67.6	58
India	1357.6	1708
Maldives	0.6	3
Nepal	32.3	45
Pakistan	695.0	892
Sri Lanka	80.8	171
Indus Basin	21.8	12

1976	1977	1978	1979	1980
0.0	0.1	0.2	0.2	0.3
24.5	25.3	51.0	55.6	64.8
35.9	46.0	48.7	48.8	32.0
33.0	33.6	49.9	77.7	125.0
30.0	45.2	55.4	59.5	96.5
166.5	158.2	191.7	232.6	88.9
65.4	61.8	71.7	66.8	72.8
71.8	87.6	92.8	92.6	105.2
40.1	57.0	92.5	97.0	103.0
26.2	33.3	122.1	97.5	126.0
194.6	202.1	235.4	296.1	568.8
63.3	50.5	17.9	74.5	56.0
49.3	41.6	48.0	56.9	96.6
39.2	36.5	41.6	115.1	220.6
41.9	35.0	29.2	35.4	45.7
13.9	19.8	20.5	27.8	27.9
4.8	5.7	4.5	4.1	4.7
1.1	1.1	2.3	2.3	2.3
3.1	5.4	3.6	3.3	5.6
2.1	1.5	3.2	0.7	1.5
4.3	5.0	7.1	9.1	17.7
2.7	3.3	2.6	2.9	3.2
3.4	3.2	1.4	1.4	3.7
2.6	2.1	2.1	1.8	6.2
7.2	4.4	3.7	2.2	8.6
4.4	4.0	4.5	5.7	9.7
3.8	3.5	2.8	2.3	3.4
2.6	2.1	1.2	1.8	4.7
3.5	2.0	3.0	3.9	6.6
–	–	-0.3	–	-1.9
29.9	26.9	17.1	14.0	13.9
990.8	*1019.6*	*1258.3*	*1522.6*	*1950.5*
30.9	28.2	28.5	42.8	18.4
71.2	93.5	145.9	156.6	170.0
110.6	79.5	113.3	106.8	85.4
8.2	11.2	7.7	-27.1	-9.7
76.6	50.2	71.4	54.1	90.1
75.8	55.2	44.9	69.6	46.4
2.7	2.0	4.1	1.9	2.3
63.5	85.3	78.9	92.5	111.7
17.0	11.9	28.4	34.8	43.1
41.3	48.0	43.0	30.5	30.5
74.1	96.6	142.7	199.6	203.1
103.8	90.2	65.6	94.6	82.2
12.9	8.0	10.6	14.3	9.8
-0.3	0.0	-14.5	6.6	15.3
18.4	15.7	18.7	18.9	5.3
706.7	*675.4*	*789.2*	*896.2*	*904.0*
72.7	73.0	81.8	119.4	190.7
1770.2	***1767.9***	***2129.2***	***2538.2***	***3045.2***
170.5	82.9	100.5	104.5	156.6
-12.6	35.2	128.0	5.9	30.9
7.3	72.0	43.5	17.8	8.4
643.4	797.4	899.7	1184.7	892.2
519.9	461.8	598.3	1124.2	1271.9
1.9	2.8	3.1	2.2	10.2
33.1	77.9	182.0	91.9	286.2
48.2	57.7	25.2	171.6	176.2
1.8	1.5	2.0	0.4	0.9
7.6	16.6	15.2	11.4	15.5
522.0	678.7	619.9	1585.2	1646.7
1.1	36.7	4.2	7.0	4.2
259.2	259.8	269.0	230.1	425.3
170.2	102.2	96.2	59.1	89.5
27.2	25.1	136.5	176.2	167.6
2400.7	*2708.0*	*3123.2*	*4772.1*	*5182.2*
78.5	100.7	94.9	107.9	32.3
532.1	764.9	989.6	1156.0	1262.5
3.2	2.9	3.2	5.8	8.3
71.0	101.6	273.8	363.7	308.7
1823.6	1105.9	1338.6	1370.1	2256.2
4.4	2.4	8.2	6.5	21.4
50.2	80.0	76.8	136.8	163.1
1276.5	545.9	669.5	604.9	1122.3
165.0	187.4	323.9	322.7	439.8
33.0	-3.0	-3.0	-3.0	-3.0

	1974	1975	1976	1977	1978	1979	1980
South Asia Unall.	2.3	4.8	8.3	3.5	4.2	28.4	1.0
TOTAL	*2840.4*	*3992.1*	*4045.7*	*2892.2*	*3779.6*	*4099.8*	*5612.6*
FAR EAST ASIA							
Brunei	0.2	0.1	0.1	0.1	0.1	0.1	0.0
China	–	–	–	–	–	16.9	66.1
Hong Kong	1.0	-1.1	2.7	2.1	2.3	11.9	10.9
Indonesia	663.2	691.7	668.8	515.5	635.3	720.8	949.5
Kampuchea	307.8	81.9	0.7	0.3	0.3	108.2	281.2
Korea, Rep.	252.3	249.8	218.1	238.6	164.3	133.8	139.0
Laos	60.1	38.8	28.5	32.4	71.8	59.1	40.9
Macao	0.0	0.0	–	–	–	0.0	4.4
Malaysia	69.7	100.3	63.3	71.2	80.2	125.1	135.0
Philippines	158.5	179.9	186.8	182.7	249.3	267.4	300.0
Singapore	21.5	12.8	12.3	13.2	6.7	5.5	14.0
Taiwan	-17.8	-19.8	-20.8	16.7	6.4	7.2	-3.6
Thailand	72.0	87.1	169.2	132.6	260.2	392.6	418.4
Viet Nam, Soc. Rep.	706.5	350.3	185.6	247.6	369.5	336.5	228.5
Mekong Delta Project	4.0	7.1	0.3	0.3	0.9	0.5	–
Far East Asia Unall.	24.1	61.6	41.1	42.0	33.2	37.8	13.8
TOTAL	*2323.1*	*1840.8*	*1557.1*	*1495.3*	*1880.5*	*2224.0*	*2598.7*
Asia Unspecified	33.4	33.8	51.6	21.8	41.6	220.9	127.6
ASIA TOTAL	***6691.2***	***7886.4***	***8054.6***	***7117.3***	***8824.9***	***11316.3***	***13520.7***
OCEANIA							
Cook Islands	5.8	5.6	6.9	7.5	7.0	7.8	10.7
Fiji	14.9	19.4	23.3	23.2	26.5	31.0	36.1
Kiribati	5.7	5.7	4.1	6.2	10.7	9.1	19.2
Nauru	–	0.0	–	0.0	–	0.0	0.0
New Caledonia	62.1	64.7	46.5	78.1	115.0	148.7	198.0
Niue Island	2.9	2.3	2.9	3.4	4.2	5.0	3.7
Pacific Islands (U.S.)	75.3	81.3	89.7	91.7	101.2	111.7	109.3
Papua New Guinea	263.2	305.4	240.6	255.4	296.2	284.3	325.9
Polynesia, French	37.7	71.7	77.7	83.2	90.6	143.9	159.5
Solomon Islands (Br.)	12.0	22.3	19.9	16.8	26.6	26.5	44.5
Tokelau Islands	0.9	0.2	1.2	1.2	1.0	1.8	1.9
Tonga	3.0	3.4	4.7	6.8	9.6	23.9	16.4
Tuvalu	–	0.1	3.0	2.4	2.9	4.1	4.9
Vanuatu	16.2	12.6	31.0	14.6	18.8	38.4	44.0
Wallis & Futuna	4.8	2.2	4.9	3.7	2.5	7.7	8.3
Western Samoa	5.6	13.4	11.7	20.6	20.2	29.9	25.7
Tom Oceania Unall.	0.5	0.6	–	8.3	21.4	–	–
Oceania Unallocated	2.5	3.7	3.4	5.3	23.6	9.5	16.4
TOTAL	*512.9*	*614.6*	*571.2*	*628.2*	*777.9*	*883.3*	*1024.4*
LDC's Unspecified	1059.6	1258.4	1054.0	1652.3	1672.2	2121.0	1835.5
TOTAL,ALL LDC'S	***14067.0***	***18542.9***	***17889.9***	***18979.2***	***22369.9***	***27045.5***	***31466.9***
INCOME GROUPS							
LLDCS	2158.5	3299.4	2950.7	3347.8	4165.4	5017.6	6074.0
OTHER LICS	5655.0	7296.2	7040.4	6543.8	7604.2	7383.3	9551.2
CHINA	–	–	–	–	–	16.9	66.1
MICS	3981.3	5256.8	5610.1	6010.9	7337.3	10633.1	12164.6
NICS	554.2	512.9	491.9	553.5	434.7	525.7	478.8
OPEC11	243.0	412.5	263.9	383.2	414.5	266.7	383.0
UNALLOCATED	1475.1	1765.2	1533.0	2140.0	2413.7	3202.2	2749.2

	1974	1975	1976	1977	1978	1979	1980
EUROPE							
Cyprus	6.2	18.6	11.2	5.3	20.2	10.0	30.4
Gibraltar	0.6	2.8	1.9	7.1	27.5	0.9	1.1
Greece	26.4	10.4	69.4	31.5	35.3	28.4	9.9
Malta	13.1	29.6	12.6	17.1	11.2	2.1	3.4
Portugal	–	20.2	137.5	150.1	103.4	160.1	140.4
Spain	11.6	13.5	15.3	27.5	28.9	20.9	33.0
Turkey	71.2	44.9	186.7	42.4	179.9	659.8	771.9
Yugoslavia	272.3	2.1	2.7	4.9	6.1	16.2	8.1
Europe Unallocated	1.4	7.0	6.1	6.3	5.1	9.9	7.4
TOTAL	*402.8*	*149.1*	*443.4*	*292.1*	*417.6*	*908.2*	*1005.7*
NORTH OF SAHARA							
Algeria	180.6	142.0	141.8	104.1	99.7	125.5	121.3
Egypt	251.7	769.3	1122.4	1267.1	1271.2	1690.0	1370.5
Libya	10.4	0.5	6.4	5.2	4.0	1.9	9.9
Morocco	160.0	202.8	196.1	236.0	206.4	211.1	232.2
Tunisia	124.2	196.5	211.3	213.8	275.0	148.2	474.2
North of Sahara Unall.	2.7	6.2	6.0	6.1	8.1	2.5	0.4
TOTAL	*729.5*	*1317.2*	*1684.0*	*1832.4*	*1864.4*	*2179.2*	*2208.5*
SOUTH OF SAHARA							
Angola	0.2	2.4	18.5	7.4	31.9	45.8	57.7
Benin	36.8	28.6	31.5	12.7	78.9	42.6	57.8
Botswana	40.7	36.9	41.1	41.3	134.1	103.5	112.8
Burundi	22.3	35.3	32.9	43.8	44.1	68.9	89.8
Cameroon	72.1	118.7	114.8	124.4	213.9	179.6	134.1
Cape Verde	–	9.8	13.4	26.0	31.5	52.3	39.8
Central African Rep.	25.9	36.4	24.9	34.1	26.2	51.2	99.2
Chad	35.0	32.2	57.0	57.5	77.3	38.5	21.4
Comoros	28.5	20.2	7.6	0.3	0.3	9.1	15.2
Congo	36.3	42.0	44.0	30.9	30.5	42.5	64.0
Djibouti	34.6	34.6	26.4	29.8	20.1	22.8	35.5
Equatorial Guinea	–	–	–	–	–	0.1	5.7
Ethiopia	79.1	88.5	53.9	51.2	70.4	64.1	79.9
Gabon	30.7	60.7	28.4	24.5	48.7	27.9	58.7
Gambia	5.3	6.7	16.5	9.2	16.4	37.5	36.2
Ghana	42.4	134.4	68.8	97.1	128.0	82.5	133.4
Guinea	8.1	11.5	11.4	13.0	16.4	49.1	57.3
Guinea-Bissau	0.1	15.7	23.3	27.0	52.6	30.9	43.0
Ivory Coast	110.4	152.5	92.9	118.3	76.1	170.5	172.1
Kenya	212.5	158.2	171.7	209.6	286.4	560.2	325.1
Lesotho	12.5	21.3	32.8	40.1	28.5	89.6	79.0
Liberia	21.6	10.3	27.3	31.4	31.9	65.8	52.7
Madagascar	41.5	54.1	35.5	52.3	75.7	88.9	95.7
Malawi	57.4	59.2	36.3	63.1	216.6	126.7	84.4
Mali	60.8	90.4	89.0	91.1	96.8	186.8	109.2
Mauritania	27.0	28.7	37.4	34.0	35.6	67.5	64.0
Mauritius	10.8	23.7	9.8	7.7	9.6	25.2	44.6
Mayotte	–	–	–	6.9	14.6	20.8	58.7
Mozambique	0.9	20.3	74.5	108.0	70.4	123.8	123.9
Niger	90.8	89.1	80.9	83.7	118.1	190.5	123.8
Nigeria	98.2	35.8	41.8	18.2	28.6	27.9	37.9
Reunion	314.8	404.7	411.5	450.8	566.1	702.2	754.4
Rwanda	34.6	67.1	66.2	79.8	111.6	125.6	145.1
St. Helena	3.0	3.0	3.1	4.2	8.3	7.4	8.1
Sao Tome & Principe	–	–	0.6	2.4	0.9	1.3	2.5
Senegal	97.4	116.9	105.3	109.8	138.3	192.9	205.9
Seychelles	5.2	19.4	6.0	14.7	9.3	12.8	14.2
Sierra Leone	9.3	17.2	8.9	19.6	28.6	60.1	57.0
Somalia	10.8	27.2	18.5	29.9	57.6	77.4	234.4
Sudan	43.0	72.0	56.5	77.0	273.9	273.4	624.2
Swaziland	14.2	12.5	9.7	35.5	45.8	16.8	21.3
Tanzania	211.5	263.4	266.1	481.3	590.9	733.2	674.3
Togo	22.5	30.7	35.4	101.7	31.8	43.4	104.1
Uganda	11.7	3.8	4.2	3.7	9.0	26.3	80.0
Upper Volta	56.7	71.5	68.4	102.2	146.3	201.3	170.4
Zaire	296.9	172.8	219.0	240.2	323.0	261.3	377.8
Zambia	49.1	56.8	90.8	119.2	262.2	231.9	276.0
Zimbabwe	3.0	3.9	6.7	6.3	9.0	13.7	196.4
East African Community	7.0	15.2	10.8	6.9	11.4	3.8	4.7
DOM/TOM Unallocated	–	–	4.0	46.6	–	–	–
EAMA Unallocated	85.1	78.4	-107.7	97.2	146.6	136.6	140.0
South of Sahara Unall.	41.4	12.7	89.6	44.2	45.7	84.0	33.0
TOTAL	*2559.4*	*2907.2*	*2717.8*	*3567.7*	*4926.2*	*5898.3*	*6635.8*
Africa Unspecified	90.6	62.6	87.5	89.5	133.6	104.9	97.9
AFRICA TOTAL	***3379.5***	***4287.1***	***4489.3***	***5489.5***	***6924.2***	***8182.3***	***8942.2***
N.& C. AMERICA							
Bahamas	0.1	0.1	0.2	0.1	0.7	0.3	0.2
Barbados	0.9	3.9	2.3	1.9	2.5	1.7	1.7
Belize	12.4	6.0	16.8	2.0	20.6	12.0	6.3

	1974	197
Bermuda	0.0	0.
Costa Rica	37.0	12
Cuba	25.9	39.
Dominican Republic	19.0	16
El Salvador	4.9	25.
Guadeloupe	169.6	236
Guatemala	7.9	29.
Haiti	21.3	24
Honduras	53.8	18.
Jamaica	21.8	13
Martinique	183.4	269.
Mexico	31.9	12
Netherlands Antilles	23.9	24.
Nicaragua	49.8	28
Panama	31.8	32
St. Pierre & Miquelon	7.9	16
Trinidad & Tobago	6.0	10.
Anguilla	–	1
Antigua	5.4	4
Cayman Islands	1.3	1
Dominica	2.6	5
Grenada	1.9	4
Montserrat	1.7	4
St. Kitts-Nevis	2.5	3
St. Lucia	4.8	3
St. Vincent	2.1	3
Turks & Caicos Isl.	2.4	3
Virgin Islands (BR)	2.2	2
West Indies Unall.	0.4	10
DOM/TOM Unallocated	–	
N.& C. America Unall.	11.2	19
TOTAL	*747.4*	*888*
SOUTH AMERICA		
Argentina	9.8	9
Bolivia	86.7	43
Brazil	102.4	87
Chile	82.5	125
Colombia	75.7	70
Ecuador	13.2	36
Falkland Islands	5.8	0
Guiana, French	54.4	72
Guyana	3.8	6
Paraguay	12.4	19
Peru	63.6	71
Surinam	43.2	50
Uruguay	3.6	15
Venezuela	9.8	6
South America Unall.	3.9	14
TOTAL	*570.8*	*629*
America Unspecified	59.9	61
AMERICA TOTAL	***1378.1***	***1578***
MIDDLE EAST		
Bahrain	0.7	0
Iran	20.8	9
Iraq	1.3	75
Israel	120.4	557
Jordan	101.4	116
Kuwait	0.1	0
Lebanon	13.6	11
Oman	0.7	0
Qatar	–	0
Saudi Arabia	1.0	0
Syria	56.4	103
United Arab Emirates	0.0	0
Yemen	21.2	23
Yemen, Dem.	7.5	5
Middle East Unall.	7.3	11
TOTAL	*352.3*	*915*
SOUTH ASIA		
Afghanistan	36.0	31
Bangladesh	441.2	832
Bhutan	0.3	0
Burma	47.9	49
India	862.0	1227
Maldives	0.1	1
Nepal	21.4	27
Pakistan	349.2	593
Sri Lanka	78.0	156
Indus Basin	12.7	9

1976	1977	1978	1979	1980
0.0	0.0	0.0	0.0	0.1
29.2	18.9	16.2	46.5	25.0
20.5	27.6	12.3	5.0	2.5
36.3	16.7	33.5	59.0	83.1
24.6	11.8	23.6	28.7	81.7
238.2	245.1	321.9	423.9	478.2
74.1	31.6	26.0	34.0	24.4
64.3	64.9	45.2	53.4	46.9
37.2	37.1	33.2	53.5	114.0
33.7	69.0	112.1	61.3	84.8
262.9	289.7	387.4	504.0	593.9
9.5	16.1	58.4	41.5	51.0
45.6	43.4	47.9	57.7	92.6
12.9	6.3	53.0	68.2	165.2
15.8	17.6	24.8	24.6	7.5
12.8	15.5	23.0	31.8	32.4
0.9	1.0	0.9	0.5	1.8
1.1	1.3	3.1	2.0	2.4
8.5	1.3	1.9	3.4	2.5
0.8	0.9	1.1	0.3	0.4
3.1	2.1	13.6	6.9	6.0
1.8	0.2	0.3	0.6	0.3
2.9	1.3	1.7	2.8	2.0
3.9	1.8	1.4	0.7	2.5
8.3	2.2	0.9	11.3	1.7
2.5	1.3	3.8	13.3	1.3
4.2	3.1	3.2	3.0	12.3
1.8	1.1	2.1	2.0	3.8
4.9	0.9	1.6	6.0	2.5
–	–	–	–	–
43.9	14.8	13.9	33.0	45.6
1025.4	*948.4*	*1291.7*	*1592.8*	*1976.5*
10.0	12.2	38.3	19.3	25.8
36.9	85.2	121.3	207.8	67.7
48.7	123.8	102.1	116.2	221.5
75.0	37.7	31.0	46.5	42.9
87.0	50.8	52.5	54.7	128.6
23.3	48.9	19.3	26.5	51.2
1.0	4.4	3.2	1.0	1.0
75.6	95.8	107.8	130.1	0.0
4.2	16.3	69.3	13.2	169.4
11.5	22.6	21.8	72.6	82.3
111.2	127.5	159.0	256.6	203.1
227.0	96.5	228.7	195.3	269.1
3.3	4.8	4.3	30.7	7.3
4.5	5.1	9.4	10.5	16.3
14.2	14.9	17.5	18.8	16.9
733.0	*746.5*	*985.4*	*1199.7*	*1303.0*
58.9	35.2	40.7	40.9	30.4
1817.4	**1730.0**	**2317.8**	**2833.3**	**3309.9**
1.7	1.6	1.1	0.8	0.7
105.5	10.1	13.5	22.1	39.3
1.6	56.6	3.3	3.5	5.8
1508.6	840.3	902.8	826.6	528.9
186.0	129.0	186.4	144.2	161.0
0.2	0.6	0.7	0.6	7.5
16.7	42.2	39.3	22.3	20.6
0.9	0.8	0.8	1.2	7.3
0.1	0.2	0.1	0.1	0.4
0.5	0.7	2.5	6.7	8.9
120.6	182.1	155.3	160.2	70.9
0.6	1.3	0.7	1.1	1.9
31.2	81.3	46.6	98.8	201.2
3.0	8.4	13.8	4.0	5.2
13.3	15.7	20.7	44.4	9.7
1990.7	*1370.8*	*1387.6*	*1336.7*	*1069.3*
44.5	59.3	55.6	25.4	7.9
626.9	544.6	1011.7	758.4	1301.7
1.4	0.7	0.7	0.7	1.1
45.9	294.9	154.1	414.3	129.1
772.5	987.1	1161.6	1277.2	1296.5
0.9	7.5	1.8	1.4	3.7
61.1	58.6	65.0	129.8	112.9
757.4	501.7	666.2	473.6	377.0
174.4	187.1	318.5	444.5	383.9
32.5	0.0	–	–	–

	1974	1975	1976	1977	1978	1979	1980
South Asia Unall.	8.6	0.6	4.9	3.6	4.0	5.3	0.5
TOTAL	*1857.2*	*2928.7*	*2522.4*	*2645.1*	*3439.1*	*3530.3*	*3614.1*
FAR EAST ASIA							
Brunei	0.1	0.1	0.1	0.1	0.1	0.1	0.0
China	–	–	–	–	–	4.7	489.5
Hong Kong	3.6	1.5	1.5	2.2	2.4	3.7	4.9
Indonesia	688.6	479.6	607.8	928.0	733.2	1425.1	1483.3
Kampuchea	195.8	41.1	0.3	0.2	0.3	26.7	47.3
Korea, Rep.	306.9	113.0	273.5	143.9	319.8	85.4	309.2
Laos	73.4	33.5	26.7	24.4	40.7	18.7	45.3
Macao	–	–	0.0	–	–	0.0	2.5
Malaysia	112.1	92.0	76.5	83.8	81.0	141.7	193.2
Philippines	251.0	166.5	141.8	161.9	445.5	293.8	400.5
Singapore	37.8	5.4	4.5	5.8	11.4	15.0	29.0
Taiwan	1.4	2.0	0.7	3.4	5.6	5.1	2.7
Thailand	199.9	97.3	53.2	200.9	287.6	513.2	382.8
Viet Nam, Soc. Rep.	809.2	305.7	153.3	262.6	199.1	206.5	223.8
Mekong Delta Project	6.3	2.3	0.1	7.1	0.0	–	–
Far East Asia Unall.	13.0	33.7	14.5	37.4	38.4	34.5	21.2
TOTAL	*2699.2*	*1373.9*	*1354.2*	*1861.4*	*2165.0*	*2774.2*	*3635.2*
Asia Unspecified	33.1	32.7	26.4	20.2	27.8	41.6	43.1
ASIA TOTAL	***4941.8***	***5250.5***	***5893.7***	***5897.4***	***7019.5***	***7682.7***	***8361.6***
OCEANIA							
Cook Islands	5.8	5.5	8.0	5.8	6.6	8.5	8.7
Fiji	15.7	25.7	13.9	19.7	40.0	26.4	25.5
Kiribati	3.6	6.3	6.5	11.1	11.7	45.8	11.5
Nauru	–	–	0.0	–	–	–	–
New Caledonia	47.0	77.4	51.0	74.3	102.6	146.3	172.8
Niue Island	3.3	2.4	3.3	3.0	3.2	4.3	1.7
Pacific Islands (U.S.)	68.9	100.5	79.2	112.9	98.0	149.6	124.9
Papua New Guinea	284.0	281.6	295.3	252.6	280.1	292.6	308.1
Polynesia, French	37.2	76.5	72.5	86.3	77.4	141.4	175.1
Solomon Islands (Br.)	20.3	18.8	20.9	18.9	60.7	13.5	18.8
Tokelau Islands	0.9	0.6	0.7	0.9	0.9	1.8	0.2
Tonga	4.8	2.3	5.3	10.5	19.4	11.5	13.8
Tuvalu	–	–	2.0	5.0	2.9	12.5	2.4
Vanuatu	16.7	15.1	25.8	11.8	21.6	39.0	70.7
Wallis & Futuna	5.0	2.0	4.6	3.5	1.5	7.2	9.7
Western Samoa	4.8	9.3	2.4	12.6	21.0	14.3	14.7
Tom Oceania Unall.	0.5	2.7	–	–	19.2	–	–
Oceania Unallocated	3.9	3.2	6.9	6.4	2.9	10.5	13.7
TOTAL	*522.1*	*629.6*	*598.1*	*635.2*	*769.7*	*925.0*	*972.4*
LDC's Unspecified	990.7	799.3	920.8	1022.6	1348.2	1530.4	1851.1
TOTAL,ALL LDC'S	***11615.0***	***12694.3***	***14162.6***	***15066.9***	***18797.0***	***22061.9***	***24442.9***
INCOME GROUPS							
LLDCS	1498.6	2074.3	1894.6	2230.3	3499.4	3683.3	4717.5
OTHER LICS	4125.2	4439.1	4504.6	5518.4	5829.8	7656.8	7246.3
CHINA	–	–	–	–	–	4.7	489.5
MICS	3539.6	4388.4	5639.8	5064.2	6668.9	7872.1	8514.9
NICS	804.2	277.5	573.1	521.2	711.8	511.6	835.6
OPEC11	267.8	332.8	312.9	257.4	201.8	226.4	321.2
UNALLOCATED	1379.7	1182.2	1237.7	1475.4	1885.3	2107.0	2317.9

	1974	1975	1976	1977	1978	1979	1980
EUROPE							
Cyprus	21.1	44.0	46.4	57.5	41.2	22.3	60.6
Gibraltar	0.6	2.8	1.9	7.1	27.5	0.9	1.1
Greece	28.2	12.1	71.9	32.7	37.1	90.8	33.5
Malta	23.9	31.0	14.7	18.0	83.9	29.3	14.0
Portugal	–	22.3	144.3	170.7	105.3	179.4	144.4
Spain	12.6	14.5	16.3	27.7	29.5	23.8	34.7
Turkey	80.1	105.8	228.6	50.8	199.2	966.6	1268.0
Yugoslavia	274.2	3.6	4.3	7.0	8.8	19.0	10.5
Europe Unallocated	1.4	8.5	6.1	6.4	8.7	13.8	8.7
TOTAL	*441.9*	*244.5*	*534.5*	*377.8*	*541.2*	*1345.9*	*1575.5*
NORTH OF SAHARA							
Algeria	218.6	207.5	154.1	162.1	111.1	134.6	225.2
Egypt	1340.3	3539.2	2504.1	3832.2	2058.2	1974.7	1817.7
Libya	13.6	4.6	10.3	11.1	11.8	19.8	16.7
Morocco	278.0	291.9	290.8	346.5	298.1	1042.6	399.9
Tunisia	216.5	333.2	280.9	357.4	362.6	218.6	570.6
North of Sahara Unall.	2.7	6.3	6.1	6.2	8.1	2.6	0.5
TOTAL	*2069.7*	*4382.7*	*3246.3*	*4715.6*	*2849.9*	*3392.9*	*3030.6*
SOUTH OF SAHARA							
Angola	0.3	3.2	25.5	49.6	45.1	64.3	86.9
Benin	46.0	47.3	66.8	75.9	130.4	83.3	103.4
Botswana	48.1	59.4	52.7	59.1	153.8	127.7	152.1
Burundi	39.1	61.2	70.7	88.0	84.6	132.0	177.7
Cameroon	81.6	172.2	186.4	231.4	283.8	236.7	216.4
Cape Verde	0.5	16.7	30.6	38.9	48.8	60.3	76.1
Central African Rep.	33.7	57.4	34.1	61.6	62.4	88.9	129.9
Chad	80.4	84.5	123.6	88.8	155.3	50.6	35.2
Comoros	28.6	20.9	32.0	22.7	19.8	56.3	39.0
Congo	42.5	57.7	109.7	47.0	48.8	55.7	145.3
Djibouti	34.6	34.8	26.4	44.4	86.7	32.0	109.2
Equatorial Guinea	17.4	0.7	-1.5	0.9	0.6	4.2	19.7
Ethiopia	160.6	210.6	132.1	182.3	117.9	145.3	227.2
Gabon	51.1	76.5	39.3	32.0	75.4	32.4	65.7
Gambia	16.4	9.2	35.7	40.0	37.2	68.5	104.7
Ghana	58.5	171.3	116.7	215.4	162.5	119.6	236.3
Guinea	31.9	42.2	39.2	57.4	100.5	105.0	148.5
Guinea-Bissau	3.4	30.0	43.4	48.8	78.6	65.3	68.1
Ivory Coast	139.1	162.9	133.1	143.0	103.1	188.8	183.4
Kenya	254.7	198.4	237.2	312.2	456.1	672.5	442.8
Lesotho	26.9	38.7	53.1	82.9	64.1	128.0	131.5
Liberia	29.5	22.7	35.2	63.1	97.1	81.9	72.4
Madagascar	89.7	73.4	93.2	105.7	161.2	210.7	237.7
Malawi	73.1	85.4	69.5	147.6	266.7	185.2	143.3
Mali	126.5	172.3	212.2	182.7	183.0	269.3	204.2
Mauritania	133.1	81.3	242.4	144.0	209.6	442.8	264.9
Mauritius	22.1	39.0	20.4	20.6	13.6	29.2	77.7
Mayotte	–	–	–	6.9	14.6	20.8	58.7
Mozambique	1.0	29.4	110.9	137.3	96.3	188.9	184.2
Niger	132.8	126.5	196.1	126.0	187.3	254.8	201.5
Nigeria	111.8	49.6	53.6	30.8	48.3	47.4	61.6
Reunion	314.9	411.3	420.5	460.4	581.4	713.7	780.7
Rwanda	53.4	109.5	121.2	162.3	141.1	166.3	210.1
St. Helena	3.0	3.0	3.1	4.2	8.3	7.4	8.1
Sao Tome & Principe	–	0.8	11.6	4.2	14.1	3.6	4.4
Senegal	193.6	171.2	159.9	169.3	271.4	362.1	327.1
Seychelles	5.3	19.6	6.5	15.4	16.4	13.9	15.4
Sierra Leone	14.9	33.8	17.2	58.7	42.7	113.7	79.3
Somalia	133.6	174.2	167.5	465.7	127.1	264.1	501.7
Sudan	217.1	425.3	415.6	483.1	785.2	598.1	1265.0
Swaziland	23.1	23.0	14.5	45.9	82.0	32.3	35.6
Tanzania	305.4	323.5	409.1	637.8	762.1	877.2	938.3
Togo	37.1	45.1	69.2	150.9	61.7	86.3	147.6
Uganda	38.5	88.8	19.9	37.4	35.1	75.5	221.8
Upper Volta	107.7	114.5	139.7	144.0	207.4	257.1	250.8
Zaire	332.4	248.4	328.4	287.0	421.4	430.5	544.9
Zambia	66.8	63.4	105.7	145.6	314.1	354.9	322.4
Zimbabwe	3.0	4.0	6.8	6.3	9.0	13.8	257.4
East African Community	7.0	15.2	10.8	6.9	11.4	3.8	4.7
DOM/TOM Unallocated	–	–	4.0	46.6	–	–	–
EAMA Unallocated	85.1	78.4	-92.0	97.2	146.6	136.6	140.0
South of Sahara Unall.	65.2	44.5	119.6	57.1	74.0	98.7	114.9
TOTAL	*3922.1*	*4632.8*	*5078.7*	*6372.8*	*7705.3*	*8857.5*	*10575.4*
Africa Unspecified	112.9	68.5	90.1	108.3	176.7	180.6	131.4
AFRICA TOTAL	***6104.6***	***9084.0***	***8415.1***	***11196.8***	***10731.8***	***12431.1***	***13737.4***
N.& C. AMERICA							
Bahamas	0.6	0.7	0.9	0.7	2.8	1.3	2.0
Barbados	2.6	15.2	12.8	5.9	7.0	16.8	6.1
Belize	23.3	7.9	20.1	11.9	26.5	12.5	9.8

	1974	197
Bermuda	0.0	0.
Costa Rica	42.4	48.
Cuba	30.7	46.
Dominican Republic	56.9	54.
El Salvador	46.5	59.
Guadeloupe	173.4	240.
Guatemala	29.3	93.
Haiti	35.1	95.
Honduras	103.5	54.
Jamaica	24.3	35.
Martinique	183.4	273.
Mexico	89.8	60.
Netherlands Antilles	33.9	32.
Nicaragua	61.8	48.
Panama	47.4	77.
St. Pierre & Miquelon	7.9	16.
Trinidad & Tobago	10.6	11.
Anguilla	–	1.
Antigua	6.7	4.
Cayman Islands	1.4	2.
Dominica	6.1	6.
Grenada	3.7	6.
Montserrat	2.6	4.
St. Kitts-Nevis	4.7	3.
St. Lucia	8.4	6.
St. Vincent	2.5	4.
Turks & Caicos Isl.	2.4	3.
Virgin Islands (BR)	2.2	2.
West Indies Unall.	0.4	11.
DOM/TOM Unallocated	–	
N.& C. America Unall.	11.2	19.
TOTAL	*1055.8*	*1349.*
SOUTH AMERICA		
Argentina	67.2	42.
Bolivia	138.1	114.
Brazil	131.0	172.
Chile	103.0	160.
Colombia	92.7	115.
Ecuador	37.9	45.
Falkland Islands	5.8	0.
Guiana, French	54.4	72.
Guyana	5.3	14.
Paraguay	74.8	30.
Peru	113.1	82.
Surinam	54.7	52.
Uruguay	21.6	24.
Venezuela	13.4	9.
South America Unall.	3.9	16.
TOTAL	*917.0*	*952.*
America Unspecified	74.1	119.
AMERICA TOTAL	***2046.9***	***2421.***
MIDDLE EAST		
Bahrain	33.7	20.
Iran	29.3	20.
Iraq	7.3	113.
Israel	121.4	558.
Jordan	338.2	498.
Kuwait	1.3	1.
Lebanon	130.1	19.
Oman	151.6	193.
Qatar	0.6	1.
Saudi Arabia	5.0	6.
Syria	726.0	1127.
United Arab Emirates	7.4	4.
Yemen	162.4	238.
Yemen, Dem.	67.5	110.
Middle East Unall.	24.0	25.
TOTAL	*1805.7*	*2939.*
SOUTH ASIA		
Afghanistan	101.8	140.
Bangladesh	757.9	1317.
Bhutan	0.6	1.
Burma	111.2	119.
India	1703.0	3233.
Maldives	0.5	3.
Nepal	45.4	54.
Pakistan	1306.3	808.
Sri Lanka	116.7	289.
Indus Basin	12.7	9.

Sri Lanka 116.7 289.
Indus Basin 12.7 9.

1976	1977	1978	1979	1980
0.0	0.1	0.2	0.2	0.3
65.1	92.7	48.2	97.7	64.3
30.4	41.0	34.5	29.9	37.5
78.0	24.5	100.1	226.5	125.6
49.4	87.9	40.2	81.6	143.8
243.0	250.0	331.1	427.9	498.9
150.8	98.2	30.3	38.8	105.6
102.1	107.9	130.3	90.6	79.9
183.3	62.6	130.8	124.6	225.1
45.8	103.4	146.4	135.9	128.4
269.7	297.1	398.2	504.0	612.7
22.1	35.5	70.3	82.7	116.4
46.9	44.4	52.6	58.2	104.3
62.2	27.3	86.7	173.0	262.1
21.3	19.1	45.8	46.7	46.5
12.8	15.5	23.0	31.8	32.4
2.5	7.0	11.5	3.3	4.4
1.1	1.3	3.1	2.0	2.4
9.7	3.6	3.3	3.7	5.1
1.3	1.7	2.5	0.4	0.7
4.1	6.1	16.1	15.5	14.7
2.7	1.0	5.0	1.1	2.6
3.2	2.0	1.8	3.0	3.0
5.3	1.9	5.7	0.9	3.7
8.7	6.4	2.8	11.7	11.5
4.2	6.5	5.8	13.5	8.7
4.5	3.1	3.5	3.2	12.7
1.9	1.1	4.3	2.1	5.6
5.4	1.7	1.6	6.0	2.5
–	1.1	2.0	–	-6.3
43.9	16.9	13.9	40.0	45.6
1515.0	*1387.2*	*1787.8*	*2286.8*	*2718.2*
17.8	68.7	95.8	28.9	36.9
98.5	123.1	303.4	287.7	115.3
112.9	245.2	114.0	194.5	353.6
130.7	47.6	36.1	52.6	49.8
210.9	99.2	111.8	151.7	243.3
44.7	112.3	77.2	110.0	146.5
1.0	4.4	3.2	1.0	1.0
77.9	101.7	111.8	132.1	8.3
11.3	71.7	134.3	29.7	178.4
38.0	35.1	40.2	114.0	114.5
186.7	137.1	189.0	317.2	289.4
228.9	97.2	233.6	201.1	273.5
6.8	7.6	7.4	33.5	11.0
6.0	7.4	13.0	15.1	20.8
14.2	19.0	17.5	18.8	16.9
1186.0	*1177.1*	*1488.4*	*1687.8*	*1859.1*
82.8	53.1	88.5	146.0	152.1
2783.8	***2617.4***	***3364.6***	***4120.7***	***4729.4***
167.7	190.2	40.4	90.0	120.6
109.3	19.5	47.8	23.9	39.4
5.0	60.8	8.8	10.2	10.5
1511.1	840.7	903.2	826.9	529.1
594.3	560.0	1778.7	588.5	1372.4
2.0	2.9	3.1	2.3	10.3
36.6	248.3	102.6	513.3	449.2
81.8	273.2	435.1	88.8	69.1
1.0	1.6	2.1	0.4	1.0
7.7	15.2	15.1	10.9	15.5
676.6	1022.9	2382.5	784.7	2009.4
1.2	36.7	4.3	2.7	4.3
423.6	443.3	581.7	351.3	541.3
202.3	151.9	73.0	92.5	153.1
27.0	16.2	136.6	194.4	174.1
3846.9	*3883.3*	*6515.1*	*3580.7*	*5499.1*
140.9	244.4	139.8	151.5	17.3
891.2	1116.9	1479.6	1266.2	2132.8
3.6	3.0	3.1	5.3	14.7
129.4	365.9	269.9	552.0	300.4
1834.9	2142.1	2351.1	2706.8	2822.9
8.6	8.8	15.1	9.2	23.1
179.1	132.8	187.4	219.3	269.9
1872.0	912.2	1319.3	973.1	1220.2
248.8	307.3	407.4	566.6	689.0
32.5	0.0	–	–	–

	1974	1975	1976	1977	1978	1979	1980
South Asia Unall.	8.6	0.6	12.2	3.6	230.5	27.3	0.5
TOTAL	*4164.7*	*5978.4*	*5353.0*	*5236.9*	*6403.3*	*6477.1*	*7490.9*
FAR EAST ASIA							
Brunei	0.1	0.1	0.1	0.1	0.1	0.1	0.0
China	–	–	–	–	–	4.8	533.4
Hong Kong	3.8	1.8	1.7	2.2	2.7	12.3	12.2
Indonesia	792.3	520.4	712.6	1049.5	915.4	1634.1	1733.3
Kampuchea	198.3	42.8	0.5	0.3	0.3	114.2	261.1
Korea, Rep.	318.6	134.4	404.1	161.6	329.2	95.6	320.6
Laos	81.4	37.3	30.6	38.2	73.7	65.5	82.3
Macao	0.0	0.0	0.0	–	–	0.0	6.9
Malaysia	118.0	201.1	89.4	106.0	91.5	199.9	234.6
Philippines	279.9	176.7	188.3	194.2	514.7	399.4	446.4
Singapore	39.4	7.6	5.5	6.9	12.9	16.7	33.5
Taiwan	1.4	2.0	82.9	3.4	37.4	17.7	49.6
Thailand	219.1	110.7	174.1	249.6	398.1	670.8	493.4
Viet Nam, Soc. Rep.	834.4	491.6	171.8	309.2	371.2	324.6	283.3
Mekong Delta Project	6.3	2.3	0.1	7.1	0.0	–	–
Far East Asia Unall.	20.0	59.4	40.2	54.7	40.0	35.6	21.2
TOTAL	*2913.1*	*1788.3*	*1901.9*	*2182.9*	*2787.3*	*3591.5*	*4511.9*
Asia Unspecified	41.7	37.1	43.4	28.8	43.9	87.9	90.2
ASIA TOTAL	***8925.2***	***10742.7***	***11145.2***	***11331.8***	***15749.5***	***13737.1***	***17592.0***
OCEANIA							
Cook Islands	5.9	5.7	8.4	6.0	6.9	9.0	10.4
Fiji	16.4	27.3	16.3	23.4	69.1	35.2	29.3
Kiribati	3.7	6.4	8.5	12.5	11.9	46.1	12.6
Nauru	–	–	0.0	–	–	0.0	–
New Caledonia	47.0	80.6	53.7	74.3	102.6	146.3	172.8
Niue Island	3.3	2.4	3.4	3.1	3.3	4.5	2.1
Pacific Islands (U.S.)	69.1	100.7	79.8	113.4	98.6	150.2	125.6
Papua New Guinea	284.9	283.6	324.7	274.4	334.2	302.7	348.4
Polynesia, French	37.2	76.6	72.5	86.3	77.4	141.5	177.8
Solomon Islands (Br.)	20.6	19.5	24.9	26.5	65.8	16.7	32.5
Tokelau Islands	0.9	0.6	0.7	0.9	1.0	1.8	0.2
Tonga	4.9	2.7	6.1	13.0	23.5	15.3	14.6
Tuvalu	–	0.1	2.1	5.1	3.2	12.5	3.5
Vanuatu	16.9	15.6	26.2	12.6	22.0	39.7	72.9
Wallis & Futuna	5.4	2.0	4.6	3.5	1.5	7.2	10.6
Western Samoa	6.5	17.8	9.6	21.9	33.0	29.1	25.6
Tom Oceania Unall.	0.5	2.7	–	–	19.2	–	–
Oceania Unallocated	3.9	3.2	6.9	6.4	2.9	10.5	13.7
TOTAL	*527.3*	*647.5*	*648.5*	*683.1*	*876.1*	*968.3*	*1052.6*
LDC's Unspecified	1415.1	1341.2	1336.6	2039.6	2142.5	2755.5	2471.3
TOTAL,ALL LDC'S	***19461.0***	***24481.7***	***24863.7***	***28246.4***	***33405.7***	***35358.6***	***41158.3***
INCOME GROUPS							
LLDCS	2962.6	4315.0	4456.1	5502.0	6465.1	6339.2	8670.4
OTHER LICS	7639.8	10198.9	8984.0	10725.4	9943.2	11755.4	12269.4
CHINA	–	–	–	–	–	4.8	533.4
MICS	5610.2	7135.4	8369.6	8219.3	12620.3	12377.5	14601.4
NICS	966.1	473.9	883.9	761.4	842.9	761.5	1145.9
OPEC11	385.5	490.7	380.3	461.6	369.7	362.2	555.8
UNALLOCATED	1896.8	1867.8	1789.8	2576.8	3164.5	3758.1	3381.9

	1974	1975	1976	1977	1978	1979	1980
EUROPE							
Cyprus	-6.4	12.9	13.7	98.2	47.4	0.5	37.0
Gibraltar	9.9	4.1	10.2	16.4	9.8	14.6	15.4
Greece	319.0	302.9	493.8	298.5	197.2	209.7	674.9
Malta	27.2	32.3	46.0	20.7	47.1	19.0	18.3
Portugal	65.6	200.9	339.9	424.7	1095.6	731.9	292.6
Spain	1055.4	1135.2	770.9	1196.9	1154.2	1547.4	1289.9
Turkey	341.9	221.1	381.7	693.8	956.8	1452.0	1345.3
Yugoslavia	132.2	319.8	471.4	864.7	747.8	1257.3	971.5
Europe Unallocated	38.2	108.8	137.1	185.7	387.6	1231.3	1717.7
TOTAL	*1982.9*	*2338.0*	*2664.8*	*3799.4*	*4643.6*	*6463.6*	*6362.6*
NORTH OF SAHARA							
Algeria	654.6	1872.8	1727.4	2289.3	3804.0	1435.1	1445.9
Egypt	123.3	360.0	638.8	967.6	1232.5	1492.0	1987.4
Libya	99.5	-671.0	220.7	222.6	456.7	1225.4	1020.5
Morocco	48.4	386.7	485.0	338.3	837.9	561.7	552.9
Tunisia	152.6	116.4	273.4	260.1	369.0	354.1	215.7
North of Sahara Unall.	43.2	44.3	18.5	15.8	11.2	26.0	6.1
TOTAL	*1121.5*	*2109.2*	*3363.7*	*4093.7*	*6711.3*	*5094.4*	*5228.6*
SOUTH OF SAHARA							
Angola	36.9	36.5	40.6	-14.1	23.6	90.5	183.1
Benin	16.9	34.4	25.5	30.5	36.3	57.8	331.9
Botswana	-3.3	70.4	44.4	27.6	5.0	108.7	27.0
Burundi	19.0	28.3	25.0	33.3	39.1	43.7	59.8
Cameroon	87.5	65.0	158.3	259.1	226.2	474.4	604.8
Cape Verde	-0.1	2.0	6.8	15.8	25.0	27.2	39.0
Central African Rep.	18.0	30.4	25.2	30.8	30.3	55.2	93.4
Chad	36.7	31.5	45.1	55.5	84.5	49.0	19.5
Comoros	27.3	15.7	8.5	1.8	3.7	6.3	14.3
Congo	32.1	18.8	125.6	39.1	53.1	34.2	46.6
Djibouti	27.9	33.2	28.4	33.1	28.8	17.8	31.9
Equatorial Guinea	–	-1.8	-1.8	-3.8	0.7	-0.7	1.2
Ethiopia	69.4	67.5	71.2	54.2	51.0	121.0	92.2
Gabon	89.3	116.8	110.5	278.9	76.4	-57.2	-36.4
Gambia	5.5	3.6	6.4	19.0	18.1	17.0	38.3
Ghana	37.9	31.2	37.8	106.1	103.3	85.1	115.1
Guinea	0.2	-8.2	-1.0	5.3	26.3	9.2	71.7
Guinea-Bissau	-1.7	7.9	13.1	26.9	39.9	37.9	37.1
Ivory Coast	109.1	125.1	362.4	490.7	510.8	473.7	771.0
Kenya	124.2	95.5	290.6	459.0	340.2	534.1	367.2
Lesotho	12.6	14.9	18.0	21.0	30.6	41.5	59.6
Liberia	392.8	637.4	293.4	691.9	674.2	284.4	349.8
Madagascar	35.9	30.6	25.6	17.7	60.1	165.5	284.8
Malawi	36.6	67.8	57.2	80.3	68.2	138.9	93.9
Mali	62.6	55.5	51.9	61.2	104.6	103.2	133.0
Mauritania	24.4	15.3	20.1	35.7	27.5	13.2	42.1
Mauritius	24.7	13.6	8.4	17.4	24.2	45.2	34.0
Mayotte	–	–	–	6.9	12.9	18.2	22.7
Mozambique	9.8	-8.4	70.4	61.1	82.7	116.3	287.2
Niger	80.0	88.9	117.1	93.2	133.5	189.8	172.4
Nigeria	-63.6	642.0	123.3	358.3	588.5	637.0	1022.7
Reunion	243.5	301.3	341.7	360.7	435.2	455.4	547.9
Rwanda	31.6	54.0	57.1	60.7	77.3	88.8	96.7
St. Helena	2.6	2.8	2.8	3.8	7.1	8.4	8.8
Sao Tome & Principe	–	0.0	0.8	1.6	1.8	1.4	1.2
Senegal	90.0	87.9	124.0	124.7	181.6	180.6	340.9
Seychelles	10.5	15.7	9.2	10.1	19.6	28.8	21.2
Sierra Leone	-0.6	12.6	16.8	26.6	23.3	33.3	57.7
Somalia	-4.5	33.8	26.3	129.0	61.5	98.6	211.1
Sudan	89.3	335.4	218.6	211.0	267.0	182.3	352.1
Swaziland	11.4	11.2	10.5	25.6	37.0	44.4	35.7
Tanzania	139.0	224.1	270.0	313.6	402.7	591.9	681.9
Togo	32.4	37.6	47.7	97.0	201.3	141.0	110.3
Uganda	-2.8	-2.1	30.3	9.2	-143.4	13.5	60.1
Upper Volta	52.0	52.4	60.4	73.0	97.3	148.9	164.9
Zaire	442.9	563.1	404.3	397.2	571.7	602.9	623.2
Zambia	134.1	259.4	51.1	147.9	267.6	361.3	226.5
Zimbabwe	34.1	28.1	33.7	32.9	29.0	64.5	118.1
East African Community	16.0	21.9	19.2	6.7	12.5	3.4	5.5
DOM/TOM Unallocated	-21.2	13.7	1.3	24.9	–	–	–
EAMA Unallocated	140.2	206.0	12.8	93.8	132.3	139.5	94.7
South of Sahara Unall.	48.3	124.9	82.4	99.5	-52.0	103.3	285.1
TOTAL	*2837.0*	*4744.9*	*4028.7*	*5642.9*	*6159.3*	*7229.9*	*9454.3*
Africa Unspecified	106.8	790.1	565.5	132.7	1583.9	1286.1	421.0
AFRICA TOTAL	***4065.3***	***7644.2***	***7957.9***	***9869.3***	***14454.4***	***13610.3***	***15103.9***
N.& C. AMERICA							
Bahamas	162.4	261.0	557.9	151.7	615.9	746.6	58.0
Barbados	5.7	-14.1	22.9	0.4	8.3	37.7	4.5
Belize	4.5	11.2	7.8	5.3	11.5	19.2	13.4

	1974	197
Bermuda	1715.0	820.
Costa Rica	14.4	15
Cuba	32.1	157
Dominican Republic	17.1	36.
El Salvador	14.7	34
Guadeloupe	123.8	173
Guatemala	26.4	33
Haiti	7.7	22
Honduras	14.9	27
Jamaica	45.9	65
Martinique	127.4	196
Mexico	1145.9	1127
Netherlands Antilles	166.9	409
Nicaragua	21.7	39
Panama	197.5	584
St. Pierre & Miquelon	9.7	17
Trinidad & Tobago	22.7	8
Anguilla	–	1
Antigua	2.7	1
Cayman Islands	69.9	27
Dominica	2.7	3
Grenada	1.5	1
Montserrat	2.6	4
St. Kitts-Nevis	3.5	1
St. Lucia	6.9	8
St. Vincent	3.3	5
Turks & Caicos Isl.	2.4	1
Virgin Islands (BR)	-4.3	3
West Indies Unall.	4.7	-5
DOM/TOM Unallocated	–	
N.& C. America Unall.	164.6	36
TOTAL	*4136.7*	*4118*
SOUTH AMERICA		
Argentina	80.8	282
Bolivia	45.5	69
Brazil	2657.2	2295
Chile	233.5	-259
Colombia	44.1	135
Ecuador	6.5	16
Falkland Islands	2.8	3
Guiana, French	45.3	47
Guyana	14.8	21
Paraguay	10.0	14
Peru	739.9	538
Surinam	49.3	52
Uruguay	-3.9	43
Venezuela	-184.3	531
South America Unall.	76.5	26
TOTAL	*3818.2*	*3819*
America Unspecified	825.8	1054
AMERICA TOTAL	***8780.7***	***8993***
MIDDLE EAST		
Bahrain	-6.3	-16
Iran	-739.8	416
Iraq	45.8	230
Israel	560.5	846
Jordan	74.3	106
Kuwait	-13.8	-32
Lebanon	40.5	47
Oman	30.5	281
Qatar	6.0	75
Saudi Arabia	83.9	-69
Syria	25.2	100
United Arab Emirates	139.2	244
Yemen	26.7	19
Yemen, Dem.	7.3	12
Middle East Unall.	-5918.1	1961
TOTAL	*-5637.9*	*4225*
SOUTH ASIA		
Afghanistan	18.1	28
Bangladesh	351.8	694
Bhutan	0.7	0
Burma	60.3	22
India	576.5	820
Maldives	0.6	4
Nepal	20.7	29
Pakistan	324.8	244
Sri Lanka	71.7	30
Indus Basin	19.8	4

1976	1977	1978	1979	1980
685.3	-477.1	-155.1	775.8	945.8
21.1	44.6	62.1	53.1	73.1
347.4	63.0	179.5	8.1	19.7
34.3	-5.5	-18.1	85.6	52.1
17.3	13.0	48.3	31.5	73.2
196.0	201.2	235.3	289.3	167.0
74.3	74.6	86.3	64.6	69.3
30.5	40.0	51.4	84.5	78.4
33.2	29.4	22.4	66.4	108.0
-66.6	5.4	42.7	58.5	90.2
220.3	238.4	284.6	333.4	733.6
1052.6	1557.0	2274.8	2929.1	3790.4
270.0	603.0	847.6	107.8	195.1
31.6	24.9	29.6	76.4	129.0
302.7	543.9	530.9	625.2	673.6
16.2	20.1	20.1	29.0	27.7
-13.0	-21.1	98.2	64.5	64.4
1.1	1.1	2.3	2.3	2.3
2.6	4.4	4.6	3.1	2.6
12.2	146.2	150.2	349.9	278.7
2.4	3.5	5.9	8.0	8.1
1.4	2.1	0.7	0.4	0.5
3.1	2.9	1.2	1.3	3.1
1.9	1.3	1.6	1.6	2.7
5.6	4.6	1.3	1.8	3.5
3.6	2.7	3.9	5.5	3.0
2.5	2.3	1.6	1.5	1.3
3.3	2.7	-2.4	9.2	65.1
-48.2	29.9	26.8	23.1	73.7
–	-1.2	-0.3	-0.1	–
30.2	217.3	37.1	45.4	636.3
3863.5	*3531.8*	*5510.7*	*6939.1*	*8447.4*
426.8	337.9	1081.3	1918.0	2671.1
78.0	102.2	137.1	336.6	16.6
3478.6	2118.6	4746.3	4688.4	3742.1
-73.8	-162.7	88.8	255.2	370.6
175.9	133.9	257.2	375.4	587.5
98.3	143.8	324.8	563.1	141.9
2.7	2.0	4.1	1.9	2.3
66.6	88.4	85.2	90.4	109.3
50.1	12.7	25.7	12.4	7.4
35.6	42.3	32.8	59.5	39.7
318.5	247.1	318.3	780.8	428.4
102.6	93.7	63.5	93.0	75.0
21.6	9.8	9.1	47.2	63.5
-355.6	820.2	1416.1	605.2	1314.3
27.9	1017.3	31.2	35.9	99.9
4453.8	*5007.1*	*8621.3*	*9863.0*	*9669.6*
1098.7	1918.1	3555.6	3469.7	2814.3
9416.0	***10457.0***	***17687.6***	***20271.7***	***20931.3***
-4.3	0.9	139.2	28.4	-68.9
3.6	1706.7	2892.2	49.8	546.7
-80.2	-64.3	200.2	120.4	172.9
955.9	1098.7	1390.2	1689.0	1274.3
143.3	106.9	146.3	245.1	309.1
-19.9	24.1	54.4	108.9	71.8
6.5	-9.5	87.6	58.5	144.0
140.1	-5.1	26.5	0.7	16.7
81.6	33.3	251.3	30.4	-55.4
158.3	211.5	414.0	363.6	179.6
78.1	78.0	26.7	48.7	12.8
346.0	53.3	390.2	407.9	196.9
14.4	39.8	47.5	108.4	143.1
8.6	6.3	15.7	33.6	124.9
1336.6	555.8	58.5	1842.1	-3212.9
3168.6	*3836.3*	*6140.4*	*5135.6*	*-144.5*
32.7	27.4	32.7	68.2	13.4
324.2	391.0	677.7	772.8	856.0
1.0	0.6	0.7	1.2	1.7
42.5	58.8	237.7	413.2	324.6
725.9	385.1	531.5	629.0	780.9
2.0	2.7	5.3	1.3	1.7
29.1	37.6	40.2	86.1	82.7
379.4	364.8	384.4	453.6	472.0
81.1	111.1	204.4	232.5	329.6
30.0	-8.0	-8.0	-11.0	-8.0

	1974	1975	1976	1977	1978	1979	1980
South Asia Unall.	3.7	8.4	3.1	8.2	7.6	15.4	3.0
TOTAL	*1448.7*	*1886.8*	*1650.9*	*1379.3*	*2114.2*	*2662.4*	*2857.6*
FAR EAST ASIA							
Brunei	1.8	-2.8	-51.1	-2.1	4.9	77.6	-18.7
China	–	–	–	–	–	116.4	286.2
Hong Kong	87.0	166.3	422.0	267.0	169.8	1034.2	880.2
Indonesia	900.3	2401.4	2362.9	586.7	1183.2	128.3	1309.2
Kampuchea	305.1	78.8	1.0	0.3	0.4	24.9	48.6
Korea, Rep.	414.3	745.7	1012.6	1037.6	1096.6	1102.3	571.9
Laos	60.3	32.5	26.0	27.3	43.0	26.7	15.8
Macao	-0.2	0.1	5.0	-1.9	-1.9	-2.8	-0.2
Malaysia	213.4	240.4	218.8	133.5	107.3	596.6	508.4
Philippines	288.2	261.2	941.5	565.8	848.4	812.0	612.7
Singapore	139.9	99.4	161.3	214.2	304.9	531.8	662.0
Taiwan	322.4	370.3	130.9	46.3	24.3	421.9	455.7
Thailand	97.6	102.4	41.5	160.3	416.7	684.2	780.2
Viet Nam, Soc. Rep.	705.1	284.6	161.4	257.6	297.3	339.5	124.5
Mekong Delta Project	4.0	7.1	0.3	0.3	0.9	0.5	–
Far East Asia Unall.	214.0	12.5	8.1	23.3	35.0	17.9	9.3
TOTAL	*3753.2*	*4800.0*	*5442.5*	*3316.0*	*4518.2*	*5913.0*	*6246.4*
Asia Unspecified	789.9	378.4	255.3	643.2	145.8	752.1	-1377.2
ASIA TOTAL	***353.9***	***11290.4***	***10516.8***	***9174.9***	***12931.1***	***14462.2***	***7581.7***
OCEANIA							
Cook Islands	5.6	5.4	6.5	8.2	6.4	7.3	10.7
Fiji	28.7	10.0	30.7	35.3	38.9	45.7	53.1
Kiribati	5.5	5.5	3.8	6.1	9.9	8.8	18.6
Nauru	-1.0	-0.9	-0.7	7.6	0.0	6.9	-2.1
New Caledonia	69.3	90.4	60.1	82.8	128.0	155.8	214.3
Niue Island	2.9	2.3	2.8	3.4	4.2	4.8	3.4
Pacific Islands (U.S.)	75.0	81.0	86.2	89.5	100.6	119.3	109.4
Papua New Guinea	321.4	276.7	271.2	246.4	310.7	303.2	346.1
Polynesia, French	42.0	78.8	86.2	92.6	99.2	155.6	155.6
Solomon Islands (Br.)	12.2	24.9	18.0	16.3	25.6	22.9	31.1
Tokelau Islands	0.9	0.2	1.2	1.2	0.9	1.8	1.8
Tonga	2.9	2.9	3.7	5.0	8.4	20.7	12.6
Tuvalu	–	–	2.9	2.4	2.5	4.1	4.5
Vanuatu	19.2	16.0	40.7	14.4	23.3	42.4	41.7
Wallis & Futuna	4.8	1.9	4.9	3.7	2.5	7.7	8.3
Western Samoa	4.4	8.8	7.2	14.9	14.4	24.3	13.2
Tom Oceania Unall.	0.5	0.6	–	8.3	21.4	–	–
Oceania Unallocated	6.2	35.0	20.2	1.7	31.7	3.6	18.9
TOTAL	*600.5*	*639.4*	*645.4*	*639.7*	*828.6*	*934.8*	*1041.1*
LDC's Unspecified	2170.6	6001.9	6364.9	7918.1	9525.3	9253.9	11527.7
TOTAL,ALL LDC'S	***17953.9***	***36907.0***	***37565.7***	***41858.3***	***60070.6***	***64996.6***	***62548.3***
INCOME GROUPS							
LLDCS	1182.3	2060.7	1652.7	1940.4	2386.7	3337.4	4180.8
OTHER LICS	4379.5	5879.9	5854.8	4834.9	6480.1	6121.6	8370.1
CHINA	–	–	–	–	–	116.4	286.2
MICS	7051.8	8356.1	9043.1	8109.1	12486.8	15958.5	15595.2
NICS	6419.7	7046.8	8760.7	8363.3	12892.8	16371.9	16002.5
OPEC11	187.0	2731.8	2290.7	5719.3	10280.2	4852.8	4998.6
UNALLOCATED	-1266.3	10831.7	9963.8	12891.4	15543.8	18238.0	13115.0

	1974	1975	1976	1977	1978	1979	1980
EUROPE							
Cyprus	18.1	39.7	51.4	145.9	74.6	19.9	66.9
Gibraltar	9.9	4.1	10.2	16.4	9.8	14.6	15.4
Greece	333.2	328.5	523.4	324.6	207.8	286.1	768.9
Malta	36.6	40.3	65.2	21.3	47.0	41.6	31.3
Portugal	65.6	199.9	373.4	491.1	1147.0	818.0	398.5
Spain	1120.0	1156.4	885.2	1187.8	1159.7	1543.1	1272.4
Turkey	465.3	419.6	653.4	907.5	1356.2	1850.9	1877.6
Yugoslavia	325.5	525.3	718.2	969.0	903.2	1531.9	1174.7
Europe Unallocated	38.2	109.2	137.1	185.8	391.2	1235.2	1718.9
TOTAL	*2412.2*	*2822.9*	*3417.5*	*4249.2*	*5296.6*	*7341.4*	*7324.7*
NORTH OF SAHARA							
Algeria	764.2	1982.6	1828.2	2362.7	3871.9	1506.6	1546.6
Egypt	1233.7	3412.3	2353.6	3088.9	2763.3	2058.2	2352.8
Libya	102.7	-666.8	224.6	228.4	464.5	1228.3	1036.4
Morocco	130.3	602.1	613.0	540.6	1091.3	1145.5	1071.3
Tunisia	212.0	245.3	394.7	350.5	444.3	474.6	370.0
North of Sahara Unall.	43.2	44.4	18.6	15.9	11.2	26.1	6.2
TOTAL	*2486.2*	*5619.8*	*5432.7*	*6587.0*	*8646.5*	*6439.3*	*6383.3*
SOUTH OF SAHARA							
Angola	37.0	37.3	47.6	25.6	41.8	108.2	199.9
Benin	33.0	59.7	51.0	56.0	70.6	96.8	390.0
Botswana	9.0	85.9	53.6	39.8	21.4	140.4	53.4
Burundi	37.4	51.4	45.2	53.9	75.2	94.2	117.6
Cameroon	114.9	148.8	221.5	331.4	340.1	596.0	735.0
Cape Verde	-0.1	8.5	24.1	26.4	33.2	33.4	64.4
Central African Rep.	36.2	54.5	37.9	42.8	57.9	92.8	129.4
Chad	81.8	69.4	65.0	89.0	132.6	79.2	34.7
Comoros	27.5	20.0	25.8	17.2	14.3	16.7	43.3
Congo	49.7	37.5	157.3	58.4	106.7	63.0	83.6
Djibouti	28.6	33.5	28.4	46.7	95.7	21.9	145.4
Equatorial Guinea	15.9	0.4	-1.4	-2.9	1.3	1.9	10.0
Ethiopia	109.3	131.6	137.1	105.6	130.6	220.9	210.4
Gabon	89.6	149.0	118.3	284.5	88.1	-43.7	-27.2
Gambia	12.0	8.5	12.9	30.4	38.5	41.1	81.9
Ghana	47.3	51.1	67.8	158.1	188.9	193.1	223.5
Guinea	37.9	2.9	5.7	22.3	133.9	59.7	135.4
Guinea-Bissau	1.5	18.5	23.8	38.4	53.2	56.7	67.0
Ivory Coast	164.0	193.8	416.1	568.0	617.2	551.8	918.4
Kenya	177.7	194.8	399.0	550.9	462.2	654.3	531.1
Lesotho	20.9	30.3	30.1	39.1	51.9	62.1	90.2
Liberia	403.9	652.5	308.2	711.2	711.1	356.8	411.9
Madagascar	75.2	94.1	61.7	54.0	118.5	222.3	394.2
Malawi	48.0	84.9	77.3	114.3	122.2	210.5	177.4
Mali	120.1	144.3	87.5	113.6	179.4	207.1	254.0
Mauritania	92.0	41.3	190.9	176.8	214.4	163.0	148.6
Mauritius	34.7	30.9	18.3	36.0	58.7	60.8	56.5
Mayotte	–	–	–	6.9	12.9	18.2	22.7
Mozambique	9.9	0.6	106.1	75.5	112.5	157.9	331.8
Niger	134.8	149.0	168.4	130.5	219.1	264.1	255.7
Nigeria	-13.8	685.3	169.4	416.0	649.8	686.1	1087.1
Reunion	247.6	310.0	348.6	362.6	440.6	456.5	556.3
Rwanda	46.6	91.1	80.6	95.5	123.8	148.6	155.6
St. Helena	2.6	2.8	2.8	3.8	7.1	8.4	8.8
Sao Tome & Principe	–	0.8	11.7	3.1	4.1	3.1	3.9
Senegal	168.7	145.6	175.7	189.8	298.4	350.2	448.1
Seychelles	10.6	15.9	9.7	10.7	20.2	32.2	27.8
Sierra Leone	8.8	24.8	25.8	41.5	50.0	60.5	92.9
Somalia	105.8	177.9	121.9	359.5	211.2	255.9	540.7
Sudan	349.5	652.3	650.8	421.1	520.8	633.2	768.2
Swaziland	15.0	19.5	21.1	37.6	54.4	78.8	70.1
Tanzania	169.3	324.5	337.3	420.4	516.3	744.4	838.4
Togo	48.1	55.7	72.0	120.6	267.1	210.8	180.9
Uganda	21.7	44.5	50.0	30.0	-129.2	42.8	138.9
Upper Volta	99.4	88.3	85.4	111.4	160.8	214.7	227.9
Zaire	517.7	643.4	489.2	512.3	707.1	732.5	775.8
Zambia	184.8	325.0	128.9	205.7	315.6	449.4	318.1
Zimbabwe	29.5	23.4	29.5	29.4	26.8	61.5	163.6
East African Community	16.0	21.9	19.2	6.7	15.5	3.4	5.5
DOM/TOM Unallocated	-21.2	13.7	1.3	24.9	–	–	–
EAMA Unallocated	140.2	208.1	19.5	93.8	132.3	139.5	94.7
South of Sahara Unall.	68.0	157.2	111.5	112.4	-29.0	108.3	327.4
TOTAL	*4264.5*	*6616.6*	*5947.0*	*7609.2*	*8867.8*	*10221.8*	*13120.8*
Africa Unspecified	114.9	800.4	579.7	152.6	1630.1	1416.6	459.0
AFRICA TOTAL	***6865.6***	***13036.7***	***11959.4***	***14348.8***	***19144.4***	***18077.7***	***19963.1***
N.& C. AMERICA							
Bahamas	162.9	261.5	558.3	153.6	617.4	748.0	62.6
Barbados	6.5	-11.3	27.6	11.0	14.9	45.7	19.1
Belize	6.5	13.9	11.2	9.1	18.1	19.7	17.9

	1974	1975
Bermuda	1715.0	820.
Costa Rica	54.3	60.
Cuba	36.8	164.
Dominican Republic	25.7	53.
El Salvador	41.5	98.
Guadeloupe	125.5	180.
Guatemala	39.1	82.
Haiti	12.5	56.
Honduras	37.6	89.
Jamaica	55.1	93.
Martinique	129.1	200.
Mexico	1414.3	1388.
Netherlands Antilles	170.6	421.
Nicaragua	50.0	92.
Panama	223.7	645.
St. Pierre & Miquelon	9.7	17.
Trinidad & Tobago	30.9	16.
Anguilla	–	1.
Antigua	3.0	2.
Cayman Islands	70.0	28.
Dominica	4.0	8.
Grenada	1.9	2.
Montserrat	2.7	4.
St. Kitts-Nevis	3.6	1.
St. Lucia	7.8	10.
St. Vincent	3.8	6.
Turks & Caicos Isl.	2.4	1.
Virgin Islands (BR)	-4.3	3.
West Indies Unall.	4.7	-4.
DOM/TOM Unallocated	–	
N.& C. America Unall.	164.6	36.
TOTAL	*4611.7*	*4847.*
SOUTH AMERICA		
Argentina	231.7	330.
Bolivia	69.7	101.
Brazil	3118.3	2723.
Chile	237.3	-227.
Colombia	165.9	246.
Ecuador	36.9	69.
Falkland Islands	2.8	3.
Guiana, French	47.9	53.
Guyana	52.1	37.
Paraguay	33.0	44.
Peru	757.1	590.
Surinam	55.1	56.
Uruguay	20.4	58.
Venezuela	-168.6	538.
South America Unall.	76.5	27.
TOTAL	*4735.9*	*4654.*
America Unspecified	860.9	1109.
AMERICA TOTAL	***10208.5***	***10611.***
MIDDLE EAST		
Bahrain	23.9	70.
Iran	-608.2	597.
Iraq	54.3	276.
Israel	568.3	862.
Jordan	286.0	391.
Kuwait	-12.6	-31.
Lebanon	180.1	74.
Oman	171.0	487.
Qatar	6.6	76.
Saudi Arabia	87.9	-64.
Syria	612.8	691.
United Arab Emirates	139.8	256.
Yemen	130.5	182.
Yemen, Dem.	47.2	73.
Middle East Unall.	-5899.8	1977.
TOTAL	*-4212.4*	*5923.*
SOUTH ASIA		
Afghanistan	61.5	70.
Bangladesh	529.6	1064.
Bhutan	1.0	2.
Burma	65.5	48.
India	1319.6	1693.
Maldives	1.0	5.
Nepal	33.8	46.
Pakistan	760.7	842.
Sri Lanka	117.4	144.
Indus Basin	19.8	4.

1976	1977	1978	1979	1980
685.3	-477.0	-155.0	775.9	946.0
89.5	119.5	121.8	104.8	147.3
357.3	79.4	210.7	32.9	40.6
48.4	80.2	35.2	128.0	155.7
62.7	62.7	102.5	77.7	134.9
200.0	201.8	238.3	290.6	170.8
128.1	156.5	171.5	134.0	136.6
70.1	88.0	94.5	128.7	120.7
71.7	97.5	125.3	143.2	198.3
-12.1	67.0	116.4	90.4	216.4
227.6	238.8	287.4	334.6	738.6
1340.3	1867.5	2499.7	3379.1	4446.5
274.7	605.0	851.2	110.7	204.8
81.3	67.9	57.9	119.7	240.1
360.2	588.9	592.9	669.3	740.6
16.2	20.1	20.1	29.0	27.7
-4.0	-11.3	104.8	74.2	67.8
1.1	1.1	2.3	2.3	2.3
3.4	5.5	5.6	3.3	6.5
14.2	146.7	152.9	350.1	279.2
4.6	5.0	6.5	8.8	17.4
2.7	3.3	2.7	2.9	3.7
3.4	3.2	1.4	1.4	3.9
2.6	2.3	2.2	1.8	6.2
7.8	6.8	3.8	2.2	9.7
4.4	4.0	4.6	5.7	10.7
2.6	2.3	1.6	1.6	1.8
3.4	2.8	-2.1	9.3	67.0
-47.8	30.7	26.8	23.1	73.7
–	-1.2	-0.3	-0.1	-1.9
36.8	217.3	39.9	48.4	789.0
4633.5	*4456.2*	*6373.4*	*7897.0*	*10102.0*
518.4	426.7	1187.1	2002.4	2718.4
124.7	170.0	232.0	430.6	157.0
3739.4	2425.6	5030.6	5085.7	4210.2
-60.9	-123.2	129.0	288.6	400.0
252.5	238.7	332.7	506.3	831.2
141.0	212.6	365.7	630.2	239.0
2.7	2.0	4.1	1.9	2.3
68.3	88.6	86.5	92.3	111.7
61.7	19.7	52.0	42.4	48.6
64.6	71.2	68.1	93.0	74.8
368.8	432.3	380.4	868.4	622.1
104.9	106.5	66.8	94.6	80.1
46.7	13.8	16.5	61.5	79.0
-340.2	802.7	1399.2	575.4	1287.9
27.9	1017.3	31.2	35.9	99.9
5120.7	*5904.4*	*9382.0*	*10809.0*	*10962.1*
1125.4	1962.3	3640.4	3576.4	2959.7
10879.5	***12322.8***	***19395.8***	***22282.4***	***24023.9***
231.4	149.9	238.7	134.1	87.0
58.3	1750.7	2904.6	11.2	498.6
-56.4	-36.7	213.9	130.9	171.8
966.3	1096.4	1393.9	1686.8	1271.1
573.3	468.2	659.1	1301.7	1539.7
-17.8	26.4	56.8	110.6	74.5
24.7	38.3	245.5	148.2	432.3
189.8	60.6	62.5	177.2	289.1
82.4	34.6	253.3	30.7	-54.9
165.5	226.0	426.7	367.9	186.1
594.9	756.8	642.0	1598.2	1650.7
349.0	88.7	409.7	409.4	204.7
262.4	277.2	334.6	289.9	508.6
169.8	111.5	104.0	88.0	222.6
1351.0	566.7	175.7	1992.1	-3048.4
4944.6	*5615.4*	*8121.0*	*8476.9*	*4033.6*
76.5	100.6	95.6	129.1	34.3
536.6	771.9	1000.3	1190.4	1256.6
3.2	2.9	3.2	5.8	8.3
73.1	106.1	358.1	518.1	402.7
1835.1	1048.9	1313.7	1288.2	2493.3
5.8	3.9	9.7	6.8	21.2
49.9	82.3	77.8	140.4	161.4
1382.1	627.9	754.0	692.5	1286.7
152.1	180.1	315.4	322.5	476.1
30.0	-8.0	-8.0	-11.0	-8.0

	1974	1975	1976	1977	1978	1979	1980
South Asia Unall.	3.7	8.4	8.1	8.2	7.6	37.4	3.0
TOTAL	*2913.6*	*3931.1*	*4152.5*	*2924.8*	*3927.5*	*4320.1*	*6135.5*
FAR EAST ASIA							
Brunei	1.8	-2.8	-51.0	-2.1	4.9	77.7	-18.7
China	–	–	–	–	–	129.0	323.6
Hong Kong	107.5	169.4	423.6	264.8	171.1	1053.4	899.3
Indonesia	1049.0	2625.5	2697.7	907.8	1446.6	430.1	1759.8
Kampuchea	307.4	81.1	1.2	0.4	0.5	108.2	281.2
Korea, Rep.	588.6	1076.2	1455.3	1380.5	1539.6	1570.7	823.1
Laos	63.1	38.8	30.4	33.0	72.2	59.5	39.9
Macao	-0.2	0.1	5.0	-1.9	-1.9	-2.8	4.2
Malaysia	268.4	311.0	306.6	240.3	204.1	718.1	623.5
Philippines	383.8	401.4	1085.2	715.8	1061.3	1153.0	968.6
Singapore	155.9	122.3	171.2	214.9	364.4	527.0	672.4
Taiwan	354.7	373.2	117.9	61.6	19.6	419.5	438.9
Thailand	141.0	187.9	207.3	284.4	643.3	946.3	1112.5
Viet Nam, Soc. Rep.	709.4	355.1	186.2	305.2	458.5	446.3	201.7
Mekong Delta Project	4.0	7.1	0.3	0.3	0.9	0.5	–
Far East Asia Unall.	221.1	38.2	33.8	40.6	36.6	19.0	9.3
TOTAL	*4355.4*	*5784.6*	*6671.0*	*4445.5*	*6009.0*	*7656.3*	*8139.9*
Asia Unspecified	798.5	362.1	287.0	649.7	161.9	915.6	-1310.6
ASIA TOTAL	***3855.2***	***16000.7***	***16054.5***	***13635.5***	***18231.9***	***21368.0***	***16997.9***
OCEANIA							
Cook Islands	5.8	5.6	6.9	8.5	6.7	7.8	11.4
Fiji	36.1	18.2	38.7	43.6	43.6	60.7	77.6
Kiribati	5.7	5.7	4.1	6.3	10.7	9.1	19.2
Nauru	-1.0	-0.9	-0.7	7.6	0.0	6.9	-2.1
New Caledonia	69.3	90.3	65.2	84.0	128.4	155.7	215.0
Niue Island	2.9	2.3	2.9	3.5	4.3	5.0	3.7
Pacific Islands (U.S.)	75.3	81.3	86.7	90.1	101.2	120.0	110.2
Papua New Guinea	338.6	297.3	284.5	263.1	336.0	327.4	394.3
Polynesia, French	43.5	79.6	86.8	92.8	99.2	155.6	155.6
Solomon Islands (Br.)	12.5	25.6	19.0	17.0	28.1	26.4	44.6
Tokelau Islands	0.9	0.2	1.2	1.2	1.0	1.8	1.9
Tonga	3.0	3.4	4.7	6.9	9.9	24.2	16.1
Tuvalu	–	0.1	3.0	2.4	2.9	4.1	4.9
Vanuatu	19.5	16.5	41.2	16.5	23.7	43.1	42.4
Wallis & Futuna	4.8	2.2	5.0	3.7	2.5	7.7	8.3
Western Samoa	5.7	13.4	11.6	24.4	23.3	33.5	25.1
Tom Oceania Unall.	0.5	0.6	–	8.3	21.4	–	–
Oceania Unallocated	6.2	35.0	20.2	1.7	33.7	3.6	18.9
TOTAL	*629.2*	*676.3*	*680.9*	*681.4*	*876.5*	*992.5*	*1147.0*
LDC's Unspecified	2571.5	6589.1	7204.2	9348.1	10466.7	10222.6	12054.0
TOTAL,ALL LDC'S	***26542.2***	***49737.3***	***50196.1***	***54585.7***	***73411.9***	***80284.6***	***81510.6***
INCOME GROUPS							
LLDCS	2387.4	3850.9	3387.5	3853.0	4553.1	5787.2	7173.4
OTHER LICS	7249.3	11247.1	10717.0	8997.8	10772.1	9247.1	13427.2
CHINA	–	–	–	–	–	129.0	323.6
MICS	9366.4	11516.0	12308.7	11706.2	16616.7	22154.2	23349.4
NICS	7815.2	8392.9	10266.2	9614.0	14229.9	18216.9	17823.4
OPEC11	492.5	3184.3	2552.9	5980.6	10454.3	4957.4	5163.5
UNALLOCATED	-768.6	11546.2	10963.8	14434.0	16785.8	19792.7	14250.2

	1974	1975	1976	1977	1978	1979	1980
EUROPE							
Cyprus	15.3	25.5	37.1	46.6	24.4	12.3	20.9
Gibraltar	–	–	–	–	–	–	–
Greece	1.8	1.7	2.5	1.2	1.8	24.0	20.6
Malta	1.1	0.8	2.4	0.7	0.4	11.7	9.6
Portugal	–	1.1	5.3	20.9	2.1	14.1	4.0
Spain	1.0	0.9	1.0	0.3	0.5	1.0	1.7
Turkey	22.2	47.9	93.0	63.5	24.0	126.0	20.7
Yugoslavia	1.4	1.5	1.7	2.1	2.7	2.8	2.4
Europe Unallocated	–	0.4	–	0.1	3.7	4.0	1.2
TOTAL	*42.6*	*79.8*	*142.9*	*135.3*	*59.5*	*195.8*	*81.3*
NORTH OF SAHARA							
Algeria	22.5	23.0	11.3	16.2	18.2	9.1	16.9
Egypt	54.3	97.1	348.2	1114.7	898.5	272.5	195.7
Libya	3.2	4.1	3.9	5.9	7.8	2.9	6.8
Morocco	24.8	8.7	15.9	35.2	63.6	60.1	66.0
Tunisia	29.4	33.8	37.1	19.6	13.9	20.1	25.5
North of Sahara Unall.	–	0.1	0.1	0.1	–	0.1	0.1
TOTAL	*134.2*	*166.8*	*416.5*	*1191.6*	*1002.0*	*364.9*	*311.0*
SOUTH OF SAHARA							
Angola	0.1	0.8	7.0	39.7	18.2	17.7	16.2
Benin	14.7	25.3	23.4	22.0	30.9	33.9	52.9
Botswana	6.7	12.8	7.0	9.4	13.9	26.1	22.6
Burundi	15.7	21.7	18.6	19.1	33.8	49.0	53.9
Cameroon	14.3	43.3	44.2	44.1	57.2	74.0	70.9
Cape Verde	–	6.6	16.8	10.2	8.2	6.3	23.4
Central African Rep.	18.2	23.3	12.4	12.0	21.6	31.1	33.8
Chad	31.8	33.3	17.7	33.5	48.1	30.3	15.1
Comoros	0.2	4.2	13.7	7.6	7.0	7.5	12.5
Congo	16.7	18.3	22.9	12.5	25.8	31.5	21.7
Djibouti	0.7	0.3	–	3.5	6.9	4.1	8.6
Equatorial Guinea	0.9	1.0	0.4	0.9	0.6	2.6	8.1
Ethiopia	40.2	60.4	67.7	55.1	83.5	103.8	120.4
Gabon	1.9	2.8	2.2	4.0	7.0	9.9	6.7
Gambia	5.4	4.6	4.4	6.9	13.2	19.1	30.9
Ghana	10.9	21.3	30.0	39.3	38.3	63.7	59.3
Guinea	2.2	3.9	7.1	14.5	43.3	37.3	56.8
Guinea-Bissau	1.2	7.4	6.9	11.5	11.4	17.0	23.7
Ivory Coast	24.4	28.9	32.5	31.1	45.6	22.9	58.5
Kenya	18.2	24.2	24.7	41.4	60.8	66.8	119.6
Lesotho	8.3	15.5	12.1	18.1	20.9	20.2	30.6
Liberia	8.4	10.4	5.7	12.0	26.0	35.5	28.7
Madagascar	31.8	50.5	34.0	27.6	50.3	40.6	91.4
Malawi	11.2	16.8	17.1	25.3	42.1	49.7	67.7
Mali	47.9	63.5	32.7	40.8	64.9	89.3	103.4
Mauritania	26.0	24.3	36.3	33.9	69.8	74.5	36.0
Mauritius	10.5	13.6	6.4	9.9	25.7	7.9	7.8
Mayotte	–	–	–	–	–	–	–
Mozambique	0.1	9.1	35.6	14.3	29.8	31.4	34.1
Niger	53.4	46.6	45.3	34.5	62.7	56.8	63.6
Nigeria	17.5	15.0	7.1	14.1	19.1	16.2	18.3
Reunion	4.2	8.7	6.9	2.0	5.5	1.1	8.4
Rwanda	15.0	28.9	22.3	30.0	45.2	59.3	57.5
St. Helena	–	–	–	–	–	–	–
Sao Tome & Principe	–	0.8	11.0	1.6	2.3	1.6	2.7
Senegal	38.0	48.7	36.1	31.7	94.5	157.2	79.1
Seychelles	0.1	0.2	0.5	0.6	0.7	2.3	3.4
Sierra Leone	6.0	8.3	7.5	14.2	26.8	21.1	29.8
Somalia	31.8	56.9	51.5	49.8	49.5	62.7	166.3
Sudan	58.6	64.2	89.7	69.2	129.7	128.0	192.2
Swaziland	3.9	8.0	6.1	7.8	11.6	18.6	17.4
Tanzania	22.3	60.6	55.0	75.9	90.8	127.4	127.5
Togo	14.0	16.3	20.0	21.8	35.9	40.8	38.8
Uganda	10.2	14.3	10.5	15.4	9.8	25.3	69.9
Upper Volta	40.5	35.7	23.0	38.6	62.8	66.3	61.2
Zaire	27.4	50.4	44.9	89.7	112.9	122.9	105.7
Zambia	4.2	19.3	6.6	13.0	20.1	55.7	61.6
Zimbabwe	0.0	0.1	0.1	–	0.8	–	47.0
East African Community	–	–	–	–	–	–	–
DOM/TOM Unallocated	–	–	–	–	–	–	–
EAMA Unallocated	–	2.1	6.7	–	–	–	–
South of Sahara Unall.	19.6	31.3	29.2	12.9	16.3	1.8	42.3
TOTAL	*735.1*	*1063.9*	*1019.5*	*1122.6*	*1701.3*	*1968.7*	*2408.2*
Africa Unspecified	0.1	0.5	0.1	16.3	37.0	75.7	29.3
AFRICA TOTAL	***869.4***	***1231.2***	***1436.1***	***2330.4***	***2740.3***	***2409.4***	***2748.5***
N.& C. AMERICA							
Bahamas	0.5	0.5	0.5	0.5	1.2	1.1	2.0
Barbados	0.9	2.7	3.5	2.6	3.8	7.1	12.0
Belize	1.5	2.1	3.1	3.7	6.5	0.5	3.6

	1974	1975
Bermuda	–	
Costa Rica	9.3	13.
Cuba	4.7	6.
Dominican Republic	10.1	14.
El Salvador	21.9	29.
Guadeloupe	1.7	7.
Guatemala	6.4	13.
Haiti	4.9	34.
Honduras	12.3	24.
Jamaica	7.2	7.
Martinique	1.7	4.
Mexico	37.7	52.
Netherlands Antilles	3.7	11.
Nicaragua	23.0	23.
Panama	10.9	13.
St. Pierre & Miquelon	0.0	
Trinidad & Tobago	3.5	2.
Anguilla	–	0.
Antigua	0.3	0.
Cayman Islands	0.1	1.
Dominica	0.9	4.
Grenada	0.3	1.
Montserrat	0.1	0.
St. Kitts-Nevis	0.1	0.
St. Lucia	0.6	1.
St. Vincent	0.4	0.
Turks & Caicos Isl.	0.1	0.
Virgin Islands (BR)	0.0	0.
West Indies Unall.	–	0.
DOM/TOM Unallocated	–	
N.& C. America Unall.	–	
TOTAL	*164.9*	*272.*
SOUTH AMERICA		
Argentina	24.0	18.
Bolivia	24.8	24.
Brazil	50.7	49.
Chile	15.6	23.
Colombia	38.4	24.
Ecuador	25.0	45.
Falkland Islands	–	
Guiana, French	2.6	0.
Guyana	3.6	2.
Paraguay	19.9	24.
Peru	18.4	21.
Surinam	5.8	4.
Uruguay	9.5	11.
Venezuela	6.3	17.
South America Unall.	–	1.
TOTAL	*244.6*	*269.*
America Unspecified	26.2	34.
AMERICA TOTAL	***435.7***	***577.***
MIDDLE EAST		
Bahrain	0.6	1.
Iran	8.6	10.
Iraq	6.1	8.
Israel	2.5	1.
Jordan	18.6	20.
Kuwait	1.2	1.
Lebanon	11.7	7.
Oman	0.6	1.
Qatar	0.6	1
Saudi Arabia	3.9	5.
Syria	14.3	26.
United Arab Emirates	0.5	0.
Yemen	22.8	23.
Yemen, Dem.	17.3	14.
Middle East Unall.	18.4	16.
TOTAL	*127.7*	*138.*
SOUTH ASIA		
Afghanistan	14.8	21.
Bangladesh	142.6	252.
Bhutan	0.3	1.
Burma	7.5	29.
India	520.5	685.
Maldives	0.4	1.
Nepal	11.7	16
Pakistan	101.5	95.
Sri Lanka	22.5	51.
Indus Basin	–	

	1976	1977	1978	1979	1980
	–	0.1	0.1	0.1	0.2
	12.8	10.8	16.9	30.0	42.1
	9.9	16.4	31.3	14.9	20.9
	13.1	23.1	40.4	39.8	66.8
	17.3	25.2	29.1	32.9	47.0
	4.0	0.6	3.0	1.3	3.8
	21.6	24.6	45.5	33.4	39.3
	39.6	48.1	43.1	44.2	42.3
	17.1	34.1	58.7	55.3	55.4
	8.3	10.6	24.3	16.9	32.5
	7.3	0.4	2.8	1.2	5.0
	53.4	44.8	9.5	25.1	1.0
	4.6	2.0	3.6	2.9	9.6
	20.6	17.8	15.2	40.3	104.0
	14.6	12.1	10.5	17.7	27.5
	–	–	–	–	–
	2.3	5.0	3.8	3.7	3.2
	–	–	–	–	–
	0.5	1.0	0.9	0.2	3.0
	1.1	0.5	2.8	0.2	0.5
	2.2	1.4	1.1	0.8	9.4
	1.4	1.3	1.9	2.5	2.7
	0.3	0.3	0.2	0.1	0.5
	0.7	0.8	0.5	0.2	3.5
	2.2	1.7	2.4	0.4	6.0
	0.8	1.2	0.6	0.2	7.8
	0.1	0.0	0.1	0.2	0.4
	0.1	0.1	0.1	0.1	1.8
	0.4	0.8	–	–	–
	–	–	0.1	–	-1.9
	–	–	1.7	0.0	1.3
	263.2	*291.7*	*361.4*	*373.2*	*553.1*
	24.3	19.3	18.8	24.4	-13.6
	21.0	36.0	60.3	51.3	71.0
	32.4	21.7	35.3	37.6	21.6
	3.6	9.1	21.7	7.5	3.5
	19.0	18.8	19.7	24.6	58.3
	38.6	32.3	21.3	19.6	23.1
	–	–	–	–	–
	1.7	0.2	1.3	1.9	2.4
	2.4	4.8	10.7	18.9	30.6
	23.9	22.8	22.2	13.8	5.3
	19.8	24.2	22.6	24.4	26.6
	2.4	2.8	3.3	1.5	5.1
	9.9	5.9	8.4	9.8	4.5
	16.2	10.4	3.9	0.6	0.2
	–	–	–	–	–
	215.1	*208.3*	*249.5*	*236.1*	*238.5*
	19.4	23.8	28.4	59.2	128.6
	497.7	***523.8***	***639.2***	***668.5***	***920.3***
	0.7	0.9	7.8	6.0	8.1
	3.7	9.4	8.4	1.8	0.1
	3.4	4.2	5.5	6.6	4.8
	2.5	0.4	0.3	0.3	0.2
	23.5	24.4	35.7	45.5	46.4
	1.8	2.3	2.5	1.7	2.7
	11.9	25.4	36.0	25.0	19.1
	1.7	7.8	7.8	2.0	7.5
	0.9	1.4	2.0	0.3	0.6
	7.2	14.5	12.7	4.3	6.5
	27.9	35.0	36.0	39.3	30.2
	0.5	2.6	3.6	1.5	2.5
	48.8	41.0	42.8	42.9	54.5
	20.9	29.7	48.0	43.9	46.4
	14.5	10.9	117.2	150.0	164.5
	169.8	*209.9*	*366.1*	*370.9*	*394.0*
	29.1	51.5	44.4	52.5	19.4
	201.3	215.9	296.3	367.7	362.1
	2.2	2.3	2.5	4.7	6.6
	31.7	47.0	117.0	104.6	77.4
	595.8	490.6	449.5	577.8	1521.7
	0.9	1.1	1.3	2.0	4.4
	20.8	38.0	35.5	50.9	72.3
	103.0	165.1	222.4	163.9	418.4
	39.2	62.8	104.0	86.2	87.6
	–	–	–	–	–

	1974	1975	1976	1977	1978	1979	1980
South Asia Unall.	–	–	5.0	–	–	22.0	–
TOTAL	*821.9*	*1154.7*	*1028.8*	*1074.2*	*1272.8*	*1432.2*	*2569.9*
FAR EAST ASIA							
Brunei	0.0	0.0	0.0	0.0	0.0	0.0	0.0
China	–	–	–	–	–	12.6	43.9
Hong Kong	0.2	0.2	0.2	0.1	0.3	8.7	7.3
Indonesia	123.4	165.1	145.0	87.4	66.9	84.1	94.3
Kampuchea	2.2	2.3	0.2	0.1	0.1	83.3	231.6
Korea, Rep.	31.6	36.5	37.0	46.2	15.2	13.7	10.8
Laos	2.8	6.3	4.4	5.7	29.2	27.7	24.1
Macao	0.0	0.0	–	–	–	–	4.4
Malaysia	6.8	7.4	3.5	4.4	4.6	29.7	19.3
Philippines	25.5	19.9	25.8	38.8	84.7	94.0	91.0
Singapore	1.8	2.8	2.4	1.9	1.5	1.7	4.0
Taiwan	-0.2	-0.2	-0.2	-0.2	0.7	-0.2	-0.2
Thailand	8.5	16.2	22.8	48.8	109.2	110.2	103.4
Viet Nam, Soc. Rep.	4.4	30.4	18.6	47.6	161.2	106.8	70.1
Mekong Delta Project	–	–	–	–	–	–	–
Far East Asia Unall.	7.0	25.7	25.7	17.3	1.6	1.0	–
TOTAL	*214.1*	*312.6*	*285.3*	*298.0*	*475.1*	*573.4*	*704.0*
Asia Unspecified	8.6	4.3	11.2	6.5	16.1	46.4	46.3
ASIA TOTAL	***1172.2***	***1610.2***	***1495.2***	***1588.5***	***2130.1***	***2422.8***	***3714.1***
OCEANIA							
Cook Islands	0.1	0.2	0.5	0.3	0.3	0.5	0.8
Fiji	0.7	1.7	2.4	3.8	2.6	5.1	4.5
Kiribati	0.2	0.1	0.3	0.2	0.7	0.3	0.6
Nauru	–	–	–	–	–	0.0	–
New Caledonia	0.0	0.0	0.0	1.4	0.8	0.5	0.3
Niue Island	0.0	0.0	0.1	0.1	0.1	0.2	0.3
Pacific Islands (U.S.)	0.2	0.3	0.6	0.6	0.6	0.7	0.8
Papua New Guinea	5.7	7.8	8.3	14.0	25.3	12.8	38.6
Polynesia, French	1.5	0.8	0.6	0.2	0.0	0.0	–
Solomon Islands (Br.)	0.4	0.7	1.0	0.8	2.5	3.4	13.5
Tokelau Islands	–	–	–	0.0	0.0	0.0	0.1
Tonga	0.1	0.5	1.1	1.9	1.6	3.5	3.5
Tuvalu	–	0.1	0.0	0.0	0.3	0.1	0.4
Vanuatu	0.3	0.5	0.5	2.1	0.4	0.7	0.7
Wallis & Futuna	0.0	0.4	0.1	0.1	–	–	–
Western Samoa	1.3	4.6	4.4	9.5	8.9	9.2	12.0
Tom Oceania Unall.	–	–	–	–	–	–	–
Oceania Unallocated	–	–	–	–	–	–	–
TOTAL	*10.6*	*17.6*	*19.8*	*34.9*	*44.1*	*37.0*	*75.8*
LDC's Unspecified	287.2	319.1	275.5	345.8	385.9	461.6	181.0
TOTAL,ALL LDC'S	***2817.8***	***3835.2***	***3867.2***	***4958.7***	***5999.2***	***6195.0***	***7721.0***
INCOME GROUPS							
LLDCS	654.3	981.7	927.3	1041.9	1445.0	1692.1	2030.0
OTHER LICS	1020.5	1428.4	1569.1	2390.4	2596.9	2166.2	3433.7
CHINA	–	–	–	–	–	12.6	43.9
MICS	546.1	704.1	733.5	830.6	1168.5	1291.2	1490.2
NICS	150.0	165.0	159.9	158.1	88.3	152.8	59.6
OPEC11	79.8	119.5	89.6	103.2	92.8	58.3	70.9
UNALLOCATED	367.1	436.5	387.7	434.6	607.9	821.8	592.7

	1974	1975	1976	1977	1978	1979	1980
EUROPE							
Cyprus	24.5	26.5	37.7	47.7	27.2	18.4	29.1
Gibraltar	–	–	–	–	–	–	–
Greece	12.6	25.6	29.6	26.1	10.6	65.4	94.0
Malta	0.6	0.4	1.9	0.4	-0.1	11.2	9.2
Portugal	–	-2.1	33.5	51.4	43.9	86.1	105.9
Spain	39.2	12.7	14.4	-9.1	-3.3	-6.2	-17.4
Turkey	123.4	174.9	234.6	188.7	172.3	398.9	264.5
Yugoslavia	91.6	148.5	145.5	104.4	149.9	274.6	203.1
Europe Unallocated	–	0.4	–	0.1	3.7	4.0	1.2
TOTAL	*292.0*	*386.9*	*497.1*	*409.6*	*404.2*	*852.3*	*689.6*
NORTH OF SAHARA							
Algeria	28.3	63.7	71.2	77.7	66.6	73.7	56.4
Egypt	59.2	130.7	414.4	1157.7	955.2	417.0	360.6
Libya	3.2	4.1	3.9	5.9	7.8	2.9	15.9
Morocco	73.5	107.7	70.6	92.9	186.7	189.6	115.5
Tunisia	51.8	59.5	69.0	67.7	49.1	72.5	82.3
North of Sahara Unall.	–	0.1	0.1	0.1	–	0.1	0.1
TOTAL	*216.0*	*365.8*	*629.1*	*1401.9*	*1265.4*	*755.8*	*630.9*
SOUTH OF SAHARA							
Angola	0.1	0.8	7.0	39.7	18.2	17.7	16.2
Benin	14.9	25.4	24.5	25.5	34.3	36.9	56.3
Botswana	12.4	15.5	9.1	12.3	16.4	31.6	26.4
Burundi	15.4	22.0	20.1	20.2	34.0	48.8	54.2
Cameroon	24.8	66.4	55.2	63.2	110.6	109.5	106.0
Cape Verde	–	6.6	16.8	10.2	8.2	6.3	23.4
Central African Rep.	18.2	23.8	12.7	12.0	21.6	31.0	34.0
Chad	32.4	34.1	18.4	33.5	48.1	30.3	15.1
Comoros	0.2	4.2	13.7	7.6	7.0	7.5	12.5
Congo	17.6	18.8	27.6	15.9	42.6	24.8	22.2
Djibouti	0.7	0.3	–	3.5	6.9	4.1	8.6
Equatorial Guinea	0.9	1.0	0.4	0.9	0.6	2.6	8.8
Ethiopia	38.9	62.9	65.9	51.4	79.6	99.8	118.3
Gabon	0.3	5.9	4.7	5.6	11.7	13.5	9.2
Gambia	5.4	4.6	4.4	6.9	13.2	19.9	36.6
Ghana	9.4	19.9	30.0	52.0	67.1	91.4	83.2
Guinea	0.4	5.2	5.0	14.1	42.5	47.6	63.6
Guinea-Bissau	1.2	7.4	6.9	11.5	11.4	17.0	28.5
Ivory Coast	54.9	68.7	53.7	77.2	106.3	78.1	147.5
Kenya	53.4	99.3	108.5	91.9	122.0	120.2	163.8
Lesotho	8.3	15.5	12.1	18.1	21.2	20.2	30.6
Liberia	11.1	13.1	14.8	19.3	36.9	57.6	53.0
Madagascar	32.0	63.5	36.0	35.3	54.4	43.0	91.4
Malawi	11.4	17.1	20.1	34.0	54.0	71.5	83.5
Mali	47.8	63.3	32.6	41.3	67.5	93.6	103.7
Mauritania	16.8	3.2	36.7	35.1	69.8	81.2	36.7
Mauritius	10.0	17.3	9.9	18.7	34.5	15.6	22.5
Mayotte	–	–	–	–	–	–	–
Mozambique	0.1	9.1	35.6	14.3	29.8	31.6	34.3
Niger	53.9	46.8	45.2	34.3	68.4	74.3	81.5
Nigeria	49.8	43.3	46.2	57.7	59.3	49.1	64.4
Reunion	4.2	8.7	6.9	2.0	5.5	1.1	8.4
Rwanda	15.0	28.9	22.3	30.3	45.4	59.3	57.6
St. Helena	–	–	–	–	–	–	–
Sao Tome & Principe	–	0.8	11.0	1.6	2.3	1.6	2.7
Senegal	39.6	56.3	42.6	43.0	103.1	168.1	105.2
Seychelles	0.1	0.2	0.5	0.6	0.7	2.5	5.8
Sierra Leone	9.4	12.2	8.7	15.0	26.7	23.2	33.2
Somalia	32.4	58.4	51.6	49.8	49.5	62.6	201.1
Sudan	60.9	76.3	116.4	71.1	135.7	167.7	196.3
Swaziland	3.6	8.3	10.6	12.0	17.4	34.4	34.4
Tanzania	30.4	100.2	66.7	99.9	112.7	148.9	149.1
Togo	14.0	16.2	20.7	23.6	65.8	69.8	70.6
Uganda	10.4	15.2	14.0	17.9	10.3	28.4	71.7
Upper Volta	41.3	35.7	24.0	38.5	63.5	65.8	63.0
Zaire	24.2	60.0	63.8	115.1	135.4	124.9	129.1
Zambia	49.6	65.6	77.8	57.8	48.1	78.6	91.6
Zimbabwe	-4.5	-4.6	-4.2	-3.5	-2.1	-3.0	40.6
East African Community	–	–	–	–	3.0	–	–
DOM/TOM Unallocated	–	–	–	–	–	–	–
EAMA Unallocated	–	2.1	6.7	–	–	–	–
South of Sahara Unall.	19.6	31.3	29.2	12.9	23.0	5.1	42.3
TOTAL	*892.9*	*1356.5*	*1343.3*	*1450.5*	*2143.6*	*2415.2*	*2938.5*
Africa Unspecified	1.3	2.3	1.9	17.6	41.0	80.8	33.9
AFRICA TOTAL	***1110.2***	***1724.7***	***1974.2***	***2870.0***	***3449.9***	***3251.7***	***3603.4***
N.& C. AMERICA							
Bahamas	0.5	0.5	0.5	2.0	1.4	1.5	4.6
Barbados	0.9	2.8	4.8	10.6	6.5	8.0	14.6
Belize	2.0	2.7	3.4	3.9	6.7	0.5	4.4

	1974	197[illegible]
Bermuda	–	
Costa Rica	20.0	27
Cuba	4.7	6
Dominican Republic	8.6	16
El Salvador	26.8	41
Guadeloupe	1.7	7
Guatemala	12.7	18
Haiti	4.9	34
Honduras	17.7	35
Jamaica	9.2	16
Martinique	1.7	4
Mexico	268.4	253
Netherlands Antilles	3.7	11
Nicaragua	28.3	33
Panama	26.2	37
St. Pierre & Miquelon	0.0	
Trinidad & Tobago	8.2	7
Anguilla	–	0
Antigua	0.3	0
Cayman Islands	0.1	1
Dominica	1.3	4
Grenada	0.4	1
Montserrat	0.1	0
St. Kitts-Nevis	0.1	0
St. Lucia	0.9	2
St. Vincent	0.5	0
Turks & Caicos Isl.	0.1	0
Virgin Islands (BR)	0.0	0
West Indies Unall.	–	0
DOM/TOM Unallocated	–	
N.& C. America Unall.	–	
TOTAL	*449.9*	*57[illegible]*
SOUTH AMERICA		
Argentina	100.9	47
Bolivia	24.2	32
Brazil	433.6	404
Chile	3.8	32
Colombia	121.8	110
Ecuador	30.4	52
Falkland Islands	–	
Guiana, French	2.6	[illegible]
Guyana	7.2	[illegible]
Paraguay	23.0	3[illegible]
Peru	17.2	3[illegible]
Surinam	5.8	[illegible]
Uruguay	24.3	1[illegible]
Venezuela	15.6	[illegible]
South America Unall.	–	[illegible]
TOTAL	*810.2*	*78[illegible]*
America Unspecified	35.1	5[illegible]
AMERICA TOTAL	***1295.3***	***141[illegible]***
MIDDLE EAST		
Bahrain	0.6	[illegible]
Iran	131.5	18[illegible]
Iraq	10.2	1[illegible]
Israel	7.7	1[illegible]
Jordan	18.6	2[illegible]
Kuwait	1.2	
Lebanon	11.7	1[illegible]
Oman	0.9	[illegible]
Qatar	0.6	
Saudi Arabia	3.9	[illegible]
Syria	14.3	2[illegible]
United Arab Emirates	0.5	[illegible]
Yemen	22.8	2[illegible]
Yemen, Dem.	17.3	1[illegible]
Middle East Unall.	18.4	1[illegible]
TOTAL	*260.3*	*34[illegible]*
SOUTH ASIA		
Afghanistan	14.8	2[illegible]
Bangladesh	143.0	30[illegible]
Bhutan	0.3	
Burma	5.2	2[illegible]
India	508.1	66[illegible]
Maldives	0.4	
Nepal	13.0	1[illegible]
Pakistan	99.1	14[illegible]
Sri Lanka	24.7	5[illegible]
Indus Basin	–	

Sri Lanka 24.7 5[illegible]
Indus Basin –

1976	1977	1978	1979	1980
–	0.1	0.1	0.1	0.2
42.3	50.6	49.2	51.7	74.2
9.9	16.4	31.3	14.9	20.9
14.1	25.7	38.9	41.4	102.6
24.6	32.0	40.7	46.2	61.6
4.0	0.6	3.0	1.3	3.8
24.4	59.4	66.5	69.4	67.3
39.6	48.1	43.1	44.2	42.3
27.8	53.7	85.3	76.8	90.2
29.5	29.1	69.5	31.9	93.2
7.3	0.4	2.8	1.2	5.0
246.8	310.5	224.8	450.0	656.2
4.6	2.0	3.6	2.9	9.6
35.6	31.2	18.9	42.3	111.1
36.8	26.3	44.6	44.1	67.0
–	–	–	–	–
8.9	9.8	6.6	9.8	3.5
–	–	–	–	–
0.8	1.1	0.9	0.2	3.9
1.9	0.5	2.7	0.2	0.5
2.2	1.5	0.6	0.8	9.4
1.4	1.3	1.9	2.5	3.2
0.3	0.3	0.2	0.1	0.8
0.8	1.0	0.6	0.2	3.5
2.2	2.2	2.4	0.4	6.2
0.8	1.3	0.7	0.2	7.8
0.1	0.0	0.1	0.2	0.4
0.1	0.1	0.3	0.1	1.9
0.4	0.8	–	–	–
–	–	0.1	–	-1.9
–	–	2.8	3.1	5.7
575.6	*722.3*	*756.7*	*945.8*	*1473.6*
91.7	88.7	105.6	84.4	47.3
42.2	67.8	94.9	94.0	140.3
260.8	307.0	281.5	381.9	462.5
13.0	39.5	40.2	33.4	29.4
76.6	104.8	75.5	130.9	243.7
42.7	43.8	40.9	67.1	97.1
–	–	–	–	–
1.7	0.2	1.3	1.9	2.4
6.6	7.1	16.4	30.0	41.2
29.0	28.9	35.3	33.5	35.1
32.4	55.2	41.7	87.6	193.7
2.4	2.8	3.3	1.5	5.1
25.1	4.0	7.5	14.2	15.6
15.5	-17.5	-22.3	-29.8	-26.4
–	–	–	–	–
639.5	*732.3*	*721.7*	*930.6*	*1287.0*
26.7	44.1	79.5	106.7	145.4
1241.8	***1498.8***	***1557.9***	***1983.1***	***2906.0***
0.7	0.9	7.8	8.0	8.1
54.7	44.0	-13.6	-38.7	-48.1
24.4	29.5	15.7	12.5	1.0
10.4	-2.3	3.8	-2.2	-3.2
23.5	24.4	45.2	71.2	102.3
2.1	2.3	2.5	1.7	2.7
10.3	23.4	34.0	41.1	46.1
4.0	8.4	11.9	7.7	13.2
0.9	1.4	2.0	0.3	0.6
7.2	14.5	12.7	4.3	6.5
50.9	80.7	66.5	92.8	83.1
1.7	2.6	8.8	1.5	7.8
48.8	41.0	42.8	45.3	73.3
20.9	29.7	48.0	43.9	58.7
14.5	10.9	117.2	150.0	164.5
274.8	*311.4*	*405.0*	*439.4*	*516.6*
29.1	51.5	44.4	52.5	19.4
201.4	215.9	295.8	404.3	350.5
2.2	2.3	2.5	4.7	6.6
30.6	47.3	120.3	104.8	78.1
606.8	530.0	563.3	635.7	1611.3
0.9	1.1	1.3	2.0	4.4
20.7	40.1	36.0	50.7	71.9
162.0	204.0	271.9	215.8	450.0
40.1	61.4	104.9	85.5	90.4
–	–	–	–	–

	1974	1975	1976	1977	1978	1979	1980
South Asia Unall.	–	–	5.0	–	–	22.0	–
TOTAL	*808.7*	*1238.8*	*1098.8*	*1153.6*	*1440.5*	*1577.9*	*2682.5*
FAR EAST ASIA							
Brunei	0.0	0.0	0.0	0.0	0.0	0.0	0.0
China	–	–	–	–	–	12.6	37.4
Hong Kong	17.0	1.3	1.5	-2.1	1.3	19.2	19.0
Indonesia	147.6	224.0	312.9	291.8	235.0	296.8	439.7
Kampuchea	2.2	2.3	0.2	0.1	0.1	83.3	231.6
Korea, Rep.	155.3	330.5	416.0	294.5	390.2	448.2	240.2
Laos	2.8	6.3	4.4	5.7	29.2	27.7	24.1
Macao	0.0	0.0	–	–	–	–	4.4
Malaysia	55.1	68.8	81.7	99.3	87.8	116.3	105.5
Philippines	78.5	140.2	143.8	150.0	212.8	338.0	352.3
Singapore	16.0	22.9	9.9	0.7	59.5	-4.8	9.9
Taiwan	32.3	2.9	-13.0	-18.5	-24.5	-23.9	-18.0
Thailand	43.4	85.5	90.3	123.8	224.8	259.0	322.3
Viet Nam, Soc. Rep.	4.4	30.5	18.6	47.6	161.2	106.7	70.7
Mekong Delta Project	–	–	–	–	–	–	–
Far East Asia Unall.	7.0	25.7	25.7	17.3	1.6	1.0	–
TOTAL	*561.6*	*940.8*	*1092.0*	*1010.3*	*1379.0*	*1680.2*	*1839.1*
Asia Unspecified	8.6	4.3	11.2	6.5	16.1	46.4	46.3
ASIA TOTAL	***1639.2***	***2532.4***	***2476.8***	***2481.8***	***3240.6***	***3743.7***	***5084.5***
OCEANIA							
Cook Islands	0.1	0.2	0.5	0.3	0.3	0.5	0.8
Fiji	7.4	8.3	8.0	8.3	4.7	15.0	24.5
Kiribati	0.2	0.1	0.3	0.2	0.7	0.3	0.6
Nauru	–	–	–	–	–	0.0	–
New Caledonia	0.0	0.0	5.2	1.1	0.4	-0.2	0.8
Niue Island	0.0	0.0	0.1	0.1	0.1	0.2	0.3
Pacific Islands (U.S.)	0.2	0.3	0.6	0.6	0.6	0.7	0.8
Papua New Guinea	17.2	20.6	13.3	16.6	25.2	22.1	47.8
Polynesia, French	1.5	0.8	0.6	0.2	0.0	0.0	–
Solomon Islands (Br.)	0.4	0.7	1.0	0.8	2.5	3.4	13.5
Tokelau Islands	–	–	–	0.0	0.0	0.0	0.1
Tonga	0.1	0.5	1.1	1.9	1.6	3.5	3.5
Tuvalu	–	0.1	0.0	0.0	0.3	0.1	0.4
Vanuatu	0.3	0.5	0.5	2.1	0.4	0.7	0.7
Wallis & Futuna	0.0	0.4	0.1	0.1	–	–	–
Western Samoa	1.3	4.6	4.4	9.5	8.9	9.2	12.0
Tom Oceania Unall.	–	–	–	–	–	–	–
Oceania Unallocated	–	–	–	–	–	–	–
TOTAL	*28.7*	*37.0*	*35.5*	*41.7*	*45.9*	*55.6*	*105.4*
LDC's Unspecified	287.2	326.1	318.5	595.8	385.9	468.5	181.0
TOTAL,ALL LDC'S	***4652.6***	***6418.5***	***6544.0***	***7897.6***	***9084.3***	***10355.0***	***12569.8***
INCOME GROUPS							
LLDCS	671.8	1100.5	975.0	1084.9	1496.2	1853.4	2170.2
OTHER LICS	1060.1	1634.0	1991.5	2830.6	3151.9	2786.0	4241.3
CHINA	–	–	–	–	–	12.6	37.4
MICS	1150.6	1630.6	1672.4	1912.6	2390.5	2931.6	3577.1
NICS	1166.9	1247.8	1236.6	1153.6	1239.4	1774.8	1802.7
OPEC11	225.9	340.7	228.7	209.7	132.6	108.9	122.7
UNALLOCATED	377.3	464.9	439.8	706.2	673.7	887.5	618.5

SECTION B

INDIVIDUAL COUNTRY TABLES

TABLEAUX PAR PAYS

AFGHANISTAN

DISBURSEMENTS, UNLESS OTHERWISE STATE

	1977	1978	1979	1980	1977	1978	1979	1980		197
TOTAL RECEIPTS NET					**TOTAL ODA NET**				**TOTAL ODA GROSS**	
DAC COUNTRIES										
Australia	0.7	1.0	0.2	0.1	0.7	1.0	0.2	0.1	Australia	0.
Austria	0.1	0.1	0.1	0.3	0.1	0.1	0.1	0.3	Austria	0
Belgium	0.0	0.1	0.2	0.5	0.0	0.1	0.0	–	Belgium	0.
Canada	0.3	4.2	7.5	2.1	0.3	4.2	6.0	2.2	Canada	0.
Denmark	0.1	0.4	0.0	1.8	0.1	0.4	0.0	1.8	Denmark	0.
Finland	–	–	0.1	0.0	–	–	0.1	0.0	Finland	
France	–	–	0.2	0.7	–	–	–	0.7	France	
Germany, Fed. Rep.	2.4	6.1	12.9	1.3	2.3	5.8	12.9	1.4	Germany, Fed. Rep.	7
Italy	0.1	0.1	0.1	0.0	0.1	0.1	0.1	0.0	Italy	0.
Japan	5.8	4.9	11.9	0.4	6.1	4.9	11.9	0.4	Japan	6.
Netherlands	1.6	1.7	0.2	0.2	1.6	1.7	0.2	0.2	Netherlands	1
New Zealand	0.0	–	–	–	0.0	–	–	–	New Zealand	0
Norway	0.1	–	-0.4	–	0.1	–	–	–	Norway	0
Sweden	0.9	0.7	-0.1	0.9	0.9	0.5	–	1.1	Sweden	0.
Switzerland	0.5	0.7	0.6	0.2	0.5	0.7	0.6	0.2	Switzerland	0.
United Kingdom	3.0	1.8	2.9	1.1	3.0	1.7	2.9	1.1	United Kingdom	3.
United States	12.0	11.0	32.0	4.0	12.0	11.0	12.0	2.0	United States	13
TOTAL	*27.4*	*32.7*	*68.2*	*13.4*	*27.6*	*32.0*	*47.0*	*11.4*	*TOTAL*	*34.*
MULTILATERAL										
AF.D.F.	–	–	–	–	–	–	–	–	AF.D.F.	
AF.D.B.	–	–	–	–	–	–	–	–	AF.D.B.	
AS.D.B.	2.9	8.0	6.3	4.4	2.9	8.0	6.3	4.4	AS.D.B.	2
CAR.D.B.	–	–	–	–	–	–	–	–	CAR.D.B.	
E.E.C.	0.4	1.6	0.0	–	0.4	1.6	0.0	–	E.E.C.	0
IBRD	–	–	–	–	–	–	–	–	IBRD	
IDA	24.7	14.5	12.3	5.6	24.7	14.5	12.3	5.6	IDA	24
I.D.B.	–	–	–	–	–	–	–	–	I.D.B.	
IFAD	–	–	–	–	–	–	–	–	IFAD	
I.F.C.	–	–	–	–	–	–	–	–	I.F.C.	
IMF TRUST FUND	–	–	–	–	–	–	–	–	IMF TRUST FUND	
U.N. AGENCIES	–	–	–	–	–	–	–	–	U.N. AGENCIES	
UNDP	5.5	6.2	8.5	6.3	5.5	6.2	8.5	6.3	UNDP	5
UNTA	1.9	2.1	2.3	0.1	1.9	2.1	2.3	0.1	UNTA	1.
UNICEF	2.0	3.0	4.1	3.3	2.0	3.0	4.1	3.3	UNICEF	2
UNRWA	–	–	–	–	–	–	–	–	UNRWA	
WFP	7.9	6.6	16.7	-1.5	7.9	6.6	16.7	-1.5	WFP	7
UNHCR	–	–	–	–	–	–	–	–	UNHCR	
Other Multilateral	2.5	2.4	2.3	1.2	2.5	2.4	2.3	1.2	Other Multilateral	2
Arab OPEC Agencies	3.8	–	–	–	3.8	–	–	–	Arab OPEC Agencies	3.
TOTAL	*51.5*	*44.4*	*52.5*	*19.4*	*51.5*	*44.4*	*52.5*	*19.4*	*TOTAL*	*51*
OPEC COUNTRIES	*21.6*	*18.5*	*8.5*	*1.5*	*21.6*	*18.5*	*8.5*	*1.5*	*OPEC COUNTRIES*	*21.*
E.E.C.+ MEMBERS	*7.4*	*11.8*	*16.4*	*5.6*	*7.4*	*11.3*	*16.1*	*5.2*	*E.E.C.+ MEMBERS*	*12.*
TOTAL	***100.6***	***95.6***	***129.1***	***34.3***	***100.7***	***94.9***	***107.9***	***32.3***	***TOTAL***	***107***

	1977	1978	1979	1980	1977	1978	1979	1980		197
ODA LOANS GROSS					**ODA LOANS NET**				**GRANTS**	
DAC COUNTRIES										
Australia	–	–	–	–	–	–	–	–	Australia	0.
Austria	–	–	–	–	–	–	–	–	Austria	0.
Belgium	–	–	–	–	–	–	–	–	Belgium	0
Canada	–	–	–	–	–	-1.1	–	–	Canada	0.
Denmark	–	–	–	–	0.0	–	-0.1	–	Denmark	0
Finland	–	–	–	–	–	–	–	–	Finland	
France	–	–	–	–	–	–	–	–	France	
Germany, Fed. Rep.	1.5	2.8	8.8	1.2	-3.7	-2.3	5.6	-4.4	Germany, Fed. Rep.	6.
Italy	–	–	–	–	–	–	–	–	Italy	0.
Japan	–	–	–	–	-0.2	-0.2	-0.2	-0.2	Japan	6.
Netherlands	–	–	–	–	–	–	–	–	Netherlands	1
New Zealand	–	–	–	–	–	–	–	–	New Zealand	0
Norway	–	–	–	–	–	–	–	–	Norway	0.
Sweden	–	–	–	–	–	–	–	–	Sweden	0.
Switzerland	–	–	–	–	–	–	–	–	Switzerland	0.
United Kingdom	0.8	–	–	–	0.6	-0.1	0.0	-0.4	United Kingdom	2.
United States	4.0	6.0	–	–	3.0	4.0	-1.0	-1.0	United States	9.
TOTAL	*6.2*	*8.8*	*8.8*	*1.2*	*-0.3*	*0.2*	*4.3*	*-6.0*	*TOTAL*	*27.*
MULTILATERAL	*31.3*	*22.7*	*18.8*	*10.3*	*31.3*	*22.5*	*18.5*	*10.0*	*MULTILATERAL*	*20.*
OPEC COUNTRIES	*21.5*	*13.4*	*8.3*	*1.5*	*21.5*	*13.4*	*8.3*	*1.5*	*OPEC COUNTRIES*	*0.*
E.E.C.+ MEMBERS	*2.2*	*2.8*	*8.8*	*1.2*	*-3.1*	*-2.4*	*5.5*	*-4.8*	*E.E.C.+ MEMBERS*	*10.*
TOTAL	***59.0***	***45.0***	***35.9***	***13.0***	***52.5***	***36.2***	***31.1***	***5.4***	***TOTAL***	***48.***

	1977	1978	1979	1980	1977	1978	1979	1980		197
TOTAL OFFICIAL GROSS					**TOTAL OFFICIAL NET**				**TOTAL OOF GROSS**	
DAC COUNTRIES										
Australia	0.7	1.0	0.2	0.1	0.7	1.0	0.2	0.1	Australia	
Austria	0.1	0.1	0.1	0.3	0.1	0.1	0.1	0.3	Austria	
Belgium	0.0	0.1	0.0	–	0.0	0.1	0.0	–	Belgium	
Canada	0.3	5.3	7.5	2.2	0.3	4.2	7.5	2.1	Canada	
Denmark	0.1	0.4	0.1	1.8	0.1	0.4	0.0	1.8	Denmark	
Finland	–	–	0.1	0.0	–	–	0.1	0.0	Finland	
France	–	–	–	0.7	–	–	–	0.7	France	
Germany, Fed. Rep.	7.4	11.0	16.1	6.9	2.3	5.8	12.9	1.3	Germany, Fed. Rep.	
Italy	0.1	0.1	0.1	0.0	0.1	0.1	0.1	0.0	Italy	
Japan	6.3	5.1	12.1	0.6	6.1	4.9	11.9	0.4	Japan	
Netherlands	1.6	1.7	0.2	0.2	1.6	1.7	0.2	0.2	Netherlands	
New Zealand	0.0	–	–	–	0.0	–	–	–	New Zealand	
Norway	0.1	–	–	–	0.1	–	–	–	Norway	
Sweden	0.9	0.5	–	1.1	0.9	0.5	–	1.1	Sweden	
Switzerland	0.5	0.7	0.6	0.2	0.5	0.7	0.6	0.2	Switzerland	
United Kingdom	3.1	1.8	2.9	1.6	3.0	1.7	2.9	1.1	United Kingdom	
United States	13.0	13.0	33.0	5.0	12.0	11.0	32.0	4.0	United States	
TOTAL	*34.1*	*40.6*	*72.9*	*20.7*	*27.6*	*32.0*	*68.4*	*13.2*	*TOTAL*	
MULTILATERAL	*51.5*	*44.6*	*52.7*	*19.7*	*51.5*	*44.4*	*52.5*	*19.4*	*MULTILATERAL*	
OPEC COUNTRIES	*21.6*	*18.5*	*8.5*	*1.5*	*21.6*	*18.5*	*8.5*	*1.5*	*OPEC COUNTRIES*	
E.E.C.+ MEMBERS	*12.7*	*16.6*	*19.4*	*11.2*	*7.4*	*11.3*	*16.1*	*5.1*	*E.E.C.+ MEMBERS*	
TOTAL	***107.2***	***103.7***	***134.2***	***41.9***	***100.7***	***94.9***	***129.4***	***34.1***	***TOTAL***	

1978	1979	1980	1977	1978	1979	1980
			ODA COMMITMENTS			
1.0	0.2	0.1	1.0	0.9	0.1	–
0.1	0.1	0.3	–	–	–	–
0.1	0.0	–	–	–	–	–
5.3	6.0	2.2	11.1	10.0	–	0.2
0.4	0.1	1.8	0.5	10.3	1.1	–
–	0.1	0.0	–	–	0.1	–
–	–	0.7	–	–	–	0.7
11.0	16.1	6.9	8.1	10.9	11.5	5.1
0.1	0.1	0.0	0.1	0.1	0.1	0.0
5.1	12.1	0.6	5.6	12.4	5.7	0.3
1.7	0.2	0.2	3.2	0.6	3.0	0.2
–	–	–	–	–	–	–
–	–	–	–	–	–	–
0.5	–	1.1	0.3	–	–	–
0.7	0.6	0.2	–	–	1.1	–
1.8	2.9	1.6	3.0	1.1	2.2	1.3
13.0	13.0	3.0	26.5	9.3	0.5	0.1
40.6	*51.5*	*18.7*	*59.3*	*55.6*	*25.4*	*7.9*
–	–	–	–	–	–	–
–	–	–	–	–	–	–
8.2	6.5	4.7	14.7	1.7	20.1	–
–	–	–	–	–	–	–
1.6	0.0	–	0.3	0.7	0.6	–
–	–	–	–	–	–	–
14.5	12.3	5.6	18.0	56.5	55.1	–
–	–	–	–	–	–	–
–	–	–	–	–	12.9	–
–	–	–	–	–	–	–
–	–	–	–	–	–	–
–	–	–	19.8	20.3	33.9	9.4
6.2	8.5	6.3	–	–	–	–
2.1	2.3	0.1	–	–	–	–
3.0	4.1	3.3	–	–	–	–
–	–	–	–	–	–	–
6.6	16.7	-1.5	–	–	–	–
–	–	–	–	–	–	–
2.4	2.3	1.2	–	–	–	–
–	–	–	3.8	–	3.6	–
44.6	*52.7*	*19.7*	*56.5*	*79.2*	*126.2*	*9.4*
18.5	*8.5*	*1.5*	*128.6*	*5.0*	–	–
16.6	*19.4*	*11.2*	*15.1*	*23.8*	*18.5*	*7.2*
103.7	***112.7***	***39.9***	***244.4***	***139.8***	***151.5***	***17.2***
			TECH. COOP. GRANTS			
1.0	0.2	0.1	0.4	0.3	0.2	0.1
0.1	0.1	0.3	0.1	0.1	0.1	0.2
0.1	0.0	–	0.0	0.1	0.0	–
5.3	6.0	2.2	0.0	–	–	–
0.4	0.1	1.8	0.1	0.4	0.1	0.1
–	0.1	0.0	–	–	0.1	0.0
–	–	0.7	–	–	–	0.7
8.1	7.3	5.8	5.9	8.1	7.3	5.8
0.1	0.1	0.0	0.1	0.1	0.1	0.0
5.1	12.1	0.6	1.7	1.8	1.5	0.3
1.7	0.2	0.2	1.0	0.4	0.2	0.2
–	–	–	0.0	–	–	–
–	–	–	0.1	–	–	–
0.5	–	1.1	0.3	0.3	–	–
0.7	0.6	0.2	0.0	0.0	0.0	0.2
1.8	2.9	1.6	0.7	0.9	1.0	0.6
7.0	13.0	3.0	6.0	5.0	10.0	3.0
31.8	*42.7*	*17.5*	*16.2*	*17.5*	*20.6*	*10.9*
21.9	*34.0*	*9.4*	*12.0*	*13.7*	*17.2*	*9.4*
5.1	*0.2*	*0.0*	–	–	–	–
13.8	*10.6*	*10.0*	*7.7*	*9.9*	*8.7*	*7.3*
58.8	***76.8***	***26.9***	***28.2***	***31.1***	***37.8***	***20.3***
			TOTAL OOF NET			
–	–	–	–	–	–	–
–	–	–	–	–	–	–
–	–	–	–	–	–	–
–	1.4	–	–	–	1.4	-0.1
–	–	–	–	–	–	–
–	–	–	–	–	–	–
–	–	–	–	–	–	–
–	–	–	–	–	–	-0.1
–	–	–	–	–	–	–
–	–	–	–	–	–	–
–	–	–	–	–	–	–
–	–	–	–	–	–	–
–	–	–	–	–	–	–
–	–	–	–	–	–	–
–	–	–	–	–	–	–
–	–	–	–	–	–	–
–	20.0	2.0	–	–	20.0	2.0
–	*21.4*	*2.0*	–	–	*21.4*	*1.8*
–	–	–	–	–	–	–
–	–	–	–	–	–	–
–	–	–	–	–	–	*-0.1*
–	***21.4***	***2.0***	–	–	***21.4***	***1.8***

MAIN AID AGGREGATES

	1977	1978	1979	1980
DAC COUNTRIES COMBINED				
PRIVATE SECTOR NET	-0.2	0.7	-0.2	0.2
Direct Investment	-0.2	–	1.2	–
Portfolio Invest.	0.1	0.1	-0.9	0.2
Export Credits	0.0	0.6	-0.6	0.0
OFFICIAL & PRIVATE				
GROSS:				
Contractual Lending	6.7	11.7	31.2	4.4
Export Credits Tot.	0.5	2.8	22.4	3.3
Export Credits Priv	0.5	2.8	0.9	1.3
OTHER NET DATA				
Contractual Lending	-0.3	0.8	25.1	-4.3
Export Credits Tot.	0.0	0.6	20.9	1.8
(Bank Sector Loans)	–	–	2.0	-1.0
ODA CONCESSIONALITY				
Total:Grant Element	97.0	97.0	98.0	99.0
Loans:Grant Element	68.0	84.0	81.0	67.0
OTHER SOURCES				
CMEA Countr.(Gross)	46.5	43.8	38.2	284.0
Intra LDCS Exc.OPEC	–	–	–	–
Other	–	–	–	–
ALL SOURCE COMMITMENTS				
TOTAL BILATERAL	187.8	84.7	26.8	7.9
of which				
OPEC (ODA)	128.6	5.0	–	–
CMEA (ODA)	12.2	21.2	472.0	353.1
TOTAL MULTILAT.(ODA)	56.5	79.2	126.2	9.4
TOTAL BIL.& MULTIL.	244.4	163.9	153.0	17.3
of which				
ODA Grants	74.0	71.4	57.2	17.1
ODA Loans	170.4	68.4	94.4	0.1
ODA CONCESSIONALITY				
Total: Grant Element	63.0	91.0	88.0	99.0
Loans: Grant Element	48.0	82.0	80.0	67.0

INDEBTEDNESS

	1977	1978	1979	1980
TOTAL DEBT DISBURSED	***961.8***	***1110.6***	***1174.1***	
Debt to DAC Countries	196.0	213.0	250.0	
ODA	180.0	197.0	206.0	
Total Export Credits	16.0	16.0	44.0	
Other Private Market	–	–	–	
International Org.	63.0	89.0	107.2	
CMEA	635.8	717.1	724.3	
Other	67.1	91.5	92.6	
TOTAL DEBT SERVICE	***38.3***	***54.5***	***14.0***	
Paid to DAC Countries	13.2	15.8	12.5	
ODA	10.4	11.2	7.5	
Total Export Credits	2.8	4.6	5.0	
Other Private Market	–	–	–	
International Org.	0.4	0.6	0.9	
CMEA	22.2	31.3	0.6	
Other	2.5	6.8	–	

ECONOMIC INDICATORS

	1977	1978	1979	1980
GNP Curr. Prices, $M	–	–	–	–
Real GNP, 1976=100	–	–	–	–
GNP/Cap Curr. Prices,$	–	–	–	–
GNP/cap Atlas Basis, $	–	–	–	–
Real GNP/Cap, 1976=100	–	–	–	–
Population, Million	14.8	15.2	15.5	15.9
Curr.A/C Deficit(-),$M	–	–	–	–
BOP Exp. & Transf.,$M	–	–	–	–
Exp. to OECD CIF, $M	155.1	137.8	173.3	170.6
of which				
Manufact.	44.5	52.6	62.1	80.8
Imp. from OECD FOB, $M	253.5	241.4	274.3	202.7
Reserves ex. Gold, $M	275.8	390.6	441.2	371.2

	1977	1978	1979	1980	1977	1978	1979	1980
TOTAL RECEIPTS NET					**TOTAL ODA NET**			
DAC COUNTRIES								
Australia	–	0.0	0.0	0.1	–	0.0	0.0	0.1
Austria	50.3	274.0	2.1	-3.6	0.1	0.2	0.2	0.5
Belgium	237.2	717.0	107.1	-137.8	2.1	2.2	3.4	4.1
Canada	83.1	69.1	-26.3	-9.2	3.7	1.1	0.8	0.2
Denmark	0.7	36.3	-0.1	51.7	0.1	0.0	0.1	0.0
Finland	–	–	–	–	–	–	–	–
France	451.4	657.2	210.6	356.6	64.5	65.9	75.4	75.3
Germany, Fed. Rep.	280.1	539.9	162.8	581.3	26.8	29.0	9.9	28.6
Italy	449.9	520.6	272.8	231.6	0.9	0.4	0.8	0.5
Japan	492.1	788.3	315.2	77.8	14.3	19.5	6.0	4.8
Netherlands	0.1	–	153.6	195.2	0.1	–	0.2	0.6
New Zealand	–	–	–	–	–	–	–	–
Norway	0.2	0.2	–	0.3	0.1	0.2	–	0.3
Sweden	11.4	9.4	4.9	20.0	0.7	1.0	1.6	2.4
Switzerland	200.2	76.8	129.8	-39.9	0.2	0.1	0.2	0.5
United Kingdom	0.9	3.3	-45.4	-3.2	0.3	0.2	0.1	0.8
United States	32.0	112.0	148.0	125.0	-1.0	-1.0	-1.0	-1.0
TOTAL	*2289.3*	*3804.0*	*1435.1*	*1446.0*	*112.7*	*118.8*	*97.6*	*117.6*
MULTILATERAL								
AF.D.F.	–	–	–	–	–	–	–	–
AF.D.B.	1.7	1.5	1.1	1.2	–	–	–	–
AS.D.B.	–	–	–	–	–	–	–	–
CAR.D.B.	–	–	–	–	–	–	–	–
E.E.C.	–	0.7	0.1	0.6	–	0.7	0.1	0.6
IBRD	52.2	49.6	39.8	25.5	–	–	–	–
IDA	–	–	–	–	–	–	–	–
I.D.B.	–	–	–	–	–	–	–	–
IFAD	–	–	–	–	–	–	–	–
I.F.C.	–	–	–	–	–	–	–	–
IMF TRUST FUND	–	–	–	–	–	–	–	–
U.N. AGENCIES	–	–	–	–	–	–	–	–
UNDP	1.6	4.2	5.2	6.2	1.6	4.2	5.2	6.2
UNTA	0.4	0.1	0.1	0.1	0.4	0.1	0.1	0.1
UNICEF	0.3	0.9	0.3	0.3	0.3	0.9	0.3	0.3
UNRWA	–	–	–	–	–	–	–	–
WFP	10.0	2.4	2.2	10.1	10.0	2.4	2.2	10.1
UNHCR	–	0.0	0.0	0.0	–	0.0	0.0	0.0
Other Multilateral	3.8	3.9	0.1	0.4	3.8	3.9	0.1	0.4
Arab OPEC Agencies	7.7	3.4	24.9	12.1	–	6.1	1.2	-0.8
TOTAL	*77.7*	*66.6*	*73.7*	*56.4*	*16.2*	*18.2*	*9.1*	*16.9*
OPEC COUNTRIES	*-4.3*	*1.3*	*-2.3*	*44.2*	*-4.3*	*-4.5*	*-2.3*	*44.2*
E.E.C.+ MEMBERS	*1420.1*	*2474.9*	*861.6*	*1276.1*	*94.8*	*98.4*	*90.0*	*110.5*
TOTAL	***2362.7***	***3871.9***	***1506.6***	***1546.6***	***124.6***	***132.5***	***104.5***	***178.8***

TOTAL ODA GROSS	197
Australia	
Austria	0
Belgium	2
Canada	3.
Denmark	0.
Finland	
France	73
Germany, Fed. Rep.	27
Italy	1
Japan	14.
Netherlands	0
New Zealand	
Norway	0
Sweden	0
Switzerland	0.
United Kingdom	0.
United States	
TOTAL	*123.*
AF.D.F.	
AF.D.B.	
AS.D.B.	
CAR.D.B.	
E.E.C.	
IBRD	
IDA	
I.D.B.	
IFAD	
I.F.C.	
IMF TRUST FUND	
U.N. AGENCIES	
UNDP	1
UNTA	0
UNICEF	0.
UNRWA	
WFP	10
UNHCR	
Other Multilateral	3
Arab OPEC Agencies	
TOTAL	*16*
OPEC COUNTRIES	
E.E.C.+ MEMBERS	*104.*
TOTAL	***139***

	1977	1978	1979	1980	1977	1978	1979	1980
ODA LOANS GROSS					**ODA LOANS NET**			
DAC COUNTRIES								
Australia	–	–	–	–	–	–	–	–
Austria	–	–	–	–	–	–	–	–
Belgium	–	–	–	–	–	–	–	–
Canada	2.3	0.7	0.8	0.2	2.3	0.7	0.7	0.2
Denmark	0.1	0.0	0.1	–	0.1	0.0	0.1	-0.2
Finland	–	–	–	–	–	–	–	–
France	0.5	0.1	–	–	-8.4	-12.5	-11.3	-14.1
Germany, Fed. Rep.	22.4	23.0	3.9	19.7	22.3	22.9	3.8	19.7
Italy	–	–	–	–	-0.6	-0.6	-0.8	-0.6
Japan	14.0	19.1	5.4	2.5	14.0	19.1	5.4	2.5
Netherlands	–	–	–	–	–	–	–	–
New Zealand	–	–	–	–	–	–	–	–
Norway	–	–	–	–	–	–	–	–
Sweden	–	–	–	–	–	–	–	–
Switzerland	–	–	–	–	–	–	–	–
United Kingdom	–	–	–	–	–	–	–	–
United States	–	–	–	–	-1.0	-1.0	-1.0	-1.0
TOTAL	*39.3*	*43.0*	*10.1*	*22.4*	*28.6*	*28.6*	*-3.1*	*6.5*
MULTILATERAL	–	*6.1*	*2.2*	*0.2*	–	*6.1*	*1.2*	*-0.8*
OPEC COUNTRIES	–	–	–	–	*-4.3*	*-4.5*	*-2.3*	–
E.E.C.+ MEMBERS	*23.0*	*23.1*	*3.9*	*19.7*	*13.4*	*9.8*	*-8.2*	*4.8*
TOTAL	***39.3***	***49.1***	***12.3***	***22.7***	***24.3***	***30.2***	***-4.2***	***5.8***

GRANTS	197
Australia	
Austria	0.
Belgium	2
Canada	1.
Denmark	
Finland	
France	72.
Germany, Fed. Rep.	4.
Italy	1.
Japan	0.
Netherlands	0.
New Zealand	
Norway	0.
Sweden	0.
Switzerland	0.
United Kingdom	0.
United States	
TOTAL	*84.*
MULTILATERAL	*16.*
OPEC COUNTRIES	
E.E.C.+ MEMBERS	*81.*
TOTAL	***100.***

	1977	1978	1979	1980	1977	1978	1979	1980
TOTAL OFFICIAL GROSS					**TOTAL OFFICIAL NET**			
DAC COUNTRIES								
Australia	–	0.0	0.0	0.1	–	0.0	0.0	0.1
Austria	0.1	0.2	0.2	0.5	-0.8	-1.5	-1.6	-1.1
Belgium	2.1	2.2	3.4	4.1	2.1	2.2	3.4	4.1
Canada	29.4	89.3	0.8	23.0	28.1	86.9	0.8	13.2
Denmark	0.1	0.2	0.1	0.2	0.1	0.2	0.1	0.0
Finland	–	–	–	–	–	–	–	–
France	73.4	78.5	86.7	97.3	64.5	62.4	68.4	83.3
Germany, Fed. Rep.	27.2	111.0	63.7	65.0	27.1	107.0	51.4	46.6
Italy	1.5	1.1	1.6	89.5	0.9	0.4	0.8	88.9
Japan	226.5	384.8	218.3	29.8	226.5	384.8	218.3	-12.3
Netherlands	0.1	–	0.2	0.6	0.1	–	0.2	0.6
New Zealand	–	–	–	–	–	–	–	–
Norway	0.1	0.2	–	0.3	0.1	0.2	–	0.3
Sweden	0.7	1.0	1.6	2.4	0.7	1.0	1.6	2.4
Switzerland	0.2	0.1	0.2	0.5	0.2	0.1	0.2	0.5
United Kingdom	0.3	0.2	0.1	0.8	0.3	0.2	0.1	0.8
United States	45.0	125.0	166.0	150.0	32.0	112.0	148.0	125.0
TOTAL	*406.5*	*793.7*	*542.8*	*464.0*	*381.6*	*755.9*	*491.6*	*352.2*
MULTILATERAL	*78.1*	*78.9*	*87.4*	*97.1*	*77.7*	*66.6*	*73.7*	*56.4*
OPEC COUNTRIES	–	*5.8*	–	*44.2*	*-4.3*	*1.3*	*-2.3*	*44.2*
E.E.C.+ MEMBERS	*104.6*	*193.8*	*155.9*	*258.1*	*95.0*	*173.1*	*124.5*	*224.8*
TOTAL	***484.6***	***878.4***	***630.2***	***605.3***	***455.0***	***823.8***	***563.1***	***452.9***

TOTAL OOF GROSS	197
Australia	
Austria	
Belgium	
Canada	25.
Denmark	
Finland	
France	
Germany, Fed. Rep.	0.
Italy	
Japan	212.
Netherlands	
New Zealand	
Norway	
Sweden	
Switzerland	
United Kingdom	
United States	45.
TOTAL	*283.*
MULTILATERAL	*61.*
OPEC COUNTRIES	
E.E.C.+ MEMBERS	*0.*
TOTAL	***345.***

1978	1979	1980	1977	1978	1979	1980
			ODA COMMITMENTS			
0.0	0.0	0.1	–	0.0	0.0	0.1
0.2	0.2	0.5	–	–	–	0.0
2.2	3.4	4.1	2.8	3.2	3.9	5.1
1.1	0.8	0.2	0.8	0.3	0.0	0.1
0.0	0.1	0.2	–	–	–	–
–	–	–	–	–	–	0.3
78.5	86.7	89.4	75.0	83.1	88.9	97.8
29.1	10.0	28.6	4.2	6.8	25.3	8.7
1.1	1.6	1.1	1.5	1.1	1.6	1.1
19.5	6.0	4.8	14.1	0.5	4.1	2.5
–	0.2	0.6	0.1	–	0.2	3.1
–	–	–	–	–	–	–
0.2	–	0.3	–	–	–	0.3
1.0	1.6	2.4	–	0.4	1.4	1.1
0.1	0.2	0.5	–	–	–	0.5
0.2	0.1	0.8	0.3	0.2	0.1	0.8
–	–	–	5.4	4.1	–	–
133.1	*110.8*	*133.5*	*104.1*	*99.7*	*125.5*	*121.3*
–	–	–	–	–	–	–
–	–	–	–	–	–	–
–	–	–	–	–	–	–
–	–	–	–	–	–	–
0.7	0.1	0.6	–	–	1.3	32.6
–	–	–	–	–	–	–
–	–	–	–	–	–	–
–	–	–	–	–	–	–
–	–	–	–	–	–	–
–	–	–	–	–	–	–
–	–	–	–	–	–	–
–	–	–	16.2	11.5	7.9	17.0
4.2	5.2	6.2	–	–	–	–
0.1	0.1	0.1	–	–	–	–
0.9	0.3	0.3	–	–	–	–
–	–	–	–	–	–	–
2.4	2.2	10.1	–	–	–	–
0.0	0.0	0.0	–	–	–	–
3.9	0.1	0.4	–	–	–	–
6.1	2.2	0.2	41.9	–	–	–
18.2	*10.1*	*17.9*	*58.1*	*11.5*	*9.2*	*49.6*
–	–	*44.2*	–	–	–	*54.2*
111.7	*102.2*	*125.4*	*83.8*	*94.3*	*121.2*	*149.2*
151.4	***120.9***	***195.7***	***162.1***	***111.1***	***134.6***	***225.2***
			TECH. COOP. GRANTS			
0.0	0.0	0.1	–	0.0	0.0	–
0.2	0.2	0.5	0.1	0.2	0.2	0.4
2.2	3.4	4.1	2.1	1.9	3.2	3.6
0.4	0.0	0.0	0.7	0.2	–	0.0
0.0	–	0.2	–	0.0	–	–
–	–	–	–	–	–	–
78.4	86.7	89.4	61.2	65.0	69.9	74.9
6.1	6.1	8.9	4.6	5.8	6.1	8.2
1.1	1.6	1.1	1.5	1.1	1.6	0.6
0.4	0.6	2.3	0.3	0.4	0.6	1.0
–	0.2	0.6	0.1	–	0.1	0.1
–	–	–	–	–	–	–
0.2	–	0.3	–	0.0	–	–
1.0	1.6	2.4	–	0.7	0.4	0.2
0.1	0.2	0.5	0.0	0.0	0.0	–
0.2	0.1	0.8	0.3	0.2	0.1	0.1
–	–	–	–	–	–	–
90.2	*100.7*	*111.1*	*70.8*	*75.5*	*82.2*	*89.0*
12.1	*7.9*	*17.7*	*6.1*	*9.1*	*5.7*	*17.0*
–	–	*44.2*	–	–	–	–
88.6	*98.2*	*105.7*	*69.7*	*74.0*	*81.1*	*87.5*
102.3	***108.6***	***173.0***	***76.9***	***84.6***	***87.9***	***106.1***
			TOTAL OOF NET			
–	–	–	–	–	–	–
–	–	–	-0.9	-1.6	-1.8	-1.6
–	–	–	–	–	–	–
88.2	–	22.8	24.4	85.8	–	13.0
0.2	–	–	0.0	0.2	–	–
–	–	–	–	–	–	–
–	–	8.0	–	-3.5	-7.0	8.0
81.9	53.7	36.4	0.2	78.0	41.5	18.0
–	–	88.4	–	–	–	88.4
365.3	212.3	25.0	212.2	365.3	212.3	-17.1
–	–	–	–	–	–	–
–	–	–	–	–	–	–
–	–	–	–	–	–	–
–	–	–	–	–	–	–
–	–	–	–	–	–	–
–	–	–	–	–	–	–
125.0	166.0	150.0	33.0	113.0	149.0	126.0
660.5	*432.0*	*330.5*	*268.9*	*637.1*	*394.0*	*234.6*
60.7	*77.3*	*79.2*	*61.6*	*48.4*	*64.6*	*39.5*
5.8	–	–	–	*5.8*	–	–
82.0	*53.7*	*132.7*	*0.2*	*74.7*	*34.5*	*114.3*
727.0	***509.3***	***409.7***	***330.4***	***691.3***	***458.6***	***274.1***

MAIN AID AGGREGATES

	1977	1978	1979	1980
DAC COUNTRIES COMBINED				
PRIVATE SECTOR NET	1907.7	3048.1	943.5	1093.8
Direct Investment	19.4	6.0	6.4	16.3
Portfolio Invest.	86.8	924.0	377.1	228.6
Export Credits	1801.5	2118.1	560.0	848.8
OFFICIAL & PRIVATE				
GROSS:				
Contractual Lending	2943.2	3850.6	2340.0	2749.9
Export Credits Tot.	2903.8	3807.4	2328.6	2718.2
Export Credits Priv	2620.9	3147.1	1897.9	2397.0
OTHER NET DATA				
Contractual Lending	2099.0	2783.8	950.9	1089.9
Export Credits Tot.	2070.2	2758.8	959.9	1075.6
(Bank Sector Loans)	384.0	1446.0	960.0	146.0
ODA CONCESSIONALITY				
Total:Grant Element	92.0	100.0	88.0	100.0
Loans:Grant Element	46.0	–	34.0	–
OTHER SOURCES				
CMEA Countr.(Gross)	55.3	64.4	65.8	68.2
Intra LDCS Exc.OPEC	–	–	–	–
Other	–	–	–	–
ALL SOURCE COMMITMENTS				
TOTAL BILATERAL	819.1	1682.1	1216.7	319.2
of which				
OPEC (ODA)	–	–	–	54.2
CMEA (ODA)	–	–	–	–
TOTAL MULTILAT.(ODA)	58.1	11.5	9.2	49.6
TOTAL BIL.& MULTIL.	877.2	1693.5	1225.9	368.9
of which				
ODA Grants	106.5	111.1	111.9	204.3
ODA Loans	55.7	–	22.8	20.9
ODA CONCESSIONALITY				
Total: Grant Element	76.0	100.0	88.0	100.0
Loans: Grant Element	32.0	–	34.0	–

INDEBTEDNESS

	1977	1978	1979	1980
TOTAL DEBT DISBURSED	***10065.5***	***14884.4***	***17447.3***	
Debt to DAC Countries	8890.0	13151.0	15449.0	
ODA	344.0	429.0	435.0	
Total Export Credits	6198.0	8324.0	10296.0	
Other Private Market	2348.0	4398.0	4718.0	
International Org.	141.3	191.1	245.0	
CMEA	405.5	440.4	532.3	
Other	628.8	1101.9	1220.9	
TOTAL DEBT SERVICE	***1408.7***	***2036.8***	***3270.7***	
Paid to DAC Countries	1322.6	1912.7	3035.9	
ODA	13.6	26.0	23.7	
Total Export Credits	1109.0	1434.6	1950.9	
Other Private Market	200.0	452.1	1061.3	
International Org.	9.8	20.2	31.3	
CMEA	37.3	43.5	61.1	
Other	39.0	60.4	142.4	

ECONOMIC INDICATORS

	1977	1978	1979	1980
GNP Curr. Prices, $M	19506.5	24990.7	31220.0	39725.6
Real GNP, 1976=100	106.0	115.0	126.0	130.0
GNP/Cap Curr. Prices,$	1143.0	1417.0	1709.0	2099.0
GNP/cap Atlas Basis, $	1380.3	1555.0	1772.2	1924.3
Real GNP/Cap, 1976=100	103.0	108.0	114.0	113.0
Population, Million	17.1	17.6	18.3	18.9
Curr.A/C Deficit(-),$M	-2328.0	-3559.0	-1739.0	219.0
BOP Exp. & Transf.,$M	6661.0	7031.0	10402.0	14769.0
Exp. to OECD CIF, $M	5857.1	6620.0	9857.6	13694.3
of which				
Manufact.	36.4	48.6	56.7	39.9
Imp. from OECD FOB, $M	5976.8	6565.0	6986.0	8747.8
Reserves ex. Gold, $M	1683.6	1980.5	2658.8	3772.6

TOTAL RECEIPTS NET	1977	1978	1979	1980
DAC COUNTRIES				
Australia	–	–	–	–
Austria	–	–	0.2	0.2
Belgium	0.2	0.2	8.2	2.1
Canada	–	–	–	–
Denmark	0.1	2.0	1.3	2.3
Finland	–	–	–	0.0
France	-6.6	-11.6	0.9	67.6
Germany, Fed. Rep.	0.0	0.3	0.5	0.8
Italy	-0.2	2.7	43.7	43.2
Japan	0.0	0.0	0.0	–
Netherlands	4.7	10.7	2.3	8.0
New Zealand	–	–	–	–
Norway	-1.0	0.0	-0.5	-0.1
Sweden	-1.6	19.6	39.6	36.8
Switzerland	-3.5	-2.1	-0.5	-3.1
United Kingdom	-5.2	1.9	-6.1	18.3
United States	-1.0	–	1.0	7.0
TOTAL	*-14.1*	*23.6*	*90.5*	*183.1*
MULTILATERAL				
AF.D.F.	–	–	–	–
AF.D.B.	–	–	–	–
AS.D.B.	–	–	–	–
CAR.D.B.	–	–	–	–
E.E.C.	2.0	5.6	0.6	1.0
IBRD	–	–	–	–
IDA	–	–	–	–
I.D.B.	–	–	–	–
IFAD	–	–	–	–
I.F.C.	–	–	–	–
IMF TRUST FUND	–	–	–	–
U.N. AGENCIES	–	–	–	–
UNDP	0.4	2.6	2.7	4.1
UNTA	0.2	0.2	0.3	0.2
UNICEF	3.3	1.3	4.7	3.2
UNRWA	–	–	–	–
WFP	6.3	4.6	5.0	3.1
UNHCR	14.2	3.8	4.3	4.5
Other Multilateral	0.2	0.2	0.0	0.2
Arab OPEC Agencies	13.2	–	–	–
TOTAL	*39.7*	*18.2*	*17.7*	*16.2*
OPEC COUNTRIES	–	–	–	*0.6*
E.E.C.+ MEMBERS	*-4.9*	*11.8*	*51.3*	*143.2*
TOTAL	***25.7***	***41.8***	***108.2***	***199.9***

TOTAL ODA NET	1977	1978	1979	1980
Australia	–	–	–	–
Austria	–	–	0.2	0.2
Belgium	0.4	0.5	4.0	0.5
Canada	–	–	–	–
Denmark	0.1	2.0	1.3	2.3
Finland	–	–	–	0.0
France	–	–	–	0.2
Germany, Fed. Rep.	0.0	0.2	0.5	0.2
Italy	0.6	0.6	0.2	0.2
Japan	–	0.0	0.0	–
Netherlands	4.7	10.7	2.3	8.0
New Zealand	–	–	–	–
Norway	0.3	–	–	0.1
Sweden	1.6	13.6	18.7	16.9
Switzerland	0.2	0.1	0.1	0.2
United Kingdom	–	0.2	0.1	0.0
United States	–	1.0	2.0	7.0
TOTAL	*7.9*	*28.9*	*29.4*	*35.8*
AF.D.F.	–	–	–	–
AF.D.B.	–	–	–	–
AS.D.B.	–	–	–	–
CAR.D.B.	–	–	–	–
E.E.C.	2.0	5.6	0.6	1.0
IBRD	–	–	–	–
IDA	–	–	–	–
I.D.B.	–	–	–	–
IFAD	–	–	–	–
I.F.C.	–	–	–	–
IMF TRUST FUND	–	–	–	–
U.N. AGENCIES	–	–	–	–
UNDP	0.4	2.6	2.7	4.1
UNTA	0.2	0.2	0.3	0.2
UNICEF	3.3	1.3	4.7	3.2
UNRWA	–	–	–	–
WFP	6.3	4.6	5.0	3.1
UNHCR	14.2	3.8	4.3	4.5
Other Multilateral	0.2	0.2	0.0	0.2
Arab OPEC Agencies	13.2	–	–	–
TOTAL	*39.7*	*18.2*	*17.7*	*16.2*
OPEC COUNTRIES	–	–	–	*0.6*
E.E.C.+ MEMBERS	*7.8*	*19.8*	*9.0*	*12.4*
TOTAL	***47.7***	***47.0***	***47.1***	***52.6***

TOTAL ODA GROSS	197
Australia	
Austria	
Belgium	0
Canada	
Denmark	0
Finland	
France	
Germany, Fed. Rep.	0
Italy	0
Japan	
Netherlands	4
New Zealand	
Norway	0
Sweden	1
Switzerland	0
United Kingdom	
United States	
TOTAL	*7*
AF.D.F.	
AF.D.B.	
AS.D.B.	
CAR.D.B.	
E.E.C.	2
IBRD	
IDA	
I.D.B.	
IFAD	
I.F.C.	
IMF TRUST FUND	
U.N. AGENCIES	
UNDP	0
UNTA	0
UNICEF	3
UNRWA	
WFP	6
UNHCR	14
Other Multilateral	0
Arab OPEC Agencies	13
TOTAL	*39*
OPEC COUNTRIES	
E.E.C.+ MEMBERS	*7*
TOTAL	***47***

ODA LOANS GROSS	1977	1978	1979	1980
DAC COUNTRIES				
Australia	–	–	–	–
Austria	–	–	–	–
Belgium	–	–	3.4	–
Canada	–	–	–	–
Denmark	–	–	–	–
Finland	–	–	–	–
France	–	–	–	–
Germany, Fed. Rep.	–	–	–	–
Italy	–	–	–	–
Japan	–	–	–	–
Netherlands	2.7	1.5	0.0	5.6
New Zealand	–	–	–	–
Norway	–	–	–	–
Sweden	–	–	–	–
Switzerland	–	–	–	–
United Kingdom	–	–	–	–
United States	–	–	–	–
TOTAL	*2.7*	*1.5*	*3.4*	*5.6*
MULTILATERAL	*13.2*	–	–	–
OPEC COUNTRIES	–	–	–	–
E.E.C.+ MEMBERS	*2.7*	*1.5*	*3.4*	*5.6*
TOTAL	***16.0***	***1.5***	***3.4***	***5.6***

ODA LOANS NET	1977	1978	1979	1980
Australia	–	–	–	–
Austria	–	–	–	–
Belgium	–	–	3.4	–
Canada	–	–	–	–
Denmark	–	–	–	–
Finland	–	–	–	–
France	–	–	–	–
Germany, Fed. Rep.	–	–	–	–
Italy	–	–	–	–
Japan	–	–	–	–
Netherlands	2.7	1.5	0.0	4.9
New Zealand	–	–	–	–
Norway	–	–	–	–
Sweden	–	–	–	–
Switzerland	–	–	–	–
United Kingdom	–	–	–	–
United States	–	–	–	–
TOTAL	*2.7*	*1.5*	*3.4*	*4.9*
MULTILATERAL	*13.2*	–	–	–
OPEC COUNTRIES	–	–	–	–
E.E.C.+ MEMBERS	*2.7*	*1.5*	*3.4*	*4.9*
TOTAL	***16.0***	***1.5***	***3.4***	***4.9***

GRANTS	197
Australia	
Austria	
Belgium	0
Canada	
Denmark	0
Finland	
France	
Germany, Fed. Rep.	0
Italy	0
Japan	
Netherlands	2
New Zealand	
Norway	0
Sweden	1
Switzerland	0
United Kingdom	
United States	
TOTAL	*5*
MULTILATERAL	*26*
OPEC COUNTRIES	
E.E.C.+ MEMBERS	*5*
TOTAL	***31.***

TOTAL OFFICIAL GROSS	1977	1978	1979	1980
DAC COUNTRIES				
Australia	–	–	–	–
Austria	–	–	0.2	0.2
Belgium	0.4	0.5	4.0	0.5
Canada	–	–	–	–
Denmark	0.1	2.0	1.3	2.3
Finland	–	–	–	0.0
France	–	–	–	6.6
Germany, Fed. Rep.	0.0	0.3	0.5	0.2
Italy	0.6	0.6	0.2	0.2
Japan	–	0.0	0.0	–
Netherlands	4.7	10.7	2.3	8.6
New Zealand	–	–	–	–
Norway	0.3	–	–	0.1
Sweden	1.6	13.6	18.7	16.9
Switzerland	0.2	0.1	0.1	0.2
United Kingdom	–	0.2	0.1	0.0
United States	–	1.0	2.0	7.0
TOTAL	*8.0*	*29.0*	*29.4*	*42.8*
MULTILATERAL	*39.7*	*18.2*	*17.7*	*16.2*
OPEC COUNTRIES	–	–	–	*0.6*
E.E.C.+ MEMBERS	*7.9*	*19.9*	*9.0*	*19.3*
TOTAL	***47.7***	***47.2***	***47.1***	***59.6***

TOTAL OFFICIAL NET	1977	1978	1979	1980
Australia	–	–	–	–
Austria	–	–	0.2	0.2
Belgium	0.4	0.5	4.0	0.5
Canada	–	–	–	–
Denmark	0.1	2.0	1.3	2.3
Finland	–	–	–	0.0
France	–	–	–	6.6
Germany, Fed. Rep.	0.0	0.3	0.5	0.2
Italy	0.6	0.6	0.2	0.2
Japan	–	0.0	0.0	–
Netherlands	4.7	10.7	2.3	8.0
New Zealand	–	–	–	–
Norway	0.3	–	–	0.1
Sweden	1.6	13.6	18.7	16.9
Switzerland	0.2	0.1	0.1	0.2
United Kingdom	–	0.2	0.1	0.0
United States	-1.0	–	1.0	7.0
TOTAL	*7.0*	*28.0*	*28.4*	*42.2*
MULTILATERAL	*39.7*	*18.2*	*17.7*	*16.2*
OPEC COUNTRIES	–	–	–	*0.6*
E.E.C.+ MEMBERS	*7.9*	*19.9*	*9.0*	*18.7*
TOTAL	***46.7***	***46.2***	***46.1***	***59.0***

TOTAL OOF GROSS	197
Australia	
Austria	
Belgium	
Canada	
Denmark	
Finland	
France	
Germany, Fed. Rep.	0.
Italy	
Japan	
Netherlands	
New Zealand	
Norway	
Sweden	
Switzerland	
United Kingdom	
United States	
TOTAL	*0.*
MULTILATERAL	
OPEC COUNTRIES	
E.E.C.+ MEMBERS	*0.*
TOTAL	***0.***

1978	1979	1980	1977	1978	1979	1980
			ODA COMMITMENTS			
–	–	–	–	–	–	–
–	0.2	0.2	–	0.3	0.3	0.0
0.5	4.0	0.5	–	–	3.4	–
–	–	–	–	–	–	0.0
2.0	1.3	2.3	0.1	2.4	5.4	0.4
–	–	0.0	–	–	–	0.0
–	–	0.2	–	–	–	0.2
0.2	0.5	0.2	–	0.2	0.5	0.8
0.6	0.2	0.2	0.6	0.6	0.2	0.2
0.0	0.0	–	–	0.0	0.0	–
10.7	2.3	8.6	6.5	7.3	12.2	12.0
–	–	–	–	–	–	–
–	–	0.1	–	–	–	–
13.6	18.7	16.9	–	19.9	22.4	38.5
0.1	0.1	0.2	–	–	–	0.2
0.2	0.1	0.0	–	0.2	0.1	0.0
1.0	2.0	7.0	0.2	1.0	1.3	5.3
28.9	*29.4*	*36.4*	*7.4*	*31.9*	*45.8*	*57.7*
–	–	–	–	–	–	–
–	–	–	–	–	–	–
–	–	–	–	–	–	–
–	–	–	–	–	–	–
5.6	0.6	1.0	4.5	0.7	1.4	0.3
–	–	–	–	–	–	–
–	–	–	–	–	–	–
–	–	–	–	–	–	–
–	–	–	–	–	–	–
–	–	–	–	–	–	–
–	–	–	–	–	–	–
–	–	–	24.5	12.6	17.1	15.3
2.6	2.7	4.1	–	–	–	–
0.2	0.3	0.2	–	–	–	–
1.3	4.7	3.2	–	–	–	–
–	–	–	–	–	–	–
4.6	5.0	3.1	–	–	–	–
3.8	4.3	4.5	–	–	–	–
0.2	0.0	0.2	–	–	–	–
–	–	–	13.2	–	–	13.0
18.2	*17.7*	*16.2*	*42.2*	*13.2*	*18.5*	*28.5*
–	–	*0.6*	–	–	–	*0.6*
19.8	*9.0*	*13.0*	*11.7*	*11.3*	*23.3*	*13.8*
47.0	***47.1***	***53.2***	***49.6***	***45.1***	***64.3***	***86.9***
			TECH. COOP. GRANTS			
–	–	–	–	–	–	–
–	0.2	0.2	–	–	0.2	0.2
0.5	0.6	0.5	–	0.0	0.2	0.2
–	–	–	–	–	–	–
2.0	1.3	2.3	0.1	1.9	1.3	2.3
–	–	0.0	–	–	–	–
–	–	0.2	–	–	–	0.2
0.2	0.5	0.2	-0.2	0.1	0.3	0.2
0.6	0.2	0.2	0.6	0.6	0.2	0.2
0.0	0.0	–	–	0.0	0.0	–
9.2	2.2	3.1	0.0	0.0	0.2	0.2
–	–	–	–	–	–	–
–	–	0.1	–	–	–	0.0
13.6	18.7	16.9	–	–	–	0.1
0.1	0.1	0.2	–	0.0	0.0	–
0.2	0.1	0.0	–	–	0.1	0.0
1.0	2.0	7.0	–	–	–	–
27.4	*26.0*	*30.9*	*0.5*	*2.7*	*2.4*	*3.5*
18.2	*17.7*	*16.2*	*18.2*	*8.0*	*12.1*	*15.3*
–	–	*0.6*	–	–	–	–
18.2	*5.5*	*7.4*	*0.5*	*2.7*	*2.1*	*3.2*
45.5	***43.7***	***47.7***	***18.7***	***10.6***	***14.4***	***18.8***
			TOTAL OOF NET			
–	–	–	–	–	–	–
–	–	–	–	–	–	–
–	–	–	–	–	–	–
–	–	–	–	–	–	–
–	–	–	–	–	–	–
–	–	–	–	–	–	–
–	–	6.4	–	–	–	6.4
0.1	–	–	0.1	0.1	–	–
–	–	–	–	–	–	–
–	–	–	–	–	–	–
–	–	–	–	–	–	–
–	–	–	–	–	–	–
–	–	–	–	–	–	–
–	–	–	–	–	–	–
–	–	–	–	–	–	–
–	–	–	–	–	–	–
–	–	–	-1.0	-1.0	-1.0	–
0.1	–	*6.4*	*-0.9*	*-0.9*	*-1.0*	*6.4*
–	–	–	–	–	–	–
–	–	–	–	–	–	–
0.1	–	*6.4*	*0.1*	*0.1*	–	*6.4*
0.1	–	***6.4***	***-0.9***	***-0.9***	***-1.0***	***6.4***

MAIN AID AGGREGATES

	1977	1978	1979	1980
DAC COUNTRIES COMBINED				
PRIVATE SECTOR NET	-21.1	-4.3	62.1	140.9
Direct Investment	–	1.9	2.0	36.4
Portfolio Invest.	0.4	-1.8	1.1	7.9
Export Credits	-21.4	-4.4	59.0	96.7
OFFICIAL & PRIVATE				
GROSS:				
Contractual Lending	9.3	20.4	92.8	189.2
Export Credits Tot.	6.5	18.8	89.4	177.3
Export Credits Priv	6.5	18.8	89.4	177.3
OTHER NET DATA				
Contractual Lending	-19.6	-3.8	61.5	107.9
Export Credits Tot.	-22.4	-5.4	58.0	96.7
(Bank Sector Loans)	-12.0	4.0	-18.0	10.0
ODA CONCESSIONALITY				
Total:Grant Element	63.0	100.0	94.0	98.0
Loans:Grant Element	33.0	–	83.0	60.0
OTHER SOURCES				
CMEA Countr.(Gross)	3.0	3.5	4.1	4.5
Intra LDCS Exc.OPEC	–	–	–	–
Other	–	–	–	–
ALL SOURCE COMMITMENTS				
TOTAL BILATERAL	7.4	31.9	45.8	143.3
of which				
OPEC (ODA)	–	–	–	0.6
CMEA (ODA)	–	1.0	0.1	–
TOTAL MULTILAT.(ODA)	42.2	13.2	18.5	28.5
TOTAL BIL.& MULTIL.	49.6	45.1	64.3	171.9
of which				
ODA Grants	32.3	45.1	49.0	71.1
ODA Loans	17.3	–	15.4	15.8
ODA CONCESSIONALITY				
Total: Grant Element	86.0	100.0	96.0	90.0
Loans: Grant Element	62.0	–	83.0	45.0

INDEBTEDNESS

	1977	1978	1979	1980
TOTAL DEBT DISBURSED	***120.0***	***124.0***	***186.0***	
Debt to DAC Countries	120.0	124.0	186.0	
ODA	3.0	5.0	9.0	
Total Export Credits	117.0	119.0	177.0	
Other Private Market	–	–	–	
International Org.	–	–	–	
CMEA	–	–	–	
Other	–	–	–	
TOTAL DEBT SERVICE	***27.9***	***36.8***	***48.3***	
Paid to DAC Countries	27.9	36.8	48.3	
ODA	–	0.1	0.1	
Total Export Credits	27.9	36.7	48.2	
Other Private Market	–	–	–	
International Org.	–	–	–	
CMEA	–	–	–	
Other	–	–	–	

ECONOMIC INDICATORS

	1977	1978	1979	1980
GNP Curr. Prices, $M	2871.1	2741.5	2800.6	2878.5
Real GNP, 1976=100	102.0	106.0	109.0	111.0
GNP/Cap Curr. Prices,$	437.0	407.0	405.0	406.0
GNP/cap Atlas Basis, $	364.3	397.8	430.6	469.7
Real GNP/Cap, 1976=100	99.0	101.0	101.0	101.0
Population, Million	6.6	6.7	6.9	7.1
Curr.A/C Deficit(-),$M	–	–	–	–
BOP Exp. & Transf.,$M	–	–	–	–
Exp. to OECD CIF, $M	409.2	344.6	489.3	797.9
of which				
Manufact.	0.8	12.2	3.7	4.5
Imp. from OECD FOB, $M	477.1	489.0	667.0	969.1
Reserves ex. Gold, $M	–	–	–	–

TOTAL RECEIPTS NET

	1977	1978	1979	1980
DAC COUNTRIES				
Australia	-0.1	-0.2	0.1	2.9
Austria	5.7	-1.0	-3.5	-3.2
Belgium	17.2	64.2	62.5	114.3
Canada	43.6	32.3	19.2	34.9
Denmark	1.6	1.2	28.3	1.6
Finland	-1.0	36.0	-8.7	-3.4
France	12.1	105.5	146.0	293.1
Germany, Fed. Rep.	-12.0	241.9	142.6	151.8
Italy	24.7	69.4	-22.2	61.9
Japan	21.9	36.9	199.0	84.9
Netherlands	1.1	-10.8	33.8	309.9
New Zealand	0.1	0.0	–	–
Norway	-0.1	-0.6	-0.3	0.5
Sweden	-0.6	10.0	4.7	19.8
Switzerland	15.6	12.2	-0.7	329.8
United Kingdom	50.3	73.4	104.2	39.4
United States	158.0	411.0	1213.0	1233.0
TOTAL	*337.9*	*1081.3*	*1918.0*	*2671.1*
MULTILATERAL				
AF.D.F.	–	–	–	–
AF.D.B.	–	–	–	–
AS.D.B.	–	–	–	–
CAR.D.B.	–	–	–	–
E.E.C.	–	–	0.3	–
IBRD	0.4	8.9	15.3	36.7
IDA	–	–	–	–
I.D.B.	76.4	88.6	49.5	-0.1
IFAD	–	–	–	–
I.F.C.	4.2	0.7	10.0	0.1
IMF TRUST FUND	–	–	–	–
U.N. AGENCIES	–	–	–	–
UNDP	3.5	3.6	5.8	5.7
UNTA	0.5	0.5	0.8	0.3
UNICEF	–	–	–	–
UNRWA	–	–	–	–
WFP	–	–	0.0	–
UNHCR	3.4	2.9	2.5	3.3
Other Multilateral	0.4	0.4	0.3	1.3
Arab OPEC Agencies	–	–	–	–
TOTAL	*88.7*	*105.6*	*84.4*	*47.3*
OPEC COUNTRIES	–	*0.3*	–	–
E.E.C.+ MEMBERS	*94.8*	*544.8*	*495.4*	*971.9*
TOTAL	***426.7***	***1187.1***	***2002.4***	***2718.4***

TOTAL ODA NET

	1977	1978	1979	1980
Australia	0.0	–	–	–
Austria	0.1	0.1	0.1	0.5
Belgium	0.4	0.4	0.2	0.4
Canada	0.0	0.0	0.0	0.0
Denmark	0.1	0.5	0.1	0.1
Finland	–	–	–	–
France	–	–	–	1.3
Germany, Fed. Rep.	10.0	10.3	14.0	18.1
Italy	0.5	0.6	0.8	1.0
Japan	1.8	1.9	4.7	7.5
Netherlands	1.1	0.7	2.3	3.0
New Zealand	–	–	–	–
Norway	–	–	–	0.0
Sweden	–	–	–	0.9
Switzerland	0.0	0.3	0.2	0.2
United Kingdom	0.0	0.0	0.0	0.1
United States	-5.0	-5.0	-4.0	-1.0
TOTAL	*8.9*	*9.8*	*18.4*	*32.1*
AF.D.F.	–	–	–	–
AF.D.B.	–	–	–	–
AS.D.B.	–	–	–	–
CAR.D.B.	–	–	–	–
E.E.C.	–	–	0.3	–
IBRD	–	–	–	–
IDA	–	–	–	–
I.D.B.	11.5	11.4	14.7	-24.2
IFAD	–	–	–	–
I.F.C.	–	–	–	–
IMF TRUST FUND	–	–	–	–
U.N. AGENCIES	–	–	–	–
UNDP	3.5	3.6	5.8	5.7
UNTA	0.5	0.5	0.8	0.3
UNICEF	–	–	–	–
UNRWA	–	–	–	–
WFP	–	–	0.0	–
UNHCR	3.4	2.9	2.5	3.3
Other Multilateral	0.4	0.4	0.3	1.3
Arab OPEC Agencies	–	–	–	–
TOTAL	*19.3*	*18.8*	*24.4*	*-13.6*
OPEC COUNTRIES	–	–	–	–
E.E.C.+ MEMBERS	*12.1*	*12.5*	*17.7*	*23.9*
TOTAL	***28.2***	***28.5***	***42.8***	***18.4***

TOTAL ODA GROSS

	1977
Australia	0.0
Austria	0.1
Belgium	0.4
Canada	–
Denmark	0.
Finland	–
France	–
Germany, Fed. Rep.	10.0
Italy	0.5
Japan	1.8
Netherlands	1.1
New Zealand	–
Norway	–
Sweden	–
Switzerland	0.0
United Kingdom	0.0
United States	–
TOTAL	*14.0*
AF.D.F.	–
AF.D.B.	–
AS.D.B.	–
CAR.D.B.	–
E.E.C.	–
IBRD	–
IDA	–
I.D.B.	17.
IFAD	–
I.F.C.	–
IMF TRUST FUND	–
U.N. AGENCIES	–
UNDP	3.5
UNTA	0.5
UNICEF	–
UNRWA	–
WFP	–
UNHCR	3.4
Other Multilateral	0.4
Arab OPEC Agencies	–
TOTAL	*25.4*
OPEC COUNTRIES	–
E.E.C.+ MEMBERS	*12.*
TOTAL	***39.4***

ODA LOANS GROSS

	1977	1978	1979	1980
DAC COUNTRIES				
Australia	–	–	–	–
Austria	–	–	–	0.4
Belgium	–	–	–	–
Canada	–	–	–	–
Denmark	–	–	–	–
Finland	–	–	–	–
France	–	–	–	–
Germany, Fed. Rep.	3.1	0.5	0.3	1.4
Italy	–	–	–	–
Japan	–	–	1.7	5.0
Netherlands	–	–	–	–
New Zealand	–	–	–	–
Norway	–	–	–	–
Sweden	–	–	–	–
Switzerland	–	–	–	–
United Kingdom	–	–	–	–
United States	–	–	–	–
TOTAL	*3.1*	*0.5*	*2.0*	*6.7*
MULTILATERAL	*17.7*	*19.1*	*25.6*	*12.7*
OPEC COUNTRIES	–	–	–	–
E.E.C.+ MEMBERS	*3.1*	*0.5*	*0.3*	*1.4*
TOTAL	***20.8***	***19.6***	***27.6***	***19.4***

ODA LOANS NET

	1977	1978	1979	1980
Australia	–	–	–	–
Austria	0.0	–	–	0.4
Belgium	–	–	–	–
Canada	0.0	0.0	0.0	0.0
Denmark	–	–	–	–
Finland	–	–	–	–
France	–	–	–	–
Germany, Fed. Rep.	3.1	0.4	0.3	1.4
Italy	–	–	–	–
Japan	–	–	1.7	5.0
Netherlands	–	–	–	–
New Zealand	–	–	–	–
Norway	–	–	–	–
Sweden	–	–	–	–
Switzerland	–	–	–	–
United Kingdom	–	–	–	–
United States	-5.0	-3.0	-2.0	-1.0
TOTAL	*-2.0*	*-2.6*	–	*5.7*
MULTILATERAL	*11.5*	*11.4*	*14.7*	*-24.2*
OPEC COUNTRIES	–	–	–	–
E.E.C.+ MEMBERS	*3.1*	*0.4*	*0.3*	*1.4*
TOTAL	***9.6***	***8.8***	***14.7***	***-18.5***

GRANTS

	1977
Australia	0.
Austria	0.
Belgium	0.4
Canada	–
Denmark	0.
Finland	–
France	–
Germany, Fed. Rep.	6.
Italy	0.
Japan	1.
Netherlands	1.
New Zealand	–
Norway	–
Sweden	–
Switzerland	0.
United Kingdom	0.
United States	–
TOTAL	*10.*
MULTILATERAL	*7.*
OPEC COUNTRIES	–
E.E.C.+ MEMBERS	*9.*
TOTAL	***18.***

TOTAL OFFICIAL GROSS

	1977	1978	1979	1980
DAC COUNTRIES				
Australia	0.0	–	–	–
Austria	0.1	0.1	0.1	0.5
Belgium	0.4	0.4	0.2	0.4
Canada	45.0	31.3	22.6	40.3
Denmark	0.1	0.5	0.1	0.1
Finland	–	–	–	–
France	–	–	–	1.3
Germany, Fed. Rep.	13.0	46.3	14.3	53.6
Italy	0.5	0.6	0.8	7.0
Japan	1.8	1.9	4.7	7.5
Netherlands	1.1	0.7	2.3	3.0
New Zealand	0.1	–	–	–
Norway	–	–	–	0.0
Sweden	–	–	–	0.9
Switzerland	0.0	0.3	0.2	0.2
United Kingdom	0.0	0.0	0.0	0.1
United States	21.0	17.0	18.0	22.0
TOTAL	*83.0*	*99.1*	*63.4*	*136.9*
MULTILATERAL	*146.6*	*168.9*	*153.5*	*234.0*
OPEC COUNTRIES	–	*0.3*	–	–
E.E.C.+ MEMBERS	*15.0*	*48.5*	*18.0*	*65.4*
TOTAL	***229.6***	***268.3***	***216.9***	***370.9***

TOTAL OFFICIAL NET

	1977	1978	1979	1980
Australia	0.0	–	–	–
Austria	-0.9	-1.0	-1.0	-0.6
Belgium	0.4	0.4	0.2	0.4
Canada	44.0	29.6	20.2	35.7
Denmark	0.1	0.5	0.1	0.1
Finland	–	–	–	–
France	–	–	–	1.3
Germany, Fed. Rep.	-5.3	31.6	-3.7	38.0
Italy	0.5	0.6	0.8	7.0
Japan	1.8	1.9	4.7	7.5
Netherlands	1.1	0.7	2.3	3.0
New Zealand	0.1	–	–	–
Norway	–	–	–	0.0
Sweden	–	–	–	0.9
Switzerland	0.0	0.3	0.2	0.2
United Kingdom	0.0	0.0	0.0	0.1
United States	-10.0	-15.0	-13.0	-9.0
TOTAL	*31.8*	*49.6*	*10.9*	*84.4*
MULTILATERAL	*88.7*	*105.6*	*84.4*	*47.3*
OPEC COUNTRIES	–	*0.3*	–	–
E.E.C.+ MEMBERS	*-3.2*	*33.8*	*0.0*	*49.7*
TOTAL	***120.5***	***155.4***	***95.3***	***131.7***

TOTAL OOF GROSS

	1977
Australia	–
Austria	–
Belgium	–
Canada	45.
Denmark	–
Finland	–
France	–
Germany, Fed. Rep.	2.
Italy	–
Japan	–
Netherlands	–
New Zealand	0.
Norway	–
Sweden	–
Switzerland	–
United Kingdom	–
United States	21.
TOTAL	*69.*
MULTILATERAL	*121.*
OPEC COUNTRIES	–
E.E.C.+ MEMBERS	*2.*
TOTAL	***190.***

1978	1979	1980	1977	1978	1979	1980
			ODA COMMITMENTS			
–	–	–	–	–	–	–
0.1	0.1	0.5	–	–	–	0.4
0.4	0.2	0.4	–	–	–	–
–	–	–	–	–	–	–
0.5	0.1	0.1	0.1	–	–	–
–	–	–	–	–	–	–
–	–	1.3	–	–	–	0.9
10.4	14.0	18.1	8.9	27.4	12.3	17.0
0.6	0.8	1.0	0.5	0.6	0.8	1.0
1.9	4.7	7.5	2.0	9.3	3.5	2.9
0.7	2.3	3.0	0.6	1.0	2.7	3.4
–	–	–	–	–	–	–
–	–	0.0	–	–	–	–
–	–	0.9	–	–	–	–
0.3	0.2	0.2	–	–	–	0.2
0.0	0.0	0.1	0.0	0.0	0.0	0.1
-2.0	-2.0	–	–	–	–	–
12.9	*20.5*	*33.1*	*12.2*	*38.3*	*19.3*	*25.8*
–	–	–	–	–	–	–
–	–	–	–	–	–	–
–	–	–	–	–	–	–
–	–	–	–	–	–	–
–	0.3	–	–	0.2	0.1	0.5
–	–	–	–	–	–	–
–	–	–	–	–	–	–
19.1	25.6	12.7	48.8	50.0	–	–
–	–	–	–	–	–	–
–	–	–	–	–	–	–
–	–	–	–	–	–	–
–	–	–	7.7	7.4	9.4	10.6
3.6	5.8	5.7	–	–	–	–
0.5	0.8	0.3	–	–	–	–
–	–	–	–	–	–	–
–	–	–	–	–	–	–
–	0.0	–	–	–	–	–
2.9	2.5	3.3	–	–	–	–
0.4	0.3	1.3	–	–	–	–
–	–	–	–	–	–	–
26.5	*35.3*	*23.3*	*56.5*	*57.5*	*9.5*	*11.0*
–	–	–	–	–	–	–
12.6	*17.7*	*23.9*	*10.2*	*29.2*	*15.9*	*22.8*
39.3	***55.7***	***56.4***	***68.7***	***95.8***	***28.9***	***36.9***
			TECH. COOP. GRANTS			
–	–	–	–	–	–	–
0.1	0.1	0.2	0.1	0.1	0.1	0.2
0.4	0.2	0.4	0.2	0.1	0.2	0.2
–	–	–	–	–	–	–
0.5	0.1	0.1	0.1	0.1	0.1	0.1
–	–	–	–	–	–	–
–	–	1.3	–	–	–	1.3
9.9	13.7	16.8	6.7	9.3	13.7	16.8
0.6	0.8	1.0	0.5	0.6	0.8	1.0
1.9	3.0	2.6	1.5	1.9	3.0	2.6
0.7	2.3	3.0	1.0	0.5	2.3	2.4
–	–	–	–	–	–	–
–	–	0.0	–	–	–	0.0
–	–	0.9	–	–	–	–
0.3	0.2	0.2	–	0.0	–	–
0.0	0.0	0.1	0.0	0.0	0.0	0.1
-2.0	-2.0	–	–	–	–	–
12.4	*18.4*	*26.4*	*10.1*	*12.6*	*20.1*	*24.4*
7.4	*9.7*	*10.6*	*7.7*	*7.4*	*9.4*	*10.6*
–	–	–	–	–	–	–
12.1	*17.4*	*22.5*	*8.5*	*10.6*	*17.0*	*21.7*
19.8	***28.1***	***37.0***	***17.9***	***20.0***	***29.5***	***35.0***
			TOTAL OOF NET			
–	–	–	–	–	–	–
–	–	–	-0.9	-1.1	-1.1	-1.2
–	–	–	–	–	–	–
31.3	22.6	40.3	44.0	29.6	20.2	35.7
–	–	–	–	–	–	–
–	–	–	–	–	–	–
–	–	–	–	–	–	–
36.0	0.3	35.5	-15.3	21.3	-17.7	19.8
–	–	6.0	–	–	–	6.0
–	–	–	–	–	–	–
–	–	–	–	–	–	–
–	–	–	0.1	–	–	–
–	–	–	–	–	–	–
–	–	–	–	–	–	–
–	–	–	–	–	–	–
–	–	–	–	–	–	–
19.0	20.0	22.0	-5.0	-10.0	-9.0	-8.0
86.3	*42.9*	*103.8*	*22.9*	*39.8*	*-7.6*	*52.4*
142.5	*118.3*	*210.7*	*69.5*	*86.8*	*60.1*	*60.9*
0.3	–	–	–	*0.3*	–	–
36.0	*0.3*	*41.5*	*-15.3*	*21.3*	*-17.7*	*25.8*
229.0	***161.2***	***314.5***	***92.3***	***126.9***	***52.5***	***113.3***

MAIN AID AGGREGATES

	1977	1978	1979	1980
DAC COUNTRIES COMBINED				
PRIVATE SECTOR NET	306.2	1031.7	1907.1	2586.7
Direct Investment	213.1	310.0	666.8	880.5
Portfolio Invest.	-7.5	561.1	1223.7	1153.6
Export Credits	100.6	160.6	16.6	552.7
OFFICIAL & PRIVATE				
GROSS:				
Contractual Lending	440.5	622.6	497.3	1232.2
Export Credits Tot.	437.4	622.2	495.3	1225.5
Export Credits Priv	368.4	535.9	452.4	1121.7
OTHER NET DATA				
Contractual Lending	121.5	197.8	9.0	610.8
Export Credits Tot.	133.1	200.5	9.0	605.1
(Bank Sector Loans)	463.0	1488.0	2631.0	2525.0
ODA CONCESSIONALITY				
Total:Grant Element	100.0	57.0	100.0	99.0
Loans:Grant Element	–	33.0	–	37.0
OTHER SOURCES				
CMEA Countr.(Gross)	13.8	20.2	27.5	17.5
Intra LDCS Exc.OPEC	–	–	–	–
Other	–	–	–	–
ALL SOURCE COMMITMENTS				
TOTAL BILATERAL	28.7	99.3	146.9	766.1
of which				
OPEC (ODA)	–	–	–	–
CMEA (ODA)	–	–	–	–
TOTAL MULTILAT.(ODA)	56.5	57.5	9.5	11.0
TOTAL BIL.& MULTIL.	85.3	156.8	156.4	777.1
of which				
ODA Grants	19.9	21.3	28.9	36.5
ODA Loans	48.8	74.6	–	0.4
ODA CONCESSIONALITY				
Total: Grant Element	100.0	56.0	68.0	99.0
Loans: Grant Element	–	44.0	50.0	37.0

INDEBTEDNESS

	1977	1978	1979	1980
TOTAL DEBT DISBURSED	***6133.1***	***7893.1***	***11327.5***	
Debt to DAC Countries	5206.0	6643.0	9095.0	
ODA	120.0	128.0	133.0	
Total Export Credits	2044.0	2775.0	3000.0	
Other Private Market	3042.0	3740.0	5962.0	
International Org.	718.3	904.4	1001.7	
CMEA	61.7	180.2	266.2	
Other	147.1	165.5	964.6	
TOTAL DEBT SERVICE	***1381.2***	***2212.0***	***1832.3***	
Paid to DAC Countries	1187.8	1993.7	1511.0	
ODA	8.1	7.7	8.3	
Total Export Credits	533.7	553.7	635.1	
Other Private Market	646.0	1432.3	867.6	
International Org.	105.1	126.9	136.3	
CMEA	16.5	18.3	37.8	
Other	71.8	73.1	147.2	

ECONOMIC INDICATORS

	1977	1978	1979	1980
GNP Curr. Prices, $M	51487.1	56415.5	106148.9	142031.8
Real GNP, 1976=100	104.0	101.0	107.0	108.0
GNP/Cap Curr. Prices,$	1944.0	2097.0	3886.0	5120.0
GNP/cap Atlas Basis, $	1916.2	1949.8	2208.3	2394.8
Real GNP/Cap, 1976=100	103.0	98.0	102.0	101.0
Population, Million	26.5	26.9	27.3	27.7
Curr.A/C Deficit(-),$M	1287.0	1838.0	-537.0	-4686.0
BOP Exp. & Transf.,$M	6773.0	7885.0	9950.0	11233.0
Exp. to OECD CIF, $M	3501.8	4397.5	5022.7	4098.1
of which				
Manufact.	527.3	779.7	774.7	768.8
Imp. from OECD FOB, $M	2637.0	2995.8	5704.4	7573.1
Reserves ex. Gold, $M	3154.0	4966.0	9388.0	6719.0

	1977	1978	1979	1980	1977	1978	1979	1980
TOTAL RECEIPTS NET					**TOTAL ODA NET**			
DAC COUNTRIES								
Australia	1.5	-0.7	0.0	–	0.0	–	–	–
Austria	–	–	–	–	–	–	–	–
Belgium	2.8	6.2	-6.1	-9.6	0.0	–	–	–
Canada	-0.6	0.8	-0.6	-0.8	–	–	–	–
Denmark	–	–	–	–	–	–	–	–
Finland	–	–	–	–	–	–	–	–
France	-3.9	183.9	452.7	-331.3	–	–	–	–
Germany, Fed. Rep.	2.6	-152.6	-12.6	-29.2	0.0	0.0	0.0	0.0
Italy	-1.8	-9.1	-2.1	10.8	–	–	–	–
Japan	-23.8	3.5	-21.3	-2.8	–	–	–	–
Netherlands	-3.7	0.1	13.6	-19.6	0.1	0.1	0.1	0.0
New Zealand	0.0	0.0	–	–	–	–	–	–
Norway	0.1	-0.3	-0.3	3.1	–	–	–	–
Sweden	–	–	–	0.3	–	–	–	–
Switzerland	-0.1	-0.2	–	40.1	0.0	–	–	–
United Kingdom	-8.6	-12.7	27.2	1.9	0.0	0.1	0.1	0.2
United States	187.0	597.0	296.0	395.0	–	–	–	–
TOTAL	*151.7*	*615.9*	*746.6*	*58.0*	*0.2*	*0.1*	*0.3*	*0.2*
MULTILATERAL								
AF.D.F.	–	–	–	–	–	–	–	–
AF.D.B.	–	–	–	–	–	–	–	–
AS.D.B.	–	–	–	–	–	–	–	–
CAR.D.B.	1.1	0.2	–	0.4	–	–	–	0.1
E.E.C.	–	0.3	0.1	0.1	–	0.3	0.1	0.1
IBRD	0.4	0.1	0.3	1.9	–	–	–	–
IDA	–	–	–	–	–	–	–	–
I.D.B.	–	0.4	0.3	1.0	–	0.4	0.3	0.6
IFAD	–	–	–	–	–	–	–	–
I.F.C.	–	–	–	–	–	–	–	–
IMF TRUST FUND	–	–	–	–	–	–	–	–
U.N. AGENCIES	–	–	–	–	–	–	–	–
UNDP	0.3	0.3	0.4	1.0	0.3	0.3	0.4	1.0
UNTA	0.0	0.1	0.2	0.1	0.0	0.1	0.2	0.1
UNICEF	–	–	–	–	–	–	–	–
UNRWA	–	–	–	–	–	–	–	–
WFP	–	–	–	–	–	–	–	–
UNHCR	–	–	–	–	–	–	–	–
Other Multilateral	0.2	0.1	0.2	0.1	0.2	0.1	0.2	0.1
Arab OPEC Agencies	–	–	–	–	–	–	–	–
TOTAL	*2.0*	*1.4*	*1.5*	*4.6*	*0.5*	*1.2*	*1.1*	*2.0*
OPEC COUNTRIES	–	–	–	–	–	–	–	–
E.E.C.+ MEMBERS	*-12.5*	*16.0*	*472.9*	*-376.9*	*0.1*	*0.4*	*0.4*	*0.3*
TOTAL	***153.6***	***617.4***	***748.0***	***62.6***	***0.6***	***1.3***	***1.4***	***2.1***
ODA LOANS GROSS					**ODA LOANS NET**			
DAC COUNTRIES								
Australia	–	–	–	–	–	–	–	–
Austria	–	–	–	–	–	–	–	–
Belgium	–	–	–	–	–	–	–	–
Canada	–	–	–	–	–	–	–	–
Denmark	–	–	–	–	–	–	–	–
Finland	–	–	–	–	–	–	–	–
France	–	–	–	–	–	–	–	–
Germany, Fed. Rep.	–	–	–	–	–	–	–	–
Italy	–	–	–	–	–	–	–	–
Japan	–	–	–	–	–	–	–	–
Netherlands	–	–	–	–	–	–	–	–
New Zealand	–	–	–	–	–	–	–	–
Norway	–	–	–	–	–	–	–	–
Sweden	–	–	–	–	–	–	–	–
Switzerland	–	–	–	–	–	–	–	–
United Kingdom	–	–	–	–	–	–	–	–
United States	–	–	–	–	–	–	–	–
TOTAL	–	–	–	–	–	–	–	–
MULTILATERAL	–	–	–	*0.1*	–	–	–	*0.1*
OPEC COUNTRIES	–	–	–	–	–	–	–	–
E.E.C.+ MEMBERS	–	–	–	–	–	–	–	–
TOTAL	–	–	–	***0.1***	–	–	–	***0.1***
TOTAL OFFICIAL GROSS					**TOTAL OFFICIAL NET**			
DAC COUNTRIES								
Australia	0.0	–	–	–	0.0	–	–	–
Austria	–	–	–	–	–	–	–	–
Belgium	0.0	–	–	–	0.0	–	–	–
Canada	–	1.5	–	–	-0.6	0.8	-0.6	-0.8
Denmark	–	–	–	–	–	–	–	–
Finland	–	–	–	–	–	–	–	–
France	–	–	–	–	–	–	–	–
Germany, Fed. Rep.	0.0	0.0	0.0	0.0	0.0	0.0	0.0	0.0
Italy	–	–	–	–	–	–	–	–
Japan	–	–	–	–	–	–	–	–
Netherlands	0.1	0.1	0.1	0.0	0.1	0.1	0.1	0.0
New Zealand	0.0	–	–	–	0.0	–	–	–
Norway	–	–	–	–	–	–	–	–
Sweden	–	–	–	–	–	–	–	–
Switzerland	0.0	–	–	–	0.0	–	–	–
United Kingdom	0.0	0.1	0.1	0.2	0.0	0.1	0.1	0.2
United States	–	–	–	–	-21.0	-1.0	-3.0	-2.0
TOTAL	*0.2*	*1.6*	*0.3*	*0.2*	*-21.4*	*-0.1*	*-3.4*	*-2.6*
MULTILATERAL	*1.9*	*1.4*	*1.7*	*5.2*	*1.9*	*1.4*	*1.5*	*4.6*
OPEC COUNTRIES	–	–	–	–	–	–	–	–
E.E.C.+ MEMBERS	*0.1*	*0.4*	*0.4*	*0.3*	*0.1*	*0.4*	*0.4*	*0.3*
TOTAL	***2.1***	***3.1***	***2.0***	***5.3***	***-19.5***	***1.4***	***-1.9***	***2.0***

	197
TOTAL ODA GROSS	
Australia	0.
Austria	
Belgium	0.
Canada	
Denmark	
Finland	
France	
Germany, Fed. Rep.	0.
Italy	
Japan	
Netherlands	0.
New Zealand	
Norway	
Sweden	
Switzerland	0.
United Kingdom	0.
United States	
TOTAL	*0.*
AF.D.F.	
AF.D.B.	
AS.D.B.	
CAR.D.B.	
E.E.C.	
IBRD	
IDA	
I.D.B.	
IFAD	
I.F.C.	
IMF TRUST FUND	
U.N. AGENCIES	
UNDP	0.
UNTA	0.
UNICEF	
UNRWA	
WFP	
UNHCR	
Other Multilateral	0.
Arab OPEC Agencies	
TOTAL	*0.*
OPEC COUNTRIES	
E.E.C.+ MEMBERS	*0.*
TOTAL	***0.***
GRANTS	
Australia	0.
Austria	
Belgium	0
Canada	
Denmark	
Finland	
France	
Germany, Fed. Rep.	0.
Italy	
Japan	
Netherlands	0.
New Zealand	
Norway	
Sweden	
Switzerland	0.
United Kingdom	0.
United States	
TOTAL	*0.*
MULTILATERAL	*0.*
OPEC COUNTRIES	
E.E.C.+ MEMBERS	*0.*
TOTAL	***0.***
TOTAL OOF GROSS	
Australia	
Austria	
Belgium	
Canada	
Denmark	
Finland	
France	
Germany, Fed. Rep.	
Italy	
Japan	
Netherlands	
New Zealand	0.
Norway	
Sweden	
Switzerland	
United Kingdom	
United States	
TOTAL	*0.*
MULTILATERAL	*1.*
OPEC COUNTRIES	
E.E.C.+ MEMBERS	
TOTAL	***1.***

1978	1979	1980	1977	1978	1979	1980
			ODA COMMITMENTS			
–	–	–	0.0	–	–	–
–	–	–	–	–	–	–
–	–	–	–	–	–	–
–	–	–	–	0.5	–	0.0
–	–	–	–	–	–	–
–	–	–	–	–	–	–
–	–	–	–	–	–	–
0.0	0.0	0.0	0.0	0.0	0.0	0.0
–	–	–	–	–	–	–
–	–	–	–	–	–	–
0.1	0.1	0.0	0.1	0.1	0.1	0.0
–	–	–	–	–	–	–
–	–	–	–	–	–	–
–	–	–	–	–	–	–
–	–	–	–	–	–	–
0.1	0.1	0.2	0.0	0.1	0.1	0.2
–	–	–	–	–	–	–
0.1	*0.3*	*0.2*	*0.1*	*0.7*	*0.3*	*0.2*
–	–	–	–	–	–	–
–	–	–	–	–	–	–
–	–	–	–	–	–	–
–	–	0.1	–	0.7	–	–
0.3	0.1	0.1	0.1	1.0	0.4	0.6
–	–	–	–	–	–	–
–	–	–	–	–	–	–
0.4	0.3	0.6	–	–	–	–
–	–	–	–	–	–	–
–	–	–	–	–	–	–
–	–	–	–	–	–	–
–	–	–	0.5	0.5	0.7	1.2
0.3	0.4	1.0	–	–	–	–
0.1	0.2	0.1	–	–	–	–
–	–	–	–	–	–	–
–	–	–	–	–	–	–
–	–	–	–	–	–	–
–	–	–	–	–	–	–
0.1	0.2	0.1	–	–	–	–
–	–	–	–	–	–	–
1.2	*1.1*	*2.0*	*0.6*	*2.2*	*1.0*	*1.8*
–	–	–	–	–	–	–
0.4	*0.4*	*0.3*	*0.2*	*1.1*	*0.6*	*0.8*
1.3	***1.4***	***2.1***	***0.7***	***2.8***	***1.3***	***2.0***
			TECH. COOP. GRANTS			
–	–	–	0.0	–	–	–
–	–	–	–	–	–	–
–	–	–	0.0	–	–	–
–	–	–	–	–	–	–
–	–	–	–	–	–	–
–	–	–	–	–	–	–
–	–	–	–	–	–	–
0.0	0.0	0.0	0.0	0.0	0.0	0.0
–	–	–	–	–	–	–
–	–	–	–	–	–	–
0.1	0.1	0.0	0.1	0.1	0.1	0.0
–	–	–	–	–	–	–
–	–	–	–	–	–	–
–	–	–	–	–	–	–
–	–	–	–	–	–	–
0.1	0.1	0.2	0.0	0.1	0.1	0.2
–	–	–	–	–	–	–
0.1	*0.3*	*0.2*	*0.2*	*0.1*	*0.3*	*0.2*
1.2	*1.1*	*1.9*	*0.5*	*0.9*	*1.0*	*1.2*
–	–	–	–	–	–	–
0.4	*0.4*	*0.3*	*0.1*	*0.1*	*0.3*	*0.2*
1.3	***1.4***	***2.1***	***0.6***	***1.0***	***1.3***	***1.4***
			TOTAL OOF NET			
–	–	–	–	–	–	–
–	–	–	–	–	–	–
–	–	–	–	–	–	–
1.5	–	–	-0.6	0.8	-0.6	-0.8
–	–	–	–	–	–	–
–	–	–	–	–	–	–
–	–	–	–	–	–	–
–	–	–	–	–	–	–
–	–	–	–	–	–	–
–	–	–	–	–	–	–
–	–	–	–	–	–	–
–	–	–	0.0	–	–	–
–	–	–	–	–	–	–
–	–	–	–	–	–	–
–	–	–	–	–	–	–
–	–	–	–	–	–	–
–	–	–	-21.0	-1.0	-3.0	-2.0
1.5	–	–	*-21.6*	*-0.2*	*-3.6*	*-2.8*
0.3	*0.6*	*3.2*	*1.5*	*0.3*	*0.3*	*2.6*
–	–	–	–	–	–	–
–	–	–	–	–	–	–
1.8	***0.6***	***3.2***	***-20.1***	***0.1***	***-3.3***	***-0.2***

MAIN AID AGGREGATES

	1977	1978	1979	1980
DAC COUNTRIES COMBINED				
PRIVATE SECTOR NET	173.1	616.0	750.0	60.6
Direct Investment	151.5	539.8	295.5	462.5
Portfolio Invest.	49.1	82.5	444.9	-441.1
Export Credits	-27.5	-6.3	9.6	39.2
OFFICIAL & PRIVATE				
GROSS:				
Contractual Lending	18.7	2.8	31.6	60.0
Export Credits Tot.	18.7	2.8	31.6	60.0
Export Credits Priv	18.7	1.3	31.6	60.0
OTHER NET DATA				
Contractual Lending	-49.1	-6.5	6.0	36.4
Export Credits Tot.	-49.1	-6.5	6.0	36.4
(Bank Sector Loans)	–	–	–	47.0
ODA CONCESSIONALITY				
Total:Grant Element	100.0	100.0	100.0	100.0
Loans:Grant Element	–	–	–	–
OTHER SOURCES				
CMEA Countr.(Gross)	–	–	–	–
Intra LDCS Exc.OPEC	–	–	–	–
Other	–	–	–	–
ALL SOURCE COMMITMENTS				
TOTAL BILATERAL	0.2	0.7	0.3	8.0
of which				
OPEC (ODA)	–	–	–	–
CMEA (ODA)	–	–	–	–
TOTAL MULTILAT.(ODA)	0.6	2.2	1.0	1.8
TOTAL BIL.& MULTIL.	0.7	2.8	1.3	9.8
of which				
ODA Grants	0.7	1.3	1.3	1.4
ODA Loans	–	1.6	–	0.6
ODA CONCESSIONALITY				
Total: Grant Element	100.0	100.0	100.0	100.0
Loans: Grant Element	–	–	–	–

INDEBTEDNESS

	1977	1978	1979	1980
TOTAL DEBT DISBURSED	***39.0***	***65.0***	***65.0***	
Debt to DAC Countries	39.0	65.0	65.0	
ODA	–	–	–	
Total Export Credits	28.0	54.0	55.0	
Other Private Market	11.0	11.0	10.0	
International Org.	–	–	–	
CMEA	–	–	–	
Other	–	–	–	
TOTAL DEBT SERVICE	***50.2***	***28.5***	***32.8***	
Paid to DAC Countries	50.2	28.5	32.8	
ODA	–	–	–	
Total Export Credits	48.7	27.0	30.8	
Other Private Market	1.5	1.5	2.0	
International Org.	–	–	–	
CMEA	–	–	–	
Other	–	–	–	

ECONOMIC INDICATORS

	1977	1978	1979	1980
GNP Curr. Prices, $M	482.8	524.7	635.2	804.1
Real GNP, 1976=100	109.0	111.0	125.0	141.0
GNP/Cap Curr. Prices,$	2204.0	2311.0	2714.0	3336.0
GNP/cap Atlas Basis, $	2213.8	2340.3	2771.5	3301.0
Real GNP/Cap, 1976=100	105.0	103.0	113.0	123.0
Population, Million	0.2	0.2	0.2	0.2
Curr.A/C Deficit(-),$M	54.0	26.0	-6.0	-34.0
BOP Exp. & Transf.,$M	704.0	827.0	937.0	1145.0
Exp. to OECD CIF, $M	1395.3	1484.7	2299.6	2483.6
of which				
Manufact.	94.8	148.4	150.8	160.3
Imp. from OECD FOB, $M	349.6	565.9	564.1	656.2
Reserves ex. Gold, $M	67.1	58.1	77.5	92.1

	TOTAL RECEIPTS NET 1977	1978	1979	1980	TOTAL ODA NET 1977	1978	1979	1980	TOTAL ODA GROSS 197
DAC COUNTRIES									
Australia	6.4	16.2	35.3	13.5	6.4	16.2	35.0	13.3	6
Austria	0.0	0.1	0.1	0.1	0.0	0.1	0.1	0.1	0
Belgium	5.0	0.3	14.7	8.9	4.9	0.2	14.7	8.8	4
Canada	42.1	77.6	59.2	57.1	42.1	77.6	59.2	57.1	42.
Denmark	9.6	23.6	20.3	28.9	9.6	23.6	20.3	28.9	9.
Finland	2.0	0.2	0.4	2.1	2.0	0.2	0.4	2.1	2.
France	12.0	14.6	18.9	23.3	9.6	8.4	11.6	20.5	9
Germany, Fed. Rep.	53.5	48.6	86.8	114.5	51.8	49.6	86.6	114.6	59
Italy	0.1	1.3	0.0	1.2	0.1	1.3	0.0	1.2	0
Japan	65.9	120.5	204.8	220.6	65.9	119.6	206.3	215.1	65.
Netherlands	27.1	63.6	45.9	53.2	27.1	63.6	45.9	53.2	27.
New Zealand	0.4	0.2	0.2	0.2	0.4	0.2	0.2	0.2	0
Norway	17.1	15.5	23.7	23.4	17.1	15.5	23.7	23.4	17
Sweden	23.0	26.4	39.3	27.6	23.0	26.4	39.3	27.6	23
Switzerland	4.6	14.8	3.1	11.2	4.6	14.8	3.1	11.2	5
United Kingdom	41.3	89.4	63.2	96.3	38.4	84.4	71.7	99.2	38
United States	81.0	165.0	157.0	174.0	81.0	165.0	157.0	174.0	81
TOTAL	*391.0*	*677.7*	*772.8*	*856.0*	*384.0*	*666.5*	*775.0*	*850.4*	*392*
MULTILATERAL									
AF.D.F.	–	–	–	–	–	–	–	–	
AF.D.B.	–	–	–	–	–	–	–	–	
AS.D.B.	12.0	35.8	40.0	57.8	11.9	36.3	40.5	57.4	11
CAR.D.B.	–	–	–	–	–	–	–	–	
E.E.C.	44.2	29.8	22.3	33.2	44.2	29.8	22.3	33.2	44
IBRD	–	–	–	–	–	–	–	–	
IDA	88.2	103.1	162.6	155.7	88.2	103.1	162.6	155.7	88
I.D.B.	–	–	–	–	–	–	–	–	
IFAD	–	–	–	8.2	–	–	–	8.2	
I.F.C.	–	–	–	0.9	–	–	–	–	
IMF TRUST FUND	15.6	48.1	49.0	41.7	15.6	48.1	49.0	41.7	15
U.N. AGENCIES	–	–	–	–	–	–	–	–	
UNDP	6.9	13.3	13.4	18.8	6.9	13.3	13.4	18.8	6
UNTA	1.3	1.8	2.4	0.7	1.3	1.8	2.4	0.7	1
UNICEF	8.7	14.6	22.2	17.8	8.7	14.6	22.2	17.8	8
UNRWA	–	–	–	–	–	–	–	–	
WFP	40.4	41.6	36.7	13.2	40.4	41.6	36.7	13.2	40
UNHCR	–	3.2	5.2	0.7	–	3.2	5.2	0.7	
Other Multilateral	-15.2	3.4	3.0	10.4	-15.2	3.4	3.0	10.4	-15
Arab OPEC Agencies	13.9	1.1	47.6	-8.7	13.9	1.1	10.5	4.2	13
TOTAL	*215.9*	*295.8*	*404.3*	*350.5*	*215.9*	*296.3*	*367.7*	*362.1*	*215*
OPEC COUNTRIES	*165.0*	*26.8*	*13.3*	*50.1*	*165.0*	*26.8*	*13.3*	*50.1*	*165*
E.E.C.+ MEMBERS	*192.6*	*271.2*	*272.0*	*359.4*	*185.6*	*260.8*	*273.0*	*359.5*	*192*
TOTAL	***771.9***	***1000.3***	***1190.4***	***1256.6***	***764.9***	***989.6***	***1156.0***	***1262.5***	***773***

	ODA LOANS GROSS 1977	1978	1979	1980	ODA LOANS NET 1977	1978	1979	1980	GRANTS 197
DAC COUNTRIES									
Australia	–	–	–	–	–	–	–	–	6
Austria	–	–	–	–	–	–	–	–	0
Belgium	4.2	–	11.9	7.7	4.2	–	11.9	7.7	0
Canada	–	–	–	–	–	-15.7	–	–	42
Denmark	3.5	4.1	4.4	10.6	3.5	4.1	-7.9	10.6	6
Finland	1.1	0.2	–	–	1.1	0.2	-2.4	–	0
France	4.8	4.8	4.4	9.0	4.8	4.8	4.4	9.0	4
Germany, Fed. Rep.	39.6	33.4	44.3	–	32.4	25.0	34.8	-371.0	19
Italy	–	–	–	–	–	–	–	–	0
Japan	45.7	95.9	161.3	172.3	45.7	95.9	161.3	172.3	20
Netherlands	7.4	2.9	5.3	2.1	7.4	-34.4	–	–	19
New Zealand	–	–	–	–	–	–	–	–	0
Norway	–	–	–	–	–	–	–	–	17
Sweden	0.0	–	–	–	0.0	-9.8	–	–	23
Switzerland	–	–	–	–	-0.8	–	–	–	5
United Kingdom	0.4	0.3	1.8	1.0	0.4	0.3	1.4	-54.0	38
United States	63.0	66.0	33.0	31.0	63.0	65.0	33.0	31.0	18
TOTAL	*169.7*	*207.5*	*266.5*	*233.7*	*161.6*	*135.3*	*236.5*	*-194.3*	*222*
MULTILATERAL	*128.5*	*188.9*	*263.0*	*266.9*	*128.5*	*188.5*	*262.5*	*266.4*	*87*
OPEC COUNTRIES	*15.0*	*16.7*	*13.3*	*31.7*	*15.0*	*16.7*	*13.3*	*30.6*	*150*
E.E.C.+ MEMBERS	*59.9*	*45.5*	*72.2*	*30.3*	*52.6*	*-0.2*	*44.5*	*-397.7*	*133*
TOTAL	***313.2***	***413.1***	***542.7***	***532.2***	***305.1***	***340.6***	***512.2***	***102.6***	***459***

	TOTAL OFFICIAL GROSS 1977	1978	1979	1980	TOTAL OFFICIAL NET 1977	1978	1979	1980	TOTAL OOF GROSS 197
DAC COUNTRIES									
Australia	6.4	16.2	35.0	13.5	6.4	16.2	35.0	13.5	
Austria	0.0	0.1	0.1	0.1	0.0	0.1	0.1	0.1	
Belgium	4.9	0.2	14.7	8.8	4.9	0.2	14.7	8.8	
Canada	42.1	93.2	59.2	57.1	42.1	77.6	59.2	57.1	
Denmark	9.6	23.6	32.7	28.9	9.6	23.6	20.3	28.9	
Finland	2.0	0.2	2.8	2.1	2.0	0.2	0.4	2.1	
France	9.6	8.4	11.6	20.5	9.6	8.4	11.6	20.5	
Germany, Fed. Rep.	60.2	59.1	97.3	488.4	52.1	47.8	86.7	116.6	
Italy	0.1	1.3	0.0	1.2	0.1	1.3	0.0	1.2	
Japan	65.9	119.6	206.3	215.1	65.9	119.6	206.3	215.1	
Netherlands	27.1	100.9	51.2	55.2	27.1	63.6	45.9	53.2	
New Zealand	0.4	0.2	0.2	0.2	0.4	0.2	0.2	0.2	
Norway	17.1	15.5	23.7	23.4	17.1	15.5	23.7	23.4	
Sweden	23.0	36.2	39.3	27.6	23.0	26.4	39.3	27.6	
Switzerland	5.4	14.8	3.1	11.2	4.6	14.8	3.1	11.2	
United Kingdom	38.4	84.4	72.1	154.1	38.4	84.4	71.7	99.2	
United States	81.0	166.0	157.0	174.0	81.0	165.0	157.0	174.0	
TOTAL	*393.2*	*739.8*	*806.3*	*1281.5*	*384.3*	*664.7*	*775.2*	*852.6*	
MULTILATERAL	*216.5*	*296.7*	*405.4*	*403.8*	*215.9*	*295.8*	*404.3*	*350.5*	
OPEC COUNTRIES	*165.0*	*26.8*	*13.3*	*51.2*	*165.0*	*26.8*	*13.3*	*50.1*	
E.E.C.+ MEMBERS	*193.9*	*307.6*	*301.9*	*790.4*	*185.9*	*259.0*	*273.2*	*361.5*	
TOTAL	***774.6***	***1063.3***	***1224.9***	***1736.5***	***765.2***	***987.3***	***1192.7***	***1253.2***	

ODA COMMITMENTS

1978	1979	1980	1977	1978	1979	1980
16.2	35.0	13.3	31.1	23.5	19.7	17.4
0.1	0.1	0.1	–	–	–	–
0.2	14.7	8.8	4.2	4.8	9.9	9.1
93.2	59.2	57.1	74.4	122.4	93.2	51.5
23.6	32.7	28.9	7.7	56.8	27.2	11.3
0.2	2.8	2.1	0.9	0.0	2.7	3.5
8.4	11.6	20.5	10.0	11.3	22.0	22.3
58.0	96.1	485.6	32.6	97.5	86.3	629.6
1.3	0.0	1.2	0.1	1.3	0.0	1.2
119.6	206.3	215.1	100.3	189.4	167.1	213.6
100.9	51.2	55.2	34.7	125.3	45.1	65.3
0.2	0.2	0.2	0.1	0.3	0.1	0.2
15.5	23.7	23.4	12.9	10.5	8.0	8.0
36.2	39.3	27.6	24.6	36.0	57.2	2.8
14.8	3.1	11.2	8.7	14.1	3.0	14.4
84.4	72.1	154.1	37.0	159.4	55.1	85.0
166.0	157.0	174.0	165.2	159.2	161.9	166.7
738.7	*805.0*	*1278.4*	*544.6*	*1011.7*	*758.4*	*1301.7*
–	–	–	–	–	–	–
–	–	–	–	–	–	–
36.6	41.0	57.9	84.8	91.5	115.9	150.9
–	–	–	–	–	–	–
29.8	22.3	33.2	19.0	37.1	31.3	58.8
–	–	–	–	–	–	–
103.1	162.6	155.7	202.0	163.0	202.0	411.7
–	–	–	–	–	–	–
–	–	8.2	–	30.0	25.7	21.9
–	–	–	–	–	–	–
48.1	49.0	41.7	–	–	–	–
–	–	–	42.1	78.0	82.9	61.7
13.3	13.4	18.8	–	–	–	–
1.8	2.4	0.7	–	–	–	–
14.6	22.2	17.8	–	–	–	–
–	–	–	–	–	–	–
41.6	36.7	13.2	–	–	–	–
3.2	5.2	0.7	–	–	–	–
3.4	3.0	10.4	–	–	–	–
1.1	10.5	4.2	24.5	7.0	18.5	41.3
296.6	*368.2*	*362.5*	*372.3*	*406.6*	*476.3*	*746.2*
26.8	*13.3*	*51.2*	*199.9*	*61.3*	*31.5*	*84.9*
306.5	*300.6*	*787.5*	*145.3*	*493.5*	*276.8*	*882.5*
1062.1	***1186.5***	***1692.1***	***1116.9***	***1479.6***	***1266.2***	***2132.8***

TECH. COOP. GRANTS

1978	1979	1980	1977	1978	1979	1980
16.2	35.0	13.3	2.2	3.0	1.9	3.3
0.1	0.1	0.1	0.0	0.1	0.1	0.1
0.2	2.8	1.2	0.2	0.2	0.3	0.5
93.2	59.2	57.1	0.2	0.1	0.0	0.1
19.5	28.3	18.3	1.8	4.5	7.4	9.8
0.0	2.8	2.1	0.0	0.0	0.1	0.1
3.6	7.2	11.5	–	–	–	0.2
24.6	51.8	485.6	4.4	10.9	15.8	12.9
1.3	0.0	1.2	0.1	0.1	0.0	0.0
23.8	45.0	42.8	2.9	5.3	5.3	6.3
98.0	45.9	53.2	7.4	4.6	6.1	9.3
0.2	0.2	0.2	0.1	0.2	0.1	0.2
15.5	23.7	23.4	0.4	0.5	1.6	1.5
36.2	39.3	27.6	0.9	1.4	1.3	1.4
14.8	3.1	11.2	0.0	0.0	–	0.7
84.1	70.3	153.2	3.1	5.5	8.1	12.1
100.0	124.0	143.0	2.0	27.0	54.0	52.0
531.2	*538.6*	*1044.7*	*25.7*	*63.4*	*102.1*	*110.5*
107.8	*105.2*	*95.7*	*2.8*	*36.3*	*46.1*	*61.7*
10.1	–	*19.5*	–	–	–	–
261.0	*228.5*	*757.2*	*16.9*	*25.7*	*37.8*	*44.8*
649.0	***643.7***	***1159.9***	***28.5***	***99.7***	***148.2***	***172.1***

TOTAL OOF NET

1978	1979	1980	1977	1978	1979	1980
–	–	0.3	–	–	–	0.3
–	–	–	–	–	–	–
–	–	–	–	–	–	–
–	–	–	–	–	–	–
–	–	–	–	–	–	–
–	–	–	–	–	–	–
–	–	–	–	–	–	–
1.1	1.2	2.9	0.3	-1.8	0.2	1.9
–	–	–	–	–	–	–
–	–	–	–	–	–	–
–	–	–	–	–	–	–
–	–	–	–	–	–	–
–	–	–	–	–	–	–
–	–	–	–	–	–	–
–	–	–	–	–	–	–
–	–	–	–	–	–	–
–	–	–	–	–	–	–
1.1	*1.2*	*3.1*	*0.3*	*-1.8*	*0.2*	*2.2*
0.1	*37.2*	*41.3*	*0.0*	*-0.5*	*36.6*	*-11.6*
–	–	–	–	–	–	–
1.1	*1.2*	*2.9*	*0.3*	*-1.8*	*0.2*	*1.9*
1.2	***38.5***	***44.4***	***0.3***	***-2.3***	***36.8***	***-9.4***

MAIN AID AGGREGATES

	1977	1978	1979	1980
DAC COUNTRIES COMBINED				
PRIVATE SECTOR NET	6.8	13.0	-2.4	3.4
Direct Investment	7.0	7.7	-8.0	5.5
Portfolio Invest.	0.2	0.0	0.5	0.4
Export Credits	-0.5	5.3	5.2	-2.5
OFFICIAL & PRIVATE				
GROSS:				
Contractual Lending	178.8	229.4	275.4	246.6
Export Credits Tot.	8.0	20.8	7.7	10.1
Export Credits Priv	8.0	20.8	7.7	10.1
OTHER NET DATA				
Contractual Lending	161.5	138.8	241.8	-194.6
Export Credits Tot.	-0.5	5.3	5.2	-2.5
(Bank Sector Loans)	8.0	2.0	-6.0	3.0
ODA CONCESSIONALITY				
Total:Grant Element	88.0	91.0	93.0	94.0
Loans:Grant Element	65.0	70.0	67.0	70.0
OTHER SOURCES				
CMEA Countr.(Gross)	19.4	16.0	11.5	11.5
Intra LDCS Exc.OPEC	–	–	–	–
Other	–	–	–	–
ALL SOURCE COMMITMENTS				
TOTAL BILATERAL	744.6	1073.0	789.9	1387.7
of which				
OPEC (ODA)	199.9	61.3	31.5	84.9
CMEA (ODA)	7.0	–	50.0	–
TOTAL MULTILAT.(ODA)	372.3	406.6	476.3	746.2
TOTAL BIL.& MULTIL.	1116.9	1479.6	1266.2	2134.0
of which				
ODA Grants	569.3	853.5	714.9	1209.0
ODA Loans	547.6	626.1	551.3	923.8
ODA CONCESSIONALITY				
Total: Grant Element	85.0	89.0	88.0	89.0
Loans: Grant Element	70.0	73.0	74.0	73.0

INDEBTEDNESS

	1977	1978	1979	1980
TOTAL DEBT DISBURSED	***2303.1***	***2738.5***	***3250.2***	
Debt to DAC Countries	1352.0	1619.0	1874.0	
ODA	1290.0	1475.0	1731.0	
Total Export Credits	50.0	131.0	119.0	
Other Private Market	12.0	13.0	24.0	
International Org.	611.0	750.4	966.2	
CMEA	124.0	139.2	151.7	
Other	216.1	230.0	258.4	
TOTAL DEBT SERVICE	***83.6***	***102.0***	***98.8***	
Paid to DAC Countries	35.9	46.0	47.1	
ODA	16.3	21.0	21.2	
Total Export Credits	14.8	15.8	18.7	
Other Private Market	4.8	9.2	7.2	
International Org.	8.2	9.9	13.4	
CMEA	20.9	31.1	25.4	
Other	18.6	14.9	12.9	

ECONOMIC INDICATORS

	1977	1978	1979	1980
GNP Curr. Prices, $M	6865.0	8697.0	9614.5	11487.3
Real GNP, 1976=100	101.0	109.0	114.0	118.0
GNP/Cap Curr. Prices,$	82.0	102.0	109.0	127.0
GNP/cap Atlas Basis, $	91.3	102.6	113.0	123.8
Real GNP/Cap, 1976=100	98.0	103.0	104.0	105.0
Population, Million	82.8	85.2	87.7	90.2
Curr.A/C Deficit(-),$M	-600.2	-843.3	-1181.0	-1491.4
BOP Exp. & Transf.,$M	662.3	810.8	1014.2	1381.2
Exp. to OECD CIF, $M	244.5	331.3	393.6	383.8
of which				
Manufact.	125.5	220.0	250.1	247.7
Imp. from OECD FOB, $M	632.5	774.0	1050.3	1111.7
Reserves ex. Gold, $M	232.7	315.2	386.2	299.7

BENIN

	TOTAL RECEIPTS NET 1977	1978	1979	1980	TOTAL ODA NET 1977	1978	1979	1980	TOTAL ODA GROSS 1977
DAC COUNTRIES									
Australia	–	–	–	–	–	–	–	–	–
Austria	–	–	–	–	–	–	–	–	–
Belgium	1.6	0.2	0.2	209.7	0.8	0.5	0.5	0.5	0.
Canada	3.1	2.3	4.9	1.5	3.1	2.3	4.9	1.5	3.
Denmark	0.5	1.7	5.3	1.6	0.5	1.7	5.3	1.6	0.
Finland	–	–	–	–	–	–	–	–	–
France	13.6	19.7	27.8	38.9	10.2	13.3	18.5	16.8	11.
Germany, Fed. Rep.	2.8	4.8	10.5	10.3	2.8	4.9	10.4	10.3	3.
Italy	-0.2	0.1	0.1	–	0.1	0.1	0.1	–	0.
Japan	0.1	0.2	0.0	0.0	0.1	0.2	0.0	0.0	0.
Netherlands	0.7	0.7	1.0	1.0	0.7	0.7	1.0	1.0	0.
New Zealand	–	–	–	–	–	–	–	–	–
Norway	–	1.9	4.0	67.3	–	1.9	4.1	2.3	–
Sweden	–	–	–	–	–	–	–	–	–
Switzerland	0.3	1.7	0.8	0.4	0.3	1.7	0.8	0.6	0.
United Kingdom	0.0	0.1	0.1	0.2	0.0	0.1	0.1	0.2	0.
United States	8.0	3.0	3.0	1.0	8.0	3.0	3.0	1.0	8.
TOTAL	*30.5*	*36.3*	*57.8*	*331.9*	*26.6*	*30.3*	*48.6*	*35.7*	*28.*
MULTILATERAL									
AF.D.F.	1.0	0.8	3.6	3.9	1.0	0.8	3.6	3.9	1.
AF.D.B.	3.5	2.5	1.2	3.4	–	–	–	–	
AS.D.B.	–	–	–	–	–	–	–	–	
CAR.D.B.	–	–	–	–	–	–	–	–	
E.E.C.	6.1	11.7	14.3	13.6	6.1	11.7	14.3	13.6	6.
IBRD	–	–	–	–	–	–	–	–	
IDA	7.0	2.4	5.5	12.2	7.0	2.4	5.5	12.2	7.
I.D.B.	–	–	–	–	–	–	–	–	
IFAD	–	–	–	–	–	–	–	–	
I.F.C.	–	–	–	–	–	–	–	–	
IMF TRUST FUND	–	6.8	–	9.5	–	6.8	–	9.5	
U.N. AGENCIES	–	–	–	–	–	–	–	–	
UNDP	2.1	2.9	4.1	4.2	2.1	2.9	4.1	4.2	2.
UNTA	0.5	0.6	0.5	0.3	0.5	0.6	0.5	0.3	0.
UNICEF	0.3	0.1	1.1	1.7	0.3	0.1	1.1	1.7	0.
UNRWA	–	–	–	–	–	–	–	–	
WFP	0.9	1.4	3.3	2.7	0.9	1.4	3.3	2.7	0
UNHCR	–	–	–	–	–	–	–	–	
Other Multilateral	0.5	0.8	0.1	2.4	0.5	0.8	0.1	2.4	0.
Arab OPEC Agencies	3.6	4.4	3.1	2.3	3.6	3.4	1.3	2.3	3.
TOTAL	*25.5*	*34.3*	*36.9*	*56.3*	*22.0*	*30.9*	*33.9*	*52.9*	*22.*
OPEC COUNTRIES	–	–	*2.1*	*1.8*	–	–	*2.1*	*1.8*	
E.E.C.+ MEMBERS	*25.1*	*38.8*	*59.3*	*275.3*	*21.2*	*32.8*	*50.1*	*43.9*	*22.*
TOTAL	***56.0***	***70.6***	***96.8***	***390.0***	***48.7***	***61.1***	***84.6***	***90.4***	***50.***

	ODA LOANS GROSS 1977	1978	1979	1980	ODA LOANS NET 1977	1978	1979	1980	GRANTS 1977
DAC COUNTRIES									
Australia	–	–	–	–	–	–	–	–	
Austria	–	–	–	–	–	–	–	–	
Belgium	–	–	–	–	–	–	–	–	0
Canada	1.3	–	–	–	1.3	-13.1	–	–	1.
Denmark	0.6	1.9	5.4	1.5	0.5	1.7	-0.7	1.5	
Finland	–	–	–	–	–	–	–	–	
France	1.2	2.1	8.0	6.6	0.2	1.6	7.5	6.1	10
Germany, Fed. Rep.	1.2	1.7	5.6	–	0.7	1.7	5.6	-14.9	2
Italy	–	–	–	–	–	–	–	–	0.
Japan	–	–	–	–	–	–	–	–	0
Netherlands	–	–	–	–	–	–	–	–	0
New Zealand	–	–	–	–	–	–	–	–	
Norway	–	–	–	–	–	–	–	–	
Sweden	–	–	–	–	–	–	–	–	
Switzerland	–	–	–	–	–	–	–	–	0
United Kingdom	–	–	–	–	–	–	–	–	0
United States	7.0	2.0	3.0	1.0	7.0	2.0	3.0	1.0	1
TOTAL	*11.3*	*7.7*	*22.0*	*9.1*	*9.7*	*-6.2*	*15.4*	*-6.3*	*16*
MULTILATERAL	*11.6*	*13.4*	*11.7*	*35.2*	*11.5*	*13.4*	*10.5*	*28.0*	*10*
OPEC COUNTRIES	–	–	*2.1*	*1.8*	–	–	*2.1*	*1.8*	
E.E.C.+ MEMBERS	*3.0*	*5.7*	*19.0*	*8.1*	*1.3*	*5.0*	*12.4*	*-7.3*	*19*
TOTAL	***22.9***	***21.1***	***35.8***	***46.1***	***21.2***	***7.2***	***27.9***	***23.5***	***27***

	TOTAL OFFICIAL GROSS 1977	1978	1979	1980	TOTAL OFFICIAL NET 1977	1978	1979	1980	TOTAL OOF GROSS 1977
DAC COUNTRIES									
Australia	–	–	–	–	–	–	–	–	
Austria	–	–	–	–	–	–	–	–	
Belgium	0.8	0.5	0.5	0.5	0.8	0.5	0.5	0.5	
Canada	3.1	15.5	4.9	1.5	3.1	2.3	4.9	1.5	
Denmark	0.6	1.9	11.4	1.6	0.5	1.7	5.3	1.6	
Finland	–	–	–	–	–	–	–	–	
France	11.2	13.8	19.0	17.2	10.1	13.2	18.4	16.7	
Germany, Fed. Rep.	3.4	5.0	10.5	25.4	2.9	4.9	10.4	10.4	0
Italy	0.1	0.1	0.1	–	0.1	0.1	0.1	–	
Japan	0.1	0.2	0.0	0.0	0.1	0.2	0.0	0.0	
Netherlands	0.7	0.7	1.0	1.0	0.7	0.7	1.0	1.0	
New Zealand	–	–	–	–	–	–	–	–	
Norway	–	1.9	4.1	2.3	–	1.9	4.1	2.3	
Sweden	–	–	–	–	–	–	–	–	
Switzerland	0.3	1.7	0.8	0.6	0.3	1.7	0.8	0.6	
United Kingdom	0.0	0.1	0.1	0.2	0.0	0.1	0.1	0.2	
United States	8.0	3.0	3.0	1.0	8.0	3.0	3.0	1.0	
TOTAL	*28.3*	*44.3*	*55.4*	*51.2*	*26.6*	*30.3*	*48.5*	*35.8*	*0*
MULTILATERAL	*25.6*	*34.4*	*38.5*	*64.3*	*25.5*	*34.3*	*36.9*	*56.3*	*3*
OPEC COUNTRIES	–	–	*2.1*	*1.8*	–	–	*2.1*	*1.8*	
E.E.C.+ MEMBERS	*23.0*	*33.6*	*56.9*	*59.4*	*21.2*	*32.8*	*50.0*	*43.9*	*0*
TOTAL	***53.9***	***78.7***	***96.0***	***117.3***	***52.1***	***64.6***	***87.5***	***93.9***	***3***

ODA COMMITMENTS

	1978	1979	1980	1977	1978	1979	1980
	–	–	–	–	–	–	–
	–	–	–	–	–	–	–
	0.5	0.5	0.5	–	–	–	–
	15.5	4.9	1.5	0.9	34.4	6.4	0.5
	1.9	11.4	1.6	–	15.0	0.1	–
	–	–	–	–	–	–	–
	13.8	19.0	17.2	7.9	10.3	24.0	12.9
	4.9	10.4	25.2	2.5	5.1	7.9	30.6
	0.1	0.1	–	0.1	0.1	0.1	–
	0.2	0.0	0.0	0.2	0.2	1.8	1.8
	0.7	1.0	1.0	0.4	2.3	0.9	3.8
	–	–	–	–	–	–	–
	1.9	4.1	2.3	–	8.3	0.8	–
	–	–	–	–	–	–	–
	1.7	0.8	0.6	–	2.1	–	0.3
	0.1	0.1	0.2	0.0	0.1	0.1	0.2
	3.0	3.0	1.0	0.8	1.1	0.4	7.9
	44.1	*55.3*	*51.0*	*12.7*	*78.9*	*42.6*	*57.8*
	0.8	3.7	3.9	14.4	5.4	10.6	9.4
	–	–	–	–	–	–	–
	–	–	–	–	–	–	–
	–	–	–	–	–	–	–
	11.7	14.3	13.6	25.1	11.2	16.5	3.4
	–	–	–	–	–	–	–
	2.4	6.6	19.5	17.2	19.3	–	17.0
	–	–	–	–	–	–	–
	–	–	–	–	–	–	–
	–	–	–	–	–	–	–
	6.8	–	9.5	–	–	–	–
	–	–	–	4.3	5.8	9.2	11.3
	2.9	4.1	4.2	–	–	–	–
	0.6	0.5	0.3	–	–	–	–
	0.1	1.1	1.7	–	–	–	–
	–	–	–	–	–	–	–
	1.4	3.3	2.7	–	–	–	–
	–	–	–	–	–	–	–
	0.8	0.1	2.4	–	–	–	–
	3.4	1.3	2.3	2.1	1.6	4.5	4.5
	30.9	*35.1*	*60.1*	*63.1*	*43.3*	*40.7*	*45.6*
	–	*2.1*	*1.8*	–	*8.2*	–	–
	33.5	*56.8*	*59.2*	*36.0*	*44.0*	*49.6*	*50.7*
	75.0	***92.5***	***113.0***	***75.9***	***130.4***	***83.3***	***103.4***

TECH. COOP. GRANTS

	1978	1979	1980	1977	1978	1979	1980
	–	–	–	–	–	–	–
	–	–	–	–	–	–	–
	0.5	0.5	0.5	0.5	0.5	0.5	0.5
	15.5	4.9	1.5	0.8	0.6	0.6	0.2
	–	6.0	0.1	–	–	–	0.1
	–	–	–	–	–	–	–
	11.7	11.0	10.7	5.8	6.2	7.4	8.0
	3.2	4.8	25.2	2.1	3.2	4.8	7.3
	0.1	0.1	–	0.1	0.1	0.1	–
	0.2	0.0	0.0	0.1	0.2	0.0	0.0
	0.7	1.0	1.0	0.7	0.6	1.0	0.9
	–	–	–	–	–	–	–
	1.9	4.1	2.3	–	–	–	–
	–	–	–	–	–	–	–
	1.7	0.8	0.6	0.1	0.1	0.1	0.1
	0.1	0.1	0.2	0.0	0.1	0.1	0.2
	1.0	–	–	–	1.0	–	–
	36.4	*33.3*	*42.0*	*10.3*	*12.5*	*14.6*	*17.3*
	17.5	*23.4*	*24.9*	*3.4*	*4.4*	*5.8*	*11.3*
	–	–	–	–	–	–	–
	27.8	*37.8*	*51.2*	*9.2*	*10.7*	*13.9*	*17.0*
	53.9	***56.7***	***66.9***	***13.7***	***16.9***	***20.4***	***28.6***

TOTAL OOF NET

	1978	1979	1980	1977	1978	1979	1980
	–	–	–	–	–	–	–
	–	–	–	–	–	–	–
	–	–	–	–	–	–	–
	–	–	–	–	–	–	–
	–	–	–	–	–	–	–
	–	–	–	–	–	–	–
	–	–	–	-0.1	-0.1	-0.1	-0.1
	0.1	0.1	0.2	0.1	0.1	0.1	0.2
	–	–	–	–	–	–	–
	–	–	–	–	–	–	–
	–	–	–	–	–	–	–
	–	–	–	–	–	–	–
	–	–	–	–	–	–	–
	–	–	–	–	–	–	–
	–	–	–	–	–	–	–
	–	–	–	–	–	–	–
	–	–	–	–	–	–	–
	0.1	*0.1*	*0.2*	*0.0*	*0.0*	*-0.1*	*0.1*
	3.5	*3.4*	*4.1*	*3.5*	*3.5*	*3.0*	*3.4*
	–	–	–	–	–	–	–
	0.1	*0.1*	*0.2*	*0.0*	*0.0*	*-0.1*	*0.1*
	3.7	***3.5***	***4.3***	***3.5***	***3.5***	***2.9***	***3.5***

MAIN AID AGGREGATES

	1977	1978	1979	1980
DAC COUNTRIES COMBINED				
PRIVATE SECTOR NET	3.9	6.0	9.3	296.2
Direct Investment	0.0	0.0	0.3	1.7
Portfolio Invest.	-0.1	–	-0.2	0.4
Export Credits	4.0	6.0	9.2	294.1
OFFICIAL & PRIVATE				
GROSS:				
Contractual Lending	17.6	18.5	40.6	304.9
Export Credits Tot.	6.2	10.6	18.5	295.7
Export Credits Priv	6.2	10.6	18.5	295.7
OTHER NET DATA				
Contractual Lending	13.7	-0.1	24.5	287.9
Export Credits Tot.	4.0	6.0	9.2	294.1
(Bank Sector Loans)	–	-1.0	3.0	6.0
ODA CONCESSIONALITY				
Total:Grant Element	99.0	98.0	76.0	100.0
Loans:Grant Element	83.0	85.0	25.0	–
OTHER SOURCES				
CMEA Countr.(Gross)	0.5	–	–	–
Intra LDCS Exc.OPEC	–	–	–	–
Other	–	–	–	–
ALL SOURCE COMMITMENTS				
TOTAL BILATERAL	17.0	92.2	42.6	58.8
of which				
OPEC (ODA)	–	8.2	–	–
CMEA (ODA)	0.6	–	–	–
TOTAL MULTILAT.(ODA)	63.1	43.3	40.7	45.6
TOTAL BIL.& MULTIL.	80.2	135.5	83.3	104.4
of which				
ODA Grants	41.5	86.9	54.1	72.5
ODA Loans	34.3	43.6	29.2	30.9
ODA CONCESSIONALITY				
Total: Grant Element	91.0	93.0	83.0	93.0
Loans: Grant Element	81.0	79.0	52.0	75.0

INDEBTEDNESS

	1977	1978	1979	1980
TOTAL DEBT DISBURSED	***134.5***	***169.1***	***225.0***	
Debt to DAC Countries	77.0	88.0	118.0	
ODA	50.0	44.0	55.0	
Total Export Credits	24.0	29.0	50.0	
Other Private Market	3.0	15.0	13.0	
International Org.	46.1	62.3	79.9	
CMEA	6.7	9.9	12.2	
Other	4.7	8.8	14.9	
TOTAL DEBT SERVICE	***10.6***	***14.2***	***17.4***	
Paid to DAC Countries	9.9	12.6	14.3	
ODA	2.7	1.0	0.8	
Total Export Credits	6.4	10.6	11.3	
Other Private Market	0.8	1.0	2.2	
International Org.	0.2	1.1	2.8	
CMEA	0.2	0.4	0.0	
Other	0.2	0.1	0.3	

ECONOMIC INDICATORS

	1977	1978	1979	1980
GNP Curr. Prices, $M	624.0	767.2	952.9	1119.7
Real GNP, 1976=100	104.0	107.0	112.0	117.0
GNP/Cap Curr. Prices,$	193.0	230.0	278.0	317.0
GNP/cap Atlas Basis, $	232.1	250.0	274.0	304.6
Real GNP/Cap, 1976=100	101.0	101.0	102.0	104.0
Population, Million	3.2	3.3	3.4	3.5
Curr.A/C Deficit(-),$M	-103.1	–	–	–
BOP Exp. & Transf.,$M	203.9	–	–	–
Exp. to OECD CIF, $M	35.8	26.4	45.6	66.2
of which				
Manufact.	1.4	1.6	3.1	3.6
Imp. from OECD FOB, $M	188.6	236.0	340.1	460.0
Reserves ex. Gold, $M	20.4	15.5	14.2	8.1

	1977	1978	1979	1980	1977	1978	1979	1980	197
TOTAL RECEIPTS NET					**TOTAL ODA NET**				**TOTAL ODA GROSS**
DAC COUNTRIES									
Australia	7.8	1.0	3.9	2.3	–	–	–	–	
Austria	–	–	–	–	–	–	–	–	
Belgium	1.0	-11.9	7.7	-8.8	–	–	–	–	
Canada	20.2	20.3	4.3	-3.0	–	–	–	–	
Denmark	–	–	–	–	–	–	–	–	
Finland	-0.1	0.0	0.0	0.0	–	–	–	–	
France	24.4	11.3	66.8	-11.8	–	–	–	–	
Germany, Fed. Rep.	-14.1	41.4	5.0	52.2	–	–	–	–	
Italy	–	–	8.6	5.3	–	–	–	–	
Japan	33.9	-25.7	-91.5	-56.0	–	–	–	–	
Netherlands	–	–	7.0	1.5	–	–	–	–	
New Zealand	0.0	0.0	–	–	–	–	–	–	
Norway	0.1	–	0.0	0.4	–	–	–	–	
Sweden	0.7	1.2	-0.1	-0.1	–	–	–	–	
Switzerland	–	–	–	–	–	–	–	–	
United Kingdom	-361.0	15.4	9.2	9.9	0.0	0.0	0.0	0.1	0
United States	-190.0	-208.0	755.0	954.0	–	–	–	–	
TOTAL	*-477.1*	*-155.1*	*775.8*	*945.8*	*0.0*	*0.0*	*0.0*	*0.1*	*0*
MULTILATERAL									
AF.D.F.	–	–	–	–	–	–	–	–	
AF.D.B.	–	–	–	–	–	–	–	–	
AS.D.B.	–	–	–	–	–	–	–	–	
CAR.D.B.	–	–	–	–	–	–	–	–	
E.E.C.	–	–	–	–	–	–	–	–	
IBRD	–	–	–	–	–	–	–	–	
IDA	–	–	–	–	–	–	–	–	
I.D.B.	–	–	–	–	–	–	–	–	
IFAD	–	–	–	–	–	–	–	–	
I.F.C.	–	–	–	–	–	–	–	–	
IMF TRUST FUND	–	–	–	–	–	–	–	–	
U.N. AGENCIES	–	–	–	–	–	–	–	–	
UNDP	0.1	0.1	0.1	0.2	0.1	0.1	0.1	0.2	0
UNTA	–	–	–	–	–	–	–	–	
UNICEF	–	–	–	–	–	–	–	–	
UNRWA	–	–	–	–	–	–	–	–	
WFP	–	–	–	–	–	–	–	–	
UNHCR	–	–	–	–	–	–	–	–	
Other Multilateral	–	–	–	–	–	–	–	–	
Arab OPEC Agencies	–	–	–	–	–	–	–	–	
TOTAL	*0.1*	*0.1*	*0.1*	*0.2*	*0.1*	*0.1*	*0.1*	*0.2*	*0*
OPEC COUNTRIES	–	–	–	–	–	–	–	–	
E.E.C.+ MEMBERS	*-349.7*	*56.2*	*104.2*	*48.2*	*0.0*	*0.0*	*0.0*	*0.1*	*0*
TOTAL	***-477.0***	***-155.0***	***775.9***	***946.0***	***0.1***	***0.2***	***0.2***	***0.3***	***0***

	1977	1978	1979	1980	1977	1978	1979	1980	197
ODA LOANS GROSS					**ODA LOANS NET**				**GRANTS**
DAC COUNTRIES									
Australia	–	–	–	–	–	–	–	–	
Austria	–	–	–	–	–	–	–	–	
Belgium	–	–	–	–	–	–	–	–	
Canada	–	–	–	–	–	–	–	–	
Denmark	–	–	–	–	–	–	–	–	
Finland	–	–	–	–	–	–	–	–	
France	–	–	–	–	–	–	–	–	
Germany, Fed. Rep.	–	–	–	–	–	–	–	–	
Italy	–	–	–	–	–	–	–	–	
Japan	–	–	–	–	–	–	–	–	
Netherlands	–	–	–	–	–	–	–	–	
New Zealand	–	–	–	–	–	–	–	–	
Norway	–	–	–	–	–	–	–	–	
Sweden	–	–	–	–	–	–	–	–	
Switzerland	–	–	–	–	–	–	–	–	
United Kingdom	–	–	–	–	–	–	–	–	0
United States	–	–	–	–	–	–	–	–	
TOTAL	–	–	–	–	–	–	–	–	*0*
MULTILATERAL	–	–	–	–	–	–	–	–	*0*
OPEC COUNTRIES	–	–	–	–	–	–	–	–	
E.E.C.+ MEMBERS	–	–	–	–	–	–	–	–	*0*
TOTAL	–	–	–	–	–	–	–	–	***0***

	1977	1978	1979	1980	1977	1978	1979	1980	197
TOTAL OFFICIAL GROSS					**TOTAL OFFICIAL NET**				**TOTAL OOF GROSS**
DAC COUNTRIES									
Australia	–	–	–	–	–	–	–	–	
Austria	–	–	–	–	–	–	–	–	
Belgium	–	–	–	–	–	–	–	–	
Canada	20.3	20.3	4.3	–	20.3	20.3	4.3	-3.0	20
Denmark	–	–	–	–	–	–	–	–	
Finland	–	–	–	–	–	–	–	–	
France	–	–	–	–	–	–	–	–	
Germany, Fed. Rep.	–	–	–	5.3	–	–	–	5.3	
Italy	–	–	–	–	–	–	–	–	
Japan	–	–	–	–	–	–	–	–	
Netherlands	–	–	–	–	–	–	–	–	
New Zealand	0.1	–	–	–	0.0	–	–	–	0
Norway	–	–	–	–	–	–	–	–	
Sweden	–	–	–	–	–	–	–	–	
Switzerland	–	–	–	–	–	–	–	–	
United Kingdom	0.0	0.0	0.0	0.1	0.0	0.0	0.0	0.1	
United States	–	–	–	–	-6.0	-2.0	-1.0	-1.0	
TOTAL	*20.4*	*20.3*	*4.3*	*5.4*	*14.2*	*18.3*	*3.3*	*1.4*	*20*
MULTILATERAL	*0.1*	*0.1*	*0.1*	*0.2*	*0.1*	*0.1*	*0.1*	*0.2*	
OPEC COUNTRIES	–	–	–	–	–	–	–	–	
E.E.C.+ MEMBERS	*0.0*	*0.0*	*0.0*	*5.4*	*0.0*	*0.0*	*0.0*	*5.4*	
TOTAL	***20.5***	***20.5***	***4.5***	***5.6***	***14.3***	***18.5***	***3.5***	***1.6***	***20***

1978	1979	1980	1977	1978	1979	1980
			ODA COMMITMENTS			
–	–	–	–	–	–	–
–	–	–	–	–	–	–
–	–	–	–	–	–	–
–	–	–	–	–	–	–
–	–	–	–	–	–	–
–	–	–	–	–	–	–
–	–	–	–	–	–	–
–	–	–	–	–	–	–
–	–	–	–	–	–	–
–	–	–	–	–	–	–
–	–	–	–	–	–	–
–	–	–	–	–	–	–
–	–	–	–	–	–	–
–	–	–	–	–	–	–
–	–	–	–	–	–	–
0.0	0.0	0.1	0.0	0.0	0.0	0.1
–	–	–	–	–	–	–
0.0	*0.0*	*0.1*	*0.0*	*0.0*	*0.0*	*0.1*
–	–	–	–	–	–	–
–	–	–	–	–	–	–
–	–	–	–	–	–	–
–	–	–	–	–	–	–
–	–	–	–	–	–	–
–	–	–	–	–	–	–
–	–	–	–	–	–	–
–	–	–	–	–	–	–
–	–	–	–	–	–	–
–	–	–	–	–	–	–
–	–	–	–	–	–	–
–	–	–	0.1	0.1	0.1	0.2
0.1	0.1	0.2	–	–	–	–
–	–	–	–	–	–	–
–	–	–	–	–	–	–
–	–	–	–	–	–	–
–	–	–	–	–	–	–
–	–	–	–	–	–	–
–	–	–	–	–	–	–
–	–	–	–	–	–	–
0.1	*0.1*	*0.2*	*0.1*	*0.1*	*0.1*	*0.2*
–	–	–	–	–	–	–
0.0	*0.0*	*0.1*	*0.0*	*0.0*	*0.0*	*0.1*
0.2	***0.2***	***0.3***	***0.1***	***0.2***	***0.2***	***0.3***
			TECH. COOP. GRANTS			
–	–	–	–	–	–	–
–	–	–	–	–	–	–
–	–	–	–	–	–	–
–	–	–	–	–	–	–
–	–	–	–	–	–	–
–	–	–	–	–	–	–
–	–	–	–	–	–	–
–	–	–	–	–	–	–
–	–	–	–	–	–	–
–	–	–	–	–	–	–
–	–	–	–	–	–	–
–	–	–	–	–	–	–
–	–	–	–	–	–	–
–	–	–	–	–	–	–
–	–	–	–	–	–	–
0.0	0.0	0.1	0.0	0.0	0.0	0.1
–	–	–	–	–	–	–
0.0	*0.0*	*0.1*	*0.0*	*0.0*	*0.0*	*0.1*
0.1	*0.1*	*0.2*	*0.1*	*0.1*	*0.1*	*0.2*
–	–	–	–	–	–	–
0.0	*0.0*	*0.1*	*0.0*	*0.0*	*0.0*	*0.1*
0.2	***0.2***	***0.3***	***0.1***	***0.2***	***0.2***	***0.3***
			TOTAL OOF NET			
–	–	–	–	–	–	–
–	–	–	–	–	–	–
–	–	–	–	–	–	–
20.3	4.3	–	20.3	20.3	4.3	-3.0
–	–	–	–	–	–	–
–	–	–	–	–	–	–
–	–	–	–	–	–	–
–	–	5.3	–	–	–	5.3
–	–	–	–	–	–	–
–	–	–	–	–	–	–
–	–	–	–	–	–	–
–	–	–	0.0	–	–	–
–	–	–	–	–	–	–
–	–	–	–	–	–	–
–	–	–	–	–	–	–
–	–	–	–	–	–	–
–	–	–	-6.0	-2.0	-1.0	-1.0
20.3	*4.3*	*5.3*	*14.2*	*18.3*	*3.3*	*1.3*
–	–	–	–	–	–	–
–	–	–	–	–	–	–
–	–	*5.3*	–	–	–	*5.3*
20.3	***4.3***	***5.3***	***14.2***	***18.3***	***3.3***	***1.3***

	1977	1978	1979	1980
MAIN AID AGGREGATES				
DAC COUNTRIES COMBINED				
PRIVATE SECTOR NET	-491.3	-173.4	772.5	944.4
Direct Investment	-401.7	40.0	746.3	810.0
Portfolio Invest.	-182.6	-172.0	-11.1	168.4
Export Credits	93.0	-41.4	37.3	-33.9
OFFICIAL & PRIVATE				
GROSS:				
Contractual Lending	169.7	64.3	129.1	41.0
Export Credits Tot.	169.7	64.3	129.1	41.0
Export Credits Priv	149.3	44.1	124.8	35.7
OTHER NET DATA				
Contractual Lending	107.3	-23.1	40.6	-32.6
Export Credits Tot.	107.3	-23.1	40.6	-32.6
(Bank Sector Loans)	–	–	–	29.0
ODA CONCESSIONALITY				
Total:Grant Element	100.0	100.0	100.0	100.0
Loans:Grant Element	–	–	–	–
OTHER SOURCES				
CMEA Countr.(Gross)	–	–	–	–
Intra LDCS Exc.OPEC	–	–	–	–
Other	–	–	–	–
ALL SOURCE COMMITMENTS				
TOTAL BILATERAL	0.2	0.0	0.0	10.6
of which				
OPEC (ODA)	–	–	–	–
CMEA (ODA)	–	–	–	–
TOTAL MULTILAT.(ODA)	0.1	0.1	0.1	0.2
TOTAL BIL.& MULTIL.	0.2	0.2	0.2	10.9
of which				
ODA Grants	0.1	0.2	0.2	0.3
ODA Loans	–	–	–	–
ODA CONCESSIONALITY				
Total: Grant Element	100.0	100.0	100.0	100.0
Loans: Grant Element	–	–	–	–
INDEBTEDNESS				
TOTAL DEBT DISBURSED	***211.0***	***295.0***	***258.0***	
Debt to DAC Countries	211.0	295.0	258.0	
ODA	–	–	–	
Total Export Credits	196.0	275.0	233.0	
Other Private Market	15.0	20.0	25.0	
International Org.	–	–	–	
CMEA	–	–	–	
Other	–	–	–	
TOTAL DEBT SERVICE	***59.7***	***165.7***	***114.9***	
Paid to DAC Countries	59.7	165.7	114.9	
ODA	–	–	–	
Total Export Credits	57.6	163.2	110.9	
Other Private Market	2.1	2.5	4.0	
International Org.	–	–	–	
CMEA	–	–	–	
Other	–	–	–	
ECONOMIC INDICATORS				
GNP Curr. Prices, $M	–	–	–	–
Real GNP, 1976=100	100.0	103.0	108.0	113.0
GNP/Cap Curr. Prices,$	–	–	–	–
GNP/cap Atlas Basis, $	7945.1	8779.3	9819.1	11047.3
Real GNP/Cap, 1976=100	98.0	101.0	104.0	107.0
Population, Million	0.1	0.1	0.1	0.1
Curr.A/C Deficit(-),$M	–	–	–	–
BOP Exp. & Transf.,$M	–	–	–	–
Exp. to OECD CIF, $M	40.3	57.4	35.0	37.1
of which				
Manufact.	7.0	16.1	6.8	8.4
Imp. from OECD FOB, $M	518.5	385.0	375.7	290.9
Reserves ex. Gold, $M	–	–	–	–

	TOTAL RECEIPTS NET 1977	1978	1979	1980	TOTAL ODA NET 1977	1978	1979	1980
DAC COUNTRIES								
Australia	0.0	0.0	–	–	0.0	–	–	–
Austria	0.6	0.6	1.4	0.4	0.6	0.6	1.4	0.4
Belgium	1.7	25.9	164.1	-4.9	2.6	3.8	4.9	1.5
Canada	-1.5	-0.5	1.1	0.6	0.1	0.9	1.2	0.9
Denmark	4.7	1.8	-0.4	3.1	4.7	1.8	0.2	3.1
Finland	1.2	-0.1	-0.2	-0.2	–	–	–	–
France	1.5	-1.6	8.8	8.9	0.0	0.8	3.0	2.1
Germany, Fed. Rep.	26.2	13.5	87.6	-30.5	12.1	12.5	19.3	21.5
Italy	3.6	0.7	0.0	-2.1	0.7	0.3	0.2	0.1
Japan	11.6	25.5	19.2	13.2	7.7	14.5	21.9	19.2
Netherlands	2.2	1.5	23.4	3.2	2.2	1.5	2.0	3.2
New Zealand	–	–	–	–	–	–	–	–
Norway	–	–	0.0	0.3	–	–	–	0.3
Sweden	0.9	4.9	-2.0	-1.3	–	–	0.3	0.8
Switzerland	11.4	0.0	1.8	1.3	1.5	1.9	3.0	3.3
United Kingdom	11.2	3.0	-4.2	-6.3	2.6	2.0	1.9	2.7
United States	27.0	62.0	36.0	31.0	23.0	45.0	46.0	40.0
TOTAL	*102.2*	*137.1*	*336.6*	*16.6*	*57.6*	*85.6*	*105.3*	*99.0*
MULTILATERAL								
AF.D.F.	–	–	–	–	–	–	–	–
AF.D.B.	–	–	–	–	–	–	–	–
AS.D.B.	–	–	–	–	–	–	–	–
CAR.D.B.	–	–	–	–	–	–	–	–
E.E.C.	0.6	0.9	1.8	1.2	0.6	0.9	1.8	1.2
IBRD	20.9	22.8	30.9	70.0	0.6	0.7	1.5	1.1
IDA	3.5	2.0	3.3	1.5	3.5	2.0	3.3	1.5
I.D.B.	35.4	40.5	46.0	32.2	24.5	30.2	32.6	31.5
IFAD	–	–	–	–	–	–	–	–
I.F.C.	0.6	2.2	-0.1	-0.2	–	–	–	–
IMF TRUST FUND	–	19.2	–	27.0	–	19.2	–	27.0
U.N. AGENCIES	–	–	–	–	–	–	–	–
UNDP	2.2	2.6	4.8	3.8	2.2	2.6	4.8	3.8
UNTA	0.3	0.4	0.6	0.2	0.3	0.4	0.6	0.2
UNICEF	0.8	0.6	0.6	0.7	0.8	0.6	0.6	0.7
UNRWA	–	–	–	–	–	–	–	–
WFP	2.5	3.0	5.8	2.7	2.5	3.0	5.8	2.7
UNHCR	–	–	–	–	–	–	–	–
Other Multilateral	1.0	0.8	0.4	1.3	1.0	0.8	0.4	1.3
Arab OPEC Agencies	–	–	–	–	–	–	–	–
TOTAL	*67.8*	*94.9*	*94.0*	*140.3*	*36.0*	*60.3*	*51.3*	*71.0*
OPEC COUNTRIES	–	–	–	–	–	–	–	–
E.E.C.+ MEMBERS	*51.7*	*45.6*	*281.1*	*-27.4*	*25.3*	*23.5*	*33.2*	*35.3*
TOTAL	***170.0***	***232.0***	***430.6***	***157.0***	***93.5***	***145.9***	***156.6***	***170.0***

	ODA LOANS GROSS 1977	1978	1979	1980	ODA LOANS NET 1977	1978	1979	1980
DAC COUNTRIES								
Australia	–	–	–	–	–	–	–	–
Austria	–	–	1.0	–	–	–	1.0	–
Belgium	1.4	2.4	2.6	–	1.4	2.4	2.6	–
Canada	–	–	–	–	–	–	–	–
Denmark	4.7	1.8	–	2.6	4.6	1.6	-0.1	2.4
Finland	–	–	–	–	–	–	–	–
France	–	–	3.0	0.1	0.0	-0.1	3.0	0.0
Germany, Fed. Rep.	5.6	2.9	8.8	8.7	5.2	2.7	7.9	8.0
Italy	–	–	–	–	–	–	–	–
Japan	3.4	3.8	8.6	6.3	3.4	3.8	8.6	6.3
Netherlands	–	–	–	–	–	–	–	–
New Zealand	–	–	–	–	–	–	–	–
Norway	–	–	–	–	–	–	–	–
Sweden	–	–	–	–	–	–	–	–
Switzerland	–	–	–	–	–	–	–	–
United Kingdom	–	–	–	–	0.0	0.0	0.0	0.0
United States	15.0	24.0	17.0	10.0	11.0	20.0	14.0	3.0
TOTAL	*30.1*	*34.8*	*40.9*	*27.6*	*25.5*	*30.4*	*36.9*	*19.7*
MULTILATERAL	*31.7*	*55.1*	*39.8*	*64.0*	*28.6*	*51.8*	*36.6*	*61.1*
OPEC COUNTRIES	–	–	–	–	–	–	–	–
E.E.C.+ MEMBERS	*11.7*	*7.1*	*14.4*	*11.4*	*11.1*	*6.6*	*13.3*	*10.4*
TOTAL	***61.8***	***89.9***	***80.7***	***91.6***	***54.1***	***82.1***	***73.5***	***80.7***

	TOTAL OFFICIAL GROSS 1977	1978	1979	1980	TOTAL OFFICIAL NET 1977	1978	1979	1980
DAC COUNTRIES								
Australia	0.0	–	–	–	0.0	–	–	–
Austria	0.6	0.6	1.4	0.4	0.6	0.6	1.4	0.4
Belgium	2.6	3.8	4.9	1.5	2.6	3.8	4.9	1.5
Canada	0.1	0.9	1.2	0.9	0.0	0.8	1.1	0.6
Denmark	4.9	2.0	0.4	3.3	4.8	1.8	0.2	3.1
Finland	–	–	–	–	–	–	–	–
France	–	0.8	3.0	2.2	0.0	0.8	3.0	2.1
Germany, Fed. Rep.	12.5	12.7	34.3	22.2	12.1	12.5	33.5	20.7
Italy	0.7	0.3	0.2	0.1	0.7	0.3	0.2	0.1
Japan	7.7	14.5	21.9	19.2	7.7	14.5	21.9	19.2
Netherlands	2.2	1.5	2.0	3.2	2.2	1.5	2.0	3.2
New Zealand	–	–	–	–	–	–	–	–
Norway	–	–	–	0.3	–	–	–	0.3
Sweden	–	–	0.3	0.8	–	–	0.3	0.8
Switzerland	1.5	1.9	3.0	3.3	1.5	1.9	3.0	3.3
United Kingdom	2.6	2.0	1.9	2.7	2.6	2.0	1.9	2.7
United States	36.0	74.0	51.0	47.0	27.0	62.0	36.0	31.0
TOTAL	*71.2*	*115.1*	*125.5*	*107.0*	*61.6*	*102.4*	*109.3*	*88.9*
MULTILATERAL	*73.2*	*101.4*	*100.2*	*147.7*	*67.8*	*94.9*	*94.0*	*140.3*
OPEC COUNTRIES	–	–	–	–	–	–	–	–
E.E.C.+ MEMBERS	*26.0*	*24.1*	*48.5*	*36.3*	*25.4*	*23.6*	*47.5*	*34.4*
TOTAL	***144.4***	***216.4***	***225.7***	***254.7***	***129.4***	***197.3***	***203.3***	***229.2***

TOTAL ODA GROSS	197
Australia	0
Austria	0
Belgium	2
Canada	0
Denmark	4
Finland	
France	
Germany, Fed. Rep.	12
Italy	0
Japan	7
Netherlands	2
New Zealand	
Norway	
Sweden	
Switzerland	1
United Kingdom	2
United States	27
TOTAL	*62*
AF.D.F.	
AF.D.B.	
AS.D.B.	
CAR.D.B.	
E.E.C.	0
IBRD	0
IDA	3
I.D.B.	27
IFAD	
I.F.C.	
IMF TRUST FUND	
U.N. AGENCIES	
UNDP	2
UNTA	0
UNICEF	0
UNRWA	
WFP	2
UNHCR	
Other Multilateral	1
Arab OPEC Agencies	
TOTAL	*39*
OPEC COUNTRIES	
E.E.C.+ MEMBERS	*25*
TOTAL	***101***

GRANTS	197
Australia	0
Austria	0
Belgium	1
Canada	0
Denmark	0
Finland	
France	
Germany, Fed. Rep.	6
Italy	0
Japan	4
Netherlands	2
New Zealand	
Norway	
Sweden	
Switzerland	1
United Kingdom	2
United States	12
TOTAL	*32*
MULTILATERAL	*4*
OPEC COUNTRIES	
E.E.C.+ MEMBERS	*14*
TOTAL	***39***

TOTAL OOF GROSS	197
Australia	
Austria	
Belgium	
Canada	
Denmark	0
Finland	
France	
Germany, Fed. Rep.	
Italy	
Japan	
Netherlands	
New Zealand	
Norway	
Sweden	
Switzerland	
United Kingdom	
United States	9
TOTAL	*9*
MULTILATERAL	*34*
OPEC COUNTRIES	
E.E.C.+ MEMBERS	*0*
TOTAL	***43***

1978	1979	1980	1977	1978	1979	1980
			ODA COMMITMENTS			
–	–	–	–	0.0	–	–
0.6	1.4	0.4	0.2	0.5	0.0	–
3.8	4.9	1.5	2.9	4.4	5.3	1.9
0.9	1.2	0.9	0.0	10.1	0.6	1.1
2.0	0.3	3.3	6.7	9.9	0.4	0.3
–	–	–	–	–	–	–
0.8	3.0	2.2	–	–	3.8	0.8
12.7	20.1	22.2	13.9	13.6	60.3	16.8
0.3	0.2	0.1	0.7	0.3	0.2	0.1
14.5	21.9	19.2	9.2	15.7	63.2	15.4
1.5	2.0	3.2	2.0	2.4	2.0	3.6
–	–	–	–	–	–	–
–	–	0.3	–	–	–	0.5
–	0.3	0.8	–	–	–	–
1.9	3.0	3.3	2.6	1.8	9.3	2.0
2.0	1.9	2.7	1.7	1.4	2.9	2.3
49.0	49.0	47.0	45.3	61.3	59.8	23.0
90.1	*109.3*	*107.0*	*85.2*	*121.3*	*207.8*	*67.7*
–	–	–	–	–	–	–
–	–	–	–	–	–	–
–	–	–	–	–	–	–
–	–	–	–	–	–	–
0.9	1.8	1.2	2.3	2.7	4.3	0.3
0.7	1.5	1.1	–	–	–	–
2.2	3.5	1.8	–	9.0	19.5	16.0
33.3	35.5	34.1	28.8	163.0	34.8	22.6
–	–	–	–	–	4.1	–
–	–	–	–	–	–	–
19.2	–	27.0	–	–	–	–
–	–	–	6.8	7.4	12.2	8.7
2.6	4.8	3.8	–	–	–	–
0.4	0.6	0.2	–	–	–	–
0.6	0.6	0.7	–	–	–	–
–	–	–	–	–	–	–
3.0	5.8	2.7	–	–	–	–
–	–	–	–	–	–	–
0.8	0.4	1.3	–	–	–	–
–	–	–	–	–	5.0	–
63.6	*54.5*	*73.9*	*37.9*	*182.1*	*79.9*	*47.6*
–	–	–	–	–	–	–
24.0	*34.3*	*36.3*	*30.2*	*34.6*	*79.2*	*26.0*
153.7	***163.8***	***180.9***	***123.1***	***303.4***	***287.7***	***115.3***
			TECH. COOP. GRANTS			
–	–	–	–	–	–	–
0.6	0.5	0.4	0.6	0.6	0.5	0.4
1.4	2.3	1.5	0.7	0.8	0.9	0.6
0.9	1.2	0.9	0.0	0.1	0.1	0.1
0.2	0.3	0.7	0.1	0.2	0.3	0.5
–	–	–	–	–	–	–
0.8	–	2.1	–	0.8	–	2.1
9.8	11.3	13.5	6.8	9.8	11.3	13.5
0.3	0.2	0.1	0.7	0.3	0.2	0.1
10.7	13.3	12.9	4.3	5.6	4.4	4.9
1.5	2.0	3.2	2.1	1.5	1.8	3.1
–	–	–	–	–	–	–
–	–	0.3	–	–	–	0.1
–	0.3	0.8	–	–	–	–
1.9	3.0	3.3	0.0	0.0	0.0	1.4
2.0	1.9	2.7	1.7	1.4	1.9	2.3
25.0	32.0	37.0	2.0	4.0	4.0	6.0
55.2	*68.4*	*79.4*	*19.0*	*25.1*	*25.5*	*35.1*
8.6	*14.7*	*9.9*	*4.3*	*4.7*	*7.1*	*8.7*
–	–	–	–	–	–	–
17.0	*19.9*	*24.9*	*12.1*	*14.8*	*16.4*	*22.2*
63.8	***83.1***	***89.2***	***23.3***	***29.8***	***32.6***	***43.8***
			TOTAL OOF NET			
–	–	–	–	–	–	–
–	–	–	–	–	–	–
–	–	–	–	–	–	–
–	–	–	-0.1	-0.2	-0.2	-0.3
0.0	0.0	–	0.1	0.0	0.0	0.0
–	–	–	–	–	–	–
–	–	–	–	–	–	–
–	14.2	–	–	–	14.2	-0.8
–	–	–	–	–	–	–
–	–	–	–	–	–	–
–	–	–	–	–	–	–
–	–	–	–	–	–	–
–	–	–	–	–	–	–
–	–	–	–	–	–	–
–	–	–	–	–	–	–
–	–	–	–	–	–	–
25.0	2.0	–	4.0	17.0	-10.0	-9.0
25.0	*16.2*	–	*4.0*	*16.8*	*4.0*	*-10.1*
37.7	*45.7*	*73.9*	*31.9*	*34.6*	*42.7*	*69.4*
–	–	–	–	–	–	–
0.0	*14.2*	–	*0.1*	*0.0*	*14.2*	*-0.9*
62.8	***61.9***	***73.9***	***35.9***	***51.4***	***46.7***	***59.2***

MAIN AID AGGREGATES

	1977	1978	1979	1980
DAC COUNTRIES COMBINED				
PRIVATE SECTOR NET	40.6	34.7	227.3	-72.2
Direct Investment	2.6	0.0	0.2	-0.7
Portfolio Invest.	2.6	7.6	77.9	-46.1
Export Credits	35.5	27.1	149.2	-25.4
OFFICIAL & PRIVATE				
GROSS:				
Contractual Lending	108.4	130.1	246.4	56.9
Export Credits Tot.	78.2	95.2	205.5	29.3
Export Credits Priv	69.2	70.2	189.3	29.3
OTHER NET DATA				
Contractual Lending	65.0	74.2	190.1	-15.9
Export Credits Tot.	39.4	43.9	153.2	-35.6
(Bank Sector Loans)	99.0	-169.0	392.0	-32.0
ODA CONCESSIONALITY				
Total:Grant Element	84.0	87.0	69.0	98.0
Loans:Grant Element	71.0	69.0	48.0	66.0
OTHER SOURCES				
CMEA Countr.(Gross)	7.5	6.0	8.0	6.0
Intra LDCS Exc.OPEC	–	–	–	–
Other	–	–	–	–
ALL SOURCE COMMITMENTS				
TOTAL BILATERAL	119.2	133.5	210.4	67.7
of which				
OPEC (ODA)	–	–	–	–
CMEA (ODA)	–	5.0	–	10.0
TOTAL MULTILAT.(ODA)	37.9	182.1	79.9	47.6
TOTAL BIL.& MULTIL.	157.1	315.6	290.3	115.3
of which				
ODA Grants	49.2	81.6	101.7	74.0
ODA Loans	73.9	221.8	186.0	41.3
ODA CONCESSIONALITY				
Total: Grant Element	84.0	84.0	73.0	92.0
Loans: Grant Element	71.0	74.0	62.0	78.0

INDEBTEDNESS

	1977	1978	1979	1980
TOTAL DEBT DISBURSED	***1439.2***	***1726.6***	***1981.9***	
Debt to DAC Countries	1013.0	1229.0	1417.0	
ODA	276.0	312.0	348.0	
Total Export Credits	198.0	292.0	415.0	
Other Private Market	539.0	625.0	654.0	
International Org.	194.9	260.4	340.2	
CMEA	28.6	32.6	30.1	
Other	202.7	204.7	194.6	
TOTAL DEBT SERVICE	***164.7***	***363.4***	***276.6***	
Paid to DAC Countries	121.1	320.5	218.6	
ODA	9.5	8.4	10.1	
Total Export Credits	43.0	58.3	77.5	
Other Private Market	68.6	253.8	131.0	
International Org.	15.3	16.5	20.1	
CMEA	4.4	7.6	8.7	
Other	23.9	18.8	29.2	

ECONOMIC INDICATORS

	1977	1978	1979	1980
GNP Curr. Prices, $M	2286.1	2871.5	4744.2	5784.7
Real GNP, 1976=100	102.0	105.0	106.0	105.0
GNP/Cap Curr. Prices,$	443.0	542.0	874.0	1038.0
GNP/cap Atlas Basis, $	475.7	510.0	546.0	573.5
Real GNP/Cap, 1976=100	99.0	99.0	98.0	94.0
Population, Million	5.2	5.3	5.4	5.6
Curr.A/C Deficit(-),$M	-129.7	-353.6	-398.9	-166.6
BOP Exp. & Transf.,$M	703.0	711.5	869.0	1066.6
Exp. to OECD CIF, $M	354.1	337.8	483.4	472.0
of which				
Manufact.	16.1	18.8	21.5	21.9
Imp. from OECD FOB, $M	445.7	546.1	467.1	397.6
Reserves ex. Gold, $M	211.1	169.8	178.2	106.1

	TOTAL RECEIPTS NET 1977	1978	1979	1980	TOTAL ODA NET 1977	1978	1979	1980	TOTAL ODA GROSS 197
DAC COUNTRIES									
Australia	0.0	0.1	0.1	0.1	0.0	0.1	0.1	0.1	0
Austria	–	0.0	–	0.0	–	0.0	–	0.0	
Belgium	0.0	–	–	0.0	0.0	–	–	–	0
Canada	2.1	2.3	2.7	2.7	2.1	2.3	2.7	2.7	2
Denmark	3.5	1.4	5.6	3.9	3.5	1.4	5.6	3.9	3
Finland	–	0.0	–	0.1	–	0.0	–	0.1	
France	–	–	–	0.2	–	–	–	0.2	
Germany, Fed. Rep.	-5.5	-47.2	49.9	-45.6	4.3	6.2	16.3	14.9	4
Italy	–	–	–	–	–	–	–	–	
Japan	0.0	0.0	0.2	0.7	0.0	0.0	0.2	0.7	0
Netherlands	1.4	1.9	2.8	3.4	1.4	1.9	2.8	3.4	1
New Zealand	–	–	–	0.0	–	–	–	0.0	
Norway	5.1	9.1	9.1	12.8	5.1	9.1	9.1	12.8	5
Sweden	10.7	13.0	14.8	13.2	10.7	13.0	14.8	13.2	10
Switzerland	0.1	0.0	–	–	0.1	0.0	–	–	0
United Kingdom	7.1	13.4	17.4	23.5	7.8	10.1	15.9	19.5	8
United States	3.0	11.0	6.0	12.0	3.0	11.0	6.0	12.0	3
TOTAL	*27.6*	*5.0*	*108.7*	*27.0*	*38.1*	*55.1*	*73.6*	*83.5*	*38*
MULTILATERAL									
AF.D.F.	0.4	1.8	3.5	2.4	0.4	1.8	3.5	2.4	0
AF.D.B.	0.1	1.1	1.4	-0.2	–	–	–	–	
AS.D.B.	–	–	–	–	–	–	–	–	
CAR.D.B.	–	–	–	–	–	–	–	–	
E.E.C.	1.1	2.0	4.9	5.9	1.1	2.0	4.9	5.9	1
IBRD	3.3	1.7	5.2	4.3	0.5	0.3	1.1	0.9	0
IDA	1.1	0.6	0.2	0.0	1.1	0.6	0.2	0.0	1
I.D.B.	–	–	–	–	–	–	–	–	
IFAD	–	–	–	–	–	–	–	–	
I.F.C.	–	–	–	0.1	–	–	–	–	
IMF TRUST FUND	–	–	–	–	–	–	–	–	
U.N. AGENCIES	–	–	–	–	–	–	–	–	
UNDP	1.3	1.5	1.7	2.3	1.3	1.5	1.7	2.3	1
UNTA	0.2	0.4	0.1	0.0	0.2	0.4	0.1	0.0	0
UNICEF	0.3	0.2	0.3	0.3	0.3	0.2	0.3	0.3	0
UNRWA	–	–	–	–	–	–	–	–	
WFP	3.6	4.5	9.6	6.4	3.6	4.5	9.6	6.4	3
UNHCR	0.6	2.3	4.0	0.8	0.6	2.3	4.0	0.8	0
Other Multilateral	0.4	0.2	0.3	1.4	0.4	0.2	0.3	1.4	0
Arab OPEC Agencies	–	0.1	0.6	2.7	–	0.1	0.6	2.2	
TOTAL	*12.3*	*16.4*	*31.6*	*26.4*	*9.4*	*13.9*	*26.1*	*22.6*	*9*
OPEC COUNTRIES	–	–	–	–	–	–	–	–	
E.E.C.+ MEMBERS	*7.6*	*-28.6*	*80.6*	*-8.7*	*18.1*	*21.5*	*45.5*	*47.8*	*18*
TOTAL	***39.8***	***21.4***	***140.4***	***53.4***	***47.5***	***69.0***	***99.7***	***106.1***	***47***

	ODA LOANS GROSS 1977	1978	1979	1980	ODA LOANS NET 1977	1978	1979	1980	GRANTS 197
DAC COUNTRIES									
Australia	–	–	–	–	–	–	–	–	0
Austria	–	–	–	–	–	–	–	–	
Belgium	–	–	–	–	–	–	–	–	0
Canada	0.5	–	–	–	0.5	-31.7	–	–	1
Denmark	0.0	0.0	3.6	1.8	0.0	0.0	3.6	-0.8	3
Finland	–	–	–	–	–	–	–	–	
France	–	–	–	–	–	–	–	–	
Germany, Fed. Rep.	2.3	3.3	3.0	0.1	2.3	3.3	-3.5	0.1	2
Italy	–	–	–	–	–	–	–	–	
Japan	–	–	–	–	–	–	–	–	0
Netherlands	–	–	–	0.1	–	–	–	0.1	1
New Zealand	–	–	–	–	–	–	–	–	
Norway	–	–	–	–	–	–	–	–	5
Sweden	0.3	0.2	–	–	0.3	-5.8	–	–	10
Switzerland	–	–	–	–	–	–	–	–	0
United Kingdom	1.6	2.4	3.7	3.9	1.4	2.1	2.7	2.8	6
United States	2.0	1.0	1.0	–	2.0	1.0	1.0	–	1
TOTAL	*6.8*	*6.9*	*11.2*	*5.9*	*6.5*	*-31.1*	*3.7*	*2.2*	*31*
MULTILATERAL	*2.0*	*2.9*	*5.3*	*5.9*	*1.9*	*2.8*	*5.3*	*5.8*	*7*
OPEC COUNTRIES	–	–	–	–	–	–	–	–	
E.E.C.+ MEMBERS	*3.9*	*5.7*	*10.2*	*6.1*	*3.7*	*5.4*	*2.7*	*2.4*	*14*
TOTAL	***8.7***	***9.8***	***16.6***	***11.8***	***8.5***	***-28.3***	***9.0***	***8.0***	***39***

	TOTAL OFFICIAL GROSS 1977	1978	1979	1980	TOTAL OFFICIAL NET 1977	1978	1979	1980	TOTAL OOF GROSS 197
DAC COUNTRIES									
Australia	0.0	0.1	0.1	0.1	0.0	0.1	0.1	0.1	
Austria	–	0.0	–	0.0	–	0.0	–	0.0	
Belgium	0.0	–	–	–	0.0	–	–	–	
Canada	2.1	34.1	2.7	2.7	2.1	2.3	2.7	2.7	
Denmark	3.5	1.4	5.6	6.6	3.5	1.4	5.6	3.9	
Finland	–	0.0	–	0.1	–	0.0	–	0.1	
France	–	–	–	0.2	–	–	–	0.2	
Germany, Fed. Rep.	4.3	6.2	22.9	14.9	-5.2	-21.6	7.1	10.3	
Italy	–	–	–	–	–	–	–	–	
Japan	0.0	0.0	0.2	0.7	0.0	0.0	0.2	0.7	
Netherlands	1.4	1.9	2.8	3.4	1.4	1.9	2.8	3.4	
New Zealand	–	–	–	0.0	–	–	–	0.0	
Norway	5.1	9.1	9.1	12.8	5.1	9.1	9.1	12.8	
Sweden	10.7	19.0	14.8	13.2	10.7	13.0	14.8	13.2	
Switzerland	0.1	0.0	–	–	0.1	0.0	–	–	
United Kingdom	8.0	10.8	16.9	26.9	7.4	9.8	15.7	24.6	
United States	3.0	11.0	6.0	12.0	3.0	11.0	6.0	12.0	
TOTAL	*38.3*	*93.6*	*81.2*	*93.5*	*28.1*	*27.0*	*64.2*	*83.9*	
MULTILATERAL	*13.4*	*19.6*	*34.9*	*32.0*	*12.3*	*16.4*	*31.6*	*26.4*	*4*
OPEC COUNTRIES	–	–	–	–	–	–	–	–	
E.E.C.+ MEMBERS	*18.3*	*22.3*	*53.1*	*57.8*	*8.1*	*-6.6*	*36.1*	*48.2*	
TOTAL	***51.8***	***113.2***	***116.1***	***125.5***	***40.4***	***43.4***	***95.9***	***110.3***	***4***

1978	1979	1980	1977	1978	1979	1980
			ODA COMMITMENTS			
0.1	0.1	0.1	0.0	0.1	0.2	0.0
0.0	–	0.0	–	–	–	–
–	–	–	–	–	–	–
34.1	2.7	2.7	3.6	33.1	4.8	1.5
1.4	5.6	6.6	1.1	6.7	1.2	0.8
0.0	–	0.1	–	0.0	–	0.1
–	–	0.2	–	–	–	0.2
6.2	22.9	14.9	4.3	7.0	28.6	36.8
–	–	–	–	–	–	–
0.0	0.2	0.7	0.0	0.1	0.3	0.8
1.9	2.8	3.4	2.6	4.2	3.7	4.6
–	–	0.0	–	–	–	–
9.1	9.1	12.8	1.6	23.1	2.6	13.6
19.0	14.8	13.2	11.9	30.8	1.7	30.7
0.0	–	–	–	–	–	–
10.4	16.9	20.6	11.9	11.4	38.3	13.6
11.0	6.0	12.0	4.4	17.6	22.1	10.1
93.1	*81.1*	*87.2*	*41.3*	*134.1*	*103.5*	*112.8*
1.8	3.5	2.5	–	–	–	–
–	–	–	–	–	–	–
–	–	–	–	–	–	–
–	–	–	–	–	–	–
2.0	4.9	5.9	10.5	10.6	4.0	2.5
0.3	1.1	0.9	–	–	–	–
0.6	0.2	0.0	–	–	–	–
–	–	–	–	–	–	–
–	–	–	–	–	–	–
–	–	–	–	–	–	–
–	–	–	–	–	–	–
–	–	–	6.3	9.1	15.9	11.2
1.5	1.7	2.3	–	–	–	–
0.4	0.1	0.0	–	–	–	–
0.2	0.3	0.3	–	–	–	–
–	–	–	–	–	–	–
4.5	9.6	6.4	–	–	–	–
2.3	4.0	0.8	–	–	–	–
0.2	0.3	1.4	–	–	–	–
0.1	0.6	2.2	1.0	–	4.2	7.3
13.9	*26.1*	*22.7*	*17.8*	*19.7*	*24.2*	*20.9*
–	–	–	–	–	–	*18.4*
21.8	*53.0*	*51.5*	*30.3*	*40.0*	*75.9*	*58.6*
107.0	***107.3***	***109.9***	***59.1***	***153.8***	***127.7***	***152.1***
			TECH. COOP. GRANTS			
0.1	0.1	0.1	0.0	0.1	0.1	0.1
0.0	–	0.0	–	0.0	–	0.0
–	–	–	0.0	–	–	–
34.1	2.7	2.7	0.7	0.9	1.1	1.4
1.4	2.0	4.8	1.0	1.3	2.0	2.2
0.0	–	0.1	–	0.0	–	0.1
–	–	0.2	–	–	–	0.2
2.9	19.9	14.9	1.9	2.9	5.3	8.1
–	–	–	–	–	–	–
0.0	0.2	0.7	0.0	0.0	0.2	0.7
1.9	2.8	3.3	1.3	1.9	2.7	2.8
–	–	0.0	–	–	–	0.0
9.1	9.1	12.8	1.6	1.9	2.3	2.7
18.7	14.8	13.2	2.4	2.0	2.7	3.1
0.0	–	–	–	–	–	–
8.0	13.2	16.7	5.4	6.4	9.5	12.4
10.0	5.0	12.0	1.0	1.0	4.0	9.0
86.2	*69.9*	*81.3*	*15.3*	*18.4*	*29.9*	*42.7*
11.0	*20.8*	*16.8*	*2.7*	*4.6*	*6.4*	*11.2*
–	–	–	–	–	–	–
16.1	*42.8*	*45.4*	*9.6*	*12.5*	*19.6*	*25.6*
97.3	***90.7***	***98.1***	***18.0***	***23.0***	***36.3***	***53.9***
			TOTAL OOF NET			
–	–	–	–	–	–	–
–	–	–	–	–	–	–
–	–	–	–	–	–	–
–	–	–	–	–	–	–
–	–	–	–	–	–	–
–	–	–	–	–	–	–
–	–	–	–	–	–	–
–	–	–	-9.6	-27.8	-9.2	-4.7
–	–	–	–	–	–	–
–	–	–	–	–	–	–
–	–	–	–	–	–	–
–	–	–	–	–	–	–
–	–	–	–	–	–	–
–	–	–	–	–	–	–
–	–	–	–	–	–	–
0.5	0.0	6.3	-0.5	-0.3	-0.1	5.1
–	–	–	–	–	–	–
0.5	*0.0*	*6.3*	*-10.0*	*-28.1*	*-9.3*	*0.4*
5.7	*8.8*	*9.4*	*2.9*	*2.5*	*5.5*	*3.8*
–	–	–	–	–	–	–
0.5	*0.0*	*6.3*	*-10.0*	*-28.1*	*-9.3*	*0.4*
6.2	***8.8***	***15.7***	***-7.1***	***-25.6***	***-3.8***	***4.2***

MAIN AID AGGREGATES

	1977	1978	1979	1980
DAC COUNTRIES COMBINED				
PRIVATE SECTOR NET	-0.5	-22.0	44.5	-56.9
Direct Investment	0.3	3.6	2.0	0.0
Portfolio Invest.	-0.5	-18.3	42.8	-55.8
Export Credits	-0.3	-7.3	-0.3	-1.1
OFFICIAL & PRIVATE				
GROSS:				
Contractual Lending	6.8	7.4	11.3	12.2
Export Credits Tot.	0.1	–	–	0.0
Export Credits Priv	0.1	–	–	0.0
OTHER NET DATA				
Contractual Lending	-3.7	-66.5	-6.0	1.5
Export Credits Tot.	-0.3	-7.3	-0.3	-1.1
(Bank Sector Loans)	12.0	6.0	30.0	-45.0
ODA CONCESSIONALITY				
Total:Grant Element	97.0	98.0	100.0	100.0
Loans:Grant Element	74.0	83.0	–	–
OTHER SOURCES				
CMEA Countr.(Gross)	–	–	–	–
Intra LDCS Exc.OPEC	–	–	–	–
Other	–	–	–	–
ALL SOURCE COMMITMENTS				
TOTAL BILATERAL	43.7	134.1	103.5	143.2
of which				
OPEC (ODA)	–	–	–	18.4
CMEA (ODA)	–	–	–	–
TOTAL MULTILAT.(ODA)	17.8	19.7	24.2	20.9
TOTAL BIL.& MULTIL.	61.5	153.8	127.7	164.1
of which				
ODA Grants	53.1	144.8	123.5	123.9
ODA Loans	6.0	9.0	4.2	28.2
ODA CONCESSIONALITY				
Total: Grant Element	97.0	99.0	98.0	90.0
Loans: Grant Element	71.0	83.0	46.0	43.0

INDEBTEDNESS

	1977	1978	1979	1980
TOTAL DEBT DISBURSED	***293.8***	***253.1***	***258.3***	
Debt to DAC Countries	231.0	184.0	181.0	
ODA	90.0	60.0	64.0	
Total Export Credits	126.0	107.0	99.0	
Other Private Market	15.0	17.0	18.0	
International Org.	60.6	66.9	75.0	
CMEA	–	–	–	
Other	2.2	2.2	2.3	
TOTAL DEBT SERVICE	***39.3***	***64.5***	***42.0***	
Paid to DAC Countries	35.0	57.3	34.0	
ODA	0.3	1.4	–	
Total Export Credits	32.7	53.9	31.5	
Other Private Market	2.0	2.0	2.5	
International Org.	4.1	7.1	7.8	
CMEA	–	–	–	
Other	0.2	0.2	0.2	

ECONOMIC INDICATORS

	1977	1978	1979	1980
GNP Curr. Prices, $M	354.9	384.7	584.8	777.6
Real GNP, 1976=100	101.0	102.0	127.0	140.0
GNP/Cap Curr. Prices,$	487.0	515.0	756.0	972.0
GNP/cap Atlas Basis, $	569.4	599.3	783.7	911.5
Real GNP/Cap, 1976=100	98.0	97.0	116.0	124.0
Population, Million	0.7	0.7	0.8	0.8
Curr.A/C Deficit(-),$M	–	–	–	–
BOP Exp. & Transf.,$M	–	–	–	–
Exp. to OECD CIF, $M	76.3	28.5	66.9	15.0
of which				
Manufact.	0.3	0.4	1.8	2.3
Imp. from OECD FOB, $M	10.1	11.2	13.1	16.7
Reserves ex. Gold, $M	100.1	150.6	267.3	343.7

	1977	1978	1979	1980	1977	1978	1979	1980	197
TOTAL RECEIPTS NET / **TOTAL ODA NET** / **TOTAL ODA GROSS**									
DAC COUNTRIES									
Australia	0.2	–	0.0	0.0	0.0	0.0	0.0	0.0	0
Austria	0.5	7.3	-2.3	-2.2	0.7	0.7	1.1	1.4	1
Belgium	44.3	339.4	190.5	104.2	1.1	0.9	1.1	1.1	1
Canada	-12.4	-11.5	-18.9	-4.3	1.2	2.1	1.9	1.5	1
Denmark	-20.7	-5.2	-6.9	-5.0	-0.3	-0.3	-0.3	-0.2	0
Finland	-0.4	6.7	-1.2	-1.2	–	0.0	0.0	–	
France	143.8	372.2	385.9	885.7	-0.9	17.8	5.1	9.2	2
Germany, Fed. Rep.	597.2	531.8	389.2	1360.7	26.7	36.3	39.6	47.8	34
Italy	13.9	-45.2	1088.2	114.0	1.3	1.4	1.7	1.2	1
Japan	665.3	1185.3	1054.8	71.4	28.3	34.5	25.5	20.5	28
Netherlands	47.6	55.0	137.3	28.6	2.2	3.2	2.8	7.0	3
New Zealand	-0.5	–	–	–	–	–	–	–	
Norway	4.0	2.9	-6.8	2.1	0.0	–	–	0.1	0
Sweden	16.6	-1.9	-10.7	596.3	–	–	0.4	–	
Switzerland	30.5	-11.6	142.5	141.6	0.5	0.7	0.7	0.6	0
United Kingdom	89.8	76.0	20.7	132.3	2.1	0.5	1.2	1.2	2
United States	499.0	2245.0	1326.0	318.0	-5.0	-22.0	-27.0	-33.0	22
TOTAL	*2118.6*	*4746.3*	*4688.4*	*3742.1*	*57.8*	*75.7*	*53.8*	*58.2*	*98*
MULTILATERAL									
AF.D.F.	–	–	–	–	–	–	–	–	
AF.D.B.	–	–	–	–	–	–	–	–	
AS.D.B.	–	–	–	–	–	–	–	–	
CAR.D.B.	–	–	–	–	–	–	–	–	
E.E.C.	0.0	0.2	0.2	–	0.0	0.2	0.2	–	0
IBRD	195.9	188.5	225.1	242.2	–	–	–	–	
IDA	–	–	–	–	–	–	–	–	
I.D.B.	91.7	90.6	153.3	130.2	11.2	23.5	18.8	2.2	34
IFAD	–	–	–	–	–	–	–	–	
I.F.C.	8.9	-9.3	-15.3	70.7	–	–	–	–	
IMF TRUST FUND	–	–	–	–	–	–	–	–	
U.N. AGENCIES	–	–	–	–	–	–	–	–	
UNDP	6.7	8.9	10.9	11.6	6.7	8.9	10.9	11.6	6
UNTA	1.0	1.5	1.2	0.3	1.0	1.5	1.2	0.3	1
UNICEF	0.2	0.2	0.3	0.6	0.2	0.2	0.3	0.6	0
UNRWA	–	–	–	–	–	–	–	–	
WFP	1.8	0.5	6.1	6.1	1.8	0.5	6.1	6.1	1
UNHCR	–	–	–	–	–	–	–	–	
Other Multilateral	0.8	0.5	0.2	0.8	0.8	0.5	0.2	0.8	0
Arab OPEC Agencies	–	–	–	–	–	–	–	–	
TOTAL	*307.0*	*281.5*	*381.9*	*462.5*	*21.7*	*35.3*	*37.6*	*21.6*	*44*
OPEC COUNTRIES	–	*2.9*	*15.4*	*5.6*	–	*2.4*	*15.4*	*5.6*	
E.E.C.+ MEMBERS	*915.9*	*1324.2*	*2205.1*	*2620.4*	*32.1*	*59.9*	*51.4*	*67.2*	*44*
TOTAL	***2425.6***	***5030.6***	***5085.7***	***4210.2***	***79.5***	***113.3***	***106.8***	***85.4***	***143***

	1977	1978	1979	1980	1977	1978	1979	1980	197
ODA LOANS GROSS / **ODA LOANS NET** / **GRANTS**									
DAC COUNTRIES									
Australia	–	–	–	–	–	–	–	–	0
Austria	0.5	0.3	0.4	0.9	0.2	0.1	0.4	0.8	0
Belgium	–	–	–	–	–	–	–	–	1
Canada	0.3	0.3	0.7	0.5	-0.1	0.0	0.4	0.1	1
Denmark	–	–	–	–	-0.3	-0.3	-0.3	-0.3	0
Finland	–	–	–	–	–	–	–	–	
France	2.3	20.3	8.2	4.4	-0.9	16.2	5.1	-0.5	
Germany, Fed. Rep.	16.0	21.9	17.4	18.5	7.8	12.0	5.6	9.2	18
Italy	–	–	–	–	–	–	–	–	1
Japan	23.1	26.2	18.4	11.3	22.8	25.9	16.7	8.4	5
Netherlands	0.4	–	–	–	-0.3	-0.1	-0.2	-0.3	2
New Zealand	–	–	–	–	–	–	–	–	
Norway	–	–	–	–	–	–	–	–	0
Sweden	–	–	–	–	–	–	–	–	
Switzerland	–	–	–	–	–	–	–	–	0
United Kingdom	1.1	0.0	–	–	1.1	-0.9	-1.0	-1.1	1
United States	18.0	8.0	5.0	–	-9.0	-26.0	-28.0	-35.0	4
TOTAL	*61.8*	*77.0*	*50.1*	*35.5*	*21.3*	*26.9*	*-1.3*	*-18.7*	*36*
MULTILATERAL	*34.3*	*50.3*	*47.7*	*33.6*	*11.2*	*23.5*	*18.8*	*2.2*	*10*
OPEC COUNTRIES	–	*2.4*	*15.4*	*5.6*	–	*2.4*	*15.4*	*5.6*	
E.E.C.+ MEMBERS	*19.9*	*42.2*	*25.6*	*22.9*	*7.3*	*26.9*	*9.1*	*6.9*	*24*
TOTAL	***96.1***	***129.6***	***113.2***	***74.7***	***32.6***	***52.7***	***32.9***	***-10.9***	***46***

	1977	1978	1979	1980	1977	1978	1979	1980	197
TOTAL OFFICIAL GROSS / **TOTAL OFFICIAL NET** / **TOTAL OOF GROSS**									
DAC COUNTRIES									
Australia	0.0	0.0	0.0	0.0	0.0	0.0	0.0	0.0	
Austria	1.0	0.9	1.1	1.5	0.6	0.5	1.0	1.3	
Belgium	1.1	0.9	1.1	1.1	1.1	0.9	1.1	1.1	
Canada	12.0	14.0	6.4	18.2	9.0	10.0	2.4	14.0	10
Denmark	0.7	0.5	0.4	0.3	-0.2	0.1	-0.6	-2.2	0
Finland	–	0.0	0.0	–	–	0.0	0.0	–	
France	5.1	27.5	10.8	16.7	1.9	23.4	7.2	11.8	2
Germany, Fed. Rep.	101.9	103.1	97.9	203.8	69.7	68.2	60.5	142.6	66
Italy	39.3	21.3	20.2	14.7	31.0	2.1	10.4	-4.7	38
Japan	50.6	176.9	160.9	107.6	33.7	155.5	136.3	76.4	22
Netherlands	3.0	3.3	3.0	7.3	2.2	3.2	2.8	7.0	
New Zealand	–	–	–	–	-0.5	–	–	–	
Norway	0.0	–	–	0.1	0.0	–	–	0.1	
Sweden	–	–	0.4	–	–	–	0.4	–	
Switzerland	0.5	0.7	0.7	0.6	0.5	0.7	0.7	0.6	
United Kingdom	2.1	1.4	2.2	2.3	2.1	0.5	1.2	1.2	
United States	137.0	94.0	151.0	181.0	32.0	-22.0	1.0	-6.0	115
TOTAL	*354.1*	*444.4*	*456.1*	*555.3*	*183.0*	*243.0*	*224.3*	*243.2*	*255*
MULTILATERAL	*499.5*	*481.2*	*570.6*	*683.4*	*307.0*	*281.5*	*381.9*	*462.5*	*454*
OPEC COUNTRIES	–	*2.9*	*15.4*	*5.6*	–	*2.9*	*15.4*	*5.6*	
E.E.C.+ MEMBERS	*153.2*	*158.1*	*135.8*	*246.3*	*107.8*	*98.6*	*82.6*	*156.9*	*108.*
TOTAL	***853.6***	***928.4***	***1042.2***	***1244.3***	***490.1***	***527.4***	***621.6***	***711.3***	***710***

1978	1979	1980	1977	1978	1979	1980
			ODA COMMITMENTS			
0.0	0.0	0.0	–	–	–	–
0.9	1.1	1.5	0.5	0.3	0.4	0.9
0.9	1.1	1.1	1.5	–	1.2	1.4
2.4	2.2	1.8	5.2	0.8	0.8	1.0
0.0	0.1	0.1	0.0	0.1	0.1	–
0.0	0.0	–	–	0.0	0.0	–
21.9	8.2	14.1	–	29.3	–	119.8
46.1	51.4	57.0	70.2	32.6	58.8	59.7
1.4	1.7	1.2	1.3	1.4	1.7	1.2
34.8	27.1	23.4	38.9	30.5	46.2	25.6
3.3	3.0	7.3	1.7	4.0	4.0	8.8
–	–	–	–	–	–	–
–	–	0.1	–	–	–	–
–	0.4	–	–	–	–	–
0.7	0.7	0.6	0.4	0.2	0.1	0.4
1.4	2.2	2.3	1.0	1.4	2.2	2.3
12.0	6.0	2.0	3.1	1.7	0.8	0.4
125.8	*105.2*	*112.5*	*123.8*	*102.1*	*116.1*	*221.5*
–	–	–	–	–	–	–
–	–	–	–	–	–	–
–	–	–	–	–	–	–
–	–	–	–	–	–	–
0.2	0.2	–	0.0	0.3	0.8	0.8
–	–	–	–	–	–	–
–	–	–	–	–	–	–
50.3	47.7	33.6	55.9	–	59.0	92.0
–	–	–	–	–	–	19.9
–	–	–	–	–	–	–
–	–	–	–	–	–	–
–	–	–	10.5	11.6	18.6	19.4
8.9	10.9	11.6	–	–	–	–
1.5	1.2	0.3	–	–	–	–
0.2	0.3	0.6	–	–	–	–
–	–	–	–	–	–	–
0.5	6.1	6.1	–	–	–	–
–	–	–	–	–	–	–
0.5	0.2	0.8	–	–	–	–
–	–	–	–	–	–	–
62.1	*66.5*	*53.0*	*66.4*	*11.9*	*78.4*	*132.1*
2.4	*15.4*	*5.6*	*55.0*	–	–	–
75.2	*67.9*	*83.1*	*75.8*	*69.0*	*68.7*	*194.0*
190.2	***187.2***	***171.0***	***245.2***	***114.0***	***194.5***	***353.6***
			TECH. COOP. GRANTS			
0.0	0.0	0.0	0.0	–	–	–
0.6	0.7	0.6	0.4	0.6	0.7	0.6
0.9	1.1	1.1	0.8	0.6	0.6	0.7
2.1	1.5	1.4	0.5	0.7	0.5	0.8
0.0	0.1	0.1	0.0	0.0	0.1	0.1
0.0	0.0	–	–	0.0	0.0	–
1.6	–	9.7	–	1.6	–	9.7
24.2	34.0	38.6	18.9	24.2	34.0	35.5
1.4	1.7	1.2	1.3	1.4	1.7	1.2
8.6	8.7	12.1	5.5	8.6	8.6	12.1
3.3	3.0	7.3	2.1	3.0	1.9	6.4
–	–	–	–	–	–	–
–	–	0.1	0.0	–	–	0.1
–	0.4	–	–	–	–	–
0.7	0.7	0.6	0.0	–	0.0	0.1
1.4	2.2	2.3	1.0	1.4	2.2	2.3
4.0	1.0	2.0	4.0	3.0	1.0	–
48.8	*55.1*	*77.0*	*34.6*	*45.0*	*51.3*	*69.4*
11.8	*18.8*	*19.4*	*8.7*	*11.1*	*12.6*	*19.4*
–	–	–	–	–	–	–
33.0	*42.3*	*60.2*	*24.2*	*32.1*	*40.5*	*55.8*
60.6	***73.9***	***96.3***	***43.3***	***56.1***	***63.8***	***88.8***
			TOTAL OOF NET			
–	–	–	–	–	–	–
–	–	–	-0.1	-0.2	-0.1	-0.1
–	–	–	–	–	–	–
11.6	4.2	16.4	7.8	7.9	0.5	12.5
0.5	0.4	0.3	0.0	0.3	-0.3	-2.0
–	–	–	–	–	–	–
5.6	2.6	2.7	2.8	5.6	2.1	2.7
57.0	46.5	146.8	43.1	32.0	20.9	94.9
19.9	18.5	13.5	29.7	0.8	8.6	-5.8
142.1	133.8	84.2	5.4	120.9	110.9	55.9
–	–	–	–	–	–	–
–	–	–	-0.5	–	–	–
–	–	–	–	–	–	–
–	–	–	–	–	–	–
–	–	–	–	–	–	–
–	–	–	–	–	–	–
82.0	145.0	179.0	37.0	–	28.0	27.0
318.6	*350.9*	*442.8*	*125.3*	*167.3*	*170.5*	*185.0*
419.1	*504.1*	*630.4*	*285.3*	*246.3*	*344.3*	*440.9*
0.5	–	–	–	*0.5*	–	–
82.9	*67.9*	*163.2*	*75.6*	*38.7*	*31.3*	*89.7*
738.2	***855.0***	***1073.2***	***410.6***	***414.1***	***514.8***	***625.9***

MAIN AID AGGREGATES

	1977	1978	1979	1980
DAC COUNTRIES COMBINED				
PRIVATE SECTOR NET	1935.5	4503.2	4464.1	3498.9
Direct Investment	1072.3	1738.2	1532.5	787.9
Portfolio Invest.	501.1	2587.0	2029.9	1020.2
Export Credits	362.2	178.1	901.7	1690.8
OFFICIAL & PRIVATE				
GROSS:				
Contractual Lending	1287.8	1172.5	2149.3	3088.5
Export Credits Tot.	1178.6	1089.2	2096.0	3018.6
Export Credits Priv	970.1	776.9	1748.3	2610.1
OTHER NET DATA				
Contractual Lending	508.8	372.3	1070.8	1857.1
Export Credits Tot.	460.2	348.1	1072.6	1877.7
(Bank Sector Loans)	1247.0	5828.0	1841.0	1386.0
ODA CONCESSIONALITY				
Total:Grant Element	71.0	72.0	82.0	73.0
Loans:Grant Element	59.0	42.0	49.0	51.0
OTHER SOURCES				
CMEA Countr.(Gross)	5.2	5.2	10.4	5.2
Intra LDCS Exc.OPEC	–	–	–	–
Other	–	–	–	–
ALL SOURCE COMMITMENTS				
TOTAL BILATERAL	320.2	413.1	572.0	452.9
of which				
OPEC (ODA)	55.0	–	–	–
CMEA (ODA)	–	–	–	–
TOTAL MULTILAT.(ODA)	66.4	11.9	78.4	132.1
TOTAL BIL.& MULTIL.	386.6	425.0	650.4	584.9
of which				
ODA Grants	46.9	64.0	75.8	104.1
ODA Loans	198.3	50.0	118.7	249.5
ODA CONCESSIONALITY				
Total: Grant Element	58.0	67.0	79.0	68.0
Loans: Grant Element	48.0	43.0	47.0	49.0

INDEBTEDNESS

	1977	1978	1979	1980
TOTAL DEBT DISBURSED	***32246.5***	***44437.7***	***50628.0***	
Debt to DAC Countries	29387.0	40773.0	46635.0	
ODA	1474.0	1533.0	1528.0	
Total Export Credits	6688.0	8118.0	9847.0	
Other Private Market	21225.0	31122.0	35260.0	
International Org.	2052.6	2383.9	2755.4	
CMEA	157.4	151.4	176.1	
Other	649.5	1129.5	1061.6	
TOTAL DEBT SERVICE	***6351.6***	***8069.3***	***10819.2***	
Paid to DAC Countries	5802.4	7487.5	10063.4	
ODA	72.5	86.3	89.0	
Total Export Credits	1008.0	1602.4	1433.5	
Other Private Market	4721.9	5798.8	8540.9	
International Org.	313.0	344.7	366.6	
CMEA	56.0	57.7	55.0	
Other	180.2	179.5	334.2	

ECONOMIC INDICATORS

	1977	1978	1979	1980
GNP Curr. Prices, $M	161319.7	188643.9	208473.5	230449.7
Real GNP, 1976=100	104.0	110.0	117.0	126.0
GNP/Cap Curr. Prices,$	1435.0	1648.0	1788.0	1941.0
GNP/cap Atlas Basis, $	1408.0	1569.9	1772.8	2049.8
Real GNP/Cap, 1976=100	102.0	106.0	111.0	117.0
Population, Million	112.4	114.4	116.5	118.7
Curr.A/C Deficit(-),$M	-5120.0	-7037.0	-10483.0	-12897.0
BOP Exp. & Transf.,$M	13513.0	14561.0	18013.0	23412.0
Exp. to OECD CIF, $M	8841.8	9124.4	11229.7	13427.4
of which				
Manufact.	1523.1	2062.4	2795.3	3168.3
Imp. from OECD FOB, $M	6563.6	7933.8	8764.2	10546.7
Reserves ex. Gold, $M	7192.0	11826.0	8966.0	5769.0

	TOTAL RECEIPTS NET 1977	1978	1979	1980	TOTAL ODA NET 1977	1978	1979	1980
DAC COUNTRIES								
Australia	2.1	6.7	11.0	19.3	2.1	6.7	7.4	14.4
Austria	–	–	–	44.0	–	–	–	–
Belgium	-0.3	–	–	3.8	–	–	–	0.0
Canada	6.2	2.7	4.4	3.7	6.2	2.7	4.4	3.7
Denmark	0.1	5.6	9.9	11.7	0.1	5.6	9.9	11.7
Finland	–	–	0.0	1.0	–	–	0.0	1.0
France	8.2	-1.0	14.7	1.8	2.5	—.3	-0.3	2.2
Germany, Fed. Rep.	12.3	16.3	91.5	-13.7	9.6	15.8	51.8	26.3
Italy	0.1	0.0	15.6	0.0	0.0	0.0	0.1	0.0
Japan	17.8	125.2	189.6	144.2	20.6	104.0	178.0	152.5
Netherlands	0.1	13.3	-6.2	1.9	0.1	13.3	0.8	1.9
New Zealand	0.2	0.1	0.1	0.0	0.2	0.1	0.1	0.0
Norway	0.0	52.4	30.2	68.0	0.0	0.6	0.9	2.4
Sweden	–	–	–	1.6	–	–	–	–
Switzerland	0.0	0.0	0.2	-5.0	0.0	0.0	0.2	0.1
United Kingdom	3.1	14.3	52.3	42.5	4.3	2.6	6.0	15.1
United States	9.0	2.0	–	–	9.0	2.0	–	–
TOTAL	*58.8*	*237.7*	*413.2*	*324.6*	*54.6*	*156.8*	*259.1*	*231.3*
MULTILATERAL								
AF.D.F.	–	–	–	–	–	–	–	–
AF.D.B.	–	–	–	–	–	–	–	–
AS.D.B.	10.6	60.9	20.9	14.1	9.6	57.6	20.6	13.4
CAR.D.B.	–	–	–	–	–	–	–	–
E.E.C.	0.6	1.4	–	–	0.6	1.4	–	–
IBRD	-0.7	–	–	–	–	–	–	–
IDA	19.3	25.0	34.8	26.1	19.3	25.0	34.8	26.1
I.D.B.	–	–	–	–	–	–	–	–
IFAD	–	–	–	–	–	–	–	–
I.F.C.	–	–	–	–	–	–	–	–
IMF TRUST FUND	7.5	23.2	23.5	19.9	7.5	23.2	23.5	19.9
U.N. AGENCIES	–	–	–	–	–	–	–	–
UNDP	4.8	4.6	7.1	9.2	4.8	4.6	7.1	9.2
UNTA	1.1	1.2	1.3	0.3	1.1	1.2	1.3	0.3
UNICEF	1.6	3.9	9.9	7.2	1.6	3.9	9.9	7.2
UNRWA	–	–	–	–	–	–	–	–
WFP	–	–	4.0	0.1	–	–	4.0	0.1
UNHCR	–	–	–	–	–	–	–	–
Other Multilateral	0.2	0.2	0.9	0.9	0.2	0.2	0.9	0.9
Arab OPEC Agencies	2.3	–	2.4	0.3	2.3	–	2.4	0.3
TOTAL	*47.3*	*120.3*	*104.8*	*78.1*	*47.0*	*117.0*	*104.6*	*77.4*
OPEC COUNTRIES	–	–	–	–	–	–	–	–
E.E.C.+ MEMBERS	*24.1*	*50.0*	*177.8*	*48.0*	*17.2*	*42.1*	*68.2*	*57.2*
TOTAL	***106.1***	***358.1***	***518.1***	***402.7***	***101.7***	***273.8***	***363.7***	***308.7***

	ODA LOANS GROSS 1977	1978	1979	1980	ODA LOANS NET 1977	1978	1979	1980
DAC COUNTRIES								
Australia	–	–	–	–	–	–	–	–
Austria	–	–	–	–	–	–	–	–
Belgium	–	–	–	–	–	–	–	–
Canada	4.8	0.2	0.9	0.9	4.8	0.2	0.9	0.9
Denmark	–	5.4	9.9	11.7	–	5.4	9.9	11.7
Finland	–	–	–	–	–	–	–	–
France	2.7	3.6	–	2.4	2.5	3.3	-0.3	2.0
Germany, Fed. Rep.	7.7	12.9	53.0	26.4	6.1	12.0	47.4	21.7
Italy	–	–	–	–	–	–	–	–
Japan	10.1	96.7	153.3	122.4	9.2	93.4	148.0	115.3
Netherlands	–	–	–	0.9	–	–	–	0.9
New Zealand	–	–	–	–	–	–	–	–
Norway	–	–	–	–	–	–	–	–
Sweden	–	–	–	–	–	–	–	–
Switzerland	–	–	–	–	–	–	–	–
United Kingdom	–	–	–	–	–	–	–	–
United States	–	–	–	–	–	–	–	–
TOTAL	*25.2*	*118.9*	*217.2*	*164.7*	*22.5*	*114.4*	*206.0*	*152.6*
MULTILATERAL	*37.9*	*105.7*	*81.3*	*58.6*	*37.9*	*105.7*	*81.3*	*58.6*
OPEC COUNTRIES	–	–	–	–	–	–	–	–
E.E.C.+ MEMBERS	*10.4*	*21.9*	*62.9*	*41.4*	*8.5*	*20.7*	*57.0*	*36.4*
TOTAL	***63.2***	***224.6***	***298.5***	***223.4***	***60.4***	***220.1***	***287.3***	***211.2***

	TOTAL OFFICIAL GROSS 1977	1978	1979	1980	TOTAL OFFICIAL NET 1977	1978	1979	1980
DAC COUNTRIES								
Australia	2.1	6.7	11.0	19.3	2.1	6.7	11.0	19.3
Austria	–	–	–	–	–	–	–	–
Belgium	–	–	–	0.0	–	–	–	0.0
Canada	6.2	2.7	4.4	3.7	6.2	2.7	4.4	3.7
Denmark	0.1	5.6	9.9	11.7	0.1	5.6	9.9	11.7
Finland	–	–	0.0	1.0	–	–	0.0	1.0
France	2.7	3.6	–	2.5	2.5	3.3	-0.3	2.2
Germany, Fed. Rep.	11.2	16.7	57.4	30.9	9.2	15.3	51.8	26.3
Italy	0.0	0.0	0.1	0.0	0.0	0.0	0.1	0.0
Japan	21.4	107.3	183.3	159.6	20.6	104.0	178.0	152.5
Netherlands	0.1	13.3	0.8	1.9	0.1	13.3	0.8	1.9
New Zealand	0.2	0.1	0.1	0.0	0.2	0.1	0.1	0.0
Norway	0.0	0.6	0.9	2.4	0.0	0.6	0.9	2.4
Sweden	–	–	–	–	–	–	–	–
Switzerland	0.0	0.0	0.2	0.1	0.0	0.0	0.2	0.1
United Kingdom	4.3	2.6	6.0	15.1	4.3	2.6	6.0	15.1
United States	9.0	2.0	–	–	9.0	2.0	–	–
TOTAL	*57.4*	*161.3*	*274.0*	*248.3*	*54.2*	*156.4*	*262.7*	*236.2*
MULTILATERAL	*48.0*	*120.3*	*104.9*	*78.1*	*47.3*	*120.3*	*104.8*	*78.1*
OPEC COUNTRIES	–	–	–	–	–	–	–	–
E.E.C.+ MEMBERS	*19.0*	*43.3*	*74.1*	*62.2*	*16.8*	*41.7*	*68.2*	*57.2*
TOTAL	***105.4***	***281.6***	***378.8***	***326.5***	***101.6***	***276.7***	***367.6***	***314.3***

	197
TOTAL ODA GROSS	
Australia	2
Austria	
Belgium	
Canada	6
Denmark	0
Finland	
France	2
Germany, Fed. Rep.	11
Italy	0
Japan	21
Netherlands	0
New Zealand	0
Norway	0
Sweden	
Switzerland	0
United Kingdom	4
United States	9
TOTAL	*57*
AF.D.F.	
AF.D.B.	
AS.D.B.	9
CAR.D.B.	
E.E.C.	0
IBRD	
IDA	19
I.D.B.	
IFAD	
I.F.C.	
IMF TRUST FUND	7
U.N. AGENCIES	
UNDP	4
UNTA	1
UNICEF	1
UNRWA	
WFP	
UNHCR	
Other Multilateral	0
Arab OPEC Agencies	2
TOTAL	*47*
OPEC COUNTRIES	
E.E.C.+ MEMBERS	*19*
TOTAL	***104***
GRANTS	
Australia	2
Austria	
Belgium	
Canada	1
Denmark	0
Finland	
France	
Germany, Fed. Rep.	3
Italy	0
Japan	11
Netherlands	0
New Zealand	0
Norway	0
Sweden	
Switzerland	0
United Kingdom	4
United States	9
TOTAL	*32*
MULTILATERAL	*9*
OPEC COUNTRIES	
E.E.C.+ MEMBERS	*8*
TOTAL	***41***
TOTAL OOF GROSS	
Australia	
Austria	
Belgium	
Canada	
Denmark	
Finland	
France	
Germany, Fed. Rep.	
Italy	
Japan	
Netherlands	
New Zealand	
Norway	
Sweden	
Switzerland	
United Kingdom	
United States	
TOTAL	
MULTILATERAL	*1*
OPEC COUNTRIES	
E.E.C.+ MEMBERS	
TOTAL	***1***

ODA COMMITMENTS

1978	1979	1980	1977	1978	1979	1980
6.7	7.4	14.4	32.5	1.7	3.3	5.4
–	–	–	–	–	–	–
–	–	0.0	–	–	–	–
2.7	4.4	3.7	3.0	5.2	0.6	0.2
5.6	9.9	11.7	0.3	5.4	17.1	6.3
–	0.0	1.0	–	–	1.8	0.8
3.6	–	2.5	4.8	–	–	15.8
16.7	57.4	30.9	14.0	39.4	206.8	25.3
0.0	0.1	0.0	0.0	0.0	0.1	0.0
107.3	183.3	159.6	227.4	95.6	172.0	35.2
13.3	0.8	1.9	12.4	1.2	0.6	5.2
0.1	0.1	0.0	0.1	0.0	0.0	0.0
0.6	0.9	2.4	–	–	0.9	8.5
–	–	–	–	–	–	–
0.0	0.2	0.1	–	–	–	0.1
2.6	6.0	15.1	0.6	5.5	6.5	16.7
2.0	–	–	–	–	4.7	9.6
161.3	*270.3*	*243.5*	*294.9*	*154.1*	*414.3*	*129.1*
–	–	–	–	–	–	–
–	–	–	–	–	–	–
57.6	20.6	13.4	25.1	65.7	37.2	50.5
–	–	–	–	–	–	–
1.4	–	–	–	–	0.8	6.8
–	–	–	–	–	–	–
25.0	34.8	26.1	31.5	33.8	74.5	90.0
–	–	–	–	–	–	–
–	–	–	–	–	–	–
–	–	–	–	–	–	–
23.2	23.5	19.9	–	–	–	–
–	–	–	7.7	9.8	23.2	17.7
4.6	7.1	9.2	–	–	–	–
1.2	1.3	0.3	–	–	–	–
3.9	9.9	7.2	–	–	–	–
–	–	–	–	–	–	–
–	4.0	0.1	–	–	–	–
–	–	–	–	–	–	–
0.2	0.9	0.9	–	–	–	–
–	2.4	0.3	6.7	6.5	2.0	6.3
117.0	*104.6*	*77.4*	*71.0*	*115.8*	*137.7*	*171.4*
–	–	–	–	–	–	–
43.3	*74.1*	*62.2*	*32.1*	*51.5*	*231.8*	*76.1*
278.3	***374.9***	***320.9***	***365.9***	***269.9***	***552.0***	***300.4***

TECH. COOP. GRANTS

1978	1979	1980	1977	1978	1979	1980
6.7	7.4	14.4	0.3	0.2	0.2	0.2
–	–	–	–	–	–	–
–	–	0.0	–	–	–	0.0
2.5	3.5	2.7	0.1	0.1	0.1	0.2
0.2	0.1	0.0	0.1	0.2	0.1	0.0
–	0.0	1.0	–	–	0.0	1.0
–	–	0.2	–	–	–	0.2
3.8	4.4	4.5	3.5	3.8	4.4	4.5
0.0	0.1	0.0	0.0	0.0	0.1	0.0
10.6	30.0	37.2	1.4	2.7	5.0	4.6
13.3	0.8	1.0	0.1	0.1	0.6	0.6
0.1	0.1	0.0	0.1	0.1	0.0	0.0
0.6	0.9	2.4	0.0	0.0	0.0	0.0
–	–	–	–	–	–	–
0.0	0.2	0.1	–	–	–	–
2.6	6.0	15.1	0.6	0.7	1.3	2.2
2.0	–	–	–	–	–	–
42.5	*53.2*	*78.7*	*6.3*	*8.0*	*11.7*	*13.5*
11.2	*23.2*	*18.8*	*8.5*	*9.8*	*19.2*	*17.7*
–	–	–	–	–	–	–
21.4	*11.2*	*20.9*	*4.4*	*4.8*	*6.3*	*7.5*
53.7	***76.4***	***97.5***	***14.8***	***17.7***	***30.9***	***31.2***

TOTAL OOF NET

1978	1979	1980	1977	1978	1979	1980
–	3.6	4.9	–	–	3.6	4.9
–	–	–	–	–	–	–
–	–	–	–	–	–	–
–	–	–	–	–	–	–
–	–	–	–	–	–	–
–	–	–	–	–	–	–
–	–	–	–	–	–	–
–	–	–	-0.4	-0.5	–	–
–	–	–	–	–	–	–
–	–	–	–	–	–	–
–	–	–	–	–	–	–
–	–	–	–	–	–	–
–	–	–	–	–	–	–
–	–	–	–	–	–	–
–	–	–	–	–	–	–
–	–	–	–	–	–	–
–	–	–	–	–	–	–
–	*3.6*	*4.9*	*-0.4*	*-0.5*	*3.6*	*4.9*
3.4	*0.3*	*0.7*	*0.3*	*3.4*	*0.3*	*0.7*
–	–	–	–	–	–	–
–	–	–	*-0.4*	*-0.5*	–	–
3.4	***4.0***	***5.6***	***-0.1***	***2.9***	***3.9***	***5.5***

MAIN AID AGGREGATES

	1977	1978	1979	1980
DAC COUNTRIES COMBINED				
PRIVATE SECTOR NET	4.5	81.4	150.5	88.5
Direct Investment	0.1	–	–	0.4
Portfolio Invest.	0.0	0.9	39.8	-38.8
Export Credits	4.5	80.5	110.7	126.9
OFFICIAL & PRIVATE				
GROSS:				
Contractual Lending	42.9	219.6	362.1	320.5
Export Credits Tot.	17.6	100.7	144.9	155.8
Export Credits Priv	17.6	100.7	141.3	150.9
OTHER NET DATA				
Contractual Lending	26.6	194.4	320.3	284.3
Export Credits Tot.	4.1	80.0	114.3	131.7
(Bank Sector Loans)	1.0	37.0	47.0	-23.0
ODA CONCESSIONALITY				
Total:Grant Element	65.0	75.0	70.0	88.0
Loans:Grant Element	55.0	63.0	65.0	59.0
OTHER SOURCES				
CMEA Countr.(Gross)	–	3.0	2.0	2.0
Intra LDCS Exc.OPEC	–	–	–	–
Other	–	–	–	–
ALL SOURCE COMMITMENTS				
TOTAL BILATERAL	294.9	154.1	423.8	129.1
of which				
OPEC (ODA)	–	–	–	–
CMEA (ODA)	–	140.0	–	–
TOTAL MULTILAT.(ODA)	71.0	115.8	137.7	171.4
TOTAL BIL.& MULTIL.	365.9	269.9	561.5	300.4
of which				
ODA Grants	71.4	61.0	86.8	116.8
ODA Loans	294.5	209.0	465.2	183.6
ODA CONCESSIONALITY				
Total: Grant Element	68.0	77.0	73.0	85.0
Loans: Grant Element	60.0	71.0	69.0	75.0

INDEBTEDNESS

	1977	1978	1979	1980
TOTAL DEBT DISBURSED	***527.3***	***848.6***	***1226.4***	
Debt to DAC Countries	345.0	574.0	806.0	
ODA	201.0	382.0	529.0	
Total Export Credits	144.0	159.0	221.0	
Other Private Market	–	33.0	56.0	
International Org.	93.8	175.2	238.0	
CMEA	61.9	71.4	152.1	
Other	26.6	28.0	30.3	
TOTAL DEBT SERVICE	***34.2***	***54.1***	***104.7***	
Paid to DAC Countries	29.2	46.8	87.6	
ODA	8.2	11.3	22.8	
Total Export Credits	21.0	33.7	46.3	
Other Private Market	–	1.8	18.5	
International Org.	0.6	1.0	2.3	
CMEA	4.2	4.6	11.8	
Other	0.3	1.6	3.0	

ECONOMIC INDICATORS

	1977	1978	1979	1980
GNP Curr. Prices, $M	4108.2	4650.1	5114.0	5579.2
Real GNP, 1976=100	105.0	112.0	118.0	128.0
GNP/Cap Curr. Prices,$	131.0	145.0	157.0	167.0
GNP/cap Atlas Basis, $	123.4	138.0	154.1	177.5
Real GNP/Cap, 1976=100	103.0	108.0	111.0	117.0
Population, Million	31.2	31.9	32.6	33.3
Curr.A/C Deficit(-),$M	-110.0	-240.4	-405.9	–
BOP Exp. & Transf.,$M	246.9	307.1	421.8	–
Exp. to OECD CIF, $M	82.4	104.1	173.7	156.6
of which				
Manufact.	3.4	13.8	11.7	5.7
Imp. from OECD FOB, $M	194.7	398.5	505.1	446.9
Reserves ex. Gold, $M	103.3	96.3	203.3	260.6

	1977	1978	1979	1980		1977	1978	1979	1980		197
TOTAL RECEIPTS NET					**TOTAL ODA NET**					**TOTAL ODA GROSS**	
DAC COUNTRIES											
Australia	–	–	–	–		–	–	–	–	Australia	
Austria	0.1	0.1	0.0	–		0.1	0.1	0.0	–	Austria	0
Belgium	21.5	21.6	25.3	28.4		16.5	20.9	25.2	27.7	Belgium	16
Canada	0.1	0.0	0.0	0.0		0.1	0.0	0.0	0.0	Canada	0
Denmark	–	0.1	0.4	0.4		–	0.1	0.4	0.4	Denmark	
Finland	–	–	–	0.2		–	–	–	0.2	Finland	
France	6.2	7.2	7.4	12.8		6.2	7.2	7.5	12.9	France	6
Germany, Fed. Rep.	3.6	6.8	6.4	10.1		3.8	6.3	6.3	10.0	Germany, Fed. Rep.	3
Italy	0.0	-0.4	-0.3	-0.4		0.2	0.3	0.2	0.2	Italy	0
Japan	–	–	–	2.2		–	–	–	2.2	Japan	
Netherlands	0.5	0.3	0.9	0.7		0.5	0.3	0.9	0.7	Netherlands	0
New Zealand	–	–	–	–		–	–	–	–	New Zealand	
Norway	–	–	–	–		–	–	–	–	Norway	
Sweden	–	–	0.9	0.3		–	–	0.9	0.3	Sweden	
Switzerland	0.5	0.7	0.7	1.1		0.5	0.7	0.7	1.1	Switzerland	0
United Kingdom	-0.1	-0.2	0.0	0.0		0.0	0.0	0.0	0.1	United Kingdom	0
United States	1.0	3.0	2.0	4.0		1.0	3.0	2.0	4.0	United States	1
TOTAL	*33.3*	*39.1*	*43.7*	*59.8*		*28.8*	*38.6*	*44.1*	*59.7*	*TOTAL*	*28*
MULTILATERAL											
AF.D.F.	1.1	1.9	0.9	4.5		1.1	1.9	0.9	4.5	AF.D.F.	1
AF.D.B.	1.5	0.2	-0.2	0.3		–	–	–	–	AF.D.B.	
AS.D.B.	–	–	–	–		–	–	–	–	AS.D.B.	
CAR.D.B.	–	–	–	–		–	–	–	–	CAR.D.B.	
E.E.C.	4.8	7.6	13.0	12.0		4.8	7.6	13.0	12.0	E.E.C.	4
IBRD	-0.4	–	–	–		–	–	–	–	IBRD	
IDA	2.5	6.9	11.3	11.6		2.5	6.9	11.3	11.6	IDA	2
I.D.B.	–	–	–	–		–	–	–	–	I.D.B.	
IFAD	–	–	–	–		–	–	–	–	IFAD	
I.F.C.	–	–	–	–		–	–	–	–	I.F.C.	
IMF TRUST FUND	2.4	7.4	7.4	6.4		2.4	7.4	7.4	6.4	IMF TRUST FUND	2
U.N. AGENCIES	–	–	–	–		–	–	–	–	U.N. AGENCIES	
UNDP	2.8	3.5	4.5	5.8		2.8	3.5	4.5	5.8	UNDP	2
UNTA	0.5	0.6	0.6	0.4		0.5	0.6	0.6	0.4	UNTA	0
UNICEF	0.6	0.9	0.9	1.1		0.6	0.9	0.9	1.1	UNICEF	0
UNRWA	–	–	–	–		–	–	–	–	UNRWA	
WFP	2.4	3.2	5.0	5.3		2.4	3.2	5.0	5.3	WFP	2
UNHCR	0.2	0.2	0.2	0.4		0.2	0.2	0.2	0.4	UNHCR	0
Other Multilateral	0.7	0.6	0.8	1.9		0.7	0.6	0.8	1.9	Other Multilateral	0
Arab OPEC Agencies	1.1	1.0	4.5	4.5		1.1	1.0	4.5	4.5	Arab OPEC Agencies	1
TOTAL	*20.2*	*34.0*	*48.8*	*54.2*		*19.1*	*33.8*	*49.0*	*53.9*	*TOTAL*	*19*
OPEC COUNTRIES	*0.4*	*2.1*	*1.7*	*3.7*		*0.4*	*2.1*	*1.7*	*3.7*	*OPEC COUNTRIES*	*0*
E.E.C.+ MEMBERS	*36.5*	*43.0*	*53.0*	*63.9*		*32.0*	*42.5*	*53.4*	*63.9*	*E.E.C.+ MEMBERS*	*32*
TOTAL	***53.9***	***75.2***	***94.2***	***117.6***		***48.2***	***74.5***	***94.8***	***117.2***	***TOTAL***	***48***

	1977	1978	1979	1980		1977	1978	1979	1980		197
ODA LOANS GROSS					**ODA LOANS NET**					**GRANTS**	
DAC COUNTRIES											
Australia	–	–	–	–		–	–	–	–	Australia	
Austria	–	–	–	–		–	–	–	–	Austria	0
Belgium	–	–	–	–		–	–	–	–	Belgium	16
Canada	–	–	–	–		–	–	–	–	Canada	0
Denmark	–	–	–	–		–	–	–	–	Denmark	
Finland	–	–	–	–		–	–	–	–	Finland	
France	0.1	0.3	0.5	1.7		0.1	0.3	0.5	1.7	France	6
Germany, Fed. Rep.	1.3	2.0	1.0	1.4		1.1	1.9	0.9	1.1	Germany, Fed. Rep.	2
Italy	–	–	–	–		–	–	–	–	Italy	0
Japan	–	–	–	–		–	–	–	–	Japan	
Netherlands	–	–	–	–		–	–	–	–	Netherlands	0
New Zealand	–	–	–	–		–	–	–	–	New Zealand	
Norway	–	–	–	–		–	–	–	–	Norway	
Sweden	–	–	–	–		–	–	–	–	Sweden	
Switzerland	–	–	–	–		–	–	–	–	Switzerland	0
United Kingdom	–	–	–	–		–	–	–	–	United Kingdom	0
United States	–	–	–	–		–	–	–	–	United States	1
TOTAL	*1.4*	*2.3*	*1.5*	*3.0*		*1.2*	*2.2*	*1.4*	*2.8*	*TOTAL*	*27*
MULTILATERAL	*6.9*	*17.1*	*24.2*	*27.0*		*6.9*	*17.1*	*24.1*	*27.0*	*MULTILATERAL*	*12*
OPEC COUNTRIES	*0.4*	*2.1*	*1.7*	*3.7*		*0.4*	*2.1*	*1.7*	*3.7*	*OPEC COUNTRIES*	
E.E.C.+ MEMBERS	*1.4*	*2.3*	*1.5*	*3.0*		*1.2*	*2.2*	*1.4*	*2.8*	*E.E.C.+ MEMBERS*	*30*
TOTAL	***8.7***	***21.4***	***27.4***	***33.7***		***8.5***	***21.3***	***27.3***	***33.4***	***TOTAL***	***39***

	1977	1978	1979	1980		1977	1978	1979	1980		197
TOTAL OFFICIAL GROSS					**TOTAL OFFICIAL NET**					**TOTAL OOF GROSS**	
DAC COUNTRIES											
Australia	–	–	–	–		–	–	–	–	Australia	
Austria	0.1	0.1	0.0	–		0.1	0.1	0.0	–	Austria	
Belgium	16.5	20.9	25.2	27.7		16.5	20.9	25.2	27.7	Belgium	
Canada	0.1	0.0	0.0	0.0		0.1	0.0	0.0	0.0	Canada	
Denmark	–	0.1	0.4	0.4		–	0.1	0.4	0.4	Denmark	
Finland	–	–	–	0.2		–	–	–	0.2	Finland	
France	6.2	7.2	7.5	12.9		6.2	7.2	7.4	12.8	France	
Germany, Fed. Rep.	3.9	6.3	6.4	10.3		3.8	6.3	6.3	10.0	Germany, Fed. Rep.	
Italy	0.2	0.3	0.2	0.2		0.2	0.3	0.2	0.2	Italy	
Japan	–	–	–	2.2		–	–	–	2.2	Japan	
Netherlands	0.5	0.3	0.9	0.7		0.5	0.3	0.9	0.7	Netherlands	
New Zealand	–	–	–	–		–	–	–	–	New Zealand	
Norway	–	–	–	–		–	–	–	–	Norway	
Sweden	–	–	0.9	0.3		–	–	0.9	0.3	Sweden	
Switzerland	0.5	0.7	0.7	1.1		0.5	0.7	0.7	1.1	Switzerland	
United Kingdom	0.0	0.0	0.0	0.1		0.0	0.0	0.0	0.1	United Kingdom	
United States	1.0	3.0	2.0	4.0		1.0	3.0	2.0	4.0	United States	
TOTAL	*28.9*	*38.7*	*44.2*	*59.9*		*28.8*	*38.6*	*44.0*	*59.6*	*TOTAL*	
MULTILATERAL	*20.6*	*34.0*	*49.0*	*54.5*		*20.2*	*34.0*	*48.8*	*54.2*	*MULTILATERAL*	*1*
OPEC COUNTRIES	*0.4*	*2.1*	*1.7*	*3.7*		*0.4*	*2.1*	*1.7*	*3.7*	*OPEC COUNTRIES*	
E.E.C.+ MEMBERS	*32.1*	*42.6*	*53.5*	*64.1*		*32.0*	*42.5*	*53.3*	*63.8*	*E.E.C.+ MEMBERS*	
TOTAL	***49.9***	***74.8***	***95.0***	***118.1***		***49.3***	***74.7***	***94.6***	***117.4***	***TOTAL***	***1***

1978	1979	1980	1977	1978	1979	1980
			ODA COMMITMENTS			
–	–	–	–	–	–	–
0.1	0.0	–	–	–	–	–
20.9	25.2	27.7	24.8	29.8	28.5	34.1
0.0	0.0	0.0	0.0	0.0	–	0.1
0.1	0.4	0.4	–	0.8	0.1	0.1
–	–	0.2	–	–	–	0.3
7.2	7.5	12.9	7.2	5.9	10.8	27.2
6.3	6.4	10.3	10.0	3.3	23.2	18.4
0.3	0.2	0.2	0.2	0.3	0.2	0.2
–	–	2.2	–	–	2.7	2.7
0.3	0.9	0.7	0.5	0.3	1.2	0.7
–	–	–	–	–	–	–
–	–	–	–	–	–	–
–	0.9	0.3	–	–	0.2	–
0.7	0.7	1.1	–	1.6	0.4	0.4
0.0	0.0	0.1	0.0	0.0	0.0	0.1
3.0	2.0	4.0	1.1	2.1	1.5	5.7
38.7	*44.2*	*59.9*	*43.8*	*44.1*	*68.9*	*89.7*
1.9	0.9	4.5	–	1.1	9.7	13.4
–	–	–	–	–	–	–
–	–	–	–	–	–	–
–	–	–	–	–	–	–
7.6	13.0	12.0	11.6	10.3	15.3	15.2
–	–	–	–	–	–	–
6.9	11.4	11.6	13.4	14.0	6.8	37.7
–	–	–	–	–	–	–
–	–	–	–	–	14.9	–
–	–	–	–	–	–	–
7.4	7.4	6.4	–	–	–	–
–	–	–	7.2	9.0	11.9	14.9
3.5	4.5	5.8	–	–	–	–
0.6	0.6	0.4	–	–	–	–
0.9	0.9	1.1	–	–	–	–
–	–	–	–	–	–	–
3.2	5.0	5.3	–	–	–	–
0.2	0.2	0.4	–	–	–	–
0.6	0.8	1.9	–	–	–	–
1.0	4.5	4.5	6.0	6.1	4.5	5.0
33.8	*49.0*	*53.9*	*38.1*	*40.4*	*63.1*	*86.1*
2.1	*1.7*	*3.7*	*6.1*	–	–	*1.8*
42.6	*53.5*	*64.1*	*54.2*	*50.7*	*79.3*	*95.8*
74.6	***95.0***	***117.5***	***88.0***	***84.6***	***132.0***	***177.7***
			TECH. COOP. GRANTS			
–	–	–	–	–	–	–
0.1	0.0	–	0.1	0.1	0.0	–
20.9	25.2	27.7	12.9	14.9	16.1	17.8
0.0	0.0	0.0	0.0	0.0	0.0	–
0.1	0.4	0.4	–	0.1	0.4	0.4
–	–	0.2	–	–	–	0.2
6.9	7.0	11.2	4.4	4.8	6.0	7.0
4.4	5.4	8.9	2.6	4.2	4.9	7.3
0.3	0.2	0.2	0.2	0.3	0.2	0.2
–	–	2.2	–	–	–	0.0
0.3	0.9	0.7	0.5	0.3	0.9	0.7
–	–	–	–	–	–	–
–	–	–	–	–	–	–
–	0.9	0.3	–	–	–	–
0.7	0.7	1.1	0.1	0.1	0.2	0.8
0.0	0.0	0.1	0.0	0.0	0.0	0.1
3.0	2.0	4.0	–	–	–	1.0
36.5	*42.7*	*56.9*	*20.8*	*24.7*	*28.8*	*35.4*
16.7	*24.9*	*26.9*	*4.8*	*5.8*	*6.9*	*14.9*
–	–	–	–	–	–	–
40.3	*52.0*	*61.1*	*20.6*	*24.5*	*28.5*	*33.3*
53.2	***67.6***	***83.8***	***25.6***	***30.4***	***35.7***	***50.2***
			TOTAL OOF NET			
–	–	–	–	–	–	–
–	–	–	–	–	–	–
–	–	–	–	–	–	–
–	–	–	–	–	–	–
–	–	–	–	–	–	–
–	–	–	–	–	–	–
–	–	–	–	–	-0.1	-0.1
–	–	–	–	–	–	–
–	–	–	–	–	–	–
–	–	–	–	–	–	–
–	–	–	–	–	–	–
–	–	–	–	–	–	–
–	–	–	–	–	–	–
–	–	–	–	–	–	–
–	–	–	–	–	–	–
–	–	–	–	–	–	–
–	–	–	–	–	–	–
–	–	–	–	–	*-0.1*	*-0.1*
0.2	–	*0.6*	*1.1*	*0.2*	*-0.2*	*0.3*
–	–	–	–	–	–	–
–	–	–	–	–	*-0.1*	*-0.1*
0.2	–	***0.6***	***1.1***	***0.2***	***-0.3***	***0.2***

	1977	1978	1979	1980
MAIN AID AGGREGATES				
DAC COUNTRIES COMBINED				
PRIVATE SECTOR NET	4.6	0.5	-0.4	0.2
Direct Investment	-0.2	0.9	-0.3	0.6
Portfolio Invest.	0.0	-0.2	-0.3	0.2
Export Credits	4.8	-0.2	0.3	-0.6
OFFICIAL & PRIVATE				
GROSS:				
Contractual Lending	6.9	3.5	2.8	3.0
Export Credits Tot.	5.5	1.2	1.3	–
Export Credits Priv	5.5	1.2	1.3	–
OTHER NET DATA				
Contractual Lending	6.0	2.0	1.6	2.1
Export Credits Tot.	4.8	-0.2	0.3	-0.6
(Bank Sector Loans)	–	1.0	1.0	3.0
ODA CONCESSIONALITY				
Total:Grant Element	98.0	99.0	100.0	91.0
Loans:Grant Element	83.0	83.0	–	43.0
OTHER SOURCES				
CMEA Countr.(Gross)	–	–	–	–
Intra LDCS Exc.OPEC	–	–	–	–
Other	–	–	–	–
ALL SOURCE COMMITMENTS				
TOTAL BILATERAL	49.9	44.3	69.8	94.0
of which				
OPEC (ODA)	6.1	–	–	1.8
CMEA (ODA)	–	–	–	–
TOTAL MULTILAT.(ODA)	38.1	40.4	63.1	86.1
TOTAL BIL.& MULTIL.	88.0	84.8	132.9	180.1
of which				
ODA Grants	60.0	58.3	95.4	105.6
ODA Loans	28.0	26.3	36.6	72.1
ODA CONCESSIONALITY				
Total: Grant Element	89.0	93.0	95.0	88.0
Loans: Grant Element	68.0	74.0	76.0	73.0
INDEBTEDNESS				
TOTAL DEBT DISBURSED	***40.3***	***54.6***	***87.1***	
Debt to DAC Countries	12.0	15.0	22.0	
ODA	3.0	6.0	7.0	
Total Export Credits	6.0	6.0	9.0	
Other Private Market	3.0	3.0	6.0	
International Org.	14.8	23.9	39.5	
CMEA	12.5	14.1	22.3	
Other	1.0	1.5	3.3	
TOTAL DEBT SERVICE	***2.8***	***4.9***	***3.5***	
Paid to DAC Countries	2.2	4.3	2.5	
ODA	0.2	0.1	0.2	
Total Export Credits	0.6	3.5	1.5	
Other Private Market	1.4	0.7	0.8	
International Org.	0.6	0.3	0.7	
CMEA	–	0.3	0.3	
Other	–	–	0.1	
ECONOMIC INDICATORS				
GNP Curr. Prices, $M	529.9	608.6	798.8	878.9
Real GNP, 1976=100	109.0	115.0	116.0	116.0
GNP/Cap Curr. Prices,$	136.0	154.0	198.0	214.0
GNP/cap Atlas Basis. $	158.3	175.6	189.4	202.7
Real GNP/Cap, 1976=100	107.0	110.0	110.0	108.0
Population, Million	3.9	3.9	4.0	4.1
Curr.A/C Deficit(-),$M	–	–	–	–
BOP Exp. & Transf.,$M	–	–	–	–
Exp. to OECD CIF, $M	76.1	74.7	87.4	105.8
of which				
Manufact.	0.2	0.7	0.5	0.4
Imp. from OECD FOB, $M	41.7	57.1	70.7	73.4
Reserves ex. Gold, $M	94.4	81.3	90.0	93.5

	1977	1978	1979	1980	1977	1978	1979	1980
TOTAL RECEIPTS NET / **TOTAL ODA NET**								
DAC COUNTRIES								
Australia	–	–	0.0	–	–	–	0.0	–
Austria	26.2	0.1	0.2	0.1	26.2	0.1	0.2	0.1
Belgium	1.5	3.4	3.2	6.2	1.8	2.5	3.2	3.6
Canada	8.3	13.3	14.6	29.6	8.7	13.4	13.5	17.8
Denmark	0.1	4.8	0.3	0.1	–	3.6	–	–
Finland	–	–	–	0.0	–	–	–	0.0
France	126.0	155.1	298.8	493.1	42.6	49.3	68.4	94.7
Germany, Fed. Rep.	20.3	39.9	93.8	20.3	20.3	36.1	76.4	25.3
Italy	5.5	-2.2	1.0	0.4	-0.2	-0.2	0.1	0.0
Japan	0.1	-1.1	0.1	0.1	0.1	0.1	0.1	0.1
Netherlands	3.9	3.7	4.4	19.6	3.9	3.2	4.4	4.1
New Zealand	–	–	–	–	–	–	–	–
Norway	9.6	1.6	2.7	2.1	9.5	1.6	2.9	2.3
Sweden	29.5	-1.6	–	-6.1	–	–	–	–
Switzerland	2.8	2.0	1.5	1.4	2.8	2.0	1.5	1.7
United Kingdom	15.4	5.2	41.0	17.9	0.8	1.6	2.2	11.9
United States	10.0	2.0	13.0	20.0	6.0	4.0	11.0	10.0
TOTAL	*259.1*	*226.2*	*474.4*	*604.8*	*122.5*	*117.2*	*183.8*	*171.4*
MULTILATERAL								
AF.D.F.	–	–	–	–	–	–	–	–
AF.D.B.	3.5	7.3	6.8	0.4	–	–	–	–
AS.D.B.	–	–	–	–	–	–	–	–
CAR.D.B.	–	–	–	–	–	–	–	–
E.E.C.	12.8	12.3	26.1	20.2	12.0	11.6	23.7	13.6
IBRD	14.3	30.8	27.2	22.6	0.2	2.5	3.2	4.8
IDA	24.6	14.1	19.6	18.7	24.6	14.1	19.6	18.7
I.D.B.	–	–	–	–	–	–	–	–
IFAD	–	–	–	–	–	–	–	–
I.F.C.	0.8	–	0.4	7.9	–	–	–	–
IMF TRUST FUND	–	18.2	13.7	11.7	–	18.2	13.7	11.7
U.N. AGENCIES	–	–	–	–	–	–	–	–
UNDP	2.3	1.7	2.2	6.7	2.3	1.7	2.2	6.7
UNTA	0.3	0.3	0.2	0.4	0.3	0.3	0.2	0.4
UNICEF	0.2	0.1	0.4	0.7	0.2	0.1	0.4	0.7
UNRWA	–	–	–	–	–	–	–	–
WFP	0.1	3.4	1.0	1.1	0.1	3.4	1.0	1.1
UNHCR	–	0.2	0.2	9.4	–	0.2	0.2	9.4
Other Multilateral	0.7	0.5	0.3	0.6	0.7	0.5	0.3	0.6
Arab OPEC Agencies	3.9	21.8	11.5	5.7	3.9	4.6	9.6	3.3
TOTAL	*63.2*	*110.6*	*109.5*	*106.0*	*44.1*	*57.2*	*74.0*	*70.9*
OPEC COUNTRIES	*9.1*	*3.2*	*12.1*	*24.1*	*9.1*	*3.2*	*12.1*	*24.1*
E.E.C.+ MEMBERS	*185.4*	*222.2*	*468.5*	*578.0*	*81.1*	*107.8*	*178.3*	*153.1*
TOTAL	***331.4***	***340.1***	***596.0***	***735.0***	***175.7***	***177.6***	***269.9***	***266.4***
ODA LOANS GROSS / **ODA LOANS NET**								
DAC COUNTRIES								
Australia	–	–	–	–	–	–	–	–
Austria	26.1	–	–	–	26.1	–	–	–
Belgium	–	–	–	–	–	–	–	–
Canada	6.9	12.2	12.7	16.4	6.9	12.2	12.7	16.4
Denmark	–	3.6	–	–	–	3.6	–	–
Finland	–	–	–	–	–	–	–	–
France	14.6	23.8	31.6	51.9	9.5	16.3	25.0	46.0
Germany, Fed. Rep.	11.6	24.7	62.5	14.0	10.1	23.5	61.3	12.6
Italy	–	–	–	–	-0.3	-0.3	-0.3	-0.3
Japan	–	–	–	–	–	–	–	–
Netherlands	0.3	0.4	–	–	0.3	0.3	–	0.0
New Zealand	–	–	–	–	–	–	–	–
Norway	–	–	–	–	–	–	–	–
Sweden	–	–	–	–	–	–	–	–
Switzerland	–	–	–	–	-1.2	–	–	–
United Kingdom	–	1.0	1.5	10.4	-0.1	0.8	1.3	10.3
United States	–	–	5.0	1.0	–	–	5.0	–
TOTAL	*59.5*	*65.7*	*113.2*	*93.7*	*51.4*	*56.4*	*105.0*	*84.8*
MULTILATERAL	*31.9*	*48.3*	*57.9*	*45.9*	*30.2*	*42.4*	*57.0*	*44.1*
OPEC COUNTRIES	*9.1*	*3.2*	*12.1*	*24.1*	*9.1*	*3.2*	*12.1*	*24.1*
E.E.C.+ MEMBERS	*28.7*	*57.2*	*107.4*	*83.3*	*21.2*	*47.2*	*98.3*	*74.0*
TOTAL	***100.6***	***117.2***	***183.3***	***163.7***	***90.7***	***102.0***	***174.1***	***153.0***
TOTAL OFFICIAL GROSS / **TOTAL OFFICIAL NET**								
DAC COUNTRIES								
Australia	–	–	0.0	–	–	–	0.0	–
Austria	26.2	0.1	0.2	0.1	26.2	0.1	0.2	0.1
Belgium	1.8	2.5	3.2	3.6	1.8	2.5	3.2	3.6
Canada	8.7	13.4	14.9	29.6	8.3	13.3	14.6	29.6
Denmark	0.1	3.8	0.1	0.0	0.1	3.8	0.1	0.0
Finland	–	–	–	0.0	–	–	–	0.0
France	66.2	121.7	147.9	149.1	60.0	80.5	119.6	140.3
Germany, Fed. Rep.	22.1	37.9	81.9	32.1	20.5	36.6	80.6	30.4
Italy	1.2	0.1	1.9	0.3	0.1	-2.0	-0.3	-2.0
Japan	0.1	0.1	0.1	0.1	0.1	0.1	0.1	0.1
Netherlands	3.9	3.8	4.4	4.1	3.9	3.7	4.4	4.0
New Zealand	–	–	–	–	–	–	–	–
Norway	9.5	1.6	2.9	2.3	9.5	1.6	2.9	2.3
Sweden	–	–	–	–	–	–	–	–
Switzerland	4.1	2.0	1.5	1.7	2.8	2.0	1.5	1.7
United Kingdom	0.8	1.9	2.4	12.0	0.8	1.6	2.2	11.9
United States	10.0	4.0	16.0	23.0	10.0	2.0	13.0	20.0
TOTAL	*154.7*	*192.8*	*277.3*	*258.0*	*144.1*	*145.7*	*242.1*	*241.9*
MULTILATERAL	*68.0*	*125.3*	*117.2*	*114.7*	*63.2*	*110.6*	*109.5*	*106.0*
OPEC COUNTRIES	*9.1*	*3.2*	*12.1*	*24.1*	*9.1*	*3.2*	*12.1*	*24.1*
E.E.C.+ MEMBERS	*111.9*	*187.1*	*271.8*	*225.4*	*99.9*	*139.1*	*235.9*	*208.4*
TOTAL	***231.8***	***321.3***	***406.6***	***396.9***	***216.4***	***259.6***	***363.7***	***372.0***

	197
TOTAL ODA GROSS	
Australia	
Austria	26
Belgium	1
Canada	8
Denmark	
Finland	
France	47
Germany, Fed. Rep.	21
Italy	0
Japan	0
Netherlands	3
New Zealand	
Norway	9
Sweden	
Switzerland	4
United Kingdom	0
United States	6
TOTAL	*130*
AF.D.F.	
AF.D.B.	
AS.D.B.	
CAR.D.B.	
E.E.C.	12
IBRD	0
IDA	25
I.D.B.	
IFAD	
I.F.C.	
IMF TRUST FUND	
U.N. AGENCIES	
UNDP	2
UNTA	0
UNICEF	0
UNRWA	
WFP	0
UNHCR	
Other Multilateral	0
Arab OPEC Agencies	3
TOTAL	*45*
OPEC COUNTRIES	*9*
E.E.C.+ MEMBERS	*88*
TOTAL	***185***
GRANTS	
Australia	
Austria	0
Belgium	1
Canada	1
Denmark	
Finland	
France	33
Germany, Fed. Rep.	10
Italy	0
Japan	0
Netherlands	3
New Zealand	
Norway	9
Sweden	
Switzerland	4
United Kingdom	0
United States	6
TOTAL	*71*
MULTILATERAL	*13*
OPEC COUNTRIES	
E.E.C.+ MEMBERS	*59*
TOTAL	***85***
TOTAL OOF GROSS	
Australia	
Austria	
Belgium	
Canada	
Denmark	0
Finland	
France	18
Germany, Fed. Rep.	0
Italy	1
Japan	
Netherlands	
New Zealand	
Norway	
Sweden	
Switzerland	
United Kingdom	
United States	4
TOTAL	*24*
MULTILATERAL	*22*
OPEC COUNTRIES	
E.E.C.+ MEMBERS	*23*
TOTAL	***46***

1978	1979	1980	1977	1978	1979	1980
			ODA COMMITMENTS			
–	0.0	–	–	–	0.0	–
0.1	0.2	0.1	26.1	0.1	0.0	–
2.5	3.2	3.6	2.5	3.6	3.5	4.4
13.4	13.5	17.8	6.6	31.2	23.0	0.6
3.6	–	–	–	3.6	–	–
–	–	0.0	–	–	–	–
56.8	75.0	100.6	46.9	61.0	102.2	61.1
37.2	77.5	26.8	17.6	83.0	17.0	23.2
0.1	0.4	0.3	0.1	0.1	0.4	0.3
0.1	0.1	0.1	0.1	0.1	0.1	0.1
3.3	4.4	4.1	3.9	5.0	4.2	4.1
–	–	–	–	–	–	–
1.6	2.9	2.3	12.5	1.2	4.3	0.0
–	–	–	–	–	–	–
2.0	1.5	1.7	3.0	2.1	0.0	1.2
1.9	2.4	12.0	0.8	8.3	15.2	29.5
4.0	11.0	11.0	4.3	14.6	9.5	9.6
126.5	*192.1*	*180.3*	*124.4*	*213.9*	*179.6*	*134.1*
–	–	–	–	–	–	–
–	–	–	–	–	–	–
–	–	–	–	–	–	–
–	–	–	–	–	–	–
12.4	24.5	15.0	5.8	27.7	14.7	4.5
2.5	3.2	4.8	7.0	–	–	–
19.3	19.6	19.1	20.0	36.0	30.0	43.1
–	–	–	–	–	–	–
–	–	–	–	–	–	11.6
–	–	–	–	–	–	–
18.2	13.7	11.7	–	–	–	–
–	–	–	3.5	6.1	4.3	18.9
1.7	2.2	6.7	–	–	–	–
0.3	0.2	0.4	–	–	–	–
0.1	0.4	0.7	–	–	–	–
–	–	–	–	–	–	–
3.4	1.0	1.1	–	–	–	–
0.2	0.2	9.4	–	–	–	–
0.5	0.3	0.6	–	–	–	–
4.6	9.6	3.3	22.0	0.0	4.5	1.2
63.1	*74.9*	*72.8*	*58.2*	*69.9*	*53.5*	*79.3*
3.2	*12.1*	*24.1*	*48.7*	–	*3.7*	*3.0*
117.8	*187.4*	*162.4*	*77.6*	*192.3*	*157.2*	*127.1*
192.8	***279.1***	***277.2***	***231.4***	***283.8***	***236.7***	***216.4***
			TECH. COOP. GRANTS			
–	0.0	–	–	–	0.0	–
0.1	0.2	0.1	0.1	0.1	0.2	0.1
2.5	3.2	3.6	1.7	2.1	2.5	2.9
1.2	0.9	1.4	1.1	0.3	0.2	0.4
–	–	–	–	–	–	–
–	–	0.0	–	–	–	0.0
33.0	43.4	48.7	24.7	27.0	34.5	38.8
12.5	15.1	12.7	10.1	12.5	15.1	12.6
0.1	0.4	0.3	0.1	0.1	0.4	0.2
0.1	0.1	0.1	0.1	0.1	0.1	0.1
2.9	4.4	4.1	3.5	2.9	3.3	3.9
–	–	–	–	–	–	–
1.6	2.9	2.3	0.1	0.2	0.4	0.3
–	–	–	–	–	–	–
2.0	1.5	1.7	0.0	0.1	0.1	0.2
0.9	0.9	1.6	0.8	0.9	0.9	1.6
4.0	6.0	10.0	2.0	3.0	3.0	6.0
60.8	*78.8*	*86.6*	*44.5*	*49.2*	*60.7*	*67.0*
14.8	*16.9*	*26.9*	*3.4*	*2.7*	*3.3*	*18.9*
–	–	–	–	–	–	–
60.6	*80.0*	*79.1*	*41.0*	*45.5*	*56.7*	*59.9*
75.6	***95.8***	***113.5***	***47.9***	***51.9***	***64.0***	***85.8***
			TOTAL OOF NET			
–	–	–	–	–	–	–
–	–	–	–	–	–	–
–	–	–	–	–	–	–
–	1.4	11.8	-0.4	-0.1	1.1	11.8
0.2	0.1	0.0	0.1	0.2	0.1	0.0
–	–	–	–	–	–	–
64.9	72.9	48.6	17.4	31.2	51.2	45.6
0.8	4.4	5.4	0.3	0.6	4.2	5.2
–	1.4	–	0.3	-1.8	-0.4	-1.9
–	–	–	–	–	–	–
0.6	–	–	–	0.5	–	-0.1
–	–	–	–	–	–	–
–	–	–	–	–	–	–
–	–	–	–	–	–	–
–	–	–	–	–	–	–
–	–	–	–	–	–	–
–	5.0	12.0	4.0	-2.0	2.0	10.0
66.4	*85.2*	*77.7*	*21.6*	*28.5*	*58.3*	*70.5*
62.2	*42.4*	*42.0*	*19.1*	*53.5*	*35.5*	*35.1*
–	–	–	–	–	–	–
69.3	*84.4*	*63.0*	*18.8*	*31.3*	*57.6*	*55.3*
128.5	***127.6***	***119.7***	***40.7***	***82.0***	***93.8***	***105.6***

	1977	1978	1979	1980
MAIN AID AGGREGATES				
DAC COUNTRIES COMBINED				
PRIVATE SECTOR NET	115.0	80.5	232.3	362.9
Direct Investment	-2.0	-1.8	7.7	69.2
Portfolio Invest.	12.3	6.3	95.2	142.5
Export Credits	104.7	76.0	129.5	151.2
OFFICIAL & PRIVATE				
GROSS:				
Contractual Lending	230.0	254.6	393.1	377.2
Export Credits Tot.	150.4	122.6	202.5	232.3
Export Credits Priv	146.4	122.6	194.7	205.8
OTHER NET DATA				
Contractual Lending	177.7	160.9	292.7	306.5
Export Credits Tot.	108.4	72.1	132.2	173.8
(Bank Sector Loans)	42.0	9.0	22.0	1.0
ODA CONCESSIONALITY				
Total:Grant Element	71.0	76.0	69.0	80.0
Loans:Grant Element	42.0	62.0	44.0	32.0
OTHER SOURCES				
CMEA Countr.(Gross)	–	–	–	–
Intra LDCS Exc.OPEC	–	–	–	–
Other	–	–	–	–
ALL SOURCE COMMITMENTS				
TOTAL BILATERAL	209.6	310.6	334.4	200.6
of which				
OPEC (ODA)	48.7	–	3.7	3.0
CMEA (ODA)	–	–	–	–
TOTAL MULTILAT.(ODA)	58.2	69.9	53.5	79.3
TOTAL BIL.& MULTIL.	267.8	380.5	387.9	279.8
of which				
ODA Grants	72.0	96.4	97.5	119.2
ODA Loans	159.3	187.4	139.2	97.2
ODA CONCESSIONALITY				
Total: Grant Element	66.0	78.0	72.0	82.0
Loans: Grant Element	50.0	67.0	53.0	58.0
INDEBTEDNESS				
TOTAL DEBT DISBURSED	***829.9***	***1136.6***	***1672.7***	
Debt to DAC Countries	549.0	747.0	1174.0	
ODA	165.0	235.0	337.0	
Total Export Credits	248.0	381.0	637.0	
Other Private Market	136.0	131.0	200.0	
International Org.	215.0	294.4	362.5	
CMEA	40.9	64.1	84.1	
Other	25.1	31.1	52.2	
TOTAL DEBT SERVICE	***78.3***	***121.9***	***176.5***	
Paid to DAC Countries	67.4	100.7	155.1	
ODA	8.0	14.6	14.9	
Total Export Credits	45.6	66.0	102.2	
Other Private Market	13.8	20.1	38.0	
International Org.	10.4	20.1	20.6	
CMEA	0.4	0.4	0.4	
Other	0.1	0.6	0.5	
ECONOMIC INDICATORS				
GNP Curr. Prices, $M	3097.5	3859.4	4971.3	5834.8
Real GNP, 1976=100	108.0	117.0	126.0	133.0
GNP/Cap Curr. Prices,$	393.0	479.0	602.0	691.0
GNP/cap Atlas Basis, $	459.2	523.0	593.7	669.8
Real GNP/Cap, 1976=100	106.0	112.0	117.0	121.0
Population, Million	7.9	8.1	8.2	8.4
Curr.A/C Deficit(-),$M	-125.9	-197.3	-158.3	–
BOP Exp. & Transf.,$M	979.0	1318.8	1718.1	–
Exp. to OECD CIF, $M	718.1	920.8	1191.1	1764.1
of which				
Manufact.	20.8	19.0	31.0	34.0
Imp. from OECD FOB, $M	606.6	796.4	1010.9	1279.4
Reserves ex. Gold, $M	42.4	52.3	125.7	188.8

	1977	1978	1979	1980	1977	1978	1979	1980
TOTAL RECEIPTS NET / **TOTAL ODA NET**								
DAC COUNTRIES								
Australia	–	–	–	–	–	–	–	–
Austria	-0.1	0.1	-0.1	0.0	0.1	0.1	0.1	0.1
Belgium	0.2	0.8	0.5	0.4	0.2	0.5	0.5	0.3
Canada	0.1	0.1	0.0	0.0	0.1	0.1	0.0	0.0
Denmark	–	–	–	–	–	–	–	–
Finland	–	–	–	–	–	–	–	–
France	28.0	25.0	44.4	74.2	27.0	24.3	41.6	69.5
Germany, Fed. Rep.	2.7	4.1	5.8	2.9	2.5	4.1	5.3	3.2
Italy	0.1	-0.2	1.0	13.8	0.2	0.2	0.1	0.1
Japan	0.0	0.1	2.1	0.3	0.0	0.1	2.1	0.3
Netherlands	0.1	0.2	0.3	0.6	0.1	0.2	0.3	0.6
New Zealand	–	–	–	–	–	–	–	–
Norway	–	–	–	–	–	–	–	–
Sweden	–	–	0.2	–	–	–	0.2	–
Switzerland	0.1	0.1	0.1	0.1	0.1	0.1	0.1	0.1
United Kingdom	-0.3	-0.1	–	–	–	–	–	–
United States	–	–	1.0	1.0	–	–	1.0	1.0
TOTAL	*30.8*	*30.3*	*55.2*	*93.4*	*30.2*	*29.7*	*51.2*	*75.1*
MULTILATERAL								
AF.D.F.	0.2	3.0	5.9	5.6	0.2	3.0	5.9	5.6
AF.D.B.	–	0.0	-0.1	0.2	–	–	–	–
AS.D.B.	–	–	–	–	–	–	–	–
CAR.D.B.	–	–	–	–	–	–	–	–
E.E.C.	4.7	5.9	11.4	11.0	4.7	5.9	11.4	11.0
IBRD	–	–	–	–	–	–	–	–
IDA	0.9	0.6	7.1	10.2	0.9	0.6	7.1	10.2
I.D.B.	–	–	–	–	–	–	–	–
IFAD	–	–	–	0.1	–	–	–	0.1
I.F.C.	–	–	–	–	–	–	–	–
IMF TRUST FUND	–	6.8	–	–	–	6.8	–	–
U.N. AGENCIES	–	–	–	–	–	–	–	–
UNDP	2.2	2.4	2.9	2.7	2.2	2.4	2.9	2.7
UNTA	0.7	0.6	0.4	0.2	0.7	0.6	0.4	0.2
UNICEF	0.6	0.7	1.8	0.6	0.6	0.7	1.8	0.6
UNRWA	–	–	–	–	–	–	–	–
WFP	0.2	1.3	1.2	1.8	0.2	1.3	1.2	1.8
UNHCR	–	0.0	0.1	0.4	–	0.0	0.1	0.4
Other Multilateral	0.7	0.3	0.2	1.3	0.7	0.3	0.2	1.3
Arab OPEC Agencies	1.8	–	–	–	1.8	–	–	–
TOTAL	*12.0*	*21.6*	*31.0*	*34.0*	*12.0*	*21.6*	*31.1*	*33.8*
OPEC COUNTRIES	–	*6.0*	*6.6*	*2.1*	–	*6.0*	*6.6*	*2.1*
E.E.C.+ MEMBERS	*35.5*	*35.8*	*63.3*	*103.0*	*34.7*	*35.2*	*59.2*	*84.6*
TOTAL	***42.8***	***57.9***	***92.8***	***129.4***	***42.1***	***57.3***	***88.9***	***111.0***
ODA LOANS GROSS / **ODA LOANS NET**								
DAC COUNTRIES								
Australia	–	–	–	–	–	–	–	–
Austria	–	–	–	–	–	–	–	–
Belgium	–	–	–	–	–	–	–	–
Canada	–	–	–	–	–	–	–	–
Denmark	–	–	–	–	–	–	–	–
Finland	–	–	–	–	–	–	–	–
France	–	0.2	–	3.3	-1.3	0.1	-1.7	3.2
Germany, Fed. Rep.	0.7	0.7	0.0	–	0.6	0.6	0.0	–
Italy	–	–	–	–	–	–	–	–
Japan	–	–	–	–	–	–	–	–
Netherlands	–	–	–	–	–	–	–	–
New Zealand	–	–	–	–	–	–	–	–
Norway	–	–	–	–	–	–	–	–
Sweden	–	–	–	–	–	–	–	–
Switzerland	–	–	–	–	–	–	–	–
United Kingdom	–	–	–	–	–	–	–	–
United States	–	–	–	–	–	–	–	–
TOTAL	*0.7*	*0.9*	*0.0*	*3.3*	*-0.7*	*0.7*	*-1.7*	*3.2*
MULTILATERAL	*2.9*	*10.4*	*13.0*	*15.9*	*2.9*	*10.4*	*13.0*	*15.8*
OPEC COUNTRIES	–	–	*1.3*	*2.1*	–	–	*1.3*	*2.1*
E.E.C.+ MEMBERS	*0.7*	*0.9*	*0.0*	*3.3*	*-0.7*	*0.7*	*-1.7*	*3.2*
TOTAL	***3.6***	***11.3***	***14.4***	***21.3***	***2.2***	***11.1***	***12.7***	***21.1***
TOTAL OFFICIAL GROSS / **TOTAL OFFICIAL NET**								
DAC COUNTRIES								
Australia	–	–	–	–	–	–	–	–
Austria	0.1	0.1	0.1	0.1	0.1	0.1	0.1	0.1
Belgium	0.2	0.5	0.5	0.3	0.2	0.5	0.5	0.3
Canada	0.1	0.1	0.0	0.0	0.1	0.1	0.0	0.0
Denmark	–	–	–	–	–	–	–	–
Finland	–	–	–	–	–	–	–	–
France	28.3	24.4	43.3	69.6	26.6	24.3	41.6	69.5
Germany, Fed. Rep.	2.7	4.2	5.3	3.2	2.6	4.1	5.3	3.2
Italy	0.2	0.2	0.1	0.1	0.2	0.2	0.1	0.1
Japan	0.0	0.1	2.1	0.3	0.0	0.1	2.1	0.3
Netherlands	0.1	0.2	0.3	0.6	0.1	0.2	0.3	0.6
New Zealand	–	–	–	–	–	–	–	–
Norway	–	–	–	–	–	–	–	–
Sweden	–	–	0.2	–	–	–	0.2	–
Switzerland	0.1	0.1	0.1	0.1	0.1	0.1	0.1	0.1
United Kingdom	–	–	–	–	–	–	–	–
United States	–	–	1.0	1.0	–	–	1.0	1.0
TOTAL	*31.7*	*29.9*	*52.9*	*75.2*	*29.9*	*29.6*	*51.2*	*75.1*
MULTILATERAL	*12.0*	*21.8*	*31.1*	*34.0*	*12.0*	*21.6*	*31.0*	*33.9*
OPEC COUNTRIES	–	*6.0*	*1.3*	*2.1*	–	*6.0*	*6.6*	*2.1*
E.E.C.+ MEMBERS	*36.3*	*35.4*	*60.9*	*84.7*	*34.5*	*35.1*	*59.2*	*84.6*
TOTAL	***43.7***	***57.7***	***85.3***	***111.4***	***41.9***	***57.2***	***88.8***	***111.2***

TOTAL ODA GROSS	19
Australia	
Austria	
Belgium	
Canada	
Denmark	
Finland	
France	2
Germany, Fed. Rep.	
Italy	
Japan	
Netherlands	
New Zealand	
Norway	
Sweden	
Switzerland	
United Kingdom	
United States	
TOTAL	3
AF.D.F.	
AF.D.B.	
AS.D.B.	
CAR.D.B.	
E.E.C.	
IBRD	
IDA	
I.D.B.	
IFAD	
I.F.C.	
IMF TRUST FUND	
U.N. AGENCIES	
UNDP	
UNTA	
UNICEF	
UNRWA	
WFP	
UNHCR	
Other Multilateral	
Arab OPEC Agencies	
TOTAL	1.
OPEC COUNTRIES	
E.E.C.+ MEMBERS	3
TOTAL	4.

GRANTS	19
Australia	
Austria	
Belgium	
Canada	
Denmark	
Finland	
France	2
Germany, Fed. Rep.	
Italy	
Japan	
Netherlands	
New Zealand	
Norway	
Sweden	
Switzerland	
United Kingdom	
United States	
TOTAL	3
MULTILATERAL	
OPEC COUNTRIES	
E.E.C.+ MEMBERS	3
TOTAL	3

TOTAL OOF GROSS	19
Australia	
Austria	
Belgium	
Canada	
Denmark	
Finland	
France	
Germany, Fed. Rep.	
Italy	
Japan	
Netherlands	
New Zealand	
Norway	
Sweden	
Switzerland	
United Kingdom	
United States	
TOTAL	
MULTILATERAL	
OPEC COUNTRIES	
E.E.C.+ MEMBERS	
TOTAL	

1978	1979	1980	1977	1978	1979	1980
			ODA COMMITMENTS			
–	–	–	–	–	–	–
0.1	0.1	0.1	–	–	–	–
0.5	0.5	0.3	–	–	–	–
0.1	0.0	0.0	0.1	0.1	–	0.1
–	–	–	–	–	–	–
–	–	–	–	–	–	–
24.4	43.3	69.6	30.3	20.5	45.1	95.7
4.2	5.3	3.2	1.8	1.2	4.8	0.7
0.2	0.1	0.1	0.2	0.2	0.1	0.1
0.1	2.1	0.3	0.0	2.5	0.0	1.0
0.2	0.3	0.6	0.1	–	0.3	0.6
–	–	–	–	–	–	–
–	–	–	–	–	–	–
–	0.2	–	–	–	–	–
0.1	0.1	0.1	–	–	–	0.1
–	–	–	–	–	–	–
–	1.0	1.0	1.5	1.8	0.8	1.1
29.9	*52.9*	*75.2*	*34.1*	*26.2*	*51.2*	*99.2*
3.0	5.9	5.6	12.8	6.2	3.9	–
–	–	–	–	–	–	–
–	–	–	–	–	–	–
–	–	–	–	–	–	–
5.9	11.4	11.0	10.4	9.1	18.5	18.3
–	–	–	–	–	–	–
0.6	7.1	10.3	–	15.5	2.5	5.4
–	–	–	–	–	–	–
–	–	0.1	–	–	2.6	–
–	–	–	–	–	–	–
6.8	–	–	–	–	–	–
–	–	–	4.3	5.3	6.6	7.0
2.4	2.9	2.7	–	–	–	–
0.6	0.4	0.2	–	–	–	–
0.7	1.8	0.6	–	–	–	–
–	–	–	–	–	–	–
1.3	1.2	1.8	–	–	–	–
0.0	0.1	0.4	–	–	–	–
0.3	0.2	1.3	–	–	–	–
–	–	–	–	–	–	–
21.6	*31.1*	*33.9*	*27.5*	*36.2*	*34.1*	*30.7*
6.0	*1.3*	*2.1*	–	–	*3.6*	–
35.4	*60.9*	*84.7*	*42.8*	*31.0*	*68.8*	*115.4*
57.5	***85.3***	***111.2***	***61.6***	***62.4***	***88.9***	***129.9***
			TECH. COOP. GRANTS			
–	–	–	–	–	–	–
0.1	0.1	0.1	0.1	0.1	0.1	0.1
0.5	0.5	0.3	0.2	0.5	0.5	0.3
0.1	0.0	0.0	0.1	0.1	0.0	0.0
–	–	–	–	–	–	–
–	–	–	–	–	–	–
24.2	43.3	66.3	14.1	16.0	20.3	23.6
3.6	5.2	3.2	1.8	3.6	5.1	3.2
0.2	0.1	0.1	0.2	0.2	0.1	0.1
0.1	2.1	0.3	0.0	0.1	0.0	0.1
0.2	0.3	0.6	0.1	0.2	0.3	0.6
–	–	–	–	–	–	–
–	–	–	–	–	–	–
–	0.2	–	–	–	–	–
0.1	0.1	0.1	0.0	0.0	0.1	–
–	–	–	–	–	–	–
–	1.0	1.0	–	–	1.0	1.0
29.0	*52.9*	*71.9*	*16.6*	*20.6*	*27.4*	*28.9*
11.2	*18.0*	*18.0*	*4.2*	*4.0*	*5.5*	*7.0*
6.0	–	–	–	–	–	–
34.5	*60.9*	*81.4*	*16.5*	*20.4*	*26.3*	*27.8*
46.2	***71.0***	***89.9***	***20.8***	***24.6***	***32.9***	***35.9***
			TOTAL OOF NET			
–	–	–	–	–	–	–
–	–	–	–	–	–	–
–	–	–	–	–	–	–
–	–	–	–	–	–	–
–	–	–	–	–	–	–
–	–	–	–	–	–	–
–	–	–	-0.4	–	–	–
–	–	–	0.2	0.0	–	–
–	–	–	–	–	–	–
–	–	–	–	–	–	–
–	–	–	–	–	–	–
–	–	–	–	–	–	–
–	–	–	–	–	–	–
–	–	–	–	–	–	–
–	–	–	–	–	–	–
–	–	–	–	–	–	–
–	–	–	–	–	–	–
–	–	–	*-0.2*	*0.0*	–	–
0.2	–	*0.2*	–	*0.0*	*-0.1*	*0.2*
–	–	–	–	–	–	–
–	–	–	*-0.2*	*0.0*	–	–
0.2	–	***0.2***	***-0.2***	***-0.1***	***-0.1***	***0.2***

MAIN AID AGGREGATES

	1977	1978	1979	1980
DAC COUNTRIES COMBINED				
PRIVATE SECTOR NET	0.9	0.7	4.0	18.3
Direct Investment	0.3	1.1	0.7	4.7
Portfolio Invest.	1.6	0.1	0.2	0.0
Export Credits	-0.9	-0.5	3.2	13.5
OFFICIAL & PRIVATE GROSS:				
Contractual Lending	2.8	3.5	3.0	17.5
Export Credits Tot.	1.9	2.7	3.0	14.2
Export Credits Priv	1.9	2.7	3.0	14.2
OTHER NET DATA				
Contractual Lending	-1.8	0.1	1.5	16.7
Export Credits Tot.	-0.9	-0.5	3.2	13.5
(Bank Sector Loans)	18.0	-17.0	1.0	-3.0
ODA CONCESSIONALITY				
Total:Grant Element	100.0	100.0	100.0	83.0
Loans:Grant Element	–	–	–	34.0
OTHER SOURCES				
CMEA Countr.(Gross)	0.4	0.2	–	–
Intra LDCS Exc.OPEC	–	–	–	–
Other	–	–	–	–
ALL SOURCE COMMITMENTS				
TOTAL BILATERAL	34.6	26.4	54.8	99.8
of which				
OPEC (ODA)	–	–	3.6	–
CMEA (ODA)	–	–	–	–
TOTAL MULTILAT.(ODA)	27.5	36.2	34.1	30.7
TOTAL BIL.& MULTIL.	62.1	62.6	88.9	130.4
of which				
ODA Grants	48.8	40.0	76.3	99.4
ODA Loans	12.8	22.4	12.6	30.5
ODA CONCESSIONALITY				
Total: Grant Element	96.0	93.0	96.0	86.0
Loans: Grant Element	83.0	82.0	72.0	34.0

INDEBTEDNESS

	1977	1978	1979	1980
TOTAL DEBT DISBURSED	***133.3***	***127.5***	***155.9***	
Debt to DAC Countries	75.0	68.0	83.0	
ODA	42.0	21.0	21.0	
Total Export Credits	30.0	44.0	57.0	
Other Private Market	3.0	3.0	5.0	
International Org.	13.5	14.7	25.9	
CMEA	10.5	10.9	11.1	
Other	34.3	33.9	35.9	
TOTAL DEBT SERVICE	***6.8***	***6.4***	***4.7***	
Paid to DAC Countries	5.9	4.0	4.6	
ODA	1.5	0.4	2.0	
Total Export Credits	4.4	3.6	2.1	
Other Private Market	–	–	0.5	
International Org.	0.3	0.1	0.1	
CMEA	–	0.0	–	
Other	0.6	2.3	0.0	

ECONOMIC INDICATORS

	1977	1978	1979	1980
GNP Curr. Prices, $M	422.5	521.2	619.6	729.8
Real GNP, 1976=100	105.0	108.0	109.0	110.0
GNP/Cap Curr. Prices,$	196.0	226.0	275.0	318.0
GNP/cap Atlas Basis, $	239.4	247.1	276.1	297.7
Real GNP/Cap, 1976=100	103.0	99.0	102.0	101.0
Population, Million	2.1	2.3	2.2	2.3
Curr.A/C Deficit(-),$M	-57.2	-76.1	-103.1	-117.7
BOP Exp. & Transf.,$M	130.5	146.9	159.9	170.9
Exp. to OECD CIF, $M	96.6	93.1	86.6	104.0
of which				
Manufact.	2.1	0.7	1.1	2.9
Imp. from OECD FOB, $M	73.7	62.6	61.4	75.4
Reserves ex. Gold, $M	25.4	24.1	44.1	55.0

	1977	1978	1979	1980	1977	1978	1979	1980	19
TOTAL RECEIPTS NET					**TOTAL ODA NET**				**TOTAL ODA GROSS**
DAC COUNTRIES									
Australia	–	–	–	–	–	–	–	–	
Austria	–	–	–	–	–	–	–	–	
Belgium	0.2	0.4	0.2	0.1	0.2	0.4	0.2	0.1	
Canada	3.9	0.2	0.2	0.2	3.9	0.2	0.2	0.2	
Denmark	0.1	0.1	-0.1	0.1	0.1	0.1	-0.1	0.1	
Finland	–	–	–	0.0	–	–	–	0.0	
France	38.4	61.9	28.6	8.7	31.5	48.5	28.9	9.8	3
Germany, Fed. Rep.	-0.1	4.0	4.6	1.9	-0.1	2.7	4.3	1.5	
Italy	-0.9	-1.0	-0.7	0.0	0.1	0.1	0.1	0.0	
Japan	–	0.0	–	–	–	0.0	–	–	
Netherlands	1.7	1.8	0.4	0.7	1.7	1.8	0.4	0.7	
New Zealand	–	–	–	–	–	–	–	–	
Norway	1.1	3.5	3.4	1.4	1.1	3.5	3.4	1.4	
Sweden	–	–	–	–	–	–	–	–	
Switzerland	0.9	1.7	1.0	0.4	0.9	1.7	1.0	0.4	
United Kingdom	1.2	-0.2	0.5	0.1	1.2	-0.2	0.1	0.1	
United States	9.0	12.0	11.0	6.0	9.0	12.0	11.0	6.0	
TOTAL	*55.5*	*84.5*	*49.0*	*19.5*	*49.6*	*70.9*	*49.4*	*20.2*	5
MULTILATERAL									
AF.D.F.	3.3	5.0	1.4	1.7	3.3	5.0	1.4	1.7	
AF.D.B.	–	–	–	–	–	–	–	–	
AS.D.B.	–	–	–	–	–	–	–	–	
CAR.D.B.	–	–	–	–	–	–	–	–	
E.E.C.	14.5	17.6	20.7	9.1	14.5	17.6	20.7	9.1	1
IBRD	–	–	–	–	–	–	–	–	
IDA	8.3	7.0	4.9	0.4	8.3	7.0	4.9	0.4	
I.D.B.	–	–	–	–	–	–	–	–	
IFAD	–	–	–	–	–	–	–	–	
I.F.C.	–	–	–	–	–	–	–	–	
IMF TRUST FUND	–	6.8	–	–	–	6.8	–	–	
U.N. AGENCIES	–	–	–	–	–	–	–	–	
UNDP	2.6	3.2	1.7	0.8	2.6	3.2	1.7	0.8	
UNTA	0.5	0.5	0.3	0.2	0.5	0.5	0.3	0.2	
UNICEF	0.6	0.6	0.4	1.1	0.6	0.6	0.4	1.1	
UNRWA	–	–	–	–	–	–	–	–	
WFP	1.1	4.4	–	1.6	1.1	4.4	–	1.6	
UNHCR	–	–	–	–	–	–	–	–	
Other Multilateral	1.5	1.9	0.9	0.3	1.5	1.9	0.9	0.3	
Arab OPEC Agencies	1.2	1.2	–	–	1.2	1.2	–	–	
TOTAL	*33.5*	*48.1*	*30.3*	*15.1*	*33.5*	*48.1*	*30.3*	*15.1*	3
OPEC COUNTRIES	–	–	–	–	–	–	–	–	
E.E.C.+ MEMBERS	*55.1*	*84.6*	*54.1*	*20.6*	*49.2*	*71.1*	*54.5*	*21.2*	5
TOTAL	***89.0***	***132.6***	***79.2***	***34.7***	***83.1***	***119.0***	***79.6***	***35.3***	8

	1977	1978	1979	1980	1977	1978	1979	1980	19
ODA LOANS GROSS					**ODA LOANS NET**				**GRANTS**
DAC COUNTRIES									
Australia	–	–	–	–	–	–	–	–	
Austria	–	–	–	–	–	–	–	–	
Belgium	–	–	–	–	–	–	–	–	
Canada	–	–	–	–	–	–	–	–	
Denmark	0.1	0.1	–	–	0.1	0.1	-1.9	–	
Finland	–	–	–	–	–	–	–	–	
France	4.8	5.8	2.2	0.4	4.3	5.3	-0.2	-0.4	2
Germany, Fed. Rep.	0.1	1.6	0.7	0.2	-0.5	0.8	0.2	0.2	
Italy	–	–	–	–	–	–	–	–	
Japan	–	–	–	–	–	–	–	–	
Netherlands	–	–	–	–	–	–	–	–	
New Zealand	–	–	–	–	–	–	–	–	
Norway	–	–	–	–	–	–	–	–	
Sweden	–	–	–	–	–	–	–	–	
Switzerland	–	–	–	–	–	–	–	–	
United Kingdom	–	–	–	–	–	–	–	–	
United States	–	–	–	–	–	–	–	–	
TOTAL	*5.0*	*7.4*	*2.8*	*0.5*	*3.9*	*6.2*	*-1.9*	*-0.2*	4
MULTILATERAL	*19.9*	*30.5*	*11.4*	*2.2*	*19.9*	*26.5*	*10.9*	*2.1*	1
OPEC COUNTRIES	–	–	–	–	–	–	–	–	
E.E.C.+ MEMBERS	*12.1*	*14.1*	*7.5*	*0.6*	*11.0*	*12.7*	*2.7*	*-0.2*	3
TOTAL	***24.9***	***37.9***	***14.2***	***2.7***	***23.8***	***32.7***	***9.0***	***1.8***	5

	1977	1978	1979	1980	1977	1978	1979	1980	19
TOTAL OFFICIAL GROSS					**TOTAL OFFICIAL NET**				**TOTAL OOF GROSS**
DAC COUNTRIES									
Australia	–	–	–	–	–	–	–	–	
Austria	–	–	–	–	–	–	–	–	
Belgium	0.2	0.4	0.2	0.1	0.2	0.4	0.2	0.1	
Canada	3.9	0.2	0.2	0.2	3.9	0.2	0.2	0.2	
Denmark	0.1	0.1	1.8	0.1	0.1	0.1	-0.1	0.1	
Finland	–	–	–	0.0	–	–	–	0.0	
France	32.0	49.0	31.3	10.5	31.4	48.5	28.8	9.7	
Germany, Fed. Rep.	0.5	3.5	4.7	2.3	-0.1	2.7	4.2	2.3	
Italy	0.1	0.1	0.1	0.0	0.1	0.1	0.1	0.0	
Japan	–	0.0	–	–	–	0.0	–	–	
Netherlands	1.7	1.8	0.4	0.7	1.7	1.8	0.4	0.7	
New Zealand	–	–	–	–	–	–	–	–	
Norway	1.1	3.5	3.4	1.4	1.1	3.5	3.4	1.4	
Sweden	–	–	–	–	–	–	–	–	
Switzerland	0.9	1.7	1.0	0.4	0.9	1.7	1.0	0.4	
United Kingdom	1.2	-0.2	0.1	0.1	1.2	-0.2	0.1	0.1	
United States	9.0	12.0	11.0	6.0	9.0	12.0	11.0	6.0	
TOTAL	*50.7*	*72.1*	*54.1*	*21.7*	*49.5*	*70.8*	*49.3*	*20.9*	
MULTILATERAL	*33.5*	*52.0*	*30.7*	*15.2*	*33.5*	*48.1*	*30.3*	*15.1*	
OPEC COUNTRIES	–	–	–	–	–	–	–	–	
E.E.C.+ MEMBERS	*50.4*	*72.4*	*59.3*	*22.9*	*49.1*	*70.9*	*54.4*	*22.0*	
TOTAL	***84.2***	***124.2***	***84.9***	***37.0***	***83.0***	***118.9***	***79.5***	***36.0***	

1978	1979	1980	1977	1978	1979	1980
			ODA COMMITMENTS			
–	–	–	–	–	–	–
–	–	–	–	–	–	–
0.4	0.2	0.1	–	–	–	–
0.2	0.2	0.2	4.1	2.0	0.9	0.1
0.1	1.8	0.1	0.3	1.8	–	–
–	–	0.0	–	–	–	0.0
49.0	31.3	10.5	28.7	30.7	30.7	14.3
3.5	4.7	1.5	1.6	17.1	1.3	1.3
0.1	0.1	0.0	0.1	0.1	0.1	0.0
0.0	–	–	–	0.0	–	–
1.8	0.4	0.7	1.8	0.7	0.6	0.6
–	–	–	–	–	–	–
3.5	3.4	1.4	6.2	1.2	–	–
–	–	–	–	–	–	–
1.7	1.0	0.4	1.1	0.7	0.0	1.1
-0.2	0.1	0.1	1.2	0.4	0.1	0.1
12.0	11.0	6.0	12.4	22.7	4.8	3.9
72.1	*54.1*	*20.9*	*57.5*	*77.3*	*38.5*	*21.4*
6.3	1.8	1.7	–	6.3	–	–
–	–	–	–	–	–	–
–	–	–	–	–	–	–
–	–	–	–	–	–	–
17.7	20.8	9.2	20.8	13.1	8.9	9.9
–	–	–	–	–	–	–
9.6	5.0	0.4	1.9	27.4	–	–
–	–	–	–	–	–	–
–	–	–	–	–	–	–
–	–	–	–	–	–	–
6.8	–	–	–	–	–	–
–	–	–	6.2	10.5	3.2	4.0
3.2	1.7	0.8	–	–	–	–
0.5	0.3	0.2	–	–	–	–
0.6	0.4	1.1	–	–	–	–
–	–	–	–	–	–	–
4.4	–	1.6	–	–	–	–
–	–	–	–	–	–	–
1.9	0.9	0.3	–	–	–	–
1.2	–	–	2.4	8.7	–	–
52.0	*30.7*	*15.2*	*31.3*	*66.0*	*12.1*	*13.8*
–	–	–	–	*12.0*	–	–
72.4	*59.3*	*22.1*	*54.5*	*63.8*	*41.7*	*26.2*
124.2	***84.9***	***36.1***	***88.8***	***155.3***	***50.6***	***35.2***
			TECH. COOP. GRANTS			
–	–	–	–	–	–	–
–	–	–	–	–	–	–
0.4	0.2	0.1	0.2	0.4	0.1	0.1
0.2	0.2	0.2	0.1	0.2	0.1	0.0
–	1.8	0.1	–	–	–	–
–	–	0.0	–	–	–	–
43.2	29.1	10.2	15.6	16.7	12.2	5.8
1.9	4.1	1.3	0.3	1.3	1.2	0.8
0.1	0.1	0.0	0.1	0.1	0.1	0.0
0.0	–	–	–	0.0	–	–
1.8	0.4	0.7	0.2	0.3	0.3	0.5
–	–	–	–	–	–	–
3.5	3.4	1.4	–	–	–	–
–	–	–	–	–	–	–
1.7	1.0	0.4	0.0	0.0	0.1	0.3
-0.2	0.1	0.1	0.0	0.1	0.1	0.1
12.0	11.0	6.0	3.0	4.0	4.0	2.0
64.7	*51.3*	*20.4*	*19.6*	*23.1*	*18.2*	*9.6*
21.6	*19.4*	*13.1*	*5.0*	*6.1*	*3.2*	*4.0*
–	–	–	–	–	–	–
58.3	*51.8*	*21.5*	*16.5*	*18.9*	*14.0*	*7.3*
86.3	***70.6***	***33.4***	***24.6***	***29.2***	***21.4***	***13.5***
			TOTAL OOF NET			
–	–	–	–	–	–	–
–	–	–	–	–	–	–
–	–	–	–	–	–	–
–	–	–	–	–	–	–
–	–	–	–	–	–	–
–	–	–	–	–	–	–
–	–	–	-0.1	-0.1	-0.1	-0.1
–	–	0.8	–	0.0	0.0	0.8
–	–	–	–	–	–	–
–	–	–	–	–	–	–
–	–	–	–	–	–	–
–	–	–	–	–	–	–
–	–	–	–	–	–	–
–	–	–	–	–	–	–
–	–	–	–	–	–	–
–	–	–	–	–	–	–
–	–	–	–	–	–	–
–	–	*0.8*	*-0.1*	*-0.1*	*-0.1*	*0.7*
–	–	–	–	–	–	–
–	–	–	–	–	–	–
–	–	*0.8*	*-0.1*	*-0.1*	*-0.1*	*0.7*
–	–	***0.8***	***-0.1***	***-0.1***	***-0.1***	***0.7***

	1977	1978	1979	1980
MAIN AID AGGREGATES				
DAC COUNTRIES COMBINED				
PRIVATE SECTOR NET	6.0	13.7	-0.3	-1.3
Direct Investment	–	0.7	–	0.0
Portfolio Invest.	0.0	0.7	0.2	-0.2
Export Credits	6.0	12.3	-0.5	-1.2
OFFICIAL & PRIVATE				
GROSS:				
Contractual Lending	15.2	22.8	5.9	1.3
Export Credits Tot.	10.2	15.4	3.1	–
Export Credits Priv	10.2	15.4	3.1	–
OTHER NET DATA				
Contractual Lending	9.7	18.4	-2.5	-0.7
Export Credits Tot.	6.0	12.3	-0.5	-1.2
(Bank Sector Loans)	1.0	-1.0	–	–
ODA CONCESSIONALITY				
Total:Grant Element	99.0	99.0	100.0	100.0
Loans:Grant Element	83.0	77.0	–	–
OTHER SOURCES				
CMEA Countr.(Gross)	–	–	–	–
Intra LDCS Exc.OPEC	–	–	–	–
Other	–	–	–	–
ALL SOURCE COMMITMENTS				
TOTAL BILATERAL	59.9	91.0	41.1	21.4
of which				
OPEC (ODA)	–	12.0	–	–
CMEA (ODA)	–	–	–	–
TOTAL MULTILAT.(ODA)	31.3	66.0	12.1	13.8
TOTAL BIL.& MULTIL.	91.2	157.0	53.2	35.2
of which				
ODA Grants	84.2	110.1	50.6	35.2
ODA Loans	4.6	45.2	–	–
ODA CONCESSIONALITY				
Total: Grant Element	98.0	93.0	100.0	100.0
Loans: Grant Element	74.0	78.0	–	–
INDEBTEDNESS				
TOTAL DEBT DISBURSED	***114.9***	***160.2***	***170.9***	
Debt to DAC Countries	52.0	72.0	73.0	
ODA	15.0	23.0	20.0	
Total Export Credits	35.0	47.0	52.0	
Other Private Market	2.0	2.0	1.0	
International Org.	48.6	75.2	86.1	
CMEA	3.0	3.3	4.0	
Other	11.3	9.6	7.7	
TOTAL DEBT SERVICE	***11.9***	***15.9***	***18.1***	
Paid to DAC Countries	8.7	12.5	12.1	
ODA	1.2	1.8	3.7	
Total Export Credits	7.2	10.4	6.8	
Other Private Market	0.3	0.3	1.6	
International Org.	0.4	0.6	3.3	
CMEA	0.5	0.4	0.4	
Other	2.4	2.4	2.3	
ECONOMIC INDICATORS				
GNP Curr. Prices, $M	534.5	664.8	558.0	502.1
Real GNP, 1976=100	101.0	103.0	71.0	68.0
GNP/Cap Curr. Prices,$	127.0	155.0	127.0	112.0
GNP/cap Atlas Basis, $	146.7	157.3	115.3	118.2
Real GNP/Cap, 1976=100	99.0	99.0	67.0	63.0
Population, Million	4.2	4.3	4.4	4.5
Curr.A/C Deficit(-),$M	-131.1	–	–	–
BOP Exp. & Transf.,$M	132.4	–	–	–
Exp. to OECD CIF, $M	82.4	51.2	64.9	60.5
of which				
Manufact.	1.2	1.4	1.4	1.9
Imp. from OECD FOB, $M	81.2	103.2	46.6	19.9
Reserves ex. Gold, $M	18.8	11.8	11.3	5.1

TOTAL RECEIPTS NET

DAC COUNTRIES	1977	1978	1979	1980
Australia	0.0	0.4	3.7	-0.2
Austria	13.0	0.2	0.2	0.2
Belgium	-2.4	-3.0	10.3	31.4
Canada	-2.4	-5.1	6.4	7.3
Denmark	-1.0	-1.1	-0.1	-0.2
Finland	0.0	0.0	–	0.0
France	-42.6	-27.8	-14.8	104.3
Germany, Fed. Rep.	-8.6	-5.4	-20.4	24.8
Italy	5.0	-0.8	-1.8	4.2
Japan	-7.2	6.2	60.1	-0.8
Netherlands	3.0	2.2	2.6	5.6
New Zealand	–	0.0	0.0	–
Norway	-2.3	-1.4	-1.3	-0.8
Sweden	-0.9	-0.8	-0.7	-0.3
Switzerland	2.6	8.7	0.8	-0.6
United Kingdom	-27.0	4.6	39.4	-2.2
United States	-92.0	112.0	171.0	198.0
TOTAL	*-162.7*	*88.8*	*255.3*	*370.6*
MULTILATERAL				
AF.D.F.	–	–	–	–
AF.D.B.	–	–	–	–
AS.D.B.	–	–	–	–
CAR.D.B.	–	–	–	–
E.E.C.	3.9	13.5	0.5	–
IBRD	5.6	10.5	6.3	4.9
IDA	-0.2	-0.2	-0.2	-0.2
I.D.B.	24.7	11.4	21.5	25.7
IFAD	–	–	–	–
I.F.C.	–	–	–	-7.7
IMF TRUST FUND	–	–	–	–
U.N. AGENCIES	–	–	–	–
UNDP	3.7	3.2	3.4	4.9
UNTA	0.4	0.5	0.4	0.2
UNICEF	0.1	0.6	0.5	0.3
UNRWA	–	–	–	–
WFP	–	–	–	–
UNHCR	0.4	0.3	0.2	0.2
Other Multilateral	0.9	0.5	0.8	1.2
Arab OPEC Agencies	–	–	–	–
TOTAL	*39.5*	*40.2*	*33.4*	*29.4*
OPEC COUNTRIES	–	–	–	–
E.E.C.+ MEMBERS	*-69.6*	*-17.8*	*15.5*	*167.9*
TOTAL	***-123.2***	***129.0***	***288.6***	***400.0***

TOTAL ODA NET

	1977	1978	1979	1980
Australia	0.0	0.0	–	0.0
Austria	0.1	0.2	0.2	0.2
Belgium	1.4	0.6	0.7	1.1
Canada	-0.2	-0.3	-0.2	-0.2
Denmark	0.1	–	0.1	0.1
Finland	–	–	–	0.0
France	-5.6	-5.3	-6.2	-4.8
Germany, Fed. Rep.	-5.4	-4.5	-14.1	-5.8
Italy	-4.8	-0.6	-0.6	-0.1
Japan	2.2	1.1	7.3	2.5
Netherlands	3.0	2.5	3.0	5.9
New Zealand	–	0.0	0.0	–
Norway	0.0	–	–	0.0
Sweden	0.0	–	–	–
Switzerland	0.3	0.7	0.5	0.5
United Kingdom	3.1	1.6	3.8	4.4
United States	8.0	-10.0	-29.0	-17.0
TOTAL	*2.2*	*-14.0*	*-34.7*	*-13.2*
AF.D.F.	–	–	–	–
AF.D.B.	–	–	–	–
AS.D.B.	–	–	–	–
CAR.D.B.	–	–	–	–
E.E.C.	3.9	13.5	0.5	–
IBRD	–	–	–	–
IDA	-0.2	-0.2	-0.2	-0.2
I.D.B.	-0.1	3.4	2.0	-3.0
IFAD	–	–	–	–
I.F.C.	–	–	–	–
IMF TRUST FUND	–	–	–	–
U.N. AGENCIES	–	–	–	–
UNDP	3.7	3.2	3.4	4.9
UNTA	0.4	0.5	0.4	0.2
UNICEF	0.1	0.6	0.5	0.3
UNRWA	–	–	–	–
WFP	–	–	–	–
UNHCR	0.4	0.3	0.2	0.2
Other Multilateral	0.9	0.5	0.8	1.2
Arab OPEC Agencies	–	–	–	–
TOTAL	*9.1*	*21.7*	*7.5*	*3.5*
OPEC COUNTRIES	–	–	–	–
E.E.C.+ MEMBERS	*-4.3*	*7.7*	*-12.9*	*0.8*
TOTAL	***11.2***	***7.7***	***-27.1***	***-9.7***

TOTAL ODA GROSS

	197[…]
Australia	0[…]
Austria	0[…]
Belgium	1[…]
Canada	0[…]
Denmark	0[…]
Finland	
France	0[…]
Germany, Fed. Rep.	9[…]
Italy	0[…]
Japan	2[…]
Netherlands	3[…]
New Zealand	
Norway	0[…]
Sweden	
Switzerland	0[…]
United Kingdom	3[…]
United States	35[…]
TOTAL	*55[…]*
AF.D.F.	
AF.D.B.	
AS.D.B.	
CAR.D.B.	
E.E.C.	3[…]
IBRD	
IDA	
I.D.B.	6[…]
IFAD	
I.F.C.	
IMF TRUST FUND	
U.N. AGENCIES	
UNDP	3[…]
UNTA	0[…]
UNICEF	0[…]
UNRWA	
WFP	
UNHCR	0[…]
Other Multilateral	0[…]
Arab OPEC Agencies	
TOTAL	*15[…]*
OPEC COUNTRIES	
E.E.C.+ MEMBERS	*21[…]*
TOTAL	***71[…]***

ODA LOANS GROSS

DAC COUNTRIES	1977	1978	1979	1980
Australia	–	–	–	–
Austria	–	–	–	–
Belgium	–	–	–	–
Canada	–	–	–	–
Denmark	–	–	–	–
Finland	–	–	–	–
France	0.1	0.1	0.1	–
Germany, Fed. Rep.	0.1	0.0	–	–
Italy	–	–	–	–
Japan	–	–	3.7	0.8
Netherlands	–	–	–	–
New Zealand	–	–	–	–
Norway	–	–	–	–
Sweden	–	–	–	–
Switzerland	–	–	–	–
United Kingdom	–	–	–	–
United States	15.0	10.0	4.0	3.0
TOTAL	*15.2*	*10.1*	*7.8*	*3.8*
MULTILATERAL	*6.5*	*11.6*	*10.7*	*5.7*
OPEC COUNTRIES	–	–	–	–
E.E.C.+ MEMBERS	*0.2*	*0.1*	*0.1*	–
TOTAL	***21.7***	***21.7***	***18.5***	***9.5***

ODA LOANS NET

	1977	1978	1979	1980
Australia	–	–	–	–
Austria	–	–	–	–
Belgium	–	–	–	–
Canada	-0.2	-0.3	-0.2	-0.3
Denmark	–	–	–	–
Finland	–	–	–	–
France	-5.6	-5.3	-6.2	-6.5
Germany, Fed. Rep.	-15.0	-16.8	-30.5	-19.8
Italy	-4.9	-0.7	-0.7	-0.7
Japan	–	-1.3	2.5	-0.4
Netherlands	–	-1.6	-0.7	-0.9
New Zealand	–	–	–	–
Norway	–	–	–	–
Sweden	0.0	–	–	–
Switzerland	–	–	–	–
United Kingdom	-0.6	-0.5	-0.7	-0.3
United States	-12.0	-20.0	-40.0	-24.0
TOTAL	*-38.3*	*-46.5*	*-76.6*	*-52.8*
MULTILATERAL	*-0.4*	*3.2*	*1.8*	*-3.2*
OPEC COUNTRIES	–	–	–	–
E.E.C.+ MEMBERS	*-26.0*	*-24.9*	*-38.8*	*-28.1*
TOTAL	***-38.6***	***-43.3***	***-74.8***	***-56.1***

GRANTS

	197[…]
Australia	0[…]
Austria	0[…]
Belgium	1[…]
Canada	0[…]
Denmark	0[…]
Finland	
France	
Germany, Fed. Rep.	9[…]
Italy	0[…]
Japan	2[…]
Netherlands	3[…]
New Zealand	
Norway	0[…]
Sweden	
Switzerland	0[…]
United Kingdom	3[…]
United States	20[…]
TOTAL	*40[…]*
MULTILATERAL	*9[…]*
OPEC COUNTRIES	
E.E.C.+ MEMBERS	*21[…]*
TOTAL	***49[…]***

TOTAL OFFICIAL GROSS

DAC COUNTRIES	1977	1978	1979	1980
Australia	0.0	0.4	3.7	0.1
Austria	0.1	0.2	0.2	0.2
Belgium	1.4	0.6	0.7	1.1
Canada	0.0	0.8	8.6	9.1
Denmark	0.1	–	0.1	0.1
Finland	–	–	–	0.0
France	0.1	0.1	0.1	1.7
Germany, Fed. Rep.	9.8	12.3	16.4	14.0
Italy	12.1	0.1	0.1	0.6
Japan	2.2	2.3	8.5	3.7
Netherlands	3.0	4.1	3.7	6.7
New Zealand	–	0.0	0.0	–
Norway	0.0	–	–	0.0
Sweden	–	–	–	–
Switzerland	0.3	0.7	0.5	0.5
United Kingdom	3.6	2.1	4.5	4.7
United States	127.0	66.0	15.0	10.0
TOTAL	*159.7*	*89.7*	*62.0*	*52.5*
MULTILATERAL	*63.5*	*65.8*	*54.4*	*58.6*
OPEC COUNTRIES	–	–	–	–
E.E.C.+ MEMBERS	*34.0*	*32.7*	*26.0*	*28.9*
TOTAL	***223.2***	***155.6***	***116.4***	***111.1***

TOTAL OFFICIAL NET

	1977	1978	1979	1980
Australia	0.0	0.4	3.7	-0.2
Austria	0.1	0.2	0.2	0.2
Belgium	0.9	-0.6	-0.6	-0.2
Canada	-2.1	-4.9	5.9	7.6
Denmark	0.1	–	0.1	0.1
Finland	–	–	–	0.0
France	-12.3	-11.9	-13.2	-11.8
Germany, Fed. Rep.	-11.5	-16.7	-33.9	-16.4
Italy	7.2	-2.4	-2.4	-1.8
Japan	2.2	1.1	7.3	2.5
Netherlands	3.0	2.2	2.6	5.6
New Zealand	–	0.0	0.0	–
Norway	0.0	–	–	0.0
Sweden	0.0	–	–	–
Switzerland	-2.0	-2.2	-0.7	-0.1
United Kingdom	3.1	1.6	3.8	4.4
United States	33.0	-22.0	-148.0	-63.0
TOTAL	*21.7*	*-55.3*	*-175.2*	*-73.2*
MULTILATERAL	*39.5*	*40.2*	*33.4*	*29.4*
OPEC COUNTRIES	–	–	–	–
E.E.C.+ MEMBERS	*-5.6*	*-14.3*	*-43.2*	*-20.2*
TOTAL	***61.1***	***-15.1***	***-141.8***	***-43.8***

TOTAL OOF GROSS

	197[…]
Australia	
Austria	
Belgium	
Canada	
Denmark	
Finland	
France	
Germany, Fed. Rep.	0[…]
Italy	12[…]
Japan	
Netherlands	
New Zealand	
Norway	
Sweden	
Switzerland	
United Kingdom	
United States	92[…]
TOTAL	*104[…]*
MULTILATERAL	*47[…]*
OPEC COUNTRIES	
E.E.C.+ MEMBERS	*12[…]*
TOTAL	***151[…]***

1978	1979	1980	1977	1978	1979	1980
			ODA COMMITMENTS			
0.0	–	0.0	0.0	–	–	–
0.2	0.2	0.2	–	–	–	–
0.6	0.7	1.1	1.8	–	–	1.4
0.1	–	0.0	0.0	0.2	0.0	–
–	0.1	0.1	0.1	0.1	0.1	0.2
–	–	0.0	–	–	–	–
0.1	0.1	1.7	–	–	–	1.5
12.3	16.4	14.0	8.6	14.6	19.3	15.4
0.1	0.1	0.6	0.1	0.1	0.1	0.6
2.3	8.5	3.7	2.5	5.1	8.3	4.1
4.1	3.7	6.7	2.5	2.3	4.2	8.7
0.0	0.0	–	0.0	0.0	–	–
–	–	0.0	–	–	–	–
–	–	–	–	–	–	–
0.7	0.5	0.5	–	–	–	0.5
2.1	4.5	4.7	3.6	2.1	4.5	4.7
20.0	15.0	10.0	18.5	6.5	9.9	5.8
42.6	*49.7*	*43.4*	*37.7*	*31.0*	*46.5*	*42.8*
–	–	–	–	–	–	–
–	–	–	–	–	–	–
–	–	–	–	–	–	–
–	–	–	–	–	–	–
13.5	0.5	–	4.4	0.1	0.8	0.2
–	–	–	–	–	–	–
–	–	–	–	–	–	–
11.6	10.7	5.7	–	–	–	–
–	–	–	–	–	–	–
–	–	–	–	–	–	–
–	–	–	–	–	–	–
–	–	–	5.5	5.1	5.3	6.7
3.2	3.4	4.9	–	–	–	–
0.5	0.4	0.2	–	–	–	–
0.6	0.5	0.3	–	–	–	–
–	–	–	–	–	–	–
–	–	–	–	–	–	–
0.3	0.2	0.2	–	–	–	–
0.5	0.8	1.2	–	–	–	–
–	–	–	–	–	–	–
30.1	*16.5*	*12.4*	*9.9*	*5.1*	*6.1*	*6.9*
–	–	–	–	–	–	–
32.7	*26.0*	*28.9*	*21.1*	*19.3*	*29.1*	*32.6*
72.7	***66.2***	***55.8***	***47.6***	***36.1***	***52.6***	***49.8***
			TECH. COOP. GRANTS			
0.0	–	0.0	0.0	–	–	–
0.2	0.2	0.2	0.1	0.2	0.2	0.2
0.6	0.7	1.1	1.1	0.5	0.6	0.6
0.1	–	0.0	0.0	–	–	–
–	0.1	0.1	0.0	–	0.0	0.1
–	–	0.0	–	–	–	0.0
–	–	1.7	–	–	–	1.7
12.3	16.4	14.0	10.2	12.2	16.3	14.0
0.1	0.1	0.6	0.1	0.1	0.1	0.6
2.3	4.8	2.9	2.2	2.3	2.5	2.7
4.1	3.7	6.7	2.9	0.9	1.5	4.9
0.0	0.0	–	–	–	0.0	–
–	–	0.0	0.0	–	–	–
–	–	–	–	–	–	–
0.7	0.5	0.5	0.0	0.0	–	–
2.1	4.5	4.7	3.6	2.1	4.5	4.7
10.0	11.0	7.0	3.0	1.0	1.0	1.0
32.5	*41.9*	*39.6*	*23.2*	*19.3*	*26.8*	*30.5*
18.5	*5.8*	*6.7*	*5.5*	*5.1*	*5.3*	*6.7*
–	–	–	–	–	–	–
32.6	*25.9*	*28.9*	*17.9*	*15.7*	*23.1*	*26.5*
51.0	***47.7***	***46.4***	***28.7***	***24.3***	***32.1***	***37.2***
			TOTAL OOF NET			
0.4	3.7	0.1	–	0.4	3.7	-0.2
–	–	–	–	–	–	–
–	–	–	-0.5	-1.2	-1.3	-1.3
0.7	8.6	9.1	-1.9	-4.7	6.2	7.9
–	–	–	–	–	–	–
–	–	–	–	–	–	–
–	–	–	-6.7	-6.6	-7.0	-7.0
–	–	–	-6.1	-12.2	-19.7	-10.6
–	–	–	12.0	-1.8	-1.8	-1.8
–	–	–	–	–	–	–
–	–	–	–	-0.2	-0.4	-0.3
–	–	–	–	–	–	–
–	–	–	–	–	–	–
–	–	–	–	–	–	–
–	–	–	-2.3	-2.9	-1.2	-0.6
–	–	–	–	–	–	–
46.0	–	–	25.0	-12.0	-119.0	-46.0
47.2	*12.3*	*9.1*	*19.5*	*-41.2*	*-140.5*	*-59.9*
35.7	*37.9*	*46.2*	*30.4*	*18.5*	*25.8*	*25.9*
–	–	–	–	–	–	–
–	–	–	*-1.3*	*-22.0*	*-30.2*	*-21.0*
82.9	***50.2***	***55.3***	***49.9***	***-22.7***	***-114.7***	***-34.1***

MAIN AID AGGREGATES

	1977	1978	1979	1980
DAC COUNTRIES COMBINED				
PRIVATE SECTOR NET	-184.3	144.1	430.5	443.8
Direct Investment	-43.1	25.9	138.7	82.9
Portfolio Invest.	-98.1	139.8	333.9	352.1
Export Credits	-43.1	-21.6	-42.1	8.7
OFFICIAL & PRIVATE GROSS:				
Contractual Lending	185.7	97.3	90.8	98.1
Export Credits Tot.	67.4	87.2	81.4	94.3
Export Credits Priv	66.4	40.0	70.7	85.2
OTHER NET DATA				
Contractual Lending	-61.9	-109.3	-259.3	-104.0
Export Credits Tot.	-94.1	-19.8	-128.3	-18.4
(Bank Sector Loans)	249.0	1031.0	982.0	1249.0
ODA CONCESSIONALITY				
Total:Grant Element	99.0	100.0	92.0	98.0
Loans:Grant Element	43.0	–	30.0	27.0
OTHER SOURCES				
CMEA Countr.(Gross)	–	–	–	–
Intra LDCS Exc.OPEC	–	–	–	–
Other	–	–	–	–
ALL SOURCE COMMITMENTS				
TOTAL BILATERAL	140.8	91.0	50.3	66.0
of which				
OPEC (ODA)	–	–	–	–
CMEA (ODA)	–	–	–	–
TOTAL MULTILAT.(ODA)	9.9	5.1	6.1	6.9
TOTAL BIL.& MULTIL.	150.6	96.1	56.4	73.0
of which				
ODA Grants	47.5	36.1	47.4	49.0
ODA Loans	0.1	–	5.2	0.8
ODA CONCESSIONALITY				
Total: Grant Element	94.0	92.0	93.0	98.0
Loans: Grant Element	62.0	44.0	30.0	27.0

INDEBTEDNESS

	1977	1978	1979	1980
TOTAL DEBT DISBURSED	***3781.1***	***5142.8***	***7049.8***	
Debt to DAC Countries	2924.0	4259.0	5550.0	
ODA	888.0	843.0	776.0	
Total Export Credits	953.0	916.0	646.0	
Other Private Market	1083.0	2500.0	4128.0	
International Org.	289.8	296.0	323.8	
CMEA	131.5	119.3	57.2	
Other	435.8	468.4	1118.8	
TOTAL DEBT SERVICE	***856.3***	***1470.5***	***1578.2***	
Paid to DAC Countries	687.0	1207.8	1218.2	
ODA	74.8	77.7	104.7	
Total Export Credits	386.9	359.9	464.8	
Other Private Market	225.3	770.2	648.7	
International Org.	42.2	68.1	37.6	
CMEA	25.7	71.1	78.4	
Other	101.4	123.5	244.1	

ECONOMIC INDICATORS

	1977	1978	1979	1980
GNP Curr. Prices, $M	13013.0	14978.6	19783.9	27167.5
Real GNP, 1976=100	109.0	118.0	128.0	137.0
GNP/Cap Curr. Prices,$	1233.0	1395.0	1812.0	2446.0
GNP/cap Atlas Basis, $	1426.5	1630.0	1892.4	2159.9
Real GNP/Cap, 1976=100	107.0	114.0	122.0	128.0
Population, Million	10.5	10.7	10.9	11.1
Curr.A/C Deficit(-),$M	-544.0	-1089.0	-1190.0	-1785.0
BOP Exp. & Transf.,$M	2667.0	3082.0	4851.0	6212.0
Exp. to OECD CIF, $M	1494.9	1856.8	2709.8	3255.7
of which				
Manufact.	41.3	50.0	66.4	84.8
Imp. from OECD FOB, $M	1191.1	1584.9	2092.9	2988.8
Reserves ex. Gold, $M	426.5	1090.1	1938.4	3123.2

TOTAL RECEIPTS NET / TOTAL ODA NET

	TOTAL RECEIPTS NET 1977	1978	1979	1980	TOTAL ODA NET 1977	1978	1979	1980
DAC COUNTRIES								
Australia	–	–	0.0	-2.1	–	–	0.0	0.1
Austria	–	–	0.1	0.1	–	–	0.1	0.1
Belgium	–	–	–	47.5	–	–	–	10.4
Canada	–	–	–	–	–	–	–	–
Denmark	–	–	13.3	0.1	–	–	–	0.0
Finland	–	–	–	0.1	–	–	–	0.1
France	–	–	–	48.4	–	–	–	–
Germany, Fed. Rep.	–	–	51.0	-363.3	–	–	1.3	6.5
Italy	–	–	0.2	48.6	–	–	0.1	0.2
Japan	–	–	39.6	290.6	–	–	2.6	4.3
Netherlands	–	–	–	–	–	–	–	–
New Zealand	–	–	–	–	–	–	–	–
Norway	–	–	–	0.5	–	–	–	0.5
Sweden	–	–	0.1	–	–	–	0.1	–
Switzerland	–	–	0.1	–	–	–	0.1	–
United Kingdom	–	–	–	110.9	–	–	–	0.1
United States	–	–	12.0	105.0	–	–	–	–
TOTAL	–	–	*116.4*	*286.2*	–	–	*4.3*	*22.2*
MULTILATERAL								
AF.D.F.	–	–	–	–	–	–	–	–
AF.D.B.	–	–	–	–	–	–	–	–
AS.D.B.	–	–	–	-6.5	–	–	–	–
CAR.D.B.	–	–	–	–	–	–	–	–
E.E.C.	–	–	–	–	–	–	–	–
IBRD	–	–	–	–	–	–	–	–
IDA	–	–	–	–	–	–	–	–
I.D.B.	–	–	–	–	–	–	–	–
IFAD	–	–	–	–	–	–	–	–
I.F.C.	–	–	–	–	–	–	–	–
IMF TRUST FUND	–	–	–	–	–	–	–	–
U.N. AGENCIES	–	–	–	–	–	–	–	–
UNDP	–	–	1.2	11.6	–	–	1.2	11.6
UNTA	–	–	1.7	0.2	–	–	1.7	0.2
UNICEF	–	–	–	0.2	–	–	–	0.2
UNRWA	–	–	–	–	–	–	–	–
WFP	–	–	3.5	7.0	–	–	3.5	7.0
UNHCR	–	–	6.2	11.6	–	–	6.2	11.6
Other Multilateral	–	–	0.1	13.3	–	–	0.1	13.3
Arab OPEC Agencies	–	–	–	–	–	–	–	–
TOTAL	–	–	*12.6*	*37.4*	–	–	*12.6*	*43.9*
OPEC COUNTRIES	–	–	–	–	–	–	–	–
E.E.C.+ MEMBERS	–	–	*64.5*	*-108.0*	–	–	*1.5*	*17.2*
TOTAL	–	–	***129.0***	***323.6***	–	–	***16.9***	***66.1***

ODA LOANS GROSS / ODA LOANS NET

	ODA LOANS GROSS 1977	1978	1979	1980	ODA LOANS NET 1977	1978	1979	1980
DAC COUNTRIES								
Australia	–	–	–	–	–	–	–	–
Austria	–	–	–	–	–	–	–	–
Belgium	–	–	–	10.3	–	–	–	10.3
Canada	–	–	–	–	–	–	–	–
Denmark	–	–	–	–	–	–	–	–
Finland	–	–	–	–	–	–	–	–
France	–	–	–	–	–	–	–	–
Germany, Fed. Rep.	–	–	–	–	–	–	–	–
Italy	–	–	–	–	–	–	–	–
Japan	–	–	–	0.9	–	–	–	0.9
Netherlands	–	–	–	–	–	–	–	–
New Zealand	–	–	–	–	–	–	–	–
Norway	–	–	–	–	–	–	–	–
Sweden	–	–	–	–	–	–	–	–
Switzerland	–	–	–	–	–	–	–	–
United Kingdom	–	–	–	–	–	–	–	–
United States	–	–	–	–	–	–	–	–
TOTAL	–	–	–	*11.2*	–	–	–	*11.2*
MULTILATERAL	–	–	–	–	–	–	–	–
OPEC COUNTRIES	–	–	–	–	–	–	–	–
E.E.C.+ MEMBERS	–	–	–	*10.3*	–	–	–	*10.3*
TOTAL	–	–	–	***11.2***	–	–	–	***11.2***

TOTAL OFFICIAL GROSS / TOTAL OFFICIAL NET

	TOTAL OFFICIAL GROSS 1977	1978	1979	1980	TOTAL OFFICIAL NET 1977	1978	1979	1980
DAC COUNTRIES								
Australia	–	–	0.0	0.1	–	–	0.0	-2.1
Austria	–	–	0.1	0.1	–	–	0.1	0.1
Belgium	–	–	–	10.4	–	–	–	10.4
Canada	–	–	–	–	–	–	–	–
Denmark	–	–	–	0.1	–	–	–	0.1
Finland	–	–	–	0.1	–	–	–	0.1
France	–	–	–	48.4	–	–	–	48.4
Germany, Fed. Rep.	–	–	1.3	6.5	–	–	1.3	6.5
Italy	–	–	0.1	0.2	–	–	0.1	0.2
Japan	–	–	2.6	407.6	–	–	2.6	407.6
Netherlands	–	–	–	–	–	–	–	–
New Zealand	–	–	–	–	–	–	–	–
Norway	–	–	–	0.5	–	–	–	0.5
Sweden	–	–	0.1	–	–	–	0.1	–
Switzerland	–	–	0.1	–	–	–	0.1	–
United Kingdom	–	–	–	0.1	–	–	–	0.1
United States	–	–	–	–	–	–	–	–
TOTAL	–	–	*4.3*	*473.9*	–	–	*4.3*	*471.7*
MULTILATERAL	–	–	*12.6*	*43.9*	–	–	*12.6*	*37.4*
OPEC COUNTRIES	–	–	–	–	–	–	–	–
E.E.C.+ MEMBERS	–	–	*1.5*	*65.6*	–	–	*1.5*	*65.6*
TOTAL	–	–	***16.9***	***517.8***	–	–	***16.9***	***509.1***

TOTAL ODA GROSS

	197
Australia	
Austria	
Belgium	
Canada	
Denmark	
Finland	
France	
Germany, Fed. Rep.	
Italy	
Japan	
Netherlands	
New Zealand	
Norway	
Sweden	
Switzerland	
United Kingdom	
United States	
TOTAL	
AF.D.F.	
AF.D.B.	
AS.D.B.	
CAR.D.B.	
E.E.C.	
IBRD	
IDA	
I.D.B.	
IFAD	
I.F.C.	
IMF TRUST FUND	
U.N. AGENCIES	
UNDP	
UNTA	
UNICEF	
UNRWA	
WFP	
UNHCR	
Other Multilateral	
Arab OPEC Agencies	
TOTAL	
OPEC COUNTRIES	
E.E.C.+ MEMBERS	
TOTAL	

GRANTS

Australia	
Austria	
Belgium	
Canada	
Denmark	
Finland	
France	
Germany, Fed. Rep.	
Italy	
Japan	
Netherlands	
New Zealand	
Norway	
Sweden	
Switzerland	
United Kingdom	
United States	
TOTAL	
MULTILATERAL	
OPEC COUNTRIES	
E.E.C.+ MEMBERS	
TOTAL	

TOTAL OOF GROSS

Australia	
Austria	
Belgium	
Canada	
Denmark	
Finland	
France	
Germany, Fed. Rep.	
Italy	
Japan	
Netherlands	
New Zealand	
Norway	
Sweden	
Switzerland	
United Kingdom	
United States	
TOTAL	
MULTILATERAL	
OPEC COUNTRIES	
E.E.C.+ MEMBERS	
TOTAL	

1978	1979	1980	1977	1978	1979	1980
			ODA COMMITMENTS			
–	0.0	0.1	–	–	–	0.2
–	0.1	0.1	–	–	–	–
–	–	10.4	–	–	–	10.3
–	–	–	–	–	–	–
–	–	0.0	–	–	–	–
–	–	0.1	–	–	–	–
–	–	–	–	–	–	–
–	1.3	6.5	–	–	1.3	7.0
–	0.1	0.2	–	–	0.1	0.2
–	2.6	4.3	–	–	3.1	471.3
–	–	–	–	–	–	–
–	–	–	–	–	–	–
–	–	0.5	–	–	–	0.5
–	0.1	–	–	–	0.2	–
–	0.1	–	–	–	–	–
–	–	0.1	–	–	–	0.1
–	–	–	–	–	–	–
–	*4.3*	*22.2*	–	–	*4.7*	*489.5*
–	–	–	–	–	–	–
–	–	–	–	–	–	–
–	–	–	–	–	–	–
–	–	–	–	–	–	–
–	–	–	–	–	0.1	–
–	–	–	–	–	–	–
–	–	–	–	–	–	–
–	–	–	–	–	–	–
–	–	–	–	–	–	–
–	–	–	–	–	–	–
–	–	–	–	–	–	–
–	–	–	–	–	–	43.9
–	1.2	11.6	–	–	–	–
–	1.7	0.2	–	–	–	–
–	–	0.2	–	–	–	–
–	–	–	–	–	–	–
–	3.5	7.0	–	–	–	–
–	6.2	11.6	–	–	–	–
–	0.1	13.3	–	–	–	–
–	–	–	–	–	–	–
–	*12.6*	*43.9*	–	–	*0.1*	*43.9*
–	–	–	–	–	–	–
–	*1.5*	*17.2*	–	–	*1.6*	*17.5*
–	***16.9***	***66.1***	–	–	***4.8***	***533.4***
			TECH. COOP. GRANTS			
–	0.0	0.1	–	–	0.0	0.1
–	0.1	0.1	–	–	0.1	0.1
–	–	0.1	–	–	–	0.1
–	–	–	–	–	–	–
–	–	0.0	–	–	–	0.0
–	–	0.1	–	–	–	–
–	–	–	–	–	–	–
–	1.3	6.5	–	–	1.3	6.5
–	0.1	0.2	–	–	0.1	0.2
–	2.6	3.4	–	–	2.6	3.4
–	–	–	–	–	–	–
–	–	–	–	–	–	–
–	–	0.5	–	–	–	0.5
–	0.1	–	–	–	0.1	–
–	0.1	–	–	–	–	–
–	–	0.1	–	–	–	0.1
–	–	–	–	–	–	–
–	*4.3*	*11.1*	–	–	*4.2*	*11.0*
–	*12.6*	*43.9*	–	–	*12.6*	*43.9*
–	–	–	–	–	–	–
–	*1.5*	*6.9*	–	–	*1.4*	*6.9*
–	***16.9***	***54.9***	–	–	***16.9***	***54.8***
			TOTAL OOF NET			
–	–	–	–	–	–	-2.2
–	–	–	–	–	–	–
–	–	–	–	–	–	–
–	–	–	–	–	–	–
–	–	0.0	–	–	–	0.0
–	–	–	–	–	–	–
–	–	48.4	–	–	–	48.4
–	–	–	–	–	–	–
–	–	–	–	–	–	–
–	–	403.3	–	–	–	403.3
–	–	–	–	–	–	–
–	–	–	–	–	–	–
–	–	–	–	–	–	–
–	–	–	–	–	–	–
–	–	–	–	–	–	–
–	–	–	–	–	–	–
–	–	–	–	–	–	–
–	–	*451.7*	–	–	–	*449.5*
–	–	–	–	–	–	*-6.5*
–	–	–	–	–	–	–
–	–	*48.4*	–	–	–	*48.4*
–	–	***451.7***	–	–	–	***443.0***

	1977	1978	1979	1980
MAIN AID AGGREGATES				
DAC COUNTRIES COMBINED				
PRIVATE SECTOR NET	–	–	112.1	-185.5
Direct Investment	–	–	0.1	23.5
Portfolio Invest.	–	–	64.4	54.8
Export Credits	–	–	47.6	-263.7
OFFICIAL & PRIVATE GROSS:				
Contractual Lending	–	–	199.7	1012.7
Export Credits Tot.	–	–	199.7	953.1
Export Credits Priv	–	–	199.7	549.8
OTHER NET DATA				
Contractual Lending	–	–	47.6	196.9
Export Credits Tot.	–	–	47.6	137.4
(Bank Sector Loans)	–	–	–	–
ODA CONCESSIONALITY				
Total:Grant Element	–	–	100.0	58.0
Loans:Grant Element	–	–	–	57.0
OTHER SOURCES				
CMEA Countr.(Gross)	–	–	–	–
Intra LDCS Exc.OPEC	–	–	–	–
Other	–	–	–	–
ALL SOURCE COMMITMENTS				
TOTAL BILATERAL	–	–	4.7	1212.0
of which				
OPEC (ODA)	–	–	–	–
CMEA (ODA)	–	–	–	–
TOTAL MULTILAT.(ODA)	–	–	0.1	43.9
TOTAL BIL.& MULTIL.	–	–	4.8	1255.9
of which				
ODA Grants	–	–	4.8	55.7
ODA Loans	–	–	–	477.8
ODA CONCESSIONALITY				
Total: Grant Element	–	–	100.0	62.0
Loans: Grant Element	–	–	–	57.0
INDEBTEDNESS				
TOTAL DEBT DISBURSED	–	–	–	
Debt to DAC Countries	–	–	–	
ODA	–	–	–	
Total Export Credits	–	–	–	
Other Private Market	–	–	–	
International Org.	–	–	–	
CMEA	–	–	–	
Other	–	–	–	
TOTAL DEBT SERVICE	–	–	–	
Paid to DAC Countries	–	–	–	
ODA	–	–	–	
Total Export Credits	–	–	–	
Other Private Market	–	–	–	
International Org.	–	–	–	
CMEA	–	–	–	
Other	–	–	–	
ECONOMIC INDICATORS				
GNP Curr. Prices, $M	–	–	–	–
Real GNP, 1976=100	–	–	–	–
GNP/Cap Curr. Prices,$	–	–	–	–
GNP/cap Atlas Basis, $	–	–	–	–
Real GNP/Cap, 1976=100	–	–	–	–
Population, Million	939.0	951.7	964.5	976.7
Curr.A/C Deficit(-),$M	–	–	–	–
BOP Exp. & Transf.,$M	–	–	–	–
Exp. to OECD CIF, $M	3151.9	4078.6	6160.2	8922.3
of which				
Manufact.	1207.9	1588.1	2479.7	3520.7
Imp. from OECD FOB, $M	4145.2	7154.5	10159.2	13403.4
Reserves ex. Gold, $M	2345.0	1557.0	2154.0	2545.0

	1977	1978	1979	1980	1977	1978	1979	1980
TOTAL RECEIPTS NET					**TOTAL ODA NET**			
DAC COUNTRIES								
Australia	–	–	–	–	–	–	–	–
Austria	0.0	-0.1	-0.2	-0.1	0.2	0.2	0.1	0.2
Belgium	0.7	2.5	8.3	28.3	1.4	0.7	2.2	2.3
Canada	4.3	13.1	10.8	5.7	4.7	5.1	6.9	5.3
Denmark	-0.1	-0.1	31.1	-0.1	-0.1	-0.1	-0.1	-0.1
Finland	–	–	1.1	0.3	–	–	0.0	0.0
France	6.1	44.8	4.6	66.0	1.2	5.8	0.3	1.2
Germany, Fed. Rep.	19.4	64.4	40.4	68.0	10.9	16.2	14.4	19.6
Italy	29.3	-3.3	-14.7	94.1	0.4	0.3	0.5	0.2
Japan	2.2	-1.9	3.2	14.6	1.5	2.2	1.9	4.3
Netherlands	11.3	7.5	18.9	27.9	9.9	7.5	8.4	10.8
New Zealand	–	–	–	–	–	–	–	–
Norway	0.0	–	-0.1	-0.1	0.0	–	–	0.0
Sweden	-0.2	–	0.5	-0.2	–	–	0.2	–
Switzerland	5.4	-1.9	-0.3	0.1	0.2	0.4	0.7	0.5
United Kingdom	9.5	7.2	2.7	-4.0	2.0	1.3	2.1	1.5
United States	46.0	125.0	269.0	287.0	-1.0	12.0	-8.0	-14.0
TOTAL	*133.9*	*257.2*	*375.4*	*587.5*	*31.4*	*51.7*	*29.4*	*31.8*
MULTILATERAL								
AF.D.F.	–	–	–	–	–	–	–	–
AF.D.B.	–	–	–	–	–	–	–	–
AS.D.B.	–	–	–	–	–	–	–	–
CAR.D.B.	–	–	–	–	–	–	–	–
E.E.C.	–	0.1	0.2	–	–	0.1	0.2	–
IBRD	44.7	35.2	87.0	152.3	–	–	–	–
IDA	-0.2	-0.2	-0.2	-0.2	-0.2	-0.2	-0.2	-0.2
I.D.B.	35.7	32.7	36.2	83.8	8.1	13.1	14.2	47.6
IFAD	–	–	–	–	–	–	–	–
I.F.C.	13.7	1.0	-2.7	-3.1	–	–	–	–
IMF TRUST FUND	–	–	–	–	–	–	–	–
U.N. AGENCIES	–	–	–	–	–	–	–	–
UNDP	2.7	3.7	5.2	5.6	2.7	3.7	5.2	5.6
UNTA	0.4	0.3	0.4	0.5	0.4	0.3	0.4	0.5
UNICEF	0.8	0.9	1.5	1.3	0.8	0.9	1.5	1.3
UNRWA	–	–	–	–	–	–	–	–
WFP	3.5	1.1	2.9	2.1	3.5	1.1	2.9	2.1
UNHCR	–	–	–	–	–	–	–	–
Other Multilateral	3.6	0.8	0.4	1.5	3.6	0.8	0.4	1.5
Arab OPEC Agencies	–	–	–	–	–	–	–	–
TOTAL	*104.8*	*75.5*	*130.9*	*243.7*	*18.8*	*19.7*	*24.6*	*58.3*
OPEC COUNTRIES	–	–	–	–	–	–	–	–
E.E.C.+ MEMBERS	*76.2*	*123.0*	*91.7*	*280.0*	*25.7*	*31.8*	*27.9*	*35.5*
TOTAL	***238.7***	***332.7***	***506.3***	***831.2***	***50.2***	***71.4***	***54.1***	***90.1***

	197
TOTAL ODA GROSS	
Australia	
Austria	0
Belgium	1
Canada	4
Denmark	0
Finland	
France	1
Germany, Fed. Rep.	12
Italy	0
Japan	1
Netherlands	10
New Zealand	
Norway	0
Sweden	
Switzerland	0
United Kingdom	2
United States	16
TOTAL	*51*
AF.D.F.	
AF.D.B.	
AS.D.B.	
CAR.D.B.	
E.E.C.	
IBRD	
IDA	
I.D.B.	15
IFAD	
I.F.C.	
IMF TRUST FUND	
U.N. AGENCIES	
UNDP	2
UNTA	0
UNICEF	0
UNRWA	
WFP	3
UNHCR	
Other Multilateral	3
Arab OPEC Agencies	
TOTAL	*26*
OPEC COUNTRIES	
E.E.C.+ MEMBERS	*28*
TOTAL	***77***

	1977	1978	1979	1980	1977	1978	1979	1980
ODA LOANS GROSS					**ODA LOANS NET**			
DAC COUNTRIES								
Australia	–	–	–	–	–	–	–	–
Austria	–	–	–	–	0.0	0.0	–	–
Belgium	0.7	–	0.9	0.9	0.7	–	0.9	0.9
Canada	1.9	2.9	4.9	4.1	1.9	2.9	4.7	3.7
Denmark	–	–	–	–	-0.1	-0.1	-0.1	-0.1
Finland	–	–	–	–	–	–	–	–
France	1.8	6.1	1.7	0.4	1.2	5.8	0.3	-1.2
Germany, Fed. Rep.	1.1	4.0	1.1	2.8	0.0	2.4	-0.9	-0.3
Italy	–	–	–	–	-0.1	-0.1	–	–
Japan	–	–	–	0.0	–	–	–	0.0
Netherlands	2.6	2.1	1.7	2.3	2.1	1.2	1.0	1.8
New Zealand	–	–	–	–	–	–	–	–
Norway	–	–	–	–	–	–	–	–
Sweden	–	–	–	–	–	–	–	–
Switzerland	–	–	–	–	–	–	–	–
United Kingdom	0.9	0.4	1.2	0.2	0.7	0.0	0.6	-0.3
United States	6.0	20.0	8.0	5.0	-11.0	6.0	-12.0	-16.0
TOTAL	*15.0*	*35.5*	*19.4*	*15.6*	*-4.7*	*18.0*	*-5.5*	*-11.6*
MULTILATERAL	*15.3*	*22.7*	*23.9*	*58.7*	*7.8*	*12.9*	*14.0*	*47.3*
OPEC COUNTRIES	–	–	–	–	–	–	–	–
E.E.C.+ MEMBERS	*7.1*	*12.6*	*6.5*	*6.5*	*4.5*	*9.1*	*1.8*	*0.7*
TOTAL	***30.3***	***58.2***	***43.3***	***74.3***	***3.1***	***30.9***	***8.5***	***35.7***

	197
GRANTS	
Australia	
Austria	0
Belgium	0
Canada	2
Denmark	0
Finland	
France	
Germany, Fed. Rep.	10
Italy	0
Japan	1
Netherlands	7
New Zealand	
Norway	0
Sweden	
Switzerland	0
United Kingdom	1
United States	10
TOTAL	*36*
MULTILATERAL	*11*
OPEC COUNTRIES	
E.E.C.+ MEMBERS	*21*
TOTAL	***47***

	1977	1978	1979	1980	1977	1978	1979	1980
TOTAL OFFICIAL GROSS					**TOTAL OFFICIAL NET**			
DAC COUNTRIES								
Australia	–	–	–	–	–	–	–	–
Austria	0.2	0.2	0.1	0.2	0.0	-0.1	-0.2	-0.1
Belgium	1.4	0.7	2.2	2.3	1.4	0.7	2.2	2.3
Canada	4.7	14.3	14.0	8.8	4.4	13.2	10.8	5.7
Denmark	0.0	0.0	0.0	0.0	-0.1	-0.1	-0.1	-0.1
Finland	–	–	0.0	0.0	–	–	0.0	0.0
France	5.3	13.6	12.8	13.8	4.7	13.3	11.4	12.2
Germany, Fed. Rep.	12.0	28.5	16.3	114.4	8.7	24.5	11.7	99.3
Italy	0.5	0.5	0.5	0.2	0.0	0.1	0.3	-0.2
Japan	1.5	2.2	1.9	4.3	1.1	1.8	1.5	3.9
Netherlands	11.8	8.5	9.0	11.3	11.3	7.5	8.4	10.8
New Zealand	–	–	–	–	–	–	–	–
Norway	0.0	–	–	0.0	0.0	–	–	0.0
Sweden	–	–	0.2	–	–	–	0.2	–
Switzerland	0.2	0.4	0.7	0.5	0.2	0.4	0.7	0.5
United Kingdom	2.1	1.7	2.6	2.0	2.0	1.3	2.1	1.5
United States	21.0	28.0	14.0	22.0	-5.0	4.0	-11.0	-3.0
TOTAL	*60.8*	*98.5*	*74.2*	*179.9*	*28.6*	*66.6*	*37.8*	*132.9*
MULTILATERAL	*165.0*	*144.5*	*208.1*	*332.1*	*104.8*	*75.5*	*130.9*	*243.7*
OPEC COUNTRIES	–	–	–	–	–	–	–	–
E.E.C.+ MEMBERS	*33.2*	*53.4*	*43.7*	*144.0*	*27.9*	*47.5*	*36.2*	*125.7*
TOTAL	***225.8***	***242.9***	***282.4***	***512.0***	***133.4***	***142.1***	***168.7***	***376.6***

	197
TOTAL OOF GROSS	
Australia	
Austria	
Belgium	
Canada	
Denmark	
Finland	
France	3
Germany, Fed. Rep.	
Italy	
Japan	
Netherlands	1
New Zealand	
Norway	
Sweden	
Switzerland	
United Kingdom	
United States	5
TOTAL	*9*
MULTILATERAL	*138*
OPEC COUNTRIES	
E.E.C.+ MEMBERS	*4*
TOTAL	***148***

1978	1979	1980	1977	1978	1979	1980
			ODA COMMITMENTS			
–	–	–	–	–	–	–
0.2	0.1	0.2	–	–	0.0	0.0
0.7	2.2	2.3	0.7	0.8	2.4	1.8
5.2	7.1	5.7	6.7	7.5	1.5	3.4
0.0	0.0	0.0	0.0	–	–	–
–	0.0	0.0	–	–	0.0	0.4
6.1	1.7	2.8	–	–	–	1.8
17.7	16.3	22.7	20.5	20.6	22.8	35.8
0.5	0.5	0.2	0.5	0.5	0.5	0.2
2.2	1.9	4.3	2.7	0.9	5.0	56.7
8.5	9.0	11.3	10.3	16.5	15.3	9.4
–	–	–	–	–	–	0.0
–	–	0.0	–	–	–	–
–	0.2	–	–	–	–	–
0.4	0.7	0.5	1.0	–	0.1	0.3
1.7	2.6	2.0	1.3	1.3	1.4	1.8
26.0	12.0	7.0	7.3	4.3	5.8	17.0
69.1	*54.3*	*59.0*	*50.8*	*52.5*	*54.7*	*128.6*
–	–	–	–	–	–	–
–	–	–	–	–	–	–
–	–	–	–	–	–	–
–	–	–	–	–	–	–
0.1	0.2	–	–	0.1	0.5	0.0
–	–	–	–	–	–	–
–	–	–	–	–	–	–
22.7	23.9	58.8	37.4	52.5	86.0	103.6
–	–	–	–	–	–	–
–	–	–	–	–	–	–
–	–	–	–	–	–	–
–	–	–	11.0	6.8	10.4	11.0
3.7	5.2	5.6	–	–	–	–
0.3	0.4	0.5	–	–	–	–
0.9	1.5	1.3	–	–	–	–
–	–	–	–	–	–	–
1.1	2.9	2.1	–	–	–	–
–	–	–	–	–	–	–
0.8	0.4	1.5	–	–	–	–
–	–	–	–	–	–	–
29.5	*34.6*	*69.8*	*48.4*	*59.3*	*96.9*	*114.6*
–	–	–	–	–	–	–
35.2	*32.5*	*41.3*	*33.2*	*39.7*	*42.9*	*50.9*
98.7	***88.9***	***128.8***	***99.2***	***111.8***	***151.7***	***243.3***
			TECH. COOP. GRANTS			
–	–	–	–	–	–	–
0.2	0.1	0.2	0.2	0.2	0.1	0.2
0.7	1.3	1.5	0.6	0.6	0.7	0.8
2.2	2.2	1.6	0.7	0.7	0.6	0.5
0.0	0.0	0.0	0.0	0.0	0.0	0.0
–	0.0	0.0	–	–	0.0	0.0
–	–	2.4	–	–	–	2.4
13.8	15.3	19.9	10.9	13.8	15.2	19.9
0.5	0.5	0.2	0.5	0.5	0.4	0.2
2.2	1.9	4.2	0.7	0.8	1.9	2.1
6.3	7.4	9.0	7.5	6.0	7.1	8.2
–	–	–	–	–	–	–
–	–	0.0	0.0	–	–	0.0
–	0.2	–	–	–	–	–
0.4	0.7	0.5	0.0	–	0.0	0.2
1.3	1.4	1.8	1.3	1.3	1.4	1.8
6.0	4.0	2.0	3.0	3.0	1.0	1.0
33.6	*34.9*	*43.4*	*25.3*	*26.8*	*28.5*	*37.4*
6.8	*10.7*	*11.1*	*7.5*	*5.7*	*7.6*	*11.0*
–	–	–	–	–	–	–
22.7	*26.1*	*34.7*	*20.7*	*22.1*	*24.8*	*33.3*
40.5	***45.6***	***54.4***	***32.8***	***32.5***	***36.0***	***48.4***
			TOTAL OOF NET			
–	–	–	–	–	–	–
–	–	–	-0.2	-0.3	-0.3	-0.3
–	–	–	–	–	–	–
9.1	6.8	3.2	-0.3	8.0	3.9	0.5
–	0.0	–	–	–	0.0	–
–	–	–	–	–	–	–
7.5	11.1	11.1	3.5	7.5	11.1	11.1
10.7	–	91.7	-2.2	8.4	-2.6	79.7
–	–	–	-0.4	-0.2	-0.2	-0.5
–	–	–	-0.3	-0.4	-0.4	-0.4
–	–	–	1.3	–	–	–
–	–	–	–	–	–	–
–	–	–	–	–	–	–
–	–	–	–	–	–	–
–	–	–	–	–	–	–
–	–	–	–	–	–	–
2.0	2.0	15.0	-4.0	-8.0	-3.0	11.0
29.4	*20.0*	*120.9*	*-2.7*	*15.0*	*8.4*	*101.0*
114.9	*173.6*	*262.3*	*86.0*	*55.8*	*106.3*	*185.4*
–	–	–	–	–	–	–
18.2	*11.1*	*102.7*	*2.2*	*15.7*	*8.3*	*90.3*
144.3	***193.5***	***383.2***	***83.3***	***70.8***	***114.7***	***286.4***

MAIN AID AGGREGATES

	1977	1978	1979	1980
DAC COUNTRIES COMBINED				
PRIVATE SECTOR NET	105.3	190.6	337.6	454.6
Direct Investment	63.4	78.7	95.7	113.4
Portfolio Invest.	-14.9	82.3	273.3	183.7
Export Credits	56.8	29.6	-31.3	157.6
OFFICIAL & PRIVATE GROSS:				
Contractual Lending	176.3	235.4	205.0	534.3
Export Credits Tot.	156.5	192.4	174.5	507.7
Export Credits Priv	151.5	170.6	165.7	397.8
OTHER NET DATA				
Contractual Lending	49.4	62.6	-28.4	247.1
Export Credits Tot.	49.6	37.2	-34.0	247.6
(Bank Sector Loans)	650.0	-397.0	480.0	570.0
ODA CONCESSIONALITY				
Total:Grant Element	87.0	86.0	94.0	64.0
Loans:Grant Element	58.0	56.0	53.0	35.0
OTHER SOURCES				
CMEA Countr.(Gross)	1.5	3.5	0.5	1.0
Intra LDCS Exc.OPEC	–	–	–	–
Other	–	–	–	–
ALL SOURCE COMMITMENTS				
TOTAL BILATERAL	59.4	192.0	94.1	213.5
of which				
OPEC (ODA)	–	–	–	–
CMEA (ODA)	–	–	–	–
TOTAL MULTILAT.(ODA)	48.4	59.3	96.9	114.6
TOTAL BIL.& MULTIL.	107.8	251.3	191.0	328.1
of which				
ODA Grants	46.3	45.1	58.8	69.6
ODA Loans	52.9	66.7	92.8	173.7
ODA CONCESSIONALITY				
Total: Grant Element	78.0	86.0	77.0	66.0
Loans: Grant Element	62.0	55.0	56.0	47.0

INDEBTEDNESS

	1977	1978	1979	1980
TOTAL DEBT DISBURSED	***2999.3***	***3166.9***	***3701.1***	
Debt to DAC Countries	2007.0	2094.0	2440.0	
ODA	889.0	908.0	908.0	
Total Export Credits	286.0	434.0	630.0	
Other Private Market	832.0	752.0	902.0	
International Org.	933.7	1016.4	1139.3	
CMEA	0.2	0.1	0.0	
Other	58.4	56.3	121.8	
TOTAL DEBT SERVICE	***403.5***	***545.2***	***711.7***	
Paid to DAC Countries	273.5	388.8	529.8	
ODA	38.6	36.0	45.3	
Total Export Credits	110.0	187.6	221.8	
Other Private Market	124.9	165.2	262.7	
International Org.	121.2	146.4	159.9	
CMEA	0.1	0.1	0.1	
Other	8.7	9.9	22.0	

ECONOMIC INDICATORS

	1977	1978	1979	1980
GNP Curr. Prices, $M	19145.0	23050.0	27837.3	32524.3
Real GNP, 1976=100	105.0	114.0	121.0	126.0
GNP/Cap Curr. Prices,$	765.0	901.0	1065.0	1219.0
GNP/cap Atlas Basis, $	828.2	949.3	1063.8	1183.6
Real GNP/Cap, 1976=100	102.0	109.0	113.0	115.0
Population, Million	25.0	25.6	26.1	26.7
Curr.A/C Deficit(-),$M	435.0	294.0	489.0	-48.0
BOP Exp. & Transf.,$M	3568.0	4175.0	4950.0	5643.0
Exp. to OECD CIF, $M	2135.9	2697.7	3209.4	3663.7
of which				
Manufact.	151.7	181.5	206.1	206.7
Imp. from OECD FOB, $M	1681.1	2146.9	2815.0	3505.0
Reserves ex. Gold, $M	1747.0	2366.0	3844.0	4831.0

	TOTAL RECEIPTS NET 1977	1978	1979	1980	TOTAL ODA NET 1977	1978	1979	1980	TOTAL ODA GROSS 1977
DAC COUNTRIES									
Australia	–	–	–	–	–	–	–	–	–
Austria	-0.1	-0.2	-0.2	–	0.0	–	–	–	0.(
Belgium	0.9	-0.3	-3.4	-4.1	0.2	0.4	0.3	0.2	0.
Canada	3.1	3.0	1.8	1.7	2.1	2.4	1.8	1.7	2.
Denmark	-0.1	–	–	–	0.0	–	–	–	0.(
Finland	–	–	–	–	–	–	–	–	–
France	31.0	70.8	37.5	119.9	28.1	40.3	45.8	48.9	30.
Germany, Fed. Rep.	4.1	-1.8	1.9	6.0	0.5	1.0	1.5	2.8	0.
Italy	5.7	-17.5	-3.3	-43.6	0.0	0.0	0.0	0.1	0.
Japan	-8.1	-1.4	-0.6	-35.3	–	–	0.0	0.0	–
Netherlands	2.8	0.4	0.3	0.5	1.5	0.4	0.3	0.5	1.
New Zealand	–	–	–	–	–	–	–	–	–
Norway	0.0	–	-0.1	0.0	0.0	–	–	0.0	0.
Sweden	–	–	–	0.8	–	–	–	0.8	–
Switzerland	0.1	0.1	0.1	-0.9	0.1	0.1	0.1	0.1	0.
United Kingdom	-0.2	-0.1	0.1	0.6	0.1	0.1	0.2	0.3	0.
United States	–	–	–	1.0	–	–	–	–	–
TOTAL	*39.1*	*53.1*	*34.2*	*46.6*	*32.7*	*44.7*	*50.1*	*55.4*	*35.*
MULTILATERAL									
AF.D.F.	–	–	–	–	–	–	–	–	–
AF.D.B.	4.6	3.3	-0.2	4.9	–	–	–	–	–
AS.D.B.	–	–	–	–	–	–	–	–	–
CAR.D.B.	–	–	–	–	–	–	–	–	–
E.E.C.	4.6	10.5	6.0	5.2	5.4	13.5	12.4	7.2	5.
IBRD	-0.4	16.6	-0.1	-2.4	–	–	–	–	–
IDA	1.5	1.3	0.7	1.1	1.5	1.3	0.7	1.1	1.
I.D.B.	–	–	–	–	–	–	–	–	–
IFAD	–	–	–	–	–	–	–	–	–
I.F.C.	–	–	–	–	–	–	–	–	–
IMF TRUST FUND	1.6	5.0	5.0	4.4	1.6	5.0	5.0	4.4	1.
U.N. AGENCIES	–	–	–	–	–	–	–	–	–
UNDP	0.7	1.0	1.5	2.4	0.7	1.0	1.5	2.4	0.
UNTA	0.5	0.6	0.8	0.1	0.5	0.6	0.8	0.1	0.
UNICEF	0.1	0.1	0.5	0.1	0.1	0.1	0.5	0.1	0.
UNRWA	–	–	–	–	–	–	–	–	–
WFP	2.1	1.9	4.2	2.6	2.1	1.9	4.2	2.6	2.
UNHCR	–	0.0	0.0	0.0	–	0.0	0.0	0.0	–
Other Multilateral	0.6	0.8	0.7	1.1	0.6	0.8	0.7	1.1	0.
Arab OPEC Agencies	–	1.4	5.6	2.8	–	1.4	5.6	2.8	
TOTAL	*15.9*	*42.6*	*24.8*	*22.2*	*12.5*	*25.8*	*31.5*	*21.7*	*12.*
OPEC COUNTRIES	*3.3*	*11.1*	*4.0*	*14.9*	*3.3*	*10.6*	*4.0*	*14.9*	*3.*
E.E.C.+ MEMBERS	*48.8*	*62.0*	*39.2*	*84.4*	*36.0*	*55.8*	*60.6*	*59.9*	*38.*
TOTAL	***58.4***	***106.7***	***63.0***	***83.7***	***48.6***	***81.1***	***85.6***	***92.1***	***51.***

	ODA LOANS GROSS 1977	1978	1979	1980	ODA LOANS NET 1977	1978	1979	1980	GRANTS 1977
DAC COUNTRIES									
Australia	–	–	–	–	–	–	–	–	
Austria	–	–	–	–	–	–	–	–	0.
Belgium	–	–	–	–	–	–	–	–	0.
Canada	1.6	1.9	1.3	1.6	1.6	1.9	1.3	1.6	0.
Denmark	–	–	–	–	–	–	–	–	0.
Finland	–	–	–	–	–	–	–	–	
France	4.7	6.4	4.7	10.9	2.2	4.7	-0.8	8.0	25.
Germany, Fed. Rep.	–	–	–	6.5	–	–	–	1.0	0.
Italy	–	–	–	–	–	–	–	–	0.
Japan	–	–	–	–	–	–	–	–	
Netherlands	1.2	0.1	0.2	0.3	1.2	0.1	0.2	0.3	0.
New Zealand	–	–	–	–	–	–	–	–	
Norway	–	–	–	–	–	–	–	–	0.
Sweden	–	–	–	–	–	–	–	–	
Switzerland	–	–	–	–	–	–	–	–	0.
United Kingdom	–	–	–	–	–	–	–	–	0.
United States	–	–	–	–	–	–	–	–	
TOTAL	*7.5*	*8.4*	*6.2*	*19.3*	*5.0*	*6.7*	*0.7*	*10.9*	*27.*
MULTILATERAL	*3.2*	*11.5*	*19.7*	*9.5*	*3.1*	*11.3*	*19.4*	*9.2*	*9.*
OPEC COUNTRIES	*3.3*	*10.6*	*9.3*	*14.9*	*3.3*	*10.6*	*9.3*	*14.9*	
E.E.C.+ MEMBERS	*6.0*	*10.3*	*13.2*	*18.9*	*3.3*	*8.3*	*7.4*	*10.2*	*32.*
TOTAL	***14.0***	***30.5***	***35.2***	***43.7***	***11.4***	***28.6***	***29.4***	***35.1***	***37.***

	TOTAL OFFICIAL GROSS 1977	1978	1979	1980	TOTAL OFFICIAL NET 1977	1978	1979	1980	TOTAL OOF GROSS 1977
DAC COUNTRIES									
Australia	–	–	–	–	–	–	–	–	
Austria	0.0	–	–	–	0.0	-0.2	–	–	
Belgium	0.2	0.4	0.3	0.2	0.2	0.4	0.3	0.2	
Canada	3.1	3.0	1.8	1.7	3.1	3.0	1.8	1.7	1.
Denmark	0.0	–	–	–	0.0	–	–	–	
Finland	–	–	–	–	–	–	–	–	
France	34.7	83.2	122.4	51.7	32.0	64.8	79.3	40.1	4.
Germany, Fed. Rep.	1.2	1.5	1.5	8.3	1.2	1.5	1.5	2.6	0.
Italy	25.2	0.0	0.0	6.0	17.3	-17.7	-7.4	-6.1	25.
Japan	–	–	0.0	0.0	–	–	0.0	0.0	
Netherlands	2.8	0.4	0.3	0.5	2.8	0.4	0.3	0.5	1.
New Zealand	–	–	–	–	–	–	–	–	
Norway	0.0	–	–	0.0	0.0	–	–	0.0	
Sweden	–	–	–	0.8	–	–	–	0.8	
Switzerland	0.1	0.1	0.1	0.1	0.1	0.1	0.1	0.1	
United Kingdom	0.1	0.1	0.2	0.3	0.1	0.1	0.2	0.3	
United States	–	–	–	1.0	–	–	–	1.0	
TOTAL	*67.5*	*88.8*	*126.7*	*70.7*	*56.9*	*52.4*	*76.2*	*41.2*	*32.*
MULTILATERAL	*19.4*	*48.3*	*42.5*	*30.2*	*15.9*	*42.6*	*24.8*	*22.2*	*6.*
OPEC COUNTRIES	*3.3*	*11.1*	*9.3*	*14.9*	*3.3*	*11.1*	*4.0*	*14.9*	
E.E.C.+ MEMBERS	*69.8*	*99.4*	*137.5*	*74.5*	*58.3*	*60.0*	*80.3*	*42.8*	*31.*
TOTAL	***90.2***	***148.1***	***178.5***	***115.8***	***76.1***	***106.1***	***105.0***	***78.3***	***39.***

1978	1979	1980	1977	1978	1979	1980
			ODA COMMITMENTS			
–	–	–	–	–	–	–
–	–	–	–	–	–	–
0.4	0.3	0.2	–	–	–	–
2.4	1.8	1.7	0.4	0.2	0.1	3.1
–	–	–	0.0	–	–	–
–	–	–	–	–	–	–
42.0	51.3	51.7	26.8	27.2	38.8	45.3
1.0	1.5	8.3	0.6	1.7	2.9	13.8
0.0	0.0	0.1	0.0	0.0	0.0	0.1
–	0.0	0.0	–	–	0.0	0.0
0.4	0.3	0.5	2.1	0.6	0.4	0.5
–	–	–	–	–	–	–
–	–	0.0	–	–	–	–
–	–	0.8	–	–	–	–
0.1	0.1	0.1	–	–	–	0.1
0.1	0.2	0.3	0.1	0.1	0.2	0.3
–	–	–	0.8	0.6	0.2	0.9
46.4	*55.6*	*63.8*	*30.9*	*30.5*	*42.5*	*64.0*
–	–	–	–	–	–	9.4
–	–	–	–	–	–	–
–	–	–	–	–	–	–
–	–	–	–	–	–	–
13.8	12.7	7.5	11.8	6.2	0.5	6.5
–	–	–	–	–	–	–
1.3	0.7	1.1	0.3	–	5.0	30.0
–	–	–	–	–	–	–
–	–	–	–	–	–	–
–	–	–	–	–	–	–
5.0	5.0	4.4	–	–	–	–
–	–	–	4.0	4.5	7.7	6.3
1.0	1.5	2.4	–	–	–	–
0.6	0.8	0.1	–	–	–	–
0.1	0.5	0.1	–	–	–	–
–	–	–	–	–	–	–
1.9	4.2	2.6	–	–	–	–
0.0	0.0	0.0	–	–	–	–
0.8	0.7	1.1	–	–	–	–
1.4	5.6	2.8	–	4.0	–	8.0
26.0	*31.8*	*22.0*	*16.1*	*14.7*	*13.2*	*60.2*
10.6	*9.3*	*14.9*	–	*3.6*	–	*21.1*
57.7	*66.4*	*68.6*	*41.5*	*35.9*	*42.8*	*66.4*
83.0	***96.6***	***100.7***	***47.0***	***48.8***	***55.7***	***145.3***
			TECH. COOP. GRANTS			
–	–	–	–	–	–	–
–	–	–	0.0	–	–	–
0.4	0.3	0.2	0.2	0.4	0.3	0.2
0.5	0.5	0.1	0.4	0.2	0.1	0.1
–	–	–	0.0	–	–	–
–	–	–	–	–	–	–
35.6	46.6	40.9	22.0	23.2	28.1	30.8
1.0	1.5	1.8	0.5	1.0	1.5	1.8
0.0	0.0	0.1	0.0	0.0	0.0	0.1
–	0.0	0.0	–	–	0.0	0.0
0.3	0.1	0.2	0.3	0.3	0.1	0.2
–	–	–	–	–	–	–
–	–	0.0	0.0	–	–	0.0
–	–	0.8	–	–	–	–
0.1	0.1	0.1	0.0	0.0	0.0	–
0.1	0.2	0.3	0.1	0.1	0.2	0.3
–	–	–	–	–	–	–
38.0	*49.4*	*44.5*	*23.6*	*25.3*	*30.4*	*33.4*
14.5	*12.1*	*12.5*	*1.9*	*2.6*	*3.5*	*6.3*
–	–	–	–	–	–	–
47.5	*53.2*	*49.7*	*23.2*	*25.1*	*30.3*	*33.3*
52.5	***61.5***	***57.0***	***25.5***	***27.9***	***33.9***	***39.7***
			TOTAL OOF NET			
–	–	–	–	–	–	–
–	–	–	–	-0.2	–	–
–	–	–	–	–	–	–
0.6	–	–	1.0	0.6	–	–
–	–	–	–	–	–	–
–	–	–	–	–	–	–
41.2	71.1	–	3.9	24.5	33.5	-8.7
0.5	–	–	0.7	0.5	–	-0.2
–	–	5.9	17.2	-17.7	-7.4	-6.2
–	–	–	–	–	–	–
–	–	–	1.3	–	–	–
–	–	–	–	–	–	–
–	–	–	–	–	–	–
–	–	–	–	–	–	–
–	–	–	–	–	–	–
–	–	–	–	–	–	–
–	–	1.0	–	–	–	1.0
42.3	*71.1*	*6.9*	*24.1*	*7.7*	*26.1*	*-14.2*
22.2	*10.7*	*8.1*	*3.4*	*16.8*	*-6.7*	*0.4*
0.5	–	–	–	*0.5*	–	–
41.7	*71.1*	*5.9*	*22.3*	*4.2*	*19.6*	*-17.2*
65.0	***81.8***	***15.1***	***27.5***	***25.0***	***19.4***	***-13.7***

MAIN AID AGGREGATES

	1977	1978	1979	1980
DAC COUNTRIES COMBINED				
PRIVATE SECTOR NET	-17.8	0.6	-42.0	5.3
Direct Investment	0.2	0.0	0.4	-0.8
Portfolio Invest.	5.8	-3.0	-18.6	39.5
Export Credits	-23.8	3.6	-23.8	-33.4
OFFICIAL & PRIVATE				
GROSS:				
Contractual Lending	87.9	113.4	114.4	94.7
Export Credits Tot.	49.2	63.3	37.1	75.4
Export Credits Priv	48.2	62.7	37.1	68.5
OTHER NET DATA				
Contractual Lending	5.3	18.1	3.0	-36.6
Export Credits Tot.	-22.7	-13.6	-31.2	-38.6
(Bank Sector Loans)	-3.0	-2.0	4.0	-3.0
ODA CONCESSIONALITY				
Total:Grant Element	98.0	100.0	100.0	89.0
Loans:Grant Element	34.0	–	–	53.0
OTHER SOURCES				
CMEA Countr.(Gross)	2.2	0.8	0.5	0.2
Intra LDCS Exc.OPEC	–	–	–	–
Other	–	–	–	–
ALL SOURCE COMMITMENTS				
TOTAL BILATERAL	57.5	86.3	48.5	98.1
of which				
OPEC (ODA)	–	3.6	–	21.1
CMEA (ODA)	31.0	0.4	–	–
TOTAL MULTILAT.(ODA)	16.1	14.7	13.2	60.2
TOTAL BIL.& MULTIL.	73.6	101.0	61.7	158.3
of which				
ODA Grants	45.5	37.1	50.5	58.1
ODA Loans	1.5	11.7	5.2	87.2
ODA CONCESSIONALITY				
Total: Grant Element	98.0	88.0	100.0	77.0
Loans: Grant Element	49.0	31.0	–	62.0

INDEBTEDNESS

	1977	1978	1979	1980
TOTAL DEBT DISBURSED	***571.8***	***742.4***	***837.1***	
Debt to DAC Countries	343.0	400.0	441.0	
ODA	71.0	88.0	89.0	
Total Export Credits	270.0	282.0	315.0	
Other Private Market	2.0	30.0	37.0	
International Org.	60.0	85.4	92.7	
CMEA	119.4	163.9	184.8	
Other	49.3	93.1	118.7	
TOTAL DEBT SERVICE	***73.2***	***101.4***	***123.7***	
Paid to DAC Countries	64.9	92.9	101.7	
ODA	2.5	3.4	8.8	
Total Export Credits	62.4	89.5	87.9	
Other Private Market	–	–	5.0	
International Org.	5.7	6.9	16.3	
CMEA	2.1	0.7	3.9	
Other	0.4	0.9	1.7	

ECONOMIC INDICATORS

	1977	1978	1979	1980
GNP Curr. Prices, $M	697.3	817.7	1053.5	1160.0
Real GNP, 1976=100	95.0	98.0	101.0	103.0
GNP/Cap Curr. Prices,$	490.0	560.0	703.0	754.0
GNP/cap Atlas Basis, $	573.8	620.8	671.6	729.6
Real GNP/Cap, 1976=100	93.0	93.0	93.0	93.0
Population, Million	1.4	1.5	1.5	1.5
Curr.A/C Deficit(-),$M	-220.0	-232.5	-142.4	-230.0
BOP Exp. & Transf.,$M	348.7	380.3	568.7	1029.2
Exp. to OECD CIF, $M	218.3	275.2	365.1	692.3
of which				
Manufact.	22.0	23.3	30.5	28.4
Imp. from OECD FOB, $M	214.5	198.8	279.4	413.4
Reserves ex. Gold, $M	13.5	9.4	42.2	85.9

	TOTAL RECEIPTS NET 1977	1978	1979	1980	TOTAL ODA NET 1977	1978	1979	1980
DAC COUNTRIES								
Australia	0.0	0.0	0.3	0.3	0.0	–	–	–
Austria	0.0	1.9	-0.7	-1.3	0.0	0.2	0.1	0.0
Belgium	0.2	4.4	4.6	1.7	0.2	0.1	0.1	0.1
Canada	0.0	3.3	3.5	0.0	0.1	0.2	–	0.1
Denmark	0.7	-0.1	3.4	-0.2	–	–	–	0.0
Finland	–	0.0	–	0.0	–	0.0	–	0.0
France	1.6	-5.1	-4.2	17.5	–	–	–	0.4
Germany, Fed. Rep.	6.7	9.9	4.6	24.1	4.2	7.9	6.8	12.7
Italy	28.1	1.1	0.6	3.9	0.1	0.2	0.6	0.3
Japan	1.2	22.5	14.9	15.9	1.4	18.8	9.6	3.6
Netherlands	1.0	1.8	2.0	13.8	1.0	1.8	2.0	1.2
New Zealand	–	–	–	–	–	–	–	–
Norway	0.1	17.9	9.9	-0.1	0.0	0.1	–	0.0
Sweden	1.6	0.7	-0.8	-1.0	–	–	–	–
Switzerland	-0.5	-0.1	4.2	1.0	0.1	0.2	0.5	0.3
United Kingdom	0.0	1.8	1.7	-7.5	1.4	0.5	0.9	1.0
United States	4.0	2.0	9.0	5.0	6.0	4.0	5.0	3.0
TOTAL	*44.6*	*62.1*	*53.1*	*73.1*	*14.5*	*34.1*	*25.5*	*22.8*
MULTILATERAL								
AF.D.F.	–	–	–	–	–	–	–	–
AF.D.B.	–	–	–	–	–	–	–	–
AS.D.B.	–	–	–	–	–	–	–	–
CAR.D.B.	–	–	–	–	–	–	–	–
E.E.C.	–	–	0.0	–	–	–	0.0	–
IBRD	20.0	16.8	14.6	22.8	–	–	–	–
IDA	0.1	0.0	0.0	0.0	0.1	0.0	0.0	0.0
I.D.B.	28.2	29.3	29.4	48.6	8.5	15.0	24.9	39.7
IFAD	–	–	–	–	–	–	–	–
I.F.C.	–	1.2	2.5	0.4	–	–	–	–
IMF TRUST FUND	–	–	–	–	–	–	–	–
U.N. AGENCIES	–	–	–	–	–	–	–	–
UNDP	0.8	0.8	1.0	1.0	0.8	0.8	1.0	1.0
UNTA	0.4	0.4	0.3	0.1	0.4	0.4	0.3	0.1
UNICEF	0.0	0.1	0.1	0.0	0.0	0.1	0.1	0.0
UNRWA	–	–	–	–	–	–	–	–
WFP	0.3	0.3	0.4	0.4	0.3	0.3	0.4	0.4
UNHCR	–	–	–	0.3	–	–	–	0.3
Other Multilateral	0.8	0.4	0.4	0.5	0.8	0.4	0.4	0.5
Arab OPEC Agencies	–	–	3.0	–	–	–	3.0	–
TOTAL	*50.6*	*49.2*	*51.7*	*74.2*	*10.8*	*16.9*	*30.0*	*42.1*
OPEC COUNTRIES	*24.4*	*10.5*	–	–	–	–	–	–
E.E.C.+ MEMBERS	*38.3*	*13.8*	*12.8*	*53.2*	*6.8*	*10.6*	*10.5*	*15.7*
TOTAL	***119.5***	***121.8***	***104.8***	***147.3***	***25.3***	***51.0***	***55.6***	***64.8***

	ODA LOANS GROSS 1977	1978	1979	1980	ODA LOANS NET 1977	1978	1979	1980
DAC COUNTRIES								
Australia	–	–	–	–	–	–	–	–
Austria	–	–	–	–	0.0	0.0	–	0.0
Belgium	–	–	–	–	–	–	–	–
Canada	–	–	–	–	–	–	–	–
Denmark	–	–	–	–	–	–	–	–
Finland	–	–	–	–	–	–	–	–
France	–	–	–	–	–	–	–	–
Germany, Fed. Rep.	0.5	5.2	3.6	8.1	0.3	5.0	3.3	7.7
Italy	–	–	–	–	–	–	–	–
Japan	0.4	17.8	8.5	2.4	0.4	17.8	8.5	2.4
Netherlands	–	–	–	–	–	–	–	–
New Zealand	–	–	–	–	–	–	–	–
Norway	–	–	–	–	–	–	–	–
Sweden	–	–	–	–	–	–	–	–
Switzerland	–	–	–	–	–	–	–	–
United Kingdom	0.4	–	0.2	0.0	0.4	-0.4	-0.2	-0.4
United States	2.0	3.0	5.0	3.0	1.0	2.0	4.0	2.0
TOTAL	*3.3*	*26.0*	*17.3*	*13.6*	*2.1*	*24.4*	*15.6*	*11.7*
MULTILATERAL	*10.7*	*17.2*	*30.3*	*41.5*	*8.5*	*14.5*	*27.9*	*38.9*
OPEC COUNTRIES	–	–	–	–	–	–	–	–
E.E.C.+ MEMBERS	*0.9*	*5.2*	*3.8*	*8.2*	*0.7*	*4.6*	*3.1*	*7.3*
TOTAL	***14.0***	***43.2***	***47.6***	***55.1***	***10.6***	***38.9***	***43.5***	***50.6***

	TOTAL OFFICIAL GROSS 1977	1978	1979	1980	TOTAL OFFICIAL NET 1977	1978	1979	1980
DAC COUNTRIES								
Australia	0.0	–	–	–	0.0	–	–	–
Austria	0.0	0.3	0.1	0.0	0.0	0.2	0.1	0.0
Belgium	0.2	0.1	0.1	0.1	0.2	0.1	0.1	0.1
Canada	0.1	3.2	3.8	0.2	0.1	3.2	3.8	0.2
Denmark	–	–	–	0.0	–	–	–	0.0
Finland	–	0.0	–	0.0	–	0.0	–	0.0
France	–	–	–	0.4	–	–	–	0.4
Germany, Fed. Rep.	4.4	8.2	7.0	13.1	4.2	7.9	6.8	12.7
Italy	0.1	0.2	0.6	0.3	0.1	0.2	0.6	0.3
Japan	1.4	18.8	9.6	3.6	1.4	18.8	9.6	3.6
Netherlands	1.0	1.8	2.0	1.2	1.0	1.8	2.0	1.2
New Zealand	–	–	–	–	–	–	–	–
Norway	0.0	0.1	–	0.0	0.0	0.1	–	0.0
Sweden	–	–	–	–	–	–	–	–
Switzerland	0.1	0.2	0.5	0.3	0.1	0.2	0.5	0.3
United Kingdom	1.4	0.9	1.3	1.4	1.4	0.5	0.9	0.5
United States	7.0	5.0	12.0	7.0	4.0	2.0	9.0	5.0
TOTAL	*15.7*	*38.7*	*37.0*	*27.6*	*12.5*	*35.1*	*33.3*	*24.3*
MULTILATERAL	*57.0*	*57.4*	*60.6*	*84.1*	*50.6*	*49.2*	*51.7*	*74.2*
OPEC COUNTRIES	*24.4*	*10.5*	–	–	*24.4*	*10.5*	–	–
E.E.C.+ MEMBERS	*7.0*	*11.2*	*11.1*	*16.5*	*6.8*	*10.6*	*10.5*	*15.2*
TOTAL	***97.1***	***106.6***	***97.6***	***111.7***	***87.5***	***94.8***	***85.0***	***98.5***

TOTAL ODA GROSS	197
Australia	0
Austria	0
Belgium	0
Canada	0
Denmark	
Finland	
France	
Germany, Fed. Rep.	4
Italy	0
Japan	1
Netherlands	1
New Zealand	
Norway	0
Sweden	
Switzerland	0
United Kingdom	1
United States	7
TOTAL	*15*
AF.D.F.	
AF.D.B.	
AS.D.B.	
CAR.D.B.	
E.E.C.	
IBRD	
IDA	0
I.D.B.	10
IFAD	
I.F.C.	
IMF TRUST FUND	
U.N. AGENCIES	
UNDP	0
UNTA	0
UNICEF	0
UNRWA	
WFP	0
UNHCR	
Other Multilateral	0
Arab OPEC Agencies	
TOTAL	*13*
OPEC COUNTRIES	
E.E.C.+ MEMBERS	*7*
TOTAL	***28***

GRANTS	197
Australia	0
Austria	0
Belgium	0
Canada	0
Denmark	
Finland	
France	
Germany, Fed. Rep.	4
Italy	0
Japan	1
Netherlands	1
New Zealand	
Norway	0
Sweden	
Switzerland	0
United Kingdom	0
United States	5
TOTAL	*12*
MULTILATERAL	*2*
OPEC COUNTRIES	
E.E.C.+ MEMBERS	*6*
TOTAL	***14***

TOTAL OOF GROSS	197
Australia	
Austria	
Belgium	
Canada	
Denmark	
Finland	
France	
Germany, Fed. Rep.	
Italy	
Japan	
Netherlands	
New Zealand	
Norway	
Sweden	
Switzerland	
United Kingdom	
United States	
TOTAL	
MULTILATERAL	*44*
OPEC COUNTRIES	*24*
E.E.C.+ MEMBERS	
TOTAL	***68***

1978	1979	1980	1977	1978	1979	1980
			ODA COMMITMENTS			
–	–	–	–	–	0.0	–
0.3	0.1	0.0	0.2	–	–	–
0.1	0.1	0.1	–	–	–	–
0.2	–	0.1	0.4	0.0	0.0	0.1
–	–	0.0	–	–	–	–
0.0	–	0.0	–	0.0	–	–
–	–	0.4	–	–	–	0.4
8.2	7.0	13.1	3.5	2.8	20.0	8.4
0.2	0.6	0.3	0.1	0.2	0.6	0.3
18.8	9.6	3.6	1.2	1.2	2.2	1.5
1.8	2.0	1.2	1.3	2.6	1.9	1.2
–	–	–	–	–	–	–
0.1	–	0.0	–	–	–	–
–	–	–	–	0.2	–	–
0.2	0.5	0.3	–	–	1.0	–
0.9	1.3	1.4	0.9	0.9	1.1	1.4
5.0	6.0	4.0	11.3	8.2	19.7	11.8
35.7	*27.2*	*24.6*	*18.9*	*16.2*	*46.5*	*25.0*
–	–	–	–	–	–	–
–	–	–	–	–	–	–
–	–	–	–	–	–	–
–	–	–	–	–	–	–
–	0.0	–	–	–	0.1	–
–	–	–	–	–	–	–
–	–	–	–	–	–	–
17.7	27.3	42.3	68.5	30.0	49.0	36.9
–	–	–	–	–	–	–
–	–	–	–	–	–	–
–	–	–	–	–	–	–
–	–	–	2.3	2.0	2.1	2.4
0.8	1.0	1.0	–	–	–	–
0.4	0.3	0.1	–	–	–	–
0.1	0.1	0.0	–	–	–	–
–	–	–	–	–	–	–
0.3	0.4	0.4	–	–	–	–
–	–	0.3	–	–	–	–
0.4	0.4	0.5	–	–	–	–
–	3.0	–	3.0	–	–	–
19.7	*32.5*	*44.7*	*73.8*	*32.0*	*51.2*	*39.3*
–	–	–	–	–	–	–
11.2	*11.1*	*16.5*	*5.7*	*6.5*	*23.8*	*11.7*
55.4	***59.7***	***69.3***	***92.7***	***48.2***	***97.7***	***64.3***
			TECH. COOP. GRANTS			
–	–	–	0.0	–	–	–
0.3	0.1	0.0	0.0	0.3	0.1	0.0
0.1	0.1	0.1	0.2	0.1	0.1	0.0
0.2	–	0.1	–	0.0	–	0.0
–	–	0.0	–	–	–	0.0
0.0	–	0.0	–	0.0	–	0.0
–	–	0.4	–	–	–	0.4
2.9	3.5	5.0	4.0	2.9	3.5	5.0
0.2	0.6	0.3	0.1	0.2	0.6	0.3
0.9	1.1	1.2	1.0	0.9	1.1	1.2
1.8	2.0	1.2	1.0	1.4	1.6	1.2
–	–	–	–	–	–	–
0.1	–	0.0	0.0	0.1	–	0.0
–	–	–	–	–	–	–
0.2	0.5	0.3	–	–	–	0.1
0.9	1.1	1.4	0.9	0.9	1.1	1.4
2.0	1.0	1.0	2.0	2.0	1.0	2.0
9.7	*9.9*	*11.0*	*9.2*	*8.9*	*9.0*	*11.6*
2.5	*2.2*	*3.2*	*2.0*	*2.1*	*1.8*	*2.4*
–	–	–	–	–	–	–
6.0	*7.3*	*8.3*	*6.1*	*5.6*	*6.9*	*8.2*
12.1	***12.1***	***14.3***	***11.1***	***11.0***	***10.8***	***14.0***
			TOTAL OOF NET			
–	–	–	–	–	–	–
–	–	–	–	–	–	–
–	–	–	–	–	–	–
3.0	3.8	0.0	–	3.0	3.8	0.0
–	–	–	–	–	–	–
–	–	–	–	–	–	–
–	–	–	–	–	–	–
–	–	–	–	–	–	–
–	–	–	–	–	–	–
–	–	–	–	–	–	–
–	–	–	–	–	–	–
–	–	–	–	–	–	–
–	–	–	–	–	–	–
–	–	–	–	–	–	–
–	–	–	–	–	–	–
–	–	–	–	–	–	-0.5
–	6.0	3.0	-2.0	-2.0	4.0	2.0
3.0	*9.8*	*3.0*	*-2.0*	*1.0*	*7.8*	*1.6*
37.7	*28.1*	*39.3*	*39.8*	*32.3*	*21.6*	*32.1*
10.5	–	–	*24.4*	*10.5*	–	–
–	–	–	–	–	–	*-0.5*
51.3	***37.9***	***42.4***	***62.2***	***43.9***	***29.4***	***33.7***

	1977	1978	1979	1980
MAIN AID AGGREGATES				
DAC COUNTRIES COMBINED				
PRIVATE SECTOR NET	32.1	27.0	19.8	48.8
Direct Investment	2.2	5.0	7.9	7.4
Portfolio Invest.	-5.6	22.6	-4.4	34.3
Export Credits	35.5	-0.6	16.3	7.1
OFFICIAL & PRIVATE				
GROSS:				
Contractual Lending	66.1	63.4	66.7	60.8
Export Credits Tot.	62.8	37.4	47.4	45.2
Export Credits Priv	62.8	34.4	39.6	44.2
OTHER NET DATA				
Contractual Lending	35.5	24.8	39.7	20.4
Export Credits Tot.	33.5	0.4	22.1	7.2
(Bank Sector Loans)	10.0	37.0	155.0	37.0
ODA CONCESSIONALITY				
Total:Grant Element	85.0	86.0	62.0	85.0
Loans:Grant Element	51.0	61.0	50.0	62.0
OTHER SOURCES				
CMEA Countr.(Gross)	4.5	–	–	–
Intra LDCS Exc.OPEC	–	–	–	–
Other	–	–	–	–
ALL SOURCE COMMITMENTS				
TOTAL BILATERAL	19.2	27.3	51.7	35.8
of which				
OPEC (ODA)	–	–	–	–
CMEA (ODA)	–	–	–	–
TOTAL MULTILAT.(ODA)	73.8	32.0	51.2	39.3
TOTAL BIL.& MULTIL.	93.0	59.3	102.8	75.1
of which				
ODA Grants	15.5	12.5	13.8	17.8
ODA Loans	77.1	35.6	83.8	46.5
ODA CONCESSIONALITY				
Total: Grant Element	69.0	72.0	64.0	72.0
Loans: Grant Element	61.0	65.0	50.0	65.0
INDEBTEDNESS				
TOTAL DEBT DISBURSED	***760.8***	***1052.3***	***1361.0***	
Debt to DAC Countries	435.0	616.0	868.0	
ODA	73.0	100.0	112.0	
Total Export Credits	92.0	115.0	138.0	
Other Private Market	270.0	401.0	618.0	
International Org.	248.6	318.0	360.0	
CMEA	3.1	2.7	2.5	
Other	74.1	115.7	130.5	
TOTAL DEBT SERVICE	***105.9***	***238.7***	***273.5***	
Paid to DAC Countries	76.3	197.0	214.3	
ODA	2.3	2.9	4.1	
Total Export Credits	35.0	39.1	32.1	
Other Private Market	39.0	155.0	178.1	
International Org.	23.4	32.0	42.1	
CMEA	0.5	0.4	0.3	
Other	5.7	9.2	16.9	
ECONOMIC INDICATORS				
GNP Curr. Prices, $M	2999.0	3523.3	4035.5	4846.6
Real GNP, 1976=100	109.0	114.0	119.0	118.0
GNP/Cap Curr. Prices,$	1454.0	1669.0	1866.0	2190.0
GNP/cap Atlas Basis, $	1348.6	1487.4	1633.9	1728.3
Real GNP/Cap, 1976=100	106.0	109.0	110.0	107.0
Population, Million	2.1	2.1	2.2	2.2
Curr.A/C Deficit(-),$M	-225.7	-363.9	-554.2	-653.8
BOP Exp. & Transf.,$M	984.8	1040.9	1127.6	1229.6
Exp. to OECD CIF, $M	661.6	714.7	870.6	831.0
of which				
Manufact.	35.6	45.0	54.3	69.0
Imp. from OECD FOB, $M	604.3	686.3	799.7	837.9
Reserves ex. Gold, $M	190.5	193.9	118.6	145.6

	TOTAL RECEIPTS NET 1977	1978	1979	1980	TOTAL ODA NET 1977	1978	1979	1980
DAC COUNTRIES								
Australia	–	-2.1	-1.0	-1.0	–	–	–	–
Austria	-3.4	-5.3	-8.2	-6.4	0.0	–	0.0	2.1
Belgium	-0.8	-6.8	-26.6	-26.0	0.1	0.0	3.5	0.0
Canada	18.1	4.9	-2.9	-5.4	4.6	1.9	0.1	–
Denmark	61.3	-7.3	-25.0	-17.6	–	0.1	0.3	0.1
Finland	1.2	-0.5	-0.4	-0.9	2.0	0.3	0.4	-0.1
France	-27.9	12.7	-15.4	26.5	–	–	–	0.5
Germany, Fed. Rep.	-1.8	-1.5	19.1	0.4	0.4	0.0	0.0	0.1
Italy	1.4	10.6	9.0	-0.3	0.2	0.3	0.4	0.5
Japan	14.1	159.8	35.7	-5.3	0.1	0.2	0.1	0.1
Netherlands	3.2	5.6	10.1	3.8	3.2	5.6	10.1	3.8
New Zealand	–	–	–	–	–	–	–	–
Norway	3.7	1.2	0.8	0.1	3.8	1.2	0.9	0.2
Sweden	8.7	9.8	1.7	12.9	15.2	7.8	8.1	3.8
Switzerland	0.1	0.0	20.0	28.8	0.1	0.1	0.1	0.0
United Kingdom	-14.9	-1.5	-9.0	10.1	–	–	–	–
United States	–	–	–	–	–	–	–	–
TOTAL	*63.0*	*179.5*	*8.1*	*19.7*	*29.7*	*17.4*	*23.9*	*11.1*
MULTILATERAL								
AF.D.F.	–	–	–	–	–	–	–	–
AF.D.B.	–	–	–	–	–	–	–	–
AS.D.B.	–	–	–	–	–	–	–	–
CAR.D.B.	–	–	–	–	–	–	–	–
E.E.C.	2.9	9.1	–	–	2.9	9.1	–	–
IBRD	–	–	–	–	–	–	–	–
IDA	–	–	–	–	–	–	–	–
I.D.B.	–	–	–	–	–	–	–	–
IFAD	–	–	–	–	–	–	–	–
I.F.C.	–	–	–	–	–	–	–	–
IMF TRUST FUND	–	–	–	–	–	–	–	–
U.N. AGENCIES	–	–	–	–	–	–	–	–
UNDP	2.5	1.9	4.3	4.0	2.5	1.9	4.3	4.0
UNTA	0.3	0.5	0.6	0.3	0.3	0.5	0.6	0.3
UNICEF	1.1	1.1	0.4	0.2	1.1	1.1	0.4	0.2
UNRWA	–	–	–	–	–	–	–	–
WFP	7.5	17.9	8.7	13.6	7.5	17.9	8.7	13.6
UNHCR	–	–	–	–	–	–	–	–
Other Multilateral	1.9	0.7	0.9	2.9	1.9	0.7	0.9	2.9
Arab OPEC Agencies	–	–	–	–	–	–	–	–
TOTAL	*16.4*	*31.3*	*14.9*	*20.9*	*16.4*	*31.3*	*14.9*	*20.9*
OPEC COUNTRIES	–	–	*10.0*	–	–	–	*10.0*	–
E.E.C.+ MEMBERS	*23.4*	*20.9*	*-37.7*	*-3.1*	*6.8*	*15.1*	*14.3*	*5.0*
TOTAL	***79.4***	***210.8***	***32.9***	***40.6***	***46.0***	***48.7***	***48.8***	***32.0***

	TOTAL ODA GROSS 197[illegible]
Australia	
Austria	[illegible]
Belgium	[illegible]
Canada	[illegible]
Denmark	
Finland	[illegible]
France	
Germany, Fed. Rep.	[illegible]
Italy	[illegible]
Japan	[illegible]
Netherlands	[illegible]
New Zealand	
Norway	[illegible]
Sweden	[illegible]
Switzerland	[illegible]
United Kingdom	
United States	
TOTAL	[illegible]
AF.D.F.	
AF.D.B.	
AS.D.B.	
CAR.D.B.	
E.E.C.	[illegible]
IBRD	
IDA	
I.D.B.	
IFAD	
I.F.C.	
IMF TRUST FUND	
U.N. AGENCIES	
UNDP	[illegible]
UNTA	[illegible]
UNICEF	[illegible]
UNRWA	
WFP	[illegible]
UNHCR	
Other Multilateral	[illegible]
Arab OPEC Agencies	
TOTAL	[illegible]
OPEC COUNTRIES	
E.E.C.+ MEMBERS	[illegible]
TOTAL	[illegible]

	ODA LOANS GROSS 1977	1978	1979	1980	ODA LOANS NET 1977	1978	1979	1980
DAC COUNTRIES								
Australia	–	–	–	–	–	–	–	–
Austria	–	–	–	2.1	–	–	–	2.1
Belgium	–	–	3.4	–	–	–	3.4	–
Canada	3.7	0.9	0.1	–	3.7	0.9	0.1	–
Denmark	–	–	–	–	–	–	–	–
Finland	1.5	0.3	0.5	0.0	1.5	0.3	0.4	-0.1
France	–	–	–	–	–	–	–	–
Germany, Fed. Rep.	–	–	–	–	–	–	–	–
Italy	–	–	–	–	–	–	–	–
Japan	–	–	–	–	–	–	–	–
Netherlands	2.1	4.4	8.6	2.5	2.1	4.4	8.6	2.5
New Zealand	–	–	–	–	–	–	–	–
Norway	–	–	–	–	–	–	–	–
Sweden	4.0	1.8	1.9	–	4.0	1.8	1.9	–
Switzerland	–	–	–	–	–	–	–	–
United Kingdom	–	–	–	–	–	–	–	–
United States	–	–	–	–	–	–	–	–
TOTAL	*11.3*	*7.3*	*14.4*	*4.6*	*11.3*	*7.3*	*14.3*	*4.5*
MULTILATERAL	–	–	–	–	–	–	–	–
OPEC COUNTRIES	–	–	–	–	–	–	–	–
E.E.C.+ MEMBERS	*2.1*	*4.4*	*12.0*	*2.5*	*2.1*	*4.4*	*12.0*	*2.5*
TOTAL	***11.3***	***7.3***	***14.4***	***4.6***	***11.3***	***7.3***	***14.3***	***4.5***

	GRANTS 197[illegible]
Australia	
Austria	[illegible]
Belgium	[illegible]
Canada	[illegible]
Denmark	
Finland	[illegible]
France	
Germany, Fed. Rep.	[illegible]
Italy	[illegible]
Japan	[illegible]
Netherlands	[illegible]
New Zealand	
Norway	[illegible]
Sweden	[illegible]
Switzerland	[illegible]
United Kingdom	
United States	
TOTAL	[illegible]
MULTILATERAL	[illegible]
OPEC COUNTRIES	
E.E.C.+ MEMBERS	[illegible]
TOTAL	[illegible]

	TOTAL OFFICIAL GROSS 1977	1978	1979	1980	TOTAL OFFICIAL NET 1977	1978	1979	1980
DAC COUNTRIES								
Australia	–	–	–	–	–	–	–	–
Austria	0.0	–	0.0	2.1	-3.4	-5.3	-8.2	-6.4
Belgium	0.1	0.0	3.5	0.0	0.1	0.0	3.5	0.0
Canada	22.0	10.0	2.7	0.7	20.3	6.1	-2.3	-5.4
Denmark	–	0.1	0.3	0.1	–	0.1	0.3	0.1
Finland	2.0	0.3	0.5	0.0	2.0	0.3	0.4	-0.1
France	–	–	–	0.5	–	–	–	0.5
Germany, Fed. Rep.	0.4	0.0	0.0	0.1	-0.2	-0.1	0.0	0.1
Italy	4.0	7.5	18.7	13.5	4.0	7.5	18.7	9.2
Japan	0.1	0.2	0.1	0.1	0.1	0.2	0.1	0.1
Netherlands	3.2	5.6	10.1	3.8	3.2	5.6	10.1	3.8
New Zealand	–	–	–	–	–	–	–	–
Norway	3.8	1.2	0.9	0.2	3.8	1.2	0.9	0.2
Sweden	15.2	7.8	8.1	3.8	15.2	7.8	8.1	3.8
Switzerland	0.1	0.1	0.1	0.0	0.1	0.1	0.1	0.0
United Kingdom	–	–	–	–	–	–	–	–
United States	–	–	–	–	–	–	–	–
TOTAL	*50.8*	*32.8*	*44.9*	*24.9*	*45.2*	*23.3*	*31.6*	*5.8*
MULTILATERAL	*16.4*	*31.3*	*14.9*	*20.9*	*16.4*	*31.3*	*14.9*	*20.9*
OPEC COUNTRIES	–	–	*10.0*	–	–	–	*10.0*	–
E.E.C.+ MEMBERS	*10.6*	*22.3*	*32.6*	*18.0*	*10.1*	*22.2*	*32.6*	*13.6*
TOTAL	***67.2***	***64.0***	***69.8***	***45.8***	***61.5***	***54.6***	***56.5***	***26.7***

	TOTAL OOF GROSS 197[illegible]
Australia	
Austria	
Belgium	
Canada	[illegible]
Denmark	
Finland	
France	
Germany, Fed. Rep.	
Italy	[illegible]
Japan	
Netherlands	
New Zealand	
Norway	
Sweden	
Switzerland	
United Kingdom	
United States	
TOTAL	[illegible]
MULTILATERAL	
OPEC COUNTRIES	
E.E.C.+ MEMBERS	[illegible]
TOTAL	[illegible]

1978	1979	1980	1977	1978	1979	1980
			ODA COMMITMENTS			
–	–	–	–	–	–	–
–	0.0	2.1	–	–	–	–
0.0	3.5	0.0	–	–	3.4	–
1.9	0.1	–	0.4	1.2	–	–
0.1	0.3	0.1	–	–	–	–
0.3	0.5	0.0	–	0.0	0.0	–
–	–	0.5	–	–	–	0.5
0.0	0.0	0.1	0.4	0.0	0.0	0.1
0.3	0.4	0.5	0.2	0.3	0.4	0.5
0.2	0.1	0.1	0.1	0.2	0.1	0.1
5.6	10.1	3.8	5.4	9.5	0.4	0.3
–	–	–	–	–	–	–
1.2	0.9	0.2	–	0.6	0.4	0.2
7.8	8.1	3.8	21.2	0.6	0.3	0.8
0.1	0.1	0.0	–	–	–	0.0
–	–	–	–	–	–	–
–	–	–	–	–	–	–
17.4	*24.0*	*11.2*	*27.6*	*12.3*	*5.0*	*2.5*
–	–	–	–	–	–	–
–	–	–	–	–	–	–
–	–	–	–	–	–	–
–	–	–	–	–	–	–
9.1	–	–	–	–	–	–
–	–	–	–	–	–	–
–	–	–	–	–	–	–
–	–	–	–	–	–	–
–	–	–	–	–	–	14.1
–	–	–	–	–	–	–
–	–	–	–	–	–	–
–	–	–	13.4	22.1	14.9	20.9
1.9	4.3	4.0	–	–	–	–
0.5	0.6	0.3	–	–	–	–
1.1	0.4	0.2	–	–	–	–
–	–	–	–	–	–	–
17.9	8.7	13.6	–	–	–	–
–	–	–	–	–	–	–
0.7	0.9	2.9	–	–	–	–
–	–	–	–	–	–	–
31.3	*14.9*	*20.9*	*13.4*	*22.1*	*14.9*	*35.0*
–	*10.0*	–	–	–	*10.0*	–
15.1	*14.3*	*5.0*	*6.0*	*9.8*	*4.2*	*1.4*
48.7	***48.9***	***32.1***	***41.0***	***34.5***	***29.9***	***37.5***
			TECH. COOP. GRANTS			
–	–	–	–	–	–	–
–	0.0	–	0.0	–	0.0	–
0.0	0.1	0.0	–	–	0.1	0.0
0.9	0.0	–	0.4	0.1	0.0	–
0.1	0.3	0.1	–	0.1	0.3	0.1
0.0	0.0	0.0	–	0.0	0.0	0.0
–	–	0.5	–	–	–	0.5
0.0	0.0	0.1	0.0	0.0	0.0	0.1
0.3	0.4	0.5	0.2	0.3	0.3	0.0
0.2	0.1	0.1	0.1	0.2	0.1	0.1
1.3	1.5	1.3	1.1	1.1	1.5	1.3
–	–	–	–	–	–	–
1.2	0.9	0.2	1.3	0.9	0.4	0.2
6.0	6.2	3.8	0.2	1.1	0.4	1.9
0.1	0.1	0.0	0.0	–	–	–
–	–	–	–	–	–	–
–	–	–	–	–	–	–
10.1	*9.6*	*6.5*	*3.3*	*3.8*	*3.1*	*4.1*
31.3	*14.9*	*20.9*	*5.9*	*4.2*	*6.1*	*20.9*
–	*10.0*	–	–	–	–	–
10.8	*2.3*	*2.4*	*1.4*	*1.5*	*2.2*	*1.9*
41.3	***34.5***	***27.4***	***9.2***	***8.0***	***9.3***	***25.0***
			TOTAL OOF NET			
–	–	–	–	–	–	–
–	–	–	-3.4	-5.3	-8.2	-8.5
–	–	–	–	–	–	–
8.2	2.7	0.7	15.7	4.2	-2.4	-5.4
–	–	–	–	–	–	–
–	–	–	–	–	–	–
–	–	–	–	–	–	–
–	–	–	-0.5	-0.2	–	–
7.2	18.3	13.0	3.8	7.2	18.3	8.7
–	–	–	–	–	–	–
–	–	–	–	–	–	–
–	–	–	–	–	–	–
–	–	–	–	–	–	–
–	–	–	–	–	–	–
–	–	–	–	–	–	–
–	–	–	–	–	–	–
–	–	–	–	–	–	–
15.4	*20.9*	*13.7*	*15.5*	*5.9*	*7.7*	*-5.3*
–	–	–	–	–	–	–
–	–	–	–	–	–	–
7.2	*18.3*	*13.0*	*3.3*	*7.0*	*18.3*	*8.7*
15.4	***20.9***	***13.7***	***15.5***	***5.9***	***7.7***	***-5.3***

	1977	1978	1979	1980
MAIN AID AGGREGATES				
DAC COUNTRIES COMBINED				
PRIVATE SECTOR NET	17.8	156.1	-23.5	14.0
Direct Investment	–	–	–	0.0
Portfolio Invest.	-25.3	59.8	43.2	-34.7
Export Credits	43.1	96.4	-66.7	48.7
OFFICIAL & PRIVATE				
GROSS:				
Contractual Lending	163.6	237.1	112.4	225.4
Export Credits Tot.	148.5	229.7	98.0	220.8
Export Credits Priv	131.1	214.4	77.1	207.1
OTHER NET DATA				
Contractual Lending	69.9	109.7	-44.7	47.9
Export Credits Tot.	55.3	102.5	-59.0	43.4
(Bank Sector Loans)	163.0	85.0	59.0	-77.0
ODA CONCESSIONALITY				
Total:Grant Element	91.0	79.0	86.0	100.0
Loans:Grant Element	77.0	60.0	80.0	–
OTHER SOURCES				
CMEA Countr.(Gross)	175.0	295.0	400.0	400.0
Intra LDCS Exc.OPEC	–	–	–	–
Other	–	–	–	–
ALL SOURCE COMMITMENTS				
TOTAL BILATERAL	34.3	22.6	33.3	16.0
of which				
OPEC (ODA)	–	–	10.0	–
CMEA (ODA)	400.0	400.0	400.0	400.0
TOTAL MULTILAT.(ODA)	13.4	22.1	14.9	35.0
TOTAL BIL.& MULTIL.	47.7	44.7	48.2	51.1
of which				
ODA Grants	30.4	28.0	26.5	23.4
ODA Loans	10.7	6.5	3.4	14.1
ODA CONCESSIONALITY				
Total: Grant Element	94.0	92.0	97.0	77.0
Loans: Grant Element	77.0	60.0	80.0	39.0
INDEBTEDNESS				
TOTAL DEBT DISBURSED	***2806.0***	***3182.0***	***3853.0***	
Debt to DAC Countries	1006.0	1082.0	1353.0	
ODA	25.0	33.0	49.0	
Total Export Credits	711.0	734.0	804.0	
Other Private Market	270.0	315.0	500.0	
International Org.	–	–	–	
CMEA	1800.0	2000.0	2300.0	
Other	–	100.0	200.0	
TOTAL DEBT SERVICE	***304.3***	***398.9***	***451.7***	
Paid to DAC Countries	154.3	203.9	246.7	
ODA	0.2	0.2	0.5	
Total Export Credits	112.1	176.2	186.2	
Other Private Market	42.0	27.5	60.0	
International Org.	–	–	–	
CMEA	150.0	175.0	200.0	
Other	–	20.0	5.0	
ECONOMIC INDICATORS				
GNP Curr. Prices, $M	–	–	–	–
Real GNP, 1976=100	–	–	–	–
GNP/Cap Curr. Prices,$	–	–	–	–
GNP/cap Atlas Basis, $	–	–	–	–
Real GNP/Cap, 1976=100	–	–	–	–
Population, Million	9.6	9.7	9.8	9.9
Curr.A/C Deficit(-),$M	–	–	–	–
BOP Exp. & Transf.,$M	–	–	–	–
Exp. to OECD CIF, $M	443.5	472.3	610.2	847.5
of which				
Manufact.	8.7	20.8	18.4	16.5
Imp. from OECD FOB, $M	1163.3	882.1	970.2	1508.8
Reserves ex. Gold, $M	–	–	–	–

	TOTAL RECEIPTS NET 1977	1978	1979	1980	TOTAL ODA NET 1977	1978	1979	1980
DAC COUNTRIES								
Australia	0.0	0.0	0.1	0.1	0.0	0.0	0.0	0.0
Austria	0.1	0.1	0.1	0.1	0.1	0.1	0.1	0.1
Belgium	2.1	9.3	0.5	-0.9	–	–	–	–
Canada	–	–	0.3	0.0	–	–	–	–
Denmark	0.0	–	–	–	0.0	–	–	–
Finland	–	0.0	–	–	–	0.0	–	–
France	6.6	2.2	4.1	4.9	–	–	0.3	4.7
Germany, Fed. Rep.	21.5	12.8	-17.3	17.6	4.5	4.4	3.8	4.2
Italy	-0.1	0.9	-0.3	-0.2	0.0	0.0	0.0	0.0
Japan	-1.3	-1.0	-0.6	-0.4	0.0	0.0	0.0	0.1
Netherlands	0.1	0.2	0.1	0.3	0.1	0.2	0.1	0.3
New Zealand	-0.3	0.1	–	–	–	–	–	–
Norway	0.1	-0.2	-0.2	-0.4	–	–	–	–
Sweden	-0.4	–	–	–	–	–	–	–
Switzerland	-0.3	0.7	0.3	2.4	0.0	0.0	0.0	–
United Kingdom	23.2	0.4	-7.5	-2.5	0.6	0.6	1.1	1.5
United States	47.0	22.0	21.0	16.0	44.0	19.0	11.0	20.0
TOTAL	*98.2*	*47.4*	*0.5*	*37.0*	*49.3*	*24.3*	*16.5*	*30.9*
MULTILATERAL								
AF.D.F.	–	–	–	–	–	–	–	–
AF.D.B.	–	–	–	–	–	–	–	–
AS.D.B.	–	–	–	–	–	–	–	–
CAR.D.B.	–	–	–	–	–	–	–	–
E.E.C.	0.1	3.4	–	–	0.1	3.4	–	–
IBRD	0.8	3.2	6.4	8.1	–	–	–	–
IDA	–	–	–	–	–	–	–	–
I.D.B.	–	–	–	–	–	–	–	–
IFAD	–	–	–	–	–	–	–	–
I.F.C.	0.3	-0.3	-0.4	0.1	–	–	–	–
IMF TRUST FUND	–	–	–	–	–	–	–	–
U.N. AGENCIES	–	–	–	–	–	–	–	–
UNDP	0.8	0.6	1.1	1.3	0.8	0.6	1.1	1.3
UNTA	0.2	0.3	0.5	0.2	0.2	0.3	0.5	0.2
UNICEF	0.1	–	–	–	0.1	–	–	–
UNRWA	–	–	–	–	–	–	–	–
WFP	3.4	5.7	4.6	3.8	3.4	5.7	4.6	3.8
UNHCR	41.2	13.4	5.6	15.0	41.2	13.4	5.6	15.0
Other Multilateral	0.9	1.1	0.5	0.7	0.9	1.1	0.5	0.7
Arab OPEC Agencies	–	–	–	–	–	–	–	–
TOTAL	*47.7*	*27.2*	*18.4*	*29.1*	*46.6*	*24.4*	*12.3*	*20.9*
OPEC COUNTRIES	–	–	*1.0*	*0.8*	–	–	*1.0*	*0.8*
E.E.C.+ MEMBERS	*53.4*	*29.1*	*-20.4*	*19.2*	*5.3*	*8.5*	*5.3*	*10.7*
TOTAL	***145.9***	***74.6***	***19.9***	***66.9***	***95.9***	***48.7***	***29.8***	***52.6***

TOTAL ODA GROSS	197
Australia	
Austria	
Belgium	
Canada	
Denmark	
Finland	
France	
Germany, Fed. Rep.	
Italy	
Japan	
Netherlands	
New Zealand	
Norway	
Sweden	
Switzerland	
United Kingdom	
United States	
TOTAL	
AF.D.F.	
AF.D.B.	
AS.D.B.	
CAR.D.B.	
E.E.C.	
IBRD	
IDA	
I.D.B.	
IFAD	
I.F.C.	
IMF TRUST FUND	
U.N. AGENCIES	
UNDP	
UNTA	
UNICEF	
UNRWA	
WFP	
UNHCR	
Other Multilateral	
Arab OPEC Agencies	
TOTAL	
OPEC COUNTRIES	
E.E.C.+ MEMBERS	
TOTAL	

	ODA LOANS GROSS 1977	1978	1979	1980	ODA LOANS NET 1977	1978	1979	1980
DAC COUNTRIES								
Australia	–	–	–	–	–	–	–	–
Austria	–	–	–	–	–	–	–	–
Belgium	–	–	–	–	–	–	–	–
Canada	–	–	–	–	–	–	–	–
Denmark	–	–	–	–	–	–	–	–
Finland	–	–	–	–	–	–	–	–
France	–	–	0.3	4.0	–	–	0.3	4.0
Germany, Fed. Rep.	3.8	3.1	2.3	1.8	3.3	2.4	1.6	1.4
Italy	–	–	–	–	–	–	–	–
Japan	–	–	–	–	–	–	–	–
Netherlands	–	–	–	–	–	–	–	–
New Zealand	–	–	–	–	–	–	–	–
Norway	–	–	–	–	–	–	–	–
Sweden	–	–	–	–	–	–	–	–
Switzerland	–	–	–	–	–	–	–	–
United Kingdom	–	–	–	–	-0.1	-0.1	-0.1	-0.2
United States	–	–	–	–	–	–	–	–
TOTAL	*3.8*	*3.1*	*2.6*	*5.8*	*3.2*	*2.3*	*1.8*	*5.2*
MULTILATERAL	–	–	–	–	–	–	–	–
OPEC COUNTRIES	–	–	*1.0*	*0.8*	–	–	*1.0*	*0.8*
E.E.C.+ MEMBERS	*3.8*	*3.1*	*2.6*	*5.8*	*3.2*	*2.3*	*1.8*	*5.2*
TOTAL	***3.8***	***3.1***	***3.7***	***6.6***	***3.2***	***2.3***	***2.8***	***6.0***

GRANTS	197
Australia	
Austria	
Belgium	
Canada	
Denmark	
Finland	
France	
Germany, Fed. Rep.	
Italy	
Japan	
Netherlands	
New Zealand	
Norway	
Sweden	
Switzerland	
United Kingdom	
United States	
TOTAL	
MULTILATERAL	
OPEC COUNTRIES	
E.E.C.+ MEMBERS	
TOTAL	

	TOTAL OFFICIAL GROSS 1977	1978	1979	1980	TOTAL OFFICIAL NET 1977	1978	1979	1980
DAC COUNTRIES								
Australia	0.0	0.0	0.0	0.0	0.0	0.0	0.0	0.0
Austria	0.1	0.1	0.1	0.1	0.1	0.1	0.1	0.1
Belgium	–	–	–	–	–	–	–	–
Canada	–	–	0.3	0.0	–	–	0.3	0.0
Denmark	0.0	–	–	–	0.0	–	–	–
Finland	–	0.0	–	–	–	0.0	–	–
France	–	–	0.3	4.7	–	–	0.3	4.7
Germany, Fed. Rep.	4.9	5.0	4.5	4.7	4.5	4.4	3.8	4.2
Italy	0.0	0.0	0.0	0.0	0.0	0.0	0.0	0.0
Japan	0.0	0.0	0.0	0.1	0.0	0.0	0.0	0.1
Netherlands	0.1	0.2	0.1	0.3	0.1	0.2	0.1	0.3
New Zealand	0.5	–	–	–	-0.3	–	–	–
Norway	–	–	–	–	–	–	–	–
Sweden	–	–	–	–	–	–	–	–
Switzerland	0.0	0.0	0.0	–	0.0	0.0	0.0	–
United Kingdom	0.7	0.7	1.2	1.6	0.6	0.6	1.1	1.5
United States	48.0	26.0	18.0	21.0	47.0	24.0	13.0	16.0
TOTAL	*54.4*	*32.1*	*24.7*	*32.5*	*52.1*	*29.3*	*18.8*	*26.9*
MULTILATERAL	*50.5*	*30.2*	*21.8*	*33.3*	*47.7*	*27.2*	*18.4*	*29.1*
OPEC COUNTRIES	–	–	*1.0*	*0.8*	–	–	*1.0*	*0.8*
E.E.C.+ MEMBERS	*5.8*	*9.3*	*6.2*	*11.3*	*5.3*	*8.5*	*5.3*	*10.7*
TOTAL	***104.9***	***62.3***	***47.5***	***66.6***	***99.8***	***56.5***	***38.2***	***56.8***

TOTAL OOF GROSS	197
Australia	
Austria	
Belgium	
Canada	
Denmark	
Finland	
France	
Germany, Fed. Rep.	
Italy	
Japan	
Netherlands	
New Zealand	
Norway	
Sweden	
Switzerland	
United Kingdom	
United States	
TOTAL	
MULTILATERAL	
OPEC COUNTRIES	
E.E.C.+ MEMBERS	
TOTAL	

1978	1979	1980	1977	1978	1979	1980
			ODA COMMITMENTS			
0.0	0.0	0.0	0.0	–	–	0.1
0.1	0.1	0.1	–	–	–	–
–	–	–	–	–	–	–
–	–	–	–	–	–	–
–	–	–	0.0	–	–	–
0.0	–	–	–	0.0	–	–
–	0.3	4.7	–	–	4.3	4.0
5.0	4.5	4.7	4.4	3.4	4.4	8.6
0.0	0.0	0.0	0.0	0.0	0.0	0.0
0.0	0.0	0.1	0.0	0.0	0.0	0.1
0.2	0.1	0.3	0.1	0.2	0.1	0.3
–	–	–	–	–	–	–
–	–	–	–	–	–	–
–	–	–	–	–	–	–
0.0	0.0	–	–	–	–	–
0.7	1.2	1.6	0.7	0.7	1.2	2.5
19.0	11.0	20.0	–	15.8	–	15.0
25.1	*17.3*	*31.5*	*5.3*	*20.2*	*10.0*	*30.4*
–	–	–	–	–	–	–
–	–	–	–	–	–	–
–	–	–	–	–	–	–
–	–	–	–	–	–	–
3.4	–	–	1.7	–	–	–
–	–	–	–	–	–	–
–	–	–	–	–	–	–
–	–	–	–	–	–	–
–	–	–	–	–	–	–
–	–	–	–	–	–	–
–	–	–	–	–	–	–
–	–	–	46.5	21.0	12.3	20.9
0.6	1.1	1.3	–	–	–	–
0.3	0.5	0.2	–	–	–	–
–	–	–	–	–	–	–
–	–	–	–	–	–	–
5.7	4.6	3.8	–	–	–	–
13.4	5.6	15.0	–	–	–	–
1.1	0.5	0.7	–	–	–	–
–	–	–	–	–	–	–
24.4	*12.3*	*20.9*	*48.2*	*21.0*	*12.3*	*20.9*
–	*1.0*	*0.8*	*3.9*	–	–	*9.2*
9.3	*6.2*	*11.3*	*6.9*	*4.3*	*10.0*	*15.3*
49.4	***30.7***	***53.2***	***57.5***	***41.2***	***22.3***	***60.6***
			TECH. COOP. GRANTS			
0.0	0.0	0.0	0.0	0.0	0.0	0.0
0.1	0.1	0.1	0.1	0.1	0.1	0.1
–	–	–	–	–	–	–
–	–	–	–	–	–	–
–	–	–	–	–	–	–
0.0	–	–	–	0.0	–	–
–	–	0.7	–	–	–	0.7
2.0	2.2	2.9	1.1	1.9	2.2	2.9
0.0	0.0	0.0	0.0	0.0	0.0	0.0
0.0	0.0	0.1	0.0	0.0	0.0	0.1
0.2	0.1	0.3	0.1	0.2	0.1	0.3
–	–	–	–	–	–	–
–	–	–	–	–	–	–
–	–	–	–	–	–	–
0.0	0.0	–	–	0.0	0.0	–
0.7	1.2	1.6	0.7	0.7	1.1	1.3
19.0	11.0	20.0	–	–	–	–
22.0	*14.7*	*25.7*	*2.0*	*3.0*	*3.6*	*5.4*
24.4	*12.3*	*20.9*	*43.2*	*15.3*	*7.7*	*20.9*
–	–	–	–	–	–	–
6.2	*3.6*	*5.5*	*1.9*	*2.8*	*3.5*	*5.2*
46.4	***27.0***	***46.6***	***45.2***	***18.3***	***11.3***	***26.3***
			TOTAL OOF NET			
–	–	–	–	–	–	–
–	–	–	–	–	–	–
–	–	–	–	–	–	–
–	0.3	0.0	–	–	0.3	0.0
–	–	–	–	–	–	–
–	–	–	–	–	–	–
–	–	–	–	–	–	–
–	–	–	–	–	0.0	–
–	–	–	–	–	–	–
–	–	–	–	–	–	–
–	–	–	–	–	–	–
–	–	–	-0.3	–	–	–
–	–	–	–	–	–	–
–	–	–	–	–	–	–
–	–	–	–	–	–	–
–	–	–	–	–	–	–
7.0	7.0	1.0	3.0	5.0	2.0	-4.0
7.0	*7.3*	*1.0*	*2.7*	*5.0*	*2.3*	*-4.0*
5.9	*9.5*	*12.3*	*1.1*	*2.9*	*6.0*	*8.2*
–	–	–	–	–	–	–
–	–	–	–	–	*0.0*	–
12.9	***16.8***	***13.4***	***3.8***	***7.9***	***8.4***	***4.2***

MAIN AID AGGREGATES

	1977	1978	1979	1980
DAC COUNTRIES COMBINED				
PRIVATE SECTOR NET	46.1	18.1	-18.2	10.1
Direct Investment	3.9	-1.0	6.3	-0.6
Portfolio Invest.	17.4	11.5	-18.0	15.2
Export Credits	24.7	7.6	-6.6	-4.5
OFFICIAL & PRIVATE				
GROSS:				
Contractual Lending	42.9	29.5	13.9	18.2
Export Credits Tot.	39.2	26.4	11.3	12.4
Export Credits Priv	34.7	19.4	3.9	11.4
OTHER NET DATA				
Contractual Lending	30.7	14.9	-2.5	-3.3
Export Credits Tot.	27.5	12.6	-4.2	-8.5
(Bank Sector Loans)	39.0	54.0	4.0	104.0
ODA CONCESSIONALITY				
Total:Grant Element	74.0	100.0	58.0	81.0
Loans:Grant Element	36.0	–	37.0	44.0
OTHER SOURCES				
CMEA Countr.(Gross)	1.0	0.2	0.1	1.8
Intra LDCS Exc.OPEC	–	–	–	–
Other	–	–	–	–
ALL SOURCE COMMITMENTS				
TOTAL BILATERAL	14.0	31.0	14.6	41.9
of which				
OPEC (ODA)	3.9	–	–	9.2
CMEA (ODA)	–	–	–	5.0
TOTAL MULTILAT.(ODA)	48.2	21.0	12.3	20.9
TOTAL BIL.& MULTIL.	62.2	52.0	26.9	62.9
of which				
ODA Grants	51.4	41.2	15.3	41.4
ODA Loans	6.1	–	7.0	19.2
ODA CONCESSIONALITY				
Total: Grant Element	92.0	100.0	82.0	80.0
Loans: Grant Element	30.0	–	37.0	38.0

INDEBTEDNESS

	1977	1978	1979	1980
TOTAL DEBT DISBURSED	***221.8***	***245.7***	***307.6***	
Debt to DAC Countries	133.0	140.0	190.0	
ODA	15.0	21.0	24.0	
Total Export Credits	33.0	49.0	60.0	
Other Private Market	85.0	70.0	106.0	
International Org.	81.2	100.7	111.9	
CMEA	–	–	–	
Other	7.5	5.0	5.7	
TOTAL DEBT SERVICE	***33.4***	***47.5***	***50.9***	
Paid to DAC Countries	24.5	34.1	38.9	
ODA	0.9	1.2	1.4	
Total Export Credits	10.1	16.9	19.0	
Other Private Market	13.5	16.0	18.5	
International Org.	7.8	9.7	11.2	
CMEA	–	–	–	
Other	1.1	3.7	0.8	

ECONOMIC INDICATORS

	1977	1978	1979	1980
GNP Curr. Prices, $M	1115.0	1428.5	1781.6	2094.6
Real GNP, 1976=100	138.0	151.2	159.5	165.8
GNP/Cap Curr. Prices,$	1818.0	2319.0	2882.0	3378.0
GNP/cap Atlas Basis, $	–	–	3168.1	3557.7
Real GNP/Cap, 1976=100	137.2	148.8	155.4	161.0
Population, Million	0.6	0.6	0.6	0.6
Curr.A/C Deficit(-),$M	-146.0	-202.2	-251.4	-284.2
BOP Exp. & Transf.,$M	579.6	680.8	921.6	1117.5
Exp. to OECD CIF, $M	200.1	294.6	275.7	341.4
of which				
Manufact.	22.6	141.3	83.7	121.8
Imp. from OECD FOB, $M	513.6	654.9	797.8	979.7
Reserves ex. Gold, $M	313.5	345.7	353.1	368.3

TOTAL RECEIPTS NET

	1977	1978	1979	1980
DAC COUNTRIES				
Australia	0.0	0.0	–	0.5
Austria	0.0	0.0	0.1	0.0
Belgium	-0.3	0.0	0.2	0.6
Canada	-0.8	-19.0	–	1.0
Denmark	0.0	0.0	-0.1	-0.1
Finland	–	–	–	0.0
France	-4.2	0.0	-1.6	4.8
Germany, Fed. Rep.	0.8	1.1	3.4	12.7
Italy	1.0	-1.0	-0.7	-0.5
Japan	-3.5	-3.4	-1.5	-1.7
Netherlands	0.6	1.4	1.3	2.3
New Zealand	–	–	–	–
Norway	–	5.3	22.5	0.6
Sweden	-0.6	-0.5	0.4	0.1
Switzerland	0.3	0.3	0.5	–
United Kingdom	0.1	0.9	0.2	-0.1
United States	1.0	-3.0	61.0	32.0
TOTAL	*-5.5*	*-18.1*	*85.6*	*52.1*
MULTILATERAL				
AF.D.F.	–	–	–	–
AF.D.B.	–	–	–	–
AS.D.B.	–	–	–	–
CAR.D.B.	–	–	–	–
E.E.C.	–	0.1	–	0.5
IBRD	5.2	2.1	3.7	36.6
IDA	0.6	5.8	0.4	0.3
I.D.B.	18.5	29.0	31.6	54.1
IFAD	–	–	–	0.7
I.F.C.	-0.3	–	–	–
IMF TRUST FUND	–	–	–	–
U.N. AGENCIES	–	–	–	–
UNDP	0.8	1.3	2.2	2.2
UNTA	0.1	0.2	0.5	0.2
UNICEF	0.1	0.3	0.6	0.5
UNRWA	–	–	–	–
WFP	–	–	0.1	2.9
UNHCR	–	–	0.0	–
Other Multilateral	0.8	0.1	0.1	1.5
Arab OPEC Agencies	–	0.1	2.1	3.0
TOTAL	*25.7*	*38.9*	*41.4*	*102.6*
OPEC COUNTRIES	*60.0*	*14.3*	*1.1*	*1.0*
E.E.C.+ MEMBERS	*-1.9*	*2.4*	*2.7*	*20.0*
TOTAL	***80.2***	***35.2***	***128.0***	***155.7***

TOTAL ODA NET

	1977	1978	1979	1980
Australia	–	–	–	–
Austria	0.0	0.0	0.1	0.0
Belgium	0.1	0.1	0.1	0.3
Canada	0.1	0.1	–	0.4
Denmark	0.0	0.0	–	–
Finland	–	–	–	0.0
France	–	–	–	3.6
Germany, Fed. Rep.	1.4	1.4	2.7	12.9
Italy	0.0	0.1	0.1	0.0
Japan	0.1	0.1	0.7	0.8
Netherlands	0.6	1.4	1.3	2.3
New Zealand	–	–	–	–
Norway	–	–	–	0.6
Sweden	–	–	0.5	–
Switzerland	–	0.0	0.0	–
United Kingdom	0.1	0.2	0.2	0.3
United States	8.0	6.0	31.0	36.0
TOTAL	*10.5*	*9.4*	*36.8*	*57.2*
AF.D.F.	–	–	–	–
AF.D.B.	–	–	–	–
AS.D.B.	–	–	–	–
CAR.D.B.	–	–	–	–
E.E.C.	–	0.1	–	0.5
IBRD	2.3	3.0	2.2	1.1
IDA	0.6	5.8	0.4	0.3
I.D.B.	18.5	29.6	31.6	53.8
IFAD	–	–	–	0.7
I.F.C.	–	–	–	–
IMF TRUST FUND	–	–	–	–
U.N. AGENCIES	–	–	–	–
UNDP	0.8	1.3	2.2	2.2
UNTA	0.1	0.2	0.5	0.2
UNICEF	0.1	0.3	0.6	0.5
UNRWA	–	–	–	–
WFP	–	–	0.1	2.9
UNHCR	–	–	0.0	–
Other Multilateral	0.8	0.1	0.1	1.5
Arab OPEC Agencies	–	0.1	2.1	3.0
TOTAL	*23.1*	*40.4*	*39.8*	*66.8*
OPEC COUNTRIES	–	–	*1.1*	*1.0*
E.E.C.+ MEMBERS	*2.2*	*3.3*	*4.5*	*19.8*
TOTAL	***33.6***	***49.9***	***77.7***	***125.0***

TOTAL ODA GROSS

	197
Australia	
Austria	
Belgium	
Canada	
Denmark	
Finland	
France	
Germany, Fed. Rep.	
Italy	
Japan	
Netherlands	
New Zealand	
Norway	
Sweden	
Switzerland	
United Kingdom	
United States	
TOTAL	
AF.D.F.	
AF.D.B.	
AS.D.B.	
CAR.D.B.	
E.E.C.	
IBRD	
IDA	
I.D.B.	
IFAD	
I.F.C.	
IMF TRUST FUND	
U.N. AGENCIES	
UNDP	
UNTA	
UNICEF	
UNRWA	
WFP	
UNHCR	
Other Multilateral	
Arab OPEC Agencies	
TOTAL	
OPEC COUNTRIES	
E.E.C.+ MEMBERS	
TOTAL	

ODA LOANS GROSS

	1977	1978	1979	1980
DAC COUNTRIES				
Australia	–	–	–	–
Austria	–	–	–	–
Belgium	–	–	–	–
Canada	0.1	–	–	0.3
Denmark	–	–	–	–
Finland	–	–	–	–
France	–	–	–	3.3
Germany, Fed. Rep.	0.3	–	0.3	7.9
Italy	–	–	–	–
Japan	–	–	–	–
Netherlands	–	–	–	–
New Zealand	–	–	–	–
Norway	–	–	–	–
Sweden	–	–	–	–
Switzerland	–	–	–	–
United Kingdom	–	–	–	–
United States	4.0	6.0	24.0	35.0
TOTAL	*4.4*	*6.0*	*24.3*	*46.4*
MULTILATERAL	*24.1*	*40.2*	*38.8*	*58.8*
OPEC COUNTRIES	–	–	–	–
E.E.C.+ MEMBERS	*0.3*	–	*0.3*	*11.1*
TOTAL	***28.5***	***46.2***	***63.1***	***105.2***

ODA LOANS NET

	1977	1978	1979	1980
Australia	–	–	–	–
Austria	–	–	–	–
Belgium	–	–	–	–
Canada	0.1	–	–	0.3
Denmark	–	–	–	–
Finland	–	–	–	–
France	–	–	–	3.3
Germany, Fed. Rep.	0.3	–	0.3	7.9
Italy	–	–	–	–
Japan	–	–	–	–
Netherlands	–	–	–	–
New Zealand	–	–	–	–
Norway	–	–	–	–
Sweden	–	–	–	–
Switzerland	–	–	–	–
United Kingdom	–	–	–	–
United States	-4.0	-3.0	13.0	27.0
TOTAL	*-3.6*	*-3.0*	*13.3*	*38.4*
MULTILATERAL	*21.4*	*37.4*	*36.0*	*56.1*
OPEC COUNTRIES	–	–	–	–
E.E.C.+ MEMBERS	*0.3*	–	*0.3*	*11.1*
TOTAL	***17.8***	***34.4***	***49.3***	***94.5***

GRANTS

	197
Australia	
Austria	
Belgium	
Canada	
Denmark	
Finland	
France	
Germany, Fed. Rep.	
Italy	
Japan	
Netherlands	
New Zealand	
Norway	
Sweden	
Switzerland	
United Kingdom	
United States	
TOTAL	
MULTILATERAL	
OPEC COUNTRIES	
E.E.C.+ MEMBERS	
TOTAL	

TOTAL OFFICIAL GROSS

	1977	1978	1979	1980
DAC COUNTRIES				
Australia	–	–	–	–
Austria	0.0	0.0	0.1	0.0
Belgium	0.1	0.1	0.1	0.3
Canada	1.6	0.3	–	1.0
Denmark	0.0	0.0	–	–
Finland	–	–	–	0.0
France	–	–	–	3.6
Germany, Fed. Rep.	1.4	1.4	2.7	12.9
Italy	0.0	0.1	0.1	0.0
Japan	0.1	0.1	0.7	0.8
Netherlands	0.6	1.4	1.3	2.3
New Zealand	–	–	–	–
Norway	–	–	–	0.6
Sweden	–	–	0.5	–
Switzerland	–	0.0	0.0	–
United Kingdom	0.1	0.2	0.2	0.3
United States	18.0	16.0	80.0	55.0
TOTAL	*21.9*	*19.7*	*85.8*	*76.8*
MULTILATERAL	*31.3*	*44.5*	*46.3*	*107.2*
OPEC COUNTRIES	*60.0*	*14.3*	*1.1*	*1.0*
E.E.C.+ MEMBERS	*2.2*	*3.3*	*4.5*	*19.8*
TOTAL	***113.3***	***78.5***	***133.2***	***184.9***

TOTAL OFFICIAL NET

	1977	1978	1979	1980
Australia	–	–	–	–
Austria	0.0	0.0	0.1	0.0
Belgium	0.1	0.1	0.1	0.3
Canada	-0.8	-19.0	–	1.0
Denmark	0.0	0.0	–	-0.1
Finland	–	–	–	0.0
France	–	–	–	3.6
Germany, Fed. Rep.	1.4	1.4	2.7	12.9
Italy	0.0	0.1	0.1	0.0
Japan	0.1	0.1	0.7	0.8
Netherlands	0.6	1.4	1.3	2.3
New Zealand	–	–	–	–
Norway	–	–	–	0.6
Sweden	–	–	0.5	–
Switzerland	–	0.0	0.0	–
United Kingdom	0.1	0.2	0.2	0.3
United States	1.0	-3.0	61.0	32.0
TOTAL	*2.6*	*-18.6*	*66.8*	*53.6*
MULTILATERAL	*25.7*	*38.9*	*41.4*	*102.6*
OPEC COUNTRIES	*60.0*	*14.3*	*1.1*	*1.0*
E.E.C.+ MEMBERS	*2.2*	*3.3*	*4.5*	*19.7*
TOTAL	***88.3***	***34.6***	***109.2***	***157.2***

TOTAL OOF GROSS

	197
Australia	
Austria	
Belgium	
Canada	
Denmark	
Finland	
France	
Germany, Fed. Rep.	
Italy	
Japan	
Netherlands	
New Zealand	
Norway	
Sweden	
Switzerland	
United Kingdom	
United States	
TOTAL	
MULTILATERAL	
OPEC COUNTRIES	
E.E.C.+ MEMBERS	
TOTAL	

1978	1979	1980	1977	1978	1979	1980
			ODA COMMITMENTS			
–	–	–	–	–	–	–
0.0	0.1	0.0	–	–	–	–
0.1	0.1	0.3	–	–	–	–
0.1	–	0.4	–	0.0	0.0	4.9
0.0	–	–	0.0	0.1	–	–
–	–	0.0	–	–	–	0.0
–	–	3.6	–	–	–	5.6
1.4	2.7	12.9	0.6	1.9	15.3	6.0
0.1	0.1	0.0	0.0	0.1	0.1	0.0
0.1	0.7	0.8	0.2	0.2	0.7	15.8
1.4	1.3	2.3	0.8	2.5	1.2	1.9
–	–	–	–	–	–	–
–	–	0.6	–	–	–	–
–	0.5	–	–	–	–	3.9
0.0	0.0	–	–	–	–	–
0.2	0.2	0.3	0.1	0.2	0.2	0.3
15.0	42.0	44.0	15.0	28.6	41.5	44.6
18.4	*47.8*	*65.2*	*16.7*	*33.5*	*59.0*	*83.1*
–	–	–	–	–	–	–
–	–	–	–	–	–	–
–	–	–	–	–	–	–
–	–	–	–	–	–	–
0.1	–	0.5	–	0.3	–	–
3.0	2.2	1.1	–	–	–	–
5.8	0.4	0.3	–	–	–	–
32.4	34.4	56.5	3.2	64.5	145.5	34.2
–	–	0.7	–	–	12.3	–
–	–	–	–	–	–	–
–	–	–	–	–	–	–
–	–	–	1.8	1.8	3.5	7.3
1.3	2.2	2.2	–	–	–	–
0.2	0.5	0.2	–	–	–	–
0.3	0.6	0.5	–	–	–	–
–	–	–	–	–	–	–
–	0.1	2.9	–	–	–	–
–	0.0	–	–	–	–	–
0.1	0.1	1.5	–	–	–	–
0.1	2.1	3.0	2.9	–	5.0	–
43.2	*42.6*	*69.5*	*7.9*	*66.6*	*166.3*	*41.5*
–	*1.1*	*1.0*	–	–	*1.1*	*1.0*
3.3	*4.5*	*19.8*	*1.5*	*5.0*	*16.8*	*13.9*
61.7	***91.5***	***135.7***	***24.5***	***100.1***	***226.5***	***125.6***
			TECH. COOP. GRANTS			
–	–	–	–	–	–	–
0.0	0.1	0.0	0.0	0.0	0.0	0.0
0.1	0.1	0.3	0.0	0.1	0.1	0.3
0.1	–	0.1	–	–	–	–
0.0	–	–	0.0	0.0	–	–
–	–	0.0	–	–	–	–
–	–	0.3	–	–	–	0.3
1.4	2.5	5.0	1.1	1.4	2.2	4.0
0.1	0.1	0.0	0.0	0.1	0.0	0.0
0.1	0.7	0.8	0.1	0.1	0.2	0.8
1.4	1.3	2.3	0.2	0.6	0.4	1.1
–	–	–	–	–	–	–
–	–	0.6	–	–	–	–
–	0.5	–	–	–	–	–
0.0	0.0	–	–	0.0	0.0	–
0.2	0.2	0.3	0.1	0.2	0.2	0.3
9.0	18.0	9.0	1.0	2.0	1.0	2.0
12.4	*23.5*	*18.7*	*2.5*	*4.6*	*4.2*	*8.7*
3.0	*3.8*	*10.7*	*1.8*	*2.9*	*3.7*	*7.3*
–	*1.1*	*1.0*	–	–	–	–
3.3	*4.2*	*8.7*	*1.4*	*2.4*	*2.9*	*5.9*
15.5	***28.4***	***30.5***	***4.3***	***7.5***	***7.8***	***16.0***
			TOTAL OOF NET			
–	–	–	–	–	–	–
–	–	–	–	–	–	–
–	–	–	–	–	–	–
0.2	–	0.6	-0.9	-19.1	–	0.6
–	–	–	–	–	–	-0.1
–	–	–	–	–	–	–
–	–	–	–	–	–	–
–	–	–	0.0	0.0	–	–
–	–	–	–	–	–	–
–	–	–	–	–	–	–
–	–	–	–	–	–	–
–	–	–	–	–	–	–
–	–	–	–	–	–	–
–	–	–	–	–	–	–
–	–	–	–	–	–	–
–	–	–	–	–	–	–
1.0	38.0	11.0	-7.0	-9.0	30.0	-4.0
1.2	*38.0*	*11.6*	*-7.9*	*-28.1*	*30.0*	*-3.5*
1.3	*3.7*	*37.7*	*2.6*	*-1.5*	*1.5*	*35.8*
14.3	–	–	*60.0*	*14.3*	–	–
–	–	–	*0.0*	*0.0*	–	*-0.1*
16.8	***41.7***	***49.3***	***54.7***	***-15.2***	***31.5***	***32.3***

MAIN AID AGGREGATES

	1977	1978	1979	1980
DAC COUNTRIES COMBINED				
PRIVATE SECTOR NET	-8.1	0.6	18.8	-1.5
Direct Investment	0.3	–	0.2	0.2
Portfolio Invest.	-0.5	3.1	7.6	-60.9
Export Credits	-7.8	-2.5	11.0	59.2
OFFICIAL & PRIVATE				
GROSS:				
Contractual Lending	12.2	18.5	87.4	124.2
Export Credits Tot.	7.8	12.5	62.1	77.8
Export Credits Priv	4.4	11.3	25.1	66.2
OTHER NET DATA				
Contractual Lending	-19.3	-33.6	54.3	94.1
Export Credits Tot.	-15.7	-30.6	40.0	55.8
(Bank Sector Loans)	54.0	30.0	42.0	11.0
ODA CONCESSIONALITY				
Total:Grant Element	91.0	77.0	75.0	70.0
Loans:Grant Element	45.0	65.0	58.0	50.0
OTHER SOURCES				
CMEA Countr.(Gross)	–	–	–	–
Intra LDCS Exc.OPEC	–	–	–	–
Other	–	–	–	–
ALL SOURCE COMMITMENTS				
TOTAL BILATERAL	17.0	33.6	90.5	99.4
of which				
OPEC (ODA)	–	–	1.1	1.0
CMEA (ODA)	–	–	–	–
TOTAL MULTILAT.(ODA)	7.9	66.6	166.3	41.5
TOTAL BIL.& MULTIL.	24.9	100.2	256.8	140.9
of which				
ODA Grants	15.9	14.1	28.9	42.0
ODA Loans	8.6	86.0	197.6	83.6
ODA CONCESSIONALITY				
Total: Grant Element	80.0	78.0	74.0	73.0
Loans: Grant Element	69.0	66.0	71.0	54.0

INDEBTEDNESS

	1977	1978	1979	1980
TOTAL DEBT DISBURSED	***772.7***	***890.6***	***962.0***	
Debt to DAC Countries	646.0	708.0	740.0	
ODA	204.0	199.0	212.0	
Total Export Credits	92.0	166.0	162.0	
Other Private Market	350.0	343.0	366.0	
International Org.	53.8	87.4	115.3	
CMEA	–	–	–	
Other	72.9	95.1	106.8	
TOTAL DEBT SERVICE	***97.0***	***105.2***	***278.9***	
Paid to DAC Countries	90.3	92.4	241.6	
ODA	12.0	15.0	16.0	
Total Export Credits	29.3	47.7	31.1	
Other Private Market	49.0	29.7	194.5	
International Org.	4.7	5.4	6.1	
CMEA	–	–	–	
Other	2.0	7.4	31.2	

ECONOMIC INDICATORS

	1977	1978	1979	1980
GNP Curr. Prices, $M	4415.4	4590.8	5321.4	6484.4
Real GNP, 1976=100	105.0	108.0	112.0	118.0
GNP/Cap Curr. Prices,$	886.0	895.0	1007.0	1192.0
GNP/cap Atlas Basis, $	874.7	937.2	1025.5	1140.9
Real GNP/Cap, 1976=100	102.0	102.0	102.0	105.0
Population, Million	5.0	5.1	5.3	5.4
Curr.A/C Deficit(-),$M	-264.7	-322.4	-365.1	–
BOP Exp. & Transf.,$M	969.9	936.3	1257.2	–
Exp. to OECD CIF, $M	758.2	706.3	876.0	930.8
of which				
Manufact.	69.8	104.6	138.1	155.7
Imp. from OECD FOB, $M	662.1	697.8	901.8	1171.3
Reserves ex. Gold, $M	180.1	154.0	238.6	201.8

	TOTAL RECEIPTS NET 1977	1978	1979	1980	TOTAL ODA NET 1977	1978	1979	1980
DAC COUNTRIES								
Australia	-0.9	-0.2	–	–	–	–	–	–
Austria	0.3	0.3	0.1	0.2	0.3	0.3	0.1	0.2
Belgium	-0.8	5.4	7.1	14.5	0.5	1.1	2.3	1.5
Canada	4.3	4.1	1.8	7.7	0.5	0.1	0.6	0.0
Denmark	1.4	1.5	0.0	3.5	–	-0.1	-0.1	0.0
Finland	-0.1	0.6	-0.1	-0.1	0.0	0.0	–	–
France	-7.0	8.6	-24.1	25.1	–	1.2	–	2.1
Germany, Fed. Rep.	30.3	55.9	19.6	-12.2	9.9	7.6	11.2	11.5
Italy	0.7	120.8	261.9	17.0	0.5	0.6	0.4	0.1
Japan	28.2	2.4	39.3	20.5	1.4	7.1	28.1	4.6
Netherlands	1.3	1.1	1.1	9.6	1.3	1.1	1.1	1.5
New Zealand	-0.1	–	–	–	–	–	–	–
Norway	0.2	32.0	17.4	19.4	–	–	–	0.1
Sweden	0.7	10.2	0.1	-2.1	–	–	0.1	–
Switzerland	3.2	19.6	5.6	3.6	0.3	0.8	0.6	0.6
United Kingdom	33.0	3.3	8.3	-10.8	3.3	2.8	3.5	1.1
United States	49.0	59.0	225.0	46.0	5.0	1.0	2.0	–
TOTAL	*143.8*	*324.8*	*563.1*	*141.9*	*22.9*	*23.5*	*50.0*	*23.3*
MULTILATERAL								
AF.D.F.	–	–	–	–	–	–	–	–
AF.D.B.	–	–	–	–	–	–	–	–
AS.D.B.	–	–	–	–	–	–	–	–
CAR.D.B.	–	–	–	–	–	–	–	–
E.E.C.	0.1	0.2	0.3	0.8	0.1	0.2	0.3	0.8
IBRD	1.7	16.7	24.8	24.2	–	–	–	–
IDA	4.8	0.7	0.1	-0.2	4.8	0.7	0.1	-0.2
I.D.B.	26.7	15.8	30.8	54.3	21.8	12.8	10.7	12.8
IFAD	–	–	–	–	–	–	–	–
I.F.C.	4.8	-0.2	2.5	8.3	–	–	–	–
IMF TRUST FUND	–	–	–	–	–	–	–	–
U.N. AGENCIES	–	–	–	–	–	–	–	–
UNDP	1.9	1.8	3.9	4.5	1.9	1.8	3.9	4.5
UNTA	0.5	0.6	0.4	0.3	0.5	0.6	0.4	0.3
UNICEF	0.1	0.2	0.3	0.7	0.1	0.2	0.3	0.7
UNRWA	–	–	–	–	–	–	–	–
WFP	1.8	4.1	3.3	2.5	1.8	4.1	3.3	2.5
UNHCR	–	–	–	–	–	–	–	–
Other Multilateral	1.5	0.9	0.8	1.8	1.5	0.9	0.8	1.8
Arab OPEC Agencies	–	–	–	–	–	–	–	–
TOTAL	*43.8*	*40.9*	*67.1*	*97.1*	*32.3*	*21.3*	*19.6*	*23.1*
OPEC COUNTRIES	*25.0*	–	–	–	–	–	–	–
E.E.C.+ MEMBERS	*59.1*	*196.9*	*274.2*	*47.4*	*15.5*	*14.5*	*18.7*	*18.5*
TOTAL	***212.6***	***365.7***	***630.2***	***239.0***	***55.2***	***44.9***	***69.6***	***46.4***

	ODA LOANS GROSS 1977	1978	1979	1980	ODA LOANS NET 1977	1978	1979	1980
DAC COUNTRIES								
Australia	–	–	–	–	–	–	–	–
Austria	–	–	–	–	–	–	–	–
Belgium	–	–	–	–	–	–	–	–
Canada	0.3	0.1	0.6	–	0.3	0.0	0.6	0.0
Denmark	–	-0.1	–	–	–	-0.1	-0.2	0.0
Finland	–	–	–	–	–	–	–	–
France	–	–	–	–	–	–	–	–
Germany, Fed. Rep.	5.1	1.9	4.5	1.7	4.1	0.8	3.2	0.4
Italy	–	–	–	–	–	–	–	–
Japan	1.1	4.7	26.5	3.8	1.1	4.1	26.5	3.8
Netherlands	0.2	–	–	–	0.2	–	–	–
New Zealand	–	–	–	–	–	–	–	–
Norway	–	–	–	–	–	–	–	–
Sweden	–	–	–	–	–	–	–	–
Switzerland	–	–	–	–	–	–	–	–
United Kingdom	2.4	2.1	2.5	0.2	2.2	1.4	1.9	-0.9
United States	3.0	–	–	–	-1.0	-4.0	-5.0	-4.0
TOTAL	*12.1*	*8.7*	*34.0*	*5.7*	*6.8*	*2.2*	*27.0*	*-0.7*
MULTILATERAL	*28.9*	*15.6*	*13.8*	*15.7*	*26.6*	*12.9*	*10.6*	*11.5*
OPEC COUNTRIES	–	–	–	–	–	–	–	–
E.E.C.+ MEMBERS	*7.7*	*3.9*	*6.9*	*1.9*	*6.5*	*2.1*	*5.0*	*-0.5*
TOTAL	***41.0***	***24.4***	***47.8***	***21.4***	***33.4***	***15.1***	***37.7***	***10.8***

	TOTAL OFFICIAL GROSS 1977	1978	1979	1980	TOTAL OFFICIAL NET 1977	1978	1979	1980
DAC COUNTRIES								
Australia	–	–	–	–	–	–	–	–
Austria	0.3	0.3	0.1	0.2	0.3	0.3	0.1	0.2
Belgium	0.5	1.1	2.3	1.5	0.5	1.1	2.3	1.5
Canada	6.1	5.8	3.2	9.3	4.7	4.3	1.8	7.8
Denmark	–	-0.1	0.1	1.6	–	-0.1	-0.1	1.6
Finland	0.0	0.0	–	–	0.0	0.0	–	–
France	–	1.2	–	2.1	–	1.2	–	2.1
Germany, Fed. Rep.	10.8	8.8	12.5	12.8	9.9	7.6	11.2	11.5
Italy	0.5	0.6	0.4	2.1	0.5	0.6	0.4	2.1
Japan	2.6	7.8	28.5	7.1	2.0	5.6	27.0	5.6
Netherlands	1.3	1.1	1.1	1.5	1.3	1.1	1.1	1.5
New Zealand	–	–	–	–	-0.1	–	–	–
Norway	–	–	–	0.1	–	–	–	0.1
Sweden	–	–	0.1	–	–	–	0.1	–
Switzerland	0.3	0.8	0.6	0.6	0.3	0.8	0.6	0.6
United Kingdom	3.6	3.4	4.0	2.2	3.3	2.8	3.5	1.1
United States	10.0	6.0	12.0	25.0	-2.0	1.0	6.0	20.0
TOTAL	*35.9*	*36.7*	*64.9*	*66.0*	*20.5*	*26.2*	*54.0*	*55.7*
MULTILATERAL	*54.3*	*51.5*	*79.3*	*114.2*	*43.8*	*40.9*	*67.1*	*97.1*
OPEC COUNTRIES	*25.0*	–	–	–	*25.0*	–	–	–
E.E.C.+ MEMBERS	*16.8*	*16.3*	*20.6*	*24.4*	*15.5*	*14.5*	*18.7*	*22.1*
TOTAL	***115.1***	***88.2***	***144.2***	***180.1***	***89.3***	***67.0***	***121.1***	***152.8***

TOTAL ODA GROSS	19[illegible]
Australia	
Austria	[illegible]
Belgium	[illegible]
Canada	[illegible]
Denmark	
Finland	[illegible]
France	
Germany, Fed. Rep.	[illegible]
Italy	[illegible]
Japan	[illegible]
Netherlands	[illegible]
New Zealand	
Norway	
Sweden	
Switzerland	[illegible]
United Kingdom	[illegible]
United States	[illegible]
TOTAL	[illegible]
AF.D.F.	
AF.D.B.	
AS.D.B.	
CAR.D.B.	
E.E.C.	[illegible]
IBRD	
IDA	[illegible]
I.D.B.	[illegible]
IFAD	
I.F.C.	
IMF TRUST FUND	
U.N. AGENCIES	
UNDP	
UNTA	[illegible]
UNICEF	[illegible]
UNRWA	
WFP	
UNHCR	
Other Multilateral	[illegible]
Arab OPEC Agencies	
TOTAL	[illegible]
OPEC COUNTRIES	
E.E.C.+ MEMBERS	[illegible]
TOTAL	[illegible]

GRANTS	19[illegible]
Australia	
Austria	[illegible]
Belgium	[illegible]
Canada	[illegible]
Denmark	
Finland	[illegible]
France	
Germany, Fed. Rep.	[illegible]
Italy	[illegible]
Japan	[illegible]
Netherlands	[illegible]
New Zealand	
Norway	
Sweden	
Switzerland	[illegible]
United Kingdom	[illegible]
United States	[illegible]
TOTAL	[illegible]
MULTILATERAL	[illegible]
OPEC COUNTRIES	
E.E.C.+ MEMBERS	[illegible]
TOTAL	[illegible]

TOTAL OOF GROSS	19[illegible]
Australia	
Austria	
Belgium	
Canada	[illegible]
Denmark	
Finland	
France	
Germany, Fed. Rep.	
Italy	
Japan	[illegible]
Netherlands	
New Zealand	
Norway	
Sweden	
Switzerland	
United Kingdom	
United States	[illegible]
TOTAL	[illegible]
MULTILATERAL	[illegible]
OPEC COUNTRIES	[illegible]
E.E.C.+ MEMBERS	
TOTAL	[illegible]

1978	1979	1980	1977	1978	1979	1980
			ODA COMMITMENTS			
–	–	–	–	–	–	–
0.3	0.1	0.2	–	–	–	–
1.1	2.3	1.5	–	1.6	2.7	1.8
0.1	0.6	0.0	0.2	0.2	0.0	0.0
-0.1	0.1	0.1	–	0.0	0.1	0.1
0.0	–	–	–	0.0	0.0	–
1.2	–	2.1	–	–	–	0.7
8.8	12.5	12.8	5.7	6.1	9.7	27.7
0.6	0.4	0.1	0.5	0.6	0.4	0.1
7.8	28.1	4.6	32.4	1.3	1.4	0.9
1.1	1.1	1.5	1.4	1.8	1.6	1.7
–	–	–	–	–	–	0.0
–	–	0.1	–	–	–	–
–	0.1	–	–	–	–	–
0.8	0.6	0.6	0.2	0.2	1.2	1.1
3.4	4.0	2.2	3.8	1.3	2.8	2.0
5.0	7.0	4.0	4.7	6.2	6.6	15.2
30.1	*56.9*	*29.6*	*48.9*	*19.3*	*26.5*	*51.2*
–	–	–	–	–	–	–
–	–	–	–	–	–	–
–	–	–	–	–	–	–
–	–	–	–	–	–	–
0.2	0.3	0.8	0.2	0.2	4.8	1.0
–	–	–	–	–	–	–
0.8	0.2	–	–	–	–	–
15.4	13.7	16.8	57.5	44.3	70.0	84.5
–	–	–	–	5.8	–	–
–	–	–	–	–	–	–
–	–	–	–	–	–	–
–	–	–	5.7	7.6	8.6	9.8
1.8	3.9	4.5	–	–	–	–
0.6	0.4	0.3	–	–	–	–
0.2	0.3	0.7	–	–	–	–
–	–	–	–	–	–	–
4.1	3.3	2.5	–	–	–	–
–	–	–	–	–	–	–
0.9	0.8	1.8	–	–	–	–
–	–	–	–	–	–	–
24.0	*22.8*	*27.3*	*63.3*	*57.9*	*83.5*	*95.3*
–	–	–	–	–	–	–
16.3	*20.6*	*20.9*	*11.5*	*11.6*	*22.1*	*35.1*
54.1	***79.7***	***56.9***	***112.3***	***77.2***	***110.0***	***146.5***
			TECH. COOP. GRANTS			
–	–	–	–	–	–	–
0.3	0.1	0.2	0.3	0.3	0.1	0.2
1.1	2.3	1.5	0.1	0.2	0.4	0.6
0.1	0.0	0.0	0.2	0.1	–	–
–	0.1	0.1	–	–	0.1	0.1
0.0	–	–	0.0	0.0	–	–
1.2	–	2.1	–	1.2	–	2.1
6.9	8.0	11.1	5.7	6.9	8.0	11.1
0.6	0.4	0.1	0.5	0.6	0.4	0.1
3.1	1.6	0.8	0.4	1.2	1.2	0.8
1.1	1.1	1.5	1.1	1.1	1.1	1.5
–	–	–	–	–	–	–
–	–	0.1	–	–	–	0.1
–	0.1	–	–	–	–	–
0.8	0.6	0.6	0.0	0.0	0.0	0.3
1.3	1.6	2.0	1.2	1.3	1.6	2.0
5.0	7.0	4.0	2.0	2.0	1.0	1.0
21.3	*22.9*	*24.0*	*11.4*	*14.8*	*13.8*	*19.7*
8.4	*9.0*	*11.6*	*3.9*	*4.1*	*5.5*	*9.8*
–	–	–	–	–	–	–
12.3	*13.7*	*19.0*	*8.6*	*11.3*	*11.4*	*17.4*
29.7	***31.9***	***35.5***	***15.3***	***18.9***	***19.2***	***29.5***
			TOTAL OOF NET			
–	–	–	–	–	–	–
–	–	–	–	–	–	–
–	–	–	–	–	–	–
5.6	2.6	9.3	4.2	4.2	1.2	7.8
–	–	1.6	–	–	–	1.6
–	–	–	–	–	–	–
–	–	–	–	–	–	–
–	–	–	–	–	–	–
–	–	2.0	–	–	–	2.0
–	0.4	2.5	0.6	-1.6	-1.1	1.0
–	–	–	–	–	–	–
–	–	–	-0.1	–	–	–
–	–	–	–	–	–	–
–	–	–	–	–	–	–
–	–	–	–	–	–	–
–	–	–	–	–	–	–
1.0	5.0	21.0	-7.0	–	4.0	20.0
6.6	*8.0*	*36.3*	*-2.3*	*2.6*	*4.1*	*32.4*
27.4	*56.5*	*86.9*	*11.4*	*19.5*	*47.4*	*74.0*
–	–	–	*25.0*	–	–	–
–	–	*3.6*	–	–	–	*3.6*
34.1	***64.5***	***123.2***	***34.1***	***22.2***	***51.5***	***106.4***

	1977	1978	1979	1980
MAIN AID AGGREGATES				
DAC COUNTRIES COMBINED				
PRIVATE SECTOR NET	123.3	298.6	509.1	86.3
Direct Investment	6.5	1.1	2.7	23.2
Portfolio Invest.	43.3	123.9	200.7	18.6
Export Credits	73.5	173.7	305.7	44.5
OFFICIAL & PRIVATE				
GROSS:				
Contractual Lending	163.6	261.0	435.6	199.0
Export Credits Tot.	151.5	251.3	399.6	190.7
Export Credits Priv	143.8	245.6	393.6	157.0
OTHER NET DATA				
Contractual Lending	78.0	178.5	336.8	76.2
Export Credits Tot.	71.1	175.3	307.8	74.4
(Bank Sector Loans)	445.0	539.0	416.0	184.0
ODA CONCESSIONALITY				
Total:Grant Element	56.0	100.0	97.0	79.0
Loans:Grant Element	35.0	–	39.0	50.0
OTHER SOURCES				
CMEA Countr.(Gross)	–	–	–	–
Intra LDCS Exc.OPEC	–	–	–	–
Other	–	–	–	–
ALL SOURCE COMMITMENTS				
TOTAL BILATERAL	54.7	56.5	56.4	62.6
of which				
OPEC (ODA)	–	–	–	–
CMEA (ODA)	–	–	–	–
TOTAL MULTILAT.(ODA)	63.3	57.9	83.5	95.3
TOTAL BIL.& MULTIL.	118.0	114.4	139.9	157.9
of which				
ODA Grants	21.8	27.1	38.7	41.2
ODA Loans	90.5	50.1	71.3	105.3
ODA CONCESSIONALITY				
Total: Grant Element	65.0	81.0	86.0	78.0
Loans: Grant Element	52.0	75.0	65.0	70.0
INDEBTEDNESS				
TOTAL DEBT DISBURSED	***1344.9***	***2075.4***	***2706.0***	
Debt to DAC Countries	1125.0	1794.0	2151.0	
ODA	145.0	158.0	182.0	
Total Export Credits	219.0	503.0	666.0	
Other Private Market	761.0	1133.0	1303.0	
International Org.	191.5	224.0	287.3	
CMEA	0.9	0.4	2.1	
Other	27.5	57.0	265.5	
TOTAL DEBT SERVICE	***158.5***	***276.9***	***821.9***	
Paid to DAC Countries	132.2	248.7	782.6	
ODA	8.9	9.7	11.1	
Total Export Credits	72.9	97.8	127.9	
Other Private Market	50.4	141.2	643.6	
International Org.	19.5	22.8	27.8	
CMEA	0.6	0.5	2.4	
Other	6.1	4.9	9.1	
ECONOMIC INDICATORS				
GNP Curr. Prices, $M	6283.7	7269.2	8873.6	10891.1
Real GNP, 1976=100	105.0	110.0	116.0	121.0
GNP/Cap Curr. Prices,$	831.0	930.0	1098.0	1303.0
GNP/cap Atlas Basis, $	924.0	1007.5	1111.8	1223.6
Real GNP/Cap, 1976=100	101.0	103.0	105.0	106.0
Population, Million	7.6	7.8	8.1	8.4
Curr.A/C Deficit(-),$M	-377.1	-730.3	-646.4	-616.2
BOP Exp. & Transf.,$M	1618.3	1752.4	2499.8	2924.9
Exp. to OECD CIF, $M	972.7	1207.2	1276.6	1570.3
of which				
Manufact.	11.1	12.4	18.3	21.6
Imp. from OECD FOB, $M	1260.5	1341.1	1631.1	1761.1
Reserves ex. Gold, $M	623.1	635.8	722.0	1013.0

TOTAL RECEIPTS NET	1977	1978	1979	1980
DAC COUNTRIES				
Australia	52.0	-8.4	68.0	9.4
Austria	46.1	5.5	1.5	6.8
Belgium	6.9	4.3	39.2	-8.7
Canada	3.7	3.0	75.1	30.9
Denmark	5.3	51.7	25.8	27.4
Finland	0.5	0.8	3.7	1.2
France	39.8	167.2	263.1	342.8
Germany, Fed. Rep.	146.6	119.8	119.9	112.4
Italy	22.5	8.9	9.6	160.3
Japan	68.0	158.8	167.5	201.5
Netherlands	13.6	7.3	14.6	37.2
New Zealand	0.1	0.1	0.0	0.0
Norway	7.3	54.1	13.7	28.9
Sweden	20.9	16.2	11.7	-13.5
Switzerland	85.6	71.6	5.8	38.6
United Kingdom	47.9	-30.3	48.7	192.1
United States	401.0	602.0	624.0	820.0
TOTAL	*967.6*	*1232.5*	*1492.0*	*1987.4*
MULTILATERAL				
AF.D.F.	–	–	–	–
AF.D.B.	4.6	2.0	10.4	-0.5
AS.D.B.	–	–	–	–
CAR.D.B.	–	–	–	–
E.E.C.	15.4	26.5	28.4	42.8
IBRD	37.3	56.5	115.3	162.1
IDA	42.1	44.6	54.9	41.4
I.D.B.	–	–	–	–
IFAD	–	–	–	–
I.F.C.	1.6	0.7	22.5	2.0
IMF TRUST FUND	23.5	72.4	73.7	62.6
U.N. AGENCIES	–	–	–	–
UNDP	5.7	6.0	9.1	8.5
UNTA	0.7	1.0	1.3	0.3
UNICEF	3.5	4.4	3.3	2.4
UNRWA	–	–	–	–
WFP	28.4	31.2	54.5	26.0
UNHCR	0.4	0.3	1.0	1.3
Other Multilateral	8.8	3.8	0.7	3.7
Arab OPEC Agencies	985.9	705.9	42.1	7.9
TOTAL	*1157.7*	*955.2*	*417.0*	*360.6*
OPEC COUNTRIES	*963.6*	*575.6*	*149.2*	*4.8*
E.E.C.+ MEMBERS	*297.9*	*355.5*	*549.4*	*906.3*
TOTAL	**3088.9**	**2763.3**	**2058.2**	**2352.8**

TOTAL ODA NET	1977	1978	1979	1980
Australia	0.0	2.7	3.1	5.8
Austria	32.0	4.4	1.1	1.8
Belgium	4.4	0.3	0.5	4.0
Canada	3.8	2.3	10.9	31.1
Denmark	5.9	7.2	10.4	3.5
Finland	0.5	0.2	1.2	1.0
France	10.5	19.1	58.6	33.0
Germany, Fed. Rep.	54.7	67.4	121.9	106.7
Italy	-0.6	-2.4	-2.9	-4.4
Japan	67.3	118.8	132.7	123.0
Netherlands	13.6	7.3	14.6	17.1
New Zealand	0.1	0.1	0.0	0.0
Norway	0.2	0.3	0.3	1.2
Sweden	0.7	0.4	0.6	0.5
Switzerland	0.1	0.2	0.2	0.9
United Kingdom	6.0	7.1	37.4	27.9
United States	418.0	625.0	621.0	834.0
TOTAL	*617.0*	*860.2*	*1011.6*	*1187.0*
AF.D.F.	–	–	–	–
AF.D.B.	–	–	–	–
AS.D.B.	–	–	–	–
CAR.D.B.	–	–	–	–
E.E.C.	15.4	26.5	28.4	32.0
IBRD	0.4	2.5	3.7	9.5
IDA	42.1	44.6	54.9	41.4
I.D.B.	–	–	–	–
IFAD	–	–	–	–
I.F.C.	–	–	–	–
IMF TRUST FUND	23.5	72.4	73.7	62.6
U.N. AGENCIES	–	–	–	–
UNDP	5.7	6.0	9.1	8.5
UNTA	0.7	1.0	1.3	0.3
UNICEF	3.5	4.4	3.3	2.4
UNRWA	–	–	–	–
WFP	28.4	31.2	54.5	26.0
UNHCR	0.4	0.3	1.0	1.3
Other Multilateral	8.8	3.8	0.7	3.7
Arab OPEC Agencies	985.9	705.9	42.1	7.9
TOTAL	*1114.7*	*898.5*	*272.5*	*195.7*
OPEC COUNTRIES	*896.2*	*508.2*	*149.2*	*4.8*
E.E.C.+ MEMBERS	*109.8*	*132.3*	*268.9*	*219.7*
TOTAL	**2627.8**	**2266.9**	**1433.3**	**1387.5**

TOTAL ODA GROSS	197
Australia	0
Austria	32
Belgium	4
Canada	3
Denmark	6
Finland	0
France	10
Germany, Fed. Rep.	66
Italy	6
Japan	67
Netherlands	13
New Zealand	0
Norway	0
Sweden	0
Switzerland	0
United Kingdom	6
United States	434
TOTAL	*652*
AF.D.F.	
AF.D.B.	
AS.D.B.	
CAR.D.B.	
E.E.C.	15
IBRD	0
IDA	42
I.D.B.	
IFAD	
I.F.C.	
IMF TRUST FUND	23
U.N. AGENCIES	
UNDP	5
UNTA	0
UNICEF	3
UNRWA	
WFP	28
UNHCR	0
Other Multilateral	8
Arab OPEC Agencies	985
TOTAL	*1114*
OPEC COUNTRIES	*90*
E.E.C.+ MEMBERS	*12*
TOTAL	**2668**

ODA LOANS GROSS	1977	1978	1979	1980
DAC COUNTRIES				
Australia	–	–	–	–
Austria	31.2	0.1	–	–
Belgium	4.2	–	–	3.4
Canada	–	–	10.7	30.9
Denmark	6.0	7.2	10.5	3.5
Finland	–	–	–	–
France	10.5	16.1	45.5	9.0
Germany, Fed. Rep.	49.9	55.2	111.2	89.8
Italy	–	–	–	–
Japan	64.6	112.2	114.7	102.0
Netherlands	2.5	0.4	7.1	11.9
New Zealand	–	–	–	–
Norway	–	–	–	–
Sweden	–	–	–	–
Switzerland	–	–	–	0.7
United Kingdom	2.0	3.7	0.2	12.7
United States	419.0	610.0	573.0	719.0
TOTAL	*589.7*	*804.8*	*872.9*	*982.9*
MULTILATERAL	*1051.8*	*825.3*	*176.0*	*123.5*
OPEC COUNTRIES	*128.3*	*80.7*	*43.1*	*22.7*
E.E.C.+ MEMBERS	*75.0*	*82.6*	*174.6*	*130.4*
TOTAL	**1769.8**	**1710.9**	**1092.0**	**1129.1**

ODA LOANS NET	1977	1978	1979	1980
Australia	–	–	–	–
Austria	31.2	0.1	–	–
Belgium	4.2	–	–	3.4
Canada	–	–	10.7	30.9
Denmark	5.7	7.0	10.1	3.0
Finland	–	–	–	–
France	10.5	15.4	44.4	7.4
Germany, Fed. Rep.	38.2	46.3	101.1	84.9
Italy	-7.4	-5.6	-6.5	-5.6
Japan	64.6	112.2	114.7	101.4
Netherlands	2.5	0.4	7.1	11.9
New Zealand	–	–	–	–
Norway	–	–	–	–
Sweden	–	–	–	–
Switzerland	–	–	–	0.7
United Kingdom	1.7	3.7	0.2	12.1
United States	403.0	583.0	546.0	692.0
TOTAL	*554.1*	*762.3*	*827.7*	*942.1*
MULTILATERAL	*1051.8*	*825.3*	*174.4*	*121.5*
OPEC COUNTRIES	*123.0*	*74.0*	*32.4*	*2.9*
E.E.C.+ MEMBERS	*55.3*	*67.1*	*156.4*	*117.1*
TOTAL	**1728.9**	**1661.6**	**1034.4**	**1066.5**

GRANTS	197
Australia	0
Austria	6
Belgium	0
Canada	3
Denmark	0
Finland	0
France	
Germany, Fed. Rep.	16
Italy	6
Japan	2
Netherlands	1
New Zealand	0
Norway	0
Sweden	0
Switzerland	0
United Kingdom	4
United States	15
TOTAL	*6*
MULTILATERAL	*62*
OPEC COUNTRIES	*77*
E.E.C.+ MEMBERS	*54*
TOTAL	**89**

TOTAL OFFICIAL GROSS	1977	1978	1979	1980
DAC COUNTRIES				
Australia	0.0	2.7	3.2	5.8
Austria	32.0	4.4	1.1	1.8
Belgium	4.4	0.3	0.5	4.0
Canada	3.8	2.3	79.9	31.1
Denmark	7.1	7.4	10.9	4.6
Finland	0.5	0.2	1.2	1.0
France	23.0	38.4	63.5	36.5
Germany, Fed. Rep.	66.4	76.3	132.0	121.3
Italy	6.8	3.2	3.6	14.7
Japan	67.3	118.8	132.7	123.5
Netherlands	13.6	7.3	14.6	17.5
New Zealand	0.1	0.1	0.0	0.0
Norway	0.2	0.3	0.3	1.2
Sweden	0.7	0.4	0.6	0.5
Switzerland	0.1	0.2	0.2	0.9
United Kingdom	6.2	7.1	37.4	28.5
United States	444.0	656.0	650.0	861.0
TOTAL	*676.2*	*925.4*	*1131.7*	*1253.9*
MULTILATERAL	*1157.7*	*955.2*	*421.4*	*370.2*
OPEC COUNTRIES	*968.9*	*582.3*	*159.9*	*24.6*
E.E.C.+ MEMBERS	*143.0*	*166.5*	*291.0*	*270.0*
TOTAL	**2802.8**	**2462.9**	**1713.0**	**1648.7**

TOTAL OFFICIAL NET	1977	1978	1979	1980
Australia	0.0	2.7	3.2	5.8
Austria	31.3	3.6	0.1	0.8
Belgium	4.4	0.3	0.5	4.0
Canada	3.8	2.3	74.8	31.1
Denmark	6.9	7.2	10.3	4.0
Finland	0.5	0.2	1.2	1.0
France	23.0	37.7	62.4	34.9
Germany, Fed. Rep.	46.6	57.5	110.4	104.0
Italy	-0.6	-2.4	-12.3	9.2
Japan	67.3	118.8	132.7	123.0
Netherlands	13.6	7.3	14.6	17.6
New Zealand	0.1	0.1	0.0	0.0
Norway	0.2	0.3	0.3	1.2
Sweden	0.7	0.4	0.6	0.5
Switzerland	0.1	0.2	0.2	0.9
United Kingdom	6.0	7.1	37.4	27.9
United States	408.0	610.0	620.0	831.0
TOTAL	*611.6*	*853.0*	*1056.4*	*1196.8*
MULTILATERAL	*1157.7*	*955.2*	*417.0*	*360.6*
OPEC COUNTRIES	*963.6*	*575.6*	*149.2*	*4.8*
E.E.C.+ MEMBERS	*115.2*	*141.0*	*251.8*	*244.3*
TOTAL	**2732.9**	**2383.8**	**1622.6**	**1562.2**

TOTAL OOF GROSS	197
Australia	
Austria	
Belgium	
Canada	
Denmark	
Finland	
France	12
Germany, Fed. Rep.	
Italy	
Japan	
Netherlands	
New Zealand	
Norway	
Sweden	
Switzerland	
United Kingdom	
United States	10
TOTAL	*2*
MULTILATERAL	*4*
OPEC COUNTRIES	*6*
E.E.C.+ MEMBERS	*1*
TOTAL	**13**

1978	1979	1980	1977	1978	1979	1980
			ODA COMMITMENTS			
2.7	3.1	5.8	2.3	5.5	3.1	5.1
4.4	1.1	1.8	31.2	0.7	0.1	0.4
0.3	0.5	4.0	4.2	–	3.4	–
2.3	10.9	31.1	6.7	66.4	0.3	0.1
7.4	10.8	4.1	0.2	18.3	0.1	14.3
0.2	1.2	1.0	0.0	0.5	4.3	3.4
19.8	59.7	34.6	29.0	30.3	53.3	85.2
76.3	132.0	111.7	101.7	100.6	215.7	126.3
3.2	3.6	1.2	6.8	3.2	3.6	7.8
118.8	132.7	123.5	133.3	33.7	123.2	65.8
7.3	14.6	17.0	21.9	17.4	21.3	21.1
0.1	0.0	0.0	0.0	0.0	0.0	0.0
0.3	0.3	1.2	1.1	1.3	0.3	0.3
0.4	0.6	0.5	–	0.4	0.7	–
0.2	0.2	0.9	–	–	9.1	0.2
7.1	37.4	28.5	4.3	3.4	45.9	10.4
652.0	648.0	861.0	924.5	989.5	1205.6	1030.1
902.7	*1056.8*	*1227.8*	*1267.1*	*1271.2*	*1690.0*	*1370.5*
–	–	–	–	9.6	9.7	9.4
–	–	–	–	–	–	–
–	–	–	–	–	–	–
–	–	–	–	–	–	–
26.5	28.4	32.0	16.3	10.6	18.9	34.6
2.5	3.7	9.5	12.0	–	–	–
44.6	55.1	41.8	54.0	164.0	69.5	331.3
–	–	–	–	–	–	–
–	–	–	–	–	–	27.8
–	–	–	–	–	–	–
72.4	73.7	62.6	–	–	–	–
–	–	–	47.5	46.7	69.8	42.3
6.0	9.1	8.5	–	–	–	–
1.0	1.3	0.3	–	–	–	–
4.4	3.3	2.4	–	–	–	–
–	–	–	–	–	–	–
31.2	54.5	26.0	–	–	–	–
0.3	1.0	1.3	–	–	–	–
3.8	0.7	3.7	–	–	–	–
705.9	43.6	9.6	1572.1	100.0	–	–
898.5	*274.2*	*197.7*	*1701.8*	*330.9*	*167.9*	*445.3*
514.9	*159.9*	*24.6*	*863.3*	*456.0*	*116.8*	*1.9*
147.9	*287.1*	*233.0*	*184.3*	*183.7*	*362.3*	*299.7*
2316.2	***1490.9***	***1450.1***	***3832.2***	***2058.2***	***1974.7***	***1817.7***
			TECH. COOP. GRANTS			
2.7	3.1	5.8	–	0.2	0.0	0.0
4.4	1.1	1.8	0.9	4.4	1.1	1.8
0.3	0.5	0.5	0.1	0.3	0.5	0.3
2.3	0.3	0.2	–	0.1	0.1	0.1
0.2	0.3	0.5	0.2	0.2	0.3	0.5
0.2	1.2	1.0	0.5	0.2	1.0	1.0
3.7	14.2	25.6	–	–	–	8.6
21.1	20.8	21.8	16.1	20.8	20.6	21.8
3.2	3.6	1.2	1.1	1.1	1.1	1.2
6.6	18.0	21.5	2.6	4.9	6.5	5.6
7.0	7.5	5.1	3.3	3.4	2.1	3.4
0.1	0.0	0.0	0.0	–	0.0	0.0
0.3	0.3	1.2	0.2	0.2	0.2	0.3
0.4	0.6	0.5	0.7	0.4	0.6	0.5
0.2	0.2	0.2	0.0	0.0	0.0	–
3.4	37.2	15.8	2.8	3.4	7.9	8.6
42.0	75.0	142.0	26.0	52.0	84.0	86.0
97.9	*183.9*	*244.8*	*54.3*	*91.6*	*126.0*	*139.7*
73.2	*98.2*	*74.3*	*19.1*	*15.5*	*15.3*	*42.3*
434.2	*116.8*	*1.9*	–	–	–	–
65.3	*112.6*	*102.6*	*23.5*	*29.1*	*32.6*	*44.4*
605.3	***398.9***	***321.0***	***73.4***	***107.1***	***141.3***	***182.0***
			TOTAL OOF NET			
–	0.0	–	–	–	0.0	–
–	–	–	-0.8	-0.9	-0.9	-1.0
–	–	–	–	–	–	–
–	69.0	–	–	–	63.9	–
0.0	0.1	0.5	1.0	0.0	0.0	0.5
–	–	–	–	–	–	–
18.6	3.8	1.9	12.5	18.6	3.8	1.9
–	–	9.7	-8.1	-9.9	-11.5	-2.7
–	–	13.6	–	–	-9.4	13.6
–	–	–	–	–	–	–
–	–	0.5	–	–	–	0.5
–	–	–	–	–	–	–
–	–	–	–	–	–	–
–	–	–	–	–	–	–
–	–	–	–	–	–	–
–	–	–	–	–	–	–
4.0	2.0	–	-10.0	-15.0	-1.0	-3.0
22.6	*74.9*	*26.2*	*-5.4*	*-7.2*	*44.7*	*9.8*
56.6	*147.2*	*172.5*	*43.1*	*56.6*	*144.5*	*164.9*
67.4	–	–	*67.4*	*67.4*	–	–
18.6	*3.9*	*37.0*	*5.4*	*8.7*	*-17.2*	*24.6*
146.7	***222.1***	***198.6***	***105.1***	***116.9***	***189.2***	***174.7***

MAIN AID AGGREGATES

	1977	1978	1979	1980
DAC COUNTRIES COMBINED				
PRIVATE SECTOR NET	356.0	379.5	435.6	790.6
Direct Investment	15.0	21.6	38.3	26.6
Portfolio Invest.	27.4	-45.2	-8.0	29.1
Export Credits	313.6	403.1	405.3	734.9
OFFICIAL & PRIVATE				
GROSS:				
Contractual Lending	1282.3	1621.3	2013.6	2211.6
Export Credits Tot.	679.0	797.8	1136.8	1225.8
Export Credits Priv	669.0	793.8	1065.8	1202.5
OTHER NET DATA				
Contractual Lending	862.3	1158.2	1277.8	1686.9
Export Credits Tot.	302.8	387.2	457.8	754.2
(Bank Sector Loans)	175.0	2.0	25.0	56.0
ODA CONCESSIONALITY				
Total:Grant Element	69.0	75.0	84.0	81.0
Loans:Grant Element	65.0	69.0	69.0	67.0
OTHER SOURCES				
CMEA Countr.(Gross)	58.0	54.5	45.2	36.6
Intra LDCS Exc.OPEC	–	–	–	–
Other	–	–	–	–
ALL SOURCE COMMITMENTS				
TOTAL BILATERAL	2130.4	1746.0	1912.9	1429.1
of which				
OPEC (ODA)	863.3	456.0	116.8	1.9
CMEA (ODA)	–	–	10.0	–
TOTAL MULTILAT.(ODA)	1701.8	330.9	167.9	445.3
TOTAL BIL.& MULTIL.	3832.2	2076.9	2080.8	1874.4
of which				
ODA Grants	1000.4	709.1	1047.0	682.0
ODA Loans	2831.9	1349.1	927.8	1135.7
ODA CONCESSIONALITY				
Total: Grant Element	61.0	79.0	86.0	82.0
Loans: Grant Element	48.0	68.0	71.0	70.0

INDEBTEDNESS

	1977	1978	1979	1980
TOTAL DEBT DISBURSED	***8345.8***	***10354.4***	***11962.5***	
Debt to DAC Countries	2878.0	4441.0	5873.0	
ODA	1504.0	2438.0	3231.0	
Total Export Credits	825.0	1352.0	2081.0	
Other Private Market	549.0	651.0	561.0	
International Org.	1540.5	2229.5	2456.4	
CMEA	641.8	626.1	571.2	
Other	3285.5	3057.9	3061.9	
TOTAL DEBT SERVICE	***1084.8***	***1221.9***	***1238.9***	
Paid to DAC Countries	435.4	849.0	1045.3	
ODA	63.1	84.0	104.5	
Total Export Credits	339.1	660.4	829.9	
Other Private Market	33.2	104.6	110.9	
International Org.	26.3	105.1	30.8	
CMEA	76.1	89.3	86.9	
Other	547.0	178.4	76.0	

ECONOMIC INDICATORS

	1977	1978	1979	1980
GNP Curr. Prices, $M	14521.2	15093.0	18887.5	25301.9
Real GNP, 1976=100	109.0	120.0	125.0	136.0
GNP/Cap Curr. Prices,$	391.0	397.0	485.0	636.0
GNP/cap Atlas Basis, $	395.1	457.2	503.5	581.8
Real GNP/Cap, 1976=100	107.0	115.0	117.0	124.0
Population, Million	37.1	38.0	38.9	39.8
Curr.A/C Deficit(-),$M	-1219.0	-1248.0	-1566.0	-525.0
BOP Exp. & Transf.,$M	4586.0	5455.0	6634.0	9254.0
Exp. to OECD CIF, $M	1182.5	1771.4	3051.1	4418.2
of which				
Manufact.	79.1	106.2	186.6	228.9
Imp. from OECD FOB, $M	3896.7	4564.8	5803.4	8035.4
Reserves ex. Gold, $M	431.0	492.0	529.0	1046.0

	TOTAL RECEIPTS NET 1977	1978	1979	1980	TOTAL ODA NET 1977	1978	1979	1980
DAC COUNTRIES								
Australia	0.0	–	–	–	0.0	–	–	–
Austria	0.0	0.0	0.0	0.0	0.0	0.0	0.0	0.0
Belgium	0.1	0.6	-0.2	0.0	0.1	0.1	0.2	0.2
Canada	0.2	0.2	0.6	2.1	0.3	0.3	0.6	2.1
Denmark	–	0.1	–	0.1	–	–	–	0.1
Finland	0.0	0.0	–	–	–	–	–	–
France	0.6	-1.1	5.8	20.3	–	–	7.4	0.5
Germany, Fed. Rep.	0.4	2.5	6.0	-1.3	1.4	1.6	2.3	1.6
Italy	-0.1	18.9	0.4	0.0	0.1	0.2	0.1	0.0
Japan	8.3	12.0	6.7	9.8	7.5	12.7	4.4	0.1
Netherlands	1.1	0.6	0.8	1.2	1.1	0.6	0.8	1.2
New Zealand	–	–	–	–	–	–	–	–
Norway	–	–	0.0	–	–	–	–	0.0
Sweden	–	–	–	0.3	–	–	–	0.3
Switzerland	0.4	0.8	-0.3	–	0.0	0.0	0.1	–
United Kingdom	-9.9	2.0	0.8	-2.1	0.5	0.8	1.0	0.6
United States	12.0	12.0	11.0	43.0	9.0	10.0	10.0	43.0
TOTAL	*13.0*	*48.3*	*31.5*	*73.3*	*20.0*	*26.3*	*26.6*	*49.5*
MULTILATERAL								
AF.D.F.	–	–	–	–	–	–	–	–
AF.D.B.	–	–	–	–	–	–	–	–
AS.D.B.	–	–	–	–	–	–	–	–
CAR.D.B.	–	–	–	–	–	–	–	–
E.E.C.	0.2	–	0.2	0.8	0.2	–	0.2	0.8
IBRD	7.3	9.0	14.6	7.5	0.1	1.8	3.2	1.5
IDA	0.8	2.0	3.0	2.8	0.8	2.0	3.0	2.8
I.D.B.	18.9	26.0	24.2	20.8	19.2	21.5	22.2	12.2
IFAD	–	–	–	–	–	–	–	–
I.F.C.	-0.1	-0.1	-0.1	–	–	–	–	–
IMF TRUST FUND	–	–	–	25.5	–	–	–	25.5
U.N. AGENCIES	–	–	–	–	–	–	–	–
UNDP	1.2	0.9	1.5	1.8	1.2	0.9	1.5	1.8
UNTA	0.2	0.4	0.3	0.1	0.2	0.4	0.3	0.1
UNICEF	0.1	0.3	0.3	0.2	0.1	0.3	0.3	0.2
UNRWA	–	–	–	–	–	–	–	–
WFP	1.8	1.2	1.9	0.6	1.8	1.2	1.9	0.6
UNHCR	–	–	–	–	–	–	–	–
Other Multilateral	0.7	0.3	0.2	1.5	0.7	0.3	0.2	1.5
Arab OPEC Agencies	0.9	0.9	–	–	0.9	0.9	–	–
TOTAL	*32.0*	*40.7*	*46.2*	*61.6*	*25.2*	*29.1*	*32.9*	*47.0*
OPEC COUNTRIES	*17.7*	*13.5*	–	–	–	–	–	–
E.E.C.+ MEMBERS	*-7.6*	*23.4*	*13.8*	*18.9*	*3.4*	*3.3*	*11.8*	*4.8*
TOTAL	***62.7***	***102.5***	***77.7***	***134.9***	***45.2***	***55.4***	***59.5***	***96.5***

	TOTAL ODA GROSS 197…
Australia	
Austria	
Belgium	
Canada	
Denmark	
Finland	
France	
Germany, Fed. Rep.	
Italy	
Japan	
Netherlands	
New Zealand	
Norway	
Sweden	
Switzerland	
United Kingdom	
United States	1…
TOTAL	*2…*
AF.D.F.	
AF.D.B.	
AS.D.B.	
CAR.D.B.	
E.E.C.	
IBRD	
IDA	
I.D.B.	2…
IFAD	
I.F.C.	
IMF TRUST FUND	
U.N. AGENCIES	
UNDP	
UNTA	
UNICEF	
UNRWA	
WFP	
UNHCR	
Other Multilateral	
Arab OPEC Agencies	
TOTAL	*2…*
OPEC COUNTRIES	
E.E.C.+ MEMBERS	
TOTAL	***4…***

	ODA LOANS GROSS 1977	1978	1979	1980	ODA LOANS NET 1977	1978	1979	1980
DAC COUNTRIES								
Australia	–	–	–	–	–	–	–	–
Austria	–	–	–	–	–	–	–	–
Belgium	–	–	–	–	–	–	–	–
Canada	–	–	0.0	1.7	-0.2	-0.1	-0.1	1.5
Denmark	–	–	–	–	–	–	–	–
Finland	–	–	–	–	–	–	–	–
France	–	–	7.4	0.3	–	–	7.4	0.3
Germany, Fed. Rep.	–	–	–	–	-0.2	-0.3	-0.2	-0.3
Italy	–	–	–	–	–	–	–	–
Japan	6.8	12.1	4.1	–	6.8	12.1	4.1	–
Netherlands	–	–	–	–	–	–	–	–
New Zealand	–	–	–	–	–	–	–	–
Norway	–	–	–	–	–	–	–	–
Sweden	–	–	–	–	–	–	–	–
Switzerland	–	–	–	–	–	–	–	–
United Kingdom	–	–	–	–	–	–	–	–
United States	1.0	3.0	1.0	14.0	–	2.0	–	13.0
TOTAL	*7.8*	*15.1*	*12.6*	*15.9*	*6.3*	*13.7*	*11.3*	*14.5*
MULTILATERAL	*22.0*	*27.5*	*29.1*	*43.2*	*21.0*	*26.0*	*27.8*	*41.9*
OPEC COUNTRIES	–	–	–	–	–	–	–	–
E.E.C.+ MEMBERS	–	–	*7.4*	*0.3*	*-0.2*	*-0.3*	*7.2*	*-0.1*
TOTAL	***29.8***	***42.6***	***41.7***	***59.2***	***27.4***	***39.7***	***39.1***	***56.4***

	GRANTS 197…
Australia	
Austria	
Belgium	
Canada	
Denmark	
Finland	
France	
Germany, Fed. Rep.	
Italy	
Japan	
Netherlands	
New Zealand	
Norway	
Sweden	
Switzerland	
United Kingdom	
United States	
TOTAL	*1…*
MULTILATERAL	
OPEC COUNTRIES	
E.E.C.+ MEMBERS	
TOTAL	***1…***

	TOTAL OFFICIAL GROSS 1977	1978	1979	1980	TOTAL OFFICIAL NET 1977	1978	1979	1980
DAC COUNTRIES								
Australia	0.0	–	–	–	0.0	–	–	–
Austria	0.0	0.0	0.0	0.0	0.0	0.0	0.0	0.0
Belgium	0.1	0.1	0.2	0.2	0.1	0.1	0.2	0.2
Canada	0.5	0.4	0.7	2.2	0.3	0.3	0.6	2.1
Denmark	–	–	–	0.1	–	–	–	0.1
Finland	–	–	–	–	–	–	–	–
France	–	–	7.4	0.5	–	–	7.4	0.5
Germany, Fed. Rep.	1.7	1.9	2.4	1.9	1.4	1.6	2.2	1.4
Italy	0.1	0.2	0.1	0.0	0.1	0.2	0.1	0.0
Japan	7.5	12.7	4.4	0.1	7.5	12.7	4.4	0.1
Netherlands	1.1	0.6	0.8	1.2	1.1	0.6	0.8	1.2
New Zealand	0.0	–	–	–	–	–	–	–
Norway	–	–	–	0.0	–	–	–	0.0
Sweden	–	–	–	0.3	–	–	–	0.3
Switzerland	0.0	0.0	0.1	–	0.0	0.0	0.1	–
United Kingdom	0.5	0.8	1.0	0.6	0.5	0.8	1.0	0.6
United States	14.0	14.0	12.0	44.0	12.0	12.0	11.0	43.0
TOTAL	*25.4*	*30.7*	*28.9*	*51.0*	*23.0*	*28.3*	*27.6*	*49.4*
MULTILATERAL	*35.1*	*44.9*	*50.4*	*66.2*	*32.0*	*40.7*	*46.2*	*61.6*
OPEC COUNTRIES	*17.7*	*13.5*	–	–	*17.7*	*13.5*	–	–
E.E.C.+ MEMBERS	*3.6*	*3.6*	*12.0*	*5.1*	*3.4*	*3.3*	*11.8*	*4.7*
TOTAL	***78.2***	***89.1***	***79.3***	***117.2***	***72.7***	***82.4***	***73.8***	***111.0***

	TOTAL OOF GROSS 197…
Australia	
Austria	
Belgium	
Canada	
Denmark	
Finland	
France	
Germany, Fed. Rep.	
Italy	
Japan	
Netherlands	
New Zealand	
Norway	
Sweden	
Switzerland	
United Kingdom	
United States	
TOTAL	
MULTILATERAL	
OPEC COUNTRIES	*1…*
E.E.C.+ MEMBERS	
TOTAL	***3…***

ODA COMMITMENTS

1978	1979	1980	1977	1978	1979	1980
–	–	–	0.0	–	–	–
0.0	0.0	0.0	–	–	–	–
0.1	0.2	0.2	–	–	–	–
0.4	0.7	2.2	1.2	2.2	9.4	0.1
–	–	0.1	–	–	–	–
–	–	–	–	–	–	–
–	7.4	0.5	–	7.2	–	0.1
1.9	2.4	1.9	2.2	1.6	4.4	1.4
0.2	0.1	0.0	0.1	0.2	0.1	0.0
12.7	4.4	0.1	0.9	0.7	0.3	0.1
0.6	0.8	1.2	0.9	0.8	1.2	1.6
–	–	–	–	–	–	–
–	–	0.0	–	–	–	–
–	–	0.3	–	–	–	–
0.0	0.1	–	0.2	–	–	–
0.8	1.0	0.6	0.5	0.8	1.0	0.6
11.0	11.0	44.0	5.8	10.2	12.3	77.9
27.7	*27.9*	*51.0*	*11.8*	*23.6*	*28.7*	*81.7*
–	–	–	–	–	–	–
–	–	–	–	–	–	–
–	–	–	–	–	–	–
–	–	–	–	–	–	–
–	0.2	0.8	0.1	0.4	0.7	0.8
1.8	3.2	1.5	–	–	–	–
2.1	3.1	2.9	6.0	–	–	–
22.8	23.4	13.4	64.3	13.2	48.0	56.9
–	–	–	–	–	–	–
–	–	–	–	–	–	–
–	–	25.5	–	–	–	–
–	–	–	4.0	3.0	4.2	4.3
0.9	1.5	1.8	–	–	–	–
0.4	0.3	0.1	–	–	–	–
0.3	0.3	0.2	–	–	–	–
–	–	–	–	–	–	–
1.2	1.9	0.6	–	–	–	–
–	–	–	–	–	–	–
0.3	0.2	1.5	–	–	–	–
0.9	–	–	1.8	–	–	–
30.5	*34.2*	*48.3*	*76.1*	*16.6*	*52.9*	*62.0*
–	–	–	–	–	–	–
3.6	*12.0*	*5.1*	*3.9*	*10.9*	*7.3*	*4.5*
58.3	***62.2***	***99.3***	***87.9***	***40.2***	***81.6***	***143.8***

TECH. COOP. GRANTS

1978	1979	1980	1977	1978	1979	1980
–	–	–	0.0	–	–	–
0.0	0.0	0.0	0.0	0.0	0.0	0.0
0.1	0.2	0.2	0.1	0.1	0.1	0.1
0.4	0.7	0.5	0.3	0.3	0.1	0.1
–	–	0.1	–	–	–	0.1
–	–	–	–	–	–	–
–	–	0.2	–	–	–	0.2
1.9	2.4	1.9	1.6	1.9	2.4	1.9
0.2	0.1	0.0	0.1	0.2	0.1	0.0
0.6	0.2	0.1	0.8	0.6	0.2	0.1
0.6	0.8	1.2	1.1	0.4	0.7	0.7
–	–	–	–	–	–	–
–	–	0.0	–	–	–	–
–	–	0.3	–	–	–	–
0.0	0.1	–	0.0	0.0	0.0	–
0.8	1.0	0.6	0.5	0.8	1.0	0.6
8.0	10.0	30.0	2.0	2.0	2.0	2.0
12.6	*15.4*	*35.1*	*6.4*	*6.2*	*6.6*	*5.8*
3.1	*5.1*	*5.1*	*2.2*	*1.9*	*2.9*	*4.3*
–	–	–	–	–	–	–
3.6	*4.6*	*4.9*	*3.4*	*3.3*	*4.2*	*3.6*
15.7	***20.4***	***40.1***	***8.7***	***8.1***	***9.5***	***10.1***

TOTAL OOF NET

1978	1979	1980	1977	1978	1979	1980
–	–	–	–	–	–	–
–	–	–	–	–	–	–
–	–	–	–	–	–	–
–	–	–	–	–	–	–
–	–	–	–	–	–	–
–	–	–	–	–	–	–
–	–	–	–	–	–	–
–	–	–	–	–	0.0	-0.1
–	–	–	–	–	–	–
–	–	–	–	–	–	–
–	–	–	–	–	–	–
–	–	–	–	–	–	–
–	–	–	–	–	–	–
–	–	–	–	–	–	–
–	–	–	–	–	–	–
–	–	–	–	–	–	–
3.0	1.0	–	3.0	2.0	1.0	–
3.0	*1.0*	–	*3.0*	*2.0*	*1.0*	*-0.1*
14.4	*16.1*	*17.9*	*6.8*	*11.6*	*13.3*	*14.6*
13.5	–	–	*17.7*	*13.5*	–	–
–	–	–	–	–	*0.0*	*-0.1*
30.8	***17.1***	***17.9***	***27.5***	***27.0***	***14.2***	***14.5***

MAIN AID AGGREGATES

	1977	1978	1979	1980
DAC COUNTRIES COMBINED				
PRIVATE SECTOR NET	-10.0	20.1	4.0	23.9
Direct Investment	1.8	0.7	2.8	11.2
Portfolio Invest.	-5.5	1.0	3.6	-2.0
Export Credits	-6.3	18.4	-2.5	14.7
OFFICIAL & PRIVATE				
GROSS:				
Contractual Lending	29.4	53.6	25.8	47.3
Export Credits Tot.	21.7	36.5	13.2	31.4
Export Credits Priv	17.7	35.5	12.2	31.4
OTHER NET DATA				
Contractual Lending	3.0	34.0	9.7	29.0
Export Credits Tot.	-3.3	18.4	-1.5	14.7
(Bank Sector Loans)	-26.0	24.0	-10.0	3.0
ODA CONCESSIONALITY				
Total:Grant Element	100.0	86.0	92.0	82.0
Loans:Grant Element	–	66.0	81.0	64.0
OTHER SOURCES				
CMEA Countr.(Gross)	–	–	–	–
Intra LDCS Exc.OPEC	–	–	–	–
Other	–	–	–	–
ALL SOURCE COMMITMENTS				
TOTAL BILATERAL	13.4	23.9	28.8	81.7
of which				
OPEC (ODA)	–	–	–	–
CMEA (ODA)	–	–	–	–
TOTAL MULTILAT.(ODA)	76.1	16.6	52.9	62.0
TOTAL BIL.& MULTIL.	89.5	40.4	81.7	143.8
of which				
ODA Grants	15.9	13.1	21.5	46.5
ODA Loans	72.1	27.1	60.1	97.3
ODA CONCESSIONALITY				
Total: Grant Element	84.0	79.0	88.0	79.0
Loans: Grant Element	76.0	74.0	78.0	72.0

INDEBTEDNESS

	1977	1978	1979	1980
TOTAL DEBT DISBURSED	***304.7***	***436.4***	***515.5***	
Debt to DAC Countries	116.0	181.0	205.0	
ODA	61.0	79.0	86.0	
Total Export Credits	24.0	52.0	69.0	
Other Private Market	31.0	50.0	50.0	
International Org.	128.1	181.4	229.2	
CMEA	–	–	–	
Other	60.6	74.0	81.3	
TOTAL DEBT SERVICE	***71.1***	***53.9***	***70.9***	
Paid to DAC Countries	60.3	39.2	47.2	
ODA	2.6	3.0	3.8	
Total Export Credits	21.4	28.6	18.1	
Other Private Market	36.3	7.6	25.3	
International Org.	9.4	11.7	15.6	
CMEA	–	–	–	
Other	1.3	3.0	8.1	

ECONOMIC INDICATORS

	1977	1978	1979	1980
GNP Curr. Prices, $M	2533.8	2817.7	3468.8	3325.6
Real GNP, 1976=100	105.0	109.0	99.0	87.0
GNP/Cap Curr. Prices,$	609.0	657.0	786.0	732.0
GNP/cap Atlas Basis, $	611.5	660.8	635.3	592.0
Real GNP/Cap, 1976=100	102.0	103.0	91.0	78.0
Population, Million	4.2	4.3	4.4	4.5
Curr.A/C Deficit(-),$M	21.3	-245.1	122.8	–
BOP Exp. & Transf.,$M	1156.6	1051.6	1492.3	–
Exp. to OECD CIF, $M	947.1	677.8	1006.3	888.0
of which				
Manufact.	100.8	135.9	167.1	124.8
Imp. from OECD FOB, $M	568.2	653.5	591.7	422.8
Reserves ex. Gold, $M	211.3	268.1	140.2	77.7

TOTAL RECEIPTS NET

	1977	1978	1979	1980
DAC COUNTRIES				
Australia	0.9	1.9	0.3	1.1
Austria	0.0	0.0	0.1	0.1
Belgium	0.4	1.1	0.2	0.1
Canada	0.4	0.6	1.2	2.5
Denmark	0.1	0.3	0.1	0.1
Finland	0.3	0.2	0.3	0.3
France	1.3	0.0	0.5	3.5
Germany, Fed. Rep.	9.5	12.3	57.6	-26.3
Italy	-3.1	0.9	3.7	47.0
Japan	–	0.4	1.1	1.5
Netherlands	10.6	4.5	5.5	3.8
New Zealand	0.0	–	–	–
Norway	0.4	0.4	1.5	1.0
Sweden	20.4	13.2	19.7	31.4
Switzerland	0.6	0.5	0.6	1.2
United Kingdom	3.6	4.7	5.8	5.2
United States	9.0	10.0	23.0	20.0
TOTAL	*54.2*	*51.0*	*121.0*	*92.2*
MULTILATERAL				
AF.D.F.	1.3	2.0	4.2	2.6
AF.D.B.	–	–	–	2.2
AS.D.B.	–	–	–	–
CAR.D.B.	–	–	–	–
E.E.C.	4.2	8.7	18.3	32.2
IBRD	-3.0	-3.1	-3.2	-3.6
IDA	33.1	32.0	46.7	27.8
I.D.B.	–	–	–	–
IFAD	–	–	–	–
I.F.C.	-0.7	-0.8	-0.8	-0.8
IMF TRUST FUND	–	14.0	10.6	9.0
U.N. AGENCIES	–	–	–	–
UNDP	3.8	4.9	7.6	12.6
UNTA	0.7	1.1	1.3	0.2
UNICEF	5.2	3.8	4.7	7.9
UNRWA	–	–	–	–
WFP	3.7	13.7	10.2	24.6
UNHCR	0.4	0.1	0.1	2.7
Other Multilateral	0.5	0.8	0.2	0.9
Arab OPEC Agencies	2.4	2.4	–	–
TOTAL	*51.4*	*79.6*	*99.8*	*118.3*
OPEC COUNTRIES	–	–	–	–
E.E.C.+ MEMBERS	*26.5*	*32.5*	*91.6*	*65.4*
TOTAL	***105.6***	***130.6***	***220.8***	***210.4***

TOTAL ODA NET

	1977	1978	1979	1980
DAC COUNTRIES				
Australia	0.9	1.9	0.3	1.1
Austria	0.0	0.0	0.1	0.1
Belgium	0.5	0.8	0.2	0.1
Canada	0.4	0.6	1.2	2.5
Denmark	0.2	0.3	0.1	0.1
Finland	0.3	0.2	0.3	0.3
France	0.4	–	–	3.2
Germany, Fed. Rep.	9.6	12.4	16.5	14.9
Italy	0.4	1.9	5.0	7.5
Japan	1.6	3.1	1.7	1.0
Netherlands	10.6	4.5	5.5	3.8
New Zealand	–	–	–	–
Norway	0.4	0.4	1.5	1.0
Sweden	20.4	13.2	19.7	31.4
Switzerland	0.6	0.5	0.6	1.2
United Kingdom	2.9	5.3	6.0	4.4
United States	10.0	11.0	12.0	19.0
TOTAL	*59.0*	*56.0*	*70.5*	*91.4*
MULTILATERAL				
AF.D.F.	1.3	2.0	4.2	2.6
AF.D.B.	–	–	–	–
AS.D.B.	–	–	–	–
CAR.D.B.	–	–	–	–
E.E.C.	4.2	8.7	18.3	32.2
IBRD	–	–	–	–
IDA	33.1	32.0	46.7	27.8
I.D.B.	–	–	–	–
IFAD	–	–	–	–
I.F.C.	–	–	–	–
IMF TRUST FUND	–	14.0	10.6	9.0
U.N. AGENCIES	–	–	–	–
UNDP	3.8	4.9	7.6	12.6
UNTA	0.7	1.1	1.3	0.2
UNICEF	5.2	3.8	4.7	7.9
UNRWA	–	–	–	–
WFP	3.7	13.7	10.2	24.6
UNHCR	0.4	0.1	0.1	2.7
Other Multilateral	0.5	0.8	0.2	0.9
Arab OPEC Agencies	2.4	2.4	–	–
TOTAL	*55.1*	*83.5*	*103.8*	*120.4*
OPEC COUNTRIES	–	–	–	–
E.E.C.+ MEMBERS	*28.6*	*33.8*	*51.6*	*66.1*
TOTAL	***114.0***	***139.5***	***174.4***	***211.8***

TOTAL ODA GROSS

	197
Australia	0.
Austria	0
Belgium	0
Canada	0
Denmark	0
Finland	0
France	0
Germany, Fed. Rep.	11
Italy	1
Japan	1
Netherlands	10
New Zealand	
Norway	0
Sweden	20
Switzerland	0
United Kingdom	3
United States	11
TOTAL	*62*
AF.D.F.	1
AF.D.B.	
AS.D.B.	
CAR.D.B.	
E.E.C.	4
IBRD	
IDA	33
I.D.B.	
IFAD	
I.F.C.	
IMF TRUST FUND	
U.N. AGENCIES	
UNDP	3
UNTA	0
UNICEF	5
UNRWA	
WFP	3
UNHCR	0
Other Multilateral	0
Arab OPEC Agencies	2
TOTAL	*55*
OPEC COUNTRIES	
E.E.C.+ MEMBERS	*31*
TOTAL	***118***

ODA LOANS GROSS

	1977	1978	1979	1980
DAC COUNTRIES				
Australia	–	–	–	–
Austria	–	–	–	–
Belgium	–	–	–	–
Canada	–	–	–	–
Denmark	–	–	–	–
Finland	–	–	–	–
France	–	–	–	–
Germany, Fed. Rep.	3.5	4.8	7.6	6.7
Italy	–	–	–	–
Japan	0.8	2.6	0.7	1.2
Netherlands	–	–	–	–
New Zealand	–	–	–	–
Norway	–	–	–	–
Sweden	0.0	0.0	–	–
Switzerland	–	–	–	–
United Kingdom	0.6	1.1	1.1	0.2
United States	3.0	1.0	–	–
TOTAL	*7.8*	*9.5*	*9.5*	*8.1*
MULTILATERAL	*37.0*	*50.8*	*61.8*	*39.7*
OPEC COUNTRIES	–	–	–	–
E.E.C.+ MEMBERS	*4.0*	*5.9*	*8.7*	*6.9*
TOTAL	***44.8***	***60.2***	***71.3***	***47.8***

ODA LOANS NET

	1977	1978	1979	1980
Australia	–	–	–	–
Austria	–	–	–	–
Belgium	–	–	–	–
Canada	–	–	–	–
Denmark	–	–	–	–
Finland	–	–	-1.8	–
France	–	–	–	–
Germany, Fed. Rep.	1.8	2.9	6.7	4.9
Italy	-1.2	-0.6	-0.7	-0.6
Japan	0.8	2.6	0.7	0.5
Netherlands	–	–	–	–
New Zealand	–	–	–	–
Norway	–	–	–	–
Sweden	0.0	-10.8	–	–
Switzerland	–	–	–	–
United Kingdom	0.4	1.0	0.9	0.0
United States	2.0	–	-1.0	-1.0
TOTAL	*3.9*	*-4.9*	*4.9*	*3.8*
MULTILATERAL	*36.8*	*50.4*	*61.5*	*39.3*
OPEC COUNTRIES	–	–	–	–
E.E.C.+ MEMBERS	*1.1*	*3.3*	*6.9*	*4.3*
TOTAL	***40.6***	***45.5***	***66.3***	***43.1***

GRANTS

	197
Australia	0
Austria	0
Belgium	0
Canada	0
Denmark	0
Finland	0
France	0
Germany, Fed. Rep.	7
Italy	1
Japan	0
Netherlands	10
New Zealand	
Norway	0
Sweden	20
Switzerland	0
United Kingdom	2
United States	8
TOTAL	*55*
MULTILATERAL	*18*
OPEC COUNTRIES	
E.E.C.+ MEMBERS	*27*
TOTAL	***73***

TOTAL OFFICIAL GROSS

	1977	1978	1979	1980
DAC COUNTRIES				
Australia	0.9	1.9	0.3	1.1
Austria	0.0	0.0	0.1	0.1
Belgium	0.5	0.8	0.2	0.1
Canada	0.4	0.6	1.2	2.5
Denmark	0.2	0.3	0.1	0.1
Finland	0.3	0.2	2.1	0.3
France	0.4	–	–	3.2
Germany, Fed. Rep.	11.2	14.2	17.5	16.7
Italy	1.6	2.5	5.7	8.1
Japan	1.6	3.1	1.7	1.7
Netherlands	10.6	4.5	5.5	3.8
New Zealand	0.1	–	–	–
Norway	0.4	0.4	1.5	1.0
Sweden	20.4	24.0	19.7	31.4
Switzerland	0.6	0.5	0.6	1.2
United Kingdom	3.0	5.5	6.1	4.5
United States	11.0	12.0	25.0	22.0
TOTAL	*63.0*	*70.4*	*87.1*	*97.7*
MULTILATERAL	*56.7*	*84.0*	*104.5*	*123.1*
OPEC COUNTRIES	–	–	–	–
E.E.C.+ MEMBERS	*31.6*	*36.4*	*53.4*	*68.7*
TOTAL	***119.7***	***154.4***	***191.6***	***220.8***

TOTAL OFFICIAL NET

	1977	1978	1979	1980
Australia	0.9	1.9	0.3	1.1
Austria	0.0	0.0	0.1	0.1
Belgium	0.5	0.8	0.2	0.1
Canada	0.4	0.6	1.2	2.5
Denmark	0.2	0.3	0.1	0.1
Finland	0.3	0.2	0.3	0.3
France	0.4	–	–	3.2
Germany, Fed. Rep.	9.5	12.3	16.5	14.8
Italy	0.0	1.0	4.9	5.9
Japan	1.6	3.1	1.7	1.0
Netherlands	10.6	4.5	5.5	3.8
New Zealand	0.0	–	–	–
Norway	0.4	0.4	1.5	1.0
Sweden	20.4	13.2	19.7	31.4
Switzerland	0.6	0.5	0.6	1.2
United Kingdom	2.9	5.3	6.0	4.4
United States	9.0	10.0	23.0	20.0
TOTAL	*57.5*	*54.0*	*81.4*	*90.7*
MULTILATERAL	*51.4*	*79.6*	*99.8*	*118.3*
OPEC COUNTRIES	–	–	–	–
E.E.C.+ MEMBERS	*28.2*	*32.9*	*51.4*	*64.4*
TOTAL	***108.9***	***133.6***	***181.2***	***209.0***

TOTAL OOF GROSS

	197
Australia	
Austria	
Belgium	
Canada	
Denmark	
Finland	
France	
Germany, Fed. Rep.	
Italy	
Japan	
Netherlands	
New Zealand	0
Norway	
Sweden	
Switzerland	
United Kingdom	
United States	
TOTAL	*0*
MULTILATERAL	*1*
OPEC COUNTRIES	
E.E.C.+ MEMBERS	
TOTAL	***1***

1978	1979	1980	1977	1978	1979	1980
			ODA COMMITMENTS			
1.9	0.3	1.1	0.1	2.2	0.9	4.4
0.0	0.1	0.1	–	–	0.0	–
0.8	0.2	0.1	–	–	–	–
0.6	1.2	2.5	0.2	0.1	0.2	3.7
0.3	0.1	0.1	0.1	0.0	0.1	0.1
0.2	2.1	0.3	0.1	0.2	2.1	0.2
–	–	3.2	–	–	–	3.2
14.2	17.5	16.7	7.3	19.0	14.4	13.7
2.5	5.7	8.1	1.6	2.5	5.7	8.1
3.1	1.7	1.7	1.0	1.1	1.1	1.0
4.5	5.5	3.8	13.8	4.0	1.3	4.7
–	–	–	–	–	–	–
0.4	1.5	1.0	0.4	0.4	1.5	0.6
24.0	19.7	31.4	17.4	28.5	18.7	21.1
0.5	0.6	1.2	–	–	0.3	1.5
5.5	6.1	4.5	2.3	3.4	4.3	4.2
12.0	13.0	20.0	6.9	9.0	13.7	13.4
70.4	*75.1*	*95.7*	*51.2*	*70.4*	*64.1*	*79.9*
2.0	4.2	2.6	13.3	–	17.2	18.8
–	–	–	–	–	–	–
–	–	–	–	–	–	–
–	–	–	–	–	–	–
8.7	18.3	32.2	41.9	16.1	39.9	21.1
–	–	–	–	–	–	–
32.4	47.1	28.2	56.9	7.0	–	40.8
–	–	–	–	–	–	–
–	–	–	–	–	–	17.7
–	–	–	–	–	–	–
14.0	10.6	9.0	–	–	–	–
–	–	–	14.2	24.3	24.1	48.9
4.9	7.6	12.6	–	–	–	–
1.1	1.3	0.2	–	–	–	–
3.8	4.7	7.9	–	–	–	–
–	–	–	–	–	–	–
13.7	10.2	24.6	–	–	–	–
0.1	0.1	2.7	–	–	–	–
0.8	0.2	0.9	–	–	–	–
2.4	–	–	4.8	–	–	–
83.8	*104.2*	*120.8*	*131.1*	*47.4*	*81.2*	*147.3*
–	–	–	–	–	–	*0.1*
36.4	*53.4*	*68.7*	*67.1*	*45.1*	*65.6*	*55.1*
154.2	***179.3***	***216.5***	***182.3***	***117.9***	***145.3***	***227.2***
			TECH. COOP. GRANTS			
1.9	0.3	1.1	0.0	–	–	–
0.0	0.1	0.1	0.0	0.0	0.1	0.1
0.8	0.2	0.1	0.4	0.4	0.2	0.1
0.6	1.2	2.5	0.1	0.1	0.2	0.1
0.3	0.1	0.1	0.1	0.2	0.1	0.1
0.2	2.1	0.3	0.3	0.2	0.2	0.2
–	–	3.2	–	–	–	3.2
9.5	9.9	10.0	5.9	5.5	7.1	7.1
2.5	5.7	8.1	1.3	2.1	2.4	2.2
0.5	0.9	0.5	0.8	0.3	0.4	0.5
4.5	5.5	3.8	1.5	1.2	1.1	1.5
–	–	–	–	–	–	–
0.4	1.5	1.0	0.4	0.4	0.4	0.3
24.0	19.7	31.4	4.7	1.4	0.5	1.0
0.5	0.6	1.2	–	–	–	–
4.3	5.0	4.4	1.3	1.1	1.7	1.6
11.0	13.0	20.0	3.0	3.0	1.0	2.0
60.9	*65.7*	*87.6*	*19.8*	*15.9*	*15.3*	*19.9*
33.0	*42.4*	*81.1*	*10.5*	*10.6*	*13.9*	*48.9*
–	–	–	–	–	–	–
30.6	*44.6*	*61.8*	*10.4*	*10.4*	*12.6*	*15.7*
94.0	***108.0***	***168.7***	***30.3***	***26.5***	***29.2***	***68.8***
			TOTAL OOF NET			
–	–	–	–	–	–	–
–	–	–	–	–	–	–
–	–	–	–	–	–	–
–	–	–	–	–	–	–
–	–	–	–	–	–	–
–	–	–	–	–	–	–
–	–	–	–	–	–	–
–	–	–	-0.1	-0.1	0.0	-0.1
–	–	–	-0.4	-0.9	-0.1	-1.5
–	–	–	–	–	–	–
–	–	–	–	–	–	–
–	–	–	0.0	–	–	–
–	–	–	–	–	–	–
–	–	–	–	–	–	–
–	–	–	–	–	–	–
–	–	–	–	–	–	–
–	12.0	2.0	-1.0	-1.0	11.0	1.0
–	*12.0*	*2.0*	*-1.5*	*-2.0*	*10.8*	*-0.6*
0.2	*0.3*	*2.3*	*-3.7*	*-3.9*	*-4.0*	*-2.2*
–	–	–	–	–	–	–
–	–	–	*-0.5*	*-1.0*	*-0.2*	*-1.6*
0.2	***12.3***	***4.3***	***-5.2***	***-5.8***	***6.8***	***-2.8***

	1977	1978	1979	1980
MAIN AID AGGREGATES				
DAC COUNTRIES COMBINED				
PRIVATE SECTOR NET	-3.3	-3.0	39.7	1.5
Direct Investment	-1.2	0.0	0.0	–
Portfolio Invest.	0.6	0.3	41.1	-40.8
Export Credits	-2.6	-3.4	-1.5	42.3
OFFICIAL & PRIVATE				
GROSS:				
Contractual Lending	11.9	13.6	22.2	58.8
Export Credits Tot.	4.1	4.2	12.8	50.7
Export Credits Priv	4.0	4.2	0.8	48.7
OTHER NET DATA				
Contractual Lending	-0.2	-10.3	14.2	45.4
Export Credits Tot.	-3.6	-5.3	9.4	41.8
(Bank Sector Loans)	1.0	-1.0	9.0	-2.0
ODA CONCESSIONALITY				
Total:Grant Element	99.0	96.0	100.0	100.0
Loans:Grant Element	43.0	83.0	–	–
OTHER SOURCES				
CMEA Countr.(Gross)	6.7	12.3	10.5	17.7
Intra LDCS Exc.OPEC	–	–	–	–
Other	–	–	–	–
ALL SOURCE COMMITMENTS				
TOTAL BILATERAL	51.3	86.5	64.1	79.9
of which				
OPEC (ODA)	–	–	–	0.1
CMEA (ODA)	40.5	57.7	99.4	37.8
TOTAL MULTILAT.(ODA)	131.1	47.4	81.2	147.3
TOTAL BIL.& MULTIL.	182.4	133.9	145.3	227.2
of which				
ODA Grants	107.2	95.9	128.1	149.9
ODA Loans	75.1	22.0	17.2	77.3
ODA CONCESSIONALITY				
Total: Grant Element	92.0	95.0	95.0	98.0
Loans: Grant Element	81.0	83.0	71.0	83.0
INDEBTEDNESS				
TOTAL DEBT DISBURSED	***476.3***	***529.5***	***593.6***	
Debt to DAC Countries	227.0	243.0	234.0	
ODA	187.0	191.0	197.0	
Total Export Credits	28.0	46.0	28.0	
Other Private Market	12.0	6.0	9.0	
International Org.	228.1	262.3	312.2	
CMEA	20.2	23.4	31.8	
Other	1.0	0.8	15.7	
TOTAL DEBT SERVICE	***32.1***	***31.9***	***26.7***	
Paid to DAC Countries	18.4	18.6	12.7	
ODA	7.6	7.4	6.2	
Total Export Credits	8.6	8.7	4.9	
Other Private Market	2.2	2.5	1.6	
International Org.	10.9	10.7	11.4	
CMEA	2.6	2.4	2.4	
Other	0.2	0.2	0.2	
ECONOMIC INDICATORS				
GNP Curr. Prices, $M	3295.9	3489.4	3846.3	4076.2
Real GNP, 1976=100	102.0	101.0	108.0	112.0
GNP/Cap Curr. Prices,$	110.0	115.0	124.0	129.0
GNP/cap Atlas Basis, $	104.1	109.0	123.4	137.2
Real GNP/Cap, 1976=100	101.0	98.0	102.0	105.0
Population, Million	29.8	30.3	30.9	31.5
Curr.A/C Deficit(-),$M	-125.9	-178.5	-151.8	-281.3
BOP Exp. & Transf.,$M	452.4	426.4	556.4	590.7
Exp. to OECD CIF, $M	233.9	216.6	301.1	286.6
of which				
Manufact.	3.5	4.5	6.0	8.3
Imp. from OECD FOB, $M	283.3	303.9	407.2	438.1
Reserves ex. Gold, $M	213.3	152.9	172.7	80.1

	TOTAL RECEIPTS NET 1977	1978	1979	1980	TOTAL ODA NET 1977	1978	1979	1980
DAC COUNTRIES								
Australia	13.8	16.5	24.8	31.9	5.1	8.7	10.3	11.2
Austria	–	–	–	–	–	–	–	–
Belgium	0.1	–	–	0.1	0.1	–	–	0.1
Canada	–	–	–	–	–	–	–	–
Denmark	0.0	–	–	–	0.0	–	–	–
Finland	–	–	–	–	–	–	–	–
France	0.4	1.9	0.7	-1.7	–	–	–	0.2
Germany, Fed. Rep.	0.1	0.4	0.5	0.9	0.1	0.4	0.5	0.9
Italy	–	–	–	0.2	–	–	–	–
Japan	3.8	0.7	0.5	3.6	0.3	0.6	0.5	3.2
Netherlands	0.2	0.3	0.6	0.5	0.2	0.3	0.6	0.5
New Zealand	9.9	12.1	5.8	4.1	3.9	4.1	5.8	4.1
Norway	–	–	0.0	0.0	–	–	–	–
Sweden	–	–	–	–	–	–	–	–
Switzerland	–	–	–	2.0	–	–	–	0.0
United Kingdom	6.0	6.1	11.9	9.6	8.8	8.9	7.3	9.5
United States	1.0	1.0	1.0	2.0	1.0	1.0	1.0	2.0
TOTAL	*35.3*	*38.9*	*45.7*	*53.1*	*19.4*	*24.0*	*25.9*	*31.7*
MULTILATERAL								
AF.D.F.	–	–	–	–	–	–	–	–
AF.D.B.	–	–	–	–	–	–	–	–
AS.D.B.	0.2	-0.3	5.6	8.2	0.1	–	–	–
CAR.D.B.	–	–	–	–	–	–	–	–
E.E.C.	1.7	0.4	4.3	9.1	1.7	0.4	3.2	2.3
IBRD	4.4	2.5	3.1	5.0	–	–	–	–
IDA	–	–	–	–	–	–	–	–
I.D.B.	–	–	–	–	–	–	–	–
IFAD	–	–	–	–	–	–	–	–
I.F.C.	–	–	–	–	–	–	–	–
IMF TRUST FUND	–	–	–	–	–	–	–	–
U.N. AGENCIES	–	–	–	–	–	–	–	–
UNDP	0.8	1.1	1.1	1.1	0.8	1.1	1.1	1.1
UNTA	0.5	0.4	0.4	0.2	0.5	0.4	0.4	0.2
UNICEF	–	–	–	–	–	–	–	–
UNRWA	–	–	–	–	–	–	–	–
WFP	0.1	0.5	0.1	0.5	0.1	0.5	0.1	0.5
UNHCR	–	–	–	–	–	–	–	–
Other Multilateral	0.6	0.2	0.3	0.5	0.6	0.2	0.3	0.5
Arab OPEC Agencies	–	–	–	–	–	–	–	–
TOTAL	*8.3*	*4.7*	*15.0*	*24.5*	*3.8*	*2.6*	*5.1*	*4.5*
OPEC COUNTRIES	–	–	–	–	–	–	–	–
E.E.C.+ MEMBERS	*8.5*	*9.0*	*18.0*	*18.6*	*10.9*	*10.0*	*11.5*	*13.4*
TOTAL	***43.6***	***43.6***	***60.7***	***77.6***	***23.2***	***26.5***	***31.0***	***36.1***
	ODA LOANS GROSS				**ODA LOANS NET**			
DAC COUNTRIES								
Australia	–	–	–	–	–	-0.1	–	-0.1
Austria	–	–	–	–	–	–	–	–
Belgium	–	–	–	–	–	–	–	–
Canada	–	–	–	–	–	–	–	–
Denmark	–	–	–	–	–	–	–	–
Finland	–	–	–	–	–	–	–	–
France	–	–	–	–	–	–	–	–
Germany, Fed. Rep.	–	–	–	–	–	–	–	–
Italy	–	–	–	–	–	–	–	–
Japan	–	–	–	–	0.0	-0.1	0.0	-0.1
Netherlands	–	–	–	–	–	–	–	–
New Zealand	–	–	–	–	–	-0.2	-1.7	–
Norway	–	–	–	–	–	–	–	–
Sweden	–	–	–	–	–	–	–	–
Switzerland	–	–	–	–	–	–	–	–
United Kingdom	5.8	4.5	3.6	3.7	5.1	3.7	2.7	2.6
United States	–	–	–	–	–	–	–	–
TOTAL	*5.8*	*4.5*	*3.6*	*3.7*	*5.1*	*3.2*	*0.9*	*2.3*
MULTILATERAL	–	–	*2.5*	*1.6*	–	–	*2.5*	*1.6*
OPEC COUNTRIES	–	–	–	–	–	–	–	–
E.E.C.+ MEMBERS	*5.8*	*4.5*	*6.1*	*5.3*	*5.1*	*3.7*	*5.2*	*4.2*
TOTAL	***5.8***	***4.5***	***6.1***	***5.3***	***5.1***	***3.2***	***3.4***	***4.0***
	TOTAL OFFICIAL GROSS				**TOTAL OFFICIAL NET**			
DAC COUNTRIES								
Australia	5.5	8.8	12.3	19.2	5.5	8.7	12.3	18.4
Austria	–	–	–	–	–	–	–	–
Belgium	0.1	–	–	0.1	0.1	–	–	0.1
Canada	–	–	–	–	–	–	–	–
Denmark	0.0	–	–	–	0.0	–	–	–
Finland	–	–	–	–	–	–	–	–
France	0.4	0.2	0.2	0.2	0.4	0.2	0.2	0.2
Germany, Fed. Rep.	0.1	0.4	0.5	0.9	0.1	0.4	0.5	0.9
Italy	–	–	–	–	–	–	–	–
Japan	0.3	0.7	0.6	3.3	0.3	0.6	0.5	3.2
Netherlands	0.2	0.3	0.6	0.5	0.2	0.3	0.6	0.5
New Zealand	9.8	4.3	7.5	4.1	4.3	4.1	5.8	4.1
Norway	–	–	–	–	–	–	–	–
Sweden	–	–	–	–	–	–	–	–
Switzerland	–	–	–	0.0	–	–	–	0.0
United Kingdom	9.5	9.8	14.7	12.3	8.8	8.4	13.4	10.1
United States	1.0	1.0	1.0	2.0	1.0	1.0	1.0	2.0
TOTAL	*27.0*	*25.5*	*37.3*	*42.5*	*20.7*	*23.6*	*34.2*	*39.4*
MULTILATERAL	*8.9*	*5.5*	*15.8*	*25.5*	*8.3*	*4.7*	*15.0*	*24.5*
OPEC COUNTRIES	–	–	–	–	–	–	–	–
E.E.C.+ MEMBERS	*12.1*	*11.0*	*20.3*	*23.0*	*11.3*	*9.6*	*18.9*	*20.8*
TOTAL	***35.9***	***31.0***	***53.1***	***68.0***	***28.9***	***28.4***	***49.2***	***63.9***

	TOTAL ODA GROSS 197
Australia	5
Austria	
Belgium	[illegible]
Canada	
Denmark	[illegible]
Finland	
France	
Germany, Fed. Rep.	[illegible]
Italy	
Japan	[illegible]
Netherlands	[illegible]
New Zealand	[illegible]
Norway	
Sweden	
Switzerland	
United Kingdom	[illegible]
United States	
TOTAL	2
AF.D.F.	
AF.D.B.	
AS.D.B.	[illegible]
CAR.D.B.	
E.E.C.	
IBRD	
IDA	
I.D.B.	
IFAD	
I.F.C.	
IMF TRUST FUND	
U.N. AGENCIES	
UNDP	[illegible]
UNTA	[illegible]
UNICEF	
UNRWA	
WFP	[illegible]
UNHCR	
Other Multilateral	[illegible]
Arab OPEC Agencies	
TOTAL	[illegible]
OPEC COUNTRIES	
E.E.C.+ MEMBERS	1
TOTAL	2
GRANTS	
Australia	5
Austria	
Belgium	[illegible]
Canada	
Denmark	[illegible]
Finland	
France	
Germany, Fed. Rep.	[illegible]
Italy	
Japan	[illegible]
Netherlands	[illegible]
New Zealand	[illegible]
Norway	
Sweden	
Switzerland	
United Kingdom	[illegible]
United States	
TOTAL	1
MULTILATERAL	[illegible]
OPEC COUNTRIES	
E.E.C.+ MEMBERS	[illegible]
TOTAL	1
TOTAL OOF GROSS	
Australia	[illegible]
Austria	
Belgium	
Canada	
Denmark	
Finland	
France	[illegible]
Germany, Fed. Rep.	
Italy	
Japan	
Netherlands	
New Zealand	5
Norway	
Sweden	
Switzerland	
United Kingdom	
United States	
TOTAL	[illegible]
MULTILATERAL	[illegible]
OPEC COUNTRIES	
E.E.C.+ MEMBERS	[illegible]
TOTAL	1

1978	1979	1980	1977	1978	1979	1980
			ODA COMMITMENTS			
8.8	10.3	11.4	9.5	17.8	6.7	5.1
–	–	–	–	–	–	–
–	–	0.1	–	–	–	–
–	–	–	–	0.1	–	–
–	–	–	0.0	–	–	0.1
–	–	–	–	–	–	–
–	–	0.2	–	–	–	0.2
0.4	0.5	0.9	0.5	0.8	0.1	2.0
–	–	–	–	–	–	–
0.7	0.6	3.3	0.3	0.8	2.9	3.6
0.3	0.6	0.5	0.2	0.5	0.6	0.5
4.3	7.5	4.1	4.3	4.6	7.8	3.4
–	–	–	–	–	–	–
–	–	–	–	–	–	–
–	–	0.0	–	–	–	0.0
9.8	8.2	10.7	3.7	14.9	5.7	7.0
1.0	1.0	2.0	1.0	0.6	2.6	3.8
25.3	*28.6*	*33.1*	*19.7*	*40.0*	*26.4*	*25.5*
–	–	–	–	–	–	–
–	–	–	–	–	–	–
–	–	–	–	0.1	0.1	–
–	–	–	–	–	–	–
0.4	3.2	2.3	1.7	26.9	6.8	1.5
–	–	–	–	–	–	–
–	–	–	–	–	–	–
–	–	–	–	–	–	–
–	–	–	–	–	–	–
–	–	–	–	–	–	–
–	–	–	–	–	–	–
–	–	–	2.0	2.2	1.9	2.2
1.1	1.1	1.1	–	–	–	–
0.4	0.4	0.2	–	–	–	–
–	–	–	–	–	–	–
–	–	–	–	–	–	–
0.5	0.1	0.5	–	–	–	–
–	–	–	–	–	–	–
0.2	0.3	0.5	–	–	–	–
–	–	–	–	–	–	–
2.6	*5.1*	*4.5*	*3.7*	*29.1*	*8.8*	*3.7*
–	–	–	–	–	–	–
10.8	*12.4*	*14.5*	*6.2*	*43.0*	*13.2*	*11.2*
27.8	***33.7***	***37.5***	***23.4***	***69.1***	***35.2***	***29.3***
			TECH. COOP. GRANTS			
8.8	10.3	11.4	1.7	2.1	2.0	2.1
–	–	–	–	–	–	–
–	–	0.1	0.1	–	–	0.1
–	–	–	–	–	–	–
–	–	–	0.0	–	–	–
–	–	–	–	–	–	–
–	–	0.2	–	–	–	0.2
0.4	0.5	0.9	0.1	0.4	0.4	0.9
–	–	–	–	–	–	–
0.7	0.6	3.3	0.3	0.7	0.5	1.0
0.3	0.6	0.5	0.2	0.3	0.6	0.5
4.3	7.5	4.1	1.0	2.8	1.3	1.7
–	–	–	–	–	–	–
–	–	–	–	–	–	–
–	–	0.0	–	–	–	–
5.3	4.6	7.0	3.7	5.3	4.6	6.9
1.0	1.0	2.0	1.0	1.0	–	2.0
20.8	*25.0*	*29.3*	*8.1*	*12.4*	*9.4*	*15.2*
2.6	*2.5*	*2.9*	*1.9*	*1.7*	*1.8*	*2.2*
–	–	–	–	–	–	–
6.3	*6.3*	*9.2*	*4.1*	*5.9*	*5.6*	*8.5*
23.3	***27.5***	***32.2***	***10.0***	***14.1***	***11.2***	***17.4***
			TOTAL OOF NET			
–	2.0	7.9	0.4	–	2.0	7.2
–	–	–	–	–	–	–
–	–	–	–	–	–	–
–	–	–	–	–	–	–
–	–	–	–	–	–	–
–	–	–	–	–	–	–
0.2	0.2	–	0.4	0.2	0.2	–
–	–	–	–	–	–	–
–	–	–	–	–	–	–
–	–	–	–	–	–	–
–	–	–	0.4	–	–	–
–	–	–	–	–	–	–
–	–	–	–	–	–	–
–	–	–	–	–	–	–
–	6.5	1.6	0.0	-0.5	6.1	0.6
–	–	–	–	–	–	–
0.2	*8.7*	*9.5*	*1.2*	*-0.3*	*8.3*	*7.8*
3.0	*10.8*	*21.0*	*4.5*	*2.2*	*9.9*	*20.0*
–	–	–	–	–	–	–
0.2	*7.9*	*8.5*	*0.4*	*-0.3*	*7.5*	*7.4*
3.2	***19.5***	***30.5***	***5.7***	***1.8***	***18.2***	***27.8***

	1977	1978	1979	1980
MAIN AID AGGREGATES				
DAC COUNTRIES COMBINED				
PRIVATE SECTOR NET	14.7	15.2	11.5	13.7
Direct Investment	17.1	12.2	10.7	11.3
Portfolio Invest.	0.4	2.7	2.2	-0.8
Export Credits	-2.8	0.3	-1.4	3.2
OFFICIAL & PRIVATE				
GROSS:				
Contractual Lending	13.2	14.6	14.4	18.8
Export Credits Tot.	6.5	9.9	4.0	13.5
Export Credits Priv	0.6	9.9	2.1	5.6
OTHER NET DATA				
Contractual Lending	3.5	3.2	7.8	13.3
Export Credits Tot.	-2.4	0.3	0.6	10.8
(Bank Sector Loans)	–	13.0	-1.0	17.0
ODA CONCESSIONALITY				
Total:Grant Element	100.0	82.0	100.0	100.0
Loans:Grant Element	–	26.0	–	–
OTHER SOURCES				
CMEA Countr.(Gross)	–	–	–	–
Intra LDCS Exc.OPEC	–	–	–	–
Other	–	–	–	–
ALL SOURCE COMMITMENTS				
TOTAL BILATERAL	26.4	46.0	29.9	76.7
of which				
OPEC (ODA)	–	–	–	–
CMEA (ODA)	–	–	–	–
TOTAL MULTILAT.(ODA)	3.7	29.1	8.8	3.7
TOTAL BIL.& MULTIL.	30.1	75.1	38.7	80.4
of which				
ODA Grants	23.4	36.1	34.3	29.3
ODA Loans	–	33.1	0.9	–
ODA CONCESSIONALITY				
Total: Grant Element	100.0	70.0	99.0	100.0
Loans: Grant Element	–	27.0	79.0	–
INDEBTEDNESS				
TOTAL DEBT DISBURSED	***87.5***	***92.4***	***118.6***	
Debt to DAC Countries	52.0	57.0	71.0	
ODA	19.0	25.0	28.0	
Total Export Credits	14.0	15.0	20.0	
Other Private Market	19.0	17.0	23.0	
International Org.	31.8	31.7	44.0	
CMEA	–	–	–	
Other	3.7	3.7	3.6	
TOTAL DEBT SERVICE	***10.4***	***17.8***	***15.2***	
Paid to DAC Countries	7.4	11.8	11.2	
ODA	1.5	2.3	2.2	
Total Export Credits	3.7	2.6	5.9	
Other Private Market	2.2	6.9	3.1	
International Org.	2.7	5.7	3.7	
CMEA	–	–	–	
Other	0.3	0.3	0.3	
ECONOMIC INDICATORS				
GNP Curr. Prices, $M	762.3	856.4	996.7	1190.0
Real GNP, 1976=100	104.0	106.0	116.0	121.0
GNP/Cap Curr. Prices,$	1274.0	1408.0	1610.0	1888.0
GNP/cap Atlas Basis, $	1320.0	1419.7	1654.9	1847.6
Real GNP/Cap, 1976=100	102.0	102.0	110.0	113.0
Population, Million	0.6	0.6	0.6	0.6
Curr.A/C Deficit(-),$M	-21.5	-37.7	-80.8	-75.7
BOP Exp. & Transf.,$M	318.4	369.4	474.0	585.0
Exp. to OECD CIF, $M	122.9	147.1	192.8	241.5
of which				
Manufact.	3.1	7.6	3.8	4.8
Imp. from OECD FOB, $M	188.6	249.1	308.4	370.6
Reserves ex. Gold, $M	147.1	134.7	136.5	167.5

	TOTAL RECEIPTS NET 1977	1978	1979	1980	TOTAL ODA NET 1977	1978	1979	1980
DAC COUNTRIES								
Australia	–	–	0.0	–	–	–	–	–
Austria	–	–	–	–	–	–	–	–
Belgium	41.4	-26.7	-53.4	-5.2	0.2	0.2	0.2	0.3
Canada	1.0	0.5	0.4	0.1	1.0	0.5	0.4	0.1
Denmark	–	–	–	–	–	–	–	–
Finland	–	–	–	0.7	–	–	–	–
France	202.0	57.4	-23.5	-64.8	19.3	28.7	20.7	40.6
Germany, Fed. Rep.	6.2	5.6	14.5	37.5	0.2	7.2	4.1	6.4
Italy	13.8	24.7	-10.1	-2.8	0.0	0.1	0.2	0.1
Japan	9.3	2.4	3.5	6.2	2.5	0.1	0.1	0.1
Netherlands	0.4	8.4	1.2	1.3	0.4	0.1	1.2	0.4
New Zealand	–	–	–	–	–	–	–	–
Norway	–	–	0.0	–	–	–	–	–
Sweden	–	–	–	–	–	–	–	–
Switzerland	0.0	0.1	0.0	-5.2	0.0	0.1	0.0	0.0
United Kingdom	0.9	4.2	11.4	-1.4	–	–	–	–
United States	4.0	–	-1.0	-3.0	–	–	–	1.0
TOTAL	*278.9*	*76.4*	*-57.2*	*-36.4*	*23.6*	*36.9*	*26.8*	*49.1*
MULTILATERAL								
AF.D.F.	–	–	–	–	–	–	–	–
AF.D.B.	1.3	5.3	5.0	4.6	–	–	–	–
AS.D.B.	–	–	–	–	–	–	–	–
CAR.D.B.	–	–	–	–	–	–	–	–
E.E.C.	1.2	3.9	6.6	3.0	1.2	4.5	7.1	3.4
IBRD	0.3	0.0	-0.9	-1.7	–	–	–	–
IDA	–	–	–	–	–	–	–	–
I.D.B.	–	–	–	–	–	–	–	–
IFAD	–	–	–	–	–	–	–	–
I.F.C.	–	–	–	–	–	–	–	–
IMF TRUST FUND	–	–	–	–	–	–	–	–
U.N. AGENCIES	–	–	–	–	–	–	–	–
UNDP	1.7	1.6	2.0	2.6	1.7	1.6	2.0	2.6
UNTA	0.5	0.5	0.4	0.0	0.5	0.5	0.4	0.0
UNICEF	0.0	0.0	0.0	0.0	0.0	0.0	0.0	0.0
UNRWA	–	–	–	–	–	–	–	–
WFP	–	–	0.4	–	–	–	0.4	–
UNHCR	0.1	0.0	0.0	0.0	0.1	0.0	0.0	0.0
Other Multilateral	0.5	0.4	0.1	0.6	0.5	0.4	0.1	0.6
Arab OPEC Agencies	–	–	–	–	–	–	–	–
TOTAL	*5.6*	*11.7*	*13.5*	*9.2*	*4.0*	*7.0*	*9.9*	*6.7*
OPEC COUNTRIES	–	–	–	–	–	–	–	–
E.E.C.+ MEMBERS	*265.9*	*77.4*	*-53.4*	*-32.3*	*21.3*	*40.7*	*33.4*	*51.2*
TOTAL	***284.5***	***88.1***	***-43.7***	***-27.2***	***27.6***	***43.9***	***36.7***	***55.8***

	ODA LOANS GROSS 1977	1978	1979	1980	ODA LOANS NET 1977	1978	1979	1980
DAC COUNTRIES								
Australia	–	–	–	–	–	–	–	–
Austria	–	–	–	–	–	–	–	–
Belgium	–	–	–	–	–	–	–	–
Canada	–	–	–	–	–	–	–	–
Denmark	–	–	–	–	–	–	–	–
Finland	–	–	–	–	–	–	–	–
France	3.1	7.1	5.4	9.7	-3.0	0.6	-2.3	5.6
Germany, Fed. Rep.	0.4	7.1	3.8	6.3	-0.4	6.6	3.5	5.5
Italy	–	–	–	–	–	–	–	–
Japan	2.4	–	–	–	2.4	–	–	–
Netherlands	–	–	1.1	0.2	–	–	1.1	0.2
New Zealand	–	–	–	–	–	–	–	–
Norway	–	–	–	–	–	–	–	–
Sweden	–	–	–	–	–	–	–	–
Switzerland	–	–	–	–	–	–	–	–
United Kingdom	–	–	–	–	–	–	–	–
United States	–	–	–	–	–	–	–	–
TOTAL	*6.0*	*14.2*	*10.3*	*16.2*	*-1.0*	*7.2*	*2.3*	*11.4*
MULTILATERAL	*1.7*	*4.3*	*6.8*	*3.6*	*1.1*	*4.2*	*6.7*	*3.3*
OPEC COUNTRIES	–	–	–	–	–	–	–	–
E.E.C.+ MEMBERS	*5.2*	*18.4*	*17.0*	*19.8*	*-2.3*	*11.4*	*9.0*	*14.6*
TOTAL	***7.6***	***18.4***	***17.0***	***19.8***	***0.1***	***11.4***	***9.0***	***14.6***

	TOTAL OFFICIAL GROSS 1977	1978	1979	1980	TOTAL OFFICIAL NET 1977	1978	1979	1980
DAC COUNTRIES								
Australia	–	–	0.0	–	–	–	0.0	–
Austria	–	–	–	–	–	–	–	–
Belgium	0.2	0.2	7.8	0.3	0.2	0.2	5.9	-0.8
Canada	1.0	0.5	0.4	0.1	1.0	0.5	0.4	0.1
Denmark	–	–	–	–	–	–	–	–
Finland	–	–	–	–	–	–	–	–
France	33.0	97.3	76.5	51.8	22.3	10.1	-33.1	-30.7
Germany, Fed. Rep.	1.1	7.6	4.4	9.3	0.3	7.2	4.1	8.5
Italy	0.0	0.1	5.2	3.8	0.0	0.1	5.2	3.8
Japan	2.5	0.1	0.1	0.1	2.5	0.1	0.1	0.1
Netherlands	0.4	0.1	1.2	1.3	0.4	0.1	1.2	1.3
New Zealand	–	–	–	–	–	–	–	–
Norway	–	–	–	–	–	–	–	–
Sweden	–	–	–	–	–	–	–	–
Switzerland	0.0	0.1	0.0	0.0	0.0	0.1	0.0	0.0
United Kingdom	–	–	–	–	–	–	–	–
United States	4.0	1.0	–	1.0	4.0	–	-1.0	-3.0
TOTAL	*42.3*	*106.9*	*95.5*	*67.8*	*30.8*	*18.3*	*-17.3*	*-20.5*
MULTILATERAL	*7.4*	*13.6*	*15.8*	*11.9*	*5.6*	*11.7*	*13.5*	*9.2*
OPEC COUNTRIES	–	–	–	–	–	–	–	–
E.E.C.+ MEMBERS	*36.6*	*109.8*	*102.2*	*70.3*	*24.5*	*21.5*	*-10.1*	*-14.9*
TOTAL	***49.7***	***120.6***	***111.2***	***79.7***	***36.4***	***30.0***	***-3.8***	***-11.4***

TOTAL ODA GROSS	197
Australia	
Austria	
Belgium	0
Canada	1
Denmark	
Finland	
France	25
Germany, Fed. Rep.	1
Italy	0
Japan	2
Netherlands	0
New Zealand	
Norway	
Sweden	
Switzerland	0
United Kingdom	
United States	
TOTAL	*3[illegible]*
AF.D.F.	
AF.D.B.	
AS.D.B.	
CAR.D.B.	
E.E.C.	[illegible]
IBRD	
IDA	
I.D.B.	
IFAD	
I.F.C.	
IMF TRUST FUND	
U.N. AGENCIES	
UNDP	[illegible]
UNTA	[illegible]
UNICEF	[illegible]
UNRWA	
WFP	
UNHCR	[illegible]
Other Multilateral	[illegible]
Arab OPEC Agencies	
TOTAL	[illegible]
OPEC COUNTRIES	
E.E.C.+ MEMBERS	*2[illegible]*
TOTAL	***3[illegible]***

GRANTS	
Australia	
Austria	
Belgium	[illegible]
Canada	[illegible]
Denmark	
Finland	
France	2[illegible]
Germany, Fed. Rep.	[illegible]
Italy	[illegible]
Japan	[illegible]
Netherlands	[illegible]
New Zealand	
Norway	
Sweden	
Switzerland	[illegible]
United Kingdom	
United States	
TOTAL	*2[illegible]*
MULTILATERAL	[illegible]
OPEC COUNTRIES	
E.E.C.+ MEMBERS	*2[illegible]*
TOTAL	***2[illegible]***

TOTAL OOF GROSS	
Australia	
Austria	
Belgium	
Canada	
Denmark	
Finland	
France	[illegible]
Germany, Fed. Rep.	[illegible]
Italy	
Japan	
Netherlands	
New Zealand	
Norway	
Sweden	
Switzerland	
United Kingdom	
United States	[illegible]
TOTAL	*1*
MULTILATERAL	[illegible]
OPEC COUNTRIES	
E.E.C.+ MEMBERS	
TOTAL	***1[illegible]***

1978	1979	1980	1977	1978	1979	1980
			ODA COMMITMENTS			
–	–	–	–	–	–	–
–	–	–	–	–	–	–
0.2	0.2	0.3	–	–	–	–
0.5	0.4	0.1	2.2	0.5	0.4	0.2
–	–	–	–	–	0.0	–
–	–	–	–	–	–	–
35.2	28.4	44.6	21.4	31.9	24.6	56.8
7.6	4.4	7.2	0.2	15.6	1.0	0.3
0.1	0.2	0.1	0.0	0.1	0.2	0.1
0.1	0.1	0.1	0.0	0.1	0.1	0.2
0.1	1.2	0.4	0.4	0.0	1.2	0.4
–	–	–	–	–	–	–
–	–	–	–	–	–	–
–	–	–	–	–	–	–
0.1	0.0	0.0	–	–	–	0.0
–	–	–	–	–	–	–
–	–	1.0	0.2	0.5	0.5	0.7
43.8	*34.8*	*53.9*	*24.5*	*48.7*	*27.9*	*58.7*
–	–	–	–	–	–	–
–	–	–	–	–	–	–
–	–	–	–	–	–	–
–	–	–	–	–	–	–
4.5	7.1	3.8	4.7	3.4	1.7	1.1
–	–	–	–	–	–	–
–	–	–	–	–	–	–
–	–	–	–	–	–	–
–	–	–	–	–	–	–
–	–	–	–	–	–	–
–	–	–	–	–	–	–
–	–	–	2.8	2.5	2.9	3.3
1.6	2.0	2.6	–	–	–	–
0.5	0.4	0.0	–	–	–	–
0.0	0.0	0.0	–	–	–	–
–	–	–	–	–	–	–
–	0.4	–	–	–	–	–
0.0	0.0	0.0	–	–	–	–
0.4	0.1	0.6	–	–	–	–
–	–	–	–	–	–	–
7.1	*10.0*	*7.1*	*7.5*	*5.9*	*4.5*	*4.4*
–	–	–	–	*20.8*	–	*2.7*
47.7	*41.4*	*56.4*	*26.8*	*51.0*	*28.7*	*58.6*
50.9	***44.8***	***61.0***	***32.0***	***75.4***	***32.4***	***65.7***
			TECH. COOP. GRANTS			
–	–	–	–	–	–	–
–	–	–	–	–	–	–
0.2	0.2	0.3	0.2	0.2	0.2	0.3
0.5	0.4	0.1	0.9	0.5	0.3	0.1
–	–	–	–	–	–	–
–	–	–	–	–	–	–
28.1	23.0	34.9	19.4	24.1	20.5	31.5
0.6	0.6	0.9	0.6	0.6	0.6	0.9
0.1	0.2	0.1	0.0	0.1	0.2	0.1
0.1	0.1	0.1	0.0	0.1	0.1	0.1
0.1	0.1	0.2	0.4	0.1	0.1	0.2
–	–	–	–	–	–	–
–	–	–	–	–	–	–
–	–	–	–	–	–	–
0.1	0.0	0.0	–	–	–	–
–	–	–	–	–	–	–
–	–	1.0	–	–	–	1.0
29.7	*24.5*	*37.7*	*21.5*	*25.6*	*21.9*	*34.3*
2.8	*3.2*	*3.5*	*2.8*	*2.5*	*2.5*	*3.3*
–	–	–	–	–	–	–
29.3	*24.4*	*36.6*	*20.6*	*25.0*	*21.5*	*33.0*
32.5	***27.7***	***41.2***	***24.3***	***28.1***	***24.4***	***37.6***
			TOTAL OOF NET			
–	0.0	–	–	–	0.0	–
–	–	–	–	–	–	–
–	7.6	–	–	–	5.7	-1.1
–	–	–	–	–	–	–
–	–	–	–	–	–	–
–	–	–	–	–	–	–
62.1	48.1	7.2	3.0	-18.6	-53.8	-71.2
0.0	–	2.1	0.2	0.0	–	2.1
–	5.0	3.7	–	–	5.0	3.7
–	–	–	–	–	–	–
–	–	0.9	–	–	–	0.9
–	–	–	–	–	–	–
–	–	–	–	–	–	–
–	–	–	–	–	–	–
–	–	–	–	–	–	–
–	–	–	–	–	–	–
1.0	–	–	4.0	–	-1.0	-4.0
63.1	*60.7*	*13.9*	*7.2*	*-18.6*	*-44.1*	*-69.6*
6.6	*5.7*	*4.9*	*1.6*	*4.7*	*3.6*	*2.4*
–	–	–	–	–	–	–
62.1	*60.7*	*13.9*	*3.2*	*-19.2*	*-43.5*	*-66.1*
69.7	***66.5***	***18.8***	***8.8***	***-13.9***	***-40.5***	***-67.2***

MAIN AID AGGREGATES

	1977	1978	1979	1980
DAC COUNTRIES COMBINED				
PRIVATE SECTOR NET	248.2	58.1	-40.0	-15.8
Direct Investment	25.6	9.1	20.2	24.6
Portfolio Invest.	24.0	25.9	-16.8	-26.5
Export Credits	198.5	23.2	-43.3	-13.9
OFFICIAL & PRIVATE				
GROSS:				
Contractual Lending	355.9	246.3	276.0	136.7
Export Credits Tot.	342.2	170.0	210.0	112.4
Export Credits Priv	338.2	169.0	205.0	106.6
OTHER NET DATA				
Contractual Lending	204.7	11.8	-85.1	-72.1
Export Credits Tot.	202.5	23.2	-39.3	-12.1
(Bank Sector Loans)	7.0	14.0	-15.0	22.0
ODA CONCESSIONALITY				
Total:Grant Element	100.0	81.0	100.0	81.0
Loans:Grant Element	–	55.0	–	27.0
OTHER SOURCES				
CMEA Countr.(Gross)	–	–	–	–
Intra LDCS Exc.OPEC	–	–	–	–
Other	–	–	–	–
ALL SOURCE COMMITMENTS				
TOTAL BILATERAL	57.1	148.1	56.8	89.0
of which				
OPEC (ODA)	–	20.8	–	2.7
CMEA (ODA)	–	–	–	–
TOTAL MULTILAT.(ODA)	7.5	5.9	4.5	4.4
TOTAL BIL.& MULTIL.	64.6	154.0	61.3	93.4
of which				
ODA Grants	28.0	31.3	30.0	47.8
ODA Loans	4.0	44.0	2.4	17.9
ODA CONCESSIONALITY				
Total: Grant Element	98.0	70.0	100.0	81.0
Loans: Grant Element	79.0	49.0	–	30.0

INDEBTEDNESS

	1977	1978	1979	1980
TOTAL DEBT DISBURSED	***1281.7***	***1546.0***	***1600.1***	
Debt to DAC Countries	1146.0	1415.0	1482.0	
ODA	55.0	74.0	72.0	
Total Export Credits	670.0	907.0	983.0	
Other Private Market	421.0	434.0	427.0	
International Org.	38.6	44.3	47.6	
CMEA	–	–	–	
Other	97.1	86.7	70.5	
TOTAL DEBT SERVICE	***240.3***	***371.7***	***493.6***	
Paid to DAC Countries	229.1	338.7	456.8	
ODA	7.8	9.9	10.6	
Total Export Credits	177.6	204.5	317.8	
Other Private Market	43.7	124.3	128.4	
International Org.	3.8	4.3	4.9	
CMEA	–	–	–	
Other	7.5	28.7	31.9	

ECONOMIC INDICATORS

	1977	1978	1979	1980
GNP Curr. Prices, $M	2594.9	2087.4	2586.5	3414.1
Real GNP, 1976=100	77.0	52.0	51.0	51.0
GNP/Cap Curr. Prices,$	4138.0	3292.0	4010.0	5196.0
GNP/cap Atlas Basis, $	5554.9	3946.2	4126.4	4436.5
Real GNP/Cap, 1976=100	77.0	51.0	49.0	48.0
Population, Million	0.6	0.6	0.6	0.7
Curr.A/C Deficit(-),$M	-33.3	37.1	209.2	–
BOP Exp. & Transf.,$M	1487.0	1482.9	2028.5	–
Exp. to OECD CIF, $M	843.2	879.7	1213.0	1677.5
of which				
Manufact.	22.9	39.8	84.0	161.0
Imp. from OECD FOB, $M	584.1	458.0	443.5	643.1
Reserves ex. Gold, $M	9.9	22.6	20.1	107.5

	TOTAL RECEIPTS NET 1977	1978	1979	1980	TOTAL ODA NET 1977	1978	1979	1980
DAC COUNTRIES								
Australia	0.1	0.1	0.0	0.0	0.1	0.1	0.0	0.0
Austria	4.7	0.0	-0.5	-1.0	0.0	0.0	0.0	0.0
Belgium	–	0.2	0.0	0.0	–	0.2	0.0	–
Canada	2.0	1.1	0.0	0.1	2.0	1.1	0.0	0.1
Denmark	0.1	0.4	0.1	0.6	0.1	0.4	0.1	0.6
Finland	0.0	–	–	0.0	0.0	–	–	0.0
France	0.0	–	2.8	3.7	–	–	–	1.1
Germany, Fed. Rep.	5.4	4.6	4.9	4.8	3.4	4.6	4.4	5.0
Italy	–	–	0.4	0.0	–	–	–	0.1
Japan	-1.2	0.0	–	0.0	0.4	0.0	–	0.0
Netherlands	0.1	0.5	2.1	0.6	0.1	0.5	2.1	0.6
New Zealand	0.0	–	–	–	–	–	–	–
Norway	–	3.3	-0.3	15.4	–	–	–	0.2
Sweden	–	–	–	–	–	–	–	–
Switzerland	–	0.1	0.1	0.0	–	0.1	0.1	0.0
United Kingdom	5.8	6.8	5.3	10.0	5.6	6.8	4.4	4.7
United States	2.0	1.0	2.0	4.0	1.0	1.0	2.0	4.0
TOTAL	*19.0*	*18.1*	*17.0*	*38.3*	*12.6*	*14.8*	*13.2*	*16.5*
MULTILATERAL								
AF.D.F.	0.5	0.5	–	–	0.5	0.5	–	–
AF.D.B.	0.0	0.1	0.8	5.7	–	–	–	–
AS.D.B.	–	–	–	–	–	–	–	–
CAR.D.B.	–	–	–	–	–	–	–	–
E.E.C.	0.2	3.1	6.1	9.4	0.2	3.1	6.1	9.4
IBRD	–	–	–	–	–	–	–	–
IDA	1.7	1.3	2.8	5.2	1.7	1.3	2.8	5.2
I.D.B.	–	–	–	–	–	–	–	–
IFAD	–	–	–	–	–	–	–	–
I.F.C.	–	–	–	–	–	–	–	–
IMF TRUST FUND	0.9	2.6	2.7	2.4	0.9	2.6	2.7	2.4
U.N. AGENCIES	–	–	–	–	–	–	–	–
UNDP	0.6	1.9	1.8	2.2	0.6	1.9	1.8	2.2
UNTA	0.2	0.4	0.4	0.1	0.2	0.4	0.4	0.1
UNICEF	0.0	0.2	0.1	0.1	0.0	0.2	0.1	0.1
UNRWA	–	–	–	–	–	–	–	–
WFP	0.8	0.7	0.6	2.3	0.8	0.7	0.6	2.3
UNHCR	–	–	0.0	0.0	–	–	0.0	0.0
Other Multilateral	0.3	1.3	2.2	2.0	0.3	1.3	2.2	2.0
Arab OPEC Agencies	1.7	1.3	2.4	7.2	1.7	1.3	2.4	7.2
TOTAL	*6.9*	*13.2*	*19.9*	*36.6*	*6.9*	*13.2*	*19.1*	*30.9*
OPEC COUNTRIES	*4.5*	*7.2*	*4.1*	*7.0*	*4.5*	*7.2*	*4.1*	*7.0*
E.E.C.+ MEMBERS	*11.6*	*15.6*	*21.7*	*29.1*	*9.4*	*15.6*	*17.1*	*21.5*
TOTAL	***30.4***	***38.5***	***41.1***	***81.9***	***24.0***	***35.2***	***36.4***	***54.4***

	ODA LOANS GROSS 1977	1978	1979	1980	ODA LOANS NET 1977	1978	1979	1980
DAC COUNTRIES								
Australia	–	–	–	–	–	–	–	–
Austria	–	–	–	–	–	–	–	–
Belgium	–	–	–	–	–	–	–	–
Canada	–	–	–	–	–	–	–	–
Denmark	–	0.3	0.0	0.6	–	0.3	0.0	0.6
Finland	–	–	–	–	–	–	–	–
France	–	–	–	–	–	–	–	–
Germany, Fed. Rep.	2.4	2.8	3.1	–	2.4	2.8	3.1	-7.6
Italy	–	–	–	–	–	–	–	–
Japan	–	–	–	–	–	–	–	–
Netherlands	–	–	–	–	–	–	–	–
New Zealand	–	–	–	–	–	–	–	–
Norway	–	–	–	–	–	–	–	–
Sweden	–	–	–	–	–	–	–	–
Switzerland	–	–	–	–	–	–	–	–
United Kingdom	0.1	0.4	–	0.2	-0.1	0.3	-0.7	-0.4
United States	–	–	–	–	–	–	–	–
TOTAL	*2.5*	*3.6*	*3.2*	*0.8*	*2.3*	*3.4*	*2.4*	*-7.4*
MULTILATERAL	*4.7*	*5.7*	*7.9*	*15.0*	*4.7*	*5.7*	*7.9*	*15.0*
OPEC COUNTRIES	*0.8*	*7.2*	*4.0*	*7.1*	*0.8*	*7.2*	*4.0*	*7.0*
E.E.C.+ MEMBERS	*2.5*	*3.6*	*3.2*	*1.0*	*2.3*	*3.4*	*2.4*	*-7.2*
TOTAL	***8.1***	***16.5***	***15.1***	***22.8***	***7.8***	***16.3***	***14.3***	***14.6***

	TOTAL OFFICIAL GROSS 1977	1978	1979	1980	TOTAL OFFICIAL NET 1977	1978	1979	1980
DAC COUNTRIES								
Australia	0.1	0.1	0.0	0.0	0.1	0.1	0.0	0.0
Austria	0.0	0.0	0.0	0.0	0.0	0.0	0.0	0.0
Belgium	–	0.2	0.0	–	–	0.2	0.0	–
Canada	2.0	1.1	0.0	0.1	2.0	1.1	0.0	0.1
Denmark	0.1	0.4	0.1	0.6	0.1	0.4	0.1	0.6
Finland	0.0	–	–	0.0	0.0	–	–	0.0
France	–	–	–	3.2	–	–	–	3.2
Germany, Fed. Rep.	4.3	4.6	4.7	12.6	4.3	4.6	4.7	5.0
Italy	–	–	–	0.1	–	–	–	0.1
Japan	0.4	0.0	–	0.0	0.4	0.0	–	0.0
Netherlands	0.1	0.5	2.1	0.6	0.1	0.5	2.1	0.6
New Zealand	0.0	–	–	–	0.0	–	–	–
Norway	–	–	–	0.2	–	–	–	0.2
Sweden	–	–	–	–	–	–	–	–
Switzerland	–	0.1	0.1	0.0	–	0.1	0.1	0.0
United Kingdom	6.0	7.0	5.9	5.3	5.7	6.8	5.2	4.5
United States	1.0	1.0	2.0	4.0	1.0	1.0	2.0	4.0
TOTAL	*14.0*	*14.9*	*15.0*	*26.7*	*13.7*	*14.8*	*14.2*	*18.4*
MULTILATERAL	*6.9*	*13.2*	*19.9*	*36.6*	*6.9*	*13.2*	*19.9*	*36.6*
OPEC COUNTRIES	*2.0*	*7.2*	*4.1*	*7.1*	*4.5*	*7.2*	*4.1*	*7.0*
E.E.C.+ MEMBERS	*10.8*	*15.8*	*18.9*	*31.8*	*10.5*	*15.6*	*18.1*	*23.5*
TOTAL	***22.9***	***35.4***	***39.0***	***70.4***	***25.1***	***35.2***	***38.2***	***62.0***

TOTAL ODA GROSS	197[7]
Australia	
Austria	
Belgium	
Canada	
Denmark	
Finland	
France	
Germany, Fed. Rep.	
Italy	
Japan	
Netherlands	
New Zealand	
Norway	
Sweden	
Switzerland	
United Kingdom	
United States	
TOTAL	
AF.D.F.	
AF.D.B.	
AS.D.B.	
CAR.D.B.	
E.E.C.	
IBRD	
IDA	
I.D.B.	
IFAD	
I.F.C.	
IMF TRUST FUND	
U.N. AGENCIES	
UNDP	
UNTA	
UNICEF	
UNRWA	
WFP	
UNHCR	
Other Multilateral	
Arab OPEC Agencies	
TOTAL	
OPEC COUNTRIES	
E.E.C.+ MEMBERS	
TOTAL	

GRANTS	
Australia	
Austria	
Belgium	
Canada	
Denmark	
Finland	
France	
Germany, Fed. Rep.	
Italy	
Japan	
Netherlands	
New Zealand	
Norway	
Sweden	
Switzerland	
United Kingdom	
United States	
TOTAL	
MULTILATERAL	
OPEC COUNTRIES	
E.E.C.+ MEMBERS	
TOTAL	

TOTAL OOF GROSS	
Australia	
Austria	
Belgium	
Canada	
Denmark	
Finland	
France	
Germany, Fed. Rep.	
Italy	
Japan	
Netherlands	
New Zealand	
Norway	
Sweden	
Switzerland	
United Kingdom	
United States	
TOTAL	
MULTILATERAL	
OPEC COUNTRIES	
E.E.C.+ MEMBERS	
TOTAL	

1978	1979	1980	1977	1978	1979	1980
			ODA COMMITMENTS			
0.1	0.0	0.0	0.1	0.0	0.0	0.0
0.0	0.0	0.0	–	–	–	–
0.2	0.0	–	–	–	–	–
1.1	0.0	0.1	3.2	0.0	0.0	0.0
0.4	0.1	0.6	–	3.7	0.1	0.1
–	–	0.0	0.0	–	–	–
–	–	1.1	–	0.3	–	1.1
4.6	4.4	12.6	2.9	5.3	2.7	16.3
–	–	0.1	–	–	–	0.1
0.0	–	0.0	–	0.0	–	1.0
0.5	2.1	0.6	0.1	0.5	4.0	4.4
–	–	–	–	–	–	–
–	–	0.2	–	–	–	0.5
–	–	–	–	–	–	–
0.1	0.1	0.0	–	–	–	0.0
7.0	5.1	5.3	1.9	3.9	25.2	4.2
1.0	2.0	4.0	1.0	2.7	5.6	8.4
14.9	*13.9*	*24.6*	*9.2*	*16.4*	*37.5*	*36.2*
0.5	–	–	–	–	6.1	18.8
–	–	–	–	–	–	–
–	–	–	–	–	–	–
–	–	–	–	–	–	–
3.1	6.1	9.4	2.5	5.9	13.1	10.9
–	–	–	–	–	–	–
1.3	2.8	5.2	–	8.5	5.0	–
–	–	–	–	–	–	–
–	–	–	–	–	–	–
–	–	–	–	–	–	–
2.6	2.7	2.4	–	–	–	–
–	–	–	2.0	4.4	5.2	6.7
1.9	1.8	2.2	–	–	–	–
0.4	0.4	0.1	–	–	–	–
0.2	0.1	0.1	–	–	–	–
–	–	–	–	–	–	–
0.7	0.6	2.3	–	–	–	–
–	0.0	0.0	–	–	–	–
1.3	2.2	2.0	–	–	–	–
1.3	2.4	7.2	1.7	2.0	1.0	6.7
13.2	*19.1*	*30.9*	*6.1*	*20.8*	*30.3*	*43.1*
7.2	*4.1*	*7.1*	*24.7*	–	*0.8*	*25.5*
15.8	*17.9*	*29.7*	*7.4*	*19.5*	*45.0*	*37.1*
35.3	***37.2***	***62.7***	***40.0***	***37.2***	***68.6***	***104.7***
			TECH. COOP. GRANTS			
0.1	0.0	0.0	0.1	0.1	0.0	0.0
0.0	0.0	0.0	0.0	0.0	0.0	0.0
0.2	0.0	–	–	–	–	–
1.1	0.0	0.1	–	–	–	–
0.1	0.1	0.1	0.1	0.1	0.1	0.1
–	–	0.0	–	–	–	0.0
–	–	1.1	–	–	–	0.4
1.8	1.3	12.6	0.2	0.5	0.7	2.8
–	–	0.1	–	–	–	0.1
0.0	–	0.0	–	0.0	–	0.0
0.5	2.1	0.6	0.1	0.2	0.1	0.2
–	–	–	–	–	–	–
–	–	0.2	–	–	–	–
–	–	–	–	–	–	–
0.1	0.1	0.0	–	–	–	–
6.5	5.1	5.0	1.6	2.2	3.1	3.6
1.0	2.0	4.0	–	–	1.0	1.0
11.4	*10.8*	*23.9*	*2.1*	*3.0*	*5.1*	*8.2*
7.5	*11.2*	*16.0*	*1.2*	*3.7*	*4.5*	*6.7*
–	*0.1*	–	–	–	–	–
12.2	*14.7*	*28.7*	*2.0*	*3.0*	*4.0*	*7.1*
18.9	***22.1***	***39.8***	***3.3***	***6.8***	***9.6***	***15.0***
			TOTAL OOF NET			
–	–	–	–	–	–	–
–	–	–	–	–	–	–
–	–	–	–	–	–	–
–	–	–	–	–	–	–
–	–	–	0.0	–	–	–
–	–	–	–	–	–	–
–	–	2.1	–	–	–	2.1
–	0.2	–	0.9	–	0.2	–
–	–	–	–	–	–	–
–	–	–	–	–	–	–
–	–	–	–	–	–	–
–	–	–	0.0	–	–	–
–	–	–	–	–	–	–
–	–	–	–	–	–	–
–	–	–	–	–	–	–
–	0.8	–	0.2	–	0.8	-0.1
–	–	–	–	–	–	–
–	*1.0*	*2.1*	*1.1*	–	*1.0*	*2.0*
0.1	*0.8*	*5.7*	*0.0*	*0.1*	*0.8*	*5.7*
–	–	–	–	–	–	–
–	*1.0*	*2.1*	*1.1*	–	*1.0*	*2.0*
0.1	***1.8***	***7.8***	***1.1***	***0.1***	***1.8***	***7.6***

MAIN AID AGGREGATES

	1977	1978	1979	1980
DAC COUNTRIES COMBINED				
PRIVATE SECTOR NET	5.3	3.3	2.8	19.9
Direct Investment	-0.6	–	2.8	0.3
Portfolio Invest.	1.0	3.3	0.2	0.0
Export Credits	4.8	0.0	-0.2	19.6
OFFICIAL & PRIVATE				
GROSS:				
Contractual Lending	8.6	3.9	4.8	23.8
Export Credits Tot.	5.0	0.3	0.6	20.9
Export Credits Priv	5.0	0.3	0.6	20.9
OTHER NET DATA				
Contractual Lending	8.2	3.4	3.3	14.1
Export Credits Tot.	4.8	0.0	-0.2	19.6
(Bank Sector Loans)	1.0	–	5.0	2.0
ODA CONCESSIONALITY				
Total:Grant Element	98.0	89.0	100.0	100.0
Loans:Grant Element	83.0	66.0	–	–
OTHER SOURCES				
CMEA Countr.(Gross)	–	–	–	–
Intra LDCS Exc.OPEC	–	–	–	–
Other	–	–	–	–
ALL SOURCE COMMITMENTS				
TOTAL BILATERAL	34.4	16.4	39.1	61.6
of which				
OPEC (ODA)	24.7	–	0.8	25.5
CMEA (ODA)	–	–	–	–
TOTAL MULTILAT.(ODA)	6.1	20.8	30.3	43.1
TOTAL BIL.& MULTIL.	40.4	37.2	69.4	104.7
of which				
ODA Grants	13.5	21.4	53.4	53.6
ODA Loans	26.5	15.9	15.2	51.1
ODA CONCESSIONALITY				
Total: Grant Element	71.0	89.0	94.0	81.0
Loans: Grant Element	57.0	74.0	75.0	61.0

INDEBTEDNESS

	1977	1978	1979	1980
TOTAL DEBT DISBURSED	***28.0***	***43.6***	***70.7***	
Debt to DAC Countries	18.0	22.0	32.0	
ODA	11.0	17.0	20.0	
Total Export Credits	7.0	5.0	12.0	
Other Private Market	–	–	–	
International Org.	8.8	13.4	20.5	
CMEA	–	–	4.1	
Other	1.2	8.2	14.2	
TOTAL DEBT SERVICE	***0.5***	***0.9***	***0.8***	
Paid to DAC Countries	0.5	0.8	0.6	
ODA	0.3	0.3	0.2	
Total Export Credits	0.2	0.5	0.4	
Other Private Market	–	–	–	
International Org.	0.0	0.1	0.1	
CMEA	–	–	–	
Other	–	0.0	0.1	

ECONOMIC INDICATORS

	1977	1978	1979	1980
GNP Curr. Prices, $M	93.9	87.4	126.2	160.4
Real GNP, 1976=100	98.0	81.0	97.0	105.0
GNP/Cap Curr. Prices,$	168.0	153.0	215.0	266.0
GNP/cap Atlas Basis, $	200.3	171.9	217.6	248.8
Real GNP/Cap, 1976=100	96.0	76.0	89.0	94.0
Population, Million	0.6	0.6	0.6	0.6
Curr.A/C Deficit(-),$M	-11.5	-56.6	-58.8	-99.4
BOP Exp. & Transf.,$M	68.1	55.5	78.2	67.3
Exp. to OECD CIF, $M	43.3	37.3	43.3	25.8
of which				
Manufact.	0.3	0.4	0.6	0.5
Imp. from OECD FOB, $M	54.1	66.8	73.3	89.9
Reserves ex. Gold, $M	24.4	26.1	1.9	5.7

	1977	1978	1979	1980	1977	1978	1979	1980
TOTAL RECEIPTS NET / **TOTAL ODA NET**								
DAC COUNTRIES								
Australia	1.5	1.3	1.9	0.7	1.5	1.3	1.9	0.7
Austria	0.2	0.3	4.6	-0.6	0.2	0.3	0.2	0.1
Belgium	0.1	0.1	0.2	0.4	0.1	0.1	0.2	0.1
Canada	13.5	15.6	18.7	16.3	13.5	15.6	15.5	13.9
Denmark	-0.6	0.2	-0.7	-0.4	-0.1	0.1	-0.7	-0.4
Finland	0.0	0.0	0.0	0.0	0.0	0.0	0.0	0.0
France	11.3	3.3	-0.2	4.5	2.0	1.3	–	3.3
Germany, Fed. Rep.	3.1	10.7	13.7	26.9	6.2	10.5	14.5	26.2
Italy	38.2	49.1	-7.4	-9.7	0.3	0.6	0.5	0.5
Japan	3.0	7.9	5.8	3.8	3.0	7.9	5.6	2.5
Netherlands	7.0	3.4	6.6	5.3	7.0	3.3	6.4	4.8
New Zealand	–	0.6	–	–	–	–	–	–
Norway	1.3	0.4	5.5	12.0	0.5	0.4	0.7	1.2
Sweden	–	–	0.5	0.4	–	–	0.5	0.4
Switzerland	0.1	0.1	0.1	0.2	0.1	0.1	0.1	0.2
United Kingdom	11.5	3.2	17.7	41.5	3.9	7.6	21.2	34.8
United States	16.0	7.0	18.0	14.0	14.0	8.0	22.0	19.0
TOTAL	*106.1*	*103.3*	*85.1*	*115.1*	*52.0*	*57.2*	*88.6*	*107.1*
MULTILATERAL								
AF.D.F.	–	–	–	–	–	–	–	–
AF.D.B.	8.2	4.1	2.9	0.6	–	–	–	–
AS.D.B.	–	–	–	–	–	–	–	–
CAR.D.B.	–	–	–	–	–	–	–	–
E.E.C.	3.2	12.2	7.4	11.8	3.2	11.1	6.8	8.6
IBRD	4.6	23.5	26.8	21.3	0.1	2.8	5.4	4.8
IDA	23.0	11.3	4.0	4.6	23.0	11.3	4.0	4.6
I.D.B.	–	–	–	–	–	–	–	–
IFAD	–	–	–	–	–	–	–	–
I.F.C.	–	–	–	–	–	–	–	–
IMF TRUST FUND	–	–	34.1	28.9	–	–	34.1	28.9
U.N. AGENCIES	–	–	–	–	–	–	–	–
UNDP	4.2	4.2	3.2	3.8	4.2	4.2	3.2	3.8
UNTA	0.5	0.5	0.3	0.3	0.5	0.5	0.3	0.3
UNICEF	0.6	0.5	0.5	0.9	0.6	0.5	0.5	0.9
UNRWA	–	–	–	–	–	–	–	–
WFP	1.8	4.3	4.2	2.5	1.8	4.3	4.2	2.5
UNHCR	0.0	0.1	0.2	0.1	0.0	0.1	0.2	0.1
Other Multilateral	1.3	1.7	0.6	0.9	1.3	1.7	0.6	0.9
Arab OPEC Agencies	4.6	4.7	7.3	7.5	4.6	1.7	4.4	3.9
TOTAL	*52.0*	*67.1*	*91.4*	*83.2*	*39.2*	*38.3*	*63.7*	*59.3*
OPEC COUNTRIES	–	*18.4*	*16.6*	*25.2*	–	*18.4*	*16.6*	*25.2*
E.E.C.+ MEMBERS	*73.7*	*82.2*	*37.3*	*80.1*	*22.5*	*34.6*	*48.9*	*77.7*
TOTAL	***158.1***	***188.9***	***193.1***	***223.5***	***91.2***	***113.9***	***168.9***	***191.6***
ODA LOANS GROSS / **ODA LOANS NET**								
DAC COUNTRIES								
Australia	–	–	–	–	–	–	–	–
Austria	–	–	–	–	–	–	–	–
Belgium	–	–	–	–	–	–	–	–
Canada	7.1	10.2	11.3	8.6	7.1	10.2	11.3	8.4
Denmark	0.0	0.1	–	0.0	-0.2	0.1	-0.7	-0.4
Finland	–	–	–	–	–	–	–	–
France	1.8	1.3	–	–	1.8	1.3	–	–
Germany, Fed. Rep.	1.0	1.1	5.7	17.4	-2.4	-2.2	1.5	12.5
Italy	–	–	–	–	–	–	–	–
Japan	–	–	–	–	-0.1	-0.1	0.0	–
Netherlands	–	–	0.2	0.4	0.0	0.0	0.2	0.3
New Zealand	–	–	–	–	–	–	–	–
Norway	–	–	–	–	–	–	–	–
Sweden	–	–	–	–	–	–	–	–
Switzerland	–	–	–	–	–	–	–	–
United Kingdom	0.1	2.7	16.8	29.3	-1.0	1.8	14.2	27.8
United States	8.0	1.0	15.0	14.0	4.0	-3.0	10.0	7.0
TOTAL	*18.0*	*16.4*	*49.0*	*69.6*	*9.2*	*8.1*	*36.5*	*55.6*
MULTILATERAL	*29.3*	*20.9*	*49.0*	*46.0*	*29.1*	*20.6*	*48.7*	*46.0*
OPEC COUNTRIES	–	*18.4*	*16.6*	*25.2*	–	*18.4*	*16.6*	*25.2*
E.E.C.+ MEMBERS	*4.4*	*10.0*	*23.4*	*50.8*	*-0.3*	*5.7*	*16.0*	*44.0*
TOTAL	***47.3***	***55.7***	***114.6***	***140.9***	***38.4***	***47.0***	***101.8***	***126.8***
TOTAL OFFICIAL GROSS / **TOTAL OFFICIAL NET**								
DAC COUNTRIES								
Australia	1.5	1.3	1.9	0.7	1.5	1.3	1.9	0.7
Austria	0.2	0.3	0.2	0.1	0.2	0.3	0.2	0.1
Belgium	0.1	0.1	0.2	0.1	0.1	0.1	0.2	0.1
Canada	13.5	15.6	18.7	16.5	13.5	15.6	18.7	16.3
Denmark	0.1	0.2	0.0	0.0	-0.1	0.2	-0.7	-0.4
Finland	0.0	0.0	0.0	0.0	0.0	0.0	0.0	0.0
France	2.0	3.8	–	3.3	2.0	3.8	–	3.3
Germany, Fed. Rep.	9.7	13.8	19.2	31.0	6.2	7.3	13.4	26.1
Italy	0.3	0.6	0.5	0.5	0.3	0.6	0.5	0.5
Japan	3.0	8.0	5.6	2.5	3.0	7.9	5.6	2.5
Netherlands	7.0	3.4	6.6	5.3	7.0	3.4	6.6	5.3
New Zealand	–	–	–	–	–	–	–	–
Norway	0.5	0.4	0.7	1.2	0.5	0.4	0.7	1.2
Sweden	–	–	0.5	0.4	–	–	0.5	0.4
Switzerland	0.1	0.1	0.1	0.2	0.1	0.1	0.1	0.2
United Kingdom	4.9	8.6	23.8	36.3	3.9	7.6	21.2	34.8
United States	22.0	12.0	27.0	26.0	16.0	7.0	19.0	14.0
TOTAL	*64.8*	*68.2*	*105.2*	*124.0*	*54.0*	*55.7*	*88.0*	*104.9*
MULTILATERAL	*54.4*	*70.1*	*94.8*	*87.0*	*52.0*	*67.1*	*91.4*	*83.2*
OPEC COUNTRIES	–	*18.4*	*16.6*	*25.2*	–	*18.4*	*16.6*	*25.2*
E.E.C.+ MEMBERS	*27.2*	*42.6*	*57.8*	*88.2*	*22.6*	*35.2*	*48.6*	*81.3*
TOTAL	***119.1***	***156.7***	***216.6***	***236.3***	***106.0***	***141.3***	***196.0***	***213.4***

	197
TOTAL ODA GROSS	
Australia	1.
Austria	0.
Belgium	0.
Canada	13.
Denmark	0.
Finland	0.
France	2.
Germany, Fed. Rep.	9.
Italy	0.
Japan	3
Netherlands	7.
New Zealand	
Norway	0.
Sweden	
Switzerland	0.
United Kingdom	4
United States	18
TOTAL	*60*
AF.D.F.	
AF.D.B.	
AS.D.B.	
CAR.D.B.	
E.E.C.	3
IBRD	0
IDA	23
I.D.B.	
IFAD	
I.F.C.	
IMF TRUST FUND	
U.N. AGENCIES	
UNDP	4
UNTA	0
UNICEF	0
UNRWA	
WFP	1
UNHCR	0
Other Multilateral	1
Arab OPEC Agencies	4
TOTAL	*39*
OPEC COUNTRIES	
E.E.C.+ MEMBERS	*27*
TOTAL	***100***
GRANTS	
Australia	1
Austria	0
Belgium	0
Canada	6
Denmark	0
Finland	0
France	0
Germany, Fed. Rep.	8
Italy	0
Japan	3
Netherlands	7
New Zealand	
Norway	0
Sweden	
Switzerland	0
United Kingdom	4
United States	10
TOTAL	*42*
MULTILATERAL	*10*
OPEC COUNTRIES	
E.E.C.+ MEMBERS	*22*
TOTAL	***52***
TOTAL OOF GROSS	
Australia	
Austria	
Belgium	
Canada	
Denmark	
Finland	
France	
Germany, Fed. Rep.	0
Italy	
Japan	
Netherlands	
New Zealand	
Norway	
Sweden	
Switzerland	
United Kingdom	
United States	4
TOTAL	*4*
MULTILATERAL	*14*
OPEC COUNTRIES	
E.E.C.+ MEMBERS	[illegible]
TOTAL	***19***

ODA COMMITMENTS

1978	1979	1980	1977	1978	1979	1980
1.3	1.9	0.7	3.1	0.6	1.2	0.5
0.3	0.2	0.1	–	0.3	–	0.0
0.1	0.2	0.1	–	–	–	–
15.6	15.5	14.1	39.7	5.4	5.5	5.1
0.1	0.0	0.0	0.0	–	–	–
0.0	0.0	0.0	–	0.0	0.0	–
1.3	–	3.3	3.2	0.3	–	2.7
13.8	18.6	31.0	19.7	41.5	39.2	80.0
0.6	0.5	0.5	0.3	0.6	0.5	0.5
8.0	5.6	2.5	5.5	9.5	2.7	3.9
3.3	6.4	4.8	8.9	7.3	5.2	4.2
–	–	–	–	–	–	–
0.4	0.7	1.2	0.2	0.3	–	0.2
–	0.5	0.4	–	–	–	–
0.1	0.1	0.2	–	–	–	0.2
8.6	23.8	36.3	4.9	50.0	7.2	7.0
12.0	27.0	26.0	11.7	12.1	21.1	29.3
65.6	*101.0*	*121.2*	*97.1*	*127.9*	*82.5*	*133.4*
–	–	–	–	–	–	9.4
–	–	–	–	–	–	–
–	–	–	–	–	–	–
–	–	–	–	–	–	–
11.1	6.8	8.6	29.2	23.3	5.3	10.8
2.8	5.4	4.8	–	–	–	–
11.7	4.3	4.7	9.0	–	19.0	54.5
–	–	–	–	–	–	–
–	–	–	–	–	–	12.2
–	–	–	–	–	–	–
–	34.1	28.9	–	–	–	–
–	–	–	8.5	11.3	9.0	8.5
4.2	3.2	3.8	–	–	–	–
0.5	0.3	0.3	–	–	–	–
0.5	0.5	0.9	–	–	–	–
–	–	–	–	–	–	–
4.3	4.2	2.5	–	–	–	–
0.1	0.2	0.1	–	–	–	–
1.7	0.6	0.9	–	–	–	–
1.7	4.4	3.9	7.8	0.0	3.7	7.5
38.6	*64.0*	*59.4*	*54.5*	*34.6*	*37.0*	*102.9*
18.4	*16.6*	*25.2*	*63.8*	–	–	–
38.9	*56.3*	*84.5*	*66.2*	*122.9*	*57.4*	*105.1*
122.6	***181.7***	***205.8***	***215.4***	***162.5***	***119.5***	***236.3***

TECH. COOP. GRANTS

1978	1979	1980	1977	1978	1979	1980
1.3	1.9	0.7	0.5	0.3	0.3	0.3
0.3	0.2	0.1	0.2	0.3	0.2	0.1
0.1	0.2	0.1	0.1	0.1	0.2	0.1
5.3	4.1	5.5	1.1	1.0	0.9	1.1
0.0	0.0	0.0	0.0	0.0	0.0	0.0
0.0	0.0	0.0	0.0	0.0	0.0	0.0
–	–	3.3	–	–	–	2.7
12.7	12.9	13.7	8.6	12.0	12.0	13.7
0.6	0.5	0.5	0.3	0.3	0.5	0.2
8.0	5.6	2.5	1.5	2.1	1.7	1.9
3.3	6.2	4.5	2.1	2.3	3.9	4.5
–	–	–	–	–	–	–
0.4	0.7	1.2	0.2	0.2	0.2	0.2
–	0.5	0.4	–	–	–	–
0.1	0.1	0.2	–	0.0	0.0	–
5.9	7.1	7.0	4.0	4.7	5.6	6.7
11.0	12.0	12.0	4.0	7.0	5.0	5.0
49.2	*52.1*	*51.5*	*22.6*	*30.4*	*30.6*	*36.4*
17.7	*15.0*	*13.3*	*6.6*	*7.1*	*4.8*	*8.5*
–	–	–	–	–	–	–
29.0	*32.9*	*33.7*	*15.1*	*19.4*	*22.2*	*27.7*
66.9	***67.1***	***64.9***	***29.2***	***37.5***	***35.4***	***44.9***

TOTAL OOF NET

1978	1979	1980	1977	1978	1979	1980
–	–	–	–	–	–	–
–	–	–	–	–	–	–
–	3.3	2.4	–	–	3.3	2.4
0.1	–	–	–	0.1	–	–
–	–	–	–	–	–	–
2.5	–	–	–	2.5	–	–
–	0.6	–	0.1	-3.1	-1.1	-0.1
–	–	–	–	–	–	–
–	–	–	–	–	–	–
0.1	0.2	0.5	–	0.1	0.2	0.5
–	–	–	–	–	–	–
–	–	–	–	–	–	–
–	–	–	–	–	–	–
–	–	–	–	–	–	–
–	–	–	–	–	–	–
–	–	–	2.0	-1.0	-3.0	-5.0
2.6	*4.1*	*2.9*	*2.1*	*-1.5*	*-0.6*	*-2.2*
31.5	*30.8*	*27.6*	*12.7*	*28.9*	*27.8*	*23.9*
–	–	–	–	–	–	–
3.7	*1.4*	*3.7*	*0.1*	*0.6*	*-0.3*	*3.6*
34.1	***34.9***	***30.5***	***14.8***	***27.4***	***27.2***	***21.7***

MAIN AID AGGREGATES

	1977	1978	1979	1980
DAC COUNTRIES COMBINED				
PRIVATE SECTOR NET	52.1	47.6	-2.9	10.2
Direct Investment	-3.5	-2.6	0.7	0.4
Portfolio Invest.	-11.0	4.7	-4.8	8.1
Export Credits	66.6	45.5	1.2	1.8
OFFICIAL & PRIVATE				
GROSS:				
Contractual Lending	88.6	88.1	79.8	120.2
Export Credits Tot.	69.6	69.0	30.0	50.1
Export Credits Priv	66.6	69.0	26.7	47.7
OTHER NET DATA				
Contractual Lending	77.9	52.1	37.1	55.2
Export Credits Tot.	67.6	44.5	1.5	-0.8
(Bank Sector Loans)	-4.0	15.0	-14.0	3.0
ODA CONCESSIONALITY				
Total:Grant Element	92.0	85.0	89.0	86.0
Loans:Grant Element	84.0	71.0	76.0	77.0
OTHER SOURCES				
CMEA Countr.(Gross)	2.3	0.2	0.1	0.1
Intra LDCS Exc.OPEC	–	–	–	–
Other	–	–	–	–
ALL SOURCE COMMITMENTS				
TOTAL BILATERAL	168.1	134.1	82.5	134.4
of which				
OPEC (ODA)	63.8	–	–	–
CMEA (ODA)	0.9	–	–	–
TOTAL MULTILAT.(ODA)	54.5	34.6	37.0	102.9
TOTAL BIL.& MULTIL.	222.6	168.7	119.6	237.3
of which				
ODA Grants	72.4	92.0	57.9	73.6
ODA Loans	143.0	70.5	61.6	162.7
ODA CONCESSIONALITY				
Total: Grant Element	77.0	88.0	88.0	84.0
Loans: Grant Element	64.0	71.0	77.0	78.0

INDEBTEDNESS

	1977	1978	1979
TOTAL DEBT DISBURSED	***791.2***	***880.0***	***968.5***
Debt to DAC Countries	596.0	677.0	733.0
ODA	395.0	434.0	485.0
Total Export Credits	201.0	243.0	248.0
Other Private Market	–	–	–
International Org.	134.2	178.4	221.7
CMEA	59.2	24.1	13.2
Other	1.8	0.5	0.6
TOTAL DEBT SERVICE	***38.1***	***59.3***	***65.3***
Paid to DAC Countries	27.9	47.9	51.6
ODA	17.5	15.4	23.4
Total Export Credits	10.4	32.5	28.2
Other Private Market	–	–	–
International Org.	6.3	9.5	13.2
CMEA	2.4	0.5	0.4
Other	1.5	1.4	0.1

ECONOMIC INDICATORS

	1977	1978	1979	1980
GNP Curr. Prices, $M	2455.6	4372.9	10139.1	15362.4
Real GNP, 1976=100	102.0	107.0	107.0	108.0
GNP/Cap Curr. Prices,$	231.0	398.0	896.0	1315.0
GNP/cap Atlas Basis, $	345.5	374.7	395.1	421.3
Real GNP/Cap, 1976=100	99.0	100.0	97.0	95.0
Population, Million	10.6	11.0	11.3	11.7
Curr.A/C Deficit(-),$M	-144.0	-109.6	181.0	-165.6
BOP Exp. & Transf.,$M	1020.6	997.2	1186.8	1281.7
Exp. to OECD CIF, $M	1066.5	1051.2	975.2	1023.2
of which				
Manufact.	9.8	17.8	12.8	14.8
Imp. from OECD FOB, $M	799.5	815.9	570.5	641.6
Reserves ex. Gold, $M	155.4	279.5	291.6	196.6

	TOTAL RECEIPTS NET 1977	1978	1979	1980	TOTAL ODA NET 1977	1978	1979	1980
DAC COUNTRIES								
Australia	0.3	0.2	0.5	0.8	–	0.0	–	–
Austria	113.7	8.0	17.2	-17.4	3.3	3.7	3.6	3.1
Belgium	-32.8	19.9	13.7	96.4	0.0	0.0	0.0	–
Canada	-3.2	2.6	-0.2	1.5	–	–	–	–
Denmark	1.8	-4.3	-4.6	2.7	–	–	–	–
Finland	-3.0	8.5	-4.7	-1.7	–	–	–	–
France	69.2	20.2	-52.9	271.0	3.2	1.0	0.9	7.2
Germany, Fed. Rep.	-21.0	-11.2	56.5	225.2	-4.1	3.2	5.5	14.2
Italy	-11.8	35.0	145.3	35.4	-0.2	0.2	0.2	0.0
Japan	210.0	15.8	-16.9	-52.0	0.1	0.1	0.2	0.1
Netherlands	11.9	11.6	15.0	107.1	0.0	0.0	0.0	0.0
New Zealand	–	0.1	–	–	–	–	–	–
Norway	0.9	-1.9	-1.7	-1.1	–	–	–	–
Sweden	-2.1	-2.0	-1.8	-0.8	–	–	–	–
Switzerland	1.3	0.5	0.0	-2.0	0.1	0.1	0.1	–
United Kingdom	13.3	17.3	16.3	32.9	–	–	–	–
United States	-50.0	77.0	28.0	-23.0	3.0	52.0	-5.0	-5.0
TOTAL	*298.5*	*197.2*	*209.7*	*675.0*	*5.4*	*60.2*	*5.5*	*19.5*
MULTILATERAL								
AF.D.F.	–	–	–	–	–	–	–	–
AF.D.B.	–	–	–	–	–	–	–	–
AS.D.B.	–	–	–	–	–	–	–	–
CAR.D.B.	–	–	–	–	–	–	–	–
E.E.C.	1.5	-3.0	60.0	68.4	–	–	21.6	17.9
IBRD	9.3	2.7	3.4	12.2	–	–	–	–
IDA	–	–	–	–	–	–	–	–
I.D.B.	–	–	–	–	–	–	–	–
IFAD	–	–	–	–	–	–	–	–
I.F.C.	14.2	9.2	-0.3	10.7	–	–	–	–
IMF TRUST FUND	–	–	–	–	–	–	–	–
U.N. AGENCIES	–	–	–	–	–	–	–	–
UNDP	0.6	1.2	1.9	2.3	0.6	1.2	1.9	2.3
UNTA	0.1	0.2	0.1	0.1	0.1	0.2	0.1	0.1
UNICEF	–	–	–	–	–	–	–	–
UNRWA	–	–	–	–	–	–	–	–
WFP	–	–	–	–	–	–	–	–
UNHCR	0.4	0.3	0.3	0.2	0.4	0.3	0.3	0.2
Other Multilateral	0.1	0.1	0.1	0.1	0.1	0.1	0.1	0.1
Arab OPEC Agencies	–	–	–	–	–	–	–	–
TOTAL	*26.1*	*10.6*	*65.4*	*94.0*	*1.2*	*1.8*	*24.0*	*20.6*
OPEC COUNTRIES	–	–	*11.0*	–	–	–	*11.0*	–
E.E.C.+ MEMBERS	*32.1*	*85.4*	*249.2*	*838.9*	*-1.0*	*4.3*	*28.2*	*39.3*
TOTAL	***324.6***	***207.8***	***286.1***	***768.9***	***6.6***	***62.0***	***40.4***	***40.1***

	ODA LOANS GROSS 1977	1978	1979	1980	ODA LOANS NET 1977	1978	1979	1980
DAC COUNTRIES								
Australia	–	–	–	–	–	–	–	–
Austria	0.2	0.1	0.2	–	0.1	0.1	0.1	-0.1
Belgium	–	–	–	–	–	–	–	–
Canada	–	–	–	–	–	–	–	–
Denmark	–	–	–	–	–	–	–	–
Finland	–	–	–	–	–	–	–	–
France	4.4	2.3	1.6	6.9	3.2	1.0	0.9	5.8
Germany, Fed. Rep.	4.7	9.9	14.9	18.2	-9.3	-6.3	-2.4	4.8
Italy	–	–	–	–	-0.4	–	–	–
Japan	–	–	–	–	–	–	–	–
Netherlands	0.1	0.0	–	–	0.0	-0.1	-0.1	-0.1
New Zealand	–	–	–	–	–	–	–	–
Norway	–	–	–	–	–	–	–	–
Sweden	–	–	–	–	–	–	–	–
Switzerland	–	–	–	–	–	–	–	–
United Kingdom	–	–	–	–	–	–	–	–
United States	8.0	57.0	–	–	6.0	55.0	-2.0	-2.0
TOTAL	*17.3*	*69.3*	*16.6*	*25.1*	*-0.4*	*49.7*	*-3.5*	*8.4*
MULTILATERAL	–	–	–	–	–	–	–	–
OPEC COUNTRIES	–	–	–	–	–	–	–	–
E.E.C.+ MEMBERS	*9.1*	*12.2*	*16.5*	*25.1*	*-6.5*	*-5.4*	*-1.6*	*10.5*
TOTAL	***17.3***	***69.3***	***16.6***	***25.1***	***-0.4***	***49.7***	***-3.5***	***8.4***

	TOTAL OFFICIAL GROSS 1977	1978	1979	1980	TOTAL OFFICIAL NET 1977	1978	1979	1980
DAC COUNTRIES								
Australia	–	0.0	–	–	–	0.0	–	–
Austria	3.3	3.8	3.7	3.2	3.3	3.7	3.6	3.1
Belgium	0.0	0.0	0.0	–	0.0	0.0	0.0	–
Canada	–	7.1	4.3	6.4	-3.1	2.6	-0.1	1.6
Denmark	–	–	–	–	–	–	–	–
Finland	–	–	–	–	–	–	–	–
France	4.4	2.3	1.6	8.3	3.2	1.0	0.9	7.2
Germany, Fed. Rep.	28.8	27.8	98.3	86.4	-3.2	-8.7	31.6	45.6
Italy	0.2	0.2	0.2	0.0	-0.2	0.2	0.2	0.0
Japan	0.1	0.1	0.2	0.1	0.1	0.1	0.2	0.1
Netherlands	0.1	0.1	0.1	0.1	0.0	0.0	0.0	0.0
New Zealand	10.4	–	–	–	–	–	–	–
Norway	–	–	–	–	–	–	–	–
Sweden	–	–	–	–	–	–	–	–
Switzerland	0.1	0.1	0.1	–	0.1	0.1	0.1	–
United Kingdom	–	–	–	–	–	–	–	–
United States	93.0	118.0	57.0	49.0	76.0	71.0	-12.0	-26.0
TOTAL	*140.4*	*159.4*	*165.4*	*153.5*	*76.1*	*69.9*	*24.4*	*31.4*
MULTILATERAL	*43.5*	*31.8*	*87.8*	*119.2*	*26.1*	*10.6*	*65.4*	*94.0*
OPEC COUNTRIES	–	–	*11.0*	–	–	–	*11.0*	–
E.E.C.+ MEMBERS	*40.9*	*34.5*	*168.1*	*172.6*	*1.3*	*-10.6*	*92.7*	*121.1*
TOTAL	***183.8***	***191.2***	***264.2***	***272.7***	***102.3***	***80.5***	***100.8***	***125.4***

TOTAL ODA GROSS	197…
Australia	
Austria	
Belgium	
Canada	
Denmark	
Finland	
France	
Germany, Fed. Rep.	
Italy	
Japan	
Netherlands	
New Zealand	
Norway	
Sweden	
Switzerland	
United Kingdom	
United States	
TOTAL	
AF.D.F.	
AF.D.B.	
AS.D.B.	
CAR.D.B.	
E.E.C.	
IBRD	
IDA	
I.D.B.	
IFAD	
I.F.C.	
IMF TRUST FUND	
U.N. AGENCIES	
UNDP	
UNTA	
UNICEF	
UNRWA	
WFP	
UNHCR	
Other Multilateral	
Arab OPEC Agencies	
TOTAL	
OPEC COUNTRIES	
E.E.C.+ MEMBERS	
TOTAL	

GRANTS	
Australia	
Austria	
Belgium	
Canada	
Denmark	
Finland	
France	
Germany, Fed. Rep.	
Italy	
Japan	
Netherlands	
New Zealand	
Norway	
Sweden	
Switzerland	
United Kingdom	
United States	
TOTAL	
MULTILATERAL	
OPEC COUNTRIES	
E.E.C.+ MEMBERS	
TOTAL	

TOTAL OOF GROSS	
Australia	
Austria	
Belgium	
Canada	
Denmark	
Finland	
France	
Germany, Fed. Rep.	
Italy	
Japan	
Netherlands	
New Zealand	
Norway	
Sweden	
Switzerland	
United Kingdom	
United States	
TOTAL	
MULTILATERAL	
OPEC COUNTRIES	
E.E.C.+ MEMBERS	
TOTAL	

GREECE

1978	1979	1980	1977	1978	1979	1980
			ODA COMMITMENTS			
0.0	–	–	–	–	–	–
3.8	3.7	3.2	0.2	0.1	0.2	–
0.0	0.0	–	–	–	–	–
–	–	–	–	–	–	–
–	–	–	–	–	–	–
–	–	–	–	–	–	–
2.3	1.6	8.3	–	5.5	5.9	1.0
19.3	22.8	27.5	31.0	29.4	22.0	8.7
0.2	0.2	0.0	0.2	0.2	0.2	0.0
0.1	0.2	0.1	0.1	0.1	0.2	0.1
0.1	0.1	0.1	0.1	0.1	0.1	0.1
–	–	–	–	–	–	–
–	–	–	–	–	–	–
–	–	–	–	–	–	–
0.1	0.1	–	–	–	–	–
–	–	–	–	–	–	–
54.0	-3.0	-3.0	–	–	–	–
79.8	*25.6*	*36.2*	*31.5*	*35.3*	*28.4*	*9.9*
–	–	–	–	–	–	–
–	–	–	–	–	–	–
–	–	–	–	–	–	–
–	–	–	–	–	–	–
–	21.6	17.9	–	–	49.0	20.9
–	–	–	–	–	–	–
–	–	–	–	–	–	–
–	–	–	–	–	–	–
–	–	–	–	–	–	–
–	–	–	–	–	–	–
–	–	–	–	–	–	–
–	–	–	1.2	1.8	2.3	2.7
1.2	1.9	2.3	–	–	–	–
0.2	0.1	0.1	–	–	–	–
–	–	–	–	–	–	–
–	–	–	–	–	–	–
–	–	–	–	–	–	–
0.3	0.3	0.2	–	–	–	–
0.1	0.1	0.1	–	–	–	–
–	–	–	–	–	–	–
1.8	*24.0*	*20.6*	*1.2*	*1.8*	*51.4*	*23.6*
–	*11.0*	–	–	–	*11.0*	–
21.9	*46.3*	*53.8*	*31.3*	*35.1*	*77.1*	*30.7*
81.6	***60.5***	***56.8***	***32.7***	***37.1***	***90.8***	***33.5***
			TECH. COOP. GRANTS			
0.0	–	–	–	–	–	–
3.7	3.5	3.2	3.2	3.7	3.5	3.2
0.0	0.0	–	0.0	0.0	0.0	–
–	–	–	–	–	–	–
–	–	–	–	–	–	–
–	–	–	–	–	–	–
–	–	1.4	–	–	–	1.4
9.5	8.0	9.3	5.2	6.2	7.8	9.3
0.2	0.2	0.0	0.2	0.2	0.2	0.0
0.1	0.2	0.1	0.1	0.1	0.2	0.1
0.1	0.1	0.1	0.1	0.1	0.1	0.1
–	–	–	–	–	–	–
–	–	–	–	–	–	–
–	–	–	–	–	–	–
0.1	0.1	–	0.0	0.0	0.0	–
–	–	–	–	–	–	–
-3.0	-3.0	-3.0	–	–	–	–
10.6	*9.0*	*11.1*	*8.7*	*10.2*	*11.7*	*14.1*
1.8	*24.0*	*20.6*	*1.2*	*1.8*	*2.3*	*2.7*
–	*11.0*	–	–	–	–	–
9.7	*29.9*	*28.8*	*5.5*	*6.4*	*8.0*	*10.8*
12.3	***43.9***	***31.7***	***9.9***	***12.0***	***14.0***	***16.8***
			TOTAL OOF NET			
–	–	–	–	–	–	–
–	–	–	–	0.0	–	–
–	–	–	–	–	–	–
7.1	4.3	6.4	-3.1	2.6	-0.1	1.6
–	–	–	–	–	–	–
–	–	–	–	–	–	–
–	–	–	–	–	–	–
8.5	75.5	58.9	0.9	-11.9	26.1	31.4
–	–	–	–	–	–	–
–	–	–	–	–	–	–
–	–	–	–	–	–	–
–	–	–	–	–	–	–
–	–	–	–	–	–	–
–	–	–	–	–	–	–
–	–	–	–	–	–	–
–	–	–	–	–	–	–
64.0	60.0	52.0	73.0	19.0	-7.0	-21.0
79.6	*139.9*	*117.3*	*70.7*	*9.7*	*19.0*	*11.9*
30.0	*63.8*	*98.6*	*25.0*	*8.9*	*41.5*	*73.3*
–	–	–	–	–	–	–
12.7	*121.8*	*118.8*	*2.3*	*-14.9*	*64.5*	*81.8*
109.7	***203.7***	***215.9***	***95.7***	***18.5***	***60.4***	***85.3***

	1977	1978	1979	1980
MAIN AID AGGREGATES				
DAC COUNTRIES COMBINED				
PRIVATE SECTOR NET	222.4	127.3	185.3	643.5
Direct Investment	-1.2	54.0	99.5	-17.1
Portfolio Invest.	31.9	73.5	-74.0	518.0
Export Credits	191.7	-0.2	159.7	142.7
OFFICIAL & PRIVATE				
GROSS:				
Contractual Lending	665.9	499.8	664.1	628.4
Export Credits Tot.	648.6	430.6	620.2	603.3
Export Credits Priv	531.3	351.0	507.6	486.0
OTHER NET DATA				
Contractual Lending	262.0	59.2	175.2	163.0
Export Credits Tot.	262.5	9.6	178.7	154.8
(Bank Sector Loans)	750.0	214.0	160.0	1100.0
ODA CONCESSIONALITY				
Total:Grant Element	71.0	71.0	76.0	100.0
Loans:Grant Element	65.0	60.0	59.0	–
OTHER SOURCES				
CMEA Countr.(Gross)	–	–	–	–
Intra LDCS Exc.OPEC	–	–	–	–
Other	–	–	–	–
ALL SOURCE COMMITMENTS				
TOTAL BILATERAL	192.8	104.9	144.4	158.8
of which				
OPEC (ODA)	–	–	11.0	–
CMEA (ODA)	–	–	–	–
TOTAL MULTILAT.(ODA)	1.2	1.8	51.4	23.6
TOTAL BIL.& MULTIL.	194.0	106.7	195.8	182.4
of which				
ODA Grants	6.7	11.6	46.4	33.5
ODA Loans	26.0	25.5	44.4	–
ODA CONCESSIONALITY				
Total: Grant Element	72.0	72.0	84.0	100.0
Loans: Grant Element	65.0	60.0	60.0	–
INDEBTEDNESS				
TOTAL DEBT DISBURSED	***4267.4***	***4658.6***	***5569.0***	
Debt to DAC Countries	3808.0	4180.0	5019.0	
ODA	159.0	234.0	238.0	
Total Export Credits	1607.0	1449.0	1590.0	
Other Private Market	2042.0	2497.0	3191.0	
International Org.	233.1	254.9	303.9	
CMEA	21.5	22.0	43.3	
Other	204.8	201.7	202.8	
TOTAL DEBT SERVICE	***865.6***	***906.5***	***1195.7***	
Paid to DAC Countries	817.0	851.8	1088.8	
ODA	23.1	26.3	28.6	
Total Export Credits	517.4	447.7	549.3	
Other Private Market	276.5	377.8	510.9	
International Org.	35.1	42.7	53.9	
CMEA	9.9	8.8	8.6	
Other	3.6	3.2	44.5	
ECONOMIC INDICATORS				
GNP Curr. Prices, $M	27011.6	32617.5	39741.2	42209.8
Real GNP, 1976=100	103.0	110.0	114.0	115.0
GNP/Cap Curr. Prices,$	2949.0	3539.0	4286.0	4524.0
GNP/cap Atlas Basis, $	3253.6	3686.8	4142.6	4522.0
Real GNP/Cap, 1976=100	103.0	108.0	112.0	112.0
Population, Million	9.2	9.2	9.3	9.3
Curr.A/C Deficit(-),$M	-1071.0	-958.0	-1888.0	-2203.0
BOP Exp. & Transf.,$M	5759.0	6887.0	8846.0	9464.0
Exp. to OECD CIF, $M	2149.5	2650.3	3594.9	3861.6
of which				
Manufact.	1050.1	1320.0	1837.7	1992.3
Imp. from OECD FOB, $M	5487.7	6157.7	7878.2	8112.8
Reserves ex. Gold, $M	861.5	999.1	951.0	1129.9

	TOTAL RECEIPTS NET 1977	1978	1979	1980	TOTAL ODA NET 1977	1978	1979	1980	TOTAL ODA GROSS	197
DAC COUNTRIES										
Australia	0.2	0.0	0.1	–	–	–	–	–	Australia	
Austria	0.7	0.9	1.0	1.1	0.7	0.9	1.0	1.1	Austria	0
Belgium	1.1	0.1	1.2	0.5	0.9	0.3	0.4	0.5	Belgium	0
Canada	21.1	2.9	-4.0	1.7	1.5	4.0	2.3	1.7	Canada	1
Denmark	1.1	0.5	-0.3	0.0	0.1	0.0	–	–	Denmark	0
Finland	–	–	–	–	–	–	–	–	Finland	
France	0.4	10.4	28.9	52.4	–	–	–	0.2	France	
Germany, Fed. Rep.	0.5	9.3	16.4	7.9	3.4	4.2	6.3	7.8	Germany, Fed. Rep.	3
Italy	20.5	13.2	1.3	0.3	0.1	0.1	0.5	0.1	Italy	0
Japan	2.3	2.0	2.3	4.4	2.2	2.2	2.0	2.7	Japan	2
Netherlands	1.7	0.7	1.2	1.7	1.7	0.7	1.2	1.7	Netherlands	1
New Zealand	–	–	–	–	–	–	–	–	New Zealand	
Norway	0.2	–	-0.3	0.0	0.2	–	–	0.0	Norway	0
Sweden	–	0.2	0.1	–	–	–	0.1	–	Sweden	
Switzerland	0.9	24.2	-6.7	-3.9	0.3	0.7	0.7	0.7	Switzerland	0
United Kingdom	-0.3	0.7	-5.4	-3.7	0.0	0.1	0.0	0.1	United Kingdom	0
United States	24.0	21.0	29.0	7.0	26.0	13.0	19.0	17.0	United States	27
TOTAL	*74.6*	*86.3*	*64.6*	*69.3*	*37.2*	*26.2*	*33.5*	*33.5*	*TOTAL*	*38*
MULTILATERAL										
AF.D.F.	–	–	–	–	–	–	–	–	AF.D.F.	
AF.D.B.	–	–	–	–	–	–	–	–	AF.D.B.	
AS.D.B.	–	–	–	–	–	–	–	–	AS.D.B.	
CAR.D.B.	–	–	–	–	–	–	–	–	CAR.D.B.	
E.E.C.	–	0.0	0.0	–	–	0.0	0.0	–	E.E.C.	
IBRD	4.1	17.9	44.1	35.4	0.1	1.9	2.7	4.1	IBRD	0
IDA	–	–	–	–	–	–	–	–	IDA	
I.D.B.	35.1	42.1	24.9	28.9	19.3	39.2	25.1	30.6	I.D.B.	21
IFAD	–	–	–	–	–	–	–	–	IFAD	
I.F.C.	15.0	2.2	-5.2	-1.6	–	–	–	–	I.F.C.	
IMF TRUST FUND	–	–	–	–	–	–	–	–	IMF TRUST FUND	
U.N. AGENCIES	–	–	–	–	–	–	–	–	U.N. AGENCIES	
UNDP	2.1	2.4	2.8	3.2	2.1	2.4	2.8	3.2	UNDP	2
UNTA	0.3	0.5	0.4	0.1	0.3	0.5	0.4	0.1	UNTA	0
UNICEF	1.4	0.9	1.1	0.5	1.4	0.9	1.1	0.5	UNICEF	1
UNRWA	–	–	–	–	–	–	–	–	UNRWA	
WFP	0.2	0.2	0.1	0.2	0.2	0.2	0.1	0.2	WFP	0
UNHCR	–	–	–	–	–	–	–	–	UNHCR	
Other Multilateral	0.3	0.4	0.3	0.5	0.3	0.4	0.3	0.5	Other Multilateral	0
Arab OPEC Agencies	0.9	–	0.9	–	0.9	–	0.9	–	Arab OPEC Agencies	0
TOTAL	*59.4*	*66.5*	*69.4*	*67.3*	*24.6*	*45.5*	*33.4*	*39.3*	*TOTAL*	*26*
OPEC COUNTRIES	*22.5*	*18.7*	–	–	–	–	–	–	*OPEC COUNTRIES*	
E.E.C.+ MEMBERS	*25.2*	*35.0*	*43.2*	*59.0*	*6.2*	*5.5*	*8.4*	*10.3*	*E.E.C.+ MEMBERS*	*6*
TOTAL	***156.5***	***171.5***	***134.0***	***136.6***	***61.8***	***71.7***	***66.8***	***72.8***	***TOTAL***	***65***

	ODA LOANS GROSS 1977	1978	1979	1980	ODA LOANS NET 1977	1978	1979	1980	GRANTS	197
DAC COUNTRIES										
Australia	–	–	–	–	–	–	–	–	Australia	
Austria	–	–	–	–	–	–	–	–	Austria	0
Belgium	–	–	–	–	–	–	–	–	Belgium	0
Canada	–	–	–	0.4	–	–	–	0.4	Canada	1
Denmark	–	–	–	–	–	–	–	–	Denmark	0
Finland	–	–	–	–	–	–	–	–	Finland	
France	–	–	–	–	–	–	–	–	France	
Germany, Fed. Rep.	–	0.0	0.9	1.5	–	0.0	0.9	1.5	Germany, Fed. Rep.	3
Italy	–	–	–	–	–	–	–	–	Italy	0
Japan	–	–	–	–	–	–	–	–	Japan	2
Netherlands	–	–	–	–	–	–	–	–	Netherlands	1
New Zealand	–	–	–	–	–	–	–	–	New Zealand	
Norway	–	–	–	–	–	–	–	–	Norway	0
Sweden	–	–	–	–	–	–	–	–	Sweden	
Switzerland	–	–	–	–	–	–	–	–	Switzerland	0
United Kingdom	–	–	–	–	–	–	–	–	United Kingdom	0
United States	3.0	1.0	3.0	5.0	2.0	–	2.0	4.0	United States	24
TOTAL	*3.0*	*1.0*	*3.9*	*6.8*	*2.0*	*0.0*	*2.9*	*5.8*	*TOTAL*	*35*
MULTILATERAL	*22.6*	*43.1*	*31.2*	*36.9*	*20.3*	*40.6*	*28.7*	*34.4*	*MULTILATERAL*	*4.*
OPEC COUNTRIES	–	–	–	–	–	–	–	–	*OPEC COUNTRIES*	
E.E.C.+ MEMBERS	–	*0.0*	*0.9*	*1.5*	–	*0.0*	*0.9*	*1.5*	*E.E.C.+ MEMBERS*	*6.*
TOTAL	***25.6***	***44.1***	***35.0***	***43.8***	***22.3***	***40.6***	***31.5***	***40.3***	***TOTAL***	***39.***

	TOTAL OFFICIAL GROSS 1977	1978	1979	1980	TOTAL OFFICIAL NET 1977	1978	1979	1980	TOTAL OOF GROSS	197
DAC COUNTRIES										
Australia	–	–	–	–	–	–	–	–	Australia	
Austria	0.7	0.9	1.0	1.1	0.7	0.9	1.0	1.1	Austria	
Belgium	0.9	0.3	0.4	0.5	0.9	0.3	0.4	0.5	Belgium	
Canada	21.1	4.0	2.3	1.7	21.1	3.1	-3.9	1.7	Canada	19.
Denmark	0.1	0.0	–	–	0.1	0.0	–	–	Denmark	
Finland	–	–	–	–	–	–	–	–	Finland	
France	–	5.6	3.8	44.6	–	5.6	3.8	44.6	France	
Germany, Fed. Rep.	3.4	4.2	6.3	7.8	3.4	4.2	6.3	7.8	Germany, Fed. Rep.	
Italy	0.1	0.1	0.5	0.1	0.1	0.1	0.5	0.1	Italy	
Japan	2.2	2.2	2.0	2.7	2.2	2.2	2.0	2.7	Japan	
Netherlands	1.7	0.7	1.2	1.7	1.7	0.7	1.2	1.7	Netherlands	
New Zealand	–	–	–	–	–	–	–	–	New Zealand	
Norway	0.2	–	–	0.0	0.2	–	–	0.0	Norway	
Sweden	–	–	0.1	–	–	–	0.1	–	Sweden	
Switzerland	0.3	0.7	0.7	0.7	0.3	0.7	0.7	0.7	Switzerland	
United Kingdom	0.0	0.1	0.0	0.1	0.0	0.1	0.0	0.1	United Kingdom	
United States	27.0	20.0	20.0	18.0	24.0	18.0	18.0	16.0	United States	
TOTAL	*57.7*	*38.8*	*38.3*	*78.9*	*54.7*	*36.0*	*30.1*	*76.9*	*TOTAL*	*19.*
MULTILATERAL	*63.4*	*72.1*	*81.0*	*78.1*	*59.4*	*66.5*	*69.4*	*67.3*	*MULTILATERAL*	*36.*
OPEC COUNTRIES	*22.5*	*18.7*	–	–	*22.5*	*18.7*	–	–	*OPEC COUNTRIES*	*22.*
E.E.C.+ MEMBERS	*6.2*	*11.1*	*12.2*	*54.7*	*6.2*	*11.1*	*12.2*	*54.7*	*E.E.C.+ MEMBERS*	
TOTAL	***143.7***	***129.7***	***119.2***	***157.0***	***136.7***	***121.2***	***99.5***	***144.2***	***TOTAL***	***78.***

ODA COMMITMENTS

1978	1979	1980	1977	1978	1979	1980
–	–	–	–	–	–	–
0.9	1.0	1.1	0.0	–	–	–
0.3	0.4	0.5	–	–	–	–
4.0	2.3	1.7	3.7	0.2	0.2	0.4
0.0	–	–	0.1	0.0	0.0	–
–	–	–	–	–	–	–
–	–	0.2	–	–	–	0.2
4.2	6.3	7.8	8.2	4.0	6.4	7.3
0.1	0.5	0.1	0.1	0.1	0.5	0.1
2.2	2.0	2.7	2.5	4.5	1.4	1.8
0.7	1.2	1.7	1.5	1.0	2.4	1.9
–	–	–	–	–	–	–
–	–	0.0	–	–	–	–
–	0.1	–	–	–	–	–
0.7	0.7	0.7	0.2	–	–	0.5
0.1	0.0	0.1	0.0	0.1	0.0	0.1
14.0	20.0	18.0	15.2	16.2	23.0	12.1
27.2	*34.5*	*34.5*	*31.6*	*26.0*	*34.0*	*24.4*
–	–	–	–	–	–	–
–	–	–	–	–	–	–
–	–	–	–	–	–	–
–	–	–	–	–	–	–
0.0	0.0	–	0.0	–	0.2	0.1
1.9	2.7	4.1	–	–	–	–
–	–	–	–	–	–	–
41.7	27.6	33.1	60.5	–	–	76.5
–	–	–	–	–	–	–
–	–	–	–	–	–	–
–	–	–	–	–	–	–
–	–	–	4.3	4.3	4.7	4.6
2.4	2.8	3.2	–	–	–	–
0.5	0.4	0.1	–	–	–	–
0.9	1.1	0.5	–	–	–	–
–	–	–	–	–	–	–
0.2	0.1	0.2	–	–	–	–
–	–	–	–	–	–	–
0.4	0.3	0.5	–	–	–	–
–	0.9	–	1.8	–	–	–
48.0	*35.9*	*41.8*	*66.6*	*4.3*	*4.8*	*81.1*
–	–	–	–	–	–	–
5.5	*8.4*	*10.3*	*9.9*	*5.2*	*9.5*	*9.6*
75.2	***70.3***	***76.3***	***98.2***	***30.3***	***38.8***	***105.6***

TECH. COOP. GRANTS

1978	1979	1980	1977	1978	1979	1980
–	–	–	–	–	–	–
0.9	1.0	1.1	0.7	0.9	1.0	1.1
0.3	0.4	0.5	0.2	0.3	0.3	0.4
4.0	2.3	1.3	0.2	0.2	0.1	0.2
0.0	–	–	0.1	0.0	–	–
–	–	–	–	–	–	–
–	–	0.2	–	–	–	0.2
4.2	5.5	6.3	2.9	3.7	4.8	5.4
0.1	0.5	0.1	0.1	0.1	0.5	0.1
2.2	2.0	2.7	2.2	2.2	1.2	1.6
0.7	1.2	1.7	1.7	0.4	1.2	1.7
–	–	–	–	–	–	–
–	–	0.0	–	–	–	–
–	0.1	–	–	–	–	–
0.7	0.7	0.7	–	0.0	0.0	–
0.1	0.0	0.1	0.0	0.1	0.0	0.1
13.0	17.0	13.0	3.0	3.0	2.0	3.0
26.2	*30.6*	*27.6*	*11.0*	*10.9*	*11.1*	*13.7*
4.8	*4.7*	*4.9*	*4.1*	*4.6*	*4.6*	*4.6*
–	–	–	–	–	–	–
5.5	*7.6*	*8.8*	*4.9*	*4.6*	*6.8*	*7.8*
31.1	***35.3***	***32.5***	***15.1***	***15.5***	***15.7***	***18.2***

TOTAL OOF NET

1978	1979	1980	1977	1978	1979	1980
–	–	–	–	–	–	–
–	–	–	–	–	–	–
–	–	–	–	–	–	–
–	–	–	19.5	-0.9	-6.2	–
–	–	–	–	–	–	–
–	–	–	–	–	–	–
5.6	3.8	44.4	–	5.6	3.8	44.4
–	–	–	–	–	–	–
–	–	–	–	–	–	–
–	–	–	–	–	–	–
–	–	–	–	–	–	–
–	–	–	–	–	–	–
–	–	–	–	–	–	–
–	–	–	–	–	–	–
–	–	–	–	–	–	–
–	–	–	–	–	–	–
6.0	–	–	-2.0	5.0	-1.0	-1.0
11.6	*3.8*	*44.4*	*17.5*	*9.7*	*-3.4*	*43.4*
24.1	*45.1*	*36.3*	*34.8*	*21.1*	*36.0*	*28.0*
18.7	–	–	*22.5*	*18.7*	–	–
5.6	*3.8*	*44.4*	–	*5.6*	*3.8*	*44.4*
54.5	***48.9***	***80.7***	***74.9***	***49.5***	***32.6***	***71.4***

MAIN AID AGGREGATES

	1977	1978	1979	1980
DAC COUNTRIES COMBINED				
PRIVATE SECTOR NET	19.9	50.3	34.6	-7.6
Direct Investment	0.7	1.9	3.4	1.6
Portfolio Invest.	-21.1	15.5	5.3	-12.1
Export Credits	40.3	32.9	25.9	2.9
OFFICIAL & PRIVATE				
GROSS:				
Contractual Lending	99.0	80.3	81.4	114.6
Export Credits Tot.	96.0	73.7	73.8	63.4
Export Credits Priv	76.5	67.7	73.8	63.4
OTHER NET DATA				
Contractual Lending	59.8	42.6	25.4	52.2
Export Credits Tot.	57.8	37.0	18.7	1.9
(Bank Sector Loans)	-14.0	68.0	-5.0	-20.0
ODA CONCESSIONALITY				
Total:Grant Element	88.0	89.0	91.0	92.0
Loans:Grant Element	73.0	62.0	65.0	65.0
OTHER SOURCES				
CMEA Countr.(Gross)	–	–	–	–
Intra LDCS Exc.OPEC	–	–	–	–
Other	–	–	–	–
ALL SOURCE COMMITMENTS				
TOTAL BILATERAL	37.8	31.6	34.0	25.2
of which				
OPEC (ODA)	–	–	–	–
CMEA (ODA)	–	–	–	–
TOTAL MULTILAT.(ODA)	66.6	4.3	4.8	81.1
TOTAL BIL.& MULTIL.	104.4	35.9	38.8	106.4
of which				
ODA Grants	21.5	23.3	30.0	24.1
ODA Loans	76.7	7.0	8.8	81.5
ODA CONCESSIONALITY				
Total: Grant Element	83.0	83.0	92.0	94.0
Loans: Grant Element	74.0	73.0	65.0	65.0

INDEBTEDNESS

	1977	1978	1979	1980
TOTAL DEBT DISBURSED	***396.8***	***578.6***	***700.5***	
Debt to DAC Countries	181.0	276.0	284.0	
ODA	69.0	68.0	71.0	
Total Export Credits	82.0	168.0	158.0	
Other Private Market	30.0	40.0	55.0	
International Org.	130.9	195.7	281.9	
CMEA	–	–	–	
Other	85.0	106.9	134.5	
TOTAL DEBT SERVICE	***45.3***	***60.6***	***94.9***	
Paid to DAC Countries	33.8	40.3	65.5	
ODA	3.0	2.0	3.0	
Total Export Credits	28.9	37.7	60.5	
Other Private Market	1.9	0.6	2.0	
International Org.	10.2	18.8	27.1	
CMEA	–	–	–	
Other	1.3	1.5	2.3	

ECONOMIC INDICATORS

	1977	1978	1979	1980
GNP Curr. Prices, $M	5448.0	6044.1	6863.0	7805.2
Real GNP, 1976=100	109.0	114.0	119.0	124.0
GNP/Cap Curr. Prices,$	846.0	912.0	1007.0	1113.0
GNP/cap Atlas Basis, $	836.2	915.7	1011.2	1112.2
Real GNP/Cap, 1976=100	106.0	108.0	110.0	111.0
Population, Million	6.4	6.6	6.8	7.0
Curr.A/C Deficit(-),$M	-37.5	-271.0	-209.0	-164.2
BOP Exp. & Transf.,$M	1463.3	1464.3	1675.4	1943.1
Exp. to OECD CIF, $M	942.9	850.4	1003.0	1057.2
of which				
Manufact.	12.7	16.2	23.0	21.2
Imp. from OECD FOB, $M	704.4	785.3	842.4	909.9
Reserves ex. Gold, $M	668.9	741.5	696.3	444.7

	TOTAL RECEIPTS NET 1977	1978	1979	1980	TOTAL ODA NET 1977	1978	1979	1980
DAC COUNTRIES								
Australia	–	–	–	–	–	–	–	–
Austria	–	–	0.0	0.0	–	–	0.0	0.0
Belgium	-5.4	-1.8	-16.8	-3.0	0.1	0.1	0.2	0.1
Canada	0.1	0.2	0.0	0.0	0.1	0.2	0.0	0.0
Denmark	0.3	–	–	–	0.3	–	–	–
Finland	–	–	0.3	0.0	–	–	0.3	0.0
France	2.6	9.1	22.5	41.8	-0.6	-4.3	3.0	9.1
Germany, Fed. Rep.	-1.5	-1.3	7.7	3.3	0.0	0.5	1.0	12.9
Italy	0.9	-0.5	-0.2	0.3	-1.1	0.1	0.4	0.2
Japan	-0.5	-1.2	-8.8	1.7	0.5	1.5	2.9	1.9
Netherlands	2.8	0.8	1.5	0.3	2.8	0.8	1.5	0.3
New Zealand	–	–	–	–	–	–	–	–
Norway	–	–	–	–	–	–	–	–
Sweden	–	–	–	–	–	–	–	–
Switzerland	-1.9	12.1	0.0	21.3	–	0.0	0.0	0.1
United Kingdom	–	–	–	–	–	–	–	–
United States	8.0	9.0	3.0	6.0	3.0	11.0	5.0	8.0
TOTAL	*5.3*	*26.3*	*9.2*	*71.7*	*5.1*	*9.9*	*14.2*	*32.5*
MULTILATERAL								
AF.D.F.	–	–	–	0.7	–	–	–	0.7
AF.D.B.	2.1	0.7	1.3	0.5	–	–	–	–
AS.D.B.	–	–	–	–	–	–	–	–
CAR.D.B.	–	–	–	–	–	–	–	–
E.E.C.	0.0	7.9	8.7	21.1	0.0	7.9	8.7	21.1
IBRD	-2.4	-2.6	-2.8	-2.9	–	–	–	–
IDA	6.3	7.4	7.8	10.2	6.3	7.4	7.8	10.2
I.D.B.	–	–	–	–	–	–	–	–
IFAD	–	–	–	–	–	–	–	–
I.F.C.	–	–	–	–	–	–	–	–
IMF TRUST FUND	–	12.5	9.3	8.1	–	12.5	9.3	8.1
U.N. AGENCIES	–	–	–	–	–	–	–	–
UNDP	3.1	6.2	6.3	7.3	3.1	6.2	6.3	7.3
UNTA	0.5	0.5	0.5	0.1	0.5	0.5	0.5	0.1
UNICEF	0.7	0.9	0.6	1.2	0.7	0.9	0.6	1.2
UNRWA	–	–	–	–	–	–	–	–
WFP	0.7	2.0	0.7	2.4	0.7	2.0	0.7	2.4
UNHCR	–	–	–	–	–	–	–	–
Other Multilateral	0.7	1.0	0.3	1.3	0.7	1.0	0.3	1.3
Arab OPEC Agencies	2.5	5.9	14.7	13.6	2.5	4.9	3.1	4.4
TOTAL	*14.1*	*42.5*	*47.6*	*63.6*	*14.5*	*43.3*	*37.3*	*56.8*
OPEC COUNTRIES	*2.9*	*65.1*	*2.9*	*0.1*	*2.9*	*7.1*	*2.9*	*0.1*
E.E.C.+ MEMBERS	*-0.4*	*14.2*	*23.4*	*63.7*	*1.5*	*5.1*	*14.7*	*43.5*
TOTAL	***22.2***	***133.9***	***59.7***	***135.4***	***22.4***	***60.3***	***54.5***	***89.5***

	ODA LOANS GROSS 1977	1978	1979	1980	ODA LOANS NET 1977	1978	1979	1980
DAC COUNTRIES								
Australia	–	–	–	–	–	–	–	–
Austria	–	–	–	–	–	–	–	–
Belgium	–	–	–	–	–	–	–	–
Canada	–	–	–	–	–	–	–	–
Denmark	–	–	–	–	–	–	–	–
Finland	–	–	–	–	–	–	–	–
France	–	–	4.5	6.7	-0.8	-4.3	3.0	5.6
Germany, Fed. Rep.	–	–	31.3	7.5	–	–	-6.4	7.5
Italy	–	–	–	–	-1.2	–	–	–
Japan	–	–	–	–	–	–	-0.1	-0.1
Netherlands	2.4	–	–	–	2.4	–	–	–
New Zealand	–	–	–	–	–	–	–	–
Norway	–	–	–	–	–	–	–	–
Sweden	–	–	–	–	–	–	–	–
Switzerland	–	–	–	–	–	–	–	–
United Kingdom	–	–	–	–	–	–	–	–
United States	3.0	5.0	6.0	6.0	2.0	5.0	5.0	5.0
TOTAL	*5.4*	*5.0*	*41.8*	*20.2*	*2.4*	*0.7*	*1.5*	*17.9*
MULTILATERAL	*8.7*	*24.5*	*20.2*	*27.9*	*8.7*	*24.5*	*20.2*	*27.9*
OPEC COUNTRIES	*2.6*	*7.0*	*2.4*	*0.6*	*2.6*	*7.0*	*2.4*	*0.0*
E.E.C.+ MEMBERS	*2.4*	–	*35.8*	*18.7*	*0.4*	*-4.3*	*-3.4*	*17.5*
TOTAL	***16.8***	***36.5***	***64.4***	***48.7***	***13.8***	***32.2***	***24.1***	***45.7***

	TOTAL OFFICIAL GROSS 1977	1978	1979	1980	TOTAL OFFICIAL NET 1977	1978	1979	1980
DAC COUNTRIES								
Australia	–	–	–	–	–	–	–	–
Austria	–	–	0.0	0.0	–	–	0.0	0.0
Belgium	0.1	0.1	0.2	0.1	-0.8	0.1	0.2	-0.4
Canada	0.1	0.2	0.0	0.0	0.1	0.2	0.0	0.0
Denmark	0.3	–	–	–	0.3	–	–	–
Finland	–	–	0.3	0.0	–	–	0.3	0.0
France	0.2	–	4.5	10.2	-0.6	-5.3	0.8	6.5
Germany, Fed. Rep.	0.0	0.5	51.1	13.4	-1.5	-1.3	1.0	11.4
Italy	5.9	0.1	0.4	0.2	3.8	0.1	0.4	0.2
Japan	0.5	1.5	3.0	2.1	0.5	1.5	2.9	1.9
Netherlands	2.8	0.8	1.5	0.3	2.8	0.8	1.5	0.3
New Zealand	–	–	–	–	–	–	–	–
Norway	–	–	–	–	–	–	–	–
Sweden	–	–	–	–	–	–	–	–
Switzerland	–	0.0	0.0	0.1	–	0.0	0.0	0.1
United Kingdom	–	–	–	–	–	–	–	–
United States	11.0	11.0	6.0	9.0	8.0	9.0	3.0	6.0
TOTAL	*20.9*	*14.2*	*66.9*	*35.4*	*12.5*	*5.0*	*10.0*	*26.0*
MULTILATERAL	*16.7*	*45.1*	*50.3*	*73.4*	*14.1*	*42.5*	*47.5*	*63.6*
OPEC COUNTRIES	*2.9*	*65.1*	*2.9*	*0.8*	*2.9*	*65.1*	*2.9*	*0.1*
E.E.C.+ MEMBERS	*9.3*	*9.4*	*66.3*	*45.2*	*3.9*	*2.3*	*12.5*	*38.9*
TOTAL	***40.4***	***124.4***	***120.2***	***109.5***	***29.5***	***112.6***	***60.5***	***89.6***

TOTAL ODA GROSS	197
Australia	
Austria	
Belgium	0.
Canada	0.
Denmark	0.
Finland	
France	0.
Germany, Fed. Rep.	0.
Italy	0.
Japan	0.
Netherlands	2.
New Zealand	
Norway	
Sweden	
Switzerland	
United Kingdom	
United States	4.
TOTAL	*8.*
AF.D.F.	
AF.D.B.	
AS.D.B.	
CAR.D.B.	
E.E.C.	0.
IBRD	
IDA	6.
I.D.B.	
IFAD	
I.F.C.	
IMF TRUST FUND	
U.N. AGENCIES	
UNDP	3.
UNTA	0.
UNICEF	0.
UNRWA	
WFP	0.
UNHCR	
Other Multilateral	0.
Arab OPEC Agencies	2.
TOTAL	*14.*
OPEC COUNTRIES	*2.*
E.E.C.+ MEMBERS	*3.*
TOTAL	***25.***

GRANTS	
Australia	
Austria	
Belgium	0.
Canada	0.
Denmark	0.
Finland	
France	0.
Germany, Fed. Rep.	0.
Italy	0.
Japan	0.
Netherlands	0.
New Zealand	
Norway	
Sweden	
Switzerland	
United Kingdom	
United States	1.
TOTAL	*2.*
MULTILATERAL	*5.*
OPEC COUNTRIES	*0.*
E.E.C.+ MEMBERS	*1.*
TOTAL	***8.***

TOTAL OOF GROSS	
Australia	
Austria	
Belgium	
Canada	
Denmark	
Finland	
France	
Germany, Fed. Rep.	
Italy	5.
Japan	
Netherlands	
New Zealand	
Norway	
Sweden	
Switzerland	
United Kingdom	
United States	7.
TOTAL	*12.*
MULTILATERAL	*2.*
OPEC COUNTRIES	
E.E.C.+ MEMBERS	*5.*
TOTAL	***15.***

1978	1979	1980	1977	1978	1979	1980
			ODA COMMITMENTS			
–	–	–	–	–	–	–
–	0.0	0.0	–	–	–	–
0.1	0.2	0.1	–	–	–	–
0.2	0.0	0.0	0.0	–	0.1	0.1
–	–	–	0.3	–	–	–
–	0.3	0.0	–	0.2	–	–
–	4.5	10.2	0.2	0.7	–	30.0
0.5	38.7	12.9	0.0	1.0	41.0	10.3
0.1	0.4	0.2	0.1	0.1	0.4	0.2
1.5	3.0	2.1	0.5	3.4	1.8	4.0
0.8	1.5	0.3	4.7	0.0	0.0	0.3
–	–	–	–	–	–	–
–	–	–	–	–	–	–
–	–	–	–	–	–	–
0.0	0.0	0.1	–	–	–	0.1
–	–	–	–	–	–	–
11.0	6.0	9.0	7.1	10.9	5.9	12.4
14.2	*54.5*	*34.8*	*13.0*	*16.4*	*49.1*	*57.3*
–	–	0.7	5.6	–	5.1	11.2
–	–	–	–	–	–	–
–	–	–	–	–	–	–
–	–	–	–	–	–	–
7.9	8.7	21.1	21.6	47.3	4.1	9.9
–	–	–	–	–	–	–
7.4	7.8	10.2	–	21.6	23.4	45.2
–	–	–	–	–	–	–
–	–	–	–	–	–	12.6
–	–	–	–	–	–	–
12.5	9.3	8.1	–	–	–	–
–	–	–	5.7	10.6	8.4	12.4
6.2	6.3	7.3	–	–	–	–
0.5	0.5	0.1	–	–	–	–
0.9	0.6	1.2	–	–	–	–
–	–	–	–	–	–	–
2.0	0.7	2.4	–	–	–	–
–	–	–	–	–	–	–
1.0	0.3	1.3	–	–	–	–
4.9	3.1	4.4	5.4	4.6	8.0	–
43.3	*37.3*	*56.8*	*38.3*	*84.1*	*49.0*	*91.2*
7.1	*2.9*	*0.8*	*6.2*	–	*6.9*	–
9.4	*53.9*	*44.7*	*27.0*	*49.2*	*45.4*	*50.6*
64.6	***94.8***	***92.4***	***57.4***	***100.5***	***105.0***	***148.5***
			TECH. COOP. GRANTS			
–	–	–	–	–	–	–
–	0.0	0.0	–	–	0.0	0.0
0.1	0.2	0.1	0.1	0.1	0.2	0.1
0.2	0.0	0.0	0.0	–	–	–
–	–	–	0.3	–	–	–
–	0.3	0.0	–	–	0.3	0.0
–	–	3.5	–	–	–	2.9
0.5	7.4	5.4	0.0	0.0	0.2	0.7
0.1	0.4	0.2	0.1	0.1	0.2	0.2
1.5	3.0	2.1	0.5	1.5	1.5	2.0
0.8	1.5	0.3	–	0.0	0.0	0.0
–	–	–	–	–	–	–
–	–	–	–	–	–	–
–	–	–	–	–	–	–
0.0	0.0	0.1	–	–	–	–
–	–	–	–	–	–	–
6.0	–	3.0	–	–	1.0	3.0
9.2	*12.7*	*14.7*	*1.0*	*1.7*	*3.3*	*8.8*
18.8	*17.2*	*28.9*	*5.0*	*8.6*	*7.8*	*12.4*
0.1	*0.5*	*0.2*	–	–	–	–
9.4	*18.1*	*26.0*	*0.6*	*0.2*	*0.6*	*3.8*
28.1	***30.4***	***43.7***	***6.0***	***10.3***	***11.1***	***21.1***
			TOTAL OOF NET			
–	–	–	–	–	–	–
–	–	–	–	–	–	–
–	–	–	-0.9	–	–	-0.5
–	–	–	–	–	–	–
–	–	–	–	–	–	–
–	–	–	–	–	–	–
–	–	–	–	-1.0	-2.2	-2.5
–	12.4	0.5	-1.6	-1.8	0.0	-1.5
–	–	–	4.9	–	–	–
–	–	–	–	–	–	–
–	–	–	–	–	–	–
–	–	–	–	–	–	–
–	–	–	–	–	–	–
–	–	–	–	–	–	–
–	–	–	–	–	–	–
–	–	–	–	–	–	–
–	–	–	5.0	-2.0	-2.0	-2.0
–	*12.4*	*0.5*	*7.4*	*-4.8*	*-4.2*	*-6.6*
1.8	*13.0*	*16.5*	*-0.3*	*-0.8*	*10.2*	*6.8*
58.0	–	–	–	*58.0*	–	–
–	*12.4*	*0.5*	*2.4*	*-2.8*	*-2.2*	*-4.6*
59.8	***25.4***	***17.1***	***7.1***	***52.4***	***6.0***	***0.2***

	1977	1978	1979	1980
MAIN AID AGGREGATES				
DAC COUNTRIES COMBINED				
PRIVATE SECTOR NET	-7.2	21.3	-0.8	45.8
Direct Investment	-1.8	0.6	-0.5	0.6
Portfolio Invest.	-0.1	2.2	-4.4	-7.1
Export Credits	-5.3	18.4	4.1	52.3
OFFICIAL & PRIVATE				
GROSS:				
Contractual Lending	32.3	38.2	89.7	81.9
Export Credits Tot.	21.1	33.2	35.5	61.2
Export Credits Priv	14.1	33.2	35.5	61.2
OTHER NET DATA				
Contractual Lending	4.6	14.3	1.4	63.6
Export Credits Tot.	-1.4	15.1	0.7	48.8
(Bank Sector Loans)	-2.0	-6.0	-3.0	9.0
ODA CONCESSIONALITY				
Total:Grant Element	68.0	100.0	67.0	61.0
Loans:Grant Element	50.0	–	57.0	31.0
OTHER SOURCES				
CMEA Countr.(Gross)	5.2	4.7	0.3	0.3
Intra LDCS Exc.OPEC	–	–	–	–
Other	–	–	–	–
ALL SOURCE COMMITMENTS				
TOTAL BILATERAL	25.0	16.4	73.8	63.3
of which				
OPEC (ODA)	6.2	–	6.9	–
CMEA (ODA)	–	–	–	–
TOTAL MULTILAT.(ODA)	38.3	84.1	49.0	91.2
TOTAL BIL.& MULTIL.	63.2	100.5	122.8	154.4
of which				
ODA Grants	32.5	48.9	25.0	39.6
ODA Loans	24.9	51.6	80.0	108.9
ODA CONCESSIONALITY				
Total: Grant Element	74.0	94.0	72.0	71.0
Loans: Grant Element	47.0	73.0	65.0	51.0
INDEBTEDNESS				
TOTAL DEBT DISBURSED	***851.1***	***963.8***	***1020.5***	
Debt to DAC Countries	227.0	321.0	373.0	
ODA	113.0	125.0	123.0	
Total Export Credits	110.0	177.0	231.0	
Other Private Market	4.0	19.0	19.0	
International Org.	79.5	93.2	103.8	
CMEA	452.7	442.3	422.2	
Other	92.0	107.3	121.6	
TOTAL DEBT SERVICE	***99.0***	***95.5***	***109.1***	
Paid to DAC Countries	39.3	39.3	41.0	
ODA	5.9	6.8	4.1	
Total Export Credits	31.6	30.7	35.2	
Other Private Market	1.8	1.8	1.7	
International Org.	8.6	9.8	9.4	
CMEA	48.6	43.4	55.1	
Other	2.5	3.0	3.6	
ECONOMIC INDICATORS				
GNP Curr. Prices, $M	1188.8	1380.2	1444.6	1483.2
Real GNP, 1976=100	95.0	101.0	101.0	104.0
GNP/Cap Curr. Prices,$	238.0	269.0	273.0	273.0
GNP/cap Atlas Basis, $	231.9	255.6	270.8	293.4
Real GNP/Cap, 1976=100	93.0	95.0	93.0	93.0
Population, Million	5.0	5.1	5.3	5.4
Curr.A/C Deficit(-),$M	–	–	–	–
BOP Exp. & Transf.,$M	–	–	–	–
Exp. to OECD CIF, $M	222.6	270.7	292.2	341.4
of which				
Manufact.	50.2	45.1	51.5	0.9
Imp. from OECD FOB, $M	136.8	190.7	179.3	245.4
Reserves ex. Gold, $M	–	–	–	–

	1977	1978	1979	1980	1977	1978	1979	1980
TOTAL RECEIPTS NET					**TOTAL ODA NET**			
DAC COUNTRIES								
Australia	0.0	0.1	0.0	0.0	0.0	0.1	0.0	0.0
Austria	0.1	–	0.2	–	0.1	–	0.2	–
Belgium	–	-0.1	-0.1	-0.2	–	0.1	0.0	0.0
Canada	1.8	3.8	5.3	3.0	1.4	2.8	5.5	4.1
Denmark	–	–	0.1	–	–	–	0.1	–
Finland	0.0	0.1	–	0.0	0.0	0.1	–	0.0
France	–	0.2	4.2	6.7	–	–	–	–
Germany, Fed. Rep.	2.7	0.1	3.8	-5.6	0.1	0.0	0.1	–
Italy	–	–	0.9	–	–	–	–	–
Japan	0.0	1.9	1.1	-0.2	0.1	0.0	1.7	0.4
Netherlands	0.1	0.2	1.6	1.8	0.1	0.2	1.6	1.8
New Zealand	0.1	0.2	0.1	0.0	0.1	0.2	0.1	0.0
Norway	0.3	–	-1.7	-1.9	–	–	–	–
Sweden	–	–	–	–	–	–	–	–
Switzerland	0.0	0.0	–	–	0.0	0.0	–	–
United Kingdom	0.6	15.2	-7.0	-0.2	-0.9	9.4	1.6	1.1
United States	7.0	4.0	4.0	4.0	6.0	5.0	5.0	5.0
TOTAL	*12.7*	*25.7*	*12.4*	*7.4*	*7.1*	*17.7*	*15.8*	*12.5*
MULTILATERAL								
AF.D.F.	–	–	–	–	–	–	–	–
AF.D.B.	–	–	–	–	–	–	–	–
AS.D.B.	–	–	–	–	–	–	–	–
CAR.D.B.	1.1	1.8	–	9.5	0.4	1.4	–	5.4
E.E.C.	–	1.0	5.0	2.9	–	1.0	5.0	2.9
IBRD	1.5	5.3	9.1	1.4	–	–	–	–
IDA	1.6	2.9	6.4	2.1	1.6	2.9	6.4	2.1
I.D.B.	–	1.6	4.7	15.1	–	1.6	4.7	15.1
IFAD	–	–	–	–	–	–	–	–
I.F.C.	–	–	2.0	–	–	–	–	–
IMF TRUST FUND	–	–	–	–	–	–	–	–
U.N. AGENCIES	–	–	–	–	–	–	–	–
UNDP	0.7	1.0	1.2	1.3	0.7	1.0	1.2	1.3
UNTA	0.2	0.2	0.3	0.1	0.2	0.2	0.3	0.1
UNICEF	0.1	0.1	0.2	0.1	0.1	0.1	0.2	0.1
UNRWA	–	–	–	–	–	–	–	–
WFP	0.1	0.4	0.0	–	0.1	0.4	0.0	–
UNHCR	–	–	–	–	–	–	–	–
Other Multilateral	0.3	0.2	0.0	0.9	0.3	0.2	0.0	0.9
Arab OPEC Agencies	1.6	2.0	1.2	7.8	1.6	2.0	1.2	2.8
TOTAL	*7.1*	*16.4*	*30.0*	*41.2*	*4.8*	*10.7*	*18.9*	*30.6*
OPEC COUNTRIES	–	*10.0*	–	–	–	–	–	–
E.E.C.+ MEMBERS	*3.4*	*16.6*	*8.5*	*5.4*	*-0.7*	*10.6*	*8.4*	*5.8*
TOTAL	***19.7***	***52.0***	***42.4***	***48.6***	***11.9***	***28.4***	***34.8***	***43.1***

TOTAL ODA GROSS	197[illegible]
Australia	[illegible]
Austria	[illegible]
Belgium	
Canada	[illegible]
Denmark	
Finland	[illegible]
France	
Germany, Fed. Rep.	[illegible]
Italy	
Japan	[illegible]
Netherlands	[illegible]
New Zealand	[illegible]
Norway	
Sweden	
Switzerland	[illegible]
United Kingdom	[illegible]
United States	[illegible]
TOTAL	[illegible]
AF.D.F.	
AF.D.B.	
AS.D.B.	
CAR.D.B.	[illegible]
E.E.C.	
IBRD	
IDA	[illegible]
I.D.B.	
IFAD	
I.F.C.	
IMF TRUST FUND	
U.N. AGENCIES	
UNDP	[illegible]
UNTA	[illegible]
UNICEF	[illegible]
UNRWA	
WFP	[illegible]
UNHCR	
Other Multilateral	[illegible]
Arab OPEC Agencies	
TOTAL	[illegible]
OPEC COUNTRIES	
E.E.C.+ MEMBERS	
TOTAL	[illegible]

	1977	1978	1979	1980	1977	1978	1979	1980
ODA LOANS GROSS					**ODA LOANS NET**			
DAC COUNTRIES								
Australia	–	–	–	–	–	–	–	–
Austria	–	–	–	–	–	–	–	–
Belgium	–	–	–	–	–	–	–	–
Canada	0.8	2.3	4.8	3.5	0.8	2.2	4.7	3.3
Denmark	–	–	–	–	–	–	–	–
Finland	–	–	–	–	–	–	–	–
France	–	–	–	–	–	–	–	–
Germany, Fed. Rep.	–	–	–	–	–	–	–	–
Italy	–	–	–	–	–	–	–	–
Japan	–	–	–	–	0.0	-0.1	–	–
Netherlands	–	–	–	1.1	–	–	–	1.1
New Zealand	–	–	–	–	–	–	–	–
Norway	–	–	–	–	–	–	–	–
Sweden	–	–	–	–	–	–	–	–
Switzerland	–	–	–	–	–	–	–	–
United Kingdom	0.7	11.1	3.9	4.1	-1.7	8.1	0.0	-0.3
United States	5.0	5.0	4.0	4.0	5.0	4.0	3.0	3.0
TOTAL	*6.5*	*18.3*	*12.6*	*12.7*	*4.0*	*14.3*	*7.6*	*7.2*
MULTILATERAL	*3.6*	*7.5*	*15.0*	*24.0*	*3.6*	*7.5*	*14.9*	*24.0*
OPEC COUNTRIES	–	–	–	–	–	–	–	–
E.E.C.+ MEMBERS	*0.7*	*11.1*	*7.1*	*6.0*	*-1.7*	*8.1*	*3.2*	*1.6*
TOTAL	***10.1***	***25.8***	***27.6***	***36.7***	***7.6***	***21.8***	***22.6***	***31.1***

GRANTS	197[illegible]
Australia	[illegible]
Austria	[illegible]
Belgium	
Canada	[illegible]
Denmark	
Finland	
France	
Germany, Fed. Rep.	
Italy	
Japan	
Netherlands	
New Zealand	
Norway	
Sweden	
Switzerland	
United Kingdom	[illegible]
United States	
TOTAL	
MULTILATERAL	
OPEC COUNTRIES	
E.E.C.+ MEMBERS	
TOTAL	

	1977	1978	1979	1980	1977	1978	1979	1980
TOTAL OFFICIAL GROSS					**TOTAL OFFICIAL NET**			
DAC COUNTRIES								
Australia	0.0	0.1	0.0	0.0	0.0	0.1	0.0	0.0
Austria	0.1	–	0.2	–	0.1	–	0.2	–
Belgium	–	0.1	0.0	0.0	–	0.1	0.0	0.0
Canada	2.5	4.5	5.7	4.2	2.0	3.9	5.3	3.1
Denmark	–	–	0.1	–	–	–	0.1	–
Finland	0.0	0.1	–	0.0	0.0	0.1	–	0.0
France	–	–	6.6	9.2	–	–	4.2	6.7
Germany, Fed. Rep.	2.2	2.3	1.2	–	2.2	2.3	0.5	-0.9
Italy	–	–	–	–	–	–	–	–
Japan	0.2	0.0	1.7	0.4	0.1	0.0	1.7	0.4
Netherlands	0.1	0.2	1.6	1.8	0.1	0.2	1.6	1.8
New Zealand	0.1	0.2	0.1	0.0	0.1	0.2	0.1	0.0
Norway	–	–	–	–	–	–	–	–
Sweden	–	–	–	–	–	–	–	–
Switzerland	0.0	0.0	–	–	0.0	0.0	–	–
United Kingdom	1.6	12.3	5.5	5.5	-0.9	9.3	1.6	1.1
United States	7.0	6.0	6.0	6.0	7.0	4.0	4.0	4.0
TOTAL	*13.7*	*25.8*	*28.7*	*27.2*	*10.7*	*20.2*	*19.2*	*16.3*
MULTILATERAL	*7.6*	*16.9*	*30.6*	*42.0*	*7.1*	*16.4*	*30.0*	*41.2*
OPEC COUNTRIES	–	*10.0*	–	–	–	*10.0*	–	–
E.E.C.+ MEMBERS	*3.8*	*15.9*	*20.1*	*19.3*	*1.4*	*12.9*	*13.0*	*11.6*
TOTAL	***21.3***	***52.7***	***59.3***	***69.2***	***17.7***	***46.5***	***49.2***	***57.4***

TOTAL OOF GROSS	197[illegible]
Australia	
Austria	
Belgium	
Canada	
Denmark	
Finland	
France	
Germany, Fed. Rep.	
Italy	
Japan	
Netherlands	
New Zealand	
Norway	
Sweden	
Switzerland	
United Kingdom	
United States	
TOTAL	
MULTILATERAL	
OPEC COUNTRIES	
E.E.C.+ MEMBERS	
TOTAL	

1978	1979	1980	1977	1978	1979	1980
			ODA COMMITMENTS			
0.1	0.0	0.0	0.0	0.0	0.0	0.0
–	0.2	–	–	–	–	–
0.1	0.0	0.0	–	–	–	–
2.9	5.6	4.2	8.9	2.3	3.2	1.3
–	0.1	–	–	0.2	0.1	0.1
0.1	–	0.0	–	0.1	–	0.0
–	–	–	–	–	–	155.1
0.0	0.1	–	0.0	0.0	0.1	0.0
–	–	–	–	–	–	–
0.0	1.7	0.4	0.1	1.9	0.1	1.4
0.2	1.6	1.8	0.1	3.6	0.1	4.6
0.2	0.1	0.0	0.0	0.2	0.0	0.0
–	–	–	–	–	–	–
–	–	–	–	–	–	–
0.0	–	–	–	–	–	–
12.3	5.5	5.5	0.9	33.3	1.7	1.4
6.0	6.0	6.0	6.3	27.7	7.9	5.5
21.8	*20.8*	*18.0*	*16.3*	*69.3*	*13.2*	*169.4*
–	–	–	–	–	–	–
–	–	–	–	–	–	–
–	–	–	–	–	–	–
1.4	–	5.4	1.1	4.6	–	–
1.0	5.0	2.9	2.0	11.8	7.2	0.7
–	–	–	–	–	–	–
2.9	6.4	2.2	–	15.0	–	–
1.6	4.7	15.1	49.5	16.0	7.7	6.0
–	–	–	–	10.0	–	–
–	–	–	–	–	–	–
–	–	–	–	–	–	–
–	–	–	1.2	1.7	1.7	2.4
1.0	1.2	1.3	–	–	–	–
0.2	0.3	0.1	–	–	–	–
0.1	0.2	0.1	–	–	–	–
–	–	–	–	–	–	–
0.4	0.0	–	–	–	–	–
–	–	–	–	–	–	–
0.2	0.0	0.9	–	–	–	–
2.0	1.2	2.8	1.6	6.0	–	–
10.7	*19.0*	*30.7*	*55.4*	*65.0*	*16.5*	*9.1*
–	–	–	–	–	–	–
13.5	*12.3*	*10.2*	*3.0*	*48.8*	*9.1*	*161.9*
32.5	***39.8***	***48.7***	***71.7***	***134.3***	***29.7***	***178.4***
			TECH. COOP. GRANTS			
0.1	0.0	0.0	0.0	0.1	0.0	0.0
–	0.2	–	0.1	–	0.2	–
0.1	0.0	0.0	–	0.1	0.0	–
0.6	0.8	0.7	0.3	0.4	0.6	0.6
–	0.1	–	–	–	0.1	–
0.1	–	0.0	0.0	0.1	–	0.0
–	–	–	–	–	–	–
0.0	0.1	–	0.1	0.0	0.1	–
–	–	–	–	–	–	–
0.0	1.7	0.4	0.1	0.0	0.0	0.3
0.2	1.6	0.7	0.1	0.2	0.1	0.1
0.2	0.1	0.0	0.0	0.1	0.0	0.0
–	–	–	–	–	–	–
–	–	–	–	–	–	–
0.0	–	–	–	–	–	–
1.2	1.7	1.4	0.9	1.2	1.2	1.4
1.0	2.0	2.0	–	1.0	1.0	1.0
3.5	*8.2*	*5.3*	*1.6*	*3.0*	*3.3*	*3.4*
3.1	*4.0*	*6.7*	*1.2*	*1.8*	*2.3*	*2.4*
–	–	–	–	–	–	–
2.5	*5.2*	*4.2*	*1.1*	*1.5*	*1.4*	*1.5*
6.6	***12.2***	***12.0***	***2.8***	***4.8***	***5.6***	***5.7***
			TOTAL OOF NET			
–	–	–	–	–	–	–
–	–	–	–	–	–	–
–	–	–	–	–	–	–
1.7	0.2	–	0.6	1.1	-0.2	-1.0
–	–	–	–	–	–	–
–	–	–	–	–	–	–
–	6.6	9.2	–	–	4.2	6.7
2.3	1.1	–	2.0	2.3	0.4	-0.9
–	–	–	–	–	–	–
–	–	–	–	–	–	–
–	–	–	–	–	–	–
–	–	–	–	–	–	–
–	–	–	–	–	–	–
–	–	–	–	–	–	–
–	–	–	–	–	–	–
–	–	–	0.0	0.0	0.0	–
–	–	–	1.0	-1.0	-1.0	-1.0
4.0	*7.9*	*9.2*	*3.6*	*2.4*	*3.4*	*3.8*
6.2	*11.6*	*11.4*	*2.2*	*5.7*	*11.1*	*10.5*
10.0	–	–	–	*10.0*	–	–
2.3	*7.7*	*9.2*	*2.0*	*2.3*	*4.6*	*5.8*
20.2	***19.5***	***20.5***	***5.8***	***18.1***	***14.5***	***14.3***

MAIN AID AGGREGATES

	1977	1978	1979	1980
DAC COUNTRIES COMBINED				
PRIVATE SECTOR NET	2.0	5.5	-6.8	-8.9
Direct Investment	0.0	–	2.0	-0.2
Portfolio Invest.	1.9	0.8	3.4	-12.3
Export Credits	0.0	4.7	-12.1	3.6
OFFICIAL & PRIVATE				
GROSS:				
Contractual Lending	27.4	39.4	23.9	42.3
Export Credits Tot.	20.9	21.0	4.7	20.4
Export Credits Priv	16.8	17.1	3.4	20.4
OTHER NET DATA				
Contractual Lending	7.6	21.4	-1.1	14.6
Export Credits Tot.	3.7	7.2	-12.9	0.7
(Bank Sector Loans)	2.0	–	2.0	13.0
ODA CONCESSIONALITY				
Total:Grant Element	84.0	58.0	81.0	97.0
Loans:Grant Element	81.0	50.0	67.0	50.0
OTHER SOURCES				
CMEA Countr.(Gross)	1.3	1.0	4.0	1.0
Intra LDCS Exc.OPEC	–	–	–	–
Other	–	–	–	–
ALL SOURCE COMMITMENTS				
TOTAL BILATERAL	16.3	71.3	13.2	171.9
of which				
OPEC (ODA)	–	–	–	–
CMEA (ODA)	–	–	–	–
TOTAL MULTILAT.(ODA)	55.4	65.0	16.5	9.1
TOTAL BIL.& MULTIL.	71.7	136.3	29.7	180.9
of which				
ODA Grants	5.4	15.0	13.5	163.9
ODA Loans	66.3	119.3	16.3	14.5
ODA CONCESSIONALITY				
Total: Grant Element	84.0	66.0	88.0	98.0
Loans: Grant Element	79.0	63.0	68.0	50.0

INDEBTEDNESS

	1977	1978	1979	1980
TOTAL DEBT DISBURSED	***380.6***	***385.3***	***492.4***	
Debt to DAC Countries	288.0	276.0	352.0	
ODA	109.0	127.0	139.0	
Total Export Credits	48.0	72.0	59.0	
Other Private Market	131.0	77.0	154.0	
International Org.	29.6	43.2	71.9	
CMEA	17.2	20.0	19.6	
Other	45.7	46.1	48.9	
TOTAL DEBT SERVICE	***45.7***	***52.7***	***95.6***	
Paid to DAC Countries	43.2	47.2	84.9	
ODA	5.8	7.3	9.2	
Total Export Credits	8.5	12.0	18.5	
Other Private Market	28.9	27.9	57.2	
International Org.	2.1	2.5	3.4	
CMEA	0.3	0.5	4.7	
Other	–	2.5	2.6	

ECONOMIC INDICATORS

	1977	1978	1979	1980
GNP Curr. Prices, $M	419.4	468.9	486.9	556.2
Real GNP, 1976=100	96.0	94.0	93.0	94.0
GNP/Cap Curr. Prices,$	535.0	596.0	616.0	701.0
GNP/cap Atlas Basis, $	562.3	590.4	629.4	693.1
Real GNP/Cap, 1976=100	95.0	93.0	91.0	92.0
Population, Million	0.8	0.8	0.8	0.8
Curr.A/C Deficit(-),$M	-97.1	-22.4	-82.9	-126.4
BOP Exp. & Transf.,$M	275.6	314.4	315.3	411.9
Exp. to OECD CIF, $M	222.7	282.0	263.4	357.0
of which				
Manufact.	48.3	11.7	9.2	16.7
Imp. from OECD FOB, $M	165.4	149.3	175.6	212.0
Reserves ex. Gold, $M	23.0	58.3	17.5	12.7

	TOTAL RECEIPTS NET 1977	1978	1979	1980	TOTAL ODA NET 1977	1978	1979	1980
DAC COUNTRIES								
Australia	–	–	–	–	–	–	–	–
Austria	0.0	0.0	0.0	3.3	0.0	0.0	0.0	0.0
Belgium	0.3	1.6	2.3	1.7	0.3	1.6	2.3	1.6
Canada	4.7	8.3	8.0	5.4	4.7	8.3	8.0	5.4
Denmark	–	–	–	–	–	–	–	–
Finland	–	–	–	–	–	–	–	–
France	3.1	3.4	2.7	14.7	2.0	2.4	1.2	7.3
Germany, Fed. Rep.	3.4	10.1	8.0	9.1	3.4	9.2	7.2	9.0
Italy	-0.4	0.2	34.4	2.5	0.0	0.0	0.1	0.0
Japan	–	-0.1	-0.1	2.2	–	–	0.0	2.2
Netherlands	0.9	1.2	1.5	1.9	0.9	1.2	1.5	1.9
New Zealand	–	–	–	–	–	–	–	–
Norway	0.0	–	-0.4	-0.7	0.0	–	–	0.0
Sweden	–	–	–	–	–	–	–	–
Switzerland	0.1	0.1	0.2	4.6	0.1	0.1	0.2	0.3
United Kingdom	0.9	0.7	0.0	-0.3	0.0	0.0	0.0	0.1
United States	27.0	26.0	28.0	34.0	28.0	27.0	28.0	35.0
TOTAL	*40.0*	*51.4*	*84.5*	*78.4*	*39.6*	*49.8*	*48.5*	*62.8*
MULTILATERAL								
AF.D.F.	–	–	–	–	–	–	–	–
AF.D.B.	–	–	–	–	–	–	–	–
AS.D.B.	–	–	–	–	–	–	–	–
CAR.D.B.	–	–	–	–	–	–	–	–
E.E.C.	–	1.7	0.4	0.7	–	1.7	0.4	0.7
IBRD	–	–	–	–	–	–	–	–
IDA	13.7	7.4	8.2	13.6	13.7	7.4	8.2	13.6
I.D.B.	21.3	16.9	15.9	8.9	21.3	16.9	15.9	8.9
IFAD	–	–	–	0.6	–	–	–	0.6
I.F.C.	–	–	–	–	–	–	–	–
IMF TRUST FUND	2.4	7.4	7.4	6.4	2.4	7.4	7.4	6.4
U.N. AGENCIES	–	–	–	–	–	–	–	–
UNDP	2.3	2.9	6.5	6.6	2.3	2.9	6.5	6.6
UNTA	0.2	0.3	0.5	0.3	0.2	0.3	0.5	0.3
UNICEF	0.5	1.5	0.7	0.7	0.5	1.5	0.7	0.7
UNRWA	–	–	–	–	–	–	–	–
WFP	1.8	3.2	3.0	2.6	1.8	3.2	3.0	2.6
UNHCR	–	–	–	–	–	–	–	–
Other Multilateral	2.8	1.8	1.8	2.0	2.8	1.8	1.8	2.0
Arab OPEC Agencies	3.2	–	–	–	3.2	–	–	–
TOTAL	*48.1*	*43.1*	*44.2*	*42.3*	*48.1*	*43.1*	*44.2*	*42.3*
OPEC COUNTRIES	–	–	–	–	–	–	–	–
E.E.C.+ MEMBERS	*8.1*	*18.8*	*49.2*	*30.3*	*6.7*	*16.0*	*12.6*	*20.6*
TOTAL	***88.0***	***94.5***	***128.7***	***120.7***	***87.6***	***92.8***	***92.6***	***105.2***

TOTAL ODA GROSS	197
Australia	
Austria	0
Belgium	0
Canada	4
Denmark	
Finland	
France	2
Germany, Fed. Rep.	3
Italy	0
Japan	
Netherlands	0
New Zealand	
Norway	0
Sweden	
Switzerland	0
United Kingdom	0
United States	28
TOTAL	*39*
AF.D.F.	
AF.D.B.	
AS.D.B.	
CAR.D.B.	
E.E.C.	
IBRD	
IDA	13
I.D.B.	21
IFAD	
I.F.C.	
IMF TRUST FUND	2
U.N. AGENCIES	
UNDP	2
UNTA	C
UNICEF	C
UNRWA	
WFP	1
UNHCR	
Other Multilateral	2
Arab OPEC Agencies	3
TOTAL	*48*
OPEC COUNTRIES	
E.E.C.+ MEMBERS	*6*
TOTAL	***88***

	ODA LOANS GROSS 1977	1978	1979	1980	ODA LOANS NET 1977	1978	1979	1980
DAC COUNTRIES								
Australia	–	–	–	–	–	–	–	–
Austria	–	–	–	–	–	–	–	–
Belgium	–	–	–	–	–	–	–	–
Canada	–	–	–	–	–	–	–	–
Denmark	–	–	–	–	–	–	–	–
Finland	–	–	–	–	–	–	–	–
France	–	–	–	2.8	–	–	–	2.8
Germany, Fed. Rep.	1.1	6.3	2.8	1.8	1.1	6.3	2.8	1.8
Italy	–	–	–	–	–	–	–	–
Japan	–	–	–	–	–	–	–	–
Netherlands	–	–	–	–	–	–	–	–
New Zealand	–	–	–	–	–	–	–	–
Norway	–	–	–	–	–	–	–	–
Sweden	–	–	–	–	–	–	–	–
Switzerland	–	–	–	–	–	–	–	–
United Kingdom	–	–	–	–	–	–	–	–
United States	12.0	11.0	10.0	10.0	12.0	11.0	10.0	10.0
TOTAL	*13.1*	*17.3*	*12.8*	*14.6*	*13.1*	*17.3*	*12.8*	*14.6*
MULTILATERAL	*40.9*	*30.5*	*31.1*	*28.8*	*40.5*	*30.0*	*30.5*	*28.1*
OPEC COUNTRIES	–	–	–	–	–	–	–	–
E.E.C.+ MEMBERS	*1.1*	*6.3*	*2.8*	*4.6*	*1.1*	*6.3*	*2.8*	*4.6*
TOTAL	***54.0***	***47.8***	***43.9***	***43.4***	***53.6***	***47.3***	***43.2***	***42.7***

GRANTS	
Australia	
Austria	
Belgium	
Canada	
Denmark	
Finland	
France	
Germany, Fed. Rep.	
Italy	
Japan	
Netherlands	
New Zealand	
Norway	
Sweden	
Switzerland	
United Kingdom	
United States	1
TOTAL	*2*
MULTILATERAL	
OPEC COUNTRIES	
E.E.C.+ MEMBERS	
TOTAL	***3***

	TOTAL OFFICIAL GROSS 1977	1978	1979	1980	TOTAL OFFICIAL NET 1977	1978	1979	1980
DAC COUNTRIES								
Australia	–	–	–	–	–	–	–	–
Austria	0.0	0.0	0.0	0.0	0.0	0.0	0.0	0.0
Belgium	0.3	1.6	2.3	1.6	0.3	1.6	2.3	1.6
Canada	4.7	8.3	8.0	5.4	4.7	8.3	8.0	5.4
Denmark	–	–	–	–	–	–	–	–
Finland	–	–	–	–	–	–	–	–
France	2.0	2.4	1.2	7.3	2.0	2.4	1.2	7.3
Germany, Fed. Rep.	3.4	9.2	7.2	9.0	3.4	9.2	7.2	9.0
Italy	0.0	0.0	0.1	0.0	0.0	0.0	0.1	0.0
Japan	–	–	0.0	2.2	–	–	0.0	2.2
Netherlands	0.9	1.2	1.5	1.9	0.9	1.2	1.5	1.9
New Zealand	–	–	–	–	–	–	–	–
Norway	0.0	–	–	0.0	0.0	–	–	0.0
Sweden	–	–	–	–	–	–	–	–
Switzerland	0.1	0.1	0.2	0.3	0.1	0.1	0.2	0.3
United Kingdom	0.0	0.0	0.0	0.1	0.0	0.0	0.0	0.1
United States	28.0	27.0	29.0	35.0	27.0	26.0	28.0	34.0
TOTAL	*39.6*	*49.8*	*49.5*	*62.8*	*38.6*	*48.8*	*48.5*	*61.8*
MULTILATERAL	*48.5*	*43.6*	*44.9*	*43.0*	*48.1*	*43.1*	*44.2*	*42.3*
OPEC COUNTRIES	–	–	–	–	–	–	–	–
E.E.C.+ MEMBERS	*6.7*	*16.0*	*12.6*	*20.6*	*6.7*	*16.0*	*12.6*	*20.6*
TOTAL	***88.0***	***93.3***	***94.3***	***105.9***	***86.6***	***91.8***	***92.6***	***104.2***

TOTAL OOF GROSS	
Australia	
Austria	
Belgium	
Canada	
Denmark	
Finland	
France	
Germany, Fed. Rep.	
Italy	
Japan	
Netherlands	
New Zealand	
Norway	
Sweden	
Switzerland	
United Kingdom	
United States	
TOTAL	
MULTILATERAL	
OPEC COUNTRIES	
E.E.C.+ MEMBERS	
TOTAL	

1978	1979	1980	1977	1978	1979	1980
			ODA COMMITMENTS			
–	–	–	–	–	–	–
0.0	0.0	0.0	–	–	–	–
1.6	2.3	1.6	–	2.4	2.7	2.0
8.3	8.0	5.4	18.8	5.4	16.0	2.7
–	–	–	–	–	–	–
–	–	–	–	–	–	–
2.4	1.2	7.3	3.1	1.7	1.8	3.6
9.2	7.2	9.0	7.8	7.3	6.0	8.7
0.0	0.1	0.0	0.0	0.0	0.1	0.0
–	0.0	2.2	–	–	2.3	2.3
1.2	1.5	1.9	1.2	1.0	1.6	2.1
–	–	–	–	–	–	–
–	–	0.0	–	–	–	–
–	–	–	–	–	–	–
0.1	0.2	0.3	–	–	–	0.4
0.0	0.0	0.1	0.0	0.0	0.0	0.1
27.0	28.0	35.0	33.9	27.4	23.1	25.1
49.8	*48.5*	*62.8*	*64.9*	*45.2*	*53.4*	*46.9*
–	–	–	–	–	–	–
–	–	–	–	–	–	–
–	–	–	–	–	–	–
–	–	–	–	–	–	–
1.7	0.4	0.7	–	3.5	0.2	8.2
–	–	–	–	–	–	–
7.4	8.2	13.6	16.6	25.0	16.5	–
17.4	16.5	9.6	15.7	43.5	4.1	9.1
–	–	0.6	–	3.5	–	–
–	–	–	–	–	–	–
7.4	7.4	6.4	–	–	–	–
–	–	–	7.6	9.6	12.4	12.2
2.9	6.5	6.6	–	–	–	–
0.3	0.5	0.3	–	–	–	–
1.5	0.7	0.7	–	–	–	–
–	–	–	–	–	–	–
3.2	3.0	2.6	–	–	–	–
–	–	–	–	–	–	–
1.8	1.8	2.0	–	–	–	–
–	–	–	3.2	–	4.0	3.5
43.6	*44.9*	*43.0*	*43.0*	*85.2*	*37.2*	*33.0*
–	–	–	–	–	–	–
16.0	*12.6*	*20.6*	*12.2*	*15.9*	*12.3*	*24.6*
93.3	***93.3***	***105.9***	***107.9***	***130.3***	***90.6***	***79.9***
			TECH. COOP. GRANTS			
–	–	–	–	–	–	–
0.0	0.0	0.0	0.0	0.0	0.0	0.0
1.6	2.3	1.6	0.3	1.3	1.2	1.3
8.3	8.0	5.4	0.2	1.4	0.9	0.9
–	–	–	–	–	–	–
–	–	–	–	–	–	–
2.4	1.2	4.5	0.2	0.1	0.2	3.3
2.9	4.5	7.1	1.6	2.1	3.8	5.9
0.0	0.1	0.0	0.0	0.0	0.1	0.0
–	0.0	2.2	–	–	0.0	0.0
1.2	1.5	1.9	0.5	0.3	0.4	0.7
–	–	–	–	–	–	–
–	–	0.0	–	–	–	–
–	–	–	–	–	–	–
0.1	0.2	0.3	–	–	–	0.0
0.0	0.0	0.1	0.0	0.0	0.0	0.0
16.0	18.0	25.0	5.0	7.0	7.0	9.0
32.5	*35.7*	*48.2*	*7.8*	*12.3*	*13.6*	*21.3*
13.1	*13.7*	*14.3*	*5.8*	*8.2*	*10.4*	*12.2*
–	–	–	–	–	–	–
9.8	*9.9*	*16.0*	*2.6*	*3.9*	*5.7*	*11.3*
45.5	***49.4***	***62.5***	***13.6***	***20.5***	***24.0***	***33.5***
			TOTAL OOF NET			
–	–	–	–	–	–	–
–	–	–	–	–	–	–
–	–	–	–	–	–	–
–	–	–	–	–	–	–
–	–	–	–	–	–	–
–	–	–	–	–	–	–
–	–	–	–	–	–	–
–	–	–	–	–	–	–
–	–	–	–	–	–	–
–	–	–	–	–	–	–
–	–	–	–	–	–	–
–	–	–	–	–	–	–
–	–	–	–	–	–	–
–	–	–	–	–	–	–
–	–	–	–	–	–	–
–	–	–	–	–	–	–
–	1.0	–	-1.0	-1.0	–	-1.0
–	*1.0*	–	*-1.0*	*-1.0*	–	*-1.0*
–	–	–	–	–	–	–
–	–	–	–	–	–	–
–	–	–	–	–	–	–
–	***1.0***	–	***-1.0***	***-1.0***	–	***-1.0***

	1977	1978	1979	1980
MAIN AID AGGREGATES				
DAC COUNTRIES COMBINED				
PRIVATE SECTOR NET	1.4	2.6	36.1	16.6
Direct Investment	0.8	1.2	2.4	0.9
Portfolio Invest.	0.0	0.8	0.3	1.9
Export Credits	0.6	0.6	33.4	13.8
OFFICIAL & PRIVATE				
GROSS:				
Contractual Lending	15.1	21.4	48.4	34.5
Export Credits Tot.	2.0	4.1	34.6	19.9
Export Credits Priv	2.0	4.1	34.6	19.9
OTHER NET DATA				
Contractual Lending	12.7	16.9	46.1	27.4
Export Credits Tot.	-0.4	-0.4	32.4	12.8
(Bank Sector Loans)	-2.0	16.0	-10.0	3.0
ODA CONCESSIONALITY				
Total:Grant Element	96.0	91.0	94.0	93.0
Loans:Grant Element	76.0	70.0	67.0	67.0
OTHER SOURCES				
CMEA Countr.(Gross)	–	–	–	–
Intra LDCS Exc.OPEC	–	–	–	–
Other	–	–	–	–
ALL SOURCE COMMITMENTS				
TOTAL BILATERAL	64.9	46.3	53.8	51.7
of which				
OPEC (ODA)	–	–	–	–
CMEA (ODA)	–	–	–	–
TOTAL MULTILAT.(ODA)	43.0	85.2	37.2	33.0
TOTAL BIL.& MULTIL.	107.9	131.5	91.0	84.7
of which				
ODA Grants	63.8	44.8	57.5	58.6
ODA Loans	44.1	85.5	33.2	21.3
ODA CONCESSIONALITY				
Total: Grant Element	91.0	88.0	87.0	93.0
Loans: Grant Element	76.0	78.0	75.0	68.0
INDEBTEDNESS				
TOTAL DEBT DISBURSED	***124.1***	***169.7***	***213.0***	
Debt to DAC Countries	54.0	70.0	91.0	
ODA	24.0	42.0	55.0	
Total Export Credits	26.0	21.0	32.0	
Other Private Market	4.0	7.0	4.0	
International Org.	70.1	99.7	122.0	
CMEA	–	–	–	
Other	–	–	–	
TOTAL DEBT SERVICE	***10.0***	***12.9***	***8.8***	
Paid to DAC Countries	9.4	12.1	7.8	
ODA	–	1.1	1.0	
Total Export Credits	9.2	9.9	5.4	
Other Private Market	0.2	1.1	1.4	
International Org.	0.6	0.8	1.0	
CMEA	–	–	–	
Other	–	–	–	
ECONOMIC INDICATORS				
GNP Curr. Prices, $M	992.0	1013.7	1121.2	1396.2
Real GNP, 1976=100	101.0	107.0	109.0	117.0
GNP/Cap Curr. Prices,$	208.0	209.0	227.0	278.0
GNP/cap Atlas Basis, $	193.4	215.8	233.7	268.2
Real GNP/Cap, 1976=100	100.0	104.0	103.0	109.0
Population, Million	4.7	4.8	4.9	5.0
Curr.A/C Deficit(-),$M	-70.0	-83.8	-116.7	-132.3
BOP Exp. & Transf.,$M	206.5	242.2	255.3	319.6
Exp. to OECD CIF, $M	233.5	268.8	306.1	366.7
of which				
Manufact.	126.2	164.8	202.5	230.8
Imp. from OECD FOB, $M	279.3	293.6	349.2	426.4
Reserves ex. Gold, $M	33.8	38.7	55.0	16.2

TOTAL RECEIPTS NET

	1977	1978	1979	1980
DAC COUNTRIES				
Australia	–	–	–	–
Austria	0.1	0.1	0.0	0.1
Belgium	0.0	0.5	1.3	9.5
Canada	1.0	7.5	3.6	9.7
Denmark	–	0.1	–	17.4
Finland	–	–	0.4	0.5
France	0.2	0.0	4.7	1.6
Germany, Fed. Rep.	4.2	3.2	18.1	-9.1
Italy	-0.5	-14.5	0.1	26.7
Japan	8.5	8.8	9.4	1.6
Netherlands	0.2	0.9	1.7	6.9
New Zealand	–	–	–	–
Norway	–	–	0.0	–
Sweden	-0.2	-0.2	-0.2	-0.3
Switzerland	-1.6	0.2	0.9	24.6
United Kingdom	1.5	-0.1	0.5	–
United States	16.0	16.0	26.0	19.0
TOTAL	*29.4*	*22.4*	*66.4*	*108.0*
MULTILATERAL				
AF.D.F.	–	–	–	–
AF.D.B.	–	–	–	–
AS.D.B.	–	–	–	–
CAR.D.B.	–	–	–	–
E.E.C.	2.5	1.7	3.2	4.6
IBRD	19.7	21.8	23.1	20.3
IDA	2.6	8.3	5.5	17.5
I.D.B.	23.7	41.8	26.1	33.7
IFAD	–	–	–	–
I.F.C.	–	7.0	3.0	-0.8
IMF TRUST FUND	–	–	9.8	8.3
U.N. AGENCIES	–	–	–	–
UNDP	1.3	1.8	2.6	3.1
UNTA	0.4	0.4	0.4	0.2
UNICEF	0.7	1.0	0.3	0.3
UNRWA	–	–	–	–
WFP	1.0	0.8	1.4	1.6
UNHCR	–	0.2	–	0.2
Other Multilateral	0.9	0.7	0.5	1.2
Arab OPEC Agencies	0.9	–	0.9	–
TOTAL	*53.7*	*85.3*	*76.8*	*90.2*
OPEC COUNTRIES	*14.4*	*17.6*	–	–
E.E.C.+ MEMBERS	*8.1*	*-8.3*	*29.5*	*57.6*
TOTAL	***97.5***	***125.3***	***143.2***	***198.3***

TOTAL ODA NET

	1977	1978	1979	1980
Australia	–	–	–	–
Austria	0.1	0.1	0.0	0.1
Belgium	0.1	0.1	0.1	0.2
Canada	1.0	7.5	3.6	4.1
Denmark	–	0.1	–	0.1
Finland	–	–	0.4	0.5
France	–	–	–	0.2
Germany, Fed. Rep.	3.0	3.4	3.5	4.9
Italy	0.0	0.1	0.0	–
Japan	2.3	4.9	4.1	7.2
Netherlands	0.2	0.9	1.7	6.9
New Zealand	–	–	–	–
Norway	–	–	–	–
Sweden	–	–	–	–
Switzerland	0.1	0.2	0.9	3.7
United Kingdom	1.0	0.6	0.5	0.8
United States	15.0	16.0	27.0	19.0
TOTAL	*22.9*	*33.9*	*41.7*	*47.7*
AF.D.F.	–	–	–	–
AF.D.B.	–	–	–	–
AS.D.B.	–	–	–	–
CAR.D.B.	–	–	–	–
E.E.C.	2.5	1.7	3.2	4.6
IBRD	0.1	2.2	4.6	2.6
IDA	2.6	8.3	5.5	17.5
I.D.B.	23.7	41.8	26.1	15.7
IFAD	–	–	–	–
I.F.C.	–	–	–	–
IMF TRUST FUND	–	–	9.8	8.3
U.N. AGENCIES	–	–	–	–
UNDP	1.3	1.8	2.6	3.1
UNTA	0.4	0.4	0.4	0.2
UNICEF	0.7	1.0	0.3	0.3
UNRWA	–	–	–	–
WFP	1.0	0.8	1.4	1.6
UNHCR	–	0.2	–	0.2
Other Multilateral	0.9	0.7	0.5	1.2
Arab OPEC Agencies	0.9	–	0.9	–
TOTAL	*34.1*	*58.7*	*55.3*	*55.4*
OPEC COUNTRIES	–	–	–	–
E.E.C.+ MEMBERS	*6.9*	*6.9*	*9.0*	*17.7*
TOTAL	***57.0***	***92.5***	***97.0***	***103.0***

TOTAL ODA GROSS

	197
Australia	
Austria	0.
Belgium	0.
Canada	1.
Denmark	
Finland	
France	
Germany, Fed. Rep.	3
Italy	0
Japan	2.
Netherlands	0.
New Zealand	
Norway	
Sweden	
Switzerland	0.
United Kingdom	1.
United States	16.
TOTAL	*23.*
AF.D.F.	
AF.D.B.	
AS.D.B.	
CAR.D.B.	
E.E.C.	2.
IBRD	0.
IDA	2.
I.D.B.	26
IFAD	
I.F.C.	
IMF TRUST FUND	
U.N. AGENCIES	
UNDP	1.
UNTA	0.
UNICEF	0.
UNRWA	
WFP	1.
UNHCR	
Other Multilateral	0.
Arab OPEC Agencies	0.
TOTAL	*37.*
OPEC COUNTRIES	
E.E.C.+ MEMBERS	*6.*
TOTAL	***61***

ODA LOANS GROSS

	1977	1978	1979	1980
DAC COUNTRIES				
Australia	–	–	–	–
Austria	–	–	–	–
Belgium	–	–	–	–
Canada	0.6	6.2	2.2	2.3
Denmark	–	–	–	–
Finland	–	–	–	–
France	–	–	–	–
Germany, Fed. Rep.	–	–	–	–
Italy	–	–	–	–
Japan	–	2.6	2.1	4.5
Netherlands	–	–	–	5.5
New Zealand	–	–	–	–
Norway	–	–	–	–
Sweden	–	–	–	–
Switzerland	–	–	–	–
United Kingdom	–	–	–	–
United States	8.0	8.0	13.0	10.0
TOTAL	*8.6*	*16.8*	*17.3*	*22.3*
MULTILATERAL	*30.3*	*55.6*	*49.8*	*47.3*
OPEC COUNTRIES	–	–	–	–
E.E.C.+ MEMBERS	–	–	–	*5.5*
TOTAL	***38.8***	***72.4***	***67.1***	***69.6***

ODA LOANS NET

	1977	1978	1979	1980
Australia	–	–	–	–
Austria	–	–	–	–
Belgium	–	–	–	–
Canada	0.6	6.2	2.2	2.3
Denmark	–	–	–	–
Finland	–	–	–	–
France	–	–	–	–
Germany, Fed. Rep.	–	–	–	–
Italy	–	–	–	–
Japan	–	2.6	2.1	4.5
Netherlands	–	–	–	5.5
New Zealand	–	–	–	–
Norway	–	–	–	–
Sweden	–	–	–	–
Switzerland	–	–	–	–
United Kingdom	–	–	–	–
United States	7.0	7.0	12.0	9.0
TOTAL	*7.6*	*15.8*	*16.3*	*21.3*
MULTILATERAL	*27.3*	*52.1*	*46.3*	*43.8*
OPEC COUNTRIES	–	–	–	–
E.E.C.+ MEMBERS	–	–	–	*5.5*
TOTAL	***34.8***	***67.9***	***62.7***	***65.1***

GRANTS

	197
Australia	
Austria	0.
Belgium	0.
Canada	0.
Denmark	
Finland	
France	
Germany, Fed. Rep.	3.
Italy	0
Japan	2.
Netherlands	0.
New Zealand	
Norway	
Sweden	
Switzerland	0.
United Kingdom	1
United States	8.
TOTAL	*15.*
MULTILATERAL	*6.*
OPEC COUNTRIES	
E.E.C.+ MEMBERS	*6.*
TOTAL	***22.***

TOTAL OFFICIAL GROSS

	1977	1978	1979	1980
DAC COUNTRIES				
Australia	–	–	–	–
Austria	0.1	0.1	0.0	0.1
Belgium	0.1	0.1	0.1	0.2
Canada	1.0	7.5	3.6	9.5
Denmark	–	0.1	–	0.1
Finland	–	–	0.4	0.5
France	–	–	–	0.2
Germany, Fed. Rep.	3.0	3.4	3.5	4.9
Italy	0.0	0.1	0.0	–
Japan	2.3	4.9	4.1	7.2
Netherlands	0.2	0.9	1.7	6.9
New Zealand	–	–	–	–
Norway	–	–	–	–
Sweden	–	–	–	–
Switzerland	0.1	0.2	0.9	3.7
United Kingdom	1.0	0.6	0.5	0.8
United States	18.0	18.0	29.0	22.0
TOTAL	*25.9*	*35.9*	*43.7*	*56.1*
MULTILATERAL	*59.4*	*91.9*	*83.5*	*98.7*
OPEC COUNTRIES	*14.4*	*17.6*	–	–
E.E.C.+ MEMBERS	*6.9*	*6.9*	*9.0*	*17.7*
TOTAL	***99.7***	***145.4***	***127.3***	***154.8***

TOTAL OFFICIAL NET

	1977	1978	1979	1980
Australia	–	–	–	–
Austria	0.1	0.1	0.0	0.1
Belgium	0.1	0.1	0.1	0.2
Canada	1.0	7.5	3.6	9.5
Denmark	–	0.1	–	0.1
Finland	–	–	0.4	0.5
France	–	–	–	0.2
Germany, Fed. Rep.	3.0	3.4	3.5	4.9
Italy	0.0	0.1	0.0	–
Japan	2.3	4.9	4.1	7.2
Netherlands	0.2	0.9	1.7	6.9
New Zealand	–	–	–	–
Norway	–	–	–	–
Sweden	–	–	–	–
Switzerland	0.1	0.2	0.9	3.7
United Kingdom	1.0	0.6	0.5	0.8
United States	16.0	16.0	26.0	19.0
TOTAL	*23.9*	*33.9*	*40.7*	*53.1*
MULTILATERAL	*53.7*	*85.3*	*76.8*	*90.2*
OPEC COUNTRIES	*14.4*	*17.6*	–	–
E.E.C.+ MEMBERS	*6.9*	*6.9*	*9.0*	*17.7*
TOTAL	***92.0***	***136.8***	***117.5***	***143.3***

TOTAL OOF GROSS

	197
Australia	
Austria	
Belgium	
Canada	
Denmark	
Finland	
France	
Germany, Fed. Rep.	
Italy	
Japan	
Netherlands	
New Zealand	
Norway	
Sweden	
Switzerland	
United Kingdom	
United States	2.
TOTAL	*2.*
MULTILATERAL	*22.*
OPEC COUNTRIES	*14.*
E.E.C.+ MEMBERS	
TOTAL	***38.***

1978	1979	1980	1977	1978	1979	1980
			ODA COMMITMENTS			
–	–	–	–	–	–	–
0.1	0.0	0.1	–	0.1	–	0.1
0.1	0.1	0.2	–	–	–	–
7.5	3.6	4.1	20.9	0.4	0.6	1.0
0.1	–	0.1	–	0.2	–	0.1
–	0.4	0.5	–	0.4	0.4	0.6
–	–	0.2	–	–	–	0.6
3.4	3.5	4.9	3.6	3.6	2.4	5.3
0.1	0.0	–	0.0	0.1	0.0	–
4.9	4.1	7.2	2.6	6.0	5.8	38.6
0.9	1.7	6.9	1.1	1.0	9.0	1.7
–	–	–	–	–	–	–
–	–	–	–	–	–	–
–	–	–	–	–	–	–
0.2	0.9	3.7	–	1.8	1.4	2.6
0.6	0.5	0.8	1.3	0.6	0.5	12.4
17.0	28.0	20.0	7.8	19.1	33.3	51.1
34.9	*42.7*	*48.7*	*37.1*	*33.2*	*53.5*	*114.0*
–	–	–	–	–	–	–
–	–	–	–	–	–	–
–	–	–	–	–	–	–
–	–	–	–	–	–	–
1.7	3.2	4.6	1.9	6.8	8.9	11.9
2.2	4.6	2.6	5.0	–	–	–
8.4	5.7	17.7	5.0	5.0	–	25.0
45.1	29.4	19.0	5.8	81.0	43.2	62.6
–	–	–	–	–	10.2	–
–	–	–	–	–	–	–
–	9.8	8.3	–	–	–	–
–	–	–	4.3	4.8	5.2	6.6
1.8	2.6	3.1	–	–	–	–
0.4	0.4	0.2	–	–	–	–
1.0	0.3	0.3	–	–	–	–
–	–	–	–	–	–	–
0.8	1.4	1.6	–	–	–	–
0.2	–	0.2	–	–	–	–
0.7	0.5	1.2	–	–	–	–
–	0.9	–	3.5	–	3.5	5.0
62.1	*58.8*	*58.9*	*25.5*	*97.6*	*71.0*	*111.2*
–	–	–	–	–	–	–
6.9	*9.0*	*17.7*	*7.8*	*12.3*	*20.8*	*32.0*
97.0	***101.5***	***107.5***	***62.6***	***130.8***	***124.6***	***225.1***
			TECH. COOP. GRANTS			
–	–	–	–	–	–	–
0.1	0.0	0.1	0.1	0.1	0.0	0.1
0.1	0.1	0.2	0.1	0.1	0.1	0.0
1.3	1.4	1.8	0.3	0.4	0.6	0.8
0.1	–	0.1	–	0.1	–	0.1
–	0.4	0.5	–	–	0.4	0.5
–	–	0.2	–	–	–	0.2
3.4	3.5	4.9	1.7	2.2	2.1	3.1
0.1	0.0	–	0.0	0.1	0.0	–
2.3	2.0	2.7	2.3	2.3	2.0	1.4
0.9	1.7	1.4	0.2	0.4	1.0	1.2
–	–	–	–	–	–	–
–	–	–	–	–	–	–
–	–	–	–	–	–	–
0.2	0.9	3.7	–	–	–	1.0
0.6	0.5	0.8	0.4	0.6	0.5	0.7
9.0	15.0	10.0	3.0	3.0	2.0	4.0
18.1	*25.4*	*26.4*	*8.0*	*9.3*	*8.6*	*13.1*
6.5	*9.0*	*11.6*	*3.3*	*4.1*	*4.4*	*6.6*
–	–	–	–	–	–	–
6.9	*9.0*	*12.2*	*2.4*	*3.5*	*3.7*	*5.3*
24.6	***34.3***	***38.0***	***11.3***	***13.3***	***13.0***	***19.7***
			TOTAL OOF NET			
–	–	–	–	–	–	–
–	–	–	–	–	–	–
–	–	–	–	–	–	–
–	–	5.4	–	–	–	5.4
–	–	–	–	–	–	–
–	–	–	–	–	–	–
–	–	–	–	–	–	–
–	–	–	–	–	–	–
–	–	–	–	–	–	–
–	–	–	–	–	–	–
–	–	–	–	–	–	–
–	–	–	–	–	–	–
–	–	–	–	–	–	–
–	–	–	–	–	–	–
–	–	–	–	–	–	–
–	–	–	–	–	–	–
1.0	1.0	2.0	1.0	–	-1.0	–
1.0	*1.0*	*7.4*	*1.0*	–	*-1.0*	*5.4*
29.8	*24.8*	*39.8*	*19.6*	*26.6*	*21.5*	*34.9*
17.6	–	–	*14.4*	*17.6*	–	–
–	–	–	–	–	–	–
48.4	***25.8***	***47.2***	***35.0***	***44.2***	***20.5***	***40.3***

	1977	1978	1979	1980
MAIN AID AGGREGATES				
DAC COUNTRIES COMBINED				
PRIVATE SECTOR NET	5.5	-11.5	25.7	54.9
Direct Investment	0.9	3.8	2.7	-4.0
Portfolio Invest.	-3.1	3.3	21.4	-5.9
Export Credits	7.7	-18.5	1.6	64.8
OFFICIAL & PRIVATE				
GROSS:				
Contractual Lending	34.1	28.3	40.4	118.4
Export Credits Tot.	25.5	11.5	23.1	95.2
Export Credits Priv	23.5	10.5	22.1	88.7
OTHER NET DATA				
Contractual Lending	16.3	-2.7	16.9	91.5
Export Credits Tot.	8.7	-18.5	1.6	69.3
(Bank Sector Loans)	16.0	49.0	38.0	-25.0
ODA CONCESSIONALITY				
Total:Grant Element	96.0	83.0	86.0	73.0
Loans:Grant Element	89.0	59.0	68.0	64.0
OTHER SOURCES				
CMEA Countr.(Gross)	–	–	–	–
Intra LDCS Exc.OPEC	–	–	–	–
Other	–	–	–	–
ALL SOURCE COMMITMENTS				
TOTAL BILATERAL	38.2	33.9	61.5	152.4
of which				
OPEC (ODA)	–	–	–	–
CMEA (ODA)	–	–	–	–
TOTAL MULTILAT.(ODA)	25.5	97.6	71.0	111.2
TOTAL BIL.& MULTIL.	63.7	131.5	132.5	263.5
of which				
ODA Grants	29.1	31.5	44.1	47.9
ODA Loans	33.5	99.3	80.5	177.3
ODA CONCESSIONALITY				
Total: Grant Element	79.0	86.0	81.0	76.0
Loans: Grant Element	75.0	68.0	74.0	70.0
INDEBTEDNESS				
TOTAL DEBT DISBURSED	***476.4***	***685.0***	***834.6***	
Debt to DAC Countries	174.0	288.0	379.0	
ODA	67.0	83.0	99.0	
Total Export Credits	22.0	105.0	103.0	
Other Private Market	85.0	100.0	177.0	
International Org.	238.4	312.0	364.3	
CMEA	–	–	–	
Other	64.0	85.0	91.3	
TOTAL DEBT SERVICE	***52.8***	***63.5***	***121.1***	
Paid to DAC Countries	23.8	26.2	75.4	
ODA	2.0	2.0	3.1	
Total Export Credits	9.0	9.3	26.6	
Other Private Market	12.8	14.9	45.7	
International Org.	24.8	31.3	39.0	
CMEA	–	–	–	
Other	4.2	6.0	6.6	
ECONOMIC INDICATORS				
GNP Curr. Prices, $M	1482.5	1740.5	2061.0	2414.5
Real GNP, 1976=100	108.0	115.0	122.0	124.0
GNP/Cap Curr. Prices,$	446.0	506.0	578.0	654.0
GNP/cap Atlas Basis, $	427.7	471.1	523.6	560.7
Real GNP/Cap, 1976=100	104.0	107.0	109.0	108.0
Population, Million	3.3	3.4	3.6	3.7
Curr.A/C Deficit(-),$M	-139.2	-170.2	-212.0	-333.8
BOP Exp. & Transf.,$M	597.6	710.8	859.6	961.8
Exp. to OECD CIF, $M	479.5	615.0	778.4	818.9
of which				
Manufact.	11.1	16.6	32.7	40.6
Imp. from OECD FOB, $M	367.3	435.5	497.5	590.5
Reserves ex. Gold, $M	179.8	184.4	209.2	149.8

	1977	1978	1979	1980	1977	1978	1979	1980
TOTAL RECEIPTS NET					**TOTAL ODA NET**			
DAC COUNTRIES								
Australia	3.8	19.7	28.5	19.5	0.0	0.0	0.0	0.1
Austria	0.0	0.5	0.0	0.1	0.0	0.0	0.0	0.1
Belgium	1.0	-7.4	-16.5	27.3	–	0.0	0.0	0.0
Canada	–	–	–	–	–	–	–	–
Denmark	–	–	–	1.8	–	–	–	–
Finland	-1.4	-1.2	-0.6	-0.2	–	–	–	–
France	0.0	62.7	1.2	36.6	–	–	–	0.4
Germany, Fed. Rep.	56.5	36.7	14.4	61.4	0.7	0.7	1.9	1.3
Italy	0.0	0.4	2.2	3.6	–	–	–	–
Japan	198.9	48.0	186.5	73.9	0.5	0.7	1.0	1.1
Netherlands	–	-8.8	0.0	-67.4	–	–	0.0	–
New Zealand	2.7	1.9	0.0	–	–	–	–	–
Norway	9.7	17.6	-0.4	0.5	–	–	–	–
Sweden	–	–	–	-2.8	–	–	–	–
Switzerland	0.8	16.5	1.4	-0.2	0.0	0.0	0.1	0.1
United Kingdom	10.2	59.2	692.4	689.2	0.8	0.5	0.1	0.5
United States	-15.0	-76.0	125.0	37.0	–	–	–	–
TOTAL	*267.0*	*169.8*	*1034.2*	*880.2*	*2.0*	*2.1*	*3.2*	*3.6*
MULTILATERAL								
AF.D.F.	–	–	–	–	–	–	–	–
AF.D.B.	–	–	–	–	–	–	–	–
AS.D.B.	-2.2	1.0	10.5	11.8	–	–	–	–
CAR.D.B.	–	–	–	–	–	–	–	–
E.E.C.	–	–	–	–	–	–	–	–
IBRD	–	–	–	–	–	–	–	–
IDA	–	–	–	–	–	–	–	–
I.D.B.	–	–	–	–	–	–	–	–
IFAD	–	–	–	–	–	–	–	–
I.F.C.	–	–	–	–	–	–	–	–
IMF TRUST FUND	–	–	–	–	–	–	–	–
U.N. AGENCIES	–	–	–	–	–	–	–	–
UNDP	–	0.1	0.1	0.1	–	0.1	0.1	0.1
UNTA	0.0	0.1	0.0	–	0.0	0.1	0.0	–
UNICEF	0.0	0.0	–	–	0.0	0.0	–	–
UNRWA	–	–	–	–	–	–	–	–
WFP	–	–	–	–	–	–	–	–
UNHCR	–	0.1	8.5	7.2	–	0.1	8.5	7.2
Other Multilateral	0.0	–	–	–	0.0	–	–	–
Arab OPEC Agencies	–	–	–	–	–	–	–	–
TOTAL	*-2.1*	*1.3*	*19.2*	*19.0*	*0.1*	*0.3*	*8.7*	*7.3*
OPEC COUNTRIES	–	–	–	–	–	–	–	–
E.E.C.+ MEMBERS	*67.6*	*142.8*	*693.8*	*752.5*	*1.4*	*1.2*	*2.0*	*2.3*
TOTAL	***264.8***	***171.1***	***1053.4***	***899.3***	***2.1***	***2.3***	***11.9***	***10.9***

	1977	1978	1979	1980	1977	1978	1979	1980
ODA LOANS GROSS					**ODA LOANS NET**			
DAC COUNTRIES								
Australia	–	–	–	–	–	–	–	–
Austria	–	–	–	–	–	–	–	–
Belgium	–	–	–	–	–	–	–	–
Canada	–	–	–	–	–	–	–	–
Denmark	–	–	–	–	–	–	–	–
Finland	–	–	–	–	–	–	–	–
France	–	–	–	–	–	–	–	–
Germany, Fed. Rep.	–	–	–	–	–	–	–	–
Italy	–	–	–	–	–	–	–	–
Japan	–	–	–	–	-0.1	-0.1	-0.1	-0.1
Netherlands	–	–	–	–	–	–	–	–
New Zealand	–	–	–	–	–	–	–	–
Norway	–	–	–	–	–	–	–	–
Sweden	–	–	–	–	–	–	–	–
Switzerland	–	–	–	–	–	–	–	–
United Kingdom	–	–	–	–	-0.1	-0.1	-0.3	-0.3
United States	–	–	–	–	–	–	–	–
TOTAL	–	–	–	–	*-0.2*	*-0.2*	*-0.4*	*-0.5*
MULTILATERAL	–	–	–	–	–	–	–	–
OPEC COUNTRIES	–	–	–	–	–	–	–	–
E.E.C.+ MEMBERS	–	–	–	–	*-0.1*	*-0.1*	*-0.3*	*-0.3*
TOTAL	–	–	–	–	***-0.2***	***-0.2***	***-0.4***	***-0.5***

	1977	1978	1979	1980	1977	1978	1979	1980
TOTAL OFFICIAL GROSS					**TOTAL OFFICIAL NET**			
DAC COUNTRIES								
Australia	0.0	0.0	1.0	0.1	0.0	0.0	1.0	-0.2
Austria	0.0	0.0	0.0	0.1	0.0	0.0	0.0	0.1
Belgium	–	0.0	0.0	0.0	–	0.0	0.0	0.0
Canada	–	–	–	–	–	–	–	–
Denmark	–	–	–	–	–	–	–	–
Finland	–	–	–	–	–	–	–	–
France	–	–	–	0.4	–	–	–	0.4
Germany, Fed. Rep.	0.7	0.7	1.9	1.3	0.7	0.7	1.9	1.3
Italy	–	–	–	–	–	–	–	–
Japan	0.6	0.8	1.1	1.2	0.5	0.7	1.0	1.1
Netherlands	–	–	0.0	–	–	–	0.0	–
New Zealand	4.4	–	–	–	1.6	–	–	–
Norway	–	–	–	–	–	–	–	–
Sweden	–	–	–	–	–	–	–	–
Switzerland	0.0	0.0	0.1	0.1	0.0	0.0	0.1	0.1
United Kingdom	0.9	0.6	0.4	0.9	0.8	0.5	0.1	0.5
United States	–	–	–	13.0	-4.0	-3.0	-5.0	9.0
TOTAL	*6.7*	*2.3*	*4.6*	*17.1*	*-0.4*	*-0.9*	*-0.8*	*12.4*
MULTILATERAL	*0.7*	*3.9*	*23.3*	*22.5*	*-2.1*	*1.3*	*19.2*	*19.0*
OPEC COUNTRIES	–	–	–	–	–	–	–	–
E.E.C.+ MEMBERS	*1.6*	*1.4*	*2.4*	*2.7*	*1.4*	*1.2*	*2.0*	*2.3*
TOTAL	***7.3***	***6.2***	***27.8***	***39.7***	***-2.5***	***0.4***	***18.4***	***31.4***

	19
TOTAL ODA GROSS	
Australia	
Austria	
Belgium	
Canada	
Denmark	
Finland	
France	
Germany, Fed. Rep.	
Italy	
Japan	
Netherlands	
New Zealand	
Norway	
Sweden	
Switzerland	
United Kingdom	
United States	
TOTAL	
AF.D.F.	
AF.D.B.	
AS.D.B.	
CAR.D.B.	
E.E.C.	
IBRD	
IDA	
I.D.B.	
IFAD	
I.F.C.	
IMF TRUST FUND	
U.N. AGENCIES	
UNDP	
UNTA	
UNICEF	
UNRWA	
WFP	
UNHCR	
Other Multilateral	
Arab OPEC Agencies	
TOTAL	
OPEC COUNTRIES	
E.E.C.+ MEMBERS	
TOTAL	
GRANTS	
Australia	
Austria	
Belgium	
Canada	
Denmark	
Finland	
France	
Germany, Fed. Rep.	
Italy	
Japan	
Netherlands	
New Zealand	
Norway	
Sweden	
Switzerland	
United Kingdom	
United States	
TOTAL	
MULTILATERAL	
OPEC COUNTRIES	
E.E.C.+ MEMBERS	
TOTAL	
TOTAL OOF GROSS	
Australia	
Austria	
Belgium	
Canada	
Denmark	
Finland	
France	
Germany, Fed. Rep.	
Italy	
Japan	
Netherlands	
New Zealand	
Norway	
Sweden	
Switzerland	
United Kingdom	
United States	
TOTAL	
MULTILATERAL	
OPEC COUNTRIES	
E.E.C.+ MEMBERS	
TOTAL	

1978	1979	1980	1977	1978	1979	1980
			ODA COMMITMENTS			
0.0	0.0	0.1	0.1	0.0	0.0	0.1
0.0	0.0	0.1	–	–	–	–
0.0	0.0	0.0	–	–	–	–
–	–	–	–	–	–	–
–	–	–	–	–	–	–
–	–	–	–	–	–	–
–	–	0.4	–	–	–	0.4
0.7	1.9	1.3	0.5	0.8	1.8	2.1
–	–	–	–	–	–	–
0.8	1.1	1.2	0.7	1.0	1.3	1.4
–	0.0	–	–	–	0.2	–
–	–	–	–	–	–	–
–	–	–	–	–	–	–
–	–	–	–	–	–	–
0.0	0.1	0.1	–	–	–	0.1
0.6	0.4	0.9	0.9	0.6	0.4	0.9
–	–	–	–	–	–	–
2.3	*3.7*	*4.1*	*2.2*	*2.4*	*3.7*	*4.9*
–	–	–	–	–	–	–
–	–	–	–	–	–	–
–	–	–	–	–	–	–
–	–	–	–	–	–	–
–	–	–	–	–	–	0.0
–	–	–	–	–	–	–
–	–	–	–	–	–	–
–	–	–	–	–	–	–
–	–	–	–	–	–	–
–	–	–	–	–	–	–
–	–	–	–	–	–	–
–	–	–	0.1	0.3	8.7	7.3
0.1	0.1	0.1	–	–	–	–
0.1	0.0	–	–	–	–	–
0.0	–	–	–	–	–	–
–	–	–	–	–	–	–
–	–	–	–	–	–	–
0.1	8.5	7.2	–	–	–	–
–	–	–	–	–	–	–
–	–	–	–	–	–	–
0.3	*8.7*	*7.3*	*0.1*	*0.3*	*8.7*	*7.3*
–	–	–	–	–	–	–
1.4	*2.4*	*2.7*	*1.4*	*1.4*	*2.3*	*3.4*
2.6	***12.3***	***11.4***	***2.2***	***2.7***	***12.3***	***12.2***
			TECH. COOP. GRANTS			
0.0	0.0	0.1	0.0	0.0	0.0	0.1
0.0	0.0	0.1	0.0	0.0	0.0	0.1
0.0	0.0	0.0	–	0.0	0.0	0.0
–	–	–	–	–	–	–
–	–	–	–	–	–	–
–	–	–	–	–	–	–
–	–	0.4	–	–	–	0.4
0.7	1.9	1.3	0.7	0.7	1.9	1.3
–	–	–	–	–	–	–
0.8	1.1	1.2	0.6	0.8	1.1	1.2
–	0.0	–	–	–	0.0	–
–	–	–	–	–	–	–
–	–	–	–	–	–	–
–	–	–	–	–	–	–
0.0	0.1	0.1	–	–	–	–
0.6	0.4	0.9	0.9	0.6	0.4	0.9
–	–	–	–	–	–	–
2.3	*3.7*	*4.1*	*2.2*	*2.3*	*3.5*	*4.0*
0.3	*8.7*	*7.3*	*0.1*	*0.3*	*8.7*	*7.3*
–	–	–	–	–	–	–
1.4	*2.4*	*2.7*	*1.6*	*1.4*	*2.4*	*2.6*
2.6	***12.3***	***11.4***	***2.3***	***2.5***	***12.2***	***11.3***
			TOTAL OOF NET			
–	0.9	–	–	–	0.9	-0.3
–	–	–	–	–	–	–
–	–	–	–	–	–	–
–	–	–	–	–	–	–
–	–	–	–	–	–	–
–	–	–	–	–	–	–
–	–	–	–	–	–	–
–	–	–	–	–	–	–
–	–	–	–	–	–	–
–	–	–	–	–	–	–
–	–	–	–	–	–	–
–	–	–	1.6	–	–	–
–	–	–	–	–	–	–
–	–	–	–	–	–	–
–	–	–	–	–	–	–
–	–	–	–	–	–	–
–	–	13.0	-4.0	-3.0	-5.0	9.0
–	*0.9*	*13.0*	*-2.4*	*-3.0*	*-4.1*	*8.7*
3.6	*14.6*	*15.3*	*-2.2*	*1.0*	*10.5*	*11.8*
–	–	–	–	–	–	–
–	–	–	–	–	–	–
3.6	***15.5***	***28.3***	***-4.6***	***-2.0***	***6.5***	***20.5***

MAIN AID AGGREGATES

	1977	1978	1979	1980
DAC COUNTRIES COMBINED				
PRIVATE SECTOR NET	267.4	170.8	1035.0	867.9
Direct Investment	144.5	252.0	342.1	362.9
Portfolio Invest.	35.9	-15.2	224.6	-177.4
Export Credits	86.9	-66.0	468.4	682.4
OFFICIAL & PRIVATE				
GROSS:				
Contractual Lending	302.0	176.4	683.6	894.8
Export Credits Tot.	302.0	176.4	683.6	894.8
Export Credits Priv	297.6	176.4	682.7	881.8
OTHER NET DATA				
Contractual Lending	84.3	-69.3	463.9	690.6
Export Credits Tot.	84.5	-69.0	464.3	691.1
(Bank Sector Loans)	–	–	–	342.0
ODA CONCESSIONALITY				
Total:Grant Element	100.0	100.0	100.0	100.0
Loans:Grant Element	–	–	–	–
OTHER SOURCES				
CMEA Countr.(Gross)	–	–	–	–
Intra LDCS Exc.OPEC	–	–	–	–
Other	–	–	–	–
ALL SOURCE COMMITMENTS				
TOTAL BILATERAL	6.6	3.3	3.7	80.1
of which				
OPEC (ODA)	–	–	–	–
CMEA (ODA)	–	–	–	–
TOTAL MULTILAT.(ODA)	0.1	0.3	8.7	7.3
TOTAL BIL.& MULTIL.	6.7	3.6	12.3	87.3
of which				
ODA Grants	2.2	2.7	12.3	12.2
ODA Loans	–	–	–	–
ODA CONCESSIONALITY				
Total: Grant Element	100.0	100.0	100.0	100.0
Loans: Grant Element	–	–	–	–

INDEBTEDNESS

	1977	1978	1979	1980
TOTAL DEBT DISBURSED	***826.1***	***1281.2***	***1868.7***	
Debt to DAC Countries	809.0	1263.0	1848.0	
ODA	3.0	3.0	3.0	
Total Export Credits	446.0	870.0	1321.0	
Other Private Market	360.0	390.0	524.0	
International Org.	17.1	18.2	20.7	
CMEA	–	–	–	
Other	–	–	–	
TOTAL DEBT SERVICE	***102.0***	***186.2***	***313.7***	
Paid to DAC Countries	97.7	181.7	308.4	
ODA	0.3	0.5	0.6	
Total Export Credits	38.3	145.9	232.3	
Other Private Market	59.1	35.3	75.5	
International Org.	4.3	4.5	5.3	
CMEA	–	–	–	
Other	–	–	–	

ECONOMIC INDICATORS

	1977	1978	1979	1980
GNP Curr. Prices, $M	13113.3	15220.4	18513.2	21758.4
Real GNP, 1976=100	110.0	121.0	131.0	143.0
GNP/Cap Curr. Prices,$	2809.0	3159.0	3728.0	4261.0
GNP/cap Atlas Basis, $	2780.6	3187.5	3643.4	4210.7
Real GNP/Cap, 1976=100	106.0	114.0	120.0	127.0
Population, Million	4.7	4.8	5.0	5.1
Curr.A/C Deficit(-),$M	–	–	–	–
BOP Exp. & Transf.,$M	–	–	–	–
Exp. to OECD CIF, $M	6736.2	8401.9	10599.8	12377.6
of which				
Manufact.	6233.4	7748.6	9726.7	11377.7
Imp. from OECD FOB, $M	5531.3	7663.8	9299.0	11437.6
Reserves ex. Gold, $M	–	–	–	–

	TOTAL RECEIPTS NET 1977	1978	1979	1980	TOTAL ODA NET 1977	1978	1979	1980
DAC COUNTRIES								
Australia	8.5	2.5	4.9	3.2	8.5	2.5	4.9	3.2
Austria	2.7	-8.4	-8.8	2.9	2.9	0.2	0.3	12.3
Belgium	0.3	0.8	14.3	-2.4	10.7	12.3	24.5	0.5
Canada	28.2	37.5	9.9	28.1	36.8	46.3	17.4	35.8
Denmark	13.0	21.3	17.2	25.2	14.0	22.3	17.9	25.8
Finland	-0.2	–	0.0	–	0.0	–	0.0	–
France	39.0	16.4	2.5	27.5	26.7	20.0	13.0	16.4
Germany, Fed. Rep.	5.5	72.0	57.8	46.9	14.9	91.2	92.2	34.6
Italy	33.3	-17.1	-11.7	25.3	20.2	-1.6	-1.3	-3.1
Japan	30.3	58.5	39.5	37.9	28.8	44.8	42.2	37.4
Netherlands	71.3	79.0	90.6	144.8	71.3	79.0	90.6	144.8
New Zealand	0.5	0.7	0.4	0.3	0.5	0.7	0.4	0.3
Norway	15.1	18.5	21.4	26.0	15.2	21.2	22.1	22.4
Sweden	49.2	51.4	73.1	62.3	55.3	52.0	73.3	69.5
Switzerland	13.0	-32.5	18.4	-13.6	4.9	9.0	19.5	16.6
United Kingdom	106.6	209.8	284.6	196.6	106.9	187.2	258.1	133.9
United States	-31.0	21.0	15.0	170.0	64.0	83.0	94.0	83.0
TOTAL	*385.1*	*531.5*	*629.0*	*780.9*	*481.6*	*670.2*	*769.0*	*633.4*
MULTILATERAL								
AF.D.F.	–	–	–	–	–	–	–	–
AF.D.B.	–	–	–	–	–	–	–	–
AS.D.B.	–	–	–	–	–	–	–	–
CAR.D.B.	–	–	–	–	–	–	–	–
E.E.C.	35.9	27.7	34.7	85.5	35.9	27.7	34.7	85.5
IBRD	36.3	123.6	76.4	116.9	–	12.5	18.1	25.9
IDA	352.1	303.3	422.3	609.1	352.1	303.3	422.3	609.1
I.D.B.	–	–	–	–	–	–	–	–
IFAD	–	–	–	9.2	–	–	–	9.2
I.F.C.	3.1	2.7	-0.4	-1.5	–	–	–	–
IMF TRUST FUND	–	–	–	684.0	–	–	–	684.0
U.N. AGENCIES	–	–	–	–	–	–	–	–
UNDP	16.2	21.7	26.8	23.9	16.2	21.7	26.8	23.9
UNTA	2.7	3.5	3.2	0.3	2.7	3.5	3.2	0.3
UNICEF	13.5	18.9	28.7	32.6	13.5	18.9	28.7	32.6
UNRWA	–	–	–	–	–	–	–	–
WFP	38.9	44.0	37.9	40.7	38.9	44.0	37.9	40.7
UNHCR	–	–	–	0.0	–	–	–	0.0
Other Multilateral	9.5	4.0	6.1	8.3	9.5	4.0	6.1	8.3
Arab OPEC Agencies	21.8	14.0	–	2.4	21.8	14.0	–	2.4
TOTAL	*530.0*	*563.3*	*635.7*	*1611.3*	*490.6*	*449.5*	*577.8*	*1521.7*
OPEC COUNTRIES	*133.8*	*218.9*	*23.4*	*101.1*	*133.8*	*218.9*	*23.4*	*101.1*
E.E.C.+ MEMBERS	*304.8*	*410.0*	*490.1*	*549.3*	*300.6*	*438.2*	*529.7*	*438.4*
TOTAL	***1048.9***	***1313.7***	***1288.2***	***2493.3***	***1105.9***	***1338.6***	***1370.1***	***2256.2***

	ODA LOANS GROSS 1977	1978	1979	1980	ODA LOANS NET 1977	1978	1979	1980
DAC COUNTRIES								
Australia	–	–	–	–	–	–	–	–
Austria	2.7	–	–	12.0	2.7	–	–	12.0
Belgium	10.5	11.9	23.9	–	9.9	11.3	23.0	-1.2
Canada	20.6	29.1	15.1	21.8	19.2	26.8	12.1	17.8
Denmark	4.2	4.2	4.1	7.5	4.2	4.2	2.7	5.8
Finland	–	–	–	–	–	–	–	–
France	31.5	26.7	21.6	21.8	26.7	20.0	13.0	14.2
Germany, Fed. Rep.	75.9	157.1	167.0	110.5	-6.6	63.1	60.7	5.0
Italy	21.8	–	–	–	20.1	-1.6	-1.8	-3.2
Japan	68.1	103.1	78.4	69.3	26.5	42.6	21.5	9.5
Netherlands	44.7	71.9	83.1	102.9	40.5	67.1	76.1	94.8
New Zealand	–	–	–	–	–	–	–	–
Norway	–	–	–	–	–	–	–	–
Sweden	2.9	0.8	–	–	2.4	-117.2	–	–
Switzerland	1.4	2.8	2.6	0.1	-30.1	2.8	2.6	0.1
United Kingdom	10.1	14.5	18.2	3.3	-22.3	-26.5	-49.1	-63.0
United States	25.0	26.0	1.0	32.0	-34.0	-45.0	-97.0	-54.0
TOTAL	*319.5*	*448.1*	*414.9*	*381.0*	*59.2*	*47.6*	*63.7*	*37.7*
MULTILATERAL	*384.2*	*340.4*	*452.5*	*1345.0*	*373.9*	*329.8*	*440.4*	*1330.5*
OPEC COUNTRIES	*133.7*	*218.9*	*45.0*	*140.4*	*133.7*	*218.9*	*23.4*	*90.0*
E.E.C.+ MEMBERS	*198.8*	*286.3*	*317.8*	*245.9*	*72.6*	*137.6*	*124.6*	*52.3*
TOTAL	***837.4***	***1007.5***	***912.4***	***1866.4***	***566.8***	***596.3***	***527.5***	***1458.2***

	TOTAL OFFICIAL GROSS 1977	1978	1979	1980	TOTAL OFFICIAL NET 1977	1978	1979	1980
DAC COUNTRIES								
Australia	8.5	2.5	4.9	3.2	8.5	2.5	4.9	3.2
Austria	2.9	0.2	0.3	12.3	2.7	-8.2	-8.6	3.1
Belgium	11.2	12.9	25.4	1.7	10.7	12.3	24.5	0.5
Canada	38.4	48.6	20.4	39.7	28.2	37.5	9.9	28.1
Denmark	14.0	22.3	19.4	27.5	14.0	22.3	17.9	25.8
Finland	0.0	–	0.0	–	0.0	–	0.0	–
France	31.5	26.7	21.6	24.0	26.7	20.0	13.0	16.4
Germany, Fed. Rep.	103.9	186.0	198.5	147.0	8.1	78.7	82.5	33.4
Italy	21.9	–	0.5	0.2	19.4	-2.4	-1.7	-3.1
Japan	70.5	105.3	99.2	97.2	28.8	44.8	42.2	37.4
Netherlands	75.5	83.8	97.6	152.9	71.3	79.0	90.6	144.8
New Zealand	0.5	0.7	0.4	0.3	0.5	0.7	0.4	0.3
Norway	15.2	21.2	22.1	22.4	15.2	21.2	22.1	22.4
Sweden	55.8	169.9	73.3	69.5	55.3	52.0	73.3	69.5
Switzerland	36.3	9.0	19.5	16.6	4.9	9.0	19.5	16.6
United Kingdom	139.4	228.2	325.3	200.2	106.9	187.2	258.1	133.9
United States	123.0	154.0	192.0	237.0	33.0	56.0	83.0	144.0
TOTAL	*748.6*	*1071.4*	*1120.2*	*1051.6*	*434.2*	*612.5*	*731.4*	*676.2*
MULTILATERAL	*608.2*	*648.0*	*724.9*	*1708.4*	*530.0*	*563.3*	*635.7*	*1611.3*
OPEC COUNTRIES	*133.8*	*218.9*	*45.0*	*151.5*	*133.8*	*218.9*	*23.4*	*101.1*
E.E.C.+ MEMBERS	*433.2*	*587.6*	*723.0*	*638.9*	*293.0*	*424.8*	*519.7*	*437.2*
TOTAL	***1490.6***	***1938.4***	***1890.1***	***2911.5***	***1098.0***	***1394.8***	***1390.5***	***2388.6***

TOTAL ODA GROSS

	197
Australia	8
Austria	2
Belgium	11.
Canada	38
Denmark	14
Finland	0
France	31
Germany, Fed. Rep.	97
Italy	21
Japan	70
Netherlands	75
New Zealand	0
Norway	15
Sweden	55
Switzerland	36
United Kingdom	139
United States	123
TOTAL	*741*
AF.D.F.	
AF.D.B.	
AS.D.B.	
CAR.D.B.	
E.E.C.	35
IBRD	
IDA	362
I.D.B.	
IFAD	
I.F.C.	
IMF TRUST FUND	
U.N. AGENCIES	
UNDP	16
UNTA	2
UNICEF	13
UNRWA	
WFP	38
UNHCR	
Other Multilateral	9
Arab OPEC Agencies	2
TOTAL	*50*
OPEC COUNTRIES	*13.*
E.E.C.+ MEMBERS	*42*
TOTAL	***137***

GRANTS

Australia	[illegible]
Austria	[illegible]
Belgium	[illegible]
Canada	1
Denmark	[illegible]
Finland	[illegible]
France	
Germany, Fed. Rep.	2
Italy	[illegible]
Japan	[illegible]
Netherlands	3
New Zealand	[illegible]
Norway	1
Sweden	5
Switzerland	3
United Kingdom	12
United States	9
TOTAL	*42*
MULTILATERAL	*11*
OPEC COUNTRIES	[illegible]
E.E.C.+ MEMBERS	*22*
TOTAL	***53***

TOTAL OOF GROSS

Australia	
Austria	
Belgium	
Canada	
Denmark	
Finland	
France	
Germany, Fed. Rep.	
Italy	
Japan	
Netherlands	
New Zealand	
Norway	
Sweden	
Switzerland	
United Kingdom	
United States	
TOTAL	
MULTILATERAL	*10*
OPEC COUNTRIES	
E.E.C.+ MEMBERS	
TOTAL	***11***

ODA COMMITMENTS

1978	1979	1980	1977	1978	1979	1980
2.5	4.9	3.2	5.9	6.9	2.1	4.5
0.2	0.3	12.3	1.4	–	9.5	–
12.9	25.4	1.7	10.5	11.1	13.9	2.1
48.6	20.4	39.7	63.1	30.5	33.4	45.5
22.3	19.4	27.5	30.5	27.1	1.4	36.3
–	0.0	–	–	–	0.0	–
26.7	21.6	24.0	47.0	6.8	–	72.8
185.2	198.5	140.1	140.6	159.4	201.5	268.8
–	0.5	0.2	0.1	–	0.5	0.2
105.3	99.2	97.2	147.8	99.5	26.3	98.5
83.8	97.6	152.9	103.1	110.9	128.6	155.1
0.7	0.4	0.3	0.5	0.7	0.1	0.7
21.2	22.1	22.4	12.9	35.1	17.4	12.6
169.9	73.3	69.5	57.3	183.9	135.6	5.1
9.0	19.5	16.6	34.7	4.1	31.9	4.6
228.2	325.3	200.2	205.8	289.2	460.4	284.2
154.0	192.0	169.0	126.1	196.2	214.6	305.6
1070.7	*1120.2*	*976.7*	*987.1*	*1161.6*	*1277.2*	*1296.5*
–	–	–	–	–	–	–
–	–	–	–	–	–	–
–	–	–	–	–	–	–
–	–	–	–	–	–	–
27.7	34.7	85.5	17.5	64.3	116.3	91.8
12.5	18.1	25.9	14.0	–	–	–
313.9	434.4	623.5	821.7	999.0	1083.6	1174.4
–	–	–	–	–	–	–
–	–	9.2	–	–	107.0	17.0
–	–	–	–	–	–	–
–	–	684.0	–	–	–	–
–	–	–	80.8	92.0	102.6	105.8
21.7	26.8	23.9	–	–	–	–
3.5	3.2	0.3	–	–	–	–
18.9	28.7	32.6	–	–	–	–
–	–	–	–	–	–	–
44.0	37.9	40.7	–	–	–	–
–	–	0.0	–	–	–	–
4.0	6.1	8.3	–	–	–	–
14.0	–	2.4	35.8	–	20.0	20.0
460.2	*589.8*	*1536.2*	*969.8*	*1155.3*	*1429.5*	*1408.9*
218.9	*45.0*	*151.5*	*185.2*	*34.2*	–	*117.4*
586.9	*723.0*	*632.0*	*555.0*	*668.9*	*922.5*	*911.3*
1749.8	***1755.0***	***2664.4***	***2142.1***	***2351.1***	***2706.8***	***2822.9***

TECH. COOP. GRANTS

1978	1979	1980	1977	1978	1979	1980
2.5	4.9	3.2	0.7	0.4	0.4	0.5
0.2	0.3	0.4	0.2	0.2	0.3	0.4
1.0	1.6	1.7	0.2	0.5	0.7	0.6
19.6	5.3	18.0	0.5	0.3	0.2	0.4
18.1	15.2	20.0	5.0	11.2	5.6	15.3
–	0.0	–	0.0	–	0.0	–
–	–	2.2	–	–	–	2.2
28.1	31.5	29.6	20.7	27.6	31.5	29.5
–	0.5	0.2	0.0	–	0.5	0.2
2.2	20.7	27.9	1.2	1.7	2.1	2.1
11.9	14.5	50.0	6.6	4.6	4.6	10.8
0.7	0.4	0.3	0.2	0.6	0.2	0.3
21.2	22.1	22.4	0.8	0.7	0.5	0.8
169.2	73.3	69.5	2.8	4.0	3.4	4.9
6.2	16.9	16.5	–	–	0.1	0.8
213.7	307.1	196.9	3.9	9.4	10.7	17.7
128.0	191.0	137.0	–	–	–	–
622.6	*705.3*	*595.7*	*42.6*	*61.1*	*60.9*	*86.4*
119.7	*137.3*	*191.2*	*41.8*	*48.0*	*64.8*	*105.8*
–	–	*11.1*	–	–	–	–
300.6	*405.2*	*386.1*	*36.3*	*53.2*	*53.6*	*76.2*
742.3	***842.6***	***798.1***	***84.4***	***109.1***	***125.6***	***192.1***

TOTAL OOF NET

1978	1979	1980	1977	1978	1979	1980
–	–	–	–	–	–	–
–	–	–	-0.2	-8.4	-8.9	-9.2
–	–	–	–	–	–	–
–	–	–	-8.6	-8.8	-7.6	-7.7
–	–	–	–	–	–	–
–	–	–	–	–	–	–
–	–	–	–	–	–	–
0.7	–	6.9	-6.8	-12.6	-9.7	-1.2
–	–	–	-0.8	-0.8	-0.4	–
–	–	–	–	–	–	–
–	–	–	–	–	–	–
–	–	–	–	–	–	–
–	–	–	–	–	–	–
–	–	–	–	–	–	–
–	–	–	–	–	–	–
–	–	–	–	–	–	–
–	–	68.0	-31.0	-27.0	-11.0	61.0
0.7	–	*74.9*	*-47.3*	*-57.6*	*-37.6*	*42.8*
187.9	*135.1*	*172.2*	*39.4*	*113.8*	*58.0*	*89.5*
–	–	–	–	–	–	–
0.7	–	*6.9*	*-7.5*	*-13.4*	*-10.1*	*-1.2*
188.6	***135.1***	***247.1***	***-7.9***	***56.2***	***20.4***	***132.4***

MAIN AID AGGREGATES

	1977	1978	1979	1980
DAC COUNTRIES COMBINED				
PRIVATE SECTOR NET	-49.1	-81.0	-102.4	104.7
Direct Investment	-36.1	18.1	48.6	55.2
Portfolio Invest.	-29.4	-33.0	-85.5	-17.1
Export Credits	16.4	-66.1	-65.5	66.6
OFFICIAL & PRIVATE				
GROSS:				
Contractual Lending	496.0	551.9	458.7	665.7
Export Credits Tot.	176.5	103.8	43.8	284.7
Export Credits Priv	169.8	103.1	43.8	209.8
OTHER NET DATA				
Contractual Lending	28.2	-76.1	-39.3	147.1
Export Credits Tot.	-22.7	-115.1	-98.0	112.5
(Bank Sector Loans)	-11.0	10.0	55.0	-33.0
ODA CONCESSIONALITY				
Total:Grant Element	83.0	90.0	92.0	85.0
Loans:Grant Element	65.0	71.0	75.0	72.0
OTHER SOURCES				
CMEA Countr.(Gross)	40.6	39.2	28.0	30.0
Intra LDCS Exc.OPEC	–	–	–	–
Other	–	–	–	–
ALL SOURCE COMMITMENTS				
TOTAL BILATERAL	1172.3	1195.7	1327.2	1482.1
of which				
OPEC (ODA)	185.2	34.2	–	117.4
CMEA (ODA)	340.9	1.0	166.0	807.3
TOTAL MULTILAT.(ODA)	969.8	1155.3	1429.5	1409.0
TOTAL BIL.& MULTIL.	2142.1	2351.1	2756.8	2891.0
of which				
ODA Grants	619.1	907.2	1131.2	843.0
ODA Loans	1523.0	1443.8	1575.5	1979.8
ODA CONCESSIONALITY				
Total: Grant Element	79.0	86.0	89.0	84.0
Loans: Grant Element	69.0	79.0	80.0	78.0

INDEBTEDNESS

	1977	1978	1979	1980
TOTAL DEBT DISBURSED	***14943.1***	***15862.1***	***16569.3***	
Debt to DAC Countries	9134.0	9548.0	9617.0	
ODA	8105.0	8770.0	8831.0	
Total Export Credits	892.0	603.0	524.0	
Other Private Market	137.0	175.0	262.0	
International Org.	4217.6	4654.4	5269.0	
CMEA	333.0	308.4	302.6	
Other	1258.4	1351.4	1380.7	
TOTAL DEBT SERVICE	***939.2***	***1058.1***	***1098.9***	
Paid to DAC Countries	694.7	752.2	763.3	
ODA	365.9	466.1	550.3	
Total Export Credits	322.7	268.7	176.9	
Other Private Market	6.1	17.4	36.1	
International Org.	141.5	164.5	173.5	
CMEA	74.1	65.8	60.4	
Other	28.9	75.6	101.6	

ECONOMIC INDICATORS

	1977	1978	1979	1980
GNP Curr. Prices, $M	105091.6	118902.4	133765.4	173305.3
Real GNP, 1976=100	108.0	115.0	110.0	118.0
GNP/Cap Curr. Prices,$	165.0	183.0	202.0	257.0
GNP/cap Atlas Basis, $	180.8	203.3	205.9	236.8
Real GNP/Cap, 1976=100	105.0	110.0	103.0	109.0
Population, Million	633.2	646.2	659.6	673.2
Curr.A/C Deficit(-),$M	1739.0	210.0	–	–
BOP Exp. & Transf.,$M	8768.0	9662.0	–	–
Exp. to OECD CIF, $M	3861.6	4292.0	5122.8	5165.1
of which				
Manufact.	1508.0	1887.8	2481.3	2612.9
Imp. from OECD FOB, $M	3302.1	4700.6	5345.5	6541.7
Reserves ex. Gold, $M	4872.0	6426.0	7432.0	6944.0

TOTAL RECEIPTS NET

	1977	1978	1979	1980
DAC COUNTRIES				
Australia	60.4	58.9	43.5	52.7
Austria	-0.3	-0.7	-0.8	65.4
Belgium	14.9	-5.0	-6.0	84.5
Canada	80.8	55.1	9.4	43.0
Denmark	3.4	–	-3.1	-10.4
Finland	–	0.0	0.2	0.5
France	103.1	-17.9	-101.9	76.7
Germany, Fed. Rep.	83.9	44.5	-26.2	20.7
Italy	10.0	-6.3	2.3	24.2
Japan	348.5	646.3	143.4	541.3
Netherlands	51.6	42.4	64.1	50.6
New Zealand	2.8	3.5	2.8	3.1
Norway	7.7	2.4	1.4	3.5
Sweden	–	43.0	–	0.3
Switzerland	3.3	12.0	37.7	51.1
United Kingdom	19.6	5.9	67.5	34.8
United States	-203.0	299.0	-106.0	267.0
TOTAL	*586.7*	*1183.2*	*128.3*	*1309.2*
MULTILATERAL				
AF.D.F.	–	–	–	–
AF.D.B.	–	–	–	–
AS.D.B.	28.7	16.6	44.8	53.0
CAR.D.B.	–	–	–	–
E.E.C.	2.7	2.2	1.3	1.4
IBRD	189.2	161.2	175.6	300.6
IDA	48.9	29.5	29.4	40.4
I.D.B.	–	–	–	–
IFAD	–	–	–	–
I.F.C.	-0.5	-4.5	-5.2	-3.8
IMF TRUST FUND	–	–	–	–
U.N. AGENCIES	–	–	–	–
UNDP	7.6	12.5	10.9	13.0
UNTA	2.2	2.4	2.1	0.4
UNICEF	3.0	4.2	7.1	10.8
UNRWA	–	–	–	–
WFP	6.0	6.8	12.2	4.6
UNHCR	–	–	16.7	9.6
Other Multilateral	4.1	4.3	1.9	9.7
Arab OPEC Agencies	–	–	–	–
TOTAL	*291.8*	*235.0*	*296.8*	*439.7*
OPEC COUNTRIES	*29.3*	*28.4*	*5.0*	*11.0*
E.E.C.+ MEMBERS	*289.1*	*65.8*	*-2.1*	*282.5*
TOTAL	**907.8**	**1446.6**	**430.1**	**1759.8**

TOTAL ODA NET

	1977	1978	1979	1980
Australia	26.7	36.0	44.2	48.1
Austria	0.6	0.4	0.4	66.6
Belgium	14.0	4.9	16.2	20.6
Canada	11.8	14.4	8.8	14.4
Denmark	-0.4	-0.2	0.2	0.1
Finland	–	0.0	0.2	0.5
France	12.7	30.7	24.8	43.5
Germany, Fed. Rep.	24.5	26.1	30.0	65.6
Italy	-1.7	-2.2	-1.4	3.3
Japan	148.4	227.6	226.9	350.0
Netherlands	44.3	43.1	75.8	85.4
New Zealand	2.7	2.8	2.8	3.1
Norway	3.5	2.7	1.5	3.7
Sweden	–	–	–	0.3
Switzerland	1.2	1.4	1.9	3.6
United Kingdom	8.7	11.3	18.7	18.4
United States	102.0	142.0	181.0	117.0
TOTAL	*398.9*	*541.0*	*631.8*	*844.2*
AF.D.F.	–	–	–	–
AF.D.B.	–	–	–	–
AS.D.B.	13.0	5.1	2.5	4.4
CAR.D.B.	–	–	–	–
E.E.C.	2.7	2.2	1.3	1.4
IBRD	–			–
IDA	48.9	29.5	29.4	40.4
I.D.B.	–	–	–	–
IFAD	–	–	–	–
I.F.C.	–	–	–	–
IMF TRUST FUND	–	–	–	–
U.N. AGENCIES	–	–	–	–
UNDP	7.6	12.5	10.9	13.0
UNTA	2.2	2.4	2.1	0.4
UNICEF	3.0	4.2	7.1	10.8
UNRWA	–	–	–	–
WFP	6.0	6.8	12.2	4.6
UNHCR	–	–	16.7	9.6
Other Multilateral	4.1	4.3	1.9	9.7
Arab OPEC Agencies	–	–	–	–
TOTAL	*87.4*	*66.9*	*84.1*	*94.3*
OPEC COUNTRIES	*29.3*	*27.4*	*5.0*	*11.0*
E.E.C.+ MEMBERS	*104.7*	*115.9*	*165.4*	*238.2*
TOTAL	**515.5**	**635.3**	**720.8**	**949.5**

TOTAL ODA GROSS

	197
Australia	26.
Austria	0.
Belgium	14.
Canada	11.
Denmark	0
Finland	
France	16
Germany, Fed. Rep.	39
Italy	3
Japan	177
Netherlands	47
New Zealand	2.
Norway	3
Sweden	
Switzerland	13
United Kingdom	9
United States	115
TOTAL	*481*
AF.D.F.	
AF.D.B.	
AS.D.B.	13
CAR.D.B.	
E.E.C.	2
IBRD	
IDA	48
I.D.B.	
IFAD	
I.F.C.	
IMF TRUST FUND	
U.N. AGENCIES	
UNDP	7
UNTA	2
UNICEF	3
UNRWA	
WFP	6
UNHCR	
Other Multilateral	4
Arab OPEC Agencies	
TOTAL	*87*
OPEC COUNTRIES	*29*
E.E.C.+ MEMBERS	*133*
TOTAL	**598**

ODA LOANS GROSS

	1977	1978	1979	1980
DAC COUNTRIES				
Australia	–	–	–	–
Austria	0.1	–	–	66.3
Belgium	9.1	–	11.1	14.5
Canada	5.5	10.7	5.7	11.3
Denmark	–	–	–	–
Finland	–	–	–	–
France	16.2	34.6	27.2	43.5
Germany, Fed. Rep.	22.5	26.4	23.5	59.4
Italy	–	–	–	9.3
Japan	153.1	237.5	242.3	366.9
Netherlands	30.8	25.1	28.3	66.0
New Zealand	–	–	–	–
Norway	–	–	–	–
Sweden	–	–	–	–
Switzerland	–	–	–	–
United Kingdom	4.3	0.7	1.8	0.3
United States	105.0	148.0	181.0	111.0
TOTAL	*346.6*	*483.0*	*520.8*	*748.5*
MULTILATERAL	*61.2*	*35.7*	*34.4*	*47.9*
OPEC COUNTRIES	*29.3*	*27.4*	*5.0*	*15.3*
E.E.C.+ MEMBERS	*82.9*	*86.8*	*91.8*	*193.0*
TOTAL	**437.0**	**546.1**	**560.2**	**811.7**

ODA LOANS NET

	1977	1978	1979	1980
Australia	–	–	–	–
Austria	0.1	–	–	66.3
Belgium	8.9	-0.1	10.7	13.8
Canada	5.5	10.7	5.7	11.3
Denmark	-0.5	-0.3	-0.3	-0.3
Finland	–	–	–	–
France	12.0	29.8	22.5	38.1
Germany, Fed. Rep.	8.0	8.4	3.5	38.4
Italy	-5.2	-2.3	-2.9	3.1
Japan	124.2	188.3	183.3	290.8
Netherlands	27.2	21.6	22.6	59.3
New Zealand	–	–	–	–
Norway	–	–	–	–
Sweden	–	–	–	–
Switzerland	-12.1	–	–	–
United Kingdom	3.5	-0.2	-1.5	-3.5
United States	92.0	126.0	159.0	82.0
TOTAL	*263.7*	*381.8*	*402.6*	*599.3*
MULTILATERAL	*61.1*	*34.6*	*31.9*	*43.7*
OPEC COUNTRIES	*29.3*	*27.4*	*5.0*	*10.4*
E.E.C.+ MEMBERS	*54.0*	*56.8*	*54.6*	*148.9*
TOTAL	**354.0**	**443.8**	**439.5**	**653.4**

GRANTS

	197
Australia	26
Austria	0
Belgium	5
Canada	6
Denmark	0
Finland	
France	0
Germany, Fed. Rep.	16
Italy	3
Japan	24
Netherlands	17
New Zealand	2
Norway	3
Sweden	
Switzerland	13
United Kingdom	5
United States	10
TOTAL	*13*
MULTILATERAL	*26*
OPEC COUNTRIES	
E.E.C.+ MEMBERS	*50*
TOTAL	**161**

TOTAL OFFICIAL GROSS

	1977	1978	1979	1980
DAC COUNTRIES				
Australia	26.7	62.9	48.2	53.0
Austria	0.6	0.4	0.4	66.6
Belgium	14.1	5.1	16.6	21.3
Canada	84.5	58.3	19.3	59.5
Denmark	0.1	0.1	0.5	0.5
Finland	–	0.0	0.2	0.5
France	18.0	38.5	37.7	51.4
Germany, Fed. Rep.	48.4	117.0	57.9	100.5
Italy	3.6	0.1	1.5	9.5
Japan	177.3	276.8	285.9	426.1
Netherlands	48.4	46.8	83.4	93.0
New Zealand	2.8	2.8	2.8	3.1
Norway	3.5	2.7	1.5	3.7
Sweden	–	–	–	0.3
Switzerland	13.3	1.4	1.9	3.6
United Kingdom	9.7	12.6	27.9	26.0
United States	198.0	200.0	208.0	149.0
TOTAL	*648.8*	*825.5*	*793.4*	*1067.6*
MULTILATERAL	*298.2*	*248.7*	*330.2*	*482.9*
OPEC COUNTRIES	*29.3*	*28.4*	*5.0*	*16.0*
E.E.C.+ MEMBERS	*144.9*	*222.4*	*226.6*	*303.5*
TOTAL	**976.3**	**1102.6**	**1128.6**	**1566.4**

TOTAL OFFICIAL NET

	1977	1978	1979	1980
Australia	26.7	62.3	45.1	48.4
Austria	0.6	0.4	0.4	66.6
Belgium	14.0	4.9	16.2	20.6
Canada	80.8	55.1	9.4	43.0
Denmark	-0.4	-0.2	0.2	0.2
Finland	–	0.0	0.2	0.5
France	13.8	33.7	33.0	46.0
Germany, Fed. Rep.	27.4	87.3	7.7	66.0
Italy	-1.7	-2.2	-1.4	3.3
Japan	148.4	227.6	226.9	350.0
Netherlands	43.7	40.6	76.6	85.8
New Zealand	2.8	2.8	2.8	3.1
Norway	3.5	2.7	1.5	3.7
Sweden	–	–	–	0.3
Switzerland	1.2	1.4	1.9	3.6
United Kingdom	8.2	11.6	24.0	20.6
United States	147.0	151.0	161.0	109.0
TOTAL	*516.0*	*678.9*	*605.2*	*870.7*
MULTILATERAL	*291.8*	*235.0*	*296.8*	*439.7*
OPEC COUNTRIES	*29.3*	*28.4*	*5.0*	*11.0*
E.E.C.+ MEMBERS	*107.7*	*177.9*	*157.3*	*243.8*
TOTAL	**837.0**	**942.4**	**906.9**	**1321.3**

TOTAL OOF GROSS

	197
Australia	
Austria	
Belgium	
Canada	7
Denmark	
Finland	
France	
Germany, Fed. Rep.	[illegible]
Italy	
Japan	
Netherlands	[illegible]
New Zealand	[illegible]
Norway	
Sweden	
Switzerland	
United Kingdom	[illegible]
United States	83
TOTAL	*16*
MULTILATERAL	*21*
OPEC COUNTRIES	
E.E.C.+ MEMBERS	*1*
TOTAL	**37**

1978	1979	1980	1977	1978	1979	1980
			ODA COMMITMENTS			
36.0	44.2	48.1	40.1	21.4	64.2	59.7
0.4	0.4	66.6	–	0.1	–	66.3
5.1	16.6	21.3	16.1	17.5	17.3	11.7
14.4	8.8	14.4	18.4	59.7	21.2	12.3
0.1	0.5	0.4	0.1	0.4	9.8	0.3
0.0	0.2	0.5	–	0.1	0.6	0.2
35.5	29.5	48.9	26.8	17.2	66.3	101.6
44.1	50.0	86.7	82.4	104.7	236.5	213.2
0.1	1.5	9.5	3.6	0.1	1.5	12.4
276.8	285.9	426.1	441.7	276.7	661.7	590.2
46.6	81.5	92.1	57.8	30.5	129.6	158.2
2.8	2.8	3.1	3.1	3.9	9.7	5.2
2.7	1.5	3.7	–	–	1.1	0.1
–	–	0.3	–	–	–	–
1.4	1.9	3.6	13.5	0.5	1.9	3.0
12.2	21.9	22.2	31.5	10.6	31.4	14.5
164.0	203.0	146.0	193.0	189.8	172.4	234.5
642.2	*750.0*	*993.4*	*928.0*	*733.2*	*1425.1*	*1483.3*
–	–	–	–	–	–	–
–	–	–	–	–	–	–
6.3	4.6	7.3	–	25.2	25.7	–
–	–	–	–	–	–	–
2.2	1.3	1.4	3.9	8.0	15.0	12.8
–	–	–	–	–	–	–
29.5	29.8	41.7	-0.6	118.9	89.0	162.0
–	–	–	–	–	–	–
–	–	–	–	–	–	26.5
–	–	–	–	–	–	–
–	–	–	–	–	–	–
–	–	–	22.8	30.1	50.9	48.1
12.5	10.9	13.0	–	–	–	–
2.4	2.1	0.4	–	–	–	–
4.2	7.1	10.8	–	–	–	–
–	–	–	–	–	–	–
6.8	12.2	4.6	–	–	–	–
–	16.7	9.6	–	–	–	–
4.3	1.9	9.7	–	–	–	–
–	–	–	–	–	10.3	–
68.1	*86.6*	*98.4*	*26.1*	*182.2*	*190.9*	*249.4*
27.4	*5.0*	*16.0*	*95.4*	–	*18.1*	*0.6*
145.9	*202.6*	*282.4*	*222.2*	*189.0*	*507.3*	*524.7*
737.7	***841.6***	***1107.8***	***1049.5***	***915.4***	***1634.1***	***1733.3***
			TECH. COOP. GRANTS			
36.0	44.2	48.1	10.7	11.8	8.4	13.7
0.4	0.4	0.3	0.6	0.4	0.4	0.3
5.1	5.5	6.7	1.8	2.5	3.0	2.5
3.7	3.1	3.1	0.2	0.3	0.3	0.5
0.1	0.5	0.4	0.1	0.1	0.5	0.4
0.0	0.2	0.5	–	0.0	0.2	0.5
0.9	2.3	5.4	–	0.0	–	5.4
17.7	26.5	27.2	16.5	17.6	24.8	27.2
0.1	1.5	0.2	0.4	0.1	0.7	0.2
39.3	43.6	59.2	16.1	25.0	23.7	32.7
21.5	53.2	26.1	15.0	20.1	19.0	23.7
2.8	2.8	3.1	0.7	1.5	2.3	1.7
2.7	1.5	3.7	0.1	0.1	0.1	0.1
–	–	0.3	–	–	–	–
1.4	1.9	3.6	0.0	0.1	0.1	1.0
11.5	20.2	21.9	5.2	7.3	9.3	10.8
16.0	22.0	35.0	5.0	9.0	13.0	23.0
159.2	*229.2*	*244.9*	*72.3*	*96.1*	*105.5*	*143.7*
32.3	*52.2*	*50.6*	*17.7*	*23.3*	*38.7*	*48.1*
–	–	*0.6*	–	–	–	–
59.1	*110.8*	*89.4*	*38.9*	*47.9*	*57.2*	*70.2*
191.5	***281.4***	***296.1***	***90.0***	***119.4***	***144.2***	***191.8***
			TOTAL OOF NET			
26.9	4.0	4.9	–	26.3	0.9	0.3
–	–	–	–	–	–	–
–	–	–	–	–	–	–
43.9	10.5	45.1	69.1	40.7	0.6	28.5
–	–	0.1	–	–	–	0.1
–	–	–	–	–	–	–
3.0	8.2	2.5	1.1	3.0	8.2	2.5
72.9	7.9	13.9	2.9	61.3	-22.3	0.4
–	–	–	–	–	–	–
–	–	–	–	–	–	–
0.2	1.9	0.9	-0.5	-2.5	0.8	0.4
–	–	–	0.1	–	–	–
–	–	–	–	–	–	–
–	–	–	–	–	–	–
–	–	–	–	–	–	–
0.4	6.0	3.8	-0.5	0.2	5.3	2.2
36.0	5.0	3.0	45.0	9.0	-20.0	-8.0
183.3	*43.4*	*74.2*	*117.1*	*138.0*	*-26.6*	*26.4*
180.6	*243.6*	*384.4*	*204.5*	*168.1*	*212.7*	*345.4*
1.0	–	–	–	*1.0*	–	–
76.5	*24.0*	*21.2*	*3.0*	*62.0*	*-8.1*	*5.6*
364.9	***287.0***	***458.6***	***321.6***	***307.1***	***186.1***	***371.8***

MAIN AID AGGREGATES

	1977	1978	1979	1980
DAC COUNTRIES COMBINED				
PRIVATE SECTOR NET	70.7	504.2	-476.9	438.5
Direct Investment	-67.4	417.7	-382.6	280.1
Portfolio Invest.	15.5	112.8	-102.8	56.8
Export Credits	122.7	-26.3	8.6	101.6
OFFICIAL & PRIVATE				
GROSS:				
Contractual Lending	921.9	993.3	981.0	1422.3
Export Credits Tot.	572.3	505.9	443.6	666.5
Export Credits Priv	408.3	327.1	416.8	599.6
OTHER NET DATA				
Contractual Lending	503.4	493.4	384.6	727.3
Export Credits Tot.	243.6	115.9	-13.1	123.3
(Bank Sector Loans)	188.0	568.0	-368.0	-31.0
ODA CONCESSIONALITY				
Total:Grant Element	64.0	68.0	67.0	66.0
Loans:Grant Element	55.0	58.0	58.0	57.0
OTHER SOURCES				
CMEA Countr.(Gross)	–	0.3	1.0	1.0
Intra LDCS Exc.OPEC	–	–	–	–
Other	–	–	–	–
ALL SOURCE COMMITMENTS				
TOTAL BILATERAL	1099.0	745.2	1469.1	1680.2
of which				
OPEC (ODA)	95.4	–	18.1	0.6
CMEA (ODA)	–	–	–	–
TOTAL MULTILAT.(ODA)	26.1	182.2	190.9	249.4
TOTAL BIL.& MULTIL.	1125.1	927.3	1660.1	1929.6
of which				
ODA Grants	221.6	213.5	383.2	367.7
ODA Loans	827.9	701.8	1250.9	1365.6
ODA CONCESSIONALITY				
Total: Grant Element	63.0	71.0	69.0	68.0
Loans: Grant Element	53.0	63.0	60.0	59.0

INDEBTEDNESS

	1977	1978	1979	1980
TOTAL DEBT DISBURSED	***12341.0***	***14522.8***	***15592.9***	
Debt to DAC Countries	9998.0	11796.0	12556.0	
ODA	4173.0	5294.0	5291.0	
Total Export Credits	3535.0	4073.0	4539.0	
Other Private Market	2290.0	2429.0	2726.0	
International Org.	983.6	1190.8	1440.3	
CMEA	1083.5	1054.3	1015.8	
Other	275.9	481.7	580.9	
TOTAL DEBT SERVICE	***1370.9***	***1643.1***	***2250.2***	
Paid to DAC Countries	1290.4	1437.1	2014.1	
ODA	149.4	198.2	231.4	
Total Export Credits	502.6	540.6	909.6	
Other Private Market	638.4	698.3	873.1	
International Org.	37.9	71.8	112.5	
CMEA	32.3	42.0	42.0	
Other	10.3	92.1	81.6	

ECONOMIC INDICATORS

	1977	1978	1979	1980
GNP Curr. Prices, $M	44173.5	48985.4	47360.6	64422.6
Real GNP, 1976=100	108.0	114.0	120.0	129.0
GNP/Cap Curr. Prices,$	323.0	350.0	331.0	440.0
GNP/cap Atlas Basis, $	299.6	333.0	370.5	422.4
Real GNP/Cap, 1976=100	105.0	109.0	112.0	117.0
Population, Million	136.4	139.6	142.9	146.2
Curr.A/C Deficit(-),$M	-74.0	-1428.0	950.0	2809.0
BOP Exp. & Transf.,$M	10929.0	11326.0	15552.0	22193.0
Exp. to OECD CIF, $M	9738.7	10544.6	14723.3	21022.2
of which				
Manufact.	99.8	159.2	232.6	315.0
Imp. from OECD FOB, $M	4185.5	4523.0	4764.2	7366.5
Reserves ex. Gold, $M	2509.0	2626.0	4062.0	5392.0

	TOTAL RECEIPTS NET 1977	1978	1979	1980	TOTAL ODA NET 1977	1978	1979	1980
DAC COUNTRIES								
Australia	0.1	-0.2	0.0	0.0	0.1	0.0	0.0	0.0
Austria	4.8	2.9	4.1	3.6	3.3	3.7	4.2	3.5
Belgium	-2.0	74.5	-33.8	-10.5	0.1	0.1	0.3	0.0
Canada	-2.0	29.4	-6.2	-12.0	–	–	–	–
Denmark	0.5	5.6	-6.2	-4.5	-0.2	-0.2	-0.2	-0.2
Finland	-1.1	0.4	1.1	-0.5	–	–	–	–
France	205.4	79.3	134.4	-137.9	-1.4	-3.2	-3.4	0.0
Germany, Fed. Rep.	-83.2	549.4	262.3	381.9	0.9	5.6	11.7	4.5
Italy	568.2	793.4	-142.2	321.5	0.3	0.6	0.2	0.3
Japan	462.2	816.5	148.4	146.9	33.6	95.3	-0.3	23.1
Netherlands	4.2	0.1	-22.0	-18.0	0.3	0.1	0.0	0.0
New Zealand	-0.3	0.2	0.0	–	0.0	0.0	–	–
Norway	0.6	-0.9	-1.7	-1.2	–	–	–	–
Sweden	51.8	7.0	-4.2	-13.7	–	–	–	–
Switzerland	36.8	44.0	-32.1	-49.1	0.0	–	0.1	0.2
United Kingdom	304.4	52.8	-215.0	-59.6	-0.2	-0.4	-0.5	-0.6
United States	156.0	438.0	-37.0	–	-11.0	-8.0	-8.0	–
TOTAL	*1706.7*	*2892.2*	*49.8*	*546.7*	*25.8*	*93.7*	*4.1*	*30.8*
MULTILATERAL								
AF.D.F.	–	–	–	–	–	–	–	–
AF.D.B.	–	–	–	–	–	–	–	–
AS.D.B.	–	–	–	–	–	–	–	–
CAR.D.B.	–	–	–	–	–	–	–	–
E.E.C.	–	–	–	–	–	–	–	–
IBRD	37.3	-19.0	-40.2	-48.2	–	–	–	–
IDA	–	–	–	–	–	–	–	–
I.D.B.	–	–	–	–	–	–	–	–
IFAD	–	–	–	–	–	–	–	–
I.F.C.	-2.7	-2.9	-0.2	–	–	–	–	–
IMF TRUST FUND	–	–	–	–	–	–	–	–
U.N. AGENCIES	–	–	–	–	–	–	–	–
UNDP	8.2	6.6	1.4	–	8.2	6.6	1.4	–
UNTA	0.2	0.4	0.2	0.0	0.2	0.4	0.2	0.0
UNICEF	–	–	0.0	0.0	–	–	0.0	0.0
UNRWA	–	–	–	–	–	–	–	–
WFP	–	–	–	–	–	–	–	–
UNHCR	–	–	–	–	–	–	–	–
Other Multilateral	1.0	1.4	0.2	0.0	1.0	1.4	0.2	0.0
Arab OPEC Agencies	–	–	–	–	–	–	–	–
TOTAL	*44.0*	*-13.6*	*-38.7*	*-48.1*	*9.4*	*8.4*	*1.8*	*0.1*
OPEC COUNTRIES	–	*26.0*	–	–	–	*26.0*	–	–
E.E.C.+ MEMBERS	*997.7*	*1554.9*	*-22.6*	*472.8*	*-0.1*	*2.7*	*8.1*	*4.0*
TOTAL	***1750.7***	***2904.6***	***11.2***	***498.6***	***35.2***	***128.0***	***5.9***	***30.9***

	ODA LOANS GROSS 1977	1978	1979	1980	ODA LOANS NET 1977	1978	1979	1980
DAC COUNTRIES								
Australia	–	–	–	–	–	–	–	–
Austria	0.2	–	–	–	0.1	-0.1	0.0	-0.7
Belgium	–	–	–	–	–	–	–	–
Canada	–	–	–	–	–	–	–	–
Denmark	–	–	–	–	-0.2	-0.2	-0.2	-0.2
Finland	–	–	–	–	–	–	–	–
France	0.0	–	–	–	-1.4	-3.2	-3.4	-3.5
Germany, Fed. Rep.	0.1	–	–	–	-5.7	-3.4	-8.3	-5.9
Italy	–	–	–	–	–	–	–	–
Japan	32.9	94.1	0.7	23.8	31.2	91.9	-1.7	21.9
Netherlands	–	–	–	–	-0.1	–	–	–
New Zealand	–	–	–	–	–	–	–	–
Norway	–	–	–	–	–	–	–	–
Sweden	–	–	–	–	–	–	–	–
Switzerland	–	–	–	–	–	–	–	–
United Kingdom	–	–	–	–	-0.5	-0.5	-0.5	-0.6
United States	–	–	–	–	-9.0	-6.0	-6.0	–
TOTAL	*33.3*	*94.1*	*0.7*	*23.8*	*14.5*	*78.6*	*-20.3*	*11.0*
MULTILATERAL	–	–	–	–	–	–	–	–
OPEC COUNTRIES	–	–	–	–	–	–	–	–
E.E.C.+ MEMBERS	*0.1*	–	–	–	*-7.8*	*-7.3*	*-12.5*	*-10.2*
TOTAL	***33.3***	***94.1***	***0.7***	***23.8***	***14.5***	***78.6***	***-20.3***	***11.0***

	TOTAL OFFICIAL GROSS 1977	1978	1979	1980	TOTAL OFFICIAL NET 1977	1978	1979	1980
DAC COUNTRIES								
Australia	0.1	0.0	0.0	0.0	0.1	0.0	0.0	0.0
Austria	6.8	3.8	4.2	4.2	4.6	2.8	4.1	3.4
Belgium	0.1	0.1	0.3	0.0	0.1	0.1	0.3	0.0
Canada	3.3	34.5	5.4	–	-1.9	29.6	-6.2	-12.0
Denmark	–	–	0.0	0.0	-0.3	-0.2	-0.2	-0.2
Finland	–	–	–	–	–	–	–	–
France	92.5	62.9	30.3	3.5	84.1	58.8	-49.5	-6.6
Germany, Fed. Rep.	7.0	9.0	20.7	199.1	-15.7	-10.6	1.5	180.2
Italy	4.0	4.2	0.2	0.3	3.7	4.1	-0.2	-1.1
Japan	129.1	241.9	16.9	25.3	127.4	239.7	14.5	23.3
Netherlands	0.5	0.1	0.0	0.0	0.3	0.1	0.0	0.0
New Zealand	0.0	0.0	–	–	-0.3	0.0	–	–
Norway	–	–	–	–	–	–	–	–
Sweden	–	–	–	–	–	–	–	–
Switzerland	0.0	–	0.1	0.2	0.0	–	0.1	0.2
United Kingdom	0.2	0.1	0.1	0.0	-0.2	-0.4	-0.5	-0.6
United States	25.0	11.0	-2.0	–	-20.0	-22.0	-159.0	–
TOTAL	*268.6*	*367.6*	*76.3*	*232.6*	*182.0*	*302.0*	*-195.2*	*186.7*
MULTILATERAL	*83.9*	*32.1*	*11.9*	*4.1*	*44.0*	*-13.6*	*-38.7*	*-48.1*
OPEC COUNTRIES	–	*26.0*	–	–	–	*26.0*	–	–
E.E.C.+ MEMBERS	*104.3*	*76.4*	*51.5*	*202.8*	*72.1*	*51.8*	*-48.7*	*171.8*
TOTAL	***352.5***	***425.7***	***88.2***	***236.6***	***226.0***	***314.4***	***-233.8***	***138.5***

TOTAL ODA GROSS	197
Australia	0.
Austria	3.
Belgium	0.
Canada	
Denmark	
Finland	
France	0.
Germany, Fed. Rep.	6.
Italy	0.
Japan	35.
Netherlands	0.
New Zealand	0.
Norway	
Sweden	
Switzerland	0.
United Kingdom	0.
United States	-2.
TOTAL	*44.*
AF.D.F.	
AF.D.B.	
AS.D.B.	
CAR.D.B.	
E.E.C.	
IBRD	
IDA	
I.D.B.	
IFAD	
I.F.C.	
IMF TRUST FUND	
U.N. AGENCIES	
UNDP	8.
UNTA	0.
UNICEF	
UNRWA	
WFP	
UNHCR	
Other Multilateral	1
Arab OPEC Agencies	
TOTAL	*9.*
OPEC COUNTRIES	
E.E.C.+ MEMBERS	*7.*
TOTAL	***53***

GRANTS	197
Australia	0.
Austria	3.
Belgium	0.
Canada	
Denmark	
Finland	
France	
Germany, Fed. Rep.	6.
Italy	0.
Japan	2.
Netherlands	0.
New Zealand	0.
Norway	
Sweden	
Switzerland	0
United Kingdom	0.
United States	-2.
TOTAL	*11.*
MULTILATERAL	*9.*
OPEC COUNTRIES	
E.E.C.+ MEMBERS	*7.*
TOTAL	***20.***

TOTAL OOF GROSS	197
Australia	
Austria	3.
Belgium	
Canada	3.
Denmark	
Finland	
France	92.
Germany, Fed. Rep.	0.
Italy	3
Japan	93.
Netherlands	
New Zealand	
Norway	
Sweden	
Switzerland	
United Kingdom	
United States	27.
TOTAL	*224.*
MULTILATERAL	*74.*
OPEC COUNTRIES	
E.E.C.+ MEMBERS	*96.*
TOTAL	***298.***

ODA COMMITMENTS

1978	1979	1980	1977	1978	1979	1980
0.0	0.0	0.0	0.0	0.0	–	0.0
3.8	4.2	4.2	0.2	–	–	–
0.1	0.3	0.0	–	–	–	–
–	–	–	–	–	–	–
–	0.0	0.0	–	–	0.0	–
–	–	–	–	–	–	–
–	–	3.5	–	–	–	3.3
9.0	20.0	10.4	6.4	8.9	19.9	10.4
0.6	0.2	0.3	0.3	0.6	0.2	0.3
97.4	2.2	25.1	2.6	3.8	1.7	25.2
0.1	0.0	0.0	0.3	0.1	0.1	0.0
0.0	–	–	–	0.0	–	0.0
–	–	–	–	–	–	–
–	–	–	–	–	–	–
–	0.1	0.2	–	–	–	0.1
0.1	0.1	0.0	0.2	0.1	0.1	0.0
-2.0	-2.0	–	–	–	0.1	–
109.2	*25.1*	*43.7*	*10.1*	*13.5*	*22.1*	*39.3*
–	–	–	–	–	–	–
–	–	–	–	–	–	–
–	–	–	–	–	–	–
–	–	–	–	–	–	–
–	–	–	–	–	–	–
–	–	–	–	–	–	–
–	–	–	–	–	–	–
–	–	–	–	–	–	–
–	–	–	–	–	–	–
–	–	–	–	–	–	–
–	–	–	–	–	–	–
–	–	–	9.4	8.4	1.8	0.1
6.6	1.4	–	–	–	–	–
0.4	0.2	0.0	–	–	–	–
–	0.0	0.0	–	–	–	–
–	–	–	–	–	–	–
–	–	–	–	–	–	–
–	–	–	–	–	–	–
1.4	0.2	0.0	–	–	–	–
–	–	–	–	–	–	–
8.4	*1.8*	*0.1*	*9.4*	*8.4*	*1.8*	*0.1*
26.0	–	–	–	*26.0*	–	–
9.9	*20.6*	*14.2*	*7.2*	*9.7*	*20.3*	*14.0*
143.5	***26.9***	***43.7***	***19.5***	***47.8***	***23.9***	***39.4***

TECH. COOP. GRANTS

1978	1979	1980	1977	1978	1979	1980
0.0	0.0	0.0	0.1	0.0	0.0	–
3.8	4.2	4.2	3.2	3.8	4.2	4.2
0.1	0.3	0.0	0.1	0.1	0.1	0.0
–	–	–	–	–	–	–
–	0.0	0.0	–	–	–	–
–	–	–	–	–	–	–
–	–	3.5	–	–	–	3.5
9.0	20.0	10.4	6.5	7.7	19.3	9.8
0.6	0.2	0.3	0.3	0.6	0.2	0.2
3.3	1.5	1.2	2.3	2.9	1.5	0.9
0.1	0.0	0.0	0.3	0.1	0.0	0.0
0.0	–	–	0.0	0.0	–	–
–	–	–	–	–	–	–
–	–	–	–	–	–	–
–	0.1	0.2	–	–	–	–
0.1	0.1	0.0	0.2	0.1	0.1	–
-2.0	-2.0	–	–	–	–	–
15.1	*24.4*	*19.8*	*13.0*	*15.3*	*25.4*	*18.6*
8.4	*1.8*	*0.1*	*9.4*	*8.4*	*1.8*	*0.1*
26.0	–	–	–	–	–	–
9.9	*20.6*	*14.2*	*7.5*	*8.6*	*19.7*	*13.4*
49.4	***26.2***	***19.9***	***22.5***	***23.6***	***27.1***	***18.6***

TOTAL OOF NET

1978	1979	1980	1977	1978	1979	1980
–	–	–	–	–	–	–
–	–	–	1.3	-0.9	-0.1	-0.1
–	–	–	–	–	–	–
34.5	5.4	–	-1.9	29.6	-6.2	-12.0
–	–	–	-0.1	–	–	–
–	–	–	–	–	–	–
62.9	30.3	–	85.5	62.0	-46.1	-6.5
–	0.7	188.7	-16.5	-16.3	-10.2	175.7
3.6	–	–	3.4	3.5	-0.4	-1.3
144.5	14.8	0.2	93.9	144.5	14.8	0.2
–	–	–	–	–	–	–
–	–	–	-0.3	–	–	–
–	–	–	–	–	–	–
–	–	–	–	–	–	–
–	–	–	–	–	–	–
–	–	–	–	–	–	–
13.0	–	–	-9.0	-14.0	-151.0	–
258.4	*51.1*	*188.9*	*156.2*	*208.3*	*-199.3*	*155.9*
23.7	*10.1*	*4.0*	*34.6*	*-21.9*	*-40.4*	*-48.2*
–	–	–	–	–	–	–
66.5	*31.0*	*188.7*	*72.3*	*49.2*	*-56.8*	*167.8*
282.2	***61.3***	***192.9***	***190.8***	***186.4***	***-239.7***	***107.7***

MAIN AID AGGREGATES

	1977	1978	1979	1980
DAC COUNTRIES COMBINED				
PRIVATE SECTOR NET	1524.7	2590.2	245.0	360.0
Direct Investment	345.7	909.1	164.4	80.9
Portfolio Invest.	382.4	548.9	125.2	-13.9
Export Credits	796.6	1132.3	-44.5	293.0
OFFICIAL & PRIVATE				
GROSS:				
Contractual Lending	2429.1	2457.8	865.3	1150.1
Export Credits Tot.	2299.7	2300.8	833.6	937.6
Export Credits Priv	2171.8	2105.2	813.4	937.4
OTHER NET DATA				
Contractual Lending	967.4	1419.2	-264.1	459.9
Export Credits Tot.	867.3	1284.9	-197.7	271.2
(Bank Sector Loans)	845.0	1390.0	-371.0	-539.0
ODA CONCESSIONALITY				
Total:Grant Element	98.0	100.0	100.0	100.0
Loans:Grant Element	31.0	–	–	–
OTHER SOURCES				
CMEA Countr.(Gross)	63.5	63.3	6.6	17.5
Intra LDCS Exc.OPEC	–	–	–	–
Other	–	–	–	–
ALL SOURCE COMMITMENTS				
TOTAL BILATERAL	119.8	156.5	22.1	39.4
of which				
OPEC (ODA)	–	26.0	–	–
CMEA (ODA)	–	–	–	–
TOTAL MULTILAT.(ODA)	9.4	8.4	1.8	0.1
TOTAL BIL.& MULTIL.	129.2	164.9	23.9	39.4
of which				
ODA Grants	19.3	47.8	23.9	15.6
ODA Loans	0.2	–	–	23.8
ODA CONCESSIONALITY				
Total: Grant Element	99.0	100.0	100.0	100.0
Loans: Grant Element	31.0	–	–	–

INDEBTEDNESS

	1977	1978	1979	1980
TOTAL DEBT DISBURSED	***8310.0***	***10937.6***	***9902.0***	
Debt to DAC Countries	6423.0	8790.0	8102.0	
ODA	187.0	304.0	258.0	
Total Export Credits	3742.0	5415.0	5344.0	
Other Private Market	2494.0	3071.0	2500.0	
International Org.	655.2	635.0	641.0	
CMEA	1203.1	1176.8	952.0	
Other	28.6	335.8	207.0	
TOTAL DEBT SERVICE	***1986.9***	***2270.8***	***1881.2***	
Paid to DAC Countries	1715.9	1914.2	1571.2	
ODA	24.7	23.2	32.2	
Total Export Credits	1523.2	1606.7	1439.0	
Other Private Market	168.0	284.3	100.0	
International Org.	86.9	98.0	70.0	
CMEA	176.5	179.5	200.0	
Other	7.6	79.1	40.0	

ECONOMIC INDICATORS

	1977	1978	1979	1980
GNP Curr. Prices, $M	75257.5	75090.5	73203.3	83480.8
Real GNP, 1976=100	100.0	91.0	79.0	71.0
GNP/Cap Curr. Prices,$	2164.0	2094.0	1980.0	2189.0
GNP/cap Atlas Basis, $	2349.0	2224.6	2036.3	1937.1
Real GNP/Cap, 1976=100	97.0	86.0	72.0	63.0
Population, Million	34.8	35.9	37.0	38.1
Curr.A/C Deficit(-),$M	5091.0	–	–	–
BOP Exp. & Transf.,$M	27985.0	–	–	–
Exp. to OECD CIF, $M	18746.1	19002.7	15205.4	10009.7
of which				
Manufact.	393.2	528.4	625.5	613.6
Imp. from OECD FOB, $M	11495.7	14124.8	5669.4	7725.8
Reserves ex. Gold, $M	12106.0	11977.0	15210.0	–

	TOTAL RECEIPTS NET 1977	1978	1979	1980	TOTAL ODA NET 1977	1978	1979	1980
DAC COUNTRIES								
Australia	–	0.0	1.6	2.4	–	0.0	–	–
Austria	-0.2	-0.1	-0.1	0.5	0.2	0.4	0.4	0.5
Belgium	0.1	-0.9	-2.8	0.4	0.2	0.1	0.1	0.1
Canada	–	–	–	0.2	–	–	–	–
Denmark	5.3	15.3	9.4	17.9	–	0.0	0.0	0.0
Finland	–	0.0	0.0	0.0	–	0.0	0.0	0.0
France	-183.7	-13.3	-11.2	-9.5	–	–	10.5	3.8
Germany, Fed. Rep.	27.4	8.9	-14.3	-21.5	0.4	0.4	0.7	0.6
Italy	-9.2	67.5	44.1	50.8	0.1	0.2	0.2	0.1
Japan	55.5	119.9	-14.8	129.2	69.5	39.3	2.1	1.6
Netherlands	0.2	0.2	0.1	0.1	0.2	0.2	0.1	0.1
New Zealand	–	0.0	–	–	–	0.0	–	–
Norway	–	–	–	-0.4	–	–	–	–
Sweden	–	0.4	2.4	-2.9	–	0.2	0.1	–
Switzerland	0.3	1.1	–	-4.6	–	–	–	0.0
United Kingdom	41.9	3.1	107.1	11.3	0.1	0.1	0.0	–
United States	-2.0	-2.0	-1.0	-1.0	-1.0	-1.0	-1.0	-1.0
TOTAL	*-64.3*	*200.2*	*120.4*	*172.9*	*69.7*	*40.0*	*13.2*	*5.7*
MULTILATERAL								
AF.D.F.	–	–	–	–	–	–	–	–
AF.D.B.	–	–	–	–	–	–	–	–
AS.D.B.	–	–	–	–	–	–	–	–
CAR.D.B.	–	–	–	–	–	–	–	–
E.E.C.	–	–	–	–	–	–	–	–
IBRD	25.3	10.2	5.9	-3.8	–	–	–	–
IDA	–	–	–	–	–	–	–	–
I.D.B.	–	–	–	–	–	–	–	–
IFAD	–	–	–	–	–	–	–	–
I.F.C.	–	–	–	–	–	–	–	–
IMF TRUST FUND	–	–	–	–	–	–	–	–
U.N. AGENCIES	–	–	–	–	–	–	–	–
UNDP	1.0	3.0	4.4	3.8	1.0	3.0	4.4	3.8
UNTA	0.7	0.6	0.5	0.1	0.7	0.6	0.5	0.1
UNICEF	–	–	–	–	–	–	–	–
UNRWA	–	–	–	–	–	–	–	–
WFP	1.2	0.2	1.1	–	1.2	0.2	1.1	–
UNHCR	–	–	–	–	–	–	–	–
Other Multilateral	1.3	1.8	0.6	0.9	1.3	1.8	0.6	0.9
Arab OPEC Agencies	–	–	–	–	–	–	–	–
TOTAL	*29.5*	*15.7*	*12.5*	*1.0*	*4.2*	*5.5*	*6.6*	*4.8*
OPEC COUNTRIES	*-1.9*	*-2.0*	*-2.0*	*-2.1*	*-1.9*	*-2.0*	*-2.0*	*-2.1*
E.E.C.+ MEMBERS	*-117.9*	*80.8*	*132.4*	*49.5*	*1.0*	*1.0*	*11.6*	*4.6*
TOTAL	***-36.7***	***213.9***	***130.9***	***171.8***	***72.0***	***43.5***	***17.8***	***8.4***

TOTAL ODA GROSS	197
Australia	
Austria	0
Belgium	0
Canada	
Denmark	
Finland	
France	
Germany, Fed. Rep.	0
Italy	0
Japan	69
Netherlands	0
New Zealand	
Norway	
Sweden	
Switzerland	
United Kingdom	0
United States	
TOTAL	*70*
AF.D.F.	
AF.D.B.	
AS.D.B.	
CAR.D.B.	
E.E.C.	
IBRD	
IDA	
I.D.B.	
IFAD	
I.F.C.	
IMF TRUST FUND	
U.N. AGENCIES	
UNDP	1
UNTA	0
UNICEF	
UNRWA	
WFP	1
UNHCR	
Other Multilateral	1
Arab OPEC Agencies	
TOTAL	*4*
OPEC COUNTRIES	
E.E.C.+ MEMBERS	*1*
TOTAL	***74***

	ODA LOANS GROSS 1977	1978	1979	1980	ODA LOANS NET 1977	1978	1979	1980
DAC COUNTRIES								
Australia	–	–	–	–	–	–	–	–
Austria	–	–	–	–	–	–	–	–
Belgium	–	–	–	–	–	–	–	–
Canada	–	–	–	–	–	–	–	–
Denmark	–	–	–	–	–	–	–	–
Finland	–	–	–	–	–	–	–	–
France	–	–	10.5	–	–	–	10.5	–
Germany, Fed. Rep.	–	–	–	–	–	–	–	–
Italy	–	–	–	–	–	–	–	–
Japan	68.0	37.5	–	–	68.0	37.5	–	–
Netherlands	–	–	–	–	–	–	–	–
New Zealand	–	–	–	–	–	–	–	–
Norway	–	–	–	–	–	–	–	–
Sweden	–	–	–	–	–	–	–	–
Switzerland	–	–	–	–	–	–	–	–
United Kingdom	–	–	–	–	–	–	–	–
United States	–	–	–	–	-1.0	-1.0	-1.0	-1.0
TOTAL	*68.0*	*37.5*	*10.5*	–	*67.0*	*36.5*	*9.5*	*-1.0*
MULTILATERAL	–	–	–	–	–	–	–	–
OPEC COUNTRIES	–	–	–	–	*-1.9*	*-2.0*	*-2.0*	*-2.1*
E.E.C.+ MEMBERS	–	–	*10.5*	–	–	–	*10.5*	–
TOTAL	***68.0***	***37.5***	***10.5***	–	***65.1***	***34.5***	***7.5***	***-3.1***

GRANTS	197
Australia	
Austria	0
Belgium	0
Canada	
Denmark	
Finland	
France	
Germany, Fed. Rep.	0
Italy	0
Japan	1
Netherlands	0
New Zealand	
Norway	
Sweden	
Switzerland	
United Kingdom	0
United States	
TOTAL	*2*
MULTILATERAL	*4*
OPEC COUNTRIES	
E.E.C.+ MEMBERS	*1*
TOTAL	***6***

	TOTAL OFFICIAL GROSS 1977	1978	1979	1980	TOTAL OFFICIAL NET 1977	1978	1979	1980
DAC COUNTRIES								
Australia	–	0.0	0.0	–	–	0.0	0.0	–
Austria	0.2	0.4	0.4	0.5	-0.2	0.4	-0.1	0.5
Belgium	0.2	0.1	0.1	0.1	0.2	0.1	0.1	0.1
Canada	–	–	–	–	–	–	–	–
Denmark	–	0.0	0.0	0.0	–	0.0	0.0	0.0
Finland	–	0.0	0.0	0.0	–	0.0	0.0	0.0
France	26.3	1.5	10.8	4.0	-161.6	1.5	10.8	4.0
Germany, Fed. Rep.	0.4	0.4	0.7	0.6	0.4	0.4	0.7	0.6
Italy	0.1	0.2	0.2	0.1	0.1	0.2	0.2	0.1
Japan	69.5	39.3	2.1	1.6	69.5	39.3	2.1	1.6
Netherlands	0.2	0.2	0.1	0.1	0.2	0.2	0.1	0.1
New Zealand	–	0.0	–	–	–	0.0	–	–
Norway	–	–	–	–	–	–	–	–
Sweden	–	0.2	0.1	–	–	0.2	0.1	–
Switzerland	–	–	–	0.0	–	–	–	0.0
United Kingdom	0.1	0.1	0.0	–	0.1	0.1	0.0	–
United States	–	–	–	–	-2.0	-2.0	-1.0	-1.0
TOTAL	*97.0*	*42.5*	*14.4*	*7.0*	*-93.3*	*40.5*	*13.0*	*6.0*
MULTILATERAL	*32.5*	*18.0*	*15.5*	*4.8*	*29.5*	*15.7*	*12.5*	*1.0*
OPEC COUNTRIES	–	–	–	–	*-1.9*	*-2.0*	*-2.0*	*-2.1*
E.E.C.+ MEMBERS	*27.3*	*2.5*	*11.9*	*4.9*	*-160.6*	*2.5*	*11.9*	*4.9*
TOTAL	***129.5***	***60.5***	***30.0***	***11.7***	***-65.7***	***54.2***	***23.4***	***4.9***

TOTAL OOF GROSS	197
Australia	
Austria	
Belgium	
Canada	
Denmark	
Finland	
France	26
Germany, Fed. Rep.	
Italy	
Japan	
Netherlands	
New Zealand	
Norway	
Sweden	
Switzerland	
United Kingdom	
United States	
TOTAL	*26*
MULTILATERAL	*28*
OPEC COUNTRIES	
E.E.C.+ MEMBERS	*26*
TOTAL	***54***

ODA COMMITMENTS

1978	1979	1980	1977	1978	1979	1980
0.0	–	–	–	0.0	–	–
0.4	0.4	0.5	–	–	–	–
0.1	0.1	0.1	–	–	–	–
–	–	–	–	–	–	–
0.0	0.0	0.0	–	–	–	–
0.0	0.0	0.0	–	0.0	0.0	0.0
–	10.5	3.8	–	–	–	3.2
0.4	0.7	0.6	0.4	0.4	0.7	0.6
0.2	0.2	0.1	0.1	0.2	0.2	0.1
39.3	2.1	1.6	55.8	2.1	2.4	1.8
0.2	0.1	0.1	0.2	0.2	0.1	0.1
0.0	–	–	–	0.0	–	–
–	–	–	–	–	–	–
0.2	0.1	–	–	0.2	0.1	–
–	–	0.0	–	–	–	0.0
0.1	0.0	–	0.1	0.1	0.0	–
–	–	–	–	–	–	–
41.0	*14.2*	*6.7*	*56.6*	*3.3*	*3.5*	*5.8*
–	–	–	–	–	–	–
–	–	–	–	–	–	–
–	–	–	–	–	–	–
–	–	–	–	–	–	–
–	–	–	–	–	–	–
–	–	–	–	–	–	–
–	–	–	–	–	–	–
–	–	–	–	–	–	–
–	–	–	–	–	–	–
–	–	–	–	–	–	–
–	–	–	–	–	–	–
–	–	–	4.2	5.5	6.6	4.8
3.0	4.4	3.8	–	–	–	–
0.6	0.5	0.1	–	–	–	–
–	–	–	–	–	–	–
–	–	–	–	–	–	–
0.2	1.1	–	–	–	–	–
–	–	–	–	–	–	–
1.8	0.6	0.9	–	–	–	–
–	–	–	–	–	–	–
5.5	*6.6*	*4.8*	*4.2*	*5.5*	*6.6*	*4.8*
–	–	–	–	–	–	–
1.0	*11.6*	*4.6*	*0.8*	*0.9*	*1.0*	*3.9*
46.5	***20.8***	***11.5***	***60.8***	***8.8***	***10.1***	***10.5***

TECH. COOP. GRANTS

1978	1979	1980	1977	1978	1979	1980
0.0	–	–	–	0.0	–	–
0.4	0.4	0.5	0.2	0.4	0.4	0.5
0.1	0.1	0.1	0.2	0.1	0.1	0.1
–	–	–	–	–	–	–
0.0	0.0	0.0	–	0.0	0.0	0.0
0.0	0.0	0.0	–	0.0	0.0	0.0
–	–	3.8	–	–	–	3.8
0.4	0.7	0.6	0.4	0.4	0.7	0.6
0.2	0.2	0.1	0.1	0.2	0.2	0.1
1.8	2.1	1.6	1.5	1.8	2.1	1.6
0.2	0.1	0.1	0.2	0.2	0.1	0.1
0.0	–	–	–	0.0	–	–
–	–	–	–	–	–	–
0.2	0.1	–	–	0.2	0.1	–
–	–	0.0	–	–	–	–
0.1	0.0	–	0.1	0.1	0.0	–
–	–	–	–	–	–	–
3.5	*3.7*	*6.7*	*2.6*	*3.5*	*3.7*	*6.7*
5.5	*6.6*	*4.8*	*3.0*	*5.3*	*5.5*	*4.8*
–	–	–	–	–	–	–
1.0	*1.1*	*4.6*	*1.0*	*1.0*	*1.1*	*4.6*
9.0	***10.3***	***11.5***	***5.6***	***8.8***	***9.2***	***11.5***

TOTAL OOF NET

1978	1979	1980	1977	1978	1979	1980
–	0.0	–	–	–	0.0	–
–	–	–	-0.4	–	-0.5	–
–	–	–	–	–	–	–
–	–	–	–	–	–	–
–	–	–	–	–	–	–
–	–	–	–	–	–	–
1.5	0.3	0.3	-161.6	1.5	0.3	0.3
–	–	–	–	–	–	–
–	–	–	–	–	–	–
–	–	–	–	–	–	–
–	–	–	–	–	–	–
–	–	–	–	–	–	–
–	–	–	–	–	–	–
–	–	–	–	–	–	–
–	–	–	–	–	–	–
–	–	–	–	–	–	–
–	–	–	-1.0	-1.0	–	–
1.5	*0.3*	*0.3*	*-163.0*	*0.5*	*-0.2*	*0.3*
12.5	*8.9*	–	*25.3*	*10.2*	*5.9*	*-3.8*
–	–	–	–	–	–	–
1.5	*0.3*	*0.3*	*-161.6*	*1.5*	*0.3*	*0.3*
14.0	***9.2***	***0.3***	***-137.7***	***10.7***	***5.7***	***-3.5***

MAIN AID AGGREGATES

	1977	1978	1979	1980
DAC COUNTRIES COMBINED				
PRIVATE SECTOR NET	29.0	159.7	107.5	166.9
Direct Investment	4.4	0.3	1.6	1.5
Portfolio Invest.	-10.5	-11.2	-10.6	-15.0
Export Credits	35.1	170.6	116.4	180.3
OFFICIAL & PRIVATE				
GROSS:				
Contractual Lending	283.5	482.9	429.0	670.4
Export Credits Tot.	189.2	443.9	418.3	670.2
Export Credits Priv	189.2	443.9	418.3	670.2
OTHER NET DATA				
Contractual Lending	-60.9	207.6	125.7	179.6
Export Credits Tot.	33.7	169.6	115.9	180.3
(Bank Sector Loans)	17.0	-26.0	-27.0	-25.0
ODA CONCESSIONALITY				
Total:Grant Element	46.0	100.0	100.0	100.0
Loans:Grant Element	44.0	–	–	–
OTHER SOURCES				
CMEA Countr.(Gross)	77.0	79.0	89.3	58.4
Intra LDCS Exc.OPEC	–	–	–	–
Other	–	–	–	–
ALL SOURCE COMMITMENTS				
TOTAL BILATERAL	56.6	4.8	3.5	5.8
of which				
OPEC (ODA)	–	–	–	–
CMEA (ODA)	50.0	–	–	–
TOTAL MULTILAT.(ODA)	4.2	5.5	6.6	4.8
TOTAL BIL.& MULTIL.	60.8	10.3	10.2	10.5
of which				
ODA Grants	6.6	8.8	10.2	10.5
ODA Loans	54.2	–	–	–
ODA CONCESSIONALITY				
Total: Grant Element	50.0	100.0	100.0	100.0
Loans: Grant Element	44.0	–	–	–

INDEBTEDNESS

	1977	1978	1979	1980
TOTAL DEBT DISBURSED	***1624.7***	***1747.3***	***2235.0***	
Debt to DAC Countries	1155.0	1243.0	1739.0	
ODA	110.0	189.0	153.0	
Total Export Credits	765.0	824.0	1376.0	
Other Private Market	280.0	230.0	210.0	
International Org.	70.5	80.7	83.0	
CMEA	345.9	373.1	368.0	
Other	53.3	50.6	45.0	
TOTAL DEBT SERVICE	***667.8***	***664.9***	***702.8***	
Paid to DAC Countries	558.3	558.8	601.0	
ODA	3.5	6.6	7.5	
Total Export Credits	544.8	430.9	543.5	
Other Private Market	10.0	121.3	50.0	
International Org.	7.7	8.8	1.8	
CMEA	91.4	90.9	–	
Other	10.5	6.4	100.0	

ECONOMIC INDICATORS

	1977	1978	1979	1980
GNP Curr. Prices, $M	18751.5	22576.3	33441.6	39034.6
Real GNP, 1976=100	108.0	124.0	176.0	187.0
GNP/Cap Curr. Prices,$	1589.0	1849.0	2647.0	2986.0
GNP/cap Atlas Basis, $	1525.8	1821.9	2706.1	3021.6
Real GNP/Cap, 1976=100	104.0	116.0	159.0	163.0
Population, Million	11.8	12.2	12.6	13.1
Curr.A/C Deficit(-),$M	3025.0	–	–	–
BOP Exp. & Transf.,$M	11599.0	–	–	–
Exp. to OECD CIF, $M	7739.9	8460.8	13615.0	19459.8
of which				
Manufact.	16.4	20.1	17.5	23.8
Imp. from OECD FOB, $M	3729.6	4334.9	7026.8	9779.9
Reserves ex. Gold, $M	6819.6	–	–	–

TOTAL RECEIPTS NET

	1977	1978	1979	1980
DAC COUNTRIES				
Australia	0.3	0.2	0.5	0.3
Austria	-0.7	-0.8	-0.8	-0.1
Belgium	-0.8	-4.4	17.5	93.9
Canada	14.1	22.4	13.5	13.5
Denmark	0.2	0.3	37.0	-8.3
Finland	–	–	–	–
France	11.9	28.5	22.4	-11.0
Germany, Fed. Rep.	46.3	68.2	39.8	100.4
Italy	-2.2	-2.2	14.9	12.1
Japan	0.1	0.1	0.1	0.1
Netherlands	0.1	15.9	13.4	1.2
New Zealand	-0.1	0.2	0.0	–
Norway	32.5	-0.6	-0.1	-4.4
Sweden	2.7	3.3	3.4	-2.5
Switzerland	0.8	1.0	-0.6	3.6
United Kingdom	12.5	-0.9	3.1	-24.3
United States	981.0	1259.0	1525.0	1100.0
TOTAL	*1098.7*	*1390.2*	*1689.0*	*1274.3*
MULTILATERAL				
AF.D.F.	–	–	–	–
AF.D.B.	–	–	–	–
AS.D.B.	–	–	–	–
CAR.D.B.	–	–	–	–
E.E.C.	–	–	–	–
IBRD	-2.5	4.1	-1.4	-2.3
IDA	–	–	–	–
I.D.B.	–	–	–	–
IFAD	–	–	–	–
I.F.C.	-0.2	-0.6	-1.0	-1.0
IMF TRUST FUND	–	–	–	–
U.N. AGENCIES	–	–	–	–
UNDP	0.2	0.0	–	–
UNTA	0.2	0.3	0.3	0.1
UNICEF	–	–	–	–
UNRWA	–	–	–	–
WFP	–	–	–	–
UNHCR	–	–	–	–
Other Multilateral	0.0	0.1	0.0	0.1
Arab OPEC Agencies	–	–	–	–
TOTAL	*-2.3*	*3.8*	*-2.2*	*-3.2*
OPEC COUNTRIES	–	–	–	–
E.E.C.+ MEMBERS	*68.1*	*105.5*	*148.0*	*163.8*
TOTAL	***1096.4***	***1393.9***	***1686.8***	***1271.1***

TOTAL ODA NET

	1977	1978	1979	1980
Australia	–	–	–	–
Austria	0.2	0.2	0.2	0.2
Belgium	0.1	0.1	0.1	0.0
Canada	–	–	–	–
Denmark	–	–	–	–
Finland	–	–	–	–
France	–	–	–	0.2
Germany, Fed. Rep.	33.1	58.4	30.3	110.0
Italy	–	0.0	0.0	–
Japan	0.1	0.1	0.1	0.1
Netherlands	0.1	0.4	0.4	1.2
New Zealand	–	–	–	–
Norway	–	–	–	–
Sweden	–	–	–	–
Switzerland	0.5	0.2	0.4	0.4
United Kingdom	–	–	–	–
United States	763.0	840.0	1153.0	780.0
TOTAL	*797.0*	*899.4*	*1184.4*	*892.1*
AF.D.F.	–	–	–	–
AF.D.B.	–	–	–	–
AS.D.B.	–	–	–	–
CAR.D.B.	–	–	–	–
E.E.C.	–	–	–	–
IBRD	–	–	–	–
IDA	–	–	–	–
I.D.B.	–	–	–	–
IFAD	–	–	–	–
I.F.C.	–	–	–	–
IMF TRUST FUND	–	–	–	–
U.N. AGENCIES	–	–	–	–
UNDP	0.2	0.0	–	–
UNTA	0.2	0.3	0.3	0.1
UNICEF	–	–	–	–
UNRWA	–	–	–	–
WFP	–	–	–	–
UNHCR	–	–	–	–
Other Multilateral	0.0	0.1	0.0	0.1
Arab OPEC Agencies	–	–	–	–
TOTAL	*0.4*	*0.3*	*0.3*	*0.2*
OPEC COUNTRIES	–	–	–	–
E.E.C.+ MEMBERS	*33.2*	*58.9*	*30.7*	*111.4*
TOTAL	***797.4***	***899.7***	***1184.7***	***892.2***

TOTAL ODA GROSS

	197[illegible]
Australia	
Austria	[illegible]
Belgium	[illegible]
Canada	
Denmark	
Finland	
France	
Germany, Fed. Rep.	48[illegible]
Italy	
Japan	[illegible]
Netherlands	[illegible]
New Zealand	
Norway	
Sweden	
Switzerland	[illegible]
United Kingdom	
United States	78[illegible]
TOTAL	*83[illegible]*
AF.D.F.	
AF.D.B.	
AS.D.B.	
CAR.D.B.	
E.E.C.	
IBRD	
IDA	
I.D.B.	
IFAD	
I.F.C.	
IMF TRUST FUND	
U.N. AGENCIES	
UNDP	[illegible]
UNTA	[illegible]
UNICEF	
UNRWA	
WFP	
UNHCR	
Other Multilateral	[illegible]
Arab OPEC Agencies	
TOTAL	[illegible]
OPEC COUNTRIES	
E.E.C.+ MEMBERS	*4[illegible]*
TOTAL	***83[illegible]***

ODA LOANS GROSS

	1977	1978	1979	1980
DAC COUNTRIES				
Australia	–	–	–	–
Austria	–	–	–	–
Belgium	–	–	–	–
Canada	–	–	–	–
Denmark	–	–	–	–
Finland	–	–	–	–
France	–	–	–	–
Germany, Fed. Rep.	43.5	74.4	46.5	124.2
Italy	–	–	–	–
Japan	–	–	–	–
Netherlands	–	–	–	–
New Zealand	–	–	–	–
Norway	–	–	–	–
Sweden	–	–	–	–
Switzerland	–	–	–	–
United Kingdom	–	–	–	–
United States	229.0	272.0	527.0	131.0
TOTAL	*272.5*	*346.4*	*573.5*	*255.2*
MULTILATERAL	–	–	–	–
OPEC COUNTRIES	–	–	–	–
E.E.C.+ MEMBERS	*43.5*	*74.4*	*46.5*	*124.2*
TOTAL	***272.5***	***346.4***	***573.5***	***255.2***

ODA LOANS NET

	1977	1978	1979	1980
Australia	–	–	–	–
Austria	–	–	–	–
Belgium	–	–	–	–
Canada	–	–	–	–
Denmark	–	–	–	–
Finland	–	–	–	–
France	–	–	–	–
Germany, Fed. Rep.	28.4	52.6	22.9	97.9
Italy	–	–	–	–
Japan	–	–	–	–
Netherlands	–	–	–	–
New Zealand	–	–	–	–
Norway	–	–	–	–
Sweden	–	–	–	–
Switzerland	–	–	–	–
United Kingdom	–	–	–	–
United States	205.0	249.0	498.0	107.0
TOTAL	*233.4*	*301.6*	*520.9*	*204.9*
MULTILATERAL	–	–	–	–
OPEC COUNTRIES	–	–	–	–
E.E.C.+ MEMBERS	*28.4*	*52.6*	*22.9*	*97.9*
TOTAL	***233.4***	***301.6***	***520.9***	***204.9***

GRANTS

	197[illegible]
Australia	
Austria	[illegible]
Belgium	[illegible]
Canada	
Denmark	
Finland	
France	
Germany, Fed. Rep.	[illegible]
Italy	
Japan	[illegible]
Netherlands	[illegible]
New Zealand	
Norway	
Sweden	
Switzerland	[illegible]
United Kingdom	
United States	55[illegible]
TOTAL	*56[illegible]*
MULTILATERAL	[illegible]
OPEC COUNTRIES	
E.E.C.+ MEMBERS	
TOTAL	***56[illegible]***

TOTAL OFFICIAL GROSS

	1977	1978	1979	1980
DAC COUNTRIES				
Australia	–	–	–	–
Austria	0.2	0.2	0.2	0.2
Belgium	0.1	0.1	0.1	0.0
Canada	17.4	26.3	17.0	17.0
Denmark	–	–	–	–
Finland	–	–	–	–
France	–	–	–	0.2
Germany, Fed. Rep.	48.2	80.1	53.9	136.8
Italy	3.0	2.4	1.0	16.9
Japan	0.1	0.1	0.1	0.1
Netherlands	0.1	0.4	0.4	1.2
New Zealand	0.1	–	–	–
Norway	–	–	–	–
Sweden	–	–	–	–
Switzerland	0.5	0.2	0.4	0.4
United Kingdom	–	–	–	–
United States	811.0	919.0	1246.0	830.0
TOTAL	*880.6*	*1028.8*	*1319.0*	*1002.8*
MULTILATERAL	*10.6*	*16.8*	*19.3*	*14.5*
OPEC COUNTRIES	–	–	–	–
E.E.C.+ MEMBERS	*51.3*	*83.0*	*55.3*	*155.1*
TOTAL	***891.3***	***1045.6***	***1338.3***	***1017.3***

TOTAL OFFICIAL NET

	1977	1978	1979	1980
Australia	–	–	–	–
Austria	-0.1	-0.2	-0.2	-0.2
Belgium	0.1	0.1	0.1	0.0
Canada	14.1	22.4	13.5	13.5
Denmark	–	–	–	–
Finland	–	–	–	–
France	–	–	–	0.2
Germany, Fed. Rep.	32.6	57.2	30.0	110.3
Italy	1.9	0.9	-0.5	14.4
Japan	0.1	0.1	0.1	0.1
Netherlands	0.1	0.2	0.4	1.2
New Zealand	-0.1	–	–	–
Norway	–	–	–	–
Sweden	–	–	–	–
Switzerland	0.5	0.2	0.4	0.4
United Kingdom	–	–	–	–
United States	763.0	871.0	1193.0	781.0
TOTAL	*812.3*	*951.9*	*1236.7*	*920.9*
MULTILATERAL	*-2.3*	*3.8*	*-2.2*	*-3.2*
OPEC COUNTRIES	–	–	–	–
E.E.C.+ MEMBERS	*34.7*	*58.3*	*29.9*	*126.1*
TOTAL	***810.0***	***955.7***	***1234.5***	***917.7***

TOTAL OOF GROSS

	197[illegible]
Australia	
Austria	
Belgium	
Canada	1[illegible]
Denmark	
Finland	
France	
Germany, Fed. Rep.	
Italy	
Japan	
Netherlands	
New Zealand	[illegible]
Norway	
Sweden	
Switzerland	
United Kingdom	
United States	2[illegible]
TOTAL	4[illegible]
MULTILATERAL	1[illegible]
OPEC COUNTRIES	
E.E.C.+ MEMBERS	
TOTAL	**5[illegible]**

1978	1979	1980	1977	1978	1979	1980
			ODA COMMITMENTS			
–	–	–	–	–	–	–
0.2	0.2	0.2	–	–	–	–
0.1	0.1	0.0	–	–	–	–
–	–	–	–	–	–	–
–	–	–	0.0	–	–	–
–	–	–	–	–	–	–
–	–	0.2	–	–	–	0.1
80.1	53.9	136.3	48.2	117.1	35.9	129.8
0.0	0.0	–	–	0.0	0.0	–
0.1	0.1	0.1	0.1	0.1	0.1	0.1
0.4	0.4	1.2	0.1	0.6	0.4	2.2
–	–	–	–	–	–	–
–	–	–	–	–	–	–
–	–	–	–	–	–	–
0.2	0.4	0.4	–	–	–	0.5
–	–	–	–	–	–	–
863.0	1182.0	804.0	791.8	785.0	790.3	396.2
944.2	*1237.0*	*942.4*	*840.3*	*902.8*	*826.6*	*528.9*
–	–	–	–	–	–	–
–	–	–	–	–	–	–
–	–	–	–	–	–	–
–	–	–	–	–	–	–
–	–	–	–	0.0	–	–
–	–	–	–	–	–	–
–	–	–	–	–	–	–
–	–	–	–	–	–	–
–	–	–	–	–	–	–
–	–	–	–	–	–	–
–	–	–	–	–	–	–
–	–	–	0.4	0.3	0.3	0.2
0.0	–	–	–	–	–	–
0.3	0.3	0.1	–	–	–	–
–	–	–	–	–	–	–
–	–	–	–	–	–	–
–	–	–	–	–	–	–
–	–	–	–	–	–	–
0.1	0.0	0.1	–	–	–	–
–	–	–	–	–	–	–
0.3	*0.3*	*0.2*	*0.4*	*0.3*	*0.3*	*0.2*
–	–	–	–	–	–	–
80.6	*54.3*	*137.7*	*48.3*	*117.7*	*36.3*	*132.1*
944.5	***1237.3***	***942.5***	***840.7***	***903.2***	***826.9***	***529.1***
			TECH. COOP. GRANTS			
–	–	–	–	–	–	–
0.2	0.2	0.2	0.2	0.2	0.2	0.2
0.1	0.1	0.0	0.1	0.1	0.1	0.0
–	–	–	–	–	–	–
–	–	–	–	–	–	–
–	–	–	–	–	–	–
–	–	0.2	–	–	–	0.2
5.8	7.4	12.1	4.7	5.3	7.4	12.1
0.0	0.0	–	–	0.0	0.0	–
0.1	0.1	0.1	0.1	0.1	0.1	0.1
0.4	0.4	1.2	0.1	0.2	0.4	1.2
–	–	–	–	–	–	–
–	–	–	–	–	–	–
–	–	–	–	–	–	–
0.2	0.4	0.4	0.0	0.0	–	–
–	–	–	–	–	–	–
591.0	655.0	673.0	–	–	–	–
597.8	*663.5*	*687.2*	*5.1*	*5.8*	*8.1*	*13.7*
0.3	*0.3*	*0.2*	*0.4*	*0.3*	*0.3*	*0.2*
–	–	–	–	–	–	–
6.2	*7.8*	*13.5*	*4.8*	*5.5*	*7.8*	*13.5*
598.1	***663.8***	***687.3***	***5.5***	***6.1***	***8.4***	***13.9***
			TOTAL OOF NET			
–	–	–	–	–	–	–
–	–	–	-0.3	-0.3	-0.4	-0.4
–	–	–	–	–	–	–
26.3	17.0	17.0	14.1	22.4	13.5	13.5
–	–	–	–	–	–	–
–	–	–	–	–	–	–
–	–	–	–	–	–	–
–	–	0.5	-0.4	-1.2	-0.3	0.4
2.4	1.0	16.9	1.9	0.8	-0.5	14.4
–	–	–	–	–	–	–
–	–	–	–	-0.2	–	–
–	–	–	-0.1	–	–	–
–	–	–	–	–	–	–
–	–	–	–	–	–	–
–	–	–	–	–	–	–
–	–	–	–	–	–	–
56.0	64.0	26.0	–	31.0	40.0	1.0
84.7	*82.0*	*60.5*	*15.2*	*52.5*	*52.3*	*28.8*
16.5	*19.0*	*14.3*	*-2.7*	*3.5*	*-2.4*	*-3.3*
–	–	–	–	–	–	–
2.4	*1.0*	*17.5*	*1.5*	*-0.6*	*-0.8*	*14.8*
101.1	***101.0***	***74.8***	***12.5***	***56.0***	***49.8***	***25.5***

MAIN AID AGGREGATES

	1977	1978	1979	1980
DAC COUNTRIES COMBINED				
PRIVATE SECTOR NET	286.5	438.3	452.3	353.4
Direct Investment	3.7	-1.4	19.7	2.9
Portfolio Invest.	232.2	423.6	284.7	368.2
Export Credits	50.6	16.1	147.8	-17.7
OFFICIAL & PRIVATE				
GROSS:				
Contractual Lending	459.9	461.0	940.8	469.1
Export Credits Tot.	184.4	114.6	367.3	213.4
Export Credits Priv	142.8	70.0	285.4	153.5
OTHER NET DATA				
Contractual Lending	299.3	370.2	721.0	216.0
Export Credits Tot.	64.3	30.0	200.4	10.8
(Bank Sector Loans)	-34.0	–	378.0	-74.0
ODA CONCESSIONALITY				
Total:Grant Element	87.0	83.0	88.0	85.0
Loans:Grant Element	65.0	59.0	66.0	36.0
OTHER SOURCES				
CMEA Countr.(Gross)	–	–	–	–
Intra LDCS Exc.OPEC	–	–	–	–
Other	–	–	–	–
ALL SOURCE COMMITMENTS				
TOTAL BILATERAL	846.7	957.0	916.2	877.6
of which				
OPEC (ODA)	–	–	–	–
CMEA (ODA)	–	–	–	–
TOTAL MULTILAT.(ODA)	0.4	0.3	0.3	0.2
TOTAL BIL.& MULTIL.	847.1	957.3	916.4	877.8
of which				
ODA Grants	530.8	532.8	534.3	412.2
ODA Loans	309.9	370.3	292.5	116.9
ODA CONCESSIONALITY				
Total: Grant Element	87.0	83.0	88.0	85.0
Loans: Grant Element	65.0	59.0	66.0	36.0

INDEBTEDNESS

	1977	1978	1979	1980
TOTAL DEBT DISBURSED	***5100.7***	***6063.9***	***7080.6***	
Debt to DAC Countries	4988.0	5948.0	6967.0	
ODA	1382.0	1872.0	2445.0	
Total Export Credits	647.0	767.0	998.0	
Other Private Market	2959.0	3309.0	3524.0	
International Org.	110.3	114.3	112.9	
CMEA	2.1	1.4	0.7	
Other	0.3	0.2	0.0	
TOTAL DEBT SERVICE	***662.5***	***743.7***	***886.9***	
Paid to DAC Countries	590.1	721.0	855.0	
ODA	67.9	62.5	86.7	
Total Export Credits	157.7	145.3	211.6	
Other Private Market	364.5	513.2	556.7	
International Org.	21.6	21.7	30.9	
CMEA	0.9	0.8	0.8	
Other	50.0	0.2	0.2	

ECONOMIC INDICATORS

	1977	1978	1979	1980
GNP Curr. Prices, $M	1436.1	1403.0	1796.5	2031.7
Real GNP, 1976=100	103.0	107.0	110.0	110.0
GNP/Cap Curr. Prices,$	397.0	379.0	474.0	524.0
GNP/cap Atlas Basis, $	3549.4	3879.5	4225.4	4498.3
Real GNP/Cap, 1976=100	101.0	103.0	103.0	100.0
Population, Million	3.6	3.7	3.8	3.9
Curr.A/C Deficit(-),$M	-1766.0	-2538.0	-2927.0	-2789.0
BOP Exp. & Transf.,$M	6463.0	7564.0	9217.0	11131.0
Exp. to OECD CIF, $M	2168.5	2888.7	3428.4	3973.1
of which				
Manufact.	651.2	820.6	1114.8	1515.4
Imp. from OECD FOB, $M	3279.0	4051.0	5041.0	4585.3
Reserves ex. Gold, $M	1521.6	2625.1	3063.5	3351.4

TOTAL RECEIPTS NET / TOTAL ODA NET

	Total Receipts Net 1977	1978	1979	1980	Total ODA Net 1977	1978	1979	1980
DAC COUNTRIES								
Australia	–	-0.2	0.0	–	–	0.0	–	–
Austria	43.8	0.2	3.9	-4.2	0.2	0.2	0.2	0.0
Belgium	126.6	149.7	110.1	-32.1	4.1	4.2	11.8	10.0
Canada	45.1	24.8	16.4	9.4	6.5	12.4	15.9	4.8
Denmark	1.1	1.2	3.1	0.2	-0.1	-0.2	-0.1	-0.1
Finland	–	–	0.0	–	–	–	0.0	–
France	195.5	224.3	264.4	645.2	55.7	51.4	86.6	118.3
Germany, Fed. Rep.	10.7	60.9	39.9	87.8	5.7	16.5	18.9	11.7
Italy	11.0	-1.8	-9.5	-2.2	0.1	0.1	0.0	0.1
Japan	18.9	11.4	-0.7	-0.3	0.2	0.3	0.1	0.2
Netherlands	1.6	1.3	31.8	22.2	1.6	1.3	1.9	2.1
New Zealand	–	0.0	–	–	–	–	–	–
Norway	6.4	-5.8	-9.3	-9.7	0.1	0.2	0.2	0.0
Sweden	–	–	0.2	0.1	–	–	–	–
Switzerland	0.1	0.1	0.2	16.4	0.1	0.1	0.2	0.3
United Kingdom	22.1	39.7	22.0	10.3	0.2	0.3	0.9	3.6
United States	8.0	5.0	1.0	28.0	1.0	-1.0	2.0	1.0
TOTAL	*490.7*	*510.8*	*473.7*	*771.0*	*75.2*	*85.7*	*138.6*	*151.9*
MULTILATERAL								
AF.D.F.	–	–	–	–	–	–	–	–
AF.D.B.	1.4	3.6	5.1	3.9	–	–	–	–
AS.D.B.	–	–	–	–	–	–	–	–
CAR.D.B.	–	–	–	–	–	–	–	–
E.E.C.	29.4	12.5	13.5	15.4	20.5	6.4	13.2	11.4
IBRD	34.9	54.8	52.8	78.3	–	4.1	3.0	1.9
IDA	3.7	0.8	–	–	3.7	0.8	–	–
I.D.B.	–	–	–	–	–	–	–	–
IFAD	–	–	–	–	–	–	–	–
I.F.C.	0.9	0.2	–	4.8	–	–	–	–
IMF TRUST FUND	–	27.1	–	37.8	–	27.1	–	37.8
U.N. AGENCIES	–	–	–	–	–	–	–	–
UNDP	3.9	3.9	4.2	3.8	3.9	3.9	4.2	3.8
UNTA	0.2	0.3	0.4	0.1	0.2	0.3	0.4	0.1
UNICEF	0.2	0.2	0.2	0.7	0.2	0.2	0.2	0.7
UNRWA	–	–	–	–	–	–	–	–
WFP	0.4	1.1	0.3	1.6	0.4	1.1	0.3	1.6
UNHCR	–	0.0	0.1	0.1	–	0.0	0.1	0.1
Other Multilateral	2.4	1.8	1.6	1.0	2.4	1.8	1.6	1.0
Arab OPEC Agencies	–	–	–	0.1	–	–	–	0.1
TOTAL	*77.2*	*106.3*	*78.1*	*147.5*	*31.1*	*45.6*	*22.9*	*58.5*
OPEC COUNTRIES	–	–	–	–	–	–	–	–
E.E.C.+ MEMBERS	*397.8*	*487.8*	*475.5*	*746.7*	*87.6*	*79.9*	*133.2*	*157.0*
TOTAL	***568.0***	***617.2***	***551.8***	***918.4***	***106.3***	***131.4***	***161.5***	***210.3***

ODA LOANS GROSS / ODA LOANS NET

	ODA Loans Gross 1977	1978	1979	1980	ODA Loans Net 1977	1978	1979	1980
DAC COUNTRIES								
Australia	–	–	–	–	–	–	–	–
Austria	–	–	0.2	–	–	–	0.2	–
Belgium	1.4	–	3.4	3.4	1.4	–	3.4	3.4
Canada	2.9	8.5	13.0	3.3	2.9	8.5	13.0	3.3
Denmark	–	–	–	–	-0.1	-0.2	-0.2	-0.1
Finland	–	–	–	–	–	–	–	–
France	20.5	15.6	28.0	33.9	12.1	4.2	18.3	22.7
Germany, Fed. Rep.	2.6	13.3	14.9	8.0	1.3	11.0	12.2	5.0
Italy	–	–	–	–	–	–	–	–
Japan	–	–	–	–	–	–	0.0	0.0
Netherlands	–	–	0.4	0.1	–	–	0.4	0.1
New Zealand	–	–	–	–	–	–	–	–
Norway	–	–	–	–	–	–	–	–
Sweden	–	–	–	–	–	–	–	–
Switzerland	–	–	–	–	–	–	–	–
United Kingdom	–	–	0.4	3.1	–	–	0.4	3.0
United States	–	–	–	–	–	–	–	–
TOTAL	*27.5*	*37.4*	*60.2*	*51.8*	*17.6*	*23.5*	*47.6*	*37.1*
MULTILATERAL	*14.9*	*35.9*	*7.6*	*48.3*	*14.0*	*34.5*	*6.2*	*46.8*
OPEC COUNTRIES	–	–	–	–	–	–	–	–
E.E.C.+ MEMBERS	*35.7*	*32.9*	*51.6*	*57.0*	*25.0*	*17.7*	*37.6*	*40.9*
TOTAL	***42.4***	***73.3***	***67.8***	***100.0***	***31.6***	***58.0***	***53.7***	***83.9***

TOTAL OFFICIAL GROSS / TOTAL OFFICIAL NET

	Total Official Gross 1977	1978	1979	1980	Total Official Net 1977	1978	1979	1980
DAC COUNTRIES								
Australia	–	0.0	0.0	–	–	0.0	0.0	–
Austria	0.2	0.2	0.2	0.0	0.2	0.2	0.2	0.0
Belgium	4.1	4.2	11.8	10.0	4.1	4.2	11.8	10.0
Canada	45.1	24.8	16.4	9.4	45.1	24.8	16.4	9.4
Denmark	1.2	1.4	3.7	1.5	1.1	1.2	3.0	0.2
Finland	–	–	0.0	–	–	–	0.0	–
France	97.5	87.5	117.9	147.2	88.7	75.2	106.5	133.1
Germany, Fed. Rep.	8.5	19.8	23.2	44.8	7.2	17.4	20.3	39.6
Italy	0.1	0.1	0.0	0.1	-2.5	-3.9	-4.0	-3.9
Japan	0.2	0.3	0.2	0.2	0.2	0.3	0.1	0.2
Netherlands	1.6	1.3	3.4	2.1	1.6	1.3	3.4	2.1
New Zealand	–	–	–	–	–	–	–	–
Norway	0.1	0.2	0.2	0.0	0.1	0.2	0.2	0.0
Sweden	–	–	–	–	–	–	–	–
Switzerland	0.1	0.1	0.2	0.3	0.1	0.1	0.2	0.3
United Kingdom	0.2	2.4	6.2	3.7	0.2	2.4	6.2	3.6
United States	11.0	7.0	4.0	31.0	8.0	5.0	1.0	28.0
TOTAL	*169.9*	*149.2*	*187.5*	*250.2*	*153.9*	*128.4*	*165.3*	*222.6*
MULTILATERAL	*83.4*	*115.2*	*90.4*	*164.7*	*77.2*	*106.3*	*78.1*	*147.5*
OPEC COUNTRIES	–	–	–	–	–	–	–	–
E.E.C.+ MEMBERS	*146.1*	*134.3*	*186.0*	*233.6*	*129.6*	*110.2*	*160.7*	*200.1*
TOTAL	***253.3***	***264.4***	***277.9***	***414.9***	***231.1***	***234.7***	***243.4***	***370.1***

TOTAL ODA GROSS / GRANTS / TOTAL OOF GROSS

	197[illegible]
TOTAL ODA GROSS	
Australia	
Austria	0[illegible]
Belgium	4[illegible]
Canada	6[illegible]
Denmark	
Finland	
France	64[illegible]
Germany, Fed. Rep.	6[illegible]
Italy	0[illegible]
Japan	0[illegible]
Netherlands	1[illegible]
New Zealand	
Norway	[illegible]
Sweden	
Switzerland	[illegible]
United Kingdom	[illegible]
United States	1[illegible]
TOTAL	*85[illegible]*
AF.D.F.	
AF.D.B.	
AS.D.B.	
CAR.D.B.	
E.E.C.	21[illegible]
IBRD	
IDA	[illegible]
I.D.B.	
IFAD	
I.F.C.	
IMF TRUST FUND	
U.N. AGENCIES	
UNDP	[illegible]
UNTA	[illegible]
UNICEF	[illegible]
UNRWA	
WFP	[illegible]
UNHCR	
Other Multilateral	[illegible]
Arab OPEC Agencies	
TOTAL	*3[illegible]*
OPEC COUNTRIES	
E.E.C.+ MEMBERS	*9[illegible]*
TOTAL	***11[illegible]***
GRANTS	
Australia	
Austria	[illegible]
Belgium	[illegible]
Canada	[illegible]
Denmark	
Finland	
France	4[illegible]
Germany, Fed. Rep.	[illegible]
Italy	[illegible]
Japan	[illegible]
Netherlands	[illegible]
New Zealand	
Norway	[illegible]
Sweden	
Switzerland	[illegible]
United Kingdom	[illegible]
United States	[illegible]
TOTAL	*5[illegible]*
MULTILATERAL	*1[illegible]*
OPEC COUNTRIES	
E.E.C.+ MEMBERS	*6[illegible]*
TOTAL	***7[illegible]***
TOTAL OOF GROSS	
Australia	
Austria	
Belgium	
Canada	3[illegible]
Denmark	
Finland	
France	3[illegible]
Germany, Fed. Rep.	
Italy	
Japan	
Netherlands	
New Zealand	
Norway	
Sweden	
Switzerland	
United Kingdom	
United States	1[illegible]
TOTAL	*8[illegible]*
MULTILATERAL	*5*
OPEC COUNTRIES	
E.E.C.+ MEMBERS	*4*
TOTAL	***13[illegible]***

1978	1979	1980	1977	1978	1979	1980
			ODA COMMITMENTS			
0.0	–	–	–	0.0	–	–
0.2	0.2	0.0	–	–	0.2	–
4.2	11.8	10.0	5.1	6.0	13.1	11.5
12.4	15.9	4.8	28.1	1.6	1.2	9.0
–	0.0	0.0	–	–	–	–
–	0.0	–	–	–	0.0	–
62.8	96.3	129.6	56.9	58.0	107.8	132.7
18.8	21.6	14.7	25.8	6.1	28.7	12.9
0.1	0.0	0.1	0.1	0.1	0.0	0.1
0.3	0.2	0.2	0.3	0.4	0.2	2.9
1.3	1.9	2.1	1.1	2.7	1.3	1.0
–	–	–	–	–	–	–
0.2	0.2	0.0	–	–	0.2	–
–	–	–	–	–	–	–
0.1	0.2	0.3	–	–	0.1	0.2
0.3	0.9	3.7	0.2	0.3	16.7	0.6
-1.0	2.0	1.0	0.8	1.1	1.0	1.1
99.6	*151.2*	*166.5*	*118.3*	*76.1*	*170.5*	*172.1*
–	–	–	–	–	–	–
–	–	–	–	–	–	–
–	–	–	–	–	–	–
–	–	–	–	–	–	–
7.7	14.7	12.9	17.8	19.6	11.6	4.1
4.1	3.0	1.9	–	–	–	–
0.8	–	–	–	–	–	–
–	–	–	–	–	–	–
–	–	–	–	–	–	–
–	–	–	–	–	–	–
27.1	–	37.8	–	–	–	–
–	–	–	7.0	7.4	6.7	7.3
3.9	4.2	3.8	–	–	–	–
0.3	0.4	0.1	–	–	–	–
0.2	0.2	0.7	–	–	–	–
–	–	–	–	–	–	–
1.1	0.3	1.6	–	–	–	–
0.0	0.1	0.1	–	–	–	–
1.8	1.6	1.0	–	–	–	–
–	–	0.1	–	–	–	–
47.0	*24.4*	*60.0*	*24.7*	*27.0*	*18.3*	*11.4*
–	–	–	–	–	–	–
95.1	*147.2*	*173.1*	*106.9*	*92.6*	*179.2*	*162.9*
146.6	***175.6***	***226.5***	***143.0***	***103.1***	***188.8***	***183.4***
			TECH. COOP. GRANTS			
0.0	–	–	–	0.0	–	–
0.2	0.0	0.0	0.2	0.2	0.0	0.0
4.2	8.4	6.6	2.4	3.5	4.6	4.7
3.9	2.9	1.5	2.0	1.5	1.2	0.8
–	0.0	0.0	–	–	0.0	0.0
–	0.0	–	–	–	0.0	–
47.2	68.3	95.7	38.7	42.9	63.1	79.5
5.5	6.7	6.7	4.3	5.5	6.7	6.1
0.1	0.0	0.1	0.1	0.1	0.0	0.1
0.3	0.2	0.2	0.2	0.3	0.2	0.2
1.3	1.5	2.1	1.6	0.9	0.8	1.0
–	–	–	–	–	–	–
0.2	0.2	0.0	0.1	0.2	0.2	0.0
–	–	–	–	–	–	–
0.1	0.2	0.3	–	0.0	0.0	–
0.3	0.5	0.6	0.2	0.3	0.5	0.6
-1.0	2.0	1.0	1.0	–	–	1.0
62.2	*91.0*	*114.8*	*50.7*	*55.3*	*77.3*	*94.1*
11.1	*16.8*	*11.7*	*6.6*	*6.3*	*6.4*	*7.3*
–	–	–	–	–	–	–
62.2	*95.6*	*116.1*	*47.2*	*53.1*	*75.8*	*92.0*
73.4	***107.8***	***126.5***	***57.3***	***61.6***	***83.7***	***101.4***
			TOTAL OOF NET			
–	0.0	–	–	–	0.0	–
–	–	–	–	–	–	–
–	–	–	–	–	–	–
12.4	0.5	4.6	38.6	12.4	0.5	4.6
1.4	3.6	1.5	1.2	1.4	3.1	0.3
–	–	–	–	–	–	–
24.7	21.6	17.7	33.0	23.8	19.9	14.9
1.0	1.6	30.0	1.5	0.9	1.4	28.0
–	–	–	-2.6	-4.0	-4.1	-4.0
–	–	–	–	–	–	–
–	1.6	–	–	–	1.6	–
–	–	–	–	–	–	–
–	–	–	–	–	–	–
–	–	–	–	–	–	–
–	–	–	–	–	–	–
2.1	5.3	–	–	2.1	5.3	–
8.0	2.0	30.0	7.0	6.0	-1.0	27.0
49.6	*36.3*	*83.7*	*78.7*	*42.7*	*26.8*	*70.7*
68.2	*66.0*	*104.7*	*46.1*	*60.7*	*55.2*	*89.0*
–	–	–	–	–	–	–
39.2	*38.8*	*60.5*	*42.0*	*30.4*	*27.6*	*43.1*
117.8	***102.3***	***188.4***	***124.9***	***103.3***	***81.9***	***159.7***

MAIN AID AGGREGATES

	1977	1978	1979	1980
DAC COUNTRIES COMBINED				
PRIVATE SECTOR NET	336.8	382.5	308.4	548.4
Direct Investment	7.8	5.5	9.2	12.1
Portfolio Invest.	4.4	87.9	126.1	371.0
Export Credits	324.6	289.0	173.0	165.3
OFFICIAL & PRIVATE				
GROSS:				
Contractual Lending	507.4	466.2	418.5	490.1
Export Credits Tot.	443.7	399.6	324.5	416.5
Export Credits Priv	395.0	379.2	322.0	354.7
OTHER NET DATA				
Contractual Lending	421.0	355.2	247.4	273.1
Export Credits Tot.	370.2	303.5	168.4	218.2
(Bank Sector Loans)	130.0	188.0	180.0	55.0
ODA CONCESSIONALITY				
Total:Grant Element	84.0	91.0	75.0	82.0
Loans:Grant Element	69.0	30.0	42.0	30.0
OTHER SOURCES				
CMEA Countr.(Gross)	–	–	–	–
Intra LDCS Exc.OPEC	–	–	–	–
Other	–	–	–	–
ALL SOURCE COMMITMENTS				
TOTAL BILATERAL	219.9	110.4	296.4	205.4
of which				
OPEC (ODA)	–	–	–	–
CMEA (ODA)	–	–	–	–
TOTAL MULTILAT.(ODA)	24.7	27.0	18.3	11.4
TOTAL BIL.& MULTIL.	244.7	137.4	314.7	216.8
of which				
ODA Grants	79.0	76.2	105.0	138.9
ODA Loans	64.0	26.9	83.8	44.5
ODA CONCESSIONALITY				
Total: Grant Element	86.0	91.0	76.0	83.0
Loans: Grant Element	70.0	30.0	42.0	30.0

INDEBTEDNESS

	1977	1978	1979	1980
TOTAL DEBT DISBURSED	***2039.3***	***3140.0***	***3919.8***	
Debt to DAC Countries	1769.0	2776.0	3484.0	
ODA	194.0	235.0	281.0	
Total Export Credits	850.0	1438.0	1785.0	
Other Private Market	725.0	1103.0	1418.0	
International Org.	229.6	346.1	419.5	
CMEA	–	–	–	
Other	40.6	18.0	16.4	
TOTAL DEBT SERVICE	***298.6***	***503.1***	***605.9***	
Paid to DAC Countries	251.2	451.2	564.8	
ODA	11.2	34.2	21.8	
Total Export Credits	124.2	214.8	271.8	
Other Private Market	115.8	202.2	271.2	
International Org.	19.8	28.2	38.5	
CMEA	–	–	–	
Other	27.6	23.8	2.6	

ECONOMIC INDICATORS

	1977	1978	1979	1980
GNP Curr. Prices, $M	6060.2	7423.8	8792.3	10172.3
Real GNP, 1976=100	103.0	114.0	120.0	124.0
GNP/Cap Curr. Prices,$	812.0	947.0	1068.0	1177.0
GNP/cap Atlas Basis, $	871.9	982.7	1070.3	1149.0
Real GNP/Cap, 1976=100	98.0	103.0	104.0	102.0
Population, Million	7.5	7.8	8.2	8.6
Curr.A/C Deficit(-),$M	-187.5	-852.7	538.4	–
BOP Exp. & Transf.,$M	2758.1	3051.0	3276.8	–
Exp. to OECD CIF, $M	2431.7	2498.3	2660.3	2631.4
of which				
Manufact.	43.2	43.1	70.3	79.8
Imp. from OECD FOB, $M	1255.6	1656.6	1858.6	2029.1
Reserves ex. Gold, $M	184.8	448.0	147.0	19.7

	1977	1978	1979	1980	1977	1978	1979	1980		197
TOTAL RECEIPTS NET					**TOTAL ODA NET**				**TOTAL ODA GROSS**	
DAC COUNTRIES										
Australia	0.1	0.1	0.1	0.2	0.1	0.1	0.1	0.2	Australia	C
Austria	–	–	0.0	0.0	–	–	0.0	0.0	Austria	
Belgium	0.0	-0.4	0.2	0.0	0.0	0.0	0.0	0.2	Belgium	C
Canada	2.7	8.2	8.0	17.0	3.9	11.0	7.5	7.7	Canada	4
Denmark	–	–	0.0	0.0	–	–	0.0	0.0	Denmark	
Finland	–	–	–	0.0	–	–	–	0.0	Finland	
France	-3.9	-0.3	6.5	1.3	–	–	0.4	0.8	France	
Germany, Fed. Rep.	-1.0	0.9	4.5	3.9	3.4	3.0	3.2	8.6	Germany, Fed. Rep.	3
Italy	-0.2	0.0	0.1	0.0	0.0	0.0	0.1	0.0	Italy	C
Japan	1.9	1.5	5.3	-2.8	0.3	0.1	0.4	0.2	Japan	C
Netherlands	5.0	22.0	28.0	34.4	5.0	22.0	28.0	34.4	Netherlands	5
New Zealand	-0.8	-0.1	0.6	0.2	0.1	0.1	0.6	0.2	New Zealand	0
Norway	–	1.7	6.4	16.1	0.0	1.7	3.6	6.0	Norway	0
Sweden	-0.4	-0.2	0.6	1.2	–	0.2	1.0	1.7	Sweden	
Switzerland	4.5	0.0	0.1	-0.5	0.0	0.0	0.1	0.0	Switzerland	C
United Kingdom	-9.5	39.4	4.2	11.2	0.7	36.7	12.5	7.7	United Kingdom	1
United States	7.0	-30.0	-6.0	8.0	9.0	23.0	23.0	16.0	United States	10
TOTAL	*5.4*	*42.7*	*58.5*	*90.2*	*22.7*	*97.8*	*80.6*	*83.5*	*TOTAL*	*24*
MULTILATERAL										
AF.D.F.	–	–	–	–	–	–	–	–	AF.D.F.	
AF.D.B.	–	–	–	–	–	–	–	–	AF.D.B.	
AS.D.B.	–	–	–	–	–	–	–	–	AS.D.B.	
CAR.D.B.	5.9	7.4	–	11.7	–	7.2	–	9.3	CAR.D.B.	
E.E.C.	0.7	2.6	4.0	4.0	0.7	2.6	4.0	4.0	E.E.C.	C
IBRD	9.5	44.0	14.4	49.8	–	–	–	–	IBRD	
IDA	–	–	–	–	–	–	–	–	IDA	
I.D.B.	11.5	9.4	8.6	16.2	8.3	8.1	7.9	14.5	I.D.B.	9
IFAD	–	–	–	–	–	–	–	–	IFAD	
I.F.C.	-0.1	-0.4	-0.2	-0.2	–	–	–	–	I.F.C.	
IMF TRUST FUND	–	–	–	–	–	–	–	–	IMF TRUST FUND	
U.N. AGENCIES	–	–	–	–	–	–	–	–	U.N. AGENCIES	
UNDP	0.7	0.9	2.2	2.9	0.7	0.9	2.2	2.9	UNDP	0
UNTA	0.2	0.2	0.3	0.2	0.2	0.2	0.3	0.2	UNTA	0
UNICEF	–	0.1	0.2	0.2	–	0.1	0.2	0.2	UNICEF	
UNRWA	–	–	–	–	–	–	–	–	UNRWA	
WFP	0.0	0.0	0.1	0.0	0.0	0.0	0.1	0.0	WFP	C
UNHCR	–	–	–	–	–	–	–	–	UNHCR	
Other Multilateral	0.8	0.2	0.3	1.0	0.8	0.2	0.3	1.0	Other Multilateral	0
Arab OPEC Agencies	–	5.0	2.0	7.5	–	5.0	2.0	0.5	Arab OPEC Agencies	
TOTAL	*29.1*	*69.5*	*31.9*	*93.2*	*10.6*	*24.3*	*16.9*	*32.5*	*TOTAL*	*11*
OPEC COUNTRIES	*32.5*	*4.3*	*–*	*33.0*	*–*	*–*	*–*	*10.0*	*OPEC COUNTRIES*	
E.E.C.+ MEMBERS	*-9.0*	*64.0*	*47.5*	*54.7*	*9.8*	*64.3*	*48.2*	*55.5*	*E.E.C.+ MEMBERS*	*10*
TOTAL	***67.0***	***116.4***	***90.4***	***216.4***	***33.3***	***122.1***	***97.5***	***126.0***	***TOTAL***	***36***

	1977	1978	1979	1980	1977	1978	1979	1980		197
ODA LOANS GROSS					**ODA LOANS NET**				**GRANTS**	
DAC COUNTRIES										
Australia	–	–	–	–	–	–	–	–	Australia	0
Austria	–	–	–	–	–	–	–	–	Austria	
Belgium	–	–	–	–	–	–	–	–	Belgium	0
Canada	2.0	1.4	7.5	8.1	1.9	1.0	7.0	7.4	Canada	2
Denmark	–	–	–	–	–	–	–	–	Denmark	
Finland	–	–	–	–	–	–	–	–	Finland	
France	–	–	0.4	0.7	–	–	0.4	0.7	France	
Germany, Fed. Rep.	0.9	0.6	0.4	5.9	0.9	0.6	0.4	5.9	Germany, Fed. Rep.	2
Italy	–	–	–	–	–	–	–	–	Italy	0
Japan	–	–	–	–	–	–	–	–	Japan	0
Netherlands	4.0	20.4	20.7	31.3	4.0	20.4	20.7	31.3	Netherlands	1
New Zealand	–	–	–	–	–	–	–	–	New Zealand	0
Norway	–	–	–	–	–	–	–	–	Norway	0
Sweden	–	–	–	–	–	–	–	–	Sweden	
Switzerland	–	–	–	–	–	–	–	–	Switzerland	0
United Kingdom	0.1	36.4	12.1	6.6	-0.7	35.5	11.1	4.7	United Kingdom	1
United States	8.0	20.0	20.0	13.0	7.0	19.0	19.0	11.0	United States	2
TOTAL	*15.1*	*78.8*	*61.1*	*65.5*	*13.1*	*76.6*	*58.6*	*60.9*	*TOTAL*	*9*
MULTILATERAL	*9.9*	*21.5*	*12.7*	*26.2*	*8.8*	*20.5*	*11.7*	*25.2*	*MULTILATERAL*	*1*
OPEC COUNTRIES	*–*	*–*	*–*	*–*	*–*	*–*	*–*	*–*	*OPEC COUNTRIES*	
E.E.C.+ MEMBERS	*5.6*	*57.8*	*35.5*	*45.5*	*4.8*	*56.9*	*34.4*	*43.6*	*E.E.C.+ MEMBERS*	*5*
TOTAL	***24.9***	***100.3***	***73.8***	***91.7***	***21.9***	***97.1***	***70.3***	***86.1***	***TOTAL***	***11***

	1977	1978	1979	1980	1977	1978	1979	1980		197
TOTAL OFFICIAL GROSS					**TOTAL OFFICIAL NET**				**TOTAL OOF GROSS**	
DAC COUNTRIES										
Australia	0.1	0.1	0.1	0.2	0.1	0.1	0.1	0.2	Australia	
Austria	–	–	0.0	0.0	–	–	0.0	0.0	Austria	
Belgium	0.0	0.0	0.0	0.2	0.0	0.0	0.0	0.2	Belgium	
Canada	4.8	12.0	10.4	20.7	2.7	8.2	8.0	16.2	Canada	0
Denmark	–	–	0.0	0.0	–	–	0.0	0.0	Denmark	
Finland	–	–	–	0.0	–	–	–	0.0	Finland	
France	–	–	0.4	0.8	–	–	0.4	0.8	France	
Germany, Fed. Rep.	3.4	3.0	3.2	8.8	3.4	3.0	3.2	8.6	Germany, Fed. Rep.	
Italy	0.0	0.0	0.1	0.0	0.0	0.0	0.1	0.0	Italy	
Japan	0.3	0.1	1.0	2.4	0.3	0.1	1.0	2.4	Japan	
Netherlands	5.0	22.0	28.0	34.4	5.0	22.0	28.0	34.4	Netherlands	
New Zealand	0.4	0.1	0.6	0.2	-0.8	0.1	0.6	0.2	New Zealand	0
Norway	0.0	1.7	3.6	6.0	0.0	1.7	3.6	6.0	Norway	
Sweden	–	0.2	1.0	1.7	–	0.2	1.0	1.7	Sweden	
Switzerland	0.0	0.0	0.1	0.0	0.0	0.0	0.1	0.0	Switzerland	
United Kingdom	1.5	37.6	13.5	11.1	0.7	36.6	12.4	9.1	United Kingdom	
United States	13.0	25.0	24.0	20.0	7.0	19.0	18.0	12.0	United States	3
TOTAL	*28.7*	*101.6*	*86.1*	*106.5*	*18.5*	*91.0*	*76.6*	*91.8*	*TOTAL*	*4.*
MULTILATERAL	*32.8*	*74.9*	*38.6*	*101.5*	*29.1*	*69.5*	*31.9*	*93.2*	*MULTILATERAL*	*21.*
OPEC COUNTRIES	*32.5*	*4.3*	*–*	*33.0*	*32.5*	*4.3*	*–*	*33.0*	*OPEC COUNTRIES*	*32.*
E.E.C.+ MEMBERS	*10.6*	*65.1*	*49.3*	*59.1*	*9.7*	*64.2*	*48.2*	*57.0*	*E.E.C.+ MEMBERS*	
TOTAL	***94.0***	***180.8***	***124.7***	***241.0***	***80.1***	***164.7***	***108.5***	***218.0***	***TOTAL***	***57.***

1978	1979	1980	1977	1978	1979	1980
			ODA COMMITMENTS			
0.1	0.1	0.2	0.1	0.0	0.1	0.2
–	0.0	0.0	–	–	–	–
0.0	0.0	0.2	–	–	–	–
11.3	8.0	8.4	11.2	10.6	3.7	3.1
–	0.0	0.0	–	0.0	0.0	–
–	–	0.0	–	–	–	0.0
–	0.4	0.8	–	–	1.2	0.2
3.0	3.2	8.6	5.5	2.4	6.9	17.1
0.0	0.1	0.0	0.0	0.0	0.1	0.0
0.1	0.4	0.2	0.4	0.1	0.4	0.2
22.0	28.0	34.4	10.3	30.5	20.4	37.7
0.1	0.6	0.2	0.1	0.1	0.2	0.1
1.7	3.6	6.0	–	4.9	5.2	1.9
0.2	1.0	1.7	–	0.2	0.5	2.4
0.0	0.1	0.0	–	–	–	0.0
37.6	13.5	9.6	1.7	50.1	5.7	3.0
24.0	24.0	18.0	39.7	13.2	17.0	19.0
99.9	*83.1*	*88.1*	*69.0*	*112.1*	*61.3*	*84.8*
–	–	–	–	–	–	–
–	–	–	–	–	–	–
–	–	–	–	–	–	–
7.2	–	9.3	–	12.0	–	2.0
2.6	4.0	4.0	11.4	2.8	5.7	3.8
–	–	–	–	–	–	–
–	–	–	–	–	–	–
9.1	8.9	15.5	18.3	10.8	22.6	23.5
–	–	–	–	–	–	–
–	–	–	–	–	–	–
–	–	–	–	–	–	–
–	–	–	1.7	1.4	3.1	4.3
0.9	2.2	2.9	–	–	–	–
0.2	0.3	0.2	–	–	–	–
0.1	0.2	0.2	–	–	–	–
–	–	–	–	–	–	–
0.0	0.1	0.0	–	–	–	–
–	–	–	–	–	–	–
0.2	0.3	1.0	–	–	–	–
5.0	2.0	0.5	3.0	7.3	–	–
25.3	*17.9*	*33.5*	*34.4*	*34.3*	*3†.4*	*33.6*
–	–	*10.0*	–	–	*43.2*	*10.0*
65.1	*49.3*	*57.4*	*29.0*	*85.8*	*40.0*	*61.8*
125.2	***101.0***	***131.6***	***103.4***	***146.4***	***135.9***	***128.4***
			TECH. COOP. GRANTS			
0.1	0.1	0.2	0.1	0.1	0.1	0.2
–	0.0	0.0	–	–	0.0	0.0
0.0	0.0	0.2	0.0	0.0	0.0	0.1
9.9	0.5	0.3	0.8	0.5	0.2	0.1
–	0.0	0.0	–	–	0.0	0.0
–	–	0.0	–	–	–	0.0
–	–	0.2	–	–	–	0.2
2.4	2.9	2.7	2.5	2.4	2.9	2.7
0.0	0.1	0.0	0.0	0.0	0.1	0.0
0.1	0.4	0.2	0.3	0.1	0.2	0.2
1.5	7.3	3.1	1.0	1.5	2.2	2.7
0.1	0.6	0.2	0.1	0.0	0.1	0.2
1.7	3.6	6.0	0.0	1.7	0.1	0.1
0.2	1.0	1.7	–	0.2	0.8	0.4
0.0	0.1	0.0	–	–	–	–
1.2	1.4	3.0	1.4	1.2	1.4	2.9
4.0	4.0	5.0	2.0	3.0	3.0	3.0
21.2	*22.0*	*22.7*	*8.2*	*10.7*	*10.9*	*12.8*
3.8	*5.2*	*7.3*	*1.7*	*1.5*	*3.0*	*4.3*
–	–	*10.0*	–	–	–	–
7.3	*13.8*	*11.9*	*4.9*	*5.1*	*6.5*	*8.5*
24.9	***27.3***	***39.9***	***9.9***	***12.2***	***13.9***	***17.0***
			TOTAL OOF NET			
–	–	–	–	–	–	–
–	–	–	–	–	–	–
–	–	–	–	–	–	–
0.7	2.3	12.4	-1.2	-2.7	0.4	8.5
–	–	–	–	–	–	–
–	–	–	–	–	–	–
–	–	–	–	–	–	–
–	–	0.2	–	–	–	0.1
–	–	–	–	–	–	–
–	0.7	2.3	–	–	0.7	2.3
–	–	–	–	–	–	–
–	–	–	-0.9	–	–	–
–	–	–	–	–	–	–
–	–	–	–	–	–	–
–	–	–	–	–	–	–
–	–	1.5	-0.1	-0.1	-0.1	1.5
1.0	–	2.0	-2.0	-4.0	-5.0	-4.0
1.7	*3.0*	*18.4*	*-4.2*	*-6.8*	*-4.0*	*8.3*
49.6	*20.7*	*68.1*	*18.5*	*45.2*	*14.9*	*60.7*
4.3	–	*23.0*	*32.5*	*4.3*	–	*23.0*
–	–	*1.7*	*-0.1*	–	*-0.1*	*1.5*
55.6	***23.7***	***109.4***	***46.8***	***42.6***	***11.0***	***92.0***

	1977	1978	1979	1980
MAIN AID AGGREGATES				
DAC COUNTRIES COMBINED				
PRIVATE SECTOR NET	-13.1	-48.3	-18.1	-1.6
Direct Investment	-6.9	-42.3	-24.0	0.1
Portfolio Invest.	-3.7	-3.2	12.9	-11.2
Export Credits	-2.5	-2.7	-7.0	9.5
OFFICIAL & PRIVATE				
GROSS:				
Contractual Lending	33.7	99.7	86.0	129.2
Export Credits Tot.	18.7	20.9	25.0	61.0
Export Credits Priv	14.6	19.2	22.0	45.4
OTHER NET DATA				
Contractual Lending	6.4	67.0	47.6	78.7
Export Credits Tot.	-6.6	-9.5	-10.9	15.3
(Bank Sector Loans)	55.0	180.0	-62.0	-32.0
ODA CONCESSIONALITY				
Total:Grant Element	67.0	49.0	65.0	63.0
Loans:Grant Element	52.0	38.0	45.0	50.0
OTHER SOURCES				
CMEA Countr.(Gross)	–	–	–	–
Intra LDCS Exc.OPEC	–	–	–	–
Other	–	–	–	–
ALL SOURCE COMMITMENTS				
TOTAL BILATERAL	69.8	112.1	130.9	98.1
of which				
OPEC (ODA)	–	–	43.2	10.0
CMEA (ODA)	8.0	–	–	–
TOTAL MULTILAT.(ODA)	34.4	34.3	31.4	33.6
TOTAL BIL.& MULTIL.	104.2	146.4	162.2	131.7
of which				
ODA Grants	30.2	24.5	28.2	40.2
ODA Loans	73.1	121.9	107.7	88.2
ODA CONCESSIONALITY				
Total: Grant Element	70.0	51.0	55.0	69.0
Loans: Grant Element	56.0	41.0	44.0	52.0
INDEBTEDNESS				
TOTAL DEBT DISBURSED	***905.8***	***1038.5***	***1173.7***	
Debt to DAC Countries	702.0	777.0	843.0	
ODA	83.0	164.0	231.0	
Total Export Credits	150.0	160.0	158.0	
Other Private Market	469.0	453.0	454.0	
International Org.	101.4	159.0	196.0	
CMEA	1.2	1.2	1.2	
Other	101.1	101.3	133.5	
TOTAL DEBT SERVICE	***150.5***	***193.3***	***222.8***	
Paid to DAC Countries	133.6	168.4	170.6	
ODA	4.7	5.7	8.5	
Total Export Credits	36.6	38.2	48.6	
Other Private Market	92.3	124.5	113.5	
International Org.	9.9	14.6	18.7	
CMEA	–	–	–	
Other	7.0	10.2	33.5	
ECONOMIC INDICATORS				
GNP Curr. Prices, $M	2861.4	2381.4	2255.5	2399.0
Real GNP, 1976=100	97.0	89.0	82.0	70.0
GNP/Cap Curr. Prices,$	1360.0	1118.0	1044.0	1096.0
GNP/cap Atlas Basis, $	1161.2	1130.0	1113.0	1030.3
Real GNP/Cap, 1976=100	96.0	87.0	79.0	67.0
Population, Million	2.1	2.1	2.2	2.2
Curr.A/C Deficit(-),$M	-24.5	-97.5	-162.9	-1150.5
BOP Exp. & Transf.,$M	1044.6	1148.0	1287.0	542.2
Exp. to OECD CIF, $M	641.6	751.9	728.7	878.5
of which				
Manufact.	258.2	20.8	58.4	23.0
Imp. from OECD FOB, $M	446.8	502.8	544.0	511.7
Reserves ex. Gold, $M	47.8	58.8	63.8	105.0

	TOTAL RECEIPTS NET 1977	1978	1979	1980	TOTAL ODA NET 1977	1978	1979	1980
DAC COUNTRIES								
Australia	0.0	-0.2	0.1	0.2	0.0	0.0	0.1	0.2
Austria	0.2	0.3	0.3	0.3	0.2	0.3	0.3	0.3
Belgium	-0.6	3.8	-2.7	3.0	0.0	0.3	0.1	0.1
Canada	–	–	–	0.5	–	–	–	–
Denmark	-0.1	0.0	0.6	3.3	-0.1	0.0	0.6	3.2
Finland	–	–	–	–	–	–	–	–
France	-0.7	12.5	-6.8	61.1	–	–	–	3.6
Germany, Fed. Rep.	21.7	22.2	24.7	28.2	23.4	19.4	19.3	24.3
Italy	0.0	0.8	2.2	4.2	0.1	0.4	0.5	0.8
Japan	3.5	6.7	17.2	53.9	3.7	7.2	5.3	5.1
Netherlands	0.3	1.9	0.1	0.7	0.3	1.9	0.1	0.7
New Zealand	-0.1	–	0.0	–	–	–	–	–
Norway	0.7	-0.1	-0.2	-0.3	–	–	–	–
Sweden	0.1	-0.1	0.3	–	0.1	–	0.4	–
Switzerland	1.8	-0.7	0.8	19.4	0.8	0.2	0.8	0.3
United Kingdom	8.1	15.3	164.4	9.6	4.4	4.4	26.9	7.8
United States	72.0	84.0	44.0	125.0	74.0	85.0	39.0	50.0
TOTAL	*106.9*	*146.3*	*245.1*	*309.1*	*106.9*	*119.0*	*93.3*	*96.3*
MULTILATERAL								
AF.D.F.	–	–	–	–	–	–	–	–
AF.D.B.	–	–	–	–	–	–	–	–
AS.D.B.	–	–	–	–	–	–	–	–
CAR.D.B.	–	–	–	–	–	–	–	–
E.E.C.	2.3	7.2	7.4	12.7	2.3	7.2	6.6	11.2
IBRD	–	–	3.7	22.3	–	–	–	–
IDA	8.5	6.2	12.7	8.9	8.5	6.2	12.7	8.9
I.D.B.	–	–	–	–	–	–	–	–
IFAD	–	–	–	–	–	–	–	–
I.F.C.	–	-0.1	9.8	25.8	–	–	–	–
IMF TRUST FUND	–	–	–	–	–	–	–	–
U.N. AGENCIES	–	–	–	–	–	–	–	–
UNDP	2.0	2.4	3.2	3.7	2.0	2.4	3.2	3.7
UNTA	0.4	0.5	0.7	0.0	0.4	0.5	0.7	0.0
UNICEF	0.5	0.3	0.4	0.5	0.5	0.3	0.4	0.5
UNRWA	–	–	–	–	–	–	–	–
WFP	3.4	2.6	11.6	6.5	3.4	2.6	11.6	6.5
UNHCR	–	–	–	–	–	–	–	–
Other Multilateral	1.0	1.4	1.0	1.9	1.0	1.4	1.0	1.9
Arab OPEC Agencies	6.3	24.7	20.7	20.0	6.3	15.1	9.3	13.7
TOTAL	*24.4*	*45.2*	*71.2*	*102.3*	*24.4*	*35.7*	*45.5*	*46.4*
OPEC COUNTRIES	*337.0*	*467.6*	*985.4*	*1128.3*	*330.5*	*443.6*	*985.4*	*1129.2*
E.E.C.+ MEMBERS	*31.0*	*63.7*	*190.0*	*122.8*	*30.4*	*33.5*	*54.2*	*51.6*
TOTAL	***468.2***	***659.1***	***1301.7***	***1539.7***	***461.8***	***598.3***	***1124.2***	***1271.9***

	ODA LOANS GROSS 1977	1978	1979	1980	ODA LOANS NET 1977	1978	1979	1980
DAC COUNTRIES								
Australia	–	–	–	–	–	–	–	–
Austria	–	–	–	–	–	–	–	–
Belgium	–	–	–	–	–	–	–	–
Canada	–	–	–	–	–	–	–	–
Denmark	0.0	–	0.5	3.2	-0.1	-0.1	0.5	3.2
Finland	–	–	–	–	–	–	–	–
France	–	–	–	1.8	–	–	–	1.8
Germany, Fed. Rep.	18.9	17.6	18.3	17.3	17.6	13.7	12.9	14.1
Italy	–	–	–	–	–	–	–	–
Japan	3.5	6.7	2.4	2.2	3.5	6.7	2.4	2.2
Netherlands	–	–	–	–	–	–	–	–
New Zealand	–	–	–	–	–	–	–	–
Norway	–	–	–	–	–	–	–	–
Sweden	–	–	–	–	–	–	–	–
Switzerland	–	–	–	–	–	–	–	–
United Kingdom	3.2	3.1	26.0	4.1	1.9	1.6	24.0	1.0
United States	28.0	28.0	22.0	25.0	26.0	25.0	19.0	23.0
TOTAL	*53.6*	*55.5*	*69.2*	*53.5*	*48.9*	*47.0*	*58.9*	*45.3*
MULTILATERAL	*14.9*	*21.3*	*22.2*	*24.2*	*14.8*	*21.2*	*22.1*	*22.8*
OPEC COUNTRIES	*30.6*	*22.2*	*39.9*	*55.9*	*30.0*	*19.5*	*36.1*	*50.0*
E.E.C.+ MEMBERS	*22.1*	*20.8*	*45.0*	*26.6*	*19.4*	*15.2*	*37.6*	*20.3*
TOTAL	***99.2***	***99.1***	***131.3***	***133.6***	***93.7***	***87.7***	***117.1***	***118.1***

	TOTAL OFFICIAL GROSS 1977	1978	1979	1980	TOTAL OFFICIAL NET 1977	1978	1979	1980
DAC COUNTRIES								
Australia	0.0	0.0	0.1	0.2	0.0	0.0	0.1	0.2
Austria	0.2	0.3	0.3	0.3	0.2	0.3	0.3	0.3
Belgium	0.0	0.3	0.1	0.1	0.0	0.3	0.1	0.1
Canada	–	–	–	–	–	–	–	–
Denmark	0.0	0.0	0.6	3.2	-0.1	0.0	0.6	3.2
Finland	–	–	–	–	–	–	–	–
France	–	–	–	3.6	–	–	–	3.6
Germany, Fed. Rep.	24.6	23.4	24.6	27.5	23.4	19.4	19.3	24.3
Italy	0.1	0.4	0.5	0.8	0.1	0.4	0.5	0.8
Japan	3.7	7.2	5.3	5.1	3.7	7.2	5.3	5.1
Netherlands	0.3	1.9	0.1	0.7	0.3	1.9	0.1	0.7
New Zealand	0.0	–	–	–	-0.1	–	–	–
Norway	–	–	–	–	–	–	–	–
Sweden	0.1	–	0.4	–	0.1	–	0.4	–
Switzerland	0.8	0.2	0.8	0.3	0.8	0.2	0.8	0.3
United Kingdom	5.8	5.9	28.9	10.9	4.4	4.4	26.9	7.8
United States	76.0	88.0	47.0	128.0	72.0	84.0	44.0	125.0
TOTAL	*111.7*	*127.5*	*108.7*	*180.6*	*104.9*	*118.0*	*98.3*	*171.3*
MULTILATERAL	*24.5*	*45.4*	*71.5*	*103.8*	*24.4*	*45.2*	*71.2*	*102.3*
OPEC COUNTRIES	*337.5*	*470.4*	*989.2*	*1136.9*	*337.0*	*467.6*	*985.4*	*1128.3*
E.E.C.+ MEMBERS	*33.1*	*39.0*	*62.3*	*59.4*	*30.4*	*33.5*	*55.0*	*53.1*
TOTAL	***473.7***	***643.3***	***1169.4***	***1421.3***	***466.2***	***630.8***	***1155.0***	***1401.9***

TOTAL ODA GROSS	197[illegible]
Australia	[illegible]
Austria	[illegible]
Belgium	[illegible]
Canada	
Denmark	[illegible]
Finland	
France	
Germany, Fed. Rep.	24[illegible]
Italy	[illegible]
Japan	[illegible]
Netherlands	[illegible]
New Zealand	
Norway	
Sweden	[illegible]
Switzerland	[illegible]
United Kingdom	[illegible]
United States	76[illegible]
TOTAL	*11[illegible]*
AF.D.F.	
AF.D.B.	
AS.D.B.	
CAR.D.B.	
E.E.C.	
IBRD	
IDA	[illegible]
I.D.B.	
IFAD	
I.F.C.	
IMF TRUST FUND	
U.N. AGENCIES	
UNDP	[illegible]
UNTA	[illegible]
UNICEF	[illegible]
UNRWA	
WFP	[illegible]
UNHCR	
Other Multilateral	
Arab OPEC Agencies	[illegible]
TOTAL	*2[illegible]*
OPEC COUNTRIES	*33[illegible]*
E.E.C.+ MEMBERS	*3[illegible]*
TOTAL	***46[illegible]***

GRANTS	
Australia	[illegible]
Austria	[illegible]
Belgium	[illegible]
Canada	
Denmark	[illegible]
Finland	
France	
Germany, Fed. Rep.	[illegible]
Italy	[illegible]
Japan	[illegible]
Netherlands	[illegible]
New Zealand	
Norway	
Sweden	[illegible]
Switzerland	[illegible]
United Kingdom	[illegible]
United States	4[illegible]
TOTAL	*5[illegible]*
MULTILATERAL	[illegible]
OPEC COUNTRIES	*30[illegible]*
E.E.C.+ MEMBERS	*1[illegible]*
TOTAL	***36[illegible]***

TOTAL OOF GROSS	
Australia	
Austria	
Belgium	
Canada	
Denmark	
Finland	
France	
Germany, Fed. Rep.	
Italy	
Japan	
Netherlands	
New Zealand	[illegible]
Norway	
Sweden	
Switzerland	
United Kingdom	
United States	
TOTAL	[illegible]
MULTILATERAL	
OPEC COUNTRIES	[illegible]
E.E.C.+ MEMBERS	
TOTAL	[illegible]

1978	1979	1980	1977	1978	1979	1980
			ODA COMMITMENTS			
0.0	0.1	0.2	–	0.0	0.0	1.9
0.3	0.3	0.3	–	–	–	–
0.3	0.1	0.1	–	–	–	–
–	–	–	–	–	–	0.0
0.0	0.6	3.2	0.0	9.1	–	–
–	–	–	–	–	–	–
–	–	3.6	9.2	–	17.1	1.8
23.4	24.6	27.5	10.3	31.0	23.4	34.4
0.4	0.5	0.8	0.1	0.4	0.5	0.8
7.2	5.3	5.1	28.1	0.5	5.8	39.2
1.9	0.1	0.7	0.4	0.2	1.2	0.3
–	–	–	–	–	–	–
–	–	–	–	–	–	–
–	0.4	–	–	–	–	–
0.2	0.8	0.3	–	0.8	0.0	0.1
5.9	28.9	10.9	2.5	11.1	26.3	6.8
88.0	42.0	52.0	78.4	133.3	69.8	75.8
127.5	*103.7*	*104.6*	*129.0*	*186.4*	*144.2*	*161.0*
–	–	–	–	–	–	–
–	–	–	–	–	–	–
–	–	–	–	–	–	–
–	–	–	–	–	–	–
7.2	6.6	11.2	3.3	4.1	14.2	15.8
–	–	–	–	–	–	–
6.4	12.8	9.1	–	14.0	–	–
–	–	–	–	–	–	–
–	–	–	–	–	–	–
–	–	–	–	–	–	–
–	–	–	–	–	–	–
–	–	–	7.2	7.2	16.9	12.6
2.4	3.2	3.7	–	–	–	–
0.5	0.7	0.0	–	–	–	–
0.3	0.4	0.5	–	–	–	–
–	–	–	–	–	–	–
2.6	11.6	6.5	–	–	–	–
–	–	–	–	–	–	–
1.4	1.0	1.9	–	–	–	–
15.1	9.3	14.8	22.2	7.1	–	–
35.8	*45.6*	*47.7*	*32.8*	*32.4*	*31.0*	*28.4*
446.4	*989.2*	*1135.0*	*398.2*	*1560.0*	*413.3*	*1183.0*
39.0	*61.5*	*57.9*	*25.8*	*55.9*	*82.8*	*59.8*
609.7	***1138.4***	***1287.4***	***560.0***	***1778.7***	***588.5***	***1372.4***
			TECH. COOP. GRANTS			
0.0	0.1	0.2	0.0	0.0	0.1	0.1
0.3	0.3	0.3	0.2	0.3	0.3	0.3
0.3	0.1	0.1	0.0	0.1	0.1	0.1
–	–	–	–	–	–	–
0.0	0.0	–	0.0	0.0	0.0	–
–	–	–	–	–	–	–
–	–	1.9	–	–	–	1.9
5.7	6.3	10.2	5.0	5.2	5.7	8.3
0.4	0.5	0.8	0.1	0.4	0.5	0.3
0.5	2.9	2.9	0.2	0.5	1.1	0.7
1.9	0.1	0.7	0.3	0.2	0.1	0.3
–	–	–	–	–	–	–
–	–	–	–	–	–	–
–	0.4	–	–	–	–	–
0.2	0.8	0.3	0.1	0.0	0.0	0.0
2.8	2.9	6.8	2.5	2.8	2.9	3.2
60.0	20.0	27.0	2.0	2.0	4.0	4.0
72.0	*34.5*	*51.1*	*10.4*	*11.5*	*14.9*	*19.1*
14.4	*23.3*	*23.6*	*3.8*	*4.6*	*5.3*	*12.6*
424.1	*949.4*	*1079.1*	–	–	–	–
18.2	*16.5*	*31.3*	*8.0*	*8.7*	*9.4*	*14.0*
510.6	***1007.2***	***1153.8***	***14.2***	***16.0***	***20.2***	***31.7***
			TOTAL OOF NET			
–	–	–	–	–	–	–
–	–	–	–	–	–	–
–	–	–	–	–	–	–
–	–	–	–	–	–	–
–	–	–	–	–	–	–
–	–	–	–	–	–	–
–	–	–	–	–	–	–
–	–	–	–	–	–	–
–	–	–	–	–	–	–
–	–	–	–	–	–	–
–	–	–	–	–	–	–
–	–	–	-0.1	–	–	–
–	–	–	–	–	–	–
–	–	–	–	–	–	–
–	–	–	–	–	–	–
–	–	–	–	–	–	–
–	5.0	76.0	-2.0	-1.0	5.0	75.0
–	*5.0*	*76.0*	*-2.1*	*-1.0*	*5.0*	*75.0*
9.6	*25.9*	*56.1*	–	*9.5*	*25.7*	*55.9*
24.0	–	*1.9*	*6.4*	*24.0*	–	*-0.8*
–	*0.8*	*1.5*	–	–	*0.8*	*1.5*
33.6	***30.9***	***133.9***	***4.4***	***32.5***	***30.7***	***130.0***

MAIN AID AGGREGATES

	1977	1978	1979	1980
DAC COUNTRIES COMBINED				
PRIVATE SECTOR NET	2.1	28.3	146.7	137.8
Direct Investment	0.6	3.9	2.8	0.9
Portfolio Invest.	0.6	-4.1	18.9	19.4
Export Credits	0.9	28.6	125.0	117.4
OFFICIAL & PRIVATE				
GROSS:				
Contractual Lending	72.9	135.4	264.7	291.0
Export Credits Tot.	19.2	79.9	195.6	237.5
Export Credits Priv	19.2	79.9	190.6	161.5
OTHER NET DATA				
Contractual Lending	47.8	74.6	188.9	237.7
Export Credits Tot.	-1.1	27.6	130.0	192.4
(Bank Sector Loans)	44.0	27.0	-4.0	39.0
ODA CONCESSIONALITY				
Total:Grant Element	77.0	83.0	68.0	77.0
Loans:Grant Element	55.0	67.0	61.0	58.0
OTHER SOURCES				
CMEA Countr.(Gross)	1.5	2.5	3.8	4.4
Intra LDCS Exc.OPEC	–	–	–	–
Other	–	–	–	–
ALL SOURCE COMMITMENTS				
TOTAL BILATERAL	527.2	1746.4	621.2	1620.9
of which				
OPEC (ODA)	398.2	1560.0	413.3	1183.0
CMEA (ODA)	–	–	–	–
TOTAL MULTILAT.(ODA)	32.8	32.4	31.1	28.4
TOTAL BIL.& MULTIL.	560.0	1778.7	652.3	1649.3
of which				
ODA Grants	372.9	1576.6	401.0	1180.6
ODA Loans	187.0	202.2	187.5	191.8
ODA CONCESSIONALITY				
Total: Grant Element	83.0	95.0	84.0	92.0
Loans: Grant Element	49.0	57.0	52.0	48.0

INDEBTEDNESS

	1977	1978	1979	1980
TOTAL DEBT DISBURSED	***769.7***	***984.3***	***1294.0***	
Debt to DAC Countries	581.0	712.0	910.0	
ODA	262.0	342.0	425.0	
Total Export Credits	177.0	142.0	220.0	
Other Private Market	142.0	228.0	265.0	
International Org.	55.8	72.7	106.4	
CMEA	–	–	–	
Other	132.9	199.7	277.6	
TOTAL DEBT SERVICE	***52.7***	***73.3***	***151.2***	
Paid to DAC Countries	45.1	61.8	132.0	
ODA	7.8	14.4	19.1	
Total Export Credits	23.3	19.4	76.0	
Other Private Market	14.0	28.0	36.9	
International Org.	0.8	1.7	3.0	
CMEA	–	–	–	
Other	6.8	9.9	16.2	

ECONOMIC INDICATORS

	1977	1978	1979	1980
GNP Curr. Prices, $M	1899.4	2376.8	2700.6	3381.3
Real GNP, 1976=100	102.0	114.0	111.0	125.0
GNP/Cap Curr. Prices,$	654.0	788.0	863.0	1042.0
GNP/cap Atlas Basis, $	1015.4	1173.0	1202.3	1416.0
Real GNP/Cap, 1976=100	99.0	107.0	101.0	109.0
Population, Million	2.9	3.0	3.1	3.2
Curr.A/C Deficit(-),$M	-516.9	-623.7	-1062.8	-935.4
BOP Exp. & Transf.,$M	1152.4	1384.2	1728.7	2364.0
Exp. to OECD CIF, $M	33.5	48.0	53.1	66.0
of which				
Manufact.	8.5	20.8	22.8	23.8
Imp. from OECD FOB, $M	784.7	860.0	1169.3	1625.2
Reserves ex. Gold, $M	643.2	885.6	1166.1	1142.8

	1977	1978	1979	1980	1977	1978	1979	1980		197
TOTAL RECEIPTS NET					**TOTAL ODA NET**				**TOTAL ODA GROSS**	
DAC COUNTRIES										
Australia	0.1	–	4.8	4.5	0.1	–	4.8	4.5	Australia	[illegible]
Austria	–	0.0	0.1	0.2	–	0.0	0.1	0.2	Austria	
Belgium	–	0.0	0.4	1.1	–	0.0	0.4	1.1	Belgium	
Canada	0.0	–	–	–	0.0	–	–	–	Canada	[illegible]
Denmark	–	–	1.0	1.4	–	–	1.0	1.4	Denmark	
Finland	–	–	0.4	0.5	–	–	0.4	0.5	Finland	
France	0.1	0.2	0.0	3.5	–	–	–	3.5	France	
Germany, Fed. Rep.	0.0	–	8.7	18.3	0.0	–	8.7	18.3	Germany, Fed. Rep.	[illegible]
Italy	–	–	–	0.2	–	–	–	0.2	Italy	
Japan	0.1	0.2	0.1	0.1	0.1	0.2	0.1	0.1	Japan	[illegible]
Netherlands	–	–	1.5	6.8	–	–	1.5	6.8	Netherlands	
New Zealand	0.1	0.0	0.1	–	0.1	0.0	0.1	–	New Zealand	[illegible]
Norway	–	–	0.9	0.2	–	–	0.9	0.2	Norway	
Sweden	–	–	4.7	6.8	–	–	4.7	6.8	Sweden	
Switzerland	0.0	0.0	0.8	3.9	0.0	0.0	0.8	3.9	Switzerland	[illegible]
United Kingdom	0.0	–	1.7	1.1	0.0	–	1.7	1.1	United Kingdom	[illegible]
United States	–	–	–	–	–	–	–	–	United States	
TOTAL	*0.3*	*0.4*	*24.9*	*48.6*	*0.2*	*0.2*	*25.0*	*48.6*	*TOTAL*	[illegible]
MULTILATERAL										
AF.D.F.	–	–	–	–	–	–	–	–	AF.D.F.	
AF.D.B.	–	–	–	–	–	–	–	–	AF.D.B.	
AS.D.B.	–	–	–	–	–	–	–	–	AS.D.B.	
CAR.D.B.	–	–	–	–	–	–	–	–	CAR.D.B.	
E.E.C.	–	–	35.6	18.8	–	–	35.6	18.8	E.E.C.	
IBRD	–	–	–	–	–	–	–	–	IBRD	
IDA	–	–	–	–	–	–	–	–	IDA	
I.D.B.	–	–	–	–	–	–	–	–	I.D.B.	
IFAD	–	–	–	–	–	–	–	–	IFAD	
I.F.C.	–	–	–	–	–	–	–	–	I.F.C.	
IMF TRUST FUND	–	–	–	–	–	–	–	–	IMF TRUST FUND	
U.N. AGENCIES	–	–	–	–	–	–	–	–	U.N. AGENCIES	
UNDP	–	–	–	15.4	–	–	–	15.4	UNDP	
UNTA	0.1	0.1	–	0.2	0.1	0.1	–	0.2	UNTA	[illegible]
UNICEF	–	–	18.4	49.0	–	–	18.4	49.0	UNICEF	
UNRWA	–	–	–	–	–	–	–	–	UNRWA	
WFP	–	–	10.9	60.9	–	–	10.9	60.9	WFP	
UNHCR	–	–	18.3	74.1	–	–	18.3	74.1	UNHCR	
Other Multilateral	–	0.0	0.1	13.3	–	0.0	0.1	13.3	Other Multilateral	
Arab OPEC Agencies	–	–	–	–	–	–	–	–	Arab OPEC Agencies	
TOTAL	*0.1*	*0.1*	*83.3*	*231.6*	*0.1*	*0.1*	*83.3*	*231.6*	*TOTAL*	[illegible]
OPEC COUNTRIES	–	–	–	*1.0*	–	–	–	*1.0*	*OPEC COUNTRIES*	
E.E.C.+ MEMBERS	*0.1*	*0.2*	*48.8*	*51.2*	*0.0*	*0.0*	*48.8*	*51.2*	*E.E.C.+ MEMBERS*	[illegible]
TOTAL	***0.4***	***0.5***	***108.2***	***281.2***	***0.3***	***0.3***	***108.2***	***281.2***	***TOTAL***	[illegible]

	1977	1978	1979	1980	1977	1978	1979	1980		197
ODA LOANS GROSS					**ODA LOANS NET**				**GRANTS**	
DAC COUNTRIES										
Australia	–	–	–	–	–	–	–	–	Australia	[illegible]
Austria	–	–	–	–	–	–	–	–	Austria	
Belgium	–	–	–	–	–	–	–	–	Belgium	
Canada	–	–	–	–	–	–	–	–	Canada	[illegible]
Denmark	–	–	–	–	–	–	–	–	Denmark	
Finland	–	–	–	–	–	–	–	–	Finland	
France	–	–	–	–	–	–	–	–	France	
Germany, Fed. Rep.	–	–	–	–	–	–	–	–	Germany, Fed. Rep.	[illegible]
Italy	–	–	–	–	–	–	–	–	Italy	
Japan	–	–	–	–	–	–	–	–	Japan	[illegible]
Netherlands	–	–	–	–	–	–	–	–	Netherlands	
New Zealand	–	–	–	–	–	–	–	–	New Zealand	[illegible]
Norway	–	–	–	–	–	–	–	–	Norway	
Sweden	–	–	–	–	–	–	–	–	Sweden	
Switzerland	–	–	–	–	–	–	–	–	Switzerland	[illegible]
United Kingdom	–	–	–	–	–	–	–	–	United Kingdom	[illegible]
United States	–	–	–	–	–	–	–	–	United States	
TOTAL	–	–	–	–	–	–	–	–	*TOTAL*	[illegible]
MULTILATERAL	–	–	–	–	–	–	–	–	*MULTILATERAL*	[illegible]
OPEC COUNTRIES	–	–	–	–	–	–	–	–	*OPEC COUNTRIES*	
E.E.C.+ MEMBERS	–	–	–	–	–	–	–	–	*E.E.C.+ MEMBERS*	[illegible]
TOTAL	–	–	–	–	–	–	–	–	***TOTAL***	[illegible]

	1977	1978	1979	1980	1977	1978	1979	1980		197
TOTAL OFFICIAL GROSS					**TOTAL OFFICIAL NET**				**TOTAL OOF GROSS**	
DAC COUNTRIES										
Australia	0.1	–	4.8	4.5	0.1	–	4.8	4.5	Australia	
Austria	–	0.0	0.1	0.2	–	0.0	0.1	0.2	Austria	
Belgium	–	0.0	0.4	1.1	–	0.0	0.4	1.1	Belgium	
Canada	0.0	–	–	–	0.0	–	–	–	Canada	
Denmark	–	–	1.0	1.4	–	–	1.0	1.4	Denmark	
Finland	–	–	0.4	0.5	–	–	0.4	0.5	Finland	
France	0.1	0.0	–	3.5	0.1	0.0	–	3.5	France	[illegible]
Germany, Fed. Rep.	0.0	–	8.7	18.3	0.0	–	8.7	18.3	Germany, Fed. Rep.	
Italy	–	–	–	0.2	–	–	–	0.2	Italy	
Japan	0.1	0.2	0.1	0.1	0.1	0.2	0.1	0.1	Japan	
Netherlands	–	–	1.5	6.8	–	–	1.5	6.8	Netherlands	
New Zealand	0.1	0.0	0.1	–	0.1	0.0	0.1	–	New Zealand	
Norway	–	–	0.9	0.2	–	–	0.9	0.2	Norway	
Sweden	–	–	4.7	6.8	–	–	4.7	6.8	Sweden	
Switzerland	0.0	0.0	0.8	3.9	0.0	0.0	0.8	3.9	Switzerland	
United Kingdom	0.0	–	1.7	1.1	0.0	–	1.7	1.1	United Kingdom	
United States	–	–	–	–	–	–	–	–	United States	
TOTAL	*0.3*	*0.2*	*25.0*	*48.6*	*0.3*	*0.2*	*25.0*	*48.6*	*TOTAL*	[illegible]
MULTILATERAL	*0.1*	*0.1*	*83.3*	*231.6*	*0.1*	*0.1*	*83.3*	*231.6*	*MULTILATERAL*	
OPEC COUNTRIES	–	–	–	*1.0*	–	–	–	*1.0*	*OPEC COUNTRIES*	
E.E.C.+ MEMBERS	*0.1*	*0.0*	*48.8*	*51.2*	*0.1*	*0.0*	*48.8*	*51.2*	*E.E.C.+ MEMBERS*	[illegible]
TOTAL	***0.4***	***0.3***	***108.2***	***281.2***	***0.4***	***0.3***	***108.2***	***281.2***	***TOTAL***	[illegible]

1978	1979	1980	1977	1978	1979	1980
			ODA COMMITMENTS			
–	4.8	4.5	–	–	6.9	5.6
0.0	0.1	0.2	–	–	–	–
0.0	0.4	1.1	–	–	–	1.4
–	–	–	0.0	–	–	–
–	1.0	1.4	–	–	1.5	–
–	0.4	0.5	–	–	0.4	0.9
–	–	3.5	–	–	–	2.4
–	8.7	18.3	0.0	–	12.1	16.8
–	–	0.2	–	–	–	0.2
0.2	0.1	0.1	0.1	0.2	0.2	0.1
–	1.5	6.8	–	–	3.0	8.1
0.0	0.1	–	–	–	0.1	–
–	0.9	0.2	–	–	0.9	0.2
–	4.7	6.8	–	–	–	6.6
0.0	0.8	3.9	–	–	–	3.9
–	1.7	1.1	0.0	–	1.7	1.1
–	–	–	0.1	0.1	0.1	0.1
0.2	*25.0*	*48.6*	*0.2*	*0.3*	*26.7*	*47.3*
–	–	–	–	–	–	–
–	–	–	–	–	–	–
–	–	–	–	–	–	–
–	–	–	–	–	–	–
–	35.6	18.8	–	–	39.9	–
–	–	–	–	–	–	–
–	–	–	–	–	–	–
–	–	–	–	–	–	–
–	–	–	–	–	–	–
–	–	–	–	–	–	–
–	–	–	–	–	–	–
–	–	–	0.1	0.1	47.6	212.8
–	–	15.4	–	–	–	–
0.1	–	0.2	–	–	–	–
–	18.4	49.0	–	–	–	–
–	–	–	–	–	–	–
–	10.9	60.9	–	–	–	–
–	18.3	74.1	–	–	–	–
0.0	0.1	13.3	–	–	–	–
–	–	–	–	–	–	–
0.1	*83.3*	*231.6*	*0.1*	*0.1*	*87.5*	*212.8*
–	–	*1.0*	–	–	–	*1.0*
0.0	*48.8*	*51.2*	*0.0*	–	*58.1*	*29.9*
0.3	***108.2***	***281.2***	***0.3***	***0.3***	***114.2***	***261.1***
			TECH. COOP. GRANTS			
–	4.8	4.5	0.1	–	–	–
0.0	0.1	0.2	–	0.0	0.0	0.0
0.0	0.4	1.1	–	0.0	0.0	0.0
–	–	–	0.0	–	–	–
–	1.0	1.4	–	–	–	–
–	0.4	0.5	–	–	–	–
–	–	3.5	–	–	–	–
–	8.7	18.3	0.0	–	1.6	5.9
–	–	0.2	–	–	–	–
0.2	0.1	0.1	0.1	0.2	0.1	0.1
–	1.5	6.8	–	–	–	–
0.0	0.1	–	0.1	–	0.0	–
–	0.9	0.2	–	–	–	–
–	4.7	6.8	–	–	–	–
0.0	0.8	3.9	0.0	0.0	0.0	0.1
–	1.7	1.1	0.0	–	–	–
–	–	–	–	–	–	–
0.2	*25.0*	*48.6*	*0.2*	*0.2*	*1.8*	*6.1*
0.1	*83.3*	*231.6*	*0.1*	*0.1*	*36.8*	*212.8*
–	–	*1.0*	–	–	–	–
0.0	*48.8*	*51.2*	*0.0*	*0.0*	*1.6*	*5.9*
0.3	***108.2***	***281.2***	***0.3***	***0.3***	***38.6***	***218.9***
			TOTAL OOF NET			
–	–	–	–	–	–	–
–	–	–	–	–	–	–
–	–	–	–	–	–	–
–	–	–	–	–	–	–
–	–	–	–	–	–	–
–	–	–	–	–	–	–
0.0	–	–	0.1	0.0	–	–
–	–	–	–	–	–	–
–	–	–	–	–	–	–
–	–	–	–	–	–	–
–	–	–	–	–	–	–
–	–	–	–	–	–	–
–	–	–	–	–	–	–
–	–	–	–	–	–	–
–	–	–	–	–	–	–
–	–	–	–	–	–	–
–	–	–	–	–	–	–
0.0	–	–	*0.1*	*0.0*	–	–
–	–	–	–	–	–	–
–	–	–	–	–	–	–
0.0	–	–	*0.1*	*0.0*	–	–
0.0	–	–	***0.1***	***0.0***	–	–

	1977	1978	1979	1980
MAIN AID AGGREGATES				
DAC COUNTRIES COMBINED				
PRIVATE SECTOR NET	0.0	0.2	0.0	0.0
Direct Investment	–	–	–	–
Portfolio Invest.	0.0	–	–	0.0
Export Credits	0.0	0.2	0.0	–
OFFICIAL & PRIVATE				
GROSS:				
Contractual Lending	0.1	0.2	–	–
Export Credits Tot.	–	0.2	–	–
Export Credits Priv	–	0.2	–	–
OTHER NET DATA				
Contractual Lending	0.1	0.2	0.0	–
Export Credits Tot.	0.0	0.2	0.0	–
(Bank Sector Loans)	–	–	–	–
ODA CONCESSIONALITY				
Total:Grant Element	87.0	89.0	99.0	99.0
Loans:Grant Element	67.0	67.0	67.0	67.0
OTHER SOURCES				
CMEA Countr.(Gross)	–	50.0	106.9	155.5
Intra LDCS Exc.OPEC	–	–	–	–
Other	–	–	–	–
ALL SOURCE COMMITMENTS				
TOTAL BILATERAL	0.2	0.3	26.7	48.3
of which				
OPEC (ODA)	–	–	–	1.0
CMEA (ODA)	–	71.9	106.9	155.3
TOTAL MULTILAT.(ODA)	0.1	0.1	87.5	212.8
TOTAL BIL.& MULTIL.	0.3	0.3	114.2	261.1
of which				
ODA Grants	0.2	0.2	114.1	261.0
ODA Loans	0.1	0.1	0.1	0.1
ODA CONCESSIONALITY				
Total: Grant Element	90.0	91.0	99.0	99.0
Loans: Grant Element	67.0	67.0	67.0	67.0
INDEBTEDNESS				
TOTAL DEBT DISBURSED	***36.0***	***249.0***	***251.0***	
Debt to DAC Countries	36.0	249.0	251.0	
ODA	31.0	243.0	245.0	
Total Export Credits	5.0	6.0	6.0	
Other Private Market	–	–	–	
International Org.	–	–	–	
CMEA	–	–	–	
Other	–	–	–	
TOTAL DEBT SERVICE	***0.1***	***0.2***	–	
Paid to DAC Countries	0.1	0.2	–	
ODA	–	–	–	
Total Export Credits	0.1	0.2	–	
Other Private Market	–	–	–	
International Org.	–	–	–	
CMEA	–	–	–	
Other	–	–	–	
ECONOMIC INDICATORS				
GNP Curr. Prices, $M	–	–	–	–
Real GNP, 1976=100	–	–	–	–
GNP/Cap Curr. Prices,$	–	–	–	–
GNP/cap Atlas Basis, $	–	–	–	–
Real GNP/Cap, 1976=100	–	–	–	–
Population, Million	7.2	6.9	6.7	6.4
Curr.A/C Deficit(-),$M	–	–	–	–
BOP Exp. & Transf.,$M	–	–	–	–
Exp. to OECD CIF, $M	0.9	1.1	0.9	1.4
of which				
Manufact.	0.3	0.4	0.4	0.6
Imp. from OECD FOB, $M	9.1	2.6	7.1	70.0
Reserves ex. Gold, $M	–	–	–	–

	TOTAL RECEIPTS NET 1977	1978	1979	1980	TOTAL ODA NET 1977	1978	1979	1980
DAC COUNTRIES								
Australia	3.0	2.0	2.9	1.9	1.6	1.9	4.1	1.8
Austria	0.2	12.6	19.9	1.1	0.3	1.5	4.6	0.8
Belgium	3.3	0.7	6.1	4.2	3.0	0.3	4.0	2.6
Canada	8.2	4.6	6.0	6.1	7.6	5.7	9.1	9.6
Denmark	11.6	13.5	16.5	18.0	12.1	14.6	16.8	18.1
Finland	2.1	1.3	1.6	2.6	2.1	1.3	1.6	2.6
France	19.1	22.3	13.1	8.1	–	5.2	3.5	4.1
Germany, Fed. Rep.	47.7	61.6	80.9	16.6	17.6	40.1	68.3	34.1
Italy	-0.5	13.2	1.2	0.0	0.0	-0.1	-0.1	-0.1
Japan	36.8	7.5	31.2	27.9	4.8	10.3	34.8	26.8
Netherlands	13.9	24.3	27.7	47.5	13.9	24.3	27.7	47.5
New Zealand	0.8	1.1	–	–	0.0	0.0	–	–
Norway	12.5	13.2	19.1	20.7	12.6	13.2	19.2	21.1
Sweden	18.1	30.6	24.5	27.5	18.0	14.3	24.4	28.4
Switzerland	31.8	1.7	6.3	-0.7	1.2	2.2	2.2	1.6
United Kingdom	238.4	119.9	260.0	144.7	14.3	40.9	47.6	38.9
United States	12.0	10.0	17.0	41.0	12.0	11.0	16.0	39.0
TOTAL	*459.0*	*340.2*	*534.1*	*367.2*	*121.2*	*186.7*	*283.8*	*276.6*
MULTILATERAL								
AF.D.F.	–	–	–	–	–	–	–	–
AF.D.B.	2.3	3.1	6.4	5.3	–	–	–	–
AS.D.B.	–	–	–	–	–	–	–	–
CAR.D.B.	–	–	–	–	–	–	–	–
E.E.C.	8.4	36.3	25.0	21.1	6.3	17.3	11.0	13.9
IBRD	43.5	38.6	36.1	29.7	0.1	0.5	3.1	1.0
IDA	17.4	15.9	21.0	71.1	17.4	15.9	21.0	71.1
I.D.B.	–	–	–	–	–	–	–	–
IFAD	–	–	–	–	–	–	–	–
I.F.C.	2.7	1.0	-0.1	3.0	–	–	–	–
IMF TRUST FUND	6.0	18.5	18.7	16.0	6.0	18.5	18.7	16.0
U.N. AGENCIES	–	–	–	–	–	–	–	–
UNDP	1.9	3.4	5.0	6.1	1.9	3.4	5.0	6.1
UNTA	0.4	0.8	0.6	0.3	0.4	0.8	0.6	0.3
UNICEF	0.6	0.6	0.4	0.8	0.6	0.6	0.4	0.8
UNRWA	–	–	–	–	–	–	–	–
WFP	–	–	2.0	3.5	–	–	2.0	3.5
UNHCR	0.7	1.7	1.7	2.2	0.7	1.7	1.7	2.2
Other Multilateral	3.0	2.0	2.5	3.9	3.0	2.0	2.5	3.9
Arab OPEC Agencies	5.1	0.1	0.8	0.7	5.1	0.1	0.8	0.7
TOTAL	*91.9*	*122.0*	*120.2*	*163.8*	*41.4*	*60.8*	*66.8*	*119.6*
OPEC COUNTRIES	–	–	*0.0*	–	–	–	*0.0*	–
E.E.C.+ MEMBERS	*342.0*	*292.0*	*430.6*	*260.2*	*67.3*	*142.6*	*178.7*	*159.1*
TOTAL	***550.9***	***462.2***	***654.3***	***531.1***	***162.6***	***247.5***	***350.6***	***396.2***

	ODA LOANS GROSS 1977	1978	1979	1980	ODA LOANS NET 1977	1978	1979	1980
DAC COUNTRIES								
Australia	–	–	–	–	–	–	–	–
Austria	–	0.3	3.4	–	–	0.3	3.4	–
Belgium	2.8	–	1.7	1.7	2.8	–	1.7	1.7
Canada	2.9	2.2	2.2	2.9	2.9	2.2	2.2	2.9
Denmark	4.8	3.4	4.0	1.1	4.6	3.2	3.7	0.9
Finland	1.8	1.0	–	–	1.8	1.0	-4.4	–
France	–	5.0	3.5	1.9	–	5.0	3.5	1.9
Germany, Fed. Rep.	5.6	26.5	49.0	12.4	4.3	25.3	47.5	10.8
Italy	–	–	–	–	-0.4	-0.4	-0.4	-0.4
Japan	2.3	7.5	19.7	11.1	2.1	6.1	18.2	9.7
Netherlands	3.3	11.1	7.0	14.3	3.3	11.1	6.8	13.8
New Zealand	–	–	–	–	–	–	–	–
Norway	–	–	–	–	–	–	–	–
Sweden	1.0	0.2	–	–	1.0	-29.2	–	–
Switzerland	–	–	–	–	-5.0	–	–	–
United Kingdom	6.3	5.0	7.7	2.0	-2.0	-2.6	-1.0	-8.3
United States	5.0	4.0	7.0	21.0	4.0	3.0	6.0	20.0
TOTAL	*35.7*	*66.0*	*105.1*	*68.3*	*19.4*	*24.8*	*87.2*	*52.9*
MULTILATERAL	*29.8*	*48.6*	*47.0*	*96.4*	*29.6*	*48.2*	*46.5*	*95.9*
OPEC COUNTRIES	–	–	–	–	–	–	–	–
E.E.C.+ MEMBERS	*23.9*	*64.2*	*75.7*	*40.4*	*13.8*	*54.8*	*64.7*	*27.5*
TOTAL	***65.5***	***114.6***	***152.0***	***164.6***	***49.0***	***73.0***	***133.7***	***148.8***

	TOTAL OFFICIAL GROSS 1977	1978	1979	1980	TOTAL OFFICIAL NET 1977	1978	1979	1980
DAC COUNTRIES								
Australia	1.6	1.9	8.0	1.8	1.6	1.8	4.9	1.7
Austria	0.3	1.5	4.6	0.8	0.3	1.5	4.6	0.8
Belgium	3.0	0.3	4.0	2.6	3.0	0.3	4.0	2.6
Canada	29.2	7.1	9.1	9.6	8.2	4.6	6.0	6.1
Denmark	12.3	14.8	17.0	18.3	11.9	14.1	16.8	18.0
Finland	2.1	1.3	6.0	2.6	2.1	1.3	1.6	2.6
France	0.0	8.4	3.6	4.1	0.0	8.4	3.6	4.1
Germany, Fed. Rep.	19.8	52.7	73.8	41.5	18.4	49.8	69.2	36.8
Italy	0.4	0.4	0.3	0.3	0.0	-0.3	-0.5	-0.5
Japan	5.0	11.7	36.3	28.2	4.8	10.3	34.8	26.8
Netherlands	13.9	24.3	27.9	47.9	13.9	24.3	27.7	47.5
New Zealand	1.4	0.0	–	–	0.8	0.0	–	–
Norway	12.6	13.2	19.2	21.1	12.6	13.2	19.2	21.1
Sweden	18.0	43.7	24.4	28.4	18.0	14.3	24.4	28.4
Switzerland	6.2	2.2	2.2	1.6	1.2	2.2	2.2	1.6
United Kingdom	27.2	60.0	68.3	72.7	16.6	49.6	59.2	61.8
United States	15.0	12.0	20.0	43.0	12.0	10.0	17.0	41.0
TOTAL	*168.1*	*255.5*	*324.8*	*324.3*	*125.3*	*205.3*	*294.7*	*300.1*
MULTILATERAL	*100.2*	*127.3*	*135.9*	*185.7*	*91.9*	*122.0*	*120.2*	*163.8*
OPEC COUNTRIES	–	–	*0.0*	–	–	–	*0.0*	–
E.E.C.+ MEMBERS	*85.0*	*197.2*	*219.9*	*208.8*	*72.2*	*182.5*	*204.9*	*191.3*
TOTAL	***268.3***	***382.8***	***460.7***	***510.0***	***217.2***	***327.3***	***415.0***	***464.0***

	TOTAL ODA GROSS 197[illegible]
Australia	1[illegible]
Austria	0[illegible]
Belgium	3[illegible]
Canada	7[illegible]
Denmark	12[illegible]
Finland	2[illegible]
France	
Germany, Fed. Rep.	18[illegible]
Italy	0[illegible]
Japan	5[illegible]
Netherlands	13[illegible]
New Zealand	0[illegible]
Norway	12[illegible]
Sweden	18[illegible]
Switzerland	6[illegible]
United Kingdom	22[illegible]
United States	13[illegible]
TOTAL	*13[illegible]*
AF.D.F.	
AF.D.B.	
AS.D.B.	
CAR.D.B.	
E.E.C.	6[illegible]
IBRD	[illegible]
IDA	17[illegible]
I.D.B.	
IFAD	
I.F.C.	
IMF TRUST FUND	6[illegible]
U.N. AGENCIES	
UNDP	[illegible]
UNTA	[illegible]
UNICEF	[illegible]
UNRWA	
WFP	
UNHCR	[illegible]
Other Multilateral	[illegible]
Arab OPEC Agencies	[illegible]
TOTAL	*4[illegible]*
OPEC COUNTRIES	
E.E.C.+ MEMBERS	*7[illegible]*
TOTAL	***17[illegible]***

	GRANTS 197[illegible]
Australia	[illegible]
Austria	[illegible]
Belgium	[illegible]
Canada	[illegible]
Denmark	[illegible]
Finland	[illegible]
France	
Germany, Fed. Rep.	1[illegible]
Italy	[illegible]
Japan	[illegible]
Netherlands	1[illegible]
New Zealand	[illegible]
Norway	1[illegible]
Sweden	1[illegible]
Switzerland	[illegible]
United Kingdom	1[illegible]
United States	[illegible]
TOTAL	*10[illegible]*
MULTILATERAL	*1[illegible]*
OPEC COUNTRIES	
E.E.C.+ MEMBERS	*5[illegible]*
TOTAL	***11[illegible]***

	TOTAL OOF GROSS 197[illegible]
Australia	
Austria	
Belgium	
Canada	2[illegible]
Denmark	
Finland	
France	[illegible]
Germany, Fed. Rep.	[illegible]
Italy	
Japan	
Netherlands	
New Zealand	[illegible]
Norway	
Sweden	
Switzerland	
United Kingdom	[illegible]
United States	[illegible]
TOTAL	*3[illegible]*
MULTILATERAL	*5[illegible]*
OPEC COUNTRIES	
E.E.C.+ MEMBERS	[illegible]
TOTAL	***8[illegible]***

1978	1979	1980	1977	1978	1979	1980
			ODA COMMITMENTS			
1.9	4.1	1.8	1.5	1.9	4.8	3.4
1.5	4.6	0.8	0.7	0.7	3.5	0.5
0.3	4.0	2.6	1.4	1.6	2.7	1.7
5.7	9.1	9.6	5.0	9.4	80.9	6.4
14.8	17.0	18.3	10.2	24.2	28.6	15.5
1.3	6.0	2.6	0.8	0.2	6.9	3.0
5.2	3.5	4.1	–	11.1	–	1.8
41.2	69.7	35.7	15.4	69.2	53.4	65.9
0.4	0.3	0.3	0.4	0.4	0.3	0.3
11.7	36.3	28.2	7.3	29.0	16.0	50.7
24.3	27.9	47.9	40.3	38.9	44.2	53.1
0.0	–	–	–	0.0	–	–
13.2	19.2	21.1	18.1	14.0	26.5	25.7
43.7	24.4	28.4	35.9	33.8	44.3	–
2.2	2.2	1.6	5.1	2.4	1.0	1.0
48.5	56.3	49.3	34.0	15.2	221.7	35.9
12.0	17.0	40.0	33.6	34.3	25.4	60.3
227.9	*301.6*	*292.0*	*209.6*	*286.4*	*560.2*	*325.1*
–	–	–	–	9.6	–	–
–	–	–	–	–	–	–
–	–	–	–	–	–	–
–	–	–	–	–	–	–
17.3	11.0	13.9	46.9	59.7	3.5	7.5
0.5	3.1	1.0	5.0	–	–	–
16.3	21.5	71.6	36.0	61.0	79.5	69.5
–	–	–	–		–	–
–	–	–	–	–	17.1	–
–	–	–	–	–	–	–
18.5	18.7	16.0	–	–	–	–
–	–	–	6.6	8.5	12.3	16.9
3.4	5.0	6.1	–	–	–	–
0.8	0.6	0.3	–	–	–	–
0.6	0.4	0.8	–	–	–	–
–	–	–	–	–	–	–
–	2.0	3.5	–	–	–	–
1.7	1.7	2.2	–	–	–	–
2.0	2.5	3.9	–	–	–	–
0.1	0.8	0.7	8.1	5.4	–	4.0
61.2	*67.3*	*120.1*	*102.6*	*144.1*	*112.3*	*97.9*
–	*0.0*	–	–	*25.7*	*0.0*	*19.9*
152.0	*189.7*	*172.0*	*148.5*	*220.3*	*354.3*	*181.5*
289.1	***368.9***	***412.1***	***312.2***	***456.1***	***672.5***	***442.8***
			TECH. COOP. GRANTS			
1.9	4.1	1.8	0.8	1.3	0.2	0.4
1.3	1.2	0.8	0.3	1.3	1.2	0.8
0.3	2.3	0.9	0.2	0.3	0.5	0.6
3.5	6.9	6.7	3.9	2.7	5.4	3.9
11.5	13.1	17.2	6.2	6.8	10.3	15.4
0.3	6.0	2.6	0.3	0.3	1.3	2.1
0.2	–	2.2	–	0.2	–	2.2
14.7	20.8	23.3	13.0	14.2	20.2	22.5
0.4	0.3	0.3	0.4	0.4	0.3	0.3
4.3	16.6	17.1	2.7	3.5	4.3	6.9
13.2	20.9	33.6	10.0	12.5	13.6	13.8
0.0	–	–	0.0	–	–	–
13.2	19.2	21.1	4.5	4.4	5.0	7.4
43.5	24.4	28.4	3.2	4.9	3.7	5.7
2.2	2.2	1.6	0.0	0.0	0.0	0.9
43.5	48.7	47.3	10.7	15.0	21.9	22.8
8.0	10.0	19.0	4.0	5.0	5.0	9.0
161.9	*196.5*	*223.8*	*60.2*	*72.8*	*92.9*	*114.5*
12.6	*20.3*	*23.7*	*6.6*	*8.5*	*10.2*	*16.9*
–	*0.0*	–	–	–	–	–
87.8	*114.1*	*131.6*	*40.4*	*49.4*	*66.8*	*77.5*
174.5	***216.9***	***247.5***	***66.8***	***81.3***	***103.1***	***131.4***
			TOTAL OOF NET			
0.0	3.9	0.1	–	-0.1	0.8	-0.1
–	–	–	–	–	–	–
–	–	–	–	–	–	–
1.4	0.0	–	0.6	-1.1	-3.1	-3.5
–	–	–	-0.3	-0.5	–	-0.1
–	–	–	–	–	–	–
3.2	0.1	–	0.0	3.2	0.1	–
11.5	4.1	5.8	0.8	9.7	0.9	2.7
–	–	–	–	-0.2	-0.3	-0.4
–	–	–	–	–	–	–
–	–	–	–	–	–	–
–	–	–	0.7	–	–	–
–	–	–	–	–	–	–
–	–	–	–	–	–	–
–	–	–	–	–	–	–
11.5	12.0	23.4	2.3	8.6	11.6	22.9
–	3.0	3.0	–	-1.0	1.0	2.0
27.6	*23.1*	*32.3*	*4.1*	*18.6*	*11.0*	*23.5*
66.1	*68.6*	*65.6*	*50.4*	*61.2*	*53.4*	*44.3*
–	–	–	–	–	–	–
45.2	*30.2*	*36.8*	*4.9*	*39.8*	*26.2*	*32.3*
93.7	***91.7***	***97.9***	***54.5***	***79.8***	***64.3***	***67.7***

MAIN AID AGGREGATES

	1977	1978	1979	1980
DAC COUNTRIES COMBINED				
PRIVATE SECTOR NET	333.7	134.8	239.3	67.1
Direct Investment	41.0	57.0	56.4	-1.9
Portfolio Invest.	0.9	8.9	26.7	-7.6
Export Credits	291.8	68.9	156.3	76.6
OFFICIAL & PRIVATE				
GROSS:				
Contractual Lending	403.8	196.7	365.8	267.2
Export Credits Tot.	362.5	115.2	245.7	174.7
Export Credits Priv	337.5	103.1	237.6	166.7
OTHER NET DATA				
Contractual Lending	315.3	112.4	254.5	153.0
Export Credits Tot.	293.0	75.4	152.8	76.7
(Bank Sector Loans)	21.0	161.0	184.0	81.0
ODA CONCESSIONALITY				
Total:Grant Element	89.0	88.0	95.0	87.0
Loans:Grant Element	66.0	72.0	77.0	66.0
OTHER SOURCES				
CMEA Countr.(Gross)	0.1	0.1	0.1	–
Intra LDCS Exc.OPEC	–	–	–	–
Other	–	–	–	–
ALL SOURCE COMMITMENTS				
TOTAL BILATERAL	251.3	332.7	573.3	387.3
of which				
OPEC (ODA)	–	25.7	0.0	19.9
CMEA (ODA)	–	–	–	–
TOTAL MULTILAT.(ODA)	102.6	144.1	112.3	97.9
TOTAL BIL.& MULTIL.	353.9	476.8	685.7	485.1
of which				
ODA Grants	164.0	197.0	452.1	229.5
ODA Loans	148.2	259.1	220.4	213.3
ODA CONCESSIONALITY				
Total: Grant Element	87.0	85.0	94.0	85.0
Loans: Grant Element	72.0	72.0	78.0	72.0

INDEBTEDNESS

	1977	1978	1979	1980
TOTAL DEBT DISBURSED	***1156.4***	***1382.3***	***1761.1***	
Debt to DAC Countries	798.0	937.0	1248.0	
ODA	325.0	394.0	489.0	
Total Export Credits	429.0	534.0	620.0	
Other Private Market	44.0	9.0	139.0	
International Org.	342.6	422.9	493.4	
CMEA	0.1	0.1	–	
Other	15.7	22.3	19.7	
TOTAL DEBT SERVICE	***99.3***	***169.7***	***183.4***	
Paid to DAC Countries	79.4	140.3	142.5	
ODA	19.5	17.6	19.3	
Total Export Credits	58.1	82.1	115.3	
Other Private Market	1.8	40.6	7.9	
International Org.	19.4	28.4	37.6	
CMEA	0.1	0.0	0.1	
Other	0.4	0.9	3.2	

ECONOMIC INDICATORS

	1977	1978	1979	1980
GNP Curr. Prices, $M	4303.9	5140.4	5871.0	6851.9
Real GNP, 1976=100	108.0	118.0	122.0	125.0
GNP/Cap Curr. Prices,$	301.0	348.0	384.0	431.0
GNP/cap Atlas Basis, $	317.5	359.3	388.7	418.1
Real GNP/Cap, 1976=100	105.0	111.0	110.0	109.0
Population, Million	14.3	14.8	15.3	15.9
Curr.A/C Deficit(-),$M	-33.8	-735.1	-551.3	-1098.4
BOP Exp. & Transf.,$M	1569.9	1568.8	1626.9	2037.9
Exp. to OECD CIF, $M	909.5	737.2	775.1	792.6
of which				
Manufact.	19.4	36.0	33.0	30.9
Imp. from OECD FOB, $M	828.0	1113.8	997.7	1289.9
Reserves ex. Gold, $M	522.4	352.6	627.7	491.7

	1977	1978	1979	1980	1977	1978	1979	1980
TOTAL RECEIPTS NET					**TOTAL ODA NET**			
DAC COUNTRIES								
Australia	0.7	0.5	1.0	0.3	0.7	0.5	0.3	0.3
Austria	-7.2	-14.6	109.2	-16.8	0.3	0.3	0.3	0.4
Belgium	-2.1	2.2	13.8	350.1	0.9	3.2	0.8	0.8
Canada	40.8	44.9	99.0	121.6	0.0	0.0	0.0	0.0
Denmark	-0.1	4.4	-0.2	-0.8	-0.1	0.0	0.0	0.0
Finland	3.2	36.6	18.7	-3.3	0.0	0.0	0.0	0.0
France	61.8	7.7	31.4	1.2	–	–	–	2.4
Germany, Fed. Rep.	86.4	43.5	193.5	109.4	24.5	11.8	18.1	14.3
Italy	6.7	-3.9	-2.9	-0.8	0.0	0.0	0.0	0.0
Japan	144.3	634.2	505.9	322.0	84.3	66.1	54.2	76.3
Netherlands	25.2	2.3	-2.6	1.3	2.2	2.3	1.4	1.3
New Zealand	1.4	-0.3	0.3	0.1	0.5	0.4	0.3	0.1
Norway	17.1	-8.2	-2.7	-17.1	0.0	–	–	–
Sweden	-1.1	4.6	-1.1	-1.1	–	–	–	–
Switzerland	256.9	37.3	-1.1	-221.2	0.1	0.1	0.1	–
United Kingdom	304.6	-18.7	-55.7	54.2	0.4	0.4	0.4	0.5
United States	99.0	324.0	196.0	-127.0	58.0	51.0	24.0	21.0
TOTAL	*1037.6*	*1096.6*	*1102.3*	*572.0*	*171.7*	*136.1*	*99.8*	*117.3*
MULTILATERAL								
AF.D.F.	–	–	–	–	–	–	–	–
AF.D.B.	–	–	–	–	–	–	–	–
AS.D.B.	68.6	70.9	57.0	51.2	1.3	-0.2	-0.2	-0.1
CAR.D.B.	–	–	–	–	–	–	–	–
E.E.C.	0.0	0.2	0.2	–	0.0	0.2	0.2	–
IBRD	191.8	294.9	390.1	188.7	19.6	3.3	4.0	0.1
IDA	8.5	3.2	-0.5	-0.6	8.5	3.2	-0.5	-0.6
I.D.B.	–	–	–	–	–	–	–	–
IFAD	–	–	–	–	–	–	–	–
I.F.C.	8.9	12.2	-8.8	-10.4	–	–	–	–
IMF TRUST FUND	–	–	–	–	–	–	–	–
U.N. AGENCIES	–	–	–	–	–	–	–	–
UNDP	1.8	2.5	3.6	3.9	1.8	2.5	3.6	3.9
UNTA	0.8	0.7	0.6	0.1	0.8	0.7	0.6	0.1
UNICEF	0.7	0.6	–	0.9	0.7	0.6	–	0.9
UNRWA	–	–	–	–	–	–	–	–
WFP	12.0	4.7	5.7	4.9	12.0	4.7	5.7	4.9
UNHCR	–	–	0.1	0.2	–	–	0.1	0.2
Other Multilateral	1.5	0.3	0.1	1.4	1.5	0.3	0.1	1.4
Arab OPEC Agencies	–	–	–	–	–	–	–	–
TOTAL	*294.5*	*390.2*	*448.2*	*240.2*	*46.2*	*15.2*	*13.7*	*10.8*
OPEC COUNTRIES	*48.4*	*52.8*	*20.2*	*10.9*	*20.8*	*12.9*	*20.2*	*10.9*
E.E.C.+ MEMBERS	*482.5*	*37.8*	*177.5*	*514.5*	*27.9*	*17.9*	*21.0*	*19.3*
TOTAL	***1380.5***	***1539.6***	***1570.7***	***823.1***	***238.6***	***164.3***	***133.8***	***139.0***
ODA LOANS GROSS					**ODA LOANS NET**			
DAC COUNTRIES								
Australia	–	–	–	–	–	–	–	–
Austria	–	–	–	–	–	0.0	0.0	0.0
Belgium	–	–	–	–	–	–	–	–
Canada	–	–	–	–	0.0	0.0	0.0	0.0
Denmark	–	–	–	–	-0.2	-0.2	-0.2	-0.2
Finland	–	–	–	–	–	–	–	–
France	–	–	–	–	–	–	–	–
Germany, Fed. Rep.	18.5	6.3	9.7	6.8	15.2	1.4	3.0	0.5
Italy	–	–	–	–	–	–	–	–
Japan	97.7	90.8	91.4	119.4	75.5	54.6	45.0	70.1
Netherlands	–	–	–	–	-0.1	-0.1	-0.1	-0.1
New Zealand	–	–	–	–	–	–	–	–
Norway	–	–	–	–	–	–	–	–
Sweden	–	–	–	–	–	–	–	–
Switzerland	–	–	–	–	–	–	–	–
United Kingdom	–	–	–	–	-0.1	-0.1	-0.1	–
United States	89.0	72.0	53.0	43.0	57.0	47.0	23.0	17.0
TOTAL	*205.2*	*169.1*	*154.0*	*169.2*	*147.3*	*102.6*	*70.6*	*87.2*
MULTILATERAL	*29.4*	*6.8*	*4.0*	*0.1*	*29.0*	*6.3*	*3.4*	*-0.8*
OPEC COUNTRIES	*20.8*	*12.9*	*20.2*	*13.4*	*20.8*	*12.9*	*20.2*	*10.9*
E.E.C.+ MEMBERS	*18.5*	*6.3*	*9.7*	*6.8*	*14.8*	*1.0*	*2.6*	*0.2*
TOTAL	***255.4***	***188.8***	***178.3***	***182.7***	***197.1***	***121.8***	***94.3***	***97.4***
TOTAL OFFICIAL GROSS					**TOTAL OFFICIAL NET**			
DAC COUNTRIES								
Australia	0.7	0.5	0.3	0.3	0.7	0.5	0.3	0.3
Austria	0.3	0.3	0.3	0.4	0.1	-0.2	-0.3	-0.2
Belgium	0.9	3.2	0.8	0.8	0.9	3.2	0.8	0.8
Canada	42.3	47.6	102.5	124.4	40.9	45.6	99.6	121.9
Denmark	0.0	0.2	0.2	0.2	-0.1	0.0	0.0	0.0
Finland	0.0	0.0	0.0	0.0	0.0	0.0	0.0	0.0
France	–	–	–	2.4	–	–	–	2.4
Germany, Fed. Rep.	62.2	54.3	92.1	74.7	50.3	41.1	71.1	53.1
Italy	0.0	0.0	0.0	0.0	0.0	0.0	0.0	0.0
Japan	106.6	102.3	100.5	125.6	83.7	65.3	53.4	75.5
Netherlands	2.3	2.4	1.5	1.4	2.2	2.3	1.4	1.3
New Zealand	1.4	0.4	0.3	0.1	1.4	0.4	0.3	0.1
Norway	0.0	–	–	–	0.0	–	–	–
Sweden	–	–	–	–	–	–	–	–
Switzerland	0.1	0.1	0.1	–	0.1	0.1	0.1	–
United Kingdom	0.4	0.5	0.5	0.5	0.4	0.4	0.4	0.5
United States	291.0	537.0	387.0	357.0	131.0	358.0	107.0	80.0
TOTAL	*508.2*	*748.8*	*686.1*	*687.8*	*311.4*	*516.6*	*334.0*	*335.7*
MULTILATERAL	*335.3*	*445.4*	*528.3*	*361.4*	*294.5*	*390.2*	*448.2*	*240.2*
OPEC COUNTRIES	*48.4*	*52.8*	*20.2*	*13.4*	*48.4*	*52.8*	*20.2*	*10.9*
E.E.C.+ MEMBERS	*66.0*	*60.8*	*95.4*	*80.1*	*53.7*	*47.2*	*74.0*	*58.1*
TOTAL	***891.8***	***1247.0***	***1234.6***	***1062.7***	***654.3***	***959.6***	***802.4***	***586.8***

	197
TOTAL ODA GROSS	
Australia	0
Austria	0
Belgium	0
Canada	
Denmark	0
Finland	0
France	
Germany, Fed. Rep.	27
Italy	0
Japan	106
Netherlands	2
New Zealand	0
Norway	0
Sweden	
Switzerland	0
United Kingdom	0
United States	90
TOTAL	*229*
AF.D.F.	
AF.D.B.	
AS.D.B.	1
CAR.D.B.	
E.E.C.	0
IBRD	19
IDA	8
I.D.B.	
IFAD	
I.F.C.	
IMF TRUST FUND	
U.N. AGENCIES	
UNDP	1
UNTA	0
UNICEF	0
UNRWA	
WFP	12
UNHCR	
Other Multilateral	1
Arab OPEC Agencies	
TOTAL	*46*
OPEC COUNTRIES	*20*
E.E.C.+ MEMBERS	*31*
TOTAL	***297***
GRANTS	
Australia	0
Austria	0
Belgium	0
Canada	
Denmark	0
Finland	0
France	
Germany, Fed. Rep.	9
Italy	0
Japan	8
Netherlands	2
New Zealand	0
Norway	0
Sweden	
Switzerland	0
United Kingdom	0
United States	1
TOTAL	*24*
MULTILATERAL	*17*
OPEC COUNTRIES	
E.E.C.+ MEMBERS	*13*
TOTAL	***41***
TOTAL OOF GROSS	
Australia	
Austria	
Belgium	
Canada	42
Denmark	
Finland	
France	
Germany, Fed. Rep.	34
Italy	
Japan	
Netherlands	
New Zealand	0
Norway	
Sweden	
Switzerland	
United Kingdom	
United States	201
TOTAL	*278*
MULTILATERAL	*288*
OPEC COUNTRIES	*27*
E.E.C.+ MEMBERS	*34*
TOTAL	***594***

1978	1979	1980	1977	1978	1979	1980
			ODA COMMITMENTS			
0.5	0.3	0.3	0.8	0.2	0.1	0.1
0.3	0.3	0.4	–	–	–	–
3.2	0.8	0.8	–	4.8	–	–
0.0	0.0	–	–	0.0	0.0	–
0.2	0.2	0.2	0.0	0.1	0.1	–
0.0	0.0	0.0	–	0.0	0.0	0.0
–	–	2.4	–	–	–	2.2
16.7	24.8	20.6	16.9	36.7	24.5	47.2
0.0	0.0	0.0	0.0	0.0	0.0	0.0
102.3	100.5	125.6	69.9	206.4	8.5	217.2
2.4	1.5	1.4	3.9	3.1	1.7	1.5
0.4	0.3	0.1	0.3	0.3	0.1	0.0
–	–	–	–	–	–	–
–	–	–	–	–	–	–
0.1	0.1	–	–	–	–	0.0
0.5	0.5	0.5	0.4	0.5	0.5	0.5
76.0	54.0	47.0	51.6	67.7	49.8	40.4
202.6	*183.2*	*199.3*	*143.9*	*319.8*	*85.4*	*309.2*
–	–	–	–	–	–	–
–	–	–	–	–	–	–
0.0	–	0.1	–	0.3	0.2	–
–	–	–	–	–	–	–
0.2	0.2	–	1.1	0.4	–	–
3.3	4.0	0.1	–	–	–	–
3.5	–	–	-0.1	–	–	–
–	–	–	–	–	–	–
–	–	–	–	–	–	–
–	–	–	–	–	–	–
–	–	–	–	–	–	–
–	–	–	16.7	8.7	10.1	11.4
2.5	3.6	3.9	–	–	–	–
0.7	0.6	0.1	–	–	–	–
0.6	–	0.9	–	–	–	–
–	–	–	–	–	–	–
4.7	5.7	4.9	–	–	–	–
–	0.1	0.2	–	–	–	–
0.3	0.1	1.4	–	–	–	–
–	–	–	–	–	–	–
15.7	*14.4*	*11.6*	*17.7*	*9.4*	*10.2*	*11.4*
12.9	*20.2*	*13.4*	–	–	–	–
23.2	*28.0*	*25.9*	*22.4*	*45.6*	*26.8*	*51.4*
231.2	***217.8***	***224.3***	***161.6***	***329.2***	***95.6***	***320.6***
			TECH. COOP. GRANTS			
0.5	0.3	0.3	0.5	0.4	0.3	0.2
0.3	0.3	0.4	0.3	0.3	0.3	0.4
3.2	0.8	0.8	0.1	0.1	0.2	0.2
0.0	0.0	–	–	0.0	0.0	–
0.2	0.2	0.2	0.0	0.2	0.2	0.2
0.0	0.0	0.0	0.0	0.0	0.0	0.0
–	–	2.4	–	–	–	2.4
10.4	15.1	13.8	8.7	8.6	15.1	13.8
0.0	0.0	0.0	0.0	0.0	0.0	0.0
11.5	9.1	6.2	5.0	8.1	7.2	6.2
2.4	1.5	1.4	2.3	2.4	1.5	1.4
0.4	0.3	0.1	0.2	0.3	0.2	0.1
–	–	–	0.0	–	–	–
–	–	–	–	–	–	–
0.1	0.1	–	0.1	0.1	0.1	–
0.5	0.5	0.5	0.4	0.5	0.5	0.5
4.0	1.0	4.0	3.0	2.0	1.0	2.0
33.5	*29.2*	*30.1*	*20.7*	*23.0*	*26.5*	*27.5*
9.0	*10.3*	*11.6*	*5.1*	*4.1*	*4.3*	*11.4*
–	–	–	–	–	–	–
16.9	*18.4*	*19.1*	*11.7*	*11.8*	*17.5*	*18.5*
42.5	***39.5***	***41.6***	***25.9***	***27.0***	***30.9***	***38.9***
			TOTAL OOF NET			
–	–	–	–	–	–	–
–	–	–	-0.2	-0.5	-0.6	-0.6
–	–	–	–	–	–	–
47.6	102.5	124.4	40.9	45.6	99.6	122.0
–	–	–	–	–	–	–
–	–	–	–	–	–	–
–	–	–	–	–	–	–
37.5	67.4	54.2	25.8	29.2	53.0	38.8
–	–	–	–	–	–	–
–	–	–	-0.7	-0.9	-0.8	-0.8
–	–	–	–	–	–	–
–	–	–	0.9	–	–	–
–	–	–	–	–	–	–
–	–	–	–	–	–	–
–	–	–	–	–	–	–
–	–	–	–	–	–	–
461.0	333.0	310.0	73.0	307.0	83.0	59.0
546.2	*502.8*	*488.6*	*139.7*	*380.4*	*234.2*	*218.4*
429.7	*513.9*	*349.8*	*248.4*	*375.0*	*434.5*	*229.4*
39.9	–	–	*27.6*	*39.9*	–	–
37.5	*67.4*	*54.2*	*25.8*	*29.2*	*53.0*	*38.8*
1015.8	***1016.7***	***838.4***	***415.7***	***795.3***	***668.7***	***447.8***

MAIN AID AGGREGATES

	1977	1978	1979	1980
DAC COUNTRIES COMBINED				
PRIVATE SECTOR NET	726.2	580.0	768.3	236.3
Direct Investment	27.8	183.6	1.2	-207.6
Portfolio Invest.	-42.4	12.8	466.0	-53.3
Export Credits	740.8	383.7	301.0	497.1
OFFICIAL & PRIVATE				
GROSS:				
Contractual Lending	1494.1	1410.0	1365.4	1956.5
Export Credits Tot.	1272.7	1222.7	1195.7	1778.3
Export Credits Priv	1010.2	694.8	708.5	1298.7
OTHER NET DATA				
Contractual Lending	1027.9	866.7	605.9	802.7
Export Credits Tot.	869.3	747.9	524.3	709.4
(Bank Sector Loans)	1250.0	390.0	1272.0	832.0
ODA CONCESSIONALITY				
Total:Grant Element	56.0	53.0	77.0	58.0
Loans:Grant Element	46.0	46.0	67.0	53.0
OTHER SOURCES				
CMEA Countr.(Gross)	–	–	–	–
Intra LDCS Exc.OPEC	–	–	–	–
Other	–	–	–	–
ALL SOURCE COMMITMENTS				
TOTAL BILATERAL	386.9	1347.1	1550.9	689.0
of which				
OPEC (ODA)	–	–	–	–
CMEA (ODA)	–	–	–	–
TOTAL MULTILAT.(ODA)	17.7	9.4	10.2	11.4
TOTAL BIL.& MULTIL.	404.7	1356.5	1561.1	700.4
of which				
ODA Grants	43.5	50.6	38.3	44.0
ODA Loans	118.1	278.6	57.3	276.6
ODA CONCESSIONALITY				
Total: Grant Element	61.0	54.0	80.0	60.0
Loans: Grant Element	46.0	46.0	67.0	53.0

INDEBTEDNESS

	1977	1978	1979	1980
TOTAL DEBT DISBURSED	***9291.8***	***12529.7***	***15635.0***	
Debt to DAC Countries	7792.0	10711.0	13043.0	
ODA	2185.0	2612.0	2441.0	
Total Export Credits	3733.0	5147.0	6115.0	
Other Private Market	1874.0	2952.0	4487.0	
International Org.	1295.1	1660.0	2109.0	
CMEA	–	–	–	
Other	204.7	158.7	483.0	
TOTAL DEBT SERVICE	***1252.5***	***1960.3***	***2906.1***	
Paid to DAC Countries	1120.4	1778.5	2652.6	
ODA	105.5	130.2	149.9	
Total Export Credits	650.2	1073.0	1613.3	
Other Private Market	364.7	575.3	889.4	
International Org.	119.8	167.5	227.4	
CMEA	–	–	–	
Other	12.3	14.2	26.1	

ECONOMIC INDICATORS

	1977	1978	1979	1980
GNP Curr. Prices, $M	35168.2	47350.4	60066.3	57670.2
Real GNP, 1976=100	110.0	123.0	130.0	123.0
GNP/Cap Curr. Prices,$	962.0	1273.0	1588.0	1499.0
GNP/cap Atlas Basis, $	1127.8	1328.1	1506.6	1523.4
Real GNP/Cap, 1976=100	108.0	118.0	124.0	115.0
Population, Million	36.6	37.2	37.8	38.5
Curr.A/C Deficit(-),$M	-50.0	-1125.0	-4193.0	-5366.0
BOP Exp. & Transf.,$M	13241.0	17597.0	19930.0	22984.0
Exp. to OECD CIF, $M	7304.5	9386.1	11037.1	11267.8
of which				
Manufact.	6102.4	8094.2	9578.2	9968.7
Imp. from OECD FOB, $M	7490.6	11080.7	13014.0	12219.0
Reserves ex. Gold, $M	2967.1	2763.9	2959.1	2924.9

	TOTAL RECEIPTS NET 1977	1978	1979	1980	TOTAL ODA NET 1977	1978	1979	1980
DAC COUNTRIES								
Australia	1.2	1.5	2.3	0.1	1.2	1.5	2.3	0.1
Austria	–	0.0	0.0	0.0	–	0.0	0.0	0.0
Belgium	0.1	0.0	0.2	0.1	0.1	0.0	0.2	0.1
Canada	2.4	–	–	–	2.4	–	–	–
Denmark	–	0.9	–	0.0	–	0.9	–	0.0
Finland	–	–	–	–	–	–	–	–
France	1.6	3.8	0.8	-0.5	1.7	3.0	0.6	0.3
Germany, Fed. Rep.	5.8	11.0	1.9	-0.3	5.8	11.0	1.9	-0.3
Italy	–	0.0	–	–	–	0.0	–	–
Japan	6.1	5.8	3.0	1.1	5.4	6.1	2.8	1.3
Netherlands	3.6	6.9	6.1	2.6	3.6	6.9	6.1	2.6
New Zealand	0.0	0.0	0.0	–	0.0	0.0	0.0	–
Norway	0.1	1.3	–	0.1	0.1	1.3	–	0.1
Sweden	6.4	9.9	12.4	12.5	6.4	9.9	12.4	12.5
Switzerland	–	0.2	0.1	0.1	–	0.2	0.1	0.1
United Kingdom	0.1	1.8	0.1	0.0	0.1	1.8	0.1	0.0
United States	–	–	–	–	–	–	–	–
TOTAL	*27.3*	*43.0*	*26.8*	*15.8*	*26.7*	*42.6*	*26.4*	*16.7*
MULTILATERAL								
AF.D.F.	–	–	–	–	–	–	–	–
AF.D.B.	–	–	–	–	–	–	–	–
AS.D.B.	0.0	2.1	1.6	0.7	0.0	2.1	1.6	0.7
CAR.D.B.	–	–	–	–	–	–	–	–
E.E.C.	–	3.3	–	0.9	–	3.3	–	0.9
IBRD	–	–	–	–	–	–	–	–
IDA	–	0.1	0.2	5.3	–	0.1	0.2	5.3
I.D.B.	–	–	–	–	–	–	–	–
IFAD	–	–	–	0.1	–	–	–	0.1
I.F.C.	–	–	–	–	–	–	–	–
IMF TRUST FUND	–	6.8	5.0	4.4	–	6.8	5.0	4.4
U.N. AGENCIES	–	–	–	–	–	–	–	–
UNDP	1.7	2.4	5.4	6.1	1.7	2.4	5.4	6.1
UNTA	0.7	0.8	0.3	0.2	0.7	0.8	0.3	0.2
UNICEF	0.1	3.1	1.4	1.7	0.1	3.1	1.4	1.7
UNRWA	–	–	–	–	–	–	–	–
WFP	0.0	6.2	5.4	-0.1	0.0	6.2	5.4	-0.1
UNHCR	0.2	3.8	4.1	3.9	0.2	3.8	4.1	3.9
Other Multilateral	0.8	0.7	0.0	0.2	0.8	0.7	0.0	0.2
Arab OPEC Agencies	2.2	–	4.2	0.7	2.2	–	4.2	0.7
TOTAL	*5.7*	*29.2*	*27.7*	*24.1*	*5.7*	*29.2*	*27.7*	*24.1*
OPEC COUNTRIES	–	–	*5.0*	–	–	–	*5.0*	–
E.E.C.+ MEMBERS	*11.2*	*27.6*	*9.0*	*2.8*	*11.3*	*26.8*	*8.8*	*3.5*
TOTAL	***33.0***	***72.2***	***59.5***	***39.9***	***32.4***	***71.8***	***59.1***	***40.9***

	ODA LOANS GROSS 1977	1978	1979	1980	ODA LOANS NET 1977	1978	1979	1980
DAC COUNTRIES								
Australia	–	–	–	–	–	–	–	–
Austria	–	–	–	–	–	–	–	–
Belgium	–	–	–	–	–	–	–	–
Canada	2.4	–	–	–	2.4	-2.2	–	–
Denmark	–	–	–	–	–	–	–	–
Finland	–	–	–	–	–	–	–	–
France	1.6	2.8	0.6	0.3	1.6	2.8	0.6	0.3
Germany, Fed. Rep.	5.8	10.7	2.3	0.6	5.3	9.9	1.8	-0.3
Italy	–	–	–	–	–	–	–	–
Japan	3.4	3.4	–	–	3.4	3.4	–	–
Netherlands	–	–	–	–	–	–	–	–
New Zealand	–	–	–	–	–	–	–	–
Norway	–	–	–	–	–	–	–	–
Sweden	–	–	–	–	–	–	–	–
Switzerland	–	–	–	–	–	–	–	–
United Kingdom	–	–	–	–	–	–	–	–
United States	–	–	–	–	–	–	–	–
TOTAL	*13.2*	*16.9*	*2.9*	*0.8*	*12.7*	*13.9*	*2.4*	*0.0*
MULTILATERAL	*2.3*	*9.1*	*11.3*	*11.1*	*2.1*	*8.9*	*11.1*	*10.9*
OPEC COUNTRIES	–	–	–	–	–	–	–	–
E.E.C.+ MEMBERS	*7.4*	*13.5*	*2.9*	*0.8*	*6.9*	*12.7*	*2.4*	*0.0*
TOTAL	***15.5***	***26.1***	***14.2***	***11.9***	***14.8***	***22.8***	***13.5***	***10.9***

	TOTAL OFFICIAL GROSS 1977	1978	1979	1980	TOTAL OFFICIAL NET 1977	1978	1979	1980
DAC COUNTRIES								
Australia	1.2	1.5	2.3	0.1	1.2	1.5	2.3	0.1
Austria	–	0.0	0.0	0.0	–	0.0	0.0	0.0
Belgium	0.1	0.0	0.2	0.1	0.1	0.0	0.2	0.1
Canada	2.4	2.2	–	–	2.4	–	–	–
Denmark	–	0.9	–	0.0	–	0.9	–	0.0
Finland	–	–	–	–	–	–	–	–
France	1.7	3.0	0.6	0.3	1.7	3.0	0.6	0.3
Germany, Fed. Rep.	6.3	11.8	2.4	0.6	5.8	11.0	1.9	-0.3
Italy	–	0.0	–	–	–	0.0	–	–
Japan	5.4	6.1	2.8	1.3	5.4	6.1	2.8	1.3
Netherlands	3.6	6.9	6.1	2.6	3.6	6.9	6.1	2.6
New Zealand	0.0	0.0	0.0	–	0.0	0.0	0.0	–
Norway	0.1	1.3	–	0.1	0.1	1.3	–	0.1
Sweden	6.4	9.9	12.4	12.5	6.4	9.9	12.4	12.5
Switzerland	–	0.2	0.1	0.1	–	0.2	0.1	0.1
United Kingdom	0.1	1.8	0.1	0.0	0.1	1.8	0.1	0.0
United States	–	–	–	–	–	–	–	–
TOTAL	*27.2*	*45.6*	*26.8*	*17.6*	*26.7*	*42.6*	*26.4*	*16.7*
MULTILATERAL	*5.9*	*29.4*	*28.0*	*24.4*	*5.7*	*29.2*	*27.7*	*24.1*
OPEC COUNTRIES	–	–	–	–	–	–	*5.0*	–
E.E.C.+ MEMBERS	*11.8*	*27.7*	*9.3*	*4.4*	*11.3*	*26.8*	*8.8*	*3.5*
TOTAL	***33.1***	***75.0***	***54.8***	***41.9***	***32.4***	***71.8***	***59.1***	***40.9***

TOTAL ODA GROSS (197…)

Australia, Austria, Belgium, Canada, Denmark, Finland, France, Germany, Fed. Rep., Italy, Japan, Netherlands, New Zealand, Norway, Sweden, Switzerland, United Kingdom, United States, *TOTAL*

AF.D.F., AF.D.B., AS.D.B., CAR.D.B., E.E.C., IBRD, IDA, I.D.B., IFAD, I.F.C., IMF TRUST FUND, U.N. AGENCIES, UNDP, UNTA, UNICEF, UNRWA, WFP, UNHCR, Other Multilateral, Arab OPEC Agencies, *TOTAL*, *OPEC COUNTRIES*, *E.E.C.+ MEMBERS*, ***TOTAL***

GRANTS

Australia, Austria, Belgium, Canada, Denmark, Finland, France, Germany, Fed. Rep., Italy, Japan, Netherlands, New Zealand, Norway, Sweden, Switzerland, United Kingdom, United States, *TOTAL*, *MULTILATERAL*, *OPEC COUNTRIES*, *E.E.C.+ MEMBERS*, ***TOTAL***

TOTAL OOF GROSS

Australia, Austria, Belgium, Canada, Denmark, Finland, France, Germany, Fed. Rep., Italy, Japan, Netherlands, New Zealand, Norway, Sweden, Switzerland, United Kingdom, United States, *TOTAL*, *MULTILATERAL*, *OPEC COUNTRIES*, *E.E.C.+ MEMBERS*, ***TOTAL***

1978	1979	1980	1977	1978	1979	1980
			ODA COMMITMENTS			
1.5	2.3	0.1	0.3	2.6	0.0	0.2
0.0	0.0	0.0	–	–	–	–
0.0	0.2	0.1	–	–	–	–
2.2	–	–	–	2.2	–	–
0.9	–	0.0	–	–	–	–
–	–	–	–	–	–	–
3.0	0.6	0.3	0.1	–	–	–
11.8	2.4	0.6	6.0	1.9	0.6	0.5
0.0	–	–	–	0.0	–	–
6.1	2.8	1.3	2.5	3.7	0.7	3.0
6.9	6.1	2.6	6.9	8.2	6.8	17.9
0.0	0.0	–	–	–	0.0	–
1.3	–	0.1	–	1.3	–	–
9.9	12.4	12.5	8.5	17.7	10.5	23.6
0.2	0.1	0.1	–	–	–	0.1
1.8	0.1	0.0	0.1	1.8	0.1	0.0
–	–	–	–	1.3	–	–
45.6	*26.8*	*17.6*	*24.4*	*40.7*	*18.7*	*45.3*
–	–	–	–	–	–	–
–	–	–	–	–	–	–
2.3	1.8	0.9	–	8.1	7.2	10.2
–	–	–	–	–	–	–
3.3	–	0.9	–	2.9	6.4	–
–	–	–	–	–	–	–
0.1	0.2	5.3	8.2	–	10.4	13.4
–	–	–	–	–	–	–
–	–	0.1	–	–	6.2	–
–	–	–	–	–	–	–
6.8	5.0	4.4	–	–	–	–
–	–	–	3.5	17.0	16.6	12.0
2.4	5.4	6.1	–	–	–	–
0.8	0.3	0.2	–	–	–	–
3.1	1.4	1.7	–	–	–	–
–	–	–	–	–	–	–
6.2	5.4	-0.1	–	–	–	–
3.8	4.1	3.9	–	–	–	–
0.7	0.0	0.2	–	–	–	–
–	4.2	0.7	2.2	5.0	–	1.5
29.4	*28.0*	*24.4*	*13.9*	*33.1*	*46.8*	*37.0*
–	–	–	–	–	–	–
27.7	*9.3*	*4.4*	*13.0*	*14.8*	*13.9*	*18.4*
75.0	***54.8***	***41.9***	***38.2***	***73.7***	***65.5***	***82.3***
			TECH. COOP. GRANTS			
1.5	2.3	0.1	0.4	0.3	0.2	0.1
0.0	0.0	0.0	–	–	0.0	0.0
0.0	0.2	0.1	0.1	0.0	0.0	0.0
2.2	–	–	0.0	–	–	–
0.9	–	0.0	–	–	–	–
–	–	–	–	–	–	–
0.2	–	–	–	–	–	–
1.1	0.1	0.0	0.4	0.1	0.1	0.0
0.0	–	–	–	0.0	–	–
2.7	2.8	1.3	0.6	0.3	0.1	0.1
6.9	6.1	2.6	0.0	0.0	0.0	0.7
0.0	0.0	–	0.0	0.0	0.0	–
1.3	–	0.1	–	–	–	–
9.9	12.4	12.5	–	0.2	0.2	1.0
0.2	0.1	0.1	–	–	–	–
1.8	0.1	0.0	0.1	0.0	0.0	0.0
–	–	–	–	–	–	–
28.7	*23.9*	*16.8*	*1.6*	*1.0*	*0.8*	*2.0*
20.3	*16.6*	*13.2*	*3.6*	*10.8*	*11.2*	*12.0*
–	–	–	–	–	–	–
14.2	*6.4*	*3.6*	*0.6*	*0.2*	*0.2*	*0.7*
48.9	***40.6***	***30.0***	***5.1***	***11.8***	***12.0***	***13.9***
			TOTAL OOF NET			
–	–	–	–	–	–	–
–	–	–	–	–	–	–
–	–	–	–	–	–	–
–	–	–	–	–	–	–
–	–	–	–	–	–	–
–	–	–	–	–	–	–
–	–	–	–	–	–	–
–	–	–	–	–	–	–
–	–	–	–	–	–	–
–	–	–	–	–	–	–
–	–	–	–	–	–	–
–	–	–	–	–	–	–
–	–	–	–	–	–	–
–	–	–	–	–	–	–
–	–	–	–	–	–	–
–	–	–	–	–	–	–
–	–	–	–	–	–	–
–	–	–	–	–	–	–
–	–	–	–	–	–	–
–	–	–	–	–	–	–
–	–	–	–	–	–	–
–	–	–	–	–	–	–

MAIN AID AGGREGATES

	1977	1978	1979	1980
DAC COUNTRIES COMBINED				
PRIVATE SECTOR NET	0.7	0.4	0.4	-0.9
Direct Investment	0.6	–	–	–
Portfolio Invest.	0.0	–	0.7	-0.3
Export Credits	0.0	0.4	-0.3	-0.6
OFFICIAL & PRIVATE				
GROSS:				
Contractual Lending	13.2	17.1	4.5	0.8
Export Credits Tot.	0.0	0.2	1.7	–
Export Credits Priv	0.0	0.2	1.7	–
OTHER NET DATA				
Contractual Lending	12.7	14.3	2.1	-0.7
Export Credits Tot.	0.0	0.4	-0.3	-0.6
(Bank Sector Loans)	–	–	–	–
ODA CONCESSIONALITY				
Total:Grant Element	96.0	100.0	100.0	100.0
Loans:Grant Element	83.0	–	–	–
OTHER SOURCES				
CMEA Countr.(Gross)	25.3	47.0	31.2	30.0
Intra LDCS Exc.OPEC	–	–	–	–
Other	–	–	–	–
ALL SOURCE COMMITMENTS				
TOTAL BILATERAL	24.4	40.7	18.7	45.3
of which				
OPEC (ODA)	–	–	–	–
CMEA (ODA)	44.6	47.0	41.2	30.0
TOTAL MULTILAT.(ODA)	13.9	33.1	46.8	37.0
TOTAL BIL.& MULTIL.	38.2	73.7	65.5	82.3
of which				
ODA Grants	22.2	60.7	41.9	57.3
ODA Loans	16.0	13.0	23.6	25.1
ODA CONCESSIONALITY				
Total: Grant Element	94.0	93.0	93.0	93.0
Loans: Grant Element	79.0	74.0	81.0	79.0

INDEBTEDNESS

	1977	1978	1979	1980
TOTAL DEBT DISBURSED	***48.0***	***77.0***	***77.0***	
Debt to DAC Countries	48.0	77.0	77.0	
ODA	44.0	72.0	72.0	
Total Export Credits	4.0	5.0	5.0	
Other Private Market	–	–	–	
International Org.	–	–	–	
CMEA	–	–	–	
Other	–	–	–	
TOTAL DEBT SERVICE	***3.0***	***2.2***	***3.3***	
Paid to DAC Countries	3.0	2.2	3.3	
ODA	1.1	1.9	1.2	
Total Export Credits	1.9	0.3	2.1	
Other Private Market	–	–	–	
International Org.	–	–	–	
CMEA	–	–	–	
Other	–	–	–	
ECONOMIC INDICATORS				
GNP Curr. Prices, $M	393.0	–	–	–
Real GNP, 1976=100	–	–	–	–
GNP/Cap Curr. Prices,$	122.0	–	–	–
GNP/cap Atlas Basis, $	–	–	–	–
Real GNP/Cap, 1976=100	–	–	–	–
Population, Million	3.2	3.3	3.3	3.4
Curr.A/C Deficit(-),$M	–	–	–	–
BOP Exp. & Transf.,$M	–	–	–	–
Exp. to OECD CIF, $M	3.5	6.3	11.4	8.3
of which				
Manufact.	1.4	1.5	2.1	1.4
Imp. from OECD FOB, $M	25.6	28.4	23.5	34.0
Reserves ex. Gold, $M	–	–	–	–

	1977	1978	1979	1980	1977	1978	1979	1980
TOTAL RECEIPTS NET					**TOTAL ODA NET**			
DAC COUNTRIES								
Australia	0.2	0.3	0.3	0.4	0.2	0.3	0.3	0.4
Austria	-0.3	-0.2	-0.2	-0.4	0.1	0.2	0.1	0.0
Belgium	-0.7	-1.0	-1.7	0.2	0.1	0.4	0.5	0.3
Canada	0.0	–	0.0	–	–	–	–	–
Denmark	0.2	0.4	0.1	0.1	0.2	0.4	0.1	0.1
Finland	0.0	0.1	0.0	0.0	0.0	0.1	0.0	0.0
France	-5.8	4.8	42.0	47.9	–	0.3	-0.2	16.4
Germany, Fed. Rep.	5.7	5.8	5.9	-1.9	2.9	2.5	3.3	3.5
Italy	-0.2	4.5	2.7	72.5	0.2	0.2	0.1	0.1
Japan	-0.1	0.3	-0.2	-0.2	0.0	0.6	0.0	0.0
Netherlands	2.9	2.3	0.4	0.3	2.9	2.3	0.4	0.3
New Zealand	0.0	0.0	–	–	–	–	–	–
Norway	0.3	14.5	-0.1	11.1	0.3	–	0.3	0.2
Sweden	0.6	0.1	–	0.2	0.6	0.1	–	–
Switzerland	0.4	54.0	0.8	0.5	0.4	1.2	0.9	0.5
United Kingdom	0.4	2.8	2.7	3.3	0.2	0.6	0.7	0.1
United States	-13.0	-1.0	6.0	10.0	20.0	13.0	12.0	3.0
TOTAL	*-9.5*	*87.6*	*58.5*	*144.0*	*28.0*	*22.1*	*18.3*	*24.9*
MULTILATERAL								
AF.D.F.	–	–	–	–	–	–	–	–
AF.D.B.	–	–	–	–	–	–	–	–
AS.D.B.	–	–	–	–	–	–	–	–
CAR.D.B.	–	–	–	–	–	–	–	–
E.E.C.	5.6	10.5	12.8	22.7	5.6	10.5	3.2	4.5
IBRD	-2.0	-2.0	6.6	7.8	–	–	–	–
IDA	–	–	–	–	–	–	–	–
I.D.B.	–	–	–	–	–	–	–	–
IFAD	–	–	–	–	–	–	–	–
I.F.C.	–	–	–	1.1	–	–	–	–
IMF TRUST FUND	–	–	–	–	–	–	–	–
U.N. AGENCIES	–	–	–	–	–	–	–	–
UNDP	0.5	0.3	0.2	1.9	0.5	0.3	0.2	1.9
UNTA	0.4	0.4	0.4	0.1	0.4	0.4	0.4	0.1
UNICEF	3.7	4.6	6.8	4.7	3.7	4.6	6.8	4.7
UNRWA	–	–	–	–	–	–	–	–
WFP	10.6	8.7	4.6	2.0	10.6	8.7	4.6	2.0
UNHCR	1.0	3.2	0.2	0.1	1.0	3.2	0.2	0.1
Other Multilateral	3.7	1.2	1.5	0.3	3.7	1.2	1.5	0.3
Arab OPEC Agencies	–	7.1	8.0	5.4	–	7.1	8.0	5.4
TOTAL	*23.4*	*34.0*	*41.1*	*46.1*	*25.4*	*36.0*	*25.0*	*19.1*
OPEC COUNTRIES	*24.4*	*123.9*	*48.6*	*242.2*	*24.4*	*123.9*	*48.6*	*242.2*
E.E.C.+ MEMBERS	*8.1*	*30.1*	*64.7*	*145.0*	*12.1*	*17.1*	*7.9*	*25.3*
TOTAL	***38.4***	***245.5***	***148.2***	***432.3***	***77.9***	***182.0***	***91.9***	***286.2***

	1977	1978	1979	1980	1977	1978	1979	1980
ODA LOANS GROSS					**ODA LOANS NET**			
DAC COUNTRIES								
Australia	–	–	–	–	–	–	–	–
Austria	–	–	–	–	0.0	0.0	-0.1	-0.1
Belgium	–	–	–	–	–	–	–	–
Canada	–	–	–	–	–	–	–	–
Denmark	–	–	–	–	–	–	–	–
Finland	–	–	–	–	–	–	–	–
France	–	–	–	10.9	-0.2	-0.4	-0.2	10.5
Germany, Fed. Rep.	–	–	0.6	0.9	–	–	0.6	0.9
Italy	–	–	–	–	–	–	–	–
Japan	–	–	–	–	–	–	–	–
Netherlands	–	–	–	–	–	–	–	–
New Zealand	–	–	–	–	–	–	–	–
Norway	–	–	–	–	–	–	–	–
Sweden	–	–	–	–	–	–	–	–
Switzerland	–	–	–	–	–	–	–	–
United Kingdom	–	–	–	–	–	–	–	–
United States	6.0	6.0	2.0	–	4.0	4.0	1.0	-1.0
TOTAL	*6.0*	*6.0*	*2.6*	*11.8*	*3.8*	*3.6*	*1.3*	*10.4*
MULTILATERAL	–	*7.1*	*8.0*	*5.4*	–	*7.1*	*8.0*	*5.4*
OPEC COUNTRIES	–	–	*5.1*	*3.4*	*-1.4*	*-0.9*	*4.4*	*3.2*
E.E.C.+ MEMBERS	–	–	*0.6*	*11.8*	*-0.2*	*-0.4*	*0.4*	*11.5*
TOTAL	***6.0***	***13.1***	***15.7***	***20.5***	***2.4***	***9.8***	***13.8***	***19.0***

	1977	1978	1979	1980	1977	1978	1979	1980
TOTAL OFFICIAL GROSS					**TOTAL OFFICIAL NET**			
DAC COUNTRIES								
Australia	0.2	0.3	0.3	0.4	0.2	0.3	0.3	0.4
Austria	0.1	0.2	0.2	0.1	0.0	0.1	0.1	0.0
Belgium	0.1	0.4	0.5	0.3	0.1	0.4	0.5	0.3
Canada	–	–	–	–	–	–	–	–
Denmark	0.2	0.4	0.1	0.1	0.2	0.4	0.1	0.1
Finland	0.0	0.1	0.0	0.0	0.0	0.1	0.0	0.0
France	0.2	0.7	–	16.7	–	0.3	-0.2	16.4
Germany, Fed. Rep.	4.0	2.6	3.3	3.5	3.2	2.4	3.3	3.5
Italy	0.2	0.2	0.1	0.1	0.2	0.2	0.1	0.1
Japan	0.0	0.6	0.0	0.0	0.0	0.6	0.0	0.0
Netherlands	2.9	2.3	0.4	0.3	2.9	2.3	0.4	0.3
New Zealand	0.0	–	–	–	0.0	–	–	–
Norway	0.3	–	0.3	0.2	0.3	–	0.3	0.2
Sweden	0.6	0.1	–	–	0.6	0.1	–	–
Switzerland	0.4	1.2	0.9	0.5	0.4	1.2	0.9	0.5
United Kingdom	0.2	0.6	0.7	0.1	0.2	0.6	0.7	0.1
United States	23.0	15.0	13.0	4.0	2.0	10.0	10.0	3.0
TOTAL	*32.3*	*24.6*	*19.6*	*26.3*	*10.3*	*18.9*	*16.3*	*24.9*
MULTILATERAL	*25.4*	*36.0*	*43.3*	*49.7*	*23.4*	*34.0*	*41.1*	*46.1*
OPEC COUNTRIES	*25.8*	*124.8*	*54.2*	*242.4*	*24.4*	*123.9*	*48.6*	*242.2*
E.E.C.+ MEMBERS	*13.4*	*17.5*	*17.6*	*43.7*	*12.4*	*17.0*	*17.4*	*43.4*
TOTAL	***83.5***	***185.4***	***117.1***	***318.4***	***58.1***	***176.8***	***106.1***	***313.2***

	197
TOTAL ODA GROSS	
Australia	0
Austria	0
Belgium	0
Canada	
Denmark	0
Finland	0
France	0
Germany, Fed. Rep.	2
Italy	0
Japan	0
Netherlands	2
New Zealand	
Norway	0
Sweden	0
Switzerland	0
United Kingdom	0
United States	22
TOTAL	*30*
AF.D.F.	
AF.D.B.	
AS.D.B.	
CAR.D.B.	
E.E.C.	5
IBRD	
IDA	
I.D.B.	
IFAD	
I.F.C.	
IMF TRUST FUND	
U.N. AGENCIES	
UNDP	0
UNTA	0
UNICEF	3
UNRWA	
WFP	10
UNHCR	1
Other Multilateral	3
Arab OPEC Agencies	
TOTAL	*25*
OPEC COUNTRIES	*25*
E.E.C.+ MEMBERS	*12*
TOTAL	***81***
GRANTS	
Australia	0
Austria	0
Belgium	0
Canada	
Denmark	0
Finland	0
France	0
Germany, Fed. Rep.	2
Italy	0
Japan	0
Netherlands	2
New Zealand	
Norway	0
Sweden	0
Switzerland	0
United Kingdom	0
United States	16
TOTAL	*24.*
MULTILATERAL	*25*
OPEC COUNTRIES	*25*
E.E.C.+ MEMBERS	*12.*
TOTAL	***75.***
TOTAL OOF GROSS	
Australia	
Austria	
Belgium	
Canada	
Denmark	
Finland	
France	
Germany, Fed. Rep.	1.
Italy	
Japan	
Netherlands	
New Zealand	0
Norway	
Sweden	
Switzerland	
United Kingdom	
United States	1
TOTAL	*2*
MULTILATERAL	
OPEC COUNTRIES	
E.E.C.+ MEMBERS	*1.*
TOTAL	***2.***

LEBANON

ODA COMMITMENTS

1978	1979	1980	1977	1978	1979	1980
0.3	0.3	0.4	0.2	0.2	–	0.6
0.2	0.2	0.1	–	–	–	–
0.4	0.5	0.3	–	–	0.9	–
–	–	–	–	–	–	–
0.4	0.1	0.1	–	–	0.1	–
0.1	0.0	0.0	–	0.1	0.0	0.0
0.7	–	16.7	0.2	0.7	14.1	15.9
2.5	3.3	3.5	11.6	2.8	2.6	2.3
0.2	0.1	0.1	0.2	0.2	0.1	0.1
0.6	0.0	0.0	0.0	0.6	0.0	0.1
2.3	0.4	0.3	4.1	1.2	0.6	0.3
–	–	–	–	–	–	–
–	0.3	0.2	–	–	–	–
0.1	–	–	0.7	–	–	–
1.2	0.9	0.5	–	–	–	0.5
0.6	0.7	0.1	0.2	0.6	0.7	0.1
15.0	13.0	4.0	25.0	32.9	3.3	0.7
24.5	*19.6*	*26.3*	*42.2*	*39.2*	*22.3*	*20.6*
–	–	–	–	–	–	–
–	–	–	–	–	–	–
–	–	–	–	–	–	–
–	–	–	–	–	–	–
10.5	3.2	4.5	3.3	4.2	4.5	4.1
–	–	–	–	–	–	–
–	–	–	–	–	–	–
–	–	–	–	–	–	–
–	–	–	–	–	–	–
–	–	–	–	–	–	–
–	–	–	–	–	–	–
–	–	–	19.8	18.4	13.7	9.2
0.3	0.2	1.9	–	–	–	–
0.4	0.4	0.1	–	–	–	–
4.6	6.8	4.7	–	–	–	–
–	–	–	–	–	–	–
8.7	4.6	2.0	–	–	–	–
3.2	0.2	0.1	–	–	–	–
1.2	1.5	0.3	–	–	–	–
7.1	8.0	5.4	38.4	–	–	9.8
36.0	*25.0*	*19.1*	*61.6*	*22.7*	*18.3*	*23.0*
124.8	*54.2*	*242.4*	*144.6*	*40.7*	*472.8*	*405.6*
17.5	*8.1*	*25.6*	*19.6*	*9.7*	*23.5*	*22.8*
185.3	***98.8***	***287.8***	***248.3***	***102.6***	***513.3***	***449.2***

TECH. COOP. GRANTS

1978	1979	1980	1977	1978	1979	1980
0.3	0.3	0.4	–	–	–	–
0.2	0.2	0.1	0.0	0.1	0.2	0.1
0.4	0.5	0.3	0.1	0.1	0.1	0.1
–	–	–	–	–	–	–
0.4	0.1	0.1	–	0.0	0.1	–
0.1	0.0	0.0	0.0	0.0	0.0	–
0.7	–	5.8	–	–	–	5.8
2.5	2.7	2.6	1.3	1.5	2.2	2.6
0.2	0.1	0.1	0.2	0.2	0.1	0.1
0.6	0.0	0.0	0.0	0.0	0.0	0.0
2.3	0.4	0.3	0.2	0.3	0.1	0.2
–	–	–	–	–	–	–
–	0.3	0.2	–	–	–	–
0.1	–	–	–	–	–	–
1.2	0.9	0.5	–	–	0.0	–
0.6	0.7	0.1	0.2	0.1	0.1	0.1
9.0	11.0	4.0	–	–	7.0	3.0
18.5	*17.0*	*14.5*	*2.0*	*2.2*	*10.0*	*12.1*
28.9	*16.9*	*13.7*	*9.3*	*9.7*	*9.1*	*9.2*
124.8	*49.2*	*239.0*	–	–	–	–
17.5	*7.5*	*13.8*	*2.0*	*2.1*	*2.7*	*8.9*
172.2	***83.1***	***267.2***	***11.3***	***12.0***	***19.1***	***21.2***

TOTAL OOF NET

1978	1979	1980	1977	1978	1979	1980
–	–	–	–	–	–	–
–	–	–	-0.1	-0.1	–	–
–	–	–	–	–	–	–
–	–	–	–	–	–	–
–	–	–	–	–	–	–
–	–	–	–	–	–	–
–	–	–	–	–	–	–
0.1	–	–	0.3	-0.1	–	0.0
–	–	–	–	–	–	–
–	–	–	–	–	–	–
–	–	–	–	–	–	–
–	–	–	0.0	–	–	–
–	–	–	–	–	–	–
–	–	–	–	–	–	–
–	–	–	–	–	–	–
–	–	–	–	–	–	–
–	–	–	-18.0	-3.0	-2.0	–
0.1	–	–	*-17.7*	*-3.2*	*-2.0*	*0.0*
–	*18.3*	*30.6*	*-2.0*	*-2.0*	*16.2*	*27.0*
–	–	–	–	–	–	–
0.1	*9.6*	*18.1*	*0.3*	*-0.1*	*9.6*	*18.1*
0.1	***18.3***	***30.6***	***-19.7***	***-5.2***	***14.2***	***27.0***

MAIN AID AGGREGATES

	1977	1978	1979	1980
DAC COUNTRIES COMBINED				
PRIVATE SECTOR NET	-19.8	68.7	42.2	119.1
Direct Investment	6.1	2.2	0.3	-13.2
Portfolio Invest.	-24.4	7.5	33.6	46.4
Export Credits	-1.5	58.9	8.3	85.9
OFFICIAL & PRIVATE				
GROSS:				
Contractual Lending	22.5	95.8	16.9	103.7
Export Credits Tot.	15.4	89.7	14.3	91.9
Export Credits Priv	14.4	89.7	14.3	91.9
OTHER NET DATA				
Contractual Lending	-15.4	59.4	7.6	96.2
Export Credits Tot.	-19.5	55.9	6.3	85.9
(Bank Sector Loans)	–	–	–	-9.0
ODA CONCESSIONALITY				
Total:Grant Element	84.0	89.0	60.0	98.0
Loans:Grant Element	57.0	46.0	41.0	43.0
OTHER SOURCES				
CMEA Countr.(Gross)	0.1	–	–	–
Intra LDCS Exc.OPEC	–	–	–	–
Other	–	–	–	–
ALL SOURCE COMMITMENTS				
TOTAL BILATERAL	186.8	80.0	495.1	426.1
of which				
OPEC (ODA)	144.6	40.7	472.8	405.6
CMEA (ODA)	0.1	–	–	–
TOTAL MULTILAT.(ODA)	61.6	22.7	18.3	23.0
TOTAL BIL.& MULTIL.	248.3	102.6	513.3	449.2
of which				
ODA Grants	177.1	65.8	498.2	429.2
ODA Loans	71.2	36.8	15.2	20.0
ODA CONCESSIONALITY				
Total: Grant Element	81.0	80.0	98.0	98.0
Loans: Grant Element	35.0	44.0	41.0	41.0

INDEBTEDNESS

	1977	1978	1979	1980
TOTAL DEBT DISBURSED	***143.2***	***185.9***	***177.2***	
Debt to DAC Countries	72.0	92.0	97.0	
ODA	16.0	20.0	22.0	
Total Export Credits	56.0	72.0	74.0	
Other Private Market	–	–	1.0	
International Org.	11.8	17.0	60.5	
CMEA	–	–	–	
Other	59.4	76.9	19.6	
TOTAL DEBT SERVICE	***48.6***	***45.7***	***24.4***	
Paid to DAC Countries	40.6	39.5	14.1	
ODA	3.2	3.6	1.2	
Total Export Credits	37.4	34.0	12.7	
Other Private Market	–	1.9	0.2	
International Org.	2.9	3.1	4.6	
CMEA	–	–	–	
Other	5.1	3.1	5.8	

ECONOMIC INDICATORS

	1977	1978	1979	1980
GNP Curr. Prices, $M	–	–	–	–
Real GNP, 1976=100	–	–	–	–
GNP/Cap Curr. Prices,$	–	–	–	–
GNP/cap Atlas Basis, $	–	–	–	–
Real GNP/Cap, 1976=100	–	–	–	–
Population, Million	2.7	2.7	2.7	2.7
Curr.A/C Deficit(-),$M	–	–	–	–
BOP Exp. & Transf.,$M	–	–	–	–
Exp. to OECD CIF, $M	103.2	94.7	108.1	148.7
of which				
Manufact.	35.2	42.2	41.9	57.8
Imp. from OECD FOB, $M	1061.3	1201.3	1806.7	2332.1
Reserves ex. Gold, $M	1568.8	1834.9	1531.5	1588.2

	1977	1978	1979	1980	1977	1978	1979	1980
TOTAL RECEIPTS NET					**TOTAL ODA NET**			
DAC COUNTRIES								
Australia	0.2	0.1	0.1	0.1	0.2	0.1	0.1	0.1
Austria	0.3	0.0	0.0	0.4	0.3	0.0	0.0	0.4
Belgium	0.1	0.2	0.2	0.2	0.1	0.2	0.2	0.2
Canada	5.0	4.0	4.1	5.8	5.0	4.0	4.1	5.8
Denmark	1.3	1.3	4.1	1.1	1.3	1.3	4.1	1.1
Finland	0.0	0.1	0.0	–	0.0	0.1	0.0	–
France	–	–	–	0.2	–	–	–	0.2
Germany, Fed. Rep.	1.7	4.1	1.9	18.1	1.3	3.7	4.1	18.0
Italy	–	–	–	–	–	–	–	–
Japan	0.0	0.5	0.0	–	0.0	0.5	0.0	–
Netherlands	0.8	1.2	2.9	3.9	0.8	1.2	2.2	3.9
New Zealand	–	–	–	0.0	–	–	–	0.0
Norway	1.3	1.1	2.0	0.1	1.3	1.1	2.0	0.1
Sweden	2.3	1.4	3.5	3.8	2.3	1.4	3.5	3.8
Switzerland	0.4	0.7	0.5	0.5	0.4	0.7	0.5	0.5
United Kingdom	3.8	11.0	13.4	9.5	3.8	9.9	14.0	9.6
United States	4.0	5.0	9.0	16.0	4.0	5.0	9.0	16.0
TOTAL	*21.0*	*30.6*	*41.5*	*59.6*	*20.7*	*29.1*	*43.7*	*59.6*
MULTILATERAL								
AF.D.F.	0.2	1.4	1.3	5.0	0.2	1.4	1.3	5.0
AF.D.B.	–	–	–	–	–	–	–	–
AS.D.B.	–	–	–	–	–	–	–	–
CAR.D.B.	–	–	–	–	–	–	–	–
E.E.C.	0.8	3.6	2.6	4.6	0.8	3.6	2.6	4.6
IBRD	–	–	–	–	–	–	–	–
IDA	5.1	2.7	2.6	3.8	5.1	2.7	2.6	3.8
I.D.B.	–	–	–	–	–	–	–	–
IFAD	–	–	–	–	–	–	–	–
I.F.C.	–	0.3	–	–	–	–	–	–
IMF TRUST FUND	0.6	2.0	1.9	1.7	0.6	2.0	1.9	1.7
U.N. AGENCIES	–	–	–	–	–	–	–	–
UNDP	1.9	1.9	2.7	3.2	1.9	1.9	2.7	3.2
UNTA	0.3	0.3	0.2	0.1	0.3	0.3	0.2	0.1
UNICEF	0.1	0.2	0.4	0.6	0.1	0.2	0.4	0.6
UNRWA	–	–	–	–	–	–	–	–
WFP	4.5	6.7	6.4	9.4	4.5	6.7	6.4	9.4
UNHCR	0.1	0.1	0.5	0.5	0.1	0.1	0.5	0.5
Other Multilateral	2.7	1.9	1.6	1.7	2.7	1.9	1.6	1.7
Arab OPEC Agencies	1.9	0.0	–	–	1.9	0.0	–	–
TOTAL	*18.1*	*21.2*	*20.2*	*30.6*	*18.1*	*20.9*	*20.2*	*30.6*
OPEC COUNTRIES	–	*0.1*	*0.3*	*0.1*	–	*0.1*	*0.3*	*0.1*
E.E.C.+ MEMBERS	*8.4*	*21.3*	*24.9*	*37.5*	*8.1*	*19.9*	*27.0*	*37.6*
TOTAL	***39.1***	***51.9***	***62.1***	***90.2***	***38.8***	***50.1***	***64.2***	***90.3***

	1977	1978	1979	1980	1977	1978	1979	1980
ODA LOANS GROSS					**ODA LOANS NET**			
DAC COUNTRIES								
Australia	–	–	–	–	–	–	–	–
Austria	–	–	–	–	–	–	–	–
Belgium	–	–	–	–	–	–	–	–
Canada	–	–	–	–	–	–	–	–
Denmark	0.1	0.1	2.9	0.1	0.1	0.1	2.9	0.1
Finland	–	–	–	–	–	–	–	–
France	–	–	–	–	–	–	–	–
Germany, Fed. Rep.	–	–	0.2	–	–	–	0.2	-0.2
Italy	–	–	–	–	–	–	–	–
Japan	–	–	–	–	–	–	–	–
Netherlands	–	–	–	–	–	–	–	–
New Zealand	–	–	–	–	–	–	–	–
Norway	–	–	–	–	–	–	–	–
Sweden	–	–	–	–	–	–	–	–
Switzerland	–	–	–	–	–	–	–	–
United Kingdom	–	–	0.1	–	0.0	0.0	0.0	-0.1
United States	–	–	–	–	–	–	–	–
TOTAL	*0.1*	*0.1*	*3.2*	*0.1*	*0.1*	*0.1*	*3.2*	*-0.2*
MULTILATERAL	*7.8*	*6.4*	*6.0*	*10.6*	*7.8*	*6.1*	*5.8*	*10.5*
OPEC COUNTRIES	–	*0.1*	*0.3*	*0.1*	–	*0.1*	*0.3*	*0.1*
E.E.C.+ MEMBERS	*0.1*	*0.1*	*3.2*	*0.1*	*0.1*	*0.1*	*3.2*	*-0.2*
TOTAL	***7.9***	***6.6***	***9.6***	***10.7***	***7.8***	***6.3***	***9.3***	***10.3***

	1977	1978	1979	1980	1977	1978	1979	1980
TOTAL OFFICIAL GROSS					**TOTAL OFFICIAL NET**			
DAC COUNTRIES								
Australia	0.2	0.1	0.1	0.1	0.2	0.1	0.1	0.1
Austria	0.3	0.0	0.0	0.4	0.3	0.0	0.0	0.4
Belgium	0.1	0.2	0.2	0.2	0.1	0.2	0.2	0.2
Canada	5.0	4.0	4.1	5.8	5.0	4.0	4.1	5.8
Denmark	1.3	1.3	4.1	1.1	1.3	1.3	4.1	1.1
Finland	0.0	0.1	0.0	–	0.0	0.1	0.0	–
France	–	–	–	0.2	–	–	–	0.2
Germany, Fed. Rep.	1.3	3.7	4.1	18.3	1.3	3.7	4.1	18.0
Italy	–	–	–	–	–	–	–	–
Japan	0.0	0.5	0.0	–	0.0	0.5	0.0	–
Netherlands	0.8	1.2	2.9	3.9	0.8	1.2	2.9	3.9
New Zealand	–	–	–	0.0	–	–	–	0.0
Norway	1.3	1.1	2.0	0.1	1.3	1.1	2.0	0.1
Sweden	2.3	1.4	3.5	3.8	2.3	1.4	3.5	3.8
Switzerland	0.4	0.7	0.5	0.5	0.4	0.7	0.5	0.5
United Kingdom	3.8	11.1	14.1	10.2	3.8	11.1	14.0	10.1
United States	4.0	5.0	9.0	16.0	4.0	5.0	9.0	16.0
TOTAL	*20.7*	*30.3*	*44.5*	*60.5*	*20.7*	*30.2*	*44.4*	*60.2*
MULTILATERAL	*18.2*	*21.5*	*20.4*	*30.7*	*18.1*	*21.2*	*20.2*	*30.6*
OPEC COUNTRIES	–	*0.1*	*0.3*	*0.1*	–	*0.1*	*0.3*	*0.1*
E.E.C.+ MEMBERS	*8.1*	*21.0*	*27.9*	*38.4*	*8.1*	*21.0*	*27.8*	*38.1*
TOTAL	***38.9***	***51.8***	***65.3***	***91.2***	***38.8***	***51.5***	***65.0***	***90.8***

	197
TOTAL ODA GROSS	
Australia	C
Austria	O
Belgium	C
Canada	5
Denmark	1
Finland	C
France	
Germany, Fed. Rep.	1
Italy	
Japan	C
Netherlands	C
New Zealand	
Norway	1
Sweden	2
Switzerland	C
United Kingdom	3
United States	4
TOTAL	*2C*
AF.D.F.	C
AF.D.B.	
AS.D.B.	
CAR.D.B.	
E.E.C.	C
IBRD	
IDA	5
I.D.B.	
IFAD	
I.F.C.	
IMF TRUST FUND	C
U.N. AGENCIES	
UNDP	1
UNTA	C
UNICEF	C
UNRWA	
WFP	4
UNHCR	C
Other Multilateral	2
Arab OPEC Agencies	1
TOTAL	*18*
OPEC COUNTRIES	
E.E.C.+ MEMBERS	*8*
TOTAL	***38***
GRANTS	
Australia	C
Austria	C
Belgium	C
Canada	5
Denmark	1
Finland	C
France	
Germany, Fed. Rep.	1
Italy	
Japan	C
Netherlands	C
New Zealand	
Norway	1
Sweden	2
Switzerland	C
United Kingdom	3
United States	4
TOTAL	*2C*
MULTILATERAL	*1C*
OPEC COUNTRIES	
E.E.C.+ MEMBERS	*8*
TOTAL	***31***
TOTAL OOF GROSS	
Australia	
Austria	
Belgium	
Canada	
Denmark	
Finland	
France	
Germany, Fed. Rep.	
Italy	
Japan	
Netherlands	
New Zealand	
Norway	
Sweden	
Switzerland	
United Kingdom	
United States	
TOTAL	
MULTILATERAL	
OPEC COUNTRIES	
E.E.C.+ MEMBERS	
TOTAL	

1978	1979	1980	1977	1978	1979	1980
			ODA COMMITMENTS			
0.1	0.1	0.1	0.1	0.0	0.2	0.2
0.0	0.0	0.4	–	–	–	0.0
0.2	0.2	0.2	–	–	–	–
4.0	4.1	5.8	15.9	1.6	2.7	8.8
1.3	4.1	1.1	1.2	0.8	0.6	0.5
0.1	0.0	–	–	–	0.0	–
–	–	0.2	–	–	–	0.1
3.7	4.1	18.3	3.5	7.5	23.7	34.5
–	–	–	–	–	–	–
0.5	0.0	–	0.0	0.5	0.0	–
1.2	2.2	3.9	1.8	3.3	5.5	2.0
–	–	0.0	–	0.1	–	0.0
1.1	2.0	0.1	3.4	0.5	–	–
1.4	3.5	3.8	4.5	1.5	0.5	7.1
0.7	0.5	0.5	1.2	–	–	0.6
10.0	14.1	9.7	1.9	2.6	46.0	4.7
5.0	9.0	16.0	6.7	10.3	10.4	20.6
29.1	*43.8*	*59.9*	*40.1*	*28.5*	*89.6*	*79.0*
1.6	1.5	5.1	13.8	5.6	–	7.2
–	–	–	–	–	–	–
–	–	–	–	–	–	–
–	–	–	–	–	–	–
3.6	2.6	4.6	7.5	7.6	8.7	1.2
–	–	–	–	–	–	–
2.8	2.6	3.8	10.0	6.0	15.0	10.0
–	–	–	–	–	–	–
–	–	–	–	–	–	6.2
–	–	–	–	–	–	–
2.0	1.9	1.7	–	–	–	–
–	–	–	9.6	11.1	11.8	15.5
1.9	2.7	3.2	–	–	–	–
0.3	0.2	0.1	–	–	–	–
0.2	0.4	0.6	–	–	–	–
–	–	–	–	–	–	–
6.7	6.4	9.4	–	–	–	–
0.1	0.5	0.5	–	–	–	–
1.9	1.6	1.7	–	–	–	–
0.0	–	–	1.9	0.0	3.0	11.4
21.2	*20.4*	*30.7*	*42.8*	*30.4*	*38.5*	*51.5*
0.1	*0.3*	*0.1*	–	*5.1*	–	*1.1*
19.9	*27.1*	*37.9*	*15.9*	*21.7*	*84.5*	*42.9*
50.4	***64.5***	***90.7***	***82.9***	***64.1***	***128.0***	***131.5***
			TECH. COOP. GRANTS			
0.1	0.1	0.1	0.2	0.1	0.1	0.1
0.0	0.0	0.4	0.3	0.0	0.0	0.4
0.2	0.2	0.2	0.1	0.2	0.2	0.2
4.0	4.1	5.8	1.4	1.3	1.0	1.3
1.2	1.2	1.0	0.7	1.2	1.2	1.0
0.1	0.0	–	0.0	0.1	0.0	–
–	–	0.2	–	–	–	0.2
3.7	3.9	18.3	1.3	3.6	3.9	5.5
–	–	–	–	–	–	–
0.5	0.0	–	0.0	0.0	0.0	–
1.2	2.2	3.9	0.8	1.1	1.5	2.2
–	–	0.0	–	–	–	0.0
1.1	2.0	0.1	0.1	0.0	0.0	–
1.4	3.5	3.8	0.2	0.9	1.1	1.9
0.7	0.5	0.5	–	–	–	0.2
10.0	13.9	9.7	1.7	2.4	3.4	4.6
5.0	9.0	16.0	1.0	1.0	2.0	5.0
29.0	*40.5*	*59.9*	*7.7*	*11.9*	*14.5*	*22.5*
14.8	*14.4*	*20.1*	*5.0*	*4.4*	*5.4*	*15.5*
–	–	–	–	–	–	–
19.8	*23.9*	*37.8*	*4.6*	*8.5*	*10.2*	*13.7*
43.8	***54.9***	***79.9***	***12.7***	***16.3***	***19.9***	***38.0***
			TOTAL OOF NET			
–	–	–	–	–	–	–
–	–	–	–	–	–	–
–	–	–	–	–	–	–
–	–	–	–	–	–	–
–	–	–	–	–	–	–
–	–	–	–	–	–	–
–	–	–	–	–	–	–
–	–	–	–	–	–	–
–	–	–	–	–	–	–
–	–	–	–	–	–	–
–	0.8	–	–	–	0.8	–
–	–	–	–	–	–	–
–	–	–	–	–	–	–
–	–	–	–	–	–	–
–	–	–	–	–	–	–
1.1	–	0.6	–	1.1	–	0.5
–	–	–	–	–	–	–
1.1	*0.8*	*0.6*	–	*1.1*	*0.8*	*0.5*
0.3	–	–	–	*0.3*	–	–
–	–	–	–	–	–	–
1.1	*0.8*	*0.6*	–	*1.1*	*0.8*	*0.5*
1.4	***0.8***	***0.6***	–	***1.4***	***0.8***	***0.5***

	1977	1978	1979	1980
MAIN AID AGGREGATES				
DAC COUNTRIES COMBINED				
PRIVATE SECTOR NET	0.3	0.4	-2.9	-0.6
Direct Investment	0.4	0.0	–	–
Portfolio Invest.	-0.1	0.4	-2.3	0.0
Export Credits	0.0	0.0	-0.6	-0.6
OFFICIAL & PRIVATE				
GROSS:				
Contractual Lending	0.1	1.2	4.0	1.0
Export Credits Tot.	–	–	–	0.4
Export Credits Priv	–	–	–	0.4
OTHER NET DATA				
Contractual Lending	0.0	1.2	3.3	-0.3
Export Credits Tot.	0.0	0.0	-0.6	-0.6
(Bank Sector Loans)	–	–	–	–
ODA CONCESSIONALITY				
Total:Grant Element	100.0	97.0	98.0	100.0
Loans:Grant Element	–	83.0	83.0	–
OTHER SOURCES				
CMEA Countr.(Gross)	–	–	–	–
Intra LDCS Exc.OPEC	–	–	–	–
Other	–	–	–	–
ALL SOURCE COMMITMENTS				
TOTAL BILATERAL	41.2	33.7	90.4	80.6
of which				
OPEC (ODA)	–	5.1	–	1.1
CMEA (ODA)	–	–	–	–
TOTAL MULTILAT.(ODA)	42.8	30.4	38.5	51.5
TOTAL BIL.& MULTIL.	84.0	64.1	128.8	132.1
of which				
ODA Grants	57.2	43.3	103.5	95.7
ODA Loans	25.7	20.8	24.5	35.8
ODA CONCESSIONALITY				
Total: Grant Element	94.0	92.0	96.0	90.0
Loans: Grant Element	82.0	76.0	80.0	66.0
INDEBTEDNESS				
TOTAL DEBT DISBURSED	***23.8***	***29.6***	***49.6***	
Debt to DAC Countries	2.0	2.0	9.0	
ODA	1.0	1.0	4.0	
Total Export Credits	1.0	1.0	3.0	
Other Private Market	–	–	2.0	
International Org.	20.2	26.0	33.9	
CMEA	–	–	–	
Other	1.6	1.6	6.7	
TOTAL DEBT SERVICE	***0.4***	***1.0***	***1.8***	
Paid to DAC Countries	0.2	0.6	1.1	
ODA	0.1	–	–	
Total Export Credits	–	0.6	0.8	
Other Private Market	0.1	–	0.3	
International Org.	0.2	0.3	0.4	
CMEA	–	–	–	
Other	0.0	0.1	0.3	
ECONOMIC INDICATORS				
GNP Curr. Prices, $M	318.6	383.4	471.2	569.0
Real GNP, 1976=100	110.0	127.0	132.0	130.0
GNP/Cap Curr. Prices,$	255.0	300.0	359.0	424.0
GNP/cap Atlas Basis, $	275.3	334.0	366.4	385.5
Real GNP/Cap, 1976=100	107.0	121.0	123.0	118.0
Population, Million	1.2	1.3	1.3	1.3
Curr.A/C Deficit(-),$M	–	–	–	–
BOP Exp. & Transf.,$M	–	–	–	–
Exp. to OECD CIF, $M	3.9	6.5	5.7	6.8
of which				
Manufact.	2.8	3.2	4.2	5.7
Imp. from OECD FOB, $M	5.0	4.7	8.5	12.7
Reserves ex. Gold, $M	–	–	–	50.3

	1977	1978	1979	1980	1977	1978	1979	1980
TOTAL RECEIPTS NET					**TOTAL ODA NET**			
DAC COUNTRIES								
Australia	0.0	–	–	–	0.0	–	–	–
Austria	–	–	0.0	–	–	–	0.0	–
Belgium	-4.8	-6.1	-11.2	-14.1	0.0	0.1	0.1	0.1
Canada	3.7	-2.0	-3.2	-9.7	–	–	–	–
Denmark	–	0.0	-17.5	20.3	–	0.0	0.0	0.0
Finland	21.3	-3.1	-3.3	25.3	0.0	–	–	0.0
France	30.5	65.5	-41.9	-42.3	–	–	–	0.8
Germany, Fed. Rep.	208.5	-2.9	-135.3	63.5	4.4	8.7	16.4	11.3
Italy	-4.8	-3.9	22.2	0.4	0.1	0.2	0.1	0.0
Japan	341.8	671.4	442.6	291.2	4.8	1.8	1.7	13.9
Netherlands	42.5	1.0	-34.4	6.3	1.9	1.0	1.0	0.9
New Zealand	–	–	–	–	–	–	–	–
Norway	10.0	8.6	25.5	8.8	0.1	–	–	0.1
Sweden	2.3	-0.1	0.9	6.3	–	–	0.2	0.3
Switzerland	-0.8	-0.6	–	-2.0	–	0.1	–	0.0
United Kingdom	17.8	0.5	27.9	35.8	0.3	0.3	1.0	0.8
United States	24.0	-54.0	12.0	-40.0	10.0	10.0	10.0	32.0
TOTAL	*691.9*	*674.2*	*284.4*	*349.8*	*21.7*	*22.0*	*30.4*	*60.0*
MULTILATERAL								
AF.D.F.	–	–	–	–	–	–	–	–
AF.D.B.	0.7	3.0	6.0	5.1	–	–	–	–
AS.D.B.	–	–	–	–	–	–	–	–
CAR.D.B.	–	–	–	–	–	–	–	–
E.E.C.	0.2	4.8	18.2	7.4	0.2	4.8	12.7	4.4
IBRD	7.6	8.5	9.9	15.6	1.0	0.7	0.7	0.7
IDA	3.2	3.5	4.9	4.9	3.2	3.5	4.9	4.9
I.D.B.	–	–	–	–	–	–	–	–
IFAD	–	–	–	–	–	–	–	–
I.F.C.	–	–	–	–	–	–	–	–
IMF TRUST FUND	3.6	11.2	11.4	9.6	3.6	11.2	11.4	9.6
U.N. AGENCIES	–	–	–	–	–	–	–	–
UNDP	1.2	1.7	1.2	1.5	1.2	1.7	1.2	1.5
UNTA	0.5	0.5	0.5	0.1	0.5	0.5	0.5	0.1
UNICEF	0.3	0.2	0.4	0.9	0.3	0.2	0.4	0.9
UNRWA	–	–	–	–	–	–	–	–
WFP	0.8	2.0	1.8	2.4	0.8	2.0	1.8	2.4
UNHCR	–	0.0	0.0	0.1	–	0.0	0.0	0.1
Other Multilateral	1.2	1.4	0.5	1.5	1.2	1.4	0.5	1.5
Arab OPEC Agencies	–	0.1	2.8	3.9	–	0.1	1.3	2.6
TOTAL	*19.3*	*36.9*	*57.6*	*53.0*	*12.0*	*26.0*	*35.5*	*28.7*
OPEC COUNTRIES	–	–	*14.8*	*9.2*	–	–	*14.8*	*9.2*
E.E.C.+ MEMBERS	*289.9*	*58.8*	*-172.0*	*77.2*	*7.0*	*15.0*	*31.3*	*18.2*
TOTAL	***711.2***	***711.1***	***356.8***	***411.9***	***33.7***	***48.0***	***80.8***	***97.9***
ODA LOANS GROSS					**ODA LOANS NET**			
DAC COUNTRIES								
Australia	–	–	–	–	–	–	–	–
Austria	–	–	–	–	–	–	–	–
Belgium	–	–	–	–	–	–	–	–
Canada	–	–	–	–	–	–	–	–
Denmark	–	–	–	–	–	–	–	–
Finland	–	–	–	–	–	–	–	–
France	–	–	–	–	–	–	–	–
Germany, Fed. Rep.	3.5	4.9	11.9	7.0	1.9	3.9	9.9	5.0
Italy	–	–	–	–	–	–	–	–
Japan	4.7	0.9	0.1	12.4	4.7	0.9	0.1	12.4
Netherlands	0.9	–	–	–	0.9	–	–	-0.1
New Zealand	–	–	–	–	–	–	–	–
Norway	–	–	–	–	–	–	–	–
Sweden	–	–	–	–	–	–	–	–
Switzerland	–	–	–	–	–	–	–	–
United Kingdom	–	–	0.4	–	0.0	0.0	0.4	0.0
United States	5.0	4.0	3.0	8.0	3.0	2.0	1.0	7.0
TOTAL	*14.2*	*9.7*	*15.4*	*27.4*	*10.5*	*6.7*	*11.3*	*24.3*
MULTILATERAL	*7.8*	*15.5*	*18.3*	*17.8*	*7.8*	*15.4*	*18.3*	*17.8*
OPEC COUNTRIES	–	–	*14.8*	*9.2*	–	–	*14.8*	*9.2*
E.E.C.+ MEMBERS	*4.4*	*5.0*	*12.3*	*7.0*	*2.8*	*3.9*	*10.2*	*4.9*
TOTAL	***22.0***	***25.2***	***48.6***	***54.4***	***18.4***	***22.1***	***44.5***	***51.3***
TOTAL OFFICIAL GROSS					**TOTAL OFFICIAL NET**			
DAC COUNTRIES								
Australia	0.0	–	–	–	0.0	–	–	–
Austria	–	–	0.0	–	–	–	0.0	–
Belgium	0.0	0.1	0.1	0.1	0.0	0.1	0.1	0.1
Canada	7.3	1.4	–	–	3.7	-2.0	-3.2	-9.7
Denmark	–	0.0	0.0	0.0	–	0.0	0.0	0.0
Finland	0.0	–	–	0.0	0.0	–	–	0.0
France	–	–	–	0.8	–	–	–	0.8
Germany, Fed. Rep.	23.2	9.7	19.0	13.6	3.5	-7.6	-5.0	3.8
Italy	0.1	0.2	0.1	0.0	-0.3	-0.3	-0.9	-0.9
Japan	4.8	1.8	1.7	13.9	4.8	1.8	1.7	13.9
Netherlands	3.3	1.0	1.0	1.0	3.3	1.0	1.0	0.8
New Zealand	–	–	–	–	–	–	–	–
Norway	0.1	–	–	0.1	0.1	–	–	0.1
Sweden	–	–	0.2	0.3	–	–	0.2	0.3
Switzerland	–	0.1	–	0.0	–	0.1	–	0.0
United Kingdom	0.3	0.3	2.5	0.8	0.3	0.3	2.5	0.8
United States	12.0	17.0	12.0	33.0	-2.0	9.0	6.0	29.0
TOTAL	*51.2*	*31.4*	*36.6*	*63.4*	*13.4*	*2.3*	*2.4*	*38.8*
MULTILATERAL	*20.9*	*39.8*	*60.3*	*55.3*	*19.3*	*36.9*	*57.6*	*53.0*
OPEC COUNTRIES	–	–	*14.8*	*9.2*	–	–	*14.8*	*9.2*
E.E.C.+ MEMBERS	*27.2*	*16.1*	*40.8*	*23.6*	*7.0*	*-1.7*	*15.9*	*12.6*
TOTAL	***72.1***	***71.2***	***111.7***	***127.9***	***32.7***	***39.3***	***74.8***	***101.0***

	197[illegible]
TOTAL ODA GROSS	
Australia	[illegible]
Austria	
Belgium	[illegible]
Canada	
Denmark	
Finland	[illegible]
France	
Germany, Fed. Rep.	[illegible]
Italy	[illegible]
Japan	[illegible]
Netherlands	[illegible]
New Zealand	
Norway	[illegible]
Sweden	
Switzerland	
United Kingdom	[illegible]
United States	[illegible]
TOTAL	[illegible]
AF.D.F.	
AF.D.B.	
AS.D.B.	
CAR.D.B.	
E.E.C.	[illegible]
IBRD	[illegible]
IDA	[illegible]
I.D.B.	
IFAD	
I.F.C.	
IMF TRUST FUND	[illegible]
U.N. AGENCIES	
UNDP	[illegible]
UNTA	[illegible]
UNICEF	[illegible]
UNRWA	
WFP	[illegible]
UNHCR	
Other Multilateral	[illegible]
Arab OPEC Agencies	
TOTAL	[illegible]
OPEC COUNTRIES	
E.E.C.+ MEMBERS	[illegible]
TOTAL	[illegible]
GRANTS	
Australia	[illegible]
Austria	
Belgium	[illegible]
Canada	
Denmark	
Finland	[illegible]
France	
Germany, Fed. Rep.	[illegible]
Italy	[illegible]
Japan	[illegible]
Netherlands	[illegible]
New Zealand	
Norway	[illegible]
Sweden	
Switzerland	
United Kingdom	[illegible]
United States	[illegible]
TOTAL	[illegible]
MULTILATERAL	[illegible]
OPEC COUNTRIES	
E.E.C.+ MEMBERS	[illegible]
TOTAL	[illegible]
TOTAL OOF GROSS	
Australia	
Austria	
Belgium	
Canada	[illegible]
Denmark	
Finland	
France	
Germany, Fed. Rep.	[illegible]
Italy	
Japan	
Netherlands	[illegible]
New Zealand	
Norway	
Sweden	
Switzerland	
United Kingdom	
United States	
TOTAL	[illegible]
MULTILATERAL	[illegible]
OPEC COUNTRIES	
E.E.C.+ MEMBERS	[illegible]
TOTAL	[illegible]

1978	1979	1980	1977	1978	1979	1980
			ODA COMMITMENTS			
–	–	–	–	–	–	–
–	0.0	–	–	–	–	–
0.1	0.1	0.1	–	–	–	–
–	–	–	–	–	–	–
0.0	0.0	0.0	–	0.0	0.1	–
–	–	0.0	–	–	–	–
–	–	0.8	–	–	–	0.7
9.7	18.4	13.3	9.2	16.3	13.2	14.3
0.2	0.1	0.0	0.1	0.2	0.1	0.0
1.8	1.7	13.9	0.1	1.1	20.1	1.6
1.0	1.0	1.0	2.1	0.9	1.0	1.1
–	–	–	–	–	–	–
–	–	0.1	–	–	–	–
–	0.2	0.3	–	–	–	–
0.1	–	0.0	–	–	–	0.0
0.3	1.0	0.8	0.3	8.2	15.5	0.8
12.0	12.0	33.0	19.5	5.2	16.0	34.2
25.0	*34.5*	*63.1*	*31.4*	*31.9*	*65.8*	*52.7*
–	–	–	–	–	–	–
–	–	–	–	–	–	–
–	–	–	–	–	–	–
–	–	–	–	–	–	–
4.9	12.7	4.4	20.7	4.4	11.6	4.0
0.7	0.7	0.7	–	–	–	–
3.5	4.9	4.9	7.0	20.0	–	4.1
–	–	–	–	–	–	–
–	–	–	–	–	–	–
–	–	–	–	–	–	–
11.2	11.4	9.6	–	–	–	–
–	–	–	4.0	5.9	4.5	6.5
1.7	1.2	1.5	–	–	–	–
0.5	0.5	0.1	–	–	–	–
0.2	0.4	0.9	–	–	–	–
–	–	–	–	–	–	–
2.0	1.8	2.4	–	–	–	–
0.0	0.0	0.1	–	–	–	–
1.4	0.5	1.5	–	–	–	–
0.1	1.3	2.6	–	6.3	–	5.0
26.1	*35.5*	*28.7*	*31.7*	*36.5*	*16.0*	*19.7*
–	*14.8*	*9.2*	–	*28.8*	–	–
16.1	*33.3*	*20.3*	*32.5*	*30.0*	*41.3*	*20.9*
51.1	***84.9***	***101.0***	***63.1***	***97.1***	***81.9***	***72.4***
			TECH. COOP. GRANTS			
–	–	–	0.0	–	–	–
–	0.0	–	–	–	0.0	–
0.1	0.1	0.1	0.0	0.1	0.1	0.1
–	–	–	–	–	–	–
0.0	0.0	0.0	–	0.0	0.0	0.0
–	–	0.0	0.0	–	–	0.0
–	–	0.8	–	–	–	0.5
4.8	6.5	6.3	2.5	4.8	6.5	6.3
0.2	0.1	0.0	0.1	0.2	0.1	0.0
0.9	1.6	1.4	0.1	0.9	1.6	1.4
1.0	1.0	1.0	0.9	0.8	0.6	0.6
–	–	–	–	–	–	–
–	–	0.1	0.1	–	–	0.0
–	0.2	0.3	–	–	–	–
0.1	–	0.0	–	–	–	–
0.3	0.6	0.8	0.3	0.3	0.6	0.8
8.0	9.0	25.0	5.0	5.0	7.0	10.0
15.3	*19.1*	*35.7*	*9.1*	*12.0*	*16.5*	*19.7*
10.7	*17.2*	*10.9*	*3.2*	*3.9*	*2.7*	*6.5*
–	–	–	–	–	–	–
11.0	*21.0*	*13.3*	*4.0*	*6.1*	*7.9*	*8.2*
25.9	***36.3***	***46.6***	***12.3***	***15.9***	***19.2***	***26.2***
			TOTAL OOF NET			
–	–	–	–	–	–	–
–	–	–	–	–	–	–
–	–	–	–	–	–	–
1.4	–	–	3.7	-2.0	-3.2	-9.7
–	–	–	–	–	0.0	–
–	–	–	–	–	–	–
–	–	–	–	–	–	–
–	0.5	0.3	-0.9	-16.2	-21.4	-7.5
–	–	–	-0.5	-0.5	-1.0	-0.9
–	–	–	–	–	–	–
–	–	–	1.4	–	–	-0.1
–	–	–	–	–	–	–
–	–	–	–	–	–	–
–	–	–	–	–	–	–
–	–	–	–	–	–	–
–	1.5	–	–	–	1.5	–
5.0	–	–	-12.0	-1.0	-4.0	-3.0
6.4	*2.0*	*0.3*	*-8.2*	*-19.7*	*-28.1*	*-21.2*
13.7	*24.8*	*26.6*	*7.3*	*10.9*	*22.1*	*24.3*
–	–	–	–	–	–	–
–	*7.5*	*3.2*	*0.1*	*-16.7*	*-15.4*	*-5.6*
20.1	***26.9***	***26.9***	***-1.0***	***-8.8***	***-6.0***	***3.0***

MAIN AID AGGREGATES

	1977	1978	1979	1980
DAC COUNTRIES COMBINED				
PRIVATE SECTOR NET	678.5	671.9	282.0	311.0
Direct Investment	170.5	144.7	41.2	66.9
Portfolio Invest.	216.9	532.3	291.4	238.9
Export Credits	291.2	-5.2	-50.6	5.1
OFFICIAL & PRIVATE				
GROSS:				
Contractual Lending	621.8	115.5	273.2	198.5
Export Credits Tot.	606.2	105.8	256.2	171.1
Export Credits Priv	581.7	99.4	255.7	170.8
OTHER NET DATA				
Contractual Lending	293.5	-18.1	-67.4	8.3
Export Credits Tot.	291.1	-10.6	-59.5	-8.4
(Bank Sector Loans)	–	–	–	281.0
ODA CONCESSIONALITY				
Total:Grant Element	82.0	76.0	69.0	89.0
Loans:Grant Element	67.0	50.0	48.0	60.0
OTHER SOURCES				
CMEA Countr.(Gross)	–	–	–	–
Intra LDCS Exc.OPEC	–	–	–	–
Other	–	–	–	–
ALL SOURCE COMMITMENTS				
TOTAL BILATERAL	38.3	61.0	70.6	57.4
of which				
OPEC (ODA)	–	28.8	–	–
CMEA (ODA)	–	–	–	–
TOTAL MULTILAT.(ODA)	31.7	36.5	16.0	19.7
TOTAL BIL.& MULTIL.	70.0	97.5	86.6	77.1
of which				
ODA Grants	33.1	26.0	42.9	48.6
ODA Loans	30.0	71.1	39.0	23.8
ODA CONCESSIONALITY				
Total: Grant Element	84.0	67.0	76.0	86.0
Loans: Grant Element	69.0	53.0	54.0	53.0

INDEBTEDNESS

	1977	1978	1979	1980
TOTAL DEBT DISBURSED	***261.8***	***318.4***	***427.6***	
Debt to DAC Countries	197.0	241.0	310.0	
ODA	105.0	119.0	132.0	
Total Export Credits	49.0	44.0	50.0	
Other Private Market	43.0	78.0	128.0	
International Org.	55.5	68.1	96.2	
CMEA	–	–	–	
Other	9.3	9.3	21.3	
TOTAL DEBT SERVICE	***27.7***	***27.3***	***76.4***	
Paid to DAC Countries	22.8	20.2	67.2	
ODA	5.2	4.8	6.4	
Total Export Credits	12.8	7.7	5.6	
Other Private Market	4.8	7.7	55.2	
International Org.	4.6	7.1	9.0	
CMEA	–	–	–	
Other	0.3	–	0.2	

ECONOMIC INDICATORS

	1977	1978	1979	1980
GNP Curr. Prices, $M	745.9	790.7	939.2	1002.0
Real GNP, 1976=100	104.0	112.0	118.0	112.0
GNP/Cap Curr. Prices,$	443.0	454.0	522.0	539.0
GNP/cap Atlas Basis, $	421.0	470.4	521.4	524.8
Real GNP/Cap, 1976=100	100.0	104.0	107.0	98.0
Population, Million	1.7	1.7	1.8	1.9
Curr.A/C Deficit(-),$M	–	–	–	–
BOP Exp. & Transf.,$M	–	–	–	–
Exp. to OECD CIF, $M	603.8	905.7	1236.3	1196.3
of which				
Manufact.	20.1	62.9	129.1	190.6
Imp. from OECD FOB, $M	4066.3	2793.5	2251.5	2371.6
Reserves ex. Gold, $M	27.3	18.0	55.0	4.1

	TOTAL RECEIPTS NET 1977	1978	1979	1980	TOTAL ODA NET 1977	1978	1979	1980	TOTAL ODA GROSS 19
DAC COUNTRIES									
Australia	–	–	–	–	–	–	–	–	
Austria	0.0	–	0.0	–	0.0	–	0.0	–	
Belgium	0.0	2.6	-0.6	4.4	0.2	0.2	0.3	0.4	
Canada	1.5	2.7	2.1	17.0	1.5	2.7	2.1	9.7	
Denmark	–	–	0.1	0.0	–	–	0.1	0.0	
Finland	–	–	–	–	–	–	–	–	
France	20.1	17.3	47.4	128.0	21.8	19.0	35.7	54.0	24
Germany, Fed. Rep.	-0.7	13.5	1.1	1.4	1.0	-0.6	0.8	-0.3	
Italy	-8.1	3.9	76.9	53.0	-0.3	0.1	-0.2	-0.2	
Japan	-1.5	7.7	24.4	21.9	2.0	5.8	20.5	17.6	
Netherlands	0.5	0.2	0.4	0.8	0.5	0.2	0.4	0.8	
New Zealand	–	–	–	–	–	–	–	–	
Norway	1.8	2.3	4.8	5.1	1.8	2.3	4.8	5.1	
Sweden	–	–	–	35.5	–	–	–	–	
Switzerland	1.9	7.5	5.8	3.4	1.9	7.5	5.8	2.5	
United Kingdom	0.3	0.3	0.2	14.4	0.2	0.3	0.2	1.3	
United States	2.0	2.0	3.0	–	2.0	2.0	3.0	–	
TOTAL	*17.7*	*60.1*	*165.5*	*284.8*	*32.6*	*39.6*	*73.5*	*90.8*	36
MULTILATERAL									
AF.D.F.	–	0.7	–	6.1	–	0.7	–	6.1	
AF.D.B.	–	–	–	–	–	–	–	–	
AS.D.B.	–	–	–	–	–	–	–	–	
CAR.D.B.	–	–	–	–	–	–	–	–	
E.E.C.	10.4	23.2	15.7	19.7	10.4	23.2	15.7	19.7	10
IBRD	-0.1	0.6	2.3	1.1	–	–	–	–	
IDA	8.8	8.4	12.4	24.5	8.8	8.4	12.4	24.5	
I.D.B.	–	–	–	–	–	–	–	–	
IFAD	–	–	–	–	–	–	–	–	
I.F.C.	7.8	3.5	–	-1.2	–	–	–	–	
IMF TRUST FUND	–	13.5	–	18.9	–	13.5	–	18.9	
U.N. AGENCIES	–	–	–	–	–	–	–	–	
UNDP	2.0	3.2	4.4	7.2	2.0	3.2	4.4	7.2	
UNTA	0.5	0.3	0.3	0.3	0.5	0.3	0.3	0.3	
UNICEF	0.3	0.3	0.8	1.2	0.3	0.3	0.8	1.2	
UNRWA	–	–	–	–	–	–	–	–	
WFP	2.1	0.2	0.8	0.8	2.1	0.2	0.8	0.8	
UNHCR	–	–	–	–	–	–	–	–	
Other Multilateral	0.5	0.4	0.9	0.9	0.5	0.4	0.9	0.9	
Arab OPEC Agencies	3.1	–	5.4	11.9	3.1	–	5.4	11.9	
TOTAL	*35.3*	*54.4*	*43.0*	*91.4*	*27.6*	*50.3*	*40.6*	*91.4*	2
OPEC COUNTRIES	*1.0*	*4.0*	*13.8*	*18.0*	*1.0*	*1.0*	*13.8*	*18.0*	
E.E.C.+ MEMBERS	*22.4*	*61.0*	*141.2*	*221.6*	*33.7*	*42.4*	*53.0*	*75.5*	3
TOTAL	**54.0**	**118.5**	**222.3**	**394.2**	**61.1**	**90.9**	**128.0**	**200.2**	6

	ODA LOANS GROSS 1977	1978	1979	1980	ODA LOANS NET 1977	1978	1979	1980	GRANTS 19
DAC COUNTRIES									
Australia	–	–	–	–	–	–	–	–	
Austria	–	–	–	–	–	–	–	–	
Belgium	–	–	–	–	–	–	–	–	
Canada	0.0	1.6	1.5	9.2	0.0	1.6	1.5	9.2	
Denmark	–	–	–	–	–	–	–	–	
Finland	–	–	–	–	–	–	–	–	
France	2.5	3.7	9.2	18.4	0.1	-2.0	6.5	16.3	2
Germany, Fed. Rep.	0.7	0.4	–	–	-0.1	-2.2	-1.3	-2.2	
Italy	–	–	–	–	-0.4	-0.4	-0.4	-0.4	
Japan	1.7	5.2	20.1	13.3	1.7	5.2	19.7	12.4	
Netherlands	–	–	–	–	–	–	–	–	
New Zealand	–	–	–	–	–	–	–	–	
Norway	–	–	–	–	–	–	–	–	
Sweden	–	–	–	–	–	–	–	–	
Switzerland	–	–	–	–	–	–	–	–	
United Kingdom	–	–	–	–	–	–	–	–	
United States	–	–	–	–	–	–	–	–	
TOTAL	*4.9*	*10.9*	*30.8*	*40.9*	*1.3*	*2.2*	*26.0*	*35.3*	3
MULTILATERAL	*12.0*	*23.1*	*18.0*	*68.2*	*11.8*	*22.7*	*17.7*	*62.0*	1
OPEC COUNTRIES	–	*1.0*	*13.8*	*18.0*	–	*1.0*	*13.8*	*18.0*	
E.E.C.+ MEMBERS	*3.2*	*4.1*	*9.2*	*20.6*	*-0.5*	*-4.6*	*4.7*	*14.3*	3
TOTAL	**16.9**	**35.0**	**62.6**	**127.0**	**13.1**	**25.9**	**57.5**	**115.3**	4

	TOTAL OFFICIAL GROSS 1977	1978	1979	1980	TOTAL OFFICIAL NET 1977	1978	1979	1980	TOTAL OOF GROSS
DAC COUNTRIES									
Australia	–	–	–	–	–	–	–	–	
Austria	0.0	–	0.0	–	0.0	–	0.0	–	
Belgium	0.2	0.2	0.3	0.4	0.2	0.2	0.3	0.4	
Canada	1.5	2.7	2.0	17.0	1.5	2.7	2.1	17.0	
Denmark	–	–	0.1	0.0	–	–	0.1	0.0	
Finland	–	–	–	–	–	–	–	–	
France	24.2	24.7	38.4	58.1	21.5	18.6	35.3	55.8	
Germany, Fed. Rep.	3.4	2.0	2.1	1.9	2.5	-0.6	0.8	-0.3	
Italy	0.1	0.5	0.2	0.1	-0.3	0.1	-0.2	-0.2	
Japan	2.0	5.8	21.0	18.6	2.0	5.8	20.5	17.6	
Netherlands	0.5	0.2	0.4	0.8	0.5	0.2	0.4	0.8	
New Zealand	–	–	–	–	–	–	–	–	
Norway	1.8	2.3	4.8	5.1	1.8	2.3	4.8	5.1	
Sweden	–	–	–	–	–	–	–	–	
Switzerland	1.9	7.5	5.8	2.5	1.9	7.5	5.8	2.5	
United Kingdom	0.2	0.3	0.2	1.3	0.2	0.3	0.2	1.3	
United States	2.0	2.0	3.0	–	2.0	2.0	3.0	–	
TOTAL	*37.7*	*48.3*	*78.3*	*105.7*	*33.8*	*39.2*	*73.1*	*99.9*	
MULTILATERAL	*35.6*	*55.1*	*43.6*	*99.1*	*35.3*	*54.4*	*43.0*	*91.4*	
OPEC COUNTRIES	*1.0*	*4.0*	*13.8*	*18.0*	*1.0*	*4.0*	*13.8*	*18.0*	
E.E.C.+ MEMBERS	*39.0*	*51.1*	*57.4*	*83.9*	*35.0*	*42.0*	*52.6*	*77.3*	
TOTAL	**74.3**	**107.4**	**135.7**	**222.8**	**70.1**	**97.6**	**129.9**	**209.2**	

ODA COMMITMENTS

1978	1979	1980	1977	1978	1979	1980
–	–	–	–	0.0	–	–
–	0.0	–	–	–	–	–
0.2	0.3	0.4	–	–	–	–
2.7	2.0	9.7	14.0	0.7	0.4	8.4
–	0.1	0.0	–	–	–	–
–	–	–	–	–	–	–
24.7	38.4	56.1	22.4	36.9	48.2	62.5
2.0	2.1	1.9	1.0	1.3	23.4	6.4
0.5	0.2	0.1	0.1	0.5	0.2	0.1
5.8	21.0	18.6	0.3	22.5	8.1	11.1
0.2	0.4	0.8	0.6	0.5	1.1	0.6
–	–	–	–	–	–	–
2.3	4.8	5.1	9.4	1.1	4.2	1.4
–	–	–	–	–	–	–
7.5	5.8	2.5	3.4	10.7	1.0	2.3
0.3	0.2	1.3	0.3	0.2	0.2	2.8
2.0	3.0	–	0.8	1.4	2.1	–
48.3	*78.3*	*96.4*	*52.3*	*75.7*	*88.9*	*95.7*
0.7	–	6.1	10.9	–	6.1	–
–	–	–	–	–	–	–
–	–	–	–	–	–	–
–	–	–	–	–	–	–
23.2	15.8	21.3	25.8	14.1	12.3	55.8
–	–	–	–	–	–	–
8.8	12.6	29.0	–	33.0	49.0	61.5
–	–	–	–	–	–	–
–	–	–	–	–	6.6	–
–	–	–	–	–	–	–
13.5	–	18.9	–	–	–	–
–	–	–	5.3	4.4	7.2	10.4
3.2	4.4	7.2	–	–	–	–
0.3	0.3	0.3	–	–	–	–
0.3	0.8	1.2	–	–	–	–
–	–	–	–	–	–	–
0.2	0.8	0.8	–	–	–	–
–	–	–	–	–	–	–
0.4	0.9	0.9	–	–	–	–
–	5.4	11.9	3.1	10.0	6.5	5.0
50.7	*40.9*	*97.6*	*45.1*	*61.5*	*87.6*	*132.6*
1.0	*13.8*	*18.0*	*8.3*	*24.0*	*34.2*	*9.4*
51.1	*57.4*	*81.8*	*50.2*	*53.4*	*85.4*	*128.2*
100.0	***133.0***	***212.0***	***105.7***	***161.2***	***210.7***	***237.7***

TECH. COOP. GRANTS

1978	1979	1980	1977	1978	1979	1980
–	–	–	–	–	–	–
–	0.0	–	0.0	–	0.0	–
0.2	0.3	0.4	0.1	0.2	0.3	0.4
1.2	0.5	0.5	0.4	0.5	0.4	0.3
–	0.1	0.0	–	–	0.1	0.0
–	–	–	–	–	–	–
21.0	29.2	37.7	19.4	16.1	26.1	35.1
1.6	2.1	1.9	1.1	1.6	2.1	1.9
0.5	0.2	0.1	0.1	0.5	0.2	0.1
0.6	0.9	5.3	0.3	0.6	0.8	0.7
0.2	0.4	0.8	0.4	0.2	0.2	0.7
–	–	–	–	–	–	–
2.3	4.8	5.1	0.4	0.4	0.4	0.4
–	–	–	–	–	–	–
7.5	5.8	2.5	0.2	0.3	0.3	1.5
0.3	0.2	1.3	0.1	0.2	0.2	0.5
2.0	3.0	–	–	–	–	–
37.4	*47.5*	*55.5*	*22.4*	*20.6*	*31.2*	*41.5*
27.6	*22.9*	*29.4*	*3.2*	*4.2*	*6.4*	*10.4*
–	–	–	–	–	–	–
47.0	*48.2*	*61.2*	*21.1*	*18.8*	*29.2*	*38.6*
65.0	***70.5***	***85.0***	***25.7***	***24.8***	***37.5***	***51.9***

TOTAL OOF NET

1978	1979	1980	1977	1978	1979	1980
–	–	–	–	–	–	–
–	–	–	–	–	–	–
–	–	–	–	–	–	–
–	–	7.3	–	–	–	7.3
–	–	–	–	–	–	–
–	–	–	–	–	–	–
–	–	2.1	-0.3	-0.4	-0.4	1.8
–	–	–	1.6	–	–	–
–	–	–	–	–	–	–
–	–	–	–	–	–	–
–	–	–	–	–	–	–
–	–	–	–	–	–	–
–	–	–	–	–	–	–
–	–	–	–	–	–	–
–	–	–	–	–	–	–
–	–	–	–	–	–	–
–	–	–	–	–	–	–
–	–	*9.3*	*1.3*	*-0.4*	*-0.4*	*9.1*
4.4	*2.7*	*1.5*	*7.7*	*4.1*	*2.3*	*-0.1*
3.0	–	–	–	*3.0*	–	–
–	–	*2.1*	*1.3*	*-0.4*	*-0.4*	*1.8*
7.4	***2.7***	***10.9***	***9.0***	***6.7***	***1.9***	***9.0***

MAIN AID AGGREGATES

	1977	1978	1979	1980
DAC COUNTRIES COMBINED				
PRIVATE SECTOR NET	-16.1	20.9	92.4	185.0
Direct Investment	-5.5	0.6	-0.6	-0.8
Portfolio Invest.	4.8	-0.3	-19.9	17.7
Export Credits	-15.4	20.7	112.9	168.1
OFFICIAL & PRIVATE				
GROSS:				
Contractual Lending	7.5	38.1	160.9	233.5
Export Credits Tot.	1.0	27.2	130.1	190.6
Export Credits Priv	1.0	27.2	130.1	183.3
OTHER NET DATA				
Contractual Lending	-12.8	22.5	138.5	212.4
Export Credits Tot.	-15.4	20.7	112.9	175.4
(Bank Sector Loans)	5.0	–	27.0	8.0
ODA CONCESSIONALITY				
Total:Grant Element	97.0	67.0	80.0	79.0
Loans:Grant Element	90.0	38.0	52.0	50.0
OTHER SOURCES				
CMEA Countr.(Gross)	0.7	0.6	2.9	2.0
Intra LDCS Exc.OPEC	–	–	–	–
Other	–	–	–	–
ALL SOURCE COMMITMENTS				
TOTAL BILATERAL	61.8	122.6	124.6	105.0
of which				
OPEC (ODA)	8.3	24.0	34.2	9.4
CMEA (ODA)	14.0	2.8	0.4	–
TOTAL MULTILAT.(ODA)	45.1	61.5	87.6	132.6
TOTAL BIL.& MULTIL.	106.9	184.1	212.2	237.7
of which				
ODA Grants	71.3	54.8	70.2	114.5
ODA Loans	34.5	106.4	140.5	123.1
ODA CONCESSIONALITY				
Total: Grant Element	88.0	69.0	74.0	83.0
Loans: Grant Element	68.0	53.0	61.0	65.0

INDEBTEDNESS

	1977	1978	1979	1980
TOTAL DEBT DISBURSED	***215.7***	***322.0***	***599.5***	
Debt to DAC Countries	97.0	178.0	368.0	
ODA	71.0	83.0	105.0	
Total Export Credits	24.0	78.0	203.0	
Other Private Market	2.0	17.0	60.0	
International Org.	107.6	131.5	154.3	
CMEA	9.9	11.3	12.3	
Other	1.3	1.2	64.8	
TOTAL DEBT SERVICE	***23.2***	***26.1***	***39.5***	
Paid to DAC Countries	19.4	21.4	34.3	
ODA	4.4	11.7	7.2	
Total Export Credits	14.6	8.7	21.4	
Other Private Market	0.4	1.0	5.7	
International Org.	2.8	3.6	3.8	
CMEA	0.9	0.9	1.0	
Other	0.1	0.1	0.3	

ECONOMIC INDICATORS

	1977	1978	1979	1980
GNP Curr. Prices, $M	1873.8	2121.9	2752.7	3213.0
Real GNP, 1976=100	102.0	99.0	109.0	110.0
GNP/Cap Curr. Prices,$	233.0	257.0	324.0	368.0
GNP/cap Atlas Basis, $	275.8	280.5	325.2	347.8
Real GNP/Cap, 1976=100	99.0	94.0	100.0	99.0
Population, Million	8.0	8.3	8.5	8.7
Curr.A/C Deficit(-),$M	-91.0	-156.0	-523.0	–
BOP Exp. & Transf.,$M	386.0	444.0	466.0	–
Exp. to OECD CIF, $M	326.2	317.0	285.5	365.4
of which				
Manufact.	25.3	23.4	28.1	26.9
Imp. from OECD FOB, $M	201.0	247.3	460.2	496.9
Reserves ex. Gold, $M	68.9	59.2	5.0	–

	TOTAL RECEIPTS NET 1977	1978	1979	1980	TOTAL ODA NET 1977	1978	1979	1980
DAC COUNTRIES								
Australia	0.1	0.1	0.1	0.1	0.1	0.1	0.1	0.1
Austria	0.0	0.0	0.0	0.0	0.0	0.0	0.0	0.0
Belgium	0.3	0.0	0.0	1.0	0.1	0.0	0.0	0.0
Canada	14.8	12.7	13.3	9.0	14.8	12.7	13.3	9.0
Denmark	4.0	1.5	2.2	6.0	4.0	1.5	2.2	6.0
Finland	0.0	0.0	0.0	0.1	0.0	0.0	0.0	0.1
France	0.0	0.0	0.7	0.8	–	–	–	0.4
Germany, Fed. Rep.	8.4	14.6	30.9	20.3	8.1	11.9	28.6	13.2
Italy	-0.2	0.1	-0.1	0.0	–	0.0	0.0	–
Japan	1.1	10.9	7.8	11.2	1.1	2.7	6.9	11.6
Netherlands	2.8	2.2	5.6	7.0	2.8	2.2	4.5	7.0
New Zealand	0.5	-0.6	0.1	0.0	–	0.0	0.1	0.0
Norway	-0.1	–	-0.1	-0.1	–	–	–	–
Sweden	–	–	1.9	0.3	–	–	0.1	–
Switzerland	0.0	0.0	0.0	-0.3	0.0	0.0	0.0	0.0
United Kingdom	44.6	21.7	73.4	35.5	19.2	20.2	33.2	25.4
United States	4.0	5.0	3.0	3.0	4.0	5.0	3.0	3.0
TOTAL	*80.3*	*68.2*	*138.9*	*93.9*	*54.1*	*56.4*	*92.0*	*75.6*
MULTILATERAL								
AF.D.F.	0.5	1.5	2.0	10.9	0.5	1.5	2.0	10.9
AF.D.B.	3.8	2.4	7.8	6.2	–	–	–	–
AS.D.B.	–	–	–	–	–	–	–	–
CAR.D.B.	–	–	–	–	–	–	–	–
E.E.C.	5.2	12.8	17.6	24.9	5.2	8.9	12.7	20.6
IBRD	4.7	2.6	12.8	7.6	2.3	2.5	7.4	4.2
IDA	10.8	17.9	13.9	14.3	10.8	17.9	13.9	14.3
I.D.B.	–	–	–	–	–	–	–	–
IFAD	–	–	–	–	–	–	–	–
I.F.C.	2.5	5.5	3.7	1.8	–	–	–	–
IMF TRUST FUND	1.9	5.8	6.0	5.0	1.9	5.8	6.0	5.0
U.N. AGENCIES	–	–	–	–	–	–	–	–
UNDP	1.9	2.4	3.6	4.9	1.9	2.4	3.6	4.9
UNTA	0.2	0.3	0.2	0.0	0.2	0.3	0.2	0.0
UNICEF	0.4	0.5	0.6	0.8	0.4	0.5	0.6	0.8
UNRWA	–	–	–	–	–	–	–	–
WFP	1.4	2.0	3.1	3.2	1.4	2.0	3.1	3.2
UNHCR	–	–	–	–	–	–	–	–
Other Multilateral	0.7	0.3	0.3	2.6	0.7	0.3	0.3	2.6
Arab OPEC Agencies	–	–	–	1.3	–	–	–	1.3
TOTAL	*34.0*	*54.0*	*71.5*	*83.5*	*25.3*	*42.1*	*49.7*	*67.7*
OPEC COUNTRIES	–	–	–	–	–	–	–	–
E.E.C.+ MEMBERS	*65.0*	*52.8*	*130.4*	*95.5*	*39.2*	*44.7*	*81.3*	*72.5*
TOTAL	***114.3***	***122.2***	***210.5***	***177.4***	***79.4***	***98.5***	***141.8***	***143.4***

	ODA LOANS GROSS 1977	1978	1979	1980	ODA LOANS NET 1977	1978	1979	1980
DAC COUNTRIES								
Australia	–	–	–	–	–	–	–	–
Austria	–	–	–	–	–	–	–	–
Belgium	–	–	–	–	–	–	–	–
Canada	13.7	–	–	–	13.7	-34.3	–	–
Denmark	3.7	0.9	0.5	4.4	3.2	0.3	-15.3	4.4
Finland	–	–	–	–	–	–	–	–
France	–	–	–	–	–	–	–	–
Germany, Fed. Rep.	6.8	6.1	6.9	–	6.0	5.7	-21.8	–
Italy	–	–	–	–	–	–	–	–
Japan	–	1.1	4.8	8.8	–	1.1	4.8	8.8
Netherlands	0.8	0.1	2.5	4.6	0.8	0.1	2.5	4.6
New Zealand	–	–	–	–	–	–	–	–
Norway	–	–	–	–	–	–	–	–
Sweden	–	–	–	–	–	–	–	–
Switzerland	–	–	–	–	–	–	–	–
United Kingdom	7.4	3.2	3.9	2.7	5.0	0.8	-0.2	-1.2
United States	4.0	4.0	2.0	1.0	4.0	4.0	2.0	1.0
TOTAL	*36.2*	*15.3*	*20.7*	*21.5*	*32.7*	*-22.4*	*-27.9*	*17.6*
MULTILATERAL	*16.5*	*28.6*	*32.9*	*41.9*	*16.4*	*28.3*	*32.3*	*41.0*
OPEC COUNTRIES	–	–	–	–	–	–	–	–
E.E.C.+ MEMBERS	*19.4*	*10.9*	*17.0*	*17.1*	*15.9*	*7.5*	*-31.6*	*13.2*
TOTAL	***52.8***	***43.9***	***53.6***	***63.4***	***49.1***	***5.9***	***4.4***	***58.6***

	TOTAL OFFICIAL GROSS 1977	1978	1979	1980	TOTAL OFFICIAL NET 1977	1978	1979	1980
DAC COUNTRIES								
Australia	0.1	0.1	0.1	0.1	0.1	0.1	0.1	0.1
Austria	0.0	0.0	0.0	0.0	0.0	0.0	0.0	0.0
Belgium	0.1	0.0	0.0	0.0	0.1	0.0	0.0	0.0
Canada	14.8	47.0	13.3	9.0	14.8	12.7	13.3	9.0
Denmark	4.4	2.0	17.9	6.0	4.0	1.5	2.2	6.0
Finland	0.0	0.0	0.0	0.1	0.0	0.0	0.0	0.1
France	–	–	–	0.4	–	–	–	0.4
Germany, Fed. Rep.	8.8	15.3	57.6	18.5	8.1	14.9	28.9	18.0
Italy	–	0.0	0.0	–	–	0.0	0.0	–
Japan	1.1	2.7	6.9	11.6	1.1	2.7	6.9	11.6
Netherlands	2.8	2.2	5.6	7.0	2.8	2.2	5.6	7.0
New Zealand	1.0	0.0	0.1	0.0	0.5	0.0	0.1	0.0
Norway	–	–	–	–	–	–	–	–
Sweden	–	–	0.1	–	–	–	0.1	–
Switzerland	0.0	0.0	0.0	0.0	0.0	0.0	0.0	0.0
United Kingdom	22.2	30.7	52.6	38.3	19.9	28.1	48.0	33.8
United States	4.0	5.0	3.0	3.0	4.0	5.0	3.0	3.0
TOTAL	*59.3*	*105.3*	*157.3*	*93.9*	*55.3*	*67.4*	*108.3*	*88.9*
MULTILATERAL	*34.5*	*54.8*	*73.3*	*85.9*	*34.0*	*54.0*	*71.5*	*83.5*
OPEC COUNTRIES	–	–	–	–	–	–	–	–
E.E.C.+ MEMBERS	*43.4*	*63.1*	*151.4*	*95.1*	*39.9*	*59.5*	*102.4*	*90.1*
TOTAL	***93.8***	***160.1***	***230.6***	***179.8***	***89.3***	***121.3***	***179.8***	***172.4***

	TOTAL ODA GROSS 19
Australia	
Austria	
Belgium	
Canada	1
Denmark	
Finland	
France	
Germany, Fed. Rep.	
Italy	
Japan	
Netherlands	
New Zealand	
Norway	
Sweden	
Switzerland	
United Kingdom	2
United States	
TOTAL	5
AF.D.F.	
AF.D.B.	
AS.D.B.	
CAR.D.B.	
E.E.C.	
IBRD	
IDA	1
I.D.B.	
IFAD	
I.F.C.	
IMF TRUST FUND	
U.N. AGENCIES	
UNDP	
UNTA	
UNICEF	
UNRWA	
WFP	
UNHCR	
Other Multilateral	
Arab OPEC Agencies	
TOTAL	2
OPEC COUNTRIES	
E.E.C.+ MEMBERS	4
TOTAL	8

	GRANTS 19
Australia	
Austria	
Belgium	
Canada	
Denmark	
Finland	
France	
Germany, Fed. Rep.	
Italy	
Japan	
Netherlands	
New Zealand	
Norway	
Sweden	
Switzerland	
United Kingdom	1
United States	
TOTAL	2
MULTILATERAL	
OPEC COUNTRIES	
E.E.C.+ MEMBERS	2
TOTAL	3

	TOTAL OOF GROSS 19
Australia	
Austria	
Belgium	
Canada	
Denmark	
Finland	
France	
Germany, Fed. Rep.	
Italy	
Japan	
Netherlands	
New Zealand	
Norway	
Sweden	
Switzerland	
United Kingdom	
United States	
TOTAL	
MULTILATERAL	
OPEC COUNTRIES	
E.E.C.+ MEMBERS	
TOTAL	1

ODA COMMITMENTS

1978	1979	1980	1977	1978	1979	1980
0.1	0.1	0.1	0.1	0.0	0.1	0.1
0.0	0.0	0.0	–	–	–	–
0.0	0.0	0.0	–	–	–	–
47.0	13.3	9.0	36.8	71.4	12.4	2.1
2.0	17.9	6.0	0.8	17.4	2.9	9.7
0.0	0.0	0.1	0.0	0.0	0.0	–
–	–	0.4			–	4.9
12.3	57.2	13.2	3.7	23.5	80.1	12.3
0.0	0.0	–	–	0.0	0.0	–
2.7	6.9	11.6	1.3	23.8	3.4	5.2
2.2	4.5	7.0	3.5	9.6	2.9	3.0
0.0	0.1	0.0	–	0.0	0.0	–
–	–	–	–	–	–	–
–	0.1	–	–	–	–	–
0.0	0.0	0.0	–	–	–	0.0
22.5	37.4	29.3	16.3	70.4	21.5	32.8
5.0	3.0	3.0	0.7	0.5	3.4	14.3
94.1	*140.6*	*79.6*	*63.1*	*216.6*	*126.7*	*84.4*
1.4	2.0	10.9	5.6	–	9.7	16.6
–	–	–	–	–	–	–
–	–	–	–	–	–	–
–	–	–	–	–	–	–
8.9	12.7	20.6	39.0	12.0	26.5	17.1
2.5	7.4	4.2	8.0	–	–	–
18.2	14.5	15.1	25.4	32.7	14.5	13.8
–	–	–	–	–	–	–
–	–	–	–	–	–	–
–	–	–	–	–	–	–
5.8	6.0	5.0	–	–	–	–
–	–	–	4.6	5.5	7.8	11.5
2.4	3.6	4.9	–	–	–	–
0.3	0.2	0.0	–	–	–	–
0.5	0.6	0.8	–	–	–	–
–	–	–	–	–	–	–
2.0	3.1	3.2	–	–	–	–
–	–	–	–	–	–	–
0.3	0.3	2.6	–	–	–	–
–	–	1.3	1.8	–	–	–
42.3	*50.3*	*68.5*	*84.4*	*50.1*	*58.5*	*58.9*
–	–	–	–	–	–	–
48.1	*129.8*	*76.4*	*63.3*	*132.9*	*133.9*	*79.8*
136.5	**190.9**	**148.1**	**147.6**	**266.7**	**185.2**	**143.3**

TECH. COOP. GRANTS

1978	1979	1980	1977	1978	1979	1980
0.1	0.1	0.1	0.1	0.1	0.1	0.1
0.0	0.0	0.0	0.0	0.0	0.0	0.0
0.0	0.0	0.0	0.1	0.0	0.0	0.0
47.0	13.3	9.0	1.0	1.1	1.3	1.3
1.2	17.4	1.6	0.4	0.5	1.5	1.6
0.0	0.0	0.1	0.0	0.0	0.0	0.1
–	–	0.4	–	–	–	0.4
6.2	50.3	13.2	2.0	6.2	5.7	4.8
0.0	0.0	–	–	0.0	0.0	–
1.7	2.0	2.7	1.1	1.7	2.0	2.4
2.2	2.0	2.4	1.9	2.1	1.9	2.0
0.0	0.1	0.0	–	–	0.1	0.0
–	–	–	–	–	–	–
–	0.1	–	–	–	–	–
0.0	0.0	0.0	–	–	–	–
19.4	33.5	26.6	7.7	7.8	11.6	14.6
1.0	1.0	2.0	–	1.0	1.0	1.0
78.8	*119.9*	*58.1*	*14.3*	*20.5*	*25.3*	*28.1*
13.8	*17.4*	*26.7*	*3.2*	*3.5*	*4.7*	*11.5*
–	–	–	–	–	–	–
37.2	*112.9*	*59.4*	*12.1*	*16.6*	*20.7*	*23.3*
92.6	**137.4**	**84.7**	**17.6**	**24.0**	**30.0**	**39.6**

TOTAL OOF NET

1978	1979	1980	1977	1978	1979	1980
–	–	–	–	–	–	–
–	–	–	–	–	–	–
–	–	–	–	–	–	–
–	–	–	–	–	–	–
–	–	–	–	–	–	–
–	–	–	–	–	–	–
–	–	–	–	–	–	–
3.0	0.4	5.3	–	3.0	0.4	4.9
–	–	–	–	–	–	–
–	–	–	–	–	–	–
–	1.1	–	–	–	1.1	–
–	–	–	0.5	–	–	–
–	–	–	–	–	–	–
–	–	–	–	–	–	–
–	–	–	–	–	–	–
8.1	15.2	9.0	0.7	7.9	14.8	8.4
–	–	–	–	–	–	–
11.1	*16.7*	*14.3*	*1.3*	*10.9*	*16.3*	*13.3*
12.5	*23.0*	*17.4*	*8.7*	*11.9*	*21.8*	*15.8*
–	–	–	–	–	–	–
15.0	*21.5*	*18.7*	*0.7*	*14.8*	*21.2*	*17.6*
23.6	**39.7**	**31.7**	**9.9**	**22.8**	**38.1**	**29.1**

MAIN AID AGGREGATES

	1977	1978	1979	1980
DAC COUNTRIES COMBINED				
PRIVATE SECTOR NET	25.0	0.8	30.6	4.9
Direct Investment	24.7	-7.8	11.0	-0.2
Portfolio Invest.	-0.5	0.5	2.4	2.8
Export Credits	0.8	8.2	17.2	2.4
OFFICIAL & PRIVATE				
GROSS:				
Contractual Lending	44.5	42.6	57.9	50.5
Export Credits Tot.	7.5	16.1	20.5	17.4
Export Credits Priv	6.5	16.1	20.5	14.6
OTHER NET DATA				
Contractual Lending	34.8	-3.3	5.6	33.2
Export Credits Tot.	1.3	8.2	17.2	4.8
(Bank Sector Loans)	-12.0	39.0	28.0	27.0
ODA CONCESSIONALITY				
Total:Grant Element	84.0	90.0	96.0	92.0
Loans:Grant Element	77.0	61.0	38.0	71.0
OTHER SOURCES				
CMEA Countr.(Gross)	–	–	–	–
Intra LDCS Exc.OPEC	–	–	–	–
Other	–	–	–	–
ALL SOURCE COMMITMENTS				
TOTAL BILATERAL	80.4	223.5	138.2	111.7
of which				
OPEC (ODA)	–	–	–	–
CMEA (ODA)	–	–	–	–
TOTAL MULTILAT.(ODA)	84.4	50.1	58.5	58.9
TOTAL BIL.& MULTIL.	164.8	273.6	196.7	170.6
of which				
ODA Grants	53.1	182.6	153.8	87.0
ODA Loans	94.5	84.1	31.4	56.3
ODA CONCESSIONALITY				
Total: Grant Element	84.0	90.0	95.0	91.0
Loans: Grant Element	74.0	71.0	73.0	78.0

INDEBTEDNESS

	1977	1978	1979	1980
TOTAL DEBT DISBURSED	***362.8***	***432.2***	***512.8***	
Debt to DAC Countries	240.0	273.0	310.0	
ODA	178.0	169.0	141.0	
Total Export Credits	28.0	55.0	85.0	
Other Private Market	34.0	49.0	84.0	
International Org.	97.4	133.0	177.1	
CMEA	–	–	–	
Other	25.4	26.2	25.7	
TOTAL DEBT SERVICE	***18.0***	***24.5***	***33.0***	
Paid to DAC Countries	15.1	18.7	25.6	
ODA	6.0	6.4	3.9	
Total Export Credits	5.9	5.7	11.5	
Other Private Market	3.2	6.6	10.2	
International Org.	1.3	3.5	4.2	
CMEA	–	–	–	
Other	1.6	2.3	3.3	

ECONOMIC INDICATORS

	1977	1978	1979	1980
GNP Curr. Prices, $M	826.5	1059.2	1243.0	1489.7
Real GNP, 1976=100	108.0	118.0	121.0	123.0
GNP/Cap Curr. Prices,$	148.0	186.0	213.0	250.0
GNP/cap Atlas Basis, $	174.4	200.0	217.2	233.9
Real GNP/Cap, 1976=100	106.0	113.0	113.0	112.0
Population, Million	5.6	5.7	5.8	6.0
Curr.A/C Deficit(-),$M	-57.4	-166.3	-252.3	-204.3
BOP Exp. & Transf.,$M	249.5	242.7	274.6	366.1
Exp. to OECD CIF, $M	157.1	168.9	188.6	210.3
of which				
Manufact.	2.3	3.0	4.2	7.3
Imp. from OECD FOB, $M	85.4	121.5	157.1	149.1
Reserves ex. Gold, $M	87.5	74.8	69.5	68.4

	1977	1978	1979	1980	1977	1978	1979	1980	19
	TOTAL RECEIPTS NET				**TOTAL ODA NET**				**TOTAL ODA GROSS**
DAC COUNTRIES									
Australia	10.5	10.3	20.3	26.1	5.2	6.7	5.2	7.3	
Austria	0.6	0.1	0.1	0.1	0.6	0.1	0.1	0.1	
Belgium	2.3	-0.2	1.3	4.3	2.2	1.2	2.6	2.2	
Canada	1.8	2.3	1.4	16.0	2.7	2.3	1.4	1.0	
Denmark	0.8	-0.5	-0.3	-0.3	-0.1	-0.2	-0.3	-0.1	
Finland	–	–	0.1	0.2	–	–	0.1	0.2	
France	21.3	-44.0	327.0	166.6	0.6	0.4	-0.3	0.3	
Germany, Fed. Rep.	47.9	38.2	15.1	16.4	2.5	3.0	3.7	6.5	
Italy	-0.8	0.8	2.8	0.1	–	–	0.1	0.0	
Japan	46.0	211.6	209.2	167.3	29.5	48.0	74.6	65.6	3
Netherlands	0.6	0.6	0.8	0.6	0.6	0.6	0.8	0.6	
New Zealand	3.6	2.2	0.9	0.7	1.4	1.5	0.8	0.7	
Norway	-0.1	–	-0.7	-1.1	0.0	–	–	0.1	
Sweden	3.6	-4.5	-6.1	-6.4	–	–	–	–	
Switzerland	-0.3	-0.5	-0.1	1.3	0.0	0.2	0.0	0.0	
United Kingdom	130.8	-89.3	29.9	62.5	11.3	0.1	0.4	20.8	1
United States	-135.0	-20.0	-5.0	54.0	3.0	3.0	1.0	1.0	
TOTAL	*133.5*	*107.3*	*596.6*	*508.4*	*59.2*	*66.8*	*90.3*	*106.2*	*6*
MULTILATERAL									
AF.D.F.	–	–	–	–	–	–	–	–	
AF.D.B.	–	–	–	–	–	–	–	–	
AS.D.B.	65.6	33.4	21.4	30.3	0.3	0.2	-0.1	0.1	
CAR.D.B.	–	–	–	–	–	–	–	–	
E.E.C.	–	–	0.1	–	–	–	0.1	–	
IBRD	29.8	48.1	64.8	56.1	–	–	–	–	
IDA	–	–	–	–	–	–	–	–	
I.D.B.	–	–	–	–	–	–	–	–	
IFAD	–	–	–	–	–	–	–	–	
I.F.C.	-0.2	-0.2	-0.1	–	–	–	–	–	
IMF TRUST FUND	–	–	–	–	–	–	–	–	
U.N. AGENCIES	–	–	–	–	–	–	–	–	
UNDP	1.4	2.5	3.8	3.9	1.4	2.5	3.8	3.9	
UNTA	0.7	0.6	0.7	0.2	0.7	0.6	0.7	0.2	
UNICEF	0.2	0.3	0.7	0.8	0.2	0.3	0.7	0.8	
UNRWA	–	–	–	–	–	–	–	–	
WFP	–	–	0.2	–	–	–	0.2	–	
UNHCR	0.6	0.5	23.7	12.7	0.6	0.5	23.7	12.7	
Other Multilateral	1.2	0.4	0.7	1.6	1.2	0.4	0.7	1.6	
Arab OPEC Agencies	–	2.1	0.4	–	–	–	–	–	
TOTAL	*99.3*	*87.8*	*116.3*	*105.5*	*4.4*	*4.6*	*29.7*	*19.3*	
OPEC COUNTRIES	*7.5*	*9.1*	*5.2*	*9.5*	*7.5*	*8.9*	*5.2*	*9.5*	
E.E.C.+ MEMBERS	*202.9*	*-94.3*	*376.7*	*250.3*	*16.9*	*5.1*	*7.2*	*30.3*	*1*
TOTAL	***240.3***	***204.1***	***718.1***	***623.5***	***71.2***	***80.2***	***125.1***	***135.0***	***7***

	1977	1978	1979	1980	1977	1978	1979	1980	19
	ODA LOANS GROSS				**ODA LOANS NET**				**GRANTS**
DAC COUNTRIES									
Australia	–	–	–	–	–	–	–	–	
Austria	0.5	–	–	–	0.5	–	–	–	
Belgium	–	–	–	–	–	–	–	–	
Canada	2.0	2.2	1.5	0.9	1.8	1.9	1.1	0.6	
Denmark	–	–	–	–	-0.3	-0.3	-0.3	-0.3	
Finland	–	–	–	–	–	–	–	–	
France	0.6	0.9	–	–	0.4	0.4	-0.3	-0.6	
Germany, Fed. Rep.	–	0.1	–	1.7	-1.3	-1.9	-2.2	-0.6	
Italy	–	–	–	–	–	–	–	–	
Japan	29.0	43.8	74.1	68.5	24.1	37.4	64.6	52.9	
Netherlands	0.1	–	–	0.0	0.1	-0.1	-0.1	-0.1	
New Zealand	–	–	–	–	–	–	–	–	
Norway	–	–	–	–	–	–	–	–	
Sweden	–	–	–	–	–	–	–	–	
Switzerland	–	–	–	–	–	–	–	–	
United Kingdom	9.7	0.3	0.3	18.8	8.8	-2.4	-2.7	15.1	
United States	–	–	1.0	–	–	–	–	–	
TOTAL	*41.9*	*47.3*	*76.9*	*89.8*	*34.0*	*35.0*	*60.1*	*67.0*	*2*
MULTILATERAL	*0.2*	*0.3*	–	–	*0.1*	*0.2*	*-0.1*	*-0.1*	
OPEC COUNTRIES	*7.5*	*8.9*	*5.2*	*9.2*	*7.5*	*8.9*	*5.2*	*7.6*	
E.E.C.+ MEMBERS	*10.5*	*1.3*	*0.3*	*20.4*	*7.6*	*-4.3*	*-5.6*	*13.5*	
TOTAL	***49.7***	***56.5***	***82.1***	***99.0***	***41.7***	***44.1***	***65.1***	***74.5***	***2***

	1977	1978	1979	1980	1977	1978	1979	1980	19
	TOTAL OFFICIAL GROSS				**TOTAL OFFICIAL NET**				**TOTAL OOF GROSS**
DAC COUNTRIES									
Australia	5.2	6.7	5.2	7.3	5.2	6.7	5.2	7.3	
Austria	0.6	0.1	0.1	0.1	0.6	0.1	0.1	0.1	
Belgium	2.2	1.2	2.6	2.2	2.2	1.2	2.6	2.2	
Canada	2.8	2.5	1.7	1.3	2.3	2.3	1.4	1.0	
Denmark	0.2	0.1	0.1	0.2	-0.1	-0.3	-0.2	-0.1	
Finland	–	–	0.1	0.2	–	–	0.1	0.2	
France	0.8	0.9	–	1.1	0.6	0.4	-0.3	0.4	
Germany, Fed. Rep.	25.5	28.0	18.3	17.3	22.7	21.8	8.7	6.9	2
Italy	–	–	0.1	0.0	–	–	0.1	0.0	
Japan	34.4	54.4	84.1	81.2	29.5	48.0	74.6	65.6	
Netherlands	0.6	0.7	0.9	0.7	0.6	0.6	0.8	0.6	
New Zealand	4.4	1.5	0.8	0.7	2.9	1.5	0.8	0.7	
Norway	0.0	–	–	0.1	0.0	–	–	0.1	
Sweden	–	–	–	–	–	–	–	–	
Switzerland	0.0	0.2	0.0	0.0	0.0	0.2	0.0	0.0	
United Kingdom	12.2	2.9	3.5	24.5	10.7	0.1	0.3	20.7	
United States	14.0	3.0	2.0	1.0	10.0	-16.0	-3.0	-4.0	1
TOTAL	*102.9*	*102.2*	*119.5*	*137.8*	*86.9*	*66.6*	*91.2*	*101.6*	*3*
MULTILATERAL	*117.8*	*111.2*	*140.6*	*137.3*	*99.3*	*87.8*	*116.3*	*105.5*	*11*
OPEC COUNTRIES	*7.5*	*9.1*	*5.2*	*11.1*	*7.5*	*9.1*	*5.2*	*9.5*	
E.E.C.+ MEMBERS	*41.4*	*33.8*	*25.6*	*46.0*	*36.5*	*23.9*	*12.1*	*30.7*	*2*
TOTAL	***228.2***	***222.4***	***265.3***	***286.2***	***193.8***	***163.4***	***212.7***	***216.7***	***14***

1978	1979	1980	1977	1978	1979	1980
			ODA COMMITMENTS			
6.7	5.2	7.3	7.8	4.2	7.7	1.1
0.1	0.1	0.1	0.0	–	–	0.0
1.2	2.6	2.2	3.1	1.6	3.1	2.7
2.5	1.7	1.3	2.6	0.4	1.7	0.3
0.1	0.0	0.2	0.1	0.1	0.2	0.1
–	0.1	0.2	–	0.1	0.1	–
0.9	–	0.9	0.2	–	–	0.8
4.9	5.9	8.7	4.3	7.3	11.1	8.0
–	0.1	0.0	–	–	0.1	0.0
54.4	84.1	81.2	52.1	60.2	92.1	171.1
0.7	0.9	0.7	0.4	1.2	0.9	0.7
1.5	0.8	0.7	0.5	1.7	0.4	0.8
–	–	0.1	–	–	–	–
–	–	–	–	–	–	–
0.2	0.0	0.0	–	–	–	0.3
2.9	3.5	24.5	11.2	2.6	23.0	6.1
3.0	2.0	1.0	1.6	1.7	1.4	1.2
79.1	*107.1*	*129.0*	*83.8*	*81.0*	*141.7*	*193.2*
–	–	–	–	–	–	–
–	–	–	–	–	–	–
0.3	–	0.3	–	0.4	0.2	–
–	–	–	–	–	–	–
–	0.1	–	–	–	0.1	–
–	–	–	–	–	–	–
–	–	–	–	–	–	–
–	–	–	–	–	–	–
–	–	–	–	–	–	–
–	–	–	–	–	–	–
–	–	–	–	–	–	–
–	–	–	4.2	4.4	29.7	19.2
2.5	3.8	3.9	–	–	–	–
0.6	0.7	0.2	–	–	–	–
0.3	0.7	0.8	–	–	–	–
–	–	–	–	–	–	–
–	0.2	–	–	–	–	–
0.5	23.7	12.7	–	–	–	–
0.4	0.7	1.6	–	–	–	–
–	–	–	–	0.9	–	–
4.7	*29.8*	*19.4*	*4.2*	*5.6*	*30.0*	*19.2*
8.9	*5.2*	*11.1*	*18.0*	*5.0*	*28.2*	*22.3*
10.7	*13.1*	*37.2*	*19.2*	*12.7*	*38.4*	*18.4*
92.6	***142.1***	***159.6***	***106.0***	***91.5***	***199.9***	***234.6***
			TECH. COOP. GRANTS			
6.7	5.2	7.3	3.9	5.8	4.2	4.8
0.1	0.1	0.1	0.1	0.1	0.1	0.1
1.2	2.6	2.2	1.6	1.0	1.6	1.8
0.4	0.2	0.4	0.7	0.3	0.2	0.1
0.1	0.0	0.2	0.2	0.1	0.0	0.2
–	0.1	0.2	–	–	0.1	0.2
–	–	0.9	–	–	–	0.9
4.9	5.9	7.0	3.8	4.6	5.8	7.0
–	0.1	0.0	–	–	0.1	0.0
10.6	10.0	12.7	5.3	7.8	9.9	12.6
0.7	0.9	0.7	0.5	0.7	0.9	0.7
1.5	0.8	0.7	1.3	1.2	0.7	0.5
–	–	0.1	0.0	–	–	0.1
–	–	–	–	–	–	–
0.2	0.0	0.0	–	0.1	0.0	0.0
2.6	3.1	5.8	2.5	2.6	3.1	5.1
3.0	1.0	1.0	3.0	3.0	1.0	1.0
31.8	*30.2*	*39.2*	*23.0*	*27.1*	*27.7*	*35.0*
4.4	*29.8*	*19.4*	*4.3*	*4.4*	*29.6*	*19.2*
–	–	*1.9*	–	–	–	–
9.4	*12.8*	*16.7*	*8.5*	*9.0*	*11.6*	*15.6*
36.1	***60.0***	***60.6***	***27.3***	***31.5***	***57.3***	***54.1***
			TOTAL OOF NET			
–	–	–	–	–	–	–
–	–	–	–	–	–	–
–	–	–	–	–	–	–
–	–	–	-0.4	–	–	–
–	0.1	0.0	–	0.0	0.1	0.0
–	–	–	–	–	–	–
–	–	0.2	–	–	–	0.2
23.1	12.4	8.6	20.3	18.9	5.0	0.4
–	–	–	–	–	–	–
–	–	–	–	–	–	–
–	–	–	–	–	–	–
–	–	–	1.5	–	–	–
–	–	–	–	–	–	–
–	–	–	–	–	–	–
–	–	–	–	–	–	–
–	–	–	-0.6	-0.1	-0.1	-0.2
–	–	–	7.0	-19.0	-4.0	-5.0
23.1	*12.4*	*8.8*	*27.7*	*-0.2*	*1.0*	*-4.6*
106.5	*110.8*	*117.9*	*94.9*	*83.2*	*86.6*	*86.3*
0.2	–	–	–	*0.2*	–	–
23.1	*12.4*	*8.8*	*19.6*	*18.8*	*5.0*	*0.4*
129.8	***123.2***	***126.7***	***122.5***	***83.2***	***87.6***	***81.7***

	1977	1978	1979	1980
MAIN AID AGGREGATES				
DAC COUNTRIES COMBINED				
PRIVATE SECTOR NET	46.6	40.7	505.4	406.8
Direct Investment	134.0	-5.3	77.2	176.5
Portfolio Invest.	-123.5	56.2	64.8	21.6
Export Credits	36.1	-10.3	363.4	208.7
OFFICIAL & PRIVATE				
GROSS:				
Contractual Lending	177.7	191.8	562.0	426.1
Export Credits Tot.	135.7	144.5	485.1	336.2
Export Credits Priv	100.0	121.4	472.7	327.5
OTHER NET DATA				
Contractual Lending	97.8	24.5	424.5	271.1
Export Credits Tot.	64.4	-10.4	364.4	204.1
(Bank Sector Loans)	156.0	128.0	71.0	142.0
ODA CONCESSIONALITY				
Total:Grant Element	62.0	63.0	58.0	54.0
Loans:Grant Element	44.0	41.0	41.0	43.0
OTHER SOURCES				
CMEA Countr.(Gross)	–	–	–	–
Intra LDCS Exc.OPEC	–	–	–	–
Other	–	–	–	–
ALL SOURCE COMMITMENTS				
TOTAL BILATERAL	120.1	102.8	170.0	345.9
of which				
OPEC (ODA)	18.0	5.0	28.2	22.3
CMEA (ODA)	–	–	–	–
TOTAL MULTILAT.(ODA)	4.2	5.6	30.0	19.2
TOTAL BIL.& MULTIL.	124.3	108.3	199.9	365.1
of which				
ODA Grants	31.4	34.6	71.5	57.7
ODA Loans	74.6	56.9	128.4	176.9
ODA CONCESSIONALITY				
Total: Grant Element	58.0	63.0	63.0	56.0
Loans: Grant Element	40.0	41.0	43.0	41.0
INDEBTEDNESS				
TOTAL DEBT DISBURSED	***2644.1***	***3184.1***	***3615.2***	
Debt to DAC Countries	2098.0	2445.0	2905.0	
ODA	332.0	455.0	453.0	
Total Export Credits	859.0	982.0	1086.0	
Other Private Market	907.0	1008.0	1366.0	
International Org.	491.7	573.2	659.1	
CMEA	–	–	–	
Other	54.3	165.9	51.2	
TOTAL DEBT SERVICE	***500.5***	***761.9***	***649.3***	
Paid to DAC Countries	446.6	689.7	565.6	
ODA	18.3	27.2	34.3	
Total Export Credits	115.4	151.9	168.6	
Other Private Market	312.9	510.6	362.7	
International Org.	52.0	69.8	80.9	
CMEA	–	–	–	
Other	1.9	2.4	2.8	
ECONOMIC INDICATORS				
GNP Curr. Prices, $M	12657.9	15091.1	19564.5	22695.9
Real GNP, 1976=100	107.0	114.0	124.0	134.0
GNP/Cap Curr. Prices,$	1007.0	1174.0	1489.0	1689.0
GNP/cap Atlas Basis, $	1118.0	1254.7	1449.0	1668.1
Real GNP/Cap, 1976=100	104.0	109.0	116.0	123.0
Population, Million	12.6	12.8	13.1	13.4
Curr.A/C Deficit(-),$M	422.0	82.0	1065.0	-492.0
BOP Exp. & Transf.,$M	6839.0	8315.0	12265.0	14455.0
Exp. to OECD CIF, $M	4831.5	5621.9	8496.7	9339.0
of which				
Manufact.	853.9	1135.6	1556.9	1962.6
Imp. from OECD FOB, $M	2403.4	3297.8	4267.3	5617.1
Reserves ex. Gold, $M	2784.0	3243.0	3915.0	4387.0

MALI

	1977	1978	1979	1980	1977	1978	1979	1980	197
TOTAL RECEIPTS NET / **TOTAL ODA NET** / **TOTAL ODA GROSS**									
DAC COUNTRIES									
Australia	–	–	–	–	–	–	–	–	
Austria	0.4	0.0	0.0	0.0	0.4	0.0	0.0	0.0	C
Belgium	1.9	1.7	3.1	1.9	1.9	1.5	2.9	1.8	1
Canada	3.6	4.4	8.0	12.8	3.6	4.4	8.0	12.8	3
Denmark	–	–	–	–	–	–	–	–	
Finland	–	–	–	–	–	–	–	–	
France	26.9	34.0	37.6	46.7	25.1	32.4	30.5	44.6	25
Germany, Fed. Rep.	15.1	32.3	29.8	26.5	16.0	22.1	27.7	27.0	16
Italy	-0.1	0.0	0.0	0.1	0.1	0.0	0.0	0.1	C
Japan	0.2	6.1	1.9	4.1	0.2	6.1	1.9	4.1	C
Netherlands	5.9	8.4	5.4	12.5	5.9	8.4	5.4	12.5	5
New Zealand	–	–	–	–	–	–	–	–	
Norway	0.0	1.7	0.5	0.6	0.0	1.7	0.5	0.6	C
Sweden	–	–	–	–	–	–	–	–	
Switzerland	1.3	1.3	1.9	4.3	1.3	1.3	1.9	4.1	1
United Kingdom	0.0	-0.2	1.0	0.5	0.5	0.3	1.0	0.5	C
United States	6.0	15.0	14.0	23.0	6.0	15.0	14.0	23.0	6
TOTAL	*61.2*	*104.6*	*103.2*	*133.0*	*60.9*	*93.0*	*93.9*	*131.4*	*62*
MULTILATERAL									
AF.D.F.	3.9	0.7	6.8	7.0	3.9	0.7	6.8	7.0	3
AF.D.B.	0.5	2.0	1.6	1.1	–	–	–	–	
AS.D.B.	–	–	–	–	–	–	–	–	
CAR.D.B.	–	–	–	–	–	–	–	–	
E.E.C.	12.0	15.8	31.3	41.6	12.0	15.8	31.3	41.6	12
IBRD	–	–	–	–	–	–	–	–	
IDA	12.7	14.5	20.5	18.8	12.7	14.5	20.5	18.8	12
I.D.B.	–	–	–	–	–	–	–	–	
IFAD	–	–	–	–	–	–	–	–	
I.F.C.	–	0.6	–	–	–	–	–	–	
IMF TRUST FUND	–	11.4	8.7	7.3	–	11.4	8.7	7.3	
U.N. AGENCIES	–	–	–	–	–	–	–	–	
UNDP	3.1	3.4	5.4	6.5	3.1	3.4	5.4	6.5	3
UNTA	0.6	1.1	0.5	0.2	0.6	1.1	0.5	0.2	6
UNICEF	0.3	1.1	1.2	1.6	0.3	1.1	1.2	1.6	C
UNRWA	–	–	–	–	–	–	–	–	
WFP	1.5	5.5	5.9	4.5	1.5	5.5	5.9	4.5	1
UNHCR	–	–	–	0.0	–	–	–	0.0	
Other Multilateral	2.3	5.1	5.7	5.9	2.3	5.1	5.7	5.9	2
Arab OPEC Agencies	4.6	6.5	6.2	9.5	4.6	6.5	3.5	10.3	4
TOTAL	*41.3*	*67.5*	*93.6*	*103.7*	*40.8*	*64.9*	*89.3*	*103.4*	*40*
OPEC COUNTRIES	*11.2*	*7.4*	*10.3*	*17.3*	*11.2*	*3.7*	*10.3*	*17.3*	*1*
E.E.C.+ MEMBERS	*61.7*	*91.9*	*108.2*	*129.8*	*61.3*	*80.4*	*98.8*	*128.2*	*62*
TOTAL	***113.6***	***179.4***	***207.1***	***254.0***	***112.8***	***161.6***	***193.4***	***252.1***	***114***

	1977	1978	1979	1980	1977	1978	1979	1980	197
ODA LOANS GROSS / **ODA LOANS NET** / **GRANTS**									
DAC COUNTRIES									
Australia	–	–	–	–	–	–	–	–	
Austria	–	–	–	–	–	–	–	–	C
Belgium	–	–	–	–	–	–	–	–	1
Canada	0.4	–	–	–	0.4	-1.7	–	–	3
Denmark	–	–	–	–	–	–	–	–	
Finland	–	–	–	–	–	–	–	–	
France	5.2	8.2	7.4	10.6	4.4	7.5	6.5	10.2	20
Germany, Fed. Rep.	7.3	11.8	3.1	–	6.9	11.5	-58.9	–	S
Italy	–	–	–	–	–	–	–	–	C
Japan	–	–	–	–	–	–	–	–	C
Netherlands	–	–	–	–	–	–	–	–	5
New Zealand	–	–	–	–	–	–	–	–	
Norway	–	–	–	–	–	–	–	–	C
Sweden	–	–	–	–	–	–	–	–	
Switzerland	–	–	–	–	–	–	–	–	1
United Kingdom	–	–	–	–	–	–	–	–	C
United States	–	1.0	–	1.0	–	1.0	–	1.0	6
TOTAL	*12.9*	*21.0*	*10.5*	*11.6*	*11.7*	*18.3*	*-52.4*	*11.2*	*49*
MULTILATERAL	*21.2*	*35.2*	*40.9*	*47.4*	*21.1*	*33.0*	*40.3*	*47.1*	*19*
OPEC COUNTRIES	*6.2*	*3.5*	*9.1*	*13.2*	*6.2*	*3.5*	*9.1*	*13.2*	*5*
E.E.C.+ MEMBERS	*12.5*	*20.0*	*11.4*	*14.3*	*11.3*	*19.0*	*-51.5*	*13.9*	*50*
TOTAL	***40.3***	***59.7***	***60.5***	***72.2***	***39.0***	***54.8***	***-3.1***	***71.5***	***73***

	1977	1978	1979	1980	1977	1978	1979	1980	197
TOTAL OFFICIAL GROSS / **TOTAL OFFICIAL NET** / **TOTAL OOF GROSS**									
DAC COUNTRIES									
Australia	–	–	–	–	–	–	–	–	
Austria	0.4	0.0	0.0	0.0	0.4	0.0	0.0	0.0	
Belgium	1.9	1.5	2.9	1.8	1.9	1.5	2.9	1.8	
Canada	3.6	6.1	8.0	12.8	3.6	4.4	8.0	12.8	
Denmark	–	–	–	–	–	–	–	–	
Finland	–	–	–	–	–	–	–	–	
France	25.9	35.1	35.4	45.9	24.0	34.3	34.3	45.0	
Germany, Fed. Rep.	16.4	22.4	89.7	27.0	16.0	22.1	27.7	27.0	
Italy	0.1	0.0	0.0	0.1	0.1	0.0	0.0	0.1	
Japan	0.2	6.1	1.9	4.1	0.2	6.1	1.9	4.1	
Netherlands	5.9	8.4	5.4	12.5	5.9	8.4	5.4	12.5	
New Zealand	–	–	–	–	–	–	–	–	
Norway	0.0	1.7	0.5	0.6	0.0	1.7	0.5	0.6	
Sweden	–	–	–	–	–	–	–	–	
Switzerland	1.3	1.3	1.9	4.1	1.3	1.3	1.9	4.1	
United Kingdom	0.5	0.3	1.0	0.5	0.5	0.3	1.0	0.5	
United States	6.0	15.0	14.0	23.0	6.0	15.0	14.0	23.0	
TOTAL	*62.0*	*97.8*	*160.8*	*132.6*	*59.8*	*94.9*	*97.7*	*131.8*	
MULTILATERAL	*41.4*	*69.7*	*94.5*	*106.8*	*41.3*	*67.5*	*93.6*	*103.7*	*C*
OPEC COUNTRIES	*11.2*	*7.4*	*10.3*	*17.3*	*11.2*	*7.4*	*10.3*	*17.3*	
E.E.C.+ MEMBERS	*62.5*	*83.4*	*165.8*	*129.5*	*60.2*	*82.3*	*102.6*	*128.7*	
TOTAL	***114.7***	***174.9***	***265.6***	***256.6***	***112.2***	***169.8***	***201.6***	***252.7***	***C***

1978	1979	1980
–	–	–
0.0	0.0	0.0
1.5	2.9	1.8
6.1	8.0	12.8
–	–	–
–	–	–
33.1	31.4	45.0
22.4	89.7	27.0
0.0	0.0	0.1
6.1	1.9	4.1
8.4	5.4	12.5
–	–	–
1.7	0.5	0.6
–	–	–
1.3	1.9	4.1
0.3	1.0	0.5
15.0	14.0	23.0
95.8	*156.8*	*131.8*
2.7	7.3	7.2
–	–	–
–	–	–
–	–	–
15.8	31.3	41.6
–	–	–
14.6	20.6	18.9
–	–	–
–	–	–
–	–	–
11.4	8.7	7.3
–	–	–
3.4	5.4	6.5
1.1	0.5	0.2
1.1	1.2	1.6
–	–	–
5.5	5.9	4.5
–	–	0.0
5.1	5.7	5.9
6.5	3.5	10.3
67.1	*90.0*	*103.8*
3.7	*10.3*	*17.3*
81.4	*161.8*	*128.6*
166.5	***257.0***	***252.8***
–	–	–
0.0	0.0	0.0
1.5	2.9	1.8
6.1	8.0	12.8
–	–	–
–	–	–
24.9	24.0	34.4
10.5	86.6	27.0
0.0	0.0	0.1
6.1	1.9	4.1
8.4	5.4	12.5
–	–	–
1.7	0.5	0.6
–	–	–
1.3	1.9	4.1
0.3	1.0	0.5
14.0	14.0	22.0
74.7	*146.3*	*120.2*
31.9	*49.0*	*56.4*
0.2	*1.2*	*4.1*
61.3	*150.4*	*114.3*
106.9	***196.5***	***180.6***
–	–	–
–	–	–
–	–	–
–	–	–
–	–	–
–	–	–
2.0	4.0	0.9
–	–	–
–	–	–
–	–	–
–	–	–
–	–	–
–	–	–
–	–	–
–	–	–
–	–	–
–	–	–
2.0	*4.0*	*0.9*
2.6	*4.5*	*3.0*
3.8	–	–
2.0	*4.0*	*0.9*
8.4	***8.5***	***3.9***

ODA COMMITMENTS

1977	1978	1979	1980
–	–	–	–
–	–	–	–
2.5	2.0	3.5	2.3
15.6	10.8	4.0	2.8
–	–	–	0.1
–	–	–	–
24.2	26.0	26.5	40.7
27.3	26.5	127.7	14.6
0.1	0.0	0.0	0.1
1.7	4.3	5.1	6.2
6.5	3.9	4.6	14.6
–	–	–	–
–	0.6	0.3	0.0
–	–	–	–
2.7	–	3.3	4.1
0.3	0.3	1.0	0.5
10.3	22.5	10.9	23.1
91.1	*96.8*	*186.8*	*109.2*
12.1	10.2	5.7	12.9
–	–	–	–
–	–	–	–
–	–	–	–
7.7	38.0	21.5	10.0
–	–	–	–
35.5	4.5	16.5	8.0
–	–	–	–
–	–	–	–
–	–	–	–
–	–	–	–
7.7	16.2	18.7	18.5
–	–	–	–
–	–	–	–
–	–	–	–
–	–	–	–
–	–	–	–
–	–	–	–
–	–	–	–
8.6	3.5	15.1	16.0
71.5	*72.3*	*77.5*	*65.4*
20.0	*13.9*	*5.0*	*29.6*
68.5	*96.6*	*184.7*	*82.9*
182.7	***183.0***	***269.3***	***204.2***

TECH. COOP. GRANTS

1977	1978	1979	1980
–	–	–	–
0.4	0.0	0.0	0.0
0.4	0.5	0.9	0.8
1.2	1.0	0.8	0.8
–	–	–	–
–	–	–	–
11.5	11.7	15.4	16.3
3.9	6.0	8.2	21.0
0.1	0.0	0.0	0.1
0.2	0.4	1.8	1.2
0.4	0.7	1.2	2.4
–	–	–	–
0.0	0.0	0.0	–
–	–	–	–
0.0	0.0	0.1	0.6
0.3	0.3	0.4	0.5
1.0	4.0	8.0	19.0
19.3	*24.7*	*36.8*	*62.8*
6.3	*10.6*	*12.8*	*18.5*
–	–	–	–
16.5	*19.2*	*26.0*	*41.2*
25.6	***35.4***	***49.5***	***81.4***

TOTAL OOF NET

1977	1978	1979	1980
–	–	–	–
–	–	–	–
–	–	–	–
–	–	–	–
–	–	–	–
–	–	–	–
-1.1	1.9	3.8	0.5
–	–	–	–
–	–	–	–
–	–	–	–
–	–	–	–
–	–	–	–
–	–	–	–
–	–	–	–
–	–	–	–
–	–	–	–
–	–	–	–
-1.1	*1.9*	*3.8*	*0.5*
0.5	*2.6*	*4.3*	*0.2*
–	*3.8*	–	–
-1.1	*1.9*	*3.8*	*0.5*
-0.6	***8.2***	***8.1***	***0.7***

MAIN AID AGGREGATES

	1977	1978	1979	1980
DAC COUNTRIES COMBINED				
PRIVATE SECTOR NET	1.4	9.6	5.6	1.2
Direct Investment	0.1	0.2	-1.3	-0.2
Portfolio Invest.	0.1	0.5	-0.6	0.5
Export Credits	1.3	9.0	7.4	0.9
OFFICIAL & PRIVATE				
GROSS:				
Contractual Lending	19.9	35.8	24.9	15.3
Export Credits Tot.	7.0	12.8	10.4	2.8
Export Credits Priv	7.0	12.8	10.4	2.8
OTHER NET DATA				
Contractual Lending	11.9	29.2	-41.2	12.5
Export Credits Tot.	1.3	9.0	7.4	0.9
(Bank Sector Loans)	–	1.0	-1.0	–
ODA CONCESSIONALITY				
Total:Grant Element	97.0	94.0	98.0	99.0
Loans:Grant Element	83.0	70.0	29.0	68.0
OTHER SOURCES				
CMEA Countr.(Gross)	1.2	2.0	1.0	1.0
Intra LDCS Exc.OPEC	–	–	–	–
Other	–	–	–	–
ALL SOURCE COMMITMENTS				
TOTAL BILATERAL	120.2	118.2	202.5	138.8
of which				
OPEC (ODA)	20.0	13.9	5.0	29.6
CMEA (ODA)	–	0.6	–	0.5
TOTAL MULTILAT.(ODA)	71.5	72.3	77.5	65.4
TOTAL BIL.& MULTIL.	191.7	190.5	280.0	204.2
of which				
ODA Grants	95.0	131.2	220.9	140.2
ODA Loans	87.6	51.8	48.4	64.0
ODA CONCESSIONALITY				
Total: Grant Element	88.0	91.0	94.0	85.0
Loans: Grant Element	75.0	68.0	65.0	54.0

INDEBTEDNESS

	1977	1978	1979	1980
TOTAL DEBT DISBURSED	***458.7***	***541.3***	***549.3***	
Debt to DAC Countries	96.0	139.0	89.0	
ODA	54.0	81.0	22.0	
Total Export Credits	42.0	47.0	54.0	
Other Private Market	–	11.0	13.0	
International Org.	82.7	103.3	141.3	
CMEA	245.4	263.1	269.3	
Other	34.7	35.8	49.7	
TOTAL DEBT SERVICE	***12.4***	***17.5***	***20.3***	
Paid to DAC Countries	8.9	12.4	15.7	
ODA	1.5	1.8	2.1	
Total Export Credits	7.4	10.0	13.0	
Other Private Market	–	0.6	0.6	
International Org.	1.0	3.1	1.4	
CMEA	0.1	0.1	0.6	
Other	2.4	1.9	2.6	

ECONOMIC INDICATORS

	1977	1978	1979	1980
GNP Curr. Prices, $M	806.2	949.3	1242.0	1416.9
Real GNP, 1976=100	107.0	105.0	117.0	115.0
GNP/Cap Curr. Prices,$	126.0	144.0	183.0	204.0
GNP/cap Atlas Basis, $	153.4	157.6	183.9	192.7
Real GNP/Cap, 1976=100	104.0	100.0	107.0	103.0
Population, Million	6.4	6.6	6.8	6.9
Curr.A/C Deficit(-),$M	-57.5	-128.4	-208.5	–
BOP Exp. & Transf.,$M	168.7	163.8	225.8	–
Exp. to OECD CIF, $M	87.3	74.8	98.6	117.2
of which				
Manufact.	0.8	1.6	0.9	1.8
Imp. from OECD FOB, $M	114.5	136.6	174.6	205.3
Reserves ex. Gold, $M	5.4	8.2	6.0	14.5

	TOTAL RECEIPTS NET 1977	1978	1979	1980	TOTAL ODA NET 1977	1978	1979	1980
DAC COUNTRIES								
Australia	0.0	–	–	–	0.0	–	–	–
Austria	-2.1	-4.9	-5.3	-5.5	0.0	0.0	0.1	0.1
Belgium	0.8	0.9	1.0	0.3	0.8	0.9	1.0	0.3
Canada	5.8	1.2	0.8	0.9	5.8	1.2	0.8	0.9
Denmark	–	–	–	–	–	–	–	–
Finland	–	0.1	–	0.1	–	0.1	–	0.1
France	21.0	5.5	0.5	10.6	8.2	12.7	16.9	20.1
Germany, Fed. Rep.	5.6	16.1	9.0	11.7	5.3	16.2	9.1	11.8
Italy	0.6	0.2	2.2	4.6	–	–	–	0.0
Japan	2.3	0.1	0.1	0.1	2.3	0.1	0.2	0.1
Netherlands	0.0	1.9	0.6	4.7	0.0	1.9	0.6	4.7
New Zealand	–	–	–	–	–	–	–	–
Norway	–	–	0.3	0.0	–	–	0.3	–
Sweden	–	–	–	–	–	–	–	–
Switzerland	0.5	0.5	0.6	-0.4	0.5	0.5	0.6	0.5
United Kingdom	-0.6	1.0	-1.5	0.2	0.0	1.0	-0.1	0.1
United States	2.0	5.0	5.0	15.0	2.0	5.0	6.0	15.0
TOTAL	*35.7*	*27.5*	*13.2*	*42.1*	*24.8*	*39.6*	*35.4*	*53.5*
MULTILATERAL								
AF.D.F.	1.0	1.6	1.5	5.4	1.0	1.6	1.5	5.4
AF.D.B.	1.2	0.0	0.3	-0.5	–	–	–	–
AS.D.B.	–	–	–	–	–	–	–	–
CAR.D.B.	–	–	–	–	–	–	–	–
E.E.C.	11.3	28.5	58.5	7.5	11.3	28.5	58.5	7.5
IBRD	–	–	–	–	–	–	–	–
IDA	5.7	5.5	4.2	3.9	5.7	5.5	4.2	3.9
I.D.B.	–	–	–	–	–	–	–	–
IFAD	–	–	–	–	–	–	–	–
I.F.C.	–	–	–	–	–	–	–	–
IMF TRUST FUND	1.6	5.0	3.2	6.3	1.6	5.0	3.2	6.3
U.N. AGENCIES	–	–	–	–	–	–	–	–
UNDP	0.8	0.8	1.5	2.6	0.8	0.8	1.5	2.6
UNTA	0.5	0.7	0.6	0.3	0.5	0.7	0.6	0.3
UNICEF	0.1	0.3	0.4	0.4	0.1	0.3	0.4	0.4
UNRWA	–	–	–	–	–	–	–	–
WFP	1.7	1.7	3.3	6.1	1.7	1.7	3.3	6.1
UNHCR	–	–	–	–	–	–	–	–
Other Multilateral	1.1	3.3	1.1	0.9	1.1	3.3	1.1	0.9
Arab OPEC Agencies	10.1	22.4	6.6	3.9	10.1	22.4	0.2	2.8
TOTAL	*35.1*	*69.8*	*81.2*	*36.7*	*33.9*	*69.8*	*74.5*	*36.0*
OPEC COUNTRIES	*106.0*	*117.2*	*68.7*	*69.8*	*106.0*	*107.4*	*68.7*	*69.8*
E.E.C.+ MEMBERS	*38.6*	*54.0*	*70.2*	*39.5*	*25.6*	*61.1*	*86.0*	*44.5*
TOTAL	***176.8***	***214.5***	***163.0***	***148.6***	***164.7***	***216.7***	***178.6***	***159.3***

	ODA LOANS GROSS 1977	1978	1979	1980	ODA LOANS NET 1977	1978	1979	1980
DAC COUNTRIES								
Australia	–	–	–	–	–	–	–	–
Austria	–	–	–	–	–	–	–	–
Belgium	–	–	–	–	–	–	–	–
Canada	3.2	0.2	0.1	0.1	3.2	0.2	0.1	0.1
Denmark	–	–	–	–	–	–	–	–
Finland	–	–	–	–	–	–	–	–
France	2.1	0.4	0.7	0.6	-2.6	-2.5	-0.6	-1.2
Germany, Fed. Rep.	2.1	11.7	0.7	2.3	2.1	11.7	0.7	2.0
Italy	–	–	–	–	–	–	–	–
Japan	–	–	–	–	–	–	0.0	-0.3
Netherlands	–	–	–	–	–	–	–	–
New Zealand	–	–	–	–	–	–	–	–
Norway	–	–	–	–	–	–	–	–
Sweden	–	–	–	–	–	–	–	–
Switzerland	–	–	–	–	–	–	–	–
United Kingdom	–	–	–	–	–	–	–	–
United States	–	–	–	–	–	–	–	–
TOTAL	*7.4*	*12.3*	*1.5*	*2.9*	*2.7*	*9.4*	*0.2*	*0.6*
MULTILATERAL	*18.4*	*34.5*	*9.3*	*18.5*	*17.9*	*34.0*	*8.7*	*17.9*
OPEC COUNTRIES	*13.5*	*7.4*	*59.3*	*47.7*	*13.5*	*7.4*	*59.3*	*47.2*
E.E.C.+ MEMBERS	*4.2*	*12.1*	*1.4*	*2.8*	*-0.8*	*8.9*	*-0.3*	*0.5*
TOTAL	***39.2***	***54.2***	***70.1***	***69.1***	***34.1***	***50.8***	***68.2***	***65.7***

	TOTAL OFFICIAL GROSS 1977	1978	1979	1980	TOTAL OFFICIAL NET 1977	1978	1979	1980
DAC COUNTRIES								
Australia	0.0	–	–	–	0.0	–	–	–
Austria	0.0	0.0	0.1	0.1	0.0	0.0	0.1	0.1
Belgium	0.8	0.9	1.0	0.3	0.8	0.9	1.0	0.3
Canada	5.8	1.2	0.8	0.9	5.8	1.2	0.8	0.9
Denmark	–	–	–	–	–	–	–	–
Finland	–	0.1	–	0.1	–	0.1	–	0.1
France	12.9	15.6	18.2	21.9	8.1	12.6	16.7	19.9
Germany, Fed. Rep.	5.3	16.2	9.1	12.1	5.3	16.2	9.1	11.8
Italy	–	–	–	0.0	–	–	–	0.0
Japan	2.3	0.1	0.2	0.3	2.3	0.1	0.2	0.1
Netherlands	0.0	1.9	0.6	4.7	0.0	1.9	0.6	4.7
New Zealand	–	–	–	–	–	–	–	–
Norway	–	–	0.3	–	–	–	0.3	–
Sweden	–	–	–	–	–	–	–	–
Switzerland	0.5	0.5	0.6	0.5	0.5	0.5	0.6	0.5
United Kingdom	0.0	1.0	-0.1	0.1	0.0	1.0	-0.1	0.1
United States	2.0	5.0	6.0	15.0	2.0	5.0	5.0	15.0
TOTAL	*29.5*	*42.5*	*36.8*	*55.9*	*24.7*	*39.4*	*34.3*	*53.3*
MULTILATERAL	*35.6*	*70.4*	*81.9*	*37.5*	*35.1*	*69.8*	*81.2*	*36.7*
OPEC COUNTRIES	*106.0*	*117.2*	*68.7*	*70.3*	*106.0*	*117.2*	*68.7*	*69.8*
E.E.C.+ MEMBERS	*30.5*	*64.3*	*87.6*	*46.8*	*25.5*	*61.0*	*85.8*	*44.3*
TOTAL	***171.0***	***230.1***	***187.4***	***163.7***	***165.8***	***226.4***	***184.1***	***159.8***

	TOTAL ODA GROSS 19
Australia	
Austria	
Belgium	
Canada	
Denmark	
Finland	
France	
Germany, Fed. Rep.	
Italy	
Japan	
Netherlands	
New Zealand	
Norway	
Sweden	
Switzerland	
United Kingdom	
United States	
TOTAL	
AF.D.F.	
AF.D.B.	
AS.D.B.	
CAR.D.B.	
E.E.C.	
IBRD	
IDA	
I.D.B.	
IFAD	
I.F.C.	
IMF TRUST FUND	
U.N. AGENCIES	
UNDP	
UNTA	
UNICEF	
UNRWA	
WFP	
UNHCR	
Other Multilateral	
Arab OPEC Agencies	
TOTAL	
OPEC COUNTRIES	
E.E.C.+ MEMBERS	
TOTAL	

	GRANTS
Australia	
Austria	
Belgium	
Canada	
Denmark	
Finland	
France	
Germany, Fed. Rep.	
Italy	
Japan	
Netherlands	
New Zealand	
Norway	
Sweden	
Switzerland	
United Kingdom	
United States	
TOTAL	
MULTILATERAL	
OPEC COUNTRIES	
E.E.C.+ MEMBERS	
TOTAL	

	TOTAL OOF GROSS
Australia	
Austria	
Belgium	
Canada	
Denmark	
Finland	
France	
Germany, Fed. Rep.	
Italy	
Japan	
Netherlands	
New Zealand	
Norway	
Sweden	
Switzerland	
United Kingdom	
United States	
TOTAL	
MULTILATERAL	
OPEC COUNTRIES	
E.E.C.+ MEMBERS	
TOTAL	

1978	1979	1980	1977	1978	1979	1980
			ODA COMMITMENTS			
–	–	–	–	–	–	–
0.0	0.1	0.1	–	0.0	0.0	0.0
0.9	1.0	0.3	–	–	1.2	–
1.2	0.8	0.9	6.9	2.2	0.8	0.4
–	–	–	–	–	–	–
0.1	–	0.1	–	0.1	–	0.1
15.6	18.2	21.9	12.0	15.4	19.7	22.3
16.2	9.1	12.1	8.2	7.2	27.6	7.5
–	–	0.0	–	–	–	0.0
0.1	0.2	0.3	2.3	0.1	0.2	16.3
1.9	0.6	4.7	0.9	0.6	8.9	7.1
–	–	–	–	–	–	–
–	0.3	–	–	–	0.6	–
–	–	–	–	–	–	–
0.5	0.6	0.5	0.0	–	0.6	0.4
1.0	-0.1	0.1	0.0	1.0	–	0.1
5.0	6.0	15.0	3.7	9.0	8.0	10.0
42.5	*36.8*	*55.9*	*34.0*	*35.6*	*67.5*	*64.0*
1.6	1.5	5.4	–	12.4	4.9	–
–	–	–	–	–	–	–
–	–	–	–	–	–	–
–	–	–	–	–	–	–
28.7	58.8	7.8	7.9	20.1	61.2	19.3
–	–	–	–	–	–	–
5.7	4.4	4.1	3.5	–	8.0	14.5
–	–	–	–	–	–	–
–	–	–	–	–	–	9.7
–	–	–	–	–	–	–
5.0	3.2	6.3	–	–	–	–
–	–	–	4.2	6.8	7.0	10.3
0.8	1.5	2.6	–	–	–	–
0.7	0.6	0.3	–	–	–	–
0.3	0.4	0.4	–	–	–	–
–	–	–	–	–	–	–
1.7	3.3	6.1	–	–	–	–
–	–	–	–	–	–	–
3.3	1.1	0.9	–	–	–	–
22.4	0.2	2.8	1.9	5.2	36.2	11.5
70.3	*75.1*	*36.6*	*17.5*	*44.6*	*117.2*	*65.2*
107.4	*68.7*	*70.3*	*92.5*	*129.4*	*258.0*	*135.7*
64.3	*87.6*	*46.8*	*29.0*	*44.3*	*118.5*	*56.2*
220.1	***180.5***	***162.8***	***144.0***	***209.6***	***442.8***	***264.9***
			TECH. COOP. GRANTS			
–	–	–	–	–	–	–
0.0	0.1	0.1	0.0	0.0	0.1	0.1
0.9	1.0	0.3	0.1	0.0	0.1	0.1
1.0	0.7	0.8	1.1	0.9	0.7	0.4
–	–	–	–	–	–	–
0.1	–	0.1	–	–	–	–
15.2	17.5	21.4	9.0	9.0	11.6	14.3
4.5	8.4	9.8	1.0	2.2	5.2	3.9
–	–	0.0	–	–	–	0.0
0.1	0.2	0.3	0.0	0.1	0.2	0.3
1.9	0.6	4.7	0.0	0.2	0.0	0.5
–	–	–	–	–	–	–
–	0.3	–	–	–	–	–
–	–	–	–	–	–	–
0.5	0.6	0.5	0.0	0.0	–	–
1.0	-0.1	0.1	0.0	0.1	0.1	0.1
5.0	6.0	15.0	–	1.0	3.0	5.0
30.2	*35.3*	*53.0*	*11.3*	*13.4*	*20.9*	*24.6*
35.8	*65.8*	*18.1*	*2.6*	*5.2*	*3.6*	*10.3*
100.0	*9.4*	*22.6*	–	–	–	–
52.2	*86.2*	*44.0*	*10.1*	*11.5*	*16.9*	*18.8*
166.0	***110.4***	***93.7***	***13.8***	***18.6***	***24.5***	***34.8***
			TOTAL OOF NET			
–	–	–	–	–	–	–
–	–	–	–	–	–	–
–	–	–	–	–	–	–
–	–	–	–	–	–	–
–	–	–	–	–	–	–
–	–	–	–	–	–	–
–	–	–	-0.1	-0.1	-0.1	-0.2
–	–	–	–	–	–	–
–	–	–	–	–	–	–
–	–	–	–	–	–	–
–	–	–	–	–	–	–
–	–	–	–	–	–	–
–	–	–	–	–	–	–
–	–	–	–	–	–	–
–	–	–	–	–	–	–
–	–	–	–	–	–	–
–	–	–	–	–	-1.0	–
–	–	–	*-0.1*	*-0.1*	*-1.1*	*-0.2*
0.2	*6.9*	*0.9*	*1.2*	*0.0*	*6.7*	*0.7*
9.8	–	–	–	*9.8*	–	–
–	–	–	*-0.1*	*-0.1*	*-0.1*	*-0.2*
10.0	***6.9***	***0.9***	***1.1***	***9.7***	***5.5***	***0.5***

MAIN AID AGGREGATES

	1977	1978	1979	1980
DAC COUNTRIES COMBINED				
PRIVATE SECTOR NET	11.0	-11.9	-21.1	-11.2
Direct Investment	0.7	-6.0	-5.4	-3.2
Portfolio Invest.	-2.8	4.6	-1.6	1.7
Export Credits	13.2	-10.5	-14.0	-9.7
OFFICIAL & PRIVATE				
GROSS:				
Contractual Lending	35.6	17.9	9.3	10.6
Export Credits Tot.	28.2	5.5	7.8	7.7
Export Credits Priv	28.2	5.5	7.8	7.7
OTHER NET DATA				
Contractual Lending	15.7	-1.2	-15.0	-9.3
Export Credits Tot.	13.2	-10.5	-15.0	-9.7
(Bank Sector Loans)	8.0	7.0	-11.0	-4.0
ODA CONCESSIONALITY				
Total:Grant Element	98.0	100.0	98.0	86.0
Loans:Grant Element	83.0	–	77.0	45.0
OTHER SOURCES				
CMEA Countr.(Gross)	1.0	0.6	–	–
Intra LDCS Exc.OPEC	–	–	–	–
Other	–	–	–	–
ALL SOURCE COMMITMENTS				
TOTAL BILATERAL	126.5	167.0	361.2	204.2
of which				
OPEC (ODA)	92.5	129.4	258.0	135.7
CMEA (ODA)	2.0	–	–	–
TOTAL MULTILAT.(ODA)	17.5	44.6	117.2	65.2
TOTAL BIL.& MULTIL.	144.0	211.6	478.5	269.4
of which				
ODA Grants	135.4	162.8	141.3	152.2
ODA Loans	8.6	46.8	301.5	112.7
ODA CONCESSIONALITY				
Total: Grant Element	98.0	95.0	65.0	83.0
Loans: Grant Element	80.0	80.0	48.0	56.0

INDEBTEDNESS

	1977	1978	1979	1980
TOTAL DEBT DISBURSED	***456.4***	***570.6***	***581.3***	
Debt to DAC Countries	178.0	229.0	172.0	
ODA	26.0	42.0	44.0	
Total Export Credits	75.0	87.0	70.0	
Other Private Market	77.0	100.0	58.0	
International Org.	61.2	92.0	98.6	
CMEA	8.6	9.0	18.0	
Other	208.6	240.6	292.7	
TOTAL DEBT SERVICE	***42.0***	***31.9***	***75.3***	
Paid to DAC Countries	30.3	24.0	66.9	
ODA	4.8	3.8	2.5	
Total Export Credits	12.4	16.2	22.1	
Other Private Market	13.1	4.0	42.3	
International Org.	0.8	1.6	3.6	
CMEA	–	–	–	
Other	10.9	6.3	4.8	

ECONOMIC INDICATORS

	1977	1978	1979	1980
GNP Curr. Prices, $M	409.4	421.5	488.0	510.8
Real GNP, 1976=100	95.0	94.0	98.0	100.0
GNP/Cap Curr. Prices,$	272.0	272.0	307.0	312.0
GNP/cap Atlas Basis, $	264.2	271.2	299.5	322.7
Real GNP/Cap, 1976=100	93.0	89.0	90.0	89.0
Population, Million	1.5	1.5	1.6	1.6
Curr.A/C Deficit(-),$M	-245.1	-240.5	-239.4	–
BOP Exp. & Transf.,$M	182.7	155.7	198.6	–
Exp. to OECD CIF, $M	208.5	150.4	206.0	249.4
of which				
Manufact.	1.2	0.7	1.2	0.7
Imp. from OECD FOB, $M	202.1	161.7	185.0	235.8
Reserves ex. Gold, $M	50.0	79.5	113.7	139.9

	TOTAL RECEIPTS NET 1977	1978	1979	1980	TOTAL ODA NET 1977	1978	1979	1980
DAC COUNTRIES								
Australia	0.1	6.2	-0.1	-0.7	0.0	0.0	0.0	–
Austria	-1.4	-3.0	-2.4	-2.5	0.4	0.2	0.4	0.4
Belgium	-1.5	151.2	275.1	214.8	0.2	0.3	0.4	0.5
Canada	18.9	-5.1	-5.5	-0.4	–	–	–	–
Denmark	13.5	8.9	20.5	-4.6	0.0	0.0	0.7	0.1
Finland	-0.2	0.2	-0.1	-0.1	–	–	0.0	–
France	43.6	278.8	380.8	466.5	-0.6	-2.9	19.0	15.0
Germany, Fed. Rep.	237.7	26.0	-59.1	47.9	6.2	7.8	7.8	15.4
Italy	6.8	14.8	103.5	-21.1	-0.8	-0.2	0.1	1.2
Japan	154.3	321.0	-123.8	492.9	5.2	4.7	5.4	7.5
Netherlands	1.0	-14.5	-16.2	47.9	0.7	0.7	1.2	1.7
New Zealand	0.2	-1.1	–	–	–	–	–	–
Norway	44.3	-7.1	-6.8	13.8	–	–	–	–
Sweden	65.0	-22.1	-3.6	30.2	–	0.2	–	0.6
Switzerland	11.5	-22.1	42.3	-2.4	0.0	0.0	0.0	–
United Kingdom	22.0	-2.2	20.4	55.0	1.5	1.6	2.5	3.7
United States	941.0	1545.0	2304.0	2453.0	-7.0	-4.0	12.0	9.0
TOTAL	*1557.0*	*2274.8*	*2929.1*	*3790.4*	*5.8*	*8.4*	*49.4*	*55.0*
MULTILATERAL								
AF.D.F.	–	–	–	–	–	–	–	–
AF.D.B.	–	–	–	–	–	–	–	–
AS.D.B.	–	–	–	–	–	–	–	–
CAR.D.B.	–	–	–	–	–	–	–	–
E.E.C.	–	–	0.1	–	–	–	0.1	–
IBRD	151.7	106.7	249.7	332.7	–	–	–	–
IDA	–	–	–	–	–	–	–	–
I.D.B.	143.2	85.2	125.5	170.2	30.6	-2.4	4.5	-12.0
IFAD	–	–	–	0.1	–	–	–	0.1
I.F.C.	1.5	21.0	54.2	140.2	–	–	–	–
IMF TRUST FUND	–	–	–	–	–	–	–	–
U.N. AGENCIES	–	–	–	–	–	–	–	–
UNDP	3.0	3.2	5.5	5.7	3.0	3.2	5.5	5.7
UNTA	0.5	0.6	0.5	0.4	0.5	0.6	0.5	0.4
UNICEF	0.1	0.4	0.6	0.5	0.1	0.4	0.6	0.5
UNRWA	–	–	–	–	–	–	–	–
WFP	7.7	4.7	11.1	3.1	7.7	4.7	11.1	3.1
UNHCR	0.0	–	–	–	0.0	–	–	–
Other Multilateral	2.8	2.9	2.8	3.2	2.8	2.9	2.8	3.2
Arab OPEC Agencies	–	–	–	–	–	–	–	–
TOTAL	*310.5*	*224.8*	*450.0*	*656.2*	*44.8*	*9.5*	*25.1*	*1.0*
OPEC COUNTRIES	–	*0.2*	–	–	–	–	–	–
E.E.C.+ MEMBERS	*323.3*	*462.9*	*725.1*	*806.6*	*7.2*	*7.3*	*31.7*	*37.5*
TOTAL	***1867.5***	***2499.7***	***3379.1***	***4446.5***	***50.5***	***17.9***	***74.5***	***56.0***

TOTAL ODA GROSS	197
Australia	0
Austria	0.
Belgium	0.
Canada	
Denmark	0.
Finland	
France	2.
Germany, Fed. Rep.	6.
Italy	0.
Japan	5.
Netherlands	0.
New Zealand	
Norway	
Sweden	
Switzerland	0.
United Kingdom	1.
United States	-4.
TOTAL	*13.*
AF.D.F.	
AF.D.B.	
AS.D.B.	
CAR.D.B.	
E.E.C.	
IBRD	
IDA	
I.D.B.	44.
IFAD	
I.F.C.	
IMF TRUST FUND	
U.N. AGENCIES	
UNDP	3.
UNTA	0.
UNICEF	0.
UNRWA	
WFP	7.
UNHCR	0.
Other Multilateral	2.
Arab OPEC Agencies	
TOTAL	*58.*
OPEC COUNTRIES	
E.E.C.+ MEMBERS	*11.*
TOTAL	***71.***

	ODA LOANS GROSS 1977	1978	1979	1980	ODA LOANS NET 1977	1978	1979	1980
DAC COUNTRIES								
Australia	–	–	–	–	–	–	–	–
Austria	0.1	–	–	–	0.1	0.0	-0.1	-0.7
Belgium	–	–	–	–	–	–	–	–
Canada	–	–	–	–	–	–	–	–
Denmark	–	–	–	–	–	–	–	–
Finland	–	–	–	–	–	–	–	–
France	2.8	1.2	22.2	14.2	-0.6	-3.0	19.0	9.6
Germany, Fed. Rep.	0.0	–	0.1	0.4	0.0	–	0.1	0.4
Italy	–	–	–	–	-1.2	-1.0	-0.9	–
Japan	–	–	1.1	1.9	0.0	-0.2	1.1	1.9
Netherlands	–	–	–	–	–	–	–	–
New Zealand	–	–	–	–	–	–	–	–
Norway	–	–	–	–	–	–	–	–
Sweden	–	–	–	–	–	–	–	–
Switzerland	–	–	–	–	–	–	–	–
United Kingdom	–	–	–	–	–	–	–	–
United States	–	–	–	–	-3.0	-3.0	-3.0	-2.0
TOTAL	*2.9*	*1.2*	*23.4*	*16.5*	*-4.7*	*-7.3*	*16.2*	*9.3*
MULTILATERAL	*44.1*	*14.0*	*21.8*	*7.7*	*30.6*	*-2.4*	*4.5*	*-11.9*
OPEC COUNTRIES	–	–	–	–	–	–	–	–
E.E.C.+ MEMBERS	*2.8*	*1.2*	*22.3*	*14.6*	*-1.8*	*-4.0*	*18.2*	*10.1*
TOTAL	***47.0***	***15.2***	***45.2***	***24.2***	***25.9***	***-9.7***	***20.7***	***-2.6***

GRANTS	197
Australia	0
Austria	0
Belgium	0
Canada	
Denmark	0.
Finland	
France	
Germany, Fed. Rep.	6
Italy	0
Japan	5
Netherlands	0
New Zealand	
Norway	
Sweden	
Switzerland	0
United Kingdom	1
United States	-4
TOTAL	*10*
MULTILATERAL	*14*
OPEC COUNTRIES	
E.E.C.+ MEMBERS	*9*
TOTAL	***24***

	TOTAL OFFICIAL GROSS 1977	1978	1979	1980	TOTAL OFFICIAL NET 1977	1978	1979	1980
DAC COUNTRIES								
Australia	0.0	6.9	0.0	–	0.0	6.5	-0.4	-0.8
Austria	0.4	0.2	0.5	1.1	-0.2	-0.5	0.4	0.4
Belgium	0.2	0.3	0.4	0.5	0.2	0.3	0.4	0.5
Canada	26.3	3.4	3.8	–	17.1	-5.3	-4.4	–
Denmark	0.0	0.0	0.7	0.1	0.0	0.0	0.7	0.1
Finland	–	–	0.0	–	–	–	0.0	–
France	2.8	1.3	22.2	19.5	-0.6	-2.9	19.0	15.0
Germany, Fed. Rep.	31.0	25.9	12.5	40.1	19.6	6.6	-21.8	29.0
Italy	0.4	7.3	92.8	25.4	-4.2	2.1	88.8	-66.2
Japan	67.0	96.0	40.9	86.4	48.7	63.2	-178.1	61.3
Netherlands	0.7	0.7	1.2	1.7	0.7	0.7	1.2	1.7
New Zealand	1.2	–	–	–	0.2	–	–	–
Norway	–	–	–	–	–	–	–	–
Sweden	–	0.2	–	0.6	–	0.2	–	0.6
Switzerland	0.0	0.0	0.0	–	0.0	0.0	0.0	–
United Kingdom	1.5	1.6	2.5	3.7	1.5	1.6	2.5	3.7
United States	117.0	67.0	170.0	259.0	77.0	20.0	106.0	181.0
TOTAL	*248.5*	*210.9*	*347.6*	*438.1*	*159.9*	*92.5*	*14.3*	*226.2*
MULTILATERAL	*404.4*	*344.5*	*587.7*	*806.4*	*310.5*	*224.8*	*450.0*	*656.2*
OPEC COUNTRIES	–	*0.2*	–	–	–	*0.2*	–	–
E.E.C.+ MEMBERS	*36.6*	*37.1*	*132.4*	*91.0*	*17.1*	*8.4*	*90.8*	*-16.2*
TOTAL	***652.9***	***555.5***	***935.3***	***1244.5***	***470.4***	***317.4***	***464.2***	***882.3***

TOTAL OOF GROSS	197
Australia	
Austria	
Belgium	
Canada	26.
Denmark	
Finland	
France	
Germany, Fed. Rep.	24
Italy	
Japan	61.
Netherlands	
New Zealand	1
Norway	
Sweden	
Switzerland	
United Kingdom	
United States	121
TOTAL	*235*
MULTILATERAL	*346*
OPEC COUNTRIES	
E.E.C.+ MEMBERS	*24*
TOTAL	***581***

ODA COMMITMENTS

1978	1979	1980	1977	1978	1979	1980
0.0	0.0	–	–	–	–	–
0.2	0.5	1.1	0.1	–	–	–
0.3	0.4	0.5	–	–	–	–
–	–	–	–	–	–	–
0.0	0.7	0.1	0.0	–	–	–
–	0.0	–	–	–	0.0	–
1.3	22.2	19.5	–	44.0	11.4	4.2
7.8	7.8	15.4	8.9	6.0	8.5	15.7
0.8	0.9	1.2	0.4	0.8	0.9	1.2
4.9	5.4	7.5	4.4	5.1	6.1	8.3
0.7	1.2	1.7	0.9	0.9	1.1	11.2
–	–	–	–	–	–	–
–	–	–	–	–	–	–
0.2	–	0.6	–	–	–	–
0.0	0.0	–	–	–	–	–
1.6	2.5	3.7	1.5	1.6	2.5	3.7
-1.0	15.0	11.0	–	–	10.9	6.8
16.9	*56.6*	*62.2*	*16.1*	*58.4*	*41.5*	*51.0*
–	–	–	–	–	–	–
–	–	–	–	–	–	–
–	–	–	–	–	–	–
–	–	–	–	–	–	–
–	0.1	–	–	0.0	8.5	0.1
–	–	–	–	–	–	–
–	–	–	–	–	–	–
14.0	21.8	7.6	5.2	–	12.2	30.0
–	–	0.1	–	–	–	22.3
–	–	–	–	–	–	–
–	–	–	–	–	–	–
–	–	–	14.1	11.9	20.5	13.0
3.2	5.5	5.7	–	–	–	–
0.6	0.5	0.4	–	–	–	–
0.4	0.6	0.5	–	–	–	–
–	–	–	–	–	–	–
4.7	11.1	3.1	–	–	–	–
–	–	–	–	–	–	–
2.9	2.8	3.2	–	–	–	–
–	–	–	–	–	–	–
25.9	*42.4*	*20.6*	*19.3*	*11.9*	*41.3*	*65.4*
–	–	–	–	–	–	–
12.6	*35.7*	*42.0*	*11.6*	*53.3*	*33.0*	*36.1*
42.8	***99.0***	***82.9***	***35.5***	***70.3***	***82.7***	***116.4***

TECH. COOP. GRANTS

1978	1979	1980	1977	1978	1979	1980
0.0	0.0	–	0.0	0.0	0.0	–
0.2	0.5	1.1	0.3	0.2	0.5	1.1
0.3	0.4	0.5	0.2	0.2	0.3	0.3
–	–	–	–	–	–	–
0.0	0.7	0.1	0.0	0.0	0.7	0.1
–	0.0	–	–	–	0.0	–
0.1	–	5.4	–	0.1	–	5.4
7.8	7.7	14.9	5.9	7.8	7.7	14.9
0.8	0.9	1.2	0.4	0.8	0.9	1.2
4.9	4.3	5.6	3.8	4.3	4.1	5.6
0.7	1.2	1.7	0.7	0.7	1.2	1.7
–	–	–	–	–	–	–
–	–	–	–	–	–	–
0.2	–	0.6	–	0.2	–	0.6
0.0	0.0	–	–	0.0	0.0	–
1.6	2.5	3.7	1.5	1.6	2.5	3.7
-1.0	15.0	11.0	–	–	–	–
15.7	*33.2*	*45.7*	*12.8*	*16.0*	*17.9*	*34.4*
11.9	*20.6*	*13.0*	*6.5*	*7.1*	*9.4*	*13.0*
–	–	–	–	–	–	–
11.4	*13.5*	*27.4*	*8.7*	*11.3*	*13.3*	*27.2*
27.6	***53.8***	***58.6***	***19.3***	***23.1***	***27.3***	***47.4***

TOTAL OOF NET

1978	1979	1980	1977	1978	1979	1980
6.9	0.0	–	–	6.4	-0.4	-0.8
–	–	–	-0.6	-0.6	–	–
–	–	–	–	–	–	–
3.4	3.8	–	17.1	-5.3	-4.4	–
–	–	0.1	–	–	–	0.1
–	–	–	–	–	–	–
–	–	–	–	–	–	–
18.0	4.8	24.7	13.4	-1.2	-29.6	13.6
6.5	91.9	24.2	-3.4	2.3	88.7	-67.4
91.2	35.5	78.9	43.5	58.5	-183.5	53.8
–	–	–	–	–	–	–
–	–	–	0.2	–	–	–
–	–	–	–	–	–	–
–	–	–	–	–	–	–
–	–	–	–	–	–	–
–	–	–	–	–	–	–
68.0	155.0	248.0	84.0	24.0	94.0	172.0
194.0	*291.0*	*375.9*	*154.2*	*84.1*	*-35.2*	*171.2*
318.6	*545.3*	*785.7*	*265.7*	*215.3*	*424.9*	*655.1*
0.2	–	–	–	*0.2*	–	–
24.5	*96.7*	*49.0*	*10.0*	*1.1*	*59.1*	*-53.7*
512.8	***836.3***	***1161.6***	***419.9***	***299.5***	***389.7***	***826.3***

MAIN AID AGGREGATES

	1977	1978	1979	1980
DAC COUNTRIES COMBINED				
PRIVATE SECTOR NET	1397.1	2182.3	2914.8	3564.2
Direct Investment	343.9	494.8	1046.9	2001.3
Portfolio Invest.	991.8	1704.0	1675.5	1378.0
Export Credits	61.3	-16.6	192.5	184.9
OFFICIAL & PRIVATE				
GROSS:				
Contractual Lending	731.1	644.1	1044.8	1223.6
Export Credits Tot.	728.0	642.9	1021.2	1207.0
Export Credits Priv	493.1	448.9	730.4	831.1
OTHER NET DATA				
Contractual Lending	210.8	60.2	173.5	365.4
Export Credits Tot.	219.0	67.6	157.1	356.2
(Bank Sector Loans)	1928.0	3624.0	3397.0	2673.0
ODA CONCESSIONALITY				
Total:Grant Element	99.0	74.0	83.0	90.0
Loans:Grant Element	35.0	65.0	45.0	48.0
OTHER SOURCES				
CMEA Countr.(Gross)	–	–	–	–
Intra LDCS Exc.OPEC	–	–	–	–
Other	–	–	–	–
ALL SOURCE COMMITMENTS				
TOTAL BILATERAL	692.0	349.0	507.1	742.2
of which				
OPEC (ODA)	–	–	–	–
CMEA (ODA)	–	–	–	–
TOTAL MULTILAT.(ODA)	19.3	11.9	41.3	65.4
TOTAL BIL.& MULTIL.	711.3	360.9	548.3	807.6
of which				
ODA Grants	30.1	26.3	58.0	53.3
ODA Loans	5.3	44.0	24.8	63.1
ODA CONCESSIONALITY				
Total: Grant Element	85.0	78.0	90.0	75.0
Loans: Grant Element	41.0	65.0	45.0	41.0

INDEBTEDNESS

	1977	1978	1979	1980
TOTAL DEBT DISBURSED	***25612.5***	***30534.3***	***34480.4***	
Debt to DAC Countries	22854.0	27072.0	31126.0	
ODA	108.0	106.0	120.0	
Total Export Credits	2677.0	3103.0	3635.0	
Other Private Market	20069.0	23863.0	27371.0	
International Org.	2094.6	2364.8	2725.9	
CMEA	4.2	4.3	4.3	
Other	659.6	1093.2	624.2	
TOTAL DEBT SERVICE	***5226.9***	***7000.8***	***11039.7***	
Paid to DAC Countries	4839.7	6491.7	10664.9	
ODA	13.1	14.6	12.7	
Total Export Credits	1026.9	758.0	1119.5	
Other Private Market	3799.7	5719.1	9532.7	
International Org.	233.8	295.3	328.0	
CMEA	0.9	0.0	–	
Other	152.6	213.9	46.7	

ECONOMIC INDICATORS

	1977	1978	1979	1980
GNP Curr. Prices, $M	72229.0	90727.9	117798.2	162650.8
Real GNP, 1976=100	103.0	110.0	119.0	128.0
GNP/Cap Curr. Prices,$	1169.0	1426.0	1798.0	2411.0
GNP/cap Atlas Basis, $	1489.2	1657.4	1876.4	2134.7
Real GNP/Cap, 1976=100	100.0	104.0	109.0	113.0
Population, Million	61.8	63.6	65.5	67.5
Curr.A/C Deficit(-),$M	-1870.0	-3261.0	-5569.0	-8006.0
BOP Exp. & Transf.,$M	8365.0	11528.0	16147.0	24893.0
Exp. to OECD CIF, $M	5840.1	7422.0	10814.7	16905.4
of which				
Manufact.	2272.7	2983.0	3750.7	4081.1
Imp. from OECD FOB, $M	6660.5	9336.6	13254.6	20299.5
Reserves ex. Gold, $M	1649.0	1842.0	2033.0	2832.0

	TOTAL RECEIPTS NET 1977	1978	1979	1980	TOTAL ODA NET 1977	1978	1979	1980
DAC COUNTRIES								
Australia	–	–	–	–	–	–	–	–
Austria	0.1	0.0	0.1	0.1	0.1	0.0	0.1	0.1
Belgium	7.2	36.3	35.8	33.0	12.3	14.3	15.6	14.2
Canada	4.7	5.4	4.0	5.1	4.7	4.6	1.5	4.3
Denmark	0.1	-0.2	-0.1	-0.1	-0.1	0.0	0.1	0.0
Finland	–	–	–	0.0	–	–	–	0.0
France	245.8	350.8	359.6	475.1	79.2	104.7	85.6	134.7
Germany, Fed. Rep.	23.8	37.4	85.1	-31.4	19.1	31.3	42.9	9.7
Italy	1.6	249.1	-5.7	29.6	1.0	1.1	0.9	0.7
Japan	12.8	33.8	58.7	4.5	12.6	0.8	1.6	4.1
Netherlands	0.3	0.5	16.9	0.8	0.3	0.5	0.5	0.8
New Zealand	0.1	-0.1	–	–	–	–	–	–
Norway	-0.1	–	-1.7	-1.6	–	–	–	0.1
Sweden	–	–	1.8	2.3	–	–	–	–
Switzerland	0.5	0.8	1.3	3.1	0.4	0.1	0.2	0.0
United Kingdom	13.4	111.9	-6.1	-0.4	0.1	0.1	0.1	0.2
United States	28.0	12.0	12.0	33.0	29.0	23.0	20.0	19.0
TOTAL	*338.3*	*837.9*	*561.7*	*552.9*	*158.7*	*180.4*	*168.8*	*187.8*
MULTILATERAL								
AF.D.F.	–	–	–	–	–	–	–	–
AF.D.B.	3.1	6.5	-1.0	7.7	–	–	–	–
AS.D.B.	–	–	–	–	–	–	–	–
CAR.D.B.	–	–	–	–	–	–	–	–
E.E.C.	–	0.1	0.1	15.1	–	0.1	0.1	11.7
IBRD	50.9	51.5	112.3	35.0	–	–	–	–
IDA	3.2	0.0	0.1	0.7	3.2	0.0	0.1	0.7
I.D.B.	–	–	–	–	–	–	–	–
IFAD	–	–	–	4.1	–	–	–	4.1
I.F.C.	3.6	4.3	–	3.1	–	–	–	–
IMF TRUST FUND	14.1	43.5	44.3	37.6	14.1	43.5	44.3	37.6
U.N. AGENCIES	–	–	–	–	–	–	–	–
UNDP	3.6	4.4	4.8	4.9	3.6	4.4	4.8	4.9
UNTA	0.3	0.4	0.3	0.4	0.3	0.4	0.3	0.4
UNICEF	0.5	0.7	1.4	1.5	0.5	0.7	1.4	1.5
UNRWA	–	–	–	–	–	–	–	–
WFP	3.0	4.8	4.3	–	3.0	4.8	4.3	–
UNHCR	–	–	–	–	–	–	–	–
Other Multilateral	0.2	0.1	0.1	1.6	0.2	0.1	0.1	1.6
Arab OPEC Agencies	10.3	70.5	22.9	3.8	10.3	9.7	4.8	3.6
TOTAL	*92.9*	*186.7*	*189.6*	*115.5*	*35.2*	*63.6*	*60.1*	*66.0*
OPEC COUNTRIES	*109.4*	*66.7*	*394.2*	*402.8*	*80.0*	*32.5*	*394.2*	*400.8*
E.E.C.+ MEMBERS	*292.3*	*786.0*	*485.6*	*521.6*	*111.9*	*152.0*	*145.6*	*171.8*
TOTAL	***540.6***	***1091.3***	***1145.5***	***1071.3***	***273.9***	***276.4***	***623.2***	***654.5***

	ODA LOANS GROSS 1977	1978	1979	1980	ODA LOANS NET 1977	1978	1979	1980
DAC COUNTRIES								
Australia	–	–	–	–	–	–	–	–
Austria	–	–	–	–	–	–	–	–
Belgium	1.4	–	–	–	1.4	–	–	–
Canada	0.9	0.9	0.0	1.9	0.9	0.9	-0.1	1.9
Denmark	–	–	–	–	-0.1	-0.1	-0.1	-0.1
Finland	–	–	–	–	–	–	–	–
France	45.7	49.3	28.6	70.0	34.2	47.2	16.0	53.7
Germany, Fed. Rep.	16.6	30.3	40.2	15.3	11.6	22.9	33.7	1.6
Italy	–	–	–	–	-0.6	-0.6	-1.2	-1.2
Japan	11.2	–	–	0.4	11.2	–	–	0.4
Netherlands	–	–	–	–	–	–	–	–
New Zealand	–	–	–	–	–	–	–	–
Norway	–	–	–	–	–	–	–	–
Sweden	–	–	–	–	–	–	–	–
Switzerland	–	–	–	–	–	–	–	–
United Kingdom	–	–	–	–	–	–	–	–
United States	14.0	11.0	12.0	10.0	10.0	7.0	6.0	3.0
TOTAL	*89.8*	*91.5*	*80.8*	*97.6*	*68.6*	*77.3*	*54.3*	*59.2*
MULTILATERAL	*27.8*	*53.3*	*49.8*	*57.3*	*27.6*	*53.2*	*49.1*	*56.6*
OPEC COUNTRIES	*16.8*	*25.6*	*320.5*	*344.7*	*15.0*	*23.8*	*317.4*	*340.6*
E.E.C.+ MEMBERS	*63.7*	*79.6*	*68.8*	*95.9*	*46.5*	*69.4*	*48.3*	*64.5*
TOTAL	***134.3***	***170.4***	***451.1***	***499.6***	***111.2***	***154.3***	***420.8***	***456.3***

	TOTAL OFFICIAL GROSS 1977	1978	1979	1980	TOTAL OFFICIAL NET 1977	1978	1979	1980
DAC COUNTRIES								
Australia	–	–	–	–	–	–	–	–
Austria	0.1	0.0	0.1	0.1	0.1	0.0	0.1	0.1
Belgium	12.3	14.3	15.6	14.2	12.3	14.3	15.6	14.2
Canada	4.7	5.5	4.3	5.3	4.7	5.4	4.0	5.1
Denmark	–	0.1	0.2	0.1	-0.1	0.0	0.1	0.0
Finland	–	–	–	0.0	–	–	–	0.0
France	90.7	107.0	101.0	165.1	79.2	104.9	88.3	148.8
Germany, Fed. Rep.	24.1	38.7	49.4	23.4	19.1	31.3	42.9	9.7
Italy	4.3	1.8	2.1	1.9	2.4	-0.5	0.9	-0.2
Japan	12.6	0.8	1.6	4.1	12.6	0.8	1.6	4.1
Netherlands	0.3	0.5	0.5	0.8	0.3	0.5	0.5	0.8
New Zealand	0.1	–	–	–	0.1	–	–	–
Norway	–	–	–	0.1	–	–	–	0.1
Sweden	–	–	–	–	–	–	–	–
Switzerland	0.4	0.1	0.2	0.0	0.4	0.1	0.2	0.0
United Kingdom	0.1	0.1	0.1	0.2	0.1	0.1	0.1	0.2
United States	50.0	33.0	28.0	44.0	27.0	12.0	3.0	31.0
TOTAL	*199.7*	*201.7*	*203.0*	*259.1*	*158.1*	*168.7*	*157.0*	*213.8*
MULTILATERAL	*110.7*	*208.2*	*226.6*	*182.5*	*92.9*	*186.7*	*189.6*	*115.5*
OPEC COUNTRIES	*111.2*	*75.5*	*397.4*	*410.7*	*109.4*	*66.7*	*394.2*	*402.8*
E.E.C.+ MEMBERS	*131.8*	*162.4*	*168.9*	*220.7*	*113.3*	*150.6*	*148.3*	*188.5*
TOTAL	***421.6***	***485.4***	***827.0***	***852.4***	***360.4***	***422.1***	***740.9***	***732.1***

TOTAL ODA GROSS

	197[illegible]
Australia	
Austria	[illegible]
Belgium	[illegible]
Canada	[illegible]
Denmark	
Finland	
France	[illegible]
Germany, Fed. Rep.	[illegible]
Italy	[illegible]
Japan	[illegible]
Netherlands	[illegible]
New Zealand	
Norway	
Sweden	
Switzerland	[illegible]
United Kingdom	[illegible]
United States	[illegible]
TOTAL	[illegible]
AF.D.F.	
AF.D.B.	
AS.D.B.	
CAR.D.B.	
E.E.C.	
IBRD	
IDA	[illegible]
I.D.B.	
IFAD	
I.F.C.	
IMF TRUST FUND	[illegible]
U.N. AGENCIES	
UNDP	[illegible]
UNTA	[illegible]
UNICEF	[illegible]
UNRWA	
WFP	[illegible]
UNHCR	
Other Multilateral	[illegible]
Arab OPEC Agencies	[illegible]
TOTAL	[illegible]
OPEC COUNTRIES	[illegible]
E.E.C.+ MEMBERS	[illegible]
TOTAL	[illegible]

GRANTS

	197[illegible]
Australia	
Austria	[illegible]
Belgium	[illegible]
Canada	[illegible]
Denmark	
Finland	
France	[illegible]
Germany, Fed. Rep.	[illegible]
Italy	[illegible]
Japan	
Netherlands	[illegible]
New Zealand	
Norway	
Sweden	
Switzerland	[illegible]
United Kingdom	[illegible]
United States	[illegible]
TOTAL	[illegible]
MULTILATERAL	[illegible]
OPEC COUNTRIES	[illegible]
E.E.C.+ MEMBERS	[illegible]
TOTAL	[illegible]

TOTAL OOF GROSS

	197[illegible]
Australia	
Austria	
Belgium	
Canada	
Denmark	
Finland	
France	
Germany, Fed. Rep.	
Italy	[illegible]
Japan	
Netherlands	
New Zealand	[illegible]
Norway	
Sweden	
Switzerland	
United Kingdom	
United States	[illegible]
TOTAL	[illegible]
MULTILATERAL	[illegible]
OPEC COUNTRIES	[illegible]
E.E.C.+ MEMBERS	[illegible]
TOTAL	[illegible]

1978 (cont.)	1979 (cont.)	1980 (cont.)	1977	1978	1979	1980
			ODA COMMITMENTS			
–	–	–	–	–	–	–
0.0	0.1	0.1	–	–	–	0.0
14.3	15.6	14.2	20.7	20.3	17.7	17.5
4.6	1.5	4.4	6.3	3.4	1.5	9.3
0.1	0.2	0.1	–	0.1	0.1	0.1
–	–	0.0	–	–	–	–
106.8	98.2	151.0	106.0	130.4	92.9	165.8
38.7	49.4	23.4	66.8	13.1	65.9	10.1
1.8	2.1	1.9	1.6	1.8	2.1	1.9
0.8	1.6	4.1	1.6	0.9	4.1	2.1
0.5	0.5	0.8	1.9	0.5	0.1	0.2
–	–	–	–	–	–	–
–	–	0.1	–	–	0.2	–
–	–	–	–	–	–	–
0.1	0.2	0.0	–	–	–	0.0
0.1	0.1	0.2	0.1	0.1	0.1	0.2
27.0	26.0	26.0	31.1	35.9	26.3	25.1
194.5	195.4	226.2	236.0	206.4	211.1	232.2
–	–	–	–	–	–	–
–	–	–	–	–	–	–
–	–	–	–	–	–	–
–	–	–	–	–	–	–
0.1	0.1	11.7	–	–	43.0	76.0
–	–	–	–	–	–	–
0.2	0.2	0.9	–	–	–	–
–	–	–	–	–	–	–
–	–	4.1	–	–	25.8	–
–	–	–	–	–	–	–
43.5	44.3	37.6	–	–	–	–
–	–	–	7.6	10.3	10.9	8.3
4.4	4.8	4.9	–	–	–	–
0.4	0.3	0.4	–	–	–	–
0.7	1.4	1.5	–	–	–	–
–	–	–	–	–	–	–
4.8	4.3	–	–	–	–	–
–	–	–	–	–	–	–
0.1	0.1	1.6	–	–	–	–
9.7	5.3	4.1	3.0	2.0	5.0	18.5
63.7	60.7	66.7	10.6	12.3	84.6	102.8
34.3	397.4	404.9	99.9	79.4	746.9	64.9
162.2	166.1	203.1	197.1	166.2	221.9	271.7
292.5	653.5	697.8	346.5	298.1	1042.6	399.9

1978 (cont.)	1979 (cont.)	1980 (cont.)	1977	1978	1979	1980
			TECH. COOP. GRANTS			
–	–	–	–	–	–	–
0.0	0.1	0.1	0.1	0.0	0.1	0.1
14.3	15.6	14.2	10.2	13.5	15.1	13.1
3.6	1.6	2.5	3.7	3.4	1.4	2.4
0.1	0.2	0.1	–	0.1	–	0.1
–	–	0.0	–	–	–	0.0
57.5	69.6	81.0	44.6	57.4	69.6	80.9
8.4	9.2	8.1	7.4	8.4	9.2	8.1
1.8	2.1	1.9	1.6	1.8	2.1	1.9
0.8	1.6	3.7	1.4	0.8	1.6	1.5
0.5	0.5	0.8	0.3	0.4	0.1	0.2
–	–	–	–	–	–	–
–	–	0.1	–	–	–	–
–	–	–	–	–	–	–
0.1	0.2	0.0	0.1	0.0	–	–
0.1	0.1	0.2	0.1	0.1	0.1	0.2
16.0	14.0	16.0	3.0	3.0	2.0	6.0
103.0	114.6	128.6	72.5	88.7	101.2	114.4
10.4	11.0	9.4	4.6	5.5	6.6	8.3
8.7	76.9	60.2	–	–	–	–
82.6	97.3	107.3	64.3	81.5	96.1	104.4
122.1	202.4	198.2	77.1	94.3	107.7	122.7

1978 (cont.)	1979 (cont.)	1980 (cont.)	1977	1978	1979	1980
			TOTAL OOF NET			
–	–	–	–	–	–	–
–	–	–	–	–	–	–
–	–	–	–	–	–	–
1.0	2.8	0.9	–	0.8	2.5	0.7
–	0.0	–	–	–	0.0	–
–	–	–	–	–	–	–
0.2	2.8	14.1	–	0.2	2.7	14.1
–	–	–	–	–	–	–
–	–	–	1.4	-1.6	–	-0.8
–	–	–	–	–	–	–
–	–	–	–	–	–	–
–	–	–	0.1	–	–	–
–	–	–	–	–	–	–
–	–	–	–	–	–	–
–	–	–	–	–	–	–
–	–	–	–	–	–	–
6.0	2.0	18.0	-2.0	-11.0	-17.0	12.0
7.2	7.6	33.0	-0.5	-11.6	-11.8	26.0
144.5	165.9	115.8	57.6	123.2	129.5	49.5
41.2	–	5.8	29.4	34.2	–	2.1
0.2	2.8	17.5	1.4	-1.4	2.7	16.7
192.9	173.5	154.6	86.5	145.8	117.7	77.6

MAIN AID AGGREGATES

	1977	1978	1979	1980
DAC COUNTRIES COMBINED				
PRIVATE SECTOR NET	180.2	669.2	404.6	339.2
Direct Investment	8.4	15.4	6.8	19.4
Portfolio Invest.	56.9	153.2	260.3	48.0
Export Credits	115.0	500.6	137.6	271.8
OFFICIAL & PRIVATE				
GROSS:				
Contractual Lending	345.0	740.7	415.2	857.5
Export Credits Tot.	252.5	648.9	331.6	745.8
Export Credits Priv	235.4	642.0	326.8	727.0
OTHER NET DATA				
Contractual Lending	183.0	566.3	180.1	357.0
Export Credits Tot.	113.1	488.8	123.2	283.7
(Bank Sector Loans)	304.0	257.0	263.0	27.0
ODA CONCESSIONALITY				
Total:Grant Element	75.0	81.0	82.0	81.0
Loans:Grant Element	55.0	53.0	59.0	55.0
OTHER SOURCES				
CMEA Countr.(Gross)	3.8	7.5	10.8	12.8
Intra LDCS Exc.OPEC	–	–	–	–
Other	–	–	–	–
ALL SOURCE COMMITMENTS				
TOTAL BILATERAL	338.8	294.6	965.8	325.1
of which				
OPEC (ODA)	99.9	79.4	746.9	64.9
CMEA (ODA)	–	310.0	–	–
TOTAL MULTILAT.(ODA)	10.6	12.3	84.6	102.8
TOTAL BIL.& MULTIL.	349.4	306.9	1050.4	427.9
of which				
ODA Grants	127.9	143.6	229.8	219.2
ODA Loans	218.6	154.5	812.9	180.7
ODA CONCESSIONALITY				
Total: Grant Element	70.0	71.0	60.0	82.0
Loans: Grant Element	52.0	45.0	48.0	51.0

INDEBTEDNESS

	1977	1978	1979	1980
TOTAL DEBT DISBURSED	**4154.4**	**5355.2**	**6620.8**	
Debt to DAC Countries	2919.0	3915.0	4864.0	
ODA	749.0	923.0	1009.0	
Total Export Credits	874.0	1016.0	1260.0	
Other Private Market	1296.0	1976.0	2595.0	
International Org.	409.9	516.0	646.1	
CMEA	23.6	19.9	15.6	
Other	802.0	904.3	1095.1	
TOTAL DEBT SERVICE	**314.8**	**641.8**	**937.3**	
Paid to DAC Countries	247.4	534.8	771.4	
ODA	32.4	28.3	47.5	
Total Export Credits	146.4	207.3	282.0	
Other Private Market	68.6	299.2	441.9	
International Org.	42.9	55.8	81.0	
CMEA	2.4	4.5	4.8	
Other	22.1	46.7	80.1	

ECONOMIC INDICATORS

	1977	1978	1979	1980
GNP Curr. Prices, $M	10863.4	13111.6	15477.4	17686.1
Real GNP, 1976=100	106.0	109.0	112.0	118.0
GNP/Cap Curr. Prices,$	593.0	693.0	792.0	876.0
GNP/cap Atlas Basis, $	672.7	721.5	780.7	864.1
Real GNP/Cap, 1976=100	102.0	102.0	102.0	104.0
Population, Million	18.3	18.9	19.5	20.2
Curr.A/C Deficit(-),$M	-1872.0	-1397.0	-1565.0	-1534.0
BOP Exp. & Transf.,$M	2415.0	2864.0	3603.0	4273.0
Exp. to OECD CIF, $M	1251.7	1435.2	1842.5	2147.1
of which				
Manufact.	220.4	287.9	372.3	399.2
Imp. from OECD FOB, $M	2557.1	2531.0	3158.0	2954.2
Reserves ex. Gold, $M	505.0	618.0	557.0	399.0

	TOTAL RECEIPTS NET 1977	1978	1979	1980	TOTAL ODA NET 1977	1978	1979	1980	TOTAL ODA GROSS 197
DAC COUNTRIES									
Australia	1.1	–	0.4	–	1.1	–	0.4	–	1.
Austria	-0.1	0.0	-0.1	0.0	–	0.0	0.0	0.0	
Belgium	2.2	-0.6	-0.6	0.1	0.4	0.2	0.3	0.8	0.
Canada	0.1	1.8	2.2	1.3	0.1	1.8	2.2	1.3	0.
Denmark	8.6	7.9	12.0	11.4	8.6	7.9	12.0	11.4	8.
Finland	2.8	2.0	5.0	5.1	2.8	2.0	2.9	3.2	2.
France	-2.3	1.8	-2.9	38.4	–	–	–	0.8	
Germany, Fed. Rep.	2.5	4.7	-4.4	9.7	0.3	0.4	1.5	2.3	0
Italy	1.2	2.5	2.7	115.2	1.4	2.1	2.2	3.2	1.
Japan	1.7	-0.3	8.1	19.0	2.1	–	–	5.1	2
Netherlands	3.4	6.6	10.0	18.3	3.4	6.6	10.0	18.3	3.
New Zealand	0.0	0.0	–	–	–	–	–	–	
Norway	6.1	8.4	8.6	10.0	6.2	8.4	9.0	10.5	6
Sweden	26.4	26.4	40.4	37.6	26.4	25.6	40.3	35.8	26.
Switzerland	-0.8	0.1	-0.3	2.3	0.3	0.2	1.1	2.3	0
United Kingdom	0.2	12.5	11.1	8.7	5.1	11.2	13.5	10.8	5.
United States	8.0	9.0	24.0	10.0	8.0	9.0	19.0	9.0	8.
TOTAL	*61.1*	*82.7*	*116.3*	*287.2*	*65.9*	*75.3*	*114.3*	*114.8*	*65*
MULTILATERAL									
AF.D.F.	–	1.0	0.4	1.9	–	1.0	0.4	1.9	
AF.D.B.	–	–	0.2	0.2	–	–	–	–	
AS.D.B.	–	–	–	–	–	–	–	–	
CAR.D.B.	–	–	–	–	–	–	–	–	
E.E.C.	1.3	6.5	5.2	7.0	1.3	6.5	5.2	7.0	1
IBRD	–	–	–	–	–	–	–	–	
IDA	–	–	–	–	–	–	–	–	
I.D.B.	–	–	–	–	–	–	–	–	
IFAD	–	–	–	–	–	–	–	–	
I.F.C.	–	–	–	–	–	–	–	–	
IMF TRUST FUND	–	–	–	–	–	–	–	–	
U.N. AGENCIES	–	–	–	–	–	–	–	–	
UNDP	2.1	2.7	4.0	4.9	2.1	2.7	4.0	4.9	2.
UNTA	0.8	0.6	0.2	0.3	0.8	0.6	0.2	0.3	0
UNICEF	1.2	1.7	2.2	1.6	1.2	1.7	2.2	1.6	1
UNRWA	–	–	–	–	–	–	–	–	
WFP	2.1	9.5	8.3	9.8	2.1	9.5	8.3	9.8	2
UNHCR	3.1	3.6	4.4	4.7	3.1	3.6	4.4	4.7	3
Other Multilateral	0.5	1.0	1.8	2.3	0.5	1.0	1.8	2.3	0
Arab OPEC Agencies	3.3	3.3	5.0	1.8	3.3	3.3	5.0	1.8	3
TOTAL	*14.3*	*29.8*	*31.6*	*34.3*	*14.3*	*29.8*	*31.4*	*34.1*	*14*
OPEC COUNTRIES	*0.1*	–	*10.0*	*10.3*	*0.1*	–	*10.0*	*10.3*	*0*
E.E.C.+ MEMBERS	*17.1*	*41.9*	*33.1*	*208.9*	*20.4*	*34.7*	*44.6*	*54.7*	*20*
TOTAL	***75.5***	***112.5***	***157.9***	***331.8***	***80.3***	***105.1***	***155.7***	***159.2***	***80***

	ODA LOANS GROSS 1977	1978	1979	1980	ODA LOANS NET 1977	1978	1979	1980	GRANTS 197
DAC COUNTRIES									
Australia	–	–	–	–	–	–	–	–	1
Austria	–	–	–	–	–	–	–	–	
Belgium	–	–	–	–	–	–	–	–	0
Canada	–	–	–	–	–	–	–	–	0
Denmark	–	–	2.4	3.0	–	–	2.4	3.0	8
Finland	–	–	–	–	–	–	–	–	2
France	–	–	–	–	–	–	–	–	
Germany, Fed. Rep.	–	–	–	–	–	–	–	–	0
Italy	–	–	–	–	–	–	–	–	1
Japan	–	–	–	4.4	–	–	–	4.4	2
Netherlands	0.6	0.4	6.4	10.7	0.6	0.4	6.4	10.7	2
New Zealand	–	–	–	–	–	–	–	–	
Norway	–	–	–	–	–	–	–	–	6
Sweden	–	–	–	–	–	–	–	–	26
Switzerland	–	–	–	–	–	–	–	–	0
United Kingdom	3.8	6.3	12.4	4.6	3.8	6.3	12.4	4.6	1
United States	–	–	5.0	9.0	–	–	5.0	9.0	8
TOTAL	*4.4*	*6.7*	*26.1*	*31.7*	*4.4*	*6.7*	*26.1*	*31.7*	*61*
MULTILATERAL	*3.3*	*4.2*	*5.4*	*3.6*	*3.3*	*4.2*	*5.4*	*3.6*	*11*
OPEC COUNTRIES	–	–	*10.0*	*10.3*	–	–	*10.0*	*10.3*	*0*
E.E.C.+ MEMBERS	*4.4*	*6.7*	*21.1*	*18.3*	*4.4*	*6.7*	*21.1*	*18.3*	*16*
TOTAL	***7.7***	***10.9***	***41.5***	***45.6***	***7.7***	***10.9***	***41.5***	***45.6***	***72***

	TOTAL OFFICIAL GROSS 1977	1978	1979	1980	TOTAL OFFICIAL NET 1977	1978	1979	1980	TOTAL OOF GROSS 197
DAC COUNTRIES									
Australia	1.1	–	0.4	–	1.1	–	0.4	–	
Austria	–	0.0	0.0	0.0	-0.1	0.0	-0.1	0.0	
Belgium	0.4	0.2	0.3	0.8	0.4	0.2	0.3	0.8	
Canada	0.1	1.8	2.2	1.3	0.1	1.8	2.2	1.3	
Denmark	8.6	7.9	12.0	11.4	8.6	7.9	12.0	11.4	
Finland	2.8	2.0	2.9	3.2	2.8	2.0	2.9	3.2	
France	–	–	–	0.8	–	–	–	0.8	
Germany, Fed. Rep.	0.3	39.4	55.6	45.8	-3.2	29.6	46.4	33.7	
Italy	1.4	2.1	2.2	3.2	1.4	2.1	2.2	3.2	
Japan	2.1	–	–	5.1	2.1	–	–	5.1	
Netherlands	3.4	6.6	10.0	18.3	3.4	6.6	10.0	18.3	
New Zealand	0.0	–	–	–	0.0	–	–	–	0
Norway	6.2	8.4	9.0	10.5	6.2	8.4	9.0	10.5	
Sweden	26.4	25.6	40.3	35.8	26.4	25.6	40.3	35.8	
Switzerland	0.3	0.2	1.1	2.3	0.3	0.2	1.1	2.3	
United Kingdom	5.1	11.2	13.5	10.8	5.1	11.2	13.5	10.8	
United States	8.0	9.0	24.0	10.0	8.0	9.0	24.0	10.0	
TOTAL	*66.0*	*114.4*	*173.5*	*159.3*	*62.4*	*104.5*	*164.1*	*147.1*	*0*
MULTILATERAL	*14.3*	*29.8*	*31.6*	*34.3*	*14.3*	*29.8*	*31.6*	*34.3*	
OPEC COUNTRIES	*0.1*	–	*10.0*	*10.3*	*0.1*	–	*10.0*	*10.3*	
E.E.C.+ MEMBERS	*20.4*	*73.8*	*98.7*	*98.1*	*16.9*	*64.0*	*89.4*	*86.0*	
TOTAL	***80.3***	***144.2***	***215.1***	***203.8***	***76.7***	***134.3***	***205.7***	***191.7***	***0***

ODA COMMITMENTS

1978	1979	1980	1977	1978	1979	1980
–	0.4	–	–	–	0.4	–
0.0	0.0	0.0	–	–	–	–
0.2	0.3	0.8	–	–	–	–
1.8	2.2	1.3	2.2	2.6	–	1.3
7.9	12.0	11.4	22.3	10.0	2.1	16.1
2.0	2.9	3.2	0.1	7.8	0.0	3.2
–	–	0.8	–	0.4	–	11.9
0.4	1.5	2.3	0.3	0.4	1.7	3.0
2.1	2.2	3.2	1.4	2.1	2.2	3.2
–	–	5.1	0.9	–	0.6	4.4
6.6	10.0	18.3	12.2	8.4	15.3	23.2
–	–	–	–	–	–	–
8.4	9.0	10.5	11.4	1.5	12.6	22.6
25.6	40.3	35.8	50.9	9.5	69.2	12.5
0.2	1.1	2.3	–	–	2.7	1.6
11.2	13.5	10.8	1.3	19.3	1.1	6.2
9.0	19.0	9.0	5.2	8.4	16.1	14.8
75.3	*114.3*	*114.8*	*108.0*	*70.4*	*123.8*	*123.9*
1.0	0.4	1.9	8.9	0.6	19.4	19.9
–	–	–	–	–	–	–
–	–	–	–	–	–	–
–	–	–	–	–	–	–
6.5	5.2	7.0	4.0	6.2	8.5	3.1
–	–	–	–	–	–	–
–	–	–	–	–	–	–
–	–	–	–	–	–	–
–	–	–	–	–	–	–
–	–	–	–	–	–	–
–	–	–	–	–	–	–
–	–	–	9.7	19.1	20.9	23.5
2.7	4.0	4.9	–	–	–	–
0.6	0.2	0.3	–	–	–	–
1.7	2.2	1.6	–	–	–	–
–	–	–	–	–	–	–
9.5	8.3	9.8	–	–	–	–
3.6	4.4	4.7	–	–	–	–
1.0	1.8	2.3	–	–	–	–
3.3	5.0	1.8	6.6	–	5.0	3.5
29.8	*31.4*	*34.1*	*29.2*	*25.9*	*53.8*	*50.0*
–	*10.0*	*10.3*	*0.1*	–	*11.4*	*10.3*
34.7	*44.6*	*54.7*	*41.5*	*46.7*	*30.8*	*66.6*
105.1	***155.7***	***159.2***	***137.3***	***96.3***	***189.0***	***184.2***

TECH. COOP. GRANTS

1978	1979	1980	1977	1978	1979	1980
–	0.4	–	–	–	–	–
0.0	0.0	0.0	–	0.0	0.0	0.0
0.2	0.3	0.8	0.1	0.0	0.1	0.2
1.8	2.2	1.3	–	–	–	–
7.9	9.6	8.4	1.8	7.0	4.9	6.0
2.0	2.9	3.2	0.0	1.9	2.9	3.2
–	–	0.8	–	–	–	0.5
0.4	1.5	2.3	0.0	0.2	1.5	2.1
2.1	2.2	3.2	1.4	2.1	2.2	3.2
–	–	0.7	–	–	–	0.0
6.2	3.7	7.6	0.2	1.1	1.2	1.7
–	–	–	–	–	–	–
8.4	9.0	10.5	–	0.1	0.8	1.4
25.6	40.3	35.8	1.0	3.8	6.2	4.0
0.2	1.1	2.3	–	–	–	0.3
4.9	1.1	6.2	0.1	0.1	0.9	1.6
9.0	14.0	–	–	1.0	–	–
68.6	*88.2*	*83.1*	*4.7*	*17.4*	*20.6*	*24.1*
25.6	*26.1*	*30.5*	*7.6*	*9.6*	*12.6*	*23.5*
–	–	–	–	–	–	–
28.0	*23.4*	*36.3*	*3.7*	*10.5*	*10.8*	*15.1*
94.1	***114.2***	***113.6***	***12.3***	***26.9***	***33.2***	***47.6***

TOTAL OOF NET

1978	1979	1980	1977	1978	1979	1980
–	–	–	–	–	–	–
–	–	–	-0.1	-0.1	-0.1	–
–	–	–	–	–	–	–
–	–	–	–	–	–	–
–	–	–	–	–	–	–
–	–	–	–	–	–	–
–	–	–	–	–	–	–
39.1	54.2	43.5	-3.5	29.3	44.9	31.3
–	–	–	–	–	–	–
–	–	–	–	–	–	–
–	–	–	–	–	–	–
–	–	–	0.0	–	–	–
–	–	–	–	–	–	–
–	–	–	–	–	–	–
–	–	–	–	–	–	–
–	–	–	–	–	–	–
–	5.0	1.0	–	–	5.0	1.0
39.1	*59.2*	*44.5*	*-3.6*	*29.2*	*49.8*	*32.3*
–	*0.2*	*0.2*	–	–	*0.2*	*0.2*
–	–	–	–	–	–	–
39.1	*54.2*	*43.5*	*-3.5*	*29.3*	*44.9*	*31.3*
39.1	***59.4***	***44.7***	***-3.6***	***29.2***	***50.0***	***32.6***

MAIN AID AGGREGATES

	1977	1978	1979	1980
DAC COUNTRIES COMBINED				
PRIVATE SECTOR NET	-1.2	-21.8	-47.8	140.1
Direct Investment	–	2.0	2.4	3.4
Portfolio Invest.	5.5	4.7	-6.0	14.7
Export Credits	-6.7	-28.5	-44.2	122.0
OFFICIAL & PRIVATE				
GROSS:				
Contractual Lending	14.5	53.4	103.5	234.6
Export Credits Tot.	10.1	36.9	68.0	202.9
Export Credits Priv	10.0	7.6	18.2	158.4
OTHER NET DATA				
Contractual Lending	-5.9	7.4	31.7	186.0
Export Credits Tot.	-10.3	0.7	5.5	154.3
(Bank Sector Loans)	7.0	16.0	-9.0	-5.0
ODA CONCESSIONALITY				
Total:Grant Element	98.0	94.0	97.0	90.0
Loans:Grant Element	83.0	79.0	77.0	69.0
OTHER SOURCES				
CMEA Countr.(Gross)	3.3	1.8	1.9	4.3
Intra LDCS Exc.OPEC	–	–	–	–
Other	–	–	–	–
ALL SOURCE COMMITMENTS				
TOTAL BILATERAL	108.1	113.0	135.1	172.5
of which				
OPEC (ODA)	0.1	–	11.4	10.3
CMEA (ODA)	2.2	–	0.4	2.8
TOTAL MULTILAT.(ODA)	29.2	25.9	53.8	50.0
TOTAL BIL.& MULTIL.	137.3	138.8	189.0	222.5
of which				
ODA Grants	110.9	75.8	141.1	111.3
ODA Loans	26.4	20.4	47.9	72.9
ODA CONCESSIONALITY				
Total: Grant Element	96.0	95.0	93.0	88.0
Loans: Grant Element	78.0	79.0	75.0	70.0

INDEBTEDNESS

	1977	1978	1979	1980
TOTAL DEBT DISBURSED	***87.0***	***155.0***	***268.0***	
Debt to DAC Countries	87.0	155.0	268.0	
ODA	4.0	12.0	40.0	
Total Export Credits	83.0	143.0	228.0	
Other Private Market	–	–	–	
International Org.	–	–	–	
CMEA	–	–	–	
Other	–	–	–	
TOTAL DEBT SERVICE	***16.6***	***12.5***	***20.2***	
Paid to DAC Countries	16.6	12.5	20.2	
ODA	–	–	–	
Total Export Credits	16.6	12.5	20.2	
Other Private Market	–	–	–	
International Org.	–	–	–	
CMEA	–	–	–	
Other	–	–	–	

ECONOMIC INDICATORS

	1977	1978	1979	1980
GNP Curr. Prices, $M	2433.6	2380.3	2422.1	2804.6
Real GNP, 1976=100	100.0	101.0	103.0	104.0
GNP/Cap Curr. Prices,$	251.0	239.0	237.0	267.0
GNP/cap Atlas Basis, $	220.9	232.9	249.6	268.0
Real GNP/Cap, 1976=100	98.0	96.0	95.0	93.0
Population, Million	9.7	9.9	10.2	10.5
Curr.A/C Deficit(-),$M	–	–	–	–
BOP Exp. & Transf.,$M	–	–	–	–
Exp. to OECD CIF, $M	278.9	198.4	232.8	262.5
of which				
Manufact.	2.2	4.0	5.2	3.4
Imp. from OECD FOB, $M	235.6	273.9	211.3	377.8
Reserves ex. Gold, $M	–	–	–	–

TOTAL RECEIPTS NET / TOTAL ODA NET

	TOTAL RECEIPTS NET 1977	1978	1979	1980	TOTAL ODA NET 1977	1978	1979	1980
DAC COUNTRIES								
Australia	0.8	0.8	0.9	1.4	0.8	0.8	0.9	1.4
Austria	0.1	0.1	0.1	0.1	0.1	0.1	0.1	0.1
Belgium	0.1	0.0	0.1	0.1	0.1	0.0	0.1	0.1
Canada	2.0	2.4	5.2	4.3	2.0	2.4	5.2	4.3
Denmark	1.3	0.3	0.3	0.7	1.3	0.3	0.3	0.7
Finland	–	0.0	0.0	0.1	–	0.0	0.0	0.1
France	0.1	–	–	0.3	–	–	–	0.3
Germany, Fed. Rep.	5.0	8.1	17.5	18.5	4.9	8.1	17.1	18.8
Italy	–	–	0.0	–	–	–	0.0	–
Japan	4.7	10.1	22.9	23.3	4.7	9.5	19.7	24.3
Netherlands	1.9	0.8	4.3	1.5	1.9	0.8	4.3	1.5
New Zealand	0.3	0.5	0.4	0.6	0.4	0.5	0.4	0.6
Norway	0.4	0.6	0.4	0.3	0.4	0.6	0.4	0.3
Sweden	–	–	0.1	–	–	–	0.1	–
Switzerland	3.7	4.3	5.5	8.1	3.7	4.3	5.5	8.1
United Kingdom	7.3	8.3	23.7	15.7	7.3	8.3	23.5	15.6
United States	10.0	4.0	5.0	8.0	10.0	4.0	5.0	8.0
TOTAL	*37.6*	*40.2*	*86.1*	*82.7*	*37.5*	*39.6*	*82.4*	*84.0*
MULTILATERAL								
AF.D.F.	–	–	–	–	–	–	–	–
AF.D.B.	–	–	–	–	–	–	–	–
AS.D.B.	6.2	5.3	6.6	9.0	6.4	5.5	6.8	9.2
CAR.D.B.	–	–	–	–	–	–	–	–
E.E.C.	0.1	0.4	0.0	–	0.1	0.4	0.0	–
IBRD	–	–	–	–	–	–	–	–
IDA	12.2	11.0	18.6	25.0	12.2	11.0	18.6	25.0
I.D.B.	–	–	–	–	–	–	–	–
IFAD	–	–	–	0.0	–	–	–	0.0
I.F.C.	2.3	0.7	–	-0.1	–	–	–	–
IMF TRUST FUND	1.8	5.4	5.4	4.7	1.8	5.4	5.4	4.7
U.N. AGENCIES	–	–	–	–	–	–	–	–
UNDP	5.8	6.1	8.1	8.3	5.8	6.1	8.1	8.3
UNTA	1.2	1.4	1.3	0.2	1.2	1.4	1.3	0.2
UNICEF	1.4	2.0	3.1	3.6	1.4	2.0	3.1	3.6
UNRWA	–	–	–	–	–	–	–	–
WFP	2.3	2.6	4.5	14.9	2.3	2.6	4.5	14.9
UNHCR	–	–	–	–	–	–	–	–
Other Multilateral	2.8	1.0	3.1	6.3	2.8	1.0	3.1	6.3
Arab OPEC Agencies	4.2	–	–	–	4.2	–	–	–
TOTAL	*40.1*	*36.0*	*50.7*	*71.9*	*38.0*	*35.5*	*50.9*	*72.3*
OPEC COUNTRIES	*4.6*	*1.6*	*3.5*	*6.8*	*4.6*	*1.6*	*3.5*	*6.8*
E.E.C.+ MEMBERS	*15.7*	*17.9*	*45.7*	*36.7*	*15.5*	*17.9*	*45.1*	*37.0*
TOTAL	***82.3***	***77.8***	***140.4***	***161.4***	***80.0***	***76.8***	***136.8***	***163.1***

TOTAL ODA GROSS

	197
Australia	0
Austria	0
Belgium	0
Canada	2
Denmark	1
Finland	
France	
Germany, Fed. Rep.	5
Italy	
Japan	4
Netherlands	1
New Zealand	0
Norway	0
Sweden	
Switzerland	5
United Kingdom	7
United States	10
TOTAL	*40*
AF.D.F.	
AF.D.B.	
AS.D.B.	7
CAR.D.B.	
E.E.C.	0
IBRD	
IDA	12
I.D.B.	
IFAD	
I.F.C.	
IMF TRUST FUND	1
U.N. AGENCIES	
UNDP	[illegible]
UNTA	1
UNICEF	1
UNRWA	
WFP	2
UNHCR	
Other Multilateral	[illegible]
Arab OPEC Agencies	4
TOTAL	*3*
OPEC COUNTRIES	*4*
E.E.C.+ MEMBERS	*15*
TOTAL	***8***

ODA LOANS GROSS / ODA LOANS NET

	ODA LOANS GROSS 1977	1978	1979	1980	ODA LOANS NET 1977	1978	1979	1980
DAC COUNTRIES								
Australia	–	–	–	–	–	–	–	–
Austria	–	–	–	–	–	–	–	–
Belgium	–	–	–	–	–	–	–	–
Canada	–	–	–	–	–	-2.2	–	–
Denmark	1.3	0.2	–	0.5	1.3	0.2	–	-3.0
Finland	–	–	–	–	–	–	–	–
France	–	–	–	–	–	–	–	–
Germany, Fed. Rep.	0.1	0.8	7.5	0.1	–	0.7	7.5	-12.0
Italy	–	–	–	–	–	–	–	–
Japan	–	0.7	5.6	4.2	-0.1	0.5	5.4	4.0
Netherlands	–	–	–	–	–	–	–	–
New Zealand	–	–	–	–	–	–	–	–
Norway	–	–	–	–	–	–	–	–
Sweden	–	–	–	–	–	–	–	–
Switzerland	–	–	–	–	-2.1	–	–	–
United Kingdom	-0.1	–	–	–	-0.3	-0.1	–	-0.3
United States	–	–	–	–	–	–	–	–
TOTAL	*1.3*	*1.7*	*13.1*	*4.8*	*-1.2*	*-0.9*	*12.9*	*-11.3*
MULTILATERAL	*23.9*	*23.1*	*32.2*	*39.9*	*23.3*	*21.9*	*30.8*	*38.3*
OPEC COUNTRIES	*4.5*	*1.6*	*3.5*	*6.8*	*4.5*	*1.6*	*3.5*	*6.8*
E.E.C.+ MEMBERS	*1.3*	*1.0*	*7.5*	*0.6*	*1.0*	*0.8*	*7.5*	*-15.3*
TOTAL	***29.7***	***26.4***	***48.8***	***51.5***	***26.6***	***22.7***	***47.3***	***33.8***

GRANTS

	197
Australia	[illegible]
Austria	[illegible]
Belgium	[illegible]
Canada	[illegible]
Denmark	[illegible]
Finland	
France	
Germany, Fed. Rep.	[illegible]
Italy	
Japan	[illegible]
Netherlands	
New Zealand	[illegible]
Norway	[illegible]
Sweden	
Switzerland	[illegible]
United Kingdom	
United States	1
TOTAL	*3*
MULTILATERAL	*1*
OPEC COUNTRIES	[illegible]
E.E.C.+ MEMBERS	*1*
TOTAL	***5***

TOTAL OFFICIAL GROSS / TOTAL OFFICIAL NET

	TOTAL OFFICIAL GROSS 1977	1978	1979	1980	TOTAL OFFICIAL NET 1977	1978	1979	1980
DAC COUNTRIES								
Australia	0.8	0.8	0.9	1.4	0.8	0.8	0.9	1.4
Austria	0.1	0.1	0.1	0.1	0.1	0.1	0.1	0.1
Belgium	0.1	0.0	0.1	0.1	0.1	0.0	0.1	0.1
Canada	2.0	4.6	5.2	4.3	2.0	2.4	5.2	4.3
Denmark	1.3	0.3	0.3	4.2	1.3	0.3	0.3	0.7
Finland	–	0.0	0.0	0.1	–	0.0	0.0	0.1
France	–	–	–	0.3	–	–	–	0.3
Germany, Fed. Rep.	5.0	8.2	17.1	30.9	4.9	8.1	17.1	18.8
Italy	–	–	0.0	–	–	–	0.0	–
Japan	4.8	9.7	19.8	24.4	4.7	9.5	19.7	24.3
Netherlands	1.9	0.8	4.3	1.5	1.9	0.8	4.3	1.5
New Zealand	0.4	0.5	0.4	0.6	0.3	0.5	0.4	0.6
Norway	0.4	0.6	0.4	0.3	0.4	0.6	0.4	0.3
Sweden	–	–	0.1	–	–	–	0.1	–
Switzerland	5.7	4.3	5.5	8.1	3.7	4.3	5.5	8.1
United Kingdom	7.5	8.5	23.5	15.9	7.3	8.3	23.5	15.6
United States	10.0	4.0	5.0	8.0	10.0	4.0	5.0	8.0
TOTAL	*40.0*	*42.2*	*82.5*	*100.1*	*37.4*	*39.6*	*82.4*	*84.0*
MULTILATERAL	*40.9*	*37.4*	*52.3*	*73.8*	*40.1*	*36.0*	*50.7*	*71.9*
OPEC COUNTRIES	*4.6*	*1.6*	*3.5*	*6.8*	*4.6*	*1.6*	*3.5*	*6.8*
E.E.C.+ MEMBERS	*15.8*	*18.1*	*45.1*	*52.9*	*15.5*	*17.9*	*45.1*	*37.0*
TOTAL	***85.5***	***81.2***	***138.4***	***180.8***	***82.1***	***77.3***	***136.6***	***162.7***

TOTAL OOF GROSS

	197
Australia	
Austria	
Belgium	
Canada	
Denmark	
Finland	
France	
Germany, Fed. Rep.	
Italy	
Japan	
Netherlands	
New Zealand	
Norway	
Sweden	
Switzerland	
United Kingdom	
United States	
TOTAL	
MULTILATERAL	
OPEC COUNTRIES	
E.E.C.+ MEMBERS	
TOTAL	

1978	1979	1980
0.8	0.9	1.4
0.1	0.1	0.1
0.0	0.1	0.1
4.6	5.2	4.3
0.3	0.3	4.2
0.0	0.0	0.1
–	–	0.3
8.2	17.1	30.9
–	0.0	–
9.7	19.8	24.4
0.8	4.3	1.5
0.5	0.4	0.6
0.6	0.4	0.3
–	0.1	–
4.3	5.5	8.1
8.5	23.5	15.9
4.0	5.0	8.0
42.2	*82.5*	*100.1*
–	–	–
–	–	–
6.7	8.1	10.8
–	–	–
0.4	0.0	–
–	–	–
11.0	18.6	25.0
–	–	–
–	–	0.0
–	–	–
5.4	5.4	4.7
–	–	–
6.1	8.1	8.3
1.4	1.3	0.2
2.0	3.1	3.6
–	–	–
2.6	4.5	14.9
–	–	–
1.0	3.1	6.3
–	–	–
36.7	*52.2*	*73.8*
1.6	*3.5*	*6.8*
18.1	*45.1*	*52.9*
80.5	***138.3***	***180.8***

ODA COMMITMENTS

1977	1978	1979	1980
0.7	3.1	1.0	1.4
–	0.7	–	–
–	–	–	–
14.9	7.4	0.9	13.8
0.0	0.5	0.5	0.2
–	0.0	0.0	0.0
–	–	–	0.3
7.4	12.2	16.1	27.1
–	–	0.0	–
4.3	22.6	19.6	29.6
1.6	1.3	3.9	1.5
0.2	0.8	0.3	0.4
–	–	0.2	1.9
–	–	–	–
10.7	2.5	7.1	5.2
8.5	3.2	66.7	6.5
10.3	10.7	13.5	25.0
58.6	*65.0*	*129.8*	*112.9*
–	–	–	–
–	–	–	–
23.5	25.4	31.4	38.5
–	–	–	–
0.1	4.0	0.0	5.3
–	–	–	–
33.0	63.9	25.8	66.1
–	–	–	–
–	13.0	–	12.5
–	–	–	–
–	–	–	–
13.5	13.2	20.1	33.3
–	–	–	–
–	–	–	–
–	–	–	–
–	–	–	–
–	–	–	–
–	–	–	–
–	–	–	–
4.2	3.0	5.0	1.3
74.2	*122.4*	*82.3*	*157.0*
–	–	*7.2*	–
17.6	*21.2*	*87.2*	*41.0*
132.8	***187.5***	***219.3***	***269.9***

1978	1979	1980
0.8	0.9	1.4
0.1	0.1	0.1
0.0	0.1	0.1
4.6	5.2	4.3
0.1	0.3	3.7
0.0	0.0	0.1
–	–	0.3
7.4	9.6	30.8
–	0.0	–
9.0	14.3	20.2
0.8	4.3	1.5
0.5	0.4	0.6
0.6	0.4	0.3
–	0.1	–
4.3	5.5	8.1
8.5	23.5	15.9
4.0	5.0	8.0
40.5	*69.4*	*95.3*
13.6	*20.1*	*33.9*
–	–	–
17.1	*37.6*	*52.3*
54.1	***89.5***	***129.3***

TECH. COOP. GRANTS

1977	1978	1979	1980
0.7	0.7	0.6	0.6
0.1	0.1	0.1	0.1
0.1	0.0	0.1	0.1
0.1	0.2	0.1	0.5
0.1	0.1	0.3	0.2
–	0.0	0.0	0.0
–	–	–	0.2
4.9	7.4	9.6	11.1
–	–	0.0	–
2.7	4.3	3.3	3.6
0.6	0.5	0.5	0.5
0.2	0.2	0.2	0.2
0.1	0.1	0.1	0.1
–	–	–	–
0.2	0.2	0.3	3.0
2.2	2.4	4.4	5.0
3.0	4.0	3.0	7.0
14.8	*20.1*	*22.5*	*32.1*
12.4	*10.6*	*15.6*	*33.3*
–	–	–	–
7.7	*10.3*	*14.8*	*17.0*
27.1	***30.6***	***38.1***	***65.4***

1978	1979	1980
–	–	–
–	–	–
–	–	–
–	–	–
–	–	–
–	–	–
–	–	–
–	–	–
–	–	–
–	–	–
–	–	–
–	–	–
–	–	–
–	–	–
–	–	–
–	–	–
–	–	–
–	–	–
0.7	*0.1*	–
–	–	–
–	–	–
0.7	***0.1***	–

TOTAL OOF NET

1977	1978	1979	1980
–	–	–	–
–	–	–	–
–	–	–	–
–	–	–	–
–	–	–	–
–	–	–	–
–	–	–	–
–	–	–	–
–	–	–	–
–	–	–	–
–	–	–	–
-0.1	–	–	–
–	–	–	–
–	–	–	–
–	–	–	–
–	–	–	–
–	–	–	–
-0.1	–	–	–
2.1	*0.5*	*-0.2*	*-0.3*
–	–	–	–
–	–	–	–
2.1	***0.5***	***-0.2***	***-0.3***

MAIN AID AGGREGATES

	1977	1978	1979	1980
DAC COUNTRIES COMBINED				
PRIVATE SECTOR NET	0.2	0.6	3.8	-1.3
Direct Investment	–	0.4	0.3	0.3
Portfolio Invest.	0.1	–	0.3	-0.3
Export Credits	0.1	0.1	3.1	-1.3
OFFICIAL & PRIVATE				
GROSS:				
Contractual Lending	1.7	1.9	17.4	12.7
Export Credits Tot.	0.4	0.2	4.3	7.9
Export Credits Priv	0.4	0.2	4.3	7.9
OTHER NET DATA				
Contractual Lending	-1.1	-0.7	16.1	-12.6
Export Credits Tot.	0.1	0.1	3.1	-1.3
(Bank Sector Loans)	–	–	–	–
ODA CONCESSIONALITY				
Total:Grant Element	100.0	95.0	100.0	100.0
Loans:Grant Element	–	71.0	–	–
OTHER SOURCES				
CMEA Countr.(Gross)	0.8	–	0.1	0.1
Intra LDCS Exc.OPEC	–	–	–	–
Other	–	–	–	–
ALL SOURCE COMMITMENTS				
TOTAL BILATERAL	58.6	65.0	137.0	112.9
of which				
OPEC (ODA)	–	–	7.2	–
CMEA (ODA)	0.8	4.2	–	–
TOTAL MULTILAT.(ODA)	74.2	122.4	82.3	157.0
TOTAL BIL.& MULTIL.	132.8	187.5	219.3	269.9
of which				
ODA Grants	72.2	72.8	150.3	151.5
ODA Loans	60.7	114.6	68.9	118.4
ODA CONCESSIONALITY				
Total: Grant Element	90.0	88.0	91.0	92.0
Loans: Grant Element	79.0	80.0	75.0	80.0

INDEBTEDNESS

	1977	1978	1979	1980
TOTAL DEBT DISBURSED	***71.3***	***98.2***	***141.4***	
Debt to DAC Countries	15.0	24.0	39.0	
ODA	14.0	16.0	29.0	
Total Export Credits	1.0	8.0	10.0	
Other Private Market	–	–	–	
International Org.	50.9	67.3	92.4	
CMEA	–	–	–	
Other	5.4	6.9	10.0	
TOTAL DEBT SERVICE	***2.4***	***3.0***	***5.3***	
Paid to DAC Countries	0.9	0.5	2.3	
ODA	0.6	0.5	0.3	
Total Export Credits	0.3	–	2.0	
Other Private Market	–	–	–	
International Org.	1.4	2.3	2.8	
CMEA	–	–	–	
Other	0.1	0.2	0.2	

ECONOMIC INDICATORS

	1977	1978	1979	1980
GNP Curr. Prices, $M	1407.9	1612.7	1795.2	2029.9
Real GNP, 1976=100	103.0	104.0	108.0	107.0
GNP/Cap Curr. Prices,$	105.0	118.0	128.0	142.0
GNP/cap Atlas Basis, $	112.3	119.0	131.4	138.4
Real GNP/Cap, 1976=100	100.0	99.0	101.0	97.0
Population, Million	13.3	13.6	14.0	14.3
Curr.A/C Deficit(-),$M	–	–	–	–
BOP Exp. & Transf.,$M	–	–	–	–
Exp. to OECD CIF, $M	20.0	24.1	33.9	34.4
of which				
Manufact.	8.6	11.3	22.4	27.1
Imp. from OECD FOB, $M	38.0	56.0	49.9	76.1
Reserves ex. Gold, $M	142.2	147.4	164.0	189.1

1978	1979	1980
0.1	–	0.3
0.0	0.9	0.1
–	0.1	0.6
–	–	0.5
1.2	6.3	5.8
0.2	1.1	1.1
0.3	0.1	2.3
0.4	6.4	12.1
–	–	–
–	0.9	0.5
–	8.1	7.7
0.1	2.3	0.5
0.3	0.5	0.3
4.0	19.0	5.0
6.6	*46.9*	*37.6*
1.9	*15.8*	*29.4*
–	*1.0*	–
2.5	*21.9*	*34.7*
8.5	***63.7***	***67.0***

1977	1978	1979	1980
–	–	–	–
–	–	–	0.1
–	–	–	0.3
–	–	–	0.4
0.9	1.2	5.1	3.8
0.1	0.2	0.1	0.6
0.2	0.3	0.1	0.1
0.0	0.3	0.2	1.8
–	–	–	–
–	–	0.0	0.0
–	–	–	–
0.0	–	–	0.1
0.7	0.3	0.3	0.1
2.0	3.0	2.0	2.0
3.8	*5.3*	*7.8*	*9.8*
1.6	*1.6*	*9.9*	*14.0*
–	–	–	–
1.6	*2.0*	*5.7*	*6.8*
5.4	***6.8***	***17.7***	***23.8***

1978	1979	1980
–	–	–
–	–	–
–	–	–
–	–	–
–	–	–
–	–	–
–	–	–
–	–	5.0
–	–	–
–	–	–
–	–	–
–	–	–
–	–	–
–	–	–
–	–	–
–	–	–
3.0	–	2.0
3.0	–	*7.0*
7.3	*7.9*	*12.1*
9.4	–	–
–	–	*5.0*
19.7	***7.9***	***19.1***

TOTAL OOF NET

1977	1978	1979	1980
–	–	–	–
–	–	–	–
–	–	–	–
–	–	–	–
–	–	–	–
–	–	–	–
–	–	–	–
–	–	–	5.0
–	–	–	–
–	–	–	–
–	–	–	–
–	–	–	–
–	–	–	–
–	–	–	–
–	–	–	–
–	–	–	–
6.0	2.0	-1.0	2.0
6.0	*2.0*	*-1.0*	*7.0*
13.4	*3.8*	*2.0*	*7.1*
11.9	*9.4*	–	–
–	–	–	*5.0*
31.2	***15.1***	***1.0***	***14.1***

	1977	1978	1979	1980
ODA	[illegible]	[illegible]	[illegible]	
Total Export Credits	36.0	64.0	40.0	
Other Private Market	410.0	414.0	385.0	
International Org.	215.3	243.9	317.1	
CMEA	–	–	–	
Other	90.5	133.9	154.3	
TOTAL DEBT SERVICE	***107.2***	***107.9***	***66.5***	
Paid to DAC Countries	81.4	79.6	37.9	
ODA	4.1	4.4	3.6	
Total Export Credits	20.6	26.9	12.5	
Other Private Market	56.7	48.3	21.8	
International Org.	19.0	19.2	21.9	
CMEA	–	–	–	
Other	6.7	9.1	6.6	

ECONOMIC INDICATORS

	1977	1978	1979	1980
GNP Curr. Prices, $M	2028.1	1936.0	1476.3	2079.4
Real GNP, 1976=100	99.0	93.0	68.0	77.0
GNP/Cap Curr. Prices,$	839.0	774.0	571.0	778.0
GNP/cap Atlas Basis, $	809.9	784.0	607.4	722.4
Real GNP/Cap, 1976=100	96.0	87.0	62.0	67.0
Population, Million	2.4	2.5	2.6	2.7
Curr.A/C Deficit(-),$M	-191.9	-34.4	89.7	–
BOP Exp. & Transf.,$M	734.0	732.0	684.4	–
Exp. to OECD CIF, $M	506.2	480.0	490.4	415.5
of which				
Manufact.	19.4	21.5	14.8	20.4
Imp. from OECD FOB, $M	438.9	324.1	148.7	346.5
Reserves ex. Gold, $M	148.3	50.8	–	–

NICARAGUA

	1977	1978	1979	1980	1977	1978	1979	1980	197
TOTAL RECEIPTS NET					**TOTAL ODA NET**				**TOTAL ODA GROSS**
DAC COUNTRIES									
Australia	–	–	–	–	–	–	–	–	
Austria	–	0.0	0.2	0.7	–	0.0	0.2	0.7	
Belgium	–	1.9	-0.5	0.2	–	–	0.9	0.3	
Canada	0.6	0.1	–	0.3	0.6	0.1	–	0.3	0.
Denmark	0.0	0.0	0.9	0.1	–	0.0	0.9	0.1	
Finland	–	–	0.2	0.5	–	–	0.1	0.6	
France	-2.4	0.6	0.8	1.9	–	–	–	0.5	
Germany, Fed. Rep.	7.5	0.6	22.1	7.9	3.1	1.0	17.8	8.3	3.
Italy	0.0	0.2	1.4	1.1	0.1	0.2	1.1	1.1	0.
Japan	0.5	-0.2	6.4	11.9	0.2	0.3	5.5	2.3	0.
Netherlands	0.0	0.4	6.4	14.6	0.0	0.4	6.4	14.6	0.
New Zealand	–	–	–	–	–	–	–	–	
Norway	1.3	–	0.9	0.5	–	–	0.9	0.5	
Sweden	–	–	8.1	7.7	–	–	8.1	7.7	
Switzerland	0.3	-0.4	2.1	0.5	0.1	0.1	2.3	0.5	0
United Kingdom	-2.9	0.5	-0.5	-1.9	0.7	0.4	0.5	0.3	0
United States	20.0	26.0	28.0	83.0	14.0	24.0	29.0	79.0	15
TOTAL	*24.9*	*29.6*	*76.4*	*129.0*	*18.7*	*26.5*	*73.8*	*116.6*	*20*
MULTILATERAL									
AF.D.F.	–	–	–	–	–	–	–	–	
AF.D.B.	–	–	–	–	–	–	–	–	
AS.D.B.	–	–	–	–	–	–	–	–	
CAR.D.B.	–	–	–	–	–	–	–	–	
E.E.C.	0.0	0.4	5.8	14.6	0.0	0.4	5.8	14.6	0
IBRD	11.4	5.1	4.4	7.9	–	–	–	–	
IDA	3.1	0.8	0.1	18.6	3.1	0.8	0.1	18.6	3
I.D.B.	14.6	11.3	29.3	34.2	12.7	12.5	30.7	35.0	14
IFAD	–	–	–	11.8	–	–	–	11.8	
I.F.C.	0.1	-0.1	-1.0	–	–	–	–	–	
IMF TRUST FUND	–	–	–	–	–	–	–	–	
U.N. AGENCIES	–	–	–	–	–	–	–	–	
UNDP	0.8	0.7	0.6	2.1	0.8	0.7	0.6	2.1	0
UNTA	0.5	0.4	0.8	0.1	0.5	0.4	0.8	0.1	0
UNICEF	0.1	0.2	0.3	0.9	0.1	0.2	0.3	0.9	0
UNRWA	–	–	–	–	–	–	–	–	
WFP	0.4	–	0.2	5.5	0.4	–	0.2	5.5	0
UNHCR	–	–	1.3	3.0	–	–	1.3	3.0	
Other Multilateral	0.2	0.3	0.6	2.5	0.2	0.3	0.6	2.5	0
Arab OPEC Agencies	–	–	–	10.0	–	–	–	10.0	
TOTAL	*31.2*	*18.9*	*42.3*	*111.1*	*17.8*	*15.2*	*40.3*	*104.0*	*19*
OPEC COUNTRIES	*11.9*	*9.4*	*1.0*	–	–	–	*1.0*	–	
E.E.C.+ MEMBERS	*2.2*	*4.5*	*36.3*	*38.5*	*4.0*	*2.3*	*33.5*	*39.7*	*4*
TOTAL	**67.9**	**57.9**	**119.7**	**240.1**	**36.5**	**41.6**	**115.1**	**220.6**	**40**

NIGER

	1977	1978	1979	1980	1977	1978	1979	1980	197
TOTAL RECEIPTS NET					**TOTAL ODA NET**				**TOTAL ODA GROSS**
DAC COUNTRIES									
Australia	–	–	–	–	–	–	–	–	
Austria	0.1	0.1	0.0	0.0	0.1	0.1	0.0	0.0	0.
Belgium	2.2	3.8	6.7	10.2	2.2	3.8	6.6	10.1	2.
Canada	2.8	3.2	2.5	3.7	2.8	3.2	2.5	3.7	2.
Denmark	0.6	1.5	0.3	0.2	0.6	1.5	0.3	0.2	0
Finland	–	–	–	–	–	–	–	–	
France	53.2	66.0	93.2	124.3	22.2	29.2	41.1	48.5	24
Germany, Fed. Rep.	11.4	16.3	33.4	19.4	11.9	16.2	30.3	21.5	12
Italy	-0.1	1.5	4.1	-0.9	0.1	0.0	0.1	0.2	0
Japan	14.0	27.3	20.9	1.1	10.4	9.8	16.5	6.3	10
Netherlands	1.1	2.6	4.0	3.3	1.1	2.6	4.0	3.3	1
New Zealand	–	–	–	–	–	–	–	–	
Norway	0.2	1.1	1.0	0.4	0.2	1.1	1.0	0.4	0
Sweden	–	–	4.5	0.1	–	–	0.1	–	
Switzerland	0.5	1.4	1.2	1.5	0.5	1.4	1.2	1.5	0
United Kingdom	0.4	-0.1	2.0	0.1	0.4	-0.1	2.0	0.1	0
United States	7.0	9.0	16.0	9.0	7.0	9.0	11.0	9.0	7
TOTAL	*93.2*	*133.5*	*189.8*	*172.5*	*59.4*	*77.7*	*116.7*	*105.0*	*61*
MULTILATERAL									
AF.D.F.	1.2	0.8	0.1	4.1	1.2	0.8	0.1	4.1	1
AF.D.B.	-0.1	0.9	6.3	4.6	–	–	–	–	
AS.D.B.	–	–	–	–	–	–	–	–	
CAR.D.B.	–	–	–	–	–	–	–	–	
E.E.C.	17.9	32.7	30.2	11.5	17.9	32.7	29.1	9.3	17
IBRD	–	–	–	–	–	–	–	–	
IDA	6.3	8.5	11.6	18.1	6.3	8.5	11.6	18.1	6
I.D.B.	–	–	–	–	–	–	–	–	
IFAD	–	–	–	–	–	–	–	–	
I.F.C.	–	–	–	–	–	–	–	–	
IMF TRUST FUND	–	6.8	–	9.5	–	6.8	–	9.5	
U.N. AGENCIES	–	–	–	–	–	–	–	–	
UNDP	2.4	3.0	4.0	5.2	2.4	3.0	4.0	5.2	2
UNTA	0.4	0.4	0.7	0.2	0.4	0.4	0.7	0.2	0
UNICEF	0.2	0.7	1.2	0.8	0.2	0.7	1.2	0.8	0
UNRWA	–	–	–	–	–	–	–	–	
WFP	0.9	3.1	2.4	4.6	0.9	3.1	2.4	4.6	0
UNHCR	–	0.0	0.0	0.0	–	0.0	0.0	0.0	
Other Multilateral	2.4	1.3	1.8	5.0	2.4	1.3	1.8	5.0	2
Arab OPEC Agencies	2.9	10.3	16.0	18.1	2.9	5.5	5.9	7.0	2
TOTAL	*34.3*	*68.4*	*74.3*	*81.5*	*34.5*	*62.7*	*56.8*	*63.6*	*34*
OPEC COUNTRIES	*2.9*	*17.3*	*0.1*	*1.7*	*2.9*	*16.2*	*0.1*	*1.7*	*2*
E.E.C.+ MEMBERS	*86.6*	*124.2*	*173.8*	*168.1*	*56.3*	*85.9*	*113.5*	*93.2*	*58*
TOTAL	**130.5**	**219.1**	**264.1**	**255.7**	**96.7**	**156.5**	**173.5**	**170.2**	**99**

	1977	1978	1979	1980	1977	1978	1979	1980	197
ODA LOANS GROSS					**ODA LOANS NET**				**GRANTS**
DAC COUNTRIES									
Australia	–	–	–	–	–	–	–	–	
Austria	–	–	–	–	–	–	–	–	0
Belgium	–	–	–	1.7	–	–	–	1.7	2
Canada	-0.4	–	–	–	-0.4	-35.2	–	–	3
Denmark	0.5	1.2	0.0	–	0.5	1.2	0.0	–	0
Finland	–	–	–	–	–	–	–	–	
France	5.5	11.5	12.1	13.3	3.2	8.4	9.7	11.0	19
Germany, Fed. Rep.	6.2	5.4	4.9	–	5.9	5.0	-32.1	–	6
Italy	–	–	–	–	–	–	–	–	0
Japan	8.8	6.4	13.1	5.4	8.8	6.4	13.1	5.4	
Netherlands	–	–	–	–	–	–	–	–	
New Zealand	–	–	–	–	–	–	–	–	
Norway	–	–	–	–	–	–	–	–	0
Sweden	–	–	–	–	–	–	–	–	
Switzerland	–	–	–	–	–	–	–	–	0
United Kingdom	–	–	–	–	–	–	–	–	0
United States	–	–	–	–	–	–	–	–	
TOTAL	*20.5*	*24.5*	*30.1*	*20.4*	*18.0*	*-14.1*	*-9.2*	*18.1*	*4*
MULTILATERAL	*10.4*	*21.2*	*18.9*	*38.8*	*10.4*	*21.1*	*18.8*	*38.7*	*2*
OPEC COUNTRIES	*2.9*	*0.3*	*0.1*	–	*2.9*	*0.3*	*0.1*	–	
E.E.C.+ MEMBERS	*12.2*	*18.1*	*18.2*	*15.0*	*9.7*	*14.7*	*-21.2*	*12.7*	*4*
TOTAL	**33.8**	**46.0**	**49.1**	**59.2**	**31.3**	**7.2**	**9.7**	**56.8**	**6**

	1977	1978	1979	1980	1977	1978	1979	1980	197
TOTAL OFFICIAL GROSS					**TOTAL OFFICIAL NET**				**TOTAL OOF GROSS**
DAC COUNTRIES									
Australia	–	–	–	–	–	–	–	–	
Austria	0.1	0.1	0.0	0.0	0.1	0.1	0.0	0.0	
Belgium	2.2	3.8	6.6	10.1	2.2	3.8	6.6	10.1	
Canada	2.8	38.4	2.5	3.7	2.8	3.2	2.5	3.7	
Denmark	0.6	1.5	0.3	0.2	0.6	1.5	0.3	0.2	
Finland	–	–	–	–	–	–	–	–	
France	32.6	42.0	45.5	63.8	30.1	38.8	40.4	55.4	
Germany, Fed. Rep.	12.1	16.6	67.3	21.5	11.5	16.0	29.2	20.7	
Italy	0.1	0.0	0.1	0.2	0.1	0.0	0.1	0.2	
Japan	10.4	9.8	16.5	6.3	10.4	9.8	16.5	6.3	
Netherlands	1.1	2.6	4.0	3.3	1.1	2.6	4.0	3.3	
New Zealand	–	–	–	–	–	–	–	–	
Norway	0.2	1.1	1.0	0.4	0.2	1.1	1.0	0.4	
Sweden	–	–	0.1	–	–	–	0.1	–	
Switzerland	0.5	1.4	1.2	1.5	0.5	1.4	1.2	1.5	
United Kingdom	0.4	-0.1	2.0	0.1	0.4	-0.1	2.0	0.1	
United States	7.0	9.0	16.0	9.0	7.0	9.0	16.0	9.0	
TOTAL	*70.0*	*126.1*	*163.0*	*120.3*	*66.9*	*87.0*	*119.8*	*111.0*	
MULTILATERAL	*34.5*	*68.6*	*74.5*	*93.3*	*34.3*	*68.4*	*74.3*	*81.5*	
OPEC COUNTRIES	*2.9*	*17.3*	*0.1*	*1.7*	*2.9*	*17.3*	*0.1*	*1.7*	
E.E.C.+ MEMBERS	*66.9*	*99.0*	*155.9*	*110.8*	*63.8*	*95.2*	*112.7*	*101.5*	
TOTAL	**107.4**	**212.0**	**237.7**	**215.3**	**104.1**	**172.7**	**194.2**	**194.2**	

1978	1979	1980	1977	1978	1979	1980
			ODA COMMITMENTS			
–	–	–	–	–	–	–
0.1	0.0	0.0	–	–	–	–
3.8	6.6	10.1	3.1	5.6	7.7	12.1
38.4	2.5	3.7	14.4	40.4	1.1	1.0
1.5	0.3	0.2	0.3	0.0	2.0	8.9
–	–	–	–	–	–	–
32.3	43.5	50.8	19.4	23.3	37.3	57.4
16.6	67.3	21.5	19.2	22.2	106.6	16.6
0.0	0.1	0.2	0.1	0.0	0.1	0.2
9.8	16.5	6.3	14.9	7.0	17.2	9.9
2.6	4.0	3.3	4.1	0.4	4.7	1.7
–	–	–	–	–	–	–
1.1	1.0	0.4	–	–	0.4	1.0
–	0.1	–	–	–	–	–
1.4	1.2	1.5	0.1	2.6	2.0	1.4
-0.1	2.0	0.1	0.4	0.2	2.0	0.1
9.0	11.0	9.0	7.9	16.3	9.5	13.6
116.4	*156.0*	*107.3*	*83.7*	*118.1*	*190.5*	*123.8*
0.9	0.1	4.2	3.0	–	–	0.7
–	–	–	–	–	–	–
–	–	–	–	–	–	–
–	–	–	–	–	–	–
32.7	29.1	9.3	24.6	20.0	7.5	15.5
–	–	–	–	–	–	–
8.5	11.7	18.2	-0.1	24.5	42.0	16.7
–	–	–	–	–	–	–
–	–	–	–	–	–	12.4
–	–	–	–	–	–	–
6.8	–	9.5	–	–	–	–
–	–	–	6.2	8.5	10.0	15.7
3.0	4.0	5.2	–	–	–	–
0.4	0.7	0.2	–	–	–	–
0.7	1.2	0.8	–	–	–	–
–	–	–	–	–	–	–
3.1	2.4	4.6	–	–	–	–
0.0	0.0	0.0	–	–	–	–
1.3	1.8	5.0	–	–	–	–
5.5	5.9	7.0	8.6	0.4	4.9	4.0
62.8	*56.8*	*63.7*	*42.3*	*53.4*	*64.3*	*64.9*
16.2	*0.1*	*1.7*	–	*15.9*	–	*12.8*
89.3	*152.9*	*95.5*	*71.0*	*71.8*	*167.7*	*112.4*
195.3	***213.0***	***172.7***	***126.0***	***187.3***	***254.8***	***201.5***
			TECH. COOP. GRANTS			
–	–	–	–	–	–	–
0.1	0.0	0.0	0.1	0.1	0.0	0.0
3.8	6.6	8.4	1.3	2.2	3.0	2.9
38.4	2.5	3.7	1.1	1.3	0.8	0.9
0.3	0.3	0.2	0.1	0.2	0.3	0.2
–	–	–	–	–	–	–
20.8	31.4	37.5	12.8	14.7	18.4	22.9
11.2	62.4	21.5	4.3	7.0	7.7	13.4
0.0	0.1	0.2	0.1	0.0	0.1	0.2
3.4	3.4	1.0	0.2	1.0	0.6	1.0
2.6	4.0	3.3	0.2	0.4	0.6	0.9
–	–	–	–	–	–	–
1.1	1.0	0.4	–	–	–	–
–	0.1	–	–	–	0.1	–
1.4	1.2	1.5	0.1	0.0	0.0	0.5
-0.1	2.0	0.1	0.0	0.0	0.1	0.1
9.0	11.0	9.0	5.0	6.0	8.0	8.0
91.8	*125.9*	*86.9*	*25.2*	*33.1*	*39.7*	*51.0*
41.6	*38.0*	*24.9*	*5.3*	*5.4*	*7.6*	*15.7*
15.9	–	*1.7*	–	–	–	–
71.2	*134.7*	*80.5*	*18.8*	*24.7*	*30.2*	*40.6*
149.3	***163.9***	***113.5***	***30.5***	***38.4***	***47.3***	***66.7***
			TOTAL OOF NET			
–	–	–	–	–	–	–
–	–	–	–	–	–	–
–	–	–	–	–	–	–
–	–	–	–	–	–	–
–	–	–	–	–	–	–
–	–	–	–	–	–	–
9.7	2.0	13.0	7.9	9.6	-0.7	6.9
–	–	–	-0.4	-0.2	-1.1	-0.9
–	–	–	–	–	–	–
–	–	–	–	–	–	–
–	–	–	–	–	–	–
–	–	–	–	–	–	–
–	–	–	–	–	–	–
–	–	–	–	–	–	–
–	–	–	–	–	–	–
–	–	–	–	–	–	–
–	5.0	–	–	–	5.0	–
9.7	*7.0*	*13.0*	*7.5*	*9.4*	*3.2*	*6.0*
5.8	*17.7*	*29.6*	*-0.1*	*5.7*	*17.5*	*17.9*
1.1	–	–	–	*1.1*	–	–
9.7	*3.0*	*15.3*	*7.5*	*9.4*	*-0.8*	*8.3*
16.6	***24.7***	***42.6***	***7.3***	***16.2***	***20.7***	***24.0***

MAIN AID AGGREGATES

	1977	1978	1979	1980
DAC COUNTRIES COMBINED				
PRIVATE SECTOR NET	26.4	46.4	69.9	61.5
Direct Investment	3.5	19.9	8.8	-5.0
Portfolio Invest.	2.9	2.9	3.9	33.3
Export Credits	20.0	23.7	57.3	33.1
OFFICIAL & PRIVATE				
GROSS:				
Contractual Lending	59.4	70.0	108.0	76.8
Export Credits Tot.	30.8	35.8	75.9	43.4
Export Credits Priv	30.8	35.8	70.9	43.4
OTHER NET DATA				
Contractual Lending	45.5	18.9	51.2	57.3
Export Credits Tot.	20.0	23.7	62.3	33.1
(Bank Sector Loans)	1.0	5.0	65.0	19.0
ODA CONCESSIONALITY				
Total:Grant Element	87.0	97.0	93.0	82.0
Loans:Grant Element	54.0	65.0	35.0	46.0
OTHER SOURCES				
CMEA Countr.(Gross)	–	–	–	–
Intra LDCS Exc.OPEC	–	–	–	–
Other	–	–	–	–
ALL SOURCE COMMITMENTS				
TOTAL BILATERAL	112.2	162.8	198.0	194.6
of which				
OPEC (ODA)	–	15.9	–	12.8
CMEA (ODA)	–	–	–	–
TOTAL MULTILAT.(ODA)	42.3	53.4	64.3	64.9
TOTAL BIL.& MULTIL.	154.5	216.1	262.3	259.5
of which				
ODA Grants	90.2	152.5	188.6	116.4
ODA Loans	35.8	34.8	66.3	85.1
ODA CONCESSIONALITY				
Total: Grant Element	85.0	97.0	91.0	82.0
Loans: Grant Element	54.0	74.0	65.0	62.0

INDEBTEDNESS

	1977	1978	1979	1980
TOTAL DEBT DISBURSED	***206.8***	***302.2***	***405.2***	
Debt to DAC Countries	158.0	229.0	281.0	
ODA	102.0	82.0	51.0	
Total Export Credits	55.0	134.0	215.0	
Other Private Market	1.0	13.0	15.0	
International Org.	35.7	57.2	82.7	
CMEA	5.9	8.0	28.7	
Other	7.2	8.0	12.8	
TOTAL DEBT SERVICE	***17.7***	***28.1***	***45.8***	
Paid to DAC Countries	16.5	27.2	44.0	
ODA	2.7	5.8	5.2	
Total Export Credits	13.5	21.1	36.5	
Other Private Market	0.3	0.3	2.3	
International Org.	0.8	0.7	1.2	
CMEA	–	–	–	
Other	0.3	0.1	0.5	

ECONOMIC INDICATORS

	1977	1978	1979	1980
GNP Curr. Prices, $M	881.7	1222.3	1547.1	1806.9
Real GNP, 1976=100	106.0	120.0	130.0	137.0
GNP/Cap Curr. Prices,$	181.0	243.0	299.0	339.0
GNP/cap Atlas Basis, $	220.8	259.2	296.4	330.9
Real GNP/Cap, 1976=100	103.0	113.0	119.0	122.0
Population, Million	4.9	5.0	5.2	5.3
Curr.A/C Deficit(-),$M	–	–	–	–
BOP Exp. & Transf.,$M	–	–	–	–
Exp. to OECD CIF, $M	106.0	146.8	333.2	484.8
of which				
Manufact.	46.7	45.3	168.1	441.4
Imp. from OECD FOB, $M	166.2	240.5	335.8	338.6
Reserves ex. Gold, $M	101.1	128.4	131.7	125.9

	TOTAL RECEIPTS NET 1977	1978	1979	1980	TOTAL ODA NET 1977	1978	1979	1980
DAC COUNTRIES								
Australia	0.2	0.4	0.3	0.3	0.2	0.2	0.3	0.3
Austria	0.6	0.3	6.3	108.3	0.7	0.3	0.8	0.5
Belgium	0.5	5.7	10.2	27.1	0.1	0.6	0.5	0.5
Canada	3.3	1.3	0.7	1.4	3.3	1.3	0.7	0.3
Denmark	9.0	10.7	65.6	9.9	0.4	-0.2	-0.1	0.3
Finland	0.3	0.1	0.1	0.1	0.3	0.1	0.1	0.1
France	1.5	166.3	23.8	199.9	–	–	–	4.8
Germany, Fed. Rep.	18.9	46.6	12.9	400.5	1.7	1.6	0.8	2.3
Italy	34.2	103.8	109.5	162.9	-0.4	-0.3	-0.3	0.2
Japan	17.3	-38.1	3.2	6.4	10.9	9.7	1.5	0.3
Netherlands	11.1	-1.5	15.0	-28.2	4.3	2.7	2.5	3.4
New Zealand	–	–	–	–	–	–	–	–
Norway	0.0	1.8	51.3	-2.9	2.1	1.8	1.2	0.4
Sweden	-0.3	3.1	–	-0.2	–	0.2	–	0.3
Switzerland	-13.2	36.7	18.0	-24.2	0.0	0.0	0.0	–
United Kingdom	294.1	204.3	403.1	75.3	5.2	5.7	2.7	4.7
United States	-19.0	47.0	-83.0	86.0	–	–	–	-1.0
TOTAL	*358.3*	*588.5*	*637.0*	*1022.7*	*28.7*	*23.7*	*10.6*	*17.3*
MULTILATERAL								
AF.D.F.	–	–	–	–	–	–	–	–
AF.D.B.	-0.3	2.3	-0.6	-0.4	–	–	–	–
AS.D.B.	–	–	–	–	–	–	–	–
CAR.D.B.	–	–	–	–	–	–	–	–
E.E.C.	0.2	4.0	3.0	4.6	0.2	4.0	0.2	0.7
IBRD	44.2	37.7	31.1	38.4	–	–	–	–
IDA	2.1	-0.2	-0.4	-0.4	2.1	-0.2	-0.4	-0.4
I.D.B.	–	–	–	–	–	–	–	–
IFAD	–	–	–	–	–	–	–	–
I.F.C.	-0.2	0.2	-0.3	4.2	–	–	–	–
IMF TRUST FUND	–	–	–	–	–	–	–	–
U.N. AGENCIES	–	–	–	–	–	–	–	–
UNDP	8.3	10.9	12.8	13.2	8.3	10.9	12.8	13.2
UNTA	0.7	0.8	1.0	0.2	0.7	0.8	1.0	0.2
UNICEF	1.4	0.8	0.9	2.2	1.4	0.8	0.9	2.2
UNRWA	–	–	–	–	–	–	–	–
WFP	0.1	–	0.0	–	0.1	–	0.0	–
UNHCR	0.1	0.2	0.6	0.7	0.1	0.2	0.6	0.7
Other Multilateral	1.3	2.6	1.1	1.7	1.3	2.6	1.1	1.7
Arab OPEC Agencies	–	–	–	–	–	–	–	–
TOTAL	*57.7*	*59.3*	*49.1*	*64.4*	*14.1*	*19.1*	*16.2*	*18.3*
OPEC COUNTRIES	–	*2.0*	–	–	–	–	–	–
E.E.C.+ MEMBERS	*369.3*	*540.0*	*643.2*	*852.0*	*11.4*	*14.0*	*6.3*	*16.9*
TOTAL	***416.0***	***649.8***	***686.1***	***1087.1***	***42.8***	***42.7***	***26.8***	***35.7***

	ODA LOANS GROSS 1977	1978	1979	1980	ODA LOANS NET 1977	1978	1979	1980
DAC COUNTRIES								
Australia	–	–	–	–	–	–	–	–
Austria	0.5	–	0.3	–	0.4	–	0.3	–
Belgium	–	–	–	–	–	–	–	–
Canada	1.7	0.3	0.3	–	1.4	-0.1	-0.1	-0.2
Denmark	0.3	–	–	–	0.3	-0.2	-0.2	-0.2
Finland	–	–	–	–	–	–	–	–
France	–	–	–	–	–	–	–	–
Germany, Fed. Rep.	0.8	0.1	1.9	0.6	-2.9	-2.3	-6.1	-3.6
Italy	–	–	–	–	-0.9	-1.0	-1.0	-0.5
Japan	11.2	9.5	2.7	2.8	10.0	8.0	0.2	-1.0
Netherlands	–	0.3	–	–	-0.5	-0.2	-0.8	-0.9
New Zealand	–	–	–	–	–	–	–	–
Norway	–	–	–	–	–	–	–	–
Sweden	–	–	–	–	–	–	–	–
Switzerland	–	–	–	–	–	–	–	–
United Kingdom	2.1	0.6	–	–	-3.9	-4.0	-8.0	-6.8
United States	–	–	–	–	-1.0	-1.0	-1.0	-1.0
TOTAL	*16.6*	*10.6*	*5.2*	*3.4*	*3.0*	*-0.8*	*-16.7*	*-14.1*
MULTILATERAL	*2.5*	*0.2*	–	–	*2.1*	*-0.2*	*-0.4*	*-0.4*
OPEC COUNTRIES	–	–	–	–	–	–	–	–
E.E.C.+ MEMBERS	*3.2*	*0.9*	*1.9*	*0.6*	*-7.8*	*-7.8*	*-16.1*	*-11.9*
TOTAL	***19.1***	***10.8***	***5.2***	***3.4***	***5.1***	***-1.0***	***-17.1***	***-14.5***

	TOTAL OFFICIAL GROSS 1977	1978	1979	1980	TOTAL OFFICIAL NET 1977	1978	1979	1980
DAC COUNTRIES								
Australia	0.2	0.2	0.3	0.3	0.2	0.2	0.3	0.3
Austria	0.7	0.3	0.8	0.5	0.6	0.3	0.8	0.5
Belgium	0.1	0.6	0.5	0.5	0.1	0.6	0.5	0.5
Canada	3.6	1.6	1.1	0.5	3.3	1.3	0.7	0.3
Denmark	0.6	0.9	0.4	0.6	0.6	0.6	0.1	0.4
Finland	0.3	0.1	0.1	0.1	0.3	0.1	0.1	0.1
France	–	0.9	7.1	37.1	–	-5.3	3.2	37.1
Germany, Fed. Rep.	6.5	4.0	15.6	26.5	2.3	0.9	7.6	20.8
Italy	0.5	0.7	1.2	6.6	-0.4	-0.3	0.3	6.1
Japan	12.0	11.2	4.0	4.0	10.9	9.7	1.5	0.3
Netherlands	4.7	3.2	3.3	4.2	4.3	2.7	2.5	3.4
New Zealand	–	–	–	–	–	–	–	–
Norway	2.1	1.8	1.2	0.4	2.1	1.8	1.2	0.4
Sweden	–	0.2	–	0.3	–	0.2	–	0.3
Switzerland	0.0	0.0	0.0	–	0.0	0.0	0.0	–
United Kingdom	11.2	18.8	10.8	11.5	4.8	8.8	2.3	3.9
United States	1.0	1.0	1.0	–	-7.0	-6.0	-3.0	-3.0
TOTAL	*43.5*	*45.4*	*47.4*	*93.1*	*21.9*	*15.6*	*18.0*	*71.3*
MULTILATERAL	*76.0*	*78.9*	*70.8*	*90.0*	*57.7*	*59.3*	*49.1*	*64.4*
OPEC COUNTRIES	–	*2.0*	–	–	–	*2.0*	–	–
E.E.C.+ MEMBERS	*23.8*	*33.0*	*42.0*	*91.5*	*11.7*	*12.0*	*19.5*	*76.8*
TOTAL	***119.5***	***126.4***	***118.2***	***183.0***	***79.7***	***76.8***	***67.1***	***135.7***

TOTAL ODA GROSS

	19
Australia	
Austria	
Belgium	
Canada	
Denmark	
Finland	
France	
Germany, Fed. Rep.	
Italy	
Japan	
Netherlands	
New Zealand	
Norway	
Sweden	
Switzerland	
United Kingdom	
United States	
TOTAL	
AF.D.F.	
AF.D.B.	
AS.D.B.	
CAR.D.B.	
E.E.C.	
IBRD	
IDA	
I.D.B.	
IFAD	
I.F.C.	
IMF TRUST FUND	
U.N. AGENCIES	
UNDP	
UNTA	
UNICEF	
UNRWA	
WFP	
UNHCR	
Other Multilateral	
Arab OPEC Agencies	
TOTAL	
OPEC COUNTRIES	
E.E.C.+ MEMBERS	
TOTAL	

GRANTS

Australia	
Austria	
Belgium	
Canada	
Denmark	
Finland	
France	
Germany, Fed. Rep.	
Italy	
Japan	
Netherlands	
New Zealand	
Norway	
Sweden	
Switzerland	
United Kingdom	
United States	
TOTAL	
MULTILATERAL	
OPEC COUNTRIES	
E.E.C.+ MEMBERS	
TOTAL	

TOTAL OOF GROSS

Australia	
Austria	
Belgium	
Canada	
Denmark	
Finland	
France	
Germany, Fed. Rep.	
Italy	
Japan	
Netherlands	
New Zealand	
Norway	
Sweden	
Switzerland	
United Kingdom	
United States	
TOTAL	
MULTILATERAL	
OPEC COUNTRIES	
E.E.C.+ MEMBERS	
TOTAL	

1978	1979	1980	1977	1978	1979	1980
			ODA COMMITMENTS			
0.2	0.3	0.3	0.1	0.1	0.2	0.3
0.3	0.8	0.5	0.5	0.3	0.4	–
0.6	0.5	0.5	–	–	–	–
1.6	1.1	0.5	0.5	0.5	0.1	0.1
0.0	0.1	0.5	0.1	0.1	0.1	–
0.1	0.1	0.1	0.3	0.1	0.1	0.0
–	–	4.8	–	–	–	4.8
4.0	8.7	6.5	3.7	3.6	9.9	13.5
0.7	0.7	0.7	0.5	0.7	0.7	0.7
11.2	4.0	4.0	1.0	9.9	1.5	3.3
3.2	3.3	4.2	2.6	3.1	3.6	4.3
–	–	–	–	–	–	–
1.8	1.2	0.4	–	0.4	0.3	–
0.2	–	0.3	–	0.2	0.3	–
0.0	0.0	–	–	–	–	–
10.3	10.8	11.5	9.0	9.7	10.8	11.1
1.0	1.0	–	–	–	–	0.0
35.1	*32.5*	*34.8*	*18.2*	*28.6*	*27.9*	*37.9*
–	–	–	–	–	–	–
–	–	–	–	–	–	–
–	–	–	–	–	–	–
–	–	–	–	–	–	–
4.0	0.2	0.7	0.8	4.4	3.1	5.7
–	–	–	–	–	–	–
0.2	–	–	–	–	–	–
–	–	–	–	–	–	–
–	–	–	–	–	–	–
–	–	–	–	–	–	–
–	–	–	–	–	–	–
–	–	–	11.8	15.3	16.4	18.0
10.9	12.8	13.2	–	–	–	–
0.8	1.0	0.2	–	–	–	–
0.8	0.9	2.2	–	–	–	–
–	–	–	–	–	–	–
–	0.0	–	–	–	–	–
0.2	0.6	0.7	–	–	–	–
2.6	1.1	1.7	–	–	–	–
–	–	–	–	0.0	–	–
19.5	*16.6*	*18.7*	*12.6*	*19.7*	*19.5*	*23.7*
–	–	–	–	–	–	–
22.7	*24.3*	*29.4*	*16.7*	*21.5*	*28.2*	*40.0*
54.6	***49.1***	***53.5***	***30.8***	***48.3***	***47.4***	***61.6***
			TECH. COOP. GRANTS			
0.2	0.3	0.3	0.2	0.2	0.3	0.3
0.3	0.5	0.5	0.3	0.3	0.5	0.5
0.6	0.5	0.5	0.1	0.6	0.5	0.5
1.4	0.8	0.5	0.4	0.4	0.1	0.0
0.0	0.1	0.5	0.1	0.0	0.1	0.5
0.1	0.1	0.1	0.3	0.1	0.1	0.1
–	–	4.8	–	–	–	4.8
3.9	6.8	5.9	4.6	3.9	6.4	5.6
0.7	0.7	0.7	0.5	0.7	0.7	0.7
1.7	1.3	1.3	0.9	1.7	1.3	1.3
2.9	3.3	4.2	4.7	2.9	3.2	4.0
–	–	–	–	–	–	–
1.8	1.2	0.4	0.1	0.3	0.3	0.0
0.2	–	0.3	–	0.2	–	0.1
0.0	0.0	–	–	0.0	0.0	–
9.7	10.8	11.5	6.8	9.7	10.8	11.1
1.0	1.0	–	1.0	1.0	1.0	–
24.5	*27.3*	*31.4*	*19.9*	*21.9*	*25.1*	*29.5*
19.3	*16.6*	*18.7*	*11.8*	*15.3*	*16.4*	*18.0*
–	–	–	–	–	–	–
21.8	*22.4*	*28.8*	*16.8*	*17.8*	*21.7*	*27.2*
43.8	***43.9***	***50.2***	***31.6***	***37.2***	***41.5***	***47.5***
			TOTAL OOF NET			
–	–	–	–	–	–	–
–	–	–	-0.1	0.0	–	–
–	–	–	–	–	–	–
–	–	–	–	–	–	–
0.8	0.4	0.1	0.2	0.8	0.2	0.1
–	–	–	–	–	–	–
0.9	7.1	32.3	–	-5.3	3.2	32.3
–	6.9	20.0	0.6	-0.7	6.9	18.5
–	0.6	5.9	–	–	0.6	5.9
–	–	–	–	–	–	–
–	–	–	–	–	–	–
–	–	–	–	–	–	–
–	–	–	–	–	–	–
–	–	–	–	–	–	–
–	–	–	–	–	–	–
8.6	–	–	-0.4	3.1	-0.5	-0.8
–	–	–	-7.0	-6.0	-3.0	-2.0
10.3	*14.9*	*58.3*	*-6.8*	*-8.1*	*7.4*	*54.0*
59.5	*54.2*	*71.2*	*43.7*	*40.2*	*32.9*	*46.1*
2.0	–	–	–	*2.0*	–	–
10.3	*17.7*	*62.1*	*0.3*	*-2.0*	*13.2*	*59.9*
71.7	***69.1***	***129.5***	***36.9***	***34.1***	***40.3***	***100.1***

	1977	1978	1979	1980
MAIN AID AGGREGATES				
DAC COUNTRIES COMBINED				
PRIVATE SECTOR NET	336.4	573.0	619.0	951.4
Direct Investment	285.3	164.2	-48.8	92.2
Portfolio Invest.	-13.1	178.9	76.4	463.6
Export Credits	64.2	229.9	591.4	395.5
OFFICIAL & PRIVATE GROSS:				
Contractual Lending	303.8	485.9	810.6	857.8
Export Credits Tot.	285.9	464.9	791.2	802.0
Export Credits Priv	285.9	464.9	790.6	796.1
OTHER NET DATA				
Contractual Lending	60.5	221.0	582.1	435.4
Export Credits Tot.	57.1	223.8	589.0	399.4
(Bank Sector Loans)	34.0	887.0	604.0	378.0
ODA CONCESSIONALITY				
Total:Grant Element	98.0	82.0	99.0	96.0
Loans:Grant Element	35.0	36.0	45.0	32.0
OTHER SOURCES				
CMEA Countr.(Gross)	0.4	0.2	–	–
Intra LDCS Exc.OPEC	–	–	–	–
Other	–	–	–	–
ALL SOURCE COMMITMENTS				
TOTAL BILATERAL	20.6	38.1	36.6	170.9
of which				
OPEC (ODA)	–	–	–	–
CMEA (ODA)	–	–	50.0	–
TOTAL MULTILAT.(ODA)	12.6	19.7	19.5	23.7
TOTAL BIL.& MULTIL.	33.2	57.8	56.1	194.6
of which				
ODA Grants	30.4	40.1	47.1	59.8
ODA Loans	0.5	8.2	0.3	1.8
ODA CONCESSIONALITY				
Total: Grant Element	98.0	89.0	99.0	98.0
Loans: Grant Element	35.0	36.0	45.0	32.0
INDEBTEDNESS				
TOTAL DEBT DISBURSED	***1565.9***	***2893.7***	***4549.3***	
Debt to DAC Countries	1110.0	2394.0	3954.0	
ODA	384.0	427.0	402.0	
Total Export Credits	711.0	967.0	1527.0	
Other Private Market	15.0	1000.0	2025.0	
International Org.	450.6	492.1	525.7	
CMEA	2.7	7.6	69.6	
Other	2.6	–	–	
TOTAL DEBT SERVICE	***535.0***	***606.6***	***729.3***	
Paid to DAC Countries	479.4	551.8	656.5	
ODA	21.5	21.8	35.3	
Total Export Credits	445.5	501.9	526.0	
Other Private Market	12.4	28.1	95.2	
International Org.	50.0	53.1	67.7	
CMEA	0.4	1.7	5.1	
Other	5.2	–	–	
ECONOMIC INDICATORS				
GNP Curr. Prices, $M	49634.1	58811.0	75378.3	91992.3
Real GNP, 1976=100	104.0	110.0	116.0	121.0
GNP/Cap Curr. Prices,$	631.0	730.0	912.0	1085.0
GNP/cap Atlas Basis, $	734.1	814.8	909.5	1009.1
Real GNP/Cap, 1976=100	101.0	105.0	108.0	110.0
Population, Million	78.6	80.6	82.6	84.7
Curr.A/C Deficit(-),$M	-1012.0	-3767.0	1714.0	3083.0
BOP Exp. & Transf.,$M	13349.0	11684.0	18034.0	25399.0
Exp. to OECD CIF, $M	10509.6	9678.0	16614.7	23884.1
of which				
Manufact.	35.6	65.3	67.3	53.4
Imp. from OECD FOB, $M	7887.3	8639.2	6886.0	12161.1
Reserves ex. Gold, $M	4232.0	1887.0	5548.0	10235.0

	TOTAL RECEIPTS NET 1977	1978	1979	1980	TOTAL ODA NET 1977	1978	1979	1980
DAC COUNTRIES								
Australia	3.1	11.8	8.9	6.7	3.1	3.6	5.6	6.6
Austria	-0.4	-0.7	-0.8	-0.8	0.4	0.2	0.1	0.1
Belgium	-4.4	2.2	2.9	3.8	0.1	4.8	5.2	5.0
Canada	71.4	72.3	53.9	26.6	67.5	73.2	55.7	28.4
Denmark	1.8	2.9	28.3	5.3	1.8	2.9	25.1	2.7
Finland	–	–	0.0	0.1	–	–	0.0	0.1
France	31.3	43.3	16.4	47.1	21.7	25.0	14.8	14.2
Germany, Fed. Rep.	37.4	41.7	25.7	109.5	38.5	42.6	19.1	25.7
Italy	16.3	20.7	12.0	33.5	4.6	7.0	-0.5	-2.9
Japan	42.7	47.7	172.7	109.3	28.7	46.9	168.3	112.4
Netherlands	28.7	36.9	23.6	31.2	28.7	36.9	23.6	31.2
New Zealand	0.1	0.0	0.0	0.0	0.1	0.0	0.0	0.0
Norway	7.6	13.2	13.4	16.4	7.4	13.2	13.4	16.5
Sweden	2.3	10.0	9.7	12.2	2.3	10.0	9.7	12.2
Switzerland	0.6	-10.7	0.4	-46.4	3.8	3.3	0.5	1.3
United Kingdom	30.2	37.0	57.4	55.2	25.0	30.1	48.1	43.7
United States	96.0	56.0	29.0	62.0	88.0	80.0	29.0	42.0
TOTAL	*364.8*	*384.4*	*453.6*	*472.0*	*321.8*	*379.4*	*417.8*	*339.2*
MULTILATERAL								
AF.D.F.	–	–	–	–	–	–	–	–
AF.D.B.	–	–	–	–	–	–	–	–
AS.D.B.	49.8	47.0	67.6	45.5	22.5	8.8	14.5	20.7
CAR.D.B.	–	–	–	–	–	–	–	–
E.E.C.	8.9	14.2	18.5	13.8	8.9	14.2	18.5	13.8
IBRD	9.1	5.0	5.9	-9.7	0.8	9.3	13.9	5.3
IDA	74.3	54.8	72.7	70.3	74.3	54.8	72.7	70.3
I.D.B.	–	–	–	–	–	–	–	–
IFAD	–	–	–	2.6	–	–	–	2.6
I.F.C.	-0.7	-0.4	6.1	11.8	–	–	–	–
IMF TRUST FUND	29.4	90.4	–	171.0	29.4	90.4	–	171.0
U.N. AGENCIES	–	–	–	–	–	–	–	–
UNDP	6.2	7.9	11.0	11.2	6.2	7.9	11.0	11.2
UNTA	0.9	1.5	1.3	0.2	0.9	1.5	1.3	0.2
UNICEF	3.6	5.3	9.9	11.4	3.6	5.3	9.9	11.4
UNRWA	–	–	–	–	–	–	–	–
WFP	4.0	8.3	9.4	33.5	4.0	8.3	9.4	33.5
UNHCR	–	–	4.9	68.6	–	–	4.9	68.6
Other Multilateral	3.9	2.0	3.0	6.4	3.9	2.0	3.0	6.4
Arab OPEC Agencies	14.8	35.9	5.4	13.4	10.7	19.9	4.9	3.4
TOTAL	*204.0*	*271.9*	*215.8*	*450.0*	*165.1*	*222.4*	*164.0*	*418.4*
OPEC COUNTRIES	*59.1*	*97.7*	*23.1*	*364.7*	*59.1*	*67.7*	*23.1*	*364.7*
E.E.C.+ MEMBERS	*150.2*	*198.9*	*184.8*	*299.6*	*129.3*	*163.3*	*153.9*	*133.4*
TOTAL	***627.9***	***754.0***	***692.5***	***1286.7***	***545.9***	***669.5***	***604.9***	***1122.3***

	ODA LOANS GROSS 1977	1978	1979	1980	ODA LOANS NET 1977	1978	1979	1980
DAC COUNTRIES								
Australia	–	–	–	–	–	–	–	–
Austria	–	–	–	–	–	–	-0.1	-0.1
Belgium	–	4.8	5.1	5.1	-0.2	4.5	4.8	4.5
Canada	55.9	70.7	52.7	26.7	55.6	69.3	51.7	25.3
Denmark	1.8	2.8	25.0	2.6	1.8	2.8	23.6	2.6
Finland	–	–	–	–	–	–	–	–
France	31.9	23.9	14.4	15.6	20.7	22.8	13.2	13.7
Germany, Fed. Rep.	78.4	83.5	25.6	57.4	32.5	35.7	10.8	12.6
Italy	12.4	11.8	–	–	3.1	7.0	-3.0	-2.9
Japan	46.3	66.0	160.6	104.2	24.4	39.5	144.6	83.8
Netherlands	14.5	26.3	16.1	18.7	12.2	25.1	14.1	16.7
New Zealand	–	–	–	–	–	–	–	–
Norway	–	–	–	–	–	–	–	–
Sweden	–	–	–	–	0.0	-5.5	–	–
Switzerland	3.0	3.0	0.0	–	-5.6	3.0	0.0	–
United Kingdom	13.5	14.3	3.1	1.4	-6.6	9.4	-7.5	-6.4
United States	118.0	105.0	76.0	80.0	83.0	78.0	47.0	49.0
TOTAL	*375.6*	*412.0*	*378.5*	*311.7*	*220.9*	*291.6*	*299.1*	*198.8*
MULTILATERAL	*140.4*	*186.7*	*110.2*	*277.3*	*137.4*	*183.3*	*105.9*	*272.8*
OPEC COUNTRIES	*49.1*	*32.7*	*14.1*	*38.5*	*49.1*	*32.7*	*11.1*	*35.6*
E.E.C.+ MEMBERS	*152.4*	*167.3*	*89.2*	*100.8*	*63.4*	*107.3*	*55.9*	*40.8*
TOTAL	***565.1***	***631.4***	***502.8***	***627.5***	***407.3***	***507.6***	***416.1***	***507.2***

	TOTAL OFFICIAL GROSS 1977	1978	1979	1980	TOTAL OFFICIAL NET 1977	1978	1979	1980
DAC COUNTRIES								
Australia	3.1	11.8	8.9	6.7	3.1	11.8	8.9	6.7
Austria	0.4	0.2	0.2	0.2	-0.4	-0.7	-0.8	-0.8
Belgium	0.3	5.0	5.5	5.6	-0.3	4.6	5.2	5.0
Canada	73.8	74.7	56.7	29.8	71.4	72.3	53.9	26.6
Denmark	1.8	2.9	29.1	5.3	1.8	2.9	27.6	5.3
Finland	–	–	0.0	0.1	–	–	0.0	0.1
France	32.9	26.1	16.0	16.1	16.6	22.5	14.8	14.2
Germany, Fed. Rep.	84.4	90.4	33.9	92.4	37.6	39.6	19.1	46.8
Italy	21.0	11.8	2.6	7.0	11.4	6.3	-1.2	3.0
Japan	50.6	73.4	184.3	132.8	28.7	46.9	168.3	112.4
Netherlands	31.0	38.0	25.5	33.2	28.7	36.9	23.6	31.2
New Zealand	0.1	0.0	0.0	0.0	0.1	0.0	0.0	0.0
Norway	7.4	13.2	13.4	16.5	7.4	13.2	13.4	16.5
Sweden	2.4	15.5	9.7	12.2	2.3	10.0	9.7	12.2
Switzerland	12.4	3.3	0.5	1.3	1.9	2.7	0.5	1.3
United Kingdom	45.1	34.9	58.8	51.5	25.0	30.1	48.1	43.7
United States	160.0	107.0	84.0	99.0	96.0	56.0	30.0	55.0
TOTAL	*526.6*	*508.2*	*529.1*	*509.8*	*331.2*	*355.0*	*421.2*	*379.3*
MULTILATERAL	*229.9*	*303.0*	*277.2*	*526.6*	*204.0*	*271.9*	*215.8*	*450.0*
OPEC COUNTRIES	*59.1*	*97.7*	*26.1*	*367.6*	*59.1*	*97.7*	*23.1*	*364.7*
E.E.C.+ MEMBERS	*225.4*	*223.3*	*189.8*	*225.0*	*129.5*	*157.0*	*155.7*	*163.0*
TOTAL	***815.6***	***908.9***	***832.3***	***1404.0***	***594.3***	***724.6***	***660.1***	***1194.0***

TOTAL ODA GROSS	197
Australia	[illegible]
Austria	[illegible]
Belgium	[illegible]
Canada	67
Denmark	[illegible]
Finland	
France	32
Germany, Fed. Rep.	84
Italy	13
Japan	56
Netherlands	31
New Zealand	[illegible]
Norway	[illegible]
Sweden	[illegible]
Switzerland	12
United Kingdom	45
United States	123
TOTAL	*47*
AF.D.F.	
AF.D.B.	
AS.D.B.	2
CAR.D.B.	
E.E.C.	[illegible]
IBRD	[illegible]
IDA	76
I.D.B.	
IFAD	
I.F.C.	
IMF TRUST FUND	29
U.N. AGENCIES	
UNDP	[illegible]
UNTA	[illegible]
UNICEF	
UNRWA	
WFP	[illegible]
UNHCR	
Other Multilateral	[illegible]
Arab OPEC Agencies	1
TOTAL	*16*
OPEC COUNTRIES	*5*
E.E.C.+ MEMBERS	*21*
TOTAL	***70.***

GRANTS	
Australia	[illegible]
Austria	[illegible]
Belgium	[illegible]
Canada	1
Denmark	[illegible]
Finland	
France	
Germany, Fed. Rep.	[illegible]
Italy	
Japan	[illegible]
Netherlands	1
New Zealand	[illegible]
Norway	
Sweden	[illegible]
Switzerland	[illegible]
United Kingdom	3
United States	[illegible]
TOTAL	*10*
MULTILATERAL	*2.*
OPEC COUNTRIES	*1*
E.E.C.+ MEMBERS	*6*
TOTAL	***13***

TOTAL OOF GROSS	
Australia	
Austria	
Belgium	
Canada	[illegible]
Denmark	
Finland	
France	
Germany, Fed. Rep.	
Italy	
Japan	
Netherlands	
New Zealand	
Norway	
Sweden	
Switzerland	
United Kingdom	
United States	3
TOTAL	*5*
MULTILATERAL	*6*
OPEC COUNTRIES	
E.E.C.+ MEMBERS	
TOTAL	***11***

1978	1979	1980	1977	1978	1979	1980
			ODA COMMITMENTS			
3.6	5.6	6.6	4.5	4.9	4.2	8.6
0.2	0.2	0.2	0.1	–	–	–
5.0	5.5	5.6	4.2	4.8	–	5.1
74.6	56.7	29.8	79.6	127.3	93.6	15.9
2.9	26.5	2.7	0.0	1.4	23.8	–
–	0.0	0.1	–	–	0.0	0.1
26.1	16.0	16.1	35.9	20.0	21.7	10.5
90.4	33.9	70.4	73.9	136.0	38.4	46.0
11.8	2.6	0.0	13.9	11.8	2.6	0.0
73.4	184.3	132.8	104.2	141.7	159.8	138.0
38.0	25.5	33.2	31.9	38.7	39.6	42.4
0.0	0.0	0.0	0.0	0.0	–	0.1
13.2	13.4	16.5	–	11.9	12.4	13.2
15.5	9.7	12.2	6.8	6.0	18.7	11.5
3.3	0.5	1.3	12.2	3.0	0.5	0.9
34.9	58.8	51.5	31.9	129.0	17.4	36.6
107.0	58.0	73.0	102.7	29.7	41.0	48.0
499.8	*497.2*	*452.0*	*501.7*	*666.2*	*473.6*	*377.0*
–	–	–	–	–	–	–
–	–	–	–	–	–	–
9.6	15.4	21.6	71.0	86.7	114.4	122.0
–	–	–	–	–	–	–
14.2	18.5	13.8	10.1	12.4	17.2	18.8
9.3	13.9	5.3	10.0	–	–	–
57.4	76.1	73.9	154.4	131.0	154.0	138.7
–	–	–	–	–	–	–
–	–	2.6	–	–	47.6	12.5
–	–	–	–	–	–	–
90.4	–	171.0	–	–	–	–
–	–	–	18.6	25.0	39.5	131.4
7.9	11.0	11.2	–	–	–	–
1.5	1.3	0.2	–	–	–	–
5.3	9.9	11.4	–	–	–	–
–	–	–	–	–	–	–
8.3	9.4	33.5	–	–	–	–
–	4.9	68.6	–	–	–	–
2.0	3.0	6.4	–	–	–	–
19.9	4.9	3.4	11.0	13.0	5.5	11.2
225.8	*168.3*	*423.0*	*275.1*	*268.1*	*378.2*	*434.5*
67.7	*26.1*	*367.6*	*135.5*	*385.0*	*121.4*	*408.7*
223.3	*187.3*	*193.4*	*201.7*	*354.1*	*160.6*	*159.4*
793.3	***691.6***	***1242.6***	***912.2***	***1319.3***	***973.1***	***1220.2***
			TECH. COOP. GRANTS			
3.6	5.6	6.6	1.9	0.9	0.4	0.4
0.2	0.2	0.2	0.4	0.2	0.2	0.2
0.2	0.3	0.5	0.2	0.2	0.3	0.3
3.9	4.0	3.1	0.3	0.2	0.1	0.3
0.1	1.5	0.1	0.1	0.1	0.1	0.1
–	0.0	0.1	–	–	0.0	–
2.2	1.7	0.5	–	–	–	0.5
7.0	8.3	13.1	6.0	4.8	4.8	5.7
0.1	2.6	0.0	0.0	0.1	0.3	0.0
7.4	23.8	28.6	1.4	1.6	3.0	4.3
11.7	9.5	14.6	2.6	2.7	2.7	2.8
0.0	0.0	0.0	0.0	0.0	0.0	0.0
13.2	13.4	16.5	0.1	0.1	0.1	0.2
15.5	9.7	12.2	–	0.2	0.1	0.2
0.3	0.5	1.3	–	–	0.0	0.3
20.7	55.7	50.1	2.7	2.1	3.1	4.9
2.0	-18.0	-7.0	–	2.0	1.0	2.0
87.8	*118.7*	*140.4*	*15.7*	*15.0*	*16.2*	*22.1*
39.1	*58.1*	*145.6*	*14.9*	*16.7*	*30.1*	*131.4*
35.0	*12.0*	*329.1*	–	–	–	–
56.0	*98.0*	*92.6*	*11.6*	*10.0*	*11.3*	*14.3*
161.9	***188.7***	***615.1***	***30.6***	***31.7***	***46.4***	***153.5***
			TOTAL OOF NET			
8.3	3.3	0.2	–	8.3	3.3	0.2
–	–	–	-0.8	-0.9	-0.9	-0.9
–	–	–	-0.4	-0.2	–	–
0.1	–	–	3.9	-0.9	-1.8	-1.8
0.1	2.6	2.7	–	0.1	2.6	2.7
–	–	–	–	–	–	–
–	–	–	-5.1	-2.4	–	–
–	–	22.0	-1.0	-3.0	–	21.1
–	–	7.0	6.8	-0.7	-0.8	5.9
–	–	–	–	–	–	–
–	–	–	–	–	–	–
–	–	–	–	–	–	–
–	–	–	–	–	–	–
–	–	–	–	–	–	–
–	–	–	-1.9	-0.6	–	–
–	–	–	–	–	–	–
–	26.0	26.0	8.0	-24.0	1.0	13.0
8.4	*31.8*	*57.8*	*9.5*	*-24.4*	*3.4*	*40.1*
77.2	*108.9*	*103.7*	*39.0*	*49.6*	*51.8*	*31.6*
30.0	–	–	–	*30.0*	–	–
0.1	*2.6*	*31.6*	*0.3*	*-6.3*	*1.8*	*29.6*
115.6	***140.8***	***161.4***	***48.4***	***55.1***	***55.2***	***71.7***

MAIN AID AGGREGATES

	1977	1978	1979	1980
DAC COUNTRIES COMBINED				
PRIVATE SECTOR NET	33.6	29.4	32.4	92.7
Direct Investment	10.2	11.4	8.5	0.8
Portfolio Invest.	-1.9	6.3	7.4	40.8
Export Credits	25.3	11.7	16.5	51.1
OFFICIAL & PRIVATE				
GROSS:				
Contractual Lending	513.3	498.4	474.4	564.4
Export Credits Tot.	127.1	86.3	93.3	242.2
Export Credits Priv	87.6	78.0	64.1	195.0
OTHER NET DATA				
Contractual Lending	255.6	278.9	319.1	290.0
Export Credits Tot.	33.2	-9.6	17.4	81.8
(Bank Sector Loans)	53.0	41.0	-30.0	117.0
ODA CONCESSIONALITY				
Total:Grant Element	74.0	81.0	77.0	80.0
Loans:Grant Element	67.0	70.0	68.0	66.0
OTHER SOURCES				
CMEA Countr.(Gross)	74.4	94.9	132.0	88.8
Intra LDCS Exc.OPEC	–	–	–	–
Other	–	–	–	–
ALL SOURCE COMMITMENTS				
TOTAL BILATERAL	671.8	1081.8	628.7	809.8
of which				
OPEC (ODA)	135.5	385.0	121.4	408.7
CMEA (ODA)	22.0	–	–	–
TOTAL MULTILAT.(ODA)	275.1	268.1	378.2	434.5
TOTAL BIL.& MULTIL.	946.8	1349.8	1006.8	1244.3
of which				
ODA Grants	137.6	304.1	214.0	635.1
ODA Loans	774.6	1015.2	759.2	585.1
ODA CONCESSIONALITY				
Total: Grant Element	72.0	75.0	76.0	86.0
Loans: Grant Element	66.0	68.0	69.0	70.0

INDEBTEDNESS

	1977	1978	1979	1980
TOTAL DEBT DISBURSED	***6850.4***	***7612.4***	***8158.9***	
Debt to DAC Countries	4349.0	4869.0	5100.0	
ODA	3816.0	4233.0	4490.0	
Total Export Credits	433.0	475.0	420.0	
Other Private Market	100.0	161.0	190.0	
International Org.	1144.8	1277.7	1412.0	
CMEA	251.0	337.2	415.4	
Other	1105.5	1128.5	1231.5	
TOTAL DEBT SERVICE	***391.2***	***441.8***	***498.6***	
Paid to DAC Countries	281.7	308.0	327.4	
ODA	160.0	155.8	154.7	
Total Export Credits	101.7	129.2	117.4	
Other Private Market	20.0	23.0	55.3	
International Org.	65.0	80.6	108.6	
CMEA	19.7	25.5	26.0	
Other	24.8	27.6	36.6	

ECONOMIC INDICATORS

	1977	1978	1979	1980
GNP Curr. Prices, $M	15468.9	18467.8	20764.0	25045.5
Real GNP, 1976=100	104.0	112.0	118.0	127.0
GNP/Cap Curr. Prices,$	206.0	238.0	260.0	304.0
GNP/cap Atlas Basis, $	213.5	239.0	265.6	302.7
Real GNP/Cap, 1976=100	100.0	105.0	107.0	112.0
Population, Million	74.9	77.3	79.7	82.2
Curr.A/C Deficit(-),$M	-840.0	-820.0	-1286.0	-1165.0
BOP Exp. & Transf.,$M	2349.0	3256.0	4107.0	5529.0
Exp. to OECD CIF, $M	552.0	717.7	1005.6	1101.5
of which				
Manufact.	342.4	477.1	688.7	718.2
Imp. from OECD FOB, $M	1572.1	1851.2	2459.9	2729.0
Reserves ex. Gold, $M	449.0	408.0	213.0	496.0

	1977	1978	1979	1980	1977	1978	1979	1980
TOTAL RECEIPTS NET					**TOTAL ODA NET**			
DAC COUNTRIES								
Australia	1.3	-0.9	0.2	–	–	–	–	–
Austria	0.0	0.0	–	–	0.0	0.0	–	–
Belgium	-13.2	10.9	39.2	-30.0	0.1	0.1	0.1	0.1
Canada	58.7	1.0	-3.1	-4.9	–	–	–	–
Denmark	–	0.4	1.0	–	–	–	–	–
Finland	–	–	–	0.0	–	–	–	0.0
France	28.9	36.7	-35.3	250.2	–	–	–	0.3
Germany, Fed. Rep.	-9.5	-62.6	-29.3	48.5	0.3	0.9	0.7	0.8
Italy	-19.5	-2.6	2.4	0.6	0.0	0.0	0.1	–
Japan	138.3	403.8	313.2	127.4	0.3	0.3	1.3	1.6
Netherlands	0.1	14.1	14.0	-16.3	0.1	0.2	0.5	0.3
New Zealand	0.1	0.0	–	–	–	–	–	–
Norway	35.0	–	0.0	0.0	–	–	–	–
Sweden	26.7	–	3.6	-6.9	–	–	–	–
Switzerland	–	0.0	0.0	–	–	0.0	0.0	–
United Kingdom	-14.9	8.1	6.5	11.1	0.1	0.2	0.1	0.2
United States	312.0	122.0	313.0	294.0	22.0	17.0	15.0	15.0
TOTAL	*543.9*	*530.9*	*625.2*	*673.6*	*22.9*	*18.7*	*17.7*	*18.3*
MULTILATERAL								
AF.D.F.	–	–	–	–	–	–	–	–
AF.D.B.	–	–	–	–	–	–	–	–
AS.D.B.	–	–	–	–	–	–	–	–
CAR.D.B.	–	–	–	–	–	–	–	–
E.E.C.	–	0.3	0.1	–	–	0.3	0.1	–
IBRD	11.6	7.7	11.0	14.9	–	–	–	–
IDA	–	–	–	2.6	–	–	–	2.6
I.D.B.	13.3	30.4	28.7	45.2	10.6	8.3	14.9	20.7
IFAD	–	–	–	–	–	–	–	–
I.F.C.	-0.1	4.2	1.6	0.1	–	–	–	–
IMF TRUST FUND	–	–	–	–	–	–	–	–
U.N. AGENCIES	–	–	–	–	–	–	–	–
UNDP	0.9	1.3	1.4	1.7	0.9	1.3	1.4	1.7
UNTA	0.4	0.4	0.3	0.2	0.4	0.4	0.3	0.2
UNICEF	0.1	0.2	0.1	0.2	0.1	0.2	0.1	0.2
UNRWA	–	–	–	–	–	–	–	–
WFP	–	–	0.3	0.1	–	–	0.3	0.1
UNHCR	–	–	–	–	–	–	–	–
Other Multilateral	0.2	0.2	0.6	1.9	0.2	0.2	0.6	1.9
Arab OPEC Agencies	–	–	–	–	–	–	–	–
TOTAL	*26.3*	*44.6*	*44.1*	*67.0*	*12.1*	*10.5*	*17.7*	*27.5*
OPEC COUNTRIES	*18.7*	*17.5*	–	–	–	–	–	–
E.E.C.+ MEMBERS	*-28.1*	*5.2*	*-1.5*	*264.1*	*0.6*	*1.6*	*1.6*	*1.6*
TOTAL	***588.9***	***592.9***	***669.3***	***740.6***	***35.0***	***29.2***	***35.4***	***45.7***

	1977	1978	1979	1980	1977	1978	1979	1980
ODA LOANS GROSS					**ODA LOANS NET**			
DAC COUNTRIES								
Australia	–	–	–	–	–	–	–	–
Austria	–	–	–	–	0.0	0.0	–	–
Belgium	–	–	–	–	–	–	–	–
Canada	–	–	–	–	–	–	–	–
Denmark	–	–	–	–	–	–	–	–
Finland	–	–	–	–	–	–	–	–
France	–	–	–	–	–	–	–	–
Germany, Fed. Rep.	–	0.4	0.1	–	–	0.4	0.1	–
Italy	–	–	–	–	–	–	–	–
Japan	–	–	–	–	–	–	–	–
Netherlands	–	–	–	–	–	–	–	–
New Zealand	–	–	–	–	–	–	–	–
Norway	–	–	–	–	–	–	–	–
Sweden	–	–	–	–	–	–	–	–
Switzerland	–	–	–	–	–	–	–	–
United Kingdom	–	–	–	–	–	–	–	–
United States	10.0	9.0	9.0	10.0	8.0	7.0	7.0	8.0
TOTAL	*10.0*	*9.4*	*9.1*	*10.0*	*8.0*	*7.4*	*7.1*	*8.0*
MULTILATERAL	*13.3*	*9.6*	*17.5*	*26.1*	*10.6*	*6.8*	*14.7*	*23.0*
OPEC COUNTRIES	–	–	–	–	–	–	–	–
E.E.C.+ MEMBERS	–	*0.4*	*0.1*	–	–	*0.4*	*0.1*	–
TOTAL	***23.3***	***19.0***	***26.6***	***36.1***	***18.6***	***14.2***	***21.8***	***31.0***

	1977	1978	1979	1980	1977	1978	1979	1980
TOTAL OFFICIAL GROSS					**TOTAL OFFICIAL NET**			
DAC COUNTRIES								
Australia	–	–	–	–	–	–	–	–
Austria	0.0	0.0	–	–	0.0	0.0	–	–
Belgium	0.1	0.1	0.1	0.1	0.1	0.1	0.1	0.1
Canada	119.7	5.7	1.3	1.2	58.7	1.0	-3.1	-4.9
Denmark	–	–	–	–	–	–	–	–
Finland	–	–	–	0.0	–	–	–	0.0
France	–	–	–	0.3	–	–	–	0.3
Germany, Fed. Rep.	0.3	0.9	0.7	0.8	-0.5	-5.7	0.7	0.8
Italy	0.0	0.0	0.1	–	0.0	0.0	0.1	–
Japan	0.3	0.3	1.3	1.6	0.3	0.3	1.3	1.6
Netherlands	0.1	0.2	0.5	0.3	0.1	0.2	0.5	0.3
New Zealand	0.1	–	–	–	0.1	–	–	–
Norway	–	–	–	–	–	–	–	–
Sweden	–	–	–	–	–	–	–	–
Switzerland	–	0.0	0.0	–	–	0.0	0.0	–
United Kingdom	0.1	0.2	0.1	0.2	0.1	0.2	0.1	0.2
United States	27.0	24.0	93.0	392.0	8.0	5.0	-9.0	-12.0
TOTAL	*147.7*	*31.4*	*97.0*	*396.5*	*66.8*	*1.1*	*-9.4*	*-13.6*
MULTILATERAL	*31.7*	*51.7*	*52.1*	*75.7*	*26.3*	*44.6*	*44.1*	*66.9*
OPEC COUNTRIES	*18.7*	*17.5*	–	–	*18.7*	*17.5*	–	–
E.E.C.+ MEMBERS	*0.6*	*1.6*	*1.6*	*1.6*	*-0.3*	*-4.9*	*1.6*	*1.6*
TOTAL	***198.2***	***100.5***	***149.1***	***472.2***	***111.8***	***63.1***	***34.7***	***53.3***

	197
TOTAL ODA GROSS	
Australia	
Austria	0
Belgium	0
Canada	
Denmark	
Finland	
France	
Germany, Fed. Rep.	0
Italy	0
Japan	0
Netherlands	0
New Zealand	
Norway	
Sweden	
Switzerland	
United Kingdom	0
United States	24
TOTAL	*24*
AF.D.F.	
AF.D.B.	
AS.D.B.	
CAR.D.B.	
E.E.C.	
IBRD	
IDA	
I.D.B.	13
IFAD	
I.F.C.	
IMF TRUST FUND	
U.N. AGENCIES	
UNDP	0
UNTA	0
UNICEF	0
UNRWA	
WFP	
UNHCR	
Other Multilateral	0
Arab OPEC Agencies	
TOTAL	*14*
OPEC COUNTRIES	
E.E.C.+ MEMBERS	*C*
TOTAL	***39***
GRANTS	
Australia	
Austria	0
Belgium	0
Canada	
Denmark	
Finland	
France	
Germany, Fed. Rep.	0
Italy	0
Japan	0
Netherlands	0
New Zealand	
Norway	
Sweden	
Switzerland	
United Kingdom	0
United States	14
TOTAL	*14*
MULTILATERAL	*1*
OPEC COUNTRIES	
E.E.C.+ MEMBERS	*C*
TOTAL	***16***
TOTAL OOF GROSS	
Australia	
Austria	
Belgium	
Canada	119
Denmark	
Finland	
France	
Germany, Fed. Rep.	
Italy	
Japan	
Netherlands	
New Zealand	0
Norway	
Sweden	
Switzerland	
United Kingdom	
United States	3
TOTAL	*122*
MULTILATERAL	*16*
OPEC COUNTRIES	*18*
E.E.C.+ MEMBERS	
TOTAL	***158***

1978	1979	1980	1977	1978	1979	1980
			ODA COMMITMENTS			
–	–	–	–	–	–	–
0.0	–	–	–	–	–	–
0.1	0.1	0.1	–	–	–	–
–	–	–	–	–	–	0.0
–	–	–	–	–	–	–
–	–	0.0	–	–	–	0.0
–	–	0.3	–	–	–	–
0.9	0.7	0.8	0.2	0.7	1.9	1.0
0.0	0.1	–	0.0	0.0	0.1	–
0.3	1.3	1.6	0.3	0.4	1.5	4.1
0.2	0.5	0.3	0.2	0.2	0.4	0.3
–	–	–	–	–	–	–
–	–	–	–	–	–	–
–	–	–	–	–	–	–
0.0	0.0	–	–	–	–	–
0.2	0.1	0.2	0.1	0.2	0.1	0.2
19.0	17.0	17.0	16.8	23.3	20.6	1.9
20.7	*19.7*	*20.3*	*17.6*	*24.8*	*24.5*	*7.5*
–	–	–	–	–	–	–
–	–	–	–	–	–	–
–	–	–	–	–	–	–
–	–	–	–	–	–	–
0.3	0.1	–	–	0.1	0.1	0.0
–	–	–	–	–	–	–
–	–	2.9	–	–	–	–
11.1	17.7	23.5	–	19.0	19.4	34.9
–	–	–	–	–	–	–
–	–	–	–	–	–	–
–	–	–	–	–	–	–
–	–	–	1.5	2.0	2.7	4.1
1.3	1.4	1.7	–	–	–	–
0.4	0.3	0.2	–	–	–	–
0.2	0.1	0.2	–	–	–	–
–	–	–	–	–	–	–
–	0.3	0.1	–	–	–	–
–	–	–	–	–	–	–
0.2	0.6	1.9	–	–	–	–
–	–	–	–	–	–	–
13.3	*20.5*	*30.5*	*1.5*	*21.1*	*22.2*	*39.0*
–	–	–	–	–	–	–
1.6	*1.6*	*1.6*	*0.4*	*1.2*	*2.6*	*1.5*
34.0	***40.2***	***50.8***	***19.1***	***45.8***	***46.7***	***46.5***
			TECH. COOP. GRANTS			
–	–	–	–	–	–	–
0.0	–	–	0.0	0.0	–	–
0.1	0.1	0.1	0.1	0.1	0.0	0.1
–	–	–	–	–	–	–
–	–	–	–	–	–	–
–	–	0.0	–	–	–	0.0
–	–	0.3	–	–	–	0.3
0.4	0.6	0.8	0.3	0.4	0.6	0.8
0.0	0.1	–	0.0	0.0	0.1	–
0.3	1.3	1.6	0.3	0.3	1.3	1.6
0.2	0.5	0.3	0.1	0.2	0.3	0.3
–	–	–	–	–	–	–
–	–	–	–	–	–	–
–	–	–	–	–	–	–
0.0	0.0	–	–	–	0.0	–
0.2	0.1	0.2	0.1	0.2	0.1	0.2
10.0	8.0	7.0	1.0	2.0	1.0	1.0
11.3	*10.7*	*10.3*	*1.9*	*3.2*	*3.4*	*4.3*
3.7	*3.0*	*4.4*	*1.5*	*3.5*	*2.6*	*4.1*
–	–	–	–	–	–	–
1.2	*1.5*	*1.6*	*0.6*	*0.9*	*1.2*	*1.6*
15.0	***13.6***	***14.7***	***3.4***	***6.7***	***6.1***	***8.4***
			TOTAL OOF NET			
–	–	–	–	–	–	–
–	–	–	–	0.0	–	–
–	–	–	–	–	–	–
5.7	1.3	1.2	58.7	1.0	-3.1	-4.9
–	–	–	–	–	–	–
–	–	–	–	–	–	–
–	–	–	–	–	–	–
–	–	–	-0.9	-6.5	–	–
–	–	–	–	–	–	–
–	–	–	–	–	–	–
–	–	–	–	–	–	–
–	–	–	0.1	–	–	–
–	–	–	–	–	–	–
–	–	–	–	–	–	–
–	–	–	–	–	–	–
–	–	–	–	–	–	–
5.0	76.0	375.0	-14.0	-12.0	-24.0	-27.0
10.7	*77.3*	*376.2*	*43.9*	*-17.6*	*-27.1*	*-31.9*
38.3	*31.7*	*45.2*	*14.2*	*34.0*	*26.4*	*39.5*
17.5	–	–	*18.7*	*17.5*	–	–
–	–	–	*-0.9*	*-6.5*	–	–
66.5	***108.9***	***421.4***	***76.8***	***33.9***	***-0.7***	***7.6***

MAIN AID AGGREGATES

	1977	1978	1979	1980
DAC COUNTRIES COMBINED				
PRIVATE SECTOR NET	477.1	529.8	634.6	687.3
Direct Investment	278.9	214.1	449.8	367.9
Portfolio Invest.	127.0	374.4	231.7	295.3
Export Credits	71.2	-58.7	-47.0	24.1
OFFICIAL & PRIVATE				
GROSS:				
Contractual Lending	304.0	52.7	133.0	508.4
Export Credits Tot.	294.0	43.2	51.0	123.4
Export Credits Priv	171.2	32.5	46.7	122.2
OTHER NET DATA				
Contractual Lending	123.1	-68.9	-67.0	0.1
Export Credits Tot.	115.1	-76.3	-61.1	13.1
(Bank Sector Loans)	–	–	–	4.0
ODA CONCESSIONALITY				
Total:Grant Element	73.0	69.0	75.0	100.0
Loans:Grant Element	61.0	62.0	62.0	–
OTHER SOURCES				
CMEA Countr.(Gross)	–	–	–	–
Intra LDCS Exc.OPEC	–	–	–	–
Other	–	–	–	–
ALL SOURCE COMMITMENTS				
TOTAL BILATERAL	121.7	31.3	25.4	40.8
of which				
OPEC (ODA)	–	–	–	–
CMEA (ODA)	–	–	–	–
TOTAL MULTILAT.(ODA)	1.5	21.1	22.2	39.0
TOTAL BIL.& MULTIL.	123.2	52.3	47.5	79.8
of which				
ODA Grants	6.9	6.8	11.3	11.6
ODA Loans	12.2	39.0	35.4	34.9
ODA CONCESSIONALITY				
Total: Grant Element	73.0	71.0	72.0	72.0
Loans: Grant Element	61.0	63.0	64.0	63.0

INDEBTEDNESS

	1977	1978	1979	1980
TOTAL DEBT DISBURSED	***1354.7***	***1905.6***	***2106.4***	
Debt to DAC Countries	1077.0	1533.0	1695.0	
ODA	108.0	114.0	121.0	
Total Export Credits	61.0	68.0	67.0	
Other Private Market	908.0	1351.0	1507.0	
International Org.	192.2	229.6	268.0	
CMEA	–	–	–	
Other	85.5	143.0	143.4	
TOTAL DEBT SERVICE	***166.2***	***572.5***	***393.7***	
Paid to DAC Countries	143.7	536.0	345.2	
ODA	3.0	4.0	5.0	
Total Export Credits	17.4	18.2	18.1	
Other Private Market	123.3	513.8	322.1	
International Org.	16.1	20.8	26.4	
CMEA	–	–	–	
Other	6.4	15.7	22.1	

ECONOMIC INDICATORS

	1977	1978	1979	1980
GNP Curr. Prices, $M	2109.8	2409.4	2761.0	3193.0
Real GNP, 1976=100	104.0	112.0	117.0	123.0
GNP/Cap Curr. Prices,$	1230.0	1373.0	1539.0	1740.0
GNP/cap Atlas Basis, $	1226.8	1389.2	1545.2	1727.6
Real GNP/Cap, 1976=100	101.0	107.0	110.0	112.0
Population, Million	1.7	1.8	1.8	1.8
Curr.A/C Deficit(-),$M	-183.0	-240.5	-356.2	–
BOP Exp. & Transf.,$M	1388.4	1741.2	2107.7	–
Exp. to OECD CIF, $M	517.7	623.1	887.8	844.1
of which				
Manufact.	128.8	162.2	190.3	158.7
Imp. from OECD FOB, $M	2175.0	2562.2	2200.4	3022.7
Reserves ex. Gold, $M	70.9	150.4	118.8	117.4

	TOTAL RECEIPTS NET 1977	1978	1979	1980	TOTAL ODA NET 1977	1978	1979	1980
DAC COUNTRIES								
Australia	262.1	291.3	286.1	324.2	239.9	266.9	260.3	276.0
Austria	0.4	0.4	0.5	0.4	0.4	0.4	0.5	0.4
Belgium	0.1	0.3	0.0	0.2	0.0	–	–	–
Canada	0.0	0.0	0.0	0.2	0.0	0.0	0.0	0.2
Denmark	–	–	–	–	–	–	–	–
Finland	–	–	0.0	0.0	–	–	0.0	0.0
France	0.1	–	–	0.3	–	–	–	0.3
Germany, Fed. Rep.	2.0	2.2	6.0	6.3	0.5	0.6	0.8	3.4
Italy	–	0.0	-0.3	–	–	0.0	–	–
Japan	-7.6	4.7	0.7	1.0	-2.2	-0.9	4.5	1.8
Netherlands	0.2	0.1	0.2	0.3	0.2	0.1	0.2	0.3
New Zealand	4.8	6.4	2.8	2.3	1.9	2.9	2.3	2.3
Norway	0.5	0.4	0.6	1.6	0.5	0.4	0.6	1.6
Sweden	–	–	–	–	–	–	–	–
Switzerland	–	–	–	–	–	–	–	–
United Kingdom	1.7	4.9	6.7	9.3	0.1	0.4	0.3	0.5
United States	-18.0	–	–	–	–	–	–	–
TOTAL	*246.4*	*310.7*	*303.2*	*346.1*	*241.4*	*270.9*	*269.4*	*286.8*
MULTILATERAL								
AF.D.F.	–	–	–	–	–	–	–	–
AF.D.B.	–	–	–	–	–	–	–	–
AS.D.B.	3.5	4.6	5.4	13.1	3.5	4.6	2.4	7.4
CAR.D.B.	–	–	–	–	–	–	–	–
E.E.C.	–	1.6	2.7	3.9	–	1.6	0.2	0.3
IBRD	2.6	-0.1	3.9	-0.2	–	–	–	–
IDA	7.7	5.5	6.4	12.5	7.7	5.5	6.4	12.5
I.D.B.	–	–	–	–	–	–	–	–
IFAD	–	–	–	–	–	–	–	–
I.F.C.	–	–	–	–	–	–	–	–
IMF TRUST FUND	–	10.4	–	14.6	–	10.4	–	14.6
U.N. AGENCIES	–	–	–	–	–	–	–	–
UNDP	1.4	1.7	2.2	2.6	1.4	1.7	2.2	2.6
UNTA	0.5	0.8	0.9	0.0	0.5	0.8	0.9	0.0
UNICEF	0.1	0.1	0.1	0.4	0.1	0.1	0.1	0.4
UNRWA	–	–	–	–	–	–	–	–
WFP	–	–	0.1	–	–	–	0.1	–
UNHCR	–	0.1	–	0.2	–	0.1	–	0.2
Other Multilateral	0.8	0.6	0.4	0.7	0.8	0.6	0.4	0.7
Arab OPEC Agencies	–	–	–	–	–	–	–	–
TOTAL	*16.6*	*25.2*	*22.1*	*47.8*	*14.0*	*25.3*	*12.8*	*38.6*
OPEC COUNTRIES	–	–	*2.2*	*0.4*	–	–	*2.2*	*0.4*
E.E.C.+ MEMBERS	*4.1*	*9.1*	*15.1*	*20.3*	*0.8*	*2.8*	*1.5*	*4.8*
TOTAL	**263.1**	**336.0**	**327.4**	**394.3**	**255.4**	**296.2**	**284.3**	**325.9**

	ODA LOANS GROSS 1977	1978	1979	1980	ODA LOANS NET 1977	1978	1979	1980
DAC COUNTRIES								
Australia	–	4.6	–	–	-2.9	1.5	-3.2	-3.4
Austria	–	–	–	–	–	–	–	–
Belgium	–	–	–	–	–	–	–	–
Canada	–	–	–	–	–	–	–	–
Denmark	–	–	–	–	–	–	–	–
Finland	–	–	–	–	–	–	–	–
France	–	–	–	–	–	–	–	–
Germany, Fed. Rep.	–	–	–	1.3	–	–	–	1.3
Italy	–	–	–	–	–	–	–	–
Japan	1.2	0.5	5.4	3.9	-3.7	-1.5	3.9	1.1
Netherlands	–	–	–	–	–	–	–	–
New Zealand	–	–	–	–	–	–	–	–
Norway	–	–	–	–	–	–	–	–
Sweden	–	–	–	–	–	–	–	–
Switzerland	–	–	–	–	–	–	–	–
United Kingdom	–	0.3	–	–	–	0.3	–	–
United States	–	–	–	–	–	–	–	–
TOTAL	*1.2*	*5.4*	*5.4*	*5.2*	*-6.5*	*0.3*	*0.7*	*-1.1*
MULTILATERAL	*11.6*	*21.2*	*9.6*	*35.2*	*11.1*	*20.5*	*8.8*	*34.4*
OPEC COUNTRIES	–	–	*2.2*	*0.4*	–	–	*2.2*	*0.4*
E.E.C.+ MEMBERS	–	*0.3*	–	*1.3*	–	*0.3*	–	*1.3*
TOTAL	**12.8**	**26.6**	**17.2**	**40.9**	**4.5**	**20.8**	**11.7**	**33.7**

	TOTAL OFFICIAL GROSS 1977	1978	1979	1980	TOTAL OFFICIAL NET 1977	1978	1979	1980
DAC COUNTRIES								
Australia	242.8	270.0	268.2	280.4	239.9	266.9	264.5	276.0
Austria	0.4	0.4	0.5	0.4	0.4	0.4	0.5	0.4
Belgium	0.0	–	–	–	0.0	–	–	–
Canada	0.0	0.0	0.0	0.2	0.0	0.0	0.0	0.2
Denmark	–	–	–	–	–	–	–	–
Finland	–	–	0.0	0.0	–	–	0.0	0.0
France	–	–	–	0.3	–	–	–	0.3
Germany, Fed. Rep.	0.5	0.8	6.3	7.7	0.5	0.8	6.3	7.7
Italy	–	0.0	–	–	–	0.0	–	–
Japan	2.7	1.1	6.0	4.7	-2.2	-0.9	4.5	1.8
Netherlands	0.2	0.1	0.2	0.3	0.2	0.1	0.2	0.3
New Zealand	7.4	2.9	2.3	2.3	4.2	2.9	2.3	2.3
Norway	0.5	0.4	0.6	1.6	0.5	0.4	0.6	1.6
Sweden	–	–	–	–	–	–	–	–
Switzerland	–	–	–	–	–	–	–	–
United Kingdom	1.4	4.6	6.7	8.7	1.4	4.6	6.7	8.7
United States	–	–	–	–	-18.0	–	–	–
TOTAL	*255.9*	*280.4*	*290.7*	*306.6*	*227.0*	*275.3*	*285.5*	*299.3*
MULTILATERAL	*18.5*	*27.5*	*24.5*	*50.8*	*16.6*	*25.2*	*22.1*	*47.8*
OPEC COUNTRIES	–	–	*2.2*	*0.4*	–	–	*2.2*	*0.4*
E.E.C.+ MEMBERS	*2.1*	*7.2*	*15.9*	*21.0*	*2.1*	*7.2*	*15.9*	*21.0*
TOTAL	**274.4**	**307.8**	**317.4**	**357.8**	**243.6**	**300.5**	**309.8**	**347.6**

TOTAL ODA GROSS	197
Australia	242
Austria	0
Belgium	0
Canada	0
Denmark	
Finland	
France	
Germany, Fed. Rep.	0
Italy	
Japan	2
Netherlands	0
New Zealand	1
Norway	0
Sweden	
Switzerland	
United Kingdom	0
United States	
TOTAL	*249*
AF.D.F.	
AF.D.B.	
AS.D.B.	4
CAR.D.B.	
E.E.C.	
IBRD	
IDA	7
I.D.B.	
IFAD	
I.F.C.	
IMF TRUST FUND	
U.N. AGENCIES	
UNDP	1
UNTA	0
UNICEF	0
UNRWA	
WFP	
UNHCR	
Other Multilateral	0
Arab OPEC Agencies	
TOTAL	*14*
OPEC COUNTRIES	
E.E.C.+ MEMBERS	*0*
TOTAL	**263**

GRANTS	197
Australia	242
Austria	0
Belgium	0
Canada	0
Denmark	
Finland	
France	
Germany, Fed. Rep.	0
Italy	
Japan	1
Netherlands	0
New Zealand	1
Norway	0
Sweden	
Switzerland	
United Kingdom	0
United States	
TOTAL	*247*
MULTILATERAL	*3*
OPEC COUNTRIES	
E.E.C.+ MEMBERS	*0*
TOTAL	**250**

TOTAL OOF GROSS	197
Australia	
Austria	
Belgium	
Canada	
Denmark	
Finland	
France	
Germany, Fed. Rep.	
Italy	
Japan	
Netherlands	
New Zealand	5
Norway	
Sweden	
Switzerland	
United Kingdom	1
United States	
TOTAL	*6*
MULTILATERAL	*4*
OPEC COUNTRIES	
E.E.C.+ MEMBERS	*1*
TOTAL	**10**

1978	1979	1980	1977	1978	1979	1980
			ODA COMMITMENTS			
270.0	263.5	279.5	248.7	270.5	265.7	283.2
0.4	0.5	0.4	–	–	–	–
–	–	–	–	–	–	–
0.0	0.0	0.2	–	0.0	–	0.2
–	–	–	–	–	–	0.1
–	0.0	0.0	–	–	0.0	0.0
–	–	0.3	–	–	–	0.3
0.6	0.8	3.4	0.1	0.7	4.5	8.0
0.0	–	–	–	0.0	–	–
1.1	6.0	4.7	2.4	2.6	20.3	4.8
0.1	0.2	0.3	0.2	0.2	0.4	0.3
2.9	2.3	2.3	0.7	2.5	0.8	2.9
0.4	0.6	1.6	0.5	1.4	0.4	7.8
–	–	–	–	–	–	–
–	–	–	–	–	–	–
0.4	0.3	0.5	0.1	2.3	0.3	0.5
–	–	–	–	–	–	0.0
276.0	*274.1*	*293.1*	*252.6*	*280.1*	*292.6*	*308.1*
–	–	–	–	–	–	–
–	–	–	–	–	–	–
5.3	3.1	8.1	–	12.6	6.2	8.0
–	–	–	–	–	–	–
1.6	0.2	0.3	–	14.6	0.2	3.4
–	–	–	–	–	–	–
5.5	6.5	12.6	19.0	20.0	–	25.0
–	–	–	–	–	–	–
–	–	–	–	–	–	–
–	–	–	–	–	–	–
10.4	–	14.6	–	–	–	–
–	–	–	2.8	3.3	3.8	3.9
1.7	2.2	2.6	–	–	–	–
0.8	0.9	0.0	–	–	–	–
0.1	0.1	0.4	–	–	–	–
–	–	–	–	–	–	–
–	0.1	–	–	–	–	–
0.1	–	0.2	–	–	–	–
0.6	0.4	0.7	–	–	–	–
–	–	–	–	–	–	–
26.0	*13.6*	*39.5*	*21.8*	*50.5*	*10.1*	*40.3*
–	*2.2*	*0.4*	–	*3.6*	–	–
2.8	*1.5*	*4.8*	*0.4*	*17.8*	*5.4*	*12.5*
302.0	***289.8***	***333.1***	***274.4***	***334.2***	***302.7***	***348.4***
			TECH. COOP. GRANTS			
265.4	263.5	279.5	1.7	2.5	2.0	4.1
0.4	0.5	0.4	0.4	0.4	0.5	0.4
–	–	–	0.0	–	–	–
0.0	0.0	0.2	–	–	–	–
–	–	–	–	–	–	–
–	0.0	0.0	–	–	0.0	0.0
–	–	0.3	–	–	–	0.3
0.6	0.8	2.1	0.5	0.6	0.8	2.1
0.0	–	–	–	0.0	–	–
0.6	0.6	0.7	1.0	0.6	0.6	0.7
0.1	0.2	0.3	0.2	0.1	0.2	0.3
2.9	2.3	2.3	0.7	1.1	0.9	1.0
0.4	0.6	1.6	0.5	0.4	0.4	0.1
–	–	–	–	–	–	–
–	–	–	–	–	–	–
0.1	0.3	0.5	0.1	0.1	0.3	0.5
–	–	–	–	–	–	–
270.6	*268.7*	*287.9*	*5.1*	*5.9*	*5.6*	*9.5*
4.8	*3.9*	*4.3*	*3.0*	*3.3*	*3.7*	*3.9*
–	–	–	–	–	–	–
2.5	*1.5*	*3.5*	*0.8*	*0.9*	*1.3*	*3.1*
275.5	***272.6***	***292.2***	***8.0***	***9.1***	***9.3***	***13.4***
			TOTAL OOF NET			
–	4.7	0.9	–	–	4.2	0.0
–	–	–	–	–	–	–
–	–	–	–	–	–	–
–	–	–	–	–	–	–
–	–	–	–	–	–	–
–	–	–	–	–	–	–
–	–	–	–	–	–	–
0.2	5.5	4.3	–	0.2	5.5	4.3
–	–	–	–	–	–	–
–	–	–	–	–	–	–
–	–	–	–	–	–	–
–	–	–	2.3	–	–	–
–	–	–	–	–	–	–
–	–	–	–	–	–	–
–	–	–	–	–	–	–
4.2	6.4	8.2	1.3	4.2	6.4	8.2
–	–	–	-18.0	–	–	–
4.4	*16.6*	*13.5*	*-14.4*	*4.4*	*16.1*	*12.5*
1.4	*11.0*	*11.3*	*2.6*	*-0.1*	*9.4*	*9.1*
–	–	–	–	–	–	–
4.4	*14.4*	*16.2*	*1.3*	*4.4*	*14.4*	*16.2*
5.8	***27.5***	***24.7***	***-11.8***	***4.3***	***25.5***	***21.6***

	1977	1978	1979	1980
MAIN AID AGGREGATES				
DAC COUNTRIES COMBINED				
PRIVATE SECTOR NET	19.5	35.5	17.6	46.8
Direct Investment	23.4	33.0	19.3	40.4
Portfolio Invest.	1.6	1.4	-0.6	6.4
Export Credits	-5.6	1.1	-1.0	0.0
OFFICIAL & PRIVATE				
GROSS:				
Contractual Lending	9.0	21.7	23.6	22.1
Export Credits Tot.	6.5	11.9	6.3	4.3
Export Credits Priv	1.0	11.9	1.6	3.4
OTHER NET DATA				
Contractual Lending	-26.6	5.7	15.8	11.4
Export Credits Tot.	-21.3	1.1	3.2	-0.1
(Bank Sector Loans)	-19.0	51.0	-13.0	-10.0
ODA CONCESSIONALITY				
Total:Grant Element	99.0	99.0	96.0	98.0
Loans:Grant Element	31.0	56.0	52.0	59.0
OTHER SOURCES				
CMEA Countr.(Gross)	–	–	–	–
Intra LDCS Exc.OPEC	–	–	–	–
Other	–	–	–	–
ALL SOURCE COMMITMENTS				
TOTAL BILATERAL	258.1	288.6	292.8	354.6
of which				
OPEC (ODA)	–	3.6	–	–
CMEA (ODA)	–	–	–	–
TOTAL MULTILAT.(ODA)	21.8	50.5	10.1	40.3
TOTAL BIL.& MULTIL.	279.9	339.1	302.9	394.9
of which				
ODA Grants	254.2	282.8	277.1	305.9
ODA Loans	20.2	51.5	25.6	42.5
ODA CONCESSIONALITY				
Total: Grant Element	98.0	95.0	96.0	97.0
Loans: Grant Element	80.0	66.0	58.0	74.0
INDEBTEDNESS				
TOTAL DEBT DISBURSED	***354.9***	***397.9***	***402.5***	
Debt to DAC Countries	264.0	291.0	283.0	
ODA	26.0	31.0	30.0	
Total Export Credits	7.0	21.0	19.0	
Other Private Market	231.0	239.0	234.0	
International Org.	90.9	106.9	119.5	
CMEA	–	–	–	
Other	–	–	–	
TOTAL DEBT SERVICE	***50.8***	***39.0***	***53.1***	
Paid to DAC Countries	45.3	32.3	45.5	
ODA	5.5	5.2	5.1	
Total Export Credits	20.3	6.1	7.6	
Other Private Market	19.5	21.0	32.8	
International Org.	5.5	6.7	7.6	
CMEA	–	–	–	
Other	–	–	–	
ECONOMIC INDICATORS				
GNP Curr. Prices, $M	1640.6	1835.7	2223.3	2427.6
Real GNP, 1976=100	95.0	103.0	105.0	102.0
GNP/Cap Curr. Prices,$	584.0	639.0	756.0	807.0
GNP/cap Atlas Basis, $	617.1	699.7	758.1	783.5
Real GNP/Cap, 1976=100	93.0	98.0	98.0	93.0
Population, Million	2.8	2.9	2.9	3.0
Curr.A/C Deficit(-),$M	–	–	–	–
BOP Exp. & Transf.,$M	–	–	–	–
Exp. to OECD CIF, $M	693.2	706.9	937.5	1024.5
of which				
Manufact.	15.3	7.4	12.8	13.7
Imp. from OECD FOB, $M	362.9	478.6	603.7	723.3
Reserves ex. Gold, $M	426.6	404.7	503.6	423.4

	1977	1978	1979	1980	1977	1978	1979	1980	197
TOTAL RECEIPTS NET / **TOTAL ODA NET** / **TOTAL ODA GROSS**									
DAC COUNTRIES									
Australia	–	–	–	–	–	–	–	–	
Austria	0.1	0.1	0.1	0.1	0.1	0.1	0.1	0.1	0
Belgium	0.0	0.3	0.1	0.1	0.0	0.3	0.1	0.1	0
Canada	0.2	2.7	0.0	0.0	0.0	0.0	0.0	0.0	
Denmark	–	–	–	0.0	–	–	–	0.0	
Finland	–	–	–	–	–	–	–	–	
France	-1.0	0.0	17.6	10.4	–	–	–	0.4	
Germany, Fed. Rep.	22.9	12.2	32.9	-8.5	4.2	3.4	4.6	4.7	5
Italy	-1.8	-1.2	-1.1	1.1	0.2	0.1	0.1	0.0	0
Japan	17.0	14.9	8.4	18.5	14.7	12.5	7.2	16.5	14
Netherlands	0.2	0.3	0.5	15.8	0.2	0.3	0.5	1.2	0
New Zealand	–	–	–	–	–	–	–	–	
Norway	0.1	–	0.0	–	0.1	–	–	0.0	0
Sweden	–	0.3	0.4	-0.3	–	–	–	–	
Switzerland	0.4	0.7	1.2	1.8	0.5	0.7	1.6	1.7	0
United Kingdom	0.3	0.6	-1.4	1.7	0.3	0.4	0.6	0.6	0
United States	4.0	2.0	1.0	-1.0	5.0	3.0	2.0	–	6
TOTAL	*42.3*	*32.8*	*59.5*	*39.7*	*25.2*	*20.8*	*16.7*	*25.3*	*27*
MULTILATERAL									
AF.D.F.	–	–	–	–	–	–	–	–	
AF.D.B.	–	–	–	–	–	–	–	–	
AS.D.B.	–	–	–	–	–	–	–	–	
CAR.D.B.	–	–	–	–	–	–	–	–	
E.E.C.	–	0.0	0.1	–	–	0.0	0.1	–	
IBRD	6.4	7.2	15.6	28.8	0.1	1.2	1.7	0.8	0
IDA	5.1	5.1	3.3	–	5.1	5.1	3.3	–	5
I.D.B.	15.8	20.0	11.7	2.0	16.0	12.9	5.9	0.1	18
IFAD	–	–	–	–	–	–	–	–	
I.F.C.	–	–	–	–	–	–	–	–	
IMF TRUST FUND	–	–	–	–	–	–	–	–	
U.N. AGENCIES	–	–	–	–	–	–	–	–	
UNDP	1.0	1.7	1.7	2.2	1.0	1.7	1.7	2.2	1
UNTA	0.1	0.2	0.3	0.2	0.1	0.2	0.3	0.2	0
UNICEF	0.1	0.7	–	0.7	0.1	0.7	–	0.7	0
UNRWA	–	–	–	–	–	–	–	–	
WFP	0.2	0.2	0.7	0.6	0.2	0.2	0.7	0.6	0
UNHCR	–	–	–	–	–	–	–	–	
Other Multilateral	0.1	0.2	0.1	0.8	0.1	0.2	0.1	0.8	0
Arab OPEC Agencies	–	–	–	–	–	–	–	–	
TOTAL	*28.9*	*35.3*	*33.5*	*35.1*	*22.8*	*22.2*	*13.8*	*5.3*	*25*
OPEC COUNTRIES	–	–	–	–	–	–	–	–	
E.E.C.+ MEMBERS	*20.7*	*12.2*	*48.6*	*20.6*	*4.9*	*4.5*	*5.9*	*7.1*	*5*
TOTAL	***71.2***	***68.1***	***93.0***	***74.8***	***48.0***	***43.0***	***30.5***	***30.5***	***52***

	1977	1978	1979	1980	1977	1978	1979	1980	197
ODA LOANS GROSS / **ODA LOANS NET** / **GRANTS**									
DAC COUNTRIES									
Australia	–	–	–	–	–	–	–	–	
Austria	–	–	–	–	–	–	–	–	0
Belgium	–	–	–	–	–	–	–	–	0
Canada	–	–	–	–	0.0	0.0	0.0	0.0	
Denmark	–	–	–	–	–	–	–	–	
Finland	–	–	–	–	–	–	–	–	
France	–	–	–	–	–	–	–	–	
Germany, Fed. Rep.	1.6	1.6	2.4	2.2	0.8	0.0	1.1	0.4	3
Italy	–	–	–	–	–	–	–	–	0
Japan	13.2	7.5	1.2	3.9	13.2	7.2	-0.4	1.1	1
Netherlands	–	–	–	–	–	–	–	–	0
New Zealand	–	–	–	–	–	–	–	–	
Norway	–	–	–	–	–	–	–	–	0
Sweden	–	–	–	–	–	–	–	–	
Switzerland	–	–	–	–	–	–	–	–	0
United Kingdom	–	–	–	–	–	–	–	–	0
United States	2.0	3.0	2.0	–	1.0	1.0	–	-2.0	4
TOTAL	*16.8*	*12.1*	*5.6*	*6.0*	*14.9*	*8.2*	*0.7*	*-0.6*	*10*
MULTILATERAL	*23.8*	*23.8*	*16.5*	*7.1*	*21.2*	*18.5*	*10.6*	*0.6*	*1*
OPEC COUNTRIES	–	–	–	–	–	–	–	–	
E.E.C.+ MEMBERS	*1.6*	*1.6*	*2.4*	*2.2*	*0.8*	*0.0*	*1.1*	*0.4*	*4*
TOTAL	***40.6***	***36.0***	***22.1***	***13.2***	***36.2***	***26.8***	***11.3***	***0.0***	***11***

	1977	1978	1979	1980	1977	1978	1979	1980	197
TOTAL OFFICIAL GROSS / **TOTAL OFFICIAL NET** / **TOTAL OOF GROSS**									
DAC COUNTRIES									
Australia	–	–	–	–	–	–	–	–	
Austria	0.1	0.1	0.1	0.1	0.1	0.1	0.1	0.1	
Belgium	0.0	0.3	0.1	0.1	0.0	0.3	0.1	0.1	
Canada	–	6.7	–	–	0.0	2.7	0.0	0.0	
Denmark	–	–	–	0.0	–	–	–	0.0	
Finland	–	–	–	–	–	–	–	–	
France	–	–	16.3	0.4	–	–	16.3	0.4	
Germany, Fed. Rep.	5.0	5.1	12.3	7.1	4.2	3.4	10.5	4.2	
Italy	0.2	0.1	0.1	0.0	-0.1	-0.1	-0.2	-0.3	
Japan	14.7	12.8	8.7	19.2	14.7	12.5	7.2	16.5	
Netherlands	0.2	0.3	0.5	1.2	0.2	0.3	0.5	1.2	
New Zealand	–	–	–	–	–	–	–	–	
Norway	0.1	–	–	0.0	0.1	–	–	0.0	
Sweden	–	–	–	–	–	–	–	–	
Switzerland	0.5	0.7	1.6	1.7	0.5	0.7	1.6	1.7	
United Kingdom	0.3	0.4	0.6	0.6	0.3	0.4	0.6	0.6	
United States	6.0	5.0	4.0	2.0	4.0	2.0	1.0	-1.0	
TOTAL	*27.1*	*31.4*	*44.2*	*32.4*	*23.9*	*22.3*	*37.5*	*23.4*	
MULTILATERAL	*32.5*	*41.6*	*40.2*	*43.2*	*28.9*	*35.3*	*33.5*	*35.1*	*7*
OPEC COUNTRIES	–	–	–	–	–	–	–	–	
E.E.C.+ MEMBERS	*5.8*	*6.2*	*29.9*	*9.4*	*4.6*	*4.3*	*27.7*	*6.2*	
TOTAL	***59.6***	***73.0***	***84.4***	***75.6***	***52.8***	***57.6***	***70.9***	***58.5***	***7***

ODA COMMITMENTS

1978	1979	1980	1977	1978	1979	1980
–	–	–	–	–	–	–
0.1	0.1	0.1	–	–	–	–
0.3	0.1	0.1	–	–	–	–
–	–	–	–	–	–	–
–	–	0.0	–	–	–	–
–	–	–	–	–	–	–
–	–	0.4	–	–	–	0.4
5.1	5.9	6.5	4.9	10.1	13.1	7.6
0.1	0.1	0.0	0.2	0.1	0.1	0.0
12.8	8.7	19.2	12.9	6.5	49.1	68.8
0.3	0.5	1.2	1.4	0.9	0.3	1.4
–	–	–	–	–	–	–
–	–	0.0	–	–	–	–
–	–	–	–	–	–	–
0.7	1.6	1.7	0.7	0.7	0.9	0.9
0.4	0.6	0.6	0.3	0.4	0.6	0.6
5.0	4.0	2.0	2.2	3.1	8.6	2.7
24.7	*21.5*	*31.9*	*22.6*	*21.8*	*72.6*	*82.3*
–	–	–	–	–	–	–
–	–	–	–	–	–	–
–	–	–	–	–	–	–
–	–	–	–	–	–	–
0.0	0.1	–	–	0.1	0.1	0.5
1.2	1.7	0.8	–	–	–	–
5.3	3.6	–	–	–	–	–
18.0	11.6	6.6	10.9	15.4	27.9	27.4
–	–	–	–	–	7.8	–
–	–	–	–	–	–	–
–	–	–	–	–	–	–
–	–	–	1.6	2.9	2.8	4.4
1.7	1.7	2.2	–	–	–	–
0.2	0.3	0.2	–	–	–	–
0.7	–	0.7	–	–	–	–
–	–	–	–	–	–	–
0.2	0.7	0.6	–	–	–	–
–	–	–	–	–	–	–
0.2	0.1	0.8	–	–	–	–
–	–	–	–	–	2.9	–
27.5	*19.7*	*11.8*	*12.5*	*18.4*	*41.4*	*32.3*
–	–	–	–	–	–	–
6.2	*7.2*	*8.9*	*6.8*	*11.6*	*14.1*	*10.4*
52.2	***41.2***	***43.6***	***35.1***	***40.2***	***114.0***	***114.5***

TECH. COOP. GRANTS

1978	1979	1980	1977	1978	1979	1980
–	–	–	–	–	–	–
0.1	0.1	0.1	0.1	0.1	0.1	0.1
0.3	0.1	0.1	0.0	0.0	0.1	0.1
–	–	–	–	–	–	–
–	–	0.0	–	–	–	0.0
–	–	–	–	–	–	–
–	–	0.4	–	–	–	0.4
3.4	3.5	4.3	3.4	3.4	3.5	4.3
0.1	0.1	0.0	0.2	0.1	0.1	0.0
5.3	7.6	15.4	1.5	2.8	4.1	7.5
0.3	0.5	1.2	0.2	0.3	0.4	1.1
–	–	–	–	–	–	–
–	–	0.0	0.1	–	–	0.0
–	–	–	–	–	–	–
0.7	1.6	1.7	0.1	0.1	0.5	0.4
0.4	0.6	0.6	0.3	0.4	0.6	0.6
2.0	2.0	2.0	3.0	2.0	1.0	2.0
12.5	*15.9*	*25.8*	*8.9*	*9.1*	*10.3*	*16.5*
3.7	*3.2*	*4.7*	*1.4*	*3.5*	*2.4*	*4.4*
–	–	–	–	–	–	–
4.5	*4.8*	*6.7*	*4.1*	*4.2*	*4.6*	*6.6*
16.2	***19.1***	***30.5***	***10.2***	***12.6***	***12.7***	***20.9***

TOTAL OOF NET

1978	1979	1980	1977	1978	1979	1980
–	–	–	–	–	–	–
–	–	–	–	–	–	–
–	–	–	–	–	–	–
6.7	–	–	–	2.7	–	–
–	–	–	–	–	–	–
–	–	–	–	–	–	–
–	16.3	–	–	–	16.3	–
–	6.4	0.6	–	–	5.9	-0.5
–	–	–	-0.3	-0.2	-0.3	-0.3
–	–	–	–	–	–	–
–	–	–	–	–	–	–
–	–	–	–	–	–	–
–	–	–	–	–	–	–
–	–	–	–	–	–	–
–	–	–	–	–	–	–
–	–	–	–	–	–	–
–	–	–	-1.0	-1.0	-1.0	-1.0
6.7	*22.7*	*0.6*	*-1.3*	*1.5*	*20.8*	*-1.8*
14.1	*20.5*	*31.4*	*6.1*	*13.1*	*19.7*	*29.8*
–	–	–	–	–	–	–
–	*22.7*	*0.6*	*-0.3*	*-0.2*	*21.8*	*-0.8*
20.8	***43.2***	***31.9***	***4.8***	***14.6***	***40.5***	***28.0***

MAIN AID AGGREGATES

	1977	1978	1979	1980
DAC COUNTRIES COMBINED				
PRIVATE SECTOR NET	18.4	10.5	22.0	16.2
Direct Investment	2.8	5.1	4.0	2.5
Portfolio Invest.	0.6	1.6	19.2	-9.8
Export Credits	15.1	3.9	-1.2	23.5
OFFICIAL & PRIVATE				
GROSS:				
Contractual Lending	37.5	30.4	42.9	42.2
Export Credits Tot.	20.7	18.3	21.1	35.6
Export Credits Priv	20.7	11.5	14.6	35.6
OTHER NET DATA				
Contractual Lending	28.7	13.6	20.3	21.1
Export Credits Tot.	14.1	5.4	3.3	21.1
(Bank Sector Loans)	-6.0	33.0	28.0	67.0
ODA CONCESSIONALITY				
Total:Grant Element	80.0	88.0	67.0	64.0
Loans:Grant Element	45.0	60.0	49.0	43.0
OTHER SOURCES				
CMEA Countr.(Gross)	–	–	–	–
Intra LDCS Exc.OPEC	–	–	–	–
Other	–	–	–	–
ALL SOURCE COMMITMENTS				
TOTAL BILATERAL	27.7	21.8	74.7	118.8
of which				
OPEC (ODA)	–	–	–	–
CMEA (ODA)	–	–	–	–
TOTAL MULTILAT.(ODA)	12.5	18.4	41.4	32.3
TOTAL BIL.& MULTIL.	40.1	40.2	116.1	151.1
of which				
ODA Grants	16.0	18.4	29.3	35.0
ODA Loans	19.0	21.8	84.8	79.6
ODA CONCESSIONALITY				
Total: Grant Element	79.0	83.0	67.0	68.0
Loans: Grant Element	66.0	64.0	56.0	54.0

INDEBTEDNESS

	1977	1978	1979	1980
TOTAL DEBT DISBURSED	***369.4***	***490.8***	***605.9***	
Debt to DAC Countries	156.0	229.0	278.0	
ODA	88.0	110.0	106.0	
Total Export Credits	30.0	57.0	113.0	
Other Private Market	38.0	62.0	59.0	
International Org.	96.7	124.4	157.1	
CMEA	–	–	–	
Other	116.8	137.3	170.8	
TOTAL DEBT SERVICE	***37.0***	***40.2***	***68.3***	
Paid to DAC Countries	23.8	23.8	45.3	
ODA	3.9	5.8	7.4	
Total Export Credits	7.7	10.2	27.8	
Other Private Market	12.2	7.8	10.1	
International Org.	4.6	6.0	8.6	
CMEA	–	–	–	
Other	8.6	10.3	14.5	

ECONOMIC INDICATORS

	1977	1978	1979	1980
GNP Curr. Prices, $M	2055.9	2499.4	3398.3	4315.1
Real GNP, 1976=100	112.0	123.0	140.0	156.0
GNP/Cap Curr. Prices,$	732.0	865.0	1142.0	1409.0
GNP/cap Atlas Basis, $	833.2	956.4	1142.2	1342.4
Real GNP/Cap, 1976=100	109.0	116.0	128.0	138.0
Population, Million	2.8	2.9	3.0	3.1
Curr.A/C Deficit(-),$M	-59.4	-118.0	-210.3	-283.8
BOP Exp. & Transf.,$M	420.2	489.7	596.8	695.6
Exp. to OECD CIF, $M	262.2	323.9	554.7	395.8
of which				
Manufact.	25.9	32.1	33.2	25.1
Imp. from OECD FOB, $M	181.7	232.2	314.4	351.7
Reserves ex. Gold, $M	267.8	448.7	609.1	761.9

	TOTAL RECEIPTS NET 1977	1978	1979	1980	TOTAL ODA NET 1977	1978	1979	1980	TOTAL ODA GROSS 197
DAC COUNTRIES									
Australia	3.9	-0.2	1.1	-0.2	0.0	0.0	0.0	0.0	0
Austria	0.2	0.2	0.3	0.2	0.2	0.2	0.3	0.2	0
Belgium	-9.0	133.4	-1.2	0.4	2.8	3.8	3.8	4.6	2
Canada	8.1	-2.0	12.5	2.2	7.7	3.7	3.7	2.0	7
Denmark	-0.4	0.4	1.2	6.1	0.2	1.1	1.0	0.9	0
Finland	-1.8	-4.3	-2.8	-2.8	-0.1	-0.2	-0.1	-0.1	0
France	9.6	2.8	-26.5	44.9	2.7	0.0	6.4	5.2	2
Germany, Fed. Rep.	37.7	60.3	110.8	-14.8	24.3	40.6	49.6	58.6	25
Italy	17.5	17.6	98.0	245.1	0.6	0.8	0.9	0.5	0
Japan	-1.4	27.6	16.0	-36.1	0.6	11.5	30.4	11.1	4
Netherlands	7.3	12.7	27.2	18.7	7.3	12.8	29.1	34.3	7
New Zealand	0.4	0.3	0.4	0.4	0.4	0.3	0.4	0.4	0
Norway	1.3	-2.1	13.1	-0.1	0.1	0.1	0.4	0.8	[illegible]
Sweden	45.8	7.4	-1.8	-4.0	–	–	0.1	0.8	
Switzerland	3.5	-7.1	88.1	60.3	4.7	3.1	2.4	2.9	4
United Kingdom	31.4	5.5	-21.6	-26.9	6.0	1.4	1.9	1.7	6
United States	93.0	66.0	466.0	135.0	15.0	41.0	45.0	53.0	17
TOTAL	*247.1*	*318.3*	*780.8*	*428.4*	*72.4*	*120.1*	*175.1*	*176.6*	*80*
MULTILATERAL									
AF.D.F.	–	–	–	–	–	–	–	–	
AF.D.B.	–	–	–	–	–	–	–	–	
AS.D.B.	–	–	–	–	–	–	–	–	
CAR.D.B.	–	–	–	–	–	–	–	–	
E.E.C.	3.5	1.7	3.4	1.2	3.5	1.7	3.4	1.2	3
IBRD	22.9	14.7	49.0	124.8	–	–	–	–	
IDA	–	–	–	–	–	–	–	–	
I.D.B.	16.6	17.2	24.0	57.6	12.8	11.3	10.8	14.6	16
IFAD	–	–	–	–	–	–	–	–	
I.F.C.	4.3	-1.5	1.0	-0.6	–	–	–	–	
IMF TRUST FUND	–	–	–	–	–	–	–	–	
U.N. AGENCIES	–	–	–	–	–	–	–	–	
UNDP	2.3	2.9	3.8	3.4	2.3	2.9	3.8	3.4	2
UNTA	0.4	0.8	0.6	0.2	0.4	0.8	0.6	0.2	0
UNICEF	0.4	0.5	0.9	1.3	0.4	0.5	0.9	1.3	0
UNRWA	–	–	–	–	–	–	–	–	
WFP	3.0	3.6	3.2	2.6	3.0	3.6	3.2	2.6	3
UNHCR	0.3	0.2	0.1	0.3	0.3	0.2	0.1	0.3	0
Other Multilateral	1.6	1.7	1.7	2.9	1.6	1.7	1.7	2.9	1
Arab OPEC Agencies	–	–	–	–	–	–	–	–	
TOTAL	*55.2*	*41.7*	*87.6*	*193.7*	*24.2*	*22.6*	*24.4*	*26.6*	*28*
OPEC COUNTRIES	*130.0*	*20.4*	–	–	–	–	–	–	
E.E.C.+ MEMBERS	*97.6*	*234.3*	*191.3*	*274.7*	*47.3*	*62.1*	*96.1*	*106.9*	*49*
TOTAL	***432.3***	***380.4***	***868.4***	***622.1***	***96.6***	***142.7***	***199.6***	***203.1***	***108***

	ODA LOANS GROSS 1977	1978	1979	1980	ODA LOANS NET 1977	1978	1979	1980	GRANTS 197
DAC COUNTRIES									
Australia	–	–	–	–	–	–	–	–	0
Austria	–	–	–	–	–	–	–	–	0
Belgium	–	1.6	1.7	2.6	–	1.6	1.7	2.6	2
Canada	4.6	0.2	0.0	–	4.6	0.2	0.0	–	3
Denmark	–	–	–	–	-0.3	-0.3	-0.3	-0.3	0
Finland	0.0	–	–	–	-0.1	-0.2	-0.1	-0.1	0
France	2.9	0.4	6.4	3.4	2.7	-0.3	6.4	2.7	
Germany, Fed. Rep.	8.0	26.3	32.4	38.4	6.5	21.8	29.1	35.1	17
Italy	–	–	–	–	–	–	–	–	6
Japan	0.1	14.1	27.7	10.8	-3.8	6.6	22.3	4.2	4
Netherlands	0.5	6.4	11.1	21.5	0.2	6.1	10.3	21.5	7
New Zealand	–	–	–	–	–	–	–	–	0
Norway	–	–	–	–	–	–	–	–	0
Sweden	–	–	–	–	–	–	–	–	
Switzerland	3.3	1.1	–	–	3.3	1.1	–	–	1
United Kingdom	5.2	0.1	0.1	0.1	5.0	0.0	0.1	-0.4	1
United States	11.0	35.0	21.0	33.0	9.0	32.0	21.0	29.0	6
TOTAL	*35.5*	*85.3*	*100.5*	*109.7*	*27.1*	*68.6*	*90.4*	*94.2*	*45*
MULTILATERAL	*16.7*	*16.6*	*17.6*	*21.2*	*12.8*	*11.0*	*10.7*	*14.0*	*11*
OPEC COUNTRIES	–	–	–	–	–	–	–	–	
E.E.C.+ MEMBERS	*16.5*	*34.9*	*51.8*	*66.0*	*14.1*	*28.9*	*47.3*	*61.1*	*33*
TOTAL	***52.2***	***101.9***	***118.1***	***130.9***	***39.9***	***79.6***	***101.1***	***108.2***	***56***

	TOTAL OFFICIAL GROSS 1977	1978	1979	1980	TOTAL OFFICIAL NET 1977	1978	1979	1980	TOTAL OOF GROSS 197
DAC COUNTRIES									
Australia	0.0	0.0	1.3	0.0	0.0	0.0	1.1	-0.2	
Austria	0.2	0.2	0.3	0.2	0.2	0.2	0.3	0.2	
Belgium	2.8	3.8	3.8	10.1	2.8	3.8	3.8	10.1	
Canada	18.1	3.7	13.1	9.3	14.7	3.7	12.5	1.7	10
Denmark	0.4	1.4	1.4	1.2	0.2	1.1	1.1	0.9	
Finland	0.1	0.0	0.0	0.0	-0.1	-0.2	-0.1	-0.1	
France	2.9	1.2	6.7	13.1	2.7	0.5	6.7	12.5	
Germany, Fed. Rep.	25.8	50.1	59.5	62.9	24.2	44.8	55.1	58.6	
Italy	16.7	37.9	97.4	3.2	16.7	35.3	96.9	-4.3	16
Japan	4.5	19.0	35.9	17.6	0.6	11.5	30.4	11.1	
Netherlands	8.0	13.5	30.2	34.3	7.3	12.7	27.2	34.3	0
New Zealand	0.4	0.3	0.4	0.4	0.4	0.3	0.4	0.4	
Norway	0.1	0.1	0.4	0.8	0.1	0.1	0.4	0.8	
Sweden	–	–	0.1	0.8	–	–	0.1	0.8	
Switzerland	4.7	3.1	7.0	2.9	4.7	3.1	7.0	2.9	
United Kingdom	6.2	1.6	1.9	2.2	6.0	1.4	1.9	1.7	
United States	117.0	121.0	158.0	98.0	84.0	63.0	85.0	8.0	100
TOTAL	*207.8*	*256.8*	*417.1*	*256.9*	*164.5*	*181.2*	*329.4*	*139.2*	*127*
MULTILATERAL	*74.0*	*64.1*	*112.3*	*221.8*	*55.2*	*41.7*	*87.6*	*193.7*	*45*
OPEC COUNTRIES	*130.0*	*20.4*	–	–	*130.0*	*20.4*	–	–	*130*
E.E.C.+ MEMBERS	*66.4*	*111.1*	*204.1*	*128.2*	*63.4*	*101.2*	*195.8*	*114.9*	*16*
TOTAL	***411.8***	***341.3***	***529.4***	***478.7***	***349.7***	***243.3***	***417.0***	***332.9***	***302***

ODA COMMITMENTS

1978	1979	1980	1977	1978	1979	1980
0.0	0.0	0.0	0.0	0.0	–	0.0
0.2	0.3	0.2	–	0.0	0.0	–
3.8	3.8	4.6	5.4	3.2	4.0	5.1
3.7	3.7	2.0	11.0	5.4	2.1	2.5
1.4	1.4	1.2	2.4	0.7	1.4	0.2
0.0	0.0	0.0	–	0.0	2.6	0.0
0.7	6.4	5.8	–	–	–	1.7
45.1	53.0	62.0	68.0	24.4	110.5	67.9
0.8	0.9	0.5	0.6	0.8	0.9	0.5
19.0	35.9	17.6	5.0	32.2	11.7	50.1
13.1	29.9	34.3	9.6	26.2	60.3	10.0
0.3	0.4	0.4	0.2	0.5	0.1	0.6
0.1	0.4	0.8	–	–	0.6	0.9
–	0.1	0.8	–	–	–	–
3.1	2.4	2.9	1.6	1.1	5.5	0.6
1.6	1.9	2.2	1.1	1.5	1.8	2.1
44.0	45.0	57.0	22.7	63.0	55.1	60.9
136.8	*185.2*	*192.1*	*127.5*	*159.0*	*256.6*	*203.1*
–	–	–	–	–	–	–
–	–	–	–	–	–	–
–	–	–	–	–	–	–
–	–	–	–	–	–	–
1.7	3.4	1.2	1.7	2.1	4.4	6.0
–	–	–	–	–	–	–
–	–	–	–	–	–	–
16.9	17.7	21.8	–	18.2	46.0	57.5
–	–	–	–	–	–	12.1
–	–	–	–	–	–	–
–	–	–	–	–	–	–
–	–	–	7.9	9.7	10.3	10.8
2.9	3.8	3.4	–	–	–	–
0.8	0.6	0.2	–	–	–	–
0.5	0.9	1.3	–	–	–	–
–	–	–	–	–	–	–
3.6	3.2	2.6	–	–	–	–
0.2	0.1	0.3	–	–	–	–
1.7	1.7	2.9	–	–	–	–
–	–	–	–	–	–	–
28.2	*31.3*	*33.8*	*9.6*	*30.1*	*60.7*	*86.3*
–	–	–	–	–	–	–
68.0	*100.6*	*111.7*	*88.6*	*58.9*	*183.4*	*93.3*
165.0	**216.6**	**225.9**	**137.1**	**189.0**	**317.2**	**289.4**

TECH. COOP. GRANTS

1978	1979	1980	1977	1978	1979	1980
0.0	0.0	0.0	0.0	0.0	0.0	0.0
0.2	0.3	0.2	0.2	0.2	0.3	0.2
2.2	2.0	2.0	1.5	1.0	1.1	1.3
3.5	3.7	2.0	1.0	1.3	0.9	0.6
1.4	1.4	1.2	0.4	0.9	1.4	1.2
0.0	0.0	0.0	0.1	0.0	0.0	0.0
0.3	–	2.5	–	0.3	–	2.5
18.8	20.5	23.6	17.8	18.8	20.0	23.5
0.8	0.9	0.5	0.6	0.8	0.9	0.5
4.9	8.1	6.9	4.4	4.9	5.7	6.7
6.7	18.8	12.8	5.1	6.4	8.7	12.4
0.3	0.4	0.4	0.3	0.2	0.3	0.3
0.1	0.4	0.8	–	0.1	0.1	0.0
–	0.1	0.8	–	–	–	–
2.0	2.4	2.9	0.1	0.1	0.2	1.1
1.5	1.8	2.1	1.1	1.3	1.6	1.9
9.0	24.0	24.0	2.0	3.0	3.0	3.0
51.5	*84.7*	*82.4*	*34.5*	*39.2*	*44.1*	*55.1*
11.6	*13.7*	*12.6*	*5.0*	*6.4*	*7.2*	*10.8*
–	–	–	–	–	–	–
33.2	*48.8*	*45.7*	*26.5*	*29.4*	*33.7*	*43.2*
63.1	**98.4**	**94.9**	**39.5**	**45.6**	**51.3**	**65.9**

TOTAL OOF NET

1978	1979	1980	1977	1978	1979	1980
–	1.2	–	–	–	1.1	-0.2
–	–	–	–	–	–	–
–	–	5.5	–	–	–	5.5
–	9.4	7.3	7.0	–	8.7	-0.3
0.0	0.1	–	–	0.0	0.1	–
–	–	–	–	–	–	–
0.5	0.3	7.3	–	0.5	0.3	7.3
5.0	6.5	0.9	-0.1	4.3	5.4	0.0
37.2	96.5	2.8	16.2	34.5	96.0	-4.7
–	–	–	–	–	–	–
0.4	0.2	–	0.1	-0.1	-1.9	–
–	–	–	–	–	–	–
–	–	–	–	–	–	–
–	–	–	–	–	–	–
–	4.7	0.0	–	–	4.6	0.0
–	–	–	–	–	–	–
77.0	113.0	41.0	69.0	22.0	40.0	-45.0
120.0	*231.9*	*64.8*	*92.1*	*61.2*	*154.2*	*-37.4*
35.9	*80.9*	*188.0*	*31.1*	*19.1*	*63.2*	*167.2*
20.4	–	–	*130.0*	*20.4*	–	–
43.0	*103.6*	*16.5*	*16.1*	*39.2*	*99.8*	*8.0*
176.3	**312.9**	**252.8**	**253.1**	**100.6**	**217.4**	**129.7**

MAIN AID AGGREGATES

	1977	1978	1979	1980
DAC COUNTRIES COMBINED				
PRIVATE SECTOR NET	82.6	137.1	451.4	289.2
Direct Investment	48.1	66.3	325.7	98.1
Portfolio Invest.	-61.2	-48.0	99.3	-155.3
Export Credits	95.7	118.8	26.4	346.5
OFFICIAL & PRIVATE				
GROSS:				
Contractual Lending	389.3	492.5	476.1	722.2
Export Credits Tot.	337.1	406.2	319.5	598.8
Export Credits Priv	226.8	287.1	143.7	547.7
OTHER NET DATA				
Contractual Lending	214.9	248.5	271.1	403.3
Export Credits Tot.	171.5	179.5	165.5	295.3
(Bank Sector Loans)	167.0	5.0	-70.0	-163.0
ODA CONCESSIONALITY				
Total:Grant Element	75.0	70.0	69.0	72.0
Loans:Grant Element	57.0	48.0	53.0	54.0
OTHER SOURCES				
CMEA Countr.(Gross)	10.2	4.2	1.0	1.0
Intra LDCS Exc.OPEC	–	–	–	–
Other	–	–	–	–
ALL SOURCE COMMITMENTS				
TOTAL BILATERAL	243.4	339.1	604.9	277.8
of which				
OPEC (ODA)	–	–	–	–
CMEA (ODA)	0.8	–	–	–
TOTAL MULTILAT.(ODA)	9.6	30.1	60.7	86.3
TOTAL BIL.& MULTIL.	253.0	369.2	665.5	364.2
of which				
ODA Grants	64.3	80.1	104.1	97.8
ODA Loans	72.8	109.0	213.2	191.6
ODA CONCESSIONALITY				
Total: Grant Element	74.0	72.0	70.0	70.0
Loans: Grant Element	58.0	48.0	54.0	55.0

INDEBTEDNESS

	1977	1978	1979	1980
TOTAL DEBT DISBURSED	***5144.0***	***6056.1***	***6784.5***	
Debt to DAC Countries	3753.0	3955.0	4878.0	
ODA	255.0	368.0	442.0	
Total Export Credits	1370.0	1753.0	1690.0	
Other Private Market	2128.0	1834.0	2746.0	
International Org.	220.1	257.8	331.4	
CMEA	602.2	705.1	709.0	
Other	568.8	1138.2	866.1	
TOTAL DEBT SERVICE	***695.6***	***764.7***	***1061.5***	
Paid to DAC Countries	557.6	589.5	766.7	
ODA	15.5	25.1	12.6	
Total Export Credits	245.0	251.4	312.2	
Other Private Market	297.1	313.0	441.9	
International Org.	28.9	35.9	41.8	
CMEA	35.6	39.5	37.1	
Other	73.5	99.8	215.9	

ECONOMIC INDICATORS

	1977	1978	1979	1980
GNP Curr. Prices, $M	13227.4	11222.8	14383.4	18417.6
Real GNP, 1976=100	99.0	98.0	101.0	105.0
GNP/Cap Curr. Prices,$	814.0	672.0	838.0	1044.0
GNP/cap Atlas Basis, $	757.6	783.1	846.9	934.7
Real GNP/Cap, 1976=100	97.0	93.0	93.0	94.0
Population, Million	16.2	16.7	17.1	17.6
Curr.A/C Deficit(-),$M	-971.0	-245.0	496.0	–
BOP Exp. & Transf.,$M	2149.0	2416.0	4126.0	–
Exp. to OECD CIF, $M	1259.5	1433.7	2450.7	2811.6
of which				
Manufact.	44.7	86.2	154.5	166.2
Imp. from OECD FOB, $M	1112.1	1053.3	1727.1	2338.8
Reserves ex. Gold, $M	356.8	389.7	1520.7	1978.8

	TOTAL RECEIPTS NET 1977	1978	1979	1980	TOTAL ODA NET 1977	1978	1979	1980
DAC COUNTRIES								
Australia	8.8	5.0	8.9	9.2	7.9	7.2	7.6	9.8
Austria	0.0	-0.1	0.7	-5.8	0.1	0.1	0.8	0.6
Belgium	0.6	0.9	3.9	219.8	1.8	0.9	0.2	17.2
Canada	-1.0	5.6	3.9	-1.2	1.4	1.7	0.2	0.2
Denmark	1.7	3.5	0.8	2.9	1.2	3.5	0.2	2.5
Finland	0.6	-0.1	-0.3	19.6	0.1	0.0	0.1	0.5
France	112.3	76.1	-16.9	-18.8	–	–	–	5.6
Germany, Fed. Rep.	-13.3	14.3	26.8	35.4	7.5	10.3	11.0	11.7
Italy	2.8	122.1	3.7	-2.1	0.3	0.1	0.2	0.0
Japan	122.1	460.9	331.6	262.6	30.6	66.5	89.2	94.4
Netherlands	3.6	-9.8	21.8	5.3	3.6	3.6	3.8	5.3
New Zealand	1.5	2.1	1.6	1.2	2.7	3.1	1.6	1.2
Norway	1.2	0.4	2.0	2.8	0.4	0.4	0.7	1.3
Sweden	–	–	-0.4	-0.9	–	–	–	–
Switzerland	0.9	-0.4	8.6	-1.4	0.1	–	0.2	0.1
United Kingdom	64.0	1.8	-9.4	-32.0	0.3	0.4	0.6	5.1
United States	260.0	166.0	425.0	116.0	86.0	67.0	54.0	50.0
TOTAL	*565.8*	*848.4*	*812.0*	*612.7*	*143.9*	*164.7*	*170.4*	*205.4*
MULTILATERAL								
AF.D.F.	–	–	–	–	–	–	–	–
AF.D.B.	–	–	–	–	–	–	–	–
AS.D.B.	28.3	-6.7	69.7	79.0	2.1	0.0	0.5	7.0
CAR.D.B.	–	–	–	–	–	–	–	–
E.E.C.	2.0	1.5	7.8	1.0	2.0	1.5	7.8	1.0
IBRD	90.8	142.6	185.4	195.5	3.2	2.8	6.0	8.2
IDA	1.9	0.9	2.5	1.7	1.9	0.9	2.5	1.7
I.D.B.	–	–	–	–	–	–	–	–
IFAD	–	–	0.0	1.3	–	–	0.0	1.3
I.F.C.	-2.5	-4.9	-4.5	2.1	–	–	–	–
IMF TRUST FUND	19.4	59.7	60.6	51.7	19.4	59.7	60.6	51.7
U.N. AGENCIES	–	–	–	–	–	–	–	–
UNDP	3.6	5.0	5.7	5.0	3.6	5.0	5.7	5.0
UNTA	0.9	0.8	1.0	0.4	0.9	0.8	1.0	0.4
UNICEF	1.4	1.8	2.7	2.3	1.4	1.8	2.7	2.3
UNRWA	–	–	–	–	–	–	–	–
WFP	1.7	2.9	4.7	6.3	1.7	2.9	4.7	6.3
UNHCR	–	–	2.0	3.6	–	–	2.0	3.6
Other Multilateral	2.6	1.8	0.4	1.9	2.6	1.8	0.4	1.9
Arab OPEC Agencies	–	7.6	–	0.8	–	7.6	–	0.8
TOTAL	*150.0*	*212.8*	*338.0*	*352.3*	*38.8*	*84.7*	*94.0*	*91.0*
OPEC COUNTRIES	–	–	*3.0*	*3.6*	–	–	*3.0*	*3.6*
E.E.C.+ MEMBERS	*173.7*	*210.4*	*38.3*	*211.6*	*16.7*	*20.2*	*23.8*	*48.4*
TOTAL	***715.8***	***1061.3***	***1153.0***	***968.6***	***182.7***	***249.3***	***267.4***	***300.0***

	ODA LOANS GROSS 1977	1978	1979	1980	ODA LOANS NET 1977	1978	1979	1980
DAC COUNTRIES								
Australia	–	–	–	–	–	–	–	–
Austria	0.1	–	–	–	0.1	–	–	–
Belgium	1.4	–	–	15.4	1.3	-0.1	-0.1	15.3
Canada	1.3	1.4	0.0	–	1.3	1.4	0.0	–
Denmark	1.3	3.7	0.2	2.5	1.1	3.4	-0.1	2.2
Finland	–	–	–	–	–	–	–	–
France	–	–	–	5.0	–	–	–	5.0
Germany, Fed. Rep.	2.2	2.7	0.4	0.4	1.0	0.9	-1.9	-1.8
Italy	–	–	–	–	–	–	–	–
Japan	19.9	48.1	68.4	73.9	16.8	41.3	57.3	58.7
Netherlands	–	–	–	–	–	–	–	–
New Zealand	–	–	–	–	–	–	–	–
Norway	–	–	–	–	–	–	–	–
Sweden	–	–	–	–	–	–	–	–
Switzerland	–	–	–	–	–	–	–	–
United Kingdom	–	–	–	4.5	–	–	–	4.5
United States	36.0	40.0	37.0	22.0	31.0	38.0	28.0	19.0
TOTAL	*62.1*	*95.9*	*106.0*	*123.6*	*52.6*	*84.9*	*83.1*	*102.8*
MULTILATERAL	*26.2*	*71.2*	*69.8*	*70.5*	*26.0*	*71.0*	*69.6*	*70.0*
OPEC COUNTRIES	–	–	*3.0*	*3.6*	–	–	*3.0*	*3.6*
E.E.C.+ MEMBERS	*4.8*	*6.4*	*0.6*	*27.7*	*3.4*	*4.3*	*-2.1*	*25.1*
TOTAL	***88.3***	***167.1***	***178.9***	***197.7***	***78.6***	***156.0***	***155.7***	***176.4***

	TOTAL OFFICIAL GROSS 1977	1978	1979	1980	TOTAL OFFICIAL NET 1977	1978	1979	1980
DAC COUNTRIES								
Australia	7.9	7.2	7.6	9.8	7.9	7.2	7.6	9.8
Austria	0.1	0.1	0.8	0.6	0.1	0.1	0.8	-5.6
Belgium	1.9	0.9	0.3	17.3	1.8	0.9	0.2	17.2
Canada	4.3	11.5	6.8	1.8	-1.0	5.6	3.9	-1.2
Denmark	1.8	3.8	1.4	2.8	1.7	3.5	0.8	2.0
Finland	0.1	0.0	0.1	0.5	0.1	0.0	0.1	0.5
France	–	–	–	5.6	–	–	–	5.6
Germany, Fed. Rep.	10.9	12.6	22.5	15.0	0.7	0.0	7.8	3.8
Italy	5.9	4.3	3.3	0.0	5.9	4.3	2.0	-1.6
Japan	37.9	75.8	100.3	109.6	34.8	55.3	89.2	94.4
Netherlands	3.6	3.6	3.8	5.3	3.6	3.6	3.8	5.3
New Zealand	4.6	3.1	1.6	1.2	1.5	3.1	1.6	1.2
Norway	0.4	0.4	0.7	1.3	0.4	0.4	0.7	1.3
Sweden	–	–	–	–	–	–	–	–
Switzerland	0.1	–	0.2	0.1	0.1	–	0.2	0.1
United Kingdom	0.3	0.4	1.6	7.4	0.3	0.4	1.6	7.4
United States	197.0	185.0	198.0	80.0	143.0	125.0	144.0	34.0
TOTAL	*276.6*	*308.6*	*349.1*	*258.2*	*200.8*	*209.3*	*264.3*	*174.2*
MULTILATERAL	*175.6*	*249.6*	*381.0*	*403.9*	*150.0*	*212.8*	*338.0*	*352.3*
OPEC COUNTRIES	–	–	*3.0*	*3.6*	–	–	*3.0*	*3.6*
E.E.C.+ MEMBERS	*26.3*	*27.1*	*40.7*	*54.4*	*16.0*	*14.1*	*24.0*	*40.7*
TOTAL	***452.1***	***558.2***	***733.2***	***665.7***	***350.8***	***422.1***	***605.3***	***530.0***

TOTAL ODA GROSS	197
Australia	7
Austria	0
Belgium	1
Canada	1
Denmark	1
Finland	0
France	
Germany, Fed. Rep.	8
Italy	0
Japan	33
Netherlands	3
New Zealand	2
Norway	0
Sweden	
Switzerland	0
United Kingdom	0
United States	91
TOTAL	*153*
AF.D.F.	
AF.D.B.	
AS.D.B.	2
CAR.D.B.	
E.E.C.	2
IBRD	3
IDA	1
I.D.B.	
IFAD	
I.F.C.	
IMF TRUST FUND	19
U.N. AGENCIES	
UNDP	3
UNTA	0
UNICEF	1
UNRWA	
WFP	1
UNHCR	
Other Multilateral	2
Arab OPEC Agencies	
TOTAL	*38*
OPEC COUNTRIES	
E.E.C.+ MEMBERS	*18*
TOTAL	***192***

GRANTS	
Australia	[illegible]
Austria	[illegible]
Belgium	[illegible]
Canada	[illegible]
Denmark	[illegible]
Finland	[illegible]
France	
Germany, Fed. Rep.	[illegible]
Italy	[illegible]
Japan	13
Netherlands	[illegible]
New Zealand	[illegible]
Norway	[illegible]
Sweden	
Switzerland	[illegible]
United Kingdom	[illegible]
United States	5
TOTAL	*9*
MULTILATERAL	*1*
OPEC COUNTRIES	
E.E.C.+ MEMBERS	*1*
TOTAL	***10***

TOTAL OOF GROSS	
Australia	
Austria	
Belgium	
Canada	[illegible]
Denmark	[illegible]
Finland	
France	
Germany, Fed. Rep.	
Italy	[illegible]
Japan	
Netherlands	
New Zealand	
Norway	
Sweden	
Switzerland	
United Kingdom	
United States	10
TOTAL	*12*
MULTILATERAL	*13*
OPEC COUNTRIES	
E.E.C.+ MEMBERS	
TOTAL	***25***

1978	1979	1980	1977	1978	1979	1980
			ODA COMMITMENTS			
7.2	7.6	9.8	2.2	31.7	8.1	23.9
0.1	0.8	0.6	0.1	0.4	0.4	0.2
0.9	0.3	17.3	1.4	–	–	17.8
1.7	0.2	0.2	0.1	0.2	0.2	0.9
3.8	0.5	2.7	0.2	7.4	0.2	0.2
0.0	0.1	0.5	–	0.0	0.7	0.2
–	–	5.6	–	–	18.8	0.5
12.1	13.4	13.9	8.1	20.5	61.0	20.9
0.1	0.2	0.0	0.3	0.1	0.2	0.0
73.3	100.3	109.6	59.7	298.2	124.4	213.0
3.6	3.8	5.3	4.6	5.2	5.5	5.4
3.1	1.6	1.2	0.0	3.7	0.4	1.9
0.4	0.7	1.3	0.2	0.4	1.6	0.6
–	–	–	–	–	–	–
–	0.2	0.1	–	–	–	0.1
0.4	0.6	5.1	0.3	0.4	0.8	15.7
69.0	63.0	53.0	84.7	77.2	71.6	99.2
175.6	*193.4*	*226.3*	*161.9*	*445.5*	*293.8*	*400.5*
–	–	–	–	–	–	–
–	–	–	–	–	–	–
0.2	0.7	7.3	–	14.2	16.0	20.0
–	–	–	–	–	–	–
1.5	7.8	1.0	1.7	0.3	7.6	6.4
2.8	6.0	8.2	–	–	–	–
0.9	2.5	1.7	–	28.0	62.0	–
–	–	–	–	–	–	–
–	0.0	1.3	–	10.0	–	–
–	–	–	–	–	–	–
59.7	60.6	51.7	–	–	–	–
–	–	–	10.2	12.2	16.5	19.4
5.0	5.7	5.0	–	–	–	–
0.8	1.0	0.4	–	–	–	–
1.8	2.7	2.3	–	–	–	–
–	–	–	–	–	–	–
2.9	4.7	6.3	–	–	–	–
–	2.0	3.6	–	–	–	–
1.8	0.4	1.9	–	–	–	–
7.6	–	0.8	8.3	4.5	3.5	–
84.8	*94.1*	*91.3*	*20.1*	*69.3*	*105.6*	*45.9*
–	*3.0*	*3.6*	*12.2*	–	–	–
22.4	*26.6*	*51.0*	*16.6*	*34.0*	*94.0*	*66.9*
260.5	***290.5***	***321.1***	***194.2***	***514.7***	***399.4***	***446.4***
			TECH. COOP. GRANTS			
7.2	7.6	9.8	0.6	1.0	0.7	2.1
0.1	0.8	0.6	0.1	0.1	0.8	0.6
0.9	0.3	1.9	0.1	0.3	0.3	0.5
0.3	0.2	0.2	0.0	0.1	0.1	0.0
0.1	0.3	0.3	0.1	0.1	0.3	0.3
0.0	0.1	0.5	0.1	0.0	0.1	0.5
–	–	0.7	–	–	–	0.7
9.4	13.0	13.5	6.5	9.4	9.7	13.5
0.1	0.2	0.0	0.3	0.1	0.2	0.0
25.2	31.9	35.7	11.1	15.4	17.7	17.8
3.6	3.8	5.3	3.4	3.2	3.1	4.5
3.1	1.6	1.2	0.4	0.7	1.1	1.2
0.4	0.7	1.3	0.0	0.4	0.6	0.8
–	–	–	–	–	–	–
–	0.2	0.1	–	–	–	–
0.4	0.6	0.7	0.3	0.4	0.5	0.7
29.0	26.0	31.0	13.0	10.0	7.0	8.0
79.7	*87.3*	*102.7*	*35.7*	*41.2*	*42.3*	*51.0*
13.7	*24.3*	*20.8*	*9.0*	*9.3*	*11.9*	*19.4*
–	–	–	–	–	–	–
16.0	*26.0*	*23.3*	*10.6*	*13.5*	*14.1*	*20.1*
93.4	***111.7***	***123.4***	***44.7***	***50.5***	***54.1***	***70.5***
			TOTAL OOF NET			
–	0.0	–	–	–	0.0	–
–	–	–	–	–	–	-6.2
–	–	–	–	–	–	–
9.8	6.6	1.6	-2.4	3.9	3.7	-1.4
0.0	0.9	0.1	0.5	0.0	0.6	-0.4
–	–	–	–	–	–	–
–	–	–	–	–	–	–
0.5	9.1	1.1	-6.8	-10.3	-3.2	-7.9
4.2	3.1	–	5.6	4.2	1.8	-1.7
2.5	–	–	4.2	-11.1	–	–
–	–	–	–	–	–	–
–	–	–	-1.2	–	–	–
–	–	–	–	–	–	–
–	–	–	–	–	–	–
–	–	–	–	–	–	–
–	1.0	2.2	–	–	1.0	2.2
116.0	135.0	27.0	57.0	58.0	90.0	-16.0
133.0	*155.7*	*32.0*	*56.9*	*44.6*	*93.9*	*-31.3*
164.8	*286.9*	*312.6*	*111.3*	*128.1*	*244.0*	*261.3*
–	–	–	–	–	–	–
4.7	*14.1*	*3.4*	*-0.8*	*-6.1*	*0.2*	*-7.7*
297.8	***442.6***	***344.6***	***168.1***	***172.8***	***337.9***	***230.0***

	1977	1978	1979	1980
MAIN AID AGGREGATES				
DAC COUNTRIES COMBINED				
PRIVATE SECTOR NET	365.0	639.1	547.7	438.6
Direct Investment	116.2	143.9	329.7	124.7
Portfolio Invest.	48.0	229.6	246.3	31.8
Export Credits	200.7	265.6	-28.3	282.1
OFFICIAL & PRIVATE				
GROSS:				
Contractual Lending	525.9	682.5	466.2	654.2
Export Credits Tot.	455.6	586.1	357.6	528.1
Export Credits Priv	340.6	453.6	204.5	498.7
OTHER NET DATA				
Contractual Lending	310.2	395.2	148.7	353.6
Export Credits Tot.	249.5	310.0	63.5	249.3
(Bank Sector Loans)	305.0	796.0	169.0	462.0
ODA CONCESSIONALITY				
Total:Grant Element	77.0	66.0	68.0	77.0
Loans:Grant Element	54.0	54.0	51.0	61.0
OTHER SOURCES				
CMEA Countr.(Gross)	8.0	9.0	9.0	5.0
Intra LDCS Exc.OPEC	–	–	–	–
Other	–	–	–	–
ALL SOURCE COMMITMENTS				
TOTAL BILATERAL	281.8	534.1	319.4	439.8
of which				
OPEC (ODA)	12.2	–	–	–
CMEA (ODA)	–	–	–	–
TOTAL MULTILAT.(ODA)	20.1	69.3	105.6	45.9
TOTAL BIL.& MULTIL.	301.9	603.4	425.1	485.7
of which				
ODA Grants	94.2	133.0	126.1	194.8
ODA Loans	100.0	381.8	273.3	251.6
ODA CONCESSIONALITY				
Total: Grant Element	75.0	68.0	71.0	79.0
Loans: Grant Element	52.0	57.0	59.0	63.0
INDEBTEDNESS				
TOTAL DEBT DISBURSED	***4911.5***	***6231.0***	***7155.2***	
Debt to DAC Countries	4149.0	5367.0	6031.0	
ODA	561.0	770.0	755.0	
Total Export Credits	1532.0	1866.0	2222.0	
Other Private Market	2056.0	2731.0	3054.0	
International Org.	588.6	769.3	1026.9	
CMEA	–	–	10.9	
Other	173.9	94.7	86.4	
TOTAL DEBT SERVICE	***534.8***	***1164.2***	***1285.4***	
Paid to DAC Countries	462.5	1067.1	1090.8	
ODA	24.4	30.1	44.7	
Total Export Credits	293.1	379.0	455.7	
Other Private Market	145.0	658.0	590.4	
International Org.	59.8	89.0	119.2	
CMEA	–	–	0.5	
Other	12.5	8.1	74.9	
ECONOMIC INDICATORS				
GNP Curr. Prices, $M	20802.3	24555.0	29908.6	35918.1
Real GNP, 1976=100	106.0	115.0	122.0	127.0
GNP/Cap Curr. Prices,$	467.0	538.0	639.0	750.0
GNP/cap Atlas Basis, $	505.5	573.4	643.9	717.4
Real GNP/Cap, 1976=100	103.0	109.0	113.0	115.0
Population, Million	44.5	45.6	46.7	47.9
Curr.A/C Deficit(-),$M	-944.0	-1272.0	-1691.0	-2187.0
BOP Exp. & Transf.,$M	4304.0	5047.0	6405.0	8162.0
Exp. to OECD CIF, $M	2817.6	3386.1	4542.4	5365.7
of which				
Manufact.	632.7	984.5	1378.0	1742.6
Imp. from OECD FOB, $M	2742.0	3619.5	4435.3	4934.4
Reserves ex. Gold, $M	1479.0	1763.0	2250.0	2846.0

	TOTAL RECEIPTS NET 1977	1978	1979	1980	TOTAL ODA NET 1977	1978	1979	1980
DAC COUNTRIES								
Australia	0.1	–	0.1	0.1	–	–	–	–
Austria	0.1	0.1	0.1	0.1	0.1	0.1	0.1	0.1
Belgium	4.1	104.1	39.6	3.5	0.8	0.1	0.0	–
Canada	6.3	7.3	5.2	1.1	7.1	3.9	2.4	–
Denmark	22.2	-2.9	6.8	1.9	–	0.1	0.1	0.1
Finland	-3.4	-4.8	-4.6	1.2	0.0	–	–	–
France	115.0	89.4	332.0	333.8	-6.5	–	0.6	2.3
Germany, Fed. Rep.	36.9	262.9	55.8	11.3	2.0	5.8	29.0	24.4
Italy	2.2	0.1	0.6	8.2	–	–	–	0.1
Japan	1.6	3.4	98.2	-1.9	–	0.1	–	0.1
Netherlands	0.2	24.6	32.5	34.0	0.2	1.5	2.1	1.3
New Zealand	0.6	-0.2	–	–	–	–	–	–
Norway	19.7	3.6	10.9	9.8	7.5	5.0	7.4	6.1
Sweden	3.5	15.4	7.6	0.9	3.5	3.3	9.4	3.6
Switzerland	9.3	36.8	27.7	-18.2	4.2	0.6	0.3	0.2
United Kingdom	11.4	41.1	-4.5	3.8	0.0	0.2	0.6	0.8
United States	195.0	515.0	124.0	-97.0	70.0	45.0	70.0	69.0
TOTAL	*424.7*	*1095.6*	*731.9*	*292.6*	*88.7*	*65.7*	*122.0*	*108.1*
MULTILATERAL								
AF.D.F.	–	–	–	–	–	–	–	–
AF.D.B.	–	–	–	–	–	–	–	–
AS.D.B.	–	–	–	–	–	–	–	–
CAR.D.B.	–	–	–	–	–	–	–	–
E.E.C.	52.6	38.0	56.2	56.0	18.7	0.2	11.1	0.5
IBRD	-3.4	3.9	26.9	46.4	–	–	–	–
IDA	–	–	–	–	–	–	–	–
I.D.B.	–	–	–	–	–	–	–	–
IFAD	–	–	–	–	–	–	–	–
I.F.C.	–	–	–	–	–	–	–	–
IMF TRUST FUND	–	–	–	–	–	–	–	–
U.N. AGENCIES	–	–	–	–	–	–	–	–
UNDP	0.2	0.7	1.3	1.2	0.2	0.7	1.3	1.2
UNTA	0.1	0.1	0.2	0.3	0.1	0.1	0.2	0.3
UNICEF	–	–	0.1	–	–	–	0.1	–
UNRWA	–	–	–	–	–	–	–	–
WFP	1.7	0.4	-0.1	–	1.7	0.4	-0.1	–
UNHCR	0.2	0.6	1.0	1.1	0.2	0.6	1.0	1.1
Other Multilateral	0.1	0.0	0.6	0.9	0.1	0.0	0.6	0.9
Arab OPEC Agencies	–	–	–	–	–	–	–	–
TOTAL	*51.4*	*43.9*	*86.2*	*105.9*	*20.9*	*2.1*	*14.1*	*4.0*
OPEC COUNTRIES	*15.0*	*7.5*	–	–	–	–	–	–
E.E.C.+ MEMBERS	*244.5*	*557.3*	*519.0*	*452.5*	*15.1*	*7.9*	*43.5*	*29.4*
TOTAL	***491.1***	***1147.0***	***818.0***	***398.5***	***109.6***	***67.8***	***136.1***	***112.2***

	ODA LOANS GROSS 1977	1978	1979	1980	ODA LOANS NET 1977	1978	1979	1980
DAC COUNTRIES								
Australia	–	–	–	–	–	–	–	–
Austria	–	–	–	–	–	–	–	–
Belgium	–	–	–	–	–	–	–	–
Canada	–	–	–	–	–	–	–	–
Denmark	–	–	–	–	–	–	–	–
Finland	–	–	–	–	–	–	–	–
France	–	–	0.6	0.4	-6.5	–	0.6	0.4
Germany, Fed. Rep.	2.3	2.8	23.9	18.7	-2.7	-2.0	18.6	13.4
Italy	–	–	–	–	–	–	–	–
Japan	–	–	–	–	–	–	–	–
Netherlands	–	–	0.8	0.1	–	–	0.8	0.1
New Zealand	–	–	–	–	–	–	–	–
Norway	–	–	–	–	–	–	–	–
Sweden	–	–	–	–	–	–	–	–
Switzerland	3.9	–	–	–	3.9	–	–	–
United Kingdom	–	–	–	–	–	–	–	–
United States	69.0	51.0	58.0	55.0	64.0	43.0	48.0	43.0
TOTAL	*75.2*	*53.8*	*83.3*	*74.2*	*58.7*	*41.0*	*68.0*	*57.0*
MULTILATERAL	–	–	–	–	–	–	–	–
OPEC COUNTRIES	–	–	–	–	–	–	–	–
E.E.C.+ MEMBERS	*2.3*	*2.8*	*25.3*	*19.2*	*-9.2*	*-2.0*	*20.0*	*14.0*
TOTAL	***75.2***	***53.8***	***83.3***	***74.2***	***58.7***	***41.0***	***68.0***	***57.0***

	TOTAL OFFICIAL GROSS 1977	1978	1979	1980	TOTAL OFFICIAL NET 1977	1978	1979	1980
DAC COUNTRIES								
Australia	–	–	–	–	–	–	–	–
Austria	0.1	0.1	0.1	0.1	0.1	0.1	0.1	0.1
Belgium	0.8	0.1	0.0	–	0.8	0.1	0.0	–
Canada	7.1	7.9	5.8	1.7	6.4	7.3	5.2	1.1
Denmark	–	0.1	0.1	0.1	–	0.1	0.1	0.1
Finland	0.0	–	–	–	0.0	–	–	–
France	–	–	0.6	2.3	-6.5	–	0.6	2.3
Germany, Fed. Rep.	7.0	10.8	38.9	29.7	-0.9	4.5	31.4	21.9
Italy	–	–	–	0.2	–	–	–	0.2
Japan	–	0.1	84.7	5.6	–	0.1	84.7	5.6
Netherlands	0.2	24.6	2.1	1.3	0.2	24.6	2.1	1.3
New Zealand	1.0	–	–	–	0.6	–	–	–
Norway	10.8	5.0	9.3	8.2	10.8	5.0	9.3	8.2
Sweden	3.5	14.4	9.4	3.6	3.5	14.4	9.4	3.6
Switzerland	4.2	0.6	0.3	0.2	4.2	0.6	0.3	0.2
United Kingdom	0.0	20.0	0.6	0.8	0.0	20.0	0.6	0.8
United States	194.0	553.0	240.0	107.0	167.0	477.0	94.0	-100.0
TOTAL	*228.5*	*636.6*	*391.9*	*160.7*	*186.1*	*553.6*	*237.8*	*-54.7*
MULTILATERAL	*54.9*	*47.6*	*95.7*	*123.0*	*51.4*	*43.9*	*86.1*	*105.9*
OPEC COUNTRIES	*15.0*	*7.5*	–	–	*15.0*	*7.5*	–	–
E.E.C.+ MEMBERS	*60.5*	*93.6*	*101.0*	*98.0*	*46.2*	*87.2*	*91.0*	*82.5*
TOTAL	***298.4***	***691.7***	***487.6***	***283.7***	***252.5***	***605.0***	***324.0***	***51.2***

	TOTAL ODA GROSS 197[illegible]
Australia	
Austria	[illegible]
Belgium	[illegible]
Canada	[illegible]
Denmark	
Finland	[illegible]
France	
Germany, Fed. Rep.	[illegible]
Italy	
Japan	
Netherlands	[illegible]
New Zealand	
Norway	[illegible]
Sweden	[illegible]
Switzerland	[illegible]
United Kingdom	[illegible]
United States	[illegible]
TOTAL	[illegible]
AF.D.F.	
AF.D.B.	
AS.D.B.	
CAR.D.B.	
E.E.C.	[illegible]
IBRD	
IDA	
I.D.B.	
IFAD	
I.F.C.	
IMF TRUST FUND	
U.N. AGENCIES	
UNDP	[illegible]
UNTA	[illegible]
UNICEF	
UNRWA	
WFP	[illegible]
UNHCR	[illegible]
Other Multilateral	[illegible]
Arab OPEC Agencies	
TOTAL	[illegible]
OPEC COUNTRIES	
E.E.C.+ MEMBERS	[illegible]
TOTAL	[illegible]

	GRANTS 197[illegible]
Australia	
Austria	[illegible]
Belgium	[illegible]
Canada	
Denmark	
Finland	[illegible]
France	
Germany, Fed. Rep.	[illegible]
Italy	
Japan	
Netherlands	[illegible]
New Zealand	
Norway	[illegible]
Sweden	[illegible]
Switzerland	[illegible]
United Kingdom	[illegible]
United States	[illegible]
TOTAL	[illegible]
MULTILATERAL	[illegible]
OPEC COUNTRIES	
E.E.C.+ MEMBERS	[illegible]
TOTAL	[illegible]

	TOTAL OOF GROSS 197[illegible]
Australia	
Austria	
Belgium	
Canada	
Denmark	
Finland	
France	
Germany, Fed. Rep.	
Italy	
Japan	
Netherlands	
New Zealand	[illegible]
Norway	[illegible]
Sweden	
Switzerland	
United Kingdom	
United States	[illegible]
TOTAL	[illegible]
MULTILATERAL	[illegible]
OPEC COUNTRIES	[illegible]
E.E.C.+ MEMBERS	[illegible]
TOTAL	[illegible]

ODA COMMITMENTS

1978	1979	1980	1977	1978	1979	1980
–	–	–	–	–	–	–
0.1	0.1	0.1	–	–	–	–
0.1	0.0	–	–	–	–	–
3.9	2.4	–	7.1	4.4	2.6	–
0.1	0.1	0.1	–	–	0.1	–
–	–	–	0.0	–	–	–
–	0.6	2.3	–	–	7.1	1.8
10.6	34.3	29.7	38.5	32.9	72.4	38.5
–	–	0.1	–	–	–	0.1
0.1	–	0.1	–	0.1	–	0.2
1.5	2.1	1.3	6.0	1.0	2.2	11.3
–	–	–	–	–	–	–
5.0	7.4	6.1	1.7	7.1	14.6	6.4
3.3	9.4	3.6	6.1	7.5	0.7	–
0.6	0.3	0.2	5.6	–	–	0.2
0.2	0.6	0.8	0.0	9.8	0.6	0.8
53.0	80.0	81.0	85.0	40.8	59.9	81.4
78.5	*137.2*	*125.4*	*150.1*	*103.4*	*160.1*	*140.4*
–	–	–	–	–	–	–
–	–	–	–	–	–	–
–	–	–	–	–	–	–
–	–	–	–	–	–	–
0.2	11.1	0.5	18.4	–	16.3	0.5
–	–	–	–	–	–	–
–	–	–	–	–	–	–
–	–	–	–	–	–	–
–	–	–	–	–	–	–
–	–	–	–	–	–	–
–	–	–	2.2	1.9	3.0	3.6
0.7	1.3	1.2	–	–	–	–
0.1	0.2	0.3	–	–	–	–
–	0.1	–	–	–	–	–
–	–	–	–	–	–	–
0.4	-0.1	–	–	–	–	–
0.6	1.0	1.1	–	–	–	–
0.0	0.6	0.9	–	–	–	–
–	–	–	–	–	–	–
2.1	*14.1*	*4.0*	*20.6*	*1.9*	*19.4*	*4.0*
–	–	–	–	–	–	–
12.7	*48.8*	*34.7*	*62.9*	*43.7*	*98.7*	*52.8*
80.6	**151.3**	**129.4**	**170.7**	**105.3**	**179.4**	**144.5**

TECH. COOP. GRANTS

1978	1979	1980	1977	1978	1979	1980
–	–	–	–	–	–	–
0.1	0.1	0.1	0.1	0.1	0.1	0.1
0.1	0.0	–	0.0	0.0	0.0	–
3.9	2.4	–	–	–	–	–
0.1	0.1	0.1	–	–	–	–
–	–	–	–	–	–	–
–	–	1.9	–	–	–	1.9
7.8	10.4	11.0	4.7	7.8	10.3	10.9
–	–	0.1	–	–	–	0.1
0.1	–	0.1	–	0.1	–	0.1
1.5	1.3	1.2	0.2	0.4	0.3	0.3
–	–	–	–	–	–	–
5.0	7.4	6.1	0.9	1.2	0.7	0.9
3.3	9.4	3.6	0.8	2.2	1.6	2.2
0.6	0.3	0.2	0.0	0.0	0.0	0.1
0.2	0.6	0.8	0.0	0.2	0.6	0.7
2.0	22.0	26.0	1.0	1.0	1.0	6.0
24.7	*53.9*	*51.2*	*7.7*	*13.0*	*14.5*	*23.3*
2.1	*14.1*	*4.0*	*0.6*	*1.5*	*3.1*	*3.6*
–	–	–	–	–	–	–
9.9	*23.5*	*15.5*	*5.0*	*8.5*	*11.2*	*13.9*
26.9	**68.0**	**55.2**	**8.2**	**14.5**	**17.6**	**26.9**

TOTAL OOF NET

1978	1979	1980	1977	1978	1979	1980
–	–	–	–	–	–	–
–	–	–	–	–	–	–
–	–	–	–	–	–	–
4.0	3.4	1.7	-0.7	3.3	2.8	1.1
–	–	–	–	–	–	–
–	–	–	–	–	–	–
–	–	–	–	–	–	–
0.2	4.6	–	-2.8	-1.4	2.4	-2.5
–	–	0.1	–	–	–	0.1
–	84.7	5.5	–	–	84.7	5.5
23.1	–	–	–	23.1	–	–
–	–	–	0.6	–	–	–
–	2.0	2.0	3.3	–	2.0	2.0
11.1	–	–	–	11.1	–	–
–	–	–	–	–	–	–
19.8	–	–	–	19.8	–	–
500.0	160.0	26.0	97.0	432.0	24.0	-169.0
558.1	*254.8*	*35.3*	*97.4*	*487.9*	*115.9*	*-162.9*
45.5	*81.6*	*119.0*	*30.5*	*41.7*	*72.1*	*101.9*
7.5	–	–	*15.0*	*7.5*	–	–
80.9	*52.2*	*63.3*	*31.1*	*79.3*	*47.5*	*53.1*
611.1	**336.3**	**154.3**	**142.9**	**537.2**	**187.9**	**-61.0**

MAIN AID AGGREGATES

	1977	1978	1979	1980
DAC COUNTRIES COMBINED				
PRIVATE SECTOR NET	238.6	542.0	494.1	347.4
Direct Investment	38.5	49.5	75.6	76.4
Portfolio Invest.	46.0	395.3	360.4	314.2
Export Credits	154.2	97.2	58.0	-43.2
OFFICIAL & PRIVATE				
GROSS:				
Contractual Lending	507.1	772.0	556.6	281.9
Export Credits Tot.	428.6	375.2	470.9	205.7
Export Credits Priv	308.6	160.1	218.6	172.4
OTHER NET DATA				
Contractual Lending	310.2	626.1	241.9	-149.1
Export Credits Tot.	248.3	242.1	171.7	-207.9
(Bank Sector Loans)	226.0	718.0	569.0	215.0
ODA CONCESSIONALITY				
Total:Grant Element	59.0	51.0	57.0	64.0
Loans:Grant Element	47.0	31.0	36.0	32.0
OTHER SOURCES				
CMEA Countr.(Gross)	–	–	–	–
Intra LDCS Exc.OPEC	–	–	–	–
Other	–	–	–	–
ALL SOURCE COMMITMENTS				
TOTAL BILATERAL	586.7	449.5	341.8	211.1
of which				
OPEC (ODA)	–	–	–	–
CMEA (ODA)	–	–	–	–
TOTAL MULTILAT.(ODA)	20.6	1.9	19.4	4.0
TOTAL BIL.& MULTIL.	607.3	451.4	361.1	215.1
of which				
ODA Grants	51.4	32.6	75.2	70.0
ODA Loans	119.2	72.7	104.2	74.5
ODA CONCESSIONALITY				
Total: Grant Element	64.0	52.0	61.0	65.0
Loans: Grant Element	47.0	31.0	36.0	32.0

INDEBTEDNESS

	1977	1978	1979	1980
TOTAL DEBT DISBURSED	***2215.4***	***3397.2***	***4673.9***	
Debt to DAC Countries	1952.0	2994.0	4187.0	
ODA	151.0	194.0	567.0	
Total Export Credits	1039.0	1912.0	1809.0	
Other Private Market	762.0	888.0	1811.0	
International Org.	150.1	284.2	370.5	
CMEA	–	–	–	
Other	113.3	118.9	116.3	
TOTAL DEBT SERVICE	***394.1***	***449.0***	***798.0***	
Paid to DAC Countries	372.2	411.9	725.2	
ODA	12.9	27.8	24.4	
Total Export Credits	175.7	217.6	411.0	
Other Private Market	183.6	166.5	289.8	
International Org.	10.8	23.6	39.0	
CMEA	–	–	–	
Other	11.1	13.5	33.8	

ECONOMIC INDICATORS

	1977	1978	1979	1980
GNP Curr. Prices, $M	16236.9	17594.4	19849.2	23746.6
Real GNP, 1976=100	105.0	108.0	111.0	117.0
GNP/Cap Curr. Prices,$	1683.0	1811.0	2031.0	2414.0
GNP/cap Atlas Basis, $	1696.7	1853.0	2062.6	2352.1
Real GNP/Cap, 1976=100	104.0	106.0	109.0	114.0
Population, Million	9.6	9.7	9.8	9.8
Curr.A/C Deficit(-),$M	-958.0	-464.0	-60.0	-1085.0
BOP Exp. & Transf.,$M	4607.0	5576.0	7805.0	9837.0
Exp. to OECD CIF, $M	1746.8	2151.8	3184.1	3902.8
of which				
Manufact.	1180.4	1541.2	2230.2	2734.3
Imp. from OECD FOB, $M	3653.1	3860.4	4912.9	6496.9
Reserves ex. Gold, $M	366.0	871.0	931.0	795.0

	1977	1978	1979	1980	1977	1978	1979	1980
TOTAL RECEIPTS NET					**TOTAL ODA NET**			
DAC COUNTRIES								
Australia	–	–	–	–	–	–	–	–
Austria	0.6	0.2	0.1	0.1	0.6	0.2	0.1	0.1
Belgium	28.4	34.9	35.1	35.8	28.6	36.3	35.5	36.2
Canada	6.6	7.1	4.8	5.7	6.6	7.1	4.8	5.7
Denmark	0.2	0.3	–	–	0.2	0.3	–	–
Finland	–	–	–	–	–	–	–	–
France	6.9	9.2	11.7	15.8	6.9	9.2	11.7	15.8
Germany, Fed. Rep.	12.2	12.3	18.2	16.7	12.1	12.3	17.2	16.8
Italy	-0.6	-0.2	-0.5	-0.1	0.1	0.0	0.0	–
Japan	0.4	2.0	5.4	5.8	0.4	2.0	5.2	5.1
Netherlands	1.6	2.0	3.8	4.6	1.6	2.0	3.8	4.6
New Zealand	–	–	–	–	–	–	–	–
Norway	0.0	–	–	–	0.0	–	–	–
Sweden	–	–	0.7	–	–	–	0.7	–
Switzerland	1.4	6.5	4.4	5.2	1.4	6.5	4.4	5.2
United Kingdom	0.1	0.1	–	0.0	0.1	0.1	–	0.0
United States	3.0	3.0	5.0	7.0	3.0	3.0	5.0	7.0
TOTAL	*60.7*	*77.3*	*88.8*	*96.7*	*61.4*	*78.9*	*88.4*	*96.6*
MULTILATERAL								
AF.D.F.	2.1	5.8	5.1	1.9	2.1	5.8	5.1	1.9
AF.D.B.	–	–	–	0.3	–	–	–	–
AS.D.B.	–	–	–	–	–	–	–	–
CAR.D.B.	–	–	–	–	–	–	–	–
E.E.C.	11.1	22.6	24.1	21.4	11.1	22.6	24.1	21.4
IBRD	–	–	–	–	–	–	–	–
IDA	9.4	6.5	10.9	10.2	9.4	6.5	10.9	10.2
I.D.B.	–	–	–	–	–	–	–	–
IFAD	–	–	–	–	–	–	–	–
I.F.C.	0.3	0.2	–	-0.1	–	–	–	–
IMF TRUST FUND	–	–	7.5	6.3	–	–	7.5	6.3
U.N. AGENCIES	–	–	–	–	–	–	–	–
UNDP	3.0	3.6	4.4	5.2	3.0	3.6	4.4	5.2
UNTA	0.6	0.8	0.7	0.1	0.6	0.8	0.7	0.1
UNICEF	1.1	1.1	1.7	2.0	1.1	1.1	1.7	2.0
UNRWA	–	–	–	–	–	–	–	–
WFP	0.5	0.7	1.3	2.6	0.5	0.7	1.3	2.6
UNHCR	0.2	0.1	0.3	0.2	0.2	0.1	0.3	0.2
Other Multilateral	1.2	1.0	1.0	1.6	1.2	1.0	1.0	1.6
Arab OPEC Agencies	0.9	2.9	2.3	6.0	0.9	2.9	2.3	6.0
TOTAL	*30.3*	*45.4*	*59.3*	*57.6*	*30.0*	*45.2*	*59.3*	*57.5*
OPEC COUNTRIES	*4.5*	*1.2*	*0.6*	*1.3*	*4.5*	*1.2*	*0.6*	*1.3*
E.E.C.+ MEMBERS	*59.8*	*81.0*	*92.4*	*94.3*	*60.5*	*82.7*	*92.4*	*94.8*
TOTAL	***95.5***	***123.8***	***148.6***	***155.6***	***95.9***	***125.3***	***148.3***	***155.3***

	1977	1978	1979	1980	1977	1978	1979	1980
ODA LOANS GROSS					**ODA LOANS NET**			
DAC COUNTRIES								
Australia	–	–	–	–	–	–	–	–
Austria	–	–	–	–	–	–	–	–
Belgium	–	–	–	–	–	–	–	–
Canada	–	–	–	–	–	–	–	–
Denmark	–	–	–	–	–	–	–	–
Finland	–	–	–	–	–	–	–	–
France	–	0.2	0.3	4.6	–	0.2	0.3	4.6
Germany, Fed. Rep.	4.8	3.2	0.9	0.1	4.6	3.1	-14.3	0.1
Italy	–	–	–	–	–	–	–	–
Japan	0.3	0.0	1.1	0.3	0.3	0.0	1.1	0.3
Netherlands	–	–	–	–	–	–	–	–
New Zealand	–	–	–	–	–	–	–	–
Norway	–	–	–	–	–	–	–	–
Sweden	–	–	–	–	–	–	–	–
Switzerland	–	–	–	–	–	–	–	–
United Kingdom	–	–	–	–	–	–	–	–
United States	–	–	–	–	–	–	–	–
TOTAL	*5.1*	*3.4*	*2.3*	*4.9*	*4.9*	*3.4*	*-12.9*	*4.9*
MULTILATERAL	*12.3*	*17.1*	*27.0*	*27.1*	*12.3*	*17.0*	*27.0*	*26.9*
OPEC COUNTRIES	*4.4*	*1.2*	*0.6*	*1.3*	*4.4*	*1.2*	*0.6*	*1.3*
E.E.C.+ MEMBERS	*4.8*	*5.3*	*2.4*	*7.2*	*4.6*	*5.2*	*-12.8*	*7.2*
TOTAL	***21.8***	***21.7***	***29.8***	***33.3***	***21.7***	***21.6***	***14.6***	***33.1***

	1977	1978	1979	1980	1977	1978	1979	1980
TOTAL OFFICIAL GROSS					**TOTAL OFFICIAL NET**			
DAC COUNTRIES								
Australia	–	–	–	–	–	–	–	–
Austria	0.6	0.2	0.1	0.1	0.6	0.2	0.1	0.1
Belgium	28.6	36.3	35.5	36.2	28.6	36.3	35.5	36.2
Canada	6.6	7.1	4.8	5.7	6.6	7.1	4.8	5.7
Denmark	0.2	0.3	–	–	0.2	0.3	–	–
Finland	–	–	–	–	–	–	–	–
France	6.9	9.2	11.7	15.8	6.9	9.2	11.7	15.8
Germany, Fed. Rep.	12.2	12.3	32.4	16.8	12.1	12.3	17.2	16.8
Italy	0.1	0.0	0.0	–	0.1	0.0	0.0	–
Japan	0.4	2.0	5.2	5.1	0.4	2.0	5.2	5.1
Netherlands	1.6	2.0	3.8	4.6	1.6	2.0	3.8	4.6
New Zealand	–	–	–	–	–	–	–	–
Norway	0.0	–	–	–	0.0	–	–	–
Sweden	–	–	0.7	–	–	–	0.7	–
Switzerland	1.4	6.5	4.4	5.2	1.4	6.5	4.4	5.2
United Kingdom	0.1	0.1	–	0.0	0.1	0.1	–	0.0
United States	3.0	3.0	5.0	7.0	3.0	3.0	5.0	7.0
TOTAL	*61.6*	*79.0*	*103.6*	*96.6*	*61.4*	*78.9*	*88.4*	*96.6*
MULTILATERAL	*30.3*	*45.4*	*59.3*	*57.9*	*30.3*	*45.4*	*59.3*	*57.6*
OPEC COUNTRIES	*4.5*	*1.2*	*0.6*	*1.3*	*4.5*	*1.2*	*0.6*	*1.3*
E.E.C.+ MEMBERS	*60.7*	*82.7*	*107.5*	*94.8*	*60.5*	*82.7*	*92.4*	*94.8*
TOTAL	***96.4***	***125.6***	***163.5***	***155.7***	***96.2***	***125.5***	***148.3***	***155.5***

	197
TOTAL ODA GROSS	
Australia	
Austria	
Belgium	
Canada	
Denmark	
Finland	
France	
Germany, Fed. Rep.	
Italy	
Japan	
Netherlands	
New Zealand	
Norway	
Sweden	
Switzerland	
United Kingdom	
United States	
TOTAL	
AF.D.F.	
AF.D.B.	
AS.D.B.	
CAR.D.B.	
E.E.C.	
IBRD	
IDA	
I.D.B.	
IFAD	
I.F.C.	
IMF TRUST FUND	
U.N. AGENCIES	
UNDP	
UNTA	
UNICEF	
UNRWA	
WFP	
UNHCR	
Other Multilateral	
Arab OPEC Agencies	
TOTAL	
OPEC COUNTRIES	
E.E.C.+ MEMBERS	
TOTAL	
GRANTS	
Australia	
Austria	
Belgium	
Canada	
Denmark	
Finland	
France	
Germany, Fed. Rep.	
Italy	
Japan	
Netherlands	
New Zealand	
Norway	
Sweden	
Switzerland	
United Kingdom	
United States	
TOTAL	
MULTILATERAL	
OPEC COUNTRIES	
E.E.C.+ MEMBERS	
TOTAL	
TOTAL OOF GROSS	
Australia	
Austria	
Belgium	
Canada	
Denmark	
Finland	
France	
Germany, Fed. Rep.	
Italy	
Japan	
Netherlands	
New Zealand	
Norway	
Sweden	
Switzerland	
United Kingdom	
United States	
TOTAL	
MULTILATERAL	
OPEC COUNTRIES	
E.E.C.+ MEMBERS	
TOTAL	

1978	1979	1980	1977	1978	1979	1980
			ODA COMMITMENTS			
–	–	–	–	–	–	–
0.2	0.1	0.1	0.1	–	–	–
36.3	35.5	36.2	39.5	51.7	40.1	44.6
7.1	4.8	5.7	7.8	15.6	4.4	4.1
0.3	–	–	0.5	0.0	–	–
–	–	–	–	–	–	–
9.2	11.7	15.8	12.8	16.4	15.9	23.6
12.3	32.4	16.8	12.1	5.9	43.2	50.0
0.0	0.0	–	0.1	0.0	0.0	–
2.0	5.2	5.1	1.2	5.2	5.3	6.7
2.0	3.8	4.6	1.7	4.1	6.2	3.7
–	–	–	–	–	–	–
–	–	–	–	–	–	–
–	0.7	–	–	–	0.2	–
6.5	4.4	5.2	2.4	9.2	3.9	6.9
0.1	–	0.0	0.1	0.1	–	0.0
3.0	5.0	7.0	1.7	3.4	6.4	5.5
79.0	*103.6*	*96.6*	*79.8*	*111.6*	*125.6*	*145.1*
5.8	5.1	1.9	5.3	2.8	5.2	15.8
–	–	–	–	–	–	–
–	–	–	–	–	–	–
–	–	–	–	–	–	–
22.6	24.1	21.4	41.4	4.3	7.4	6.0
–	–	–	–	–	–	–
6.5	10.9	10.3	14.0	15.0	13.8	28.5
–	–	–	–	–	–	–
–	–	–	–	–	–	–
–	–	–	–	–	–	–
–	7.5	6.3	–	–	–	–
–	–	–	6.6	7.4	9.4	11.7
3.6	4.4	5.2	–	–	–	–
0.8	0.7	0.1	–	–	–	–
1.1	1.7	2.0	–	–	–	–
–	–	–	–	–	–	–
0.7	1.3	2.6	–	–	–	–
0.1	0.3	0.2	–	–	–	–
1.0	1.0	1.6	–	–	–	–
2.9	2.3	6.0	15.1	–	4.5	3.0
45.2	*59.3*	*57.6*	*82.4*	*29.5*	*40.3*	*65.0*
1.2	*0.6*	*1.3*	*0.1*	–	*0.4*	–
82.7	*107.5*	*94.8*	*108.1*	*82.5*	*112.8*	*127.8*
125.4	***163.5***	***155.5***	***162.3***	***141.1***	***166.3***	***210.1***
			TECH. COOP. GRANTS			
–	–	–	–	–	–	–
0.2	0.1	0.1	0.6	0.2	0.1	0.1
36.3	35.5	36.2	17.8	18.2	19.9	20.4
7.1	4.8	5.7	1.8	1.7	1.5	1.5
0.3	–	–	0.2	0.3	–	–
–	–	–	–	–	–	–
9.0	11.4	11.3	4.5	4.4	6.0	6.8
9.1	31.5	16.7	7.4	9.1	11.5	12.2
0.0	0.0	–	0.1	0.0	0.0	–
2.0	4.1	4.9	0.1	0.1	0.1	0.1
2.0	3.8	4.6	1.6	1.9	2.6	2.0
–	–	–	–	–	–	–
–	–	–	0.0	–	–	–
–	0.7	–	–	–	–	–
6.5	4.4	5.2	0.1	0.1	0.1	1.3
0.1	–	0.0	0.1	0.1	–	0.0
3.0	5.0	7.0	1.0	–	1.0	1.0
75.6	*101.3*	*91.6*	*35.2*	*36.1*	*42.8*	*45.4*
28.1	*32.3*	*30.6*	*6.0*	*6.7*	*8.1*	*11.7*
–	–	–	–	–	–	–
77.4	*105.2*	*87.6*	*31.6*	*34.0*	*40.0*	*41.4*
103.7	***133.6***	***122.2***	***41.2***	***42.8***	***50.9***	***57.2***
			TOTAL OOF NET			
–	–	–	–	–	–	–
–	–	–	–	–	–	–
–	–	–	–	–	–	–
–	–	–	–	–	–	–
–	–	–	–	–	–	–
–	–	–	–	–	–	–
–	–	–	–	–	–	–
–	–	–	–	–	–	–
–	–	–	–	–	–	–
–	–	–	–	–	–	–
–	–	–	–	–	–	–
–	–	–	–	–	–	–
–	–	–	–	–	–	–
–	–	–	–	–	–	–
–	–	–	–	–	–	–
–	–	–	–	–	–	–
–	–	–	–	–	–	–
–	–	–	–	–	–	–
0.2	–	*0.3*	*0.3*	*0.2*	–	*0.2*
–	–	–	–	–	–	–
–	–	–	–	–	–	–
0.2	–	***0.3***	***0.3***	***0.2***	–	***0.2***

MAIN AID AGGREGATES

	1977	1978	1979	1980
DAC COUNTRIES COMBINED				
PRIVATE SECTOR NET	-0.7	-1.6	0.4	0.2
Direct Investment	0.1	-0.7	0.4	0.2
Portfolio Invest.	0.0	-0.2	-0.5	-0.2
Export Credits	-0.8	-0.8	0.5	0.2
OFFICIAL & PRIVATE GROSS:				
Contractual Lending	5.4	3.4	3.8	5.8
Export Credits Tot.	0.3	0.0	1.5	0.9
Export Credits Priv	0.3	0.0	1.5	0.9
OTHER NET DATA				
Contractual Lending	4.1	2.6	-12.4	5.1
Export Credits Tot.	-0.8	-0.8	0.5	0.2
(Bank Sector Loans)	–	–	1.0	2.0
ODA CONCESSIONALITY				
Total:Grant Element	95.0	96.0	99.0	95.0
Loans:Grant Element	29.0	36.0	55.0	42.0
OTHER SOURCES				
CMEA Countr.(Gross)	–	–	–	–
Intra LDCS Exc.OPEC	–	–	–	–
Other	–	–	–	–
ALL SOURCE COMMITMENTS				
TOTAL BILATERAL	80.1	111.9	126.3	145.1
of which				
OPEC (ODA)	0.1	–	0.4	–
CMEA (ODA)	–	–	–	–
TOTAL MULTILAT.(ODA)	82.4	29.5	40.3	65.0
TOTAL BIL.& MULTIL.	162.5	141.4	166.6	210.1
of which				
ODA Grants	116.1	116.7	140.5	150.1
ODA Loans	46.2	24.4	25.7	60.0
ODA CONCESSIONALITY				
Total: Grant Element	90.0	94.0	96.0	92.0
Loans: Grant Element	65.0	70.0	75.0	72.0

INDEBTEDNESS

	1977	1978	1979	1980
TOTAL DEBT DISBURSED	***73.5***	***98.9***	***116.9***	
Debt to DAC Countries	18.0	24.0	10.0	
ODA	14.0	22.0	8.0	
Total Export Credits	4.0	2.0	2.0	
Other Private Market	–	–	–	
International Org.	37.1	53.5	74.5	
CMEA	10.6	12.1	22.9	
Other	7.8	9.2	9.6	
TOTAL DEBT SERVICE	***2.2***	***2.6***	***2.4***	
Paid to DAC Countries	1.8	2.2	1.9	
ODA	0.4	0.1	0.5	
Total Export Credits	1.3	1.8	1.3	
Other Private Market	0.1	0.3	0.1	
International Org.	0.3	0.3	0.4	
CMEA	–	–	–	
Other	0.0	0.1	0.1	

ECONOMIC INDICATORS

	1977	1978	1979	1980
GNP Curr. Prices, $M	766.8	818.0	956.4	1047.1
Real GNP, 1976=100	105.0	104.0	105.0	107.0
GNP/Cap Curr. Prices,$	164.0	170.0	193.0	205.0
GNP/cap Atlas Basis, $	171.5	177.2	188.5	203.7
Real GNP/Cap, 1976=100	102.0	98.0	96.0	95.0
Population, Million	4.7	4.8	4.9	5.1
Curr.A/C Deficit(-),$M	-46.7	-139.4	-77.6	-172.4
BOP Exp. & Transf.,$M	140.8	131.8	241.0	182.0
Exp. to OECD CIF, $M	94.3	106.8	136.6	129.8
of which				
Manufact.	0.2	0.5	0.3	0.5
Imp. from OECD FOB, $M	55.3	87.5	103.9	118.9
Reserves ex. Gold, $M	82.9	87.6	152.3	186.6

SENEGAL

	TOTAL RECEIPTS NET 1977	1978	1979	1980	TOTAL ODA NET 1977	1978	1979	1980
DAC COUNTRIES								
Australia	0.0	0.0	–	–	0.0	0.0	–	–
Austria	0.2	0.2	0.1	0.2	0.2	0.2	0.1	0.2
Belgium	7.8	17.7	2.5	9.9	3.5	5.0	7.7	6.4
Canada	6.4	12.0	13.7	6.4	6.4	10.5	9.2	6.8
Denmark	1.0	1.2	-1.2	-0.2	1.1	0.0	0.0	0.0
Finland	–	–	–	0.1	–	–	–	0.1
France	69.4	125.4	106.7	248.1	54.7	76.7	81.3	107.7
Germany, Fed. Rep.	8.3	0.7	11.8	5.2	8.1	5.8	11.7	11.9
Italy	10.2	1.4	4.7	-4.1	1.8	0.2	0.3	0.1
Japan	0.9	1.9	2.4	3.2	1.2	1.5	3.4	4.6
Netherlands	0.8	2.9	2.3	5.0	0.8	2.9	2.3	5.0
New Zealand	–	–	–	–	–	–	–	–
Norway	0.2	2.3	1.1	34.5	0.3	2.3	1.5	0.2
Sweden	3.6	-0.7	-0.7	-0.8	–	–	–	–
Switzerland	1.0	1.0	2.3	0.2	1.0	1.0	2.3	2.5
United Kingdom	5.0	0.4	6.0	-0.8	0.3	1.5	2.1	0.5
United States	10.0	15.0	29.0	34.0	10.0	14.0	27.0	36.0
TOTAL	*124.7*	*181.6*	*180.6*	*340.9*	*89.3*	*121.6*	*148.8*	*181.9*
MULTILATERAL								
AF.D.F.	2.8	2.0	0.2	0.4	2.8	2.0	0.2	0.4
AF.D.B.	-0.2	6.6	6.0	6.2	–	–	–	–
AS.D.B.	–	–	–	–	–	–	–	–
CAR.D.B.	–	–	–	–	–	–	–	–
E.E.C.	10.2	47.2	108.3	24.0	10.7	47.8	108.5	24.2
IBRD	14.5	5.0	8.5	16.0	2.1	2.2	3.4	6.7
IDA	7.5	8.9	16.0	11.9	7.5	8.9	16.0	11.9
I.D.B.	–	–	–	–	–	–	–	–
IFAD	–	–	–	–	–	–	–	–
I.F.C.	-0.3	-0.1	–	0.5	–	–	–	–
IMF TRUST FUND	–	17.7	13.3	11.3	–	17.7	13.3	11.3
U.N. AGENCIES	–	–	–	–	–	–	–	–
UNDP	1.9	1.9	2.5	3.0	1.9	1.9	2.5	3.0
UNTA	0.4	0.4	0.5	0.2	0.4	0.4	0.5	0.2
UNICEF	0.2	0.6	0.8	1.0	0.2	0.6	0.8	1.0
UNRWA	–	–	–	–	–	–	–	–
WFP	2.5	6.4	3.5	6.9	2.5	6.4	3.5	6.9
UNHCR	0.1	0.1	0.2	0.2	0.1	0.1	0.2	0.2
Other Multilateral	1.6	3.6	3.7	3.8	1.6	3.6	3.7	3.8
Arab OPEC Agencies	1.7	2.8	4.5	19.7	1.7	2.8	4.5	9.4
TOTAL	*43.0*	*103.1*	*168.1*	*105.2*	*31.7*	*94.5*	*157.2*	*79.1*
OPEC COUNTRIES	*22.0*	*13.7*	*1.4*	*2.1*	*2.0*	*10.7*	*1.4*	*2.1*
E.E.C.+ MEMBERS	*112.6*	*197.0*	*241.1*	*287.1*	*80.9*	*139.9*	*213.9*	*155.7*
TOTAL	***189.8***	***298.4***	***350.2***	***448.1***	***122.9***	***226.8***	***307.4***	***263.0***

TOTAL ODA GROSS	197
Australia	0
Austria	0
Belgium	3
Canada	6
Denmark	1
Finland	
France	57
Germany, Fed. Rep.	8
Italy	1
Japan	1
Netherlands	0
New Zealand	
Norway	0
Sweden	
Switzerland	1
United Kingdom	0
United States	10
TOTAL	*93*
AF.D.F.	2
AF.D.B.	
AS.D.B.	
CAR.D.B.	
E.E.C.	10
IBRD	2
IDA	7
I.D.B.	
IFAD	
I.F.C.	
IMF TRUST FUND	
U.N. AGENCIES	
UNDP	1
UNTA	0
UNICEF	0
UNRWA	
WFP	2
UNHCR	0
Other Multilateral	1
Arab OPEC Agencies	1
TOTAL	*31*
OPEC COUNTRIES	*2*
E.E.C.+ MEMBERS	*84*
TOTAL	***127***

	ODA LOANS GROSS 1977	1978	1979	1980	ODA LOANS NET 1977	1978	1979	1980
DAC COUNTRIES								
Australia	–	–	–	–	–	–	–	–
Austria	–	–	–	–	–	–	–	–
Belgium	–	–	–	–	–	–	–	–
Canada	2.1	3.0	2.0	0.1	2.1	3.0	2.0	0.1
Denmark	1.2	0.1	0.0	0.1	1.1	0.0	-0.1	-0.1
Finland	–	–	–	–	–	–	–	–
France	14.1	16.1	12.7	15.1	10.9	13.2	9.7	11.4
Germany, Fed. Rep.	3.6	0.8	2.9	2.8	3.1	0.8	2.9	2.8
Italy	–	–	–	–	–	–	–	–
Japan	–	0.4	–	–	-0.1	0.3	-0.1	-0.4
Netherlands	–	–	–	–	–	–	–	–
New Zealand	–	–	–	–	–	–	–	–
Norway	–	–	–	–	–	–	–	–
Sweden	–	–	–	–	–	–	–	–
Switzerland	–	–	–	–	–	–	–	–
United Kingdom	–	–	2.1	–	–	–	2.1	–
United States	–	–	–	–	–	–	–	–
TOTAL	*20.9*	*20.4*	*19.7*	*18.1*	*17.0*	*17.3*	*16.5*	*13.8*
MULTILATERAL	*16.1*	*34.9*	*133.5*	*48.6*	*15.9*	*34.6*	*132.2*	*48.4*
OPEC COUNTRIES	*2.0*	*3.0*	*1.3*	*1.1*	*2.0*	*3.0*	*1.3*	*1.1*
E.E.C.+ MEMBERS	*20.7*	*18.1*	*113.7*	*26.7*	*16.8*	*15.0*	*109.4*	*22.8*
TOTAL	***39.0***	***58.3***	***154.5***	***67.8***	***34.9***	***54.9***	***150.0***	***63.2***

GRANTS	197
Australia	0
Austria	0
Belgium	3
Canada	4
Denmark	
Finland	
France	43
Germany, Fed. Rep.	5
Italy	1.
Japan	1
Netherlands	0
New Zealand	
Norway	0.
Sweden	
Switzerland	1
United Kingdom	0
United States	10
TOTAL	*72*
MULTILATERAL	*15.*
OPEC COUNTRIES	
E.E.C.+ MEMBERS	*64*
TOTAL	***88***

	TOTAL OFFICIAL GROSS 1977	1978	1979	1980	TOTAL OFFICIAL NET 1977	1978	1979	1980
DAC COUNTRIES								
Australia	0.0	0.0	–	–	0.0	0.0	–	–
Austria	0.2	0.2	0.1	0.2	0.2	0.2	0.1	0.2
Belgium	3.5	5.0	7.7	6.4	3.5	5.0	7.7	6.4
Canada	6.4	12.0	13.8	6.8	6.4	12.0	13.7	6.4
Denmark	1.2	0.1	0.1	0.2	1.1	0.0	0.0	–
Finland	–	–	–	0.1	–	–	–	0.1
France	59.2	100.9	89.3	199.4	55.5	97.5	85.3	194.0
Germany, Fed. Rep.	8.6	5.8	11.7	12.1	6.6	4.1	9.7	11.1
Italy	3.1	0.2	0.3	0.1	2.7	-0.6	-0.9	-1.2
Japan	1.3	1.6	3.5	5.0	1.2	1.5	3.4	4.6
Netherlands	0.8	2.9	2.3	5.0	0.8	2.9	2.3	5.0
New Zealand	–	–	–	–	–	–	–	–
Norway	0.3	2.3	1.5	0.2	0.3	2.3	1.5	0.2
Sweden	–	–	–	–	–	–	–	–
Switzerland	1.0	1.0	2.3	2.5	1.0	1.0	2.3	2.5
United Kingdom	0.3	1.5	2.1	0.5	0.3	1.5	2.1	0.5
United States	10.0	15.0	29.0	36.0	10.0	15.0	29.0	34.0
TOTAL	*95.7*	*148.5*	*163.6*	*274.5*	*89.6*	*142.4*	*156.1*	*263.6*
MULTILATERAL	*44.8*	*105.9*	*172.4*	*108.2*	*43.0*	*103.1*	*168.1*	*105.2*
OPEC COUNTRIES	*22.0*	*13.7*	*1.4*	*2.1*	*22.0*	*13.7*	*1.4*	*2.1*
E.E.C.+ MEMBERS	*87.4*	*164.2*	*223.1*	*248.0*	*80.7*	*157.6*	*214.5*	*239.7*
TOTAL	***162.5***	***268.2***	***337.4***	***384.8***	***154.6***	***259.3***	***325.7***	***370.9***

TOTAL OOF GROSS	197
Australia	
Austria	
Belgium	
Canada	
Denmark	
Finland	
France	1.
Germany, Fed. Rep.	
Italy	1.
Japan	
Netherlands	
New Zealand	
Norway	
Sweden	
Switzerland	
United Kingdom	
United States	
TOTAL	*2.*
MULTILATERAL	*12.*
OPEC COUNTRIES	*20.*
E.E.C.+ MEMBERS	*2.*
TOTAL	***35.***

ODA COMMITMENTS

1978	1979	1980	1977	1978	1979	1980
0.0	–	–	0.0	–	–	–
0.2	0.1	0.2	–	–	–	0.0
5.0	7.7	6.4	4.9	7.2	8.9	7.9
10.5	9.2	6.8	11.6	9.6	2.8	2.8
0.1	0.1	0.2	–	0.2	0.0	9.8
–	–	0.1	–	–	–	0.4
79.6	84.3	111.4	62.2	73.6	93.9	115.2
5.8	11.7	11.9	10.8	11.3	38.0	10.0
0.2	0.3	0.1	1.8	0.2	0.3	0.1
1.6	3.5	5.0	0.1	4.9	18.0	1.5
2.9	2.3	5.0	4.3	1.3	1.9	12.7
–	–	–	–	–	–	–
2.3	1.5	0.2	–	3.1	–	–
–	–	–	–	–	–	–
1.0	2.3	2.5	1.6	0.7	3.7	7.6
1.5	2.1	0.5	0.3	1.5	2.1	0.5
14.0	27.0	36.0	12.2	24.9	23.4	37.3
124.7	*152.0*	*186.2*	*109.8*	*138.3*	*192.9*	*205.9*
2.0	0.2	0.4	–	2.6	4.9	1.2
–	–	–	–	–	–	–
–	–	–	–	–	–	–
–	–	–	–	–	–	–
47.9	109.7	24.3	28.1	39.3	109.1	22.2
2.2	3.4	6.7	14.0	–	–	–
9.1	16.2	12.1	–	25.4	24.5	76.7
–	–	–	–	–	–	–
–	–	–	–	–	13.7	–
–	–	–	–	–	–	–
17.7	13.3	11.3	–	–	–	–
–	–	–	6.8	13.0	11.3	15.2
1.9	2.5	3.0	–	–	–	–
0.4	0.5	0.2	–	–	–	–
0.6	0.8	1.0	–	–	–	–
–	–	–	–	–	–	–
6.4	3.5	6.9	–	–	–	–
0.1	0.2	0.2	–	–	–	–
3.6	3.7	3.8	–	–	–	–
2.8	4.5	9.4	10.6	4.0	–	5.0
94.7	*158.5*	*79.3*	*59.5*	*84.3*	*163.4*	*120.3*
10.7	*1.4*	*2.1*	–	*48.8*	*5.8*	*1.0*
142.9	*218.1*	*159.6*	*112.4*	*134.3*	*254.2*	*178.4*
230.1	***312.0***	***267.6***	***169.3***	***271.4***	***362.1***	***327.1***

TECH. COOP. GRANTS

1978	1979	1980	1977	1978	1979	1980
0.0	–	–	0.0	0.0	–	–
0.2	0.1	0.2	0.2	0.2	0.1	0.2
5.0	7.7	6.4	3.0	3.5	5.1	5.6
7.4	7.2	6.7	1.9	2.5	1.8	0.4
–	0.1	0.1	–	–	0.1	0.1
–	–	0.1	–	–	–	0.1
63.5	71.6	96.3	39.5	56.5	66.7	82.7
5.0	8.8	9.1	2.9	4.5	5.0	7.4
0.2	0.3	0.1	0.3	0.2	0.3	0.1
1.2	3.5	5.0	0.1	1.1	0.3	0.4
2.9	2.3	5.0	0.8	1.3	0.7	0.8
–	–	–	–	–	–	–
2.3	1.5	0.2	0.1	0.1	0.1	0.0
–	–	–	–	–	–	–
1.0	2.3	2.5	0.0	–	–	0.8
1.5	0.0	0.5	0.3	0.3	0.4	0.5
14.0	27.0	36.0	2.0	6.0	11.0	15.0
104.3	*132.3*	*168.1*	*51.1*	*76.2*	*91.5*	*114.3*
59.9	*25.0*	*30.7*	*4.3*	*6.7*	*7.8*	*15.2*
7.7	*0.1*	*1.0*	–	–	–	–
124.9	*104.4*	*132.9*	*46.8*	*66.2*	*78.2*	*97.2*
171.8	***157.4***	***199.8***	***55.4***	***82.8***	***99.3***	***129.4***

TOTAL OOF NET

1978	1979	1980	1977	1978	1979	1980
–	–	–	–	–	–	–
–	–	–	–	–	–	–
–	–	–	–	–	–	–
1.6	4.6	0.0	–	1.6	4.5	-0.5
–	–	0.0	–	–	–	0.0
–	–	–	–	–	–	–
21.3	5.0	88.1	0.8	20.8	4.0	86.3
–	–	0.2	-1.5	-1.7	-2.0	-0.8
–	–	–	0.9	-0.8	-1.2	-1.3
–	–	–	–	–	–	–
–	–	–	–	–	–	–
–	–	–	–	–	–	–
–	–	–	–	–	–	–
–	–	–	–	–	–	–
–	–	–	–	–	–	–
–	–	–	–	–	–	–
1.0	2.0	–	–	1.0	2.0	-2.0
23.9	*11.6*	*88.4*	*0.3*	*20.9*	*7.4*	*81.8*
11.2	*13.8*	*28.9*	*11.4*	*8.7*	*10.9*	*26.1*
3.0	–	–	*20.0*	*3.0*	–	–
21.3	*5.0*	*88.3*	*-0.2*	*17.7*	*0.6*	*84.0*
38.1	***25.5***	***117.2***	***31.7***	***32.6***	***18.3***	***107.9***

MAIN AID AGGREGATES

	1977	1978	1979	1980
DAC COUNTRIES COMBINED				
PRIVATE SECTOR NET	35.2	39.1	24.5	77.2
Direct Investment	3.4	-4.5	3.9	1.9
Portfolio Invest.	-2.6	7.1	18.4	-0.2
Export Credits	34.4	36.5	2.2	75.6
OFFICIAL & PRIVATE				
GROSS:				
Contractual Lending	85.6	107.8	66.1	212.9
Export Credits Tot.	62.2	66.1	41.4	106.4
Export Credits Priv	62.2	63.6	34.8	106.4
OTHER NET DATA				
Contractual Lending	51.7	74.7	26.0	171.1
Export Credits Tot.	33.0	36.6	5.7	70.9
(Bank Sector Loans)	-1.0	3.0	11.0	-27.0
ODA CONCESSIONALITY				
Total:Grant Element	87.0	98.0	88.0	93.0
Loans:Grant Element	46.0	56.0	48.0	62.0
OTHER SOURCES				
CMEA Countr.(Gross)	–	–	–	–
Intra LDCS Exc.OPEC	–	–	–	–
Other	–	–	–	–
ALL SOURCE COMMITMENTS				
TOTAL BILATERAL	129.3	212.1	212.8	289.7
of which				
OPEC (ODA)	–	48.8	5.8	1.0
CMEA (ODA)	–	–	–	–
TOTAL MULTILAT.(ODA)	59.5	84.3	163.4	120.3
TOTAL BIL.& MULTIL.	188.8	296.4	376.3	410.0
of which				
ODA Grants	102.5	192.0	178.3	198.1
ODA Loans	66.8	79.4	183.8	129.0
ODA CONCESSIONALITY				
Total: Grant Element	81.0	87.0	87.0	90.0
Loans: Grant Element	50.0	58.0	58.0	71.0

INDEBTEDNESS

	1977	1978	1979	1980
TOTAL DEBT DISBURSED	***476.6***	***755.0***	***878.4***	
Debt to DAC Countries	322.0	546.0	617.0	
ODA	100.0	134.0	151.0	
Total Export Credits	132.0	224.0	281.0	
Other Private Market	90.0	188.0	185.0	
International Org.	103.6	135.6	167.2	
CMEA	8.2	9.8	10.3	
Other	42.8	63.6	84.0	
TOTAL DEBT SERVICE	***67.0***	***112.3***	***155.6***	
Paid to DAC Countries	56.1	87.0	127.2	
ODA	4.2	6.4	7.4	
Total Export Credits	32.6	36.0	52.1	
Other Private Market	19.3	44.6	67.7	
International Org.	3.6	5.9	9.0	
CMEA	0.6	0.6	0.6	
Other	6.7	18.8	18.8	

ECONOMIC INDICATORS

	1977	1978	1979	1980
GNP Curr. Prices, $M	1943.7	2034.2	2524.4	2598.2
Real GNP, 1976=100	101.0	92.0	102.0	95.0
GNP/Cap Curr. Prices,$	370.0	378.0	457.0	458.0
GNP/cap Atlas Basis, $	405.3	388.8	454.8	451.3
Real GNP/Cap, 1976=100	98.0	88.0	94.0	86.0
Population, Million	5.2	5.4	5.5	5.7
Curr.A/C Deficit(-),$M	-158.8	–	–	–
BOP Exp. & Transf.,$M	880.5	–	–	–
Exp. to OECD CIF, $M	452.2	307.7	389.5	324.9
of which				
Manufact.	7.5	6.9	8.7	14.9
Imp. from OECD FOB, $M	522.1	565.5	690.5	739.6
Reserves ex. Gold, $M	33.7	18.8	19.1	8.1

	TOTAL RECEIPTS NET 1977	1978	1979	1980	TOTAL ODA NET 1977	1978	1979	1980
DAC COUNTRIES								
Australia	0.1	0.0	0.0	0.0	0.1	0.0	0.0	0.0
Austria	0.0	–	0.1	0.0	0.0	–	0.1	0.0
Belgium	-1.4	-1.9	0.0	0.1	0.0	0.0	0.0	0.1
Canada	0.0	0.2	0.3	0.3	0.0	0.2	0.3	0.3
Denmark	0.0	0.1	0.5	2.4	0.0	0.1	0.5	2.4
Finland	–	0.0	0.0	0.1	–	0.0	0.0	0.1
France	0.8	-3.2	-0.2	5.0	–	–	–	3.5
Germany, Fed. Rep.	5.7	4.8	5.6	15.4	4.8	4.3	5.3	14.7
Italy	-2.5	2.9	-0.6	-1.2	0.0	0.0	0.0	0.0
Japan	0.0	0.0	0.2	18.0	0.0	0.0	0.2	18.0
Netherlands	0.4	3.0	11.6	4.4	0.4	2.8	10.9	4.2
New Zealand	0.0	0.0	0.0	0.1	0.0	0.0	0.0	0.1
Norway	–	2.8	0.0	-0.2	–	–	–	0.0
Sweden	–	-0.1	0.3	0.4	–	–	0.3	0.4
Switzerland	0.0	0.0	0.0	-1.6	0.0	0.0	0.0	–
United Kingdom	8.4	5.8	10.5	5.7	2.6	1.9	4.5	5.0
United States	15.0	9.0	5.0	9.0	4.0	4.0	6.0	8.0
TOTAL	*26.6*	*23.3*	*33.3*	*57.7*	*12.0*	*13.5*	*28.2*	*56.8*
MULTILATERAL								
AF.D.F.	–	–	0.1	1.2	–	–	0.1	1.2
AF.D.B.	1.5	0.1	0.5	1.8	–	–	–	–
AS.D.B.	–	–	–	–	–	–	–	–
CAR.D.B.	–	–	–	–	–	–	–	–
E.E.C.	4.6	2.9	3.1	7.7	4.6	2.9	3.1	7.7
IBRD	-0.7	-0.2	1.6	1.5	–	–	–	–
IDA	2.0	10.2	2.1	2.3	2.0	10.2	2.1	2.3
I.D.B.	–	–	–	–	–	–	–	–
IFAD	–	–	–	0.7	–	–	–	0.7
I.F.C.	–	–	–	–	–	–	–	–
IMF TRUST FUND	3.1	9.6	9.7	8.5	3.1	9.6	9.7	8.5
U.N. AGENCIES	–	–	–	–	–	–	–	–
UNDP	1.7	2.0	2.8	3.4	1.7	2.0	2.8	3.4
UNTA	0.3	0.4	0.3	0.2	0.3	0.4	0.3	0.2
UNICEF	0.1	0.2	0.1	0.5	0.1	0.2	0.1	0.5
UNRWA	–	–	–	–	–	–	–	–
WFP	0.1	0.1	0.8	1.5	0.1	0.1	0.8	1.5
UNHCR	0.0	0.1	0.1	0.2	0.0	0.1	0.1	0.2
Other Multilateral	1.1	1.0	0.6	1.0	1.1	1.0	0.6	1.0
Arab OPEC Agencies	1.1	0.4	1.3	2.6	1.1	0.4	1.3	2.6
TOTAL	*15.0*	*26.7*	*23.2*	*33.1*	*14.2*	*26.8*	*21.1*	*29.8*
OPEC COUNTRIES	–	–	*4.0*	*2.0*	–	–	*4.0*	*2.0*
E.E.C.+ MEMBERS	*16.0*	*14.3*	*30.4*	*39.4*	*12.5*	*12.1*	*24.3*	*37.6*
TOTAL	***41.5***	***50.0***	***60.5***	***92.9***	***26.2***	***40.3***	***53.2***	***88.6***

	ODA LOANS GROSS 1977	1978	1979	1980	ODA LOANS NET 1977	1978	1979	1980
DAC COUNTRIES								
Australia	–	–	–	–	–	–	–	–
Austria	–	–	–	–	–	–	–	–
Belgium	–	–	–	–	–	–	–	–
Canada	–	–	–	–	–	–	–	–
Denmark	–	–	0.4	2.2	–	–	0.4	2.2
Finland	–	–	–	–	–	–	–	–
France	–	–	–	2.8	–	–	–	2.8
Germany, Fed. Rep.	2.9	1.6	3.4	9.6	2.5	0.6	2.0	9.4
Italy	–	–	–	–	–	–	–	–
Japan	–	–	–	15.3	–	–	–	15.3
Netherlands	–	0.2	5.0	0.0	–	0.2	5.0	0.0
New Zealand	–	–	–	–	–	–	–	–
Norway	–	–	–	–	–	–	–	–
Sweden	–	–	–	–	–	–	–	–
Switzerland	–	–	–	–	–	–	–	–
United Kingdom	0.2	0.6	0.2	0.2	-0.3	-0.1	-1.8	-1.4
United States	1.0	1.0	1.0	2.0	1.0	–	1.0	1.0
TOTAL	*4.1*	*3.4*	*10.0*	*32.1*	*3.2*	*0.7*	*6.6*	*29.3*
MULTILATERAL	*6.2*	*20.2*	*13.2*	*15.8*	*6.2*	*20.2*	*13.2*	*15.7*
OPEC COUNTRIES	–	–	–	–	–	–	–	–
E.E.C.+ MEMBERS	*3.1*	*2.4*	*9.0*	*15.3*	*2.2*	*0.7*	*5.6*	*13.5*
TOTAL	***10.3***	***23.6***	***23.1***	***47.9***	***9.4***	***20.9***	***19.8***	***45.0***

	TOTAL OFFICIAL GROSS 1977	1978	1979	1980	TOTAL OFFICIAL NET 1977	1978	1979	1980
DAC COUNTRIES								
Australia	0.1	0.0	0.0	0.0	0.1	0.0	0.0	0.0
Austria	0.0	–	0.1	0.0	0.0	–	0.1	0.0
Belgium	0.0	0.5	0.0	2.5	0.0	0.4	0.0	2.5
Canada	0.0	0.2	0.3	0.3	0.0	0.2	0.3	0.3
Denmark	0.0	0.1	0.5	2.4	0.0	0.1	0.5	2.4
Finland	–	0.0	0.0	0.1	–	0.0	0.0	0.1
France	–	3.6	–	5.7	–	3.6	-0.2	5.0
Germany, Fed. Rep.	6.0	7.0	7.0	16.6	5.6	4.8	5.2	16.2
Italy	0.0	1.4	0.0	0.0	0.0	0.8	0.0	0.0
Japan	0.0	0.0	0.2	18.0	0.0	0.0	0.2	18.0
Netherlands	0.4	3.0	11.6	4.4	0.4	3.0	11.6	4.4
New Zealand	0.0	0.0	0.0	0.1	0.0	0.0	0.0	0.1
Norway	–	–	–	0.0	–	–	–	0.0
Sweden	–	–	0.3	0.4	–	–	0.3	0.4
Switzerland	0.0	0.0	0.0	–	0.0	0.0	0.0	–
United Kingdom	3.1	2.6	6.4	6.6	2.6	1.9	4.5	5.0
United States	25.0	10.0	6.0	10.0	15.0	9.0	5.0	9.0
TOTAL	*34.7*	*28.4*	*32.5*	*67.1*	*23.8*	*23.9*	*27.5*	*63.4*
MULTILATERAL	*15.8*	*27.5*	*24.1*	*33.9*	*15.0*	*26.7*	*23.2*	*33.1*
OPEC COUNTRIES	–	–	*4.0*	*2.0*	–	–	*4.0*	*2.0*
E.E.C.+ MEMBERS	*14.2*	*21.0*	*28.6*	*45.9*	*13.2*	*17.5*	*24.6*	*43.3*
TOTAL	***50.5***	***55.9***	***60.6***	***102.9***	***38.7***	***50.5***	***54.7***	***98.6***

TOTAL ODA GROSS	197
Australia	
Austria	
Belgium	
Canada	
Denmark	
Finland	
France	
Germany, Fed. Rep.	
Italy	
Japan	
Netherlands	
New Zealand	
Norway	
Sweden	
Switzerland	
United Kingdom	
United States	
TOTAL	
AF.D.F.	
AF.D.B.	
AS.D.B.	
CAR.D.B.	
E.E.C.	
IBRD	
IDA	
I.D.B.	
IFAD	
I.F.C.	
IMF TRUST FUND	
U.N. AGENCIES	
UNDP	
UNTA	
UNICEF	
UNRWA	
WFP	
UNHCR	
Other Multilateral	
Arab OPEC Agencies	
TOTAL	
OPEC COUNTRIES	
E.E.C.+ MEMBERS	
TOTAL	

GRANTS	
Australia	
Austria	
Belgium	
Canada	
Denmark	
Finland	
France	
Germany, Fed. Rep.	
Italy	
Japan	
Netherlands	
New Zealand	
Norway	
Sweden	
Switzerland	
United Kingdom	
United States	
TOTAL	
MULTILATERAL	
OPEC COUNTRIES	
E.E.C.+ MEMBERS	
TOTAL	

TOTAL OOF GROSS	
Australia	
Austria	
Belgium	
Canada	
Denmark	
Finland	
France	
Germany, Fed. Rep.	
Italy	
Japan	
Netherlands	
New Zealand	
Norway	
Sweden	
Switzerland	
United Kingdom	
United States	2
TOTAL	2
MULTILATERAL	
OPEC COUNTRIES	
E.E.C.+ MEMBERS	
TOTAL	

1978	1979	1980	1977	1978	1979	1980
			ODA COMMITMENTS			
0.0	0.0	0.0	0.0	0.0	–	0.0
–	0.1	0.0	–	–	–	–
0.0	0.0	0.1	–	–	–	–
0.2	0.3	0.3	0.7	0.1	0.3	0.3
0.1	0.5	2.4	0.0	3.7	0.7	0.1
0.0	0.0	0.1	–	0.0	0.0	0.1
–	–	3.5	–	–	–	8.1
5.4	6.7	14.9	4.6	7.7	28.7	20.9
0.0	0.0	0.0	0.0	0.0	0.0	0.0
0.0	0.2	18.0	0.0	0.0	9.3	10.2
2.8	10.9	4.2	7.4	8.6	6.4	2.4
0.0	0.0	0.1	–	0.0	0.0	0.0
–	–	0.0	–	–	–	–
–	0.3	0.4	–	–	–	–
0.0	0.0	–	–	–	–	–
2.6	6.4	6.6	2.9	2.0	6.9	6.4
5.0	6.0	9.0	4.0	6.4	7.6	8.5
16.2	*31.5*	*59.6*	*19.6*	*28.6*	*60.1*	*57.0*
–	0.1	1.2	5.6	6.3	9.7	–
–	–	–	–	–	–	–
–	–	–	–	–	–	–
–	–	–	–	–	–	–
2.9	3.1	7.7	14.9	4.1	18.2	3.5
–	–	–	–	–	–	–
10.2	2.1	2.4	8.2	–	2.5	–
–	–	–	–	–	–	–
–	–	0.7	–	–	12.7	–
–	–	–	–	–	–	–
9.6	9.7	8.5	–	–	–	–
–	–	–	3.3	3.7	4.9	6.8
2.0	2.8	3.4	–	–	–	–
0.4	0.3	0.2	–	–	–	–
0.2	0.1	0.5	–	–	–	–
–	–	–	–	–	–	–
0.1	0.8	1.5	–	–	–	–
0.1	0.1	0.2	–	–	–	–
1.0	0.6	1.0	–	–	–	–
0.4	1.3	2.6	7.1	0.0	1.6	9.5
26.8	*21.1*	*29.8*	*39.1*	*14.0*	*49.6*	*19.8*
–	*4.0*	*2.0*	–	–	*4.0*	*2.4*
13.9	*27.6*	*39.4*	*29.8*	*26.1*	*61.0*	*41.5*
43.0	***56.6***	***91.4***	***58.7***	***42.7***	***113.7***	***79.3***
			TECH. COOP. GRANTS			
0.0	0.0	0.0	0.1	0.0	0.0	0.0
–	0.1	0.0	0.0	–	0.1	0.0
0.0	0.0	0.1	0.0	0.0	0.0	0.1
0.2	0.3	0.3	–	0.1	0.3	0.3
0.1	0.0	0.2	0.0	0.1	0.0	0.2
0.0	0.0	0.1	–	0.0	0.0	0.1
–	–	0.7	–	–	–	0.7
3.8	3.3	5.3	2.3	3.8	3.3	5.3
0.0	0.0	0.0	0.0	0.0	0.0	0.0
0.0	0.2	2.7	0.0	0.0	0.2	0.3
2.6	6.0	4.1	0.4	0.6	0.6	0.8
0.0	0.0	0.1	0.0	–	0.0	0.0
–	–	0.0	–	–	–	0.0
–	0.3	0.4	–	–	–	–
0.0	0.0	–	–	–	–	–
2.0	6.3	6.4	2.2	2.0	3.3	4.2
4.0	5.0	7.0	2.0	3.0	3.0	4.0
12.8	*21.5*	*27.5*	*7.1*	*9.6*	*10.9*	*16.1*
6.6	*7.9*	*14.1*	*3.2*	*3.5*	*4.0*	*6.8*
–	*4.0*	*2.0*	–	–	–	–
11.4	*18.7*	*24.2*	*5.0*	*6.4*	*7.3*	*11.3*
19.4	***33.5***	***43.6***	***10.4***	***13.2***	***14.9***	***22.9***
			TOTAL OOF NET			
–	–	–	–	–	–	–
–	–	–	–	–	–	–
0.5	–	2.5	–	0.4	–	2.5
–	–	–	–	–	–	–
–	–	–	–	–	–	–
–	–	–	–	–	–	–
3.6	–	2.2	–	3.6	-0.2	1.5
1.6	0.3	1.6	0.7	0.5	0.0	1.5
1.3	–	–	–	0.8	0.0	0.0
–	–	–	–	–	–	–
0.2	0.6	0.2	–	0.2	0.6	0.2
–	–	–	–	–	–	–
–	–	–	–	–	–	–
–	–	–	–	–	–	–
–	–	–	–	–	–	–
–	–	–	–	–	–	–
5.0	–	1.0	11.0	5.0	-1.0	1.0
12.2	*1.0*	*7.5*	*11.7*	*10.4*	*-0.7*	*6.6*
0.7	*3.0*	*4.0*	*0.8*	*-0.1*	*2.1*	*3.3*
–	–	–	–	–	–	–
7.2	*1.0*	*6.5*	*0.7*	*5.4*	*0.3*	*5.6*
12.9	***4.0***	***11.5***	***12.5***	***10.3***	***1.5***	***10.0***

	1977	1978	1979	1980
MAIN AID AGGREGATES				
DAC COUNTRIES COMBINED				
PRIVATE SECTOR NET	2.8	-0.6	5.8	-5.7
Direct Investment	6.8	3.8	6.0	0.3
Portfolio Invest.	0.0	-1.0	0.9	-0.9
Export Credits	-3.9	-3.4	-1.1	-5.1
OFFICIAL & PRIVATE				
GROSS:				
Contractual Lending	26.1	21.8	11.0	40.4
Export Credits Tot.	6.3	11.6	0.1	0.8
Export Credits Priv	0.3	6.2	0.1	0.8
OTHER NET DATA				
Contractual Lending	11.0	7.6	4.9	30.8
Export Credits Tot.	-7.9	1.3	-2.1	-5.1
(Bank Sector Loans)	4.0	5.0	2.0	-6.0
ODA CONCESSIONALITY				
Total:Grant Element	96.0	92.0	82.0	79.0
Loans:Grant Element	75.0	68.0	71.0	59.0
OTHER SOURCES				
CMEA Countr.(Gross)	0.2	0.1	–	0.1
Intra LDCS Exc.OPEC	–	–	–	–
Other	–	–	–	–
ALL SOURCE COMMITMENTS				
TOTAL BILATERAL	35.0	37.2	65.8	64.8
of which				
OPEC (ODA)	–	–	4.0	2.4
CMEA (ODA)	–	–	–	–
TOTAL MULTILAT.(ODA)	39.1	14.0	49.6	19.8
TOTAL BIL.& MULTIL.	74.0	51.2	115.4	84.6
of which				
ODA Grants	34.2	29.7	50.0	41.0
ODA Loans	24.5	12.9	63.7	38.3
ODA CONCESSIONALITY				
Total: Grant Element	88.0	92.0	86.0	77.0
Loans: Grant Element	70.0	75.0	75.0	55.0
INDEBTEDNESS				
TOTAL DEBT DISBURSED	***207.3***	***312.7***	***330.3***	
Debt to DAC Countries	153.0	240.0	248.0	
ODA	49.0	61.0	72.0	
Total Export Credits	90.0	152.0	150.0	
Other Private Market	14.0	27.0	26.0	
International Org.	37.7	51.6	57.6	
CMEA	15.5	20.4	24.1	
Other	1.1	0.7	0.6	
TOTAL DEBT SERVICE	***28.3***	***34.9***	***52.0***	
Paid to DAC Countries	25.3	31.7	47.2	
ODA	1.6	2.3	2.6	
Total Export Credits	20.7	27.1	35.0	
Other Private Market	3.0	2.3	9.6	
International Org.	2.2	2.2	3.6	
CMEA	0.4	0.5	0.9	
Other	0.4	0.6	0.3	
ECONOMIC INDICATORS				
GNP Curr. Prices, $M	639.6	759.0	864.9	966.3
Real GNP, 1976=100	102.0	101.0	103.0	104.0
GNP/Cap Curr. Prices,$	199.0	230.0	255.0	278.0
GNP/cap Atlas Basis, $	227.7	237.2	254.6	272.8
Real GNP/Cap, 1976=100	99.0	96.0	95.0	93.0
Population, Million	3.2	3.3	3.4	3.5
Curr.A/C Deficit(-),$M	-62.2	-127.7	-195.2	–
BOP Exp. & Transf.,$M	167.3	213.4	250.9	–
Exp. to OECD CIF, $M	167.8	158.1	183.5	175.2
of which				
Manufact.	0.6	0.7	1.0	0.9
Imp. from OECD FOB, $M	100.6	168.5	181.7	249.4
Reserves ex. Gold, $M	33.4	34.8	46.7	30.6

	1977	1978	1979	1980	1977	1978	1979	1980
TOTAL RECEIPTS NET					**TOTAL ODA NET**			
DAC COUNTRIES								
Australia	8.5	19.2	14.4	21.1	1.2	1.0	0.7	1.1
Austria	0.0	–	–	0.0	0.0	–	–	0.0
Belgium	0.1	-0.7	3.1	4.6	–	–	–	0.0
Canada	-0.3	-0.1	3.9	0.1	–	–	–	–
Denmark	-2.8	-3.0	-2.8	-2.4	–	–	–	–
Finland	-2.0	-1.9	-1.9	-1.9	–	0.0	0.0	0.0
France	11.9	35.5	-17.9	60.4	–	–	–	1.5
Germany, Fed. Rep.	16.2	23.3	-7.3	110.2	1.6	1.8	3.2	4.6
Italy	–	0.2	0.3	4.9	–	–	–	–
Japan	98.2	98.2	285.8	121.5	8.8	3.6	1.5	3.8
Netherlands	0.4	6.0	0.4	-12.5	0.4	0.2	0.4	0.1
New Zealand	0.6	2.2	0.4	0.1	0.2	0.2	0.1	0.1
Norway	20.0	31.1	58.8	41.5	–	–	–	–
Sweden	–	0.1	–	0.9	–	–	–	–
Switzerland	-1.3	-0.7	-0.1	7.5	–	–	–	–
United Kingdom	50.7	4.5	64.7	-5.2	-0.9	-1.6	-2.1	-1.8
United States	14.0	91.0	130.0	311.0	–	–	–	–
TOTAL	*214.2*	*304.9*	*531.8*	*662.0*	*11.3*	*5.2*	*3.8*	*9.4*
MULTILATERAL								
AF.D.F.	–	–	–	–	–	–	–	–
AF.D.B.	–	–	–	–	–	–	–	–
AS.D.B.	-1.0	41.2	-3.6	7.2	0.8	–	–	–
CAR.D.B.	–	–	–	–	–	–	–	–
E.E.C.	–	–	0.1	–	–	–	0.1	–
IBRD	0.6	16.8	-2.9	-1.4	–	–	–	–
IDA	–	–	–	–	–	–	–	–
I.D.B.	–	–	–	–	–	–	–	–
IFAD	–	–	–	–	–	–	–	–
I.F.C.	–	–	–	–	–	–	–	–
IMF TRUST FUND	–	–	–	–	–	–	–	–
U.N. AGENCIES	–	–	–	–	–	–	–	–
UNDP	0.7	1.0	1.0	1.4	0.7	1.0	1.0	1.4
UNTA	0.3	0.2	0.2	0.0	0.3	0.2	0.2	0.0
UNICEF	–	–	–	–	–	–	–	–
UNRWA	–	–	–	–	–	–	–	–
WFP	0.0	0.3	0.0	–	0.0	0.3	0.0	–
UNHCR	–	–	0.5	2.5	–	–	0.5	2.5
Other Multilateral	0.1	0.1	0.0	0.1	0.1	0.1	0.0	0.1
Arab OPEC Agencies	–	–	–	–	–	–	–	–
TOTAL	*0.7*	*59.5*	*-4.8*	*9.9*	*1.9*	*1.5*	*1.7*	*4.0*
OPEC COUNTRIES	–	–	–	*0.5*	–	–	–	*0.5*
E.E.C.+ MEMBERS	*76.5*	*65.9*	*40.6*	*160.1*	*1.1*	*0.4*	*1.6*	*4.4*
TOTAL	**214.9**	**364.4**	**527.0**	**672.4**	**13.2**	**6.7**	**5.5**	**14.0**

	197
TOTAL ODA GROSS	
Australia	1
Austria	0
Belgium	
Canada	
Denmark	
Finland	
France	
Germany, Fed. Rep.	1
Italy	
Japan	9
Netherlands	0
New Zealand	0
Norway	
Sweden	
Switzerland	
United Kingdom	0
United States	
TOTAL	*13*
AF.D.F.	
AF.D.B.	
AS.D.B.	0
CAR.D.B.	
E.E.C.	
IBRD	
IDA	
I.D.B.	
IFAD	
I.F.C.	
IMF TRUST FUND	
U.N. AGENCIES	
UNDP	0
UNTA	0
UNICEF	
UNRWA	
WFP	0
UNHCR	
Other Multilateral	0
Arab OPEC Agencies	
TOTAL	*1*
OPEC COUNTRIES	
E.E.C.+ MEMBERS	*2*
TOTAL	**15**

	1977	1978	1979	1980	1977	1978	1979	1980
ODA LOANS GROSS					**ODA LOANS NET**			
DAC COUNTRIES								
Australia	–	–	–	–	–	–	–	–
Austria	–	–	–	–	–	–	–	–
Belgium	–	–	–	–	–	–	–	–
Canada	–	–	–	–	–	–	–	–
Denmark	–	–	–	–	–	–	–	–
Finland	–	–	–	–	–	–	–	–
France	–	–	–	–	–	–	–	–
Germany, Fed. Rep.	–	–	–	0.5	–	–	–	0.5
Italy	–	–	–	–	–	–	–	–
Japan	7.6	2.2	0.4	2.0	6.7	-0.6	-4.0	-2.3
Netherlands	–	–	–	–	–	–	–	–
New Zealand	–	–	–	–	–	–	–	–
Norway	–	–	–	–	–	–	–	–
Sweden	–	–	–	–	–	–	–	–
Switzerland	–	–	–	–	–	–	–	–
United Kingdom	–	–	–	–	-1.5	-4.5	-3.4	-3.2
United States	–	–	–	–	–	–	–	–
TOTAL	*7.6*	*2.2*	*0.4*	*2.5*	*5.3*	*-5.1*	*-7.4*	*-5.0*
MULTILATERAL	*0.8*	–	–	–	*0.8*	–	–	–
OPEC COUNTRIES	–	–	–	–	–	–	–	–
E.E.C.+ MEMBERS	–	–	–	*0.5*	*-1.5*	*-4.5*	*-3.4*	*-2.7*
TOTAL	**8.4**	**2.2**	**0.4**	**2.5**	**6.0**	**-5.1**	**-7.4**	**-5.0**

	197
GRANTS	
Australia	1
Austria	0
Belgium	
Canada	
Denmark	
Finland	
France	
Germany, Fed. Rep.	1
Italy	
Japan	2
Netherlands	0
New Zealand	0
Norway	
Sweden	
Switzerland	
United Kingdom	0
United States	
TOTAL	*6*
MULTILATERAL	*1*
OPEC COUNTRIES	
E.E.C.+ MEMBERS	*2*
TOTAL	**7**

	1977	1978	1979	1980	1977	1978	1979	1980
TOTAL OFFICIAL GROSS					**TOTAL OFFICIAL NET**			
DAC COUNTRIES								
Australia	1.2	1.0	0.7	1.1	1.2	1.0	0.7	1.1
Austria	0.0	–	–	0.0	0.0	–	–	0.0
Belgium	–	–	–	0.0	–	–	–	0.0
Canada	–	–	3.9	2.5	–	–	3.9	0.1
Denmark	–	–	–	–	–	–	–	–
Finland	–	0.0	0.0	0.0	–	0.0	0.0	0.0
France	–	–	–	1.5	–	–	–	1.5
Germany, Fed. Rep.	1.6	1.8	3.2	9.5	1.1	1.1	2.2	7.4
Italy	–	–	–	–	–	–	–	–
Japan	9.7	6.4	5.9	8.0	8.8	3.6	1.5	3.8
Netherlands	0.4	0.2	0.4	0.1	0.4	0.2	0.4	0.1
New Zealand	4.5	0.2	0.1	0.1	0.2	0.2	0.1	0.1
Norway	–	–	–	–	–	–	–	–
Sweden	–	–	–	–	–	–	–	–
Switzerland	–	–	–	–	–	–	–	–
United Kingdom	0.6	2.9	1.3	1.4	-1.3	-2.1	-2.6	-6.3
United States	–	43.0	110.0	45.0	-3.0	39.0	93.0	25.0
TOTAL	*17.9*	*55.5*	*125.5*	*69.3*	*7.3*	*43.1*	*99.2*	*32.8*
MULTILATERAL	*12.3*	*71.5*	*7.9*	*23.5*	*0.7*	*59.5*	*-4.8*	*9.9*
OPEC COUNTRIES	–	–	–	*0.5*	–	–	–	*0.5*
E.E.C.+ MEMBERS	*2.6*	*4.9*	*5.0*	*12.5*	*0.1*	*-0.7*	*0.1*	*2.7*
TOTAL	**30.1**	**127.0**	**133.4**	**93.3**	**8.0**	**102.6**	**94.5**	**43.2**

	197
TOTAL OOF GROSS	
Australia	
Austria	
Belgium	
Canada	
Denmark	
Finland	
France	
Germany, Fed. Rep.	
Italy	
Japan	
Netherlands	
New Zealand	4
Norway	
Sweden	
Switzerland	
United Kingdom	
United States	
TOTAL	*4.*
MULTILATERAL	*10*
OPEC COUNTRIES	
E.E.C.+ MEMBERS	
TOTAL	**14.**

ODA COMMITMENTS

1978	1979	1980	1977	1978	1979	1980
1.0	0.7	1.1	0.7	0.6	3.1	3.4
–	–	0.0	–	–	–	–
–	–	0.0	–	–	–	–
–	–	–	–	–	–	1.7
–	–	–	–	–	–	–
0.0	0.0	0.0	–	0.0	0.0	–
–	–	1.5	–	–	–	1.4
1.8	3.2	4.6	1.6	2.1	3.3	12.1
–	–	–	–	–	–	–
6.4	5.9	8.0	2.6	5.3	7.0	8.8
0.2	0.4	0.1	0.2	0.4	0.3	0.1
0.2	0.1	0.1	0.0	0.1	–	0.1
–	–	–	–	–	–	–
–	–	–	–	–	–	–
–	–	–	–	–	–	–
2.9	1.3	1.4	0.6	2.9	1.3	1.4
–	–	–	0.1	–	–	–
12.5	*11.6*	*16.9*	*5.8*	*11.4*	*15.0*	*29.0*
–	–	–	–	–	–	–
–	–	–	–	–	–	–
–	–	–	–	–	–	–
–	–	–	–	–	–	–
–	0.1	–	–	–	0.1	–
–	–	–	–	–	–	–
–	–	–	–	–	–	–
–	–	–	–	–	–	–
–	–	–	–	–	–	–
–	–	–	–	–	–	–
–	–	–	–	–	–	–
–	–	–	1.1	1.5	1.6	4.0
1.0	1.0	1.4	–	–	–	–
0.2	0.2	0.0	–	–	–	–
–	–	–	–	–	–	–
–	–	–	–	–	–	–
0.3	0.0	–	–	–	–	–
–	0.5	2.5	–	–	–	–
0.1	0.0	0.1	–	–	–	–
–	–	–	–	–	–	–
1.5	*1.7*	*4.0*	*1.1*	*1.5*	*1.7*	*4.0*
–	–	*0.5*	–	–	–	*0.5*
4.9	*5.0*	*7.6*	*2.4*	*5.3*	*5.0*	*14.9*
14.0	***13.3***	***21.4***	***6.9***	***12.9***	***16.7***	***33.5***

TECH. COOP. GRANTS

1978	1979	1980	1977	1978	1979	1980
1.0	0.7	1.1	1.0	1.0	0.7	1.1
–	–	0.0	0.0	–	–	0.0
–	–	0.0	–	–	–	0.0
–	–	–	–	–	–	–
–	–	–	–	–	–	–
0.0	0.0	0.0	–	0.0	0.0	0.0
–	–	1.5	–	–	–	1.5
1.8	3.2	4.0	1.6	1.8	3.2	3.6
–	–	–	–	–	–	–
4.2	5.5	6.1	2.1	4.2	5.5	6.0
0.2	0.4	0.1	0.4	0.2	0.4	0.1
0.2	0.1	0.1	0.2	0.2	0.1	0.1
–	–	–	–	–	–	–
–	–	–	–	–	–	–
–	–	–	–	–	–	–
2.9	1.3	1.4	0.6	2.9	1.3	1.4
–	–	–	–	–	–	–
10.3	*11.2*	*14.4*	*5.8*	*10.3*	*11.1*	*13.8*
1.5	*1.7*	*4.0*	*1.1*	*1.2*	*1.7*	*4.0*
–	–	*0.5*	–	–	–	–
4.9	*5.0*	*7.0*	*2.6*	*4.9*	*4.9*	*6.5*
11.8	***12.9***	***18.9***	***6.9***	***11.5***	***12.7***	***17.8***

TOTAL OOF NET

1978	1979	1980	1977	1978	1979	1980
–	–	–	–	–	–	–
–	–	–	–	–	–	–
–	–	–	–	–	–	–
–	3.9	2.5	–	–	3.9	0.1
–	–	–	–	–	–	–
–	–	–	–	–	–	–
–	–	–	–	–	–	–
–	–	4.9	-0.6	-0.7	-1.0	2.8
–	–	–	–	–	–	–
–	–	–	–	–	–	–
–	–	–	–	–	–	–
–	–	–	–	–	–	–
–	–	–	–	–	–	–
–	–	–	–	–	–	–
–	–	–	–	–	–	–
–	–	–	-0.4	-0.5	-0.5	-4.5
43.0	110.0	45.0	-3.0	39.0	93.0	25.0
43.0	*113.9*	*52.4*	*-4.0*	*37.9*	*95.4*	*23.4*
70.0	*6.2*	*19.5*	*-1.2*	*58.0*	*-6.5*	*5.8*
–	–	–	–	–	–	–
–	–	*4.9*	*-1.0*	*-1.1*	*-1.5*	*-1.7*
113.0	***120.1***	***71.9***	***-5.2***	***95.9***	***88.9***	***29.3***

MAIN AID AGGREGATES

	1977	1978	1979	1980
DAC COUNTRIES COMBINED				
PRIVATE SECTOR NET	206.9	261.8	432.6	629.2
Direct Investment	85.5	147.2	354.5	570.0
Portfolio Invest.	100.3	127.3	-10.8	17.9
Export Credits	21.1	-12.7	88.9	41.3
OFFICIAL & PRIVATE				
GROSS:				
Contractual Lending	83.5	109.0	280.5	182.7
Export Credits Tot.	75.9	106.9	280.0	180.2
Export Credits Priv	71.6	63.9	166.1	127.8
OTHER NET DATA				
Contractual Lending	22.4	20.0	177.0	59.8
Export Credits Tot.	17.6	25.7	185.2	69.2
(Bank Sector Loans)	–	–	–	321.0
ODA CONCESSIONALITY				
Total:Grant Element	98.0	97.0	100.0	100.0
Loans:Grant Element	57.0	38.0	–	–
OTHER SOURCES				
CMEA Countr.(Gross)	–	–	–	–
Intra LDCS Exc.OPEC	–	–	–	–
Other	–	–	–	–
ALL SOURCE COMMITMENTS				
TOTAL BILATERAL	10.1	11.4	177.9	67.1
of which				
OPEC (ODA)	–	–	–	0.5
CMEA (ODA)	–	–	–	–
TOTAL MULTILAT.(ODA)	1.1	1.5	1.7	4.0
TOTAL BIL.& MULTIL.	11.1	12.9	179.6	71.1
of which				
ODA Grants	6.7	12.5	16.2	31.6
ODA Loans	0.2	0.5	0.4	2.0
ODA CONCESSIONALITY				
Total: Grant Element	98.0	97.0	100.0	100.0
Loans: Grant Element	57.0	38.0	–	–

INDEBTEDNESS

	1977	1978	1979	1980
TOTAL DEBT DISBURSED	***1087.3***	***1292.1***	***1816.3***	
Debt to DAC Countries	921.0	1104.0	1635.0	
ODA	92.0	108.0	94.0	
Total Export Credits	415.0	539.0	736.0	
Other Private Market	414.0	457.0	805.0	
International Org.	166.3	180.9	174.4	
CMEA	–	–	–	
Other	–	7.2	6.9	
TOTAL DEBT SERVICE	***134.6***	***325.9***	***301.8***	
Paid to DAC Countries	110.6	299.4	271.4	
ODA	5.5	11.5	11.7	
Total Export Credits	82.3	237.0	152.7	
Other Private Market	22.8	50.9	107.0	
International Org.	24.0	26.5	28.7	
CMEA	–	–	–	
Other	–	–	1.7	

ECONOMIC INDICATORS

	1977	1978	1979	1980
GNP Curr. Prices, $M	6469.4	7668.6	8931.8	10376.8
Real GNP, 1976=100	109.0	118.0	129.0	143.0
GNP/Cap Curr. Prices,$	2804.0	3285.0	3783.0	4341.0
GNP/cap Atlas Basis, $	2785.1	3213.5	3767.2	4477.6
Real GNP/Cap, 1976=100	107.0	115.0	125.0	136.0
Population, Million	2.3	2.3	2.4	2.4
Curr.A/C Deficit(-),$M	-319.0	-617.0	-893.0	-1572.0
BOP Exp. & Transf.,$M	11101.0	13544.0	18231.0	24337.0
Exp. to OECD CIF, $M	2923.3	3406.4	5208.0	6513.9
of which				
Manufact.	1608.9	1914.9	2759.5	3520.3
Imp. from OECD FOB, $M	4352.2	5716.1	7631.6	10446.5
Reserves ex. Gold, $M	3857.7	5302.7	5818.5	6566.8

TOTAL RECEIPTS NET

	1977	1978	1979	1980
DAC COUNTRIES				
Australia	–	–	0.3	0.1
Austria	0.0	–	–	–
Belgium	0.1	-0.1	0.4	0.3
Canada	0.2	0.0	–	2.4
Denmark	0.0	–	0.0	0.0
Finland	0.0	0.0	0.0	0.5
France	-0.1	-1.0	-0.2	1.6
Germany, Fed. Rep.	9.6	20.0	9.8	27.4
Italy	109.3	23.5	76.5	70.2
Japan	0.0	0.1	0.2	0.4
Netherlands	3.2	1.4	2.8	3.2
New Zealand	–	–	–	–
Norway	0.1	–	8.6	0.7
Sweden	3.4	2.7	5.0	6.8
Switzerland	0.2	0.3	0.2	1.6
United Kingdom	–	1.5	-24.9	36.1
United States	3.0	13.0	20.0	60.0
TOTAL	*129.0*	*61.5*	*98.6*	*211.1*
MULTILATERAL				
AF.D.F.	1.0	1.3	1.5	1.5
AF.D.B.	0.0	0.0	-0.2	–
AS.D.B.	–	–	–	–
CAR.D.B.	–	–	–	–
E.E.C.	19.3	12.7	18.2	37.0
IBRD	–	–	–	–
IDA	9.4	9.4	6.8	9.7
I.D.B.	–	–	–	–
IFAD	–	–	–	0.3
I.F.C.	–	–	–	–
IMF TRUST FUND	–	–	–	13.8
U.N. AGENCIES	–	–	–	–
UNDP	3.3	3.8	4.4	4.7
UNTA	1.4	1.6	1.2	0.4
UNICEF	0.9	1.3	1.5	3.3
UNRWA	–	–	–	–
WFP	6.0	9.4	11.5	19.5
UNHCR	–	0.5	5.3	58.5
Other Multilateral	1.8	1.4	1.8	2.2
Arab OPEC Agencies	6.8	8.3	10.6	50.2
TOTAL	*49.8*	*49.5*	*62.6*	*201.1*
OPEC COUNTRIES	*180.6*	*100.3*	*94.8*	*128.5*
E.E.C.+ MEMBERS	*141.5*	*58.0*	*82.6*	*175.7*
TOTAL	***359.5***	***211.2***	***255.9***	***540.7***

TOTAL ODA NET

	1977	1978	1979	1980
Australia	–	–	0.3	0.1
Austria	0.0	–	–	–
Belgium	0.0	0.0	0.4	0.4
Canada	0.2	0.0	–	2.4
Denmark	0.0	–	0.0	0.0
Finland	0.0	0.0	0.0	0.5
France	–	–	0.0	1.6
Germany, Fed. Rep.	6.6	20.0	11.0	27.9
Italy	8.2	7.4	7.3	27.4
Japan	0.0	0.1	0.2	0.4
Netherlands	3.2	1.4	2.8	3.2
New Zealand	–	–	–	–
Norway	0.2	–	–	0.7
Sweden	3.4	2.7	5.0	6.8
Switzerland	0.2	0.3	0.2	1.6
United Kingdom	0.3	1.9	2.8	6.7
United States	3.0	13.0	20.0	60.0
TOTAL	*25.2*	*46.8*	*49.8*	*139.4*
AF.D.F.	1.0	1.3	1.5	1.5
AF.D.B.	–	–	–	–
AS.D.B.	–	–	–	–
CAR.D.B.	–	–	–	–
E.E.C.	19.3	12.7	18.2	37.0
IBRD	–	–	–	–
IDA	9.4	9.4	6.8	9.7
I.D.B.	–	–	–	–
IFAD	–	–	–	0.3
I.F.C.	–	–	–	–
IMF TRUST FUND	–	–	–	13.8
U.N. AGENCIES	–	–	–	–
UNDP	3.3	3.8	4.4	4.7
UNTA	1.4	1.6	1.2	0.4
UNICEF	0.9	1.3	1.5	3.3
UNRWA	–	–	–	–
WFP	6.0	9.4	11.5	19.5
UNHCR	–	0.5	5.3	58.5
Other Multilateral	1.8	1.4	1.8	2.2
Arab OPEC Agencies	6.8	8.3	10.6	15.4
TOTAL	*49.8*	*49.5*	*62.7*	*166.3*
OPEC COUNTRIES	*180.6*	*100.3*	*94.8*	*128.5*
E.E.C.+ MEMBERS	*37.6*	*43.4*	*42.4*	*104.0*
TOTAL	***255.7***	***196.7***	***207.4***	***434.3***

TOTAL ODA GROSS

	197
Australia	
Austria	0.
Belgium	0.
Canada	0.
Denmark	0.
Finland	0.
France	
Germany, Fed. Rep.	7.
Italy	8.
Japan	0.
Netherlands	3.
New Zealand	
Norway	0.
Sweden	3.
Switzerland	0.
United Kingdom	0.
United States	3.
TOTAL	*25.*
AF.D.F.	1.
AF.D.B.	
AS.D.B.	
CAR.D.B.	
E.E.C.	19
IBRD	
IDA	9
I.D.B.	
IFAD	
I.F.C.	
IMF TRUST FUND	
U.N. AGENCIES	
UNDP	3
UNTA	1
UNICEF	0
UNRWA	
WFP	6
UNHCR	
Other Multilateral	1
Arab OPEC Agencies	6
TOTAL	*49*
OPEC COUNTRIES	*180*
E.E.C.+ MEMBERS	*38*
TOTAL	***256***

ODA LOANS GROSS

	1977	1978	1979	1980
DAC COUNTRIES				
Australia	–	–	–	–
Austria	–	–	–	–
Belgium	–	–	–	–
Canada	–	–	–	–
Denmark	–	–	–	–
Finland	–	–	–	–
France	–	–	0.0	–
Germany, Fed. Rep.	0.0	14.1	0.8	–
Italy	–	–	–	4.4
Japan	–	–	–	–
Netherlands	–	–	–	–
New Zealand	–	–	–	–
Norway	–	–	–	–
Sweden	–	–	–	–
Switzerland	–	–	–	–
United Kingdom	–	–	–	–
United States	–	7.0	11.0	18.0
TOTAL	*0.0*	*21.1*	*11.8*	*22.4*
MULTILATERAL	*16.1*	*18.7*	*19.0*	*40.6*
OPEC COUNTRIES	*128.1*	*60.3*	*63.4*	*44.0*
E.E.C.+ MEMBERS	*0.0*	*14.1*	*0.8*	*4.4*
TOTAL	***144.3***	***100.1***	***94.3***	***107.0***

ODA LOANS NET

	1977	1978	1979	1980
Australia	–	–	–	–
Austria	–	–	–	–
Belgium	–	–	–	–
Canada	–	–	–	–
Denmark	–	–	–	–
Finland	–	–	–	–
France	–	–	0.0	–
Germany, Fed. Rep.	-0.3	13.4	0.8	-39.1
Italy	-0.3	-0.7	-0.4	4.4
Japan	–	–	–	–
Netherlands	–	–	–	–
New Zealand	–	–	–	–
Norway	–	–	–	–
Sweden	–	–	–	–
Switzerland	–	–	–	–
United Kingdom	–	–	–	–
United States	–	7.0	10.0	17.0
TOTAL	*-0.6*	*19.7*	*10.5*	*-17.7*
MULTILATERAL	*16.0*	*18.6*	*18.9*	*40.5*
OPEC COUNTRIES	*128.1*	*60.3*	*63.4*	*43.5*
E.E.C.+ MEMBERS	*-0.6*	*12.7*	*0.5*	*-34.7*
TOTAL	***143.5***	***98.5***	***92.8***	***66.3***

GRANTS

	197
Australia	
Austria	0
Belgium	0
Canada	0
Denmark	0
Finland	0
France	
Germany, Fed. Rep.	6
Italy	8
Japan	0
Netherlands	3
New Zealand	
Norway	0
Sweden	3
Switzerland	0
United Kingdom	0
United States	3
TOTAL	*25*
MULTILATERAL	*33*
OPEC COUNTRIES	*52*
E.E.C.+ MEMBERS	*38*
TOTAL	***112***

TOTAL OFFICIAL GROSS

	1977	1978	1979	1980
DAC COUNTRIES				
Australia	–	–	0.3	0.1
Austria	0.0	–	–	–
Belgium	0.0	0.0	0.4	0.4
Canada	0.2	0.0	–	2.4
Denmark	0.0	–	0.0	0.0
Finland	0.0	0.0	0.0	0.5
France	0.1	0.5	0.0	1.6
Germany, Fed. Rep.	9.4	20.7	11.0	67.0
Italy	8.5	8.1	7.7	27.4
Japan	0.0	0.1	0.2	0.4
Netherlands	3.2	1.4	2.8	3.2
New Zealand	–	–	–	–
Norway	0.2	–	–	0.7
Sweden	3.4	2.7	5.0	6.8
Switzerland	0.2	0.3	0.2	1.6
United Kingdom	0.3	1.9	2.8	6.7
United States	3.0	13.0	21.0	61.0
TOTAL	*28.5*	*48.8*	*51.2*	*179.6*
MULTILATERAL	*49.9*	*49.7*	*62.9*	*201.2*
OPEC COUNTRIES	*180.6*	*100.3*	*94.8*	*129.0*
E.E.C.+ MEMBERS	*40.9*	*45.3*	*42.8*	*143.1*
TOTAL	***259.1***	***198.8***	***208.9***	***509.8***

TOTAL OFFICIAL NET

	1977	1978	1979	1980
Australia	–	–	0.3	0.1
Austria	0.0	–	–	–
Belgium	0.0	0.0	0.4	0.4
Canada	0.2	0.0	–	2.4
Denmark	0.0	–	0.0	0.0
Finland	0.0	0.0	0.0	0.5
France	0.1	0.5	0.0	1.6
Germany, Fed. Rep.	9.1	20.0	9.8	27.5
Italy	8.2	7.4	7.3	27.4
Japan	0.0	0.1	0.2	0.4
Netherlands	3.2	1.4	2.8	3.2
New Zealand	–	–	–	–
Norway	0.2	–	–	0.7
Sweden	3.4	2.7	5.0	6.8
Switzerland	0.2	0.3	0.2	1.6
United Kingdom	0.3	1.9	2.8	6.7
United States	3.0	13.0	20.0	60.0
TOTAL	*27.8*	*47.3*	*48.7*	*139.1*
MULTILATERAL	*49.8*	*49.5*	*62.6*	*201.1*
OPEC COUNTRIES	*180.6*	*100.3*	*94.8*	*128.5*
E.E.C.+ MEMBERS	*40.2*	*43.9*	*41.3*	*103.7*
TOTAL	***258.3***	***197.1***	***206.1***	***468.8***

TOTAL OOF GROSS

	197
Australia	
Austria	
Belgium	
Canada	
Denmark	
Finland	
France	0
Germany, Fed. Rep.	2
Italy	
Japan	
Netherlands	
New Zealand	
Norway	
Sweden	
Switzerland	
United Kingdom	
United States	
TOTAL	2
MULTILATERAL	0
OPEC COUNTRIES	
E.E.C.+ MEMBERS	2
TOTAL	2

ODA COMMITMENTS

1978	1979	1980	1977	1978	1979	1980
–	0.3	0.1	–	0.1	0.2	1.9
–	–	–	–	–	–	–
0.0	0.4	0.4	–	–	–	–
0.0	–	2.4	0.2	–	0.0	2.6
–	0.0	0.0	0.0	0.1	–	1.2
0.0	0.0	0.5	–	0.0	0.0	0.7
–	0.0	1.6	–	–	–	2.0
20.7	11.0	67.0	12.3	22.9	31.5	97.8
8.1	7.7	27.4	8.5	8.1	7.7	29.6
0.1	0.2	0.4	0.0	0.1	0.2	0.4
1.4	2.8	3.2	4.4	2.7	3.8	3.2
–	–	–	–	–	–	–
–	–	0.7	–	–	0.5	0.4
2.7	5.0	6.8	3.4	0.4	–	13.3
0.3	0.2	1.6	–	–	–	1.6
1.9	2.8	6.7	0.3	4.2	7.1	5.0
13.0	21.0	61.0	0.8	19.0	26.5	74.7
48.3	*51.2*	*179.6*	*29.9*	*57.6*	*77.4*	*234.4*
1.3	1.5	1.5	7.2	16.3	19.4	–
–	–	–	–	–	–	–
–	–	–	–	–	–	–
–	–	–	–	–	–	–
12.7	18.2	37.0	9.6	2.9	13.7	37.6
–	–	–	–	–	–	–
9.5	6.9	9.8	20.0	14.5	30.5	6.0
–	–	–	–	–	–	–
–	–	0.3	–	–	17.4	–
–	–	–	–	–	–	–
–	–	13.8	–	–	–	–
–	–	–	13.3	17.9	25.6	88.6
3.8	4.4	4.7	–	–	–	–
1.6	1.2	0.4	–	–	–	–
1.3	1.5	3.3	–	–	–	–
–	–	–	–	–	–	–
9.4	11.5	19.5	–	–	–	–
0.5	5.3	58.5	–	–	–	–
1.4	1.8	2.2	–	–	–	–
8.3	10.6	15.4	39.0	3.0	8.8	12.8
49.6	*62.9*	*166.4*	*89.0*	*54.6*	*115.4*	*145.0*
100.3	*94.8*	*129.0*	*346.8*	*15.0*	*71.2*	*122.4*
44.8	*42.8*	*143.1*	*35.1*	*40.7*	*63.7*	*176.3*
198.2	***208.9***	***474.9***	***465.7***	***127.1***	***264.1***	***501.7***

TECH. COOP. GRANTS

1978	1979	1980	1977	1978	1979	1980
–	0.3	0.1	–	–	0.0	–
–	–	–	0.0	–	–	–
0.0	0.4	0.4	0.0	0.0	0.1	0.3
0.0	–	2.4	–	–	–	–
–	0.0	0.0	–	–	0.0	0.0
0.0	0.0	0.5	0.0	0.0	0.0	0.3
–	–	1.6	–	–	–	1.1
6.6	10.2	67.0	5.2	6.2	9.3	9.4
8.1	7.7	22.9	6.7	6.3	7.5	6.5
0.1	0.2	0.4	0.0	0.1	0.2	0.4
1.4	2.8	3.2	0.1	0.1	0.1	0.1
–	–	–	–	–	–	–
–	–	0.7	–	–	–	–
2.7	5.0	6.8	–	–	–	0.1
0.3	0.2	1.6	–	–	–	–
1.9	2.8	6.7	0.2	0.2	0.7	1.6
6.0	10.0	43.0	–	–	–	4.0
27.2	*39.4*	*157.1*	*12.2*	*13.0*	*17.9*	*23.9*
30.9	*43.8*	*125.8*	*7.3*	*8.5*	*14.2*	*88.6*
40.1	*31.4*	*85.0*	–	–	–	–
30.7	*42.0*	*138.7*	*12.1*	*12.8*	*17.7*	*19.1*
98.1	***114.6***	***367.9***	***19.4***	***21.5***	***32.1***	***112.5***

TOTAL OOF NET

1978	1979	1980	1977	1978	1979	1980
–	–	–	–	–	–	–
–	–	–	–	–	–	–
–	–	–	–	–	–	–
–	–	–	–	–	–	–
–	–	–	–	–	–	–
–	–	–	–	–	–	–
0.5	–	–	0.1	0.5	–	–
–	–	–	2.5	–	-1.2	-0.3
–	–	–	–	–	–	–
–	–	–	–	–	–	–
–	–	–	–	–	–	–
–	–	–	–	–	–	–
–	–	–	–	–	–	–
–	–	–	–	–	–	–
–	–	–	–	–	–	–
–	–	–	–	–	–	–
–	–	–	–	–	–	–
0.5	–	–	*2.6*	*0.5*	*-1.2*	*-0.3*
0.1	*0.0*	*34.9*	*0.0*	*0.0*	*-0.2*	*34.9*
–	–	–	–	–	–	–
0.5	–	–	*2.6*	*0.5*	*-1.2*	*-0.3*
0.6	***0.0***	***34.9***	***2.6***	***0.5***	***-1.3***	***34.6***

MAIN AID AGGREGATES

	1977	1978	1979	1980
DAC COUNTRIES COMBINED				
PRIVATE SECTOR NET	101.2	14.1	49.9	71.9
Direct Investment	56.6	-0.1	0.0	0.0
Portfolio Invest.	0.0	-1.4	0.0	0.0
Export Credits	44.6	15.7	49.9	72.0
OFFICIAL & PRIVATE GROSS:				
Contractual Lending	50.2	45.2	95.6	122.0
Export Credits Tot.	47.6	23.6	83.8	99.6
Export Credits Priv	47.6	23.6	83.8	99.6
OTHER NET DATA				
Contractual Lending	46.6	35.9	59.2	54.0
Export Credits Tot.	44.6	15.7	49.9	72.0
(Bank Sector Loans)	6.0	-6.0	–	–
ODA CONCESSIONALITY				
Total:Grant Element	98.0	92.0	95.0	97.0
Loans:Grant Element	83.0	77.0	67.0	67.0
OTHER SOURCES				
CMEA Countr.(Gross)	6.6	–	–	–
Intra LDCS Exc.OPEC	–	–	–	–
Other	–	–	–	–
ALL SOURCE COMMITMENTS				
TOTAL BILATERAL	376.7	73.1	148.7	356.7
of which				
OPEC (ODA)	346.8	15.0	71.2	122.4
CMEA (ODA)	0.6	–	–	–
TOTAL MULTILAT.(ODA)	89.0	54.6	115.4	145.0
TOTAL BIL.& MULTIL.	465.7	127.6	264.1	501.7
of which				
ODA Grants	148.8	59.3	177.1	430.4
ODA Loans	316.9	67.9	87.0	71.3
ODA CONCESSIONALITY				
Total: Grant Element	59.0	83.0	93.0	93.0
Loans: Grant Element	40.0	68.0	76.0	59.0

INDEBTEDNESS

	1977	1978	1979	1980
TOTAL DEBT DISBURSED	***405.3***	***529.8***	***643.9***	
Debt to DAC Countries	60.0	85.0	112.0	
ODA	38.0	63.0	76.0	
Total Export Credits	19.0	19.0	35.0	
Other Private Market	3.0	3.0	1.0	
International Org.	70.0	95.5	124.2	
CMEA	177.7	203.2	203.1	
Other	97.6	146.1	204.6	
TOTAL DEBT SERVICE	***5.5***	***7.9***	***7.0***	
Paid to DAC Countries	3.7	5.7	5.4	
ODA	0.9	2.0	1.5	
Total Export Credits	2.3	3.3	3.9	
Other Private Market	0.5	0.4	–	
International Org.	0.6	0.9	0.7	
CMEA	1.0	1.0	0.5	
Other	0.3	0.3	0.4	

ECONOMIC INDICATORS

	1977	1978	1979	1980
GNP Curr. Prices, $M	1000.4	1195.9	1349.6	1517.6
Real GNP, 1976=100	108.0	118.0	120.0	123.0
GNP/Cap Curr. Prices,$	273.0	319.0	352.0	387.0
GNP/cap Atlas Basis, $	283.8	324.9	352.5	383.0
Real GNP/Cap, 1976=100	105.0	112.0	112.0	112.0
Population, Million	3.7	3.7	3.8	3.9
Curr.A/C Deficit(-),$M	-138.7	-92.7	-263.7	-278.7
BOP Exp. & Transf.,$M	106.2	229.7	189.2	261.8
Exp. to OECD CIF, $M	29.3	20.2	37.2	27.6
of which				
Manufact.	0.7	0.9	3.9	1.5
Imp. from OECD FOB, $M	147.9	211.4	273.5	371.3
Reserves ex. Gold, $M	120.0	126.3	43.8	14.6

	1977	1978	1979	1980	1977	1978	1979	1980		197
TOTAL RECEIPTS NET					**TOTAL ODA NET**				**TOTAL ODA GROSS**	
DAC COUNTRIES										
Australia	-7.1	-6.2	0.1	0.0	–	–	–	–	Australia	
Austria	0.2	1.5	0.7	1.8	0.1	0.2	0.2	0.2	Austria	0
Belgium	13.1	122.8	305.0	369.0	0.0	0.0	0.0	–	Belgium	0
Canada	-4.9	0.2	12.0	-6.0	–	–	–	–	Canada	
Denmark	0.0	-0.8	-0.9	0.5	–	–	–	–	Denmark	
Finland	0.4	1.6	0.1	0.0	–	–	–	–	Finland	
France	86.5	260.7	95.2	311.0	–	-7.1	-7.5	-6.3	France	
Germany, Fed. Rep.	743.1	262.5	32.2	227.9	8.5	18.6	3.9	24.4	Germany, Fed. Rep.	15
Italy	1.5	1.7	114.0	-8.9	1.6	1.1	0.9	0.0	Italy	1
Japan	96.2	159.8	292.1	161.5	0.1	0.2	0.3	1.2	Japan	0
Netherlands	40.5	86.4	145.1	157.9	0.0	0.0	0.1	0.1	Netherlands	0
New Zealand	3.0	0.9	–	–	–	–	–	–	New Zealand	
Norway	0.9	-2.5	-4.0	2.9	–	–	–	–	Norway	
Sweden	0.2	-0.1	-0.5	7.4	–	–	–	–	Sweden	
Switzerland	5.6	0.5	11.5	-13.1	0.0	0.0	0.0	0.1	Switzerland	0
United Kingdom	44.6	113.3	11.9	21.8	–	–	–	–	United Kingdom	
United States	173.0	152.0	533.0	56.0	-9.0	-3.0	-5.0	2.0	United States	-8
TOTAL	*1196.9*	*1154.2*	*1547.4*	*1289.9*	*1.4*	*9.9*	*-7.0*	*21.7*	*TOTAL*	*9*
MULTILATERAL										
AF.D.F.	–	–	–	–	–	–	–	–	AF.D.F.	
AF.D.B.	–	–	–	–	–	–	–	–	AF.D.B.	
AS.D.B.	–	–	–	–	–	–	–	–	AS.D.B.	
CAR.D.B.	–	–	–	–	–	–	–	–	CAR.D.B.	
E.E.C.	–	–	–	–	–	–	–	–	E.E.C.	
IBRD	-9.1	-5.9	-7.4	-19.1	–	–	–	–	IBRD	
IDA	–	–	–	–	–	–	–	–	IDA	
I.D.B.	–	–	–	–	–	–	–	–	I.D.B.	
IFAD	–	–	–	–	–	–	–	–	IFAD	
I.F.C.	-0.3	2.0	0.2	–	–	–	–	–	I.F.C.	
IMF TRUST FUND	–	–	–	–	–	–	–	–	IMF TRUST FUND	
U.N. AGENCIES	–	–	–	–	–	–	–	–	U.N. AGENCIES	
UNDP	–	–	–	–	–	–	–	–	UNDP	
UNTA	0.0	0.1	0.1	0.1	0.0	0.1	0.1	0.1	UNTA	[illegible]
UNICEF	–	–	–	–	–	–	–	–	UNICEF	
UNRWA	–	–	–	–	–	–	–	–	UNRWA	
WFP	–	–	–	–	–	–	–	–	WFP	
UNHCR	0.2	0.4	0.9	1.6	0.2	0.4	0.9	1.6	UNHCR	0
Other Multilateral	0.0	0.1	0.0	–	0.0	0.1	0.0	–	Other Multilateral	[illegible]
Arab OPEC Agencies	–	–	–	–	–	–	–	–	Arab OPEC Agencies	
TOTAL	*-9.1*	*-3.3*	*-6.2*	*-17.4*	*0.3*	*0.5*	*1.0*	*1.7*	*TOTAL*	[illegible]
OPEC COUNTRIES	–	*8.8*	*2.0*	–	–	–	*2.0*	–	*OPEC COUNTRIES*	
E.E.C.+ MEMBERS	*929.4*	*846.6*	*702.5*	*1079.3*	*10.2*	*12.5*	*-2.6*	*18.2*	*E.E.C.+ MEMBERS*	*16*
TOTAL	***1187.8***	***1159.7***	***1543.1***	***1272.5***	***1.7***	***10.4***	***-4.1***	***23.3***	***TOTAL***	***9***
ODA LOANS GROSS					**ODA LOANS NET**				**GRANTS**	
DAC COUNTRIES										
Australia	–	–	–	–	–	–	–	–	Australia	
Austria	–	–	–	–	0.0	–	–	-0.1	Austria	0
Belgium	–	–	–	–	–	–	–	–	Belgium	[illegible]
Canada	–	–	–	–	–	–	–	–	Canada	
Denmark	–	–	–	–	–	–	–	–	Denmark	
Finland	–	–	–	–	–	–	–	–	Finland	
France	–	–	–	–	–	-7.1	-7.5	-7.6	France	
Germany, Fed. Rep.	–	0.4	2.3	4.7	-6.6	0.4	-14.5	-3.8	Germany, Fed. Rep.	15
Italy	–	–	–	–	–	–	–	–	Italy	[illegible]
Japan	–	–	0.2	1.1	–	–	0.2	1.1	Japan	[illegible]
Netherlands	–	–	–	–	–	–	–	–	Netherlands	0
New Zealand	–	–	–	–	–	–	–	–	New Zealand	
Norway	–	–	–	–	–	–	–	–	Norway	
Sweden	–	–	–	–	–	–	–	–	Sweden	
Switzerland	–	–	–	–	–	–	–	–	Switzerland	[illegible]
United Kingdom	–	–	–	–	–	–	–	–	United Kingdom	
United States	–	–	–	–	-1.0	-1.0	–	–	United States	-8
TOTAL	–	*0.4*	*2.4*	*5.8*	*-7.7*	*-7.7*	*-21.9*	*-10.4*	*TOTAL*	[illegible]
MULTILATERAL	–	–	–	–	–	–	–	–	*MULTILATERAL*	[illegible]
OPEC COUNTRIES	–	–	–	–	–	–	–	–	*OPEC COUNTRIES*	
E.E.C.+ MEMBERS	–	*0.4*	*2.3*	*4.7*	*-6.6*	*-6.7*	*-22.0*	*-11.4*	*E.E.C.+ MEMBERS*	*16*
TOTAL	–	***0.4***	***2.4***	***5.8***	***-7.7***	***-7.7***	***-21.9***	***-10.4***	***TOTAL***	[illegible]
TOTAL OFFICIAL GROSS					**TOTAL OFFICIAL NET**				**TOTAL OOF GROSS**	
DAC COUNTRIES										
Australia	–	–	–	–	–	–	–	–	Australia	
Austria	0.1	0.2	0.4	0.3	0.1	0.1	0.4	0.2	Austria	
Belgium	0.0	0.0	0.0	–	0.0	0.0	0.0	–	Belgium	
Canada	–	3.6	15.3	0.3	-4.7	0.3	12.0	-6.0	Canada	
Denmark	–	–	–	–	–	–	–	–	Denmark	
Finland	–	–	–	–	–	–	–	–	Finland	
France	–	–	–	1.3	–	-7.1	-7.5	-6.3	France	
Germany, Fed. Rep.	36.2	53.3	46.3	69.0	-9.5	23.3	-33.9	6.5	Germany, Fed. Rep.	2
Italy	1.6	1.1	0.9	0.0	1.6	1.1	0.9	-2.3	Italy	
Japan	0.1	0.2	0.3	1.2	0.1	0.2	0.3	1.2	Japan	
Netherlands	0.0	0.0	0.1	0.1	0.0	0.0	0.1	0.1	Netherlands	
New Zealand	5.6	–	–	–	3.0	–	–	–	New Zealand	[illegible]
Norway	–	–	–	–	–	–	–	–	Norway	
Sweden	–	–	–	–	–	–	–	–	Sweden	
Switzerland	0.0	0.0	0.0	0.1	0.0	0.0	0.0	0.1	Switzerland	
United Kingdom	–	–	–	–	–	–	–	–	United Kingdom	
United States	72.0	87.0	136.0	65.0	38.0	65.0	66.0	-14.0	United States	8
TOTAL	*115.6*	*145.3*	*199.3*	*137.3*	*28.8*	*82.9*	*38.2*	*-20.6*	*TOTAL*	*10*
MULTILATERAL	*12.0*	*18.8*	*16.4*	*9.7*	*-9.1*	*-3.4*	*-6.2*	*-17.4*	*MULTILATERAL*	*1*
OPEC COUNTRIES	–	*8.8*	*2.0*	–	–	*8.8*	*2.0*	–	*OPEC COUNTRIES*	
E.E.C.+ MEMBERS	*37.8*	*54.4*	*47.3*	*70.4*	*-7.8*	*17.3*	*-40.5*	*-2.1*	*E.E.C.+ MEMBERS*	*2*
TOTAL	***127.6***	***173.0***	***217.7***	***146.9***	***19.6***	***88.3***	***34.0***	***-38.0***	***TOTAL***	***11***

ODA COMMITMENTS

1978	1979	1980	1977	1978	1979	1980
–	–	–	–	–	–	–
0.2	0.2	0.3	–	–	–	–
0.0	0.0	–	–	–	–	–
–	–	–	–	–	–	–
–	–	–	–	–	–	–
–	–	–	–	–	–	–
–	–	1.3	–	–	–	1.3
18.6	20.7	32.9	15.7	20.6	19.2	30.4
1.1	0.9	0.0	1.6	1.1	0.9	0.0
0.2	0.3	1.2	0.2	0.3	0.4	1.2
0.0	0.1	0.1	0.0	–	0.1	–
–	–	–	–	–	–	–
–	–	–	–	–	–	–
–	–	–	–	–	–	–
0.0	0.0	0.1	–	–	–	0.1
–	–	–	–	–	–	–
-2.0	-5.0	2.0	10.0	7.0	0.3	–
18.0	*17.3*	*37.8*	*27.5*	*28.9*	*20.9*	*33.0*
–	–	–	–	–	–	–
–	–	–	–	–	–	–
–	–	–	–	–	–	–
–	–	–	–	–	–	–
–	–	–	–	–	–	–
–	–	–	–	–	–	–
–	–	–	–	–	–	–
–	–	–	–	–	–	–
–	–	–	–	–	–	–
–	–	–	–	–	–	–
–	–	–	–	–	–	–
–	–	–	0.3	0.5	1.0	1.7
–	–	–	–	–	–	–
0.1	0.1	0.1	–	–	–	–
–	–	–	–	–	–	–
–	–	–	–	–	–	–
–	–	–	–	–	–	–
0.4	0.9	1.6	–	–	–	–
0.1	0.0	–	–	–	–	–
–	–	–	–	–	–	–
0.5	*1.0*	*1.7*	*0.3*	*0.5*	*1.0*	*1.7*
–	*2.0*	–	–	–	*2.0*	–
19.6	*21.7*	*34.3*	*17.3*	*21.7*	*20.2*	*31.8*
18.5	***20.2***	***39.5***	***27.7***	***29.5***	***23.8***	***34.7***

TECH. COOP. GRANTS

1978	1979	1980	1977	1978	1979	1980
–	–	–	–	–	–	–
0.2	0.2	0.3	0.1	0.2	0.2	0.3
0.0	0.0	–	0.0	0.0	0.0	–
–	–	–	–	–	–	–
–	–	–	–	–	–	–
–	–	–	–	–	–	–
–	–	1.3	–	–	–	1.3
18.2	18.5	28.2	15.1	18.2	18.4	28.2
1.1	0.9	0.0	1.6	1.1	0.9	0.0
0.2	0.2	0.1	0.1	0.2	0.2	0.1
0.0	0.1	0.1	0.0	–	–	–
–	–	–	–	–	–	–
–	–	–	–	–	–	–
–	–	–	–	–	–	–
0.0	0.0	0.1	0.0	0.0	0.0	–
–	–	–	–	–	–	–
-2.0	-5.0	2.0	–	–	–	–
17.6	*14.9*	*32.1*	*17.1*	*19.6*	*19.7*	*29.9*
0.5	*1.0*	*1.7*	*0.3*	*0.5*	*1.0*	*1.7*
–	*2.0*	–	–	–	–	–
19.3	*19.5*	*29.6*	*16.8*	*19.2*	*19.3*	*29.5*
18.2	***17.8***	***33.7***	***17.3***	***20.1***	***20.7***	***31.6***

TOTAL OOF NET

1978	1979	1980	1977	1978	1979	1980
–	–	–	–	–	–	–
–	0.2	–	–	0.0	0.2	–
–	–	–	–	–	–	–
3.6	15.3	0.3	-4.7	0.3	12.0	-6.0
–	–	–	–	–	–	–
–	–	–	–	–	–	–
–	–	–	–	–	–	–
34.8	25.5	36.2	-18.0	4.7	-37.9	-17.9
–	–	–	–	–	–	-2.4
–	–	–	–	–	–	–
–	–	–	–	–	–	–
–	–	–	3.0	–	–	–
–	–	–	–	–	–	–
–	–	–	–	–	–	–
–	–	–	–	–	–	–
–	–	–	–	–	–	–
89.0	141.0	63.0	47.0	68.0	71.0	-16.0
127.3	*182.0*	*99.4*	*27.4*	*72.9*	*45.3*	*-42.3*
18.3	*15.5*	*8.0*	*-9.4*	*-3.9*	*-7.2*	*-19.1*
8.8	–	–	–	*8.8*	–	–
34.8	*25.5*	*36.2*	*-18.0*	*4.7*	*-37.9*	*-20.3*
154.4	***197.5***	***107.4***	***18.0***	***77.9***	***38.1***	***-61.4***

MAIN AID AGGREGATES

	1977	1978	1979	1980
DAC COUNTRIES COMBINED				
PRIVATE SECTOR NET	1168.2	1071.4	1509.1	1310.5
Direct Investment	428.0	527.3	1232.5	485.6
Portfolio Invest.	623.9	474.9	363.5	680.5
Export Credits	116.3	69.2	-86.9	144.4
OFFICIAL & PRIVATE				
GROSS:				
Contractual Lending	447.6	455.6	325.6	545.4
Export Credits Tot.	447.6	455.0	322.3	537.7
Export Credits Priv	341.0	327.9	141.2	440.2
OTHER NET DATA				
Contractual Lending	136.0	134.4	-63.5	91.7
Export Credits Tot.	149.7	145.3	-31.4	108.2
(Bank Sector Loans)	2518.0	204.0	1331.0	1617.0
ODA CONCESSIONALITY				
Total:Grant Element	100.0	100.0	99.0	97.0
Loans:Grant Element	–	–	50.0	32.0
OTHER SOURCES				
CMEA Countr.(Gross)	–	–	–	–
Intra LDCS Exc.OPEC	–	–	–	–
Other	–	–	–	–
ALL SOURCE COMMITMENTS				
TOTAL BILATERAL	149.2	109.4	129.6	213.4
of which				
OPEC (ODA)	–	–	2.0	–
CMEA (ODA)	–	–	–	–
TOTAL MULTILAT.(ODA)	0.3	0.5	1.0	1.7
TOTAL BIL.& MULTIL.	149.5	109.9	130.5	215.1
of which				
ODA Grants	27.7	29.5	23.6	33.6
ODA Loans	–	–	0.2	1.1
ODA CONCESSIONALITY				
Total: Grant Element	100.0	100.0	99.0	97.0
Loans: Grant Element	–	–	50.0	32.0

INDEBTEDNESS

	1977	1978	1979	1980
TOTAL DEBT DISBURSED	***10944.3***	***13090.1***	***15011.1***	
Debt to DAC Countries	9279.0	11286.0	13059.0	
ODA	132.0	149.0	131.0	
Total Export Credits	1887.0	2084.0	2396.0	
Other Private Market	7260.0	9053.0	10532.0	
International Org.	480.5	524.3	508.5	
CMEA	–	–	–	
Other	1184.8	1279.8	1443.6	
TOTAL DEBT SERVICE	***1596.9***	***3022.0***	***3199.0***	
Paid to DAC Countries	1326.7	2697.2	2665.0	
ODA	23.9	15.7	36.0	
Total Export Credits	386.3	386.4	506.3	
Other Private Market	916.5	2295.1	2122.7	
International Org.	56.2	69.2	80.9	
CMEA	–	–	–	
Other	214.0	255.6	453.1	

ECONOMIC INDICATORS

	1977	1978	1979	1980
GNP Curr. Prices, $M	119076.7	145954.5	195813.7	207246.6
Real GNP, 1976=100	102.0	105.0	106.0	106.0
GNP/Cap Curr. Prices,$	3278.0	3979.0	5287.0	5544.0
GNP/cap Atlas Basis, $	4163.3	4543.0	4924.0	5345.0
Real GNP/Cap, 1976=100	101.0	103.0	103.0	102.0
Population, Million	36.3	36.7	37.0	37.4
Curr.A/C Deficit(-),$M	-2190.0	1790.0	1503.0	-4627.0
BOP Exp. & Transf.,$M	18569.0	23990.0	31706.0	36122.0
Exp. to OECD CIF, $M	8028.6	10062.4	12851.0	14989.5
of which				
Manufact.	5105.7	6716.6	8491.9	9823.5
Imp. from OECD FOB, $M	9822.2	10026.0	13661.7	16418.8
Reserves ex. Gold, $M	5977.0	10112.0	13224.0	11863.0

	TOTAL RECEIPTS NET 1977	1978	1979	1980	TOTAL ODA NET 1977	1978	1979	1980
DAC COUNTRIES								
Australia	2.6	5.9	5.0	3.6	2.5	5.9	5.0	3.6
Austria	0.0	0.0	0.1	0.1	0.0	0.0	0.1	0.1
Belgium	2.1	-3.8	0.4	3.7	0.0	0.1	0.5	0.3
Canada	16.0	25.2	17.3	29.3	16.2	25.2	17.3	29.3
Denmark	0.9	2.0	0.0	5.3	0.9	2.0	0.0	5.2
Finland	–	0.1	0.2	0.4	–	0.1	0.2	0.4
France	-14.4	-3.4	2.7	8.2	0.7	2.9	6.2	6.5
Germany, Fed. Rep.	7.0	30.9	29.9	19.1	9.6	33.5	31.3	19.1
Italy	0.5	0.7	0.5	19.8	0.8	-0.1	0.1	0.1
Japan	21.7	35.6	38.1	46.2	18.6	39.5	40.0	44.8
Netherlands	12.0	32.2	21.2	24.2	12.0	32.1	21.2	22.7
New Zealand	0.2	0.2	0.1	0.1	0.2	0.2	0.1	0.1
Norway	3.9	4.4	8.4	11.3	3.8	5.2	7.9	11.4
Sweden	11.7	13.7	35.4	23.3	11.7	13.7	35.4	23.1
Switzerland	0.2	3.5	1.9	2.9	0.2	0.3	0.7	1.2
United Kingdom	9.8	16.2	31.5	77.2	5.1	14.9	26.0	73.3
United States	37.0	41.0	40.0	55.0	37.0	41.0	40.0	55.0
TOTAL	*111.1*	*204.4*	*232.5*	*329.6*	*119.4*	*216.3*	*232.0*	*296.1*
MULTILATERAL								
AF.D.F.	–	–	–	–	–	–	–	–
AF.D.B.	–	–	–	–	–	–	–	–
AS.D.B.	9.5	25.9	8.2	4.6	9.2	24.0	9.2	5.8
CAR.D.B.	–	–	–	–	–	–	–	–
E.E.C.	6.0	6.3	4.4	6.8	6.0	6.3	4.4	6.8
IBRD	-1.7	-1.1	-0.6	-1.9	–	–	–	–
IDA	11.1	11.2	12.4	19.7	11.1	11.2	12.4	19.7
I.D.B.	–	–	–	–	–	–	–	–
IFAD	–	–	1.2	1.8	–	–	1.2	1.8
I.F.C.	–	0.1	0.9	5.9	–	–	–	–
IMF TRUST FUND	–	50.8	38.4	32.7	–	50.8	38.4	32.7
U.N. AGENCIES	–	–	–	–	–	–	–	–
UNDP	4.0	4.8	6.3	7.7	4.0	4.8	6.3	7.7
UNTA	1.1	1.3	1.8	0.3	1.1	1.3	1.8	0.3
UNICEF	1.4	1.9	3.6	6.3	1.4	1.9	3.6	6.3
UNRWA	–	–	–	–	–	–	–	–
WFP	18.2	0.5	4.3	1.9	18.2	0.5	4.3	1.9
UNHCR	–	–	–	–	–	–	–	–
Other Multilateral	3.7	2.1	3.8	3.8	3.7	2.1	3.8	3.8
Arab OPEC Agencies	8.1	1.0	0.8	1.0	8.1	1.0	0.8	1.0
TOTAL	*61.4*	*104.9*	*85.5*	*90.4*	*62.8*	*104.0*	*86.2*	*87.6*
OPEC COUNTRIES	*7.7*	*6.1*	*4.5*	*56.1*	*5.2*	*3.6*	*4.5*	*56.1*
E.E.C.+ MEMBERS	*23.8*	*81.2*	*90.5*	*164.2*	*35.2*	*91.6*	*89.7*	*133.9*
TOTAL	***180.1***	***315.4***	***322.5***	***476.1***	***187.4***	***323.9***	***322.7***	***439.8***

	ODA LOANS GROSS 1977	1978	1979	1980	ODA LOANS NET 1977	1978	1979	1980
DAC COUNTRIES								
Australia	–	–	–	–	–	–	–	–
Austria	–	–	–	–	–	–	–	–
Belgium	–	–	–	–	–	–	–	–
Canada	5.6	10.9	10.6	24.2	5.5	10.7	10.5	24.0
Denmark	0.3	1.0	0.1	4.1	0.1	0.8	-0.3	3.7
Finland	–	–	–	–	–	–	–	–
France	0.9	1.5	5.5	6.4	0.7	1.2	5.1	5.9
Germany, Fed. Rep.	7.6	23.3	21.8	8.3	4.5	20.4	18.5	4.8
Italy	–	–	–	–	-0.2	-0.2	-0.1	–
Japan	15.8	29.7	21.2	18.9	13.7	27.8	18.3	15.1
Netherlands	3.8	22.7	11.8	11.9	3.8	22.7	11.8	11.9
New Zealand	–	–	–	–	–	–	–	–
Norway	–	–	–	–	–	–	–	–
Sweden	–	–	–	–	–	–	–	–
Switzerland	–	–	–	–	–	–	–	–
United Kingdom	0.1	0.0	–	–	-1.8	-1.1	-4.0	-3.2
United States	36.0	38.0	38.0	47.0	33.0	35.0	35.0	43.0
TOTAL	*70.1*	*126.9*	*109.1*	*120.7*	*59.3*	*117.3*	*94.8*	*105.1*
MULTILATERAL	*28.5*	*88.0*	*63.2*	*61.7*	*27.9*	*87.0*	*62.0*	*60.2*
OPEC COUNTRIES	*5.2*	*3.6*	*3.5*	*8.0*	*5.2*	*3.6*	*3.5*	*6.1*
E.E.C.+ MEMBERS	*12.8*	*48.4*	*39.2*	*30.6*	*7.1*	*43.7*	*31.0*	*23.0*
TOTAL	***103.8***	***218.6***	***175.8***	***190.3***	***92.3***	***207.9***	***160.2***	***171.4***

	TOTAL OFFICIAL GROSS 1977	1978	1979	1980	TOTAL OFFICIAL NET 1977	1978	1979	1980
DAC COUNTRIES								
Australia	2.5	5.9	5.0	3.6	2.5	5.9	5.0	3.6
Austria	0.0	0.0	0.1	0.1	0.0	0.0	0.1	0.1
Belgium	0.0	0.1	0.5	0.3	0.0	0.1	0.5	0.3
Canada	16.3	25.4	17.4	29.5	16.0	25.2	17.3	29.3
Denmark	1.1	2.2	0.4	5.7	0.9	2.0	0.0	5.3
Finland	–	0.1	0.2	0.4	–	0.1	0.2	0.4
France	0.9	3.2	6.6	7.0	0.7	2.9	6.2	6.5
Germany, Fed. Rep.	12.8	36.3	34.7	22.7	9.1	32.9	30.7	18.5
Italy	1.0	0.1	0.2	0.1	0.8	-0.1	0.1	0.1
Japan	20.7	41.3	42.9	48.6	18.6	39.5	40.0	44.8
Netherlands	12.0	32.2	21.2	24.2	12.0	32.2	21.2	24.2
New Zealand	0.2	0.2	0.1	0.1	0.2	0.2	0.1	0.1
Norway	3.8	5.2	7.9	11.4	3.8	5.2	7.9	11.4
Sweden	11.7	13.7	35.4	23.1	11.7	13.7	35.4	23.1
Switzerland	0.2	0.3	0.7	1.2	0.2	0.3	0.7	1.2
United Kingdom	7.0	16.0	30.0	76.4	5.1	14.9	26.0	73.3
United States	40.0	44.0	43.0	59.0	37.0	41.0	40.0	55.0
TOTAL	*130.3*	*226.1*	*246.3*	*313.3*	*118.7*	*215.8*	*231.3*	*297.0*
MULTILATERAL	*66.8*	*110.5*	*91.0*	*95.2*	*61.4*	*104.9*	*85.5*	*90.4*
OPEC COUNTRIES	*7.7*	*6.1*	*4.5*	*58.0*	*7.7*	*6.1*	*4.5*	*56.1*
E.E.C.+ MEMBERS	*40.8*	*96.5*	*98.0*	*143.1*	*34.6*	*91.2*	*89.1*	*134.8*
TOTAL	***204.7***	***342.7***	***341.7***	***466.5***	***187.8***	***326.9***	***321.3***	***443.5***

TOTAL ODA GROSS

	197
Australia	2
Austria	[illegible]
Belgium	[illegible]
Canada	16
Denmark	1
Finland	
France	[illegible]
Germany, Fed. Rep.	12
Italy	1
Japan	20
Netherlands	12
New Zealand	[illegible]
Norway	3
Sweden	11
Switzerland	[illegible]
United Kingdom	7
United States	40
TOTAL	*13*
AF.D.F.	
AF.D.B.	
AS.D.B.	[illegible]
CAR.D.B.	
E.E.C.	[illegible]
IBRD	
IDA	1
I.D.B.	
IFAD	
I.F.C.	
IMF TRUST FUND	
U.N. AGENCIES	
UNDP	[illegible]
UNTA	
UNICEF	
UNRWA	
WFP	1
UNHCR	
Other Multilateral	[illegible]
Arab OPEC Agencies	[illegible]
TOTAL	*6.*
OPEC COUNTRIES	[illegible]
E.E.C.+ MEMBERS	*4*
TOTAL	***19***

GRANTS

Australia	[illegible]
Austria	[illegible]
Belgium	[illegible]
Canada	1
Denmark	[illegible]
Finland	
France	
Germany, Fed. Rep.	
Italy	
Japan	[illegible]
Netherlands	[illegible]
New Zealand	[illegible]
Norway	
Sweden	1
Switzerland	
United Kingdom	[illegible]
United States	[illegible]
TOTAL	*6*
MULTILATERAL	*3*
OPEC COUNTRIES	
E.E.C.+ MEMBERS	*2*
TOTAL	***9***

TOTAL OOF GROSS

Australia	
Austria	
Belgium	
Canada	
Denmark	
Finland	
France	
Germany, Fed. Rep.	
Italy	
Japan	
Netherlands	
New Zealand	
Norway	
Sweden	
Switzerland	
United Kingdom	
United States	
TOTAL	
MULTILATERAL	
OPEC COUNTRIES	
E.E.C.+ MEMBERS	
TOTAL	

1978	1979	1980	1977	1978	1979	1980
			ODA COMMITMENTS			
5.9	5.0	3.6	7.2	6.1	6.2	4.6
0.0	0.1	0.1	–	–	–	–
0.1	0.5	0.3	–	–	–	–
25.4	17.4	29.5	28.5	29.3	10.4	66.1
2.2	0.4	5.6	0.8	0.4	6.4	2.6
0.1	0.2	0.4	–	0.1	0.2	0.9
3.2	6.6	7.0	–	1.7	11.4	2.2
36.3	34.7	22.7	12.2	41.9	34.8	23.0
0.1	0.2	0.1	1.0	0.1	0.2	0.1
41.3	42.9	48.6	25.8	67.4	43.5	101.0
32.1	21.2	22.7	20.7	42.4	28.9	47.9
0.2	0.1	0.1	0.3	0.1	–	0.0
5.2	7.9	11.4	2.0	4.1	12.3	7.9
13.7	35.4	23.1	31.2	2.5	21.1	47.8
0.3	0.7	1.2	0.3	0.2	9.4	1.8
16.0	30.0	76.4	25.2	49.9	223.9	20.2
44.0	43.0	59.0	31.9	72.4	35.8	58.1
225.9	*246.3*	*311.7*	*187.1*	*318.5*	*444.5*	*383.9*
–	–	–	–	–	–	–
–	–	–	–	–	–	–
24.9	10.4	7.0	41.5	34.2	25.8	47.8
–	–	–	–	–	–	–
6.3	4.4	6.8	6.0	6.7	7.8	25.2
–	–	–	–	–	–	–
11.2	12.4	19.9	41.2	25.4	67.7	184.2
–	–	–	–	–	–	–
–	1.2	1.8	–	12.0	–	14.5
–	–	–	–	–	–	–
50.8	38.4	32.7	–	–	–	–
–	–	–	28.4	10.6	19.9	20.0
4.8	6.3	7.7	–	–	–	–
1.3	1.8	0.3	–	–	–	–
1.9	3.6	6.3	–	–	–	–
–	–	–	–	–	–	–
0.5	4.3	1.9	–	–	–	–
–	–	–	–	–	–	–
2.1	3.8	3.8	–	–	–	–
1.0	0.8	1.0	3.2	–	–	6.0
105.0	*87.4*	*89.0*	*120.2*	*88.9*	*121.1*	*297.6*
3.6	*4.5*	*58.0*	–	–	*1.0*	*7.5*
96.3	*98.0*	*141.6*	*65.8*	*143.1*	*313.4*	*121.0*
334.5	***338.2***	***458.7***	***307.3***	***407.4***	***566.6***	***689.0***
			TECH. COOP. GRANTS			
5.9	5.0	3.6	0.6	0.7	0.5	0.5
0.0	0.1	0.1	0.0	0.0	0.1	0.1
0.1	0.5	0.3	–	0.0	0.0	0.1
14.5	6.8	5.3	0.1	0.1	0.2	0.4
1.2	0.3	1.5	0.8	0.7	0.3	1.5
0.1	0.2	0.4	–	0.1	0.0	0.4
1.7	1.1	0.6	–	–	–	0.6
13.1	12.9	14.4	4.8	10.5	11.2	14.4
0.1	0.2	0.1	0.0	0.1	0.2	0.1
11.6	21.7	29.7	2.4	3.1	4.0	3.1
9.4	9.4	10.9	3.0	3.5	4.1	5.4
0.2	0.1	0.1	0.1	0.1	0.0	0.1
5.2	7.9	11.4	0.2	0.3	0.4	0.5
13.7	35.4	23.1	0.4	1.1	1.2	1.2
0.3	0.7	1.2	0.0	0.0	0.2	0.2
16.0	30.0	76.4	1.3	3.6	7.5	8.7
6.0	5.0	12.0	1.0	–	1.0	2.0
99.0	*137.2*	*191.0*	*14.7*	*23.8*	*30.9*	*39.3*
17.0	*24.3*	*27.3*	*10.8*	*10.1*	*15.5*	*20.0*
–	*1.0*	*50.0*	–	–	–	–
47.9	*58.7*	*110.9*	*10.0*	*18.3*	*23.3*	*30.8*
116.0	***162.5***	***268.3***	***25.4***	***33.9***	***46.4***	***59.3***
			TOTAL OOF NET			
–	–	–	–	–	–	–
–	–	–	–	–	–	–
–	–	–	–	–	–	–
–	–	–	-0.2	-0.1	–	–
–	–	0.1	–	–	–	0.0
–	–	–	–	–	–	–
–	–	–	–	–	–	–
–	–	–	-0.5	-0.6	-0.6	-0.6
–	–	–	–	–	–	–
–	–	–	–	–	–	–
0.2	–	1.5	–	0.2	–	1.5
–	–	–	–	–	–	–
–	–	–	–	–	–	–
–	–	–	–	–	–	–
–	–	–	–	–	–	–
–	–	–	–	–	–	–
–	–	–	–	–	–	–
0.2	–	*1.6*	*-0.7*	*-0.5*	*-0.6*	*0.9*
5.5	*3.5*	*6.3*	*-1.3*	*0.9*	*-0.7*	*2.8*
2.5	–	*0.0*	*2.5*	*2.5*	–	*0.0*
0.2	–	*1.6*	*-0.5*	*-0.4*	*-0.6*	*0.9*
8.2	***3.5***	***7.9***	***0.5***	***3.0***	***-1.4***	***3.7***

MAIN AID AGGREGATES

	1977	1978	1979	1980
DAC COUNTRIES COMBINED				
PRIVATE SECTOR NET	-7.7	-11.4	1.2	32.6
Direct Investment	5.5	2.8	6.6	5.9
Portfolio Invest.	0.3	-2.3	0.2	0.4
Export Credits	-13.5	-11.9	-5.6	26.3
OFFICIAL & PRIVATE				
GROSS:				
Contractual Lending	93.3	136.7	119.0	157.7
Export Credits Tot.	23.2	9.6	9.9	35.4
Export Credits Priv	23.2	9.6	9.9	35.4
OTHER NET DATA				
Contractual Lending	45.2	104.9	88.5	132.3
Export Credits Tot.	-13.6	-12.0	-5.6	26.3
(Bank Sector Loans)	-2.0	–	–	18.0
ODA CONCESSIONALITY				
Total:Grant Element	88.0	82.0	92.0	84.0
Loans:Grant Element	67.0	67.0	69.0	70.0
OTHER SOURCES				
CMEA Countr.(Gross)	5.7	2.1	1.7	0.1
Intra LDCS Exc.OPEC	–	–	–	–
Other	–	–	–	–
ALL SOURCE COMMITMENTS				
TOTAL BILATERAL	187.1	318.7	445.5	391.5
of which				
OPEC (ODA)	–	–	1.0	7.5
CMEA (ODA)	–	10.0	1.0	–
TOTAL MULTILAT.(ODA)	120.2	88.9	121.1	297.6
TOTAL BIL.& MULTIL.	307.3	407.6	566.6	689.1
of which				
ODA Grants	153.2	162.0	368.7	225.1
ODA Loans	154.1	245.4	197.9	464.0
ODA CONCESSIONALITY				
Total: Grant Element	87.0	82.0	91.0	83.0
Loans: Grant Element	74.0	71.0	75.0	75.0

INDEBTEDNESS

	1977	1978	1979	1980
TOTAL DEBT DISBURSED	***798.1***	***980.8***	***1094.9***	
Debt to DAC Countries	529.0	667.0	764.0	
ODA	450.0	624.0	701.0	
Total Export Credits	75.0	42.0	63.0	
Other Private Market	4.0	1.0	–	
International Org.	132.8	168.1	188.0	
CMEA	69.3	66.0	56.7	
Other	67.0	79.7	86.1	
TOTAL DEBT SERVICE	***136.7***	***89.1***	***81.6***	
Paid to DAC Countries	91.8	57.1	48.3	
ODA	19.7	21.9	25.1	
Total Export Credits	64.0	31.0	22.4	
Other Private Market	8.1	4.2	0.8	
International Org.	9.2	10.2	10.6	
CMEA	26.2	13.2	12.1	
Other	9.6	8.6	10.6	

ECONOMIC INDICATORS

	1977	1978	1979	1980
GNP Curr. Prices, $M	2699.3	2718.3	3334.0	4103.1
Real GNP, 1976=100	102.0	111.0	117.0	129.0
GNP/Cap Curr. Prices,$	192.0	190.0	229.0	276.0
GNP/cap Atlas Basis, $	176.4	202.7	227.5	269.1
Real GNP/Cap, 1976=100	100.0	107.0	111.0	121.0
Population, Million	14.1	14.3	14.5	14.8
Curr.A/C Deficit(-),$M	77.1	-122.9	-372.4	-799.5
BOP Exp. & Transf.,$M	860.8	992.7	1222.2	1476.4
Exp. to OECD CIF, $M	393.4	418.0	532.6	570.7
of which				
Manufact.	23.3	54.1	90.4	151.2
Imp. from OECD FOB, $M	313.5	525.2	581.8	778.6
Reserves ex. Gold, $M	293.0	397.0	517.0	246.0

	TOTAL RECEIPTS NET 1977	1978	1979	1980	TOTAL ODA NET 1977	1978	1979	1980	TOTAL ODA GROSS 197
DAC COUNTRIES									
Australia	0.1	0.8	1.3	1.9	0.1	0.8	1.3	1.9	0.
Austria	19.2	-4.0	-4.2	-7.4	0.1	0.2	0.3	0.8	0.
Belgium	104.0	-8.0	-2.4	-3.0	0.2	0.5	1.2	2.0	0.
Canada	0.0	0.8	7.3	2.0	0.3	0.9	1.8	1.7	0.
Denmark	11.3	2.1	-0.5	39.6	1.3	1.1	2.4	22.4	1.
Finland	0.1	0.1	0.5	0.8	0.1	0.1	0.5	0.8	0.
France	3.8	88.6	1.4	19.2	–	–	1.2	7.7	
Germany, Fed. Rep.	14.4	51.2	69.0	84.4	14.5	38.2	41.5	62.4	15.
Italy	-12.2	37.5	-15.6	56.0	-0.6	0.5	1.1	-1.7	0
Japan	1.6	54.2	15.3	2.8	2.0	23.2	21.5	10.9	2
Netherlands	39.7	23.4	23.4	45.7	19.9	16.0	19.2	45.6	20.
New Zealand	–	–	–	–	–	–	–	–	
Norway	4.9	6.5	38.8	5.7	4.6	6.5	4.0	5.6	4
Sweden	0.3	0.6	0.7	-1.8	0.5	1.2	2.6	1.3	0
Switzerland	34.0	4.9	0.6	0.2	0.4	0.4	0.5	0.3	0
United Kingdom	-16.1	-0.6	24.9	41.0	8.7	13.6	27.1	49.8	8
United States	6.0	9.0	22.0	65.0	4.0	10.0	23.0	60.0	5.
TOTAL	*211.0*	*267.0*	*182.3*	*352.1*	*55.8*	*113.0*	*149.3*	*271.6*	*59*
MULTILATERAL									
AF.D.F.	0.0	2.2	0.3	–	0.0	2.2	0.3	–	0
AF.D.B.	1.5	0.1	0.0	0.2	–	–	–	–	
AS.D.B.	–	–	–	–	–	–	–	–	
CAR.D.B.	–	–	–	–	–	–	–	–	
E.E.C.	1.6	11.5	22.3	56.3	1.6	11.5	22.3	56.3	1
IBRD	-6.8	-6.0	-5.2	-2.8	–	–	–	1.3	
IDA	25.3	30.8	26.4	36.6	25.3	30.8	26.4	36.6	27
I.D.B.	–	–	–	–	–	–	–	–	
IFAD	–	–	0.2	1.8	–	–	0.2	1.8	
I.F.C.	2.2	9.7	7.9	1.5	–	–	–	–	
IMF TRUST FUND	–	37.3	28.3	24.0	–	37.3	28.3	24.0	
U.N. AGENCIES	–	–	–	–	–	–	–	–	
UNDP	7.5	7.0	7.3	10.7	7.5	7.0	7.3	10.7	7
UNTA	1.4	1.9	1.9	0.4	1.4	1.9	1.9	0.4	1
UNICEF	2.0	3.2	4.4	6.4	2.0	3.2	4.4	6.4	2
UNRWA	–	–	–	–	–	–	–	–	
WFP	12.2	9.4	13.3	10.5	12.2	9.4	13.3	10.5	12
UNHCR	1.6	3.3	4.3	15.0	1.6	3.3	4.3	15.0	1
Other Multilateral	2.0	4.6	3.8	6.7	2.0	4.6	3.8	6.7	2
Arab OPEC Agencies	20.6	20.8	52.6	29.2	15.6	18.5	15.6	22.7	15
TOTAL	*71.1*	*135.7*	*167.7*	*196.3*	*69.2*	*129.7*	*128.0*	*192.2*	*71*
OPEC COUNTRIES	*139.0*	*118.2*	*283.2*	*219.7*	*106.0*	*95.0*	*283.2*	*219.2*	*110*
E.E.C.+ MEMBERS	*146.4*	*205.6*	*122.3*	*339.3*	*45.6*	*81.2*	*116.0*	*244.6*	*47*
TOTAL	***421.1***	***520.9***	***633.2***	***768.2***	***231.0***	***337.7***	***560.5***	***682.9***	***241***

	ODA LOANS GROSS 1977	1978	1979	1980	ODA LOANS NET 1977	1978	1979	1980	GRANTS 197
DAC COUNTRIES									
Australia	–	–	–	–	–	–	–	–	0
Austria	–	–	–	0.1	–	–	–	0.1	C
Belgium	–	–	–	–	–	–	–	–	C
Canada	–	–	–	–	–	–	–	–	0
Denmark	0.6	0.2	0.3	20.8	0.6	0.2	-7.3	20.8	0
Finland	–	–	–	–	–	–	–	–	0
France	–	–	1.2	5.2	–	–	1.2	5.2	
Germany, Fed. Rep.	4.1	14.1	11.7	6.0	3.2	14.1	11.7	-137.6	11
Italy	–	–	–	–	-1.1	–	–	-1.9	0
Japan	–	18.4	15.0	3.7	–	18.4	15.0	3.7	2
Netherlands	4.6	3.0	0.5	2.9	4.3	-12.8	0.2	–	15
New Zealand	–	–	–	–	–	–	–	–	
Norway	–	–	–	–	–	–	–	–	4
Sweden	0.2	–	–	–	-0.2	-10.3	–	–	C
Switzerland	–	–	–	–	–	–	–	–	C
United Kingdom	2.0	1.6	0.7	0.6	1.9	1.6	-1.7	-0.5	6
United States	5.0	10.0	19.0	5.0	4.0	9.0	18.0	5.0	
TOTAL	*16.5*	*47.2*	*48.4*	*44.1*	*12.7*	*20.1*	*37.1*	*-105.3*	*43*
MULTILATERAL	*43.0*	*97.9*	*72.5*	*89.4*	*40.9*	*95.2*	*71.6*	*87.6*	*28*
OPEC COUNTRIES	*25.0*	*51.0*	*273.2*	*153.0*	*20.7*	*45.7*	*270.8*	*150.2*	*85*
E.E.C.+ MEMBERS	*11.3*	*25.3*	*15.1*	*36.7*	*9.0*	*9.3*	*4.9*	*-112.7*	*36*
TOTAL	***84.5***	***196.1***	***394.1***	***286.6***	***74.3***	***161.0***	***379.5***	***132.5***	***156***

	TOTAL OFFICIAL GROSS 1977	1978	1979	1980	TOTAL OFFICIAL NET 1977	1978	1979	1980	TOTAL OOF GROSS 197
DAC COUNTRIES									
Australia	0.1	0.8	1.3	1.9	0.1	0.8	1.3	1.9	
Austria	7.1	0.2	0.3	0.8	5.3	-0.9	-0.8	-2.7	[illegible]
Belgium	0.2	0.5	1.2	2.0	0.2	0.5	1.2	2.0	
Canada	0.3	0.9	7.6	2.3	0.3	0.9	7.6	2.3	
Denmark	1.4	1.6	10.7	22.9	1.4	1.6	3.1	22.8	[illegible]
Finland	0.1	0.1	0.5	0.8	0.1	0.1	0.5	0.8	
France	–	–	1.2	7.7	–	–	1.2	7.7	
Germany, Fed. Rep.	16.0	38.6	42.5	230.3	15.0	38.6	42.5	84.8	[illegible]
Italy	6.7	0.5	16.1	85.6	5.6	0.5	16.1	79.6	[illegible]
Japan	2.0	23.2	21.5	10.9	2.0	23.2	21.5	10.9	
Netherlands	20.2	31.8	20.2	48.6	19.9	16.0	19.9	45.7	
New Zealand	–	–	–	–	–	–	–	–	
Norway	4.6	6.5	4.0	5.6	4.6	6.5	4.0	5.6	
Sweden	0.9	11.5	2.6	1.3	0.5	1.2	2.6	1.3	
Switzerland	0.4	0.4	0.5	1.6	0.4	0.4	0.5	1.6	
United Kingdom	8.8	13.6	29.5	52.5	8.7	13.6	27.1	51.5	
United States	8.0	11.0	24.0	69.0	6.0	9.0	22.0	65.0	[illegible]
TOTAL	*76.5*	*141.1*	*183.9*	*543.8*	*70.0*	*111.8*	*170.4*	*380.9*	*1[illegible]*
MULTILATERAL	*80.3*	*145.2*	*177.0*	*262.1*	*71.1*	*135.7*	*167.7*	*196.3*	[illegible]
OPEC COUNTRIES	*143.4*	*123.4*	*285.5*	*222.6*	*139.0*	*118.2*	*283.2*	*219.7*	*3.*
E.E.C.+ MEMBERS	*54.9*	*98.1*	*143.7*	*506.0*	*52.5*	*82.2*	*133.4*	*350.4*	[illegible]
TOTAL	***300.2***	***409.7***	***646.4***	***1028.4***	***280.1***	***365.7***	***621.3***	***796.9***	***5[illegible]***

	1978	1979	1980	1977	1978	1979	1980
				ODA COMMITMENTS			
	0.8	1.3	1.9	0.6	0.9	1.6	5.7
	0.2	0.3	0.8	–	0.1	–	0.5
	0.5	1.2	2.0	–	–	1.6	2.5
	0.9	1.8	1.7	1.0	0.1	2.3	12.1
	1.1	10.0	22.4	2.3	14.5	0.9	24.4
	0.1	0.5	0.8	–	0.2	0.8	2.4
	–	1.2	7.7	–	0.2	7.1	20.3
	38.2	41.5	206.0	14.3	90.5	79.6	266.1
	0.5	1.1	0.2	0.5	0.5	1.1	0.2
	23.2	21.5	10.9	3.5	30.6	9.9	8.4
	31.8	19.8	48.5	32.0	40.1	47.6	30.1
	–	–	–	–	–	–	–
	6.5	4.0	5.6	0.7	11.8	–	8.5
	11.5	2.6	1.3	0.7	11.5	0.1	1.2
	0.4	0.5	0.3	0.1	–	–	0.3
	13.6	29.5	50.8	5.2	62.9	20.8	158.7
	11.0	24.0	60.0	16.2	10.1	100.1	83.0
	140.1	*160.5*	*421.0*	*77.0*	*273.9*	*273.4*	*624.2*
	2.2	0.3	–	–	8.4	–	19.5
	–	–	–	–	–	–	–
	–	–	–	–	–	–	–
	–	–	–	–	–	–	–
	11.5	22.3	56.3	15.1	23.8	49.0	89.0
	–	–	1.3	12.0	–	–	–
	33.5	26.6	36.9	25.0	78.0	55.6	170.0
	–	–	–	–	–	–	–
	–	0.2	1.8	–	–	15.4	15.2
	–	–	–	–	–	–	–
	37.3	28.3	24.0	–	–	–	–
	–	–	–	26.6	29.4	35.0	49.5
	7.0	7.3	10.7	–	–	–	–
	1.9	1.9	0.4	–	–	–	–
	3.2	4.4	6.4	–	–	–	–
	–	–	–	–	–	–	–
	9.4	13.3	10.5	–	–	–	–
	3.3	4.3	15.0	–	–	–	–
	4.6	3.8	6.7	–	–	–	–
	18.5	16.4	24.2	29.5	9.5	–	28.0
	132.4	*129.0*	*194.0*	*108.2*	*149.1*	*154.9*	*371.1*
	100.3	*285.5*	*222.0*	*297.9*	*362.2*	*169.8*	*269.7*
	97.1	*126.2*	*394.0*	*69.3*	*232.6*	*207.5*	*591.2*
	372.8	***575.0***	***837.0***	***483.1***	***785.2***	***598.1***	***1265.0***
				TECH. COOP. GRANTS			
	0.8	1.3	1.9	0.0	0.1	0.1	0.1
	0.2	0.3	0.7	0.1	0.2	0.3	0.7
	0.5	1.2	2.0	0.2	0.3	0.6	0.8
	0.9	1.8	1.7	–	–	–	–
	0.9	9.7	1.6	0.7	0.8	2.1	1.6
	0.1	0.5	0.8	0.1	0.1	0.5	0.8
	–	–	2.6	–	–	–	2.4
	24.1	29.8	200.0	11.3	23.3	17.1	24.0
	0.5	1.1	0.2	0.5	0.5	1.0	0.2
	4.8	6.5	7.3	1.4	1.6	0.7	1.4
	28.8	19.0	45.6	3.9	4.6	8.4	10.1
	–	–	–	–	–	–	–
	6.5	4.0	5.6	0.5	2.1	2.4	0.3
	11.5	2.6	1.3	–	–	–	0.1
	0.4	0.5	0.3	0.0	0.0	0.0	–
	12.0	28.8	50.3	4.6	6.8	11.2	15.2
	1.0	5.0	55.0	–	–	3.0	6.0
	92.9	*112.1*	*376.9*	*23.3*	*40.3*	*47.4*	*63.4*
	34.5	*56.5*	*104.5*	*14.4*	*20.0*	*21.7*	*49.5*
	49.3	*12.3*	*69.0*	–	–	–	–
	71.9	*111.1*	*357.3*	*21.1*	*36.2*	*40.4*	*54.2*
	176.7	***180.9***	***550.4***	***37.7***	***60.3***	***69.1***	***112.9***
				TOTAL OOF NET			
	–	–	–	–	–	–	–
	–	–	–	5.2	-1.0	-1.2	-3.4
	–	–	–	–	–	–	–
	–	5.9	0.6	–	–	5.9	0.6
	0.5	0.7	0.5	0.1	0.5	0.7	0.5
	–	–	–	–	–	–	–
	–	–	–	–	–	–	–
	0.4	1.1	24.3	0.6	0.4	1.0	22.4
	–	15.1	85.4	6.2	–	15.1	81.3
	–	–	–	–	–	–	–
	–	0.6	0.1	–	–	0.6	0.1
	–	–	–	–	–	–	–
	–	–	–	–	–	–	–
	–	–	–	–	–	–	–
	–	–	1.3	–	–	–	1.3
	–	–	1.7	–	–	–	1.7
	–	–	9.0	2.0	-1.0	-1.0	5.0
	1.0	*23.4*	*122.9*	*14.2*	*-1.1*	*21.1*	*109.3*
	12.8	*48.0*	*68.1*	*1.9*	*6.0*	*39.7*	*4.1*
	23.2	–	*0.6*	*33.0*	*23.2*	–	*0.6*
	1.0	*17.5*	*112.0*	*6.9*	*0.9*	*17.4*	*105.9*
	36.9	***71.4***	***191.5***	***49.0***	***28.1***	***60.8***	***114.0***

MAIN AID AGGREGATES

	1977	1978	1979	1980
DAC COUNTRIES COMBINED				
PRIVATE SECTOR NET	141.0	155.1	11.9	-28.7
Direct Investment	8.3	6.0	-2.7	7.9
Portfolio Invest.	-13.1	-1.7	11.7	-36.6
Export Credits	145.9	150.9	2.8	0.1
OFFICIAL & PRIVATE				
GROSS:				
Contractual Lending	256.6	301.2	144.7	247.4
Export Credits Tot.	233.2	253.0	93.9	81.0
Export Credits Priv	223.2	253.0	73.0	80.4
OTHER NET DATA				
Contractual Lending	172.8	169.8	61.1	4.1
Export Credits Tot.	153.1	148.8	21.6	-6.8
(Bank Sector Loans)	-3.0	25.0	24.0	-19.0
ODA CONCESSIONALITY				
Total:Grant Element	90.0	92.0	96.0	97.0
Loans:Grant Element	61.0	77.0	62.0	65.0
OTHER SOURCES				
CMEA Countr.(Gross)	2.6	3.6	3.9	10.6
Intra LDCS Exc.OPEC	–	–	–	–
Other	–	–	–	–
ALL SOURCE COMMITMENTS				
TOTAL BILATERAL	394.8	643.5	460.5	1088.3
of which				
OPEC (ODA)	297.9	362.2	169.8	269.7
CMEA (ODA)	–	–	–	–
TOTAL MULTILAT.(ODA)	108.2	149.1	154.9	371.1
TOTAL BIL.& MULTIL.	503.1	792.6	615.5	1459.4
of which				
ODA Grants	291.9	232.3	343.4	772.3
ODA Loans	191.2	552.9	254.7	492.7
ODA CONCESSIONALITY				
Total: Grant Element	81.0	68.0	81.0	85.0
Loans: Grant Element	54.0	54.0	57.0	61.0

INDEBTEDNESS

	1977	1978	1979	1980
TOTAL DEBT DISBURSED	***2118.1***	***2576.9***	***2633.6***	
Debt to DAC Countries	935.0	1097.0	1012.0	
ODA	161.0	209.0	251.0	
Total Export Credits	554.0	708.0	644.0	
Other Private Market	220.0	180.0	117.0	
International Org.	296.3	359.2	398.1	
CMEA	158.5	160.3	141.6	
Other	728.3	960.4	1081.9	
TOTAL DEBT SERVICE	***143.1***	***137.7***	***293.4***	
Paid to DAC Countries	99.0	86.6	130.9	
ODA	5.4	2.0	5.6	
Total Export Credits	70.0	76.8	92.3	
Other Private Market	23.6	7.8	33.0	
International Org.	14.6	16.3	33.1	
CMEA	7.5	4.1	24.0	
Other	22.0	30.6	105.4	

ECONOMIC INDICATORS

	1977	1978	1979	1980
GNP Curr. Prices, $M	6674.0	7162.3	7515.1	7644.4
Real GNP, 1976=100	107.0	113.0	111.0	109.0
GNP/Cap Curr. Prices,$	394.0	412.0	420.0	416.0
GNP/cap Atlas Basis, $	396.5	436.6	451.2	470.4
Real GNP/Cap, 1976=100	104.0	107.0	102.0	97.0
Population, Million	16.9	17.4	17.9	18.4
Curr.A/C Deficit(-),$M	-94.1	-107.5	-239.0	–
BOP Exp. & Transf.,$M	824.1	809.1	848.8	–
Exp. to OECD CIF, $M	383.1	400.8	346.2	360.5
of which				
Manufact.	4.6	9.5	9.3	14.4
Imp. from OECD FOB, $M	820.4	882.2	799.4	962.2
Reserves ex. Gold, $M	23.2	28.4	67.4	48.7

	TOTAL RECEIPTS NET 1977	1978	1979	1980	TOTAL ODA NET 1977	1978	1979	1980	TOTAL ODA GROSS 197
DAC COUNTRIES									
Australia	0.0	0.1	0.1	0.1	0.0	0.1	0.1	0.1	0.
Austria	0.0	0.0	0.0	0.0	0.0	0.0	0.0	0.0	0.
Belgium	0.0	0.0	0.1	0.1	0.0	0.0	0.1	0.0	0.
Canada	2.2	1.5	1.3	1.4	2.2	1.5	1.3	1.4	2.
Denmark	1.8	0.7	0.7	0.4	1.8	0.7	0.7	0.4	1.
Finland	0.0	–	0.0	–	0.0	–	0.0	–	0.
France	–	–	–	0.1	–	–	–	0.1	
Germany, Fed. Rep.	1.1	12.9	15.9	2.6	1.1	12.8	13.0	2.5	1.
Italy	–	–	–	–	–	–	–	–	
Japan	1.9	0.5	1.6	0.4	0.1	0.2	0.3	0.4	0.
Netherlands	0.4	0.9	0.8	1.2	0.4	0.9	0.8	1.2	0.
New Zealand	–	0.0	0.0	0.0	–	0.0	0.0	0.0	
Norway	0.3	0.4	–	0.1	0.3	0.4	–	0.1	0.
Sweden	1.0	3.1	1.4	1.5	1.0	3.1	0.8	1.6	1.
Switzerland	–	–	0.0	–	–	–	0.0	–	
United Kingdom	15.8	15.9	20.5	16.7	13.5	12.3	12.7	13.5	15.
United States	1.0	1.0	2.0	11.0	1.0	1.0	2.0	11.0	1.
TOTAL	*25.6*	*37.0*	*44.4*	*35.7*	*21.6*	*33.1*	*31.8*	*32.5*	*23.*
MULTILATERAL									
AF.D.F.	0.1	-0.1	0.0	0.0	0.1	-0.1	0.0	0.0	0.
AF.D.B.	0.9	0.4	5.2	1.9	–	–	–	–	
AS.D.B.	–	–	–	–	–	–	–	–	
CAR.D.B.	–	–	–	–	–	–	–	–	
E.E.C.	2.0	7.4	16.2	16.3	2.0	7.4	10.4	7.7	2.
IBRD	3.3	4.7	2.1	1.3	–	–	–	–	
IDA	2.0	1.2	0.7	0.3	2.0	1.2	0.7	0.3	2.
I.D.B.	–	–	–	–	–	–	–	–	
IFAD	–	–	–	–	–	–	–	–	
I.F.C.	–	0.7	2.8	5.2	–	–	–	–	
IMF TRUST FUND	–	–	3.1	2.7	–	–	3.1	2.7	
U.N. AGENCIES	–	–	–	–	–	–	–	–	
UNDP	0.8	0.7	0.6	1.6	0.8	0.7	0.6	1.6	0.
UNTA	0.3	0.2	0.2	0.3	0.3	0.2	0.2	0.3	0.
UNICEF	0.2	0.2	0.2	0.5	0.2	0.2	0.2	0.5	0.
UNRWA	–	–	–	–	–	–	–	–	
WFP	0.3	0.7	0.9	0.8	0.3	0.7	0.9	0.8	0.
UNHCR	–	0.0	0.4	1.2	–	0.0	0.4	1.2	
Other Multilateral	2.2	1.3	2.1	2.4	2.2	1.3	2.1	2.4	2.
Arab OPEC Agencies	–	–	–	–	–	–	–	–	
TOTAL	*12.0*	*17.4*	*34.4*	*34.4*	*7.8*	*11.6*	*18.6*	*17.4*	*7.*
OPEC COUNTRIES	–	–	–	–	–	–	–	–	
E.E.C.+ MEMBERS	*21.1*	*37.8*	*54.1*	*37.4*	*18.8*	*34.2*	*37.6*	*25.5*	*21.*
TOTAL	***37.6***	***54.4***	***78.8***	***70.1***	***29.4***	***44.6***	***50.4***	***49.9***	***31.***

	ODA LOANS GROSS 1977	1978	1979	1980	ODA LOANS NET 1977	1978	1979	1980	GRANTS 197
DAC COUNTRIES									
Australia	–	–	–	–	–	–	–	–	0
Austria	–	–	–	–	–	–	–	–	0
Belgium	–	–	–	–	–	–	–	–	0
Canada	0.4	0.4	0.2	0.2	0.4	0.4	0.2	0.2	1
Denmark	1.2	0.2	–	–	1.2	0.2	-0.2	-0.1	0
Finland	–	–	–	–	–	–	–	–	0
France	–	–	–	–	–	–	–	–	
Germany, Fed. Rep.	–	11.6	11.9	0.9	–	11.6	11.9	0.9	1
Italy	–	–	–	–	–	–	–	–	
Japan	–	–	–	–	–	–	–	–	0
Netherlands	–	–	–	–	–	–	–	–	0
New Zealand	–	–	–	–	–	–	–	–	
Norway	–	–	–	–	–	–	–	–	0
Sweden	–	–	–	–	–	–	–	–	1
Switzerland	–	–	–	–	–	–	–	–	
United Kingdom	13.3	10.5	9.6	9.2	11.0	9.7	8.5	7.7	2
United States	–	–	–	4.0	–	–	–	4.0	1
TOTAL	*14.9*	*22.6*	*21.7*	*14.2*	*12.6*	*21.8*	*20.5*	*12.6*	*8*
MULTILATERAL	*2.1*	*3.5*	*6.2*	*3.1*	*2.1*	*3.4*	*6.1*	*3.0*	*5*
OPEC COUNTRIES	–	–	–	–	–	–	–	–	
E.E.C.+ MEMBERS	*14.4*	*24.5*	*23.8*	*10.1*	*12.2*	*23.7*	*22.6*	*8.5*	*6*
TOTAL	***17.0***	***26.1***	***27.9***	***17.4***	***14.7***	***25.2***	***26.6***	***15.6***	***14***

	TOTAL OFFICIAL GROSS 1977	1978	1979	1980	TOTAL OFFICIAL NET 1977	1978	1979	1980	TOTAL OOF GROSS 197
DAC COUNTRIES									
Australia	0.0	0.1	0.1	0.1	0.0	0.1	0.1	0.1	
Austria	0.0	0.0	0.0	0.0	0.0	0.0	0.0	0.0	
Belgium	0.0	0.0	0.1	0.0	0.0	0.0	0.1	0.0	
Canada	2.2	1.5	1.3	1.4	2.2	1.5	1.3	1.4	
Denmark	1.8	0.7	0.9	0.6	1.8	0.7	0.7	0.4	
Finland	0.0	–	0.0	–	0.0	–	0.0	–	
France	–	–	–	0.1	–	–	–	0.1	
Germany, Fed. Rep.	1.1	12.8	14.1	4.5	1.1	12.8	14.1	4.5	
Italy	–	–	–	–	–	–	–	–	
Japan	0.1	0.2	0.3	0.4	0.1	0.2	0.3	0.4	
Netherlands	0.4	0.9	0.8	1.2	0.4	0.9	0.8	1.2	
New Zealand	–	0.0	0.0	0.0	–	0.0	0.0	0.0	
Norway	0.3	0.4	–	0.1	0.3	0.4	–	0.1	
Sweden	1.0	3.1	0.8	1.6	1.0	3.1	0.8	1.6	
Switzerland	–	–	0.0	–	–	–	0.0	–	
United Kingdom	15.7	16.7	17.7	15.1	11.9	15.9	16.6	13.6	
United States	1.0	1.0	2.0	11.0	1.0	1.0	2.0	11.0	
TOTAL	*23.8*	*37.5*	*38.0*	*36.2*	*20.0*	*36.7*	*36.8*	*34.5*	
MULTILATERAL	*12.6*	*18.4*	*35.4*	*35.6*	*12.0*	*17.4*	*34.4*	*34.4*	*4*
OPEC COUNTRIES	–	–	–	–	–	–	–	–	
E.E.C.+ MEMBERS	*21.0*	*38.6*	*49.7*	*37.8*	*17.2*	*37.8*	*48.4*	*36.1*	
TOTAL	***36.4***	***55.9***	***73.4***	***71.8***	***32.0***	***54.1***	***71.2***	***69.0***	***4***

1978	1979	1980	1977	1978	1979	1980
			ODA COMMITMENTS			
0.1	0.1	0.1	0.0	0.1	0.0	0.1
0.0	0.0	0.0	–	–	–	–
0.0	0.1	0.0	–	–	–	–
1.5	1.3	1.4	1.7	1.3	0.8	0.6
0.7	0.9	0.6	0.8	0.4	0.6	0.5
–	0.0	–	–	–	0.0	–
–	–	0.1	–	–	–	0.0
12.8	13.0	2.5	0.6	24.7	2.8	2.6
–	–	–	–	–	–	–
0.2	0.3	0.4	0.1	0.2	0.4	0.5
0.9	0.8	1.2	1.1	0.8	0.8	1.4
0.0	0.0	0.0	–	0.0	–	0.0
0.4	–	0.1	0.2	–	0.2	–
3.1	0.8	1.6	2.7	0.8	–	–
–	0.0	–	–	–	–	–
13.1	13.8	15.0	26.7	2.6	3.6	5.8
1.0	2.0	11.0	1.4	14.9	7.6	9.8
33.9	*33.0*	*34.2*	*35.5*	*45.8*	*16.8*	*21.3*
–	0.1	–	–	9.6	–	–
–	–	–	–	–	–	–
–	–	–	–	–	–	–
–	–	–	–	–	–	–
7.4	10.4	7.7	6.6	23.4	11.2	7.6
–	–	–	–	–	–	–
1.2	0.7	0.3	–	–	–	–
–	–	–	–	–	–	–
–	–	–	–	–	–	–
–	–	–	–	–	–	–
–	3.1	2.7	–	–	–	–
–	–	–	3.8	3.1	4.4	6.7
0.7	0.6	1.6	–	–	–	–
0.2	0.2	0.3	–	–	–	–
0.2	0.2	0.5	–	–	–	–
–	–	–	–	–	–	–
0.7	0.9	0.8	–	–	–	–
0.0	0.4	1.2	–	–	–	–
1.3	2.1	2.4	–	–	–	–
–	–	–	–	–	–	–
11.7	*18.7*	*17.5*	*10.4*	*36.1*	*15.5*	*14.3*
–	–	–	–	–	–	–
35.0	*38.9*	*27.1*	*35.9*	*52.0*	*18.9*	*18.0*
45.6	***51.7***	***51.7***	***45.9***	***82.0***	***32.3***	***35.6***
			TECH. COOP. GRANTS			
0.1	0.1	0.1	0.0	0.1	0.1	0.1
0.0	0.0	0.0	0.0	0.0	0.0	0.0
0.0	0.1	0.0	0.0	0.0	0.1	0.0
1.1	1.1	1.3	0.7	0.8	0.6	0.6
0.5	0.9	0.6	0.7	0.5	0.9	0.6
–	0.0	–	0.0	–	0.0	–
–	–	0.1	–	–	–	0.1
1.3	1.1	1.6	1.1	1.3	1.1	1.6
–	–	–	–	–	–	–
0.2	0.3	0.4	0.1	0.2	0.3	0.4
0.9	0.8	1.2	0.4	0.9	0.8	1.0
0.0	0.0	0.0	–	–	0.0	0.0
0.4	–	0.1	0.1	0.1	–	0.0
3.1	0.8	1.6	–	0.6	0.2	0.2
–	0.0	–	–	–	–	–
2.6	4.2	5.8	2.1	2.6	3.6	5.8
1.0	2.0	7.0	1.0	1.0	2.0	6.0
11.3	*11.3*	*19.9*	*6.2*	*8.1*	*9.6*	*16.6*
8.2	*12.5*	*14.4*	*3.5*	*2.4*	*3.5*	*6.7*
–	–	–	–	–	–	–
10.5	*15.1*	*17.0*	*4.2*	*5.3*	*6.3*	*9.2*
19.5	***23.8***	***34.3***	***9.7***	***10.5***	***13.1***	***23.3***
			TOTAL OOF NET			
–	–	–	–	–	–	–
–	–	–	–	–	–	–
–	–	–	–	–	–	–
–	–	–	–	–	–	–
–	–	–	–	–	–	–
–	–	–	–	–	–	–
–	–	–	–	–	–	–
–	1.1	2.0	–	–	1.1	2.0
–	–	–	–	–	–	–
–	–	–	–	–	–	–
–	–	–	–	–	–	–
–	–	–	–	–	–	–
–	–	–	–	–	–	–
–	–	–	–	–	–	–
–	–	–	–	–	–	–
3.6	3.9	0.0	-1.6	3.6	3.9	0.0
–	–	–	–	–	–	–
3.6	*5.0*	*2.0*	*-1.6*	*3.6*	*5.0*	*2.0*
6.7	*16.7*	*18.1*	*4.2*	*5.8*	*15.8*	*17.0*
–	–	–	–	–	–	–
3.6	*10.8*	*10.6*	*-1.6*	*3.6*	*10.8*	*10.6*
10.3	***21.7***	***20.1***	***2.7***	***9.4***	***20.8***	***19.0***

MAIN AID AGGREGATES

	1977	1978	1979	1980
DAC COUNTRIES COMBINED				
PRIVATE SECTOR NET	5.6	0.3	7.6	1.2
Direct Investment	5.2	0.3	5.3	–
Portfolio Invest.	–	0.0	1.8	-2.0
Export Credits	0.4	–	0.5	3.2
OFFICIAL & PRIVATE				
GROSS:				
Contractual Lending	15.3	26.2	27.4	20.1
Export Credits Tot.	0.4	–	0.7	3.8
Export Credits Priv	0.4	–	0.7	3.8
OTHER NET DATA				
Contractual Lending	11.5	25.4	25.9	17.8
Export Credits Tot.	0.4	–	0.5	3.2
(Bank Sector Loans)	–	16.0	6.0	-4.0
ODA CONCESSIONALITY				
Total:Grant Element	63.0	80.0	91.0	100.0
Loans:Grant Element	33.0	67.0	71.0	–
OTHER SOURCES				
CMEA Countr.(Gross)	–	–	–	–
Intra LDCS Exc.OPEC	–	–	–	–
Other	–	–	–	–
ALL SOURCE COMMITMENTS				
TOTAL BILATERAL	37.2	45.8	16.9	21.3
of which				
OPEC (ODA)	–	–	–	–
CMEA (ODA)	–	–	–	–
TOTAL MULTILAT.(ODA)	10.4	36.1	15.6	14.3
TOTAL BIL.& MULTIL.	47.6	82.0	32.4	35.6
of which				
ODA Grants	21.2	27.4	27.3	34.2
ODA Loans	24.7	54.6	5.0	1.4
ODA CONCESSIONALITY				
Total: Grant Element	74.0	74.0	95.0	100.0
Loans: Grant Element	33.0	61.0	71.0	–

INDEBTEDNESS

	1977	1978	1979	1980
TOTAL DEBT DISBURSED	***54.7***	***131.2***	***181.1***	
Debt to DAC Countries	30.0	98.0	131.0	
ODA	28.0	56.0	82.0	
Total Export Credits	2.0	14.0	21.0	
Other Private Market	–	28.0	28.0	
International Org.	24.2	32.7	49.7	
CMEA	–	–	–	
Other	0.6	0.5	0.4	
TOTAL DEBT SERVICE	***4.9***	***5.8***	***11.8***	
Paid to DAC Countries	3.3	3.1	8.5	
ODA	2.8	1.8	3.0	
Total Export Credits	0.5	1.0	2.6	
Other Private Market	–	0.3	2.9	
International Org.	1.5	2.6	3.2	
CMEA	–	–	–	
Other	0.1	0.1	0.1	

ECONOMIC INDICATORS

	1977	1978	1979	1980
GNP Curr. Prices, $M	249.2	283.2	333.5	404.1
Real GNP, 1976=100	103.0	105.0	115.0	114.0
GNP/Cap Curr. Prices,$	488.0	539.0	616.0	725.0
GNP/cap Atlas Basis, $	524.7	561.2	645.7	679.2
Real GNP/Cap, 1976=100	100.0	99.0	105.0	102.0
Population, Million	0.5	0.5	0.5	0.6
Curr.A/C Deficit(-),$M	–	–	–	–
BOP Exp. & Transf.,$M	–	–	–	–
Exp. to OECD CIF, $M	73.1	128.4	149.3	124.5
of which				
Manufact.	0.3	1.8	7.1	5.5
Imp. from OECD FOB, $M	5.6	21.7	12.9	13.2
Reserves ex. Gold, $M	94.7	116.9	117.3	161.6

	TOTAL RECEIPTS NET 1977	1978	1979	1980	TOTAL ODA NET 1977	1978	1979	1980
DAC COUNTRIES								
Australia	–	0.1	0.0	0.0	–	0.1	0.0	0.0
Austria	0.3	0.4	0.4	0.4	0.3	0.4	0.4	0.4
Belgium	0.3	0.3	3.3	2.5	0.0	0.7	0.8	3.1
Canada	48.4	-22.3	-1.3	-21.4	–	–	–	–
Denmark	0.1	–	0.0	–	–	–	–	0.0
Finland	-0.3	-0.4	-0.1	-0.3	–	0.0	0.2	0.2
France	6.7	5.3	-20.2	-7.9	–	0.2	-0.4	10.4
Germany, Fed. Rep.	0.1	17.7	-1.3	26.9	1.8	12.1	9.0	25.4
Italy	-17.1	5.7	-1.6	-4.9	2.0	0.2	0.1	0.1
Japan	3.7	0.3	-1.9	-0.4	0.8	1.5	1.2	1.4
Netherlands	0.2	1.6	1.2	0.4	0.2	1.6	1.2	0.4
New Zealand	–	–	–	–	–	–	–	–
Norway	–	–	–	-1.6	–	–	–	–
Sweden	-0.2	-1.9	0.1	-0.4	–	–	–	–
Switzerland	0.2	-1.6	-0.9	-0.3	0.4	0.5	0.5	0.6
United Kingdom	-3.2	0.5	0.0	0.7	0.1	0.1	0.3	0.7
United States	39.0	21.0	71.0	19.0	40.0	18.0	76.0	19.0
TOTAL	*78.0*	*26.7*	*48.7*	*12.8*	*45.6*	*35.1*	*89.2*	*61.7*
MULTILATERAL								
AF.D.F.	–	–	–	–	–	–	–	–
AF.D.B.	–	–	–	–	–	–	–	–
AS.D.B.	–	–	–	–	–	–	–	–
CAR.D.B.	–	–	–	–	–	–	–	–
E.E.C.	2.1	6.2	2.9	1.3	2.1	6.2	2.9	1.3
IBRD	45.7	30.6	55.2	57.2	–	0.1	1.7	4.3
IDA	9.0	8.9	1.6	1.6	9.0	8.9	1.6	1.6
I.D.B.	–	–	–	–	–	–	–	–
IFAD	–	–	–	–	–	–	–	–
I.F.C.	–	–	–	–	–	–	–	–
IMF TRUST FUND	–	–	–	–	–	–	–	–
U.N. AGENCIES	–	–	–	–	–	–	–	–
UNDP	2.1	2.5	4.1	4.4	2.1	2.5	4.1	4.4
UNTA	0.8	0.6	0.8	0.2	0.8	0.6	0.8	0.2
UNICEF	0.5	0.5	0.6	0.3	0.5	0.5	0.6	0.3
UNRWA	–	–	–	–	–	–	–	–
WFP	13.3	8.0	17.2	12.8	13.3	8.0	17.2	12.8
UNHCR	–	–	0.0	0.0	–	–	0.0	0.0
Other Multilateral	0.7	0.5	0.6	1.0	0.7	0.5	0.6	1.0
Arab OPEC Agencies	6.6	8.6	9.8	4.4	6.6	8.6	9.8	4.4
TOTAL	*80.7*	*66.5*	*92.8*	*83.1*	*35.0*	*36.0*	*39.3*	*30.2*
OPEC COUNTRIES	*598.0*	*548.8*	*1456.7*	*1554.8*	*598.0*	*548.8*	*1456.7*	*1554.8*
E.E.C.+ MEMBERS	*-10.9*	*37.4*	*-15.7*	*19.1*	*6.1*	*20.9*	*13.8*	*41.4*
TOTAL	***756.8***	***642.0***	***1598.2***	***1650.7***	***678.7***	***619.9***	***1585.2***	***1646.7***

	ODA LOANS GROSS 1977	1978	1979	1980	ODA LOANS NET 1977	1978	1979	1980
DAC COUNTRIES								
Australia	–	–	–	–	–	–	–	–
Austria	–	–	–	–	–	–	–	–
Belgium	–	–	–	2.6	–	–	–	2.6
Canada	–	–	–	–	–	–	–	–
Denmark	–	–	–	–	–	–	–	–
Finland	–	–	–	–	–	–	–	–
France	–	–	–	6.1	–	–	-0.4	5.7
Germany, Fed. Rep.	–	5.4	4.0	18.4	-0.1	5.3	3.9	18.3
Italy	–	–	–	–	–	–	–	–
Japan	–	0.5	0.2	0.3	–	0.5	0.2	0.3
Netherlands	–	–	–	–	–	–	–	–
New Zealand	–	–	–	–	–	–	–	–
Norway	–	–	–	–	–	–	–	–
Sweden	–	–	–	–	–	–	–	–
Switzerland	–	–	–	–	–	–	–	–
United Kingdom	–	–	–	–	–	–	–	–
United States	41.0	20.0	75.0	19.0	41.0	17.0	72.0	14.0
TOTAL	*41.0*	*25.9*	*79.2*	*46.3*	*40.9*	*22.8*	*75.6*	*40.8*
MULTILATERAL	*15.7*	*17.7*	*13.9*	*10.8*	*15.5*	*17.6*	*13.0*	*10.2*
OPEC COUNTRIES	*67.4*	*46.1*	*26.6*	*24.1*	*65.6*	*43.3*	*21.7*	*19.0*
E.E.C.+ MEMBERS	*–*	*5.4*	*4.0*	*27.1*	*-0.1*	*5.3*	*3.5*	*26.5*
TOTAL	***124.1***	***89.7***	***119.6***	***81.2***	***122.1***	***83.7***	***110.4***	***69.9***

	TOTAL OFFICIAL GROSS 1977	1978	1979	1980	TOTAL OFFICIAL NET 1977	1978	1979	1980
DAC COUNTRIES								
Australia	–	0.1	0.0	0.0	–	0.1	0.0	0.0
Austria	0.3	0.4	0.4	0.4	0.3	0.4	0.4	0.4
Belgium	0.0	0.7	0.8	3.1	0.0	0.7	0.8	3.1
Canada	–	–	–	–	–	–	–	–
Denmark	–	–	0.0	0.0	–	–	0.0	–
Finland	–	0.0	0.2	0.2	–	0.0	0.2	0.2
France	–	0.2	–	10.8	–	0.2	-0.4	10.4
Germany, Fed. Rep.	1.9	12.9	9.2	25.6	1.8	12.3	8.9	25.4
Italy	2.0	0.2	0.1	0.1	1.2	-0.7	-0.8	-0.7
Japan	0.8	1.5	1.2	1.4	0.8	1.5	1.2	1.4
Netherlands	0.2	1.6	1.2	0.4	0.2	1.6	1.2	0.4
New Zealand	–	–	–	–	–	–	–	–
Norway	–	–	–	–	–	–	–	–
Sweden	–	–	–	–	–	–	–	–
Switzerland	0.4	0.5	0.5	0.6	0.4	0.5	0.5	0.6
United Kingdom	0.1	0.1	0.3	0.7	0.1	0.1	0.3	0.7
United States	40.0	21.0	79.0	24.0	40.0	18.0	76.0	19.0
TOTAL	*45.7*	*38.9*	*92.7*	*67.3*	*44.8*	*34.5*	*88.2*	*60.9*
MULTILATERAL	*80.9*	*68.1*	*95.0*	*86.3*	*80.7*	*66.5*	*92.8*	*83.1*
OPEC COUNTRIES	*599.8*	*551.6*	*1461.6*	*1559.9*	*598.0*	*548.8*	*1456.7*	*1554.8*
E.E.C.+ MEMBERS	*6.3*	*21.8*	*14.4*	*42.0*	*5.3*	*20.3*	*12.9*	*40.6*
TOTAL	***726.4***	***658.6***	***1649.4***	***1713.5***	***723.6***	***649.8***	***1637.7***	***1698.8***

	TOTAL ODA GROSS 197[…]
Australia	–
Austria	0.[…]
Belgium	0.[…]
Canada	
Denmark	–
Finland	–
France	
Germany, Fed. Rep.	1.[…]
Italy	2.[…]
Japan	0.[…]
Netherlands	0.[…]
New Zealand	
Norway	
Sweden	
Switzerland	0.[…]
United Kingdom	0.[…]
United States	40.[…]
TOTAL	*45.[…]*
AF.D.F.	
AF.D.B.	
AS.D.B.	
CAR.D.B.	
E.E.C.	2.[…]
IBRD	
IDA	9.[…]
I.D.B.	
IFAD	
I.F.C.	
IMF TRUST FUND	
U.N. AGENCIES	
UNDP	2.[…]
UNTA	0.[…]
UNICEF	0.[…]
UNRWA	
WFP	13.[…]
UNHCR	
Other Multilateral	0.[…]
Arab OPEC Agencies	6[…]
TOTAL	*35.[…]*
OPEC COUNTRIES	*599.[…]*
E.E.C.+ MEMBERS	*6.[…]*
TOTAL	***680.[…]***

	GRANTS 197[…]
Australia	
Austria	0[…]
Belgium	0[…]
Canada	
Denmark	
Finland	
France	
Germany, Fed. Rep.	1[…]
Italy	2[…]
Japan	0[…]
Netherlands	0[…]
New Zealand	
Norway	
Sweden	
Switzerland	0[…]
United Kingdom	0[…]
United States	-1[…]
TOTAL	*4[…]*
MULTILATERAL	*19[…]*
OPEC COUNTRIES	*532[…]*
E.E.C.+ MEMBERS	*6[…]*
TOTAL	***556[…]***

	TOTAL OOF GROSS 197[…]
Australia	
Austria	
Belgium	
Canada	
Denmark	
Finland	
France	
Germany, Fed. Rep.	
Italy	
Japan	
Netherlands	
New Zealand	
Norway	
Sweden	
Switzerland	
United Kingdom	
United States	
TOTAL	
MULTILATERAL	*45[…]*
OPEC COUNTRIES	
E.E.C.+ MEMBERS	
TOTAL	***45[…]***

1978	1979	1980	1977	1978	1979	1980
			ODA COMMITMENTS			
0.1	0.0	0.0	–	0.0	–	0.0
0.4	0.4	0.4	–	0.2	–	–
0.7	0.8	3.1	–	–	2.6	–
–	–	–	–	–	–	–
–	–	0.0	–	–	–	–
0.0	0.2	0.2	–	0.2	–	0.0
0.2	–	10.8	10.2	–	–	4.6
12.2	9.2	25.6	66.6	48.2	54.3	61.5
0.2	0.1	0.1	2.0	0.2	0.1	0.1
1.5	1.2	1.4	1.0	1.2	1.1	1.5
1.6	1.2	0.4	2.6	0.1	0.2	2.0
–	–	–	–	–	–	–
–	–	–	–	–	–	–
–	–	–	–	–	–	–
0.5	0.5	0.6	–	–	–	0.6
0.1	0.3	0.7	0.1	0.1	0.3	0.7
21.0	79.0	24.0	99.7	105.3	101.8	–
38.2	*92.7*	*67.3*	*182.1*	*155.3*	*160.2*	*70.9*
–	–	–	–	–	–	–
–	–	–	–	–	–	–
–	–	–	–	–	–	–
–	–	–	–	–	–	–
6.2	2.9	1.3	1.0	0.1	23.8	7.6
0.1	1.7	4.3	–	–	–	–
9.0	1.7	1.7	–	–	–	–
–	–	–	–	–	–	–
–	–	–	–	–	–	–
–	–	–	–	–	–	–
–	–	–	–	–	–	–
–	–	–	17.4	12.2	23.4	18.7
2.5	4.1	4.4	–	–	–	–
0.6	0.8	0.2	–	–	–	–
0.5	0.6	0.3	–	–	–	–
–	–	–	–	–	–	–
8.0	17.2	12.8	–	–	–	–
–	0.0	0.0	–	–	–	–
0.5	0.6	1.0	–	–	–	–
8.6	10.5	4.9	20.9	6.3	2.0	6.4
36.1	*40.1*	*30.8*	*39.4*	*18.5*	*49.1*	*32.7*
551.6	*1461.6*	*1559.9*	*801.4*	*2208.7*	*575.4*	*1905.7*
21.0	*14.3*	*42.0*	*82.5*	*48.6*	*81.1*	*76.5*
626.0	***1594.5***	***1658.0***	***1022.9***	***2382.5***	***784.7***	***2009.4***
			TECH. COOP. GRANTS			
0.1	0.0	0.0	–	0.0	–	0.0
0.4	0.4	0.4	0.3	0.4	0.4	0.4
0.7	0.8	0.6	0.0	0.7	0.8	0.6
–	–	–	–	–	–	–
–	–	0.0	–	–	–	0.0
0.0	0.2	0.2	–	0.0	0.2	0.2
0.2	–	4.7	–	0.2	–	4.7
6.8	5.2	7.2	1.9	6.8	5.2	7.2
0.2	0.1	0.1	0.1	0.2	0.1	0.1
1.1	1.0	1.2	0.8	1.1	1.0	1.2
1.6	1.2	0.4	0.2	0.1	0.2	0.2
–	–	–	–	–	–	–
–	–	–	–	–	–	–
–	–	–	–	–	–	–
0.5	0.5	0.6	–	–	0.0	–
0.1	0.3	0.7	0.1	0.1	0.3	0.7
1.0	4.0	5.0	1.0	3.0	3.0	5.0
12.3	*13.5*	*20.9*	*4.4*	*12.4*	*11.0*	*20.2*
18.4	*26.3*	*20.0*	*4.1*	*4.2*	*6.1*	*18.7*
505.5	*1435.0*	*1535.8*	–	–	–	–
15.6	*10.4*	*14.9*	*2.2*	*8.0*	*6.4*	*13.4*
536.2	***1474.8***	***1576.8***	***8.5***	***16.6***	***17.1***	***38.9***
			TOTAL OOF NET			
–	–	–	–	–	–	–
–	–	–	–	–	–	–
–	–	–	–	–	–	–
–	–	–	–	–	–	–
–	0.0	–	–	–	0.0	0.0
–	–	–	–	–	–	–
–	–	–	–	–	–	–
0.7	–	–	–	0.3	-0.1	0.0
–	–	–	-0.8	-0.8	-0.8	-0.8
–	–	–	–	–	–	–
–	–	–	–	–	–	–
–	–	–	–	–	–	–
–	–	–	–	–	–	–
–	–	–	–	–	–	–
–	–	–	–	–	–	–
–	–	–	–	–	–	–
–	–	–	–	–	–	–
0.7	*0.0*	–	*-0.8*	*-0.6*	*-0.9*	*-0.8*
31.9	*54.9*	*55.5*	*45.7*	*30.5*	*53.5*	*53.0*
–	–	–	–	–	–	–
0.7	*0.0*	–	*-0.8*	*-0.6*	*-0.9*	*-0.8*
32.7	***55.0***	***55.5***	***44.9***	***29.9***	***52.5***	***52.1***

MAIN AID AGGREGATES

	1977	1978	1979	1980
DAC COUNTRIES COMBINED				
PRIVATE SECTOR NET	33.2	-7.8	-39.5	-48.0
Direct Investment	0.1	–	0.0	0.0
Portfolio Invest.	0.2	-1.6	-9.9	-0.3
Export Credits	33.0	-6.2	-29.6	-47.7
OFFICIAL & PRIVATE				
GROSS:				
Contractual Lending	156.9	83.1	108.4	62.3
Export Credits Tot.	115.9	56.5	29.2	15.9
Export Credits Priv	115.9	56.5	29.2	15.9
OTHER NET DATA				
Contractual Lending	73.1	16.0	45.1	-7.7
Export Credits Tot.	33.0	-7.0	-30.5	-48.5
(Bank Sector Loans)	-8.0	-13.0	6.0	-4.0
ODA CONCESSIONALITY				
Total:Grant Element	69.0	71.0	72.0	74.0
Loans:Grant Element	65.0	66.0	67.0	66.0
OTHER SOURCES				
CMEA Countr.(Gross)	73.5	71.5	78.3	63.9
Intra LDCS Exc.OPEC	–	–	–	–
Other	–	–	–	–
ALL SOURCE COMMITMENTS				
TOTAL BILATERAL	983.5	2364.0	735.6	1976.6
of which				
OPEC (ODA)	801.4	2208.7	575.4	1905.7
CMEA (ODA)	–	50.0	–	–
TOTAL MULTILAT.(ODA)	39.4	18.5	49.1	32.7
TOTAL BIL.& MULTIL.	1022.9	2382.5	784.7	2009.4
of which				
ODA Grants	791.6	2154.0	604.9	1949.7
ODA Loans	231.3	228.5	179.8	59.7
ODA CONCESSIONALITY				
Total: Grant Element	90.0	96.0	91.0	98.0
Loans: Grant Element	57.0	60.0	61.0	63.0

INDEBTEDNESS

	1977	1978	1979	1980
TOTAL DEBT DISBURSED	***1558.1***	***2050.7***	***2423.3***	
Debt to DAC Countries	299.0	385.0	411.0	
ODA	97.0	124.0	200.0	
Total Export Credits	180.0	220.0	183.0	
Other Private Market	22.0	41.0	28.0	
International Org.	136.2	179.0	249.4	
CMEA	664.6	791.5	783.2	
Other	458.3	695.2	979.8	
TOTAL DEBT SERVICE	***140.4***	***320.8***	***389.3***	
Paid to DAC Countries	79.1	89.9	102.8	
ODA	0.5	5.8	7.6	
Total Export Credits	75.8	77.2	86.1	
Other Private Market	2.8	6.9	9.1	
International Org.	4.7	8.9	16.0	
CMEA	48.9	117.4	155.2	
Other	7.7	104.6	115.3	

ECONOMIC INDICATORS

	1977	1978	1979	1980
GNP Curr. Prices, $M	7003.5	8401.5	10005.8	12387.5
Real GNP, 1976=100	97.0	106.0	111.0	122.0
GNP/Cap Curr. Prices,$	874.0	1010.0	1158.0	1379.0
GNP/cap Atlas Basis, $	950.8	1070.8	1165.3	1340.3
Real GNP/Cap, 1976=100	94.0	99.0	99.0	104.0
Population, Million	8.0	8.3	8.6	9.0
Curr.A/C Deficit(-),$M	-1294.0	-1233.0	-1541.0	-2159.0
BOP Exp. & Transf.,$M	1544.0	1514.0	2229.0	2705.0
Exp. to OECD CIF, $M	816.9	835.1	1156.4	1422.0
of which				
Manufact.	10.3	16.1	16.0	22.7
Imp. from OECD FOB, $M	1535.8	1517.3	2209.5	2595.1
Reserves ex. Gold, $M	484.0	382.0	581.0	337.0

	1977	1978	1979	1980	1977	1978	1979	1980
TOTAL RECEIPTS NET					**TOTAL ODA NET**			
DAC COUNTRIES								
Australia	0.4	-0.4	–	–	–	–	–	–
Austria	0.0	0.4	0.5	0.8	0.0	0.4	0.5	0.8
Belgium	-4.9	-9.0	-0.8	0.8	–	0.0	0.0	0.0
Canada	–	–	–	0.9	–	–	–	–
Denmark	–	–	–	–	–	–	–	–
Finland	–	–	–	–	–	–	–	–
France	16.3	1.0	12.0	-3.4	–	–	–	–
Germany, Fed. Rep.	15.8	22.3	14.1	-60.0	2.0	5.9	4.1	2.6
Italy	-13.2	0.5	1.0	2.4	–	–	–	–
Japan	29.1	-45.3	-7.2	110.5	-11.0	-11.4	-9.7	–
Netherlands	–	–	10.5	41.7	–	–	–	–
New Zealand	0.2	0.3	–	–	–	–	–	–
Norway	–	–	–	–	–	–	–	–
Sweden	4.2	1.3	0.1	-1.8	–	–	–	–
Switzerland	-12.2	4.7	109.3	0.7	0.0	0.0	0.0	–
United Kingdom	-9.4	-2.4	3.6	-24.8	–	–	–	–
United States	20.0	51.0	279.0	388.0	-8.0	-9.0	-9.0	-8.0
TOTAL	*46.3*	*24.3*	*421.9*	*455.7*	*-16.9*	*-14.1*	*-14.1*	*-4.6*
MULTILATERAL								
AF.D.F.	–	–	–	–	–	–	–	–
AF.D.B.	–	–	–	–	–	–	–	–
AS.D.B.	-4.4	-6.0	-6.4	–	–	–	–	–
CAR.D.B.	–	–	–	–	–	–	–	–
E.E.C.	–	–	–	–	–	–	–	–
IBRD	-12.9	-18.4	-16.7	-17.1	–	–	–	–
IDA	-0.2	-0.2	-0.2	-0.2	-0.2	-0.2	-0.2	-0.2
I.D.B.	–	–	–	–	–	–	–	–
IFAD	–	–	–	–	–	–	–	–
I.F.C.	-1.0	-0.7	-0.7	-0.7	–	–	–	–
IMF TRUST FUND	–	–	–	–	–	–	–	–
U.N. AGENCIES	–	–	–	–	–	–	–	–
UNDP	–	0.0	–	–	–	0.0	–	–
UNTA	–	0.9	–	–	–	0.9	–	–
UNICEF	–	–	–	–	–	–	–	–
UNRWA	–	–	–	–	–	–	–	–
WFP	–	–	–	–	–	–	–	–
UNHCR	–	–	–	–	–	–	–	–
Other Multilateral	–	–	–	–	–	–	–	–
Arab OPEC Agencies	–	–	–	–	–	–	–	–
TOTAL	*-18.5*	*-24.5*	*-23.9*	*-18.0*	*-0.2*	*0.7*	*-0.2*	*-0.2*
OPEC COUNTRIES	*33.8*	*19.7*	*21.5*	*1.2*	*33.8*	*19.7*	*21.5*	*1.2*
E.E.C.+ MEMBERS	*4.6*	*12.4*	*40.2*	*-43.4*	*2.0*	*6.0*	*4.1*	*2.6*
TOTAL	***61.6***	***19.6***	***419.5***	***438.9***	***16.7***	***6.4***	***7.2***	***-3.6***

	1977	1978	1979	1980	1977	1978	1979	1980
ODA LOANS GROSS					**ODA LOANS NET**			
DAC COUNTRIES								
Australia	–	–	–	–	–	–	–	–
Austria	–	–	–	–	–	–	–	–
Belgium	–	–	–	–	–	–	–	–
Canada	–	–	–	–	–	–	–	–
Denmark	–	–	–	–	–	–	–	–
Finland	–	–	–	–	–	–	–	–
France	–	–	–	–	–	–	–	–
Germany, Fed. Rep.	–	–	–	–	–	–	–	–
Italy	–	–	–	–	–	–	–	–
Japan	–	–	–	–	-11.0	-11.4	-9.7	–
Netherlands	–	–	–	–	–	–	–	–
New Zealand	–	–	–	–	–	–	–	–
Norway	–	–	–	–	–	–	–	–
Sweden	–	–	–	–	–	–	–	–
Switzerland	–	–	–	–	–	–	–	–
United Kingdom	–	–	–	–	–	–	–	–
United States	–	–	–	–	-5.0	-6.0	-5.0	-5.0
TOTAL	–	–	–	–	*-16.0*	*-17.4*	*-14.7*	*-5.0*
MULTILATERAL	–	–	–	–	*-0.2*	*-0.2*	*-0.2*	*-0.2*
OPEC COUNTRIES	*33.8*	*19.7*	*21.5*	*2.7*	*33.8*	*19.7*	*21.5*	*-0.8*
E.E.C.+ MEMBERS	–	–	–	–	–	–	–	–
TOTAL	***33.8***	***19.7***	***21.5***	***2.7***	***17.6***	***2.1***	***6.6***	***-6.0***

	1977	1978	1979	1980	1977	1978	1979	1980
TOTAL OFFICIAL GROSS					**TOTAL OFFICIAL NET**			
DAC COUNTRIES								
Australia	–	–	–	–	–	–	–	–
Austria	0.0	0.4	0.5	0.8	0.0	0.4	0.5	0.8
Belgium	–	0.0	0.0	0.0	–	0.0	0.0	0.0
Canada	–	–	–	–	–	–	–	–
Denmark	–	–	–	–	–	–	–	–
Finland	–	–	–	–	–	–	–	–
France	–	–	–	0.2	–	–	–	0.2
Germany, Fed. Rep.	31.4	6.6	4.1	2.6	26.4	-1.2	-4.4	-5.0
Italy	–	–	–	–	–	–	–	–
Japan	–	–	–	–	-13.2	-14.3	-12.5	-2.6
Netherlands	–	–	–	–	–	–	–	–
New Zealand	0.4	–	–	–	0.2	–	–	–
Norway	–	–	–	–	–	–	–	–
Sweden	–	–	–	–	–	–	–	–
Switzerland	0.0	0.0	0.0	–	0.0	0.0	0.0	–
United Kingdom	–	–	–	–	–	–	–	–
United States	111.0	80.0	207.0	450.0	85.0	57.0	179.0	412.0
TOTAL	*142.8*	*87.0*	*211.6*	*453.6*	*98.4*	*42.0*	*162.7*	*405.3*
MULTILATERAL	*4.4*	*1.1*	–	–	*-18.5*	*-24.5*	*-23.9*	*-18.0*
OPEC COUNTRIES	*33.8*	*19.7*	*21.5*	*4.7*	*33.8*	*19.7*	*21.5*	*1.2*
E.E.C.+ MEMBERS	*31.4*	*6.6*	*4.1*	*2.7*	*26.4*	*-1.2*	*-4.4*	*-4.8*
TOTAL	***181.0***	***107.8***	***233.1***	***458.3***	***113.8***	***37.2***	***160.2***	***388.5***

	197
TOTAL ODA GROSS	
Australia	
Austria	0.
Belgium	
Canada	
Denmark	
Finland	
France	
Germany, Fed. Rep.	2.
Italy	
Japan	
Netherlands	
New Zealand	
Norway	
Sweden	
Switzerland	0.
United Kingdom	
United States	-3.
TOTAL	*-0.*
AF.D.F.	
AF.D.B.	
AS.D.B.	
CAR.D.B.	
E.E.C.	
IBRD	
IDA	
I.D.B.	
IFAD	
I.F.C.	
IMF TRUST FUND	
U.N. AGENCIES	
UNDP	
UNTA	
UNICEF	
UNRWA	
WFP	
UNHCR	
Other Multilateral	
Arab OPEC Agencies	
TOTAL	
OPEC COUNTRIES	*33.*
E.E.C.+ MEMBERS	*2.*
TOTAL	***32.***
GRANTS	
Australia	
Austria	0.
Belgium	
Canada	
Denmark	
Finland	
France	
Germany, Fed. Rep.	2.
Italy	
Japan	
Netherlands	
New Zealand	
Norway	
Sweden	
Switzerland	0.
United Kingdom	
United States	-3.
TOTAL	*-0.*
MULTILATERAL	
OPEC COUNTRIES	
E.E.C.+ MEMBERS	*2.*
TOTAL	***-0.***
TOTAL OOF GROSS	
Australia	
Austria	
Belgium	
Canada	
Denmark	
Finland	
France	
Germany, Fed. Rep.	29.
Italy	
Japan	
Netherlands	
New Zealand	0.
Norway	
Sweden	
Switzerland	
United Kingdom	
United States	114.
TOTAL	*143*
MULTILATERAL	*4*
OPEC COUNTRIES	
E.E.C.+ MEMBERS	*29*
TOTAL	***148***

ODA COMMITMENTS

1978	1979	1980	1977	1978	1979	1980
–	–	–	–	–	–	–
0.4	0.5	0.8	–	–	–	–
0.0	0.0	0.0	–	–	–	–
–	–	–	–	–	–	–
–	–	–	–	–	–	–
–	–	–	–	–	–	–
–	–	–	–	–	–	–
5.9	4.1	2.6	3.4	5.6	2.9	2.7
–	–	–	–	–	–	–
–	–	–	–	–	–	–
–	–	–	–	–	–	–
–	–	–	–	–	–	–
–	–	–	–	–	–	–
–	–	–	–	–	–	–
0.0	0.0	–	–	–	–	–
–	–	–	–	–	2.2	–
-3.0	-4.0	-3.0	–	–	–	–
3.4	*0.6*	*0.4*	*3.4*	*5.6*	*5.1*	*2.7*
–	–	–	–	–	–	–
–	–	–	–	–	–	–
–	–	–	–	–	–	–
–	–	–	–	–	–	–
–	–	–	–	–	–	–
–	–	–	–	–	–	–
–	–	–	–	–	–	–
–	–	–	–	–	–	–
–	–	–	–	–	–	–
–	–	–	–	–	–	–
–	–	–	–	–	–	–
–	–	–	–	0.9	12.6	–
0.0	–	–	–	–	–	–
0.9	–	–	–	–	–	–
–	–	–	–	–	–	–
–	–	–	–	–	–	–
–	–	–	–	–	–	–
–	–	–	–	–	–	–
–	–	–	–	–	–	–
–	–	–	–	–	–	–
0.9	–	–	–	*0.9*	*12.6*	–
19.7	*21.5*	*4.7*	–	*30.9*	–	*46.9*
6.0	*4.1*	*2.6*	*3.4*	*5.6*	*5.1*	*2.7*
23.9	***22.1***	***5.1***	***3.4***	***37.4***	***17.7***	***49.6***

TECH. COOP. GRANTS

1978	1979	1980	1977	1978	1979	1980
–	–	–	–	–	–	–
0.4	0.5	0.8	0.0	0.4	0.5	0.8
0.0	0.0	0.0	–	0.0	0.0	0.0
–	–	–	–	–	–	–
–	–	–	–	–	–	–
–	–	–	–	–	–	–
–	–	–	–	–	–	–
5.9	4.1	2.6	1.5	2.7	2.5	1.5
–	–	–	–	–	–	–
–	–	–	–	–	–	–
–	–	–	–	–	–	–
–	–	–	–	–	–	–
–	–	–	–	–	–	–
–	–	–	–	–	–	–
0.0	0.0	–	0.0	0.0	0.0	–
–	–	–	–	–	–	–
-3.0	-4.0	-3.0	–	–	–	6.0
3.4	*0.6*	*0.4*	*1.5*	*3.2*	*3.0*	*8.4*
0.9	–	–	–	*0.9*	–	–
–	–	*2.0*	–	–	–	–
6.0	*4.1*	*2.6*	*1.5*	*2.7*	*2.5*	*1.5*
4.2	***0.6***	***2.4***	***1.5***	***4.0***	***3.0***	***8.4***

TOTAL OOF NET

1978	1979	1980	1977	1978	1979	1980
–	–	–	–	–	–	–
–	–	–	–	–	–	–
–	–	–	–	–	–	–
–	–	–	–	–	–	–
–	–	–	–	–	–	–
–	–	–	–	–	–	–
–	–	0.2	–	–	–	0.2
0.6	–	–	24.4	-7.1	-8.5	-7.6
–	–	–	–	–	–	–
–	–	–	-2.2	-2.9	-2.7	-2.6
–	–	–	–	–	–	–
–	–	–	0.2	–	–	–
–	–	–	–	–	–	–
–	–	–	–	–	–	–
–	–	–	–	–	–	–
–	–	–	–	–	–	–
83.0	211.0	453.0	93.0	66.0	188.0	420.0
83.6	*211.0*	*453.2*	*115.3*	*56.0*	*176.8*	*409.9*
0.2	–	–	*-18.3*	*-25.2*	*-23.8*	*-17.8*
–	–	–	–	–	–	–
0.6	–	*0.2*	*24.4*	*-7.1*	*-8.5*	*-7.4*
83.8	***211.0***	***453.2***	***97.1***	***30.9***	***153.0***	***392.1***

MAIN AID AGGREGATES

	1977	1978	1979	1980
DAC COUNTRIES COMBINED				
PRIVATE SECTOR NET	-52.1	-17.6	259.3	50.4
Direct Investment	18.7	27.8	66.6	162.5
Portfolio Invest.	-54.2	8.1	95.4	-125.0
Export Credits	-16.6	-53.5	97.2	12.9
OFFICIAL & PRIVATE				
GROSS:				
Contractual Lending	363.9	298.3	557.5	728.1
Export Credits Tot.	363.9	298.3	557.5	727.9
Export Credits Priv	220.2	214.7	346.5	274.9
OTHER NET DATA				
Contractual Lending	82.7	-14.9	259.3	417.8
Export Credits Tot.	101.0	5.4	276.8	425.4
(Bank Sector Loans)	790.0	-52.0	-263.0	469.0
ODA CONCESSIONALITY				
Total:Grant Element	100.0	100.0	100.0	100.0
Loans:Grant Element	–	–	–	–
OTHER SOURCES				
CMEA Countr.(Gross)	–	–	–	–
Intra LDCS Exc.OPEC	–	–	–	–
Other	–	–	–	–
ALL SOURCE COMMITMENTS				
TOTAL BILATERAL	125.9	283.1	571.8	161.6
of which				
OPEC (ODA)	–	30.9	–	46.9
CMEA (ODA)	–	–	–	–
TOTAL MULTILAT.(ODA)	–	0.9	12.6	–
TOTAL BIL.& MULTIL.	125.9	284.0	584.4	161.6
of which				
ODA Grants	3.4	6.5	17.7	4.7
ODA Loans	–	30.9	–	44.9
ODA CONCESSIONALITY				
Total: Grant Element	100.0	44.0	100.0	38.0
Loans: Grant Element	–	32.0	–	32.0

INDEBTEDNESS

	1977	1978	1979	1980
TOTAL DEBT DISBURSED	***2954.7***	***3545.3***	***3926.6***	
Debt to DAC Countries	2626.0	3205.0	3500.0	
ODA	102.0	114.0	83.0	
Total Export Credits	1660.0	2047.0	2405.0	
Other Private Market	864.0	1044.0	1012.0	
International Org.	303.8	279.2	256.0	
CMEA	–	–	–	
Other	24.8	61.1	170.6	
TOTAL DEBT SERVICE	***567.3***	***862.5***	***951.1***	
Paid to DAC Countries	522.6	807.4	867.9	
ODA	23.2	25.9	22.3	
Total Export Credits	331.4	477.9	434.1	
Other Private Market	168.0	303.6	411.5	
International Org.	44.5	52.0	47.0	
CMEA	–	–	–	
Other	0.2	3.1	36.2	

ECONOMIC INDICATORS

	1977	1978	1979	1980
GNP Curr. Prices, $M	21363.2	26121.3	32304.2	40207.5
Real GNP, 1976=100	109.0	125.0	135.0	144.0
GNP/Cap Curr. Prices,$	1282.0	1538.0	1866.0	2278.0
GNP/cap Atlas Basis, $	1375.3	1649.3	1896.5	2162.6
Real GNP/Cap, 1976=100	107.0	120.0	127.0	133.0
Population, Million	16.7	17.0	17.3	17.6
Curr.A/C Deficit(-),$M	931.0	1677.0	103.0	–
BOP Exp. & Transf.,$M	10885.0	14447.0	18227.0	–
Exp. to OECD CIF, $M	6704.2	9568.4	11978.9	13671.9
of which				
Manufact.	5491.8	8114.3	10336.4	12001.3
Imp. from OECD FOB, $M	5025.8	6880.7	8917.3	10931.7
Reserves ex. Gold, $M	–	–	–	–

	1977	1978	1979	1980	1977	1978	1979	1980
	TOTAL RECEIPTS NET				**TOTAL ODA NET**			
DAC COUNTRIES								
Australia	1.6	2.8	2.2	5.6	1.6	2.8	2.2	5.6
Austria	0.2	0.2	0.4	13.7	0.2	0.2	0.4	2.9
Belgium	13.0	6.2	16.9	18.7	0.2	4.8	5.3	2.5
Canada	9.7	50.2	41.2	14.3	9.7	29.0	28.6	19.4
Denmark	35.1	38.1	50.1	37.1	35.0	37.6	39.7	32.2
Finland	8.9	9.9	13.2	19.9	8.9	9.9	13.2	17.7
France	6.5	7.0	0.7	13.5	–	–	–	7.0
Germany, Fed. Rep.	34.9	63.3	87.3	81.3	29.6	55.4	79.9	74.5
Italy	4.7	-5.8	27.3	32.1	-0.4	-0.2	-0.4	0.5
Japan	12.6	23.0	28.6	33.2	2.4	10.0	23.6	39.3
Netherlands	45.6	63.4	94.4	88.7	45.6	50.9	77.5	83.2
New Zealand	0.2	0.6	0.7	1.1	0.4	0.7	0.7	1.1
Norway	26.4	30.7	38.7	52.2	25.7	30.7	35.1	44.2
Sweden	57.4	64.2	105.2	87.2	57.4	64.2	93.4	78.1
Switzerland	0.7	1.5	3.1	13.9	0.7	2.0	3.1	14.0
United Kingdom	26.3	33.6	59.9	141.5	10.4	18.6	45.1	73.2
United States	30.0	14.0	22.0	28.0	30.0	16.0	10.0	28.0
TOTAL	*313.5*	*402.6*	*591.9*	*681.9*	*257.3*	*332.3*	*457.4*	*523.1*
MULTILATERAL								
AF.D.F.	1.5	0.6	4.7	8.0	1.5	0.6	4.7	8.0
AF.D.B.	1.2	1.1	1.5	1.3	–	–	–	–
AS.D.B.	–	–	–	–	–	–	–	–
CAR.D.B.	–	–	–	–	–	–	–	–
E.E.C.	10.6	19.9	29.2	25.1	10.6	19.9	29.2	25.1
IBRD	26.1	25.4	29.8	29.4	3.3	10.5	11.1	12.3
IDA	36.5	24.0	38.4	34.4	36.5	24.0	38.4	34.4
I.D.B.	–	–	–	–	–	–	–	–
IFAD	–	–	0.9	1.3	–	–	0.9	1.3
I.F.C.	–	–	–	2.6	–	–	–	–
IMF TRUST FUND	5.3	16.2	16.4	14.1	5.3	16.2	16.4	14.1
U.N. AGENCIES	–	–	–	–	–	–	–	–
UNDP	4.1	5.7	7.6	10.1	4.1	5.7	7.6	10.1
UNTA	0.5	1.1	0.8	0.5	0.5	1.1	0.8	0.5
UNICEF	2.2	4.7	5.0	4.0	2.2	4.7	5.0	4.0
UNRWA	–	–	–	–	–	–	–	–
WFP	1.7	1.0	5.3	3.7	1.7	1.0	5.3	3.7
UNHCR	2.5	3.3	4.0	6.2	2.5	3.3	4.0	6.2
Other Multilateral	1.9	2.7	2.8	3.8	1.9	2.7	2.8	3.8
Arab OPEC Agencies	5.9	7.0	2.7	4.7	5.9	1.1	1.2	4.1
TOTAL	*99.9*	*112.7*	*148.9*	*149.1*	*75.9*	*90.8*	*127.4*	*127.5*
OPEC COUNTRIES	*6.9*	*1.0*	*3.6*	*7.4*	*6.9*	*1.0*	*3.6*	*7.4*
E.E.C.+ MEMBERS	*176.6*	*225.7*	*365.8*	*437.9*	*131.0*	*186.9*	*276.3*	*298.1*
TOTAL	***420.4***	***516.3***	***744.4***	***838.4***	***340.1***	***424.1***	***588.3***	***658.0***
	ODA LOANS GROSS				**ODA LOANS NET**			
DAC COUNTRIES								
Australia	–	–	–	–	–	–	–	–
Austria	–	0.0	–	2.3	–	0.0	–	2.3
Belgium	–	4.0	3.4	0.9	–	4.0	3.4	0.9
Canada	2.4	–	–	–	2.4	-63.1	–	–
Denmark	28.4	18.5	20.9	9.6	28.1	17.9	-10.4	9.6
Finland	4.8	1.8	–	–	3.7	1.8	-20.5	–
France	–	–	–	5.4	–	–	–	5.4
Germany, Fed. Rep.	11.8	33.9	39.7	0.0	11.4	33.0	39.1	-134.5
Italy	–	–	–	–	-1.2	-1.3	-1.3	-1.3
Japan	–	7.4	10.2	26.8	-0.3	6.8	9.7	25.9
Netherlands	10.0	3.4	5.3	5.8	10.0	-40.7	1.3	1.7
New Zealand	–	–	–	–	–	–	–	–
Norway	–	–	–	–	–	–	–	–
Sweden	–	–	–	–	-0.3	-50.3	–	–
Switzerland	–	–	–	–	–	–	–	–
United Kingdom	–	–	–	–	-1.3	-1.2	-1.5	-1.3
United States	14.0	6.0	–	8.0	13.0	5.0	-1.0	7.0
TOTAL	*71.3*	*75.1*	*79.5*	*58.7*	*65.4*	*-88.0*	*18.8*	*-84.3*
MULTILATERAL	*55.4*	*54.8*	*79.5*	*77.9*	*52.5*	*54.5*	*79.0*	*77.2*
OPEC COUNTRIES	*6.9*	*1.0*	*3.6*	*7.8*	*6.9*	*1.0*	*3.6*	*7.4*
E.E.C.+ MEMBERS	*50.2*	*61.9*	*75.6*	*24.7*	*46.9*	*13.9*	*36.8*	*-116.5*
TOTAL	***133.6***	***130.9***	***162.6***	***144.4***	***124.7***	***-32.5***	***101.3***	***0.3***
	TOTAL OFFICIAL GROSS				**TOTAL OFFICIAL NET**			
DAC COUNTRIES								
Australia	1.6	2.8	2.2	5.6	1.6	2.8	2.2	5.6
Austria	0.2	0.2	0.4	2.9	0.2	0.2	0.4	2.9
Belgium	0.2	4.8	5.3	2.5	0.2	4.8	5.3	2.5
Canada	9.7	113.4	41.2	20.1	9.7	50.2	41.2	14.3
Denmark	35.5	38.2	71.0	32.2	35.1	37.6	39.7	32.2
Finland	10.0	9.9	33.8	17.7	8.9	9.9	13.2	17.7
France	–	–	–	7.0	–	–	–	7.0
Germany, Fed. Rep.	30.7	56.9	80.5	216.7	30.3	56.0	79.8	81.3
Italy	0.9	1.6	1.0	6.3	-1.4	-0.5	-1.2	4.2
Japan	2.7	10.6	24.0	40.2	2.4	10.0	23.6	39.3
Netherlands	45.6	94.9	81.9	87.8	45.6	50.9	77.9	83.7
New Zealand	0.5	0.7	0.7	1.1	0.2	0.7	0.7	1.1
Norway	26.6	30.7	35.1	44.2	26.6	30.7	35.1	44.2
Sweden	57.7	114.4	93.4	78.1	57.4	64.2	93.4	78.1
Switzerland	0.7	2.0	3.1	14.0	0.7	2.0	3.1	14.0
United Kingdom	11.7	19.9	51.1	74.7	10.4	18.7	49.6	73.4
United States	31.0	17.0	23.0	29.0	30.0	14.0	22.0	28.0
TOTAL	*265.3*	*517.9*	*547.7*	*679.9*	*257.8*	*352.0*	*486.0*	*529.3*
MULTILATERAL	*104.7*	*115.7*	*153.6*	*155.5*	*99.9*	*112.7*	*148.9*	*149.1*
OPEC COUNTRIES	*6.9*	*1.0*	*3.6*	*7.8*	*6.9*	*1.0*	*3.6*	*7.4*
E.E.C.+ MEMBERS	*135.2*	*236.2*	*320.0*	*452.3*	*130.9*	*187.4*	*280.3*	*309.4*
TOTAL	***376.9***	***634.6***	***704.8***	***843.1***	***364.7***	***465.7***	***638.5***	***685.8***

	197
TOTAL ODA GROSS	
Australia	1.
Austria	0.
Belgium	0.
Canada	9.
Denmark	35.
Finland	10.
France	
Germany, Fed. Rep.	30.
Italy	0.
Japan	2.
Netherlands	45.
New Zealand	0.
Norway	25.
Sweden	57.
Switzerland	0.
United Kingdom	11.
United States	31.
TOTAL	*263.*
AF.D.F.	1.
AF.D.B.	
AS.D.B.	
CAR.D.B.	
E.E.C.	10.
IBRD	3.
IDA	39
I.D.B.	
IFAD	
I.F.C.	
IMF TRUST FUND	5.
U.N. AGENCIES	
UNDP	4.
UNTA	0.
UNICEF	2.
UNRWA	
WFP	1.
UNHCR	2.
Other Multilateral	1.
Arab OPEC Agencies	5.
TOTAL	*78.*
OPEC COUNTRIES	*6.*
E.E.C.+ MEMBERS	*134.*
TOTAL	***349.***
GRANTS	
Australia	1
Austria	0.
Belgium	0.
Canada	7.
Denmark	6.
Finland	5.
France	
Germany, Fed. Rep.	18
Italy	0.
Japan	2.
Netherlands	35.
New Zealand	0
Norway	25
Sweden	57
Switzerland	0
United Kingdom	11
United States	17.
TOTAL	*191*
MULTILATERAL	*23*
OPEC COUNTRIES	
E.E.C.+ MEMBERS	*84*
TOTAL	***215***
TOTAL OOF GROSS	
Australia	
Austria	
Belgium	
Canada	
Denmark	0
Finland	
France	
Germany, Fed. Rep.	0
Italy	0
Japan	
Netherlands	
New Zealand	0
Norway	0
Sweden	
Switzerland	
United Kingdom	
United States	
TOTAL	*2.*
MULTILATERAL	*25.*
OPEC COUNTRIES	
E.E.C.+ MEMBERS	*1.*
TOTAL	***27***

1978	1979	1980	1977	1978	1979	1980
			ODA COMMITMENTS			
2.8	2.2	5.6	2.8	3.5	4.3	8.8
0.2	0.4	2.9	–	0.3	0.2	0.0
4.8	5.3	2.5	2.1	1.6	6.6	6.3
92.1	28.6	19.4	92.4	110.0	47.2	9.1
38.2	71.0	32.2	28.2	78.8	66.9	41.7
9.9	33.8	17.7	8.7	7.5	35.6	31.4
–	–	7.0	–	–	11.8	8.1
56.3	80.5	209.0	36.4	62.0	78.8	267.4
1.1	1.0	1.8	0.8	1.1	1.0	2.3
10.6	24.0	40.2	3.8	23.6	27.6	66.4
94.9	81.5	87.3	71.2	123.8	76.1	107.0
0.7	0.7	1.1	0.3	0.8	0.4	1.7
30.7	35.1	44.2	19.7	10.1	48.4	31.6
114.4	93.4	78.1	181.6	72.2	185.9	16.6
2.0	3.1	14.0	0.1	6.1	1.7	12.9
19.8	46.5	74.5	8.4	69.5	117.1	30.6
17.0	11.0	29.0	24.9	20.0	23.9	32.5
495.4	*518.1*	*666.2*	*481.3*	*590.9*	*733.2*	*674.3*
0.6	4.7	8.0	8.9	14.6	9.7	13.4
–	–	–	–	–	–	–
–	–	–	–	–	–	–
–	–	–	–	–	–	–
19.9	29.2	25.1	62.5	21.5	25.8	25.1
10.5	11.1	12.3	11.5	–	–	–
24.4	39.0	35.0	49.2	99.5	53.0	149.3
–	–	–	–	–	–	–
–	0.9	1.3	–	12.0	–	–
–	–	–	–	–	–	–
16.2	16.4	14.1	–	–	–	–
–	–	–	12.8	18.5	25.5	28.3
5.7	7.6	10.1	–	–	–	–
1.1	0.8	0.5	–	–	–	–
4.7	5.0	4.0	–	–	–	–
–	–	–	–	–	–	–
1.0	5.3	3.7	–	–	–	–
3.3	4.0	6.2	–	–	–	–
2.7	2.8	3.8	–	–	–	–
1.1	1.2	4.1	5.5	5.1	–	10.0
91.1	*127.9*	*128.1*	*150.4*	*171.2*	*114.0*	*226.1*
1.0	*3.6*	*7.8*	*6.1*	–	*30.0*	*38.0*
234.9	*315.0*	*439.3*	*209.6*	*358.3*	*383.9*	*488.5*
587.5	***649.6***	***802.1***	***637.8***	***762.1***	***877.2***	***938.3***
			TECH. COOP. GRANTS			
2.8	2.2	5.6	0.5	0.5	0.3	0.5
0.2	0.4	0.6	0.2	0.2	0.4	0.6
0.8	1.9	1.6	0.2	0.3	0.2	0.5
92.1	28.6	19.4	1.6	1.6	1.5	2.4
19.7	50.1	22.6	3.9	6.4	12.2	19.0
8.0	33.8	17.7	5.2	6.7	11.3	9.3
–	–	1.6	–	–	–	0.8
22.4	40.8	209.0	17.3	21.1	27.2	28.0
1.1	1.0	1.8	0.8	1.1	1.0	0.5
3.2	13.8	13.3	2.7	2.4	2.9	3.1
91.5	76.2	81.5	11.6	16.7	19.5	19.6
0.7	0.7	1.1	0.4	–	0.5	0.3
30.7	35.1	44.2	10.6	11.2	10.4	12.3
114.4	93.4	78.1	5.7	5.8	8.1	18.2
2.0	3.1	14.0	0.3	0.5	0.6	1.6
19.8	46.5	74.5	4.2	7.1	15.0	20.4
11.0	11.0	21.0	4.0	7.0	7.0	11.0
420.3	*438.6*	*607.4*	*69.0*	*88.6*	*118.0*	*148.0*
36.3	*48.4*	*50.3*	*11.1*	*17.5*	*20.2*	*28.3*
–	–	–	–	–	–	–
173.0	*239.4*	*414.6*	*37.9*	*52.7*	*75.0*	*88.7*
456.6	***487.0***	***657.7***	***80.2***	***106.0***	***138.2***	***176.2***
			TOTAL OOF NET			
–	–	–	–	–	–	–
–	–	–	–	–	–	–
–	–	–	–	–	–	–
21.2	12.6	0.7	–	21.2	12.6	-5.1
–	–	0.0	0.1	0.0	–	0.0
–	–	–	–	–	–	–
–	–	–	–	–	–	–
0.6	0.0	7.7	0.7	0.6	-0.1	6.8
0.5	–	4.6	-1.0	-0.3	-0.8	3.7
–	–	–	–	–	–	–
–	0.5	0.5	–	–	0.5	0.5
–	–	–	-0.2	–	–	–
–	–	–	0.9	–	–	–
–	–	–	–	–	–	–
–	–	–	–	–	–	–
0.1	4.6	0.2	–	0.1	4.6	0.2
–	12.0	–	–	-2.0	12.0	–
22.5	*29.6*	*13.7*	*0.6*	*19.7*	*28.6*	*6.2*
24.6	*25.7*	*27.4*	*24.0*	*21.9*	*21.6*	*21.6*
–	–	–	–	–	–	–
1.3	*5.0*	*13.0*	*-0.2*	*0.4*	*4.1*	*11.3*
47.1	***55.2***	***41.0***	***24.5***	***41.6***	***50.2***	***27.8***

	1977	1978	1979	1980
MAIN AID AGGREGATES				
DAC COUNTRIES COMBINED				
PRIVATE SECTOR NET	55.7	50.7	105.9	152.6
Direct Investment	2.9	6.1	8.0	-0.4
Portfolio Invest.	-0.2	1.3	-0.7	5.0
Export Credits	53.0	43.3	98.6	148.0
OFFICIAL & PRIVATE				
GROSS:				
Contractual Lending	156.9	168.2	247.3	262.8
Export Credits Tot.	83.7	92.4	162.8	195.6
Export Credits Priv	83.6	70.6	138.3	190.3
OTHER NET DATA				
Contractual Lending	118.9	-25.1	146.0	69.9
Export Credits Tot.	52.8	62.2	122.3	146.7
(Bank Sector Loans)	3.0	49.0	36.0	-8.0
ODA CONCESSIONALITY				
Total:Grant Element	97.0	97.0	98.0	96.0
Loans:Grant Element	81.0	77.0	76.0	72.0
OTHER SOURCES				
CMEA Countr.(Gross)	2.5	3.5	1.2	0.2
Intra LDCS Exc.OPEC	–	–	–	–
Other	–	–	–	–
ALL SOURCE COMMITMENTS				
TOTAL BILATERAL	487.7	633.5	799.4	731.4
of which				
OPEC (ODA)	6.1	–	30.0	38.0
CMEA (ODA)	19.0	10.2	–	–
TOTAL MULTILAT.(ODA)	150.4	171.2	114.0	226.1
TOTAL BIL.& MULTIL.	638.1	804.7	913.4	957.5
of which				
ODA Grants	472.6	553.5	722.7	623.9
ODA Loans	165.3	208.6	154.5	314.4
ODA CONCESSIONALITY				
Total: Grant Element	94.0	95.0	94.0	90.0
Loans: Grant Element	75.0	79.0	72.0	65.0
INDEBTEDNESS				
TOTAL DEBT DISBURSED	***1176.1***	***1275.8***	***1487.2***	
Debt to DAC Countries	566.0	602.0	727.0	
ODA	412.0	352.0	367.0	
Total Export Credits	130.0	219.0	333.0	
Other Private Market	24.0	31.0	27.0	
International Org.	286.7	346.1	420.1	
CMEA	314.3	317.3	320.1	
Other	9.2	10.4	20.0	
TOTAL DEBT SERVICE	***45.0***	***51.4***	***100.1***	
Paid to DAC Countries	29.7	34.4	77.7	
ODA	8.7	10.5	8.1	
Total Export Credits	19.1	21.4	68.0	
Other Private Market	1.9	2.5	1.6	
International Org.	14.1	15.6	20.2	
CMEA	0.9	0.9	1.2	
Other	0.3	0.5	0.9	

ECONOMIC INDICATORS

	1977	1978	1979	1980
GNP Curr. Prices, $M	3422.9	4107.0	4243.4	4863.6
Real GNP, 1976=100	104.0	108.0	111.0	110.0
GNP/Cap Curr. Prices,$	208.0	242.0	241.0	268.0
GNP/cap Atlas Basis, $	218.4	235.5	252.7	263.7
Real GNP/Cap, 1976=100	101.0	101.0	100.0	96.0
Population, Million	16.4	17.0	17.5	18.1
Curr.A/C Deficit(-),$M	-167.7	-619.5	-489.8	-655.9
BOP Exp. & Transf.,$M	677.8	651.1	723.8	730.2
Exp. to OECD CIF, $M	394.8	389.8	396.0	372.5
of which				
Manufact.	15.7	20.2	35.9	41.2
Imp. from OECD FOB, $M	501.6	806.5	733.8	853.7
Reserves ex. Gold, $M	281.8	99.9	68.0	20.3

	1977	1978	1979	1980	1977	1978	1979	1980
	TOTAL RECEIPTS NET				**TOTAL ODA NET**			
DAC COUNTRIES								
Australia	7.5	12.0	15.6	11.3	7.9	12.4	11.6	8.7
Austria	-2.0	30.7	-1.4	-1.9	0.2	8.1	0.6	0.1
Belgium	-4.9	-4.6	-2.8	7.0	0.2	0.5	0.4	1.9
Canada	-0.4	7.9	8.5	11.3	0.3	0.9	5.3	8.0
Denmark	-4.5	68.6	8.4	33.7	1.4	0.8	12.3	0.7
Finland	0.0	0.0	0.2	0.2	0.0	0.0	0.2	0.2
France	-6.0	-3.9	81.4	1.0	–	–	5.8	3.5
Germany, Fed. Rep.	40.5	58.7	89.5	115.8	6.8	6.1	42.5	56.1
Italy	-0.6	0.4	-21.0	5.5	0.0	0.1	0.8	2.0
Japan	72.0	228.7	338.8	274.7	51.8	103.8	179.9	189.6
Netherlands	2.2	1.8	4.3	29.0	2.2	1.8	4.3	3.8
New Zealand	2.5	2.7	1.7	2.2	2.2	1.9	1.7	2.2
Norway	0.3	1.1	1.5	1.4	0.3	1.1	1.5	1.5
Sweden	-0.1	-0.1	2.3	21.0	–	–	0.5	–
Switzerland	-1.6	-2.6	5.4	7.5	0.3	0.5	1.3	3.1
United Kingdom	26.5	11.3	9.0	70.5	2.0	2.4	3.9	7.7
United States	29.0	4.0	143.0	190.0	8.0	9.0	7.0	16.0
TOTAL	*160.3*	*416.7*	*684.2*	*780.2*	*83.6*	*149.2*	*279.3*	*305.0*
MULTILATERAL								
AF.D.F.	–	–	–	–	–	–	–	–
AF.D.B.	–	–	–	–	–	–	–	–
AS.D.B.	30.9	44.2	30.2	76.0	0.8	3.0	2.7	1.8
CAR.D.B.	–	–	–	–	–	–	–	–
E.E.C.	0.1	0.3	0.9	2.1	0.1	0.3	0.9	2.1
IBRD	47.0	86.8	119.0	117.2	1.7	7.4	4.7	2.5
IDA	8.8	5.1	3.5	4.1	8.8	5.1	3.5	4.1
I.D.B.	–	–	–	–	–	–	–	–
IFAD	–	–	0.3	0.3	–	–	0.3	0.3
I.F.C.	-0.3	-5.1	7.1	30.0	–	–	–	–
IMF TRUST FUND	16.7	51.6	52.5	44.7	16.7	51.6	52.5	44.7
U.N. AGENCIES	–	–	–	–	–	–	–	–
UNDP	2.4	3.2	4.5	8.6	2.4	3.2	4.5	8.6
UNTA	1.5	1.7	1.5	0.3	1.5	1.7	1.5	0.3
UNICEF	1.2	2.3	3.2	2.9	1.2	2.3	3.2	2.9
UNRWA	–	–	–	–	–	–	–	–
WFP	–	1.6	3.1	0.0	–	1.6	3.1	0.0
UNHCR	13.5	31.6	31.1	31.2	13.5	31.6	31.1	31.2
Other Multilateral	1.9	1.4	1.5	3.6	1.9	1.4	1.5	3.6
Arab OPEC Agencies	–	–	0.6	1.3	–	–	0.6	1.3
TOTAL	*123.8*	*224.8*	*259.0*	*322.2*	*48.8*	*109.2*	*110.2*	*103.4*
OPEC COUNTRIES	*0.3*	*1.8*	*3.1*	*10.1*	*0.3*	*1.8*	*3.1*	*10.1*
E.E.C.+ MEMBERS	*53.1*	*132.5*	*169.7*	*264.7*	*12.7*	*11.9*	*70.7*	*77.7*
TOTAL	***284.4***	***643.3***	***946.3***	***1112.5***	***132.6***	***260.2***	***392.6***	***418.4***

	1977	1978	1979	1980	1977	1978	1979	1980
	ODA LOANS GROSS				**ODA LOANS NET**			
DAC COUNTRIES								
Australia	–	–	–	–	–	–	–	–
Austria	–	8.0	0.5	–	–	8.0	0.5	–
Belgium	–	–	–	–	–	–	–	–
Canada	–	0.6	5.1	7.7	0.0	0.5	5.0	7.7
Denmark	0.6	0.4	11.5	–	0.6	0.4	11.3	-0.2
Finland	–	–	–	–	–	–	–	–
France	–	–	5.8	1.2	–	–	5.8	1.2
Germany, Fed. Rep.	4.8	3.1	23.3	49.0	-0.4	-2.8	16.6	42.9
Italy	–	–	–	–	–	–	–	–
Japan	43.1	86.5	145.3	126.6	36.5	77.6	136.9	119.3
Netherlands	–	–	–	–	–	–	–	–
New Zealand	–	–	–	–	–	–	–	–
Norway	–	–	–	–	–	–	–	–
Sweden	–	–	–	–	–	–	–	–
Switzerland	–	–	–	1.2	–	–	–	1.2
United Kingdom	0.9	1.1	1.7	3.0	0.9	1.1	1.7	3.0
United States	3.0	4.0	2.0	2.0	3.0	3.0	1.0	1.0
TOTAL	*52.3*	*103.7*	*195.0*	*190.6*	*40.5*	*87.9*	*178.6*	*175.9*
MULTILATERAL	*27.5*	*67.1*	*64.4*	*54.4*	*27.5*	*67.1*	*64.3*	*54.1*
OPEC COUNTRIES	*0.3*	*1.8*	*3.1*	*10.1*	*0.3*	*1.8*	*3.1*	*10.1*
E.E.C.+ MEMBERS	*6.2*	*4.7*	*42.2*	*53.2*	*1.0*	*-1.2*	*35.3*	*46.8*
TOTAL	***80.1***	***172.5***	***262.5***	***255.1***	***68.3***	***156.7***	***246.0***	***240.1***

	1977	1978	1979	1980	1977	1978	1979	1980
	TOTAL OFFICIAL GROSS				**TOTAL OFFICIAL NET**			
DAC COUNTRIES								
Australia	7.9	12.4	11.6	8.7	7.9	12.4	11.6	8.7
Austria	0.2	8.1	0.6	0.1	-1.3	7.0	-0.6	-1.1
Belgium	0.2	0.5	0.4	1.9	0.2	0.5	0.4	1.9
Canada	0.3	10.8	9.5	12.0	0.3	10.8	8.5	11.1
Denmark	1.4	0.8	12.6	1.5	1.4	0.8	12.3	1.3
Finland	0.0	0.0	0.2	0.2	0.0	0.0	0.2	0.2
France	–	–	5.8	3.5	–	–	5.8	3.5
Germany, Fed. Rep.	20.0	21.9	57.8	62.6	11.6	11.7	48.0	53.1
Italy	0.0	0.1	0.8	2.0	0.0	0.1	0.8	2.0
Japan	59.4	127.2	188.8	275.8	52.8	118.3	180.4	266.9
Netherlands	2.2	1.8	4.3	3.8	2.2	1.8	4.3	3.8
New Zealand	2.7	1.9	1.7	2.2	2.5	1.9	1.7	2.2
Norway	0.3	1.1	1.5	1.5	0.3	1.1	1.5	1.5
Sweden	–	–	0.5	–	–	–	0.5	–
Switzerland	0.3	0.5	1.3	3.1	0.3	0.5	1.3	3.1
United Kingdom	2.4	2.5	10.7	11.0	2.3	2.4	10.5	10.8
United States	54.0	18.0	97.0	45.0	49.0	12.0	89.0	30.0
TOTAL	*151.4*	*207.5*	*404.8*	*434.9*	*129.4*	*181.1*	*376.0*	*398.9*
MULTILATERAL	*150.8*	*262.6*	*292.2*	*360.5*	*123.8*	*224.8*	*259.0*	*322.2*
OPEC COUNTRIES	*0.3*	*1.8*	*3.1*	*10.1*	*0.3*	*1.8*	*3.1*	*10.1*
E.E.C.+ MEMBERS	*26.3*	*27.9*	*93.1*	*88.4*	*17.8*	*17.5*	*82.8*	*78.5*
TOTAL	***302.4***	***471.9***	***700.1***	***805.6***	***253.5***	***407.6***	***638.0***	***731.2***

	197
TOTAL ODA GROSS	
Australia	7.
Austria	0.
Belgium	0.
Canada	0.
Denmark	1.
Finland	0.
France	
Germany, Fed. Rep.	12.
Italy	0.
Japan	58.
Netherlands	2.
New Zealand	2.
Norway	0.
Sweden	
Switzerland	0.
United Kingdom	2.
United States	8.
TOTAL	*95.*
AF.D.F.	
AF.D.B.	
AS.D.B.	0.
CAR.D.B.	
E.E.C.	0.
IBRD	1.
IDA	8.
I.D.B.	
IFAD	
I.F.C.	
IMF TRUST FUND	16.
U.N. AGENCIES	
UNDP	2.
UNTA	1.
UNICEF	1.
UNRWA	
WFP	
UNHCR	13.
Other Multilateral	1.
Arab OPEC Agencies	
TOTAL	*48.*
OPEC COUNTRIES	*0.*
E.E.C.+ MEMBERS	*17.*
TOTAL	***144.***
GRANTS	
Australia	7
Austria	0
Belgium	0
Canada	0
Denmark	0
Finland	0
France	
Germany, Fed. Rep.	7
Italy	0.
Japan	15
Netherlands	2
New Zealand	2
Norway	0
Sweden	
Switzerland	0
United Kingdom	1
United States	5
TOTAL	*43*
MULTILATERAL	*21*
OPEC COUNTRIES	
E.E.C.+ MEMBERS	*11*
TOTAL	***64***
TOTAL OOF GROSS	
Australia	
Austria	
Belgium	
Canada	
Denmark	
Finland	
France	
Germany, Fed. Rep.	8
Italy	
Japan	1
Netherlands	
New Zealand	0
Norway	
Sweden	
Switzerland	
United Kingdom	0
United States	46
TOTAL	*56*
MULTILATERAL	*102*
OPEC COUNTRIES	
E.E.C.+ MEMBERS	*8*
TOTAL	***158***

1978	1979	1980	1977	1978	1979	1980
			ODA COMMITMENTS			
12.4	11.6	8.7	14.0	10.4	2.3	9.9
8.1	0.6	0.1	–	8.3	0.5	0.0
0.5	0.4	1.9	–	–	–	2.4
0.9	5.3	8.0	0.3	15.4	0.2	2.0
0.8	12.6	0.9	0.7	1.8	11.7	0.6
0.0	0.2	0.2	–	0.1	0.0	0.4
–	5.8	3.5	–	–	6.2	5.9
11.9	49.2	62.3	17.6	11.0	156.5	22.8
0.1	0.8	2.0	0.0	0.1	0.8	2.0
112.7	188.3	196.9	150.0	223.3	292.2	286.3
1.8	4.3	3.8	3.3	2.1	5.8	7.9
1.9	1.7	2.2	0.5	0.8	2.0	1.0
1.1	1.5	1.5	0.3	3.5	0.3	2.9
–	0.5	–	–	–	–	–
0.5	1.3	3.1	0.2	0.9	8.3	1.3
2.4	3.9	7.7	1.1	1.3	–	4.7
10.0	8.0	17.0	12.9	8.7	26.4	32.9
165.0	*295.7*	*319.6*	*200.9*	*287.6*	*513.2*	*382.8*
–	–	–	–	–	–	–
–	–	–	–	–	–	–
3.0	2.7	1.8	–	14.5	15.3	20.0
–	–	–	–	–	–	–
0.3	0.9	2.1	0.2	3.5	8.6	21.5
7.4	4.7	2.5	–	–	–	–
5.1	3.6	4.4	–	33.1	60.0	–
–	–	–	–	–	–	–
–	0.3	0.3	–	17.5	–	14.5
–	–	–	–	–	–	–
51.6	52.5	44.7	–	–	–	–
–	–	–	20.5	41.9	45.0	46.6
3.2	4.5	8.6	–	–	–	–
1.7	1.5	0.3	–	–	–	–
2.3	3.2	2.9	–	–	–	–
–	–	–	–	–	–	–
1.6	3.1	0.0	–	–	–	–
31.6	31.1	31.2	–	–	–	–
1.4	1.5	3.6	–	–	–	–
–	0.6	1.3	7.0	–	7.0	8.0
109.2	*110.2*	*103.7*	*27.8*	*110.5*	*135.9*	*110.6*
1.8	*3.1*	*10.1*	*20.9*	–	*21.7*	–
17.7	*77.7*	*84.1*	*22.9*	*19.8*	*189.6*	*67.7*
276.0	***409.0***	***433.4***	***249.6***	***398.1***	***670.8***	***493.4***
			TECH. COOP. GRANTS			
12.4	11.6	8.7	3.1	4.4	4.6	3.3
0.1	0.2	0.1	0.2	0.1	0.2	0.1
0.5	0.4	1.9	0.2	0.3	0.4	0.5
0.4	0.3	0.3	0.2	0.1	0.2	0.1
0.4	1.0	0.9	0.5	0.4	0.9	0.9
0.0	0.2	0.2	0.0	0.0	0.2	0.1
–	–	2.3	–	–	–	2.3
8.9	25.9	13.2	7.0	8.3	9.2	13.1
0.1	0.8	2.0	0.0	0.1	0.1	0.1
26.1	43.0	70.2	11.1	20.0	20.1	26.2
1.8	4.3	3.8	1.8	1.5	2.3	3.3
1.9	1.7	2.2	1.6	1.7	1.4	1.3
1.1	1.5	1.5	0.3	0.2	0.3	0.3
–	0.5	–	–	–	–	–
0.5	1.3	1.9	0.1	0.1	0.4	0.3
1.3	2.2	4.7	1.1	1.3	2.1	4.7
6.0	6.0	15.0	4.0	4.0	4.0	–
61.3	*100.7*	*129.0*	*31.2*	*42.3*	*46.2*	*56.6*
42.2	*45.9*	*49.3*	*21.1*	*40.3*	*41.9*	*46.6*
–	–	–	–	–	–	–
13.1	*35.5*	*31.0*	*10.6*	*11.8*	*15.0*	*24.9*
103.5	***146.6***	***178.3***	***52.3***	***82.6***	***88.1***	***103.2***
			TOTAL OOF NET			
–	0.0	–	–	–	0.0	–
–	–	–	-1.5	-1.1	-1.2	-1.2
–	–	–	–	–	–	–
9.9	4.2	4.0	–	9.9	3.2	3.1
–	0.0	0.6	–	–	–	0.6
–	–	–	–	–	–	–
–	–	–	–	–	–	–
10.0	8.6	0.4	4.8	5.6	5.4	-3.0
–	–	–	–	–	–	–
14.5	0.5	79.0	1.0	14.5	0.5	77.3
–	–	–	–	–	–	–
–	–	–	0.3	–	–	–
–	–	–	–	–	–	–
–	–	–	–	–	–	–
–	–	–	–	–	–	–
0.1	6.8	3.4	0.3	0.0	6.6	3.2
8.0	89.0	28.0	41.0	3.0	82.0	14.0
42.5	*109.0*	*115.3*	*45.8*	*31.9*	*96.6*	*93.9*
153.4	*182.0*	*256.9*	*75.1*	*115.5*	*148.8*	*218.9*
–	–	–	–	–	–	–
10.1	*15.4*	*4.3*	*5.1*	*5.6*	*12.1*	*0.8*
195.9	***291.1***	***372.2***	***120.9***	***147.4***	***245.4***	***312.8***

	1977	1978	1979	1980
MAIN AID AGGREGATES				
DAC COUNTRIES COMBINED				
PRIVATE SECTOR NET	30.8	235.6	308.3	381.3
Direct Investment	42.4	38.4	38.1	216.9
Portfolio Invest.	-9.1	125.3	205.2	34.5
Export Credits	-2.5	72.0	64.9	129.9
OFFICIAL & PRIVATE				
GROSS:				
Contractual Lending	212.9	354.5	498.4	583.3
Export Credits Tot.	155.2	249.7	295.5	387.3
Export Credits Priv	104.6	208.3	194.3	277.4
OTHER NET DATA				
Contractual Lending	83.8	191.8	340.1	399.8
Export Credits Tot.	39.1	103.3	154.0	218.8
(Bank Sector Loans)	90.0	206.0	399.0	245.0
ODA CONCESSIONALITY				
Total:Grant Element	64.0	65.0	65.0	73.0
Loans:Grant Element	51.0	52.0	54.0	57.0
OTHER SOURCES				
CMEA Countr.(Gross)	–	–	–	–
Intra LDCS Exc.OPEC	–	–	–	–
Other	–	–	–	–
ALL SOURCE COMMITMENTS				
TOTAL BILATERAL	269.9	321.6	738.0	467.9
of which				
OPEC (ODA)	20.9	–	21.7	–
CMEA (ODA)	–	–	–	–
TOTAL MULTILAT.(ODA)	27.8	110.5	135.9	110.6
TOTAL BIL.& MULTIL.	297.6	432.1	873.8	578.5
of which				
ODA Grants	73.9	122.5	176.6	213.4
ODA Loans	175.8	275.7	494.2	280.0
ODA CONCESSIONALITY				
Total: Grant Element	65.0	70.0	69.0	75.0
Loans: Grant Element	50.0	57.0	57.0	57.0
INDEBTEDNESS				
TOTAL DEBT DISBURSED	***1814.6***	***2580.5***	***3712.8***	
Debt to DAC Countries	1211.0	1937.0	2912.0	
ODA	297.0	468.0	574.0	
Total Export Credits	414.0	479.0	824.0	
Other Private Market	500.0	990.0	1514.0	
International Org.	502.7	640.9	796.5	
CMEA	–	–	–	
Other	100.9	2.5	4.3	
TOTAL DEBT SERVICE	***551.0***	***754.7***	***1007.0***	
Paid to DAC Countries	444.3	680.6	881.5	
ODA	20.9	28.1	32.0	
Total Export Credits	148.4	168.1	222.1	
Other Private Market	275.0	484.4	627.4	
International Org.	56.4	73.8	95.2	
CMEA	–	–	–	
Other	50.2	0.3	30.3	
ECONOMIC INDICATORS				
GNP Curr. Prices, $M	19166.7	22841.3	26759.4	32198.7
Real GNP, 1976=100	106.0	116.0	122.0	129.0
GNP/Cap Curr. Prices,$	440.0	513.0	588.0	693.0
GNP/cap Atlas Basis, $	466.4	533.8	595.2	670.3
Real GNP/Cap, 1976=100	104.0	111.0	114.0	118.0
Population, Million	43.5	44.5	45.5	46.5
Curr.A/C Deficit(-),$M	-1122.0	-1191.0	-2130.0	-2422.0
BOP Exp. & Transf.,$M	4200.0	5135.0	6684.0	8441.0
Exp. to OECD CIF, $M	2091.9	2652.0	3478.5	4064.1
of which				
Manufact.	383.9	547.9	733.8	859.9
Imp. from OECD FOB, $M	2712.3	3102.6	3994.9	4526.4
Reserves ex. Gold, $M	1813.0	2009.0	1843.0	1560.0

	TOTAL RECEIPTS NET 1977	1978	1979	1980	TOTAL ODA NET 1977	1978	1979	1980
DAC COUNTRIES								
Australia	–	–	–	–	–	–	–	–
Austria	3.0	0.7	-1.4	-0.5	–	1.1	0.0	0.0
Belgium	27.6	54.8	1.2	0.2	0.5	0.3	0.4	0.4
Canada	1.5	4.6	8.0	0.6	1.5	4.6	8.0	0.6
Denmark	0.8	1.6	8.9	8.3	0.8	1.6	8.9	7.1
Finland	–	–	–	0.0	–	–	–	0.0
France	42.4	89.0	72.7	92.2	13.3	17.3	17.7	21.6
Germany, Fed. Rep.	20.8	47.2	34.5	17.8	22.5	38.9	27.6	17.2
Italy	-0.3	0.6	9.2	0.2	0.1	0.0	0.1	0.0
Japan	0.1	0.2	0.0	1.3	0.1	0.2	0.0	1.3
Netherlands	0.4	1.2	0.9	0.5	0.4	1.2	0.9	0.5
New Zealand	–	–	–	–	–	–	–	–
Norway	0.1	0.2	–	0.0	0.1	0.2	–	–
Sweden	–	-0.1	-0.6	-1.2	–	–	–	–
Switzerland	0.1	0.3	7.3	-1.0	0.1	0.3	0.1	0.2
United Kingdom	-2.4	0.3	-5.7	-11.1	0.1	0.1	0.1	0.2
United States	3.0	1.0	6.0	3.0	3.0	1.0	5.0	3.0
TOTAL	*97.0*	*201.3*	*141.0*	*110.2*	*42.4*	*66.5*	*68.9*	*52.1*
MULTILATERAL								
AF.D.F.	2.8	1.9	6.2	4.8	2.8	1.9	6.2	4.8
AF.D.B.	1.8	5.6	0.0	1.7	–	–	–	–
AS.D.B.	–	–	–	–	–	–	–	–
CAR.D.B.	–	–	–	–	–	–	–	–
E.E.C.	6.9	22.8	27.0	20.0	6.9	14.1	17.6	7.6
IBRD	–	15.6	19.7	17.7	–	–	–	–
IDA	5.7	6.8	7.5	12.5	5.7	6.8	7.5	12.5
I.D.B.	–	–	–	–	–	–	–	–
IFAD	–	–	–	–	–	–	–	–
I.F.C.	–	–	–	–	–	–	–	–
IMF TRUST FUND	–	7.8	6.0	5.0	–	7.8	6.0	5.0
U.N. AGENCIES	–	–	–	–	–	–	–	–
UNDP	1.3	2.2	2.0	3.1	1.3	2.2	2.0	3.1
UNTA	0.5	0.4	0.4	0.1	0.5	0.4	0.4	0.1
UNICEF	0.1	0.2	0.4	0.3	0.1	0.2	0.4	0.3
UNRWA	–	–	–	–	–	–	–	–
WFP	4.2	2.0	0.5	1.2	4.2	2.0	0.5	1.2
UNHCR	–	–	0.0	0.0	–	–	0.0	0.0
Other Multilateral	0.4	0.6	0.2	0.8	0.4	0.6	0.2	0.8
Arab OPEC Agencies	–	–	–	3.5	–	–	–	3.5
TOTAL	*23.6*	*65.8*	*69.8*	*70.6*	*21.8*	*35.9*	*40.8*	*38.8*
OPEC COUNTRIES	–	–	–	*0.0*	–	–	–	*0.0*
E.E.C.+ MEMBERS	*96.1*	*217.3*	*148.8*	*128.1*	*44.4*	*73.4*	*73.4*	*54.6*
TOTAL	***120.6***	***267.1***	***210.8***	***180.9***	***64.2***	***102.5***	***109.7***	***91.0***

TOTAL ODA GROSS	197
Australia	
Austria	
Belgium	0.
Canada	1.
Denmark	0.
Finland	
France	14.
Germany, Fed. Rep.	23.
Italy	0.
Japan	0.
Netherlands	0.
New Zealand	
Norway	0.
Sweden	
Switzerland	0.
United Kingdom	0.
United States	3.
TOTAL	*43.*
AF.D.F.	2.
AF.D.B.	
AS.D.B.	
CAR.D.B.	
E.E.C.	6.
IBRD	
IDA	5.
I.D.B.	
IFAD	
I.F.C.	
IMF TRUST FUND	
U.N. AGENCIES	
UNDP	1.
UNTA	0.
UNICEF	0.
UNRWA	
WFP	4.
UNHCR	
Other Multilateral	0.
Arab OPEC Agencies	
TOTAL	*21.*
OPEC COUNTRIES	
E.E.C.+ MEMBERS	*45.*
TOTAL	***65.***

	ODA LOANS GROSS 1977	1978	1979	1980	ODA LOANS NET 1977	1978	1979	1980
DAC COUNTRIES								
Australia	–	–	–	–	–	–	–	–
Austria	–	1.1	0.0	–	–	1.1	0.0	–
Belgium	–	–	–	–	–	–	–	–
Canada	0.5	3.3	7.5	0.5	0.5	3.3	7.5	0.5
Denmark	0.8	1.6	8.8	7.1	0.8	1.6	8.8	7.1
Finland	–	–	–	–	–	–	–	–
France	0.7	6.1	4.1	7.1	-0.1	5.5	3.2	5.8
Germany, Fed. Rep.	17.1	31.7	19.5	12.5	16.4	30.0	17.4	7.7
Italy	–	–	–	–	–	–	–	–
Japan	–	–	–	–	–	–	–	–
Netherlands	–	–	–	–	–	–	–	–
New Zealand	–	–	–	–	–	–	–	–
Norway	–	–	–	–	–	–	–	–
Sweden	–	–	–	–	–	–	–	–
Switzerland	–	–	–	–	–	–	–	–
United Kingdom	–	–	–	–	–	–	–	–
United States	–	–	–	–	–	–	–	–
TOTAL	*19.0*	*43.7*	*40.0*	*27.2*	*17.6*	*41.4*	*36.9*	*21.1*
MULTILATERAL	*10.1*	*19.8*	*26.9*	*25.9*	*10.1*	*19.8*	*26.8*	*25.8*
OPEC COUNTRIES	–	–	–	–	–	–	–	–
E.E.C.+ MEMBERS	*20.1*	*42.7*	*39.6*	*26.8*	*18.7*	*40.5*	*36.6*	*20.7*
TOTAL	***29.1***	***63.5***	***66.8***	***53.1***	***27.6***	***61.2***	***63.7***	***46.9***

GRANTS	197
Australia	
Austria	
Belgium	0
Canada	1
Denmark	
Finland	
France	13
Germany, Fed. Rep.	6
Italy	0
Japan	0
Netherlands	0
New Zealand	
Norway	0
Sweden	
Switzerland	0
United Kingdom	0
United States	3
TOTAL	*24*
MULTILATERAL	*11*
OPEC COUNTRIES	
E.E.C.+ MEMBERS	*25*
TOTAL	***36***

	TOTAL OFFICIAL GROSS 1977	1978	1979	1980	TOTAL OFFICIAL NET 1977	1978	1979	1980
DAC COUNTRIES								
Australia	–	–	–	–	–	–	–	–
Austria	–	1.1	0.0	0.0	-0.3	0.7	0.0	0.0
Belgium	0.5	0.3	1.1	4.6	0.5	0.3	1.1	4.3
Canada	1.5	4.6	8.0	0.6	1.5	4.6	8.0	0.6
Denmark	0.8	1.6	8.9	8.3	0.8	1.6	8.9	8.3
Finland	–	–	–	0.0	–	–	–	0.0
France	14.1	20.4	32.4	89.2	13.3	19.7	31.3	78.1
Germany, Fed. Rep.	23.1	40.5	40.4	27.0	22.2	38.7	32.6	19.9
Italy	0.1	0.0	0.1	0.0	0.1	0.0	0.1	0.0
Japan	0.1	0.2	0.0	1.3	0.1	0.2	0.0	1.3
Netherlands	0.4	1.2	0.9	0.5	0.4	1.2	0.9	0.5
New Zealand	–	–	–	–	–	–	–	–
Norway	0.1	0.2	–	–	0.1	0.2	–	–
Sweden	–	–	–	–	–	–	–	–
Switzerland	0.1	0.3	7.3	2.3	0.1	0.3	7.3	2.3
United Kingdom	0.1	0.1	0.1	0.2	0.1	0.1	0.1	0.2
United States	3.0	1.0	6.0	5.0	3.0	1.0	6.0	3.0
TOTAL	*43.9*	*71.3*	*105.2*	*139.0*	*41.7*	*68.4*	*96.2*	*118.5*
MULTILATERAL	*23.9*	*65.9*	*70.2*	*70.8*	*23.6*	*65.8*	*69.8*	*70.6*
OPEC COUNTRIES	–	–	–	–	–	–	–	*0.0*
E.E.C.+ MEMBERS	*45.9*	*86.8*	*110.8*	*149.8*	*44.1*	*84.2*	*101.9*	*131.3*
TOTAL	***67.8***	***137.2***	***175.4***	***209.8***	***65.3***	***134.1***	***166.1***	***189.2***

TOTAL OOF GROSS	197
Australia	
Austria	
Belgium	
Canada	
Denmark	
Finland	
France	
Germany, Fed. Rep.	
Italy	
Japan	
Netherlands	
New Zealand	
Norway	
Sweden	
Switzerland	
United Kingdom	
United States	
TOTAL	
MULTILATERAL	*2*
OPEC COUNTRIES	
E.E.C.+ MEMBERS	
TOTAL	***2***

ODA COMMITMENTS

1978	1979	1980	1977	1978	1979	1980
–	–	–	–	–	–	–
1.1	0.0	0.0	–	1.1	0.0	–
0.3	0.4	0.4	–	–	–	–
4.6	8.0	0.6	12.7	0.8	0.1	0.3
1.6	8.9	7.1	3.3	–	7.6	7.1
–	–	0.0	–	–	–	–
17.9	18.6	22.9	11.8	13.3	15.9	34.9
40.5	29.8	22.0	68.4	11.8	12.9	52.9
0.0	0.1	0.0	0.1	0.0	0.1	0.0
0.2	0.0	1.3	0.2	0.2	1.4	1.8
1.2	0.9	0.5	1.4	0.6	0.5	0.6
–	–	–	–	–	–	–
0.2	–	–	–	–	–	–
–	–	–	–	–	–	–
0.3	0.1	0.2	–	0.1	–	0.1
0.1	0.1	0.2	0.1	0.1	0.1	0.2
1.0	5.0	3.0	3.8	3.8	4.7	6.1
68.8	*72.0*	*58.2*	*101.7*	*31.8*	*43.4*	*104.1*
1.9	6.2	4.8	–	12.8	9.7	9.4
–	–	–	–	–	–	–
–	–	–	–	–	–	–
–	–	–	–	–	–	–
14.1	17.6	7.6	18.8	5.9	5.1	7.2
–	–	–	–	–	–	–
6.8	7.6	12.5	24.0	5.8	16.2	11.0
–	–	–	–	–	–	–
–	–	–	–	–	–	–
–	–	–	–	–	–	–
7.8	6.0	5.0	–	–	–	–
–	–	–	6.4	5.4	3.5	5.5
2.2	2.0	3.1	–	–	–	–
0.4	0.4	0.1	–	–	–	–
0.2	0.4	0.3	–	–	–	–
–	–	–	–	–	–	–
2.0	0.5	1.2	–	–	–	–
–	0.0	0.0	–	–	–	–
0.6	0.2	0.8	–	–	–	–
–	–	3.5	–	–	3.5	–
35.9	*40.9*	*38.9*	*49.1*	*29.9*	*38.0*	*33.0*
–	–	–	–	–	*4.9*	*10.6*
75.7	*76.4*	*60.7*	*103.9*	*31.8*	*42.3*	*102.9*
104.7	***112.8***	***97.1***	***150.9***	***61.7***	***86.3***	***147.6***

TECH. COOP. GRANTS

1978	1979	1980	1977	1978	1979	1980
–	–	–	–	–	–	–
–	0.0	0.0	–	–	0.0	0.0
0.3	0.4	0.4	0.5	0.2	0.3	0.4
1.3	0.5	0.1	0.4	0.2	0.1	0.0
0.0	0.0	–	–	0.0	0.0	–
–	–	0.0	–	–	–	0.0
11.8	14.5	15.8	8.2	8.5	10.6	12.1
8.9	10.3	9.6	6.1	7.9	10.3	9.6
0.0	0.1	0.0	0.1	0.0	0.1	0.0
0.2	0.0	1.3	0.1	0.2	0.0	0.0
1.2	0.9	0.5	0.4	0.4	0.5	0.4
–	–	–	–	–	–	–
0.2	–	–	–	0.0	–	–
–	–	–	–	–	–	–
0.3	0.1	0.2	–	–	0.0	–
0.1	0.1	0.2	0.1	0.1	0.1	0.2
1.0	5.0	3.0	1.0	1.0	–	2.0
25.1	*32.0*	*31.0*	*16.7*	*18.5*	*22.0*	*24.6*
16.1	*14.0*	*13.0*	*2.2*	*3.4*	*3.0*	*5.5*
–	–	–	–	–	–	–
32.9	*36.8*	*34.0*	*15.2*	*17.1*	*21.9*	*22.5*
41.2	***46.0***	***44.0***	***18.9***	***21.8***	***25.0***	***30.1***

TOTAL OOF NET

1978	1979	1980	1977	1978	1979	1980
–	–	–	–	–	–	–
–	–	–	-0.3	-0.4	–	–
–	0.7	4.2	–	–	0.7	3.9
–	–	–	–	–	–	–
–	–	1.2	–	–	–	1.2
–	–	–	–	–	–	–
2.5	13.8	66.3	0.0	2.4	13.6	56.5
–	10.6	5.0	-0.3	-0.2	4.9	2.6
–	–	–	–	–	–	–
–	–	–	–	–	–	–
–	–	–	–	–	–	–
–	–	–	–	–	–	–
–	–	–	–	–	–	–
–	–	–	–	–	–	–
–	7.2	2.2	–	–	7.2	2.2
–	–	–	–	–	–	–
–	1.0	2.0	–	–	1.0	–
2.5	*33.2*	*80.8*	*-0.7*	*1.8*	*27.3*	*66.4*
29.9	*29.4*	*31.9*	*1.8*	*29.8*	*29.0*	*31.8*
–	–	–	–	–	–	–
11.1	*34.4*	*89.1*	*-0.4*	*10.9*	*28.5*	*76.6*
32.4	***62.6***	***112.7***	***1.1***	***31.7***	***56.4***	***98.2***

MAIN AID AGGREGATES

	1977	1978	1979	1980
DAC COUNTRIES COMBINED				
PRIVATE SECTOR NET	55.3	133.0	44.8	-8.2
Direct Investment	0.7	0.1	-0.1	-1.4
Portfolio Invest.	4.2	23.6	5.0	-0.3
Export Credits	50.3	109.3	39.9	-6.5
OFFICIAL & PRIVATE				
GROSS:				
Contractual Lending	85.6	172.4	135.1	146.7
Export Credits Tot.	66.6	126.2	61.9	38.7
Export Credits Priv	66.6	126.2	61.9	38.7
OTHER NET DATA				
Contractual Lending	67.2	152.5	104.1	81.0
Export Credits Tot.	50.0	108.9	39.9	-8.5
(Bank Sector Loans)	15.0	48.0	38.0	-12.0
ODA CONCESSIONALITY				
Total:Grant Element	67.0	95.0	92.0	74.0
Loans:Grant Element	56.0	35.0	67.0	53.0
OTHER SOURCES				
CMEA Countr.(Gross)	–	–	–	–
Intra LDCS Exc.OPEC	–	–	–	–
Other	–	–	–	–
ALL SOURCE COMMITMENTS				
TOTAL BILATERAL	102.4	37.1	177.7	118.0
of which				
OPEC (ODA)	–	–	4.9	10.6
CMEA (ODA)	–	–	–	–
TOTAL MULTILAT.(ODA)	49.1	29.9	38.0	33.0
TOTAL BIL.& MULTIL.	151.6	67.0	215.7	151.0
of which				
ODA Grants	47.4	40.8	46.5	55.5
ODA Loans	103.5	20.9	39.9	92.2
ODA CONCESSIONALITY				
Total: Grant Element	75.0	92.0	89.0	75.0
Loans: Grant Element	66.0	78.0	76.0	60.0

INDEBTEDNESS

	1977	1978	1979	1980
TOTAL DEBT DISBURSED	***331.9***	***729.6***	***858.7***	
Debt to DAC Countries	291.0	632.0	706.0	
ODA	73.0	125.0	165.0	
Total Export Credits	202.0	347.0	391.0	
Other Private Market	16.0	160.0	150.0	
International Org.	28.3	59.2	87.6	
CMEA	–	–	–	
Other	12.5	38.5	65.2	
TOTAL DEBT SERVICE	***27.9***	***46.9***	***73.7***	
Paid to DAC Countries	22.9	42.5	68.5	
ODA	1.9	3.4	4.7	
Total Export Credits	20.4	35.9	45.8	
Other Private Market	0.6	3.2	18.0	
International Org.	0.4	0.9	1.1	
CMEA	–	–	–	
Other	4.6	3.5	4.1	

ECONOMIC INDICATORS

	1977	1978	1979	1980
GNP Curr. Prices, $M	772.2	877.9	991.0	1008.5
Real GNP, 1976=100	104.0	114.0	115.0	111.0
GNP/Cap Curr. Prices,$	335.0	371.0	409.0	407.0
GNP/cap Atlas Basis, $	327.3	374.5	401.5	410.7
Real GNP/Cap, 1976=100	101.0	108.0	107.0	100.0
Population, Million	2.3	2.4	2.4	2.5
Curr.A/C Deficit(-),$M	-117.5	-289.4	–	–
BOP Exp. & Transf.,$M	234.1	306.6	–	–
Exp. to OECD CIF, $M	158.6	184.5	203.2	257.8
of which				
Manufact.	3.4	11.3	5.6	3.1
Imp. from OECD FOB, $M	226.8	404.0	392.6	413.3
Reserves ex. Gold, $M	46.2	70.0	65.5	77.6

	TOTAL RECEIPTS NET 1977	1978	1979	1980	TOTAL ODA NET 1977	1978	1979	1980
DAC COUNTRIES								
Australia	0.0	–	0.0	0.0	0.0	0.0	0.0	0.0
Austria	–	18.8	0.0	–	–	–	0.0	–
Belgium	0.0	0.1	0.0	5.4	0.0	0.1	–	0.1
Canada	0.0	0.3	41.0	36.2	0.0	0.3	-0.1	-0.3
Denmark	–	–	0.0	–	–	–	0.0	–
Finland	–	–	–	0.0	–	–	–	0.0
France	2.6	1.5	-3.2	1.5	–	–	–	0.5
Germany, Fed. Rep.	-0.1	19.5	-3.9	1.0	0.1	0.1	0.1	0.4
Italy	0.1	0.1	–	21.1	0.0	–	–	–
Japan	0.0	47.8	65.2	2.2	0.1	0.1	0.2	0.1
Netherlands	0.4	0.2	0.1	0.4	0.4	0.2	0.1	0.4
New Zealand	-0.3	-0.1	0.0	0.0	–	0.0	0.0	0.0
Norway	-1.1	–	–	–	–	–	–	–
Sweden	–	–	–	–	–	–	–	–
Switzerland	0.0	0.0	-0.1	0.0	0.0	0.0	-0.1	0.0
United Kingdom	5.1	10.0	31.2	32.6	0.0	-0.1	0.2	0.3
United States	-28.0	–	-66.0	-36.0	–	–	–	–
TOTAL	*-21.1*	*98.2*	*64.5*	*64.4*	*0.7*	*0.7*	*0.5*	*1.4*
MULTILATERAL								
AF.D.F.	–	–	–	–	–	–	–	–
AF.D.B.	–	–	–	–	–	–	–	–
AS.D.B.	–	–	–	–	–	–	–	–
CAR.D.B.	0.0	-0.9	–	1.0	–	–	–	–
E.E.C.	0.1	1.1	7.3	1.3	0.1	1.1	1.7	0.5
IBRD	4.8	2.5	-0.9	-1.4	–	–	–	–
IDA	–	–	–	–	–	–	–	–
I.D.B.	3.4	1.5	0.7	0.1	3.4	1.3	0.7	0.1
IFAD	–	–	–	–	–	–	–	–
I.F.C.	–	1.0	1.4	-0.1	–	–	–	–
IMF TRUST FUND	–	–	–	–	–	–	–	–
U.N. AGENCIES	–	–	–	–	–	–	–	–
UNDP	1.1	1.2	1.0	1.8	1.1	1.2	1.0	1.8
UNTA	0.1	0.2	0.2	–	0.1	0.2	0.2	–
UNICEF	–	–	–	–	–	–	–	–
UNRWA	–	–	–	–	–	–	–	–
WFP	–	–	–	–	–	–	–	–
UNHCR	–	–	–	–	–	–	–	–
Other Multilateral	0.3	0.0	0.1	0.8	0.3	0.0	0.1	0.8
Arab OPEC Agencies	–	–	–	–	–	–	–	–
TOTAL	*9.8*	*6.6*	*9.8*	*3.4*	*5.0*	*3.8*	*3.7*	*3.2*
OPEC COUNTRIES	–	–	–	–	–	–	–	–
E.E.C.+ MEMBERS	*8.3*	*32.4*	*31.5*	*63.2*	*0.6*	*1.3*	*2.1*	*2.1*
TOTAL	***-11.3***	***104.8***	***74.2***	***67.8***	***5.7***	***4.5***	***4.1***	***4.7***

	ODA LOANS GROSS 1977	1978	1979	1980	ODA LOANS NET 1977	1978	1979	1980
DAC COUNTRIES								
Australia	–	–	–	–	–	–	–	–
Austria	–	–	–	–	–	–	–	–
Belgium	–	–	–	–	–	–	–	–
Canada	0.3	0.4	0.2	0.0	0.0	0.3	-0.2	-0.3
Denmark	–	–	–	–	–	–	–	–
Finland	–	–	–	–	–	–	–	–
France	–	–	–	–	–	–	–	–
Germany, Fed. Rep.	–	–	–	–	–	–	–	–
Italy	–	–	–	–	–	–	–	–
Japan	–	–	–	–	–	–	–	–
Netherlands	–	–	–	–	–	–	–	–
New Zealand	–	–	–	–	–	–	–	–
Norway	–	–	–	–	–	–	–	–
Sweden	–	–	–	–	–	–	–	–
Switzerland	–	–	–	–	–	–	–	–
United Kingdom	–	–	–	–	-0.3	-0.3	-0.1	-0.1
United States	–	–	–	–	–	–	–	–
TOTAL	*0.3*	*0.4*	*0.2*	*0.0*	*-0.3*	*0.0*	*-0.4*	*-0.5*
MULTILATERAL	*3.8*	*0.9*	*1.1*	*0.6*	*3.4*	*0.5*	*0.6*	*0.1*
OPEC COUNTRIES	–	–	–	–	–	–	–	–
E.E.C.+ MEMBERS	–	–	–	–	*-0.3*	*-0.3*	*-0.1*	*-0.1*
TOTAL	***4.1***	***1.3***	***1.3***	***0.6***	***3.1***	***0.5***	***0.2***	***-0.3***

	TOTAL OFFICIAL GROSS 1977	1978	1979	1980	TOTAL OFFICIAL NET 1977	1978	1979	1980
DAC COUNTRIES								
Australia	0.0	0.0	0.0	0.0	0.0	0.0	0.0	0.0
Austria	–	–	0.0	–	–	–	0.0	–
Belgium	0.0	0.1	–	0.1	0.0	0.1	–	0.1
Canada	0.3	0.5	41.4	36.5	0.0	0.3	41.0	36.2
Denmark	–	–	0.0	–	–	–	0.0	–
Finland	–	–	–	0.0	–	–	–	0.0
France	–	–	–	0.5	–	–	–	0.5
Germany, Fed. Rep.	0.1	0.1	0.1	0.4	0.1	0.1	0.1	0.4
Italy	0.0	–	–	–	0.0	–	–	–
Japan	0.1	0.1	0.2	6.6	0.1	0.1	0.2	6.6
Netherlands	0.4	0.2	0.1	0.4	0.4	0.2	0.1	0.4
New Zealand	2.5	0.0	0.0	0.0	-0.3	0.0	0.0	0.0
Norway	–	–	–	–	–	–	–	–
Sweden	–	–	–	–	–	–	–	–
Switzerland	0.0	0.0	-0.1	0.0	0.0	0.0	-0.1	0.0
United Kingdom	0.3	0.2	0.3	0.4	0.0	-0.1	0.2	0.3
United States	–	–	32.0	93.0	-1.0	-2.0	29.0	89.0
TOTAL	*3.8*	*1.1*	*74.2*	*137.9*	*-0.6*	*-1.3*	*70.6*	*133.5*
MULTILATERAL	*12.7*	*10.9*	*14.9*	*9.7*	*9.8*	*6.6*	*9.8*	*3.5*
OPEC COUNTRIES	–	–	–	–	–	–	–	–
E.E.C.+ MEMBERS	*0.9*	*1.6*	*7.8*	*3.0*	*0.6*	*1.3*	*7.7*	*2.8*
TOTAL	***16.5***	***12.0***	***89.0***	***147.6***	***9.2***	***5.3***	***80.4***	***136.9***

TOTAL ODA GROSS

	197[illegible]
Australia	0.
Austria	
Belgium	0
Canada	0
Denmark	
Finland	
France	
Germany, Fed. Rep.	0
Italy	0
Japan	0
Netherlands	0
New Zealand	
Norway	
Sweden	
Switzerland	0
United Kingdom	0
United States	
TOTAL	*1*
AF.D.F.	
AF.D.B.	
AS.D.B.	
CAR.D.B.	
E.E.C.	0
IBRD	
IDA	
I.D.B.	3
IFAD	
I.F.C.	
IMF TRUST FUND	
U.N. AGENCIES	
UNDP	1
UNTA	0
UNICEF	
UNRWA	
WFP	
UNHCR	
Other Multilateral	[illegible]
Arab OPEC Agencies	
TOTAL	*5*
OPEC COUNTRIES	
E.E.C.+ MEMBERS	[illegible]
TOTAL	***6***

GRANTS

	197[illegible]
Australia	[illegible]
Austria	
Belgium	[illegible]
Canada	[illegible]
Denmark	
Finland	
France	
Germany, Fed. Rep.	[illegible]
Italy	[illegible]
Japan	[illegible]
Netherlands	[illegible]
New Zealand	
Norway	
Sweden	
Switzerland	[illegible]
United Kingdom	[illegible]
United States	
TOTAL	
MULTILATERAL	
OPEC COUNTRIES	
E.E.C.+ MEMBERS	[illegible]
TOTAL	[illegible]

TOTAL OOF GROSS

	197[illegible]
Australia	
Austria	
Belgium	
Canada	
Denmark	
Finland	
France	
Germany, Fed. Rep.	
Italy	
Japan	
Netherlands	
New Zealand	
Norway	
Sweden	
Switzerland	
United Kingdom	
United States	
TOTAL	
MULTILATERAL	
OPEC COUNTRIES	
E.E.C.+ MEMBERS	
TOTAL	

ODA COMMITMENTS

1978	1979	1980	1977	1978	1979	1980
–	–	–	–	–	–	–
70.9	2.0	0.5	0.0	70.8	0.6	0.3
12.1	15.8	16.7	16.8	18.7	17.9	18.4
18.4	10.6	8.1	2.9	0.3	1.7	0.1
0.1	1.3	0.2	0.1	–	–	–
–	–	–	–	–	–	–
69.6	65.7	86.9	61.1	71.7	35.7	159.3
56.9	49.7	35.9	66.5	57.3	4.9	245.0
0.7	0.4	1.4	4.2	0.7	0.4	1.4
16.5	7.4	5.5	15.9	1.6	41.4	2.4
8.5	10.4	8.8	8.9	8.9	2.4	10.0
–	–	–	–	–	–	–
–	–	–	–	–	–	–
7.4	7.6	6.8	8.9	7.1	13.1	–
0.3	0.8	0.9	4.3	0.4	0.9	0.0
0.5	0.2	0.2	-0.2	0.1	0.2	0.2
14.0	11.0	17.0	24.5	37.6	29.1	37.2
275.8	*182.8*	*188.7*	*213.8*	*275.0*	*148.2*	*474.2*
–	–	–	–	–	–	–
–	–	–	–	–	–	–
–	–	–	–	–	–	–
–	–	–	–	–	–	–
0.4	4.3	1.0	0.4	–	8.4	41.7
–	–	–	–	–	–	–
1.8	0.2	1.0	–	–	–	–
–	–	–	–	–	–	–
–	–	–	–	–	–	18.8
–	–	–	–	–	–	–
–	–	–	–	–	–	–
–	–	–	13.8	10.1	15.3	16.9
2.8	3.7	3.4	–	–	–	–
0.8	0.7	0.3	–	–	–	–
1.0	1.0	0.3	–	–	–	–
–	–	–	–	–	–	–
3.6	8.1	9.7	–	–	–	–
–	–	–	–	–	–	–
1.9	1.8	3.3	–	–	–	–
2.8	1.0	7.2	7.1	6.0	18.0	18.9
15.1	*20.7*	*26.2*	*21.3*	*16.1*	*41.6*	*96.4*
29.7	*54.6*	*58.6*	*122.4*	*71.5*	*28.7*	–
148.6	*147.7*	*151.0*	*157.7*	*157.4*	*69.8*	*475.9*
320.5	***258.1***	***273.5***	***357.4***	***362.6***	***218.6***	***570.6***

TECH. COOP. GRANTS

–	–	–	–	–	–	–
1.3	1.2	0.5	0.3	1.3	1.2	0.5
12.1	14.1	15.0	5.6	7.5	8.1	9.1
0.7	0.5	1.3	0.4	0.3	0.1	0.0
–	–	–	0.1	–	–	–
–	–	–	–	–	–	–
34.3	33.8	43.0	26.5	30.7	33.4	34.2
8.0	9.5	12.5	8.2	8.0	9.5	12.5
0.7	0.4	1.4	0.8	0.4	0.4	0.3
1.4	1.8	2.1	0.8	1.4	1.8	2.1
2.2	3.3	3.1	1.1	1.2	1.8	1.9
–	–	–	–	–	–	–
–	–	–	–	–	–	–
5.2	5.8	4.6	0.5	1.1	0.8	0.7
0.3	0.5	0.7	0.0	0.0	0.0	0.1
0.1	0.2	0.2	-0.2	0.1	0.2	0.2
5.0	–	-3.0	3.0	3.0	3.0	5.0
71.1	*71.0*	*81.3*	*47.1*	*55.0*	*60.2*	*66.5*
10.5	*19.5*	*18.0*	*7.0*	*6.5*	*7.2*	*16.9*
–	*7.0*	–	–	–	–	–
57.7	*65.5*	*76.1*	*42.1*	*47.9*	*53.3*	*58.1*
81.6	***97.5***	***99.2***	***54.1***	***61.5***	***67.4***	***83.5***

TOTAL OOF NET

–	–	–	–	–	–	–
–	–	–	8.2	-3.1	-4.1	-4.3
–	–	–	–	–	–	–
1.0	–	–	–	1.0	–	-0.1
–	0.0	–	–	–	0.0	–
–	–	–	–	–	–	–
12.0	2.2	–	-15.7	-22.3	-60.1	-84.3
–	–	–	0.0	0.0	0.0	0.0
–	6.0	75.2	-1.1	-1.9	4.1	72.9
–	–	6.4	–	–	–	6.4
1.0	0.3	–	-0.1	0.5	-0.1	-0.3
–	–	–	–	–	–	–
–	–	–	–	–	–	–
–	–	–	–	–	–	–
–	–	–	–	–	–	–
–	–	–	–	–	–	–
–	–	12.0	13.0	-1.0	-1.0	12.0
14.0	*8.5*	*93.7*	*4.3*	*-26.8*	*-61.3*	*2.3*
47.5	*85.4*	*78.4*	*48.1*	*35.2*	*52.3*	*56.9*
3.0	–	*22.3*	*4.3*	*2.4*	–	*21.9*
13.0	*8.5*	*90.6*	*-16.9*	*-23.7*	*-56.2*	*3.6*
64.5	***93.9***	***194.4***	***56.7***	***10.8***	***-9.0***	***81.1***

MAIN AID AGGREGATES

	1977	1978	1979	1980
DAC COUNTRIES COMBINED				
PRIVATE SECTOR NET	91.6	143.1	264.4	55.8
Direct Investment	3.1	8.9	14.8	32.8
Portfolio Invest.	29.6	82.2	35.5	-66.0
Export Credits	58.9	52.0	214.1	88.9
OFFICIAL & PRIVATE				
GROSS:				
Contractual Lending	334.3	390.3	440.2	404.3
Export Credits Tot.	202.3	172.6	325.9	296.8
Export Credits Priv	177.0	171.6	319.9	203.2
OTHER NET DATA				
Contractual Lending	162.8	206.9	232.8	167.6
Export Credits Tot.	80.1	47.1	213.0	175.8
(Bank Sector Loans)	109.0	169.0	175.0	-88.0
ODA CONCESSIONALITY				
Total:Grant Element	67.0	66.0	80.0	54.0
Loans:Grant Element	48.0	49.0	50.0	44.0
OTHER SOURCES				
CMEA Countr.(Gross)	4.1	4.8	13.3	11.8
Intra LDCS Exc.OPEC	–	–	–	–
Other	–	–	–	–
ALL SOURCE COMMITMENTS				
TOTAL BILATERAL	347.3	360.7	241.2	568.4
of which				
OPEC (ODA)	122.4	71.5	28.7	–
CMEA (ODA)	40.0	–	–	–
TOTAL MULTILAT.(ODA)	21.3	16.1	41.6	96.4
TOTAL BIL.& MULTIL.	368.7	376.9	282.8	664.8
of which				
ODA Grants	92.8	104.0	119.2	108.5
ODA Loans	264.6	258.6	99.4	462.1
ODA CONCESSIONALITY				
Total: Grant Element	60.0	61.0	74.0	55.0
Loans: Grant Element	46.0	46.0	43.0	43.0

INDEBTEDNESS

	1977	1978	1979	1980
TOTAL DEBT DISBURSED	***2009.5***	***2760.3***	***3281.6***	
Debt to DAC Countries	1540.0	2201.0	2570.0	
ODA	800.0	978.0	1087.0	
Total Export Credits	444.0	570.0	714.0	
Other Private Market	296.0	653.0	769.0	
International Org.	276.0	319.4	425.9	
CMEA	9.4	9.4	26.8	
Other	184.2	230.4	258.9	
TOTAL DEBT SERVICE	***187.5***	***251.1***	***392.9***	
Paid to DAC Countries	149.8	197.9	317.2	
ODA	31.1	42.7	56.7	
Total Export Credits	101.7	116.7	157.8	
Other Private Market	17.0	38.5	102.7	
International Org.	26.9	30.9	48.1	
CMEA	2.1	5.3	2.1	
Other	8.7	17.0	25.5	

ECONOMIC INDICATORS

	1977	1978	1979	1980
GNP Curr. Prices, $M	5054.8	5957.9	7231.5	8437.0
Real GNP, 1976=100	104.0	114.0	123.0	131.0
GNP/Cap Curr. Prices,$	859.0	987.0	1167.0	1327.0
GNP/cap Atlas Basis, $	891.9	1018.4	1162.6	1312.7
Real GNP/Cap, 1976=100	102.0	108.0	114.0	118.0
Population, Million	5.9	6.0	6.2	6.4
Curr.A/C Deficit(-),$M	-631.0	-511.0	-366.0	–
BOP Exp. & Transf.,$M	1494.0	1874.0	2875.0	–
Exp. to OECD CIF, $M	786.9	867.6	1400.9	2023.5
of which				
Manufact.	304.1	359.1	517.1	702.0
Imp. from OECD FOB, $M	1409.1	1739.7	2211.4	2777.3
Reserves ex. Gold, $M	351.2	443.0	579.3	590.1

TOTAL RECEIPTS NET / TOTAL ODA NET

	Total receipts net 1977	1978	1979	1980	Total ODA net 1977	1978	1979	1980
DAC COUNTRIES								
Australia	0.1	0.0	0.1	0.0	0.1	0.0	–	–
Austria	72.2	16.9	8.1	41.4	2.7	3.8	8.8	27.2
Belgium	0.0	16.0	157.1	69.3	-0.6	7.3	6.0	9.3
Canada	12.0	45.0	24.8	1.3	–	–	–	1.3
Denmark	19.4	1.9	0.6	0.2	1.8	0.8	0.1	0.0
Finland	6.1	-0.1	44.2	5.4	–	0.0	–	2.0
France	41.3	134.9	171.4	192.1	1.1	2.3	-3.0	33.2
Germany, Fed. Rep.	178.1	333.5	655.9	505.7	31.5	156.9	342.1	326.7
Italy	48.2	15.4	103.4	16.3	-3.9	0.4	0.2	0.6
Japan	59.8	24.1	-5.6	50.9	5.7	5.1	4.1	5.4
Netherlands	1.8	6.4	14.2	38.1	1.8	6.4	4.2	2.5
New Zealand	-0.2	-0.1	–	–	–	–	–	–
Norway	2.4	3.4	35.4	19.9	0.7	0.1	11.0	10.7
Sweden	1.5	2.6	-0.4	11.7	-0.2	0.5	0.1	11.8
Switzerland	107.8	365.2	-3.7	-4.3	-0.8	1.2	-1.0	-0.5
United Kingdom	185.3	2.7	-1.4	89.1	2.2	-0.8	-4.9	18.7
United States	-42.0	-11.0	248.0	308.0	-17.0	-30.0	91.0	265.0
TOTAL	*693.8*	*956.8*	*1452.0*	*1345.3*	*24.9*	*154.0*	*458.8*	*713.8*
MULTILATERAL								
AF.D.F.	–	–	–	–	–	–	–	–
AF.D.B.	–	–	–	–	–	–	–	–
AS.D.B.	–	–	–	–	–	–	–	–
CAR.D.B.	–	–	–	–	–	–	–	–
E.E.C.	39.1	13.8	103.1	14.4	37.3	6.6	104.6	-2.0
IBRD	120.3	136.1	242.3	267.5	–	–	–	–
IDA	17.7	7.4	1.8	-0.9	17.7	7.4	1.8	-0.9
I.D.B.	–	–	–	–	–	–	–	–
IFAD	–	–	–	–	–	–	–	–
I.F.C.	-0.6	-11.2	-0.5	2.8	–	–	–	–
IMF TRUST FUND	–	–	–	–	–	–	–	–
U.N. AGENCIES	–	–	–	–	–	–	–	–
UNDP	4.1	5.4	6.8	6.2	4.1	5.4	6.8	6.2
UNTA	0.5	0.2	0.4	0.3	0.5	0.2	0.4	0.3
UNICEF	0.2	0.5	0.4	0.3	0.2	0.5	0.4	0.3
UNRWA	–	–	–	–	–	–	–	–
WFP	2.4	1.2	3.1	6.5	2.4	1.2	3.1	6.5
UNHCR	0.0	0.0	0.0	0.1	0.0	0.0	0.0	0.1
Other Multilateral	1.2	2.7	1.4	2.8	1.2	2.7	1.4	2.8
Arab OPEC Agencies	3.7	16.2	40.1	-35.5	–	–	7.5	7.5
TOTAL	*188.7*	*172.3*	*398.9*	*264.5*	*63.5*	*24.0*	*126.0*	*20.7*
OPEC COUNTRIES	*25.0*	*227.0*	*–*	*267.9*	*5.0*	*–*	*–*	*267.9*
E.E.C.+ MEMBERS	*513.2*	*524.6*	*1204.1*	*925.3*	*71.1*	*179.9*	*449.4*	*388.9*
TOTAL	***907.5***	***1356.2***	***1850.9***	***1877.6***	***93.4***	***178.0***	***584.8***	***1002.4***

ODA LOANS GROSS / ODA LOANS NET

	ODA loans gross 1977	1978	1979	1980	ODA loans net 1977	1978	1979	1980
DAC COUNTRIES								
Australia	–	–	–	–	–	–	–	–
Austria	–	–	4.4	22.0	–	–	4.4	22.0
Belgium	–	8.0	6.8	10.3	-0.7	7.1	5.9	9.2
Canada	–	–	–	1.3	–	–	–	1.3
Denmark	2.0	0.7	–	–	1.7	0.7	–	–
Finland	–	–	–	2.0	–	–	–	2.0
France	3.1	2.9	3.5	34.8	1.1	2.3	-3.0	31.7
Germany, Fed. Rep.	41.3	139.2	376.9	313.6	18.8	139.2	323.6	309.5
Italy	1.8	–	–	–	-4.4	–	–	–
Japan	5.6	8.3	2.6	7.2	4.2	3.3	2.2	3.8
Netherlands	1.6	2.8	3.1	2.5	0.7	2.8	1.9	1.2
New Zealand	–	–	–	–	–	–	–	–
Norway	–	–	–	–	–	–	–	–
Sweden	0.1	0.5	–	11.8	-0.2	0.5	–	11.8
Switzerland	–	0.4	0.1	–	-1.2	0.3	-1.7	-1.0
United Kingdom	4.9	0.4	0.2	17.6	1.3	-1.5	-5.7	17.6
United States	6.0	1.0	60.0	129.0	-13.0	-25.0	55.0	98.0
TOTAL	*66.3*	*164.1*	*457.6*	*552.1*	*8.3*	*129.6*	*382.6*	*507.1*
MULTILATERAL	*61.9*	*21.0*	*123.3*	*14.3*	*55.0*	*12.7*	*114.0*	*4.6*
OPEC COUNTRIES	*–*	*–*	*–*	*267.9*	*–*	*–*	*–*	*267.9*
E.E.C.+ MEMBERS	*97.8*	*166.5*	*503.4*	*385.3*	*55.8*	*155.9*	*427.4*	*367.2*
TOTAL	***128.2***	***185.1***	***580.9***	***834.2***	***63.3***	***142.3***	***496.6***	***779.5***

TOTAL OFFICIAL GROSS / TOTAL OFFICIAL NET

	Total official gross 1977	1978	1979	1980	Total official net 1977	1978	1979	1980
DAC COUNTRIES								
Australia	0.1	0.0	–	–	0.1	0.0	–	–
Austria	2.7	3.8	8.8	27.2	2.7	3.8	8.8	27.2
Belgium	0.1	19.9	10.0	23.9	-0.6	18.3	8.3	22.9
Canada	20.0	44.1	26.6	45.0	11.8	43.4	26.5	1.3
Denmark	2.1	1.9	0.6	0.2	1.8	1.9	0.6	0.2
Finland	–	0.0	–	2.0	–	0.0	–	2.0
France	3.1	2.9	52.9	74.1	1.1	2.3	42.4	70.9
Germany, Fed. Rep.	67.4	257.4	633.8	510.7	44.1	255.4	490.0	506.2
Italy	6.8	13.1	0.2	0.6	0.6	13.1	0.2	0.6
Japan	7.1	10.8	23.8	33.4	4.9	4.7	22.9	25.9
Netherlands	2.6	6.4	5.3	30.4	1.8	6.4	4.2	29.1
New Zealand	0.1	–	–	–	-0.2	–	–	–
Norway	0.7	0.1	11.0	10.7	0.7	0.1	11.0	10.7
Sweden	0.1	0.5	0.1	11.8	-0.2	0.5	0.1	11.8
Switzerland	0.4	2.6	49.8	9.4	-0.8	2.5	42.8	8.4
United Kingdom	5.7	1.1	9.0	18.7	2.2	-0.8	3.0	18.7
United States	35.0	81.0	253.0	427.0	8.0	36.0	195.0	353.0
TOTAL	*154.0*	*445.5*	*1085.1*	*1225.2*	*77.9*	*387.6*	*856.0*	*1088.9*
MULTILATERAL	*231.2*	*232.4*	*483.9*	*406.2*	*188.7*	*172.3*	*398.9*	*264.5*
OPEC COUNTRIES	*25.0*	*227.0*	*–*	*267.9*	*25.0*	*227.0*	*–*	*267.9*
E.E.C.+ MEMBERS	*133.1*	*325.5*	*826.4*	*685.6*	*90.1*	*310.4*	*651.9*	*663.0*
TOTAL	***410.3***	***904.9***	***1569.0***	***1899.2***	***291.6***	***786.9***	***1255.0***	***1621.2***

TOTAL ODA GROSS

	197
Australia	0
Austria	2
Belgium	0
Canada	
Denmark	2
Finland	
France	3
Germany, Fed. Rep.	53
Italy	2
Japan	7
Netherlands	2
New Zealand	
Norway	0
Sweden	0
Switzerland	0
United Kingdom	5
United States	2
TOTAL	*83*
AF.D.F.	
AF.D.B.	
AS.D.B.	
CAR.D.B.	
E.E.C.	43
IBRD	
IDA	18
I.D.B.	
IFAD	
I.F.C.	
IMF TRUST FUND	
U.N. AGENCIES	
UNDP	4
UNTA	0
UNICEF	0
UNRWA	
WFP	2
UNHCR	0
Other Multilateral	1
Arab OPEC Agencies	
TOTAL	*70*
OPEC COUNTRIES	*5*
E.E.C.+ MEMBERS	*113*
TOTAL	***158***

GRANTS

	197
Australia	0
Austria	2
Belgium	0
Canada	
Denmark	0
Finland	
France	
Germany, Fed. Rep.	12
Italy	0
Japan	1
Netherlands	1
New Zealand	
Norway	0
Sweden	
Switzerland	0
United Kingdom	0
United States	-4
TOTAL	*16*
MULTILATERAL	*8*
OPEC COUNTRIES	*5*
E.E.C.+ MEMBERS	*15*
TOTAL	***30***

TOTAL OOF GROSS

	197
Australia	
Austria	
Belgium	
Canada	20
Denmark	
Finland	
France	
Germany, Fed. Rep.	13
Italy	4
Japan	
Netherlands	
New Zealand	0
Norway	
Sweden	
Switzerland	
United Kingdom	
United States	33
TOTAL	*71*
MULTILATERAL	*160*
OPEC COUNTRIES	*20*
E.E.C.+ MEMBERS	*20*
TOTAL	***252***

1978	1979	1980	1977	1978	1979	1980
			ODA COMMITMENTS			
0.0	–	–	–	–	–	–
3.8	8.8	27.2	0.1	–	4.4	22.0
8.1	6.9	10.3	2.8	4.8	6.8	10.3
–	–	1.3	–	–	10.1	10.3
0.8	0.1	0.0	0.1	–	–	–
0.0	–	2.0	–	0.0	2.1	3.8
2.9	3.5	36.3	7.5	–	23.5	38.7
156.9	395.4	330.8	24.9	164.3	461.4	300.2
0.4	0.2	0.6	0.5	0.4	0.2	0.6
10.1	4.5	8.8	1.7	7.6	2.2	7.4
6.4	5.3	3.8	3.6	0.7	4.3	3.4
–	–	–	–	–	–	–
0.1	11.0	10.7	–	–	11.8	0.1
0.5	0.1	11.8	–	0.1	–	11.8
1.3	0.8	0.5	–	1.0	–	0.0
1.1	1.1	18.7	0.8	0.7	32.7	64.9
-4.0	96.0	296.0	0.5	0.4	100.3	298.3
188.5	*533.8*	*758.9*	*42.4*	*179.9*	*659.8*	*771.9*
–	–	–	–	–	–	–
–	–	–	–	–	–	–
–	–	–	–	–	–	–
–	–	–	–	–	–	–
13.9	112.9	6.5	–	9.3	153.5	188.0
–	–	–	–	–	–	–
8.4	2.9	0.3	–	–	–	–
–	–	–	–	–	–	–
–	–	–	–	–	–	–
–	–	–	–	–	–	–
–	–	–	–	–	–	–
–	–	–	8.4	10.0	12.1	16.2
5.4	6.8	6.2	–	–	–	–
0.2	0.4	0.3	–	–	–	–
0.5	0.4	0.3	–	–	–	–
–	–	–	–	–	–	–
1.2	3.1	6.5	–	–	–	–
0.0	0.0	0.1	–	–	–	–
2.7	1.4	2.8	–	–	–	–
–	7.5	7.5	–	–	15.0	4.0
32.3	*135.4*	*30.4*	*8.4*	*19.3*	*180.6*	*208.1*
–	–	*267.9*	–	–	*126.2*	*288.1*
190.5	*525.4*	*407.0*	*40.1*	*180.1*	*682.5*	*606.0*
220.8	***669.2***	***1057.1***	***50.8***	***199.2***	***966.6***	***1268.0***
			TECH. COOP. GRANTS			
0.0	–	–	–	–	–	–
3.8	4.4	5.2	2.7	3.8	4.4	5.2
0.2	0.1	0.0	0.1	0.1	0.1	0.0
–	–	–	–	–	–	–
0.2	0.1	0.0	0.1	0.1	0.0	0.0
0.0	–	0.0	–	–	–	–
–	–	1.5	–	–	–	1.5
17.7	18.5	17.2	11.9	16.7	18.5	17.2
0.4	0.2	0.6	0.5	0.4	0.2	0.6
1.8	1.9	1.6	1.5	1.8	1.9	1.6
3.6	2.3	1.3	0.7	0.8	1.0	0.8
–	–	–	–	–	–	–
0.1	11.0	10.7	0.1	0.1	0.0	0.5
0.1	0.1	–	–	–	–	–
0.9	0.7	0.5	0.0	0.1	0.0	–
0.7	0.9	1.1	0.4	0.6	0.9	1.0
-5.0	36.0	167.0	–	–	–	–
24.4	*76.2*	*206.8*	*17.9*	*24.4*	*27.0*	*28.4*
11.3	*12.1*	*16.2*	*6.0*	*8.8*	*8.9*	*16.2*
–	–	–	–	–	–	–
24.0	*22.0*	*21.7*	*13.7*	*18.7*	*20.6*	*21.2*
35.7	***88.2***	***222.9***	***24.0***	***33.2***	***35.9***	***44.5***
			TOTAL OOF NET			
–	–	–	–	–	–	–
–	–	–	–	–	–	–
11.7	3.1	13.6	–	11.0	2.3	13.6
44.1	26.6	43.7	11.8	43.4	26.5	–
1.1	0.5	0.2	–	1.1	0.5	0.2
–	–	–	–	–	–	–
–	49.4	37.8	–	–	45.4	37.7
100.5	238.4	179.9	12.7	98.5	147.9	179.5
12.7	–	–	4.5	12.7	–	–
0.6	19.4	24.6	-0.8	-0.4	18.9	20.6
–	–	26.6	–	–	–	26.6
–	–	–	-0.2	–	–	–
–	–	–	–	–	–	–
–	–	–	–	–	–	–
1.3	49.0	8.9	–	1.3	43.8	8.9
–	7.9	–	–	–	7.9	–
85.0	157.0	131.0	25.0	66.0	104.0	88.0
257.0	*551.4*	*466.3*	*53.0*	*233.6*	*397.2*	*375.1*
200.1	*348.4*	*375.8*	*125.2*	*148.3*	*272.9*	*243.7*
227.0	–	–	*20.0*	*227.0*	–	–
135.0	*301.0*	*278.6*	*19.0*	*130.5*	*202.5*	*274.1*
684.1	***899.8***	***842.1***	***198.2***	***608.9***	***670.2***	***618.8***

MAIN AID AGGREGATES

	1977	1978	1979	1980
DAC COUNTRIES COMBINED				
PRIVATE SECTOR NET	615.9	569.3	596.0	256.4
Direct Investment	-19.4	5.1	8.2	-14.5
Portfolio Invest.	24.0	-29.5	163.7	-80.0
Export Credits	611.3	593.7	424.0	350.9
OFFICIAL & PRIVATE				
GROSS:				
Contractual Lending	968.2	1191.0	1769.6	1567.0
Export Credits Tot.	883.9	820.6	813.7	579.2
Export Credits Priv	830.8	769.9	760.6	548.6
OTHER NET DATA				
Contractual Lending	672.6	956.9	1203.9	1233.0
Export Credits Tot.	646.8	623.4	474.4	334.5
(Bank Sector Loans)	-158.0	148.0	878.0	394.0
ODA CONCESSIONALITY				
Total:Grant Element	78.0	66.0	59.0	65.0
Loans:Grant Element	61.0	62.0	54.0	54.0
OTHER SOURCES				
CMEA Countr.(Gross)	37.8	40.5	45.1	43.9
Intra LDCS Exc.OPEC	–	–	–	–
Other	–	–	–	–
ALL SOURCE COMMITMENTS				
TOTAL BILATERAL	266.4	750.1	1000.4	1416.7
of which				
OPEC (ODA)	–	–	126.2	288.1
CMEA (ODA)	–	–	53.0	–
TOTAL MULTILAT.(ODA)	8.4	19.3	180.6	208.1
TOTAL BIL.& MULTIL.	274.9	769.4	1181.0	1624.8
of which				
ODA Grants	27.3	33.7	85.8	214.2
ODA Loans	23.5	165.6	880.8	1053.8
ODA CONCESSIONALITY				
Total: Grant Element	82.0	67.0	57.0	56.0
Loans: Grant Element	61.0	61.0	53.0	45.0

INDEBTEDNESS

	1977	1978	1979	1980
TOTAL DEBT DISBURSED	***5294.6***	***7315.6***	***11829.1***	
Debt to DAC Countries	3780.0	5200.0	9313.0	
ODA	1758.0	2059.0	2614.0	
Total Export Credits	1388.0	2286.0	2950.0	
Other Private Market	634.0	855.0	3749.0	
International Org.	1201.1	1462.3	1796.3	
CMEA	258.7	334.4	455.3	
Other	54.9	318.9	264.5	
TOTAL DEBT SERVICE	***447.6***	***647.7***	***924.1***	
Paid to DAC Countries	309.9	414.1	565.3	
ODA	100.3	56.2	56.5	
Total Export Credits	144.0	255.2	368.1	
Other Private Market	65.6	102.7	140.7	
International Org.	91.6	122.5	172.3	
CMEA	37.6	39.8	53.7	
Other	8.5	71.3	132.8	

ECONOMIC INDICATORS

	1977	1978	1979	1980
GNP Curr. Prices, $M	48478.2	53142.2	61142.9	59106.0
Real GNP, 1976=100	103.0	106.0	106.0	105.0
GNP/Cap Curr. Prices,$	1152.0	1231.0	1382.0	1303.0
GNP/cap Atlas Basis, $	1217.1	1310.8	1379.5	1456.8
Real GNP/Cap, 1976=100	101.0	101.0	98.0	95.0
Population, Million	42.1	43.1	44.2	45.4
Curr.A/C Deficit(-),$M	-3242.0	-1238.0	-1020.0	-2778.0
BOP Exp. & Transf.,$M	3656.0	4166.0	5070.0	6374.0
Exp. to OECD CIF, $M	1333.7	1524.3	1802.6	1895.1
of which				
Manufact.	355.1	384.2	492.7	483.4
Imp. from OECD FOB, $M	3544.8	2788.6	3102.1	3724.1
Reserves ex. Gold, $M	620.0	833.0	767.0	1274.0

	1977	1978	1979	1980	1977	1978	1979	1980
	TOTAL RECEIPTS NET				**TOTAL ODA NET**			
DAC COUNTRIES								
Australia	0.2	0.1	0.4	1.8	0.2	0.1	0.4	1.8
Austria	0.0	0.3	0.0	0.1	0.0	0.3	0.0	0.1
Belgium	0.0	0.0	-0.4	0.2	0.0	0.1	0.0	0.2
Canada	0.5	0.3	0.1	0.9	0.5	0.3	0.1	0.9
Denmark	-0.3	0.0	1.4	1.7	-0.3	0.0	1.4	1.7
Finland	–	–	0.0	0.2	–	–	0.0	0.2
France	0.5	4.2	-0.4	12.6	–	–	–	4.1
Germany, Fed. Rep.	4.8	2.4	4.6	3.6	0.8	3.1	2.5	5.7
Italy	6.5	-155.2	-5.1	-5.7	0.2	0.2	0.8	0.1
Japan	0.7	0.5	0.3	0.0	0.7	0.5	0.3	0.0
Netherlands	0.8	0.7	3.1	4.3	0.8	0.7	3.1	4.3
New Zealand	–	–	–	–	–	–	–	–
Norway	–	–	0.9	0.4	–	–	0.9	0.4
Sweden	–	–	1.4	2.4	–	–	1.4	2.4
Switzerland	0.0	0.1	0.5	0.7	0.0	0.1	0.5	0.7
United Kingdom	-4.6	3.2	6.7	24.0	0.8	2.2	4.7	6.7
United States	–	–	–	13.0	–	–	–	13.0
TOTAL	*9.2*	*-143.4*	*13.5*	*60.1*	*3.8*	*7.5*	*16.1*	*42.3*
MULTILATERAL								
AF.D.F.	–	–	–	–	–	–	–	–
AF.D.B.	3.1	0.8	3.8	2.5	–	–	–	–
AS.D.B.	–	–	–	–	–	–	–	–
CAR.D.B.	–	–	–	–	–	–	–	–
E.E.C.	4.4	0.8	11.3	25.1	4.4	0.8	11.3	25.1
IBRD	-0.6	-0.3	-0.7	-0.7	–	–	–	–
IDA	1.0	1.5	1.0	0.7	1.0	1.5	1.0	0.7
I.D.B.	–	–	–	–	–	–	–	–
IFAD	–	–	–	–	–	–	–	–
I.F.C.	–	–	–	–	–	–	–	–
IMF TRUST FUND	–	–	–	29.2	–	–	–	29.2
U.N. AGENCIES	–	–	–	–	–	–	–	–
UNDP	2.8	3.8	3.6	3.3	2.8	3.8	3.6	3.3
UNTA	0.6	0.8	0.8	0.3	0.6	0.8	0.8	0.3
UNICEF	0.3	0.4	0.9	3.1	0.3	0.4	0.9	3.1
UNRWA	–	–	–	–	–	–	–	–
WFP	0.7	1.6	3.3	4.9	0.7	1.6	3.3	4.9
UNHCR	0.1	0.1	4.2	2.9	0.1	0.1	4.2	2.9
Other Multilateral	0.5	0.6	0.2	0.4	0.5	0.6	0.2	0.4
Arab OPEC Agencies	5.1	0.3	0.1	0.1	5.1	0.3	0.1	0.1
TOTAL	*17.9*	*10.3*	*28.4*	*71.7*	*15.4*	*9.8*	*25.3*	*69.9*
OPEC COUNTRIES	*3.0*	*4.0*	*0.9*	*7.0*	*3.0*	*4.0*	*0.9*	*7.0*
E.E.C.+ MEMBERS	*12.1*	*-144.0*	*21.2*	*65.8*	*6.7*	*7.0*	*23.8*	*48.0*
TOTAL	***30.0***	***-129.2***	***42.8***	***138.9***	***22.2***	***21.3***	***42.3***	***119.2***

	1977	1978	1979	1980	1977	1978	1979	1980
	ODA LOANS GROSS				**ODA LOANS NET**			
DAC COUNTRIES								
Australia	–	–	–	–	–	–	–	–
Austria	–	–	–	–	–	–	–	–
Belgium	–	–	–	–	–	–	–	–
Canada	0.2	–	–	–	0.2	-2.0	–	–
Denmark	–	–	–	–	-0.3	–	-7.7	–
Finland	–	–	–	–	–	–	–	–
France	–	–	–	1.8	–	–	–	1.8
Germany, Fed. Rep.	2.1	1.1	0.1	–	-0.5	1.1	0.1	-0.6
Italy	–	–	–	–	–	–	–	–
Japan	0.7	–	–	–	0.5	-0.1	-0.3	-0.1
Netherlands	–	–	0.1	–	–	–	-3.5	–
New Zealand	–	–	–	–	–	–	–	–
Norway	–	–	–	–	–	–	–	–
Sweden	–	–	–	–	–	–	–	–
Switzerland	–	–	–	–	–	–	–	–
United Kingdom	–	–	–	–	–	–	–	–
United States	–	–	–	–	–	–	–	–
TOTAL	*3.0*	*1.1*	*0.3*	*1.8*	*-0.2*	*-1.1*	*-11.4*	*1.0*
MULTILATERAL	*5.7*	*1.7*	*1.3*	*30.3*	*5.6*	*1.5*	*1.0*	*30.0*
OPEC COUNTRIES	*2.9*	*3.6*	*0.7*	*5.8*	*2.9*	*3.6*	*0.7*	*5.8*
E.E.C.+ MEMBERS	*2.1*	*1.1*	*0.3*	*1.8*	*-0.8*	*1.1*	*-11.1*	*1.1*
TOTAL	***11.6***	***6.4***	***2.3***	***37.9***	***8.3***	***4.0***	***-9.7***	***36.8***

	1977	1978	1979	1980	1977	1978	1979	1980
	TOTAL OFFICIAL GROSS				**TOTAL OFFICIAL NET**			
DAC COUNTRIES								
Australia	0.2	0.1	0.4	1.8	0.2	0.1	0.4	1.8
Austria	0.0	0.3	0.0	0.1	0.0	0.3	0.0	0.1
Belgium	0.0	0.1	0.0	0.2	0.0	0.1	0.0	0.2
Canada	0.5	2.4	0.1	0.9	0.5	0.3	0.1	0.9
Denmark	0.0	0.0	9.1	1.7	-0.3	0.0	1.4	1.7
Finland	–	–	0.0	0.2	–	–	0.0	0.2
France	–	–	–	4.1	–	–	–	4.1
Germany, Fed. Rep.	3.4	3.1	2.5	6.4	0.8	3.0	2.5	5.7
Italy	0.2	0.2	0.8	0.1	0.2	0.2	0.8	0.1
Japan	0.9	0.6	0.7	0.1	0.7	0.5	0.3	0.0
Netherlands	0.8	0.7	6.7	4.3	0.8	0.7	3.1	4.3
New Zealand	–	–	–	–	–	–	–	–
Norway	–	–	0.9	0.4	–	–	0.9	0.4
Sweden	–	–	1.4	2.4	–	–	1.4	2.4
Switzerland	0.0	0.1	0.5	0.7	0.0	0.1	0.5	0.7
United Kingdom	0.8	2.2	4.7	6.7	0.7	2.1	4.7	6.7
United States	–	–	–	13.0	–	–	–	13.0
TOTAL	*7.0*	*9.7*	*27.8*	*43.0*	*3.7*	*7.4*	*16.1*	*42.3*
MULTILATERAL	*18.8*	*10.9*	*30.0*	*73.3*	*17.9*	*10.3*	*28.4*	*71.7*
OPEC COUNTRIES	*3.0*	*4.0*	*0.9*	*7.0*	*3.0*	*4.0*	*0.9*	*7.0*
E.E.C.+ MEMBERS	*9.7*	*7.0*	*35.2*	*48.6*	*6.6*	*6.8*	*23.8*	*48.0*
TOTAL	***28.8***	***24.5***	***58.7***	***123.3***	***24.5***	***21.6***	***45.4***	***121.0***

	197[illegible]
TOTAL ODA GROSS	
Australia	0.[illegible]
Austria	0.[illegible]
Belgium	0.[illegible]
Canada	0.[illegible]
Denmark	0.[illegible]
Finland	-
France	-
Germany, Fed. Rep.	3.[illegible]
Italy	0.[illegible]
Japan	0.[illegible]
Netherlands	0.[illegible]
New Zealand	-
Norway	-
Sweden	-
Switzerland	0.[illegible]
United Kingdom	0.[illegible]
United States	-
TOTAL	*7.[illegible]*
AF.D.F.	-
AF.D.B.	-
AS.D.B.	-
CAR.D.B.	-
E.E.C.	4.[illegible]
IBRD	-
IDA	1.[illegible]
I.D.B.	-
IFAD	-
I.F.C.	-
IMF TRUST FUND	-
U.N. AGENCIES	-
UNDP	2.[illegible]
UNTA	0.[illegible]
UNICEF	0.[illegible]
UNRWA	-
WFP	0.[illegible]
UNHCR	0.[illegible]
Other Multilateral	0.[illegible]
Arab OPEC Agencies	5.[illegible]
TOTAL	*15.[illegible]*
OPEC COUNTRIES	*3.[illegible]*
E.E.C.+ MEMBERS	*9.[illegible]*
TOTAL	***25.[illegible]***
GRANTS	
Australia	0.[illegible]
Austria	0.[illegible]
Belgium	0.[illegible]
Canada	0.[illegible]
Denmark	0.[illegible]
Finland	-
France	-
Germany, Fed. Rep.	1.[illegible]
Italy	0.[illegible]
Japan	0.[illegible]
Netherlands	0.[illegible]
New Zealand	-
Norway	-
Sweden	-
Switzerland	0.[illegible]
United Kingdom	0.[illegible]
United States	-
TOTAL	*4.[illegible]*
MULTILATERAL	*9.[illegible]*
OPEC COUNTRIES	*0.[illegible]*
E.E.C.+ MEMBERS	*7.[illegible]*
TOTAL	***13.[illegible]***
TOTAL OOF GROSS	
Australia	-
Austria	-
Belgium	-
Canada	-
Denmark	-
Finland	-
France	-
Germany, Fed. Rep.	0.[illegible]
Italy	-
Japan	-
Netherlands	-
New Zealand	-
Norway	-
Sweden	-
Switzerland	-
United Kingdom	-
United States	-
TOTAL	*0.[illegible]*
MULTILATERAL	*3.[illegible]*
OPEC COUNTRIES	-
E.E.C.+ MEMBERS	*0.[illegible]*
TOTAL	***3.[illegible]***

1978	1979	1980	1977	1978	1979	1980
			ODA COMMITMENTS			
0.1	0.4	1.8	0.1	0.1	1.3	4.7
0.3	0.0	0.1	–	0.0	–	–
0.1	0.0	0.2	–	–	–	–
2.4	0.1	0.9	0.3	2.5	0.1	1.5
0.0	9.1	1.7	0.0	–	–	1.4
–	0.0	0.2	–	–	0.0	0.1
–	–	4.1	–	–	–	13.7
3.1	2.5	6.4	1.2	1.8	3.6	14.2
0.2	0.8	0.1	0.2	0.2	0.8	0.1
0.6	0.7	0.1	0.2	1.2	0.7	0.6
0.7	6.7	4.3	0.8	1.1	8.5	21.7
–	–	–	–	–	–	0.0
–	0.9	0.4	–	–	0.9	0.4
–	1.4	2.4	–	–	–	2.6
0.1	0.5	0.7	–	–	–	0.7
2.2	4.7	6.7	0.8	2.2	7.3	13.4
–	–	13.0	–	–	3.0	4.8
9.7	*27.8*	*43.0*	*3.7*	*9.0*	*26.3*	*80.0*
–	–	–	–	–	–	9.4
–	–	–	–	–	–	–
–	–	–	–	–	–	–
–	–	–	–	–	–	–
0.8	11.3	25.1	8.5	0.9	36.2	25.0
–	–	–	–	–	–	–
1.7	1.3	1.1	–	–	–	80.7
–	–	–	–	–	–	–
–	–	–	–	–	–	–
–	–	–	–	–	–	–
–	–	29.2	–	–	–	–
–	–	–	5.0	7.3	13.0	14.8
3.8	3.6	3.3	–	–	–	–
0.8	0.8	0.3	–	–	–	–
0.4	0.9	3.1	–	–	–	–
–	–	–	–	–	–	–
1.6	3.3	4.9	–	–	–	–
0.1	4.2	2.9	–	–	–	–
0.6	0.2	0.4	–	–	–	–
0.3	0.1	0.1	5.1	11.4	–	5.0
10.0	*25.6*	*70.3*	*18.5*	*19.6*	*49.2*	*134.9*
4.0	*0.9*	*7.0*	*15.2*	*6.5*	–	*6.9*
7.0	*35.2*	*48.6*	*11.5*	*6.1*	*56.5*	*89.6*
23.7	***54.2***	***120.3***	***37.4***	***35.1***	***75.5***	***221.8***
			TECH. COOP. GRANTS			
0.1	0.4	1.8	0.2	0.1	0.1	0.3
0.3	0.0	0.1	0.0	0.3	0.0	0.1
0.1	0.0	0.2	0.0	0.0	0.0	0.0
2.4	0.1	0.9	0.3	0.3	0.1	0.1
0.0	9.1	1.7	0.0	0.0	0.0	0.5
–	0.0	0.2	–	–	0.0	0.0
–	–	2.4	–	–	–	1.0
2.0	2.4	6.4	1.0	2.0	1.9	4.6
0.2	0.8	0.1	0.2	0.2	0.8	0.1
0.6	0.7	0.1	0.2	0.6	0.2	0.1
0.7	6.6	4.3	0.7	0.5	0.6	0.5
–	–	–	–	–	–	–
–	0.9	0.4	–	–	0.0	–
–	1.4	2.4	–	–	–	–
0.1	0.5	0.7	–	–	–	–
2.2	4.7	6.7	0.8	2.2	3.1	3.8
–	–	13.0	–	–	–	–
8.6	*27.5*	*41.3*	*3.5*	*6.3*	*6.8*	*11.1*
8.3	*24.3*	*39.9*	*4.3*	*5.7*	*9.7*	*14.8*
0.3	*0.1*	*1.3*	–	–	–	–
5.9	*34.9*	*46.8*	*2.7*	*4.9*	*6.4*	*10.5*
17.3	***52.0***	***82.4***	***7.7***	***12.0***	***16.4***	***25.9***
			TOTAL OOF NET			
–	–	–	–	–	–	–
–	–	–	–	–	–	–
–	–	–	–	–	–	–
–	–	–	–	–	–	–
–	–	–	–	–	–	–
–	–	–	–	–	–	–
–	–	–	–	–	–	–
–	–	–	0.0	0.0	–	–
–	–	–	–	–	–	–
–	–	–	–	–	–	–
–	–	–	–	–	–	–
–	–	–	–	–	–	–
–	–	–	–	–	–	–
–	–	–	–	–	–	–
–	–	–	–	–	–	–
–	–	–	-0.1	-0.1	–	–
–	–	–	–	–	–	–
–	–	–	*-0.1*	*-0.2*	–	–
0.9	*4.4*	*3.0*	*2.5*	*0.5*	*3.1*	*1.8*
–	–	–	–	–	–	–
–	–	–	*-0.1*	*-0.2*	–	–
0.9	***4.4***	***3.0***	***2.3***	***0.3***	***3.1***	***1.8***

	1977	1978	1979	1980
MAIN AID AGGREGATES				
DAC COUNTRIES COMBINED				
PRIVATE SECTOR NET	5.5	-150.8	-2.6	17.9
Direct Investment	–	2.0	2.0	–
Portfolio Invest.	–	–	3.2	-0.9
Export Credits	5.5	-152.7	-7.8	18.7
OFFICIAL & PRIVATE GROSS:				
Contractual Lending	16.8	8.9	4.4	29.7
Export Credits Tot.	13.8	7.9	4.1	27.9
Export Credits Priv	13.8	7.9	4.1	27.9
OTHER NET DATA				
Contractual Lending	5.2	-154.0	-19.2	19.7
Export Credits Tot.	5.5	-152.7	-7.8	18.7
(Bank Sector Loans)	1.0	-1.0	2.0	7.0
ODA CONCESSIONALITY				
Total:Grant Element	100.0	100.0	100.0	94.0
Loans:Grant Element	–	–	–	56.0
OTHER SOURCES				
CMEA Countr.(Gross)	0.6	0.5	0.5	0.1
Intra LDCS Exc.OPEC	–	–	–	–
Other	–	–	–	–
ALL SOURCE COMMITMENTS				
TOTAL BILATERAL	18.9	15.5	26.3	86.9
of which				
OPEC (ODA)	15.2	6.5	–	6.9
CMEA (ODA)	–	–	–	–
TOTAL MULTILAT.(ODA)	18.5	19.6	49.2	134.9
TOTAL BIL.& MULTIL.	37.4	35.1	75.5	221.8
of which				
ODA Grants	17.6	17.4	75.5	102.8
ODA Loans	19.8	17.6	–	119.0
ODA CONCESSIONALITY				
Total: Grant Element	73.0	66.0	100.0	88.0
Loans: Grant Element	49.0	32.0	–	76.0
INDEBTEDNESS				
TOTAL DEBT DISBURSED	***250.7***	***286.3***	***284.6***	
Debt to DAC Countries	123.0	136.0	126.0	
ODA	88.0	99.0	92.0	
Total Export Credits	32.0	30.0	32.0	
Other Private Market	3.0	7.0	2.0	
International Org.	68.0	72.5	71.2	
CMEA	46.7	45.7	35.0	
Other	12.9	32.0	52.5	
TOTAL DEBT SERVICE	***23.0***	***7.7***	***35.6***	
Paid to DAC Countries	15.6	3.9	11.2	
ODA	4.3	0.3	0.7	
Total Export Credits	10.6	3.3	9.3	
Other Private Market	0.7	0.3	1.2	
International Org.	1.8	1.6	5.0	
CMEA	2.9	2.0	10.4	
Other	2.7	0.2	9.0	
ECONOMIC INDICATORS				
GNP Curr. Prices, $M	5868.4	8351.8	9268.5	10231.5
Real GNP, 1976=100	101.0	96.0	88.0	82.0
GNP/Cap Curr. Prices,$	487.0	673.0	724.0	775.0
GNP/cap Atlas Basis, $	302.4	299.7	290.0	284.4
Real GNP/Cap, 1976=100	98.0	90.0	80.0	73.0
Population, Million	12.0	12.4	12.8	13.2
Curr.A/C Deficit(-),$M	66.1	-136.2	14.7	-101.7
BOP Exp. & Transf.,$M	556.1	337.4	414.2	335.6
Exp. to OECD CIF, $M	491.8	340.4	386.5	424.9
of which				
Manufact.	1.8	54.4	1.1	1.4
Imp. from OECD FOB, $M	170.1	173.7	61.5	180.3
Reserves ex. Gold, $M	47.2	52.7	22.8	16.8

	TOTAL RECEIPTS NET 1977	1978	1979	1980	TOTAL ODA NET 1977	1978	1979	1980	TOTAL ODA GROSS 197
DAC COUNTRIES									
Australia	0.1	–	–	–	0.1	–	–	–	0
Austria	0.5	0.5	1.3	0.6	0.5	0.5	1.3	0.6	0
Belgium	0.7	1.0	2.1	1.6	0.7	1.0	2.2	1.6	0
Canada	1.2	3.6	13.3	8.2	1.2	3.6	13.3	8.2	1
Denmark	0.1	0.3	0.6	3.9	0.1	0.3	0.6	3.4	0
Finland	–	–	–	–	–	–	–	–	
France	28.3	33.4	52.4	67.9	28.3	32.7	35.7	55.9	29
Germany, Fed. Rep.	13.8	16.7	27.8	32.2	13.6	16.7	27.7	31.3	13
Italy	0.1	0.1	0.2	0.3	0.1	0.1	0.1	0.0	0
Japan	0.3	0.3	0.1	1.9	0.2	0.3	0.1	1.9	0
Netherlands	7.7	18.4	24.8	18.1	7.7	18.4	24.8	18.1	7
New Zealand	–	–	–	–	–	–	–	–	
Norway	2.2	0.1	1.4	0.2	2.2	0.1	1.4	0.2	2
Sweden	–	–	–	–	–	–	–	–	
Switzerland	3.0	2.9	1.7	2.0	3.0	2.9	1.7	2.0	3
United Kingdom	0.1	0.1	0.1	0.2	0.1	0.1	0.1	0.2	0
United States	15.0	20.0	23.0	28.0	14.0	20.0	23.0	28.0	14
TOTAL	*73.0*	*97.3*	*148.9*	*164.9*	*71.7*	*96.6*	*132.0*	*151.1*	*73*
MULTILATERAL									
AF.D.F.	1.2	1.9	4.3	10.9	1.2	1.9	4.3	10.9	1
AF.D.B.	-0.1	0.8	-0.4	-0.4	–	–	–	–	
AS.D.B.	–	–	–	–	–	–	–	–	
CAR.D.B.	–	–	–	–	–	–	–	–	
E.E.C.	14.4	25.1	20.8	10.5	14.4	25.2	20.9	10.6	14
IBRD	–	–	–	–	–	–	–	–	
IDA	12.7	14.8	19.6	11.8	12.7	14.8	19.6	11.8	12
I.D.B.	–	–	–	–	–	–	–	–	
IFAD	–	–	–	–	–	–	–	–	
I.F.C.	–	–	–	0.5	–	–	–	–	
IMF TRUST FUND	–	6.8	5.0	4.4	–	6.8	5.0	4.4	
U.N. AGENCIES	–	–	–	–	–	–	–	–	
UNDP	3.4	3.1	4.2	6.2	3.4	3.1	4.2	6.2	3
UNTA	0.6	0.8	0.5	0.2	0.6	0.8	0.5	0.2	0
UNICEF	0.7	0.5	1.4	1.6	0.7	0.5	1.4	1.6	0
UNRWA	–	–	–	–	–	–	–	–	
WFP	1.2	5.6	3.3	5.9	1.2	5.6	3.3	5.9	1
UNHCR	–	–	–	–	–	–	–	–	
Other Multilateral	1.6	2.6	2.2	2.9	1.6	2.6	2.2	2.9	1
Arab OPEC Agencies	3.0	1.5	4.9	8.8	3.0	1.5	4.9	6.9	3
TOTAL	*38.5*	*63.5*	*65.8*	*63.0*	*38.6*	*62.8*	*66.3*	*61.2*	*38*
OPEC COUNTRIES	–	–	–	–	–	–	–	–	
E.E.C.+ MEMBERS	*65.2*	*95.0*	*128.8*	*134.6*	*65.0*	*94.4*	*112.0*	*120.9*	*66*
TOTAL	***111.4***	***160.8***	***214.7***	***227.9***	***110.3***	***159.4***	***198.4***	***212.3***	***112***

	ODA LOANS GROSS 1977	1978	1979	1980	ODA LOANS NET 1977	1978	1979	1980	GRANTS 197
DAC COUNTRIES									
Australia	–	–	–	–	–	–	–	–	0?
Austria	–	–	0.0	–	–	–	0.0	–	0?
Belgium	–	–	–	–	–	–	–	–	0?
Canada	0.2	–	–	–	0.2	-0.9	–	–	1
Denmark	0.0	–	–	3.0	0.0	–	-3.8	3.0	0?
Finland	–	–	–	–	–	–	–	–	
France	4.8	6.9	4.8	18.3	3.3	5.1	2.5	15.7	25
Germany, Fed. Rep.	4.5	3.4	0.3	–	4.3	3.1	-32.8	-0.8	9
Italy	–	–	–	–	–	–	–	–	6?
Japan	–	–	–	–	–	–	–	–	0?
Netherlands	1.8	1.1	2.6	1.5	1.8	-2.5	0.2	0.1	5
New Zealand	–	–	–	–	–	–	–	–	
Norway	–	–	–	–	–	–	–	–	2
Sweden	–	–	–	–	–	–	–	–	
Switzerland	–	–	–	–	–	–	–	–	3
United Kingdom	–	–	–	–	–	–	–	–	0?
United States	–	–	–	–	–	–	–	–	14
TOTAL	*11.4*	*11.4*	*7.8*	*22.8*	*9.7*	*4.8*	*-33.9*	*17.9*	*6.*
MULTILATERAL	*21.3*	*26.3*	*34.9*	*34.0*	*21.3*	*25.5*	*34.2*	*33.9*	*1.*
OPEC COUNTRIES	–	–	–	–	–	–	–	–	
E.E.C.+ MEMBERS	*15.6*	*11.9*	*8.1*	*22.8*	*13.9*	*6.3*	*-33.6*	*17.9*	*5.*
TOTAL	***32.6***	***37.7***	***42.7***	***56.8***	***30.9***	***30.3***	***0.3***	***51.8***	***7.***

	TOTAL OFFICIAL GROSS 1977	1978	1979	1980	TOTAL OFFICIAL NET 1977	1978	1979	1980	TOTAL OOF GROSS
DAC COUNTRIES									
Australia	0.1	–	–	–	0.1	–	–	–	
Austria	0.5	0.5	1.3	0.6	0.5	0.5	1.3	0.6	
Belgium	0.7	1.0	2.2	1.6	0.7	1.0	2.2	1.6	
Canada	1.2	4.5	13.3	8.2	1.2	3.6	13.3	8.2	
Denmark	0.1	0.3	4.4	3.4	0.1	0.3	0.6	3.4	
Finland	–	–	–	–	–	–	–	–	
France	29.8	34.5	38.0	70.3	28.2	32.6	35.6	67.5	
Germany, Fed. Rep.	13.8	16.9	60.9	32.1	13.6	16.7	27.7	31.3	
Italy	0.1	0.1	0.1	0.0	0.1	0.1	0.1	0.0	
Japan	0.2	0.3	0.1	1.9	0.2	0.3	0.1	1.9	
Netherlands	7.7	22.0	27.2	19.5	7.7	18.4	24.8	18.1	
New Zealand	–	–	–	–	–	–	–	–	
Norway	2.2	0.1	1.4	0.2	2.2	0.1	1.4	0.2	
Sweden	–	–	–	–	–	–	–	–	
Switzerland	3.0	2.9	1.7	2.0	3.0	2.9	1.7	2.0	
United Kingdom	0.1	0.1	0.1	0.2	0.1	0.1	0.1	0.2	
United States	15.0	20.0	23.0	28.0	15.0	20.0	23.0	28.0	
TOTAL	*74.4*	*103.2*	*173.7*	*167.9*	*72.6*	*96.5*	*131.9*	*162.8*	
MULTILATERAL	*38.7*	*64.7*	*67.1*	*63.6*	*38.5*	*63.5*	*65.8*	*63.0*	
OPEC COUNTRIES	–	–	–	–	–	–	–	–	
E.E.C.+ MEMBERS	*66.8*	*100.1*	*153.7*	*137.7*	*64.9*	*94.3*	*111.8*	*132.5*	
TOTAL	***113.1***	***167.9***	***240.8***	***231.5***	***111.1***	***160.1***	***197.8***	***225.8***	

E.E.C.+ MEMBERS

TOTAL

ODA COMMITMENTS

1978	1979	1980	1977	1978	1979	1980
–	–	–	–	–	–	–
0.5	1.3	0.6	0.2	0.3	0.1	0.2
1.0	2.2	1.6	–	1.6	2.3	–
4.5	13.3	8.2	19.1	38.9	0.2	2.2
0.3	4.4	3.4	–	3.6	3.8	0.5
–	–	–	–	–	–	–
34.5	38.0	58.5	23.7	31.2	41.3	75.9
16.9	60.9	32.1	17.6	11.1	106.0	22.6
0.1	0.1	0.0	0.1	0.1	0.1	0.0
0.3	0.1	1.9	0.2	0.3	2.0	0.1
22.0	27.2	19.5	19.8	35.7	22.9	32.2
–	–	–	–	–	–	–
0.1	1.4	0.2	2.9	–	0.5	–
–	–	–	–	–	–	–
2.9	1.7	2.0	6.7	1.6	0.6	0.5
0.1	0.1	0.2	0.1	0.1	0.1	0.2
20.0	23.0	28.0	11.8	21.9	21.3	36.0
103.2	*173.7*	*156.1*	*102.2*	*146.3*	*201.3*	*170.4*
2.7	5.1	10.9	5.6	17.4	15.2	0.7
–	–	–	–	–	–	–
–	–	–	–	–	–	–
–	–	–	–	–	–	–
25.2	20.9	10.6	11.7	17.5	16.4	36.0
–	–	–	–	–	–	–
14.8	19.6	11.8	12.8	8.2	11.0	21.0
–	–	–	–	–	–	–
–	–	–	–	–	–	–
–	–	–	–	–	–	–
6.8	5.0	4.4	–	–	–	–
–	–	–	7.4	12.6	11.7	16.7
3.1	4.2	6.2	–	–	–	–
0.8	0.5	0.2	–	–	–	–
0.5	1.4	1.6	–	–	–	–
–	–	–	–	–	–	–
5.6	3.3	5.9	–	–	–	–
–	–	–	–	–	–	–
2.6	2.2	2.9	–	–	–	–
1.5	4.9	6.9	4.4	5.4	1.6	6.0
63.6	*67.1*	*61.2*	*41.8*	*61.1*	*55.8*	*80.4*
–	–	–	–	–	–	–
100.1	*153.7*	*125.9*	*73.1*	*100.8*	*192.9*	*167.4*
166.7	***240.8***	***217.3***	***144.0***	***207.4***	***257.1***	***250.8***

TECH. COOP. GRANTS

1978	1979	1980	1977	1978	1979	1980
–	–	–	–	–	–	–
0.5	1.3	0.6	0.5	0.5	1.3	0.6
1.0	2.2	1.6	0.6	0.6	0.5	1.0
4.5	13.3	8.2	0.6	0.3	0.2	0.2
0.3	4.4	0.4	0.1	0.3	0.6	0.4
–	–	–	–	–	–	–
27.6	33.2	40.2	15.9	18.4	21.9	24.3
13.6	60.6	32.1	7.9	11.1	13.5	15.6
0.1	0.1	0.0	0.1	0.1	0.1	0.0
0.3	0.1	1.9	0.2	0.3	0.1	0.1
20.9	24.6	18.0	3.5	7.5	7.8	8.3
–	–	–	–	–	–	–
0.1	1.4	0.2	–	0.0	0.2	0.0
–	–	–	–	–	–	–
2.9	1.7	2.0	0.1	0.1	0.1	0.4
0.1	0.1	0.2	0.1	0.1	0.1	0.2
20.0	23.0	28.0	2.0	3.0	6.0	11.0
91.8	*165.9*	*133.2*	*31.4*	*42.1*	*52.4*	*62.2*
37.3	*32.2*	*27.3*	*6.2*	*7.0*	*8.4*	*16.7*
–	–	–	–	–	–	–
88.2	*145.6*	*103.1*	*28.1*	*37.9*	*44.5*	*49.9*
129.1	***198.1***	***160.5***	***37.6***	***49.1***	***60.7***	***78.9***

TOTAL OOF NET

1978	1979	1980	1977	1978	1979	1980
–	–	–	–	–	–	–
–	–	–	–	–	–	–
–	–	–	–	–	–	–
–	–	–	–	–	–	–
–	–	0.0	–	–	–	0.0
–	–	–	–	–	–	–
–	–	11.9	-0.1	-0.1	-0.1	11.6
–	–	–	–	–	–	–
–	–	–	–	–	–	–
–	–	–	–	–	–	–
–	–	–	–	–	–	–
–	–	–	–	–	–	–
–	–	–	–	–	–	–
–	–	–	–	–	–	–
–	–	–	–	–	–	–
–	–	–	–	–	–	–
–	–	–	1.0	–	–	–
–	–	*11.9*	*0.9*	*-0.1*	*-0.1*	*11.6*
1.1	–	*2.4*	*-0.2*	*0.7*	*-0.5*	*1.8*
–	–	–	–	–	–	–
–	–	*11.9*	*-0.1*	*-0.2*	*-0.2*	*11.5*
1.1	–	***14.2***	***0.8***	***0.6***	***-0.6***	***13.5***

MAIN AID AGGREGATES

	1977	1978	1979	1980
DAC COUNTRIES COMBINED				
PRIVATE SECTOR NET	0.4	0.7	16.9	2.2
Direct Investment	-0.1	0.0	0.0	-0.2
Portfolio Invest.	–	-0.5	14.4	-0.5
Export Credits	0.4	1.2	2.6	2.8
OFFICIAL & PRIVATE				
GROSS:				
Contractual Lending	14.5	14.2	10.8	37.9
Export Credits Tot.	3.1	2.9	3.0	3.2
Export Credits Priv	2.1	2.9	3.0	3.2
OTHER NET DATA				
Contractual Lending	11.0	5.9	-31.4	32.4
Export Credits Tot.	1.4	1.2	2.6	2.8
(Bank Sector Loans)	4.0	-3.0	-1.0	–
ODA CONCESSIONALITY				
Total:Grant Element	98.0	100.0	99.0	91.0
Loans:Grant Element	83.0	–	72.0	52.0
OTHER SOURCES				
CMEA Countr.(Gross)	–	–	–	–
Intra LDCS Exc.OPEC	–	–	–	–
Other	–	–	–	–
ALL SOURCE COMMITMENTS				
TOTAL BILATERAL	110.5	155.1	201.3	189.1
of which				
OPEC (ODA)	–	–	–	–
CMEA (ODA)	–	–	–	–
TOTAL MULTILAT.(ODA)	41.8	61.1	55.8	80.4
TOTAL BIL.& MULTIL.	152.3	216.2	257.1	269.4
of which				
ODA Grants	113.5	176.4	222.2	175.8
ODA Loans	30.6	31.0	34.8	75.0
ODA CONCESSIONALITY				
Total: Grant Element	96.0	96.0	97.0	90.0
Loans: Grant Element	80.0	79.0	78.0	62.0

INDEBTEDNESS

	1977	1978	1979	1980
TOTAL DEBT DISBURSED	***132.2***	***189.2***	***212.6***	
Debt to DAC Countries	60.0	90.0	70.0	
ODA	52.0	64.0	27.0	
Total Export Credits	8.0	24.0	27.0	
Other Private Market	–	2.0	16.0	
International Org.	61.2	88.0	128.0	
CMEA	6.1	6.1	9.4	
Other	4.9	5.1	5.2	
TOTAL DEBT SERVICE	***6.9***	***9.1***	***9.4***	
Paid to DAC Countries	5.3	7.2	7.2	
ODA	2.0	3.1	3.9	
Total Export Credits	3.3	3.6	1.5	
Other Private Market	–	0.5	1.8	
International Org.	1.4	1.7	1.9	
CMEA	–	–	–	
Other	0.2	0.2	0.2	

ECONOMIC INDICATORS

	1977	1978	1979	1980
GNP Curr. Prices, $M	694.8	867.8	1010.2	1143.9
Real GNP, 1976=100	96.0	101.0	102.0	105.0
GNP/Cap Curr. Prices,$	127.0	156.0	179.0	199.0
GNP/cap Atlas Basis, $	147.0	164.0	176.8	194.3
Real GNP/Cap, 1976=100	94.0	98.0	97.0	98.0
Population, Million	5.5	5.6	5.6	5.7
Curr.A/C Deficit(-),$M	-183.8	-215.5	–	–
BOP Exp. & Transf.,$M	158.7	191.0	–	–
Exp. to OECD CIF, $M	40.1	34.0	35.4	62.2
of which				
Manufact.	0.8	1.2	1.4	1.4
Imp. from OECD FOB, $M	128.5	142.7	150.8	191.6
Reserves ex. Gold, $M	56.2	36.3	61.5	68.1

	1977	1978	1979	1980	1977	1978	1979	1980		1977
TOTAL RECEIPTS NET					**TOTAL ODA NET**				**TOTAL ODA GROSS**	
DAC COUNTRIES										
Australia	–	–	–	0.0	–	–	–	–	Australia	–
Austria	0.0	0.0	0.0	0.0	0.0	0.0	0.0	0.0	Austria	0.
Belgium	0.6	-1.5	4.4	-0.4	0.1	0.2	0.1	0.3	Belgium	0.
Canada	–	–	–	1.3	–	–	–	–	Canada	–
Denmark	0.6	–	17.1	2.1	0.0	–	0.0	0.0	Denmark	0.
Finland	–	–	–	0.0	–	–	–	0.0	Finland	–
France	4.6	2.6	19.2	39.1	–	–	–	0.5	France	–
Germany, Fed. Rep.	4.1	9.3	-3.1	7.9	2.3	3.0	2.7	2.9	Germany, Fed. Rep.	2.
Italy	-1.3	-4.7	0.0	4.1	-0.4	-0.4	-0.5	0.3	Italy	0.
Japan	0.2	-2.3	-3.0	2.4	0.2	0.2	0.6	1.1	Japan	0.
Netherlands	-0.2	1.2	0.4	0.2	-0.2	1.2	0.4	0.2	Netherlands	0.
New Zealand	–	–	–	–	–	–	–	–	New Zealand	–
Norway	–	–	0.0	0.6	–	–	–	–	Norway	–
Sweden	0.2	–	–	-0.1	–	–	–	–	Sweden	–
Switzerland	-0.2	-0.2	0.1	0.4	0.0	0.0	0.0	–	Switzerland	0.
United Kingdom	5.1	3.6	2.1	-0.1	0.1	0.1	0.1	0.1	United Kingdom	0.
United States	-4.0	1.0	10.0	6.0	–	-2.0	1.0	–	United States	2.
TOTAL	*9.8*	*9.1*	*47.2*	*63.5*	*2.1*	*2.2*	*4.4*	*5.3*	*TOTAL*	*5.*
MULTILATERAL										
AF.D.F.	–	–	–	–	–	–	–	–	AF.D.F.	–
AF.D.B.	–	–	–	–	–	–	–	–	AF.D.B.	–
AS.D.B.	–	–	–	–	–	–	–	–	AS.D.B.	–
CAR.D.B.	–	–	–	–	–	–	–	–	CAR.D.B.	–
E.E.C.	0.0	0.5	0.1	–	0.0	0.5	0.1	–	E.E.C.	0.
IBRD	-3.6	-1.9	0.1	-1.5	–	–	–	–	IBRD	–
IDA	–	–	–	–	–	–	–	–	IDA	–
I.D.B.	5.1	5.1	7.8	9.7	3.4	5.0	7.0	1.0	I.D.B.	5.
IFAD	–	–	–	–	–	–	–	–	IFAD	–
I.F.C.	–	0.9	3.5	3.9	–	–	–	–	I.F.C.	–
IMF TRUST FUND	–	–	–	–	–	–	–	–	IMF TRUST FUND	–
U.N. AGENCIES	–	–	–	–	–	–	–	–	U.N. AGENCIES	–
UNDP	1.8	1.7	2.0	2.5	1.8	1.7	2.0	2.5	UNDP	1.
UNTA	0.3	0.3	0.3	0.2	0.3	0.3	0.3	0.2	UNTA	0.
UNICEF	0.0	–	–	–	0.0	–	–	–	UNICEF	0.
UNRWA	–	–	–	–	–	–	–	–	UNRWA	
WFP	–	0.5	0.1	0.2	–	0.5	0.1	0.2	WFP	
UNHCR	–	–	–	–	–	–	–	–	UNHCR	
Other Multilateral	0.3	0.4	0.3	0.6	0.3	0.4	0.3	0.6	Other Multilateral	0.
Arab OPEC Agencies	–	–	–	–	–	–	–	–	Arab OPEC Agencies	
TOTAL	*4.0*	*7.5*	*14.2*	*15.6*	*5.9*	*8.4*	*9.8*	*4.5*	*TOTAL*	*7.*
OPEC COUNTRIES	–	–	–	–	–	–	–	–	*OPEC COUNTRIES*	
E.E.C.+ MEMBERS	*13.6*	*11.0*	*40.2*	*52.8*	*1.9*	*4.4*	*2.9*	*4.2*	*E.E.C.+ MEMBERS*	*2.*
TOTAL	***13.8***	***16.5***	***61.5***	***79.0***	***8.0***	***10.6***	***14.3***	***9.8***	***TOTAL***	***12.***
ODA LOANS GROSS					**ODA LOANS NET**				**GRANTS**	
DAC COUNTRIES										
Australia	–	–	–	–	–	–	–	–	Australia	
Austria	–	–	–	–	–	–	–	–	Austria	0.
Belgium	–	–	–	–	–	–	–	–	Belgium	0.
Canada	–	–	–	–	–	–	–	–	Canada	
Denmark	–	–	–	–	–	–	–	–	Denmark	0.
Finland	–	–	–	–	–	–	–	–	Finland	
France	–	–	–	–	–	–	–	–	France	
Germany, Fed. Rep.	0.1	0.2	–	0.0	0.1	0.2	–	0.0	Germany, Fed. Rep.	2.
Italy	–	–	–	–	-0.6	-0.6	-0.6	0.0	Italy	0.
Japan	–	–	–	–	–	–	–	–	Japan	0.
Netherlands	–	–	–	–	-0.4	-0.5	-0.6	-0.5	Netherlands	0.
New Zealand	–	–	–	–	–	–	–	–	New Zealand	
Norway	–	–	–	–	–	–	–	–	Norway	
Sweden	–	–	–	–	–	–	–	–	Sweden	
Switzerland	–	–	–	–	–	–	–	–	Switzerland	0
United Kingdom	–	–	–	–	–	–	–	–	United Kingdom	0.
United States	1.0	1.0	3.0	3.0	-1.0	-2.0	–	–	United States	1.
TOTAL	*1.1*	*1.2*	*3.0*	*3.0*	*-1.9*	*-2.9*	*-1.1*	*-0.5*	*TOTAL*	*4.*
MULTILATERAL	*5.0*	*7.4*	*9.4*	*3.6*	*3.4*	*5.0*	*7.0*	*0.9*	*MULTILATERAL*	*2.*
OPEC COUNTRIES	–	–	–	–	–	–	–	–	*OPEC COUNTRIES*	
E.E.C.+ MEMBERS	*0.1*	*0.2*	–	*0.0*	*-0.8*	*-0.9*	*-1.1*	*-0.5*	*E.E.C.+ MEMBERS*	*2.*
TOTAL	***6.1***	***8.6***	***12.4***	***6.6***	***1.6***	***2.1***	***5.9***	***0.4***	***TOTAL***	***6.***
TOTAL OFFICIAL GROSS					**TOTAL OFFICIAL NET**				**TOTAL OOF GROSS**	
DAC COUNTRIES										
Australia	–	–	–	–	–	–	–	–	Australia	
Austria	0.0	0.0	0.0	0.0	0.0	0.0	0.0	0.0	Austria	
Belgium	0.1	0.2	0.1	0.3	0.1	0.2	0.1	0.3	Belgium	
Canada	–	–	–	1.3	–	–	–	1.3	Canada	
Denmark	0.0	–	0.0	0.0	0.0	–	0.0	0.0	Denmark	
Finland	–	–	–	0.0	–	–	–	0.0	Finland	
France	–	–	–	0.5	–	–	–	0.5	France	
Germany, Fed. Rep.	2.3	3.0	2.7	2.9	2.3	3.0	2.7	2.9	Germany, Fed. Rep.	
Italy	0.2	0.2	0.1	0.3	-0.4	-1.1	-1.2	-0.4	Italy	
Japan	0.2	0.2	0.6	1.1	0.2	0.2	0.6	1.1	Japan	
Netherlands	0.2	1.7	0.9	0.6	-0.2	1.2	0.4	0.2	Netherlands	
New Zealand	–	–	–	–	–	–	–	–	New Zealand	
Norway	–	–	–	–	–	–	–	–	Norway	
Sweden	–	–	–	–	–	–	–	–	Sweden	
Switzerland	0.0	0.0	0.0	–	0.0	0.0	0.0	–	Switzerland	
United Kingdom	0.1	0.1	0.1	0.1	0.1	0.1	0.1	0.1	United Kingdom	
United States	2.0	1.0	4.0	3.0	-1.0	-3.0	1.0	–	United States	
TOTAL	*5.0*	*6.3*	*8.6*	*10.2*	*1.1*	*0.4*	*3.7*	*5.9*	*TOTAL*	
MULTILATERAL	*15.7*	*20.4*	*27.3*	*28.0*	*4.0*	*7.5*	*14.2*	*15.6*	*MULTILATERAL*	*8.*
OPEC COUNTRIES	–	–	–	–	–	–	–	–	*OPEC COUNTRIES*	
E.E.C.+ MEMBERS	*2.9*	*5.5*	*4.1*	*4.7*	*1.9*	*3.7*	*2.2*	*3.5*	*E.E.C.+ MEMBERS*	
TOTAL	***20.7***	***26.7***	***35.9***	***38.2***	***5.1***	***7.9***	***17.9***	***21.5***	***TOTAL***	***8***

1978	1979	1980
–	–	–
0.0	0.0	0.0
0.2	0.1	0.3
–	–	–
–	0.0	0.0
–	–	0.0
–	–	0.5
3.0	2.7	2.9
0.2	0.1	0.3
0.2	0.6	1.1
1.7	0.9	0.6
–	–	–
–	–	–
–	–	–
0.0	0.0	–
0.1	0.1	0.1
1.0	4.0	3.0
6.3	*8.6*	*8.8*
–	–	–
–	–	–
–	–	–
–	–	–
0.5	0.1	–
–	–	–
–	–	–
7.4	9.4	3.7
–	–	–
–	–	–
–	–	–
–	–	–
1.7	2.0	2.5
0.3	0.3	0.2
–	–	–
–	–	–
0.5	0.1	0.2
–	–	–
0.4	0.3	0.6
–	–	–
10.8	*12.2*	*7.2*
–	–	–
5.5	*4.1*	*4.7*
17.1	***20.8***	***16.0***

–	–	–
0.0	0.0	0.0
0.2	0.1	0.3
–	–	–
–	0.0	0.0
–	–	0.0
–	–	0.5
2.8	2.7	2.9
0.2	0.1	0.3
0.2	0.6	1.1
1.7	0.9	0.6
–	–	–
–	–	–
–	–	–
0.0	0.0	–
0.1	0.1	0.1
–	1.0	–
5.1	*5.6*	*5.8*
3.4	*2.8*	*3.6*
–	–	–
5.4	*4.1*	*4.7*
8.5	***8.4***	***9.4***

–	–	–
–	–	–
–	–	–
–	–	1.3
–	–	–
–	–	–
–	–	–
–	–	–
–	–	–
–	–	–
–	–	–
–	–	–
–	–	–
–	–	–
–	–	–
–	–	–
–	–	–
–	–	*1.3*
9.6	*15.1*	*20.8*
–	–	–
–	–	–
9.6	***15.1***	***22.1***

ODA COMMITMENTS

1977	1978	1979	1980
–	–	–	–
–	–	–	–
–	–	–	–
–	–	–	–
0.0	–	–	0.1
–	–	–	–
–	–	–	0.5
3.4	2.8	28.8	4.3
0.2	0.2	0.1	0.3
0.2	0.3	0.7	1.3
0.3	0.6	0.4	0.7
–	–	–	–
–	–	–	–
–	–	–	–
–	–	–	–
0.1	0.1	0.1	0.1
0.6	0.5	0.7	–
4.8	*4.3*	*30.7*	*7.3*
–	–	–	–
–	–	–	–
–	–	–	–
–	–	–	–
0.3	0.2	0.1	0.2
–	–	–	–
–	–	–	–
–	–	–	–
–	–	–	–
–	–	–	–
–	–	–	–
2.5	2.9	2.7	3.5
–	–	–	–
–	–	–	–
–	–	–	–
–	–	–	–
–	–	–	–
–	–	–	–
–	–	–	–
–	–	–	–
2.8	*3.1*	*2.7*	*3.7*
–	–	–	–
4.3	*3.8*	*29.4*	*6.2*
7.6	***7.4***	***33.4***	***11.0***

TECH. COOP. GRANTS

1977	1978	1979	1980
–	–	–	–
0.0	0.0	0.0	0.0
0.1	0.1	0.1	0.2
–	–	–	–
0.0	–	0.0	0.0
–	–	–	0.0
–	–	–	0.5
2.2	2.8	2.7	2.9
0.2	0.2	0.1	0.3
0.2	0.2	0.6	1.1
0.2	0.4	0.2	0.5
–	–	–	–
–	–	–	–
–	–	–	–
–	0.0	0.0	–
0.1	0.1	0.1	0.1
1.0	–	–	–
3.9	*3.7*	*3.8*	*5.6*
2.5	*2.4*	*2.6*	*3.5*
–	–	–	–
2.7	*3.4*	*3.2*	*4.5*
6.4	***6.1***	***6.4***	***9.1***

TOTAL OOF NET

1977	1978	1979	1980
–	–	–	–
–	–	–	–
–	–	–	–
–	–	–	1.3
–	–	–	–
–	–	–	–
–	–	–	–
–	–	–	–
–	-0.7	-0.7	-0.7
–	–	–	–
–	–	–	–
–	–	–	–
–	–	–	–
–	–	–	–
–	–	–	–
–	–	–	–
-1.0	-1.0	–	–
-1.0	*-1.7*	*-0.7*	*0.6*
-1.9	*-0.9*	*4.4*	*11.1*
–	–	–	–
–	*-0.7*	*-0.7*	*-0.7*
-2.9	***-2.7***	***3.7***	***11.7***

MAIN AID AGGREGATES

	1977	1978	1979	1980
DAC COUNTRIES COMBINED				
PRIVATE SECTOR NET	8.7	8.6	43.5	57.6
Direct Investment	4.1	2.1	3.4	4.5
Portfolio Invest.	-2.8	8.8	10.8	14.3
Export Credits	7.4	-2.3	29.3	38.7
OFFICIAL & PRIVATE				
GROSS:				
Contractual Lending	16.7	17.6	42.8	60.2
Export Credits Tot.	15.7	16.4	39.8	57.2
Export Credits Priv	15.7	16.4	39.8	55.9
OTHER NET DATA				
Contractual Lending	4.6	-7.0	27.5	38.8
Export Credits Tot.	6.4	-4.0	28.6	39.3
(Bank Sector Loans)	10.0	1.0	75.0	62.0
ODA CONCESSIONALITY				
Total:Grant Element	100.0	100.0	40.0	100.0
Loans:Grant Element	–	–	30.0	–
OTHER SOURCES				
CMEA Countr.(Gross)	9.5	–	–	–
Intra LDCS Exc.OPEC	–	–	–	–
Other	–	–	–	–
ALL SOURCE COMMITMENTS				
TOTAL BILATERAL	4.8	4.3	30.7	23.6
of which				
OPEC (ODA)	–	–	–	–
CMEA (ODA)	–	–	–	–
TOTAL MULTILAT.(ODA)	2.8	3.1	2.7	3.7
TOTAL BIL.& MULTIL.	7.6	7.4	33.5	27.3
of which				
ODA Grants	7.6	7.4	7.3	11.0
ODA Loans	–	–	26.2	–
ODA CONCESSIONALITY				
Total: Grant Element	100.0	100.0	45.0	100.0
Loans: Grant Element	–	–	30.0	–

INDEBTEDNESS

	1977	1978	1979	1980
TOTAL DEBT DISBURSED	***749.5***	***815.2***	***994.5***	
Debt to DAC Countries	534.0	523.0	605.0	
ODA	72.0	69.0	67.0	
Total Export Credits	55.0	71.0	97.0	
Other Private Market	407.0	383.0	441.0	
International Org.	123.6	145.4	167.4	
CMEA	0.4	0.2	0.1	
Other	91.5	146.7	222.0	
TOTAL DEBT SERVICE	***248.5***	***436.6***	***146.6***	
Paid to DAC Countries	190.1	380.4	102.1	
ODA	4.4	5.4	6.4	
Total Export Credits	13.5	17.6	29.9	
Other Private Market	172.2	357.4	65.8	
International Org.	20.7	22.5	24.1	
CMEA	0.3	0.2	0.1	
Other	37.4	33.4	20.3	

ECONOMIC INDICATORS

	1977	1978	1979	1980
GNP Curr. Prices, $M	4125.1	4916.2	6905.2	9737.0
Real GNP, 1976=100	102.0	108.0	118.0	123.0
GNP/Cap Curr. Prices,$	1438.0	1704.0	2377.0	3330.0
GNP/cap Atlas Basis, $	1874.9	2123.6	2496.1	2819.5
Real GNP/Cap, 1976=100	101.0	107.0	116.0	120.0
Population, Million	2.9	2.9	2.9	2.9
Curr.A/C Deficit(-),$M	-164.7	-132.7	-322.1	–
BOP Exp. & Transf.,$M	822.1	932.8	1250.0	–
Exp. to OECD CIF, $M	385.3	436.7	461.6	494.1
of which				
Manufact.	200.5	245.9	281.5	276.9
Imp. from OECD FOB, $M	282.3	336.6	478.9	670.9
Reserves ex. Gold, $M	306.6	287.2	380.8	472.6

	1977	1978	1979	1980	1977	1978	1979	1980	197
	TOTAL RECEIPTS NET				**TOTAL ODA NET**				**TOTAL ODA GROSS**
DAC COUNTRIES									
Australia	3.9	5.1	0.6	0.1	3.9	5.1	0.6	0.1	3.
Austria	0.1	0.1	36.9	1.4	0.1	0.1	10.4	1.4	0.
Belgium	1.4	2.7	50.9	4.2	1.4	3.1	14.9	2.1	1.
Canada	–	5.5	0.0	–	–	5.5	0.0	–	
Denmark	27.4	32.8	15.8	12.8	12.0	32.8	15.8	12.8	12.
Finland	1.4	0.4	4.3	10.1	1.4	0.4	4.3	10.1	1.
France	64.6	23.8	15.8	-18.3	25.3	23.8	44.9	15.1	25.
Germany, Fed. Rep.	2.0	27.4	-12.2	12.9	1.6	8.5	0.8	0.3	1.
Italy	0.2	0.6	51.0	-3.6	0.2	0.6	0.8	0.1	0.
Japan	14.6	87.9	44.4	3.7	12.5	28.5	38.7	3.7	12.
Netherlands	22.3	9.4	4.0	4.4	22.3	9.4	4.0	4.4	22.
New Zealand	0.1	0.1	0.1	0.0	0.1	0.1	0.1	0.0	0.
Norway	3.7	9.7	14.1	6.8	3.3	9.9	14.1	7.2	3.
Sweden	113.0	88.2	69.7	87.2	113.0	77.0	63.6	91.9	113.
Switzerland	0.9	0.9	0.6	0.2	0.9	0.9	0.6	0.2	0.
United Kingdom	2.1	2.8	43.6	2.6	2.1	2.8	15.9	2.6	2.
United States	–	–	–	–	–	–	–	–	
TOTAL	*257.6*	*297.3*	*339.4*	*124.5*	*200.0*	*208.3*	*229.5*	*151.9*	*200.*
MULTILATERAL									
AF.D.F.	–	–	–	–	–	–	–	–	
AF.D.B.	–	–	–	–	–	–	–	–	
AS.D.B.	0.0	-0.1	2.2	7.4	0.0	-0.1	2.3	6.8	
CAR.D.B.	–	–	–	–	–	–	–	–	
E.E.C.	13.9	49.6	12.0	3.2	13.9	49.6	12.0	3.2	13.
IBRD	–	–	–	–	–	–	–	–	
IDA	–	–	18.8	6.0	–	–	18.8	6.0	
I.D.B.	–	–	–	–	–	–	–	–	
IFAD	–	–	–	–	–	–	–	–	
I.F.C.	–	–	–	–	–	–	–	–	
IMF TRUST FUND	–	32.2	–	–	–	32.2	–	–	
U.N. AGENCIES	–	–	–	–	–	–	–	–	
UNDP	0.4	12.9	5.0	8.8	0.4	12.9	5.0	8.8	0.
UNTA	2.0	2.3	1.5	0.4	2.0	2.3	1.5	0.4	2.
UNICEF	0.2	14.6	12.3	10.1	0.2	14.6	12.3	10.1	0.
UNRWA	–	–	–	–	–	–	–	–	
WFP	30.1	40.8	46.1	25.1	30.1	40.8	46.1	25.1	30.
UNHCR	0.5	2.7	4.8	4.4	0.5	2.7	4.8	4.4	0.
Other Multilateral	0.7	1.6	3.0	4.1	0.7	1.6	3.0	4.1	0.
Arab OPEC Agencies	–	4.6	1.0	1.2	–	4.6	1.0	1.2	
TOTAL	*47.6*	*161.2*	*106.7*	*70.7*	*47.6*	*161.2*	*106.8*	*70.1*	*47.*
OPEC COUNTRIES	–	–	*0.1*	*6.5*	–	–	*0.1*	*6.5*	
E.E.C.+ MEMBERS	*133.9*	*149.1*	*180.8*	*18.3*	*78.8*	*130.5*	*109.2*	*40.5*	*78.*
TOTAL	***305.2***	***458.5***	***446.3***	***201.7***	***247.6***	***369.5***	***336.5***	***228.5***	***247.***

	1977	1978	1979	1980	1977	1978	1979	1980	197
	ODA LOANS GROSS				**ODA LOANS NET**				**GRANTS**
DAC COUNTRIES									
Australia	–	–	–	–	–	–	–	–	3.
Austria	–	–	9.8	–	–	–	9.8	–	0.
Belgium	–	–	8.5	–	–	–	8.5	–	1.
Canada	–	–	–	–	–	–	–	–	–
Denmark	0.3	20.2	8.5	7.6	0.3	20.2	8.5	7.6	11.
Finland	0.8	–	–	–	0.8	–	-14.1	–	0.
France	10.6	15.1	26.8	8.9	10.6	15.1	26.8	8.9	14.
Germany, Fed. Rep.	–	–	–	–	–	–	–	–	1.
Italy	–	–	–	–	–	–	–	–	0.
Japan	–	12.2	31.0	2.7	–	7.8	27.1	2.7	12.
Netherlands	–	–	–	–	–	–	–	–	22.
New Zealand	–	–	–	–	–	–	–	–	0.
Norway	–	–	–	–	–	–	–	–	3.
Sweden	–	–	–	–	–	–	–	–	113.
Switzerland	–	–	–	–	–	–	–	–	0.
United Kingdom	–	–	–	–	–	–	–	–	2.
United States	–	–	–	–	–	–	–	–	–
TOTAL	*11.7*	*47.5*	*84.7*	*19.2*	*11.7*	*43.1*	*66.6*	*19.2*	*188.*
MULTILATERAL	–	*36.7*	*22.2*	*14.5*	*0.0*	*36.6*	*22.0*	*14.1*	*47.*
OPEC COUNTRIES	–	–	–	*6.4*	–	–	–	*6.4*	–
E.E.C.+ MEMBERS	*10.9*	*35.3*	*43.8*	*16.4*	*10.9*	*35.3*	*43.8*	*16.4*	*67.*
TOTAL	***11.7***	***84.3***	***106.9***	***40.1***	***11.6***	***79.8***	***88.6***	***39.7***	***236.***

	1977	1978	1979	1980	1977	1978	1979	1980	197
	TOTAL OFFICIAL GROSS				**TOTAL OFFICIAL NET**				**TOTAL OOF GROSS**
DAC COUNTRIES									
Australia	3.9	5.1	0.6	0.1	3.9	5.1	0.6	0.1	–
Austria	0.1	0.1	10.4	1.4	0.1	0.1	10.4	1.4	–
Belgium	1.4	3.1	14.9	2.1	1.4	3.1	14.9	2.1	–
Canada	–	5.5	0.0	–	–	5.5	0.0	–	–
Denmark	12.0	32.8	15.8	12.8	12.0	32.8	15.8	12.8	–
Finland	1.4	0.4	18.4	10.1	1.4	0.4	4.3	10.1	–
France	25.8	23.8	44.9	15.0	25.8	23.8	44.9	15.1	0.5
Germany, Fed. Rep.	1.6	8.5	0.8	0.3	1.6	8.5	0.8	0.3	–
Italy	0.2	0.6	20.8	0.1	0.2	0.6	20.6	-1.9	–
Japan	12.5	32.9	42.7	3.7	12.5	28.5	38.7	3.7	–
Netherlands	22.3	9.4	4.0	4.4	22.3	9.4	4.0	4.4	–
New Zealand	0.1	0.1	0.1	0.0	0.1	0.1	0.1	0.0	–
Norway	3.3	9.9	14.1	7.2	3.3	9.9	14.1	7.2	–
Sweden	113.0	77.0	63.6	91.9	113.0	77.0	63.6	91.9	–
Switzerland	0.9	0.9	0.6	0.2	0.9	0.9	0.6	0.2	–
United Kingdom	2.1	2.8	15.9	2.6	2.1	2.8	15.9	2.6	–
United States	–	–	–	–	–	–	–	–	–
TOTAL	*200.5*	*212.7*	*267.6*	*151.9*	*200.5*	*208.3*	*249.3*	*149.9*	*0.5*
MULTILATERAL	*47.7*	*161.3*	*106.9*	*71.1*	*47.6*	*161.2*	*106.7*	*70.7*	–
OPEC COUNTRIES	–	–	*0.1*	*6.5*	–	–	*0.1*	*6.5*	–
E.E.C.+ MEMBERS	*79.3*	*130.5*	*129.2*	*40.5*	*79.3*	*130.5*	*128.9*	*38.5*	*0.5*
TOTAL	***248.2***	***374.0***	***374.7***	***229.5***	***248.1***	***369.5***	***356.1***	***227.1***	***0.5***

1978	1979	1980	1977	1978	1979	1980
			ODA COMMITMENTS			
5.1	0.6	0.1	6.2	0.5	1.0	–
0.1	10.4	1.4	–	–	9.8	–
3.1	14.9	2.1	1.8	7.6	12.5	2.6
5.5	0.0	–	6.6	–	–	–
32.8	15.8	12.8	7.6	25.0	7.8	0.1
0.4	18.4	10.1	0.5	10.0	14.7	15.0
23.8	44.9	15.0	44.4	–	3.8	2.3
8.5	0.8	0.3	5.5	8.6	0.8	0.3
0.6	0.8	0.1	0.2	0.6	0.8	10.1
32.9	42.7	3.7	0.9	68.4	20.3	1.1
9.4	4.0	4.4	25.7	34.4	18.2	8.9
0.1	0.1	0.0	–	0.1	0.0	–
9.9	14.1	7.2	–	29.2	4.3	8.8
77.0	63.6	91.9	160.7	10.8	93.8	173.8
0.9	0.6	0.2	0.1	–	0.1	0.2
2.8	15.9	2.6	2.1	2.8	18.2	0.3
–	–	–	0.4	1.0	0.4	0.4
212.7	*247.6*	*151.9*	*262.6*	*199.1*	*206.5*	*223.8*
–	–	–	–	–	–	–
–	–	–	–	–	–	–
–	2.5	7.2	–	0.1	–	–
–	–	–	–	–	–	–
49.6	12.0	3.2	12.8	19.9	34.8	0.2
–	–	–	–	–	–	–
–	18.8	6.0	–	60.0	–	–
–	–	–	–	–	–	–
–	–	–	–	–	–	–
–	–	–	–	–	–	–
32.2	–	–	–	–	–	–
–	–	–	33.8	75.0	72.8	52.8
12.9	5.0	8.8	–	–	–	–
2.3	1.5	0.4	–	–	–	–
14.6	12.3	10.1	–	–	–	–
–	–	–	–	–	–	–
40.8	46.1	25.1	–	–	–	–
2.7	4.8	4.4	–	–	–	–
1.6	3.0	4.1	–	–	–	–
4.6	1.0	1.2	–	17.0	–	–
161.3	*106.9*	*70.5*	*46.6*	*172.1*	*107.6*	*53.1*
–	*0.1*	*6.5*	–	–	*10.5*	*6.4*
130.5	*109.2*	*40.5*	*100.1*	*99.0*	*96.9*	*24.7*
374.0	***354.7***	***228.9***	***309.2***	***371.2***	***324.6***	***283.3***
			TECH. COOP. GRANTS			
5.1	0.6	0.1	1.5	0.8	0.3	0.1
0.1	0.6	1.4	0.1	0.1	0.5	1.4
3.1	6.4	2.1	0.1	2.5	2.4	1.4
5.5	0.0	–	–	–	–	–
12.6	7.3	5.3	0.1	0.0	0.0	0.1
0.4	18.4	10.1	0.4	0.3	4.1	3.7
8.7	18.1	6.2	–	–	–	2.4
8.5	0.8	0.3	0.9	0.8	0.3	0.2
0.6	0.8	0.1	0.2	0.1	–	–
20.7	11.6	1.0	0.8	1.2	1.4	1.0
9.4	4.0	4.4	0.2	0.1	0.2	0.3
0.1	0.1	0.0	0.1	0.1	0.1	0.0
9.9	14.1	7.2	0.3	0.1	1.6	0.0
77.0	63.6	91.9	20.8	24.6	16.9	19.3
0.9	0.6	0.2	0.0	0.0	0.0	0.0
2.8	15.9	2.6	0.2	0.3	0.5	0.3
–	–	–	–	–	–	–
165.2	*162.9*	*132.7*	*25.5*	*31.0*	*28.1*	*30.1*
124.6	*84.8*	*56.1*	*3.7*	*34.2*	*26.6*	*52.8*
–	*0.1*	*0.1*	–	–	–	–
95.2	*65.4*	*24.1*	*1.6*	*3.9*	*3.4*	*4.6*
289.8	***247.8***	***188.9***	***29.3***	***65.2***	***54.8***	***82.9***
			TOTAL OOF NET			
–	–	–	–	–	–	–
–	–	–	–	–	–	–
–	–	–	–	–	–	–
–	–	–	–	–	–	–
–	–	–	–	–	–	–
–	–	–	–	–	–	–
–	–	–	0.5	–	–	–
–	–	–	–	–	–	–
–	20.0	–	–	–	19.8	-2.0
–	–	–	–	–	–	–
–	–	–	–	–	–	–
–	–	–	–	–	–	–
–	–	–	–	–	–	–
–	–	–	–	–	–	–
–	–	–	–	–	–	–
–	–	–	–	–	–	–
–	–	–	–	–	–	–
–	*20.0*	–	*0.5*	–	*19.8*	*-2.0*
–	–	*0.6*	–	*0.0*	*-0.1*	*0.6*
–	–	–	–	–	–	–
–	*20.0*	–	*0.5*	–	*19.8*	*-2.0*
–	***20.0***	***0.6***	***0.5***	***0.0***	***19.7***	***-1.4***

MAIN AID AGGREGATES

	1977	1978	1979	1980
DAC COUNTRIES COMBINED				
PRIVATE SECTOR NET	57.1	89.0	90.2	-25.4
Direct Investment	0.0	–	-0.1	–
Portfolio Invest.	41.2	78.0	-26.0	-27.0
Export Credits	15.9	11.0	116.3	1.6
OFFICIAL & PRIVATE				
GROSS:				
Contractual Lending	28.0	58.9	228.8	42.5
Export Credits Tot.	15.9	11.4	144.2	23.3
Export Credits Priv	15.9	11.4	124.2	23.3
OTHER NET DATA				
Contractual Lending	28.0	54.1	202.6	18.8
Export Credits Tot.	15.9	11.0	136.0	-0.4
(Bank Sector Loans)	30.0	104.0	–	10.0
ODA CONCESSIONALITY				
Total:Grant Element	94.0	88.0	93.0	96.0
Loans:Grant Element	53.0	63.0	60.0	35.0
OTHER SOURCES				
CMEA Countr.(Gross)	642.0	669.8	892.0	892.0
Intra LDCS Exc.OPEC	–	–	–	–
Other	–	–	–	–
ALL SOURCE COMMITMENTS				
TOTAL BILATERAL	262.6	229.1	237.0	230.2
of which				
OPEC (ODA)	–	–	10.5	6.4
CMEA (ODA)	642.0	669.8	892.0	892.0
TOTAL MULTILAT.(ODA)	46.6	172.1	107.6	53.1
TOTAL BIL.& MULTIL.	309.2	401.2	344.6	283.3
of which				
ODA Grants	280.3	228.9	280.0	263.9
ODA Loans	28.9	142.3	44.6	19.4
ODA CONCESSIONALITY				
Total: Grant Element	95.0	89.0	94.0	96.0
Loans: Grant Element	53.0	71.0	57.0	43.0

INDEBTEDNESS

	1977	1978	1979	1980
TOTAL DEBT DISBURSED	***535.0***	***1010.0***	***2133.0***	
Debt to DAC Countries	285.0	360.0	693.0	
ODA	204.0	286.0	338.0	
Total Export Credits	81.0	74.0	355.0	
Other Private Market	–	–	–	
International Org.	–	–	180.0	
CMEA	200.0	600.0	900.0	
Other	50.0	50.0	360.0	
TOTAL DEBT SERVICE	***20.4***	***7.1***	***67.4***	
Paid to DAC Countries	16.4	7.1	50.4	
ODA	–	6.4	7.4	
Total Export Credits	16.4	0.7	43.0	
Other Private Market	–	–	–	
International Org.	–	–	–	
CMEA	–	–	15.0	
Other	4.0	–	2.0	

ECONOMIC INDICATORS

	1977	1978	1979	1980
GNP Curr. Prices, $M	–	–	–	–
Real GNP, 1976=100	–	–	–	–
GNP/Cap Curr. Prices,$	–	–	–	–
GNP/cap Atlas Basis, $	–	–	–	–
Real GNP/Cap, 1976=100	–	–	–	–
Population, Million	–	–	–	–
Curr.A/C Deficit(-),$M	–	–	–	–
BOP Exp. & Transf.,$M	–	–	–	–
Exp. to OECD CIF, $M	84.4	65.6	65.4	65.0
of which				
Manufact.	5.9	7.7	8.7	9.4
Imp. from OECD FOB, $M	379.7	592.2	520.9	455.6
Reserves ex. Gold, $M	–	–	–	–

TOTAL RECEIPTS NET

	1977	1978	1979	1980
DAC COUNTRIES				
Australia	0.0	–	–	–
Austria	0.0	–	–	–
Belgium	0.0	-0.1	-0.1	-0.1
Canada	–	–	–	9.1
Denmark	–	-0.6	-1.1	-1.0
Finland	–	0.7	-0.2	-0.2
France	0.2	5.0	22.5	38.5
Germany, Fed. Rep.	20.6	7.4	15.1	16.4
Italy	2.8	8.1	42.6	13.3
Japan	1.0	2.1	2.3	11.5
Netherlands	6.0	14.1	15.2	19.6
New Zealand	0.0	0.2	–	–
Norway	0.3	-0.7	-1.0	-0.4
Sweden	–	–	–	4.2
Switzerland	0.1	0.1	0.2	4.0
United Kingdom	1.8	4.2	3.8	13.2
United States	7.0	7.0	9.0	15.0
TOTAL	*39.8*	*47.5*	*108.4*	*143.1*
MULTILATERAL				
AF.D.F.	–	–	–	–
AF.D.B.	–	–	–	–
AS.D.B.	–	–	–	–
CAR.D.B.	–	–	–	–
E.E.C.	–	1.5	1.8	3.9
IBRD	–	–	–	–
IDA	16.8	22.2	13.7	22.2
I.D.B.	–	–	–	–
IFAD	–	–	–	–
I.F.C.	–	–	2.4	–
IMF TRUST FUND	–	–	–	–
U.N. AGENCIES	–	–	–	–
UNDP	5.2	5.3	7.0	9.8
UNTA	1.2	1.6	1.3	0.3
UNICEF	2.0	0.6	1.6	1.0
UNRWA	–	–	–	–
WFP	3.2	2.4	4.0	2.1
UNHCR	–	0.1	–	–
Other Multilateral	2.1	2.4	1.4	3.4
Arab OPEC Agencies	10.6	6.9	12.2	30.7
TOTAL	*41.0*	*42.7*	*45.3*	*73.3*
OPEC COUNTRIES	*196.5*	*244.4*	*136.2*	*292.2*
E.E.C.+ MEMBERS	*31.4*	*39.5*	*99.8*	*103.9*
TOTAL	***277.2***	***334.6***	***289.9***	***508.6***

TOTAL ODA NET

	1977	1978	1979	1980
Australia	0.0	–	–	–
Austria	0.0	–	–	–
Belgium	0.0	–	–	–
Canada	–	–	–	–
Denmark	–	–	–	0.0
Finland	–	0.0	0.1	–
France	–	1.0	2.6	4.4
Germany, Fed. Rep.	15.2	9.3	16.5	20.3
Italy	2.8	0.6	1.0	0.6
Japan	1.1	2.3	2.2	10.1
Netherlands	6.0	14.1	15.2	19.6
New Zealand	–	–	–	–
Norway	0.3	0.3	0.3	–
Sweden	–	–	–	–
Switzerland	0.1	0.1	0.2	2.2
United Kingdom	1.6	2.5	3.8	6.3
United States	7.0	7.0	9.0	15.0
TOTAL	*34.2*	*37.1*	*51.0*	*78.5*
AF.D.F.	–	–	–	–
AF.D.B.	–	–	–	–
AS.D.B.	–	–	–	–
CAR.D.B.	–	–	–	–
E.E.C.	–	1.5	1.8	3.9
IBRD	–	–	–	–
IDA	16.8	22.2	13.7	22.2
I.D.B.	–	–	–	–
IFAD	–	–	–	–
I.F.C.	–	–	–	–
IMF TRUST FUND	–	–	–	–
U.N. AGENCIES	–	–	–	–
UNDP	5.2	5.3	7.0	9.8
UNTA	1.2	1.6	1.3	0.3
UNICEF	2.0	0.6	1.6	1.0
UNRWA	–	–	–	–
WFP	3.2	2.4	4.0	2.1
UNHCR	–	0.1	–	–
Other Multilateral	2.1	2.4	1.4	3.4
Arab OPEC Agencies	10.6	6.9	12.2	11.9
TOTAL	*41.0*	*42.7*	*42.9*	*54.5*
OPEC COUNTRIES	*184.6*	*189.1*	*136.2*	*292.2*
E.E.C.+ MEMBERS	*25.6*	*28.9*	*40.9*	*55.2*
TOTAL	***259.8***	***269.0***	***230.1***	***425.3***

TOTAL ODA GROSS

	197
Australia	0
Austria	0
Belgium	0
Canada	
Denmark	
Finland	
France	
Germany, Fed. Rep.	15
Italy	2
Japan	1
Netherlands	6
New Zealand	
Norway	0
Sweden	
Switzerland	0
United Kingdom	1
United States	7
TOTAL	*34*
AF.D.F.	
AF.D.B.	
AS.D.B.	
CAR.D.B.	
E.E.C.	
IBRD	
IDA	16
I.D.B.	
IFAD	
I.F.C.	
IMF TRUST FUND	
U.N. AGENCIES	
UNDP	5
UNTA	1
UNICEF	2
UNRWA	
WFP	3
UNHCR	
Other Multilateral	2
Arab OPEC Agencies	10
TOTAL	*41*
OPEC COUNTRIES	*184*
E.E.C.+ MEMBERS	*25*
TOTAL	***26***

ODA LOANS GROSS

	1977	1978	1979	1980
DAC COUNTRIES				
Australia	–	–	–	–
Austria	–	–	–	–
Belgium	–	–	–	–
Canada	–	–	–	–
Denmark	–	–	–	–
Finland	–	–	–	–
France	–	0.9	2.6	3.3
Germany, Fed. Rep.	10.3	2.0	2.8	–
Italy	–	–	–	–
Japan	–	0.4	0.1	6.9
Netherlands	1.5	3.0	1.9	9.5
New Zealand	–	–	–	–
Norway	–	–	–	–
Sweden	–	–	–	–
Switzerland	–	–	–	–
United Kingdom	–	–	–	–
United States	–	1.0	–	–
TOTAL	*11.7*	*7.3*	*7.4*	*19.7*
MULTILATERAL	*27.3*	*28.8*	*23.3*	*35.1*
OPEC COUNTRIES	*19.6*	*51.1*	*30.7*	*79.9*
E.E.C.+ MEMBERS	*11.7*	*5.9*	*7.3*	*12.8*
TOTAL	***58.6***	***87.2***	***61.3***	***134.8***

ODA LOANS NET

	1977	1978	1979	1980
Australia	–	–	–	–
Austria	–	–	–	–
Belgium	–	–	–	–
Canada	–	–	–	–
Denmark	–	–	–	–
Finland	–	–	–	–
France	–	0.9	2.6	3.3
Germany, Fed. Rep.	10.3	1.5	2.4	-92.0
Italy	–	–	–	–
Japan	–	0.4	0.1	6.9
Netherlands	1.5	3.0	1.9	9.5
New Zealand	–	–	–	–
Norway	–	–	–	–
Sweden	–	–	–	–
Switzerland	–	–	–	–
United Kingdom	–	–	–	–
United States	–	1.0	–	–
TOTAL	*11.7*	*6.9*	*7.0*	*-72.3*
MULTILATERAL	*27.3*	*28.8*	*22.9*	*33.9*
OPEC COUNTRIES	*19.3*	*50.5*	*30.4*	*79.0*
E.E.C.+ MEMBERS	*11.7*	*5.4*	*6.9*	*-79.1*
TOTAL	***58.3***	***86.2***	***60.3***	***40.6***

GRANTS

	197
Australia	0
Austria	0
Belgium	0
Canada	
Denmark	
Finland	
France	
Germany, Fed. Rep.	4
Italy	2
Japan	1
Netherlands	4
New Zealand	
Norway	0
Sweden	
Switzerland	0
United Kingdom	1
United States	7
TOTAL	*22*
MULTILATERAL	*1*
OPEC COUNTRIES	*16*
E.E.C.+ MEMBERS	*1.*
TOTAL	***20***

TOTAL OFFICIAL GROSS

	1977	1978	1979	1980
DAC COUNTRIES				
Australia	0.0	–	–	–
Austria	0.0	–	–	–
Belgium	0.0	–	–	–
Canada	–	–	–	9.1
Denmark	–	–	–	0.0
Finland	–	0.0	0.1	–
France	–	1.0	2.6	4.4
Germany, Fed. Rep.	15.2	9.7	16.8	112.3
Italy	2.8	0.6	1.0	0.6
Japan	1.1	2.3	2.2	10.1
Netherlands	6.0	14.1	15.2	19.6
New Zealand	0.1	–	–	–
Norway	0.3	0.3	0.3	–
Sweden	–	–	–	–
Switzerland	0.1	0.1	0.2	2.2
United Kingdom	1.6	2.5	3.8	6.3
United States	7.0	7.0	9.0	15.0
TOTAL	*34.2*	*37.6*	*51.3*	*179.6*
MULTILATERAL	*41.0*	*42.7*	*42.8*	*74.6*
OPEC COUNTRIES	*196.8*	*245.1*	*136.6*	*293.1*
E.E.C.+ MEMBERS	*25.6*	*29.3*	*41.3*	*147.1*
TOTAL	***272.0***	***325.4***	***230.7***	***547.2***

TOTAL OFFICIAL NET

	1977	1978	1979	1980
Australia	0.0	–	–	–
Austria	0.0	–	–	–
Belgium	0.0	–	–	–
Canada	–	–	–	9.1
Denmark	–	0.0	–	0.0
Finland	–	0.0	0.1	–
France	–	1.0	2.6	4.4
Germany, Fed. Rep.	15.2	9.3	16.5	20.3
Italy	2.8	0.6	1.0	0.6
Japan	1.1	2.3	2.2	10.1
Netherlands	6.0	14.1	15.2	19.6
New Zealand	0.0	–	–	–
Norway	0.3	0.3	0.3	–
Sweden	–	–	–	–
Switzerland	0.1	0.1	0.2	2.2
United Kingdom	1.6	2.5	3.8	6.3
United States	7.0	7.0	9.0	15.0
TOTAL	*34.1*	*37.1*	*51.0*	*87.6*
MULTILATERAL	*41.0*	*42.7*	*45.3*	*73.3*
OPEC COUNTRIES	*196.5*	*244.4*	*136.2*	*292.2*
E.E.C.+ MEMBERS	*25.6*	*28.9*	*40.9*	*55.2*
TOTAL	***271.6***	***324.2***	***232.5***	***453.1***

TOTAL OOF GROSS

	197
Australia	
Austria	
Belgium	
Canada	
Denmark	
Finland	
France	
Germany, Fed. Rep.	
Italy	
Japan	
Netherlands	
New Zealand	0
Norway	
Sweden	
Switzerland	
United Kingdom	
United States	
TOTAL	*0*
MULTILATERAL	
OPEC COUNTRIES	*1*
E.E.C.+ MEMBERS	
TOTAL	***1***

1978	1979	1980	1977	1978	1979	1980
			ODA COMMITMENTS			
–	–	–	–	–	–	–
–	–	–	–	–	–	–
–	–	–	–	–	–	–
–	–	–	–	–	–	0.0
–	–	0.0	–	0.0	–	–
0.0	0.1	–	–	0.0	–	–
1.0	2.6	4.4	7.1	–	–	0.9
9.7	16.8	112.3	19.9	9.3	13.4	150.9
0.6	1.0	0.6	2.8	0.6	1.0	0.6
2.3	2.2	10.1	15.9	2.6	40.2	2.7
14.1	15.2	19.6	18.1	22.4	22.4	19.2
–	–	–	–	–	–	–
0.3	0.3	–	–	–	0.3	–
–	–	–	–	–	–	–
0.1	0.2	2.2	0.6	–	–	1.8
2.5	3.8	6.3	1.6	2.5	3.8	6.3
7.0	9.0	15.0	15.3	9.3	17.7	18.8
37.6	*51.3*	*170.5*	*81.3*	*46.6*	*98.8*	*201.2*
–	–	–	–	–	–	–
–	–	–	–	–	–	–
–	–	–	–	–	–	–
–	–	–	–	–	–	–
1.5	1.8	3.9	1.8	0.9	3.4	–
–	–	–	–	–	–	–
22.2	13.7	22.2	16.0	39.0	30.0	39.1
–	–	–	–	–	–	–
–	–	–	–	–	12.3	13.5
–	–	–	–	–	–	–
–	–	–	–	–	–	–
–	–	–	13.6	12.3	15.2	16.6
5.3	7.0	9.8	–	–	–	–
1.6	1.3	0.3	–	–	–	–
0.6	1.6	1.0	–	–	–	–
–	–	–	–	–	–	–
2.4	4.0	2.1	–	–	–	–
0.1	–	–	–	–	–	–
2.4	1.4	3.4	–	–	–	–
6.9	9.7	13.1	51.6	0.5	8.7	11.1
42.7	*40.4*	*55.8*	*83.0*	*52.7*	*69.6*	*80.3*
189.7	*136.6*	*293.1*	*279.1*	*482.3*	*182.9*	*259.8*
29.3	*41.3*	*147.1*	*51.3*	*35.7*	*44.0*	*177.9*
270.0	***228.3***	***519.4***	***443.3***	***581.7***	***351.3***	***541.3***
			TECH. COOP. GRANTS			
–	–	–	–	–	–	–
–	–	–	0.0	–	–	–
–	–	–	0.0	–	–	–
–	–	–	–	–	–	–
–	–	0.0	–	–	–	0.0
0.0	0.1	–	–	0.0	0.1	–
0.1	–	1.1	–	–	–	1.1
7.7	14.0	112.3	4.9	7.7	7.2	11.0
0.6	1.0	0.6	0.4	0.6	1.0	0.6
1.9	2.1	3.2	0.1	0.7	0.4	1.0
11.1	13.3	10.1	4.6	8.0	9.6	5.6
–	–	–	–	–	–	–
0.3	0.3	–	0.1	0.3	0.0	–
–	–	–	–	–	–	–
0.1	0.2	2.2	0.1	0.1	0.2	0.2
2.5	3.8	6.3	1.6	2.5	3.7	6.3
6.0	9.0	15.0	3.0	3.0	6.0	10.0
30.3	*44.0*	*150.8*	*14.7*	*22.9*	*28.2*	*35.9*
13.9	*17.1*	*20.6*	*10.5*	*9.9*	*11.2*	*16.6*
138.6	*105.9*	*213.2*	–	–	–	–
23.5	*34.0*	*134.3*	*11.6*	*18.8*	*21.5*	*24.7*
182.8	***166.9***	***384.6***	***25.2***	***32.8***	***39.5***	***52.5***
			TOTAL OOF NET			
–	–	–	–	–	–	–
–	–	–	–	–	–	–
–	–	–	–	–	–	–
–	–	9.1	–	–	–	9.1
–	–	–	–	0.0	–	–
–	–	–	–	–	–	–
–	–	–	–	–	–	–
–	–	–	–	–	–	–
–	–	–	–	–	–	–
–	–	–	–	–	–	–
–	–	–	–	–	–	–
–	–	–	0.0	–	–	–
–	–	–	–	–	–	–
–	–	–	–	–	–	–
–	–	–	–	–	–	–
–	–	–	–	–	–	–
–	–	–	–	–	–	–
–	–	*9.1*	*0.0*	*0.0*	–	*9.1*
–	*2.4*	*18.8*	–	–	*2.4*	*18.8*
55.3	–	–	*11.9*	*55.3*	–	–
–	–	–	–	*0.0*	–	–
55.3	***2.4***	***27.8***	***11.8***	***55.3***	***2.4***	***27.8***

	1977	1978	1979	1980
MAIN AID AGGREGATES				
DAC COUNTRIES COMBINED				
PRIVATE SECTOR NET	5.6	10.4	57.4	55.5
Direct Investment	-0.2	2.4	0.6	-0.2
Portfolio Invest.	0.6	2.3	7.4	-0.9
Export Credits	5.2	5.8	49.4	56.7
OFFICIAL & PRIVATE				
GROSS:				
Contractual Lending	22.3	21.7	73.8	97.1
Export Credits Tot.	10.5	14.4	66.4	77.4
Export Credits Priv	10.5	14.4	66.4	68.3
OTHER NET DATA				
Contractual Lending	16.9	12.6	56.4	-6.6
Export Credits Tot.	5.1	5.8	49.4	65.7
(Bank Sector Loans)	–	5.0	4.0	7.0
ODA CONCESSIONALITY				
Total:Grant Element	84.0	100.0	80.0	100.0
Loans:Grant Element	68.0	–	60.0	–
OTHER SOURCES				
CMEA Countr.(Gross)	1.3	1.6	2.0	1.9
Intra LDCS Exc.OPEC	–	–	–	–
Other	–	–	–	–
ALL SOURCE COMMITMENTS				
TOTAL BILATERAL	360.4	528.9	281.7	472.2
of which				
OPEC (ODA)	279.1	482.3	182.9	259.8
CMEA (ODA)	–	3.8	–	–
TOTAL MULTILAT.(ODA)	83.0	52.7	69.6	80.3
TOTAL BIL.& MULTIL.	443.4	581.7	351.3	552.5
of which				
ODA Grants	274.8	175.1	208.5	430.9
ODA Loans	168.5	406.5	142.8	110.4
ODA CONCESSIONALITY				
Total: Grant Element	83.0	85.0	85.0	93.0
Loans: Grant Element	57.0	79.0	67.0	61.0
INDEBTEDNESS				
TOTAL DEBT DISBURSED	***347.7***	***495.5***	***595.8***	
Debt to DAC Countries	80.0	127.0	160.0	
ODA	74.0	97.0	110.0	
Total Export Credits	6.0	30.0	50.0	
Other Private Market	–	–	–	
International Org.	68.5	101.4	132.1	
CMEA	147.1	165.2	140.4	
Other	52.1	101.9	163.3	
TOTAL DEBT SERVICE	***8.3***	***23.5***	***53.8***	
Paid to DAC Countries	5.9	10.3	12.6	
ODA	0.8	1.4	1.0	
Total Export Credits	5.1	8.9	11.6	
Other Private Market	–	–	–	
International Org.	0.4	1.0	3.5	
CMEA	–	9.5	34.2	
Other	2.0	2.7	3.5	
ECONOMIC INDICATORS				
GNP Curr. Prices, $M	2155.6	2940.2	3343.6	4010.5
Real GNP, 1976=100	121.0	134.0	131.0	133.0
GNP/Cap Curr. Prices,$	395.0	526.0	584.0	690.0
GNP/cap Atlas Basis, $	357.0	412.0	423.0	461.0
Real GNP/Cap, 1976=100	118.0	128.0	122.0	122.0
Population, Million	5.5	5.6	5.7	5.8
Curr.A/C Deficit(-),$M	179.8	-109.6	-497.0	-623.9
BOP Exp. & Transf.,$M	1103.6	1096.1	1222.6	1421.1
Exp. to OECD CIF, $M	8.4	21.9	15.4	10.8
of which				
Manufact.	0.6	13.3	1.4	1.8
Imp. from OECD FOB, $M	416.8	536.2	760.1	876.8
Reserves ex. Gold, $M	1240.2	1459.4	1427.4	1282.6

	1977	1978	1979	1980	1977	1978	1979	1980	197
	TOTAL RECEIPTS NET				**TOTAL ODA NET**				**TOTAL ODA GROSS**
DAC COUNTRIES									
Australia	–	–	–	–	–	–	–	–	
Austria	–	–	–	0.0	–	–	–	0.0	
Belgium	–	–	–	–	–	–	–	–	
Canada	–	–	–	–	–	–	–	–	
Denmark	-1.2	2.1	0.2	-0.8	–	–	0.0	0.0	
Finland	–	–	–	–	–	–	–	–	
France	-2.1	-1.0	-2.4	-1.6	–	–	–	0.8	
Germany, Fed. Rep.	0.9	1.6	0.5	1.2	0.5	0.2	0.1	0.1	0.
Italy	1.5	0.1	30.8	123.6	0.2	0.1	0.0	0.0	0.
Japan	0.3	9.5	1.0	-1.2	0.3	9.5	1.0	-0.4	0.
Netherlands	0.1	0.1	0.0	0.0	0.1	0.1	0.0	0.0	0.
New Zealand	–	–	–	–	–	–	–	–	
Norway	0.1	–	–	–	–	–	–	–	
Sweden	–	–	–	0.5	–	–	–	0.5	
Switzerland	–	–	–	–	–	–	–	–	
United Kingdom	5.7	3.3	3.5	3.1	4.8	3.1	3.5	3.1	4.
United States	1.0	–	–	–	1.0	–	–	–	1
TOTAL	*6.3*	*15.7*	*33.6*	*124.9*	*6.9*	*12.9*	*4.7*	*4.1*	*7*
MULTILATERAL									
AF.D.F.	–	–	–	–	–	–	–	–	
AF.D.B.	–	–	–	–	–	–	–	–	
AS.D.B.	–	–	–	–	–	–	–	–	
CAR.D.B.	–	–	–	–	–	–	–	–	
E.E.C.	4.0	1.6	–	–	4.0	1.6	–	–	4
IBRD	–	–	–	–	–	–	–	–	
IDA	4.3	7.9	6.3	5.9	4.3	7.9	6.3	5.9	4
I.D.B.	–	–	–	–	–	–	–	–	
IFAD	–	–	–	–	–	–	–	–	
I.F.C.	–	–	–	–	–	–	–	–	
IMF TRUST FUND	3.6	11.2	11.4	9.6	3.6	11.2	11.4	9.6	3
U.N. AGENCIES	–	–	–	–	–	–	–	–	
UNDP	2.6	2.9	2.9	2.9	2.6	2.9	2.9	2.9	2
UNTA	1.6	1.8	1.3	0.2	1.6	1.8	1.3	0.2	1
UNICEF	0.3	1.4	1.3	2.0	0.3	1.4	1.3	2.0	0
UNRWA	–	–	–	–	–	–	–	–	
WFP	7.8	6.2	11.4	10.2	7.8	6.2	11.4	10.2	7
UNHCR	0.4	–	–	–	0.4	–	–	–	0
Other Multilateral	0.5	1.2	0.4	3.7	0.5	1.2	0.4	3.7	0
Arab OPEC Agencies	4.5	13.9	8.9	24.2	4.5	13.9	8.9	11.9	4
TOTAL	*29.7*	*48.0*	*43.9*	*58.7*	*29.7*	*48.0*	*43.9*	*46.4*	*29*
OPEC COUNTRIES	*75.6*	*40.3*	*10.5*	*39.0*	*65.6*	*35.3*	*10.5*	*39.0*	*65*
E.E.C.+ MEMBERS	*8.9*	*7.7*	*32.6*	*125.6*	*9.6*	*5.0*	*3.7*	*4.0*	*9*
TOTAL	***111.5***	***104.0***	***88.0***	***222.6***	***102.2***	***96.2***	***59.1***	***89.5***	***102***

	1977	1978	1979	1980	1977	1978	1979	1980	197
	ODA LOANS GROSS				**ODA LOANS NET**				**GRANTS**
DAC COUNTRIES									
Australia	–	–	–	–	–	–	–	–	
Austria	–	–	–	–	–	–	–	–	
Belgium	–	–	–	–	–	–	–	–	
Canada	–	–	–	–	–	–	–	–	
Denmark	–	–	–	–	–	–	–	-2.7	
Finland	–	–	–	–	–	–	–	–	
France	–	–	–	–	–	–	–	–	
Germany, Fed. Rep.	–	–	–	–	–	–	–	–	C
Italy	–	–	–	–	–	–	–	–	O
Japan	–	6.5	–	0.0	-0.1	6.4	-0.2	-0.8	O
Netherlands	–	–	–	–	–	–	–	–	C
New Zealand	–	–	–	–	–	–	–	–	
Norway	–	–	–	–	–	–	–	–	
Sweden	–	–	–	–	–	–	–	–	
Switzerland	–	–	–	–	–	–	–	–	
United Kingdom	–	–	–	–	–	–	–	–	4
United States	1.0	–	–	–	1.0	–	–	–	
TOTAL	*1.0*	*6.5*	*–*	*0.0*	*0.9*	*6.4*	*-0.2*	*-3.5*	*6*
MULTILATERAL	*12.5*	*32.9*	*31.0*	*29.1*	*12.5*	*32.9*	*29.5*	*27.4*	*1*
OPEC COUNTRIES	*15.2*	*21.2*	*6.9*	*22.6*	*15.2*	*21.2*	*6.3*	*21.0*	*5C*
E.E.C.+ MEMBERS	*–*	*–*	*–*	*–*	*–*	*–*	*–*	*-2.7*	*9*
TOTAL	***28.6***	***60.6***	***37.9***	***51.8***	***28.5***	***60.4***	***35.5***	***44.9***	***73***

	1977	1978	1979	1980	1977	1978	1979	1980	197
	TOTAL OFFICIAL GROSS				**TOTAL OFFICIAL NET**				**TOTAL OOF GROSS**
DAC COUNTRIES									
Australia	–	–	–	–	–	–	–	–	
Austria	–	–	–	0.0	–	–	–	0.0	
Belgium	–	–	–	–	–	–	–	–	
Canada	–	–	–	–	–	–	–	–	
Denmark	–	–	0.0	2.7	–	–	0.0	0.0	
Finland	–	–	–	–	–	–	–	–	
France	–	–	–	0.8	–	–	–	0.8	
Germany, Fed. Rep.	0.5	0.2	0.1	0.1	0.5	0.2	0.1	0.1	
Italy	0.2	0.1	0.0	0.0	0.2	0.1	0.0	0.0	
Japan	0.5	9.7	1.2	0.5	0.3	9.5	1.0	-0.4	
Netherlands	0 1	0.1	0.0	0.0	0.1	0.1	0.0	0.0	
New Zealand	–	–	–	–	–	–	–	–	
Norway	–	–	–	–	–	–	–	–	
Sweden	–	–	–	0.5	–	–	–	0.5	
Switzerland	–	–	–	–	–	–	–	–	
United Kingdom	4.8	3.1	3.5	3.1	4.8	3.1	3.5	3.1	
United States	1.0	–	–	–	1.0	–	–	–	
TOTAL	*7.0*	*13.1*	*4.9*	*7.6*	*6.9*	*12.9*	*4.7*	*4.1*	
MULTILATERAL	*29.7*	*48.0*	*48.4*	*60.4*	*29.7*	*48.0*	*43.9*	*58.7*	
OPEC COUNTRIES	*75.6*	*40.3*	*11.1*	*40.7*	*75.6*	*40.3*	*10.5*	*39.0*	*1*
E.E.C.+ MEMBERS	*9.6*	*5.0*	*3.7*	*6.7*	*9.6*	*5.0*	*3.7*	*4.0*	
TOTAL	***112.3***	***101.4***	***64.4***	***108.6***	***112.2***	***101.2***	***59.1***	***101.8***	***1***

ODA COMMITMENTS

1978	1979	1980	1977	1978	1979	1980
–	–	–	–	–	–	–
–	–	0.0	–	–	–	–
–	–	–	–	–	–	–
–	–	–	–	–	–	–
–	0.0	2.7	–	2.7	–	0.1
–	–	–	–	–	–	–
–	–	0.8	–	0.1	–	0.8
0.2	0.1	0.1	0.6	0.2	0.1	0.1
0.1	0.0	0.0	0.2	0.1	0.0	0.0
9.7	1.2	0.5	2.8	7.6	0.4	1.1
0.1	0.0	0.0	0.1	0.1	0.0	0.0
–	–	–	–	–	–	–
–	–	–	–	–	–	–
–	–	0.5	–	–	–	–
–	–	–	–	–	–	–
3.1	3.5	3.1	4.8	3.1	3.5	3.1
–	–	–	–	–	–	–
13.1	*4.9*	*7.6*	*8.4*	*13.8*	*4.0*	*5.2*
–	–	–	–	–	–	–
–	–	–	–	–	–	–
–	–	–	–	–	–	–
–	–	–	–	–	–	–
1.6	–	–	3.8	2.6	–	0.1
–	–	–	–	–	–	–
7.9	6.3	5.9	–	15.4	10.0	22.2
–	–	–	–	–	–	–
–	–	–	–	–	–	9.8
–	–	–	–	–	–	–
11.2	11.4	9.6	–	–	–	–
–	–	–	13.2	13.5	17.3	19.0
2.9	2.9	2.9	–	–	–	–
1.8	1.3	0.2	–	–	–	–
1.4	1.3	2.0	–	–	–	–
–	–	–	–	–	–	–
6.2	11.4	10.2	–	–	–	–
–	–	–	–	–	–	–
1.2	0.4	3.7	–	–	–	–
13.9	13.3	13.6	4.5	–	26.2	11.0
48.0	*48.4*	*48.1*	*21.5*	*31.6*	*53.5*	*62.1*
35.3	*11.1*	*40.7*	*122.0*	*27.7*	*35.0*	*85.7*
5.0	*3.7*	*6.7*	*9.4*	*8.8*	*3.7*	*4.2*
96.4	***64.3***	***96.3***	***151.9***	***73.0***	***92.5***	***153.1***

TECH. COOP. GRANTS

1978	1979	1980	1977	1978	1979	1980
–	–	–	–	–	–	–
–	–	0.0	–	–	–	0.0
–	–	–	–	–	–	–
–	–	–	–	–	–	–
–	0.0	2.7	–	–	0.0	0.0
–	–	–	–	–	–	–
–	–	0.8	–	–	–	0.8
0.2	0.1	0.1	0.0	0.2	0.1	0.1
0.1	0.0	0.0	0.2	0.0	0.0	0.0
3.2	1.2	0.4	0.1	0.2	0.3	0.4
0.1	0.0	0.0	0.1	0.1	0.0	0.0
–	–	–	–	–	–	–
–	–	–	–	–	–	–
–	–	0.5	–	–	–	–
–	–	–	–	–	–	–
3.1	3.5	3.1	4.8	3.1	1.5	1.5
–	–	–	–	–	–	–
6.6	*4.9*	*7.6*	*5.2*	*3.5*	*2.0*	*2.8*
15.1	*17.3*	*19.0*	*5.4*	*7.3*	*5.9*	*19.0*
14.2	*4.2*	*18.1*	–	–	–	–
5.0	*3.7*	*6.7*	*5.1*	*3.3*	*1.7*	*2.4*
35.9	***26.4***	***44.6***	***10.6***	***10.8***	***7.9***	***21.8***

TOTAL OOF NET

1978	1979	1980	1977	1978	1979	1980
–	–	–	–	–	–	–
–	–	–	–	–	–	–
–	–	–	–	–	–	–
–	–	–	–	–	–	–
–	0.0	0.0	–	–	0.0	0.0
–	–	–	–	–	–	–
–	–	–	–	–	–	–
–	–	–	–	–	–	–
–	–	–	–	–	–	–
–	–	–	–	–	–	–
–	–	–	–	–	–	–
–	–	–	–	–	–	–
–	–	–	–	–	–	–
–	–	–	–	–	–	–
–	–	–	–	–	–	–
–	–	–	–	–	–	–
–	–	–	–	–	–	–
–	*0.0*	*0.0*	–	–	*0.0*	*0.0*
–	–	*12.3*	–	–	–	*12.3*
5.0	–	–	*10.0*	*5.0*	–	–
–	*0.0*	*0.0*	–	–	*0.0*	*0.0*
5.0	***0.0***	***12.3***	***10.0***	***5.0***	***0.0***	***12.3***

MAIN AID AGGREGATES

	1977	1978	1979	1980
DAC COUNTRIES COMBINED				
PRIVATE SECTOR NET	-0.6	2.8	28.9	120.8
Direct Investment	1.3	–	–	–
Portfolio Invest.	0.4	0.2	-1.0	-1.5
Export Credits	-2.3	2.5	29.9	122.3
OFFICIAL & PRIVATE				
GROSS:				
Contractual Lending	3.3	11.8	33.4	130.8
Export Credits Tot.	2.3	5.3	33.3	130.8
Export Credits Priv	2.3	5.3	33.3	130.8
OTHER NET DATA				
Contractual Lending	-1.5	8.9	29.8	118.8
Export Credits Tot.	-2.3	2.5	29.9	122.3
(Bank Sector Loans)	–	–	1.0	-1.0
ODA CONCESSIONALITY				
Total:Grant Element	100.0	70.0	95.0	100.0
Loans:Grant Element	–	38.0	83.0	–
OTHER SOURCES				
CMEA Countr.(Gross)	12.4	10.8	13.3	17.4
Intra LDCS Exc.OPEC	–	–	–	–
Other	–	–	–	–
ALL SOURCE COMMITMENTS				
TOTAL BILATERAL	130.4	41.5	39.2	91.0
of which				
OPEC (ODA)	122.0	27.7	35.0	85.7
CMEA (ODA)	12.0	5.9	41.1	15.0
TOTAL MULTILAT.(ODA)	21.5	31.6	53.5	62.1
TOTAL BIL.& MULTIL.	151.9	73.0	92.7	153.1
of which				
ODA Grants	113.4	37.8	26.4	42.1
ODA Loans	38.5	35.2	66.2	111.0
ODA CONCESSIONALITY				
Total: Grant Element	88.0	76.0	62.0	68.0
Loans: Grant Element	54.0	52.0	44.0	56.0

INDEBTEDNESS

	1977	1978	1979	1980
TOTAL DEBT DISBURSED	***267.9***	***356.9***	***435.0***	
Debt to DAC Countries	19.0	27.0	24.0	
ODA	10.0	18.0	17.0	
Total Export Credits	9.0	9.0	7.0	
Other Private Market	–	–	–	
International Org.	19.9	47.0	72.8	
CMEA	181.5	217.7	243.8	
Other	47.4	65.2	94.4	
TOTAL DEBT SERVICE	***5.7***	***6.3***	***18.0***	
Paid to DAC Countries	5.3	4.5	6.0	
ODA	0.2	0.2	0.2	
Total Export Credits	5.1	4.3	5.8	
Other Private Market	–	–	–	
International Org.	0.1	0.7	3.9	
CMEA	0.2	0.8	6.0	
Other	0.1	0.3	2.0	

ECONOMIC INDICATORS

	1977	1978	1979	1980
GNP Curr. Prices, $M	625.2	725.8	862.8	998.0
Real GNP, 1976=100	125.0	138.0	153.0	159.0
GNP/Cap Curr. Prices,$	354.0	401.0	465.0	524.0
GNP/cap Atlas Basis, $	349.3	402.4	471.5	520.4
Real GNP/Cap, 1976=100	122.0	131.0	142.0	144.0
Population, Million	1.8	1.8	1.9	1.9
Curr.A/C Deficit(-),$M	-131.1	-87.1	-57.7	–
BOP Exp. & Transf.,$M	285.8	355.4	429.4	–
Exp. to OECD CIF, $M	42.1	42.7	108.7	160.0
of which				
Manufact.	0.5	1.7	1.0	3.5
Imp. from OECD FOB, $M	252.5	281.5	255.6	373.1
Reserves ex. Gold, $M	99.3	187.9	209.7	233.8

TOTAL RECEIPTS NET

	1977	1978	1979	1980
DAC COUNTRIES				
Australia	0.1	2.8	2.0	0.9
Austria	55.7	8.0	-27.3	-27.2
Belgium	67.4	12.4	-53.2	57.5
Canada	-7.8	-4.5	-5.2	10.9
Denmark	43.3	14.3	18.0	32.9
Finland	0.7	0.1	1.0	0.4
France	218.8	272.4	320.9	356.3
Germany, Fed. Rep.	184.8	216.9	105.6	124.6
Italy	-1.9	-50.5	-41.3	-27.0
Japan	74.5	107.6	83.4	15.4
Netherlands	1.4	-1.2	35.5	26.7
New Zealand	0.0	-0.2	–	0.0
Norway	4.7	14.0	-4.4	-7.2
Sweden	22.6	11.4	13.5	5.3
Switzerland	103.1	76.0	30.1	-55.0
United Kingdom	0.4	-1.4	671.9	226.9
United States	97.0	70.0	107.0	230.0
TOTAL	*864.7*	*747.8*	*1257.3*	*971.5*
MULTILATERAL				
AF.D.F.	–	–	–	–
AF.D.B.	–	–	–	–
AS.D.B.	–	–	–	–
CAR.D.B.	–	–	–	–
E.E.C.	–	–	25.1	15.0
IBRD	103.0	139.4	245.4	215.9
IDA	–	–	–	–
I.D.B.	–	–	–	–
IFAD	–	–	–	–
I.F.C.	-0.7	7.8	1.7	-30.1
IMF TRUST FUND	–	–	–	–
U.N. AGENCIES	–	–	–	–
UNDP	1.6	2.3	1.9	1.7
UNTA	0.1	0.1	0.2	0.2
UNICEF	–	–	0.1	0.1
UNRWA	–	–	–	–
WFP	–	–	0.1	0.1
UNHCR	0.2	0.2	0.1	–
Other Multilateral	0.2	0.1	0.1	0.3
Arab OPEC Agencies	–	–	–	–
TOTAL	*104.4*	*149.9*	*274.6*	*203.2*
OPEC COUNTRIES	–	*5.5*	–	–
E.E.C.+ MEMBERS	*514.2*	*462.7*	*1082.4*	*813.0*
TOTAL	***969.0***	***903.2***	***1531.9***	***1174.7***

TOTAL ODA NET

	1977	1978	1979	1980
Australia	–	–	0.1	–
Austria	1.2	1.6	2.0	2.0
Belgium	0.1	0.0	0.1	–
Canada	–	–	–	–
Denmark	–	–	0.1	–
Finland	–	–	0.0	–
France	-3.2	-3.5	-0.1	0.0
Germany, Fed. Rep.	63.1	4.1	4.1	2.9
Italy	-18.0	-12.4	-11.6	-5.7
Japan	-1.8	-3.5	-3.0	-3.3
Netherlands	2.6	0.1	0.5	0.3
New Zealand	–	–	–	0.0
Norway	–	–	1.0	–
Sweden	–	–	0.4	–
Switzerland	0.0	–	1.4	0.5
United Kingdom	–	–	–	–
United States	-39.0	-34.0	-27.0	-16.0
TOTAL	*5.0*	*-47.7*	*-32.0*	*-19.4*
AF.D.F.	–	–	–	–
AF.D.B.	–	–	–	–
AS.D.B.	–	–	–	–
CAR.D.B.	–	–	–	–
E.E.C.	–	–	0.4	–
IBRD	–	–	–	–
IDA	–	–	–	–
I.D.B.	–	–	–	–
IFAD	–	–	–	–
I.F.C.	–	–	–	–
IMF TRUST FUND	–	–	–	–
U.N. AGENCIES	–	–	–	–
UNDP	1.6	2.3	1.9	1.7
UNTA	0.1	0.1	0.2	0.2
UNICEF	–	–	0.1	0.1
UNRWA	–	–	–	–
WFP	–	–	0.1	0.1
UNHCR	0.2	0.2	0.1	–
Other Multilateral	0.2	0.1	0.1	0.3
Arab OPEC Agencies	–	–	–	–
TOTAL	*2.1*	*2.7*	*2.8*	*2.4*
OPEC COUNTRIES	–	–	–	–
E.E.C.+ MEMBERS	*44.5*	*-11.7*	*-6.5*	*-2.5*
TOTAL	***7.0***	***-45.0***	***-29.2***	***-16.9***

TOTAL ODA GROSS

	197
Australia	
Austria	1.
Belgium	0.
Canada	
Denmark	
Finland	
France	
Germany, Fed. Rep.	63.
Italy	0
Japan	0.
Netherlands	2.
New Zealand	
Norway	
Sweden	
Switzerland	0
United Kingdom	
United States	-15.
TOTAL	*52.*
AF.D.F.	
AF.D.B.	
AS.D.B.	
CAR.D.B.	
E.E.C.	
IBRD	
IDA	
I.D.B.	
IFAD	
I.F.C.	
IMF TRUST FUND	
U.N. AGENCIES	
UNDP	1
UNTA	0
UNICEF	
UNRWA	
WFP	
UNHCR	0.
Other Multilateral	0
Arab OPEC Agencies	
TOTAL	*2.*
OPEC COUNTRIES	
E.E.C.+ MEMBERS	*65.*
TOTAL	***54***

ODA LOANS GROSS

	1977	1978	1979	1980
DAC COUNTRIES				
Australia	–	–	–	–
Austria	–	–	–	–
Belgium	–	–	–	–
Canada	–	–	–	–
Denmark	–	–	–	–
Finland	–	–	–	–
France	–	–	–	–
Germany, Fed. Rep.	60.9	1.7	1.4	0.2
Italy	–	–	–	–
Japan	–	–	–	–
Netherlands	–	–	–	–
New Zealand	–	–	–	–
Norway	–	–	–	–
Sweden	–	–	–	–
Switzerland	–	–	–	–
United Kingdom	–	–	–	–
United States	–	–	–	–
TOTAL	*60.9*	*1.7*	*1.4*	*0.2*
MULTILATERAL	–	–	–	–
OPEC COUNTRIES	–	–	–	–
E.E.C.+ MEMBERS	*60.9*	*1.7*	*1.4*	*0.2*
TOTAL	***60.9***	***1.7***	***1.4***	***0.2***

ODA LOANS NET

	1977	1978	1979	1980
Australia	–	–	–	–
Austria	0.0	0.0	0.0	0.0
Belgium	–	–	–	–
Canada	–	–	–	–
Denmark	–	–	–	–
Finland	–	–	–	–
France	-3.2	-3.5	-0.1	-0.5
Germany, Fed. Rep.	60.9	1.7	0.8	0.2
Italy	-18.0	-12.4	-11.7	-10.2
Japan	-1.9	-3.7	-3.5	-3.4
Netherlands	–	–	–	–
New Zealand	–	–	–	–
Norway	–	–	–	–
Sweden	–	–	–	–
Switzerland	–	–	–	–
United Kingdom	–	–	–	–
United States	-24.0	-23.0	-19.0	-10.0
TOTAL	*13.8*	*-40.9*	*-33.5*	*-24.0*
MULTILATERAL	–	–	–	–
OPEC COUNTRIES	–	–	–	–
E.E.C.+ MEMBERS	*39.7*	*-14.2*	*-10.9*	*-10.5*
TOTAL	***13.8***	***-40.9***	***-33.5***	***-24.0***

GRANTS

	197
Australia	
Austria	1.
Belgium	0
Canada	
Denmark	
Finland	
France	
Germany, Fed. Rep.	2.
Italy	0
Japan	0.
Netherlands	2
New Zealand	
Norway	
Sweden	
Switzerland	0
United Kingdom	
United States	-15
TOTAL	*-8.*
MULTILATERAL	*2.*
OPEC COUNTRIES	
E.E.C.+ MEMBERS	*4*
TOTAL	***-6***

TOTAL OFFICIAL GROSS

	1977	1978	1979	1980
DAC COUNTRIES				
Australia	–	2.6	1.9	0.5
Austria	1.3	1.6	2.0	2.0
Belgium	0.1	0.0	0.1	–
Canada	0.4	0.8	1.7	7.3
Denmark	–	–	0.1	–
Finland	–	–	0.0	–
France	–	–	–	0.5
Germany, Fed. Rep.	113.4	35.2	9.3	4.3
Italy	7.7	7.3	18.8	51.9
Japan	0.1	0.2	0.5	0.1
Netherlands	2.6	0.1	0.5	0.3
New Zealand	0.2	–	–	0.0
Norway	–	–	1.0	–
Sweden	–	–	0.4	–
Switzerland	0.0	–	1.4	0.5
United Kingdom	–	–	–	–
United States	60.0	79.0	23.0	67.0
TOTAL	*185.7*	*126.7*	*60.8*	*134.3*
MULTILATERAL	*141.1*	*204.4*	*342.7*	*318.5*
OPEC COUNTRIES	–	*5.5*	–	–
E.E.C.+ MEMBERS	*123.7*	*42.6*	*53.9*	*71.9*
TOTAL	***326.8***	***336.6***	***403.5***	***452.9***

TOTAL OFFICIAL NET

	1977	1978	1979	1980
Australia	–	2.6	1.9	0.5
Austria	1.2	1.6	2.0	2.0
Belgium	-1.2	-1.4	-1.4	–
Canada	-7.7	-4.5	-5.2	-0.7
Denmark	–	–	0.1	–
Finland	–	–	0.0	–
France	-3.2	-3.5	-0.1	0.0
Germany, Fed. Rep.	62.2	31.0	-37.6	-78.9
Italy	-11.8	-8.0	1.9	29.8
Japan	-1.8	-3.5	-3.0	-3.3
Netherlands	1.4	-1.2	-0.9	-0.5
New Zealand	0.0	–	–	0.0
Norway	–	–	1.0	–
Sweden	–	–	0.4	–
Switzerland	0.0	–	1.4	0.5
United Kingdom	–	–	–	–
United States	23.0	40.0	-24.0	22.0
TOTAL	*62.2*	*53.0*	*-63.5*	*-28.6*
MULTILATERAL	*104.4*	*149.9*	*274.6*	*203.2*
OPEC COUNTRIES	–	*5.5*	–	–
E.E.C.+ MEMBERS	*47.4*	*16.8*	*-12.9*	*-34.6*
TOTAL	***166.6***	***208.4***	***211.1***	***174.6***

TOTAL OOF GROSS

	197
Australia	
Austria	
Belgium	
Canada	0.
Denmark	
Finland	
France	
Germany, Fed. Rep.	50
Italy	7.
Japan	
Netherlands	
New Zealand	0.
Norway	
Sweden	
Switzerland	
United Kingdom	
United States	75.
TOTAL	*133*
MULTILATERAL	*139*
OPEC COUNTRIES	
E.E.C.+ MEMBERS	*58*
TOTAL	***272***

1978	1979	1980	1977	1978	1979	1980
			ODA COMMITMENTS			
–	0.1	–	–	–	–	–
1.6	2.0	2.0	–	–	–	–
0.0	0.1	–	–	–	–	–
–	–	–	–	–	–	–
–	0.1	–	–	–	–	–
–	0.0	–	–	–	0.1	–
–	–	0.5	–	–	–	–
4.1	4.6	2.9	2.2	2.4	3.3	2.7
–	0.0	4.6	0.0	–	0.0	4.6
0.2	0.5	0.1	0.2	0.2	0.5	0.1
0.1	0.5	0.3	2.6	3.6	0.6	0.2
–	–	0.0	–	–	0.0	–
–	1.0	–	–	–	1.0	–
–	0.4	–	–	–	0.7	–
–	1.4	0.5	–	–	–	0.5
–	–	–	–	–	–	–
-11.0	-8.0	-6.0	–	–	10.0	–
-5.0	*2.8*	*4.8*	*4.9*	*6.1*	*16.2*	*8.1*
–	–	–	–	–	–	–
–	–	–	–	–	–	–
–	–	–	–	–	–	–
–	–	–	–	–	–	–
–	0.4	–	–	–	0.4	–
–	–	–	–	–	–	–
–	–	–	–	–	–	–
–	–	–	–	–	–	–
–	–	–	–	–	–	–
–	–	–	–	–	–	–
–	–	–	–	–	–	–
–	–	–	2.1	2.7	2.4	2.4
2.3	1.9	1.7	–	–	–	–
0.1	0.2	0.2	–	–	–	–
–	0.1	0.1	–	–	–	–
–	–	–	–	–	–	–
–	0.1	0.1	–	–	–	–
0.2	0.1	–	–	–	–	–
0.1	0.1	0.3	–	–	–	–
–	–	–	–	–	–	–
2.7	*2.8*	*2.4*	*2.1*	*2.7*	*2.8*	*2.4*
–	–	–	–	–	–	–
4.2	*5.8*	*8.2*	*4.8*	*5.9*	*4.3*	*7.5*
-2.4	***5.6***	***7.2***	***7.0***	***8.8***	***19.0***	***10.5***
			TECH. COOP. GRANTS			
–	0.1	–	–	–	–	–
1.6	2.0	2.0	1.3	1.6	1.7	1.7
0.0	0.1	–	0.1	0.0	0.0	–
–	–	–	–	–	–	–
–	0.1	–	–	–	–	–
–	0.0	–	–	–	–	–
–	–	0.5	–	–	–	0.5
2.4	3.3	2.7	2.2	2.4	2.8	2.7
–	0.0	4.6	0.0	–	0.0	0.1
0.2	0.5	0.1	0.1	0.2	0.1	0.1
0.1	0.5	0.3	0.1	0.1	0.2	0.1
–	–	0.0	–	–	–	0.0
–	1.0	–	–	–	–	–
–	0.4	–	–	–	–	–
–	1.4	0.5	0.0	–	–	–
–	–	–	–	–	–	–
-11.0	-8.0	-6.0	–	–	–	–
-6.8	*1.4*	*4.6*	*3.7*	*4.2*	*4.8*	*5.1*
2.7	*2.8*	*2.4*	*2.1*	*2.7*	*2.3*	*2.4*
–	–	–	–	–	–	–
2.5	*4.4*	*8.0*	*2.3*	*2.5*	*3.0*	*3.3*
-4.1	***4.2***	***7.0***	***5.8***	***6.9***	***7.1***	***7.5***
			TOTAL OOF NET			
2.6	1.8	0.5	–	2.6	1.8	0.5
–	–	–	–	–	–	–
–	–	–	-1.2	-1.4	-1.5	–
0.8	1.7	7.3	-7.7	-4.5	-5.2	-0.7
–	–	–	–	–	–	–
–	–	–	–	–	–	–
–	–	–	–	–	–	–
31.1	4.7	1.4	-0.8	26.9	-41.6	-81.8
7.3	18.8	47.3	6.2	4.4	13.5	35.5
–	–	–	–	–	–	–
–	–	–	-1.2	-1.3	-1.4	-0.7
–	–	–	0.0	–	–	–
–	–	–	–	–	–	–
–	–	–	–	–	–	–
–	–	–	–	–	–	–
–	–	–	–	–	–	–
90.0	31.0	73.0	62.0	74.0	3.0	38.0
131.8	*58.0*	*129.5*	*57.2*	*100.7*	*-31.5*	*-9.2*
201.7	*339.9*	*316.1*	*102.3*	*147.2*	*271.8*	*200.7*
5.5	–	–	–	*5.5*	–	–
38.4	*48.2*	*63.7*	*2.9*	*28.5*	*-6.4*	*-32.0*
339.0	***397.9***	***445.6***	***159.5***	***253.4***	***240.3***	***191.5***

	1977	1978	1979	1980
MAIN AID AGGREGATES				
DAC COUNTRIES COMBINED				
PRIVATE SECTOR NET	802.5	694.8	1320.8	1000.1
Direct Investment	13.8	14.3	28.3	22.6
Portfolio Invest.	263.7	521.1	352.5	585.8
Export Credits	525.0	159.4	940.1	391.8
OFFICIAL & PRIVATE				
GROSS:				
Contractual Lending	1188.4	679.4	1608.1	1186.1
Export Credits Tot.	1059.4	664.2	1601.7	1173.2
Export Credits Priv	993.8	545.9	1548.7	1056.4
OTHER NET DATA				
Contractual Lending	596.0	219.2	875.2	358.6
Export Credits Tot.	567.8	249.4	947.7	448.5
(Bank Sector Loans)	728.0	1043.0	1084.0	931.0
ODA CONCESSIONALITY				
Total:Grant Element	100.0	100.0	100.0	100.0
Loans:Grant Element	–	–	–	–
OTHER SOURCES				
CMEA Countr.(Gross)	–	–	–	–
Intra LDCS Exc.OPEC	–	–	–	–
Other	–	–	–	–
ALL SOURCE COMMITMENTS				
TOTAL BILATERAL	25.8	113.7	203.6	132.9
of which				
OPEC (ODA)	–	–	–	–
CMEA (ODA)	–	–	–	–
TOTAL MULTILAT.(ODA)	2.1	2.7	2.8	2.4
TOTAL BIL.& MULTIL.	27.9	116.4	206.4	135.3
of which				
ODA Grants	7.0	8.8	19.0	10.5
ODA Loans	–	–	–	–
ODA CONCESSIONALITY				
Total: Grant Element	100.0	100.0	100.0	100.0
Loans: Grant Element	–	–	–	–
INDEBTEDNESS				
TOTAL DEBT DISBURSED	***9132.8***	***11351.7***	***13346.4***	
Debt to DAC Countries	6091.0	7402.0	8514.0	
ODA	605.0	680.0	666.0	
Total Export Credits	2570.0	3308.0	4236.0	
Other Private Market	2916.0	3414.0	3612.0	
International Org.	762.1	910.6	1181.2	
CMEA	900.0	1300.0	2389.0	
Other	1379.8	1739.1	1262.2	
TOTAL DEBT SERVICE	***1613.7***	***1816.1***	***2536.5***	
Paid to DAC Countries	1206.6	1323.9	1798.1	
ODA	66.0	61.5	55.8	
Total Export Credits	528.1	579.6	889.6	
Other Private Market	612.5	682.8	852.7	
International Org.	87.1	117.2	145.2	
CMEA	100.0	130.0	397.4	
Other	220.0	245.0	195.8	
ECONOMIC INDICATORS				
GNP Curr. Prices, $M	40374.7	45501.9	70696.8	71931.5
Real GNP, 1976=100	108.0	118.0	125.0	129.0
GNP/Cap Curr. Prices,$	1856.0	2073.0	3193.0	3221.0
GNP/cap Atlas Basis, $	1786.9	2065.9	2367.5	2623.2
Real GNP/Cap, 1976=100	107.0	115.0	122.0	125.0
Population, Million	21.7	21.9	22.1	22.3
Curr.A/C Deficit(-),$M	-1343.0	-1278.0	-3657.0	–
BOP Exp. & Transf.,$M	10347.0	11813.0	13942.0	–
Exp. to OECD CIF, $M	2606.1	3022.7	3780.7	3994.8
of which				
Manufact.	1583.0	1848.9	2222.0	2467.8
Imp. from OECD FOB, $M	5630.9	6508.9	8442.8	8134.0
Reserves ex. Gold, $M	2044.4	2388.2	1256.6	1384.1

ZAIRE

DISBURSEMENTS, UNLESS OTHERWISE STATE

	1977	1978	1979	1980	1977	1978	1979	1980	197
TOTAL RECEIPTS NET / **TOTAL ODA NET** / **TOTAL ODA GROSS**									
DAC COUNTRIES									
Australia	–	–	–	–	–	–	–	–	
Austria	-0.1	-0.6	-1.2	-1.3	0.1	0.1	-0.2	-0.2	0.
Belgium	164.8	222.5	329.1	290.9	108.6	129.0	153.6	169.7	108.
Canada	2.4	8.0	6.6	13.2	1.8	7.5	5.8	13.5	1.
Denmark	2.1	1.3	1.3	0.9	2.1	1.3	1.3	0.9	2.
Finland	–	–	–	0.0	–	–	–	0.0	
France	99.2	174.6	65.1	236.1	15.0	24.3	24.9	39.4	15.
Germany, Fed. Rep.	44.9	23.5	9.6	39.5	14.5	15.2	19.9	36.8	14.
Italy	13.4	-1.3	82.5	-22.5	0.5	0.3	0.8	0.6	0.
Japan	0.0	12.0	24.9	34.9	2.5	1.9	27.4	39.4	3.
Netherlands	1.3	6.2	3.1	1.9	1.3	1.6	3.1	1.9	1.
New Zealand	–	–	–	–	–	–	–	–	
Norway	-5.8	-0.1	0.2	-1.5	0.1	0.2	0.3	0.2	0.
Sweden	–	11.3	0.1	-2.6	–	–	1.5	2.0	
Switzerland	0.3	1.3	1.4	2.0	0.3	1.3	1.4	0.6	0.
United Kingdom	15.2	2.9	-2.6	-16.4	0.2	0.3	4.9	1.3	0.
United States	90.0	110.0	83.0	48.0	24.0	21.0	44.0	11.0	29.
TOTAL	*397.2*	*571.7*	*602.9*	*623.2*	*170.9*	*204.0*	*288.7*	*316.8*	*176.*
MULTILATERAL									
AF.D.F.	–	–	–	–	–	–	–	–	
AF.D.B.	2.6	3.0	5.3	5.4	–	–	–	–	
AS.D.B.	–	–	–	–	–	–	–	–	
CAR.D.B.	–	–	–	–	–	–	–	–	
E.E.C.	30.2	20.0	16.7	24.9	31.4	19.0	19.3	23.0	31.
IBRD	24.0	18.5	-4.4	16.9	–	–	–	–	
IDA	32.3	26.2	26.3	19.6	32.3	26.2	26.3	19.6	32.
I.D.B.	–	–	–	–	–	–	–	–	
IFAD	–	–	–	–	–	–	–	–	
I.F.C.	–	–	3.7	-0.8	–	–	–	–	
IMF TRUST FUND	14.1	43.5	44.3	37.6	14.1	43.5	44.3	37.6	14.
U.N. AGENCIES	–	–	–	–	–	–	–	–	
UNDP	3.5	4.7	5.7	11.6	3.5	4.7	5.7	11.6	3
UNTA	1.0	1.0	0.8	0.3	1.0	1.0	0.8	0.3	1.
UNICEF	0.7	1.7	1.7	0.6	0.7	1.7	1.7	0.6	0
UNRWA	–	–	–	–	–	–	–	–	
WFP	–	2.6	5.3	2.8	–	2.6	5.3	2.8	
UNHCR	3.5	9.9	14.8	8.2	3.5	9.9	14.8	8.2	3
Other Multilateral	1.0	1.3	1.1	1.9	1.0	1.3	1.1	1.9	1.
Arab OPEC Agencies	2.2	3.1	3.7	0.3	2.2	3.1	3.7	0.3	2.
TOTAL	*115.1*	*135.4*	*124.9*	*129.1*	*89.7*	*112.9*	*122.9*	*105.7*	*89*
OPEC COUNTRIES	–	–	*4.8*	*23.5*	–	–	*4.8*	*23.5*	
E.E.C.+ MEMBERS	*340.7*	*449.9*	*504.6*	*555.3*	*173.4*	*191.1*	*227.8*	*273.4*	*173*
TOTAL	***512.3***	***707.1***	***732.5***	***775.8***	***260.6***	***316.9***	***416.4***	***446.0***	***266***

	1977	1978	1979	1980	1977	1978	1979	1980	197
ODA LOANS GROSS / **ODA LOANS NET** / **GRANTS**									
DAC COUNTRIES									
Australia	–	–	–	–	–	–	–	–	
Austria	–	–	–	–	–	–	-0.2	-0.3	0
Belgium	5.6	–	6.8	22.2	5.6	–	6.3	21.1	103
Canada	0.9	3.4	0.2	0.1	0.9	3.4	0.2	0.1	0
Denmark	–	–	–	–	–	–	–	–	2
Finland	–	–	–	–	–	–	–	–	
France	0.6	6.7	2.5	15.4	0.6	6.7	2.5	15.0	14
Germany, Fed. Rep.	5.8	5.5	10.5	26.0	5.8	3.8	9.9	25.7	8
Italy	–	–	–	–	–	–	–	–	0
Japan	1.5	0.3	21.9	32.0	0.9	0.2	21.8	31.9	1
Netherlands	–	–	–	–	–	–	–	–	1
New Zealand	–	–	–	–	–	–	–	–	
Norway	–	–	–	–	–	–	–	–	0
Sweden	–	–	–	–	–	–	–	–	
Switzerland	–	–	–	–	–	–	–	–	0
United Kingdom	–	–	–	–	–	–	–	–	0
United States	25.0	16.0	38.0	18.0	20.0	14.0	35.0	1.0	4
TOTAL	*39.3*	*31.9*	*79.9*	*113.7*	*33.8*	*28.1*	*75.4*	*94.6*	*137*
MULTILATERAL	*52.0*	*73.5*	*74.6*	*69.2*	*52.0*	*73.5*	*74.6*	*68.9*	*37*
OPEC COUNTRIES	–	–	–	–	–	–	–	–	
E.E.C.+ MEMBERS	*15.4*	*12.9*	*20.0*	*75.2*	*15.4*	*11.3*	*18.9*	*73.3*	*158*
TOTAL	***91.4***	***105.4***	***154.5***	***182.9***	***85.8***	***101.6***	***150.0***	***163.5***	***174***

	1977	1978	1979	1980	1977	1978	1979	1980	197
TOTAL OFFICIAL GROSS / **TOTAL OFFICIAL NET** / **TOTAL OOF GROSS**									
DAC COUNTRIES									
Australia	–	–	–	–	–	–	–	–	
Austria	0.1	0.1	0.1	0.1	0.0	0.0	-0.2	-0.2	
Belgium	119.8	150.9	154.2	311.6	119.8	147.2	147.8	297.0	11
Canada	2.4	8.0	6.7	13.5	2.4	8.0	6.6	13.2	0
Denmark	2.1	1.3	1.3	0.9	2.1	1.3	1.3	0.9	
Finland	–	–	–	0.0	–	–	–	0.0	
France	15.3	99.5	24.9	226.4	15.3	99.5	14.0	215.0	C
Germany, Fed. Rep.	42.2	72.1	39.0	50.5	37.3	40.9	28.1	37.7	27
Italy	32.9	30.1	0.8	0.6	30.4	26.1	-4.2	-3.3	32
Japan	3.1	2.0	27.5	39.5	2.5	1.9	27.4	39.4	
Netherlands	1.3	1.6	3.1	1.9	1.3	1.6	3.1	1.9	
New Zealand	0.0	–	–	–	–	–	–	–	C
Norway	0.1	0.2	0.3	0.2	0.1	0.2	0.3	0.2	
Sweden	–	–	1.5	2.0	–	–	1.5	2.0	
Switzerland	0.3	1.3	1.4	0.6	0.3	1.3	1.4	0.6	
United Kingdom	0.2	0.3	4.9	1.3	0.2	0.3	4.9	1.3	
United States	98.0	43.0	130.0	224.0	84.0	37.0	90.0	89.0	69
TOTAL	*317.7*	*410.5*	*395.6*	*872.8*	*295.7*	*365.3*	*322.1*	*694.5*	*14*
MULTILATERAL	*120.1*	*141.8*	*134.6*	*138.8*	*115.1*	*135.4*	*124.9*	*129.1*	*30*
OPEC COUNTRIES	–	–	*4.8*	*23.5*	–	–	*4.8*	*23.5*	
E.E.C.+ MEMBERS	*248.9*	*381.9*	*247.4*	*619.4*	*236.5*	*337.0*	*211.8*	*575.3*	*75*
TOTAL	***437.8***	***552.3***	***535.0***	***1035.1***	***410.8***	***500.6***	***451.7***	***847.1***	***17***

1978	1979	1980	1977	1978	1979	1980
			ODA COMMITMENTS			
—	—	—	—	—	—	—
0.1	0.1	0.1	0.0	—	—	—
129.0	154.2	170.8	139.3	183.2	174.1	205.1
7.5	5.8	13.5	18.5	17.9	4.3	4.5
1.3	1.3	0.9	0.0	1.5	0.2	0.1
—	—	0.0	—	—	—	—
24.3	24.9	39.8	20.5	22.3	23.6	39.0
16.9	20.5	37.0	14.7	55.3	17.1	82.1
0.3	0.8	0.6	0.5	0.3	0.8	0.6
2.0	27.5	39.5	4.6	8.0	7.1	10.3
1.6	3.1	1.9	1.2	3.8	1.6	2.1
—	—	—	—	—	—	—
0.2	0.3	0.2	0.1	—	0.3	—
—	1.5	2.0	—	—	—	—
1.3	1.4	0.6	—	—	—	0.7
0.3	4.9	1.3	0.2	0.3	0.2	5.1
23.0	47.0	28.0	40.5	30.5	32.1	28.2
207.8	*293.2*	*335.9*	*240.2*	*323.0*	*261.3*	*377.8*
—	—	—	—	6.6	14.6	10.1
—	—	—	—	—	—	—
—	—	—	—	—	—	—
—	—	—	—	—	—	—
19.0	19.3	23.3	19.1	56.7	67.6	16.1
—	—	—	—	—	—	—
26.2	26.4	19.7	18.0	9.0	46.0	55.3
—	—	—	—	—	—	—
—	—	—	—	—	—	15.5
—	—	—	—	—	—	—
43.5	44.3	37.6	—	—	—	—
—	—	—	9.7	21.1	29.3	25.2
4.7	5.7	11.6	—	—	—	—
1.0	0.8	0.3	—	—	—	—
1.7	1.7	0.6	—	—	—	—
—	—	—	—	—	—	—
2.6	5.3	2.8	—	—	—	—
9.9	14.8	8.2	—	—	—	—
1.3	1.1	1.9	—	—	—	—
3.1	3.7	0.3	—	5.0	7.0	—
112.9	*123.0*	*106.0*	*46.9*	*98.4*	*164.4*	*122.2*
—	*4.8*	*23.5*	—	—	*4.8*	*44.8*
192.8	*228.9*	*275.4*	*195.5*	*323.2*	*285.2*	*350.1*
320.7	***421.0***	***465.4***	***287.0***	***421.4***	***430.5***	***544.9***
			TECH. COOP. GRANTS			
—	—	—	—	—	—	—
0.1	0.1	0.1	0.1	0.1	0.1	0.1
129.0	147.4	148.6	72.8	92.4	101.2	106.1
4.1	5.6	13.4	0.6	0.9	1.2	0.7
1.3	1.3	0.9	2.1	1.2	1.3	0.9
—	—	0.0	—	—	—	0.0
17.6	22.4	24.4	11.3	11.6	17.0	16.2
11.4	10.0	11.0	6.8	11.2	9.9	9.7
0.3	0.8	0.6	0.5	0.3	0.6	0.6
1.7	5.6	7.4	0.8	1.7	1.0	1.7
1.6	3.1	1.9	1.0	1.6	0.5	1.9
—	—	—	—	—	—	—
0.2	0.3	0.2	0.1	0.2	0.1	0.0
—	1.5	2.0	—	—	—	—
1.3	1.4	0.6	0.0	0.0	0.1	—
0.3	4.9	1.3	0.2	0.2	0.2	0.4
7.0	9.0	10.0	2.0	5.0	3.0	7.0
175.9	*213.3*	*222.2*	*98.1*	*126.4*	*136.0*	*145.3*
39.4	*48.4*	*36.8*	*9.7*	*18.6*	*24.0*	*25.2*
—	*4.8*	*23.5*	—	—	—	—
179.8	*208.9*	*200.2*	*94.6*	*118.5*	*130.6*	*135.7*
215.3	***266.4***	***282.6***	***107.9***	***145.0***	***160.1***	***170.5***
			TOTAL OOF NET			
—	—	—	—	—	—	—
—	—	—	-0.1	-0.1	—	—
21.9	—	140.8	11.2	18.2	-5.8	127.3
0.5	0.9	—	0.6	0.5	0.7	-0.3
—	—	—	—	—	—	—
—	—	—	—	—	—	—
75.2	—	186.6	0.3	75.2	-10.8	175.6
55.2	18.5	13.5	22.8	25.7	8.2	0.9
29.8	—	—	29.9	25.8	-4.9	-3.9
—	—	—	—	—	—	—
—	—	—	—	—	—	—
—	—	—	—	—	—	—
—	—	—	—	—	—	—
—	—	—	—	—	—	—
—	—	—	—	—	—	—
—	—	—	—	—	—	—
20.0	83.0	196.0	60.0	16.0	46.0	78.0
202.7	*102.4*	*536.9*	*124.8*	*161.3*	*33.4*	*377.7*
28.9	*11.6*	*32.8*	*25.4*	*22.5*	*1.9*	*23.4*
—	—	—	—	—	—	—
189.1	*18.5*	*344.0*	*63.1*	*145.9*	*-16.0*	*301.9*
231.6	***114.0***	***569.7***	***150.2***	***183.7***	***35.3***	***401.1***

MAIN AID AGGREGATES

	1977	1978	1979	1980
DAC COUNTRIES COMBINED				
PRIVATE SECTOR NET	101.5	206.4	280.8	-71.3
Direct Investment	18.2	97.7	143.9	110.6
Portfolio Invest.	-117.6	63.5	-29.8	25.0
Export Credits	200.9	45.2	166.8	-207.0
OFFICIAL & PRIVATE				
GROSS:				
Contractual Lending	481.6	382.1	375.5	659.7
Export Credits Tot.	332.6	180.4	197.1	29.2
Export Credits Priv	301.0	147.6	193.1	9.2
OTHER NET DATA				
Contractual Lending	359.5	234.6	275.6	265.3
Export Credits Tot.	219.7	65.5	154.1	-313.9
(Bank Sector Loans)	-54.0	50.0	-38.0	-4.0
ODA CONCESSIONALITY				
Total:Grant Element	90.0	91.0	96.0	90.0
Loans:Grant Element	66.0	61.0	65.0	67.0
OTHER SOURCES				
CMEA Countr.(Gross)	—	—	—	—
Intra LDCS Exc.OPEC	—	—	—	—
Other	—	—	—	—
ALL SOURCE COMMITMENTS				
TOTAL BILATERAL	357.9	414.7	393.9	854.2
of which				
OPEC (ODA)	—	—	4.8	44.8
CMEA (ODA)	—	—	—	—
TOTAL MULTILAT.(ODA)	46.9	98.4	164.4	122.2
TOTAL BIL.& MULTIL.	404.8	513.1	558.3	976.4
of which				
ODA Grants	201.2	300.6	327.0	314.7
ODA Loans	85.9	120.7	103.5	230.2
ODA CONCESSIONALITY				
Total: Grant Element	91.0	91.0	94.0	87.0
Loans: Grant Element	69.0	64.0	76.0	68.0

INDEBTEDNESS

	1977	1978	1979	1980
TOTAL DEBT DISBURSED	***2779.7***	***3715.3***	***3956.0***	
Debt to DAC Countries	2283.0	3141.0	3362.0	
ODA	205.0	239.0	316.0	
Total Export Credits	1156.0	1985.0	2034.0	
Other Private Market	922.0	917.0	1012.0	
International Org.	191.4	261.0	284.6	
CMEA	108.2	108.2	108.2	
Other	197.1	205.0	201.2	
TOTAL DEBT SERVICE	***162.3***	***192.7***	***233.7***	
Paid to DAC Countries	150.0	178.3	203.8	
ODA	8.2	4.0	12.0	
Total Export Credits	96.8	133.9	154.3	
Other Private Market	45.0	40.4	37.5	
International Org.	9.8	13.2	24.1	
CMEA	—	—	—	
Other	2.5	1.3	5.8	

ECONOMIC INDICATORS

	1977	1978	1979	1980
GNP Curr. Prices, $M	4426.5	6307.8	5828.0	5340.4
Real GNP, 1976=100	103.0	99.0	98.0	99.0
GNP/Cap Curr. Prices,$	170.0	235.0	211.0	188.0
GNP/cap Atlas Basis, $	199.4	200.1	209.2	223.9
Real GNP/Cap, 1976=100	100.0	94.0	90.0	88.0
Population, Million	26.0	26.8	27.5	28.3
Curr.A/C Deficit(-),$M	—	—	—	—
BOP Exp. & Transf.,$M	—	—	—	—
Exp. to OECD CIF, $M	1545.6	1596.4	1824.0	2258.3
of which				
Manufact.	26.3	32.2	27.1	24.0
Imp. from OECD FOB, $M	747.2	701.5	787.7	981.5
Reserves ex. Gold, $M	133.9	125.8	206.7	204.1

ZAMBIA

	TOTAL RECEIPTS NET 1977	1978	1979	1980	TOTAL ODA NET 1977	1978	1979	1980
DAC COUNTRIES								
Australia	0.1	0.5	0.7	0.6	0.1	0.5	0.7	0.6
Austria	-0.1	0.1	1.6	2.1	0.1	0.2	1.8	2.3
Belgium	0.5	1.2	2.3	2.1	0.5	1.2	2.1	1.9
Canada	8.1	12.8	0.4	12.9	11.5	15.9	3.5	16.0
Denmark	1.6	2.3	2.8	4.0	1.6	2.3	2.8	4.0
Finland	5.2	6.0	6.8	7.6	5.2	6.0	6.8	7.6
France	3.6	43.9	1.1	2.9	–	–	–	0.8
Germany, Fed. Rep.	15.0	12.0	44.1	28.2	5.4	17.3	22.5	35.3
Italy	-17.8	13.2	19.3	4.1	-1.3	-1.3	-1.6	-1.6
Japan	-4.3	19.0	15.6	20.8	0.8	28.0	23.5	13.1
Netherlands	4.9	8.1	14.2	27.8	4.9	8.1	14.2	27.8
New Zealand	0.1	0.0	0.0	0.0	0.1	0.0	0.0	0.0
Norway	6.2	6.0	7.8	9.8	7.6	6.9	8.8	10.5
Sweden	24.3	19.4	23.9	28.0	24.3	19.4	23.9	31.1
Switzerland	-1.2	1.9	0.3	-0.4	0.1	0.1	0.3	0.2
United Kingdom	69.9	86.3	181.6	33.2	18.9	24.9	59.7	43.1
United States	32.0	35.0	39.0	43.0	16.0	35.0	43.0	41.0
TOTAL	*147.9*	*267.6*	*361.3*	*226.5*	*95.5*	*164.5*	*211.9*	*233.8*
MULTILATERAL								
AF.D.F.	–	–	–	–	–	–	–	–
AF.D.B.	4.5	1.5	2.9	5.8	–	–	–	–
AS.D.B.	–	–	–	–	–	–	–	–
CAR.D.B.	–	–	–	–	–	–	–	–
E.E.C.	7.4	11.7	10.5	23.2	7.4	11.7	10.5	20.2
IBRD	39.9	27.0	15.2	13.3	–	–	–	–
IDA	–	–	0.6	1.5	–	–	0.6	1.5
I.D.B.	–	–	–	–	–	–	–	–
IFAD	–	–	–	–	–	–	–	–
I.F.C.	0.4	-0.5	4.9	8.0	–	–	–	–
IMF TRUST FUND	–	–	29.7	25.4	–	–	29.7	25.4
U.N. AGENCIES	–	–	–	–	–	–	–	–
UNDP	2.0	1.9	2.3	4.5	2.0	1.9	2.3	4.5
UNTA	0.6	0.6	0.4	0.3	0.6	0.6	0.4	0.3
UNICEF	0.3	0.5	0.4	0.4	0.3	0.5	0.4	0.4
UNRWA	–	–	–	–	–	–	–	–
WFP	0.3	2.2	4.7	1.4	0.3	2.2	4.7	1.4
UNHCR	1.4	2.1	5.9	2.8	1.4	2.1	5.9	2.8
Other Multilateral	0.8	1.0	1.3	2.3	0.8	1.0	1.3	2.3
Arab OPEC Agencies	0.3	0.1	–	2.7	0.3	0.1	–	2.7
TOTAL	*57.8*	*48.1*	*78.6*	*91.6*	*13.0*	*20.1*	*55.7*	*61.6*
OPEC COUNTRIES	–	–	*9.5*	–	–	–	*9.5*	–
E.E.C.+ MEMBERS	*85.0*	*178.6*	*275.7*	*125.4*	*37.3*	*64.2*	*110.2*	*131.6*
TOTAL	***205.7***	***315.6***	***449.4***	***318.2***	***108.5***	***184.6***	***277.1***	***295.4***

	TOTAL ODA GROSS 197
Australia	0.
Austria	0.
Belgium	0
Canada	11.
Denmark	1.
Finland	5.
France	
Germany, Fed. Rep.	5.
Italy	0.
Japan	0.
Netherlands	4.
New Zealand	0.
Norway	7
Sweden	24.
Switzerland	0.
United Kingdom	19.
United States	16.
TOTAL	*97.*
AF.D.F.	
AF.D.B.	
AS.D.B.	
CAR.D.B.	
E.E.C.	7.
IBRD	
IDA	
I.D.B.	
IFAD	
I.F.C.	
IMF TRUST FUND	
U.N. AGENCIES	
UNDP	2
UNTA	0
UNICEF	0
UNRWA	
WFP	0
UNHCR	1
Other Multilateral	0
Arab OPEC Agencies	0
TOTAL	*13*
OPEC COUNTRIES	
E.E.C.+ MEMBERS	*39*
TOTAL	***110***

	ODA LOANS GROSS 1977	1978	1979	1980	ODA LOANS NET 1977	1978	1979	1980
DAC COUNTRIES								
Australia	–	–	–	–	–	–	–	–
Austria	–	–	–	–	0.0	–	–	–
Belgium	–	–	–	–	–	–	–	–
Canada	8.2	13.0	1.1	7.8	8.2	13.0	1.1	7.8
Denmark	–	–	–	–	-0.2	-0.2	-0.2	-0.2
Finland	0.0	2.8	0.8	–	0.0	2.8	0.8	-0.8
France	–	–	–	–	–	–	–	–
Germany, Fed. Rep.	1.8	8.2	11.7	22.6	1.6	8.0	11.5	22.3
Italy	–	–	–	–	-1.5	-1.6	-1.8	-1.7
Japan	–	26.5	22.3	12.7	–	26.5	22.3	11.7
Netherlands	1.3	4.6	7.0	16.1	1.3	4.6	7.0	16.1
New Zealand	–	–	–	–	–	–	–	–
Norway	–	–	–	–	–	–	–	–
Sweden	3.1	3.5	–	–	3.1	3.5	–	–
Switzerland	–	–	–	–	–	–	–	–
United Kingdom	0.9	4.7	37.9	14.9	0.4	4.1	36.8	13.8
United States	16.0	35.0	40.0	30.0	16.0	35.0	40.0	30.0
TOTAL	*31.3*	*98.4*	*120.8*	*104.1*	*28.9*	*95.8*	*117.4*	*99.0*
MULTILATERAL	–	*0.9*	*30.6*	*38.2*	–	*0.9*	*30.6*	*38.2*
OPEC COUNTRIES	–	–	–	–	–	–	–	–
E.E.C.+ MEMBERS	*4.0*	*18.4*	*56.9*	*62.1*	*1.6*	*15.8*	*53.6*	*58.8*
TOTAL	***31.3***	***99.3***	***151.4***	***142.3***	***28.9***	***96.7***	***148.0***	***137.2***

	GRANTS 197
Australia	0
Austria	0
Belgium	0
Canada	3
Denmark	1
Finland	5
France	
Germany, Fed. Rep.	3
Italy	0
Japan	0
Netherlands	3
New Zealand	0
Norway	7
Sweden	21
Switzerland	0
United Kingdom	18
United States	
TOTAL	*66*
MULTILATERAL	*13*
OPEC COUNTRIES	
E.E.C.+ MEMBERS	*35*
TOTAL	***79***

	TOTAL OFFICIAL GROSS 1977	1978	1979	1980	TOTAL OFFICIAL NET 1977	1978	1979	1980
DAC COUNTRIES								
Australia	0.1	0.5	0.7	0.6	0.1	0.5	0.7	0.6
Austria	0.1	0.2	1.8	2.3	-0.1	0.1	1.6	2.1
Belgium	0.5	1.2	2.1	1.9	0.5	1.2	2.1	1.9
Canada	11.5	15.9	3.5	16.0	8.1	12.8	0.4	12.9
Denmark	1.8	2.5	3.1	4.2	1.6	2.3	2.8	4.0
Finland	5.2	6.0	6.8	8.3	5.2	6.0	6.8	7.6
France	–	–	–	0.8	–	–	–	0.8
Germany, Fed. Rep.	6.1	22.0	36.7	57.2	2.5	17.8	22.7	39.7
Italy	0.2	0.3	16.2	0.1	-5.4	-4.7	10.9	-5.0
Japan	0.8	28.0	23.5	14.1	0.8	28.0	23.5	13.1
Netherlands	4.9	8.1	14.2	27.8	4.9	8.1	14.2	27.8
New Zealand	0.1	0.0	0.0	0.0	0.1	0.0	0.0	0.0
Norway	7.6	6.9	8.8	10.5	7.6	6.9	8.8	10.5
Sweden	24.3	19.4	23.9	31.1	24.3	19.4	23.9	31.1
Switzerland	0.1	0.1	0.3	0.2	0.1	0.1	0.3	0.2
United Kingdom	19.4	64.0	61.9	48.1	18.1	63.3	60.3	5.2
United States	33.0	37.0	47.0	52.0	32.0	35.0	39.0	43.0
TOTAL	*115.5*	*212.1*	*250.3*	*275.4*	*100.3*	*196.7*	*218.0*	*195.6*
MULTILATERAL	*64.6*	*56.9*	*94.8*	*106.7*	*57.8*	*48.1*	*78.6*	*91.6*
OPEC COUNTRIES	–	–	*9.5*	–	–	–	*9.5*	–
E.E.C.+ MEMBERS	*40.2*	*109.7*	*144.5*	*163.4*	*29.6*	*99.7*	*123.5*	*97.6*
TOTAL	***180.0***	***269.0***	***354.5***	***382.1***	***158.1***	***244.8***	***306.1***	***287.2***

	TOTAL OOF GROSS 197
Australia	
Austria	
Belgium	
Canada	
Denmark	
Finland	
France	
Germany, Fed. Rep.	0
Italy	
Japan	
Netherlands	
New Zealand	
Norway	
Sweden	
Switzerland	
United Kingdom	
United States	17
TOTAL	*17*
MULTILATERAL	*51*
OPEC COUNTRIES	
E.E.C.+ MEMBERS	*0*
TOTAL	***69***

ODA COMMITMENTS

1978	1979	1980	1977	1978	1979	1980
0.5	0.7	0.6	0.1	0.6	0.8	1.4
0.2	1.8	2.3	0.0	0.3	0.0	0.8
1.2	2.1	1.9	–	1.6	2.3	2.4
15.9	3.5	16.0	21.0	32.1	9.8	5.2
2.5	3.1	4.2	1.8	1.4	2.2	10.9
6.0	6.8	8.3	9.7	4.8	2.9	21.0
–	–	0.8	–	–	–	0.8
17.5	22.7	35.6	6.4	48.1	25.9	67.5
0.3	0.2	0.1	0.2	0.3	0.2	0.1
28.0	23.5	14.1	17.6	27.7	24.2	25.6
8.1	14.2	27.8	5.0	19.0	23.7	17.0
0.0	0.0	0.0	–	0.0	–	0.0
6.9	8.8	10.5	12.0	6.1	6.5	22.1
19.4	23.9	31.1	33.5	5.8	67.9	4.7
0.1	0.3	0.2	–	–	–	0.2
25.6	60.8	44.2	11.7	75.9	19.7	62.2
35.0	43.0	41.0	0.2	38.6	45.7	34.0
167.1	*215.3*	*238.9*	*119.2*	*262.2*	*231.9*	*276.0*
–	–	–	–	–	9.7	18.8
–	–	–	–	–	–	–
–	–	–	–	–	–	–
–	–	–	–	–	–	–
11.7	10.5	20.2	20.9	11.2	39.4	15.8
–	–	–	–	–	–	–
–	0.6	1.5	–	22.3	15.0	–
–	–	–	–	–	–	–
–	–	–	–	–	–	–
–	–	–	–	–	–	–
–	29.7	25.4	–	–	–	–
–	–	–	5.3	8.3	14.9	11.8
1.9	2.3	4.5	–	–	–	–
0.6	0.4	0.3	–	–	–	–
0.5	0.4	0.4	–	–	–	–
–	–	–	–	–	–	–
2.2	4.7	1.4	–	–	–	–
2.1	5.9	2.8	–	–	–	–
1.0	1.3	2.3	–	–	–	–
0.1	–	2.7	0.3	10.1	4.5	–
20.1	*55.7*	*61.6*	*26.5*	*51.9*	*83.6*	*46.4*
–	*9.5*	–	–	–	*39.5*	–
66.8	*113.5*	*134.9*	*46.0*	*157.5*	*113.4*	*176.7*
187.2	***280.5***	***300.5***	***145.6***	***314.1***	***354.9***	***322.4***

TECH. COOP. GRANTS

1978	1979	1980	1977	1978	1979	1980
0.5	0.7	0.6	0.1	0.1	0.1	0.2
0.2	1.8	2.3	0.1	0.2	1.8	2.3
1.2	2.1	1.9	0.3	0.8	1.0	1.4
3.0	2.4	8.1	3.1	2.8	2.2	3.6
2.5	3.1	4.2	1.8	2.5	3.1	4.2
3.2	6.0	8.3	2.1	2.2	4.4	4.0
–	–	0.8	–	–	–	0.8
9.3	11.0	13.1	3.8	7.7	10.7	12.3
0.3	0.2	0.1	0.2	0.3	0.2	0.1
1.4	1.2	1.4	0.8	1.4	1.2	1.4
3.5	7.2	11.8	3.6	3.4	5.3	7.3
0.0	0.0	0.0	0.0	–	0.0	0.0
6.9	8.8	10.5	2.0	2.9	2.8	3.2
15.8	23.9	31.1	7.3	8.8	8.9	10.0
0.1	0.3	0.2	–	–	–	–
20.8	22.9	29.3	11.7	12.8	19.6	25.9
–	3.0	11.0	–	–	–	–
68.8	*94.4*	*134.8*	*36.8*	*46.0*	*61.2*	*76.5*
19.2	*25.1*	*23.4*	*5.0*	*6.1*	*10.3*	*11.8*
–	*9.5*	–	–	–	–	–
48.4	*56.6*	*72.8*	*21.2*	*27.5*	*39.8*	*51.8*
87.9	***129.1***	***158.2***	***41.8***	***52.1***	***71.5***	***88.3***

TOTAL OOF NET

1978	1979	1980	1977	1978	1979	1980
–	–	–	–	–	–	–
–	–	–	-0.1	-0.2	-0.2	-0.2
–	–	–	–	–	–	–
–	–	–	-3.4	-3.2	-3.1	-3.1
–	–	–	–	–	–	–
–	–	–	–	–	–	–
–	–	–	–	–	–	–
4.6	13.9	21.6	-2.9	0.5	0.2	4.3
–	16.0	–	-4.1	-3.4	12.5	-3.4
–	–	–	–	–	–	–
–	–	–	–	–	–	–
–	–	–	–	–	–	–
–	–	–	–	–	–	–
–	–	–	–	–	–	–
–	–	–	–	–	–	–
38.4	1.1	4.0	-0.7	38.4	0.6	-37.9
2.0	4.0	11.0	16.0	–	-4.0	2.0
45.0	*35.0*	*36.5*	*4.7*	*32.2*	*6.1*	*-38.2*
36.8	*39.1*	*45.2*	*44.8*	*28.0*	*22.9*	*30.0*
–	–	–	–	–	–	–
43.0	*31.0*	*28.5*	*-7.7*	*35.5*	*13.3*	*-34.0*
81.8	***74.1***	***81.7***	***49.5***	***60.2***	***29.0***	***-8.2***

MAIN AID AGGREGATES

	1977	1978	1979	1980
DAC COUNTRIES COMBINED				
PRIVATE SECTOR NET	47.6	70.8	143.3	31.0
Direct Investment	43.0	25.9	40.8	1.8
Portfolio Invest.	-11.0	-2.4	4.3	-11.2
Export Credits	15.7	47.4	98.2	40.4
OFFICIAL & PRIVATE				
GROSS:				
Contractual Lending	133.0	242.0	284.6	256.8
Export Credits Tot.	101.1	100.6	148.8	127.3
Export Credits Priv	84.1	98.6	128.8	116.3
OTHER NET DATA				
Contractual Lending	49.3	175.3	221.7	101.1
Export Credits Tot.	25.5	37.6	100.2	32.4
(Bank Sector Loans)	-52.0	17.0	11.0	-44.0
ODA CONCESSIONALITY				
Total:Grant Element	88.0	70.0	85.0	81.0
Loans:Grant Element	70.0	62.0	61.0	63.0
OTHER SOURCES				
CMEA Countr.(Gross)	1.2	0.6	3.3	0.1
Intra LDCS Exc.OPEC	–	–	–	–
Other	–	–	–	–
ALL SOURCE COMMITMENTS				
TOTAL BILATERAL	124.4	300.6	322.9	282.1
of which				
OPEC (ODA)	–	–	39.5	–
CMEA (ODA)	–	–	–	19.2
TOTAL MULTILAT.(ODA)	26.5	51.9	83.6	46.4
TOTAL BIL.& MULTIL.	150.9	352.4	406.5	328.5
of which				
ODA Grants	98.2	65.5	196.3	155.7
ODA Loans	47.5	248.6	158.6	166.7
ODA CONCESSIONALITY				
Total: Grant Element	90.0	71.0	82.0	82.0
Loans: Grant Element	70.0	63.0	59.0	66.0

INDEBTEDNESS

	1977	1978	1979	1980
TOTAL DEBT DISBURSED	***1480.7***	***1600.4***	***1799.5***	
Debt to DAC Countries	865.0	961.0	1058.0	
ODA	113.0	241.0	354.0	
Total Export Credits	437.0	457.0	544.0	
Other Private Market	315.0	263.0	160.0	
International Org.	310.0	339.8	360.1	
CMEA	275.9	275.4	357.3	
Other	29.7	24.3	24.1	
TOTAL DEBT SERVICE	***205.1***	***230.4***	***313.0***	
Paid to DAC Countries	170.8	190.3	253.6	
ODA	5.8	7.5	11.5	
Total Export Credits	62.2	74.9	108.1	
Other Private Market	102.8	107.9	134.0	
International Org.	25.8	32.8	45.5	
CMEA	0.8	1.0	7.0	
Other	7.6	6.3	7.0	

ECONOMIC INDICATORS

	1977	1978	1979	1980
GNP Curr. Prices, $M	2286.8	2508.1	3126.1	3555.3
Real GNP, 1976=100	95.0	98.0	92.0	90.0
GNP/Cap Curr. Prices,$	437.0	464.0	560.0	616.0
GNP/cap Atlas Basis, $	511.6	545.4	537.2	558.9
Real GNP/Cap, 1976=100	92.0	92.0	83.0	79.0
Population, Million	5.2	5.4	5.6	5.8
Curr.A/C Deficit(-),$M	-232.0	-306.0	133.0	-532.0
BOP Exp. & Transf.,$M	974.0	933.0	1558.0	1373.0
Exp. to OECD CIF, $M	845.0	718.0	1264.2	1330.7
of which				
Manufact.	3.9	4.4	6.0	4.5
Imp. from OECD FOB, $M	434.1	398.0	494.9	635.9
Reserves ex. Gold, $M	66.3	51.1	80.0	78.2

	1977	1978	1979	1980	1977	1978	1979	1980	197
TOTAL RECEIPTS NET					**TOTAL ODA NET**				**TOTAL ODA GROSS**
DAC COUNTRIES									
Australia	–	–	0.2	2.3	–	–	0.2	2.3	
Austria	–	–	–	0.0	–	–	–	0.0	
Belgium	–	0.0	–	0.1	–	–	–	–	
Canada	0.0	0.1	0.0	0.0	0.0	0.1	0.0	0.0	0.
Denmark	0.1	–	–	0.9	0.1	–	–	0.9	0.
Finland	–	–	–	0.3	–	–	–	0.3	
France	-1.8	-0.7	-0.5	1.4	–	–	–	1.0	
Germany, Fed. Rep.	2.1	1.4	0.7	9.3	2.1	1.3	1.2	8.2	2.
Italy	0.1	–	–	5.2	–	–	–	2.7	
Japan	–	–	0.0	0.1	–	–	–	0.1	
Netherlands	–	–	0.3	7.7	–	–	0.3	7.7	
New Zealand	0.0	0.1	0.0	0.1	0.0	0.1	0.0	0.1	0.
Norway	–	–	–	4.5	–	–	–	4.5	
Sweden	–	–	–	11.5	–	–	–	11.5	
Switzerland	0.0	0.3	0.0	1.2	0.0	0.3	0.0	1.2	0.
United Kingdom	32.4	27.8	63.8	49.5	4.5	6.7	10.8	46.0	4.
United States	–	–	–	24.0	–	–	–	24.0	
TOTAL	*32.9*	*29.0*	*64.5*	*118.1*	*6.7*	*8.5*	*12.4*	*110.4*	*6.*
MULTILATERAL									
AF.D.F.	–	–	–	–	–	–	–	–	
AF.D.B.	–	–	–	–	–	–	–	–	
AS.D.B.	–	–	–	–	–	–	–	–	
CAR.D.B.	–	–	–	–	–	–	–	–	
E.E.C.	–	0.7	–	9.8	–	0.7	–	9.8	
IBRD	-3.5	-2.9	-3.0	-6.4	–	–	–	–	
IDA	–	–	–	–	–	–	–	–	
I.D.B.	–	–	–	–	–	–	–	–	
IFAD	–	–	–	–	–	–	–	–	
I.F.C.	–	–	–	–	–	–	–	–	
IMF TRUST FUND	–	–	–	–	–	–	–	–	
U.N. AGENCIES	–	–	–	–	–	–	–	–	
UNDP	–	0.0	–	0.4	–	0.0	–	0.4	
UNTA	–	–	–	0.0	–	–	–	0.0	
UNICEF	–	–	–	0.4	–	–	–	0.4	
UNRWA	–	–	–	–	–	–	–	–	
WFP	–	–	–	–	–	–	–	–	
UNHCR	–	–	–	32.9	–	–	–	32.9	
Other Multilateral	–	–	–	3.5	–	–	–	3.5	
Arab OPEC Agencies	–	–	–	–	–	–	–	–	
TOTAL	*-3.5*	*-2.1*	*-3.0*	*40.6*	–	*0.8*	–	*47.0*	
OPEC COUNTRIES	–	–	*0.1*	*5.0*	–	–	*0.1*	*5.0*	
E.E.C.+ MEMBERS	*32.8*	*29.2*	*64.3*	*83.8*	*6.6*	*8.7*	*12.2*	*76.2*	*6.*
TOTAL	**29.4**	**26.8**	**61.5**	**163.6**	**6.7**	**9.2**	**12.5**	**162.4**	**6.**

	1977	1978	1979	1980	1977	1978	1979	1980	197
ODA LOANS GROSS					**ODA LOANS NET**				**GRANTS**
DAC COUNTRIES									
Australia	–	–	–	–	–	–	–	–	
Austria	–	–	–	–	–	–	–	–	
Belgium	–	–	–	–	–	–	–	–	
Canada	–	–	–	–	–	–	–	–	0.
Denmark	–	–	–	–	–	–	–	–	0.
Finland	–	–	–	–	–	–	–	–	
France	–	–	–	–	–	–	–	–	
Germany, Fed. Rep.	–	–	–	0.8	–	–	–	0.8	2.
Italy	–	–	–	–	–	–	–	–	
Japan	–	–	–	–	–	–	–	–	
Netherlands	–	–	–	–	–	–	–	–	
New Zealand	–	–	–	–	–	–	–	–	0
Norway	–	–	–	–	–	–	–	–	
Sweden	–	–	–	–	–	–	–	–	
Switzerland	–	–	–	–	–	–	–	–	0
United Kingdom	–	–	–	–	–	–	–	-35.2	4
United States	–	–	–	–	–	–	–	–	
TOTAL	–	–	–	*0.8*	–	–	–	*-34.4*	*6*
MULTILATERAL	–	–	–	–	–	–	–	–	
OPEC COUNTRIES	–	–	–	–	–	–	–	–	
E.E.C.+ MEMBERS	–	–	–	*0.8*	–	–	–	*-34.4*	*6*
TOTAL	–	–	–	**0.8**	–	–	–	**-34.4**	**6**

	1977	1978	1979	1980	1977	1978	1979	1980	197
TOTAL OFFICIAL GROSS					**TOTAL OFFICIAL NET**				**TOTAL OOF GROSS**
DAC COUNTRIES									
Australia	–	–	0.2	2.3	–	–	0.2	2.3	
Austria	–	–	–	0.0	–	–	–	0.0	
Belgium	–	–	–	–	–	–	–	–	
Canada	0.0	0.1	0.0	0.0	0.0	0.1	0.0	0.0	
Denmark	0.1	–	–	0.9	0.1	–	–	0.9	
Finland	–	–	–	0.3	–	–	–	0.3	
France	–	–	–	1.0	–	–	–	1.0	
Germany, Fed. Rep.	2.1	1.3	1.2	8.2	2.1	1.3	1.2	8.2	
Italy	–	–	–	2.7	–	–	–	2.7	
Japan	–	–	–	0.1	–	–	–	0.1	
Netherlands	–	–	0.3	7.7	–	–	0.3	7.7	
New Zealand	0.0	0.1	0.0	0.1	0.0	0.1	0.0	0.1	
Norway	–	–	–	4.5	–	–	–	4.5	
Sweden	–	–	–	11.5	–	–	–	11.5	
Switzerland	0.0	0.3	0.0	1.2	0.0	0.3	0.0	1.2	
United Kingdom	4.5	6.7	10.8	84.7	4.5	6.7	10.8	49.5	
United States	–	–	–	24.0	–	–	–	24.0	
TOTAL	*6.7*	*8.5*	*12.4*	*149.1*	*6.7*	*8.5*	*12.4*	*113.9*	
MULTILATERAL	–	*0.8*	–	*47.0*	*-3.5*	*-2.1*	*-3.0*	*40.6*	
OPEC COUNTRIES	–	–	*0.1*	*5.0*	–	–	*0.1*	*5.0*	
E.E.C.+ MEMBERS	*6.6*	*8.7*	*12.2*	*114.9*	*6.6*	*8.7*	*12.2*	*79.7*	
TOTAL	**6.7**	**9.2**	**12.5**	**201.1**	**3.2**	**6.3**	**9.5**	**159.5**	

1978	1979	1980	1977	1978	1979	1980
			ODA COMMITMENTS			
–	0.2	2.3	–	–	0.2	5.7
–	–	0.0	–	–	–	–
–	–	–	–	–	–	–
0.1	0.0	0.0	0.0	0.1	0.0	0.1
–	–	0.9	0.1	–	0.8	0.3
–	–	0.3	–	–	–	4.3
–	–	1.0	–	–	–	–
1.3	1.2	8.2	1.7	2.1	1.9	41.5
–	–	2.7	–	–	–	2.7
–	–	0.1	–	–	–	2.3
–	0.3	7.7	–	–	0.1	13.9
0.1	0.0	0.1	0.0	0.1	–	0.1
–	–	4.5	–	–	–	4.5
–	–	11.5	–	–	–	7.3
0.3	0.0	1.2	–	–	–	1.7
6.7	10.8	81.2	4.5	6.7	10.8	88.8
–	–	24.0	–	–	–	23.3
8.5	*12.4*	*145.6*	*6.3*	*9.0*	*13.7*	*196.4*
–	–	–	–	–	–	–
–	–	–	–	–	–	–
–	–	–	–	–	–	–
–	–	–	–	–	–	–
0.7	–	9.8	–	–	–	18.9
–	–	–	–	–	–	–
–	–	–	–	–	–	–
–	–	–	–	–	–	–
–	–	–	–	–	–	–
–	–	–	–	–	–	–
–	–	–	–	–	–	–
–	–	–	–	0.0	–	37.2
0.0	–	0.4	–	–	–	–
–	–	0.0	–	–	–	–
–	–	0.4	–	–	–	–
–	–	–	–	–	–	–
–	–	–	–	–	–	–
–	–	32.9	–	–	–	–
–	–	3.5	–	–	–	–
–	–	–	–	–	–	–
0.8	–	*47.0*	–	*0.0*	–	*56.0*
–	*0.1*	*5.0*	–	–	*0.1*	*23.3*
8.7	*12.2*	*111.4*	*6.2*	*8.8*	*13.6*	*166.1*
9.2	***12.5***	***197.6***	***6.3***	***9.0***	***13.8***	***275.7***
			TECH. COOP. GRANTS			
–	0.2	2.3	–	–	0.2	0.2
–	–	0.0	–	–	–	–
–	–	–	–	–	–	–
0.1	0.0	0.0	0.0	0.1	0.0	0.0
–	–	0.9	0.1	–	–	0.2
–	–	0.3	–	–	–	0.0
–	–	1.0	–	–	–	–
1.3	1.2	7.4	2.1	1.3	1.2	5.2
–	–	2.7	–	–	–	0.1
–	–	0.1	–	–	–	0.1
–	0.3	7.7	–	–	0.1	1.1
0.1	0.0	0.1	0.0	0.1	0.0	0.1
–	–	4.5	–	–	–	–
–	–	11.5	–	–	–	–
0.3	0.0	1.2	0.0	0.0	–	0.0
6.7	10.8	81.2	4.5	6.7	10.8	24.1
–	–	24.0	–	–	–	2.0
8.5	*12.4*	*144.8*	*6.7*	*8.2*	*12.3*	*33.0*
0.8	–	*47.0*	–	*0.0*	–	*37.2*
–	*0.1*	*5.0*	–	–	–	–
8.7	*12.2*	*110.6*	*6.6*	*8.0*	*12.1*	*30.7*
9.2	***12.5***	***196.8***	***6.7***	***8.2***	***12.3***	***70.2***
			TOTAL OOF NET			
–	–	–	–	–	–	–
–	–	–	–	–	–	–
–	–	–	–	–	–	–
–	–	–	–	–	–	–
–	–	–	–	–	–	–
–	–	–	–	–	–	–
–	–	–	–	–	–	–
–	–	–	–	–	–	–
–	–	–	–	–	–	–
–	–	–	–	–	–	–
–	–	–	–	–	–	–
–	–	–	–	–	–	–
–	–	–	–	–	–	–
–	–	–	–	–	–	–
–	–	–	–	–	–	–
–	–	3.5	–	–	–	3.5
–	–	–	–	–	–	–
–	–	*3.5*	–	–	–	*3.5*
–	–	–	*-3.5*	*-2.9*	*-3.0*	*-6.4*
–	–	–	–	–	–	–
–	–	*3.5*	–	–	–	*3.5*
–	–	***3.5***	***-3.5***	***-2.9***	***-3.0***	***-2.9***

MAIN AID AGGREGATES

	1977	1978	1979	1980
DAC COUNTRIES COMBINED				
PRIVATE SECTOR NET	26.2	20.5	52.1	4.2
Direct Investment	27.4	21.1	52.5	1.0
Portfolio Invest.	-1.2	-0.6	-0.4	0.6
Export Credits	–	–	–	2.6
OFFICIAL & PRIVATE				
GROSS:				
Contractual Lending	–	–	–	7.0
Export Credits Tot.	–	–	–	2.7
Export Credits Priv	–	–	–	2.7
OTHER NET DATA				
Contractual Lending	–	–	–	-28.3
Export Credits Tot.	–	–	–	2.6
(Bank Sector Loans)	15.0	-24.0	-3.0	31.0
ODA CONCESSIONALITY				
Total:Grant Element	100.0	100.0	100.0	93.0
Loans:Grant Element	–	–	–	65.0
OTHER SOURCES				
CMEA Countr.(Gross)	–	–	–	–
Intra LDCS Exc.OPEC	–	–	–	–
Other	–	–	–	–
ALL SOURCE COMMITMENTS				
TOTAL BILATERAL	6.3	9.0	13.8	256.5
of which				
OPEC (ODA)	–	–	0.1	23.3
CMEA (ODA)	–	–	–	–
TOTAL MULTILAT.(ODA)	–	0.0	–	56.0
TOTAL BIL.& MULTIL.	6.3	9.0	13.8	312.5
of which				
ODA Grants	6.3	9.0	13.8	239.1
ODA Loans	–	–	–	36.6
ODA CONCESSIONALITY				
Total: Grant Element	100.0	100.0	100.0	95.0
Loans: Grant Element	–	–	–	65.0

INDEBTEDNESS

	1977	1978	1979	1980
TOTAL DEBT DISBURSED	***71.0***	***83.0***	***562.0***	
Debt to DAC Countries	11.0	13.0	499.0	
ODA	11.0	13.0	14.0	
Total Export Credits	–	–	15.0	
Other Private Market	–	–	470.0	
International Org.	–	–	8.0	
CMEA	–	–	–	
Other	60.0	70.0	55.0	
TOTAL DEBT SERVICE	***5.0***	***8.0***	***20.1***	
Paid to DAC Countries	–	–	8.9	
ODA	–	–	–	
Total Export Credits	–	–	0.3	
Other Private Market	–	–	8.6	
International Org.	–	–	3.5	
CMEA	–	–	–	
Other	5.0	8.0	7.7	

ECONOMIC INDICATORS

	1977	1978	1979	1980
GNP Curr. Prices, $M	3146.6	3326.6	3823.8	4704.9
Real GNP, 1976=100	93.0	90.0	90.0	97.0
GNP/Cap Curr. Prices,$	471.0	481.0	535.0	636.0
GNP/cap Atlas Basis, $	520.9	526.4	552.0	628.0
Real GNP/Cap, 1976=100	89.0	84.0	81.0	85.0
Population, Million	6.7	6.9	7.1	7.4
Curr.A/C Deficit(-),$M	–	–	–	–
BOP Exp. & Transf.,$M	–	–	–	–
Exp. to OECD CIF, $M	58.8	12.2	7.7	371.5
of which				
Manufact.	0.1	0.1	0.2	11.0
Imp. from OECD FOB, $M	6.6	6.3	7.3	163.9
Reserves ex. Gold, $M	–	–	–	–

	1977	1978	1979	1980	1977	1978	1979	1980
TOTAL RECEIPTS NET					**TOTAL ODA NET**			
DAC COUNTRIES								
Australia	17.5	29.6	49.2	30.6	17.5	29.6	48.9	30.3
Austria	26.1	-2.1	-2.3	10.5	2.4	2.0	2.8	5.7
Belgium	175.1	67.6	94.5	317.2	58.3	74.7	101.1	95.7
Canada	108.5	186.4	183.4	149.7	108.8	165.2	163.8	145.6
Denmark	68.8	78.5	91.7	127.4	60.1	75.6	85.1	106.5
Finland	11.3	11.1	14.6	24.0	11.3	10.5	14.9	22.0
France	234.8	395.4	383.9	581.4	173.1	211.7	245.3	360.6
Germany, Fed. Rep.	241.6	321.0	621.4	461.3	229.3	340.3	492.3	544.6
Italy	108.8	-89.5	199.3	354.2	11.4	13.1	16.8	37.1
Japan	116.6	283.1	324.3	329.3	104.9	216.6	330.2	343.5
Netherlands	174.4	233.2	271.5	308.1	154.6	213.3	248.6	302.6
New Zealand	5.5	7.5	6.3	6.1	4.8	5.6	6.2	6.1
Norway	62.7	79.6	134.9	181.6	61.7	77.3	90.5	94.5
Sweden	141.8	149.0	231.8	208.2	142.0	149.4	215.8	197.8
Switzerland	51.5	57.5	28.7	83.8	19.8	41.6	28.6	57.1
United Kingdom	132.2	211.8	283.4	458.5	117.1	196.1	262.2	328.7
United States	263.0	367.0	421.0	549.0	256.0	374.0	376.0	544.0
TOTAL	*1940.4*	*2386.7*	*3337.4*	*4180.8*	*1533.0*	*2196.6*	*2729.2*	*3222.2*
MULTILATERAL								
AF.D.F.	19.5	32.3	46.6	74.6	19.5	32.3	46.6	74.6
AF.D.B.	16.9	12.4	24.9	27.8	–	–	–	–
AS.D.B.	23.8	55.5	58.0	75.6	24.0	56.2	58.7	75.4
CAR.D.B.	–	–	–	–	–	–	–	–
E.E.C.	198.3	276.8	347.7	431.7	198.3	273.0	341.8	425.2
IBRD	20.9	17.7	35.9	31.3	6.1	13.3	19.5	18.7
IDA	350.9	355.9	463.0	478.9	350.9	355.9	463.0	478.9
I.D.B.	21.3	16.9	15.9	8.9	21.3	16.9	15.9	8.9
IFAD	–	–	1.1	12.3	–	–	1.1	12.3
I.F.C.	6.6	16.2	13.2	6.4	–	–	–	–
IMF TRUST FUND	34.6	222.5	182.8	227.5	34.6	222.5	182.8	227.5
U.N. AGENCIES	–	–	–	–	–	–	–	–
UNDP	87.0	108.7	136.2	167.4	87.0	108.7	136.2	167.4
UNTA	19.9	25.1	22.3	6.2	19.9	25.1	22.3	6.2
UNICEF	32.5	48.8	66.1	70.7	32.5	48.8	66.1	70.7
UNRWA	–	–	–	–	–	–	–	–
WFP	111.9	148.7	170.2	163.4	111.9	148.7	170.2	163.4
UNHCR	7.0	17.1	32.3	92.2	7.0	17.1	32.3	92.2
Other Multilateral	20.2	42.8	40.7	79.1	20.2	42.8	40.7	79.1
Arab OPEC Agencies	113.9	98.8	196.8	216.5	108.9	83.8	95.0	129.7
TOTAL	*1084.9*	*1496.2*	*1853.4*	*2170.2*	*1041.9*	*1445.0*	*1692.1*	*2030.0*
OPEC COUNTRIES	*827.8*	*670.2*	*596.4*	*822.3*	*772.9*	*523.9*	*596.4*	*821.8*
E.E.C.+ MEMBERS	*1334.1*	*1494.8*	*2293.3*	*3039.8*	*1002.2*	*1397.8*	*1793.3*	*2200.9*
TOTAL	***3853.0***	***4553.1***	***5787.2***	***7173.4***	***3347.8***	***4165.4***	***5017.6***	***6074.0***

TOTAL ODA GROSS	197
Australia	17.
Austria	2.
Belgium	58.
Canada	108.
Denmark	61.
Finland	12.
France	181.
Germany, Fed. Rep.	251.
Italy	16.
Japan	105.
Netherlands	154.
New Zealand	4.
Norway	61.
Sweden	142.
Switzerland	22.
United Kingdom	121.
United States	261.
TOTAL	*1585.*
AF.D.F.	19.
AF.D.B.	
AS.D.B.	24.
CAR.D.B.	
E.E.C.	198.
IBRD	6.
IDA	356.
I.D.B.	21.
IFAD	
I.F.C.	
IMF TRUST FUND	34.
U.N. AGENCIES	
UNDP	87.
UNTA	19.
UNICEF	32.
UNRWA	
WFP	111.
UNHCR	7.
Other Multilateral	20.
Arab OPEC Agencies	108.
TOTAL	*1049.*
OPEC COUNTRIES	*775.*
E.E.C.+ MEMBERS	*1044.*
TOTAL	***3409.***

	1977	1978	1979	1980	1977	1978	1979	1980
ODA LOANS GROSS					**ODA LOANS NET**			
DAC COUNTRIES								
Australia	–	–	–	–	–	–	–	–
Austria	–	0.0	0.0	2.4	–	0.0	0.0	2.4
Belgium	4.2	4.0	15.4	10.3	4.2	4.0	15.4	10.3
Canada	20.7	–	–	–	20.7	-203.3	–	–
Denmark	38.9	27.4	38.1	52.8	37.6	26.0	-48.6	43.9
Finland	5.9	2.0	–	–	4.8	2.0	-24.7	–
France	29.3	45.1	48.6	93.3	20.8	34.1	35.7	85.0
Germany, Fed. Rep.	117.6	165.8	189.5	25.6	95.6	145.1	-46.4	-799.4
Italy	–	–	–	4.4	-5.0	-2.6	-2.4	0.6
Japan	59.6	144.0	212.2	229.6	58.7	142.7	210.8	226.5
Netherlands	28.9	15.2	18.7	28.8	28.7	-85.6	3.1	18.3
New Zealand	–	–	–	–	–	0.0	-1.0	–
Norway	–	–	–	–	–	–	–	–
Sweden	0.5	0.3	–	–	-0.2	-86.9	–	–
Switzerland	–	–	–	–	-2.9	–	–	–
United Kingdom	12.8	9.0	11.2	8.6	8.0	4.6	0.8	-55.2
United States	118.0	121.0	85.0	81.0	113.0	115.0	79.0	76.0
TOTAL	*436.3*	*533.9*	*618.7*	*536.8*	*383.8*	*95.0*	*221.6*	*-391.6*
MULTILATERAL	*579.1*	*808.4*	*911.0*	*1062.4*	*571.9*	*794.6*	*899.6*	*1043.2*
OPEC COUNTRIES	*258.8*	*247.9*	*431.3*	*412.9*	*254.1*	*242.0*	*427.9*	*404.9*
E.E.C.+ MEMBERS	*244.0*	*284.8*	*339.9*	*245.1*	*202.1*	*143.6*	*-24.1*	*-675.3*
TOTAL	***1274.2***	***1590.1***	***1961.0***	***2012.0***	***1209.9***	***1131.5***	***1549.2***	***1056.5***

GRANTS	197
Australia	17.
Austria	2.
Belgium	54.
Canada	88.
Denmark	22.
Finland	6.
France	152.
Germany, Fed. Rep.	133.
Italy	16.
Japan	46.
Netherlands	126.
New Zealand	4.
Norway	61.
Sweden	142.
Switzerland	22.
United Kingdom	109.
United States	143.
TOTAL	*1149.*
MULTILATERAL	*469.*
OPEC COUNTRIES	*516.*
E.E.C.+ MEMBERS	*800.*
TOTAL	***2135.***

	1977	1978	1979	1980	1977	1978	1979	1980
TOTAL OFFICIAL GROSS					**TOTAL OFFICIAL NET**			
DAC COUNTRIES								
Australia	17.5	29.6	48.9	30.6	17.5	29.6	48.9	30.6
Austria	9.4	2.0	2.8	5.7	7.6	1.0	1.7	2.2
Belgium	58.3	74.7	101.1	95.7	57.4	74.7	100.6	95.2
Canada	108.8	389.8	183.7	155.9	108.8	186.5	183.7	150.0
Denmark	61.6	77.5	172.6	115.9	60.3	76.1	85.8	107.0
Finland	12.4	10.5	39.6	22.0	11.3	10.5	14.9	22.0
France	190.4	235.0	264.2	396.7	179.7	222.5	245.5	378.8
Germany, Fed. Rep.	257.9	367.1	747.8	1411.2	223.4	313.3	486.6	574.0
Italy	28.6	16.2	34.2	130.9	21.1	11.9	30.9	120.6
Japan	105.9	217.9	331.6	346.7	104.9	216.6	330.2	343.5
Netherlands	154.9	314.1	267.1	313.7	154.6	213.3	251.5	303.1
New Zealand	7.6	6.9	7.2	6.1	5.3	6.8	6.2	6.1
Norway	62.6	77.3	90.5	94.5	62.6	77.3	90.5	94.5
Sweden	142.7	236.6	215.8	197.8	142.0	149.4	215.8	197.8
Switzerland	22.8	41.6	28.6	58.4	19.8	41.6	28.6	58.4
United Kingdom	122.8	210.3	293.2	410.3	117.4	204.8	282.3	344.5
United States	272.0	380.0	432.0	562.0	262.0	367.0	421.0	549.0
TOTAL	*1635.9*	*2687.1*	*3261.0*	*4353.9*	*1555.9*	*2202.8*	*2824.6*	*3377.2*
MULTILATERAL	*1112.6*	*1532.3*	*1892.7*	*2351.0*	*1084.9*	*1496.2*	*1853.4*	*2170.2*
OPEC COUNTRIES	*829.9*	*676.1*	*589.5*	*830.3*	*827.8*	*670.2*	*596.4*	*822.3*
E.E.C.+ MEMBERS	*1072.8*	*1572.0*	*2228.0*	*3306.3*	*1012.3*	*1393.5*	*1830.9*	*2354.9*
TOTAL	***3578.4***	***4895.4***	***5743.1***	***7535.2***	***3468.6***	***4369.1***	***5274.4***	***6369.8***

TOTAL OOF GROSS	197
Australia	
Austria	7
Belgium	
Canada	
Denmark	0.
Finland	
France	8.
Germany, Fed. Rep.	6
Italy	12.
Japan	
Netherlands	
New Zealand	2
Norway	0.
Sweden	
Switzerland	
United Kingdom	0.
United States	11.
TOTAL	*50.*
MULTILATERAL	*63.*
OPEC COUNTRIES	*54.*
E.E.C.+ MEMBERS	*28.*
TOTAL	***168.***

1978	1979	1980	1977	1978	1979	1980
			ODA COMMITMENTS			
29.6	48.9	30.3	43.9	42.2	32.5	48.9
2.0	2.8	5.7	0.3	1.3	0.3	0.9
74.7	101.1	95.7	76.1	101.0	104.8	112.9
368.6	163.8	145.6	335.8	508.3	196.9	120.6
77.0	171.9	115.3	46.4	214.2	109.2	101.3
10.5	39.6	22.0	9.7	8.2	41.4	38.7
222.8	258.2	368.9	179.1	184.8	288.7	483.9
361.1	728.2	1369.5	270.8	486.0	957.1	1753.9
15.7	19.2	40.9	16.4	15.7	19.2	43.7
217.9	331.6	346.7	162.4	347.9	318.5	374.6
314.1	264.2	313.1	246.5	408.4	312.9	354.2
5.6	7.2	6.1	3.5	7.6	4.5	9.0
77.3	90.5	94.5	57.0	71.5	67.8	67.9
236.6	215.8	197.8	265.1	224.6	285.0	163.6
41.6	28.6	57.1	34.6	41.4	24.0	55.7
200.5	272.6	392.5	107.2	407.9	422.8	373.9
380.0	382.0	549.0	375.7	428.4	497.7	613.8
2635.4	*3126.2*	*4150.6*	*2230.3*	*3499.4*	*3683.3*	*4717.5*
36.7	48.5	75.2	116.3	103.7	136.6	180.9
–	–	–	–	–	–	–
58.2	61.2	78.2	128.2	130.9	178.4	204.3
–	–	–	–	–	–	–
273.1	341.9	425.3	426.3	346.7	392.8	449.2
13.3	19.5	18.7	31.5	–	–	–
362.7	466.5	489.3	575.0	764.0	659.6	1209.8
17.4	16.5	9.6	15.7	43.5	4.1	9.1
–	1.1	12.3	–	62.3	107.4	128.8
–	–	–	–	–	–	–
222.5	182.8	227.5	–	–	–	–
–	–	–	278.3	391.1	467.7	578.9
108.7	136.2	167.4	–	–	–	–
25.1	22.3	6.2	–	–	–	–
48.8	66.1	70.7	–	–	–	–
–	–	–	–	–	–	–
148.7	170.2	163.4	–	–	–	–
17.1	32.3	92.2	–	–	–	–
42.8	40.7	79.1	–	–	–	–
83.8	97.7	134.2	241.3	83.4	128.8	199.5
1458.8	*1703.4*	*2049.1*	*1812.6*	*1925.5*	*2075.5*	*2960.5*
529.8	*589.5*	*829.8*	*1459.0*	*1040.2*	*580.5*	*992.4*
1539.0	*2157.3*	*3121.3*	*1368.8*	*2164.6*	*2607.5*	*3673.0*
4624.0	***5419.1***	***7029.5***	***5502.0***	***6465.1***	***6339.3***	***8670.4***
			TECH. COOP. GRANTS			
29.6	48.9	30.3	5.2	6.1	4.6	6.2
2.0	2.8	3.2	2.4	1.9	2.8	3.1
70.8	85.7	85.5	35.6	41.0	45.0	48.1
368.6	163.8	145.6	11.3	12.2	10.3	11.9
49.6	133.8	62.6	9.6	16.7	29.4	38.6
8.5	39.6	22.0	5.6	7.1	12.5	11.3
177.7	209.6	275.6	85.1	93.9	109.8	138.0
195.2	538.7	1343.9	99.3	155.5	182.2	228.2
15.7	19.2	36.5	11.8	12.3	15.2	11.7
73.9	119.4	117.1	16.2	23.7	22.6	25.9
298.9	245.5	284.3	44.5	55.2	68.5	76.0
5.6	7.2	6.1	2.0	2.9	2.7	3.1
77.3	90.5	94.5	13.9	16.6	17.5	17.2
236.3	215.8	197.8	15.2	14.0	16.6	29.2
41.6	28.6	57.1	1.1	1.4	2.0	10.0
191.5	261.4	383.9	40.6	51.0	79.1	105.0
259.0	297.0	468.0	41.0	79.0	130.0	169.0
2101.6	*2507.5*	*3613.8*	*440.2*	*590.6*	*750.7*	*932.3*
650.4	*792.4*	*986.8*	*169.1*	*244.1*	*298.4*	*578.9*
281.9	*158.1*	*416.9*	–	–	–	–
1254.2	*1817.4*	*2876.2*	*326.5*	*425.6*	*529.3*	*645.5*
3033.9	***3458.1***	***5017.5***	***609.3***	***834.7***	***1049.1***	***1511.2***
			TOTAL OOF NET			
–	–	0.3	–	–	–	0.3
–	–	–	5.2	-1.0	-1.2	-3.4
–	–	–	-0.9	–	-0.5	-0.5
21.2	19.9	10.3	–	21.2	19.9	4.4
0.5	0.7	0.6	0.2	0.5	0.7	0.5
–	–	–	–	–	–	–
12.2	6.0	27.9	6.6	10.8	0.2	18.2
6.0	19.6	41.7	-5.8	-27.0	-5.7	29.5
0.5	15.1	89.9	9.7	-1.2	14.1	83.5
–	–	–	–	–	–	–
–	3.0	0.6	–	–	3.0	0.6
1.3	–	–	0.6	1.2	–	–
–	–	–	0.9	–	–	–
–	–	–	–	–	–	–
–	–	1.3	–	–	–	1.3
9.8	20.6	17.7	0.3	8.7	20.0	15.8
–	50.0	13.0	6.0	-7.0	45.0	5.0
51.6	*134.8*	*203.3*	*22.9*	*6.2*	*95.5*	*155.0*
73.5	*189.3*	*301.9*	*43.1*	*51.2*	*161.4*	*140.2*
146.3	–	*0.6*	*54.8*	*146.3*	–	*0.6*
33.0	*70.8*	*185.0*	*10.1*	*-4.4*	*37.6*	*154.0*
271.4	***324.0***	***505.8***	***120.8***	***203.8***	***256.9***	***295.8***

	1977	1978	1979	1980
MAIN AID AGGREGATES				
DAC COUNTRIES COMBINED				
PRIVATE SECTOR NET	384.5	184.0	512.8	803.6
Direct Investment	104.0	47.3	28.8	16.1
Portfolio Invest.	-6.9	-6.1	118.8	-97.2
Export Credits	287.4	142.7	365.2	884.7
OFFICIAL & PRIVATE				
GROSS:				
Contractual Lending	976.8	1131.9	1377.1	1885.5
Export Credits Tot.	510.9	568.2	711.8	1167.3
Export Credits Priv	490.1	546.4	623.7	1145.7
OTHER NET DATA				
Contractual Lending	694.1	243.9	682.3	648.1
Export Credits Tot.	298.1	153.3	444.7	884.8
(Bank Sector Loans)	38.0	108.0	188.0	11.0
ODA CONCESSIONALITY				
Total:Grant Element	93.0	94.0	95.0	95.0
Loans:Grant Element	69.0	71.0	63.0	62.0
OTHER SOURCES				
CMEA Countr.(Gross)	133.2	146.6	114.5	374.9
Intra LDCS Exc.OPEC	–	–	–	–
Other	–	–	–	–
ALL SOURCE COMMITMENTS				
TOTAL BILATERAL	3792.5	4696.7	4372.5	6066.9
of which				
OPEC (ODA)	1459.0	1040.2	580.5	992.4
CMEA (ODA)	137.3	151.8	704.5	436.4
TOTAL MULTILAT.(ODA)	1812.6	1925.5	2075.5	2960.5
TOTAL BIL.& MULTIL.	5605.1	6622.2	6448.0	9027.5
of which				
ODA Grants	3208.6	3732.1	4351.8	5506.3
ODA Loans	2293.4	2733.0	1987.5	3164.2
ODA CONCESSIONALITY				
Total: Grant Element	84.0	88.0	90.0	88.0
Loans: Grant Element	62.0	70.0	70.0	67.0
INDEBTEDNESS				
TOTAL DEBT DISBURSED	***11463.1***	***13690.9***	***15479.0***	
Debt to DAC Countries	4966.0	5884.0	6427.0	
ODA	3256.0	3560.0	3779.0	
Total Export Credits	1359.0	1935.0	2262.0	
Other Private Market	351.0	389.0	386.0	
International Org.	2462.9	3131.7	3925.6	
CMEA	2560.5	2761.0	2800.2	
Other	1473.8	1914.3	2326.2	
TOTAL DEBT SERVICE	***632.1***	***728.9***	***982.4***	
Paid to DAC Countries	392.5	441.8	542.6	
ODA	81.5	88.7	83.0	
Total Export Credits	266.4	315.2	387.3	
Other Private Market	44.6	37.9	72.3	
International Org.	72.5	89.4	129.9	
CMEA	107.5	127.8	161.2	
Other	59.6	69.9	148.7	
ECONOMIC INDICATORS				
GNP Curr. Prices, $M	42765.5	50549.3	57017.8	64153.0
Real GNP, 1976=100	103.0	109.0	113.0	114.0
GNP/Cap Curr. Prices,$	170.0	190.0	210.0	230.0
GNP/cap Atlas Basis, $	160.0	170.0	190.0	204.0
Real GNP/Cap, 1976=100	101.0	103.0	104.0	103.0
Population, Million	253.3	260.2	268.2	275.3
Curr.A/C Deficit(-),$M	-1730.1	-3270.5	-4132.3	–
BOP Exp. & Transf.,$M	6127.4	6219.9	6963.4	–
Exp. to OECD CIF, $M	3401.7	3359.0	4054.8	4387.0
of which				
Manufact.	447.8	665.2	843.6	1134.8
Imp. from OECD FOB, $M	5084.1	6206.5	6914.4	8135.0
Reserves ex. Gold, $M	3335.2	3648.8	3912.8	3597.8

	TOTAL RECEIPTS NET 1977	1978	1979	1980	TOTAL ODA NET 1977	1978	1979	1980
DAC COUNTRIES								
Australia	141.8	92.6	159.0	115.7	54.8	72.4	89.1	102.2
Austria	49.2	4.0	45.1	113.5	36.8	8.7	17.6	83.7
Belgium	221.2	292.1	438.1	388.6	148.1	162.0	233.9	214.9
Canada	251.1	251.4	226.1	214.7	182.2	220.9	168.5	200.1
Denmark	75.5	144.4	115.8	142.7	59.0	100.1	120.4	106.1
Finland	27.8	1.5	12.1	47.5	6.7	4.1	10.8	20.2
France	613.7	757.8	507.7	1335.3	254.6	322.1	377.2	439.0
Germany, Fed. Rep.	643.1	535.5	334.7	550.3	240.2	426.2	544.8	477.7
Italy	127.2	78.8	316.8	444.4	27.9	5.4	-1.3	0.2
Japan	929.3	1871.3	1340.0	1506.9	348.2	641.8	925.5	954.6
Netherlands	274.6	282.0	244.7	411.9	226.6	277.6	298.0	419.0
New Zealand	10.9	14.1	12.1	10.3	9.7	10.5	12.1	10.3
Norway	70.5	192.6	168.0	254.9	55.3	79.9	96.7	107.8
Sweden	245.9	309.4	309.5	331.9	229.0	206.6	273.4	300.2
Switzerland	134.3	55.1	88.7	33.2	16.7	28.8	38.1	40.5
United Kingdom	528.8	461.6	996.2	925.2	208.1	356.9	545.8	488.3
United States	490.0	1136.0	807.0	1543.0	807.0	1060.0	1127.0	1337.0
TOTAL	*4834.9*	*6480.1*	*6121.6*	*8370.1*	*2910.9*	*3984.0*	*4877.6*	*5301.8*
MULTILATERAL								
AF.D.F.	6.7	7.1	8.3	19.7	6.7	7.1	8.3	19.7
AF.D.B.	22.6	27.6	37.9	26.1	–	–	–	–
AS.D.B.	99.2	151.5	146.8	129.2	54.7	96.6	52.2	55.8
CAR.D.B.	2.5	1.1	–	5.5	2.4	1.5	–	5.4
E.E.C.	174.3	341.4	425.1	357.3	173.9	312.3	398.6	319.1
IBRD	359.2	452.3	470.2	681.3	4.3	30.5	48.3	53.8
IDA	653.4	565.1	743.6	968.3	653.4	565.1	743.6	968.3
I.D.B.	–	–	–	–	–	–	–	–
IFAD	–	–	1.2	14.3	–	–	1.2	14.3
I.F.C.	13.7	3.0	27.5	15.9	–	–	–	–
IMF TRUST FUND	88.8	395.7	276.3	1118.1	88.8	395.7	276.3	1118.1
U.N. AGENCIES	–	–	–	–	–	–	–	–
UNDP	66.9	101.2	113.0	153.0	66.9	101.2	113.0	153.0
UNTA	16.6	19.4	17.9	5.2	16.6	19.4	17.9	5.2
UNICEF	34.2	60.8	105.9	142.0	34.2	60.8	105.9	142.0
UNRWA	–	–	–	–	–	–	–	–
WFP	146.9	165.6	215.1	235.0	146.9	165.6	215.1	235.0
UNHCR	23.0	23.0	74.8	215.7	23.0	23.0	74.8	215.7
Other Multilateral	43.3	34.7	32.8	72.3	43.3	34.7	32.8	72.3
Arab OPEC Agencies	1079.4	802.2	89.4	82.4	1075.3	783.3	78.1	56.1
TOTAL	*2830.6*	*3151.9*	*2786.0*	*4241.3*	*2390.4*	*2596.9*	*2166.2*	*3433.7*
OPEC COUNTRIES	*1332.3*	*1140.1*	*339.5*	*815.8*	*1242.4*	*1023.4*	*339.5*	*815.8*
E.E.C.+ MEMBERS	*2658.5*	*2893.6*	*3379.0*	*4555.6*	*1338.4*	*1962.6*	*2517.4*	*2464.2*
TOTAL	***8997.8***	***10772.1***	***9247.1***	***13427.2***	***6543.8***	***7604.2***	***7383.3***	***9551.2***

	ODA LOANS GROSS 1977	1978	1979	1980	ODA LOANS NET 1977	1978	1979	1980
DAC COUNTRIES								
Australia	–	–	–	–	–	–	–	–
Austria	33.9	1.4	13.2	78.3	33.9	1.4	12.9	77.9
Belgium	32.1	16.7	60.6	47.0	31.2	15.7	58.4	43.3
Canada	109.6	145.8	120.8	137.6	107.9	142.0	116.6	131.8
Denmark	19.3	46.0	73.8	50.6	18.0	44.9	68.7	46.8
Finland	2.6	1.0	–	–	2.6	1.0	-18.5	–
France	130.2	161.1	173.7	168.5	97.4	133.8	147.9	139.8
Germany, Fed. Rep.	284.2	442.5	516.5	444.3	116.2	257.4	343.5	243.9
Italy	34.2	11.8	–	9.3	9.5	-3.6	-15.2	-9.5
Japan	368.3	671.7	863.4	874.8	271.8	523.9	716.9	703.7
Netherlands	103.9	159.5	164.8	243.1	93.7	150.0	150.0	225.1
New Zealand	0.2	–	–	–	–	–	–	–
Norway	–	–	–	–	–	–	–	–
Sweden	3.9	0.9	–	–	3.3	-151.9	–	–
Switzerland	4.4	5.8	2.6	0.8	-52.7	5.8	2.6	0.8
United Kingdom	40.5	47.8	63.4	55.1	-24.8	-9.4	-35.2	-75.8
United States	747.0	953.0	938.0	1061.0	609.0	793.0	748.0	857.0
TOTAL	*1914.3*	*2664.9*	*2990.9*	*3170.3*	*1317.0*	*1904.0*	*2296.7*	*2384.8*
MULTILATERAL	*1905.8*	*1917.4*	*1339.0*	*2363.8*	*1890.2*	*1899.2*	*1314.0*	*2328.7*
OPEC COUNTRIES	*360.9*	*393.2*	*226.5*	*347.0*	*355.6*	*386.5*	*191.2*	*266.5*
E.E.C.+ MEMBERS	*653.9*	*908.8*	*1160.3*	*1060.8*	*350.3*	*611.8*	*824.0*	*654.2*
TOTAL	***4181.0***	***4975.6***	***4556.4***	***5881.1***	***3562.8***	***4189.7***	***3801.9***	***4980.0***

	TOTAL OFFICIAL GROSS 1977	1978	1979	1980	TOTAL OFFICIAL NET 1977	1978	1979	1980
DAC COUNTRIES								
Australia	54.8	107.6	103.9	112.2	54.8	106.9	97.7	107.4
Austria	36.8	8.7	17.9	84.1	34.6	-2.1	6.7	72.6
Belgium	160.2	185.4	236.8	366.0	158.8	180.4	228.8	348.6
Canada	292.4	273.5	261.0	260.7	251.2	250.7	225.8	214.9
Denmark	61.3	101.3	128.1	114.5	59.7	99.8	122.9	110.5
Finland	6.7	4.1	29.3	20.2	6.7	4.1	10.8	20.2
France	303.2	479.3	433.8	823.6	263.7	448.4	395.2	770.8
Germany, Fed. Rep.	472.4	792.5	814.6	800.4	246.2	504.9	535.0	525.3
Italy	93.5	51.9	33.9	39.5	64.4	28.9	0.4	11.2
Japan	444.8	789.6	1072.0	1125.6	348.2	641.8	925.5	954.6
Netherlands	238.7	287.7	315.7	440.7	227.5	275.6	299.6	422.0
New Zealand	13.4	10.5	12.1	10.3	10.7	10.5	12.1	10.3
Norway	55.3	79.9	96.7	107.8	55.3	79.9	96.7	107.8
Sweden	229.5	359.4	273.4	300.2	229.0	206.6	273.4	300.2
Switzerland	73.8	28.8	45.3	42.7	14.8	28.2	45.3	42.7
United Kingdom	278.4	425.9	663.8	650.0	210.0	365.8	564.2	516.9
United States	1171.0	1291.0	1444.0	1842.0	879.0	1021.0	1141.0	1473.0
TOTAL	*3986.1*	*5277.2*	*5982.3*	*7140.3*	*3114.5*	*4251.3*	*4981.1*	*6009.1*
MULTILATERAL	*2971.7*	*3312.5*	*3021.7*	*4529.7*	*2830.6*	*3151.9*	*2786.0*	*4241.3*
OPEC COUNTRIES	*1337.6*	*1146.8*	*374.8*	*896.3*	*1332.3*	*1140.1*	*339.5*	*815.8*
E.E.C.+ MEMBERS	*1787.7*	*2672.6*	*3056.2*	*3595.9*	*1404.6*	*2245.2*	*2571.2*	*3062.7*
TOTAL	***8295.4***	***9736.6***	***9378.7***	***12566.3***	***7277.4***	***8543.3***	***8106.6***	***11066.2***

TOTAL ODA GROSS	197
Australia	54.
Austria	36.
Belgium	149.
Canada	184.
Denmark	60.
Finland	6.
France	287.
Germany, Fed. Rep.	408.
Italy	52.
Japan	444.
Netherlands	236.
New Zealand	9.
Norway	55.
Sweden	229.
Switzerland	73.
United Kingdom	273.
United States	945.
TOTAL	*3508.*
AF.D.F.	6.
AF.D.B.	
AS.D.B.	56.
CAR.D.B.	2.
E.E.C.	174.
IBRD	4.
IDA	667.
I.D.B.	
IFAD	
I.F.C.	
IMF TRUST FUND	88.
U.N. AGENCIES	
UNDP	66
UNTA	16
UNICEF	34
UNRWA	
WFP	146
UNHCR	23
Other Multilateral	43
Arab OPEC Agencies	1075
TOTAL	*2406*
OPEC COUNTRIES	*1247*
E.E.C.+ MEMBERS	*1642*
TOTAL	***7162***

GRANTS	197
Australia	54
Austria	2
Belgium	116
Canada	74
Denmark	41
Finland	4
France	157
Germany, Fed. Rep.	124
Italy	18
Japan	76
Netherlands	132
New Zealand	9
Norway	55
Sweden	225
Switzerland	69
United Kingdom	232
United States	198
TOTAL	*1593*
MULTILATERAL	*500*
OPEC COUNTRIES	*886*
E.E.C.+ MEMBERS	*988*
TOTAL	***2981***

TOTAL OOF GROSS	197
Australia	
Austria	
Belgium	11
Canada	108
Denmark	1
Finland	
France	15
Germany, Fed. Rep.	64
Italy	40
Japan	
Netherlands	2
New Zealand	3
Norway	
Sweden	
Switzerland	
United Kingdom	4
United States	226
TOTAL	*477*
MULTILATERAL	*565*
OPEC COUNTRIES	*85*
E.E.C.+ MEMBERS	*145*
TOTAL	***1133***

1978	1979	1980	1977	1978	1979	1980
			ODA COMMITMENTS			
72.4	89.1	102.2	109.9	58.0	106.4	111.8
8.7	17.9	84.1	33.4	3.2	23.2	67.3
163.0	236.1	218.6	182.4	232.9	237.2	237.6
224.7	172.7	205.9	317.3	367.7	255.8	171.5
101.2	125.4	109.9	75.6	119.9	113.3	109.0
4.1	29.3	20.2	1.4	18.9	28.9	32.4
349.4	403.0	467.6	356.6	281.4	398.5	681.4
611.3	717.8	678.1	585.6	826.5	1208.2	1117.2
20.7	13.9	18.9	30.8	20.7	13.9	38.5
789.6	1072.0	1125.6	1104.0	864.8	1291.2	1146.1
287.1	312.9	437.1	359.2	353.9	468.6	580.3
10.5	12.1	10.3	9.3	13.5	16.2	12.3
79.9	96.7	107.8	55.1	101.6	93.7	105.8
359.4	273.4	300.2	342.7	267.0	405.8	303.2
28.8	38.1	40.5	70.7	21.7	61.8	31.2
414.1	644.4	619.3	369.7	660.8	1099.4	553.1
1220.0	1317.0	1541.0	1514.7	1617.4	1834.7	1947.5
4745.0	*5571.8*	*6087.3*	*5518.4*	*5829.8*	*7656.8*	*7246.3*
7.2	8.4	19.7	25.3	60.5	82.1	59.4
–	–	–	–	–	–	–
99.6	56.5	61.2	143.6	213.7	206.5	224.0
1.5	–	5.4	4.6	4.4	–	4.4
312.8	400.1	321.4	296.3	363.4	569.1	389.6
30.5	48.3	53.8	55.0	–	–	–
579.8	761.2	994.0	1207.9	1686.3	1782.9	2429.7
–	–	–	–	–	–	–
–	1.2	14.3	–	12.0	204.7	138.4
–	–	–	–	–	–	–
395.7	276.3	1118.1	–	–	–	–
–	–	–	330.9	404.7	559.6	823.2
101.2	113.0	153.0	–	–	–	–
19.4	17.9	5.2	–	–	–	–
60.8	105.9	142.0	–	–	–	–
–	–	–	–	–	–	–
165.6	215.1	235.0	–	–	–	–
23.0	74.8	215.7	–	–	–	–
34.7	32.8	72.3	–	–	–	–
783.3	79.6	57.8	1689.3	176.5	102.3	109.0
2615.1	*2191.2*	*3468.7*	*3752.9*	*2921.5*	*3507.2*	*4177.6*
1030.1	*374.8*	*896.2*	*1454.1*	*1191.9*	*591.5*	*863.8*
2259.5	*2853.7*	*2870.8*	*2256.2*	*2859.5*	*4108.2*	*3706.7*
8390.2	***8137.9***	***10452.2***	***10725.4***	***9943.2***	***11755.5***	***12287.7***
			TECH. COOP. GRANTS			
72.4	89.1	102.2	18.7	19.3	12.7	19.1
7.3	4.7	5.8	2.9	7.3	4.5	5.6
146.3	175.5	171.5	79.1	103.0	114.9	118.9
78.9	51.8	68.3	10.4	9.9	11.8	9.0
55.2	51.7	59.3	16.5	29.5	24.9	43.0
3.1	29.3	20.2	1.2	2.9	9.5	12.2
188.3	229.3	299.1	104.8	119.7	155.4	213.7
168.8	201.3	233.8	114.5	149.9	177.8	200.1
9.0	13.9	9.7	5.6	6.0	7.4	6.5
117.9	208.6	250.8	31.8	51.1	56.4	68.1
127.6	148.1	193.9	47.3	55.5	55.5	74.1
10.5	12.1	10.3	1.9	7.0	4.3	4.1
79.9	96.7	107.8	7.0	7.1	9.6	11.5
358.5	273.4	300.2	28.9	38.9	32.0	36.0
23.0	35.5	39.8	0.4	0.6	0.8	6.2
366.3	581.0	564.2	44.5	62.6	91.7	124.8
267.0	379.0	480.0	52.0	97.0	136.0	173.0
2080.0	*2580.9*	*2916.9*	*567.2*	*767.3*	*905.1*	*1125.9*
697.7	*852.2*	*1104.9*	*186.4*	*239.1*	*344.5*	*823.2*
636.9	*148.3*	*549.3*	–	–	–	–
1350.8	*1693.4*	*1810.0*	*412.1*	*526.2*	*627.6*	*781.0*
3414.6	***3581.5***	***4571.1***	***753.6***	***1006.4***	***1249.6***	***1949.1***
			TOTAL OOF NET			
35.2	14.8	10.0	–	34.5	8.6	5.3
–		–	-2.2	-10.9	-10.9	-11.1
22.4	0.7	147.4	10.7	18.4	-5.2	133.7
48.8	88.3	54.8	69.0	29.8	57.4	14.8
0.1	2.7	4.6	0.8	-0.3	2.5	4.4
–	–	–	–	–	–	–
129.9	30.8	355.9	9.1	126.3	18.0	331.9
181.2	96.8	122.3	6.0	78.8	-9.7	47.7
31.1	20.0	20.6	36.4	23.6	1.7	11.0
–	–	–	–	–	–	–
0.7	2.7	3.6	0.9	-2.0	1.6	3.0
–	–	–	1.0	–	–	–
–	–	–	–	–	–	–
–	–	–	–	–	–	–
–	7.2	2.2	-1.9	-0.6	7.2	2.2
11.9	19.5	30.7	1.8	8.9	18.4	28.6
71.0	127.0	301.0	72.0	-39.0	14.0	136.0
532.3	*410.5*	*1053.0*	*203.6*	*267.3*	*103.5*	*707.4*
697.4	*830.4*	*1061.1*	*440.1*	*555.0*	*619.8*	*807.6*
116.7	–	*0.0*	*89.9*	*116.7*		*0.0*
413.0	*202.5*	*725.1*	*66.2*	*282.6*	*53.8*	*598.5*
1346.4	***1240.9***	***2114.1***	***733.7***	***939.1***	***723.3***	***1515.0***

	1977	1978	1979	1980
MAIN AID AGGREGATES				
DAC COUNTRIES COMBINED				
PRIVATE SECTOR NET	1720.4	2228.8	1140.4	2361.0
Direct Investment	188.9	788.0	22.6	582.5
Portfolio Invest.	149.0	763.9	105.3	349.7
Export Credits	1382.4	676.9	1012.5	1428.8
OFFICIAL & PRIVATE GROSS:				
Contractual Lending	5249.1	5300.1	6323.3	7709.6
Export Credits Tot.	3169.4	2383.1	3145.1	3785.8
Export Credits Priv	2857.0	2102.9	2922.0	3486.3
OTHER NET DATA				
Contractual Lending	2903.0	2848.2	3412.7	4521.0
Export Credits Tot.	1471.7	785.3	1060.6	1459.1
(Bank Sector Loans)	436.0	1048.0	-101.0	470.0
ODA CONCESSIONALITY				
Total:Grant Element	77.0	82.0	84.0	82.0
Loans:Grant Element	62.0	67.0	65.0	64.0
OTHER SOURCES				
CMEA Countr.(Gross)	831.3	920.7	1217.9	1217.0
Intra LDCS Exc.OPEC	–	–	–	–
Other	–	–	–	–
ALL SOURCE COMMITMENTS				
TOTAL BILATERAL	7295.2	7338.3	8821.7	9199.7
of which				
OPEC (ODA)	1454.1	1191.9	591.5	863.8
CMEA (ODA)	1024.0	896.5	1176.8	1857.4
TOTAL MULTILAT.(ODA)	3752.9	2921.5	3507.2	4177.6
TOTAL BIL.& MULTIL.	11048.1	10259.9	12328.9	13377.3
of which				
ODA Grants	3588.7	4010.5	5308.5	5265.3
ODA Loans	7136.7	5932.7	6447.0	7022.4
ODA CONCESSIONALITY				
Total: Grant Element	72.0	82.0	83.0	83.0
Loans: Grant Element	58.0	71.0	69.0	70.0
INDEBTEDNESS				
TOTAL DEBT DISBURSED	***51374.6***	***60836.0***	***68450.2***	
Debt to DAC Countries	32730.0	39665.0	44458.0	
ODA	19888.0	23971.0	25732.0	
Total Export Credits	8554.0	10748.0	12702.0	
Other Private Market	4288.0	4946.0	6024.0	
International Org.	9175.3	11096.1	12855.8	
CMEA	2850.3	3246.2	3600.0	
Other	6619.1	6828.7	7536.4	
TOTAL DEBT SERVICE	***4549.4***	***5278.9***	***6397.0***	
Paid to DAC Countries	3324.9	4105.1	5236.1	
ODA	835.1	1016.3	1185.5	
Total Export Credits	1696.0	2095.7	2703.4	
Other Private Market	793.8	993.1	1347.2	
International Org.	330.3	505.8	546.9	
CMEA	236.7	243.1	257.3	
Other	657.4	424.9	356.7	
ECONOMIC INDICATORS				
GNP Curr. Prices, $M	222924.9	252209.9	265537.8	340936.0
Real GNP, 1976=100	106.0	111.0	112.0	120.0
GNP/Cap Curr. Prices,$	210.0	230.0	240.0	301.0
GNP/cap Atlas Basis, $	200.0	220.0	240.0	273.0
Real GNP/Cap, 1976=100	103.0	106.0	105.0	110.0
Population, Million	1079.3	1104.2	1129.3	1154.7
Curr.A/C Deficit(-),$M	-1279.3	-5467.6	-5458.2	–
BOP Exp. & Transf.,$M	32180.8	35564.5	49346.2	–
Exp. to OECD CIF, $M	22181.5	23989.5	31610.6	40718.1
of which				
Manufact.	2180.8	2919.8	3961.9	4375.7
Imp. from OECD FOB, $M	22392.9	25069.3	27644.3	35666.5
Reserves ex. Gold, $M	9728.5	11483.5	14387.3	15537.3

	TOTAL RECEIPTS NET 1977	1978	1979	1980	TOTAL ODA NET 1977	1978	1979	1980
DAC COUNTRIES								
Australia	322.7	328.8	384.4	435.5	270.2	308.4	305.6	328.4
Austria	159.7	132.0	9.1	121.6	34.3	87.8	20.1	37.5
Belgium	130.7	402.6	571.4	508.1	43.3	57.1	77.8	94.3
Canada	301.4	197.1	196.8	194.1	88.8	125.6	96.5	97.9
Denmark	100.5	89.1	150.9	56.4	12.9	14.4	19.6	15.1
Finland	12.8	0.6	49.7	30.1	7.5	6.3	8.2	12.0
France	2161.3	3401.2	4134.1	5082.3	1215.8	1436.4	1738.5	2250.1
Germany, Fed. Rep.	735.6	924.5	1779.6	1731.6	298.4	545.5	805.9	851.9
Italy	137.0	479.0	413.1	743.8	-1.0	0.7	1.2	4.0
Japan	532.6	1767.7	1544.0	965.1	188.4	371.9	498.6	467.1
Netherlands	713.6	853.9	287.3	183.3	199.7	210.4	291.9	351.0
New Zealand	31.8	33.7	23.3	23.9	21.4	21.6	22.4	23.1
Norway	105.0	49.8	138.8	41.3	26.2	16.2	33.0	37.2
Sweden	174.0	47.9	38.4	78.3	55.3	38.9	51.6	67.0
Switzerland	138.8	483.6	146.7	187.4	13.9	15.2	19.1	22.0
United Kingdom	513.6	647.2	1112.0	447.3	149.2	193.9	225.7	273.6
United States	1838.0	2648.0	4979.0	4765.0	1349.0	1413.0	1862.0	1704.0
TOTAL	*8109.1*	*12486.8*	*15958.5*	*15595.2*	*3973.2*	*4863.2*	*6077.7*	*6636.4*
MULTILATERAL								
AF.D.F.	0.1	-0.1	0.1	1.6	0.1	-0.1	0.1	1.6
AF.D.B.	22.2	32.6	18.6	32.8	–	–	–	–
AS.D.B.	128.5	75.7	132.2	206.6	6.9	8.3	5.5	16.4
CAR.D.B.	18.9	18.9	–	38.9	8.4	18.1	–	28.4
E.E.C.	140.2	166.8	278.0	267.1	127.2	155.5	255.8	175.1
IBRD	761.9	928.1	1309.5	1543.6	8.6	29.1	35.0	33.0
IDA	114.1	81.9	71.5	96.5	114.1	81.9	71.5	96.5
I.D.B.	307.7	354.4	361.4	515.7	189.9	257.5	266.4	336.5
IFAD	–	–	0.3	18.2	–	–	0.3	18.2
I.F.C.	40.0	0.4	24.9	84.1	–	–	–	–
IMF TRUST FUND	52.1	246.7	221.4	290.3	52.1	246.7	221.4	290.3
U.N. AGENCIES	–	–	–	–	–	–	–	–
UNDP	75.4	90.1	116.8	142.0	75.4	90.1	116.8	142.0
UNTA	16.8	18.3	20.2	7.8	16.8	18.3	20.2	7.8
UNICEF	18.0	22.4	27.9	27.3	18.0	22.4	27.9	27.3
UNRWA	–	–	–	–	–	–	–	–
WFP	70.9	79.6	100.3	94.6	70.9	79.6	100.3	94.6
UNHCR	58.4	52.1	71.5	85.6	58.4	52.1	71.5	85.6
Other Multilateral	42.3	30.2	26.2	56.3	42.3	30.2	26.2	56.3
Arab OPEC Agencies	45.2	192.4	150.7	68.1	41.5	78.8	72.3	80.6
TOTAL	*1912.6*	*2390.5*	*2931.6*	*3577.1*	*830.6*	*1168.5*	*1291.2*	*1490.2*
OPEC COUNTRIES	*1684.4*	*1739.4*	*3264.2*	*4177.1*	*1207.1*	*1305.6*	*3264.2*	*4038.0*
E.E.C.+ MEMBERS	*4632.5*	*6964.5*	*8726.3*	*9019.9*	*2045.5*	*2613.8*	*3416.4*	*4015.1*
TOTAL	***11706.2***	***16616.7***	***22154.2***	***23349.4***	***6010.9***	***7337.3***	***10633.1***	***12164.6***

TOTAL ODA GROSS	1977
Australia	273.
Austria	34.
Belgium	44.
Canada	90.
Denmark	15.
Finland	7.
France	1309.
Germany, Fed. Rep.	382.
Italy	17.
Japan	214.
Netherlands	243.
New Zealand	21.
Norway	26.
Sweden	55.
Switzerland	16.
United Kingdom	171.
United States	1480.
TOTAL	*4402.*
AF.D.F.	0.
AF.D.B.	
AS.D.B.	7.
CAR.D.B.	8.
E.E.C.	134.
IBRD	8.
IDA	121.
I.D.B.	231
IFAD	
I.F.C.	
IMF TRUST FUND	52.
U.N. AGENCIES	
UNDP	75.
UNTA	16.
UNICEF	18.
UNRWA	
WFP	70.
UNHCR	58.
Other Multilateral	42.
Arab OPEC Agencies	41
TOTAL	*887.*
OPEC COUNTRIES	*1220.*
E.E.C.+ MEMBERS	*2317.*
TOTAL	***6510.***

	ODA LOANS GROSS 1977	1978	1979	1980	ODA LOANS NET 1977	1978	1979	1980
DAC COUNTRIES								
Australia	–	4.6	–	–	-2.9	1.3	-3.2	-3.6
Austria	27.1	77.6	7.1	24.2	26.9	77.5	6.4	23.4
Belgium	6.3	11.9	20.5	36.8	5.5	11.0	19.5	35.6
Canada	53.7	83.7	71.5	69.8	52.3	82.0	68.9	66.7
Denmark	10.4	10.5	13.6	8.5	8.2	8.2	10.8	5.8
Finland	1.5	3.1	1.2	2.0	1.4	2.8	1.0	1.0
France	197.9	217.0	223.8	365.5	104.3	138.2	121.4	254.9
Germany, Fed. Rep.	225.4	433.2	719.0	699.4	141.8	350.1	555.6	587.5
Italy	3.8	–	–	–	-15.0	-8.4	-10.1	-9.1
Japan	148.6	303.7	394.4	331.3	122.6	263.9	352.6	270.4
Netherlands	32.5	66.1	81.2	123.0	-10.8	15.3	26.1	67.3
New Zealand	–	–	–	0.5	–	-0.3	-2.5	0.5
Norway	–	–	–	–	–	–	–	–
Sweden	14.7	8.0	3.7	14.0	14.2	7.7	3.4	13.4
Switzerland	3.3	1.6	0.4	1.3	0.9	1.4	-1.5	0.3
United Kingdom	52.1	79.5	109.5	109.0	29.8	57.5	76.1	78.9
United States	488.0	595.0	942.0	619.0	357.0	451.0	784.0	454.0
TOTAL	*1265.2*	*1895.4*	*2587.7*	*2404.1*	*836.1*	*1459.1*	*2008.4*	*1847.0*
MULTILATERAL	*528.2*	*805.0*	*880.8*	*1011.6*	*471.0*	*731.8*	*807.5*	*932.8*
OPEC COUNTRIES	*181.0*	*192.7*	*494.1*	*864.0*	*167.3*	*173.3*	*470.9*	*829.2*
E.E.C.+ MEMBERS	*587.3*	*847.2*	*1324.4*	*1397.2*	*315.0*	*590.8*	*945.1*	*1063.9*
TOTAL	***1974.4***	***2893.1***	***3962.6***	***4279.7***	***1474.4***	***2364.2***	***3286.8***	***3609.1***

GRANTS	1977
Australia	273
Austria	7
Belgium	37
Canada	36
Denmark	4
Finland	6
France	1111
Germany, Fed. Rep.	156
Italy	14
Japan	65
Netherlands	210
New Zealand	21
Norway	26
Sweden	41
Switzerland	13
United Kingdom	119
United States	992
TOTAL	*3137*
MULTILATERAL	*359*
OPEC COUNTRIES	*1039*
E.E.C.+ MEMBERS	*1730*
TOTAL	***4536***

	TOTAL OFFICIAL GROSS 1977	1978	1979	1980	TOTAL OFFICIAL NET 1977	1978	1979	1980
DAC COUNTRIES								
Australia	273.5	312.1	320.5	342.8	270.6	308.9	316.7	337.0
Austria	45.8	87.9	20.8	38.3	36.8	77.2	5.7	16.5
Belgium	44.1	69.7	81.9	114.5	42.8	66.8	78.9	112.1
Canada	362.4	290.3	239.8	300.4	264.7	229.4	200.5	197.8
Denmark	17.6	21.1	28.2	20.3	15.4	18.8	24.5	15.8
Finland	7.6	6.6	8.5	13.0	7.5	6.3	8.2	12.0
France	1585.1	1932.5	2393.5	2961.1	1407.7	1694.2	2058.3	2621.5
Germany, Fed. Rep.	435.4	788.5	1299.5	1341.2	322.2	655.2	983.2	1159.7
Italy	91.9	72.7	154.2	132.9	51.8	24.8	116.9	77.9
Japan	219.6	429.3	560.9	646.8	192.5	374.4	518.2	579.9
Netherlands	246.2	263.1	349.0	433.3	202.4	210.7	291.0	376.9
New Zealand	57.7	21.9	24.9	23.9	24.6	21.6	22.4	23.9
Norway	26.2	16.2	33.0	37.2	26.2	16.2	33.0	37.2
Sweden	55.8	39.1	51.9	67.6	55.3	38.9	51.6	67.0
Switzerland	16.3	16.6	74.7	32.0	11.5	13.5	66.4	30.4
United Kingdom	173.2	272.9	298.7	328.9	147.2	244.2	263.5	254.1
United States	1997.0	2015.0	2761.0	2787.0	1524.0	1525.0	2086.0	1880.0
TOTAL	*5655.3*	*6655.7*	*8700.9*	*9621.1*	*4603.1*	*5526.0*	*7124.8*	*7799.7*
MULTILATERAL	*2285.4*	*2863.0*	*3516.1*	*4291.0*	*1912.6*	*2390.5*	*2931.6*	*3577.1*
OPEC COUNTRIES	*1698.1*	*1766.3*	*3297.6*	*4218.8*	*1684.4*	*1739.3*	*3264.2*	*4177.1*
E.E.C.+ MEMBERS	*2747.7*	*3608.8*	*4912.4*	*5628.6*	*2329.6*	*3081.5*	*4094.2*	*4885.2*
TOTAL	***9638.9***	***11285.0***	***15514.6***	***18130.8***	***8200.2***	***9655.8***	***13320.6***	***15553.9***

TOTAL OOF GROSS	1977
Australia	0
Austria	11
Belgium	
Canada	272
Denmark	2
Finland	
France	275
Germany, Fed. Rep.	53
Italy	74
Japan	5
Netherlands	3
New Zealand	36
Norway	
Sweden	
Switzerland	
United Kingdom	1
United States	517
TOTAL	*1253*
MULTILATERAL	*1397*
OPEC COUNTRIES	*477*
E.E.C.+ MEMBERS	*430*
TOTAL	***3128***

1978	1979	1980	1977	1978	1979	1980
			ODA COMMITMENTS			
311.7	308.8	332.0	292.8	344.5	298.6	337.3
87.9	20.8	38.3	27.2	81.0	6.9	23.6
58.0	78.8	95.4	63.1	64.8	82.9	97.6
127.3	99.1	101.0	138.1	130.4	76.5	63.9
16.6	22.4	17.8	12.9	35.3	17.3	13.4
6.6	8.5	13.0	10.0	5.8	9.1	27.4
1515.2	1840.8	2360.7	1598.6	1955.8	2589.3	3096.6
628.6	969.3	963.8	534.1	756.6	1311.0	1212.0
9.1	11.3	13.1	14.0	9.1	11.3	13.1
411.7	540.4	528.0	373.9	750.1	774.6	1031.2
261.2	346.9	406.6	233.8	430.6	441.1	534.8
21.9	24.9	23.1	12.7	22.1	22.4	19.5
16.2	33.0	37.2	26.0	18.7	33.0	40.0
39.1	51.9	67.6	67.2	15.2	88.5	31.4
15.3	21.0	23.1	13.9	10.4	30.2	13.5
215.9	259.2	303.7	136.6	331.9	303.4	358.1
1557.0	2020.0	1869.0	1509.5	1706.5	1776.2	1601.6
5299.5	*6657.0*	*7193.5*	*5064.2*	*6668.9*	*7872.1*	*8514.9*
–	0.2	1.6	–	22.0	9.7	32.6
–	–	–	–	–	–	–
9.3	6.5	17.6	–	41.8	37.8	49.0
18.1	–	28.4	17.1	35.9	–	15.0
165.5	266.9	187.2	148.4	252.1	441.6	563.4
29.1	35.0	33.0	12.0	–	–	–
91.3	75.2	101.3	50.3	182.3	223.5	144.1
310.2	322.3	394.4	368.3	515.6	576.6	608.3
–	0.3	18.2	–	37.5	72.5	71.1
–	–	–	–	–	–	–
246.7	221.4	290.3	–	–	–	–
–	–	–	281.8	292.7	362.9	413.6
90.1	116.8	142.0	–	–	–	–
18.3	20.2	7.8	–	–	–	–
22.4	27.9	27.3	–	–	–	–
–	–	–	–	–	–	–
79.6	100.3	94.6	–	–	–	–
52.1	71.5	85.6	–	–	–	–
30.2	26.2	56.3	–	–	–	–
78.8	73.8	83.1	165.1	55.5	93.9	89.8
1241.7	*1364.5*	*1568.8*	*1042.9*	*1435.3*	*1818.4*	*1986.8*
1325.0	*3297.6*	*4072.7*	*2112.1*	*4516.1*	*2686.9*	*4099.8*
2870.2	*3795.7*	*4348.4*	*2741.4*	*3836.2*	*5197.8*	*5889.1*
7866.2	***11319.1***	***12834.9***	***8219.3***	***12620.3***	***12377.5***	***14601.5***
			TECH. COOP. GRANTS			
307.1	308.8	332.0	12.1	17.3	15.1	18.8
10.4	13.7	14.1	7.4	10.2	13.4	13.9
46.0	58.4	58.6	27.6	35.1	40.5	41.3
43.7	27.6	31.2	17.5	14.4	10.0	11.5
6.2	8.8	9.3	4.1	5.2	7.5	9.0
3.5	7.2	11.0	2.5	2.4	5.6	6.2
1298.2	1617.1	1995.2	724.7	852.2	1074.5	1220.7
195.4	250.3	264.5	151.4	188.2	224.2	254.7
9.1	11.3	13.1	8.6	8.8	9.2	7.6
108.0	146.0	196.8	57.2	79.7	86.7	102.8
195.1	265.8	283.6	53.4	50.1	62.6	83.8
21.9	24.9	22.6	7.4	14.0	8.1	9.6
16.2	33.0	37.2	4.9	7.6	5.6	5.8
31.2	48.2	53.7	8.0	12.5	11.0	13.3
13.8	20.6	21.7	0.6	0.8	1.4	5.0
136.4	149.7	194.7	60.0	68.5	87.6	118.1
962.0	1078.0	1250.0	68.0	71.0	62.0	81.0
3404.1	*4069.3*	*4789.4*	*1215.4*	*1438.1*	*1725.1*	*2003.1*
436.7	*483.7*	*557.2*	*212.4*	*220.3*	*273.4*	*413.6*
1132.3	*2803.5*	*3208.7*	–	–	–	–
2023.0	*2471.3*	*2951.2*	*1029.9*	*1208.1*	*1506.2*	*1735.2*
4973.1	***7356.5***	***8555.2***	***1427.8***	***1658.4***	***1998.5***	***2416.7***
			TOTAL OOF NET			
0.4	11.7	10.8	0.4	0.4	11.1	8.6
–	–	–	2.5	-10.7	-14.4	-21.1
11.7	3.1	19.1	-0.5	9.8	1.0	17.8
163.0	140.8	199.4	175.9	103.7	104.0	99.9
4.5	5.8	2.5	2.5	4.4	4.8	0.7
–	–	–	–	–	–	–
417.3	552.7	600.4	192.0	257.8	319.8	371.3
159.9	330.2	377.4	23.7	109.7	177.3	307.8
63.7	142.9	119.8	52.8	24.2	115.7	73.9
17.6	20.5	118.8	4.1	2.6	19.6	112.7
1.9	2.0	26.6	2.6	0.4	-0.9	26.0
–	–	0.8	3.2	–	–	0.8
–	–	–	–	–	–	–
–	–	–	–	–	–	–
1.3	53.7	8.9	-2.3	-1.7	47.3	8.3
57.0	39.5	25.2	-1.9	50.3	37.8	-19.5
458.0	741.0	918.0	175.0	112.0	224.0	176.0
1356.2	*2043.9*	*2427.6*	*629.9*	*662.9*	*1047.1*	*1163.3*
1621.3	*2151.6*	*2722.2*	*1082.0*	*1222.0*	*1640.4*	*2086.9*
441.3	–	*146.0*	*477.3*	*433.7*	–	*139.2*
738.6	*1116.7*	*1280.2*	*284.1*	*467.8*	*677.8*	*870.0*
3418.9	***4195.5***	***5295.9***	***2189.3***	***2318.5***	***2687.5***	***3389.3***

	1977	1978	1979	1980
MAIN AID AGGREGATES				
DAC COUNTRIES COMBINED				
PRIVATE SECTOR NET	3506.0	6960.8	8833.7	7795.5
Direct Investment	1187.3	1830.1	2844.7	2859.5
Portfolio Invest.	266.6	2611.3	3395.4	1809.6
Export Credits	2052.2	2519.5	2593.6	3126.3
OFFICIAL & PRIVATE				
GROSS:				
Contractual Lending	7158.3	8455.5	10339.9	11822.5
Export Credits Tot.	5417.7	5862.9	6543.5	7944.0
Export Credits Priv	4640.1	5243.9	5708.4	6991.6
OTHER NET DATA				
Contractual Lending	3518.2	4641.4	5649.1	6136.7
Export Credits Tot.	2346.8	2656.2	3003.9	3574.3
(Bank Sector Loans)	3184.0	4261.0	5208.0	3528.0
ODA CONCESSIONALITY				
Total:Grant Element	86.0	83.0	83.0	83.0
Loans:Grant Element	58.0	56.0	54.0	52.0
OTHER SOURCES				
CMEA Countr.(Gross)	343.1	447.3	579.2	555.5
Intra LDCS Exc.OPEC	–	–	–	–
Other	–	–	–	–
ALL SOURCE COMMITMENTS				
TOTAL BILATERAL	8375.2	13110.3	12486.9	15111.9
of which				
OPEC (ODA)	2112.1	4516.1	2686.9	4099.8
CMEA (ODA)	479.9	765.4	504.5	487.0
TOTAL MULTILAT.(ODA)	1042.9	1435.3	1818.4	1986.8
TOTAL BIL.& MULTIL.	9418.1	14545.6	14305.3	17098.7
of which				
ODA Grants	5290.4	8642.2	7174.3	9855.8
ODA Loans	2928.9	3978.0	5203.2	4745.7
ODA CONCESSIONALITY				
Total: Grant Element	84.0	87.0	81.0	85.0
Loans: Grant Element	56.0	57.0	56.0	53.0
INDEBTEDNESS				
TOTAL DEBT DISBURSED	***61806.8***	***79022.9***	***98597.5***	
Debt to DAC Countries	44632.0	57619.0	73166.0	
ODA	11595.0	14182.0	16250.0	
Total Export Credits	14451.0	18580.0	22116.0	
Other Private Market	18586.0	24857.0	34800.0	
International Org.	8588.0	10516.1	12811.5	
CMEA	4000.8	4568.1	5127.3	
Other	4585.9	6319.7	7492.7	
TOTAL DEBT SERVICE	***8738.5***	***13156.1***	***15351.4***	
Paid to DAC Countries	7063.2	10893.7	12192.7	
ODA	617.4	680.6	823.8	
Total Export Credits	3489.5	4294.9	5199.2	
Other Private Market	2956.3	5918.2	6169.7	
International Org.	851.3	1108.6	1377.0	
CMEA	312.6	466.0	562.9	
Other	511.4	687.8	1218.8	
ECONOMIC INDICATORS				
GNP Curr. Prices, $M	306009.5	343315.1	411651.6	480974.0
Real GNP, 1976=100	105.0	110.0	115.0	119.0
GNP/Cap Curr. Prices,$	770.0	840.0	980.0	1117.0
GNP/cap Atlas Basis, $	790.0	870.0	960.0	1060.0
Real GNP/Cap, 1976=100	102.0	104.0	106.0	107.0
Population, Million	398.0	408.2	418.2	428.7
Curr.A/C Deficit(-),$M	-15384.4	-19078.0	-12558.1	–
BOP Exp. & Transf.,$M	78057.0	85606.4	115058.7	–
Exp. to OECD CIF, $M	54557.7	58900.5	81656.4	100896.8
of which				
Manufact.	5677.4	7094.5	9267.2	11059.0
Imp. from OECD FOB, $M	52133.9	58728.0	67840.6	83959.4
Reserves ex. Gold, $M	25840.9	28688.8	38167.6	47893.8

	TOTAL RECEIPTS NET 1977	1978	1979	1980	TOTAL ODA NET 1977	1978	1979	1980
DAC COUNTRIES								
Australia	6.8	41.8	46.4	44.9	1.9	1.6	1.2	1.4
Austria	167.3	7.2	92.2	-66.4	6.1	7.2	8.3	8.9
Belgium	106.0	799.2	832.9	1342.6	3.4	5.0	2.8	3.0
Canada	81.1	65.9	109.5	160.4	8.2	6.0	4.2	1.5
Denmark	58.7	12.5	58.2	28.5	-0.3	0.3	0.7	0.0
Finland	-7.0	81.6	-1.8	-10.2	0.0	0.0	0.1	0.0
France	778.9	1506.0	1634.6	3012.1	-8.0	5.3	18.0	32.7
Germany, Fed. Rep.	1941.4	1656.5	937.4	2370.3	141.1	106.3	131.2	169.9
Italy	29.0	22.4	1388.7	172.6	-15.5	-9.4	-7.9	-2.2
Japan	1694.2	2564.8	2557.7	1400.1	116.3	97.0	80.0	114.8
Netherlands	129.3	150.6	391.2	675.3	9.4	8.8	10.7	14.8
New Zealand	8.2	3.5	0.6	0.2	0.7	0.6	0.4	0.2
Norway	121.2	48.8	42.6	45.8	7.6	5.0	8.4	6.2
Sweden	108.3	16.7	8.2	654.3	3.5	3.6	10.2	5.1
Switzerland	420.9	150.2	362.9	167.5	4.8	1.8	2.9	1.7
United Kingdom	588.1	360.0	1545.7	1225.6	3.9	1.5	2.7	4.9
United States	2131.0	5405.0	6365.0	4779.0	58.0	71.0	29.0	38.0
TOTAL	*8363.3*	*12892.8*	*16372.0*	*16002.5*	*340.9*	*311.4*	*302.8*	*401.0*
MULTILATERAL								
AF.D.F.	–	–	–	–	–	–	–	–
AF.D.B.	–	–	–	–	–	–	–	–
AS.D.B.	61.0	107.2	57.6	70.2	2.1	-0.2	-0.2	-0.1
CAR.D.B.	–	–	–	–	–	–	–	–
E.E.C.	54.1	35.4	142.1	139.3	18.7	0.7	34.0	18.4
IBRD	627.3	737.5	1128.9	1037.2	19.6	3.3	4.0	0.1
IDA	8.3	3.0	-0.6	-0.8	8.3	3.0	-0.6	-0.8
I.D.B.	311.3	264.4	328.3	300.3	53.4	32.5	38.0	-34.0
IFAD	–	–	–	0.1	–	–	–	0.1
I.F.C.	35.7	42.9	41.0	180.5	–	–	–	–
IMF TRUST FUND	–	–	–	–	–	–	–	–
U.N. AGENCIES	–	–	–	–	–	–	–	–
UNDP	18.2	23.4	31.9	33.7	18.2	23.4	31.9	33.7
UNTA	3.4	4.9	3.7	1.8	3.4	4.9	3.7	1.8
UNICEF	1.0	1.1	1.0	2.1	1.0	1.1	1.0	2.1
UNRWA	–	–	–	–	–	–	–	–
WFP	23.1	10.6	22.9	14.2	23.1	10.6	22.9	14.2
UNHCR	4.4	4.5	13.8	16.1	4.4	4.5	13.8	16.1
Other Multilateral	5.8	4.5	4.3	8.2	5.8	4.5	4.3	8.2
Arab OPEC Agencies	–	–	–	–	–	–	–	–
TOTAL	*1153.6*	*1239.4*	*1774.8*	*1802.7*	*158.0*	*88.3*	*152.8*	*59.6*
OPEC COUNTRIES	*97.2*	*97.6*	*70.2*	*18.2*	*54.6*	*35.0*	*70.2*	*18.2*
E.E.C.+ MEMBERS	*3685.4*	*4542.8*	*6930.8*	*8966.3*	*152.6*	*118.3*	*192.1*	*241.5*
TOTAL	***9614.0***	***14229.9***	***18216.9***	***17823.4***	***553.5***	***434.7***	***525.7***	***478.8***

	ODA LOANS GROSS 1977	1978	1979	1980	ODA LOANS NET 1977	1978	1979	1980
DAC COUNTRIES								
Australia	–	–	–	–	–	–	–	–
Austria	0.8	0.4	0.6	1.3	0.4	0.1	0.4	0.3
Belgium	–	–	–	–	–	–	–	–
Canada	0.3	0.3	0.7	0.5	-0.1	-0.1	0.3	0.1
Denmark	–	–	–	–	-0.5	-0.5	-0.5	-0.5
Finland	–	–	–	–	–	–	–	–
France	9.5	23.8	32.6	25.9	-8.0	3.6	18.0	7.2
Germany, Fed. Rep.	105.5	43.4	69.8	69.4	68.3	7.6	11.5	26.7
Italy	–	–	–	–	-19.6	-13.5	-12.5	-10.2
Japan	128.4	119.1	113.2	140.7	92.0	64.5	47.4	80.6
Netherlands	0.5	0.0	0.8	0.1	-0.4	-0.3	0.4	-0.4
New Zealand	–	–	–	–	–	–	–	–
Norway	–	–	–	–	–	–	–	–
Sweden	–	–	–	–	–	–	–	–
Switzerland	3.9	–	–	–	3.9	–	–	–
United Kingdom	1.1	0.0	–	–	-0.6	-5.6	-4.8	-4.7
United States	184.0	188.0	116.0	98.0	80.0	83.0	12.0	5.0
TOTAL	*434.0*	*375.0*	*333.6*	*335.8*	*215.4*	*138.8*	*72.2*	*104.1*
MULTILATERAL	*126.3*	*90.2*	*99.1*	*54.1*	*83.0*	*38.6*	*41.2*	*-34.8*
OPEC COUNTRIES	*54.6*	*35.0*	*57.2*	*21.6*	*54.6*	*35.0*	*57.2*	*15.7*
E.E.C.+ MEMBERS	*116.6*	*67.2*	*103.2*	*95.4*	*39.2*	*-8.7*	*12.0*	*18.1*
TOTAL	***614.8***	***500.2***	***489.9***	***411.5***	***352.9***	***212.4***	***170.5***	***84.9***

	TOTAL OFFICIAL GROSS 1977	1978	1979	1980	TOTAL OFFICIAL NET 1977	1978	1979	1980
DAC COUNTRIES								
Australia	1.9	11.1	3.9	2.0	1.9	10.7	3.5	0.8
Austria	6.5	7.5	8.6	9.9	4.3	4.7	6.7	7.0
Belgium	3.4	5.0	2.8	3.0	2.2	3.6	1.3	3.0
Canada	133.0	115.7	166.4	201.1	101.8	85.5	133.6	167.6
Denmark	0.9	1.3	1.6	0.8	-0.3	0.6	0.3	-1.9
Finland	0.0	0.0	0.1	0.0	0.0	0.0	0.1	0.0
France	12.3	31.1	35.2	54.2	-5.2	10.9	20.1	35.5
Germany, Fed. Rep.	427.0	365.7	418.9	575.1	211.1	198.1	97.3	261.3
Italy	49.8	37.7	133.7	99.2	16.9	-1.9	103.0	-36.2
Japan	236.5	384.8	399.7	343.4	162.3	272.7	88.5	226.5
Netherlands	10.3	32.1	11.2	15.3	8.2	30.5	9.3	14.0
New Zealand	29.1	0.6	0.4	0.2	6.7	0.6	0.4	0.2
Norway	10.9	5.0	10.4	8.2	10.9	5.0	10.4	8.2
Sweden	3.5	14.6	10.2	5.1	3.5	14.6	10.2	5.1
Switzerland	4.8	1.8	2.9	1.7	4.8	1.8	2.9	1.7
United Kingdom	5.6	27.0	7.5	9.6	3.5	20.8	2.2	0.5
United States	1096.0	1675.0	1499.0	1615.0	612.0	1087.0	592.0	574.0
TOTAL	*2031.4*	*2716.1*	*2712.4*	*2943.9*	*1144.6*	*1745.2*	*1081.5*	*1267.5*
MULTILATERAL	*1654.5*	*1819.1*	*2413.8*	*2701.5*	*1153.6*	*1239.4*	*1774.8*	*1802.7*
OPEC COUNTRIES	*97.2*	*97.6*	*70.2*	*24.2*	*97.2*	*97.6*	*70.2*	*18.2*
E.E.C.+ MEMBERS	*569.2*	*542.4*	*763.3*	*913.6*	*290.4*	*298.0*	*375.5*	*415.5*
TOTAL	***3783.0***	***4632.8***	***5196.3***	***5669.6***	***2395.4***	***3082.3***	***2926.5***	***3088.4***

	197
TOTAL ODA GROSS	
Australia	1
Austria	6
Belgium	3
Canada	8
Denmark	0
Finland	0
France	9
Germany, Fed. Rep.	178
Italy	4
Japan	152
Netherlands	10
New Zealand	0
Norway	7
Sweden	3
Switzerland	4
United Kingdom	5
United States	162
TOTAL	*55*
AF.D.F.	
AF.D.B.	
AS.D.B.	2
CAR.D.B.	
E.E.C.	18
IBRD	19
IDA	8
I.D.B.	96
IFAD	
I.F.C.	
IMF TRUST FUND	
U.N. AGENCIES	
UNDP	18
UNTA	3
UNICEF	1
UNRWA	
WFP	23
UNHCR	4
Other Multilateral	[illegible]
Arab OPEC Agencies	
TOTAL	*20*
OPEC COUNTRIES	*54*
E.E.C.+ MEMBERS	*230*
TOTAL	***815***
GRANTS	
Australia	1
Austria	5
Belgium	3
Canada	8
Denmark	6
Finland	0
France	
Germany, Fed. Rep.	72
Italy	4
Japan	24
Netherlands	9
New Zealand	0
Norway	7
Sweden	3
Switzerland	6
United Kingdom	4
United States	-22
TOTAL	*12*
MULTILATERAL	*75*
OPEC COUNTRIES	
E.E.C.+ MEMBERS	*113*
TOTAL	***200***
TOTAL OOF GROSS	
Australia	
Austria	
Belgium	
Canada	124
Denmark	0
Finland	
France	2
Germany, Fed. Rep.	248
Italy	45
Japan	83
Netherlands	
New Zealand	28
Norway	3
Sweden	
Switzerland	
United Kingdom	
United States	934
TOTAL	*147*
MULTILATERAL	*1453*
OPEC COUNTRIES	*42*
E.E.C.+ MEMBERS	*339*
TOTAL	***2967***

1978	1979	1980	1977	1978	1979	1980
			ODA COMMITMENTS			
1.6	1.2	1.4	1.5	0.9	3.2	3.6
7.5	8.5	9.9	0.8	0.4	0.6	1.3
5.0	2.8	3.0	1.5	4.8	1.2	1.4
6.3	4.6	1.8	12.3	5.2	3.4	2.7
0.8	1.2	0.5	0.2	0.2	0.3	–
0.0	0.1	0.0	0.0	0.0	0.1	0.0
25.5	32.6	51.4	–	78.8	24.4	132.9
142.1	189.5	212.6	197.7	196.4	228.7	236.7
4.1	4.6	8.0	4.0	4.1	4.6	8.0
151.6	145.7	174.9	118.7	258.1	73.7	265.8
9.0	11.2	15.3	16.0	13.9	13.0	36.6
0.6	0.4	0.2	0.3	0.4	0.1	0.2
5.0	8.4	6.2	1.7	7.1	15.6	6.4
3.6	10.2	5.1	6.1	7.5	1.4	–
1.8	2.9	1.7	6.0	0.2	0.1	1.4
7.2	7.5	9.6	4.5	16.8	9.8	9.6
176.0	133.0	131.0	149.8	117.2	131.7	129.0
547.6	*564.3*	*632.7*	*521.2*	*711.8*	*511.6*	*835.6*
–	–	–	–	–	–	–
–	–	–		–	–	–
0.0	–	0.1	–	0.3	0.2	–
–	–	–	–	–	–	–
0.7	34.0	18.4	19.5	0.9	75.3	22.7
3.3	4.0	0.1	–	–	–	–
3.5	–	–	-0.1	–	–	–
83.4	95.1	53.9	109.9	50.0	71.2	122.0
–	–	0.1	–	–	–	42.2
–	–	–	–	–	–	–
–	–	–	–	–	–	–
–	–	–	56.0	49.0	90.2	76.0
23.4	31.9	33.7	–	–	–	–
4.9	3.7	1.8	–	–	–	–
1.1	1.0	2.1	–	–	–	–
–	–	–	–	–	–	–
10.6	22.9	14.2	–	–	–	–
4.5	13.8	16.1	–	–	–	–
4.5	4.3	8.2	–	–	–	–
–	–	–	–	–	–	–
139.9	*210.7*	*148.5*	*185.2*	*100.2*	*236.9*	*262.9*
35.0	*70.2*	*24.2*	*55.0*	*30.9*	*13.0*	*47.5*
194.2	*283.3*	*318.8*	*243.3*	*315.8*	*357.2*	*447.9*
722.5	***845.1***	***805.4***	***761.4***	***842.9***	***761.5***	***1145.9***
			TECH. COOP. GRANTS			
1.6	1.2	1.4	1.5	1.4	1.0	1.4
7.2	7.9	8.6	5.7	7.2	7.6	8.3
5.0	2.8	3.0	1.5	1.1	1.3	1.5
6.0	3.9	1.4	0.5	0.7	0.6	0.8
0.8	1.2	0.5	0.2	0.3	1.1	0.4
0.0	0.1	0.0	0.0	0.0	0.0	0.0
1.7	–	25.5	–	1.7	–	25.5
98.7	119.7	143.2	71.2	89.7	117.3	138.5
4.1	4.6	8.0	4.0	4.1	4.6	3.5
32.5	32.6	34.2	18.8	28.5	29.9	34.1
9.0	10.4	15.2	6.8	7.4	7.8	12.5
0.6	0.4	0.2	0.4	0.5	0.2	0.2
5.0	8.4	6.2	0.9	1.2	0.7	1.0
3.6	10.2	5.1	0.8	2.4	1.6	2.8
1.8	2.9	1.7	0.1	0.2	0.2	0.2
7.2	7.5	9.6	4.5	7.2	7.5	9.6
-12.0	17.0	33.0	8.0	6.0	3.0	14.0
172.6	*230.6*	*296.9*	*124.9*	*159.4*	*184.2*	*254.3*
49.7	*111.6*	*94.4*	*33.2*	*38.4*	*54.7*	*76.0*
–	*13.0*	*2.5*	–	–	–	–
127.0	*180.1*	*223.4*	*88.2*	*111.4*	*139.5*	*191.5*
222.3	***355.2***	***393.9***	***158.1***	***197.8***	***238.9***	***330.2***
			TOTAL OOF NET			
9.5	2.8	0.5	–	9.1	2.3	-0.6
–	0.2	–	-1.8	-2.5	-1.7	-1.9
–	–	–	-1.2	-1.4	-1.5	–
109.3	161.8	199.3	93.6	79.5	129.3	166.2
0.5	0.4	0.3	0.0	0.3	-0.3	-1.9
–	–	–	–	–	–	–
5.6	2.6	2.8	2.8	5.6	2.1	2.8
223.6	229.3	362.5	70.0	91.9	-33.9	91.5
33.7	129.1	91.2	32.4	7.5	110.9	-34.0
233.3	254.0	168.6	46.0	175.7	8.5	111.7
23.1	–	–	-1.2	21.8	-1.4	-0.7
–	–	–	6.1	–	–	–
–	2.0	2.0	3.3	–	2.0	2.0
11.1	–	–	–	11.1	–	–
–	–	–	–	–	–	–
19.8	–	–	-0.4	19.3	-0.5	-4.5
1499.0	1366.0	1484.0	554.0	1016.0	563.0	536.0
2168.5	*2148.1*	*2311.2*	*803.7*	*1433.8*	*778.7*	*866.5*
1679.3	*2203.1*	*2553.0*	*995.6*	*1151.1*	*1622.1*	*1743.1*
62.6	–	–	*42.6*	*62.6*	–	–
348.2	*479.9*	*594.8*	*137.8*	*179.7*	*183.4*	*174.1*
3910.3	***4351.2***	***4864.2***	***1841.8***	***2647.5***	***2400.8***	***2609.6***

MAIN AID AGGREGATES

	1977	1978	1979	1980
DAC COUNTRIES COMBINED				
PRIVATE SECTOR NET	7218.7	11147.6	15290.5	14735.0
Direct Investment	2384.9	3798.8	5446.5	5124.9
Portfolio Invest.	2490.3	6449.7	6706.7	5312.3
Export Credits	2343.5	899.1	3137.3	4297.8
OFFICIAL & PRIVATE GROSS:				
Contractual Lending	7511.8	6839.8	9732.7	11948.0
Export Credits Tot.	6942.7	6083.4	9344.3	11551.9
Export Credits Priv	5606.0	4296.3	7251.0	9301.0
OTHER NET DATA				
Contractual Lending	3362.6	2471.8	3988.2	5268.4
Export Credits Tot.	3112.8	1972.6	3956.1	5237.6
(Bank Sector Loans)	9900.0	13457.0	12022.0	12411.0
ODA CONCESSIONALITY				
Total:Grant Element	67.0	62.0	75.0	70.0
Loans:Grant Element	51.0	45.0	47.0	49.0
OTHER SOURCES				
CMEA Countr.(Gross)	19.0	25.4	37.9	22.7
Intra LDCS Exc.OPEC	–	–	–	–
Other	–	–	–	–
ALL SOURCE COMMITMENTS				
TOTAL BILATERAL	2525.0	3283.9	4349.5	3675.3
of which				
OPEC (ODA)	55.0	30.9	13.0	47.5
CMEA (ODA)	–	–	–	–
TOTAL MULTILAT.(ODA)	185.2	100.2	236.9	262.9
TOTAL BIL.& MULTIL.	2710.2	3384.1	4586.4	3938.2
of which				
ODA Grants	245.5	266.2	411.5	433.9
ODA Loans	516.0	576.7	350.0	712.0
ODA CONCESSIONALITY				
Total: Grant Element	66.0	61.0	77.0	69.0
Loans: Grant Element	48.0	45.0	48.0	47.0

INDEBTEDNESS

	1977	1978	1979	1980
TOTAL DEBT DISBURSED	***104711.9***	***134010.9***	***158282.8***	
Debt to DAC Countries	90725.0	116633.0	137661.0	
ODA	5131.0	5861.0	6004.0	
Total Export Credits	24766.0	31352.0	37090.0	
Other Private Market	60828.0	79420.0	94567.0	
International Org.	8273.7	9765.4	11407.2	
CMEA	1144.8	1657.9	2878.9	
Other	4568.4	5954.7	6335.7	
TOTAL DEBT SERVICE	***19486.4***	***26810.7***	***35893.2***	
Paid to DAC Countries	17403.7	24324.7	32616.7	
ODA	354.1	408.0	439.3	
Total Export Credits	5278.3	6479.2	7976.7	
Other Private Market	11771.3	17437.5	24200.7	
International Org.	1033.7	1270.0	1458.1	
CMEA	183.2	214.8	498.9	
Other	865.8	1001.2	1319.5	

ECONOMIC INDICATORS

	1977	1978	1979	1980
GNP Curr. Prices, $M	571622.6	681132.8	867319.6	997608.0
Real GNP, 1976=100	105.0	110.0	116.0	121.0
GNP/Cap Curr. Prices,$	1670.0	1940.0	2420.0	2734.0
GNP/cap Atlas Basis, $	1730.0	1910.0	2140.0	2382.0
Real GNP/Cap, 1976=100	102.0	105.0	109.0	111.0
Population, Million	342.3	350.2	357.9	364.3
Curr.A/C Deficit(-),$M	-10703.0	-9435.0	-25674.0	–
BOP Exp. & Transf.,$M	103160.0	127828.1	162797.2	–
Exp. to OECD CIF, $M	56383.0	69594.1	89301.5	105010.7
of which				
Manufact.	32678.7	43123.7	54503.1	61904.2
Imp. from OECD FOB, $M	62854.8	78160.5	101480.6	122616.5
Reserves ex. Gold, $M	28068.7	41070.9	45527.2	39983.7

	TOTAL RECEIPTS NET				TOTAL ODA NET			
	1977	1978	1979	1980	1977	1978	1979	1980
DAC COUNTRIES								
Australia	-1.7	-1.4	2.6	9.4	0.1	0.1	0.0	0.2
Austria	56.1	280.8	9.2	1.9	4.3	5.1	5.3	5.3
Belgium	262.0	872.6	58.1	-3.5	4.1	4.3	7.2	7.9
Canada	89.4	127.6	-0.3	-11.4	5.2	1.7	1.7	0.4
Denmark	15.0	58.3	17.0	85.7	-0.1	-0.2	-0.2	-0.2
Finland	-0.9	3.4	1.9	5.4	0.0	0.0	0.0	0.0
France	834.1	1197.4	812.1	472.3	82.4	93.1	103.2	130.1
Germany, Fed. Rep.	290.6	1701.9	810.4	1663.5	44.4	55.9	50.6	69.8
Italy	1330.9	2236.7	1289.8	1227.6	7.4	6.2	3.8	8.3
Japan	1171.8	2358.3	502.2	630.7	123.4	164.7	42.9	43.8
Netherlands	6.5	35.1	68.0	252.6	2.6	2.4	3.3	3.2
New Zealand	-2.0	2.8	0.1	–	0.0	0.0	–	–
Norway	22.0	58.6	29.7	44.5	0.1	0.2	–	0.4
Sweden	63.2	27.1	13.0	-5.8	0.7	1.2	1.8	2.4
Switzerland	236.0	171.5	118.8	-158.9	0.4	0.9	0.9	1.3
United Kingdom	508.5	81.7	154.4	9.8	3.6	2.7	3.2	1.3
United States	838.0	1068.0	966.0	775.0	-25.0	-36.0	-11.0	-4.0
TOTAL	*5719.3*	*10280.2*	*4852.8*	*4998.6*	*253.5*	*302.3*	*212.7*	*270.0*
MULTILATERAL								
AF.D.F.	–	–	–	–	–	–	–	–
AF.D.B.	3.0	6.7	6.1	5.7	–	–	–	–
AS.D.B.	–	–	–	–	–	–	–	–
CAR.D.B.	–	–	–	–	–	–	–	–
E.E.C.	1.3	4.7	6.9	4.4	1.3	5.3	7.4	4.8
IBRD	100.0	40.2	5.6	-26.2	–	–	–	–
IDA	4.8	0.7	0.1	-0.2	4.8	0.7	0.1	-0.2
I.D.B.	23.3	7.2	20.1	45.6	29.9	13.1	6.7	8.5
IFAD	–	–	–	–	–	–	–	–
I.F.C.	2.5	-3.1	2.3	8.3	–	–	–	–
IMF TRUST FUND	–	–	–	–	–	–	–	–
U.N. AGENCIES	–	–	–	–	–	–	–	–
UNDP	22.6	26.0	28.1	32.6	22.6	26.0	28.1	32.6
UNTA	2.9	2.6	2.3	0.7	2.9	2.6	2.3	0.7
UNICEF	0.4	1.1	0.7	1.0	0.4	1.1	0.7	1.0
UNRWA	–	–	–	–	–	–	–	–
WFP	13.0	6.7	7.0	12.6	13.0	6.7	7.0	12.6
UNHCR	0.1	0.1	0.0	0.1	0.1	0.1	0.0	0.1
Other Multilateral	28.0	31.1	4.9	11.5	28.0	31.1	4.9	11.5
Arab OPEC Agencies	7.7	8.6	24.9	26.6	–	6.1	1.2	-0.8
TOTAL	*209.8*	*132.6*	*108.9*	*122.7*	*103.2*	*92.8*	*58.3*	*70.9*
OPEC COUNTRIES	*51.6*	*41.5*	*-4.3*	*42.2*	*26.6*	*19.5*	*-4.3*	*42.2*
E.E.C.+ MEMBERS	*3248.8*	*6188.3*	*3216.8*	*3712.3*	*145.7*	*169.7*	*178.4*	*225.1*
TOTAL	***5980.6***	***10454.3***	***4957.4***	***5163.5***	***383.3***	***414.5***	***266.7***	***383.0***

TOTAL ODA GROSS	197
Australia	0
Austria	4
Belgium	4
Canada	5
Denmark	0
Finland	0
France	98
Germany, Fed. Rep.	52
Italy	8
Japan	125
Netherlands	2
New Zealand	0
Norway	0
Sweden	0
Switzerland	0
United Kingdom	4
United States	-3
TOTAL	*303*
AF.D.F.	
AF.D.B.	
AS.D.B.	
CAR.D.B.	
E.E.C.	1
IBRD	
IDA	4
I.D.B.	36
IFAD	
I.F.C.	
IMF TRUST FUND	
U.N. AGENCIES	
UNDP	22
UNTA	2
UNICEF	0
UNRWA	
WFP	13
UNHCR	0
Other Multilateral	28
Arab OPEC Agencies	
TOTAL	*110*
OPEC COUNTRIES	*32*
E.E.C.+ MEMBERS	*172*
TOTAL	***446***

	ODA LOANS GROSS				ODA LOANS NET			
	1977	1978	1979	1980	1977	1978	1979	1980
DAC COUNTRIES								
Australia	–	–	–	–	–	–	–	–
Austria	0.4	0.2	–	0.2	0.2	0.1	0.0	-0.6
Belgium	–	–	–	–	–	–	–	–
Canada	2.6	0.8	1.4	0.2	2.6	0.7	1.3	0.2
Denmark	0.1	-0.1	0.1	–	-0.1	-0.3	-0.3	-0.5
Finland	–	–	–	–	–	–	–	–
France	3.6	7.2	15.9	9.7	-12.8	-15.1	-6.5	-11.9
Germany, Fed. Rep.	29.4	32.0	18.1	29.2	21.7	26.9	8.2	21.3
Italy	–	–	–	–	-0.6	-0.6	-0.8	-0.6
Japan	119.2	155.4	36.7	34.5	117.5	152.6	33.3	32.6
Netherlands	0.2	–	1.1	0.2	0.1	–	1.1	0.2
New Zealand	–	–	–	–	–	–	–	–
Norway	–	–	–	–	–	–	–	–
Sweden	–	–	–	–	–	–	–	–
Switzerland	–	–	–	–	–	–	–	–
United Kingdom	2.4	2.1	2.5	0.2	1.7	0.9	1.4	-1.5
United States	3.0	–	–	–	-19.0	-33.0	-14.0	-7.0
TOTAL	*160.9*	*197.6*	*75.6*	*74.1*	*111.4*	*132.3*	*23.6*	*32.2*
MULTILATERAL	*43.0*	*32.3*	*25.0*	*21.6*	*35.8*	*23.5*	*14.6*	*9.7*
OPEC COUNTRIES	–	–	–	–	*-6.2*	*-6.5*	*-4.3*	*-2.1*
E.E.C.+ MEMBERS	*37.4*	*45.5*	*44.3*	*42.8*	*11.1*	*16.0*	*9.7*	*10.3*
TOTAL	***203.9***	***229.9***	***100.6***	***95.7***	***140.9***	***149.3***	***33.8***	***39.8***

GRANTS	197
Australia	0
Austria	4
Belgium	4
Canada	2
Denmark	
Finland	0
France	95
Germany, Fed. Rep.	22
Italy	8
Japan	5
Netherlands	2
New Zealand	0
Norway	0
Sweden	0
Switzerland	0
United Kingdom	1
United States	-6
TOTAL	*142*
MULTILATERAL	*67*
OPEC COUNTRIES	*32*
E.E.C.+ MEMBERS	*134*
TOTAL	***242***

	TOTAL OFFICIAL GROSS				TOTAL OFFICIAL NET			
	1977	1978	1979	1980	1977	1978	1979	1980
DAC COUNTRIES								
Australia	0.1	0.1	0.1	0.2	0.1	0.1	0.1	0.2
Austria	7.8	5.2	5.4	6.0	4.3	2.6	3.0	3.6
Belgium	4.1	4.3	14.9	7.9	4.1	4.3	12.9	6.7
Canada	50.2	152.7	29.2	41.4	37.0	143.5	14.4	15.9
Denmark	0.1	0.2	0.2	2.5	-0.2	-0.1	-0.2	2.0
Finland	0.0	0.0	0.0	0.0	0.0	0.0	0.0	0.0
France	245.5	262.3	208.6	167.1	29.6	154.9	0.9	50.0
Germany, Fed. Rep.	53.0	142.8	114.8	307.0	20.2	108.8	73.4	258.9
Italy	11.7	10.5	9.6	106.1	10.5	9.4	7.7	103.2
Japan	432.3	677.3	273.8	73.4	430.0	672.9	268.8	27.9
Netherlands	2.7	2.4	3.3	4.1	2.6	2.4	3.3	4.0
New Zealand	0.5	0.0	–	–	-2.0	0.0	–	–
Norway	0.1	0.2	–	0.4	0.1	0.2	–	0.4
Sweden	0.7	1.2	1.8	2.4	0.7	1.2	1.8	2.4
Switzerland	0.4	0.9	0.9	1.3	0.4	0.9	0.9	1.3
United Kingdom	4.3	3.9	4.2	3.0	3.6	2.7	3.2	1.3
United States	79.0	173.0	200.0	216.0	-20.0	80.0	3.0	169.0
TOTAL	*892.6*	*1436.9*	*866.7*	*938.6*	*521.0*	*1183.8*	*393.1*	*646.9*
MULTILATERAL	*314.0*	*244.5*	*230.4*	*272.6*	*209.8*	*132.6*	*108.9*	*122.7*
OPEC COUNTRIES	*57.8*	*48.0*	–	*44.2*	*51.6*	*41.5*	*-4.3*	*42.2*
E.E.C.+ MEMBERS	*323.2*	*431.7*	*363.1*	*602.7*	*71.7*	*287.1*	*108.1*	*430.6*
TOTAL	***1264.4***	***1729.5***	***1097.1***	***1255.4***	***782.3***	***1357.9***	***497.7***	***811.8***

TOTAL OOF GROSS	197
Australia	
Austria	3
Belgium	
Canada	45
Denmark	
Finland	
France	146
Germany, Fed. Rep.	0
Italy	3
Japan	307
Netherlands	
New Zealand	0
Norway	
Sweden	
Switzerland	
United Kingdom	
United States	82
TOTAL	*589*
MULTILATERAL	*203*
OPEC COUNTRIES	*25*
E.E.C.+ MEMBERS	*151*
TOTAL	***818***

1978	1979	1980	1977	1978	1979	1980
			ODA COMMITMENTS			
0.1	0.0	0.2	0.0	0.0	0.0	0.2
5.2	5.4	6.0	0.4	0.2	–	0.2
4.3	7.2	7.9	2.8	4.8	6.6	9.2
1.8	1.8	0.4	3.2	1.0	0.4	0.3
0.0	0.2	0.3	0.2	0.0	0.1	0.1
0.0	0.0	0.0	–	0.0	0.1	0.3
115.4	125.6	151.7	96.4	115.0	113.5	168.9
60.9	60.4	77.7	21.2	45.3	65.6	64.7
6.9	4.5	8.9	8.0	6.9	4.5	8.9
167.5	46.3	45.8	107.5	11.6	18.3	40.9
2.4	3.3	3.2	2.8	3.4	4.4	5.9
0.0	–	–	–	0.0	–	0.0
0.2	–	0.4	–	–	–	0.3
1.2	1.8	2.4	–	0.7	1.5	1.1
0.9	0.9	1.3	0.2	0.2	1.2	1.7
3.9	4.2	3.0	4.5	1.8	3.0	2.8
-3.0	3.0	3.0	10.3	10.9	7.2	15.9
367.6	*264.8*	*311.9*	*257.4*	*201.8*	*226.4*	*321.2*
–	–	–	–	–	–	–
–	–	–	–	–	–	–
–	–	–	–	–	–	–
–	–	–	–	–	–	–
5.4	7.4	5.1	4.9	3.5	22.8	34.7
–	–	–	–	–	–	–
0.8	0.2	–	–	–	–	–
21.7	16.0	18.9	57.5	44.3	70.0	84.5
–	–	–	–	5.8	–	–
–	–	–	–	–	–	–
–	–	–	–	–	–	–
–	–	–	67.1	67.6	43.0	58.5
26.0	28.1	32.6	–	–	–	–
2.6	2.3	0.7	–	–	–	–
1.1	0.7	1.0	–	–	–	–
–	–	–	–	–	–	–
6.7	7.0	12.6	–	–	–	–
0.1	0.0	0.1	–	–	–	–
31.1	4.9	11.5	–	–	–	–
6.1	2.2	0.2	41.9	–	–	–
101.6	*68.8*	*82.8*	*171.4*	*121.2*	*135.8*	*177.7*
26.0	–	*44.2*	*32.8*	*46.8*	–	*56.9*
199.1	*213.0*	*257.7*	*140.6*	*180.8*	*220.4*	*295.1*
495.2	***333.6***	***438.9***	***461.6***	***369.7***	***362.2***	***555.8***
			TECH. COOP. GRANTS			
0.1	0.0	0.2	0.1	0.1	0.0	–
5.0	5.4	5.9	4.0	5.0	5.4	5.7
4.3	7.2	7.9	3.0	2.7	4.1	4.8
1.0	0.4	0.2	1.7	0.8	0.3	0.2
0.1	0.1	0.3	–	0.0	0.1	0.1
0.0	0.0	0.0	0.0	0.0	0.0	0.0
108.3	109.7	142.0	80.6	90.9	90.4	124.1
29.0	42.4	48.5	22.6	27.1	41.5	46.9
6.9	4.5	8.9	3.4	3.5	3.5	1.6
12.1	9.6	11.2	5.9	9.7	9.1	9.6
2.4	2.3	3.0	2.3	2.4	2.1	2.4
0.0	–	–	0.0	0.0	–	–
0.2	–	0.4	–	0.0	–	0.1
1.2	1.8	2.4	–	0.9	0.5	0.2
0.9	0.9	1.3	0.0	0.0	0.0	0.3
1.8	1.8	2.8	1.9	1.8	1.8	2.1
-3.0	3.0	3.0	2.0	2.0	1.0	2.0
170.0	*189.1*	*237.8*	*127.6*	*146.8*	*159.8*	*200.0*
69.3	*43.8*	*61.1*	*54.2*	*61.4*	*36.1*	*58.5*
26.0	–	*44.2*	–	–	–	–
153.7	*168.7*	*214.9*	*113.8*	*128.3*	*143.4*	*181.9*
265.3	***232.9***	***343.2***	***181.8***	***208.3***	***196.0***	***258.5***
			TOTAL OOF NET			
–	0.0	–	–	–	0.0	–
0.1	–	–	0.0	-2.5	-2.4	-1.7
–	7.6	–	–	–	5.7	-1.1
150.9	27.4	41.0	31.8	141.7	12.6	15.6
0.2	0.0	2.2	-0.1	0.2	0.0	2.2
–	–	–	–	–	–	–
146.9	83.0	15.4	-52.8	61.8	-102.3	-80.0
81.9	54.4	229.3	-24.2	52.9	22.9	189.1
3.6	5.0	97.2	3.1	3.1	4.0	94.9
509.8	227.4	27.6	306.6	508.2	225.9	-15.9
–	–	0.9	–	–	–	0.9
–	–	–	-2.0	–	–	–
–	–	–	–	–	–	–
–	–	–	–	–	–	–
–	–	–	–	–	–	–
–	–	–	–	–	–	–
176.0	197.0	213.0	5.0	116.0	14.0	173.0
1069.3	*601.9*	*626.7*	*267.4*	*881.5*	*180.4*	*376.9*
143.0	*161.6*	*189.9*	*106.6*	*39.8*	*50.6*	*51.9*
22.0	–	–	*25.0*	*22.0*	–	–
232.6	*150.1*	*345.0*	*-74.0*	*117.4*	*-70.2*	*205.5*
1234.3	***763.6***	***816.6***	***399.0***	***943.4***	***231.0***	***428.8***

MAIN AID AGGREGATES

	1977	1978	1979	1980
DAC COUNTRIES COMBINED				
PRIVATE SECTOR NET	5198.4	9096.4	4459.7	4351.7
Direct Investment	844.0	1323.6	687.8	632.5
Portfolio Invest.	986.2	3000.1	979.4	1030.4
Export Credits	3368.2	4772.8	2792.5	2688.8
OFFICIAL & PRIVATE				
GROSS:				
Contractual Lending	7576.9	10240.6	8020.2	8420.0
Export Credits Tot.	7265.1	9894.9	7849.9	8134.2
Export Credits Priv	6826.5	8973.7	7342.7	7719.2
OTHER NET DATA				
Contractual Lending	3747.0	5786.5	2996.5	3097.9
Export Credits Tot.	3688.2	5597.9	3066.7	2956.5
(Bank Sector Loans)	4153.0	6666.0	2295.0	408.0
ODA CONCESSIONALITY				
Total:Grant Element	76.0	95.0	92.0	92.0
Loans:Grant Element	41.0	55.0	34.0	40.0
OTHER SOURCES				
CMEA Countr.(Gross)	195.8	206.7	161.7	144.1
Intra LDCS Exc.OPEC	–	–	–	–
Other	–	–	–	–
ALL SOURCE COMMITMENTS				
TOTAL BILATERAL	1203.7	2115.6	1462.5	694.5
of which				
OPEC (ODA)	32.8	46.8	–	56.9
CMEA (ODA)	50.0	–	–	–
TOTAL MULTILAT.(ODA)	171.4	121.2	135.8	177.7
TOTAL BIL.& MULTIL.	1375.1	2236.7	1598.3	872.2
of which				
ODA Grants	256.1	275.4	261.6	383.2
ODA Loans	205.4	94.3	100.6	172.6
ODA CONCESSIONALITY				
Total: Grant Element	77.0	89.0	92.0	91.0
Loans: Grant Element	43.0	65.0	50.0	65.0

INDEBTEDNESS

	1977	1978	1979	1980
TOTAL DEBT DISBURSED	***32634.8***	***46683.1***	***52388.2***	
Debt to DAC Countries	28055.0	40806.0	46772.0	
ODA	879.0	1161.0	1105.0	
Total Export Credits	16103.0	22041.0	26217.0	
Other Private Market	11073.0	17604.0	19450.0	
International Org.	1387.2	1453.9	1552.8	
CMEA	1955.3	1990.7	1854.4	
Other	1237.2	2432.5	2208.9	
TOTAL DEBT SERVICE	***7686.7***	***10272.6***	***14531.2***	
Paid to DAC Countries	7053.2	9490.2	13651.1	
ODA	66.5	97.4	87.1	
Total Export Credits	5777.4	7380.0	9180.1	
Other Private Market	1209.3	2012.8	4383.9	
International Org.	193.6	206.8	192.8	
CMEA	305.8	314.4	263.5	
Other	134.2	261.1	423.9	

ECONOMIC INDICATORS

	1977	1978	1979	1980
GNP Curr. Prices, $M	244238.4	281947.1	325722.6	353041.0
Real GNP, 1976=100	107.0	116.0	120.0	123.0
GNP/Cap Curr. Prices,$	2490.0	2780.0	3110.0	3258.0
GNP/cap Atlas Basis, $	2450.0	2750.0	3010.0	3263.0
Real GNP/Cap, 1976=100	104.0	109.0	109.0	108.0
Population, Million	98.0	101.4	104.6	108.2
Curr.A/C Deficit(-),$M	21447.6	2063.8	18829.8	–
BOP Exp. & Transf.,$M	117443.3	83065.4	111950.4	–
Exp. to OECD CIF, $M	99675.7	99972.1	135092.0	187310.4
of which				
Manufact.	667.3	1117.8	1225.0	1486.8
Imp. from OECD FOB, $M	53796.5	63872.1	64308.1	78851.5
Reserves ex. Gold, $M	60691.8	47478.6	56138.6	69311.3

	1977	1978	1979	1980	1977	1978	1979	1980
TOTAL RECEIPTS NET					**TOTAL ODA NET**			
DAC COUNTRIES								
Australia	513.5	502.9	661.4	652.2	348.8	419.5	457.9	477.3
Austria	460.8	433.0	162.0	194.8	86.5	112.8	57.7	145.5
Belgium	1175.7	2539.8	2065.0	2699.1	261.9	310.4	432.8	441.3
Canada	1744.9	1900.0	1740.0	2850.1	475.4	648.2	563.4	639.8
Denmark	334.3	486.5	534.0	545.6	147.1	217.3	247.2	253.0
Finland	47.2	100.2	121.0	130.0	26.9	22.9	38.7	60.8
France	4845.4	7566.6	7794.4	10675.0	1917.0	2350.7	2786.0	3351.3
Germany, Fed. Rep.	4266.1	5669.7	4780.2	7567.3	1028.2	1560.7	2160.8	2274.3
Italy	1818.2	2793.8	3693.0	3172.7	34.9	22.3	22.4	72.8
Japan	4535.7	8947.8	6410.0	5190.7	899.3	1531.0	1921.2	1960.8
Netherlands	1775.0	2357.0	1452.4	1822.2	643.6	789.2	962.0	1174.4
New Zealand	59.8	69.1	59.7	79.7	41.7	44.9	52.1	51.3
Norway	395.4	449.2	542.4	611.2	165.2	192.1	248.6	271.2
Sweden	1216.8	982.9	818.2	1529.7	486.0	473.0	619.0	675.3
Switzerland	3310.0	2543.2	4273.4	1792.7	69.2	100.8	109.1	170.2
United Kingdom	6443.6	9112.1	12562.7	12164.6	551.9	854.0	1162.6	1255.1
United States	8916.0	13617.0	17327.0	10871.0	2897.0	3474.0	4076.0	4366.0
TOTAL	*41858.3*	*60070.6*	*64996.6*	*62548.3*	*10080.5*	*13123.4*	*15917.5*	*17640.3*
MULTILATERAL								
AF.D.F.	26.3	39.3	55.0	95.8	26.3	39.3	55.0	95.8
AF.D.B.	65.9	83.3	92.4	97.1	–	–	–	–
AS.D.B.	313.4	389.9	394.6	476.6	88.6	160.9	116.1	149.0
CAR.D.B.	22.5	19.5	32.3	53.5	11.9	19.6	25.4	43.0
E.E.C.	597.9	883.0	1286.7	1270.3	549.2	804.6	1124.4	1013.1
IBRD	1871.4	2179.9	2953.2	3272.9	38.6	76.1	106.9	106.8
IDA	1131.5	1006.6	1277.6	1542.8	1131.5	1006.6	1277.6	1542.8
I.D.B.	687.5	707.2	782.2	893.3	299.2	331.8	335.1	325.9
IFAD	–	–	2.6	44.8	–	–	2.6	44.8
I.F.C.	97.6	58.5	108.0	295.2	–	–	–	–
IMF TRUST FUND	175.5	864.9	680.4	1635.8	175.5	864.9	680.4	1635.8
U.N. AGENCIES	–	–	–	–	–	–	–	–
UNDP	324.4	419.1	519.6	660.3	324.4	419.1	519.6	660.3
UNTA	94.5	114.1	116.4	34.9	94.5	114.1	116.4	34.9
UNICEF	127.8	167.5	210.3	246.6	127.8	167.5	210.3	246.6
UNRWA	120.0	109.6	136.2	156.9	120.0	109.6	136.2	156.9
WFP	365.8	411.2	526.4	539.1	365.8	411.2	526.4	539.1
UNHCR	103.8	123.3	250.3	464.5	103.8	123.3	250.3	464.5
Other Multilateral	268.0	385.1	454.8	384.6	268.0	385.1	454.8	384.6
Arab OPEC Agencies	1503.8	1122.4	476.0	404.9	1233.4	965.6	257.5	277.1
TOTAL	*7897.6*	*9084.3*	*10355.0*	*12569.9*	*4958.7*	*5999.2*	*6195.0*	*7721.0*
OPEC COUNTRIES	*4829.7*	*4256.9*	*4933.0*	*6392.4*	*3940.1*	*3247.2*	*4933.0*	*6105.6*
E.E.C.+ MEMBERS	*21256.2*	*31408.5*	*34168.4*	*39916.8*	*5133.8*	*6909.1*	*8898.2*	*9835.3*
TOTAL	***54585.7***	***73411.9***	***80284.6***	***81510.6***	***18979.2***	***22369.9***	***27045.5***	***31466.9***
ODA LOANS GROSS					**ODA LOANS NET**			
DAC COUNTRIES								
Australia	–	4.6	–	–	-2.9	1.3	-3.2	-3.6
Austria	62.2	79.6	20.9	106.3	61.4	79.1	19.7	103.5
Belgium	42.6	32.6	96.4	104.3	40.9	30.7	93.2	99.5
Canada	188.4	230.7	194.4	208.0	184.8	21.4	187.2	198.8
Denmark	68.7	83.9	125.5	111.8	63.3	78.4	30.0	95.6
Finland	10.0	6.0	1.2	2.0	8.8	5.8	-42.2	1.0
France	376.9	479.5	522.7	695.2	204.0	301.1	325.7	486.9
Germany, Fed. Rep.	764.3	1118.8	1515.7	1268.9	434.6	776.0	856.3	66.5
Italy	38.0	11.8	–	13.7	-30.7	-28.8	-40.9	-28.8
Japan	824.1	1393.9	1619.8	1611.9	662.6	1147.6	1361.0	1308.2
Netherlands	165.9	240.8	266.6	395.2	111.2	79.4	180.6	310.5
New Zealand	0.2	–	–	0.5	–	-0.3	-3.5	0.5
Norway	–	–	–	–		-3.3	–	–
Sweden	21.0	10.4	4.0	15.0	19.3	-235.1	3.6	14.4
Switzerland	11.7	7.4	3.0	2.1	-50.8	7.2	1.2	1.1
United Kingdom	108.9	138.4	186.6	172.9	12.4	46.2	35.8	-60.4
United States	1564.0	1865.0	2098.0	1868.0	1159.0	1414.0	1621.0	1391.0
TOTAL	*4246.8*	*5703.3*	*6654.7*	*6575.9*	*2877.6*	*3720.6*	*4625.4*	*3984.6*
MULTILATERAL	*3191.9*	*3678.3*	*3289.6*	*4529.0*	*3060.1*	*3510.2*	*3108.7*	*4292.3*
OPEC COUNTRIES	*882.4*	*916.0*	*1359.0*	*1695.5*	*852.5*	*877.4*	*1292.9*	*1564.3*
E.E.C.+ MEMBERS	*1650.0*	*2192.4*	*3003.0*	*2885.6*	*911.6*	*1359.1*	*1757.4*	*1078.4*
TOTAL	***8321.1***	***10297.5***	***11303.4***	***12800.4***	***6790.3***	***8108.1***	***9027.0***	***9841.1***
TOTAL OFFICIAL GROSS					**TOTAL OFFICIAL NET**			
DAC COUNTRIES								
Australia	352.1	468.0	490.5	502.4	349.2	463.6	479.8	488.5
Austria	109.0	113.4	59.1	148.3	90.2	85.2	27.2	106.4
Belgium	286.3	372.0	483.1	643.9	281.5	362.8	468.1	622.4
Canada	1180.1	1562.7	1601.9	2153.9	805.8	1096.2	987.3	1317.7
Denmark	157.1	228.6	352.3	279.5	150.5	222.4	254.9	258.9
Finland	28.1	23.1	82.1	61.8	26.9	22.9	38.7	60.8
France	2539.7	3241.6	3658.1	4610.4	2074.7	2813.5	3023.7	4042.4
Germany, Fed. Rep.	1732.7	2556.1	3550.5	4613.3	1098.4	1866.0	2310.9	2942.5
Italy	280.0	195.4	375.4	533.9	169.4	79.4	268.7	302.1
Japan	1457.0	2537.9	2682.0	2982.9	1255.9	2217.4	2175.2	2572.6
Netherlands	703.4	976.3	1055.7	1290.9	645.8	809.3	964.2	1204.1
New Zealand	113.5	46.5	55.8	55.6	50.5	46.1	52.4	54.2
Norway	169.5	202.1	259.1	273.2	169.5	198.7	259.1	273.2
Sweden	487.8	737.4	619.3	675.9	486.0	491.8	619.0	675.3
Switzerland	131.7	102.2	171.8	183.6	65.0	98.6	163.6	182.0
United Kingdom	813.6	1180.3	1723.2	2141.2	709.1	1076.6	1572.2	1854.4
United States	5072.0	6129.0	7039.0	7771.0	3701.0	4666.0	4924.0	5383.0
TOTAL	*15613.4*	*20672.6*	*24259.0*	*28921.4*	*12129.5*	*16616.6*	*18588.9*	*22340.5*
MULTILATERAL	*9049.7*	*10457.8*	*11981.0*	*14812.9*	*7897.6*	*9084.3*	*10355.0*	*12569.9*
OPEC COUNTRIES	*4857.2*	*4303.1*	*4999.2*	*6530.5*	*4829.7*	*4256.9*	*4933.0*	*6392.4*
E.E.C.+ MEMBERS	*7137.1*	*9669.7*	*12529.9*	*15434.7*	*5727.3*	*8113.0*	*10149.4*	*12497.1*
TOTAL	***29520.2***	***35433.5***	***41239.2***	***50264.8***	***24856.8***	***29957.8***	***33876.9***	***41302.7***

	197
TOTAL ODA GROSS	
Australia	351.
Austria	87.
Belgium	263.
Canada	479.
Denmark	152.
Finland	28.
France	2089.
Germany, Fed. Rep.	1357.
Italy	103.
Japan	1060.
Netherlands	698.
New Zealand	41.
Norway	165.
Sweden	487.
Switzerland	131.
United Kingdom	648.
United States	3302.
TOTAL	*11449.*
AF.D.F.	26.
AF.D.B.	
AS.D.B.	91.
CAR.D.B.	11.
E.E.C.	557.
IBRD	38.
IDA	1158.
I.D.B.	392.
IFAD	
I.F.C.	
IMF TRUST FUND	175.
U.N. AGENCIES	
UNDP	324.
UNTA	94.
UNICEF	127.
UNRWA	120.
WFP	365.
UNHCR	103.
Other Multilateral	268.
Arab OPEC Agencies	1233.
TOTAL	*5090.*
OPEC COUNTRIES	*3967.*
E.E.C.+ MEMBERS	*5872.*
TOTAL	***20507.***
GRANTS	
Australia	351
Austria	25
Belgium	221
Canada	290
Denmark	83
Finland	18
France	1713
Germany, Fed. Rep.	593
Italy	65
Japan	236
Netherlands	532
New Zealand	41
Norway	165
Sweden	466
Switzerland	120
United Kingdom	539
United States	1738
TOTAL	*7202*
MULTILATERAL	*1898*
OPEC COUNTRIES	*3085*
E.E.C.+ MEMBERS	*4222*
TOTAL	***12186***
TOTAL OOF GROSS	
Australia	0
Austria	21
Belgium	22
Canada	701
Denmark	4
Finland	
France	449
Germany, Fed. Rep.	374
Italy	176
Japan	396
Netherlands	5
New Zealand	71
Norway	4
Sweden	
Switzerland	
United Kingdom	165
United States	1770
TOTAL	*4163*
MULTILATERAL	*3959*
OPEC COUNTRIES	*889*
E.E.C.+ MEMBERS	*1264*
TOTAL	***9012***

E.E.C.

below the 25 per cent threshold which would make them eligible to be recorded as ODA. The main specific classes of transactions included here are official export credits, official sector equity and portfolio investment, and debt reorganisation undertaken by the official sector at non-concessional terms (irrespective of the nature or the identity of the original creditor).

A9. Funds provided by the official sector to support export credits or direct investment of the private sector are recorded in this report as part of the relevant private sector transactions. This treatment differs from that in the aggregate statistics, where these amounts are included as part of the official sector total, and the aggregate amounts for the private sector reduced correspondingly. For purposes of geographic allocation, the pertinent concept is the transactor dealing with a developing country; this country is not concerned with the sources of the transactor's funds, and its indebtedness is towards the transactor, not his sources of finance. By contrast, the aggregate statistics place emphasis on the source of funds, which governs the extent to which official policy can govern the amount, terms and distribution of transactions in which official sector resources form part of the total financing package.

A10. *Total Contractual Lending:* Bilateral and multilateral ODA and OOF loans plus guaranteed private export credits i.e., all borrowing at fixed terms other than financial credits extended by the banking sector.

A11. *Technical Co-operation Grants:* This heading covers practically all disbursements for technical co-operation, but small amounts are occasionally financed in loan form. Technical Co-operation is the provision of resources with the primary purpose of (*i*) augmenting the level of knowledge, skills, technical knowhow or productive aptitudes of the population of developing countries, i.e. increasing their stock of human intellectual capital or (*ii*) augmenting developing countries' capacity for more effective use of their existing endowment (as distinct from transfers intended to increase the stock of physical capital).

A12. *Multilateral Agencies:* For the list of multilateral agencies for which data are shown separately in this report, see the Introduction. To the extent possible, a distinction has been made between concessional and non-concessional flows from multilateral agencies. Loan disbursements for which it was not possible to make this distinction on a transaction by transaction basis have been treated as non-concessional if they were made from "ordinary capital" resources and concessional if made from a "soft window". Thus, for some agencies "total loans" are significantly larger than loans on concessional terms, and the volume of loans on concessional terms actually received by the borrowing country is correspondingly understated. The "net" multilateral disbursements concept used in this report, like the net bilateral concept, is defined as gross disbursements of grants and loans to developing countries minus repayments on earlier loans. Capital subscriptions to multilateral agencies by their developing country Members are not subtracted out.

A13. *Total Receipts, Net:* In addition to Official Development Assistance, this heading includes in particular: other official bilateral transactions which are not concessional or which, even though they have concessional elements, are primarily trade facilitating in character (i.e. "Other Official Flows"); changes in bilateral long-term assets of the private non-monetary and monetary sectors, in particular guaranteed export credits, direct private investment, portfolio investment, and to the extent they are not covered in the preceding headings, loans by private banks. Flows from the multilateral sector which are not classified as concessional are also included here.

Relationships Between the Categories Shown in the Report

A14. The total net resource flow presented for a recipient country ("net receipts") is the sum of (1 + 2 + 3 = 4) :

	DAC	MULTILATERAL ORGANISATIONS	OPEC DONORS	CMEA DONORS
1. Official Development Assistance (ODA)	By country	By agency	As a group	Not available
2. Other Official Flows (OOF)	By country	By agency	As a group	Not available
3. Private Sector Net	As a group	Not applicable	Not available	Not available
4. Total Resource Flows	By country	By agency	Incomplete	Not available
Memo:				
ODA Gross	By country	By agency	As a group	As a group
ODA Commitments	By country	By agency	As a group	As a group

A15. For any given recipient country the DAC total for "private sector net" can be broken down by country of origin by subtracting (ODA + OOF net) for the donor country concerned, from the total receipts figure against its name.

A16. "Private sector, net" is broken down for DAC Members combined into direct investment, portfolio investment and export credits (net). The transactions covered are those undertaken by residents of DAC Member countries. Portfolio investment corresponds largely, but not wholly, to transactions by the private monetary (bank) sector ("bank sector loans"). Where necessary and to the extent possible the portfolio investment data have been adjusted to transfer export credit claims to the corresponding heading. Accordingly, the coverage of portfolio investment differs in these two regards from the coverage of (bank sector loans). Further differences in coverage are as follows: (bank sector loans) includes as well as some export credit claims, loans by branches in offshore centres of banks resident in reporting countries, these being the countries which report to the Bank for International

Settlements (BIS) i.e., DAC Members other than the following countries: Australia, Finland, New Zealand and Norway. However, even if data could be obtained to reconcile these differences in coverage in principle, discrepancies would still remain in practice. The (bank sector loans) figure is an OECD Secretariat estimate based on the change in end-year claims as shown by BIS. The BIS data are computed at the exchange rate applicable at the date concerned, so that the change as computed includes the effect of changes in exchange rates. The figure thus reached is further adjusted to exclude the estimated change in claims of an original maturity of less than one year. As noted earlier, the portfolio investment figure is a direct measurement of new transactions of over one year maturity, less repayments of principal, converted to dollars at the average exchange rate for the year.

NOTE ON THE INTERPRETATION OF CERTAIN DATA

A17. In establishing the statistical data in the present report, it was the Secretariat's aim to present the fullest possible record of the resources put at the disposal of each country covered. However, there are some inconsistencies in Members' reporting. Although they are of marginal impact on the aggregate data, it was nevertheless necessary to make estimates which in some instances affect the data shown, and in others were intended to fill gaps in the data originally submitted.

A18. The following list sets out the main areas in which particuliarities of the data stemming from these causes could have some influence on their understanding or use by the reader.

Data for Country Groups

a) *Contents of the Groups*

A19. *Low-income Countries* are those whose per capita GNP in 1979, as shown in the IBRD World Atlas, was below approximately $500 (see 1979 entry in the fourth line of "Economic Indicators" in each country table). Two sub-groups of low-income countries are shown separately: those on the UN list of *Least-developed countries,* and all *other low-income* countries except China[1]. The remaining countries are subdivided into Newly Industrialising Countries (NIC's) (Argentina, Brazil, Greece, Hong Kong, Republic of Korea, Mexico, Portugal, Singapore, Spain, Taiwan, Yugoslavia); *OPEC donor countries* (Algeria, Ecuador, Gabon, Iran, Iraq, Kuwait, Libya, Nigeria, Qatar, Saudi Arabia, United Arab Emirates, Venezuela) and *"middle-income" countries.* The People's Republic of *China,* which was added to the DAC list of developing countries in 1980, is treated as a separate group for which the data, given on the country page, are not reproduced a second time. These groups have been defined purely for analytical purposes, and except for the Least-developed countries, are not internationally agreed lists.

b) *Treatment of Unallocated Amounts*

A20. Some reporting countries are unable to supply a full geographical distribution down to country level. One element here is that some commitments or disbursements in fact relate to expenditures in a given region (e.g. West Africa) or group of countries (e.g. the Least-developed countries). The data shown for countries and for groups are restricted to those which are available broken down by recipient country. Amounts reported as provided to a region or group are included as "unallocated". This heading also includes commitments and disbursements concerning expenditures on the territory of the donor country for research specific to some developing countries' problems (e.g., tropical diseases) or in the form of subsidies to nationals of developing countries, e.g., for apprenticeships, or school or university tuition; there are obvious statistical difficulties in assigning these amounts to the countries of origin of these trainees and students.

A21. In computing the share of a given country or group in a total for developing countries, the usual practice is to use as denominator the total excluding unallocated amounts. Implicit in this approach is the assumption that the percentage geographical distribution of allocated and unallocated amounts is the same.

A22. *Negative Grants.* In describing the recording methodology for grants, it was noted that the total of new grants is reduced by the amounts of a donor's local currency balances used by the donor for its own purposes. If the latter exceeds the volume of new grants, a "negative grant" is shown.

A23. *Cancellations of Commitments.* The data on commitments concern new commitments entered into during the calendar year. They exclude commitments that were cancelled in the year they were made, but not adjusted to allow for cancellations during the year are of commitments made in earlier years.

A24. *Partial Components of a Total* in the "All Sources: Commitments" block, certain components only are shown; the presentation of full detail would have lengthened processing time so greatly as to delay the appearance of the report. The total of the missing components can be established by direct subtraction from the grand total of which they are part.

A25. *Commitments and Disbursements of the UN Agencies.* Disbursement data are shown separately for each UN agency. Comparable commitment data are not available for the UN family. In the commitments table, gross disbursement data are shown as a proxy for the UN family as a group, with no entries against the individual agencies. This procedure was necessary to provide an order of magnitude of the commitments of multilateral organisations combined.

A26. *Effect of Changes in Exchange Rates.* The currency unit used through this report is the dollar. Loans are often denominated in another currency. If that currency strengthens vis-à-vis the dollar, repayments on the loan are reflected in the statistics by an increased number of dollars. This accounts for a number of cases in which cumulative repayments appear to exceed the original amount of a loan. Similarly, the weakening of a currency produces cases in which repayments, expressed in dollars, appear to be less than the original amount lent. If comparing data on changes in debt with the figures shown for net resource flows, it should be borne in mind that the debt data are converted to dollars at the end-of-period rate, whereas the flow data are converted at the annual average rate. See also paragraph 16.

A27. *Unusually High Amortization Entries for Least Developed Countries in 1978, 1979 and 1980.* These relate in practically all cases to the implementation of Retroactive Terms Adjustment

1 In the table headings, space limitations made it necesary to use abbreviations: *LLDC's* for the Least-developed countries, and *non-LLDC LIC's* for other low income countries.

in the form of forgiveness of the outstanding principal on loans. The effect of cancellation is to extend a grant, which is applied to pay off the loans concerned. Exceptionally large amortization entries (i.e., negative net loans) on ODA account for the Least-developed countries will be found to be accompanied by exceptionally high entries for the same donor, for the same year, for disbursements of grants.

A28. *ODA from IBRD.* Most IBRD lending is recorded as "Other Official Flows"; the main arm of the World Bank group for ODA is the International Development Association (IDA). Some small amounts listed against IBRD correspond in the main to Third Window lending.

A29. *Belgium's Data for Commitments.* By reason of the institutional procedures used, there is no stage at which it is possible for the Belgian authorities to identify the commitment of a grant (no problem arises in regard to loan reporting). In order not to leave blank entries in the commitments data for Belgium, the Secretariat has made estimates, by distributing the total budget allocation for grants among recipient countries in proportion to each country's receipts of gross disbursements of grants in the same year. The errors involved are usually small; certainly, they are much too small in any way to distort the figure for a recipient country's total receipts from DAC Members combined or from all sources. If analysing Belgium's commitment figures in isolation, a still closer approximation to the order of magnitude is obtained by taking an average over several years of the commitments and gross disbursements data shown for Belgian grants.

A30. *Other Official Flows from OPEC Countries/Official Flows from all Sources.* Data on Other Official Flows from OPEC countries for 1979 and 1980 are known to be incomplete. This also reduces each country's apparent receipts of OOF, from all sources, in these two years. The basic data for OPEC Members' OOF relate to gross disbursements. Very little information is available on repayments, and for most recipients, net OOF from OPEC is the same figure as for gross OOF. The distortion is limited. These programmes:

a) were relatively new, so that many OOF loans were still in their grace period during 1976-1980;

b) included several loans to central banks, usually for a term of two years, which were in practice renewed at maturity, and in one instance not repaid on the due date.

For these reasons, amortization receipts by OPEC Members were low, and the closeness of the gross and net figures in general reflects the position reasonably accurately.

A31. *Resource Flows from the European Economic Community.* The figures shown pertain to outflows from the EEC, including outflows from the European Investment Bank at market terms. The latter can be ascertained from the data in the present volume as the difference between a country's Total Net Receipts from the EEC and its receipts of ODA resources.

Note: The symbol – in the tables means nil, not available or less than half of the smallest unit shown, depending on the context.

Annexe

DEFINITIONS DES CONCEPTS UTILISES DANS CE RAPPORT

A1. Suivant la définition utilisée dans ce rapport, les *versements* représentent le transfert effectif de ressources financières d'un pays à l'autre. Ils peuvent être saisis à l'un des stades suivants : fourniture de biens et services, dépôts de sommes mises à la disposition du bénéficiaire dans un fonds ou un compte réservé, retrait de fonds par le bénéficiaire sur un compte ou un fonds réservé, paiement de factures par le donneur pour le compte du bénéficiaire, etc. Les modalités de versement tendent à varier en fonction du type d'apport financier (ou de coopération technique) en cause. Les versements sont comptabilisés soit bruts (c'est-à-dire les montants effectivement versés) ou nets (c'est-à-dire moins le remboursement du capital au titre de prêts antérieurs).

A2. On entend par *engagement* une obligation ferme, stipulée dans un contrat ou un accord similaire et étayée par l'ouverture de crédits ou l'affectation de fonds publics; par cette obligation, le gouvernement, un organisme public du pays déclarant ou un organisme multilatéral s'engage à fournir au profit du pays bénéficiaire une aide d'un montant spécifié, assortie de conditions financières spécifiées et destinée à des fins spécifiées.

A3. *Element-don :* Résume les conditions financières d'une opération : taux d'intérêt, durée de remboursement (délai jusqu'au remboursement final) et différé d'amortissement (délai jusqu'au premier remboursement du capital). Il s'agit d'une mesure de l'importance de la libéralité d'un prêt. Le bénéfice qu'en retire l'emprunteur dépend de la différence entre le taux d'intérêt dont est assorti le prêt et le taux du marché, ainsi que du nombre d'années pendant lesquelles l'emprunteur dispose des ressources. Le calcul de ce bénéfice se fait en actualisant, au taux du marché, le montant du service de la dette payée à chaque échéance. On évalue l'excès du nominal du prêt par rapport au total des valeurs actualisées. Ce montant, exprimé en pourcentage du nominal, est l'élément de «libéralité» (ou élément-don) du prêt. Le taux du marché est conventionnellement fixé à 10 %. Par conséquence, l'élément de libéralité d'un prêt à 10 % est nul; il est de 100 % dans le cas d'un don; et il se situe entre ces deux extrêmes pour un prêt libéral. De façon générale, l'élément de libéralité d'un prêt remboursable en moins de 10 ans ne pourra dépasser 25 % à moins que le taux d'intérêt ne soit très inférieur à 5 %. En multipliant la valeur nominale d'un prêt par son élément de libéralité, on obtient «l'équivalent-don» de ce prêt.

Apports de ressources : catégories et rubriques

A4. On entend par *Aide publique au développement* (APD) l'ensemble des apports de ressources qui sont fournis aux pays en développement et aux institutions multilatérales par des organismes officiels, y compris les collectivités locales, ou par les organismes gestionnaires et qui, considérés séparément, au niveau de chaque opération, répondent aux critères suivants :

- *a)* être dispensés dans le but essentiel de favoriser le développement économique et l'amélioration du niveau de vie dans les pays moins développés;
- *b)* revêtir un caractère de faveur et comporter un élément de libéralité (voir paragraphe 3) au moins égal à 25 %.

A5. *Dons :* Cette rubrique couvre les transferts, en monnaie ou en nature, qui n'impliquent aucun remboursement. Elle inclut les dons au titre des réparations et les paiements d'indemnisation effectués au niveau gouvernemental, ainsi que les dons au titre de la coopération technique. Les dons apparaissent sur une base nette, c'est-à-dire après déduction du montant de ses avoirs en monnaie locale que le pays donneur a utilisé à des fins autres que l'avancement du développement du pays bénéficiaire (exemple : financement des dépenses locales afférentes au fonctionnement des ambassades). Par ailleurs les dons sont présentés nets d'éléments tels que les recettes d'impôts en provenance des Territoires d'Outre-Mer.Sont également exclus les paiements de réparation et d'indemnisation à des particuliers, les paiements d'assurances et autres paiements similaires à des résidents de pays en développement, les dépenses encourues pour l'administration des programmes d'aide ainsi que les prêts accordés et remboursables dans les monnaies des bénéficiaires.

A6. *Prêts d'aide publique au développement :* Comprennent les prêts à plus d'un an accordés par des gouvernements et des organismes publics, remboursables en monnaies convertibles ou en nature, et qui satisfont aux critères présentés dans l'alinéa 4 ci-dessus. Les opérations de rééchelonnement des échéances (allongement de la durée de prêts initialement accordés par un gouvernement ou un organisme public) et les prêts octroyés par un gouvernement ou par un organisme public pour refinancer une dette contractée auprès du secteur privé ou du secteur public sont inclus dans cette catégorie s'ils sont notifiés comme Aide publique au développement; sinon, ils sont classés dans les Autres apports du secteur public. Les montants nets sont établis après déduction des recettes d'amortissement effectué en une monnaie autre que celle du pays bénéficiaire ou en nature.

A7. *Apports totaux du secteur public :* Il s'agit du total de l'aide publique au développement (APD) et des autres apports du secteur public (AASP). Cet aggrégat correspond aux versements (bruts ou nets) effectués par le secteur public dans son ensemble aux pays bénéficiaires étudiés.

A8. *Autres apports du secteur public (AASP).* Il s'agit des opérations entreprises par le secteur public dont le but essentiel est autre que le développement, ou qui, tout en visant de favoriser le développement sont assorties d'un élément-don en-dessous de la valeur seuil de 25 % à partir de laquelle elles auraient eu qualité d'aide publique au développement. Les principales catégories de transactions englobées dans les AASP sont les crédits publics à l'exportation, les prises de participation et les investissements de portefeuille effectués par le secteur public, et le réaménagement de la dette effectué par le secteur public aux conditions du marché (et ce, quel que soit la nature ou l'identité du créancier primitif).

A9. Les ressources mises à disposition par le secteur public afin de soutenir les crédits à l'exportation ou l'investissement direct en provenance du secteur privé sont comptabilisées dans le présent rapport comme faisant partie des opérations correspondantes du secteur privé. Cette approche diffère de celle utilisée dans les données statistiques aggrégatives. Aux fins de ces dernières, les versements de soutien sont assimilés à des opérations du secteur public, et les montants présentés pour le secteur privé sont minorés en conséquence. En effet, pour ce qui est de la répartition géographique, il convient de retenir comme unité statistique l'opérateur qui est en relation avec un pays en développement; l'emprunteur ne s'intéresse pas aux origines des capitaux que cet opérateur lui fournit, son endettement est envers lui et non envers ses sources de financement. En revanche, l'accent est placé dans les statistiques aggrégatives sur les sources des fonds, car ce sont elles qui déterminent dans quelle mesure les politiques mises en œuvre par le secteur public peuvent influer sur le montant total, les conditions et la répartition géographique des opérations dès que celles-ci englobent des ressources en provenance du secteur public.

A.10 *Total des prêts à conditions fixes.* Le total des prêts bilatéraux et multilatéraux au titre de l'APD ou des AASP, et des crédits privés garantis à l'exportation, soit, la totalité des emprunts effectués à des conditions de remboursement fixées d'avance, à l'exception des crédits financiers accordés par le secteur bancaire.

A11. *La coopération technique :* Aux fins de la notification correspond pratiquement en totalité à des versements de dons au titre de la coopération technique; toutefois, il peut arriver que de petits contrats soient passés sous la forme d'un prêt. La coopération technique se définit comme tout apport de ressources ayant pour but essentiel : (*i*) d'augmenter le niveau des connaissances, des qualifications, du savoir-faire technique ou des aptitudes productives de la population des pays en développement, c'est-à-dire d'accroître leur capital intellectuel, ou (*ii*) d'augmenter l'aptitude des pays en développement à utiliser plus efficacement les facteurs de production dont ils disposent, par opposition aux transferts destinés à accroître leur stock de capital physique.

A12. *Institutions multilatérales.* La liste des organismes multilatéraux auxquels se réfèrent les données dans le présent rapport a été présentée dans l'introduction. Dans la mesure du possible on a distingué dans les apports fournis par les organismes multilatéraux ceux qui sont assortis de conditions libérales de ceux qui interviennent aux conditions du marché. Lorsque pour certains versements de prêts il n'était pas possible d'appliquer cette distinction pour certaines transactions particulières, les versements ont été considérés comme étant à des conditions non libérales lorsqu'ils provenaient des ressources en « capital ordinaire », et à des conditions libérales lorsqu'ils venaient des « guichets spéciaux ». Ainsi, pour certaines agences, les « prêts totaux » sont plus élevés que les prêts à des conditions libérales, et le volume des prêts à des conditions libérales effectivement reçus par un pays en développement donné est sous-évalué. Dans le cas des apports des organismes multilatéraux comme dans celui des apports bilatéraux, on entend par versement « nets », le montant brut des dons et prêts versés aux pays en développement, diminué des sommes reçues de ces pays au titre du remboursement de prêts antérieurs.

A13. *Apport Total, Net.* Outre l'Aide Publique au Développement, ce total inclut en particulier : les autres transactions publiques bilatérales non assorties de conditions libérales, ou qui dans le cas contraire restent néanmoins de nature principalement commerciale; les variations des actifs à long terme bilatéraux du secteur monétaire et non monétaire; les flux en provenance des agences multilatérales qui ne sont pas considérés comme étant à des conditions libérales.

Articulation des catégories d'apports présentées dans le rapport

A14. Pour un pays bénéficiaire donné, le total net des apports de ressources est le total de (1+2+3)=4 :

	CAD	ORGANISMES MULTILATERALES	PAYS DE L'OPEP	PAYS DU CAEM
1. Aide publique au développement (APD)	Par pays	Par organisme	En tant que groupe	Non disponible
2. Autres apports du secteur public	Par pays	Par organisme	En tant que groupe	Non disponible
3. Apports nets du secteur privé	En tant que groupe	Sans objet	Non disponible	Non disponible
4. Total net des apports de ressources	Par pays	Par organisme	Incomplet	En tant que groupe
Pour mémoire :				
APD brut	Par pays	Par organisme	En tant que groupe	En tant que groupe
APD engagements	Par pays	Par organisme	En tant que groupe	En tant que groupe

A15. Le total pour l'ensemble des pays du CAD des apports nets du secteur privé peut être ventilé par pays de provenance en soustrayant du chiffre du total net des apports en provenance du pays étudié le total (APD+AASP) que l'on lira en regard de son nom dans le tableau se rapportant au pays bénéficiaire étudié.

A16. La rubrique « apports nets du secteur privé » est ventilée, pour l'ensemble des Pays membres du CAD, en investissements directs, investissements de portefeuille et crédits à l'exportation (nets). Les opérations recensées dans chaque catégorie sont celles qui sont entreprises par des opérateurs résidents des Pays membres du CAD.Les investissements de portefeuille correspondent dans une grande mesure, mais pas dans leur totalité, aux opérations du secteur monétaire (bancaire) privé, et a été ajusté dans la mesure du possible pour exclure ses créances au titre des crédits à l'exportation, lesquelles sont comprises sous la rubrique correspondante. Par conséquent, le champ de couverture des investissements de portefeuille diffère à ces deux égards de celui de la rubrique (bank sector loans : prêts du secteur bancaire). Cependant, il convient de noter d'autres particularités de la couverture de cette dernière catégorie, laquelle comprend outre certaines créances au titre des crédits à l'exportation, les prêts octroyés par des filiales dans des centres offshore de banques mères résidentes dans des pays déclarants (on entend ici par pays déclarants ceux qui effectuent des déclarations statistiques auprès de la BRI, c'est-à-dire non compris les Pays membres du DAC suivants : Australie, Finlande, Nouvelle-Zélande et Norvège). De plus, il faut garder à l'esprit que même si ces différences de champs de couverture pouvaient être reconciliées en principe, des écarts continueraient à se manifester dans la pratique. Les chiffres présentés pour les (bank sector loans) sont des estimations de la variation des statistiques du Secrétariat de l'OCDE établies à partir des statistiques relatives aux créances élaborées par le BRI. Or, les données de la BRI sont converties en dollars au taux de change constaté à la date concernée, de sorte que la variation telle qu'elle est calculée comprend l'effet des différences entre les taux de change constatés à deux fins d'année successives. La variation une fois calculée subit encore un deuxième ajustement visant à en exclure la variation (estimée) du montant des créances dont l'échéance primitive était inférieure à un an. Le chiffre montré en regard des « investissements de portefeuille » s'établit en tant que mesure directe des nouvelles opérations à échéance de plus d'un an, moins les remboursements en capital, et convertie en dollars au taux de change moyen s'appliquant à l'année étudiée.

NOTE SUR L'INTERPRETATION DE CERTAINES DONNEES

A17. Dans l'élaboration des données statistiques présentées dans ce volume, le Secrétariat s'est efforcé de présenter un tableau aussi complet que possible des ressources à la disposition de chaque pays bénéficiaire étudié. Du fait que les déclarations des Pays membres comportent certaines incohérences ou lacunes, quoique marginales, il a fallu recourir à des estimations qui influent sur le contenu des données, ou qui permettent de combler les lacunes constatées.

A18. Ci-dessous le lecteur trouvera la liste des principaux domaines où il y a lieu de signaler une particularité des données.

Données par groupes de pays

a) *Les groupes retenus*

A19. Les *pays à faible revenu* sont ceux dont le PNB par habitant en 1979, tel qu'il figure dans l'Atlas Mondial de la BIRD, était en-dessous d'environ $500 (voir le chiffre pour 1979 dans la quatrième ligne de « Indicateurs Economiques » dans chaque tableau par pays). Deux sous-catégories de pays à faible revenu sont présentées séparément, d'une part la catégorie des *« pays les moins avancés »* définie par les Nations-Unies, et d'autre part les *autres pays à faible revenu* à l'exclusion de la Chine[1]. Les pays restants sont subdivisés en *Pays en voie d'Industrialisation* (Argentine, Brésil, Grèce, Hong-Kong, République de Corée, Mexique, Portugal, Singapour, Espagne, Taïwan, Yougoslavie), Pays donateurs de l'OPEC (Algérie, Equateur, Gabon, Iran, Iraq, Koweit, Libye, Nigeria, Qatar, Arabie Saoudite, Emirats Arabes Unis, Vénézuéla) et les pays « à revenu moyen ». La République Populaire de la Chine, qui a été portée sur la liste du CAD des pays en développement en 1980 est considérée comme constituant un groupe à part pour lequel les données qui apparaissent dans le tableau pour la Chine ne sont pas reproduites une deuxième fois. Ces groupes ont été définis uniquement à des fins analytiques et à l'exception des « pays les moins avancés » ne constituent pas des classifications agréées sur le plan international.

b) *Montants « non-alloués »*

A20. Certains pays déclarants ne sont pas en mesure de ventiler la totalité de leurs apports au niveau du pays de destination, puisque les engagements ou les versements concernent des dépenses à entreprendre soit dans une région donnée (exemple : les pays de l'Afrique de l'Ouest), soit dans un groupe de pays donnés (plus particulièrement les pays les moins avancés). Ne sont présentées dans ce rapport que les données portant sur les montants à destination certaine. Les montants engagés ou versés sur base régionale ou en faveur d'une catégorie de pays ont été assimilés aux montants « non alloués », rubrique qui comporte par ailleurs des ressources engagées ou versées sur le territoire du pays donneur en faveur des ressortissants de pays en développement, telles par exemple les dépenses consacrées à des stages d'apprentissage ou de la formation en école ou universités sous forme de subventions aux ayants-droit, mais qui pour raisons statistiques ne peuvent être attribuées aux pays d'origine des étudiants ou des apprentis concernés, soit encore des recherches consacrées à certains problèmes propres à un ensemble de pays en développement (exemple : les maladies tropicales).

A21. S'agissant du calcul de la part d'un pays ou d'un groupe donné dans le total pour un ensemble des pays en développement, ou l'ensemble de ces pays, il est d'usage de retenir dans le dénominateur le total non compris des montants non alloués. On suppose, ce faisant, que la répartition géographique en pourcentage des montants alloués est la même que celle des montants non-alloués.

A22. *Dons négatifs.* Le lecteur qui se reportera à la description de la comptabilisation des dons y apprendra que les montants

1 Dans les en-têtes des tableaux, les abréviations suivantes ont dû être introduites pour des raisons techniques : *LLDC's* – les pays les moins avancés, et *non-LLDC LIC's* – les pays à faible revenu autres que les pays les moins avancés.

inscrits dans les statistiques le sont après minoration pour tenir compte des dépenses engagées à ses propres fins par un pays donneur en utilisant des avoirs en monnaie locale dont il dispose. Il peut arriver que ces montants dépassent celui des nouveaux dons accordés, d'où inscription de dons négatifs.

A23. *Annulation de l'engagement.* Les données relatives à l'engagement correspondent aux nouveaux engagements souscrits dans l'année. Elles excluent donc un engagement annulé dans la même année que celle où il a été souscrit, mais par contre aucune défalcation n'est faite pour tenir compte d'annulation en cours d'année d'un engagement souscrit pendant une année antérieure.

A24. *Composantes non exhaustives.* Il convient de mentionner que dans le sous-pavé «all sources, commitments» (engagements en provenance de toutes sources) seules certaines composantes des totaux apparaissent, ceci pour éviter certains traitements complexes qui auraient indument prolongé le délai de disponibilité de chiffres et ainsi retardé la parution du rapport. Le total des composantes manquantes peut être établi par la soustraction des composantes qui sont présentées du total dont elles font partie.

A25. *Engagements et Versements des Agences des Nations-Unies :* Les données sur les versements sont présentées séparément pour chaque agence des Nations-Unies. Des données comparables sur les engagements n'étant pas disponibles pour les Nations-Unies, on a inscrit dans les tableaux des engagements les données relatives aux versements bruts pour la famille des Nations-Unies en tant qu'ensemble, avec inscription d'un montant nul en regard des agences individuelles. Ce procédé répond à la nécessité de fournir un ordre de grandeur des engagements souscrits pour l'ensemble du secteur multilatéral.

A26. *Effets de variations du taux de change.* L'unité monétaire utilisée dans ce rapport est le dollar des Etats-Unis. Or, souvent ces prêts sont stipulés dans une autre monnaie. Si celle-ci raffermit par rapport au dollar, les remboursements se traduisent dans les données statistiques par un nombre plus important de dollars, d'où des cas où le cumul des remboursements paraît dépasser le montant primitif du prêt. De même, l'affaiblissement d'une monnaie se traduit dans les statistiques par des remboursements dont le total, exprimé en dollars, paraît être inférieur au principal. Si on effectue une comparaison des variations de la dette avec les chiffres présentés pour les apports totaux nets de ressources, il faut garder à l'esprit que les données relatives à la dette sont converties en dollars au taux s'appliquant en fin de période, tandis que les données relatives aux apports sont converties au taux annuel moyen. Voir paragraphe 16.

A27. *Montants exceptionnellement élevés d'amortissements inscrits en regard de certains pays les moins avancés en 1978, 1979 et 1980.* Il s'agit dans la quasi-totalité des cas de la mise en œuvre de «l'ajustement rétroactif des conditions» sous la forme de l'annulation de l'endettement au titre des prêts antérieurs. L'annulation correspond à l'octroi d'un don, dont l'objet est de permettre le remboursement du principal des prêts en cours. La comptabilisation de montants exceptionnellement élevés d'amortissements (soit, des prêts nets négatifs) dans les statistiques de l'Aide Publique au Développement consentie aux pays les moins avancés s'accompagne dans tous les cas de la comptabilisation d'un montant exceptionnellement élevé des dons octroyés par le même donneur, dans la même année.

A28. *APD en provenance de la Banque Mondiale.* La plupart des prêts de la Banque Mondiale sont classés sous la rubrique «Autres Apports du Secteur Public» (multilatéral); en effet, son APD est en règle générale dispensée par l'IDA. Certains montants inscrits en regard de la BIRD correspondent aux prêts mis à disposition par le mécanisme du «troisième guichet».

A29. *Engagements de la Belgique.* En raison des voies administratives utilisées, il n'existe pas de stade où les autorités Belges sont en mesure de déterminer qu'un engagement ferme d'octroi d'un don a été souscrit (ce problème n'existe pas pour la notification des prêts). Afin d'éviter de laisser en blanc les lignes relatives aux engagements de la Belgique, le Secrétariat a fait des estimations, en répartissant l'enveloppe budgétaire affectée aux dons au prorata de la part de chaque bénéficiaire dans les versements bruts des années en question. Les erreurs ainsi induites sont petites; en tout état de cause, elles ne sauraient déformer le chiffre donné pour le total des engagements au pays bénéficiaire étudié en provenance de toutes sources, ou de l'ensemble des Pays membres du CAD. S'il s'agit d'analyser les seuls chiffres de la Belgique, une meilleure estimation encore est disponible en faisant une moyenne pluriannuelle pour les engagements et versements de dons par la Belgique.

A30. *AASP en Provenance des Pays de l'OPEP/Total du Secteur Public, toutes sources confondues.* On sait que les données relatives aux autres apports du secteur public de l'ensemble des pays de l'OPEP en 1979 et 1980 sont incomplètes, ce qui a comme effet d'abaisser le montant total des AASP apparemment perçu par chaque pays bénéficiaire concerné en 1979 et 1980. De plus, les données de base pour ces apports en provenance de l'OPEP portent sur les versements bruts; peu de renseignements existent sur les remboursements, de sorte que pour la plupart des bénéficiaires, les AASP bruts de l'OPEP sont égaux aux AASP nets. L'erreur n'est pas très importante. En effet :

a) il s'agit de programmes nouveaux; de nombreux prêts d'AASP étaient toujours dans la période de franchise en 1976-1980;

b) certains prêts importants ont été consentis à des banques centrales, normalement pour une période de deux ans. Ils ont été renouvelés à leur échéance, et dans un cas, le prêt n'a pas été remboursé à son terme, ce qui revient au même du point de vue des écritures comptables.

Ces différentes raisons font que les amortissements versés au titre de l'AASP aux pays de l'OPEP représentent des sommes assez faibles, et la similitude des chiffres bruts et nets correspond en général à la situation réellement existante.

A31. *Apports de ressources en provenance de la Communauté européenne.* Les chiffres présentés englobent les dons et les prêts de la CEE ainsi que les fonds mis à disposition par la BEI assortis des conditions du marché. Ces derniers montants peuvent être déterminés à partir des renseignements dans le présent volume en calculant la différence entre le total des apports de la CEE reçus par un pays, et le montant de son APD en provenance de la CEE.

Note : signification du symbole – : néant, non disponible ou inférieur à la moitié de la plus petite unité utilisée, selon le contexte.

ENQUIRY FORM
FORMULAIRE D'INFORMATION

This publication is drawn from the OECD/DAC computerised data base and is available both on magnetic tape and in the form of microfiches. The full data base, which likewise is available on magnetic tape, contains annual financial flow data going back to 1969. For the period 1960 to 1968 the data are available in published form only and with no distinction between Official Development Assistance (ODA) and Other Official Flows (OOF).

Aggregate annual data by donor country and type of resource flow are discussed in the DAC Chairman's Annual Report, "Development Co-operation — Efforts and Policies of Members of the Development Assistance Committee", and presented in detail in the Statistical Annex to that report. This publication is also available from OECD Sales Agents.

◆

Cette publication est tirée de la base de données informatisée OECD/DAC, et est disponible soit sur bande magnétique, soit sous forme de microfiches. La base, qui est également disponible sur bande magnétique contient des données annuelles sur les flux financiers remontant jusqu'en 1969. Pour la période allant de 1960 à 1968 les données ne sont disponibles que sous forme de publication, et ce, sans distinction entre l'Aide Publique au Développement (APD) et les Autres Apports du Secteur Public (AASP).

Les données agrégées par pays donneur et par type de flux sont présentées et analysées dans le rapport annuel du Président du CAD, «Coopération pour le Développement — Efforts et politiques poursuivies par les membres du Comité d'Aide au Développement», qui comporte une annexe statistique ; cette publication est également en vente chez les distributeurs agréés.

◆

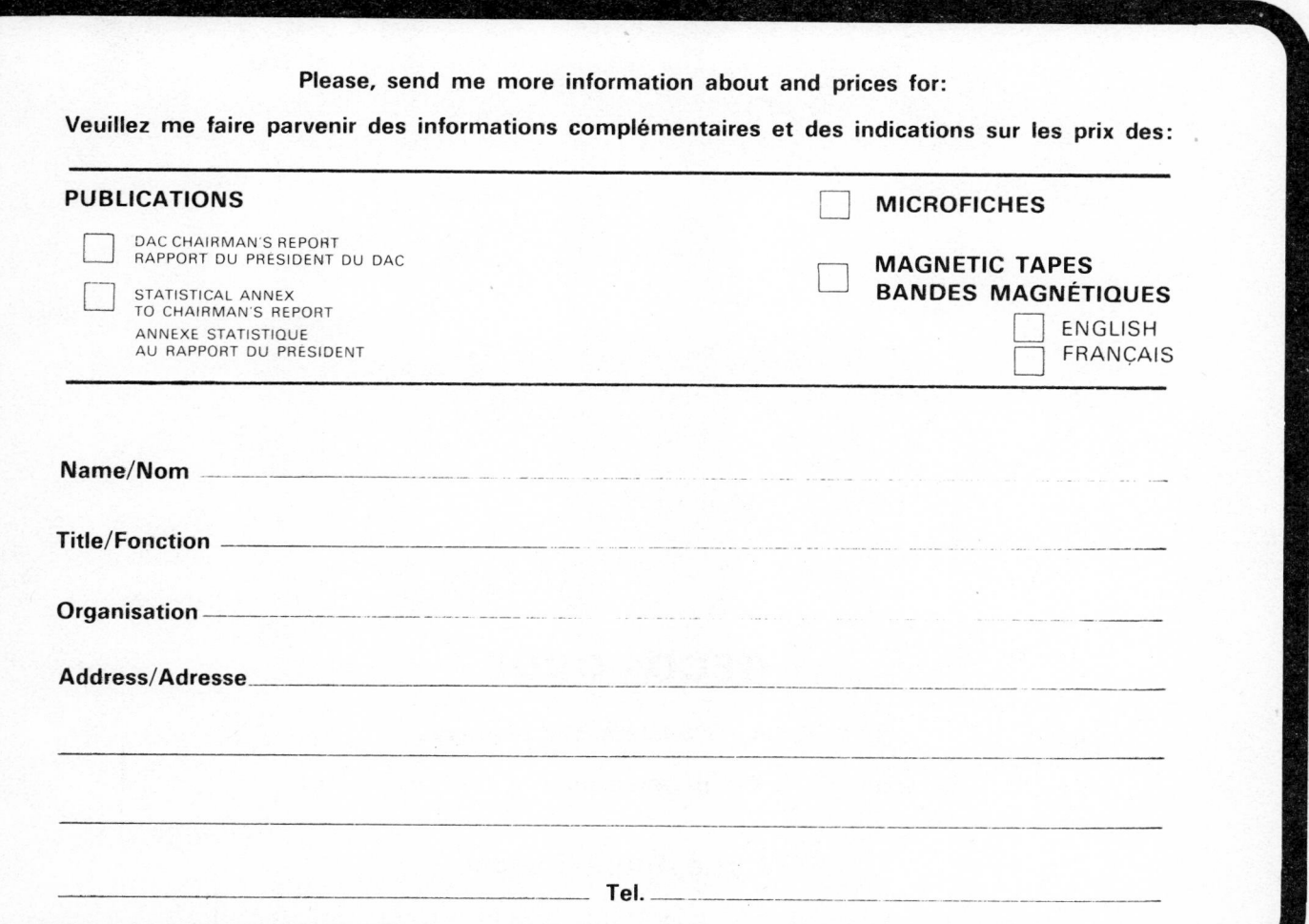

Please, send me more information about and prices for:

Veuillez me faire parvenir des informations complémentaires et des indications sur les prix des:

PUBLICATIONS

☐ DAC CHAIRMAN'S REPORT
RAPPORT DU PRESIDENT DU DAC

☐ STATISTICAL ANNEX
TO CHAIRMAN'S REPORT
ANNEXE STATISTIQUE
AU RAPPORT DU PRESIDENT

☐ **MICROFICHES**

☐ **MAGNETIC TAPES**
BANDES MAGNÉTIQUES

☐ ENGLISH
☐ FRANÇAIS

Name/Nom ______________________

Title/Fonction ______________________

Organisation ______________________

Address/Adresse ______________________

____

____

______________________ **Tel.** ______________________

OECD - OCDE

Division des Systèmes Statistiques

Direction de la Coopération pour le Développement

2, rue André-Pascal

75775 PARIS CEDEX 16 FRANCE

OECD SALES AGENTS
DÉPOSITAIRES DES PUBLICATIONS DE L'OCDE

ARGENTINA – ARGENTINE
Carlos Hirsch S.R.L., Florida 165, 4º Piso (Galería Guemes)
1333 BUENOS AIRES, Tel. 33.1787.2391 y 30.7122

AUSTRALIA – AUSTRALIE
Australia and New Zealand Book Company Pty, Ltd.,
10 Aquatic Drive, Frenchs Forest, N.S.W. 2086
P.O. Box 459, BROOKVALE, N.S.W. 2100

AUSTRIA – AUTRICHE
OECD Publications and Information Center
4 Simrockstrasse 5300 BONN. Tel. (0228) 21.60.45
Local Agent/Agent local :
Gerold and Co., Graben 31, WIEN 1. Tel. 52.22.35

BELGIUM – BELGIQUE
LCLS
35, avenue de Stalingrad, 1000 BRUXELLES. Tel. 02.512.89.74

BRAZIL – BRÉSIL
Mestre Jou S.A., Rua Guaipa 518,
Caixa Postal 24090, 05089 SAO PAULO 10. Tel. 261.1920
Rua Senador Dantas 19 s/205-6, RIO DE JANEIRO GB.
Tel. 232.07.32

CANADA
Renouf Publishing Company Limited,
2182 St. Catherine Street West,
MONTRÉAL, Que. H3H 1M7. Tel. (514)937.3519
522 West Hasting,
VANCOUVER, B.C. V6B 1L6. Tel. (604) 687.3320

DENMARK – DANEMARK
Munksgaard Export and Subscription Service
35, Nørre Søgade
DK 1370 KØBENHAVN K. Tel. +45.1.12.85.70

FINLAND – FINLANDE
Akateeminen Kirjakauppa
Keskuskatu 1, 00100 HELSINKI 10. Tel. 65.11.22

FRANCE
Bureau des Publications de l'OCDE,
2 rue André-Pascal, 75775 PARIS CEDEX 16. Tel. (1) 524.81.67
Principal correspondant :
13602 AIX-EN-PROVENCE : Librairie de l'Université.
Tel. 26.18.08

GERMANY – ALLEMAGNE
OECD Publications and Information Center
4 Simrockstrasse 5300 BONN Tel. (0228) 21.60.45

GREECE – GRÈCE
Librairie Kauffmann, 28 rue du Stade,
ATHÈNES 132. Tel. 322.21.60

HONG-KONG
Government Information Services,
Sales and Publications Office, Baskerville House, 2nd floor,
13 Duddell Street, Central. Tel. 5.214375

ICELAND – ISLANDE
Snaebjörn Jönsson and Co., h.f.,
Hafnarstraeti 4 and 9, P.O.B. 1131, REYKJAVIK.
Tel. 13133/14281/11936

INDIA – INDE
Oxford Book and Stationery Co. :
NEW DELHI-1, Scindia House. Tel. 45896
CALCUTTA 700016, 17 Park Street. Tel. 240832

INDONESIA – INDONÉSIE
PDIN-LIPI, P.O. Box 3065/JKT., JAKARTA, Tel. 583467

IRELAND – IRLANDE
TDC Publishers – Library Suppliers
12 North Frederick Street, DUBLIN 1 Tel. 744835-749677

ITALY – ITALIE
Libreria Commissionaria Sansoni :
Via Lamarmora 45, 50121 FIRENZE. Tel. 579751
Via Bartolini 29, 20155 MILANO. Tel. 365083
Sub-depositari :
Editrice e Libreria Herder,
Piazza Montecitorio 120, 00 186 ROMA. Tel. 6794628
Libreria Hoepli, Via Hoepli 5, 20121 MILANO. Tel. 865446
Libreria Lattes, Via Garibaldi 3, 10122 TORINO. Tel. 519274
La diffusione delle edizioni OCSE è inoltre assicurata dalle migliori librerie nelle città più importanti.

JAPAN – JAPON
OECD Publications and Information Center,
Landic Akasaka Bldg., 2-3-4 Akasaka,
Minato-ku, TOKYO 107 Tel. 586.2016

KOREA – CORÉE
Pan Korea Book Corporation,
P.O. Box nº 101 Kwangwhamun, SÉOUL. Tel. 72.7369

LEBANON – LIBAN
Documenta Scientifica/Redico,
Edison Building, Bliss Street, P.O. Box 5641, BEIRUT.
Tel. 354429 – 344425

MALAYSIA – MALAISIE
and/et **SINGAPORE - SINGAPOUR**
University of Malaysia Co-operative Bookshop Ltd.
P.O. Box 1127, Jalan Pantai Baru
KUALA LUMPUR. Tel. 51425, 54058, 54361

THE NETHERLANDS – PAYS-BAS
Staatsuitgeverij
Verzendboekhandel Chr. Plantijnnstraat
S-GRAVENAGE. Tel. nr. 070.789911
Voor bestellingen: Tel. 070.789208

NEW ZEALAND – NOUVELLE-ZÉLANDE
Publications Section,
Government Printing Office Bookshops:
AUCKLAND: Retail Bookshop: 25 Rutland Street,
Mail Orders: 85 Beach Road, Private Bag C.P.O.
HAMILTON: Retail: Ward Street,
Mail Orders, P.O. Box 857
WELLINGTON: Retail: Mulgrave Street (Head Office),
Cubacade World Trade Centre
Mail Orders: Private Bag
CHRISTCHURCH: Retail: 159 Hereford Street,
Mail Orders: Private Bag
DUNEDIN: Retail: Princes Street
Mail Order: P.O. Box 1104

NORWAY – NORVÈGE
J.G. TANUM A/S Karl Johansgate 43
P.O. Box 1177 Sentrum OSLO 1. Tel. (02) 80.12.60

PAKISTAN
Mirza Book Agency, 65 Shahrah Quaid-E-Azam, LAHORE 3.
Tel. 66839

PHILIPPINES
National Book Store, Inc.
Library Services Division, P.O. Box 1934, MANILA.
Tel. Nos. 49.43.06 to 09, 40.53.45, 49.45.12

PORTUGAL
Livraria Portugal, Rua do Carmo 70-74,
1117 LISBOA CODEX. Tel. 360582/3

SPAIN – ESPAGNE
Mundi-Prensa Libros, S.A.
Castello 37, Apartado 1223, MADRID-1. Tel. 275.46.55
Libreria Bastinos, Pelayo 52, BARCELONA 1. Tel. 222.06.00

SWEDEN – SUÈDE
AB CE Fritzes Kungl Hovbokhandel,
Box 16 356, S 103 27 STH, Regeringsgatan 12,
DS STOCKHOLM. Tel. 08/23.89.00

SWITZERLAND – SUISSE
OECD Publications and Information Center
4 Simrockstrasse 5300 BONN. Tel. (0228) 21.60.45
Local Agents/Agents locaux
Librairie Payot, 6 rue Grenus, 1211 GENÈVE 11. Tel. 022.31.89.50
Freihofer A.G., Weinbergstr. 109, CH-8006 ZÜRICH.
Tel. 01.3634282

TAIWAN – FORMOSE
National Book Company,
84-5 Sing Sung South Rd, Sec. 3, TAIPEI 107. Tel. 321.0698

THAILAND – THAILANDE
Suksit Siam Co., Ltd., 1715 Rama IV Rd,
Samyan, BANGKOK 5. Tel. 2511630

UNITED KINGDOM – ROYAUME-UNI
H.M. Stationery Office, P.O.B. 569,
LONDON SE1 9NH. Tel. 01.928.6977, Ext. 410 or
49 High Holborn, LONDON WC1V 6 HB (personal callers)
Branches at: EDINBURGH, BIRMINGHAM, BRISTOL,
MANCHESTER, CARDIFF, BELFAST.

UNITED STATES OF AMERICA – ÉTATS-UNIS
OECD Publications and Information Center, Suite 1207,
1750 Pennsylvania Ave., N.W. WASHINGTON, D.C.20006 – 4582
Tel. (202) 724.1857

VENEZUELA
Libreria del Este, Avda. F. Miranda 52, Edificio Galipan,
CARACAS 106. Tel. 32.23.01/33.26.04/33.24.73

YUGOSLAVIA – YOUGOSLAVIE
Jugoslovenska Knjiga, Terazije 27, P.O.B. 36, BEOGRAD.
Tel. 621.992

Les commandes provenant de pays où l'OCDE n'a pas encore désigné de dépositaire peuvent être adressées à :
OCDE, Bureau des Publications, 2, rue André-Pascal, 75775 PARIS CEDEX 16.

Orders and inquiries from countries where sales agents have not yet been appointed may be sent to:
OECD, Publications Office, 2 rue André-Pascal, 75775 PARIS CEDEX 16.

PUBLICATIONS DE L'OCDE, 2, rue André-Pascal, 75775 PARIS CEDEX 16 - Nº 42090 1981
IMPRIMÉ EN FRANCE
(43 82 01 3) ISBN 92-64-02237-6